Investment
valuation

Founded in 1807, John Wiley & Sons is the oldest independent publishing company in the United States. With offices in North America, Europe, Australia, and Asia, Wiley is globally committed to developing and marketing print and electronic products and services for our customers' professional and personal knowledge and understanding.

The Wiley Finance Series contains books written specifically for finance and investment professionals as well as sophisticated individual investors and their financial advisors. Book topics range from portfolio management to e-commerce, risk management, financial engineering, valuation and financial instruments analysis, as well as much more.

For a list of available titles, please visit our Web site at www.WileyFinance.com.

Investment
valuation

Tools and Techniques for
Determining the Value of *Any* Asset

Second Edition

ASWATH DAMODARAN
www.damodaran.com

John Wiley & Sons, Inc.

Copyright © 2002 by Aswath Damodaran. All rights reserved.

Published by John Wiley & Sons, Inc., New York.
Published simultaneously in Canada.

Library of Congress Cataloging-in-Publication Data:

Damodaran, Aswath.
    Investment valuation / Aswath Damodaran.—2nd ed.
      p. cm.—(Wiley finance)
    Includes bibliographical references and index.
    ISBN 0-471-41488-3 (cloth)
    ISBN 0-471-41490-5 (paper)
    1. Corporations—Valuation—Mathematical models. I. Title. II. Wiley finance series.
  HG4028.V3 D353 2002
  658.15—dc21   2001026890

I would like to dedicate this book to Michele, whose patience and support made it possible, and to my four children—Ryan, Brendan, Kendra, and Kiran—who provided the inspiration.

preface

This is a book about valuation—the valuation of stocks, businesses, franchises, and real assets. It is a fundamental precept of this book that any asset can be valued, albeit imprecisely in some cases. I have attempted to provide a sense of not only the differences between the models used to value different types of assets, but also the common elements in these models.

The six years between the first edition and this one have been eventful ones to say the least. We have seen the birth of a new sector—new technology—and one of the most incredible surges in value in market history as the values of these companies reached $1.4 trillion in early 2000. In the course of this market, there were many who came to the conclusion that the old valuation metrics and principles were both stodgy and inappropriate and decided to write their own rules for this new market. The past year, however, has illustrated more clearly than ever before that the basic principles of valuation have not changed. Not surprisingly, this book considers the valuation of these young companies, often with low revenues and large operating losses. In addition, we have seen the rise and fall and rise again of emerging markets as the Asian crisis devastated equity values on that continent in 1996 and 1997 and Latin America and Russia followed soon after. I spend a great deal more time talking about country risk and how best to deal with it in this edition than in the previous one.

The surge of interest in stockholder wealth maximization the world over during the 1990s also resulted in the invention of "new and better" value enhancement measures such as economic value added and cash flow return on investment. While I believe that there is little that is new or better about these approaches, they have had the salutary effect of focusing attention on value enhancement, a topic that deserves more attention than it got in the first edition.

The times seem to have also caught up with a theme that was introduced in the first edition—the notion that option pricing models could be useful in valuing businesses and equity. Real options represent not only the theme of the moment but also a fundamental change in how we view value. I spend four chapters on the topic.

Finally, the most welcome change in the past seven years is the ease with which readers can access material online. Consequently, every valuation in this book will be put on the web site that will accompany this book (www.damodaran.com), as will a significant number of datasets and spreadsheets. In fact, the valuations in the book will be updated online, allowing the book to have a much closer link to real-time valuations.

In the process of presenting and discussing the various aspects of valuation, I have tried to adhere to four basic principles. First, I have attempted to be as comprehensive as possible in covering the range of valuation models that are available to an analyst doing a valuation, while presenting the common elements in these models and providing a framework that can be used to pick the right model for any valuation scenario. Second, the models are presented with real-world examples, warts and all, so as to capture some of the problems inherent in applying these models. There is the obvious danger that some of these valuations will appear to be hopelessly wrong in hindsight, but this cost is well worth the benefits. Third, in keeping with my belief that valuation models are universal and not market-specific, illustrations from markets outside the United States are interspersed through the book. Finally, I have tried to make the book as modular as possible, enabling a reader to pick and choose sections of the book to read without a significant loss of continuity.

ASWATH DAMODARAN

New York, New York
December 2001

contents

Introduction to Valuation

Every asset, financial as well as real, has a value. The key to successfully investing in and managing these assets lies in understanding not only what the value is, but the sources of the value. Any asset can be valued, but some assets are easier to value than others, and the details of valuation will vary from case to case. Thus, the valuation of a real estate property will require different information and follow a different format than the valuation of a publicly traded stock. What is surprising, however, is not the differences in techniques across assets, but the degree of similarity in basic principles. There is uncertainty associated with valuation. Often that uncertainty comes from the asset being valued, though the valuation model may add to that uncertainty.

This chapter lays out a philosophical basis for valuation, together with a discussion of how valuation is or can be used in a variety of frameworks, from portfolio management to corporate finance.

A PHILOSOPHICAL BASIS FOR VALUATION

It was Oscar Wilde who described a cynic as one who "knows the price of everything, but the value of nothing." He could very well have been describing some analysts and many investors, a surprising number of whom subscribe to the "bigger fool" theory of investing, which argues that the value of an asset is irrelevant as long as there is a "bigger fool" around willing to buy the asset from them. While this may provide a basis for some profits, it is a dangerous game to play, since there is no guarantee that such an investor will still be around when the time to sell comes.

A postulate of sound investing is that an investor does not pay more for an asset than it's worth. This statement may seem logical and obvious, but it is forgotten and rediscovered at some time in every generation and in every market. There are those who are disingenuous enough to argue that value is in the eye of the beholder, and that any price can be justified if there are other investors willing to pay that price. That is patently absurd. Perceptions may be all that matter when the asset is a painting or a sculpture, but investors do not (and should not) buy most assets for aesthetic or emotional reasons; financial assets are acquired for the cash flows expected on them. Consequently, perceptions of value have to be backed up by reality, which implies that the price that is paid for any asset should reflect the cashflows it is expected to generate. The models of valuation described in this book attempt to relate value to the level and expected growth of these cash flows.

There are many areas in valuation where there is room for disagreement, including how to estimate true value and how long it will take for prices to adjust to true value. But there is one point on which there can be no disagreement: Asset prices cannot be justified by merely using the argument that there will be other investors around willing to pay a higher price in the future.

GENERALITIES ABOUT VALUATION

Like all analytical disciplines, valuation has developed its own set of myths over time. This section examines and debunks some of these myths.

Myth 1: Since valuation models are quantitative, valuation is objective.

Valuation is neither the science that some of its proponents make it out to be nor the objective search for true value that idealists would like it to become. The models that we use in valuation may be quantitative, but the inputs leave plenty of room for subjective judgments. Thus, the final value that we obtain from these models is colored by the bias that we bring into the process. In fact, in many valuations, the price gets set first and the valuation follows.

The obvious solution is to eliminate all bias before starting on a valuation, but this is easier said than done. Given the exposure we have to external information, analyses, and opinions about a firm, it is unlikely that we embark on most valuations without some bias. There are two ways of reducing the bias in the process. The first is to avoid taking strong public positions on the value of a firm before the valuation is complete. In far too many cases, the decision on whether a firm is under- or overvalued precedes the actual valuation,[1] leading to seriously biased analyses. The second is to minimize, prior to the valuation, the stake we have in whether the firm is under- or overvalued.

Institutional concerns also play a role in determining the extent of bias in valuation. For instance, it is an acknowledged fact that equity research analysts are more likely to make buy rather than sell recommendations[2] (i.e., they are more likely to find firms to be undervalued than overvalued). This can be traced partly to the difficulties analysts face in obtaining access and collecting information on firms that they have issued sell recommendations on, and partly to pressure that they face from portfolio managers, some of whom might have large positions in the stock. In recent years, this trend has been exacerbated by the pressure on equity research analysts to deliver investment banking business.

When using a valuation done by a third party, the biases of the analyst(s) doing the valuation should be considered before decisions are made on its basis. For instance, a self-valuation done by a target firm in a takeover is likely to be positively biased. While this does not make the valuation worthless, it suggests that the analysis should be viewed with skepticism.

---

[1] This is most visible in takeovers, where the decision to acquire a firm often seems to precede the valuation of the firm. It should come as no surprise, therefore, that the analysis almost invariably supports the decision.

[2] In most years buy recommendations outnumber sell recommendations by a margin of 10 to 1. In recent years this trend has become even stronger.

BIAS IN EQUITY RESEARCH

The lines between equity research and salesmanship blur most in periods that are characterized by "irrational exuberance." In the late 1990s, the extraordinary surge of market values in the companies that comprised the new economy saw a large number of equity research analysts, especially on the sell side, step out of their roles as analysts and become cheerleaders for these stocks. While these analysts might have been well-meaning in their recommendations, the fact that the investment banks that they worked for were leading the charge on new initial public offerings from these firms exposed them to charges of bias and worse.

In 2001, the crash in the market values of new economy stocks and the anguished cries of investors who had lost wealth in the crash created a firestorm of controversy. There were congressional hearings where legislators demanded to know what analysts knew about the companies they recommended and when the knew it, statements from the SEC about the need for impartiality in equity research, and decisions taken by some investment banks to create at least the appearance of objectivity. At the time this book went to press, both Merrill Lynch and Credit Suisse First Boston (CSFB) had decided that their equity research analysts could no longer hold stock in companies that they covered. Unfortunately, the real source of bias—the intermingling of investment banking business and investment advice—was left untouched.

Should there be government regulation of equity research? It would not be wise, since regulation tends to be heavy-handed and creates side costs that seem quickly to exceed the benefits. A much more effective response can be delivered by portfolio managers and investors. The equity research of firms that create the potential for bias should be discounted or, in egregious cases, even ignored.

Myth 2: A well-researched and well-done valuation is timeless.

The value obtained from any valuation model is affected by firm-specific as well as marketwide information. As a consequence, the value will change as new information is revealed. Given the constant flow of information into financial markets, a valuation done on a firm ages quickly and has to be updated to reflect current information. This information may be specific to the firm, affect an entire sector, or alter expectations for all firms in the market.

The most common example of firm-specific information is an earnings report that not only contains news about a firm's performance in the most recent time period but, more importantly, about the business model that the firm has adopted. The dramatic drop in value of many new economy stocks from 1999 to 2001 can be traced, at least partially, to the realization that these firms had business models that might deliver customers but not earnings, even in the long term.

In some cases, new information can affect the valuations of all firms in a sector. Thus, pharmaceutical companies that were valued highly in early 1992, on the assumption that the high growth from the 1980s would continue into the future, were valued much less in early 1993, as the prospects of health reform and price controls dimmed future prospects. With the benefit of hindsight, the valuations of these companies (and the analyst recommendations) made in 1992 can be criticized, but they were reasonable given the information available at that time.

Finally, information about the state of the economy and the level of interest rates affects all valuations in an economy. A weakening in the economy can lead to a reassessment of growth rates across the board, though the effect on earnings is likely to be largest at cyclical firms. Similarly, an increase in interest rates will affect all investments, though to varying degrees.

When analysts change their valuations, they will undoubtedly be asked to justify them, and in some cases the fact that valuations change over time is viewed as a problem. The best response may be the one that John Maynard Keynes gave when he was criticized for changing his position on a major economic issue: "When the facts change, I change my mind. And what do you do, sir?"

Myth 3: A good valuation provides a precise estimate of value.

Even at the end of the most careful and detailed valuation, there will be uncertainty about the final numbers, colored as they are by assumptions that we make about the future of the company and the economy. It is unrealistic to expect or demand absolute certainty in valuation, since cash flows and discount rates are estimated. This also means that analysts have to give themselves a reasonable margin for error in making recommendations on the basis of valuations.

The degree of precision in valuations is likely to vary widely across investments. The valuation of a large and mature company with a long financial history will usually be much more precise than the valuation of a young company in a sector in turmoil. If this latter company happens to operate in an emerging market, with additional disagreement about the future of the market thrown into the mix, the uncertainty is magnified. Later in this book, in Chapter 23, we will argue that the difficulties associated with valuation can be related to where a firm is in the life cycle. Mature firms tend to be easier to value than growth firms, and young start-up companies are more difficult to value than companies with established products and markets. The problems are not with the valuation models we use, though, but with the difficulties we run into in making estimates for the future. Many investors and analysts use the uncertainty about the future or the absence of information to justify not doing full-fledged valuations. In reality, though, the payoff to valuation is greatest in these firms.

Myth 4: The more quantitative a model, the better the valuation.

It may seem obvious that making a model more complete and complex should yield better valuations; but it is not necessarily so. As models become more complex, the number of inputs needed to value a firm tends to increase, bringing with it the potential for input errors. These problems are compounded when models become so complex that they become "black boxes" where analysts feed in numbers at one end and valuations emerge from the other. All too often when a valuation fails, the blame gets attached to the model rather than the analyst. The refrain becomes "It was not my fault. The model did it."

There are three important points on all valuation. The first is the principle of parsimony, which essentially states that you do not use more inputs than you absolutely need to value an asset. The second is that there is a trade-off between the additional benefits of building in more detail and the estimation costs (and error) with providing the detail. The third is that the models don't value companies—*you* do. In a world where the problem that we often face in valuations is not too little information but too much, separating the information that matters from the information that does not is almost as important as the valuation models and techniques that you use to value a firm.

Myth 5: To make money on valuation, you have to assume that markets are inefficient.

Implicit in the act of valuation is the assumption that markets make mistakes and that we can find these mistakes, often using information that tens of thousands of other investors have access to. Thus, it seems reasonable to say that those who believe that markets are inefficient should spend their time and resources on valuation whereas those who believe that markets are efficient should take the market price as the best estimate of value.

This statement, though, does not reflect the internal contradictions in both positions. Those who believe that markets are efficient may still feel that valuation has something to contribute, especially when they are called on to value the effect of a change in the way a firm is run or to understand why market prices change over time. Furthermore, it is not clear how markets would become efficient in the first place if investors did not attempt to find under- and over-valued stocks and trade on these valuations. In other words, a precondition for market efficiency seems to be the existence of millions of investors who believe that markets are not efficient.

On the other hand, those who believe that markets make mistakes and buy or sell stocks on that basis must believe that ultimately markets will correct these mistakes (i.e., become efficient), because that is how they make their money. This is a fairly self-serving definition of inefficiency—markets are inefficient until you take a large position in the stock that you believe to be mispriced, but they become efficient after you take the position.

It is best to approach the issue of market efficiency as a wary skeptic. Recognize that on the one hand markets make mistakes but, on the other, finding these mistakes requires a combination of skill and luck. This view of markets leads to the following conclusions: First, if something looks too good to be true—a stock looks obviously undervalued or overvalued—it is probably *not* true. Second, when the value from an analysis is significantly different from the market price, start off with the presumption that the market is correct; then you have to convince yourself that this is not the case before you conclude that something is over- or undervalued. This higher standard may lead you to be more cautious in following through on valuations, but given the difficulty of beating the market, this is not an undesirable outcome.

Myth 6: The product of valuation (i.e., the value) is what matters; the process of valuation is not important.

As valuation models are introduced in this book, there is the risk of focusing exclusively on the outcome (i.e., the value of the company and whether it is under- or overvalued), and missing some valuable insights that can be obtained from the process of the valuation. The process can tell us a great deal about the determinants of value and help us answer some fundamental questions: What is the appropriate price to pay for high growth? What is a brand name worth? How important is it to improve returns on projects? What is the effect of profit margins on value? Since the process is so informative, even those who believe that markets are efficient (and that the market price is therefore the best estimate of value) should be able to find some use for valuation models.

THE ROLE OF VALUATION

Valuation is useful in a wide range of tasks. The role it plays, however, is different in different arenas. The following section lays out the relevance of valuation in portfolio management, in acquisition analysis, and in corporate finance.

Valuation in Portfolio Management

The role that valuation plays in portfolio management is determined in large part by the investment philosophy of the investor. Valuation plays a minimal role in portfolio management for a passive investor, whereas it plays a larger role for an active investor. Even among active investors, the nature and the role of valuation are different for different types of active investment. Market timers use valuation much less than investors who pick stocks for the long term, and their focus is on market valuation rather than on firm-specific valuation. Among security selectors, valuation plays a central role in portfolio management for fundamental analysts and a peripheral role for technical analysts.

Fundamental Analysts   The underlying theme in fundamental analysis is that the true value of the firm can be related to its financial characteristics—its growth prospects, risk profile, and cash flows. Any deviation from this true value is a sign that a stock is under- or overvalued. It is a long-term investment strategy, and the assumptions underlying it are:

■ The relationship between value and the underlying financial factors can be measured.
■ The relationship is stable over time.
■ Deviations from the relationship are corrected in a reasonable time period.

Valuation is the central focus in fundamental analysis. Some analysts use discounted cash flow models to value firms, while others use multiples such as the price-earnings and price–book value ratios. Since investors using this approach hold a large number of undervalued stocks in their portfolios, their hope is that, on average, these portfolios will do better than the market.

Franchise Buyer The philosophy of a franchise buyer is best expressed by an investor who has been very successful at it—Warren Buffett. "We try to stick to businesses we believe we understand," Mr. Buffett writes.[3] "That means they must be relatively simple and stable in character. If a business is complex and subject to constant change, we're not smart enough to predict future cash flows." Franchise buyers concentrate on a few businesses they understand well and attempt to acquire undervalued firms. Often, as in the case of Mr. Buffett, franchise buyers wield influence on the management of these firms and can change financial and investment policy. As a long-term strategy, the underlying assumptions are that:

- Investors who understand a business well are in a better position to value it correctly.
- These undervalued businesses can be acquired without driving the price above the true value.

Valuation plays a key role in this philosophy, since franchise buyers are attracted to a particular business because they believe it is undervalued. They are also interested in how much additional value they can create by restructuring the business and running it right.

Chartists Chartists believe that prices are driven as much by investor psychology as by any underlying financial variables. The information available from trading—price movements, trading volume, short sales and so forth—gives an indication of investor psychology and future price movements. The assumptions here are that prices move in predictable patterns, that there are not enough marginal investors taking advantage of these patterns to eliminate them, and that the average investor in the market is driven more by emotion than by rational analysis.

While valuation does not play much of a role in charting, there are ways in which an enterprising chartist can incorporate it into analysis. For instance, valuation can be used to determine support and resistance lines[4] on price charts.

Information Traders Prices move on information about the firm. Information traders attempt to trade in advance of new information or shortly after it is revealed to financial markets, buying on good news and selling on bad. The underlying assumption is that these traders can anticipate information announcements and gauge the market reaction to them better than the average investor in the market.

For an information trader, the focus is on the relationship between information

---

[3]This is extracted from Mr. Buffett's letter to stockholders in Berkshire Hathaway for 1993.
[4]On a chart, the support line usually refers to a lower bound below which prices are unlikely to move, and the resistance line refers to the upper bound above which prices are unlikely to venture. While these levels are usually estimated using past prices, the range of values obtained from a valuation model can be used to determine these levels (i.e., the maximum value will become the resistance line and the minimum value will become the support line).

and changes in value, rather than on value per se. Thus an information trader may buy stock in even an overvalued firm if he or she believes that the next information announcement is going to cause the price to go up because it contains better than expected news. If there is a relationship between how undervalued or overvalued a company is and how its stock price reacts to new information, then valuation could play a role in investing for an information trader.

Market Timers   Market timers note, with some legitimacy, that the payoff to calling turns in markets is much greater than the returns from stock picking. They argue that it is easier to predict market movements than to select stocks and that these predictions can be based on factors that are observable.

While valuation of individual stocks may not be of any use to a market timer, market timing strategies can use valuation in at least two ways:

1. The overall market itself can be valued and compared to the current level.
2. A valuation model can be used to value all stocks, and the results from the cross section can be used to determine whether the market is over- or undervalued. For example, as the number of stocks that are overvalued, using the dividend discount model, increases relative to the number that are undervalued, there may be reason to believe that the market is overvalued.

Efficient Marketers   Efficient marketers believe that the market price at any point in time represents the best estimate of the true value of the firm, and that any attempt to exploit perceived market efficiencies will cost more than it will make in excess profits. They assume that markets aggregate information quickly and accurately, that marginal investors promptly exploit any inefficiencies, and that any inefficiencies in the market are caused by friction, such as transactions costs, and cannot be arbitraged away.

For efficient marketers, valuation is a useful exercise to determine why a stock sells for the price that it does. Since the underlying assumption is that the market price is the best estimate of the true value of the company, the objective becomes determining what assumptions about growth and risk are implied in this market price, rather than on finding under- or overvalued firms.

Valuation in Acquisition Analysis

Valuation should play a central part in acquisition analysis. The bidding firm or individual has to decide on a fair value for the target firm before making a bid, and the target firm has to determine a reasonable value for itself before deciding to accept or reject the offer.

There are also special factors to consider in takeover valuation. First, the effects of synergy on the combined value of the two firms (target plus bidding firm) have to be considered before a decision is made on the bid. Those who suggest that synergy is impossible to value and should not be considered in quantitative terms are wrong. Second, the effects on value of changing management and restructuring the target firm will have to be taken into account in deciding on a fair price. This is of particular concern in hostile takeovers.

Finally, there is a significant problem with bias in takeover valuations. Target firms may be overly optimistic in estimating value, especially when the takeovers are hostile and they are trying to convince their stockholders that the offer prices are too low. Similarly, if the bidding firm has decided for strategic reasons to do an acquisition, there may be strong pressure on the analyst to come up with an estimate of value that backs up the acquisition.

Valuation in Corporate Finance

If the objective in corporate finance is the maximization of firm value,[5] the relationship between financial decisions, corporate strategy, and firm value has to be delineated. In recent years, management consulting firms have started offering companies advice on how to increase value.[6] Their suggestions have often provided the basis for the restructuring of these firms.

The value of a firm can be directly related to decisions that it makes—on which projects it takes, on how it finances them, and on its dividend policy. Understanding this relationship is key to making value-increasing decisions and to sensible financial restructuring.

CONCLUSION

Valuation plays a key role in many areas of finance—in corporate finance, in mergers and acquisitions, and in portfolio management. The models presented in this book will provide a range of tools that analysts in each of these areas will find of use, but the cautionary note sounded in this chapter bears repeating. Valuation is not an objective exercise, and any preconceptions and biases that an analyst brings to the process will find their way into the value.

QUESTIONS AND SHORT PROBLEMS

1. The value of an investment is:
   a. The present value of the cash flows on the investment.
   b. Determined by investor perceptions about it.
   c. Determined by demand and supply.
   d. Often a subjective estimate, colored by the bias of the analyst.
   e. All of the above.
2. There are many who claim that value is based on investor perceptions, and perceptions alone, and that cash flows and earnings do not matter. This argument is flawed because:
   a. Value is determined by earnings and cash flows, and investor perceptions do not matter.
   b. Perceptions do matter, but they can change. Value must be based on something more stable.

---

[5]Most corporate financial theory is constructed on this premise.
[6]The motivation for this has been the fear of hostile takeovers. Companies have increasingly turned to "value consultants" to tell them how to restructure, increase value, and avoid being taken over.

      c. Investors are irrational. Therefore, their perceptions should not determine value.

      d. Value is determined by investor perceptions, but it is also determined by the underlying earnings and cash flows. Perceptions must be based on reality.

3. You use a valuation model to arrive at a value of $15 for a stock. The market price of the stock is $25. The difference may be explained by:

      a. A market inefficiency; the market is overvaluing the stock.

      b. The use of the wrong valuation model to value the stock.

      c. Errors in the inputs to the valuation model.

      d. All of the above.

CHAPTER 2

Approaches to Valuation

Analysts use a wide range of models in practice, ranging from the simple to the sophisticated. These models often make very different assumptions, but they do share some common characteristics and can be classified in broader terms. There are several advantages to such a classification: It makes it easier to understand where individual models fit into the big picture, why they provide different results, and when they have fundamental errors in logic.

In general terms, there are three approaches to valuation. The first, discounted cash flow (DCF) valuation, relates the value of an asset to the present value (PV) of expected future cash flows on that asset. The second, relative valuation, estimates the value of an asset by looking at the pricing of comparable assets relative to a common variable such as earnings, cash flows, book value, or sales. The third, contingent claim valuation, uses option pricing models to measure the value of assets that share option characteristics. Some of these assets are traded financial assets like warrants, and some of these options are not traded and are based on real assets, (projects, patents, and oil reserves are examples). The latter are often called real options. There can be significant differences in outcomes, depending on which approach is used. One of the objectives in this book is to explain the reasons for such differences in value across different models, and to help in choosing the right model to use for a specific task.

DISCOUNTED CASH FLOW VALUATION

While discounted cash flow valuation is only one of the three ways of approaching valuation and most valuations done in the real world are relative valuations, it is the foundation on which all other valuation approaches are built. To do relative valuation correctly, we need to understand the fundamentals of discounted cash flow valuation. To apply option pricing models to value assets, we often have to begin with a discounted cash flow valuation. This is why so much of this book focuses on discounted cash flow valuation. Anyone who understands its fundamentals will be able to analyze and use the other approaches. This section will consider the basis of this approach, a philosophical rationale for discounted cash flow valuation, and an examination of the different subapproaches to discounted cash flow valuation.

Basis for Discounted Cash Flow Valuation

This approach has its foundation in the present value rule, where the value of any asset is the present value of expected future cash flows on it.

$$\text{Value} = \sum_{t=1}^{t=n} \frac{CF_t}{(1+r)^t}$$

where n = Life of the asset
CF_t = Cash flow in period t
r = Discount rate reflecting the riskiness of the estimated cash flows

The cash flows will vary from asset to asset—dividends for stocks, coupons (interest) and the face value for bonds, and after-tax cash flows for a real project. The discount rate will be a function of the riskiness of the estimated cash flows, with higher rates for riskier assets and lower rates for safer projects.

You can in fact think of discounted cash flow valuation on a continuum. At one end of the spectrum you have the default-free zero coupon bond, with a guaranteed cash flow in the future. Discounting this cash flow at the riskless rate should yield the value of the bond. A little further up the risk spectrum are corporate bonds where the cash flows take the form of coupons and there is default risk. These bonds can be valued by discounting the cash flows at an interest rate that reflects the default risk. Moving up the risk ladder, we get to equities, where there are expected cash flows with substantial uncertainty around the expectation. The value here should be the present value of the expected cash flows at a discount rate that reflects the uncertainty.

Underpinnings of Discounted Cash Flow Valuation

In discounted cash flow valuation, we try to estimate the intrinsic value of an asset based on its fundamentals. What is intrinsic value? For lack of a better definition, consider it the value that would be attached to the firm by an all-knowing analyst, who not only estimates the expected cash flows for the firm correctly but also attaches the right discount rate to these cash flows and values them with absolute precision. Hopeless though the task of estimating intrinsic value may seem to be, especially when valuing young companies with substantial uncertainty about the future, these estimates can be different from the market prices attached to these companies. In other words, markets make mistakes. Does that mean markets are inefficient? Not quite. While market prices can deviate from intrinsic value (estimated based on fundamentals), it is expected that the two will converge sooner rather than later.

Categorizing Discounted Cash Flow Models

There are literally thousands of discounted cash flow models in existence. Investment banks or consulting firms often claim that their valuation models are better or more sophisticated than those used by their contemporaries. Ultimately, however, discounted cash flow models can vary only a couple of dimensions.

Equity Valuation, Firm Valuation, and Adjusted Present Value (APV) Valuation   There are three paths to discounted cash flow valuation: The first is to value just the equity stake in the business; the second is to value the entire firm, which includes, besides equity, the other claimholders in the firm (bondholders, preferred stockholders, etc.); and the third is to value the firm in pieces, beginning with its

operations and adding the effects on value of debt and other nonequity claims. While all three approaches discount expected cash flows, the relevant cash flows and discount rates are different under each.

The value of equity is obtained by discounting expected cash flows to equity (i.e., the residual cash flows after meeting all expenses, reinvestment needs, tax obligations, and interest and principal payments) at the cost of equity (i.e., the rate of return required by equity investors in the firm).

$$\text{Value of equity} = \sum_{t=1}^{t=n} \frac{\text{CF to equity}_t}{(1+k_e)^t}$$

where   n = Life of the asset
     CF to equity$_t$ = Expected cash flow to equity in period t
         k_e = Cost of equity

The dividend discount model is a specialized case of equity valuation, where the value of equity is the present value of expected future dividends.

The value of the firm is obtained by discounting expected cash flows to the firm (i.e., the residual cash flows after meeting all operating expenses, reinvestment needs, and taxes, but prior to any payments to either debt or equity holders) at the weighted average cost of capital (WACC), which is the cost of the different components of financing used by the firm, weighted by their market value proportions.

$$\text{Value of firm} = \sum_{t=1}^{t=n} \frac{\text{CF to firm}_t}{(1+\text{WACC})^t}$$

where   n = Life of the asset
     CF to firm$_t$ = Expected cash flow to firm in period t
    WACC = Weighted average cost of capital

The value of the firm can also be obtained by valuing each claim on the firm separately. In this approach, which is called adjusted present value (APV), we begin by valuing equity in the firm, assuming that it was financed only with equity. We then consider the value added (or taken away) by debt by considering the present value (PV) of the tax benefits that flow from debt and the expected bankruptcy costs.

Value of firm = Value of all-equity-financed firm + PV of tax benefits
+ Expected bankruptcy costs

In fact, this approach can be generalized to allow different cash flows to the firm to be discounted at different rates, given their riskiness.

While the three approaches use different definitions of cash flow and discount rates, they will yield consistent estimates of value as long as you use the same set of assumptions in valuation. The key error to avoid is mismatching cash flows and discount rates, since discounting cash flows to equity at the cost of capital will lead to an upwardly biased estimate of the value of equity, while discounting cash flows to the firm at the cost of equity will yield a downwardly biased estimate of the value of the firm. Illustration 2.1 shows the equivalence of equity and firm valuation. In Chapter 15, we will show that adjusted present value models and firm valuation models also yield the same values.

ILLUSTRATION 2.1:   Effects of Mismatching Cash Flows and Discount Rates

---

Assume that you are analyzing a company with the following cash flows for the next five years. Assume also that the cost of equity is 13.625% and the firm can borrow long term at 10%. (The tax rate for the firm is 50%.) The current market value of equity is $1,073, and the value of debt outstanding is $800.

Year	Cash Flow to Equity	Interest (Long-Term)	Cash Flow to Firm
1	$50	$40	$90
2	$60	$40	$100
3	$68	$40	$108
4	$76.2	$40	$116.2
5	$83.49	$40	$123.49
Terminal value	$1603.008		$2363.008

The cost of equity is given as an input and is 13.625%, and the after-tax cost of debt is 5%.

$$\text{Cost of debt} = \text{Pretax rate}(1 - \text{Tax rate}) = 10\%(1 - .5) = 5\%$$

Given the market values of equity and debt, we can estimate the cost of capital.

$$\text{WACC} = \text{Cost of equity}[\text{Equity}/(\text{Debt} + \text{Equity})] + \text{Cost of debt}[\text{Debt}/(\text{Debt} + \text{Equity})]$$
$$= 13.625\%(1{,}073/1{,}873) + 5\%(800/1{,}873) = 9.94\%$$

METHOD 1: DISCOUNT CASH FLOWS TO EQUITY AT COST OF EQUITY TO GET VALUE OF EQUITY

We discount cash flows to equity at the cost of equity:

$$\text{PV of equity} = 50/1.13625 + 60/1.13625^2 + 68/1.13625^3 + 76.2/1.13625^4$$
$$+ (83.49 + \$1{,}603)/1.13625^5 = \$1{,}073$$

METHOD 2: DISCOUNT CASH FLOWS TO FIRM AT COST OF CAPITAL TO GET VALUE OF FIRM

$$\text{PV of firm} = 90/1.0994 + 100/1.0994^2 + 108/1.0994^3 + 116.2/1.0994^4$$
$$+ (123.49 + \$2{,}363)/1.0994^5 = \$1{,}873$$

$$\text{PV of equity} = \text{PV of firm} - \text{Market value of debt}$$
$$= \$1{,}873 - \$800 = \$1{,}073$$

Note that the value of equity is $1,073 under both approaches. It is easy to make the mistake of discounting cash flows to equity at the cost of capital or the cash flows to the firm at the cost of equity.

ERROR 1: DISCOUNT CASH FLOWS TO EQUITY AT COST OF CAPITAL TO GET TOO HIGH A VALUE FOR EQUITY

$$\text{PV of equity} = 50/1.0994 + 60/1.0994^2 + 68/1.0994^3 + 76.2/1.0994^4$$
$$+ (83.49 + \$1{,}603)/1.0994^5 = \$1{,}248$$

ERROR 2: DISCOUNT CASH FLOWS TO FIRM AT COST OF EQUITY TO GET TOO LOW A VALUE FOR THE FIRM

$$\text{PV of firm} = 90/1.13625 + 100/1.13625^2 + 108/1.13625^3 + 116.2/1.13625^4$$
$$+ (123.49 + \$2,363)/1.13625^5 = \$1,613$$

$$\text{PV of equity} = \text{PV of firm} - \text{Market value of debt}$$
$$= \$1,612.86 - \$800 = \$813$$

The effects of using the wrong discount rate are clearly visible in the last two calculations (Error 1 and Error 2). When the cost of capital is mistakenly used to discount the cash flows to equity, the value of equity increases by $175 over its true value ($1,073). When the cash flows to the firm are erroneously discounted at the cost of equity, the value of the firm is understated by $260. It must be pointed out, though, that getting the values of equity to agree with the firm and equity valuation approaches can be much more difficult in practice than in this example. We will return to this subject in Chapters 14 and 15 and consider the assumptions that we need to make to arrive at this result.

Total Cash Flow versus Excess Cash Flow Models   The conventional discounted cash flow model values an asset by estimating the present value of all cash flows generated by that asset at the appropriate discount rate. In excess return (and excess cash flow) models, only cash flows earned in excess of the required return are viewed as value creating, and the present value of these excess cash flows can be added to the amount invested in the asset to estimate its value. To illustrate, assume that you have an asset in which you invested $100 million and that you expect to generate $12 million in after-tax cash flows in perpetuity. Assume further that the cost of capital on this investment is 10 percent. With a total cash flow model, the value of this asset can be estimated as follows:

$$\text{Value of asset} = \$12 \text{ million} /.1 = \$120 \text{ million}$$

With an excess return model, we would first compute the excess return made on this asset:

$$\text{Excess return} = \text{Cash flow earned} - \text{Cost of capital} \times \text{Capital invested in asset}$$
$$= \$12 \text{ million} - .10 \times \$100 \text{ million} = \$2 \text{ million}$$

A SIMPLE TEST OF CASH FLOWS

There is a simple test that can be employed to determine whether the cash flows being used in a valuation are cash flows to equity or cash flows to the firm. If the cash flows that are being discounted are after interest expenses (and principal payments), they are cash flows to equity and the discount rate used should be the cost of equity. If the cash flows that are discounted are before interest expenses and principal payments, they are usually cash flows to the firm. Needless to say, there are other items that need to be considered when estimating these cash flows, and they will be considered in extensive detail in the coming chapters.

We then add the present value of these excess returns to the investment in the asset:

Value of asset = Present value of excess return + Investment in the asset
= $2 million / .1 + $100 million = $120 million

Note that the answers in the two approaches are equivalent. Why, then, would we want to use an excess return model? By focusing on excess returns, this model brings home the point that it is not earnings per se that create value, but earnings in excess of a required return. Chapter 32 will consider special versions of these excess return models such as Economic Value Added (EVA). As in this simple example, with consistent assumptions, total cash flow and excess return models are equivalent.

Applicability and Limitations of Discounted Cash Flow Valuation

Discounted cash flow valuation is based on expected future cash flows and discount rates. Given these informational requirements, this approach is easiest to use for assets (firms) whose cash flows are currently positive and can be estimated with some reliability for future periods, and where a proxy for risk that can be used to obtain discount rates is available. The further we get from this idealized setting, the more difficult discounted cash flow valuation becomes. Here are some scenarios where discounted cash flow valuation might run into trouble and need to be adapted.

Firms in Trouble   A distressed firm generally has negative earnings and cash flows and expects to lose money for some time in the future. For these firms, estimating future cash flows is difficult to do, since there is a strong probability of bankruptcy. For firms that are expected to fail, discounted cash flow valuation does not work very well, since the method values the firm as a going concern providing positive cash flows to its investors. Even for firms that are expected to survive, cash flows will have to be estimated until they turn positive, since obtaining a present value of negative cash flows will yield a negative value for equity[1] or for the firm.

Cyclical Firms   The earnings and cash flows of cyclical firms tend to follow the economy—rising during economic booms and falling during recessions. If discounted cash flow valuation is used on these firms, expected future cash flows are usually smoothed out, unless the analyst wants to undertake the onerous task of predicting the timing and duration of economic recessions and recoveries. In the depths of a recession many cyclical firms look like troubled firms, with negative earnings and cash flows. Estimating future cash flows then becomes entangled with analyst predictions about when the economy will turn and how strong the upturn will be, with more optimistic analysts arriving at higher estimates of value. This is

---

[1]The protection of limited liability should ensure that no stock will sell for less than zero. The price of such a stock can never be negative.

unavoidable, but the economic biases of the analysts have to be taken into account before using these valuations.

Firms with Unutilized Assets   Discounted cash flow valuation reflects the value of all assets that produce cash flows. If a firm has assets that are unutilized (and hence do not produce any cash flows), the value of these assets will not be reflected in the value obtained from discounting expected future cash flows. The same caveat applies, in lesser degree, to underutilized assets, since their value will be understated in discounted cash flow valuation. While this is a problem, it is not insurmountable. The value of these assets can always be obtained externally[2] and added to the value obtained from discounted cash flow valuation. Alternatively, the assets can be valued as though they are used optimally.

Firms with Patents or Product Options   Firms often have unutilized patents or licenses that do not produce any current cash flows and are not expected to produce cash flows in the near future, but nevertheless are valuable. If this is the case, the value obtained from discounting expected cash flows to the firm will understate the true value of the firm. Again, the problem can be overcome, in this case by valuing these assets in the open market or by using option pricing models, and then adding the value obtained from discounted cash flow valuation.

Firms in the Process of Restructuring   Firms in the process of restructuring often sell some of their assets, acquire other assets, and change their capital structure and dividend policy. Some of them also change their ownership structure (going from publicly traded to private status and vice versa) and management compensation schemes. Each of these changes makes estimating future cash flows more difficult and affects the riskiness of the firm. Using historical data for such firms can give a misleading picture of the firm's value. However, these firms can be valued, even in the light of the major changes in investment and financing policy, if future cash flows reflect the expected effects of these changes and the discount rate is adjusted to reflect the new business and financial risk in the firm.

Firms Involved in Acquisitions   There are at least two specific issues relating to acquisitions that need to be taken into account when using discounted cash flow valuation models to value target firms. The first is the thorny one of whether there is synergy in the merger and if its value can be estimated. It can be done, though it does require assumptions about the form the synergy will take and its effect on cash flows. The second, especially in hostile takeovers, is the effect of changing management on cash flows and risk. Again, the effect of the change can and should be incorporated into the estimates of future cash flows and discount rates and hence into value.

---

[2]If these assets are traded on external markets, the market prices of these assets can be used in the valuation. If not, the cash flows can be projected, assuming full utilization of assets, and the value can be estimated.

Private Firms   The biggest problem in using discounted cash flow valuation models to value private firms is the measurement of risk (to use in estimating discount rates), since most risk/return models require that risk parameters be estimated from historical prices on the asset being analyzed. Since securities in private firms are not traded, this is not possible. One solution is to look at the riskiness of comparable firms that are publicly traded. The other is to relate the measure of risk to accounting variables, which are available for the private firm.

The point is not that discounted cash flow valuation cannot be done in these cases, but that we have to be flexible enough to deal with them. The fact is that valuation is simple for firms with well-defined assets that generate cash flows that can be easily forecasted. The real challenge in valuation is to extend the valuation framework to cover firms that vary to some extent or the other from this idealized framework. Much of this book is spent considering how to value such firms.

RELATIVE VALUATION

While we tend to focus most on discounted cash flow valuation when discussing valuation, the reality is that most valuations are relative valuations. The value of most assets, from the house you buy to the stocks you invest in, are based on how similar assets are priced in the marketplace. This section begins with a basis for relative valuation, moves on to consider the underpinnings of the model, and then considers common variants within relative valuation.

Basis for Relative Valuation

In relative valuation, the value of an asset is derived from the pricing of comparable assets, standardized using a common variable such as earnings, cash flows, book value, or revenues. One illustration of this approach is the use of an industry-average price-earnings ratio to value a firm, the assumption being that the other firms in the industry are comparable to the firm being valued and that the market, on average, prices these firms correctly. Another multiple in wide use is the price–book value ratio, with firms selling at a discount on book value relative to comparable firms being considered undervalued. The multiple of price to sales is also used to value firms, with the average price-sales ratios of firms with similar characteristics being used for comparison. While these three multiples are among the most widely used, there are others that also play a role in analysis—price to cash flows, price to dividends, and market value to replacement value (Tobin's Q), to name a few.

Underpinnings of Relative Valuation

Unlike discounted cash flow valuation, which is a search for intrinsic value, relative valuation relies much more on the market. In other words, we assume that the market is correct in the way it prices stocks on average, but that it makes errors on the pricing of individual stocks. We also assume that a comparison of multiples will allow us to identify these errors, and that these errors will be corrected over time.

The assumption that markets correct their mistakes over time is common to both discounted cash flow and relative valuation, but those who use multiples and comparables to pick stocks argue, with some basis, that errors made in pricing individual stocks in a sector are more noticeable and more likely to be corrected quickly. For instance, they would argue that a software firm that trades at a price-earnings ratio of 10 when the rest of the sector trades at 25 times earnings is clearly undervalued and that the correction toward the sector average should occur sooner rather than later. Proponents of discounted cash flow valuation would counter that this is small consolation if the entire sector is overpriced by 50 percent.

Categorizing Relative Valuation Models

Analysts and investors are endlessly inventive when it comes to using relative valuation. Some compare multiples across companies, while other compare the multiple of a company to the multiples it used to trade at in the past. While most relative valuations are based on comparables, there are some relative valuations that are based on fundamentals.

Fundamentals versus Comparables   In discounted cash flow valuation, the value of a firm is determined by its expected cash flows. Other things remaining equal, higher cash flows, lower risk, and higher growth should yield higher value. Some analysts who use multiples go back to these discounted cash flow models to extract multiples. Other analysts compare multiples across firms or time and make explicit or implicit assumptions about how firms are similar or vary on fundamentals.

Using Fundamentals   The first approach relates multiples to fundamentals about the firm being valued—growth rates in earnings and cash flows, payout ratios and risk. This approach to estimating multiples is equivalent to using discounted cash flow models, requiring the same information and yielding the same results. Its primary advantage is that it shows the relationship between multiples and firm characteristics, and allows us to explore how multiples change as these characteristics change. For instance, what will be the effect of changing profit margins on the price-sales ratio? What will happen to price-earnings ratios as growth rates decrease? What is the relationship between price–book value ratios and return on equity?

Using Comparables   The more common approach to using multiples is to compare how a firm is valued with how similar firms are priced by the market or, in some cases, with how the firm was valued in prior periods. As we will see in the later chapters, finding similar and comparable firms is often a challenge, and frequently we have to accept firms that are different from the firm being valued on one dimension or the other. When this is the case, we have to either explicitly or implicitly control for differences across firms on growth, risk, and cash flow measures. In practice, controlling for these variables can range from the naive (using industry averages) to the sophisticated (multivariate regression models where the relevant variables are identified and controlled for).

Cross-Sectional versus Time Series Comparisons In most cases, analysts price stocks on a relative basis by comparing the multiples they are trading at to the multiples at which other firms in the same business are trading at. In some cases, however, especially for mature firms with long histories, the comparison is done across time.

Cross-Sectional Comparisons When we compare the price-earnings ratio of a software firm to the average price-earnings ratio of other software firms, we are doing relative valuation and we are making cross-sectional comparisons. The conclusions can vary depending on our assumptions about the firm being valued and the comparable firms. For instance, if we assume that the firm we are valuing is similar to the average firm in the industry, we would conclude that it is cheap if it trades at a multiple that is lower than the average multiple. If, however, we assume that the firm being valued is riskier than the average firm in the industry, we might conclude that the firm should trade at a lower multiple than other firms in the business. In short, you cannot compare firms without making assumptions about their fundamentals.

Comparisons across Time If you have a mature firm with a long history, you can compare the multiple it trades at today to the multiple it used to trade at in the past. Thus, Ford Motor Company may be viewed as cheap because it trades at six times earnings, if it has historically traded at 10 times earnings. To make this comparison, however, you have to assume that your firm's fundamentals have not changed over time. For instance, you would expect a high-growth firm's price-earnings ratio to drop over time and its expected growth rate to decrease as it becomes larger. Comparing multiples across time can also be complicated by changes in interest rates and the behavior of the overall market. For instance, as interest rates fall below historical norms and the overall market increases in value, you would expect most companies to trade at much higher multiples of earnings and book value than they have historically.

Applicability and Limitations of Multiples

The allure of multiples is that they are simple and easy to relate to. They can be used to obtain estimates of value quickly for firms and assets, and are particularly useful when a large number of comparable firms are being traded on financial markets, and the market is, on average, pricing these firms correctly. They tend to be more difficult to use to value unique firms with no obvious comparables, with little or no revenues, and with negative earnings.

By the same token, multiples are also easy to misuse and manipulate, especially when comparable firms are used. Given that no two firms are exactly alike in terms of risk and growth, the definition of comparable firms is a subjective one. Consequently, a biased analyst can choose a group of comparable firms to confirm his or her biases about a firm's value. Illustration 2.2 shows an example. While this potential for bias exists with discounted cash flow valuation as well, the analyst in DCF valuation is forced to be much more explicit about the assumptions that determine the final value. With multiples, these assumptions are often left unstated.

ASSET-BASED VALUATION MODELS

There are some analysts who add a fourth approach to valuation to the three described in this chapter. They argue that you can value the individual assets owned by a firm and aggregate them to arrive at a firm value—asset-based valuation models. In fact, there are several variants on asset-based valuation models. The first is liquidation value, which is obtained by aggregating the estimated sale proceeds of the assets owned by a firm. The second is replacement cost, where you estimate what it would cost you to replace all of the assets that a firm has today.

While analysts may use asset-based valuation approaches to estimate value, they are not alternatives to discounted cash flow, relative, or option pricing models since both replacement and liquidation values have to be obtained using one or another of these approaches. Ultimately, all valuation models attempt to value assets; the differences arise in how we identify the assets and how we attach value to each asset. In liquidation valuation, we look only at assets in place and estimate their value based on what similar assets are priced at in the market. In traditional discounted cash flow valuation, we consider all assets and include expected growth potential to arrive at value. The two approaches may, in fact, yield the same values if you have a firm that has no growth assets and the market assessments of value reflect expected cash flows.

ILLUSTRATION 2.2: The Potential for Misuse with Comparable Firms

Assume that an analyst is valuing an initial public offering (IPO) of a firm that manufactures computer software. At the same time,[3] the price-earnings multiples of other publicly traded firms manufacturing software are:

Firm	Multiple
Adobe Systems	23.2
Autodesk	20.4
Broderbund	32.8
Computer Associates	18.0
Lotus Development	24.1
Microsoft	27.4
Novell	30.0
Oracle	37.8
Software Publishing	10.6
System Software	15.7
Average PE ratio	*24.0*

While the average PE ratio using the entire sample is 24, it can be changed markedly by removing a couple of firms in the group. For instance, if the two firms with the lowest PE ratios in the group (Software Publishing and System Software) are eliminated from the sample, the average PE ratio increases to 27. If the two firms with the highest PE ratios in the group (Broderbund and Oracle) are removed from the group, the average PE ratio drops to 21.

---

[3]These were the PE ratios for these firms at the end of 1992.

The other problem with using multiples based on comparable firms is that it builds in errors (overvaluation or undervaluation) that the market might be making in valuing these firms. In Illustration 2.2, for instance, if the market has overvalued all computer software firms, using the average PE ratio of these firms to value an initial public offering will lead to an overvaluation of the IPO stock. In contrast, discounted cash flow valuation is based on firm-specific growth rates and cash flows, so it is less likely to be influenced by market errors in valuation.

CONTINGENT CLAIM VALUATION

Perhaps the most significant and revolutionary development in valuation is the acceptance, at least in some cases, that the value of an asset may be greater than the present value of expected cash flows if the cash flows are contingent on the occurrence or nonoccurrence of an event. This acceptance has largely come about because of the development of option pricing models. While these models were initially used to value traded options, there has been an attempt in recent years to extend the reach of these models into more traditional valuation. There are many who argue that assets such as patents or undeveloped reserves are really options and should be valued as such, rather than with traditional discounted cash flow models.

Basis for Approach

A contingent claim or option is a claim that pays off only under certain contingencies—if the value of the underlying asset exceeds a prespecified value for a call option or is less than a prespecified value for a put option. Much work has been done in the past 20 years in developing models that value options, and these option pricing models can be used to value any assets that have optionlike features.

Figure 2.1 illustrates the payoffs on call and put options as a function of the value of the underlying asset. An option can be valued as a function of the following variables: the current value and the variance in value of the underlying asset, the strike price and the time to expiration of the option, and the riskless interest

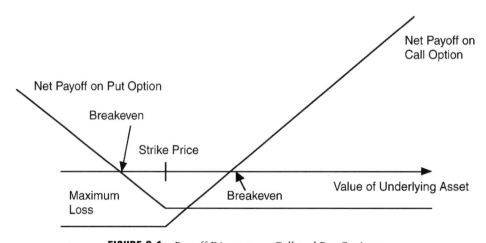

FIGURE 2.1 Payoff Diagram on Call and Put Options

rate. This was first established by Fischer Black and Myron Scholes in 1972 and has been extended and refined subsequently in numerous variants. While the Black-Scholes option pricing model ignored dividends and assumed that options would not be exercised early, it can be modified to allow for both. A discrete-time variant, the binomial option pricing model, has also been developed to price options.

An asset can be valued as an option if the payoffs are a function of the value of an underlying asset. It can be valued as a call option if when that value exceeds a prespecified level the asset is worth the difference. It can be valued as a put option if it gains value as the value of the underlying asset drops below a prespecified level, and if it is worth nothing when the underlying asset's value exceeds that specified level.

Underpinnings of Contingent Claim Valuation

The fundamental premise behind the use of option pricing models is that discounted cash flow models tend to understate the value of assets that provide payoffs that are contingent on the occurrence of an event. As a simple example, consider an undeveloped oil reserve belonging to Exxon. You could value this reserve based on expectations of oil prices in the future, but this estimate would miss the fact that the oil company will develop this reserve only if oil prices go up and will not if oil prices decline. An option pricing model would yield a value that incorporates this right.

When we use option pricing models to value assets such as patents and undeveloped natural resource reserves, we are assuming that markets are sophisticated enough to recognize such options and incorporate them into the market price. If the markets do not do so, we assume that they will eventually; the payoff to using such models comes about when this correction occurs.

Categorizing Option Pricing Models

The first categorization of options is based on whether the underlying asset is a financial asset or a real asset. Most listed options, whether they be options listed on the Chicago Board Options Exchange or callable fixed income securities, are on financial assets such as stocks and bonds. In contrast, options can be on real assets such as commodities, real estate, or even investment projects; such options are often called real options.

A second and overlapping categorization is based on whether the underlying asset is traded. The overlap occurs because most financial assets are traded, whereas relatively few real assets are traded. Options on traded assets are generally easier to value, and the inputs to the option pricing models can be obtained from financial markets. Options on nontraded assets are much more difficult to value since there are no market inputs available on the underlying assets.

Applicability and Limitations of Option Pricing Models

There are several direct examples of securities that are options—LEAPS, which are long-term equity options on trades stocks; contingent value rights, which provide protection to stockholders in companies against stock price declines; and warrants, which are long-term call options issued by firms.

There are other assets that generally are not viewed as options but still share several option characteristics. Equity, for instance, can be viewed as a call option on the value of the underlying firm, with the face value of debt representing the strike price and the term of the debt measuring the life of the option. A patent can be analyzed as a call option on a product, with the investment outlay needed to get the project going considered the strike price and the patent life becoming the time to expiration of the option.

There are limitations in using option pricing models to value long-term options on nontraded assets. The assumptions made about constant variance and dividend yields, which are not seriously contested for short-term options, are much more difficult to defend when options have long lifetimes. When the underlying asset is not traded, the inputs for the value of the underlying asset and the variance in that value cannot be extracted from financial markets and have to be estimated. Thus the final values obtained from these applications of option pricing models have much more estimation error associated with them than the values obtained in their more standard applications (to value short-term traded options).

CONCLUSION

There are three basic, though not mutually exclusive, approaches to valuation. The first is discounted cash flow valuation, where cash flows are discounted at a risk-adjusted discount rate to arrive at an estimate of value. The analysis can be done purely from the perspective of equity investors by discounting expected cash flows to equity at the cost of equity, or it can be done from the viewpoint of all claimholders in the firm, by discounting expected cash flows to the firm at the weighted average cost of capital. The second is relative valuation, where the value of the equity in a firm is based on the pricing of comparable firms relative to earnings, cash flows, book value, or sales. The third is contingent claim valuation, where an asset with the characteristics of an option is valued using an option pricing model. There should be a place for each among the tools available to any analyst interested in valuation.

QUESTIONS AND SHORT PROBLEMS

1. Discounted cash flow valuation is based on the notion that the value of an asset is the present value of the expected cash flows on that asset, discounted at a rate that reflects the riskiness of those cash flows. Specify whether the following statements about discounted cash flow valuation are true or false, assuming that all variables are constant except for the one mentioned:
   a. As the discount rate increases, the value of an asset increases.
      True _____ False _____
   b. As the expected growth rate in cash flows increases, the value of an asset increases.
      True _____ False _____
   c. As the life of an asset is lengthened, the value of that asset increases.
      True _____ False _____
   d. As the uncertainty about the expected cash flow increases, the value of an asset increases.
      True _____ False _____

    e. An asset with an infinite life (i.e., it is expected to last forever) will have an infinite value.

        True _____ False _____

2. Why might discounted cash flow valuation be difficult to do for the following types of firms?

    a. A private firm, where the owner is planning to sell the firm.

    b. A biotechnology firm with no current products or sales, but with several promising product patents in the pipeline.

    c. A cyclical firm during a recession.

    d. A troubled firm that has made significant losses and is not expected to get out of trouble for a few years.

    e. A firm that is in the process of restructuring, where it is selling some of its assets and changing its financial mix.

    f. A firm that owns a lot of valuable land that is currently unutilized.

3. The following are the projected cash flows to equity and to the firm over the next five years:

Year	CF to Equity	Int $(1 - t)$	CF to Firm
1	$250.00	$90.00	$340.00
2	$262.50	$94.50	$357.00
3	$275.63	$99.23	$374.85
4	$289.41	$104.19	$393.59
5	$303.88	$109.40	$413.27
Terminal value	$3,946.50		$6,000.00

    (The terminal value is the value of the equity or firm at the end of year 5.)

    The firm has a cost of equity of 12% and a cost of capital of 9.94%. Answer the following questions:

    a. What is the value of the equity in this firm?

    b. What is the value of the firm?

4. You are estimating the price-earnings multiple to use to value Paramount Corporation by looking at the average price-earnings multiple of comparable firms. The following are the price-earnings ratios of firms in the entertainment business.

Firm	PE Ratio
Disney (Walt)	22.09
Time Warner	36.00
King World Productions	14.10
New Line Cinema	26.70

    a. What is the average PE ratio?

    b. Would you use all the comparable firms in calculating the average? Why or why not?

    c. What assumptions are you making when you use the industry-average PE ratio to value Paramount Corporation?

CHAPTER 3

Understanding Financial Statements

Financial statements provide the fundamental information that we use to analyze and answer valuation questions. It is important, therefore, that we understand the principles governing these statements by looking at four questions:

1. How valuable are the assets of a firm? The assets of a firm can come in several forms—assets with long lives such as land and buildings, assets with shorter lives such as inventory, and intangible assets that nevertheless produce revenues for the firm such as patents and trademarks.
2. How did the firm raise the funds to finance these assets? In acquiring assets, firms can use the funds of the owners (equity) or borrowed money (debt), and the mix is likely to change as the assets age.
3. How profitable are these assets? A good investment is one that makes a return greater than the cost of funding it. To evaluate whether the investments that a firm has already made are good investments, we need to estimate what returns these investments are producing.
4. How much uncertainty (or risk) is embedded in these assets? While we have not yet directly confronted the issue of risk, estimating how much uncertainty there is in existing investments, and the implications for a firm, is clearly a first step.

This chapter will look at the way accountants would answer these questions, and why the answers might be different when doing valuation. Some of these differences can be traced to the differences in objectives: Accountants try to measure the current standing and immediate past performance of a firm, whereas valuation is much more forward-looking.

THE BASIC ACCOUNTING STATEMENTS

There are three basic accounting statements that summarize information about a firm. The first is the balance sheet, shown in Figure 3.1, which summarizes the assets owned by a firm, the value of these assets, and the mix of financing (debt and equity) used to finance these assets at a point in time.

The next is the income statement, shown in Figure 3.2, which provides information on the revenues and expenses of the firm, and the resulting income made by the firm, during a period. The period can be a quarter (if it is a quarterly income statement) or a year (if it is an annual report).

Finally, there is the statement of cash flows, shown in Figure 3.3, which speci-

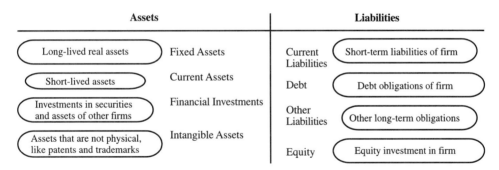

FIGURE 3.1 The Balance Sheet

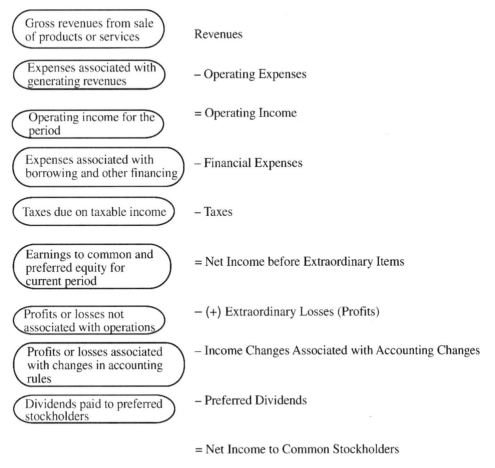

FIGURE 3.2 Income Statement

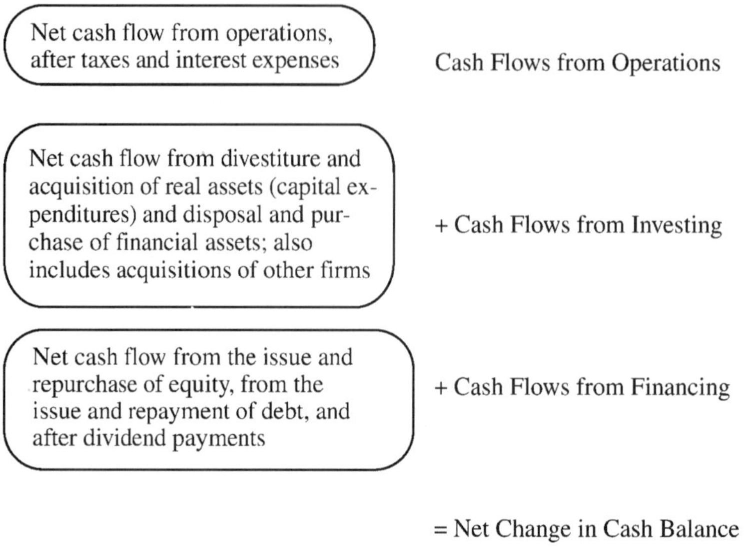

Net cash flow from operations, after taxes and interest expenses	Cash Flows from Operations
Net cash flow from divestiture and acquisition of real assets (capital expenditures) and disposal and purchase of financial assets; also includes acquisitions of other firms	+ Cash Flows from Investing
Net cash flow from the issue and repurchase of equity, from the issue and repayment of debt, and after dividend payments	+ Cash Flows from Financing

= Net Change in Cash Balance

FIGURE 3.3   Statement of Cash Flows

fies the sources and uses of cash to the firm from operating, investing, and financing activities during a period. The statement of cash flows can be viewed as an attempt to explain what the cash flows during a period were, and why the cash balance changed during the period.

ASSET MEASUREMENT AND VALUATION

When analyzing any firm, we would like to know the types of assets that it owns, the value of these assets, and the degree of uncertainty about this value. Accounting statements do a reasonably good job of categorizing the assets owned by a firm, a partial job of assessing the value of these assets, and a poor job of reporting uncertainty about asset value. This section will begin by looking at the accounting principles underlying asset categorization and measurement, and the limitations of financial statements in providing relevant information about assets.

Accounting Principles Underlying Asset Measurement

An asset is any resource that has the potential either to generate future cash inflows or to reduce future cash outflows. While that is a general definition broad enough to cover almost any kind of asset, accountants add a caveat that for a resource to be an asset a firm has to have acquired it in a prior transaction and be able to quantify future benefits with reasonable precision. The accounting view of asset value is to a great extent grounded in the notion of historical cost, which is the original cost of the asset, adjusted upward for improvements made to the asset since purchase and downward for the loss in value associated with the aging of the asset. This historical cost is called the book value. While the generally accepted accounting principles (GAAP) for valuing an asset vary across different kinds of assets, three principles underlie the way assets are valued in accounting statements:

1. *An abiding belief in book value as the best estimate of value.* Accounting estimates of asset value begin with the book value, and unless a substantial reason is given to do otherwise, accountants view the historical cost as the best estimate of the value of an asset.

2. *A distrust of market or estimated value.* When a current market value exists for an asset that is different from the book value, accounting convention seems to view this market value with suspicion. The market price of an asset is often viewed as both much too volatile and too easily manipulated to be used as an estimate of value for an asset. This suspicion runs even deeper when a value is estimated for an asset based on expected future cash flows.

3. *A preference for underestimating value rather than overestimating it.* When there is more than one approach to valuing an asset, accounting convention takes the view that the more conservative (lower) estimate of value should be used rather than the less conservative (higher) estimate of value. Thus, when both market and book value are available for an asset, accounting rules often require that you use the lesser of the two numbers.

Measuring Asset Value

The financial statement in which accountants summarize and report asset value is the balance sheet. To examine how asset value is measured, let us begin with the way assets are categorized in the balance sheet. First there are the fixed assets, which include the long-term assets of the firm, such as plant, equipment, land, and buildings. Next, we have the short-term assets of the firm, including inventory (raw materials, work in progress, and finished goods, receivables (summarizing moneys owed to the firm), and cash; these are categorized as current assets. We then have investments in the assets and securities of other firms, which are generally categorized as **financial investments**. Finally, we have what is loosely categorized as intangible assets. These include not only assets such as patents and trademarks that presumably will create future earnings and cash flows, but also uniquely accounting assets such as goodwill that arise because of acquisitions made by the firm.

Fixed Assets Generally accepted accounting principles (GAAP) in the United States require the valuation of fixed assets at historical cost, adjusted for any estimated loss in value from the aging of these assets. While in theory the adjustments for aging should reflect the loss of earning power of the asset as it ages, in practice they are much more a product of accounting rules and convention, and these adjustments are called depreciation. Depreciation methods can very broadly be categorized into straight line (where the loss in asset value is assumed to be the same every year over its lifetime) and accelerated (where the asset loses more value in the earlier years and less in the later years). While tax rules, at least in the United States, have restricted the freedom that firms have on their choices of asset life and depreciation methods, firms continue to have a significant amount of flexibility on these decisions for reporting purposes. Thus, the depreciation that is reported in the annual reports may not be, and generally is not, the same depreciation that is used in the tax statements.

Since fixed assets are valued at book value and are adjusted for depreciation provisions, the value of a fixed asset is strongly influenced by both its depreciable life and the depreciation method used. Many firms in the United States use straight-line depreciation for financial reporting while using accelerated depreciation for tax purposes, since firms can report better earnings with the former, at least in the years right after the asset is acquired.[1] In contrast, Japanese and German firms often use accelerated depreciation for both tax and financial reporting purposes, leading to reported income that is understated relative to that of their U.S. counterparts.

Current Assets   Current assets include inventory, cash, and accounts receivable. It is in this category that accountants are most amenable to the use of market value, especially in valuing marketable securities.

Accounts Receivable   Accounts receivable represent money owed by entities to the firm on the sale of products on credit. When the Home Depot sells products to building contractors and gives them a few weeks to make their payments, it is creating accounts receivable. The accounting convention is for accounts receivable to be recorded as the amount owed to the firm based on the billing at the time of the credit sale. The only major valuation and accounting issue is when the firm has to recognize accounts receivable that are not collectible. Firms can set aside a portion of their income to cover expected bad debts from credit sales, and accounts receivable will be reduced by this reserve. Alternatively, the bad debts can be recognized as they occur, and the firm can reduce the accounts receivable accordingly. There is the danger, however, that absent a decisive declaration of a bad debt, firms may continue to show as accounts receivable amounts that they know are unlikely ever to be collected.

Cash   Cash is one of the few assets for which accountants and financial analysts should agree on value. The value of a cash balance should not be open to estimation error. Having said this, we should note that fewer and fewer companies actually hold cash in the conventional sense (as currency or as demand deposits in banks). Firms often invest the cash in interest-bearing accounts or in Treasuries so as to earn a return on their investments. In either case, market value can deviate from book value, especially if the investments are long-term. While there is no real default risk in either of these investments, interest rate movements can affect their value. The valuation of marketable securities will be examined later in this section.

Inventory   Three basis approaches to valuing inventory are allowed by GAAP: first in, first out (FIFO), last in, first out (LIFO), and weighted average.

1. *First in, first out (FIFO).* Under FIFO, the cost of goods sold is based on the cost of material bought earliest in the period, while the cost of inventory is based on the cost of material bought later in the year. This results in inventory being valued close to current replacement cost. During periods of inflation, the use of FIFO will result in the lowest estimate of cost of goods sold among the three valuation approaches, and the highest net income.

---

[1]Depreciation is treated as an accounting expense. Hence, the use of straight-line depreciation (which is lower than accelerated depreciation in the first few years after an asset is acquired) will result in lower expenses and higher income.

2. *Last in, first out (LIFO)*. Under LIFO, the cost of goods sold is based on the cost of material bought toward the end of the period, resulting in costs that closely approximate current costs. The inventory, however, is valued on the basis of the cost of materials bought earlier in the year. During periods of inflation, the use of LIFO will result in the highest estimate of cost of goods sold among the three approaches, and the lowest net income.

3. *Weighted average*. Under the weighted average approach, both inventory and the cost of goods sold are based on the average cost of all material bought during the period. When inventory turns over rapidly, this approach will more closely resemble FIFO than LIFO.

Firms often adopt the LIFO approach for its tax benefits during periods of high inflation. The cost of goods sold is then higher because it is based on prices paid toward to the end of the accounting period. This, in turn, will reduce the reported taxable income and net income while increasing cash flows. Studies indicate that larger firms with rising prices for raw materials and labor, more variable inventory growth, and an absence of other tax loss carryforwards are much more likely to adopt the LIFO approach.

Given the income and cash flow effects of inventory valuation methods, it is often difficult to compare the profitability of firms that use different methods. There is, however, one way of adjusting for these differences. Firms that choose the LIFO approach to value inventories have to specify in a footnote the difference in inventory valuation between FIFO and LIFO, and this difference is termed the LIFO reserve. It can be used to adjust the beginning and ending inventories, and consequently the cost of goods sold, and to restate income based on FIFO valuation.

Investments (Financial) and Marketable Securities In the category of investments and marketable securities, accountants consider investments made by firms in the securities or assets of other firms, as well as other marketable securities including Treasury bills or bonds. The way in which these assets are valued depends on the way the investment is categorized and the motive behind the investment. In general, an investment in the securities of another firm can be categorized as a *minority passive investment*, a *minority active investment*, or a *majority active investment*, and the accounting rules vary depending on the categorization.

Minority Passive Investments If the securities or assets owned in another firm represent less than 20 percent of the overall ownership of that firm, an investment is treated as a minority passive investment. These investments have an acquisition value, which represents what the firm originally paid for the securities, and often a market value. Accounting principles require that these assets be subcategorized into one of three groups—investments that will be held to maturity, investments that are available for sale, and trading investments. The valuation principles vary for each.

■ For an investment that will be held to maturity, the valuation is at historical cost or book value, and interest or dividends from this investment are shown in the income statement.

■ For an investment that is available for sale, the valuation is at market value, but the unrealized gains or losses are shown as part of the equity in the balance sheet and not in the income statement. Thus, unrealized losses reduce the book value of the equity in the firm, and unrealized gains increase the book value of equity.

■ For a trading investment, the valuation is at market value, and the unrealized gains and losses are shown in the income statement.

Firms are allowed an element of discretion in the way they classify investments and, subsequently, in the way they value these assets. This classification ensures that firms such as investment banks, whose assets are primarily securities held in other firms for purposes of trading, revalue the bulk of these assets at market levels each period. This is called marking to market, and provides one of the few instances in which market value trumps book value in accounting statements.

Minority Active Investments   If the securities or assets owned in another firm represent between 20 percent and 50 percent of the overall ownership of that firm, an investment is treated as a minority active investment. While these investments have an initial acquisition value, a proportional share (based on ownership proportion) of the net income and losses made by the firm in which the investment was made is used to adjust the acquisition cost. In addition, the dividends received from the investment reduce the acquisition cost. This approach to valuing investments is called the equity approach.

The market value of these investments is not considered until the investment is liquidated, at which point the gain or loss from the sale relative to the adjusted acquisition cost is shown as part of the earnings in that period.

Majority Active Investments   If the securities or assets owned in another firm represent more than 50 percent of the overall ownership of that firm, an investment is treated as a majority active investment. In this case, the investment is no longer shown as a financial investment but is instead replaced by the assets and liabilities of the firm in which the investment was made. This approach leads to a consolidation of the balance sheets of the two firms, where the assets and liabilities of the two firms are merged and presented as one balance sheet.[2] The share of the equity that is owned by other investors is shown as a minority interest on the liability side of the balance sheet. A similar consolidation occurs in the other financial statements of the firm as well, with the statement of cash flows reflecting the cumulated cash inflows and outflows of the combined firm. This is in contrast to the equity approach used for minority active investments, in which only the dividends received on the investment are shown as a cash inflow in the cash flow statement.

Here again, the market value of this investment is not considered until the ownership stake is liquidated. At that point, the difference between the market price and the net value of the equity stake in the firm is treated as a gain or loss for the period.

---

[2]Firms have evaded the requirements of consolidation by keeping their share of ownership in other firms below 50 percent.

Intangible Assets Intangible assets include a wide array of assets ranging from patents and trademarks to goodwill. The accounting standards vary across intangible assets.

Patents and Trademarks Patents and trademarks are valued differently depending on whether they are generated internally or acquired. When patents and trademarks are generated from internal research, the costs incurred in developing the asset are expensed in that period, even though the asset might have a life of several accounting periods. Thus, the intangible asset is not valued in the balance sheet of the firm. In contrast, when an intangible asset is acquired from an external party, it is treated as an asset.

Intangible assets have to be amortized over their expected lives, with a maximum amortization period of 40 years. The standard practice is to use straight-line amortization. For tax purposes, however, firms are generally not allowed to amortize goodwill or other intangible assets with no specific lifetime, though recent changes in the tax law allow for some flexibility in this regard.

Goodwill Intangible assets are sometimes the by-products of acquisitions. When a firm acquires another firm, the purchase price is first allocated to tangible assets, and the excess price is then allocated to any intangible assets such as patents or trade names. Any residual becomes goodwill. While accounting principles suggest that goodwill captures the value of any intangibles that are not specifically identifiable, it is really a reflection of the difference between the book value of assets and the market value of the firm owning the assets. This approach is called purchase accounting, and it creates an intangible asset (goodwill) that is amortized over time. Until 2000, firms that did not want to see this charge against their earnings often used an alternative approach called pooling accounting, in which the purchase price never shows up in the balance sheet. Instead, the book values of the two companies involved in the merger were aggregated to create the consolidated balance of the combined firm.[3]

ILLUSTRATION 3.1: Asset Values for Boeing and the Home Depot

The following table summarizes asset values, as measured in the balance sheets of Boeing, the aerospace giant, and the Home Depot, a building supplies retailer, at the end of the 1998 financial year (in millions of dollars):

	Boeing	Home Depot
Net fixed assets	$8,589	$8,160
Goodwill	$2,312	$140
Investments and notes receivable	$41	$0
Deferred income taxes	$411	$0
Prepaid pension expense	$3,513	$0
Customer financing	$4,930	$0
Other assets	$542	$191

---

[3]The Financial Accounting Standards Board (FASB) eliminated the use of pooling and reduced the amortization period for goodwill in purchase accounting to 20 years in 2001.

Current Assets		
Cash	$2,183	$62
Short-term marketable investments	$279	$0
Accounts receivables	$3,288	$469
Current portion of customer financing	$781	$0
Deferred income taxes	$1,495	$0
Inventories	$8,349	$4,293
Other current assets	$0	$109
Total current assets	$16,375	$4,933
Total Assets	$36,672	$13,465

There are five points worth noting about these asset values:

1. *Goodwill.* Boeing, which acquired Rockwell in 1996 and McDonnell Douglas in 1997, used purchase accounting for the Rockwell acquisition and pooling for McDonnell Douglas. The goodwill on the balance sheet reflects the excess of acquisition value over book value for Rockwell and is being amortized over 30 years. With McDonnell Douglas, there is no recording of the premium paid on the acquisition among the assets.
2. *Customer financing and accounts receivable.* Boeing often either provides financing to its customers to acquire its planes or acts as the lessor on the planes. Since these contracts tend to run over several years, the present value of the payments due in future years on the financing and the lease payments is shown as customer financing. The current portion of these payments is shown as accounts receivable. The Home Depot provides credit to its customers as well, but all these payments due are shown as accounts receivable, since they are all short-term.
3. *Inventories.* Boeing values inventories using the weighted average cost method, while the Home Depot uses the FIFO approach for valuing inventories.
4. *Marketable securities.* Boeing classifies its short-term investments as trading investments and records them at market value. The Home Depot has a mix of trading, available-for-sale, and held-to-maturity investments and therefore uses a mix of book and market value to value these investments.
5. *Prepaid pension expense.* Boeing records the excess of its pension fund assets over its expected pension fund liabilities as an asset on the balance sheet.

Finally, the balance sheet for Boeing fails to report the value of a very significant asset, which is the effect of past research and development (R&D) expenses. Since accounting convention requires that these be expensed in the year that they occur and not be capitalized, the research asset does not show up in the balance sheet. Chapter 9 will consider how to capitalize research and development expenses and the effects on balance sheets.

MEASURING FINANCING MIX

The second set of questions that we would like to answer, and accounting statements to shed some light on, relate to the mix of debt and equity used by the firm, and the current values of each. The bulk of the information about these questions is provided on the liabilities side of the balance sheet and the footnotes to it.

Accounting Principles Underlying Liability and Equity Measurement

Just as with the measurement of asset value, the accounting categorization of liabilities and equity is governed by a set of fairly rigid principles. The first is a *strict cat-*

egorization of financing into either a liability or an equity based on the nature of the obligation. For an obligation to be recognized as a liability, it must meet three requirements:

1. The obligation must be expected to lead to a future cash outflow or the loss of a future cash inflow at some specified or determinable date.
2. The firm cannot avoid the obligation.
3. The transaction giving rise to the obligation has to have already happened.

In keeping with the earlier principle of conservatism in estimating asset value, accountants recognize as liabilities only cash flow obligations that cannot be avoided.

The second principle is that the value of both liabilities and equity in a firm are *better estimated using historical costs* with accounting adjustments, rather than with expected future cash flows or market value. The process by which accountants measure the value of liabilities and equities is inextricably linked to the way they value assets. Since assets are primarily valued at historical cost or at book value, both debt and equity also get measured primarily at book value. The next section will examine the accounting measurement of both liabilities and equity.

Measuring the Value of Liabilities and Equities

Accountants categorize liabilities into current liabilities, long-term debt, and long-term liabilities that are not debt or equity. Next, we will examine the way they measure each of these.

Current Liabilities Under current liabilities are categorized all obligations that the firm has coming due in the next year. These generally include:

- *Accounts payable*, representing credit received from suppliers and other vendors to the firm. The value of accounts payable represents the amounts due to these creditors. For this item, book and market value should be similar.
- *Short-term borrowing*, representing short-term loans (due in less than a year) taken to finance the operations or current asset needs of the business. Here again, the value shown represents the amounts due on such loans, and the book and market value should be similar, unless the default risk of the firm has changed dramatically since it borrowed the money.
- *Short-term portion of long-term borrowing*, representing the portion of the long-term debt or bonds that is coming due in the next year. Here again, the value shown is the actual amount due on these loans, and market and book value should converge as the due date approaches.
- *Other short-term liabilities*, which is a catchall component for any other short-term liabilities that the firm might have, including wages due to its employees and taxes due to the government.

Of all the items in the balance sheet, absent outright fraud, current liabilities should be the one for which the accounting estimates of book value and financial estimates of market value are closest.

Long-Term Debt   Long-term debt for firms can take one of two forms. It can be a long-term loan from a bank or other financial institution, or it can be a long-term bond issued to financial markets, in which case the creditors are the investors in the bond. Accountants measure the value of long-term debt by looking at the present value of payments due on the loan or bond at the time of the borrowing. For bank loans, this will be equal to the nominal value of the loan. With bonds, however, there are three possibilities: When bonds are issued at par value, for instance, the value of the long-term debt is generally measured in terms of the nominal obligation created (i.e., principal due on the borrowing). When bonds are issued at a premium or a discount on par value, the bonds are recorded at the issue price, but the premium or discount is amortized over the life of the bond. As an extreme example, companies that issue zero coupon debt have to record the debt at the issue price, which will be significantly below the principal (face value) due at maturity. The difference between the issue price and the face value is amortized each period and is treated as a noncash interest expense that is tax deductible.

In all these cases, the value of debt is unaffected by changes in interest rates during the life of the loan or bond. Note that as market interest rates rise or fall, the present value of the loan obligations should decrease or increase. This updated market value for debt is not shown on the balance sheet. If debt is retired prior to maturity, the difference between book value and the amount paid at retirement is treated as an extraordinary gain or loss in the income statement.

Finally, companies that have long-term debt denominated in nondomestic currencies have to adjust the book value of debt for changes in exchange rates. Since exchange rate changes reflect underlying changes in interest rates, it does imply that this debt is likely to be valued much nearer to market value than is debt in the domestic currency.

Other Long-Term Liabilities   Firms often have long-term obligations that are not captured in the long-term debt item. These include obligations to lessors on assets that firms have leased, to employees in the form of pension fund and health care benefits yet to be paid, and to the government in the form of taxes deferred. In the past two decades accountants have increasingly moved toward quantifying these liabilities and showing them as long-term liabilities.

Leases   Firms often choose to lease long-term assets rather than buy them. Lease payments create the same kind of obligation that interest payments on debt create, and they must be viewed in a similar light. If a firm is allowed to lease a significant portion of its assets and keep it off its financial statements, a perusal of the statements will give a very misleading view of the company's financial strength. Consequently, accounting rules have been devised to force firms to reveal the extent of their lease obligations on their books.

There are two ways of accounting for leases. In an operating lease, the lessor (or owner) transfers only the right to use the property to the lessee. At the end of the lease period, the lessee returns the property to the lessor. Since the lessee does not assume the risk of ownership, the lease expense is treated as an operating expense in the income statement and the lease does not affect the balance sheet. In a capital lease, the lessee assumes some of the risks of ownership and enjoys some of the benefits. Consequently, the lease, when signed, is recognized both as an asset and as a liability (for the lease payments) on the balance sheet. The firm gets to claim depreciation each year on the asset and also deducts the interest expense component of the lease payment each year. In general, capital leases recognize expenses sooner than equivalent operating leases.

Since firms prefer to keep leases off the books and sometimes to defer expenses, they have a strong incentive to report all leases as operating leases. Consequently the Financial Accounting Standards Board has ruled that a lease should be treated as a capital lease if it meets any one of the following four conditions:

1. The lease life exceeds 75 percent of the life of the asset.
2. There is a transfer of ownership to the lessee at the end of the lease term.
3. There is an option to purchase the asset at a bargain price at the end of the lease term.
4. The present value of the lease payments, discounted at an appropriate discount rate, exceeds 90 percent of the fair market value of the asset.

The lessor uses the same criteria for determining whether the lease is a capital or operating lease and accounts for it accordingly. If it is a capital lease, the lessor records the present value of future cash flows as revenue and recognizes expenses. The lease receivable is also shown as an asset on the balance sheet, and the interest revenue is recognized over the term of the lease as paid.

From a tax standpoint, the lessor can claim the tax benefits of the leased asset only if it is an operating lease, though the tax code uses slightly different criteria for determining whether the lease is an operating lease.[4]

Employee Benefits Employers can provide pension and health care benefits to their employees. In many cases, the obligations created by these benefits are extensive, and a failure by the firm to adequately fund these obligations needs to be revealed in financial statements.

Pension Plans In a pension plan, the firm agrees to provide certain benefits to its employees, either by specifying a defined contribution (wherein a fixed contribution is made to the plan each year by the employer, without any promises as to the benefits that will be delivered in the plan) or a defined benefit (wherein the employer promises to pay a certain benefit to the employee). In the latter case, the employer has to put sufficient money into the plan each period to meet the defined benefits.

Under a defined contribution plan, the firm meets its obligation once it has made the prespecified contribution to the plan. Under a defined benefit plan, the firm's obligations are much more difficult to estimate, since they will be determined by a number of variables, including the benefits that employees are entitled to, the

---

[4]The requirements for an operating lease in the tax code are: (1) The property can be used by someone other than the lessee at the end of the lease term, (2) the lessee cannot buy the asset using a bargain purchase option, (3) the lessor has at least 20 percent of its capital at risk, (4) the lessor has a positive cash flow from the lease independent of tax benefits, and (5) the lessee does not have an investment in the lease.

prior contributions made by the employer and the returns they have earned, and the rate of return that the employer expects to make on current contributions. As these variables change, the value of the pension fund assets can be greater than, less than, or equal to pension fund liabilities (which include the present value of promised benefits). A pension fund whose assets exceed its liabilities is an over-funded plan, whereas one whose assets are less than its liabilities is an underfunded plan, and disclosures to that effect have to be included in financial statements, generally in the footnotes.

When a pension fund is overfunded, the firm has several options. It can withdraw the excess assets from the fund, it can discontinue contributions to the plan, or it can continue to make contributions on the assumption that the overfunding is a transitory phenomenon that could well disappear by the next period. When a fund is underfunded, the firm has a liability, though accounting standards require that firms reveal only the excess of accumulated pension fund liability[5] over pension fund assets on the balance sheet.

Health Care Benefits   A firm can provide health care benefits in either of two ways—by making a fixed contribution to a health care plan without promising specific benefits (analogous to a defined contribution plan) or by promising specific health benefits and setting aside the funds to provide these benefits (analogous to a defined benefit plan). The accounting for health care benefits is very similar to the accounting for pension obligations.

Deferred Taxes   Firms often use different methods of accounting for tax and financial reporting purposes, leading to a question of how tax liabilities should be reported. Since accelerated depreciation and favorable inventory valuation methods for tax accounting purposes lead to a deferral of taxes, the taxes on the income reported in the financial statements will generally be much greater than the actual tax paid. The same principles of matching expenses to income that underlie accrual accounting suggest that the deferred income tax be recognized in the financial statements. Thus a company that pays taxes of $55,000 on its taxable income based on its tax accounting, and which would have paid taxes of $75,000 on the income reported in its financial statements, will be forced to recognize the difference ($20,000) as deferred taxes. Since the deferred taxes will be paid in later years, they will be recognized when paid.

It is worth noting that companies that actually pay more in taxes than the taxes they report in the financial statements create an asset called a deferred tax asset. This reflects the fact that the firm's earnings in future periods will be greater as the firm is given credit for the deferred taxes.

The question of whether the deferred tax liability is really a liability is an interesting one. Firms do not owe the amount categorized as deferred taxes to any entity, and treating it as a liability makes the firm look more risky than it really is. On

---

[5]The accumulated pension fund liability does not take into account the projected benefit obligation, where actuarial estimates of future benefits are made. Consequently, it is much smaller than the total pension liabilities.

the other hand, the firm will eventually have to pay its deferred taxes, and treating the amount as a liability seems to be the conservative thing to do.

Preferred Stock   When a company issues preferred stock, it generally creates an obligation to pay a fixed dividend on the stock. Accounting rules have conventionally not viewed preferred stock as debt because the failure to meet preferred dividends does not result in bankruptcy. At the same time, the fact the preferred dividends are cumulative makes them more onerous than common equity. Thus, preferred stock is a hybrid security, sharing some characteristics with equity and some with debt.

Preferred stock is valued on the balance sheet at its original issue price, with any cumulated unpaid dividends added on. Convertible preferred stock is treated similarly, but it is treated as equity on conversion.

Equity   The accounting measure of equity is a historical cost measure. The value of equity shown on the balance sheet reflects the original proceeds received by the firm when it issued the equity, augmented by any earnings made since (or reduced by losses, if any) and reduced by any dividends paid out during the period. While these three items go into what we can call the book value of equity, three other points need to be made about this estimate:

1. When companies buy back stock for short periods, with the intent of reissuing the stock or using it to cover option exercises, they are allowed to show the repurchased stock as treasury stock, which reduces the book value of equity. Firms are not allowed to keep treasury stock on the books for extended periods, and have to reduce their book value of equity by the value of repurchased stock in the case of actions such as stock buybacks. Since these buybacks occur at the current market price, they can result in significant reductions in the book value of equity.
2. Firms that have significant losses over extended periods or carry out massive stock buybacks can end up with negative book values of equity.
3. Relating back to the discussion of marketable securities, any unrealized gain or loss in marketable securities that are classified as available for sale is shown as an increase or decrease in the book value of equity in the balance sheet.

As part of their financial statements, firms provide a summary of changes in shareholders' equity during the period, where all the changes that occurred to the accounting measure of equity value are summarized.

Accounting rules still do not seem to have come to grips with the effect of warrants and equity options (such as those granted by many firms to management) on the book value of equity. If warrants are issued to financial markets, the proceeds from this issue will show up as part of the book value of equity. In the far more prevalent case where options are given or granted to management, there is no effect on the book value of equity. When the options are exercised, the cash inflows from the exercise do ultimately show up in the book value of equity, and there may be an increase in the number of shares outstanding (if the firm issues new shares). The same point can be made about convertible bonds, which are treated as debt until conversion, at which point they become part of equity. In partial defense of accountants, we must note that the effect of options outstanding is often revealed when earnings and book value are computed on a per share basis. Here, the computation is made on two bases, the first on the current number of shares outstanding (primary shares outstanding) and the second on the number of shares outstanding after all options have been exercised (fully diluted shares outstanding).

As a final point on equity, accounting rules still seem to consider preferred stock, with its fixed dividend, as equity or near-equity, largely because of the fact that preferred dividends can be deferred or cumulated without the risk of default. To the extent that there can still be a loss of control in the firm (as opposed to bankruptcy), we would argue that preferred stock shares almost as many characteristics with unsecured debt as it does with equity.

ILLUSTRATION 3.2:   Measuring Liabilities and Equity

The following table summarizes the accounting estimates of liabilities and equity at Boeing and the Home Depot for the 1998 financial year in millions of dollars:

	Boeing	Home Depot
Accounts payable and other liabilities	$10,733	$1,586
Accrued salaries and expenses	0	$1,010
Advances in excess of costs	$1,251	$0
Taxes payable	$569	$247
Short-term debt and current long-term debt	$869	$14
Total current liabilities	$13,422	$2,857
Accrued health care benefits	$4,831	0
Other long-term liabilities	0	$210
Deferred income taxes	0	$83
Long-term debt	$6,103	$1,566
Minority interests	$9	$0
Shareholder's Equity		
Par value	$5,059	$37
Additional paid-in capital	$0	$2,891
Retained earnings	$7,257	$5,812
Total shareholder's equity	$12,316	$8,740
Total liabilities	$36,672	$13,465

The most significant difference between the companies is the accrued health care liability shown by Boeing, representing the present value of expected health care obligations promised to employees in excess of health care assets. The shareholders' equity for both firms represents the book value of equity and is significantly different from the market value of equity. The follwing table summarizes the difference at the end of the 1998 (in millions of dollars):

	Boeing	Home Depot
Book value of equity	$12,316	$8,740
Market value of equity	$32,595	$85,668

One final point needs to be made about the Home Depot's liabilities. The Home Depot has substantial operating leases. Because these leases are treated as operating expenses, they do not show up in the balance sheet. Since they represent commitments to make payments in the future, we would argue that operating leases should be capitalized and treated as part of the liabilities of the firm. How best to do this will be considered later in this book, in Chapter 9.

MEASURING EARNINGS AND PROFITABILITY

How profitable is a firm? What did it earn on the assets that it invested in? These are fundamental questions we would like financial statements to answer. Accountants use the income statement to provide information about a firm's operating activities over a specific time period. The income statement is designed to measure the earnings from assets in place. This section will examine the principles underlying earnings and return measurement in accounting, and the way they are put into practice.

Accounting Principles Underlying Measurement of Earnings and Profitability

Two primary principles underlie the measurement of accounting earnings and profitability. The first is the principle of accrual accounting. In accrual accounting, the revenue from selling a good or service is recognized in the period in which the good is sold or the service is performed (in whole or substantially). A corresponding effort is made on the expense side to match expenses to revenues.[6] This is in contrast to a cash-based system of accounting, where revenues are recognized when payment is received and expenses are recorded when paid.

The second principle is the categorization of expenses into operating, financing, and capital expenses. Operating expenses are expenses that, at least in theory, provide benefits only for the current period; the cost of labor and materials expended to create products that are sold in the current period is a good example. Financing expenses are expenses arising from the nonequity financing used to raise capital for the business; the most common example is interest expenses. Capital expenses are expenses that are expected to generate benefits over multiple periods; for instance, the cost of buying land and buildings is treated as a capital expense.

Operating expenses are subtracted from revenues in the current period to arrive at a measure of operating earnings from the firm. Financing expenses are subtracted from operating earnings to estimate earnings to equity investors or net income. Capital expenses are written off over their useful lives (in terms of generating benefits) as depreciation or amortization.

Measuring Accounting Earnings and Profitability

Since income can be generated from a number of different sources, generally accepted accounting principles (GAAP) require that income statements be classified into four sections—income from continuing operations, income from discontinued operations, extraordinary gains or losses, and adjustments for changes in accounting principles.

Generally accepted accounting principles require the recognition of revenues when the service for which the firm is getting paid has been performed in full or substantially, and the firm has received in return either cash or a receivable that is both observable and measurable. Expenses linked directly to the production of revenues

---

[6]If a cost (such as an administrative cost) cannot easily be linked with particular revenues, it is usually recognized as an expense in the period in which it is consumed.

(like labor and materials) are recognized in the same period in which revenues are recognized. Any expenses that are not directly linked to the production of revenues are recognized in the period in which the firm consumes the services.

While accrual accounting is straightforward in firms that produce goods and sell them, there are special cases where accrual accounting can be complicated by the nature of the product or service being offered. For instance, firms that enter into long-term contracts with their customers are allowed to recognize revenue on the basis of the percentage of the contract that is completed. As the revenue is recognized on a percentage-of-completion basis, a corresponding proportion of the expense is also recognized. When there is considerable uncertainty about the capacity of the buyer of a good or service to pay for it, the firm providing the good or service may recognize the income only when it collects portions of the selling price under the installment method.

Reverting back to the discussion of the difference between capital and operating expenses, operating expenses should reflect only those expenses that create revenues in the current period. In practice, however, a number of expenses are classified as operating expenses that do not seem to meet this test. The first is depreciation and amortization. While the notion that capital expenditures should be written off over multiple periods is reasonable, the accounting depreciation that is computed on the original historical cost often bears little resemblance to the actual economic depreciation. The second expense is research and development expenses, which accounting standards in the United States classify as operating expenses, but which clearly provide benefits over multiple periods. The rationale used for this classification is that the benefits cannot be counted on or easily quantified.

Much of financial analysis is built around the expected future earnings of a firm, and many of these forecasts start with the current earnings. It is therefore important that we know how much of these earnings come from the ongoing operations of the firm and how much can be attributed to unusual or extraordinary events that are unlikely to recur on a regular basis. From that standpoint, it is useful that firms categorize expenses into operating and nonrecurring expenses, since it is the earnings prior to extraordinary items that should be used in forecasting. Nonrecurring items include:

- *Unusual or infrequent items*, such as gains or losses from the divestiture of an asset or division, and write-offs or restructuring costs. Companies sometimes include such items as part of operating expenses. As an example, Boeing in 1997 took a write-off of $1,400 million to adjust the value of assets it acquired in its acquisition of McDonnell Douglas, and it showed this as part of operating expenses.
- *Extraordinary items*, which are defined as events that are unusual in nature, infrequent in occurrence, and material in impact. Examples include the accounting gain associated with refinancing high-coupon debt with lower-coupon debt, and gains or losses from marketable securities that are held by the firm.
- *Losses associated with discontinued operations*, which measure both the loss from the phaseout period and any estimated loss on sale of the operations. To qualify, however, the operations have to be separable from the firm.
- *Gains or losses associated with accounting changes*, which measure earnings changes created by both accounting changes made voluntarily by the firm (such

as a change in inventory valuation) and accounting changes mandated by new accounting standards.

ILLUSTRATION 3.3:   Measures of Earnings

The following table summarizes the income statements of Boeing and the Home Depot for the 1998 financial year:

	Boeing (in $ millions)	Home Depot (in $ millons)
Sales and other operating revenues	$56,154	$30,219
– Operating costs and expenses	$51,022	$27,185
– Depreciation	$ 1,517	$ 373
– Research and development expenses	$ 1,895	$ 0
Operating income	$ 1,720	$ 2,661
+ Other income (includes interest income)	$ 130	$ 30
– Interest expenses	$ 453	$ 37
Earnings before taxes	$ 1,397	$ 2,654
– Income taxes	$ 277	$ 1,040
Net earnings (Loss)	$ 1,120	$ 1,614

Boeing's operating income is reduced by the research and development expense, which is treated as an operating expense by accountants. The Home Depot's operating expenses include operating leases. As noted earlier, the treatment of both these items skews earnings, and how best to adjust earnings when such expenses exist will be considered in Chapter 9.

Measures of Profitability   While the income statement allows us to estimate how profitable a firm is in absolute terms, it is just as important that we gauge the profitability of the firm in terms of percentage returns. Two basic ratios measure profitability. One examines the profitability relative to the capital employed to get a rate of return on investment. This can be done either from the viewpoint of just the equity investors or by looking at the entire firm. Another examines profitability relative to sales, by estimating a profit margin.

Return on Assets and Return on Capital   The *return on assets* (ROA) of a firm measures its operating efficiency in generating profits from its assets, prior to the effects of financing.

Return on assets = Earnings before interest and taxes(1 – Tax rate) / Total assets

Earnings before interest and taxes (EBIT) is the accounting measure of operating income from the income statement, and total assets refers to the assets as measured using accounting rules—that is, using book value (BV) for most assets. Alternatively, return on assets can be written as:

Return on assets = [Net income + Interest expenses(1 – Tax rate)] / Total assets

By separating the financing effects from the operating effects, the return on assets provides a cleaner measure of the true return on these assets.

ROA can also be computed on a pretax basis with no loss of generality, by using the earnings before interest and taxes and not adjusting for taxes:

$$\text{Pretax ROA} = \text{Earnings before interest and taxes/Total assets}$$

This measure is useful if the firm or division is being evaluated for purchase by an acquirer with a different tax rate.

A more useful measure of return relates the operating income to the capital invested in the firm, where capital is defined as the sum of the book value of debt and equity. This is the return on capital (ROC), and when a substantial portion of the liabilities is either current (such as accounts payable) or non-interest-bearing, this approach provides a better measure of the true return earned on capital employed in the business.

$$\text{Return on capital} = \frac{\text{EBIT}(1-t)}{\text{BV of debt} + \text{BV of equity}}$$

For both measures, the book value can be measured at the beginning of the period or as an average of beginning and ending values.

ILLUSTRATION 3.4:   Estimating Return on Capital

The following table summarizes the after-tax return on asset and return on capital estimates for Boeing and the Home Depot, using both average and beginning measures of capital in 1998:

	Boeing (in $millions)	Home Depot (in $millions)
After-tax operating income	$ 1,118	$ 1,730
Book value of capital—beginning	$19,807	$ 8,525
Book value of capital—ending	$19,288	$10,320
Book value of capital—average	$19,548	$ 9,423
Return on capital (based on average)	5.72%	18.36%
Return on capital (based on beginning)	5.64%	20.29%

Boeing had a terrible year in terms of after-tax returns. The Home Depot had a much better year in terms of those same returns.

Decomposing Return on Capital   The return on capital of a firm can be written as a function of the operating profit margin it has on its sales, and its capital turnover ratio.

$$\begin{aligned}
\text{ROC} &= \frac{\text{EBIT}(1-t)}{\text{BV of capital}} \\[2mm]
&= \frac{\text{EBIT}(1-t)}{\text{Sales}} \times \frac{\text{Sales}}{\text{BV of capital}} \\[2mm]
&= \text{After-tax operating margin} \times \text{Capital turnover ratio}
\end{aligned}$$

Thus, a firm can arrive at a high ROC by either increasing its profit margin or utilizing its capital more efficiently to increase sales. There are likely to be competitive constraints and technological constraints on increasing sales, but a firm still has some freedom within these constraints to choose the mix of profit margin and capital turnover that maximizes its ROC. The return on capital varies widely across firms in different businesses, largely as a consequence of differences in profit margins and capital turnover ratios.

 mgnroc.xls: **This is a dataset on the Web that summarizes the operating margins, turnover ratios, and returns on capital of firms in the United States, classified by industry.**

Return on Equity   While the return on capital measures the profitability of the overall firm, the return on equity (ROE) examines profitability from the perspective of the equity investor, by relating the equity investor's profits (net profit after taxes and interest expenses) to the book value of the equity investment.

$$\text{Return on equity} = \frac{\text{Net income}}{\text{Book value of common equity}}$$

Since preferred stockholders have a different type of claim on the firm than do common stockholders, the net income should be estimated after preferred dividends, and the common equity should not include the book value of preferred stock. This can be accomplished by using net income after preferred dividends in the numerator and the book value of common equity in the denominator.

Determinants of ROE   Since the ROE is based on earnings after interest payments, it is affected by the financing mix the firm uses to fund its projects. In general, a firm that borrows money to finance projects and that earns a ROC on those projects that exceeds the after-tax interest rate it pays on its debt will be able to increase its ROE by borrowing. The ROE can be written as follows:[7]

$$\text{ROE} = \text{ROC} + \frac{D}{E}\left[\text{ROC} - i(1-t)\right]$$

where ROC = EBIT(1 − t)/(BV of debt + BV of equity)
    D/E = BV of debt/ BV of equity
     i = Interest expense on debt/BV of debt
     t = Tax rate on ordinary income

The second term captures the benefit of financial leverage.

---

[7]ROC + D/E[ROC − i(1 − t)] = [NI + Int(1 − t)]/(D + E) + D/E{[NI + Int(1 − t)]/(D + E)
                  − Int(1 − t)/D}
            = {[NI + Int(1 − t)]/(D + E)}(1 + D/E) − Int(1 − t)/E
            = NI/E + Int(1 − t)/E − Int(1 − t)/E = NI/E = ROE

ILLUSTRATION 3.5:   Return on Equity Computations

The following table summarizes the return on equity for Boeing and the Home Depot in 1998:

Return Ratios	Boeing (in $millions)	Home Depot (in $millions)
Net income	$ 1,120	$1,614
Book value of equity—beginning	$12,953	$7,214
Book value of equity—ending	$12,316	$8,740
Book value of equity—average	$12,635	$7,977
Return on equity (based on average)	8.86%	20.23%
Return on equity (based on beginning)	8.65%	22.37%

The results again indicate that Boeing had a poor year in 1998, while the Home Depot reported healthier returns on equity. The returns on equity can also be estimated by decomposing into the components just specified (using the adjusted beginning-of-the-year numbers):

	Boeing (in $millions)	Home Depot (in $millions)
After-tax return on capital	5.82%	16.37%
Debt-equity ratio	35.18%	48.37%
Book interest rate (1 − Tax rate)	4.22%	4.06%
Return on equity	6.38%	22.33%

Note that a tax rate of 35% is used on both the return on capital and the book interest rate. This approach results in a return on equity that is different from the one estimated using the net income and the book value of equity.

---

 rocroe.xls: **This is a dataset on the Web that summarizes the return on capital, debt equity ratios, book interest rates, and returns on equity of firms in the United States, classified by industry.**

MEASURING RISK

How risky are the investments the firm has made over time? How much risk do equity investors in a firm face? These are two more questions that we would like to find the answers to in the course of an investment analysis. Accounting statements do not really claim to measure or quantify risk in a systematic way, other than to provide footnotes and disclosures where there might be risk embedded in the firm. This section will examine some of the ways in which accountants try to assess risk.

Accounting Principles Underlying Risk Measurement

To the extent that accounting statements and ratios do attempt to measure risk, there seem to be two common themes.

The first is that the risk being measured is the risk of default—that is, the risk that a fixed obligation, such as interest or principal due on outstanding debt, will not be met. The broader equity notion of risk, which measures the variance of actual returns around expected returns, does not seem to receive much attention.

Thus, an all-equity-financed firm with positive earnings and few or no fixed obligations will generally emerge as a low-risk firm from an accounting standpoint, in spite of the fact that its earnings are unpredictable.

The second theme is that accounting risk measures generally take a static view of risk, by looking at the capacity of a firm at a point in time to meet its obligations. For instance, when ratios are used to assess a firm's risk, the ratios are almost always based on one period's income statement and balance sheet.

Accounting Measures of Risk

Accounting measures of risk can be broadly categorized into two groups. The first is disclosures about potential obligations or losses in values that show up as footnotes on balance sheets, which are designed to alert potential or current investors to the possibility of significant losses. The second is ratios that are designed to measure both liquidity and default risk.

Disclosures in Financial Statements   In recent years, the disclosures that firms have to make about future obligations have proliferated. Consider, for instance, the case of contingent liabilities. These refer to potential liabilities that will be incurred under certain contingencies, as is the case, for instance, when a firm is the defendant in a lawsuit. The general rule that has been followed is to ignore contingent liabilities that hedge against risk, since the obligations on the contingent claim will be offset by benefits elsewhere.[8] In recent periods, however, significant losses borne by firms from supposedly hedged derivatives positions (such as options and futures) have led to FASB requirements that these derivatives be disclosed as part of a financial statement. In fact, pension fund and health care obligations have moved from mere footnotes to actual liabilities for firms.

Financial Ratios   Financial statements have long been used as the basis for estimating financial ratios that measure profitability, risk, and leverage. Earlier, the section on earnings looked at two of the profitability ratios—return on equity and return on capital. This section will look at some of the financial ratios that are often used to measure the financial risk in a firm.

Short-Term Liquidity Risk   Short-term liquidity risk arises primarily from the need to finance current operations. To the extent that the firm has to make payments to its suppliers before it gets paid for the goods and services it provides, there is a cash shortfall that has to be met, usually through short-term borrowing. Though this financing of working capital needs is done routinely in most firms, financial ratios have been devised to keep track of the extent of the firm's exposure to the risk that it will not be able to meet its short-term obligations. The two most frequently used to measure short-term liquidity risk are the current ratio and the quick ratio.

Current Ratios   The current ratio is the ratio of current assets (cash, inventory, accounts receivable) to its current liabilities (obligations coming due within the next period).

---

[8]This assumes that the hedge is set up competently. It is entirely possible that a hedge, if sloppily set up, can end up costing the firm money.

$$\text{Current ratio} = \frac{\text{Current assets}}{\text{Current liabilities}}$$

A current ratio below 1, for instance, would indicate that the firm has more obligations coming due in the next year than assets it can expect to turn to cash. That would be an indication of liquidity risk.

While traditional analysis suggests that firms maintain a current ratio of 2 or greater, there is a trade-off here between minimizing liquidity risk and tying up more and more cash in net working capital (Net working capital = Current assets – Current liabilities). In fact, it can be reasonably argued that a very high current ratio is indicative of an unhealthy firm that is having problems reducing its inventory. In recent years firms have worked at reducing their current ratios and managing their net working capital better.

Reliance on current ratios has to be tempered by a few concerns. First, the ratio can be easily manipulated by firms around the time of financial reporting dates to give the illusion of safety; second, current assets and current liabilities can change by an equal amount, but the effect on the current ratio will depend on its level before the change.[9]

Quick or Acid Test Ratios   The quick or acid test ratio is a variant of the current ratio. It distinguishes current assets that can be converted quickly into cash (cash, marketable securities) from those that cannot (inventory, accounts receivable).

$$\text{Quick ratio} = (\text{Cash} + \text{Marketable securities})/\text{Current liabilities}$$

The exclusion of accounts receivable and inventory is not a hard-and-fast rule. If there is evidence that either can be converted into cash quickly, it can, in fact, be included as part of the quick ratio.

Turnover Ratios   Turnover ratios measure the efficiency of working capital management by looking at the relationship of accounts receivable and inventory to sales and to the cost of goods sold:

$$\text{Accounts receivable turnover} = \text{Sales}/\text{Average accounts receivable}$$
$$\text{Inventory turnover} = \text{Cost of goods sold}/\text{Average inventory}$$

These statistics can be interpreted as measuring the speed with which the firm turns accounts receivable into cash or inventory into sales. These ratios are often expressed in terms of the number of days outstanding:

$$\text{Days accounts receivable outstanding} = 365/\text{Accounts receivable turnover}$$
$$\text{Days inventory held} = 365/\text{Inventory turnover}$$

A similar pair of statistics can be computed for accounts payable, relative to puchases:

$$\text{Accounts payable turnover} = \text{Purchases}/\text{Average accounts payable}$$
$$\text{Days accounts payable outstanding} = 365/\text{Accounts payable turnover}$$

---

[9]If the current assets and current liabilities increase by an equal amount, the current ratio will go down if it was greater than 1 before the increase, and go up if it was less than 1.

Since accounts receivable and inventory are assets, and accounts payable is a liability, these three statistics (standardized in terms of days outstanding) can be combined to get an estimate of how much financing the firm needs to raise to fund working capital needs.

> Required financing period = Days accounts receivable outstanding
> + Days inventory held
> − Days accounts payable outstanding

The greater the financing period for a firm, the greater is its short-term liquidity risk.

 wcdata.xls: This is a dataset on the Web that summarizes working capital ratios for firms in the United States, classified by industry.

 finratio.xls: This spreadsheet allows you to compute the working capital ratios for a firm, based upon financial statement data.

Long-Term Solvency and Default Risk   Measures of long-term solvency attempt to examine a firm's capacity to meet interest and principal payments in the long term. Clearly, the profitability ratios discussed earlier in the section are a critical component of this analysis. The ratios specifically designed to measure long-term solvency try to relate profitability to the level of debt payments in order to identify the degree of comfort with which the firm can meet these payments.

Interest Coverage Ratios   The interest coverage ratio measures the capacity of the firm to meet interest payments from predebt, pretax earnings.

$$\text{Interest coverage ratio} = \frac{\text{EBIT}}{\text{Interest expenses}}$$

The higher the interest coverage ratio, the more secure is the firm's capacity to make interest payments from earnings. This argument, however, has to be tempered by the recognition that the amount of earnings before interest and taxes is volatile and can drop significantly if the economy enters a recession. Consequently, two firms can have the same interest coverage ratio but be viewed very differently in terms of risk.

The denominator in the interest coverage ratio can be easily extended to cover other fixed obligations such as lease payments. If this is done, the ratio is called a fixed charges coverage ratio:

$$\text{Fixed charges coverage ratio} = \frac{\text{EBIT (before fixed charges)}}{\text{Fixed charges}}$$

Finally, this ratio, while stated in terms of earnings, can be restated in terms of cash flows by using earnings before interest, taxes, depreciation, and amortization (EBITDA) in the numerator and cash fixed charges in the denominator.

$$\text{Cash fixed charges coverage ratio} = \frac{\text{EBITDA}}{\text{Cash fixed charges}}$$

Both interest coverage and fixed charges coverage ratios are open to the criticism that they do not consider capital expenditures, a cash flow that may be discretionary in the very short term, but not in the long term if the firm wants to maintain growth. One way of capturing the extent of this cash flow, relative to operating cash flows, is to compute a ratio of the two:

$$\text{Operating cash flow to capital expenditures} = \frac{\text{Cash flows from operations}}{\text{Capital expenditures}}$$

While there are a number of different definitions of cash flows from operations, the most reasonable way of defining it is to measure the cash flows from continuing operations, before interest but after taxes and after meeting working capital needs.

Cash flow from operations = EBIT(1 – Tax rate) – Δ Working capital

 covratio.xls: This is a dataset on the Web that summarizes the interest coverage and fixed charges coverage ratios for firms in the United States, classified by industry.

ILLUSTRATION 3.6:   Interest and Fixed Charges Coverage Ratios

The following table summarizes interest and fixed charges coverage ratios for Boeing and the Home Depot in 1998:

	Boeing	Home Depot
EBIT	$1,720	$2,661
Interest expense	$ 453	$ 37
Interest coverage ratio	3.80	71.92
EBIT	$1,720	$2,661
Operating lease expenses	$ 215	$ 290
Interest expenses	$ 453	$ 37
Fixed charges coverage ratio	2.90	9.02
EBITDA	$3,341	$3,034
Cash fixed charges	$ 668	$ 327
Cash fixed charges coverage ratio	5.00	9.28
Cash flows from operations	$2,161	$1,662
Capital expenditures	$1,584	$2,059
Cash flows/Capital expenditures	1.36	0.81

Boeing, based on its operating income in 1998, looks riskier than the Home Depot on both the interest coverage ratio basis and fixed charges coverage ratio basis. On a cash flow basis, however, Boeing does look much better. In fact, when capital expenditures are considered, the Home Depot has a lower ratio. For Boeing, the other consideration is the fact that operating income in 1998 was depressed relative to income in earlier years, and this does have an impact on the ratios across the board. It might make more sense when computing these ratios to look at the average operating income over time.

finratio.xls: This spreadsheet allows you to compute the interest coverage and fixed charges coverage ratios for a firm based on financial statement data.

Debt Ratios   Interest coverage ratios measure the capacity of the firm to meet interest payments, but do not examine whether it can pay back the principal on outstanding debt. Debt ratios attempt to do this, by relating debt to total capital or to equity. The two most widely used debt ratios are:

$$\text{Debt to capital ratio} = \text{Debt}/(\text{Debt} + \text{Equity})$$

$$\text{Debt to equity ratio} = \text{Debt}/\text{Equity}$$

The first ratio measures debt as a proportion of the total capital of the firm and cannot exceed 100 percent. The second measures debt as a proportion of the book value of equity in the firm and can be easily derived from the first, since:

$$\text{Debt to equity ratio} = (\text{Debt}/\text{Capital ratio})/(1 - \text{Debt}/\text{Capital ratio})$$

While these ratios presume that capital is raised from only debt and equity, they can be easily adapted to include other sources of financing, such as preferred stock. While preferred stock is sometimes combined with common stock under the equity label, it is better to keep the two sources of financing separate and to compute the ratio of preferred stock to capital (which will include debt, equity, and preferred stock).

There are two close variants of debt ratios. In the first, only long-term debt is used rather than total debt, with the rationale that short-term debt is transitory and will not affect the long-term solvency of the firm.

$$\text{Long-term debt to capital ratio} = \text{Long-term debt}/(\text{Long-term debt} + \text{Equity})$$

$$\text{Long-term debt to equity ratio} = \text{Long-term debt}/\text{Equity}$$

Given the ease with which firms can roll over short-term debt and the willingness of many firms to use short-term financing to fund long-term projects, these variants can provide a misleading picture of the firm's financial leverage risk.

The second variant of debt ratios uses market value (MV) instead of book value, primarily to reflect the fact that some firms have a significantly greater capacity to borrow than their book values indicate.

$$\text{Market value debt to capital ratio} = \text{MV of debt}/(\text{MV of debt} + \text{MV of equity})$$

$$\text{Market value debt to equity ratio} = \text{MV of debt}/\text{MV of equity}$$

Many analysts disavow the use of market value in their calculations, contending that market values, in addition to being difficult to get for debt, are volatile and hence unreliable. These contentions are open to debate. It is true that the market value of debt is difficult to get for firms that do not have publicly traded bonds, but the market value of equity is not only easy to obtain, it is constantly updated to reflect marketwide and firm-specific changes. Furthermore, using the book value of debt as a proxy for market value in those cases where bonds are not traded does not significantly shift most market value–based debt ratios.[10]

---

[10]Deviations in the market value of equity from book value are likely to be much larger than deviations for debt, and are likely to dominate in most debt ratio calculations.

ILLUSTRATION 3.7:   Book Value Debt Ratios and Variants—Boeing and the Home Depot

The following table summarizes different estimates of the debt ratio for Boeing and the Home Depot, using book values of debt and equity for both firms:

	Boeing (in $millions)	Home Depot (in $millions)
Long-term debt	$ 6,103	$1,566
Short-term debt	$ 869	$ 14
Book value of equity	$12,316	$8,740
Long-term debt/Equity	49.55%	17.92%
Long-term debt/(Long-term debt + Equity)	33.13%	15.20%
Debt/Equity	56.61%	18.08%
Debt/(Debt + Equity)	36.15%	15.31%

Boeing has a much higher book value debt ratio, considering either long-term or total debt, than the Home Depot.

 dbtfund.xls: **This is a dataset on the Web that summarizes the book value debt ratios and market value debt ratios for firms in the United States, classified by industry.**

OTHER ISSUES IN ANALYZING FINANCIAL STATEMENTS

There are significant differences in accounting standards and practices across countries and these differences may color comparisons across companies.

Differences in Accounting Standards and Practices

Differences in accounting standards across countries affect the measurement of earnings. These differences, however, are not so great as they are made out to be by some analysts, and they cannot explain away radical departures from fundamental principles of valuation.[11] Choi and Levich, in a 1990 survey of accounting standards across developed markets, note that most countries subscribe to basic accounting notions of consistency, realization, and historical cost principles in preparing accounting statements. Table 3.1 summarizes accounting standards in

---

[11]At the peak of the Japanese market, there were many investors who explained away the price-earnings multiples of 60 and greater in the market by noting that Japanese firms were conservative in measuring earnings. Even after taking into account the general provisions and excess depreciation used by many of these firms to depress current earnings, the price-earnings multiples were greater than 50 for many firms, suggesting either extraordinary expected growth in the future or overvaluation.

TABLE 3.1 International Comparison of Accounting Principles

Accounting Principle	United Kingdom	United States	France	Germany	Netherlands	Sweden	Switzerland	Japan
1. Consistency—Accounting principles and methods are applied on the same basis from period to period.	Yes	Yes	Yes	Yes	Yes	PP	PP	Yes
2. Realization—Revenue is recognized when realization is reasonably assured.	Yes	Yes	Yes	Yes	Yes	Yes	PP	Yes
3. Fair presentation of the financial statement is required.	Yes	Yes	Yes	Yes	Yes	Yes	Yes	Yes
4. Historical cost convention—Departures from the historical cost convention are disclosed.	Yes	Yes	Yes	Yes	Yes	Yes	RF	Yes
5. Accounting policies—A change in accounting principles and methods without a change in circumstances is accounted for by a prior year adjustment.	Yes	No	Yes	MP	RF	MP	MP	No
6. Fixed assets—revaluation—In historical cost statements, fixed assets are stated at an amount in excess of cost, which is determined at irregular intervals.	MP	No	Yes	No	RF	PP	No	No
7. Fixed assets—revaluation—When fixed assets are stated in historical cost statements at an amount in excess of cost, depreciation based on the revaluation amount is charged to income.	Yes	No	Yes	No	Yes	Yes	No	No
8. Goodwill is amortized.	MP	Yes	Yes	Yes	M	Yes	MP	Yes
9. Finance leases are capitalized.	Yes	Yes	No	No	No	Yes	RF	No
10. Short-term marketable securities are stated at the lower of cost or market value.	Yes	Yes	Yes	Yes	Yes	Yes	Yes	Yes

(Continued)

TABLE 3.1 *(Continued)*

Accounting Principle	United Kingdom	United States	France	Germany	Netherlands	Sweden	Switzerland	Japan
11. Inventory values are stated at the lower of cost or market value.	Yes	Yes	Yes	Yes	Yes	Yes	Yes	Yes
12. Manufacturing overhead is allocated to year-end inventory.	Yes	Yes	Yes	Yes	Yes	Yes	Yes	Yes
13. Inventory is costed using FIFO.	PP	M	M	M	M	PP	PP	M
14. Long-term debt includes maturities longer than one year.	Yes	Yes	Yes	No	Yes	Yes	Yes	Yes
15. Deferred tax is recognized where accounting income and taxable income arise at different times.	Yes	Yes	Yes	No	Yes	No	No	Yes
16. Total pension fund assets and liabilities are excluded from a company's financial statements.	Yes	Yes	Yes	No	Yes	Yes	Yes	Yes
17. Research and development are expensed.	Yes	Yes	Yes	Yes	Yes	Yes	Yes	Yes
18. General purpose (purely discretionary) reserves are allowed.	No	No	Yes	Yes	Yes	Yes	Yes	Yes
19. Offsetting—Assets and liabilities are offset against each other in the balance sheet only when a legal right of offset exists.	Yes	Yes	Yes	Yes	Yes	Yes	PP	Yes
20. Unusual and extraordinary gains and losses are taken in the income statement.	Yes	Yes	Yes	Yes	Yes	Yes	Yes	Yes
21. Closing rate method of foreign currency translation is employed.	Yes	Yes	Yes	Yes	Yes	No	Yes	No

	C1	C2	C3	C4	C5	C6	C7	C8
22. Currency translation gains or losses arising from trading are reflected in current income.	Yes	Yes	MP	MP	MP	MP	MP	No
23. Excess depreciation is permitted.	Yes	No	Yes	Yes	Yes	Yes	Yes	Yes
24. Basic statements reflect a historical cost valuation (no price level adjustment).	Yes	Yes	Yes	Yes	M	Yes	Yes	Yes
25. Supplementary inflation—adjusted financial statements are adjusted.	MP	MP	No	No	MP	Yes	No	No
26. Accounting for long-term investments:								
a. Less than 20% ownership—cost method.	Yes	Yes	Yes	Yes	No	Yes	Yes	
b. 20–50% ownership—equity method.	Yes	Yes	Yes	No	Yes	MP	M	
c. More than 50% ownership—full consolidation.	Yes	Yes	Yes	Yes	Yes	Yes	Yes	
27. Both domestic and foreign subsidiaries are consolidated.	Yes	Yes	Yes	M	Yes	Yes	MP	Yes
28. Acquisitions are accounted for under the purchase cost method.	PP	PP	Yes	Yes	Yes	PP	Yes	Yes
29. Minority interest is excluded from consolidation income.	Yes	Yes	Yes	Yes	Yes	Yes	Yes	Yes
30. Minority interest is excluded from consolidated owners' equity.	Yes	Yes	Yes	Yes	Yes	Yes	Yes	Yes

Key: PP—Predominant practice
MP—Minority practice
M—Mixed practice
RF—Rarely or not found

eight major financial markets, and reveals that the common elements vastly outnumber those areas where there are differences.

The two countries that offer the strongest contrast to the United States are Germany and Japan. The key differences and their implications are: First, companies in the United States generally maintain separate tax and financial reporting books, which in turn generates items like deferred taxes to cover differences between the two books. Companies in Germany and Japan do not maintain separate books. Consequently, depreciation methods in financial reports are much more likely to be accelerated and hence to reduce stated income. Second, the requirement that a lease be capitalized and shown as a liability is much more tightly enforced in the United States. In Japan, leases are generally treated as operating leases and do not show up as liabilities in the balance sheet. In Germany, firms can capitalize leases, but they have more leeway in classifying leases as operating or capital leases than U.S. companies. Third, goodwill, once created, can be amortized over 40 years in the United States and over much shorter time periods in Germany and Japan, again depressing stated income. Fourth, reserves in the United States can be created only for specific purposes, whereas German and Japanese companies can use general reserves to equalize income across periods, leading to income being understated during the good years and overstated during bad years.

Most of these differences can be accounted and adjusted for when comparisons are made between companies in the United States and companies in other financial markets. Statistics such as price-earnings ratios, which use stated and unadjusted earnings, can be misleading when accounting standards vary widely across the companies being compared.

CONCLUSION

Financial statements remain the primary source of information for most investors and analysts. There are differences, however, in how accounting and financial analysis approach answering a number of key questions about the firm.

The first question relates to the nature and the value of the assets owned by a firm. Assets can be categorized into investments already made (assets in place) and investments yet to be made (growth assets); accounting statements provide a substantial amount of historical information about the former and very little about the latter. The focus on the original price of assets in place (book value) in accounting statements can lead to significant differences between the stated value of these assets and their market value. With growth assets, accounting rules result in low or no values for assets generated by internal research.

The second issue is the measurement of profitability. The two principles that seem to govern how profits are measured are accrual accounting—in which revenues and expenses are shown in the period where transactions occur rather than when the cash is received or paid—and the categorization of expenses into operating, financing, and capital expenses. While operating and financing expenses are shown in income statements, capital expenditures are spread over several time periods and take the form of depreciation and amortization. Accounting standards miscategorize operating leases and research and development expenses as operating expenses (when the former should be categorized as financing expenses and the latter as capital expenses).

Financial statements also deal with short-term liquidity risk and long-term default risk. While the emphasis in accounting statements is on examining the risk that firms may be unable to make payments that they have committed to make, there is very little focus on risk to equity investors.

QUESTIONS AND SHORT PROBLEMS

Coca-Cola's balance sheet for December 1998 is summarized (in millions of dollars) for problems 1 through 9:

Cash and near-cash	$1,648	Accounts payable	$3,141
Marketable securities	1049	Short-term borrowings	4,462
Accounts receivable	1,666	Other short-term liabilities	1,037
Other current assets	2,017	*Current Liabilities*	8,640
Current Assets	6,380	Long-term borrowings	687
Long-term investments	1,863	Other long-term liabilities	1,415
Depreciable fixed assets	5,486	*Noncurrent liabilities*	2,102
Nondepreciable fixed assets	199		
Accumulated depreciation	2,016	Share capital (paid-in)	3,060
Net fixed assets	3,669	Retained earnings	5,343
Other assets	7,233	*Shareholder's equity*	8,403
Total Assets	**19,145**	**Total Liabilities and Equity**	**19,145**

1. Consider the assets on Coca-Cola's balance sheet and answer the following questions:
   a. Which assets are likely to be assessed closest to market value? Explain.
   b. Coca-Cola has net fixed assets of $3,669 million. Can you estimate how much Coca-Cola paid for these assets? Is there any way to know the age of these assets?
   c. Coca-Cola seems to have far more invested in current assets than in fixed assets. Is this significant? Explain.
   d. In the early 1980s, Coca-Cola sold off its bottling operations, and the bottlers became independent companies. How would this action have impacted the assets on Coca-Cola's balance sheet? (The manufacturing plants are most likely to be part of the bottling operations.)
2. Examine the liabilities on Coca-Cola's balance sheet.
   a. How much interest-bearing debt does Coca-Cola have outstanding? (You can assume that other short-term liabilities represent sundry payables, and other long-term liabilities represent health care and pension obligations.)
   b. How much did Coca-Cola obtain in equity capital when it issued stock originally to the financial markets?
   c. Is there any significance to the fact that the retained earnings amount is much larger than the original paid-in capital?
   d. The market value of Coca-Cola's equity is $140 billion. What is the book value of equity in Coca-Cola? Why is there such a large difference between the market value of equity and the book value of equity?

3. Coca-Cola's most valuable asset is its brand name. Where in the balance sheet do you see its value? Is there any way to adjust the balance sheet to reflect the value of this asset?

4. Assume that you have been asked to analyze Coca-Cola's working capital management.
   a. Estimate the net working capital and noncash working capital for Coca-Cola.
   b. Estimate the firm's current ratio.
   c. Estimate the firm's quick ratio.
   d. Would you draw any conclusions about the riskiness of Coca-Cola as a firm by looking at these numbers? Why or why not?

Coca-Cola's income statements for 1997 and 1998 are summarized (in millions of dollars) for problems 5 through 9:

	1997	1998
Net revenues	$18,868	$18,813
Cost of goods sold	6,015	5,562
Selling, general, and administrative expenses	7,852	8,284
Earnings before interest and taxes	5,001	4,967
Interest expenses	258	277
Nonoperating gains	1,312	508
Income tax expenses	1,926	1,665
Net income	4,129	3,533
Dividends	1,387	1,480

The following questions relate to Coca-Cola's income statement.

5. How much operating income did Coca-Cola earn, before taxes, in 1998? How does this compare to how much Coca-Cola earned in 1997? What are the reasons for the difference?

6. The biggest expense for Coca-Cola is advertising, which is part of the selling, general and administrative (G&A) expenses. A large portion of these expenses is designed to build up Coca-Cola's brand name. Should advertising expenses be treated as operating expenses or are they really capital expenses? If they are to be treated as capital expenses, how would you capitalize them? (Use the capitalization of R&D as a guide.)

7. What effective tax rate did Coca-Cola have in 1998? How does it compare with what the company paid in 1997 as an effective tax rate? What might account for the difference?

8. You have been asked to assess the profitability of Coca-Cola as a firm. To that end, estimate the pretax operating and net margins in 1997 and 1998 for the firm. Are there any conclusions you would draw from the comparisons across the two years?

9. The book value of equity at Coca-Cola in 1997 was $7,274 million. The book value of interest-bearing debt was $3,875 million. Estimate:
   a. The return on equity (beginning of the year) in 1998.
   b. The pretax return on capital (beginning of the year) in 1998.
   c. The after-tax return on capital (beginning of the year) in 1998, using the effective tax rate in 1998.

10. SeeSaw Toys reported that it had a book value of equity of $1.5 billion at the end of 1998 and 100 million shares outstanding. During 1999, it bought back 10 million shares at a market price of $40 per share. The firm also reported a net income of $150 million for 1999, and paid dividends of $50 million. Estimate:

    a. The book value of equity at the end of 1999.
    b. The return on equity, using beginning book value of equity.
    c. The return on equity, using the average book value of equity.

CHAPTER 4

The Basics of Risk

When valuing assets and firms, we need to use discount rates that reflect the riskiness of the cash flows. In particular, the cost of debt has to incorporate a default spread for the default risk in the debt, and the cost of equity has to include a risk premium for equity risk. But how do we measure default and equity risk? More importantly, how do we come up with the default and equity risk premiums?

This chapter lays the foundations for analyzing risk in valuation. It presents alternative models for measuring risk and converting these risk measures into acceptable hurdle rates. It begins with a discussion of equity risk and presents the analysis in three steps. In the first step, risk is defined in statistical terms to be the variance in actual returns around an expected return. The greater this variance, the more risky an investment is perceived to be. The next step, the central one, is to decompose this risk into risk that can be diversified away by investors and risk that cannot. The third step looks at how different risk and return models in finance attempt to measure this nondiversifiable risk. It compares the most widely used model, the capital pricing asset model (CAPM), with other models and explains how and why they diverge in their measures of risk and the implications for the equity risk premium.

The final part of this chapter considers default risk and how it is measured by ratings agencies. By the end of the chapter, we should have a way of estimating the equity risk and default risk for any firm.

WHAT IS RISK?

Risk, for most of us, refers to the likelihood that in life's games of chance we will receive an outcome that we will not like. For instance, the risk of driving a car too fast is getting a speeding ticket or, worse still, getting into an accident. *Merriam-Webster's Collegiate Dictionary*, in fact, defines the verb to risk as "to expose to hazard or danger." Thus risk is perceived almost entirely in negative terms.

In finance, our definition of risk is both different and broader. Risk, as we see it, refers to the likelihood that we will receive a return on an investment that is different from the return we expect to make. Thus, risk includes not only the bad outcomes (returns that are lower than expected), but also good outcomes (returns that are higher than expected). In fact, we can refer to the former as downside risk and the latter as upside risk, but we consider both when measuring risk. In fact, the spirit of our definition of risk in finance is captured best by the Chinese symbols for risk:

The first symbol is the symbol for "danger," while the second is the symbol for "opportunity," making risk a mix of danger and opportunity. It illustrates very clearly the trade-off that every investor and business has to make—between the higher rewards that come with the opportunity and the higher risk that has to be borne as a consequence of the danger.

Much of this chapter can be viewed as an attempt to come up with a model that best measures the danger in any investment, and then attempts to convert this into the opportunity that we would need to compensate for the danger. In finance terms, we term the danger to be "risk" and the opportunity to be "expected return."

What makes the measurement of risk and expected return so challenging is that it can vary depending on whose perspective we adopt. When analyzing the risk of a firm, for instance, we can measure it from the viewpoint of the firm's managers. Alternatively, we can argue that the firm's equity is owned by its stockholders, and that it is their perspective on risk that should matter. A firm's stockholders, many of whom hold the stock as one investment in a larger portfolio, might perceive the risk in the firm very differently from the firm's managers, who might have the bulk of their capital, human and financial, invested in the firm.

This chapter will argue that risk in an investment has to be perceived through the eyes of investors in the firm. Since firms often have thousands of investors, often with very different perspectives, it can be asserted that risk has to be measured from the perspective of not just any investor in the stock, but of the marginal investor, defined to be the investor most likely to be trading on the stock at any given point in time. The objective in corporate finance is the maximization of firm value and stock price. If we want to stay true to this objective, we have to consider the viewpoint of those who set the stock prices, and they are the marginal investors.

EQUITY RISK AND EXPECTED RETURN

To demonstrate how risk is viewed in finance, risk analysis is presented here in three steps: first, defining risk in terms of the distribution of actual returns around an expected return; second, differentiating between risk that is specific to one or a few investments and risk that affects a much wider cross section of investments (in a market where the marginal investor is well diversified, it is only the latter risk, called market risk, that will be rewarded); and third, alternative models for measuring this market risk and the expected returns that go with it.

Defining Risk

Investors who buy assets expect to earn returns over the time horizon that they hold the asset. Their actual returns over this holding period may be very different from the expected returns, and it is this difference between actual and expected returns that is a source of risk. For example, assume that you are an investor with a one-year time horizon buying a one-year Treasury bill (or any other default-free one-year bond) with a 5 percent expected return. At the end of the one-year holding period, the actual return on this investment will be 5 percent, which is equal to the expected return. The return distribution for this investment is shown in Figure 4.1. This is a riskless investment.

To provide a contrast to the riskless investment, consider an investor who buys stock in a firm, say Boeing. This investor, having done her research, may conclude that she can make an expected return of 30 percent on Boeing over her one-year holding period. The actual return over this period will almost certainly not be equal to 30 percent; it might be much greater or much lower. The distribution of returns on this investment is illustrated in Figure 4.2.

In addition to the expected return, an investor now has to consider the following. First, note that the actual returns, in this case, are different from the expected return. The spread of the actual returns around the expected return is measured by the variance or standard deviation of the distribution; the greater the deviation of the actual returns from the expected return, the greater the variance. Second, the bias toward positive or negative returns is represented by the skewness of the distribution. The distribution in Figure 4.2 is positively skewed, since there is a higher probability of large positive returns than large negative returns. Third, the shape of the tails of the distribution is measured by the kurtosis of the distribution; fatter tails lead to higher kurtosis. In investment terms, this represents the tendency of the price of this investment to jump (up or down from current levels) in either direction.

In the special case where the distribution of returns is normal, investors do not have to worry about skewness and kurtosis, since there is no skewness (normal distributions are symmetric) and a normal distribution is defined to have a kurtosis of zero. Figure 4.3 illustrates the return distributions on two investments with symmetric returns.

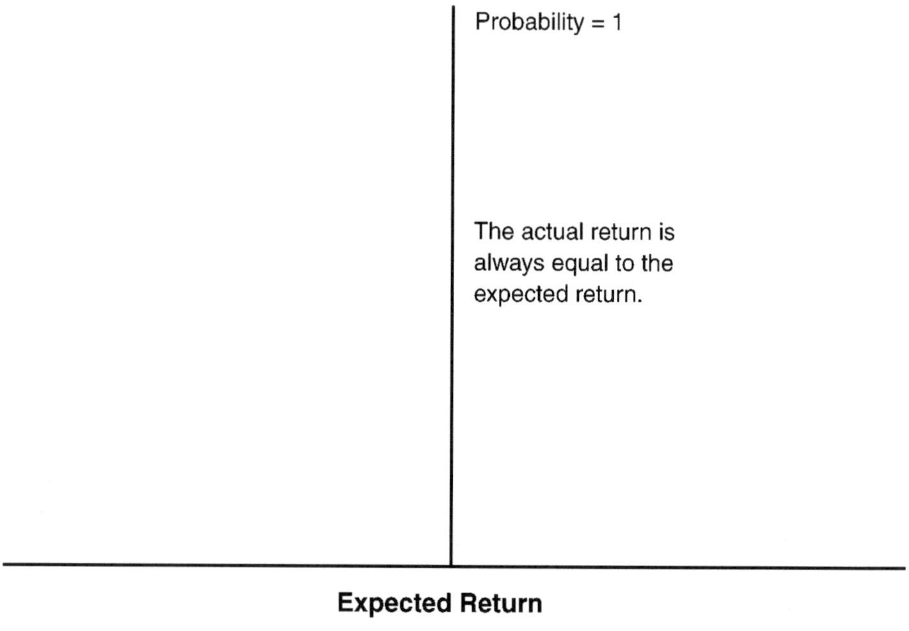

Probability = 1

The actual return is always equal to the expected return.

Expected Return

FIGURE 4.1 Probability Distribution of Returns on a Risk-Free Investment

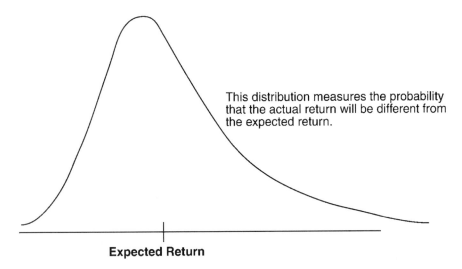

This distribution measures the probability that the actual return will be different from the expected return.

Expected Return

FIGURE 4.2   Return Distribution for Risky Investment

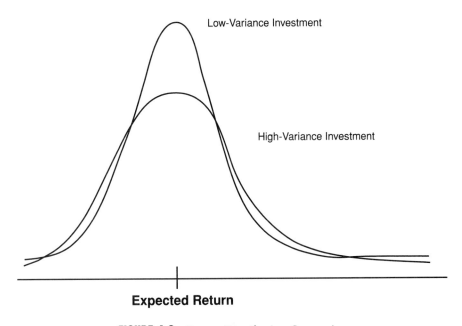

Low-Variance Investment

High-Variance Investment

Expected Return

FIGURE 4.3   Return Distribution Comparisons

When return distributions take this form, the characteristics of any investment can be measured with two variables—the expected return, which represents the opportunity in the investment, and the standard deviation or variance, which represents the danger. In this scenario, a rational investor, faced with a choice between two investments with the same standard deviation but different expected returns, will always pick the one with the higher expected return.

In the more general case, where distributions are neither symmetric nor normal, it is still conceivable that investors will choose between investments on the basis of only the expected return and the variance, if they possess utility functions that allow them to do so.[1] It is far more likely, however, that they prefer positive skewed distributions to negatively skewed ones, and distributions with a lower likelihood of jumps (lower kurtosis) over those with a higher likelihood of jumps (higher kurtosis). In this world, investors will trade off the good (higher expected returns and more positive skewness) against the bad (higher variance and kurtosis) in making investments.

In closing, it should be noted that the expected returns and variances that we run into in practice are almost always estimated using past returns rather than future returns. The assumption made when using historical variances is that past return distributions are good indicators of future return distributions. When this assumption is violated, as is the case when the asset's characteristics have changed significantly over time, the historical estimates may not be good measures of risk.

ILLUSTRATION 4.1: Calculation of Standard Deviation Using Historical Returns: Boeing and the Home Depot

We will use Boeing and the Home Depot as our investments to illustrate how standard deviations and variances are computed. To make our computations simpler, we will look at returns on an annual basis from 1991 to 1998. To begin the analysis, we first estimate returns for each company for each of these years, in percentage terms, incorporating both price appreciation and dividends into these returns:

$$\text{Return in year n} = \frac{\text{Price at end of year n} - \text{Price at beginning of year n} + \text{Dividend in year n}}{\text{Price at beginning of year n}}$$

---

[1]A utility function is a way of summarizing investor preferences into a generic term called "utility" on the basis of some choice variables. In this case, for instance, the investors' utility or satisfaction is stated as a function of wealth. By doing so, we effectively can answer questions such as, Will investors be twice as happy if they have twice as much wealth? Does each marginal increase in wealth lead to less additional utility than the prior marginal increase? In one specific form of this function, the quadratic utility function, the entire utility of an investor can be compressed into the expected wealth measure and the standard deviation in that wealth.

The following table summarizes returns on the two companies:

	Return on Boeing	Return on the Home Depot
1991	5.00%	161.00%
1992	−16.00%	50.30%
1993	7.80%	−22.00%
1994	8.70%	16.50%
1995	66.80%	3.80%
1996	35.90%	5.00%
1997	−8.10%	76.20%
1998	−33.10%	107.90%
Sum	67.00%	398.70%

We compute the average and standard deviation in these returns for the two firms, using the information in the table (there are eight years of data):

$$\text{Average return on Boeing}_{91-98} = 67.00\%/8 = 8.38\%$$

$$\text{Average return on the Home Depot}_{91-98} = 398.70\%/8 = 49.84\%$$

The variance is measured by looking at the deviations of the actual returns in each year, for each stock, from the average return. Since we consider both better-than-expected and worse-than-expected deviations in measuring variance, we square the deviations:[2]

	Return on Boeing	Return on the Home Depot	$[R_B - Average(R_B)]^2$	$[R_{HD} - Average(R_{HD})]^2$
1991	5.00%	161.00%	0.00113906	1.23571014
1992	−16.00%	50.30%	0.05941406	2.1391E-05
1993	7.80%	−22.00%	3.3063E-05	0.51606264
1994	8.70%	16.50%	1.0562E-05	0.11113889
1995	66.80%	3.80%	0.34134806	0.21194514
1996	35.90%	5.00%	0.07576256	0.20104014
1997	−8.10%	76.20%	0.02714256	0.06949814
1998	−33.10%	107.90%	0.17201756	0.33712539
Sum			0.67686750	2.68254188

Following the standard practice for estimating the variances of samples, the variances in returns at the two firms can be estimated by dividing the sum of the squared deviation columns by $(n - 1)$, where n is the number of observations in the sample; the standard deviations can be computed to be the squared root of the variances:

	Boeing	Home Depot
Variance	0.6768675/(8 − 1) = .0967	2.68254188/(8 − 1) = .3832
Standard Deviation	$\sqrt{0.0967} = .311$ or 31.1%	$\sqrt{0.3832} = .619$ or 61.9%

Based on this data, the Home Depot looks like it was two times more risky than Boeing between 1991 and 1998. What does this tell us? By itself, it provides a measure of how much each these companies' returns in the past have deviated from the average. If we assume that the past is a good indicator of the future, the Home Depot is a more risky investment than Boeing.

---

[2]If we do not square the deviations, the sum of the deviations will be zero.

optvar.xls: This is a dataset on the Web that summarizes standard deviations and variances of stocks in various sectors in the United States.

Diversifiable and Nondiversifiable Risk

Although there are many reasons why actual returns may differ from expected returns, we can group the reasons into two categories: firm-specific and marketwide. The risks that arise from firm-specific actions affect one or a few investments, while the risks arising from marketwide reasons affect many or all investments. This distinction is critical to the way we assess risk in finance.

Components of Risk   When an investor buys stock or takes an equity position in a firm, he or she is exposed to many risks. Some risk may affect only one or a few firms, and this risk is categorized as firm-specific risk. Within this category, we would consider a wide range of risks, starting with the risk that a firm may have misjudged the demand for a product from its customers; we call this project risk. For instance, consider Boeing's investment in a Super Jumbo jet. This investment is based on the assumption that airlines want a larger airplane and are willing to pay a high price for it. If Boeing has misjudged this demand, it will clearly have an impact on Boeing's earnings and value, but it should not have a significant effect on other firms in the market. The risk could also arise from competitors proving to be stronger or weaker than anticipated, called competitive risk. For instance, assume that Boeing and Airbus are competing for an order from Qantas, the Australian airline. The possibility that Airbus may win the bid is a potential source of risk to Boeing and perhaps some of its suppliers, but again, few other firms will be affected by it. Similarly, the Home Depot recently launched an online store to sell its home improvement products. Whether it succeeds is clearly important to the Home Depot and its competitors, but it is unlikely to have an impact on the rest of the market. In fact, risk measures can be extended to include risks that may affect an entire sector but are restricted to that sector; we call this sector risk. For instance, a cut in the defense budget in the United States will adversely affect all firms in the defense business, including Boeing, but there should be no significant impact on other sectors. What is common across the three risks described— project, competitive, and sector risk—is that they affect only a small subset of firms.

There is another risk that is much more pervasive and affects many if not all investments. For instance, when interest rates increase, all investments are negatively affected, albeit to different degrees. Similarly, when the economy weakens, all firms feel the effects, though cyclical firms (such as automobiles, steel, and housing) may feel it more. We term this risk market risk.

Finally, there are risks that fall in a gray area, depending on how many assets they affect. For instance, when the dollar strengthens against other currencies, it has a significant impact on the earnings and values of firms with international operations. If most firms in the market have significant international operations, it could well be categorized as market risk. If only a few do, it would be closer to firm-specific risk. Figure 4.4 summarizes the spectrum of firm-specific and market risks.

Why Diversification Reduces or Eliminates Firm-Specific Risk: An Intuitive Explanation

As an investor, you could invest all your portfolio in one asset. If you do so, you are exposed to both firm-specific and market risk. If, however, you expand your portfolio to include other assets or stocks, you are diversifying, and by doing so you can reduce

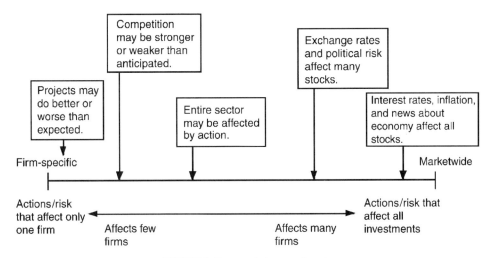

FIGURE 4.4 Breakdown of Risk

your exposure to firm-specific risk. There are two reasons why diversification reduces or, at the limit, eliminates firm-specific risk. The first is that each investment in a diversified portfolio is a much smaller percentage of that portfolio than would be the case if you were not diversified. Any action that increases or decreases the value of only that investment or a small group of investments will have only a small impact on your overall portfolio, whereas undiversified investors are much more exposed to changes in the values of the investments in their portfolios. The second reason is that the effects of firm-specific actions on the prices of individual assets in a portfolio can be either positive or negative for each asset for any period. Thus, in very large portfolios this risk will average out to zero and will not affect the overall value of the portfolio.

In contrast, the effects of marketwide movements are likely to be in the same direction for most or all investments in a portfolio, though some assets may be affected more than others. For instance, other things being equal, an increase in interest rates will lower the values of most assets in a portfolio. Being more diversified does not eliminate this risk.

A Statistical Analysis of Diversification-Reducing Risk   The effects of diversification on risk can be illustrated fairly dramatically by examining the effects of increasing the number of assets in a portfolio on portfolio variance. The variance in a portfolio is partially determined by the variances of the individual assets in the portfolio and partially by how they move together; the latter is measured statistically with a correlation coefficient or the covariance across investments in the portfolio. It is the covariance term that provides an insight into why diversification will reduce risk and by how much.

Consider a portfolio of two assets. Asset A has an expected return of μ_A and a variance in returns of σ^2_A, while asset B has an expected return of μ_B and a variance in returns of σ^2_B. The correlation in returns between the two assets, which measures how the assets move together, is ρ_{AB}. The expected returns and variances of a two-asset portfolio can be written as a function of these inputs and the proportion of the portfolio going to each asset.

$$\mu_{\text{portfolio}} = w_A \mu_A + (1 - w_A) \mu_B$$

$$\sigma^2_{\text{portfolio}} = w_A^2 \sigma_A^2 + (1 - w_A)^2 \sigma_B^2 + 2 w_A (1 - w_A) \rho_{AB} \sigma_A \sigma_B$$

where w_A = Proportion of the portfolio in asset A

The last term in the variance formulation is sometimes written in terms of the co-variance in returns between the two assets, which is:

$$\sigma_{AB} = \rho_{AB} \sigma_A \sigma_B$$

    The savings that accrue from diversification are a function of the correlation coefficient. Other things remaining equal, the higher the correlation in returns between the two assets, the smaller are the potential benefits from diversification.

Models Measuring Market Risk

While most risk and return models in use in corporate finance agree on the first two steps of the risk analysis process (i.e., that risk comes from the distribution of

---

WHY IS THE MARGINAL INVESTOR ASSUMED TO BE DIVERSIFIED?

The argument that diversification reduces an investor's exposure to risk is clear both intuitively and statistically, but risk and return models in finance go further. They look at risk through the eyes of the investor most likely to be trading on the investment at any point in time—the marginal investor. They argue that this investor, who sets prices for investments, is well diversified; thus, the only risk that he or she cares about is the risk added to a diversified portfolio or market risk. This argument can be justified simply. The risk in an investment will always be perceived to be higher for an undiversified investor than for a diversified one, since the latter does not shoulder any firm-specific risk and the former does. If both investors have the same expectations about future earnings and cash flows on an asset, the diversified investor will be willing to pay a higher price for that asset because of his or her perception of lower risk. Consequently, the asset, over time, will end up being held by diversified investors.

    This argument is powerful, especially in markets where assets can be traded easily and at low cost. Thus, it works well for a stock traded in the United States, since investors can become diversified at fairly low cost. In addition, a significant proportion of the trading in U.S. stocks is done by institutional investors, who tend to be well diversified. It becomes a more difficult argument to sustain when assets cannot be easily traded or the costs of trading are high. In these markets, the marginal investor may well be undiversified, and firm-specific risk may therefore continue to matter when looking at individual investments. For instance, real estate in most countries is still held by investors who are undiversified and have the bulk of their wealth tied up in these investments.

actual returns around the expected return and that risk should be measured from the perspective of a marginal investor who is well diversified), they part ways when it comes to measuring nondiversifiable or market risk. This section will discuss the different models that exist in finance for measuring market risk and why they differ. It begins with what still is the standard model for measuring market risk in finance—the capital asset pricing model (CAPM)—and then discusses the alternatives to this model that have developed over the past two decades. While the discussion will emphasize the differences, it will also look at what the models have in common.

Capital Asset Pricing Model   The risk and return model that has been in use the longest and is still the standard in most real-world analyses is the capital asset pricing model (CAPM). This section will examine the assumptions on which the model is based and the measures of market risk that emerge from these assumptions.

Assumptions   While diversification reduces the exposure of investors to firm-specific risk, most investors limit their diversification to holding only a few assets. Even large mutual funds rarely hold more than a few hundred stocks, and many of them hold as few as 10 to 20. There are two reasons why investors stop diversifying. One is that an investor or mutual fund manager can obtain most of the benefits of diversification from a relatively small portfolio, because the marginal benefits of diversification become smaller as the portfolio gets more diversified. Consequently, these benefits may not cover the marginal costs of diversification, which include transactions and monitoring costs. Another reason for limiting diversification is that many investors (and funds) believe they can find undervalued assets and thus choose not to hold those assets that they believe to be fairly valued or overvalued.

The capital asset pricing model assumes that there are no transaction costs, all assets are traded, and investments are infinitely divisible (i.e., you can buy any fraction of a unit of the asset). It also assumes that everyone has access to the same information and that investors therefore cannot find under- or overvalued assets in the marketplace. By making these assumptions, it allows investors to keep diversifying without additional cost. At the limit, their portfolios will not only include every traded asset in the market but will have identical weights on risky assets (based on their market value).

The fact that this portfolio includes all traded assets in the market is the reason it is called the market portfolio, which should not be a surprising result, given the benefits of diversification and the absence of transaction costs in the capital asset pricing model. If diversification reduces exposure to firm-specific risk and there are no costs associated with adding more assets to the portfolio, the logical limit to diversification is to hold a small proportion of every traded asset in the economy. If this seems abstract, consider the market portfolio to be an extremely well diversified mutual fund that holds stocks and real assets. In the CAPM, all investors will hold combinations of the riskier asset and the same mutual fund.[3]

---

[3]The significance of introducing the riskless asset into the choice mix and the implications for portfolio choice were first noted in Sharpe (1964) and Lintner (1965). Hence, the model is sometimes called the Sharpe-Lintner model.

Investor Portfolios in the CAPM   If every investor in the market holds the identical market portfolio, how exactly do investors reflect their risk aversion in their investments? In the capital asset pricing model, investors adjust for their risk preferences in their allocation decision, where they decide how much to invest in a riskless asset and how much in the market portfolio. Investors who are risk averse might choose to put much or even all of their wealth in the riskless asset. Investors who want to take more risk will invest the bulk or even all of their wealth in the market portfolio. Investors who invest all their wealth in the market portfolio and are desirous of taking on still more risk would do so by borrowing at the riskless rate and investing in the same market portfolio as everyone else.

These results are predicated on two additional assumptions. First, there exists a riskless asset, where the expected returns are known with certainty. Second, investors can lend and borrow at the riskless rate to arrive at their optimal allocations. While lending at the riskless rate can be accomplished fairly simply by buying Treasury bills or bonds, borrowing at the riskless rate might be more difficult for individuals to do. There are variations of the CAPM that allow these assumptions to be relaxed and still arrive at conclusions that are consistent with the model.

Measuring the Market Risk of an Individual Asset   The risk of any asset to an investor is the risk added by that asset to the investor's overall portfolio. In the CAPM world, where all investors hold the market portfolio, the risk to an investor of an individual asset will be the risk that this asset adds to the market portfolio. Intuitively, if an asset moves independently of the market portfolio, it will not add much risk to the market portfolio. In other words, most of the risk in this asset is firm-specific and can be diversified away. In contrast, if an asset tends to move up when the market portfolio moves up and down when it moves down, it will add risk to the market portfolio. This asset has more market risk and less firm-specific risk. Statistically, this added risk is measured by the covariance of the asset with the market portfolio.

Measuring the Nondiversifiable Risk   In a world in which investors hold a combination of only two assets—the riskless asset and the market portfolio—the risk of any individual asset will be measured relative to the market portfolio. In particular, the risk of any asset will be the risk it adds to the market portfolio. To arrive at the appropriate measure of this added risk, assume that σ_m^2 is the variance of the market portfolio prior to the addition of the new asset and that the variance of the individual asset being added to this portfolio is σ_i^2. The market value portfolio weight on this asset is w_i, and the covariance in returns between the individual asset and the market portfolio is σ_{im}. The variance of the market portfolio prior to and after the addition of the individual asset can then be written as:

Variance prior to asset i being added $= \sigma_m^2$
Variance after asset i is added $= \sigma_{m'}^2 = w_i^2 \sigma_i^2 + (1 - w_i)^2 \sigma_m^2 + 2w_i(1 - w_i)\sigma_{im}$

The market value weight on any individual asset in the market portfolio should be small, since the market portfolio includes all traded assets in the economy. Consequently, the first term in the equation should approach zero, and the second term should approach σ_m^2, leaving the third term ($\sigma_{im'}$ the covariance) as the measure of the risk added by asset i.

Standardizing Covariances   The covariance is a percentage value, and it is difficult to pass judgment on the relative risk of an investment by looking at this value. In other words, knowing that the covariance of Boeing with the market portfolio is 55 percent does not provide us a clue as to whether Boeing is riskier or safer than the average asset. We therefore standardize the risk measure by dividing the covariance of each asset with the market portfolio by the variance of the market portfolio. This yields a risk measure called the beta of the asset:

$$\text{Beta of asset } i = \frac{\text{Covariance of asset i with market portfolio}}{\text{Variance of the market portfolio}} = \frac{\sigma_{im}}{\sigma_m^2}$$

Since the covariance of the market portfolio with itself is its variance, the beta of the market portfolio (and, by extension, the average asset in it) is 1. Assets that are riskier than average (using this measure of risk) will have betas that exceed 1, and assets that are safer than average will have betas that are lower than 1. The riskless asset will have a beta of zero.

Getting Expected Returns   The fact that every investor holds some combination of the riskless asset and the market portfolio leads to the next conclusion, which is that the expected return on an asset is linearly related to the beta of the asset. In particular, the expected return on an asset can be written as a function of the risk-free rate and the beta of that asset:

$$E(R_i) = R_f + \beta_i[E(R_m) - R_f]$$

where $E(R_i)$ = Expected return on asset i
         R_f = Risk-free rate
      $E(R_m)$ = Expected return on market portfolio
         β_i = Beta of asset i

To use the capital asset pricing model, we need three inputs. While the next chapter will look at the estimation process in far more detail, each of these inputs is estimated as follows:

■ The riskless asset is defined to be an asset for which the investor knows the expected return with certainty for the time horizon of the analysis.
■ The risk premium is the premium demanded by investors for investing in the market portfolio, which includes all risky assets in the market, instead of investing in a riskless asset.
■ The beta, defined as the covariance of the asset divided by the market portfolio, measures the risk added by an investment to the market portfolio.

In summary, in the capital asset pricing model all the market risk is captured in one beta measured relative to a market portfolio, which at least in theory should include all traded assets in the marketplace held in proportion to their market value.

Arbitrage Pricing Model   The restrictive assumptions on transaction costs and private information in the capital asset pricing model, and the model's dependence on the market portfolio, have long been viewed with skepticism by both academics and practitioners. Ross (1976) suggested an alternative model for measuring risk called the arbitrage pricing model (APM).

Assumptions   If investors can invest risklessly and earn more than the riskless rate, they have found an arbitrage opportunity. The premise of the arbitrage pricing model is that investors take advantage of such arbitrage opportunities, and in the process eliminate them. If two portfolios have the same exposure to risk but offer different expected returns, investors will buy the portfolio that has the higher expected returns and sell the portfolio with the lower expected returns, and earn the difference as a riskless profit. To prevent this arbitrage from occurring, the two portfolios have to earn the same expected return.

Like the capital asset pricing model, the arbitrage pricing model begins by breaking risk down into firm-specific and market risk components. As in the capital asset pricing model, firm-specific risk covers information that affects primarily the firm. Market risk affects many or all firms and would include unanticipated changes in a number of economic variables, including gross national product, inflation, and interest rates. Incorporating both types of risk into a return model, we get:

$$R = E(R) + m + \varepsilon$$

where R is the actual return, E(R) is the expected return, m is the marketwide component of unanticipated risk, and ε is the firm-specific component. Thus, the actual return can be different from the expected return, because of either market risk or firm-specific actions.

Sources of Marketwide Risk   While both the capital asset pricing model and the arbitrage pricing model make a distinction between firm-specific and marketwide risk, they measure market risk differently. The CAPM assumes that market risk is captured in the market portfolio, whereas the arbitrage pricing model allows for multiple sources of marketwide risk and measures the sensitivity of investments to changes in each source. In general, the market component of unanticipated returns can be decomposed into economic factors:

$$R = E(R) + m + \varepsilon$$
$$= R + (\beta_1 F_1 + \beta_2 F_2 + \ldots + \beta_n F_n) + \varepsilon$$

where β_j = Sensitivity of investment to unanticipated changes in factor j
$\quad\quad$ F_j = Unanticipated changes in factor j

Note that the measure of an investment's sensitivity to any macroeconomic factor takes the form of a beta, called a factor beta. In fact, this beta has many of the same properties as the market beta in the CAPM.

Effects of Diversification   The benefits of diversification were discussed earlier, in the context of the breakdown of risk into market and firm-specific risk. The primary point of that discussion was that diversification eliminates firm-specific risk. The arbitrage pricing model uses the same argument and concludes that the return on a portfolio will not have a firm-specific component of unanticipated returns. The return on a portfolio can be written as the sum of two weighted averages—that of the anticipated returns in the portfolio and that of the market factors:

$$R_p = (w_1 R_1 + w_2 R_2 + \ldots + w_n R_n) + (w_1 \beta_{1,1} + w_2 \beta_{1,2} + \ldots + w_n \beta_{1,n})F_1 +$$
$$(w_1 \beta_{2,1} + w_2 \beta_{2,2} + \ldots + w_n \beta_{2,n})F_2 \ldots$$

where w_j = Portfolio weight on asset j (where there are n assets)
         R_j = Expected return on asset j
         $\beta_{i,j}$ = Beta on factor i for asset j

Expected Returns and Betas   The final step in this process is estimating an expected return as a function of the betas just specified. To do this, we should first note that the beta of a portfolio is the weighted average of the betas of the assets in the portfolio. This property, in conjunction with the absence of arbitrage, leads to the conclusion that expected returns should be linearly related to betas. To see why, assume that there is only one factor and three portfolios. Portfolio A has a beta of 2.0 and an expected return of 20 percent; portfolio B has a beta of 1.0 and an expected return of 12 percent; and portfolio C has a beta of 1.5 and an expected return of 14 percent. Note that investors can put half of their wealth in portfolio A and half in portfolio B and end up with portfolios with a beta of 1.5 and an expected return of 16 percent. Consequently no investor will choose to hold portfolio C until the prices of assets in that portfolio drop and the expected return increases to 16 percent. By the same rationale, the expected returns of every portfolio should be a linear function of the beta. If they were not, we could combine two other portfolios, one with a higher beta and one with a lower beta, to earn a higher return than the portfolio in question, creating an opportunity for arbitrage. This argument can be extended to multiple factors with the same results. Therefore, the expected return on an asset can be written as:

$$E(R) = R_f + \beta_1[E(R_1) - R_f] + \beta_2[E(R_2) - R_f] \ldots + \beta_K[E(R_K) - R_f]$$

where R_f = Expected return on a zero-beta portfolio
         $E(R_j)$ = Expected return on a portfolio with a factor beta of 1 for factor j, and zero for all other factors (where j = 1, 2, . . . , K factors)

The terms in the brackets can be considered to be risk premiums for each of the factors in the model.

The capital asset pricing model can be considered to be a special case of the arbitrage pricing model, where there is only one economic factor driving marketwide returns, and the market portfolio is the factor.

$$E(R) = R_f + \beta_m[E(R_m) - R_f]$$

The APM in Practice   The arbitrage pricing model requires estimates of each of the factor betas and factor risk premiums in addition to the riskless rate. In practice, these are usually estimated using historical data on asset returns and a factor analysis. Intuitively, in a factor analysis, we examine the historical data looking for common patterns that affect broad groups of assets (rather than just one sector or a few assets). A factor analysis provides two output measures:

1. It specifies the number of common factors that affected the historical return data.
2. It measures the beta of each investment relative to each of the common factors and provides an estimate of the actual risk premium earned by each factor.

The factor analysis does not, however, identify the factors in economic terms. In summary, in the arbitrage pricing model the market risk is measured relative to multiple unspecified macroeconomic variables, with the sensitivity of the investment relative to each factor being measured by a beta. The number of factors, the factor betas, and the factor risk premiums can all be estimated using the factor analysis.

Multifactor Models for Risk and Return   The arbitrage pricing model's failure to identify the factors specifically in the model may be a statistical strength, but it is an intuitive weakness. The solution seems simple: Replace the unidentified statistical factors with specific economic factors, and the resultant model should have an economic basis while still retaining much of the strength of the arbitrage pricing model. That is precisely what multifactor models try to do.

Deriving a Multifactor Model   Multifactor models generally are determined by historical data rather than by economic modeling. Once the number of factors has been identified in the arbitrage pricing model, their behavior over time can be extracted from the data. The behavior of the unnamed factors over time can then be compared to the behavior of macroeconomic variables over that same period, to see whether any of the variables is correlated, over time, with the identified factors.

For instance, Chen, Roll, and Ross (1986) suggest that the following macroeconomic variables are highly correlated with the factors that come out of factor analysis: industrial production, changes in default premium, shifts in the term structure, unanticipated inflation, and changes in the real rate of return. These variables can then be correlated with returns to come up with a model of expected returns, with firm-specific betas calculated relative to each variable.

$$E(R) = R_f + \beta_{GNP}\,[E(R_{GNP}) - R_f] + \beta_I[E(R_I) - R_f] \ldots + \beta_\delta[E(R_\delta) - R_f]$$

where β_{GNP} = Beta relative to changes in industrial production
   $E(R_{GNP})$ = Expected return on a portfolio with a beta of one on the industrial production factor and zero on all other factors
   β_I = Beta relative to changes in inflation
   $E(R_I)$ = Expected return on a portfolio with a beta of one on the inflation factor and zero on all other factors

The costs of going from the arbitrage pricing model to a macroeconomic multifactor model can be traced directly to the errors that can be made in identifying the factors. The economic factors in the model can change over time, as will the risk premium associated with each one. For instance, oil price changes were a significant economic factor driving expected returns in the 1970s but are not as significant in other time periods. Using the wrong factor or missing a significant factor in a multifactor model can lead to inferior estimates of expected return.

In summary, multifactor models, like the arbitrage pricing model, assume that market risk can be captured best using multiple macroeconomic factors and betas relative to each. Unlike the arbitrage pricing model, multifactor models do attempt to identify the macroeconomic factors that drive market risk.

Regression or Proxy Models All the models described so far begin by defining market risk in broad terms and then developing models that might best measure this market risk. All of them, however, extract their measures of market risk (betas) by looking at historical data. There is a final class of risk and return models that start with the returns, and try to explain differences in returns across stocks over long time periods, using characteristics such as a firm's market value or price multiples.[4] Proponents of these models argue that if some investments earn consistently higher returns than other investments, they must be riskier. Consequently, we could look at the characteristics that these high-return investments have in common and consider these characteristics to be indirect measures or proxies for market risk.

Fama and French (1992), in a highly influential study of the capital asset pricing model, noted that actual returns between 1963 and 1990 have been highly correlated with book-to-price ratios[5] and size. High-return investments, over this period, tended to be investments in companies with low market capitalization and high book-to-price ratios. Fama and French suggested that these measures be used as proxies for risk and reported the following regression for monthly returns on stocks on the New York Stock Exchange (NYSE):

$$R_t = 1.77\% - 0.11 \ln(MV) + 0.35 \ln(BV/MV)$$

where   ln = Natural log
           MV = Market value of equity
      BV/MV = Book value of equity/market value of equity

The values for market value of equity and book-to-price ratios for individual firms, when plugged into this regression, should yield expected monthly returns.

A COMPARATIVE ANALYSIS OF RISK AND RETURN MODELS

Figure 4.5 summarizes all the risk and return models in finance, noting their similarities in the first two steps and the differences in the way they define market risk.

As noted in Figure 4.5, all the risk and return models developed in this chapter make some assumptions in common. They all assume that only market risk is rewarded, and they derive the expected return as a function of measures of this risk. The capital asset pricing model makes the most restrictive assumptions about how markets work but arrives at the simplest model, with only one factor driving risk and requiring estimation. The arbitrage pricing model makes fewer assumptions but arrives at a more complicated model, at least in terms of the pa-

---

[4] A price multiple is obtained by dividing the market price by its earnings or its book value. Studies indicate that stocks that have low price-earnings multiples or low price–book value multiples earn higher returns than other stocks.

[5] The book-to-price ratio is the ratio of the book value of equity to the market value of equity.

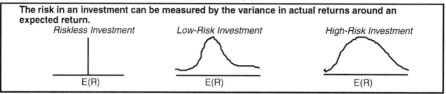

Step 1: Defining Risk

The risk in an investment can be measured by the variance in actual returns around an expected return.

Riskless Investment	Low-Risk Investment	High-Risk Investment
E(R)	E(R)	E(R)

Step 2: Differentiating between Rewarded and Unrewarded Risk

Risk that is specific to investment (firm-specific risk) can be diversified away in a diversified portfolio. 1. Each investment is a small proportion of portfolio. 2. Risk averages out across investments in portfolio.	Risk that affects all investments (market risk) cannot be diversified away since most assets are affected by it.

The marginal investor is assumed to hold a diversified portfolio. Thus, only market risk will be rewarded and priced.

Step 3: Measuring Market Risk

The CAPM	The APM	Multifactor Models	Proxy Models
If there is 1. no private information 2. no transactions cost the optimal diversified portfolio includes every traded asset. Everyone will hold this market portfolio **Market Risk = Risk added by any investment to the market portfolio**	If there are no arbitrage opportunities, then the market risk of any asset must be captured by betas relative to factors that affect all investments. **Market Risk = Risk exposures of any asset to market factors**	Since market risk affects most or all investments, it must come from macroeconomic factors. **Market Risk = Risk exposures of any asset to macroeconomic factors**	In an efficient market, differences in returns across long periods must be due to market risk differences. Looking for variables correlated with returns should then give us proxies for this risk. **Market Risk = Captured by the proxy variable(s)**
Betas of assets relative to market portfolio (from a regression)	Betas of assets relative to unspecified market factors (from a factor analysis)	Betas of assets relative to specified macroeconomic factors (from a regression)	Equation relating returns to proxy variables (from a regression)

FIGURE 4.5   Risk and Return Models in Finance

rameters that require estimation. The capital asset pricing model can be considered a specialized case of the arbitrage pricing model, where there is only one underlying factor and it is completely measured by the market index. In general, the CAPM has the advantage of being a simpler model to estimate and to use, but it will underperform the richer APM when an investment is sensitive to economic factors not well represented in the market index. For instance, oil company stocks, which derive most of their risk from oil price movements, tend to have low CAPM betas and low expected returns. Using an arbitrage pricing model, where one of the factors may measure oil and other commodity price movements, will yield a better estimate of risk and higher expected return for these firms.[6]

Which of these models works best? Is beta a good proxy for risk, and is it correlated with expected returns? The answers to these questions have been debated widely in the past two decades. The first tests of the CAPM suggested that betas

---

[6]Weston and Copeland (1992) used both approaches to estimate the cost of equity for oil companies in 1989 and came up with 14.4 percent with the CAPM and 19.1 percent using the arbitrage pricing model.

and returns were positively related, though other measures of risk (such as variance) continued to explain differences in actual returns. This discrepancy was attributed to limitations in the testing techniques. In 1977, Roll, in a seminal critique of the model's tests, suggested that since the market portfolio could never be observed, the CAPM could never be tested, and all tests of the CAPM were therefore joint tests of both the model and the market portfolio used in the tests. In other words, all that any test of the CAPM could show was that the model worked (or did not) given the proxy used for the market portfolio. It could therefore be argued that in any empirical test that claimed to reject the CAPM, the rejection could be of the proxy used for the market portfolio rather than of the model itself. Roll noted that there was no way ever to prove that the CAPM worked and thus there was no empirical basis for using the model.

Fama and French (1992) examined the relationship between betas and returns between 1963 and 1990 and concluded that there is no relationship. These results have been contested on three fronts. First, Amihud, Christensen, and Mendelson (1992) used the same data, performed different statistical tests, and showed that differences in betas did in fact explain differences in returns during the time period. Second, Kothari and Shanken (1995) estimated betas using annual data instead of the shorter intervals used in many tests, and concluded that betas do explain a significant proportion of the differences in returns across investments. Third, Chan and Lakonishok (1993) looked at a much longer time series of returns from 1926 to 1991 and found that the positive relationship between betas and returns broke down only in the period after 1982. They also found that betas are a useful guide to risk in extreme market conditions, with the riskiest firms (the 10 percent with highest betas) performing far worse than the market as a whole in the 10 worst months for the market between 1926 and 1991. (See Figure 4.6.)

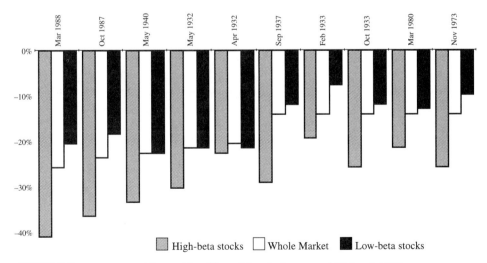

FIGURE 4.6 Returns and Betas: Ten Worst Months between 1926 and 1991
Source: Chan and Lakonishok.

While the initial tests of the APM suggested that they might provide more promise in terms of explaining differences in returns, a distinction has to be drawn between the use of these models to explain differences in past returns and their use to predict expected returns in the future. The competitors to the CAPM clearly do a much better job of explaining past returns since they do not constrain themselves to one factor, as the CAPM does. This extension to multiple factors does become more of a problem when we try to project expected returns into the future, since the betas and premiums of each of these factors now have to be estimated. Because the factor premiums and betas are themselves volatile, the estimation error may eliminate the benefits that could be gained by moving from the CAPM to more complex models. The regression models that were offered as an alternative also have an estimation problem, since the variables that work best as proxies for market risk in one period (such as market capitalization) may not be the ones that work in the next period.

Ultimately, the survival of the capital asset pricing model as the default model for risk in real-world applications is a testament to both its intuitive appeal and the failure of more complex models to deliver significant improvement in terms of estimating expected returns. It would seem that a judicious use of the capital asset pricing model, without an overreliance on historical data, is still the most effective way of dealing with risk in modern corporate finance.

MODELS OF DEFAULT RISK

The risk discussed so far in this chapter relates to cash flows on investments being different from expected cash flows. There are some investments, however, in which the cash flows are promised when the investment is made. This is the case, for instance, when you lend to a business or buy a corporate bond; the borrower may default on interest and principal payments on the borrowing. Generally speaking, borrowers with higher default risk should pay higher interest rates on their borrowing than those with lower default risk. This section examines the measurement of default risk and the relationship of default risk to interest rates on borrowing.

In contrast to the general risk and return models for equity, which evaluate the effects of market risk on expected returns, models of default risk measure the consequences of firm-specific default risk on promised returns. While diversification can be used to explain why firm-specific risk will not be priced into expected returns for equities, the same rationale cannot be applied to securities that have limited upside potential and much greater downside potential from firm-specific events. To see what is meant by limited upside potential, consider investing in the bond issued by a company. The coupons are fixed at the time of the issue, and these coupons represent the promised cash flow on the bond. The best-case scenario for you as an investor is that you receive the promised cash flows; you are not entitled to more than these cash flows even if the company is wildly successful. All other scenarios contain only bad news, though in varying degrees, with the delivered cash flows being less than the promised cash flows. Consequently, the expected return on a corporate bond is likely to reflect the firm-specific default risk of the firm issuing the bond.

Determinants of Default Risk

The default risk of a firm is a function of two variables. The first is the firm's capacity to generate cash flows from operations, and the second is its financial obligations—including interest and principal payments.[7] Firms that generate high cash flows relative to their financial obligations should have lower default risk than do firms that generate low cash flows relative to obligations. Thus, firms with significant existing investments that generate high cash flows will have lower default risk than will firms that do not have such investments.

In addition to the magnitude of a firm's cash flows, the default risk is also affected by the volatility in these cash flows. The more stability there is in cash flows, the lower is the default risk in the firm. Firms that operate in predictable and stable businesses will have lower default risk than will otherwise similar firms that operate in cyclical or volatile businesses.

Most models of default risk use financial ratios to measure the cash flow coverage (i.e., the magnitude of cash flows relative to obligations) and control for industry effects in order to evaluate the variability in cash flows.

Bond Ratings and Interest Rates

The most widely used measure of a firm's default risk is its bond rating, which is generally assigned by an independent ratings agency. The two best known are Standard & Poor's and Moody's. Thousands of companies are rated by these two agencies, and their views carry significant weight with financial markets.

The Ratings Process The process of rating a bond starts when the issuing company requests a rating from a bond ratings agency. The ratings agency then collects information from both publicly available sources, such as financial statements, and the company itself and makes a decision on the rating. If the company disagrees with the rating, it is given the opportunity to present additional information. This process is presented schematically for one ratings agency, Standard & Poor's (S&P), in Figure 4.7.

The ratings assigned by these agencies are letter ratings. A rating of AAA from Standard & Poor's and Aaa from Moody's represents the highest rating, granted to firms that are viewed as having the lowest default risk. As the default risk increases, the ratings decrease toward D for firms in default (Standard & Poor's). A rating above BBB by Standard & Poor's is categorized as above investment grade, reflecting the view of the ratings agency that there is relatively little default risk in investing in bonds issued by these firms.

Determinants of Bond Ratings The bond ratings assigned by ratings agencies are primarily based on publicly available information, though private information con-

---

[7]Financial obligation refers to any payment that the firm has legally obligated itself to make, such as interest and principal payments. It does not include discretionary cash flows, such as dividend payments or new capital expenditures, which can be deferred or delayed without legal consequences, though there may be economic consequences.

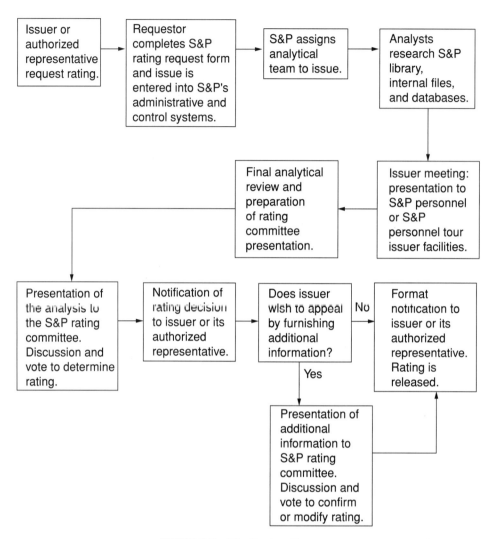

FIGURE 4.7 The Ratings Process

veyed by the firm to the rating agency does play a role. The rating assigned to a company's bonds will depend in large part on financial ratios that measure the capacity of the company to meet debt payments and generate stable and predictable cash flows. While a multitude of financial ratios exist, Table 4.1 summarizes some of the key ratios used to measure default risk.

There is a strong relationship between the bond rating a company receives and its performance on these financial ratios. Table 4.2 provides a summary of the median ratios[8] from 1997 to 1999 for different S&P ratings classes for manufacturing firms.

Not surprisingly, firms that generate income and cash flows significantly higher than debt payments, that are profitable, and that have low debt ratios are more likely to be highly rated than are firms that do not have these characteristics. There

---

[8]See the Standard & Poor's online site (www.standardandpoors.com/ratings/criteria/index.htm).

TABLE 4.1 Financial Ratios Used to Measure Default Risk

Ratio	Description
Pretax interest coverage	= (Pretax income from continuing operations + Interest expense)/ Gross interest
EBITDA interest coverage	= EBITDA/Gross interest
Funds from operations/total debt	= (Net income from continuing operations + depreciation)/Total debt
Free operating cash flow/total debt	= (Funds from operations – Capital expenditures – Change in working capital)/Total debt
Pretax return on permanent capital	= (Pretax income from continuing operations + Interest expense)/Average of beginning of the year and end of the year of long- and short-term debt, minority interest, and shareholders' equity
Operating income/ sales (%)	= (Sales – Cost of goods sold before depreciation – Selling expenses – Administrative expenses – R&D expenses)/Sales
Long-term debt capital	= Long-term debt/(Long-term debt + Equity)
Total debt/ capitalization	$= \dfrac{\text{Total debt}}{(\text{Total debt} + \text{Equity})}$

Source: Standard & Poor's.

TABLE 4.2 Three-Year (1997 to 1999) Medians

	AAA	AA	A	BBB	BB	B	CCC
EBIT int. cov. (X)	17.5	10.8	6.8	3.9	2.3	1.0	0.2
EBITDA int. cov. (X)	21.8	14.6	9.6	6.1	3.8	2.0	1.4
Funds flow % total debt	105.8	55.8	46.1	30.5	19.2	9.4	5.8
Free oper. cash flow/total debt (%)	55.4	24.6	15.6	6.6	1.9	(4.5)	(14.0)
Return on cap. (%)	28.2	22.9	19.9	14.0	11.7	7.2	0.5
Oper. inc. % sales	29.2	21.3	18.3	15.3	15.4	11.2	13.6
Long-term debt/cap. (%)	15.2	26.4	32.5	41.0	55.8	70.7	80.3
Total debt % cap.	26.9	35.6	40.1	47.4	61.3	74.6	89.4
Companies	10	34	150	234	276	240	23

Source: Standard & Poor's.
Note: Pretax interest coverage ratio and EBITDA interest coverage ratio are stated in terms of times interest earned; the other ratios are stated in percentage terms.

ratingfins.xls: This is a dataset on the Web that summarizes key financial ratios by bond rating class for the United States in the most recent period for which the data is available.

will be individual firms whose ratings are not consistent with their financial ratios, however, because the ratings agency does add subjective judgments into the final mix. Thus a firm that performs poorly on financial ratios but is expected to improve its performance dramatically over the next period may receive a higher rating than is justified by its current financials. For most firms, however, the financial ratios should provide a reasonable basis for guessing at the bond rating.

Bond Ratings and Interest Rates The interest rate on a corporate bond should be a function of its default risk, which is measured by its rating. If the rating is a good measure of the default risk, higher-rated bonds should be priced to yield lower interest rates than those of lower-rated bonds. In fact, the difference between the interest rate on a bond with default risk and a default-free government bond is the default spread. This default spread will vary by maturity of the bond and can also change from period to period, depending on economic conditions. Chapter 7 will consider how best to estimate these default spreads and how they might vary over time.

CONCLUSION

Risk, as defined in finance, is measured based on deviations of actual returns on an investment from its expected returns. There are two types of risk. The first, called equity risk, arises in investments where there are no promised cash flows, but there are expected cash flows. The second, default risk, arises on investments with promised cash flows.

On investments with equity risk, the risk is best measured by looking at the variance of actual returns around the expected returns, with greater variance indicating greater risk. This risk can be broken down into risk that affects one or a few investments, called firm-specific risk, and risk that affects many investments, refered to as market risk. When investors diversify, they can reduce their exposure to firm-specific risk. By assuming that the investors who trade at the margin are well diversified, we conclude that the risk we should be looking at with equity investments is the market risk. The different models of equity risk introduced in this chapter share this objective of measuring market risk, but they differ in the way they do it. In the capital asset pricing model, exposure to market risk is measured by a market beta, which estimates how much risk an individual investment will add to a portfolio that includes all traded assets. The arbitrage pricing model and the multifactor model allow for multiple sources of market risk and estimate betas for an investment relative to each source. Regression or proxy models for risk look for firm characteristics, such as size, that have been correlated with high returns in the past and use these to measure market risk. In all these models, the risk measures are used to estimate the expected return on an equity investment. This expected return can be considered the cost of equity for a company.

On investments with default risk, risk is measured by the likelihood that the promised cash flows might not be delivered. Investments with higher default risk should have higher interest rates, and the premium that we demand over a riskless rate is the default spread. For most U.S. companies, default risk is measured by rating agencies in the form of a company rating; these ratings determine, in large part, the interest rates at which these firms can borrow. Even in the absence of ratings, interest rates will include a default spread that reflects the lenders' assessments of default risk. These default-risk-adjusted interest rates represent the cost of borrowing or debt for a business.

QUESTIONS AND SHORT PROBLEMS

1. The following table lists the stock prices for Microsoft from 1989 to 1998. The company did not pay any dividends during the period.

Year	Price
1989	$ 1.20
1990	$ 2.09
1991	$ 4.64
1992	$ 5.34
1993	$ 5.05
1994	$ 7.64
1995	$10.97
1996	$20.66
1997	$32.31
1998	$69.34

   a. Estimate the average annual return you would have made on your investment.
   b. Estimate the standard deviation and variance in annual returns.
   c. If you were investing in Microsoft today, would you expect the historical standard deviations and variances to continue to hold? Why or why not?

2. Unicom is a regulated utility serving northern Illinois. The following table lists the stock prices and dividends on Unicom from 1989 to 1998.

Year	Price	Dividends
1989	$36.10	$3.00
1990	$33.60	$3.00
1991	$37.80	$3.00
1992	$30.90	$2.30
1993	$26.80	$1.60
1994	$24.80	$1.60
1995	$31.60	$1.60
1996	$28.50	$1.60
1997	$24.25	$1.60
1998	$35.60	$1.60

   a. Estimate the average annual return you would have made on your investment.
   b. Estimate the standard deviation and variance in annual returns.
   c. If you were investing in Unicom today, would you expect the historical standard deviations and variances to continue to hold? Why or why not?

3. The following table summarizes the annual returns you would have made on two companies—Scientific Atlanta, a satellite and data equipment manufacturer, and AT&T, the telecommunications giant—from 1989 to 1998.

Year	Scientific Atlanta	AT&T
1989	80.95%	58.26%
1990	−47.37%	−33.79%
1991	31.00%	29.88%
1992	132.44%	30.35%
1993	32.02%	2.94%
1994	25.37%	−4.29%
1995	−28.57%	28.86%
1996	0.00%	−6.36%
1997	11.67%	48.64%
1998	36.19%	23.55%

   a. Estimate the average annual return and standard deviation in annual returns in each company.
   b. Estimate the covariance and correlation in returns between the two companies.
   c. Estimate the variance of a portfolio composed, in equal parts, of the two investments.
4. You are in a world where there are only two assets, gold and stocks. You are interested in investing your money in one, the other, or both assets. Consequently you collect the following data on the returns on the two assets over the past six years.

	Gold	Stock Market
Average return	8%	20%
Standard deviation	25%	22%
Correlation	−0.4	

   a. If you were constrained to pick just one, which one would you choose?
   b. A friend argues that this is wrong. He says that you are ignoring the big payoffs that you can get on the other asset. How would you go about alleviating his concern?
   c. How would a portfolio composed of equal proportions in gold and stocks do in terms of mean and variance?
   d. You now learn that GPEC (a cartel of gold-producing countries) is going to vary the amount of gold it produces in relation to stock prices in the United States. (GPEC will produce less gold when stock markets are up and more when they are down.) What effect will this have on your portfolio? Explain.
5. You are interested in creating a portfolio of two stocks—Coca-Cola and Texas Utilities. Over the past decade, an investment in Coca-Cola stock would have earned an average annual return of 25%, with a standard deviation in returns of 36%. An investment in Texas Utilities stock would have earned an average annual return of 12%, with a standard deviation of 22%. The correlation in returns across the two stocks is 0.28.
   a. Assuming that the average return and standard deviation, estimated using past returns, will continue to hold in the future, estimate the future average returns and standard deviation of a portfolio composed 60% of Coca-Cola and 40% of Texas Utilities stock.

b. Now assume that Coca-Cola's international diversification will reduce the correlation to 0.20, while increasing Coca-Cola's standard deviation in returns to 45%. Assuming all of the other numbers remain unchanged, estimate one standard deviation of the portfolio in (a).

6. Assume that you have half your money invested in Times Mirror, the media company, and the other half invested in Unilever, the consumer product company. The expected returns and standard deviations on the two investments are:

	Times Mirror	*Unilever*
Expected return	14%	18%
Standard deviation	25%	40%

Estimate the variance of the portfolio as a function of the correlation coefficient (start with −1 and increase the correlation to +1 in 0.2 increments).

7. You have been asked to analyze the standard deviation of a portfolio composed of the following three assets:

	Expected Return	*Standard Deviation*
Sony Corporation	11%	23%
Tesoro Petroleum	9%	27%
Storage Technology	16%	50%

You have also been provided with the correlations across these three investments:

	Sony Corporation	*Tesoro Petroleum*	*Storage Technology*
Sony Corporation	1.00	−0.15	0.20
Tesoro Petroleum	−0.15	1.00	−0.25
Storage Technology	0.20	−0.25	1.00

Estimate the variance of a portfolio, equally weighted across all three assets.

8. Assume that the average variance of return for an individual security is 50 and that the average covariance is 10. What is the expected variance of a portfolio of 5, 10, 20, 50, and 100 securities? How many securities need to be held before the risk of a portfolio is only 10% more than the minimum?

9. Assume you have all your wealth (a million dollars) invested in the Vanguard 500 index fund, and that you expect to earn an annual return of 12%, with a standard deviation in returns of 25%. Since you have become more risk averse, you decide to shift $200,000 from the Vanguard 500 index fund to Treasury bills. The T-bill rate is 5%. Estimate the expected return and standard deviation of your new portfolio.

10. Every investor in the capital asset pricing model owns a combination of the market portfolio and a riskless asset. Assume that the standard deviation of the market portfolio is 30% and that the expected return on the portfolio is 15%. What proportion of the following investors' wealth would you suggest investing in the market portfolio and what proportion in the riskless asset? (The riskless asset has an expected return of 5%.)

a. An investor who desires a portfolio with no standard deviation.

b. An investor who desires a portfolio with a standard deviation of 15%.

c. An investor who desires a portfolio with a standard deviation of 30%.

d. An investor who desires a portfolio with a standard deviation of 45%.

e. An investor who desires a portfolio with an expected return of 12%.

11. The following table lists returns on the market portfolio and on Scientific Atlanta, each year from 1989 to 1998.

Year	Scientific Atlanta	Market Portfolio
1989	80.95%	31.49%
1990	−47.37%	−3.17%
1991	31.00%	30.57%
1992	132.44%	7.58%
1993	32.02%	10.36%
1994	25.37%	2.55%
1995	−28.57%	37.57%
1996	0.00%	22.68%
1997	11.67%	33.10%
1998	36.19%	28.32%

a. Estimate the covariance in returns between Scientific Atlanta and the market portfolio.

b. Estimate the variances in returns on both investments.

c. Estimate the beta for Scientific Atlanta.

12. United Airlines has a beta of 1.5. The standard deviation in the market portfolio is 22%, and United Airlines has a standard deviation of 66%.

a. Estimate the correlation between United Airlines and the market portfolio.

b. What proportion of United Airlines' risk is market risk?

13. You are using the arbitrage pricing model to estimate the expected return on Bethlehem Steel, and have derived the following estimates for the factor betas and risk premium:

Factor	Beta	Risk Premium
1	1.2	2.5%
2	0.6	1.5%
3	1.5	1.0%
4	2.2	0.8%
5	0.5	1.2%

a. Which risk factor is Bethlehem Steel most exposed to? Is there any way, within the arbitrage pricing model, to identify the risk factor?

b. If the risk-free rate is 5%, estimate the expected return on Bethlehem Steel.

c. Now assume that the beta in the capital asset pricing model for Bethlehem Steel is 1.1, and that the risk premium for the market portfolio is 5%. Estimate the expected return using the CAPM.

d. Why are the expected returns different using the two models?

14. You are using the multifactor model to estimate the expected return on Emerson Electric, and have derived the following estimates for the factor betas and risk premiums:

Macroeconomic Factor	Measure	Beta	Risk Premium $(R_{factor} - R_f)$
Level of interest rates	T-bond rate	0.5	1.8%
Term structure	T-bond rate—T-bill rate	1.4	0.6%
Inflation rate	Consumer price index	1.2	1.5%
Economic growth	Gross national product growth rate	1.8	4.2%

With a riskless rate of 6%, estimate the expected return on Emerson Electric.

15. The following equation is reproduced from the study by Fama and French of returns between 1963 and 1990.

$$R_t = 1.77 - 0.11 \ln(MV) + 0.35 \ln(BV/MV)$$

where MV is the market value of equity in hundreds of millions of dollars and BV is the book value of equity in hundreds of millions of dollars. The return is a monthly return.

a. Estimate the expected annual return on Lucent Technologies if the market value of its equity is $180 billion and the book value of its equity is $73.5 billion.

b. Lucent Technologies has a beta of 1.55. If the riskless rate is 6% and the risk premium for the market portfolio is 5.5%, estimate the expected return.

c. Why are the expected returns different under the two approaches?

CHAPTER 5

Option Pricing Theory and Models

In general, the value of any asset is the present value of the expected cash flows on that asset. This section will consider an exception to that rule when it looks at assets with two specific characteristics:

1. The assets derive their value from the values of other assets.
2. The cash flows on the assets are contingent on the occurrence of specific events.

These assets are called options, and the present value of the expected cash flows on these assets will understate their true value. This section will describe the cash flow characteristics of options, consider the factors that determine their value, and examine how best to value them.

BASICS OF OPTION PRICING

An option provides the holder with the right to buy or sell a specified quantity of an underlying asset at a fixed price (called a strike price or an exercise price) at or before the expiration date of the option. Since it is a right and not an obligation, the holder can choose not to exercise the right and allow the option to expire. There are two types of options—call options and put options.

Call and Put Options: Description and Payoff Diagrams

A call option gives the buyer of the option the right to buy the underlying asset at the strike price or the exercise price at any time prior to the expiration date of the option. The buyer pays a price for this right. If at expiration the value of the asset is less than the strike price, the option is not exercised and expires worthless. If, however, the value of the asset is greater than the strike price, the option is exercised— the buyer of the option buys the stock at the exercise price, and the difference between the asset value and the exercise price comprises the gross profit on the investment. The net profit on the investment is the difference between the gross profit and the price paid for the call initially.

A payoff diagram illustrates the cash payoff on an option at expiration. For a call, the net payoff is negative (and equal to the price paid for the call) if the value of the underlying asset is less than the strike price. If the price of the underlying asset exceeds the strike price, the gross payoff is the difference between the value of the underlying asset and the strike price, and the net payoff is the difference between the gross payoff and the price of the call. This is illustrated in Figure 5.1.

A put option gives the buyer of the option the right to sell the underlying asset at a fixed price, again called the strike or exercise price, at any time prior to the expiration date of the option. The buyer pays a price for this right. If the price of the underlying asset is greater than the strike price, the option will not be exercised and will expire worthless. But if the price of the underlying asset is less than the strike price, the owner of the put option will exercise the option and sell the stock at the strike price, claiming the difference between the strike price and the market value of the asset as the gross profit. Again, netting out the initial cost paid for the put yields the net profit from the transaction.

A put has a negative net payoff if the value of the underlying asset exceeds the strike price, and has a gross payoff equal to the difference between the strike price and the value of the underlying asset if the asset value is less than the strike price. This is summarized in Figure 5.2.

DETERMINANTS OF OPTION VALUE

The value of an option is determined by six variables relating to the underlying asset and financial markets.

1. *Current value of the underlying asset.* Options are assets that derive value from an underlying asset. Consequently, changes in the value of the underlying asset affect the value of the options on that asset. Since calls provide the right to buy the underlying asset at a fixed price, an increase in the value of the asset will increase the value of the calls. Puts, on the other hand, become less valuable as the value of the asset increases.
2. *Variance in value of the underlying asset.* The buyer of an option acquires the right to buy or sell the underlying asset at a fixed price. The higher the variance

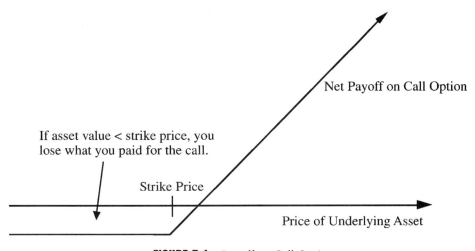

FIGURE 5.1 Payoff on Call Option

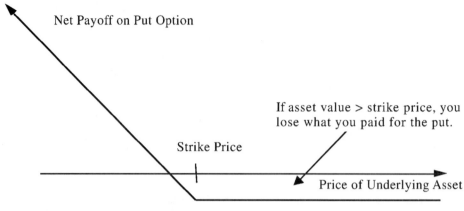

FIGURE 5.2   Payoff on Put Option

in the value of the underlying asset, the greater the value of the option.[1] This is true for both calls and puts. While it may seem counterintuitive that an increase in a risk measure (variance) should increase value, options are different from other securities since buyers of options can never lose more than the price they pay for them; in fact, they have the potential to earn significant returns from large price movements.

3. *Dividends paid on the underlying asset.* The value of the underlying asset can be expected to decrease if dividend payments are made on the asset during the life of the option. Consequently, the value of a call on the asset is a *decreasing* function of the size of expected dividend payments, and the value of a put is an *increasing* function of expected dividend payments. A more intuitive way of thinking about dividend payments, for call options, is as a cost of delaying exercise on in-the-money options. To see why, consider an option on a traded stock. Once a call option is in-the-money (i.e., the holder of the option will make a gross payoff by exercising the option), exercising the call option will provide the holder with the stock and entitle him or her to the dividends on the stock in subsequent periods. Failing to exercise the option will mean that these dividends are forgone.

4. *Strike price of the option.* A key characteristic used to describe an option is the strike price. In the case of calls, where the holder acquires the right to buy at a fixed price, the value of the call will decline as the strike price increases. In the case of puts, where the holder has the right to sell at a fixed price, the value will increase as the strike price increases.

5. *Time to expiration on the option.* Both calls and puts are more valuable the greater the time to expiration. This is because the longer time to expiration provides more time for the value of the underlying asset to move, increasing the value of both types of options. Additionally, in the case of a call, where the

---

[1]Note, though, that higher variance can reduce the value of the underlying asset. As a call option becomes more in-the-money, the more it resembles the underlying asset. For very deep in-the-money call options, higher variance can reduce the value of the option.

buyer has to pay a fixed price at expiration, the present value of this fixed price decreases as the life of the option increases, increasing the value of the call.

6. *Riskless interest rate corresponding to life of the option.* Since the buyer of an option pays the price of the option up front, an opportunity cost is involved. This cost will depend on the level of interest rates and the time to expiration of the option. The riskless interest rate also enters into the valuation of options when the present value of the exercise price is calculated, since the exercise price does not have to be paid (received) until expiration on calls (puts). Increases in the interest rate will increase the value of calls and reduce the value of puts.

Table 5.1 summarizes the variables and their predicted effects on call and put prices.

American versus European Options: Variables Relating to Early Exercise

A primary distinction between American and European options is that an American option can be exercised at any time prior to its expiration, while European options can be exercised only at expiration. The possibility of early exercise makes American options more valuable than otherwise similar European options; it also makes them more difficult to value. There is one compensating factor that enables the former to be valued using models designed for the latter. In most cases, the time premium associated with the remaining life of an option and transaction costs make early exercise suboptimal. In other words, the holders of in-the-money options generally get much more by selling the options to someone else than by exercising the options.

OPTION PRICING MODELS

Option pricing theory has made vast strides since 1972, when Fischer Black and Myron Scholes published their pathbreaking paper that provided a model for valuing dividend-protected European options. Black and Scholes used a "replicating portfolio"—a portfolio composed of the underlying asset and the risk-free asset that had the same cash flows as the option being valued—and the notion of arbitrage to come

TABLE 5.1 Summary of Variables Affecting Call and Put Prices

	Effect On	
Factor	Call Value	Put Value
Increase in underlying asset's value	Increases	Decreases
Increase in variance of underlying asset	Increases	Increases
Increase in strike price	Decreases	Increases
Increase in dividends paid	Decreases	Increases
Increase in time to expiration	Increases	Increases
Increase in interest rates	Increases	Decreases

up with their final formulation. While their derivation is mathematically complicated, there is a simpler binomial model for valuing options that draws on the same logic.

Binomial Model

The binomial option pricing model is based on a simple formulation for the asset price process in which the asset, in any time period, can move to one of two possible prices. The general formulation of a stock price process that follows the binomial path is shown in Figure 5.3. In this figure, S is the current stock price; the price moves up to Su with probability p and down to Sd with probability $1 - p$ in any time period.

Creating a Replicating Portfolio   The objective in creating a replicating portfolio is to use a combination of risk-free borrowing/lending and the underlying asset to create the same cash flows as the option being valued. The principles of arbitrage apply here, and the value of the option must be equal to the value of the replicating portfolio. In the case of the general formulation shown in Figure 5.3, where stock prices can move either up to Su or down to Sd in any time period, the replicating portfolio for a call with strike price K will involve borrowing \$B and acquiring Δ of the underlying asset, where:

$$\Delta = \text{Number of units of the underlying asset bought} = \frac{C_u - C_d}{Su - Sd}$$

where C_u = Value of the call if the stock price is Su
C_d = Value of the call if the stock price is Sd

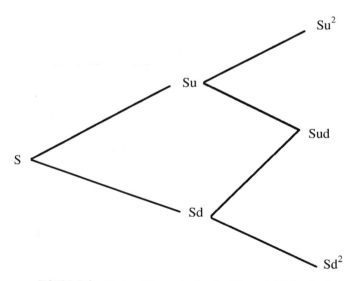

FIGURE 5.3   General Formulation for Binomial Price Path

In a multiperiod binomial process, the valuation has to proceed iteratively (i.e., starting with the final time period and moving backward in time until the current point in time). The portfolios replicating the option are created at each step and valued, providing the values for the option in that time period. The final output from the binomial option pricing model is a statement of the value of the option in terms of the replicating portfolio, composed of Δ shares (option delta) of the underlying asset and risk-free borrowing/lending.

Value of the call = Current value of underlying asset × Option delta
– Borrowing needed to replicate the option

ILLUSTRATION 5.1:   Binomial Option Valuation

Assume that the objective is to value a call with a strike price of $50, which is expected to expire in two time periods, on an underlying asset whose price currently is $50 and is expected to follow a binomial process:

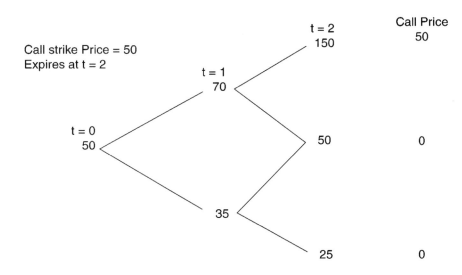

Now assume that the interest rate is 11%. In addition, define:

Δ = Number of shares in the replicating portfolio

B = Dollars of borrowing in replicating portfolio

The objective is to combined Δ shares of stock and B dollars of borrowing to replicate the cash flows from the call with a strike price of $50. This can be done iteratively, starting with the last period and working back through the binomial tree.

Step 1:   Start with the end nodes and work backward:

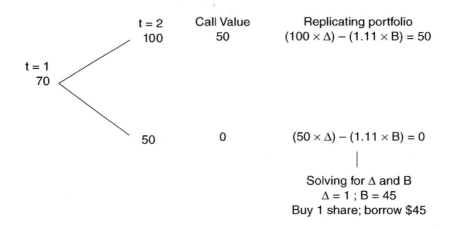

$$t = 2 \qquad \text{Call Value} \qquad \text{Replicating portfolio}$$
$$100 \qquad\qquad 50 \qquad\qquad (100 \times \Delta) - (1.11 \times B) = 50$$

t = 1
70

50   0 $(50 \times \Delta) - (1.11 \times B) = 0$

Solving for Δ and B
$\Delta = 1$; B = 45
Buy 1 share; borrow $45

Thus, if the stock price is $70 at t = 1, borrowing $45 and buying one share of the stock will give the same cash flows as buying the call. The value of the call at t = 1, if the stock price is $70, is therefore:

Value of call = Value of replicating position = $70 \Delta - B = 70 - 45 = 25$

Considering the other leg of the binomial tree at t = 1,

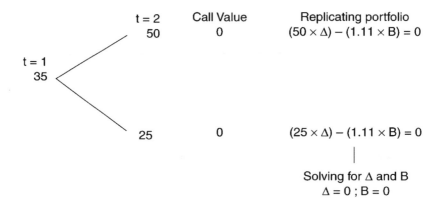

$$t = 2 \qquad \text{Call Value} \qquad \text{Replicating portfolio}$$
$$50 \qquad\qquad 0 \qquad\qquad (50 \times \Delta) - (1.11 \times B) = 0$$

t = 1
35

25   0 $(25 \times \Delta) - (1.11 \times B) = 0$

Solving for Δ and B
$\Delta = 0$; B = 0

If the stock price is $35 at t = 1, then the call is worth nothing.

Step 2: Move backward to the earlier time period and create a replicating portfolio that will provide the cash flows the option will provide.

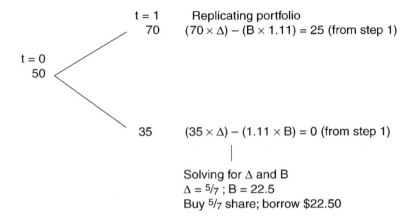

t = 1
70   Replicating portfolio
(70 × Δ) – (B × 1.11) = 25 (from step 1)

t = 0
50

35   (35 × Δ) – (1.11 × B) = 0 (from step 1)

Solving for Δ and B
Δ = 5/7 ; B = 22.5
Buy 5/7 share; borrow $22.50

In other words, borrowing $22.50 and buying five-sevenths of a share will provide the same cash flows as a call with a strike price of $50. The value of the call therefore has to be the same as the cost of creating this position.

$$\text{Value of call} = \text{Value of replicating position} = \left(\frac{5}{7}\right) \times \text{Current stock price} - \text{Borrowing}$$

$$= \left(\frac{5}{7}\right)(50) - 22.5 = \$13.21$$

The Determinants of Value   The binomial model provides insight into the determinants of option value. The value of an option is not determined by the *expected* price of the asset but by its *current* price, which, of course, reflects expectations about the future. This is a direct consequence of arbitrage. If the option value deviates from the value of the replicating portfolio, investors can create an arbitrage position (i.e., one that requires no investment, involves no risk, and delivers positive returns). To illustrate, if the portfolio that replicates the call costs more than the call does in the market, an investor could buy the call, sell the replicating portfolio, and be guaranteed the difference as a profit. The cash flows on the two positions will offset each other, leading to no cash flows in subsequent periods. The call option value also increases as the time to expiration is extended, as the price movements (u and d) increase, and with increases in the interest rate.

While the binomial model provides an intuitive feel for the determinants of option value, it requires a large number of inputs, in terms of expected future prices at each node. As time periods are made shorter in the binomial model, it becomes possible to make one of two assumptions about asset prices. It can be assumed that price changes become smaller as periods get shorter; this leads to price changes becoming infinitesimally small as time periods approach zero, leading to a continuous price process. Alternatively, it can be assumed that price changes stay large even as the period gets shorter; this leads to a jump price process, where prices can jump in any period. This section will consider the option pricing models that emerge with each of these assumptions.

Black-Scholes Model

When the price process is continuous (i.e., price changes become smaller as time periods get shorter), the binomial model for pricing options converges on the Black-Scholes model. The model, named after its cocreators, Fischer Black and Myron Scholes, allows us to estimate the value of any option using a small number of inputs, and has been shown to be remarkably robust in valuing many listed options.

The Model   While the derivation of the Black-Scholes model is far too complicated to present here, it is based on the idea of creating a portfolio of the underlying asset and the riskless asset with the same cash flows, and hence the same cost, as the option being valued. The value of a call option in the Black-Scholes model can be written as a function of the five variables:

S = Current value of the underlying asset

K = Strike price of the option

t = Life to expiration of the option

r = Riskless interest rate corresponding to the life of the option

σ^2 = Variance in the ln(value) of the underlying asset

The value of a call is then:

$$\text{Value of call} = S\,N(d_1) - K\,e^{-rt}\,N(d_2)$$

$$\text{where } d_1 = \frac{\ln\left(\frac{S}{K}\right) + \left(r + \frac{\sigma^2}{2}\right)t}{\sigma\sqrt{t}}$$

$$d_2 = d_1 - \sigma\sqrt{t}$$

Note that e^{-rt} is the present value factor, and reflects the fact that the exercise price on the call option does not have to be paid until expiration. $N(d_1)$ and $N(d_2)$ are probabilities, estimated by using a cumulative standardized normal distribution, and the values of d_1 and d_2 obtained for an option. The cumulative distribution is shown in Figure 5.4.

In approximate terms, these probabilities yield the likelihood that an option will generate positive cash flows for its owner at exercise (i.e., that $S > K$ in the case of a call option and that $K > S$ in the case of a put option). The portfolio that replicates the call option is created by buying $N(d_1)$ units of the underlying asset, and borrowing $Ke^{-rt}\,N(d_2)$. The portfolio will have the same cash flows as the call option, and thus the same value as the option. $N(d_1)$, which is the number of units of the underlying asset that are needed to create the replicating portfolio, is called the option delta.

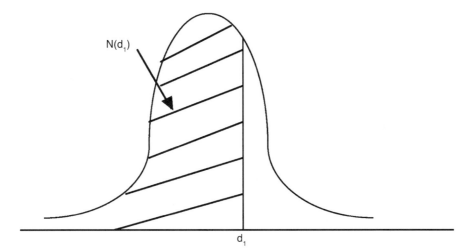

FIGURE 5.4 Cumulative Normal Distribution

A NOTE ON ESTIMATING THE INPUTS TO THE BLACK-SCHOLES MODEL

The Black-Scholes model requires inputs that are consistent on time measurement. There are two places where this affects estimates. The first relates to the fact that the model works in continuous time, rather than discrete time. That is why we use the continuous time version of present value $(\exp^{-rt})$ rather than the discrete version, $(1 + r)^{-t}$. It also means that the inputs such as the riskless rate have to be modified to make them continuous time inputs. For instance, if the one-year Treasury bond rate is 6.2 percent, the risk-free rate that is used in the Black-Scholes model should be:

$$\text{Continuous riskless rate} = \ln(1 + \text{Discrete riskless rate})$$
$$= \ln(1.062) = .06015 \text{ or } 6.015\%$$

The second relates to the period over which the inputs are estimated. For instance, the preceding rate is an annual rate. The variance that is entered into the model also has to be an annualized variance. The variance, estimated from ln(asset prices), can be annualized easily because variances are linear in time if the serial correlation is zero. Thus, if monthly or weekly prices are used to estimate variance, the variance is annualized by multiplying by 12 or 52, respectively.

ILLUSTRATION 5.2:   Valuing an Option Using the Black-Scholes Model

On April 6, 2001, Cisco Systems was trading at $13.62. We will attempt to value a July 2001 call option with a strike price of $15, trading on the CBOE on the same day for $2. The following are the other parameters of the options:

■ The annualized standard deviation in Cisco Systems stock price over the previous year was 81%. This standard deviation is estimated using weekly stock prices over the year, and the resulting number was annualized as follows:

Weekly standard deviation = 11.23%

Annualized standard deviation $= 11.23\% \times \sqrt{52} = 81\%$

■ The option expiration date is Friday, July 20, 2001. There are 103 days to expiration, and the annualized Treasury bill rate corresponding to this option life is 4.63%.

The inputs for the Black-Scholes model are as follows:

Current stock price (S) = $13.62

Strike price on the option = $15

Option life = 103/365 = 0.2822

Standard deviation in ln(stock prices) = 81%

Riskless rate = 4.63%

Inputting these numbers into the model, we get:

$$d_1 = \frac{\ln\left(\dfrac{13.62}{15.00}\right) + \left(.0463 + \dfrac{.81^2}{2}\right).2822}{.81\sqrt{.2822}} = .0212$$

$$d_2 = .0212 - .81\sqrt{.2822} = -.4091$$

Using the normal distribution, we can estimate the $N(d_1)$ and $N(d_2)$:

$$N(d_1) = .5085$$

$$N(d_2) = .3412$$

The value of the call can now be estimated:

$$\text{Value of Cisco call} = S\ N(d_1) - K\ e^{-rt}\ N(d_2)$$
$$= 13.62(.5085) - 15\ e^{-(.0463)(.2822)}(.3412) = \$1.87$$

Since the call is trading at $2, it is slightly overvalued, assuming that the estimate of standard deviation used is correct.

IMPLIED VOLATILITY

The only input on which there can be significant disagreement among investors is the variance. While the variance is often estimated by looking at historical data, the values for options that emerge from using the historical variance can be different from the market prices. For any option, there is some variance at which the estimated value will be equal to the market price. This variance is called an implied variance.

Consider the Cisco option valued in Illustration 5.2. With a standard deviation of 81 percent, the value of the call option with a strike price of $15 was estimated to be $1.87. Since the market price is higher than the calculated value, we tried higher standard deviations, and at a standard deviation 85.40 percent the value of the option is $2 (which is the market price). This is the implied standard deviation or implied volatility.

Model Limitations and Fixes   The Black-Scholes model was designed to value options that can be exercised only at maturity and whose underlying assets do not pay dividends. In addition, options are valued based on the assumption that option exercise does not affect the value of the underlying asset. In practice, assets do pay dividends, options sometimes get exercised early, and exercising an option can affect the value of the underlying asset. Adjustments exist that, while not perfect, provide partial corrections to the Black-Scholes model.

Dividends   The payment of a dividend reduces the stock price; note that on the ex-dividend day, the stock price generally declines. Consequently, call options become less valuable and put options more valuable as expected dividend payments increase. There are two ways of dealing with dividends in the Black-Scholes model:

1. *Short-term options.* One approach to dealing with dividends is to estimate the present value of expected dividends that will be paid by the underlying asset during the option life and subtract it from the current value of the asset to use as S in the model.

    Modified stock price = Current stock price
    – Present value of expected dividends
    during the life of the option

2. *Long-term options.* Since it becomes less practical to estimate the present value of dividends the longer the option life, an alternate approach can be used. If the dividend yield (y = Dividends/Current value of the asset) on the underlying asset is expected to remain unchanged during the life of the option, the Black-Scholes model can be modified to take dividends into account.

$$C = S\ e^{-yt}\ N(d_1) - K\ e^{-rt}\ N(d_2)$$

where $d_1 = \dfrac{\ln\left(\dfrac{S}{K}\right) + \left(r - y + \dfrac{\sigma^2}{2}\right)t}{\sigma\sqrt{t}}$

$d_2 = d_1 - \sigma\sqrt{t}$

From an intuitive standpoint, the adjustments have two effects. First, the value of the asset is discounted back to the present at the dividend yield to take into account the expected drop in asset value resulting from dividend payments. Second, the interest rate is offset by the dividend yield to reflect the lower carrying cost from holding the asset (in the replicating portfolio). The net effect will be a reduction in the value of calls estimated using this model.

ILLUSTRATION 5.3: Valuing a Short-Term Option with Dividend Adjustments— The Black-Scholes Correction

Assume that it is March 6, 2001, and that AT&T is trading at $20.50 a share. Consider a call option on the stock with a strike price of $20, expiring on July 20, 2001. Using past stock prices, the standard deviation in the log of stock prices for AT&T is estimated at 60%. There is one dividend, amounting to $0.15, and it will be paid in 23 days. The riskless rate is 4.63%.

Present value of expected dividend = $0.15/1.0463^{23/365} = $0.15

Dividend-adjusted stock price = $20.50 − $0.15 = $20.35

Time to expiration = 103/365 = 0.2822

Variance in ln(stock prices) = 0.6^2 = 0.36

Riskless rate = 4.63%

The value from the Black-Scholes model is:

$d_1 = 0.2548$ $\qquad\qquad$ $N(d_1) = 0.6006$

$d_2 = -0.0639$ $\qquad\qquad$ $N(d_2) = 0.4745$

Value of call = $20.35 (0.6006) − $20 $\exp^{-(0.0463)(.2822)}$(0.4745) = $2.85

The call option was trading at $2.60 on that day.

ILLUSTRATION 5.4: Valuing a Long-Term Option with Dividend Adjustments— Primes and Scores

In recent years, the CBOE has introduced longer-term call and put options on stocks. On March 6, 2001, for instance, you could have purchased an AT&T call expiring on January 17, 2003. The stock price for AT&T is $20.50 (as in the previous example). The following is the valuation of a call option with a strike price of $20. Instead of estimating the present value of dividends over the next two years, assume that AT&T's dividend yield will remain 2.51% over this period and that the risk-free rate for a two-year Treasury bond is 4.85%. The inputs to the Black-Scholes model are:

S = Current asset value = $20.50

K = Strike price = $20

Time to expiration = 1.8333 years

Standard deviation in ln(stock prices) = 60%

Riskless rate = 4.85%   Dividend yield = 2.51%

The value from the Black-Scholes model is:

$$d_1 = \frac{\ln\left(\frac{20.50}{20.00}\right) + \left(.0485 - .0251 + \frac{.6^2}{2}\right)1.8333}{.6\sqrt{1.8333}} = 0.4383 \quad N(d_1) = 0.6694$$

$$d_2 = .4383 - .6\sqrt{1.8333} = -.2387 \qquad\qquad N(d_2) = 0.4057$$

Value of call $= \$20.50 \, \exp^{-(0.0251)(1.8333)}(0.6694) - \$20 \, \exp^{-(0.0485)(1.8333)}(0.4057) = \$6.63$

The call was trading at $5.80 on March 8, 2001.

---

 stopt.xls: **This spreadsheet allows you to estimate the value of a short-term option when the expected dividends during the option life can be estimated.**

---

 ltops.xls: **This spreadsheet allows you to estimate the value of an option when the underlying asset has a constant dividend yield.**

Early Exercise   The Black-Scholes model was designed to value options that can be exercised only at expiration. Options with this characteristic are called European options. In contrast, most options that we encounter in practice can be exercised at any time until expiration. These options are called American options. As mentioned earlier, the possibility of early exercise makes American options more valuable than otherwise similar European options; it also makes them more difficult to value. In general, though, with traded options, it is almost always better to sell the option to someone else rather than exercise early, since options have a time premium (i.e., they sell for more than their exercise value). There are two exceptions. One occurs when the underlying asset pays large dividends, thus reducing the expected value of the asset. In this case, call options may be exercised *just be-*

fore an ex-dividend date, if the time premium on the options is less than the expected decline in asset value as a consequence of the dividend payment. The other exception arises when an investor holds both the underlying asset and *deep in-the-money puts* (i.e., puts with strike prices well above the current price of the underlying asset) on that asset at a time when interest rates are high. In this case, the time premium on the put may be less than the potential gain from exercising the put early and earning interest on the exercise price.

There are two basic ways of dealing with the possibility of early exercise. One is to continue to use the unadjusted Black-Scholes model and to regard the resulting value as a floor or conservative estimate of the true value. The other is to try to adjust the value of the option for the possibility of early exercise. There are two approaches for doing so. One uses the Black-Scholes model to value the option to each potential exercise date. With options on stocks, this basically requires that the investor values options to each ex-dividend day and chooses the maximum of the estimated call values. The second approach is to use a modified version of the binomial model to consider the possibility of early exercise. In this version, the up and the down movements for asset prices in each period can be estimated from the variance and the length of each period.[2]

Approach 1: Pseudo-American Valuation

Step 1: Define when dividends will be paid and how much the dividends will be.

Step 2: Value the call option to each ex-dividend date using the dividend-adjusted approach described earlier, where the stock price is reduced by the present value of expected dividends.

Step 3: Choose the maximum of the call values estimated for each ex-dividend day.

ILLUSTRATION 5.5:   Using Pseudo-American Option Valuation to Adjust for Early Exercise

---

Consider an option with a strike price of $35 on a stock trading at $40. The variance in the ln(stock prices) is 0.05, and the riskless rate is 4%. The option has a remaining life of eight months, and there are three dividends expected during this period:

Expected Dividend	Ex-Dividend Day
$0.80	In 1 month
$0.80	In 4 months
$0.80	In 7 months

The call option is first valued to just before the first ex-dividend date:

---

[2]To illustrate, if σ^2 is the variance in ln(stock prices), the up and the down movements in the binomial can be estimated as follows:

$$u = Exp\ [(r - \sigma^2/2)(T/m) + \sqrt{(\sigma^2 T/m)}]$$

$$d = Exp\ [(r - \sigma^2/2)(T/m) - \sqrt{(\sigma^2 T/m)}]$$

where u and d are the up and down movements per unit time for the binomial, T is the life of the option, and m is the number of periods within that lifetime.

$$S = \$40 \qquad K = \$35 \qquad t = 1/12 \qquad \sigma^2 = 0.05 \qquad r = 0.04$$

The value from the Black-Scholes model is:

$$\text{Value of call} = \$\, 5.131$$

The call option is then valued to before the second ex-dividend date:

$$\text{Adjusted stock price} = \$40 - \$0.80/1.04^{1/12} = \$39.20$$

$$K = \$35 \qquad t = 4/12 \qquad \sigma^2 = 0.05 \qquad r = 0.04$$

The value of the call based on these parameters is:

$$\text{Value of call} = \$5.073$$

The call option is then valued to before the third ex-dividend date:

$$\text{Adjusted stock price} = \$40 - \$0.80/1.04^{1/12} - \$0.80/1.04^{4/12} = \$38.41$$

$$K = \$35 \qquad t = 7/12 \qquad \sigma^2 = 0.05 \qquad r = 0.04$$

The value of the call based on these parameters is:

$$\text{Value of call} = \$5.128$$

The call option is then valued to expiration:

$$\text{Adjusted stock price} = \$40 - \$0.80/1.04^{1/12} - \$0.80/1.04^{4/12} - \$0.80/1.04^{7/12} = \$37.63$$

$$K = \$35 \qquad t = 8/12 \qquad \sigma^2 = 0.05 \qquad r = 0.04$$

The value of the call based on these parameters is:

$$\text{Value of call} = \$4.757$$

$$\text{Pseudo-American value of call} = \text{Maximum}\,(\$5.131, \$5.073, \$5.128, \$4.757) = \$5.131$$

Approach 2: Using the Binomial Model   The binomial model is much more capable of handling early exercise because it considers the cash flows at each time period, rather than just at expiration. The biggest limitation of the binomial model is determining what stock prices will be at the end of each period, but this can be overcome by using a variant that allows us to estimate the up and the down movements in stock prices from the estimated variance. There are four steps involved:

Step 1: If the variance in ln(stock prices) has been estimated for the Black-Scholes valuation, convert these into inputs for the binomial model:

$$u = e^{\sigma\sqrt{\text{at}} + \left(r - \frac{\sigma^2}{2}\right)dt}$$

$$d = e^{-\sigma\sqrt{\text{at}} + \left(r - \frac{\sigma^2}{2}\right)dt}$$

where u and d are the up and the down movements per unit time for the binomial, and dt is the number of periods within each year (or unit time).

Step 2: Specify the period in which the dividends will be paid and make the assumption that the price will drop by the amount of the dividend in that period.

Step 3: Value the call at each node of the tree, allowing for the possibility of early exercise just before ex-dividend dates. There will be early exercise if the remaining time premium on the option is less than the expected drop in option value as a consequence of the dividend payment.

Step 4: Value the call at time 0, using the standard binomial approach.

 bstobin.xls: **This spreadsheet allows you to estimate the parameters for a binomial model from the inputs to a Black-Scholes model.**

Impact of Exercise on Underlying Asset Value   The Black-Scholes model is based on the assumption that exercising an option does not affect the value of the underlying asset. This may be true for listed options on stocks, but it is not true for some types of options. For instance, the exercise of warrants increases the number of shares outstanding and brings fresh cash into the firm, both of which will affect the stock price.[3] The expected negative impact (dilution) of exercise will decrease the value of warrants, compared to otherwise similar call options. The adjustment for dilution to the stock price is fairly simple in the Black-Scholes valuation. The stock price is adjusted for the expected dilution from the exercise of the options. In the case of warrants, for instance:

$$\text{Dilution-adjusted } S = (S\, n_s + W\, n_w)/(n_s + n_w)$$

where S = Current value of the stock
   n_w = Number of warrants outstanding
   W = Value of warrants outstanding
   n_s = Number of shares outstanding

When the warrants are exercised, the number of shares outstanding will increase, reducing the stock price. The numerator reflects the market value of equity, including both stocks and warrants outstanding. The reduction in S will reduce the value of the call option.

There is an element of circularity in this analysis, since the value of the warrant is needed to estimate the dilution-adjusted S and the dilution-adjusted S is needed to estimate the value of the warrant. This problem can be resolved by starting the process off with an assumed value for the warrant (e.g., the exercise value or the current market price of the warrant). This will yield a value for the warrant, and this estimated value can then be used as an input to reestimate the warrant's value until there is convergence.

---

[3]Warrants are call options issued by firms, either as part of management compensation contracts or to raise equity.

FROM BLACK-SCHOLES TO BINOMIAL

The process of converting the continuous variance in a Black-Scholes model to a binomial tree is a fairly simple one. Assume, for instance, that you have an asset that is trading at $30 currently and that you estimate the annualized standard deviation in the asset value to be 40 percent; the annualized riskless rate is 5 percent. For simplicity, let us assume that the option that you are valuing has a four-year life and that each period is a year. To estimate the prices at the end of each of the four years, we begin by first estimating the up and down movements in the binomial:

$$u = \exp^{.4\sqrt{1} + \left(.05 - \frac{4^2}{2}\right)1} = 1.4477$$

$$d = \exp^{-.4\sqrt{1} + \left(.05 - \frac{.40^2}{2}\right)1} = 0.6505$$

Based on these estimates, we can obtain the prices at the end of the first node of the tree (the end of the first year):

Up price = $30(1.4477) = $43.43

Down price = $40(0.6505) = $19.52

Progressing through the rest of the tree, we obtain the following numbers:

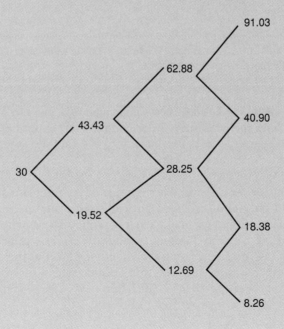

ILLUSTRATION 5.6:   Valuing a Warrant on Avatek Corporation

Avatek Corporation is a real estate firm with 19.637 million shares outstanding, trading at $0.38 a share. In March 2001 the company had 1.8 million options outstanding, with four years to expiration and with an exercise price of $2.25. The stock paid no dividends, and the standard deviation in ln(stock prices) was 93%. The four-year Treasury bond rate was 4.9%. (The warrants were trading at $0.12 apiece at the time of this analysis.)

The inputs to the warrant valuation model are as follows:

$S = (0.38 \times 19.637 + 0.12 \times 1.8)/(19.637 + 1.8) = 0.3544$

K = Exercise price on warrant = 2.25

t = Time to expiration on warrant = 4 years

r = Riskless rate corresponding to life of option = 4.9%

σ^2 = Variance in value of stock = 0.93^2

y = Dividend yield on stock = 0.0%

The results of the Black-Scholes valuation of this option are:

$$d_1 = 0.0418 \qquad\qquad N(d_1) = 0.5167$$

$$d_2 = -1.8182 \qquad\qquad N(d_2) = 0.0345$$

$$\text{Value of warrant} = 0.3544(0.5167) - 2.25\ \exp^{-(0.049)(4)}(0.0345) = \$0.12$$

The warrants were trading at $0.12 in March 2001. Since the value was equal to the price, there was no need for further iterations. If there had been a difference, we would have reestimated the adjusted stock price and warrant value.

 warrant.xls: This spreadsheet allows you to estimate the value of an option when there is a potential dilution from exercise.

The Black-Scholes Model for Valuing Puts   The value of a put can be derived from the value of a call with the same strike price and the same expiration date:

$$C - P = S - K\ e^{-rt}$$

where C is the value of the call and P is the value of the put. This relationship between the call and put values is called put-call parity, and any deviations from parity can be used by investors to make riskless profits. To see why put-call parity holds, consider selling a call and buying a put with exercise price K and expiration date t, and simultaneously buying the underlying asset at the current price S. The payoff from this position is riskless and always yields K at expiration (t). To see this, assume that the stock price at expiration is S*. The payoff on each of the positions in the portfolio can be written as follows:

Position	Payoffs at t if S*>K	Payoffs at t if S*<K
Sell call	$-(S^* - K)$	0
Buy put	0	$K - S^*$
Buy stock	S^*	S^*
Total	K	K

Since this position yields K with certainty, the cost of creating this position must be equal to the present value of K at the riskless rate (K e^{-rt}).

$$S + P - C = K\ e^{-rt}$$

$$C - P = S - K\ e^{-rt}$$

Substituting the Black-Scholes equation for the value of an equivalent call into this equation, we get:

$$\text{Value of put} = K\ e^{-rt}\ [1 - N(d_2)] - S\ e^{-yt}\ [1 - N(d_1)]$$

$$\text{where}\quad d_1 = \frac{\ln\left(\frac{S}{K}\right) + \left(r - y + \frac{\sigma^2}{2}\right)t}{\sigma\sqrt{t}}$$

$$d_2 = d_1 - \sigma\sqrt{t}$$

Thus, the replicating portfolio for a put is created by selling short $[1 - N(d_1)]$ shares of stock and investing K $e^{-rt}[1 - N(d_2)]$ in the riskless asset.

ILLUSTRATION 5.7: Valuing a Put Using Put-Call Parity: Cisco Systems and AT&T

Consider the call that valued on Cisco Systems in Illustration 5.2. The call had a strike price of $15 on the stock, had 103 days left to expiration, and was valued at $1.87. The stock was trading at $13.62, and the riskless rate was 4.63%. The put can be valued as follows:

$$\text{Put value} = C - S + K\ e^{-rt} = \$1.87 - \$13.62 + \$15\ e^{-(.0463)(.2822)} = \$3.06$$

The put was trading at $3.38.

Also, a long-term call on AT&T was valued in Illustration 5.4. The call had a strike price of $20, 1.8333 years left to expiration, and a value of $6.63. The stock was trading at $20.50 and was expected to maintain a dividend yield of 2.51% over the period. The riskless rate was 4.85%. The put value can be estimated as follows:

$$\text{Put value} = C - S\ e^{-yt} + K\ e^{-rt} = \$6.63 - \$20.5\ e^{-(.0251)(1.8333)} + \$20\ e^{-(.0485)(1.8333)} = \$5.35$$

The put was trading at $3.80. Both the call and put trade at different prices from our estimates, which may indicate that we have not correctly estimated the stock's volatility.

Jump Process Option Pricing Models

If price changes remain larger as the time periods in the binomial model are shortened, it can no longer be assumed that prices change continuously. When price changes remain large, a price process that allows for price jumps is much more realistic. Cox and Ross (1976) valued options when prices follow a pure jump process, where the jumps can only be positive. Thus, in the next interval, the stock price will either have a large positive jump with a specified probability or drift downward at a given rate.

Merton (1976) considered a distribution where there are price jumps superimposed on a continuous price process. He specified the rate at which jumps occur (λ) and the average jump size (k), measured as a percentage of the stock price. The model derived to value options with this process is called a jump diffusion model. In this model, the value of an option is determined by the five variables specified in the Black-Scholes model, and the parameters of the jump process (λ, k). Unfortunately, the estimates of the jump process parameters are so noisy for most firms that they overwhelm any advantages that accrue from using a more realistic model. These models, therefore, have seen limited use in practice.

EXTENSIONS OF OPTION PRICING

All the option pricing models described so far—the binomial, the Black-Scholes, and the jump process models—are designed to value options with clearly defined exercise prices and maturities on underlying assets that are traded. However, the options we encounter in investment analysis or valuation are often on real assets rather than financial assets. Categorized as real options, they can take much more complicated forms. This section will consider some of these variations.

Capped and Barrier Options

With a simple call option, there is no specified upper limit on the profits that can be made by the buyer of the call. Asset prices, at least in theory, can keep going up, and the payoffs increase proportionately. In some call options, though, the buyer is entitled to profits up to a specified price but not above it. For instance, consider a call option with a strike price of K_1 on an asset. In an unrestricted call option, the payoff on this option will increase as the underlying asset's price increases above

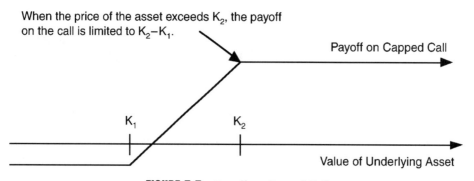

FIGURE 5.5 Payoff on Capped Call

K_1. Assume, however, that if the price reaches K_2, the payoff is capped at $(K_2 - K_1)$. The payoff diagram on this option is shown in Figure 5.5.

This option is called a capped call. Notice, also, that once the price reaches K_2, there is no longer any time premium associated with the option, and the option will therefore be exercised. Capped calls are part of a family of options called barrier options, where the payoff on and the life of the option are a function of whether the underlying asset price reaches a certain level during a specified period.

The value of a capped call is always lower than the value of the same call without the payoff limit. A simple approximation of this value can be obtained by valuing the call twice, once with the given exercise price and once with the cap, and taking the difference in the two values. In the preceding example, then, the value of the call with an exercise price of K_1 and a cap at K_2 can be written as:

$$\text{Value of capped call} = \text{Value of call } (K = K_1) - \text{Value of call } (K = K_2)$$

Barrier options can take many forms. In a knockout option, an option ceases to exist if the underlying asset reaches a certain price. In the case of a call option, this knockout price is usually set below the strike price, and this option is called a down-and-out option. In the case of a put option, the knockout price will be set above the exercise price, and this option is called an up-and-out option. Like the capped call, these options are worth less than their unrestricted counterparts. Many real options have limits on potential upside, or knockout provisions, and ignoring these limits can result in the overstatement of the value of these options.

Compound Options

Some options derive their value not from an underlying asset, but from other options. These options are called compound options. Compound options can take any of four forms—a call on a call, a put on a put, a call on a put, or a put on a call. Geske (1979) developed the analytical formulation for valuing compound options by replacing the standard normal distribution used in a simple option model with a bivariate normal distribution in the calculation.

Consider, for instance, the option to expand a project that will be discussed in Chapter 30. While we will value this option using a simple option pricing model, in reality there could be multiple stages in expansion, with each stage representing an option for the following stage. In this case, we will undervalue the option by considering it as a simple rather than a compound option.

Notwithstanding this discussion, the valuation of compound options becomes progressively more difficult as more options are added to the chain. In this case, rather than wreck the valuation on the shoals of estimation error, it may be better to accept the conservative estimate that is provided with a simple valuation model as a floor on the value.

Rainbow Options

In a simple option, the uncertainty is about the price of the underlying asset. Some options are exposed to two or more sources of uncertainty, and these options are rainbow options. Using the simple option pricing model to value such options can lead to biased estimates of value. As an example, consider an undeveloped oil reserve as an option, where the firm that owns the reserve has the right to develop the reserve. Here there are two sources of uncertainty. The first is obviously the price of oil, and the second is the quantity of oil that is in the reserve. To value this undeveloped reserve, we can make the simplifying assumption that we know the quantity of oil in the reserve with certainty. In reality, however, uncertainty about the quantity will affect the value of this option and make the decision to exercise more difficult.[4]

CONCLUSION

An option is an asset with payoffs that are contingent on the value of an underlying asset. A call option provides its holder with the right to buy the underlying asset at a fixed price, whereas a put option provides its holder with the right to sell at a fixed price, at any time before the expiration of the option. The value of an option is determined by six variables—the current value of the underlying asset, the variance in this value, the expected dividends on the asset, the strike price and life of the option, and the riskless interest rate. This is illustrated in both the binomial and the Black-Scholes models, which value options by creating replicating portfolios composed of the underlying asset and riskless lending or borrowing. These models can be used to value assets that have option like characteristics.

QUESTIONS AND SHORT PROBLEMS

1. The following are prices of options traded on Microsoft Corporation, which pays no dividends.

	Call		Put	
	K = 85	K = 90	K = 85	K = 90
One-month	2.75	1.00	4.50	7.50
Three-month	4.00	2.75	5.75	9.00
Six-month	7.75	6.00	8.00	12.00

The stock is trading at $83, and the annualized riskless rate is 3.8%. The standard deviation in log stock prices (based on historical data) is 30%.
a. Estimate the value of a three-month call with a strike price of $85.
b. Using the inputs from the Black-Scholes model, specify how you would replicate this call.
c. What is the implied standard deviation in this call?
d. Assume now that you buy a call with a strike price of $85 and sell a call with a strike price of $90. Draw the payoff diagram on this position.
e. Using put-call parity, estimate the value of a three-month put with a strike price of $85.
2. You are trying to value three-month call and put options on Merck with a strike price of $30. The stock is trading at $28.75, and the company expects to pay a

---

[4]The analogy to a listed option on a stock is the case where you do not know with certainty what the stock price is when you exercise the option. The more uncertain you are about the stock price, the more margin for error you have to give yourself when you exercise the option, to ensure that you are in fact earning a profit.

quarterly dividend per share of $0.28 in two months. The annualized riskless interest rate is 3.6%, and the standard deviation in log stock prices is 20%.

a. Estimate the value of the call and put options, using the Black-Scholes model.

b. What effect does the expected dividend payment have on call values? On put values? Why?

3. There is the possibility that the options on Merck described in the preceding problem could be exercised early.

a. Use the pseudo-American call option technique to determine whether this will affect the value of the call.

b. Why does the possibility of early exercise exist? What types of options are most likely to be exercised early?

4. You have been provided the following information on a three-month call:

$$S = 95 \quad K = 90 \quad t = 0.25 \quad r = 0.04$$
$$N(d_1) = 0.5750 \quad N(d_2) = 0.4500$$

a. If you wanted to replicate buying this call, how much money would you need to borrow?

b. If you wanted to replicate buying this call, how many shares of stock would you need to buy?

5. Go Video, a manufacturer of video recorders, was trading at $4 per share in May 1994. There were 11 million shares outstanding. At the same time, it had 550,000 one-year warrants outstanding, with a strike price of $4.25. The stock has had a standard deviation of 60%. The stock does not pay a dividend. The riskless rate is 5%.

a. Estimate the value of the warrants, ignoring dilution.

b. Estimate the value of the warrants, allowing for dilution.

c. Why does dilution reduce the value of the warrants?

6. You are trying to value a long-term call option on the NYSE Composite index, expiring in five years, with a strike price of 275. The index is currently at 250, and the annualized standard deviation in stock prices is 15%. The average dividend yield on the index is 3% and is expected to remain unchanged over the next five years. The five-year Treasury bond rate is 5%.

a. Estimate the value of the long-term call option.

b. Estimate the value of a put option with the same parameters.

c. What are the implicit assumptions you are making when you use the Black-Scholes model to value this option? Which of these assumptions are likely to be violated? What are the consequences for your valuation?

7. A new security on AT&T will entitle the investor to all dividends on AT&T over the next three years, limiting upside potential to 20% but also providing downside protection below 10%. AT&T stock is trading at $50, and three-year call and put options are traded on the exchange at the following prices:

	Call Options		Put Options	
K	1-Year	3-Year	1-Year	3-Year
45	$8.69	$13.34	$1.99	$3.55
50	$5.86	$10.89	$3.92	$5.40
55	$3.78	$8.82	$6.59	$7.63
60	$2.35	$7.11	$9.92	$10.23

How much would you be willing to pay for this security?

CHAPTER **6**

Market Efficiency— Definition, Tests, and Evidence

What is an efficient market? What does it imply for investment and valuation models? Clearly, market efficiency is a concept that is controversial and attracts strong views, pro and con, partly because of differences between individuals about what it really means, and partly because it is a core belief that in large part determines how an investor approaches investing. This chapter provides a definition of market efficiency, considers the implications of an efficient market for investors, and summarizes some of the basic approaches that are used to test investment schemes, thereby proving or disproving market efficiency. It also provides a summary of the voluminous research on whether markets are efficient.

MARKET EFFICIENCY AND INVESTMENT VALUATION

The question of whether markets are efficient, and, if not, where the inefficiencies lie, is central to investment valuation. If markets are in fact efficient, the market price provides the best estimate of value, and the process of valuation becomes one of justifying the market price. If markets are not efficient, the market price may deviate from the true value, and the process of valuation is directed toward obtaining a reasonable estimate of this value. Those who do valuation well, then, will then be able to make higher returns than other investors because of their capacity to spot under- and overvalued firms. To make these higher returns, though, markets have to correct their mistakes (i.e., become efficient) over time. Whether these corrections occur over six months or over five years can have a profound impact on which valuation approach an investor chooses to use and the time horizon that is needed for it to succeed.

There is also much that can be learned from studies of market efficiency, which highlight segments where the market seems to be inefficient. These inefficiencies can provide the basis for screening the universe of stocks to come up with a subsample that is more likely to contain undervalued stocks. Given the size of the universe of stocks, this not only saves time for the analyst, but it increases the odds significantly of finding under- and overvalued stocks. For instance, some efficiency studies suggest that stocks that are neglected by institutional investors are more likely to be undervalued and earn excess returns. A strategy that screens firms for low institutional investment (as a percentage of the outstanding stock) may yield a subsample of neglected firms, which can then be valued using valuation models to arrive at a portfolio of undervalued firms. If the research is correct, the odds of finding undervalued firms should increase in this subsample.

WHAT IS AN EFFICIENT MARKET?

An efficient market is one where the market price is an unbiased estimate of the true value of the investment. Implicit in this derivation are several key concepts:

■ Contrary to popular view, market efficiency does not require that the market price be equal to true value at every point in time. All it requires is that errors in the market price be unbiased; prices can be greater than or less than true value, as long as these deviations are random.

■ The fact that the deviations from true value are random implies, in a rough sense, that there is an equal chance that any stock is under- or overvalued at any point in time, and that these deviations are uncorrelated with any observable variable. For instance, in an efficient market, stocks with lower PE ratios should be no more or no less likely to be undervalued than stocks with high PE ratios.

■ If the deviations of market price from true value are random, it follows that no group of investors should be able to consistently find under- or overvalued stocks using any investment strategy.

Definitions of market efficiency have to be specific not only about the market that is being considered but also the investor group that is covered. It is extremely unlikely that all markets are efficient to all investors, but it is entirely possible that a particular market (for instance, the New York Stock Exchange) is efficient with respect to the average investor. It is also possible that some markets are efficient while others are not, and that a market is efficient with respect to some investors and not to others. This is a direct consequence of differential tax rates and transactions costs, which confer advantages on some investors relative to others.

Definitions of market efficiency are also linked up with assumptions about what information is available to investors and reflected in the price. For instance, a strict definition of market efficiency that assumes that all information, public as well as private, is reflected in market prices would imply that even investors with precise inside information will be unable to beat the market. One of the earliest classifications of levels of market efficiency was provided by Fama (1971), who argued that markets could be efficient at three levels, based on what information was reflected in prices. Under weak form efficiency, the current price reflects the information contained in all past prices, suggesting that charts and technical analyses that use past prices alone would not be useful in finding undervalued stocks. Under semi-strong form efficiency, the current price reflects the information contained not only in past prices but all public information (including financial statements and news reports) and no approach that is predicated on using and massaging this information would be useful in finding undervalued stocks. Under strong form efficiency, the current price reflects all information, public as well as private, and no investors will be able to find undervalued stocks consistently.

IMPLICATIONS OF MARKET EFFICIENCY

An immediate and direct implication of an efficient market is that no group of investors should be able to beat the market consistently using a common investment strategy. An efficient market would also carry negative implications for many investment strategies:

■ In an efficient market, equity research and valuation would be a costly task that would provide no benefits. The odds of finding an undervalued stock would always be 50–50, reflecting the randomness of pricing errors. At best, the benefits from information collection and equity research would cover the costs of doing the research.

■ In an efficient market, a strategy of randomly diversifying across stocks or indexing to the market, carrying little or no information cost and minimal execution costs, would be superior to any other strategy that created larger information and execution costs. There would be no value added by portfolio managers and investment strategists.

■ In an efficient market, a strategy of minimizing trading (i.e., creating a portfolio and not trading unless cash was needed) would be superior to a strategy that required frequent trading.

It is therefore no wonder that the concept of market efficiency evokes such strong reactions on the part of portfolio managers and analysts, who view it, quite rightly, as a challenge to their existence.

It is also important that there be clarity about what market efficiency does not imply. An efficient market does *not* imply that:

■ Stock prices cannot deviate from true value; in fact, there can be large deviations from true value. The only requirement is that the deviations be random.

■ No investor will beat the market in any time period. To the contrary, approximately half of all investors, prior to transactions costs, should beat the market in any period.[1]

■ No group of investors will beat the market in the long term. Given the number of investors in financial markets, the laws of probability would suggest that a fairly large number are going to beat the market consistently over long periods, not because of their investment strategies but because they are lucky. It would not, however, be consistent if a disproportionately large number[2] of these investors used the same investment strategy.

In an efficient market, the expected returns from any investment will be consistent with the risk of that investment over the long term, though there may be deviations from these expected returns in the short term.

---

[1]Since returns are positively skewed—that is, large positive returns are more likely than large negative returns (since this is bounded at –100%)—less than half of all investors will probably beat the market.

[2]One of the enduring pieces of evidence against market efficiency lies in the performance records posted by many of the investors who learned their lessons from Benjamin Graham in the 1950s. No probability statistics could ever explain the consistency and superiority of their records.

NECESSARY CONDITIONS FOR MARKET EFFICIENCY

Markets do not become efficient automatically. It is the actions of investors, sensing bargains and putting into effect schemes to beat the market, that make markets efficient. The necessary conditions for a market inefficiency to be eliminated are:

- The market inefficiency should provide the basis for a scheme to beat the market and earn excess returns. For this to hold true:
  The asset or assets that are the source of the inefficiency have to be traded.
  The transaction costs of executing the scheme have to be smaller than the expected profits from the scheme.
- There should be profit-maximizing investors who:
  Recognize the potential for excess return.
  Can replicate the beat-the-market scheme that earns the excess return.
  Have the resources to trade on the stock(s) until the inefficiency disappears.

The internal contradiction of claiming that there is no possibility of beating the market in an efficient market and requiring profit-maximizing investors to constantly seek out ways of beating the market and thus making it efficient has been explored by many. If markets were in fact efficient, investors would stop looking for inefficiencies, which would lead to markets becoming inefficient again. It makes sense to think about an efficient market as a self-correcting mechanism, where inefficiencies appear at regular intervals but disappear almost instantaneously as investors find them and trade on them.

PROPOSITIONS ABOUT MARKET EFFICIENCY

A reading of the conditions under which markets become efficient leads to general propositions about where investors are most likely to find inefficiencies in financial markets.

Proposition 1: The probability of finding inefficiencies in an asset market decreases as the ease of trading on the asset increases. To the extent that investors have difficulty trading on an asset, either because open markets do not exist or there are significant barriers to trading, inefficiencies in pricing can continue for long periods.

This proposition can be used to shed light on the differences between different asset markets. For instance, it is far easier to trade on stocks than it is on real estate, since markets are much more open, prices are in smaller units (reducing the barriers to entry for new traders), and the asset itself does not vary from transaction to transaction (one share of IBM is identical to another share, whereas one piece of real estate can be very different from another piece that is a stone's throw away). Based on these differences, there should be a greater likelihood of finding inefficiencies (both under- and overvaluation) in the real estate market.

Proposition 2: The probability of finding an inefficiency in an asset market increases as the transactions and information cost of exploiting the inefficiency increases. The cost of collecting information and trading varies widely across markets and even across investments in the same markets. As these costs increase, it pays less and less to try to exploit these inefficiencies.

Consider, for instance, the perceived wisdom that investing in "loser" stocks (i.e., stocks that have done very badly in some prior time period) should yield excess returns. This may be true in terms of raw returns, but transaction costs are likely to be much higher for these stocks since:

- They tend to be low-priced stocks, leading to higher brokerage commissions and expenses.
- The bid-ask spread, a transaction cost paid at the time of purchase, becomes a much higher fraction of the total price paid.
- Trading is often thin on these stocks, and small trades can cause prices to change, resulting in a higher buy price and a lower sell price.

Corollary 1: Investors who can estabish a cost advantage (either in information collection or transactions costs) will be more able to exploit small inefficiencies than other investors who do not possess this advantage.

There are a number of studies that look at the effect of block trades on prices and conclude that while block trades do affect prices, investors will not exploit these inefficiencies because of the number of times they will have to trade and their associated transaction costs. These concerns are unlikely to hold for a specialist on the floor of the exchange, who can trade quickly, often and at no or very low costs. It should be pointed out, however, that if the market for specialists is efficient, the value of a seat on the exchange should reflect the present value of potential benefits from being a specialist.

This corollary also suggests that investors who work at establishing a cost advantage, especially in relation to information, may be able to generate excess returns on the basis of these advantages. Thus John Templeton, who started investing in Japanese and the Asian markets well before other portfolio managers, might have been able to exploit the informational advantages he had over his peers to make excess returns on his portfolio.

Proposition 3: The speed with which an inefficiency is resolved will be directly related to how easily the scheme to exploit the inefficiency can be replicated by other investors. The ease with which a scheme can be replicated is related to the time, resources, and information needed to execute it. Since very few investors single-handedly possess the resources to eliminate an inefficiency through trading, it is much more likely that an inefficiency will disappear quickly if the scheme used to exploit the inefficiency is transparent and can be copied by other investors.

To illustrate this point, assume that stocks are consistently found to earn excess returns in the month following a stock split. Since firms announce stock splits publicly and any investor can buy stocks right after these splits, it would be surprising if this inefficiency persisted over time. This can be contrasted with the excess returns made by some arbitrage funds in index arbitrage, where index futures are bought (sold), and stocks in the index are sold short (bought). This strategy requires that investors be able to obtain information on the index and spot prices instantaneously, have the capacity (in terms of margin requirements and resources) to trade index futures and to sell short on stocks, and to have the resources to take and hold very large positions until the arbitrage unwinds. Consequently, inefficiencies in index futures pricing are likely to persist at least for the most efficient arbitrageurs, with the lowest execution costs and the speediest execution times.

TESTING MARKET EFFICIENCY

Tests of market efficiency look at the whether specific investment strategies earn excess returns. Some tests also account for transactions costs and execution feasibility. Since an excess return on an investment is the difference between the actual and expected return on that investment, there is implicit in every test of market efficiency a model for this expected return. In some cases, this expected return adjusts for risk using the capital asset pricing model or the arbitrage pricing model, and in others the expected return is based on returns on similar or equivalent investments. In every case, a test of market efficiency is a joint test of market efficiency and the efficacy of the model used for expected returns. When there is evidence of excess returns in a test of market efficiency, it can indicate that markets are inefficient or that the model used to compute expected returns is wrong or both. While this may seem to present an insoluble dilemma, if the conclusions of the study are insensitive to different model specifications, it is much more likely that the results are being driven by true market inefficiencies and not just by model misspecifications.

There are a number of different ways of testing for market efficiency, and the approach used will depend in great part on the investment scheme being tested. A scheme based on trading on information events (stock splits, earnings announcements, or acquisition announcements) is likely to be tested using an "event study" where returns around the event are scrutinized for evidence of excess returns. A scheme based on trading on an observable characteristic of a firm (price-earnings ratios, price–book value ratios, or dividend yields) is likely to be tested using a portfolio approach, where portfolios of stocks with these characteristics are created and tracked over time to see whether in fact they make excess returns. The following pages summarize the key steps involved in each of these approaches, and some potential pitfalls to watch out for when conducting or using these tests.

Event Study

An event study is designed to examine market reactions to and excess returns around specific information events. The information events can be marketwide, such as macroeconomic announcements, or firm-specifc, such as earnings or dividend announcements. The five steps in an event study are:

1. The event to be studied is clearly identified, and the date on which the event was announced pinpointed. The presumption in event studies is that the timing of the event is known with a fair degree of certainty. Since financial markets react to the information about an event rather than the event itself, most event studies are centered around the announcement date for the event.[3]

Announcement Date

_____ | _____

2. Once the event dates are known, returns are collected around these dates for each of the firms in the sample. In doing so, two decisions have to be made. First,

---

[3]In most financial transactions, the announcement date tends to precede the event date by several days and, sometimes, weeks.

the analyst has to decide whether to collect weekly, daily, or shorter-interval returns around the event. This will be decided in part by how precisely the event date is known (the more precise, the more likely it is that shorter return intervals can be used) and by how quickly information is reflected in prices (the faster the adjustment, the shorter the return interval to use). Second, the analyst has to determine how many periods of returns before and after the announcement date will be considered as part of the event window. That decision also will be determined by the precision of the event date, since more imprecise dates will require longer windows.

$$R_{-jn} \cdots\cdots\cdots \quad R_{j0} \quad \cdots\cdots\cdots R_{+jn}$$

$$\underline{\qquad}|\underline{\qquad\qquad}|\underline{\qquad\qquad}|\underline{\quad}$$

Return window: −n to +n

where R_{jt} = Returns on firm j for period t(t = −n, . . . , 0, . . . , +n)

3. The returns, by period, around the announcement date, are adjusted for market performance and risk to arrive at excess returns for each firm in the sample. For instance, if the capital asset pricing model is used to control for risk:

Excess return on period t = Return on day t − (Risk-free rate + Beta × Return on market on day t)

$$ER_{-jn} \cdots\cdots\cdots \quad ER_{j0} \quad \cdots\cdots\cdots ER_{+jn}$$

$$\underline{\qquad}|\underline{\qquad\qquad}|\underline{\qquad\qquad}|\underline{\quad}$$

Return window: −n to +n

where ER_{jt} = Excess returns on firm j for period t(t = −n, . . . , 0, . . . , +n) = $R_{jt} − E(R_{jt})$

4. The excess returns, by period, are averaged across all firms in the sample, and a standard error is computed.

$$\text{Average excess return on day t} = \sum_{j=1}^{j=N} \frac{ER_{jt}}{N}$$

$$\text{Standard error in excess return on day t} = \sum_{d=1}^{d=N} \frac{(ER_{dt} - \text{Average ER})^2}{(N-1)}$$

where N = Number of events (firms) in the event study

5. The question of whether the excess returns around the announcement are different from zero is answered by estimating the t statistic for each period, by dividing the average excess return by the standard error:

T statistic for excess return on day t = Average excess return/Standard error

If the t statistics are statistically significant,[4] the event affects returns; the sign of the excess return determines whether the effect is positive or negative.

---

[4]The standard levels of significance for t statistics are:

Level	One-Tailed	Two-Tailed
1%	2.33	2.55
5%	1.66	1.96

ILLUSTRATION 6.1:   Example of an Event Study—Effects of Option Listing on Stock Prices

Academics and practitioners have long argued about the consequences of option listing for stock price volatility. On the one hand, there are those who argue that options attract speculators and hence increase stock price volatility. On the other hand, there are others who argue that options increase the available choices for investors and increase the flow of information to financial markets, and thus lead to lower stock price volatility and higher stock prices.

One way to test these alternative hypotheses is to do an event study, examining the effects of listing options on the underlying stocks' prices. Conrad (1989) did such a study, following these steps:

Step 1: The date of the announcement that options on a particular stock would be listed on the Chicago Board Options Exchange was collected.

Step 2: The prices of the underlying stock (j) were collected for each of the 10 days prior to the option listing announcement date, for the day of the announcement, and for each of the 10 days after.

Step 3: The returns on the stock (R_{jt}) were computed for each of these trading days.

Step 4: The beta for the stock (β_j) was estimated using the returns from a time period outside the event window (using 100 trading days from before the event and 100 trading days after the event).

Step 5: The returns on the market index (R_{mt}) were computed for each of the 21 trading days.

Step 6: The excess returns were computed for each of the 21 trading days:

$$ER_{jt} = R_{jt} - \beta_j R_{mt} \qquad t = -10, -9, -8, \ldots, +8, +9, +10$$

The excess returns are cumulated for each trading day.

Step 7: The average and standard error of excess returns across all stocks with option listings were computed for each of the 21 trading days. The t statistics are computed using the averages and standard errors for each trading day. The following table summarizes the average excess returns and t statistics around option listing announcement dates:

Trading Day	Average Excess Return	Cumulative Excess Return	T Statistic
−10	0.17%	0.17%	1.30
−9	0.48%	0.65%	1.66
−8	−0.24%	0.41%	1.43
−7	0.28%	0.69%	1.62
−6	0.04%	0.73%	1.62
−5	−0.46%	0.27%	1.24
−4	−0.26%	0.01%	1.02
−3	−0.11%	−0.10%	0.93
−2	0.26%	0.16%	1.09
−1	0.29%	0.45%	1.28
0	0.01%	0.46%	1.27
1	0.17%	0.63%	1.37
2	0.14%	0.77%	1.44
3	0.04%	0.81%	1.44
4	0.18%	0.99%	1.54
5	0.56%	1.55%	1.88
6	0.22%	1.77%	1.99
7	0.05%	1.82%	2.00
8	−0.13%	1.69%	1.89
9	0.09%	1.78%	1.92
10	0.02%	1.80%	1.91

Based on these excess returns, there is no evidence of an announcement effect on the announcement day alone, but there is mild evidence of a positive effect over the entire announcement period.[5]

---

[5]The t statistics are marginally significant at the 5% level.

Portfolio Study

In some investment strategies, firms with specific characteristics are viewed as more likely to be undervalued, and therefore have excess returns, than firms without these characteristics. In these cases, the strategies can be tested by creating portfolios of firms possessing these characteristics at the beginning of a time period and then examining returns over the time period. To ensure that these results are not colored by the idiosyncracies of one time period, this analysis is repeated for a number of periods. The seven steps in doing a portfolio study are:

1. The variable on which firms will be classified is defined, using the investment strategy as a guide. This variable has to be observable, though it does not have to be numerical. Examples would include market value of equity, bond ratings, stock price, price-earnings ratios, and price–book value ratios.
2. The data on the variable is collected for every firm in the defined universe[6] at the *start* of the testing period, and firms are classified into portfolios based on the magnitude of the variable. Thus, if the price-earnings ratio is the screening variable, firms are classified on the basis of PE ratios into portfolios from lowest PE to highest PE classes. The number of classes will depend on the size of the universe, since there have to be sufficient firms in each portfolio to get some measure of diversification.
3. The returns are collected for each firm in each portfolio for the testing period, and the returns for each portfolio are computed, generally assuming that the stocks are equally weighted.
4. The beta (if using a single-factor model) or betas (if using a multifactor model) of each portfolio are estimated, either by taking the average of the betas of the individual stocks in the portfolio or by regressing the portfolio's returns against market returns over a prior time period (for instance, the year before the testing period).
5. The excess returns earned by each portfolio are computed, in conjunction with the standard error of the excess returns.
6. There are a number of statistical tests available to check whether the average excess returns are, in fact, different across the portfolios. Some of these tests are parametric[7] (they make certain distributional assumptions about excess returns), and some are nonparametric.[8]
7. As a final test, the extreme portfolios can be matched against each other to see whether there are statistically significant differences across these portfolios.

---

[6]Though there are practical limits on how big the universe can be, care should be taken to make sure that no biases enter at this stage of the process. An obvious bias would be to pick only stocks that have done well over the time period for the universe.

[7]One parametric test is an F test, which tests for equality of means across groups. This test can be conducted assuming either that the groups have the same variance or that they have different variances.

[8]An example of a nonparametric test is a rank sum test, which ranks returns across the entire sample and then sums the ranks within each group to check whether the rankings are random or systematic.

ILLUSTRATION 6.2:   Example of a Portfolio Study—Price-Earnings Ratios

Practitioners have claimed that low price-earnings ratio stocks are generally bargains and do much better than the market or stocks with high price-earnings ratios. This hypothesis can be tested using a portfolio approach:

Step 1: Using data on price-earnings ratios from the end of 1987, firms on the New York Stock Exchange were classified into five groups, the first group consisting of stocks with the lowest PE ratios and the fifth group consisting of stocks with the highest PE ratios. Firms with negative price-earnings ratios were ignored (which may bias the results).

Step 2: The returns on each portfolio were computed using data from 1988 to 1992. Stocks that went bankrupt or were delisted were assigned a return of –100%.

Step 3: The betas for each stock in each portfolio were computed using monthly returns from 1983 to 1987, and the average beta for each portfolio was estimated. The portfolios were assumed to be equally weighted.

Step 4: The returns on the market index were computed from 1988 to 1992.

Step 5: The excess returns on each portfolio were computed from 1988 to 1992. The following table summarizes the excess returns each year from 1988 to 1992 for each portfolio.

PE Class	1988	1989	1990	1991	1992	1988–1992
Lowest	3.84%	–0.83%	2.10%	6.68%	0.64%	2.61%
2	1.75%	2.26%	0.19%	1.09%	1.13%	1.56%
3	0.20%	–3.15%	–0.20%	0.17%	0.12%	–0.59%
4	–1.25%	–0.94%	–0.65%	–1.99%	–0.48%	–1.15%
Highest	–1.74%	–0.63%	–1.44%	–4.06%	–1.25%	–1.95%

Step 6: While the ranking of the returns across the portfolio classes seems to confirm our hypothesis that low-PE stocks earn a higher return, we have to consider whether the differences across portfolios are statistically significant. There are several tests available, but these are a few:

- An F test can be used to accept or reject the hypothesis that the average returns are the same across all portfolios. A high F score would lead us to conclude that the differences are too large to be random.
- A chi-squared test is a nonparametric test that can be used to test the hypothesis that the means are the same across the five portfolio classes.
- We could isolate just the lowest-PE and highest-PE stocks and estimate a t statistic that the averages are different across these two portfolios.

CARDINAL SINS IN TESTING MARKET EFFICIENCY

In the process of testing investment strategies, there are a number of pitfalls that have to be avoided. Six of them are:

1. *Using anecdotal evidence to support/reject an investment strategy.* Anecdotal evidence is a double-edged sword. It can be used to support or reject the same hypothesis. Since stock prices are noisy and all investment schemes (no matter how absurd) will succeed sometimes and fail at other times, there will always be cases where the scheme works or does not work.

2. *Testing an investment strategy on the same data and time period from which it was extracted.* This is the tool of choice for the unscrupulous investment adviser. An investment scheme is extracted from hundreds through an examination of the data for a particular time period. This investment scheme is then tested on the same time period, with predictable results. (The scheme does miraculously well and makes immense returns.)

An investment scheme should always be tested out on a time period different from the one it is extracted from or on a universe different from the one used to derive the scheme.

3. *Choosing a biased sample.* There may be bias in the sample on which the test is run. Since there are thousands of stocks that could be considered part of this universe, researchers often choose to use a smaller sample. When this choice is random, this does limited damage to the results of the study. If the choice is biased, it can provide results that are not true in the larger universe.

4. *Failure to control for market performance.* A failure to control for overall market performance can lead you to conclude that your investment scheme works just because it makes good returns (most schemes will make good returns if the overall market does well; the question is whether they made better returns than expected) or does not work just because it makes bad returns (most schemes will do badly if the overall market performs poorly). It is crucial therefore that investment schemes control for market performance during the period of the test.

5. *Failure to control for risk.* A failure to control for risk leads to a bias toward accepting high-risk investment schemes and rejecting low-risk investment schemes, since the former should make higher returns than the market and the latter lower, without implying any excess returns.

6. *Mistaking correlation for causation.* Consider the study on PE stocks cited in the earlier section. We concluded that low-PE stocks have higher excess returns than high-PE stocks. It would be a mistake to conclude that a low price-earnings ratio causes excess returns, since the high returns and the low PE ratio themselves might have been caused by the high risk associated with investing in the stock. In other words, high risk is the causative factor that leads to both the observed phenomena—low PE ratios on the one hand and high returns on the other. This insight would make us more cautious about adopting a strategy of buying low-PE stocks in the first place.

SOME LESSER SINS THAT CAN BE A PROBLEM

1. *Survival bias.* Most researchers start with an existing universe of publicly traded companies and work back through time to test investment strategies. This can create a subtle bias since it automatically eliminates firms that failed during the period, with obvious negative consequences for returns. If the investment scheme is particularly susceptible to picking firms that have high bankruptcy risk, this may lead to an overstatement of returns on the scheme.

For example, assume that the investment scheme recommends investing in stocks that have very negative earnings, using the argument that these stocks are the most likely to benefit from a turnaround. Some of the firms in this portfolio will go bankrupt, and a failure to consider these firms will overstate the returns from this strategy.

2. *Not allowing for transaction costs.* Some investment schemes are more expensive than others because of transaction costs—execution fees, bid-ask spreads, and price impact. A complete test will take these into account before it passes judgment on the strategy. This is easier said than done, because different investors have different transaction costs, and it is unclear which investor's trading cost schedule should be used in the test. Most researchers who ignore transaction costs argue that individual investors can decide for themselves, given their transaction costs, whether the excess returns justify the investment strategy.

3. *Not allowing for difficulties in execution.* Some strategies look good on paper but are difficult to execute in practice, either because of impediments to trading or because trading creates a price impact. Thus a strategy of investing in very small companies may seem to create excess returns on paper, but these excess returns may not exist in practice because the price impact is significant.

EVIDENCE ON MARKET EFFICIENCY

This section of the chapter attempts to summarize the evidence from studies of market efficiency. Without claiming to be comprehensive, the evidence is classified into four sections—the study of price changes and their time series properties, the research on the efficiency of market reaction to information announcements, the existence of return anomalies across firms and over time, and the analysis of the performance of insiders, analysts, and money managers.

TIME SERIES PROPERTIES OF PRICE CHANGES

Investors have used price charts and price patterns as tools for predicting future price movements for as long as there have been financial markets. It is not surprising, therefore, that the first studies of market efficiency focused on the relationship between price changes over time, to see if in fact such predictions were feasible. Some of this testing was spurred by the random walk theory of price movements, which contended that price changes over time followed a random walk. As the studies of the time series properties of prices have proliferated, the evidence can be classified into two categories—studies that focus on short-term (intraday, daily, and weekly price movements) price behavior and research that examines long-term (annual and five-year returns) price movements.

Short-Term Price Movements

The notion that today's price change conveys information about tomorrow's price change is deeply rooted in most investors' psyches. There are several ways in which this hypothesis can be tested in financial markets.

Serial Correlation The serial correlation measures the correlation between price changes in consecutive time periods, whether hourly, daily, or weekly, and is a measure of how much the price change in any period depends on the price change over the previous time period. A serial correlation of zero would therefore imply that price changes in consecutive time periods are uncorrelated with each other, and can thus be viewed as a rejection of the hypothesis that investors can learn about future price changes from past ones. A serial correlation that is positive and statistically significant could be viewed as evidence of price momentum in markets, and would suggest that returns in a period are more likely to be positive (negative) if the prior period's returns were positive (negative). A serial correlation that is negative and statistically significant could be evidence of price reversals, and would be consistent with a market where positive returns are more likely to follow negative returns and vice versa.

From the viewpoint of investment strategy, serial correlations can be exploited to earn excess returns. A positive serial correlation would be exploited by a strategy of buying after periods with positive returns and selling after periods with negative returns. A negative serial correlation would suggest a strategy of buying after periods with negative returns and selling after periods with positive returns. Since these strategies generate transactions costs, the correlations have to be large enough to allow investors to generate profits to cover these costs. It is therefore entirely possible that there is serial correlation in returns, without any opportunity to earn excess returns for most investors.

The earliest studies of serial correlation—Alexander (1963), Cootner (1962), and Fama (1965)—all looked at large U.S. stocks and concluded that the serial correlation in stock prices was small. Fama, for instance, found that 8 of the 30 stocks listed in the Dow had negative serial correlations and that most of the serial correlations were less than 0.05. Other studies confirm these findings not only for smaller stocks in the United States, but also for other markets. For instance, Jennergren and Korsvold (1974) report low serial correlations for the Swedish equity market, and Cootner (1961) concludes that serial correlations are low in commodity markets as well. While there may be statistical significance associated with some of these correlations, it is unlikely that there is enough correlation to generate excess returns.

The serial correlation in short period returns is affected by market liquidity and the presence of a bid-ask spread. Not all stocks in an index are liquid, and in some cases stocks may not trade during a period. When the stock trades in a subsequent period, the resulting price changes can create positive serial correlation. To see why, assume that the market is up strongly on day 1, but that three stocks in the index do not trade on that day. On day 2, if these stocks are traded, they are likely to go up in price to reflect the increase in the market the previous day. The net result is that you should expect to see positive serial correlation in daily or hourly returns in illiquid market indexes.

The bid-ask spread creates a bias in the opposite direction, if transaction prices are used to compute returns, since prices have an equal chance of ending up at the bid or the ask price. The bounce that this induces in prices—from bid to ask to bid again—will result in negative serial correlations in returns. Roll (1984) provides a simple measure of this relationship:

$$\text{Bid-ask spread} = -\sqrt{2 \text{ (Serial covariance in returns)}}$$

where the serial covariance in returns measures the covariance between return changes in consecutive time periods. For very short return intervals, this bias induced in serial correlations might dominate and create the mistaken view that price changes in consecutive time periods are negatively correlated.

Filter Rules   In a filter rule, an investor buys an investment if the price rises X percent from a previous low and holds the investment until the price drops X percent from a previous high. The magnitude of the change (X percent) that triggers the trades can vary from filter rule to filter rule, with smaller changes resulting in more transactions per period and higher transaction costs. Figure 6.1 graphs out a typical filter rule.

This strategy is based on the assumption that price changes are serially correlated and that there is price momentum (i.e., stocks that have gone up strongly in the past are more likely to keep going up than go down). Table 6.1 summarizes results—Fama and Blume (1966) and Jensen and Bennington (1970)—from a study on returns, before and after transactions costs, on a trading strategy based on filter rules ranging from 0.5 percent to 20 percent. (A 0.5 percent rule implies that a stock is bought when it rises 0.5 percent from a previous low and is sold when it falls 0.5 percent from a prior high.)

The only filter rule that beats the returns from the buy-and-hold strategy is the 0.5 percent rule, but it does so before transaction costs. This strategy creates 12,514 trades during the period which generate enough transaction costs to wipe out the principal invested by the investor. While this test is dated, it also illustrates basic problems with strategies that require frequent short-term trading. Even though these strategies may earn excess returns prior to transaction costs, adjusting for these costs can wipe out the excess returns.

One popular indicator among investors that is a variant on the filter rule is the relative strength measure, which relates recent prices on stocks or other investments

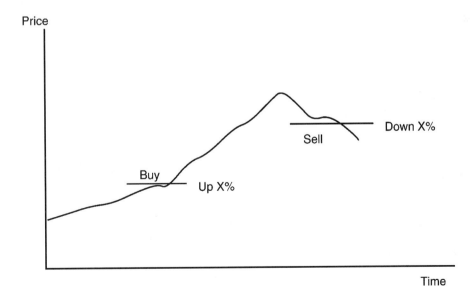

FIGURE 6.1   Filter Rule

TABLE 6.1   Returns on Filter Rule Strategies

Value of X	Return with Strategy	Return with Buy and Hold	Number of Transactions with Strategy	Return after Transaction Costs
0.5%	11.5%	10.4%	12,514	–103.6%
1.0%	5.5%	10.3%	8,660	–74.9%
2.0%	0.2%	10.3%	4,764	–45.2%
3.0%	–1.7%	10.1%	2,994	–30.5%
4.0%	0.1%	10.1%	2,013	–19.5%
5.0%	–1.9%	10.0%	1,484	–16.6%
6.0%	1.3%	9.7%	1,071	–9.4%
7.0%	0.8%	9.6%	828	–7.4%
8.0%	1.7%	9.6%	653	–5.0%
9.0%	1.9%	9.6%	539	–3.6%
10.0%	3.0%	9.6%	435	–1.4%
12.0%	5.3%	9.4%	289	2.3%
14.0%	3.9%	10.3%	224	1.4%
16.0%	4.2%	10.3%	172	2.3%
18.0%	3.6%	10.0%	139	2.0%
20.0%	4.3%	9.8%	110	3.0%

to either average prices over a specified period, say over six months, or to the price at the beginning of the period. Stocks that score high on the relative strength measure are considered good investments. This investment strategy is also based upon the assumption of price momentum.

Runs Tests   A runs test is a nonparametric variation on the serial correlation, and it is based on a count of the number of runs (i.e., sequences of price increases or decreases) in the price changes. Thus, the following time series of price changes, where U is an increase and D is a decrease, would result in the following runs:

<u>UUU</u> <u>DD</u> <u>U</u> <u>DDD</u> <u>UU</u> <u>DD</u> <u>U</u> <u>D</u> <u>UU</u> <u>DD</u> <u>U</u> <u>DD</u> <u>UUU</u> <u>DD</u> <u>UU</u> <u>D</u> <u>UU</u> <u>D</u>

There were 18 runs in this price series of 33 periods. The actual number of runs in the price series is compared against the number that can be expected in a series of this length, assuming that price changes are random.[9] If the actual number of runs is greater than the expected number, there is evidence of negative correlation in price changes. If it is lower, there is evidence of positive correlation. A 1966 study by Niederhoffer and Osborne of price changes in the Dow 30 stocks assuming daily, four-day, nine-day, and 16-day return intervals provided the following results:

---

[9]There are statistical tables that summarize the expected number of runs, assuming randomness, in a series of any length.

	Differencing Interval			
	Daily	*Four-day*	*Nine-day*	*Sixteen-day*
Actual runs	735.1	175.7	74.6	41.6
Expected runs	759.8	175.8	75.3	41.7

Based on these results, there is evidence of positive correlation in daily returns but no evidence of deviations from normality for longer return intervals.

Again, while the evidence is dated, it serves to illustrate the point that long strings of positive and negative changes are, by themselves, insufficient evidence that markets are not random, since such behavior is consistent with price changes following a random walk. It is the recurrence of these strings that can be viewed as evidence against randomness in price behavior.

Long-Term Price Movements

While most of the earlier studies of price behavior focused on shorter return intervals, more attention has been paid to price movements over longer periods (one-year to five-year periods) in recent years. Here, there is an interesting dichotomy in the results. When "long term" is defined as months rather than years, there seems to be a tendency toward positive serial correlation or price momentum. However, when "long term" is defined in terms of years, there is substantial negative correlation in the returns, suggesting that markets reverse themselves over long periods.

Fama and French (1988) examined five-year returns on stocks from 1931 to 1986 and present further evidence of this phenomenon. Studies that break down stocks on the basis of market value have found that the serial correlation is more negative in five-year returns than in one-year returns, and is much more negative for smaller stocks rather than larger stocks. Figure 6.2 summarizes one-year and five-year serial correlation from the Fama–French study by size class for stocks on the New York Stock Exchange. This phenomenon has also been examined in other markets, and the findings have been similar.

Winner and Loser Portfolios   Since there is evidence that prices reverse themselves in the long term for entire markets, it might be worth examining whether such price reversals occur on classes of stock within a market. For instance, are stocks that have gone up the most over the last period more likely to go down over the next period and vice versa? To isolate the effect of such price reversals on the extreme portfolios, DeBondt and Thaler (1985) constructed a winner portfolio of 35 stocks, which had gone up the most over the prior year, and a loser portfolio of 35 stocks, which had gone down the most over the prior year, each year from 1933 to 1978, and examined returns on these portfolios for the 60 months following the creation of the portfolio. Figure 6.3 summarizes the excess returns for winner and loser portfolios.

This analysis suggests that loser portfolios clearly outperform winner portfolios in the 60 months following creation. This evidence is consistent with market overreaction and correction in long return intervals. Jegadeesh and Titman (1993) find the same phenomenon occurring, but present interesting evidence that the win-

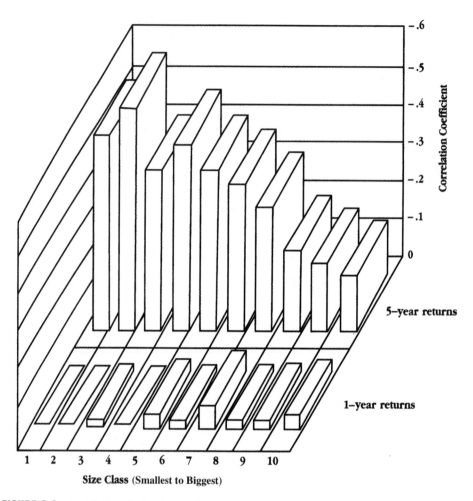

FIGURE 6.2 Serial Correlation in Stock Returns
Source: Fama and French (1988).

ner (loser) portfolios continue to go up (down) for up to eight months after they are created and it is in the subsequent periods that the reversals occur.

There are many, academics as well as practitioners, who suggest that these findings may be interesting but that they overstate potential returns on loser portfolios. For instance, loser portfolios are more likely to contain low-priced stocks (selling for less than $5), which generate higher transaction costs and are also more likely to offer heavily skewed returns (i.e., the excess returns come from a few stocks making phenomenal returns rather than from consistent performance). Furthermore, the bulk of the excess returns of loser portfolios can be attributed to low-priced stocks, and the results are sensitive to when the portfolios are created. Loser portfolios created every December earn significantly higher returns than portfolios created every June.

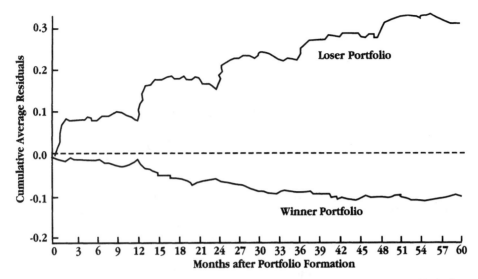

(**Average of 46 yearly replications, starting every January between 1933 and 1978**).

FIGURE 6.3 Excess Returns for Winner and Loser Portfolios
Source: DeBondt and Thaler (1985).

Speculative Bubbles, Crashes, and Panics

Historians who have examined the behavior of financial markets over time have challenged the assumption of rationality that underlies much of efficient market theory. They point to the frequency with which speculative bubbles have formed in financial markets as investors buy into fads or get-rich-quick schemes, and the crashes when these bubbles have ended, and suggest that there is nothing to prevent the recurrence of this phenomenon in today's financial markets. There is some evidence in the literature of irrationality on the part of market players.

Experimental Studies of Rationality   Some of the most interesting evidence on market efficiency and rationality in recent years has come from experimental studies. While most experimental studies suggest that traders are rational, there are some examples of irrational behavior in some of these studies.

One such study was done at the University of Arizona. In an experimental study, traders were told that a payout would be declared after each trading day, determined randomly from four possibilities—0, 8, 28, or 60 cents. The average payout was 24 cents. Thus the share's expected value on the first trading day of a 15-day experiment was $3.60 (24 cents times 15), the second day was $3.36, and so on. The traders were allowed to trade each day. The results of 60 such experiments are summarized in Figure 6.4.

There is clear evidence here of a speculative bubble forming during periods 3 to 5, where prices exceed expected values by a significant amount. The bubble ultimately bursts, and prices approach expected value by the end of the period. If this mispricing is feasible in a simple market, where every investor obtains the same information, it is clearly feasible in real financial markets, where there is much more differential information and much greater uncertainty about expected value.

It should be pointed out that some of the experiments were run with students, and some with Tucson businessmen with real-world experience. The results were similar for both groups. Furthermore, when price curbs of 15 cents were introduced, the booms lasted even longer because traders knew that prices would not fall by more than 15 cents in a period. Thus, the notion that price limits can control speculative bubbles seems misguided.

Behavioral Finance The irrationality sometimes exhibited by investors has given rise to a whole new area of finance called behavioral finance. Using evidence gathered from experimental psychology, researchers have tried to both model how investors react to information and predict how prices will change as a consequence. They have been far more successful at the first endeavor than the second. For instance, the evidence seems to suggest that:

■ Investors do not like to admit their mistakes. Consequently, they tend to hold on to losing stocks far too long, or in some cases double up their bets (investments) as stocks drop in value.
■ More information does not always lead to better investment decisions. Investors seem to suffer both from information overload and from a tendency to react to the latest piece of information. Both result in investment decisions that lower returns in the long term.

If the evidence on how investors behave is so clear-cut, you might ask, why are the predictions that emerge from these models so noisy? The answer, perhaps, is that any model that tries to forecast human foibles and irrationalities is, by its very nature, unlikely to be a stable one. Behavioral finance may emerge ultimately as a

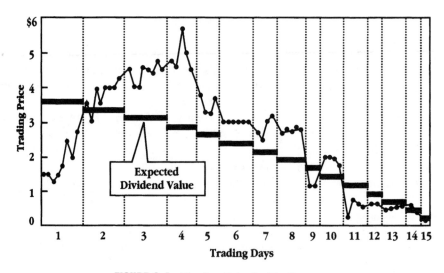

FIGURE 6.4 Trading Price by Trading Day

BEHAVORIAL FINANCE AND VALUATION

In 1999, Robert Shiller made waves in both academia and investment houses with his book titled *Irrational Exuberance*. His thesis is that investors are often not just irrational but irrational in predictable ways—overreacting to some information and buying and selling in herds. His work forms part of a growing body of theory and evidence of behavioral finance, which can be viewed as a congruence of psychology, statistics, and finance.

While the evidence presented for investor irrationality is strong, the implications for valuation are less so. You can consider discounted cash flow valuation to be the antithesis of behavioral finance, because it takes the point of view that the value of an asset is the present value of the expected cash flows generated by that asset. With this context, there are two ways in which you can look at the findings in behavioral finance:

1. Irrational behavior may explain why prices can deviate from value (as estimated in a discounted cash flow model). Consequently, it provides the foundation for the excess returns earned by rational investors who base decisions on estimated value. Implicit here is the assumption that markets ultimately recognize their irrationality and correct themselves.
2. It may also explain why discounted cash flow values can deviate from relative values (estimated using multiples). Since the relative value is estimated by looking at how the market prices similar assets, irrationalities that exist will be priced into the asset.

---

trump card in explaining why and how stock prices deviate from true value, but its role in devising investment strategy still remains questionable.

MARKET REACTION TO INFORMATION EVENTS

Some of the most powerful tests of market efficiency are event studies where market reaction to informational events (such as earnings and takeover announcements) has been scrutinized for evidence of inefficiency. While it is consistent with market efficiency for markets to react to new information, the reaction has to be instantaneous and unbiased. This point is made in Figure 6.5 by contrasting three different market reactions to information announcements.

Of the three market reactions pictured here, only the first one is consistent with an efficient market. In the second market, the information announcement is followed by a gradual increase in prices, allowing investors to make excess returns after the announcement. This is a slow learning market where some investors will make excess returns on the price drift. In the third market, the price reacts instantaneously to the announcement, but corrects itself in the days that follow, suggesting that the initial price change was an overreaction to the information. Here again, an enterprising investor could have sold short after the announcement and expected to make excess returns as a consequence of the price correction.

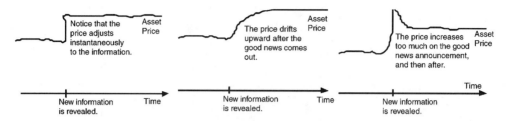

FIGURE 6.5   Information and Price Adjustment

Earnings Announcements

When firms make earnings announcements, they convey information to financial markets about their current and future prospects. The magnitude of the information, and the size of the market reaction, should depend on how much the earnings report exceeds or falls short of investor expectations. In an efficient market, there should be an instantaneous reaction to the earnings report, if it contains surprising information, and prices should increase following positive surprises and decline following negative surprises.

Since actual earnings are compared to investor expectations, one of the key parts of an earnings event study is the measurement of these expectations. Some of the earlier studies used earnings from the same quarter in the prior year as a measure of expected earnings (i.e., firms that report increases in quarter-to-quarter earnings provide positive surprises, and those which report decreases in quarter-to-quarter earnings provide negative surprises). In more recent studies, analyst estimates of earnings have been used as a proxy for expected earnings and compared to the actual earnings.

Figure 6.6 provides a graph of price reactions to earnings surprises, classified on the basis of magnitude into different classes from "most negative" earnings reports (group 1) to "most positive" earnings reports (group 10). The evidence contained in this graph is consistent with the evidence in most earnings announcement studies:

■ The earnings announcement clearly conveys valuable information to financial markets; there are positive excess returns (cumulative abnormal returns) after positive announcements and negative excess returns around negative announcements.

■ There is some evidence of a market reaction in the day immediately prior to the earnings announcement that is consistent with the nature of the announcement (i.e., prices tend to go up on the day before positive announcements and down on the day before negative announcements). This can be viewed as evidence of either insider trading, information leakage, or getting the announcement date wrong.[10]

---

[10]The *Wall Street Journal* is often used as an information source to extract announcement dates for earnings. For some firms, news of the announcement may actually cross the news wire the day before the *Wall Street Journal* announcement, leading to a misidentification of the report date and the drift in returns the day before the announcement.

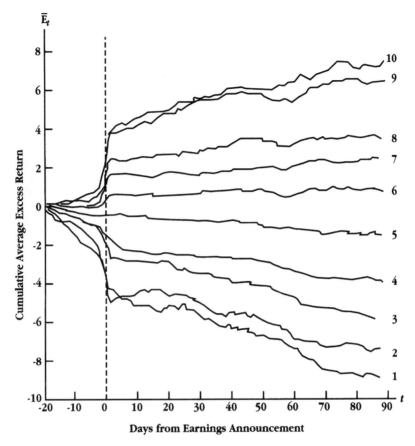

FIGURE 6.6 Price Reaction to Quarterly Earnings Report
Source: Rendleman, Jones, and Latrané (1982).

■ There is some evidence, albeit weak, of a price drift in the days following an earnings announcement. Thus a positive report evokes a positive market reaction on the announcement date, and there are mildly positive excess returns in the days following the earnings announcement. Similar conclusions emerge for negative earnings reports.

The management of a firm has some discretion on the timing of earnings reports, and there is some evidence that the timing affects expected returns. A 1989 study by Damodaran of earnings reports, classified by the day of the week that the earnings are reported, reveals that earnings and dividend reports on Fridays are much more likely to contain negative information than announcements on any other day of the week. This is shown in Figure 6.7.

There is also some evidence discussed by Chamber and Penman (1984) that earnings announcements that are delayed, relative to the expected announcement date, are much more likely to contain bad news than earnings announcements that

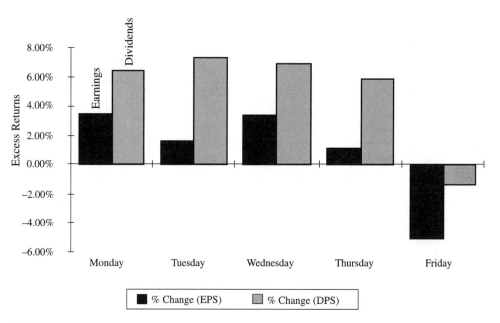

FIGURE 6.7   Earnings and Dividend Reports by Day of the Week
Source: Damodaran (1989).

are early or on time. This is graphed in Figure 6.8. Earnings announcements that are more than six days late relative to the expected announcement date are much more likely to contain bad news and evoke negative market reactions than earnings announcements that are on time or early.

Investment and Project Announcements

Firms frequently make announcements of their intentions of investing resources in projects and research and development. There is evidence that financial markets react to these announcements. The question of whether markets have a long-term or short-term perspective can be partially answered by looking at these market reactions. If financial markets are as short-term as some of their critics claim, they should react negatively to announcements by the firm that it plans to invest in research and development. The evidence suggests the contrary. Table 6.2 summarizes market reactions to various classes of investment announcements made by the firm.

This table excludes the largest investments that most firms make, which is acquisitions of other firms. Here the evidence is not so favorable. In about 55 percent of all acquisitions, the stock price of the acquiring firm drops on the announcement of the acquisition, reflecting the market's beliefs that firms tend to overpay on acquisitions.

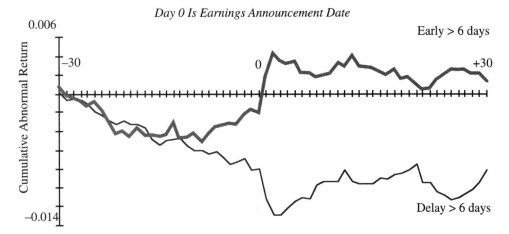

FIGURE 6.8 Cumulated Abnormal Returns and Earnings Delay
Source: Chambers and Penman (1984).

TABLE 6.2 Market Reactions to Investment Announcements

	Abnormal Returns	
Type of Announcement	On Announcement Day	In Announcement Month
Joint venture formations	0.399%	1.412%
R&D expenditures	0.251%	1.456%
Product strategies	0.440%	–0.35%
Capital expenditures	0.290%	1.499%
All announcements	0.355%	0.984%

Source: Chan, Martin, and Kensinger (1990); McConnell and Muscarella (1985).

MARKET ANOMALIES

Merriam-Webster's Collegiate Dictionary defines an anomaly as a "deviation from the common rule." Studies of market efficiency have uncovered numerous examples of market behavior that are inconsistent with existing models of risk and return and often defy rational explanation. The persistence of some of these patterns of behavior suggests that the problem, in at least some of these anomalies, lies in the models being used for risk and return rather than in the behavior of financial markets. The following section summarizes some of the more widely noticed anomalies in financial markets in the United States and elsewhere.

Anomalies Based on Firm Characteristics

There are a number of anomalies that have been related to observable firm characteristics, including the market value of equity, price-earnings ratios, and price–book value ratios.

The Small Firm Effect   Studies such as Banz (1981) and Keim (1983) have consistently found that smaller firms (in terms of market value of equity) earn higher returns than larger firms of equivalent risk, where risk is defined in terms of the market beta. Figure 6.9 summarizes returns for stocks in 10 market value classes for the period from 1927 to 1983.

The size of the small firm premium, while it has varied across time, has been generally positive. It was highest during the 1970s and early 1980s and lowest during the 1990s. The persistence of this premium has led to several possible explanations.

1. The transaction costs of investing in small stocks are significantly higher than the transaction costs of investing in larger stocks, and the premiums are estimated prior to these costs. While this is generally true, the differential transaction costs are unlikely to explain the magnitude of the premium across time, and are likely to become even less critical for longer investment horizons. The difficulties of replicating the small firm premiums that are observed in the studies in real time are illustrated in Figure 6.10, which compares the returns on a hypothetical small firm portfolio (CRSP Small Stocks) with the actual returns on a small firm mutual fund (DFA Small Stock Fund), which passively invests in small stocks.

2. The capital asset pricing model may not be the right model for risk, and betas underestimate the true risk of small stocks. Thus, the small firm premium is really a measure of the failure of beta to capture risk. The additional risk associated with small stocks may come from several sources. First, the estimation risk associated with estimates of beta for small firms is much greater than the estimation risk associated with beta estimates for larger firms. The small firm premium may be a

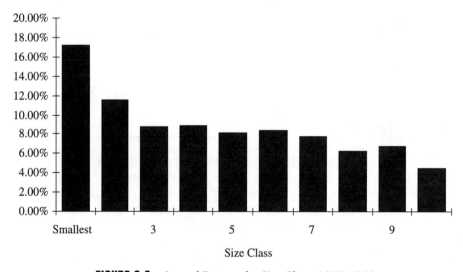

FIGURE 6.9   Annual Returns by Size Class, 1927–1983

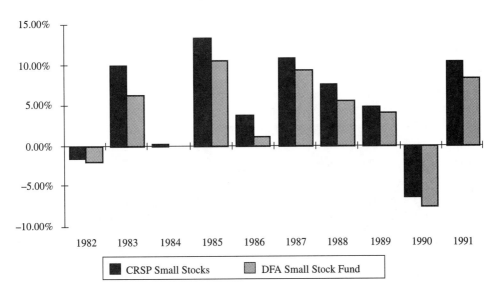

FIGURE 6.10 Returns on CRSP Small Stocks versus DFA Small Stock Fund

reward for this additional estimation risk. Second, there may be additional risk in investing in small stocks because far less information is available on these stocks. In fact, studies indicate that stocks that are neglected by analysts and institutional investors earn an excess return that parallels the small firm premium.

There is evidence of a small firm premium in markets outside the United States as well. Dimson and Marsh (1986) examined stocks in the United Kingdom from 1955 to 1984 and found that the annual returns on small stocks exceeded that on large stocks by 6 percent annually over the period. Chan, Hamao, and Lakonishok (1991) report a small firm premium of about 5 percent for Japanese stocks between 1971 and 1988.

Price-Earnings Ratios Investors have long argued that stocks with low price-earnings ratios are more likely to be undervalued and earn excess returns. For instance, Benjamin Graham, in his investment classic *The Intelligent Investor*, used low price-earnings ratios as a screen for finding undervalued stocks. Studies [Basu (1977); Basu (1983)] that have looked at the relationship between PE ratios and excess returns confirm these priors. Figure 6.11 summarizes annual returns by PE ratio classes for stocks from 1967 to 1988. Firms in the lowest PE ratio class earned an average return of 16.26 percent during the period, while firms in the highest PE ratio class earned an average return of only 6.64 percent.

The excess returns earned by low PE ratio stocks also persist in other international markets. Table 6.3 summarizes the results of studies looking at this phenomenon in markets outside the United States.

The excess returns earned by low price-earnings ratio stocks are difficult to justify using a variation of the argument used for small stocks (i.e., that the risk of low PE ratios stocks is understated in the CAPM). Low PE ratio stocks generally are characterized by low growth, large size, and stable businesses, all of which should work toward reducing their risk rather than increasing it. The only explanation that can be given for this phenomenon, which is consistent with an efficient market,

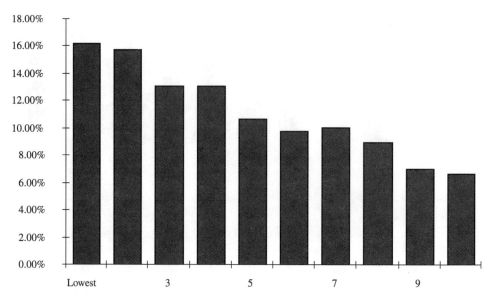

FIGURE 6.11   Annual Returns by PE Ratio Class

TABLE 6.3   Excess Returns on Low PE Ratio Stocks by Country, 1989–1994

Country	Annual Premium Earned by Lowest-PE Stocks (Bottom Quintile)
Australia	3.03%
France	6.40%
Germany	1.06%
Hong Kong	6.60%
Italy	14.16%
Japan	7.30%
Switzerland	9.02%
United Kingdom	2.40%

Annual premium: Premium earned over an index of equally weighted stocks in that market between January 1, 1989, and December 31, 1994. These numbers were obtained from a Merrill Lynch Survey of Proprietary Indices.

is that low PE ratio stocks generate large dividend yields, which would have created a larger tax burden because dividends are taxed at higher rates.

Price–Book Value Ratios   Another statistic that is widely used by investors in investment strategy is price–book value ratios. A low price–book value ratio has been considered a reliable indicator of undervaluation in firms. In studies that parallel those done on price-earnings ratios, the relationship between returns and price–book value ratios has been studied. The consistent finding from these studies is that there is a negative relationship between returns and price–book value ratios—low price–book value ratio stocks earn higher returns than high price–book value ratio stocks.

Rosenberg, Reid, and Lanstein (1985) find that the average returns on U.S. stocks are positively related to the ratio of a firm's book value to market value. Between 1973 and 1984, the strategy of picking stocks with high book-price ratios (low price-book values) yielded an excess return of 36 basis points a month. Fama and French (1992), in examining the cross section of expected stock returns between 1963 and 1990, established that the positive relationship between book-to-price ratios and average returns persists in both the univariate and multivariate tests, and is even stronger than the size effect in explaining returns. When they classified firms on the basis of book-to-price ratios into 12 portfolios, firms in the lowest book-to-price (highest price-book) class earned an average monthly return of 0.30 percent, while firms in the highest book-to-price (lowest price-book) class earned an average monthly return of 1.83 percent for the 1963–1990 period.

Chan, Hamao, and Lakonishok (1991) find that the book-to-market ratio has a strong role in explaining the cross section of average returns on Japanese stocks. Capaul, Rowley, and Sharpe (1993) extend the analysis of price–book value ratios across other international markets, and conclude that value stocks (i.e., stocks with low price–book value ratios) earned excess returns in every market that they analyzed between 1981 and 1992. Their annualized estimates of the return differential earned by stocks with low price–book value ratios, over the market index, were:

Country	*Added Return to Low Price–Book Value Portfolio*
France	3.26%
Germany	1.39%
Switzerland	1.17%
United Kingdom	1.09%
Japan	3.43%
United States	1.06%
Europe	1.30%
Global	1.88%

A caveat is in order. Fama and French pointed out that low price–book value ratios may operate as a measure of risk, since firms with prices well below book value are more likely to be in trouble and go out of business. Investors therefore have to evaluate for themselves whether the additional returns made by such firms justify the additional risk taken on by investing in them.

Temporal Anomalies

There are a number of peculiarities in return differences across calendar time that not only are difficult to rationalize but are also suggestive of inefficiencies. Furthermore, some of these temporal anomalies are related to the small firm effect described in the previous section.

January Effect Studies of returns in the United States and other major financial markets [Roll (1983); Haugen and Lakonishok (1988)] consistently reveal strong differences in return behavior across the months of the year. Figure 6.12 reports

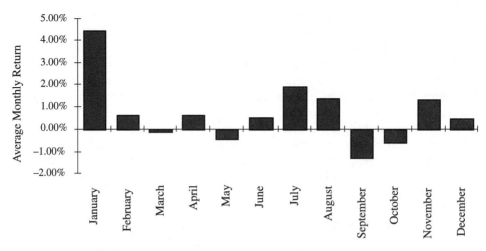

FIGURE 6.12 Average Return by Months of the Year, 1926–1983

average returns by months of the year from 1926 to 1983. Returns in January are significantly higher than returns in any other month of the year. This phenomenon is called the year-end or January effect, and it can be traced to the first two weeks in January.

The relationship between the January effect and the small firm effect [(Keum (1983) and Reinganum (1983)] adds to the complexity of this phenomenon. The January effect is much more accentuated for small firms than for larger firms, and roughly half of the small firm premium described in the prior section is earned in the first two weeks of January. Figure 6.13 graphs returns in January by size and risk class for data from 1935 to 1986.

A number of explanations have been advanced for the January effect, but few hold up to serious scrutiny. Reinganum suggested that there is tax loss selling by investors at the end of the year on stocks that have lost money to capture the capital gain, driving prices down, presumably below true value, in December, and a buying back of the same stocks in January,[11] resulting in the high returns. The fact that the January effect is accentuated for stocks that have done worse over the prior year is offered as evidence for this explanation. There are several pieces of evidence that contradict it, though. First, there are countries, like Australia, that have a different tax year but continue to have a January effect. Second, the January effect is no greater, on average, in years following bad years for the stock market than in other years.

A second rationale is that the January effect is related to institutional trading behavior around the turn of the years. It has been noted, for instance, that the ratio of buys to sells for institutions drops significantly below average in the days before

---

[11]Since wash sales rules would prevent an investor from selling and buying back the same stock within 45 days, there has to be some substitution among the stocks. Thus investor 1 sells stock A and investor 2 sells stock B, but when it comes time to buy back the stock, investor 1 buys stock B and investor 2 buys stock A.

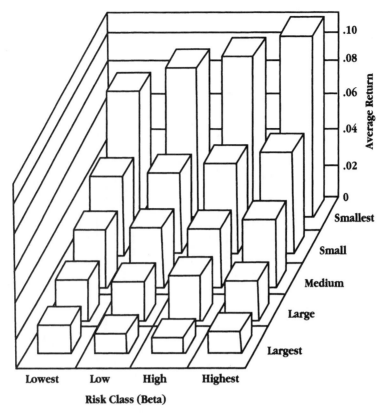

FIGURE 6.13 Returns in January by Size and Risk Class, 1935–1986
Source: Ritter and Chopra (1989).

the turn of the year and picks up to above average in the months that follow. This is illustrated in Figure 6.14. It is argued that the absence of institutional buying pushes down prices in the days before the turn of the year and pushes up prices in the days after.

The universality of the January effect is illustrated in Figure 6.15, which examines returns in January versus the other months of the year in several major financial markets, and finds strong evidence of a January effect in every market [Haugen and Lakonishok (1988); Gultekin and Gultekin (1983)].

Weekend Effect   The weekend effect is another return phenomenon that has persisted over extraordinarily long periods and over a number of international markets. It refers to the differences in returns between Mondays and other days of the week. The significance of the return difference is brought out in Figure 6.16, which graphs returns by days of the week from 1962 to 1978 [Gibbons and Hess (1981)].

The returns on Mondays are significantly negative, whereas the returns on every day of the week are not. There are a number of other findings on the Monday effect that have fleshed this out. First, the Monday effect is really a weekend effect since the bulk of the negative returns is manifested in the Friday close to Monday open returns. The intraday returns on Monday are not the culprits in creating the

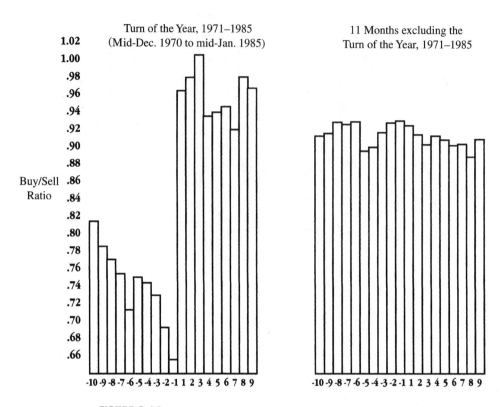

FIGURE 6.14   Institutional Buying/Selling around Year-End

negative returns. Second, the Monday effect is worse for small stocks than for larger stocks. Third, the Monday effect is no worse following three-day weekends than following two-day weekends.

There are some who have argued that the weekend effect is the result of bad news being revealed after the close of trading on Friday and during the weekend. They point to Figure 6.7, which reveals that more negative earnings reports are revealed after close of trading on Friday. Even if this were a widespread phenomenon, the return behavior would be inconsistent with a rational market, since rational investors would build the expectation of the bad news over the weekend into the price before the weekend, leading to an elimination of the weekend effect.

The weekend effect is fairly strong in most major international markets, as shown in Figure 6.17. The presence of a strong weekend effect in Japan, which allowed Saturday trading for a portion of the period studied here, indicates that there might be a more direct reason for negative returns on Mondays than bad information over the weekend.

As a final note, the negative returns on Mondays cannot be attributed to just the absence of trading over the weekend. The returns on days following trading holidays in general are characterized by positive, not negative, returns. Figure 6.18 summarizes returns on trading days following major holidays and confirms this pattern.

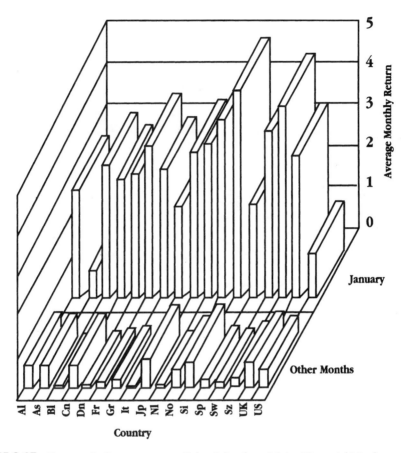

FIGURE 6.15 Returns in January versus Other Months—Major Financial Markets
Source: Gultekin and Gultekin (1983).

EVIDENCE ON INSIDERS AND INVESTMENT PROFESSIONALS

There is a sense that insiders, analysts, and portfolio managers must possess an advantage over the average investors in the market and be able to convert this advantage into excess returns. The evidence on the performance of these investors is actually surprisingly mixed.

Insider Trading

The Securities and Exchange Commission (SEC) defines an insider to be an officer or director of the firm or a major stockholder (holding more than 5 percent of the outstanding stock in the firm). Insiders are barred from trading in advance of specific information on the company and are required to file with the SEC when they buy or sell stock in the company. If it is assumed, as seems reasonable, that insiders have better information about the company and consequently better estimates of value than other investors, the decisions by insiders to buy and sell stock should affect stock

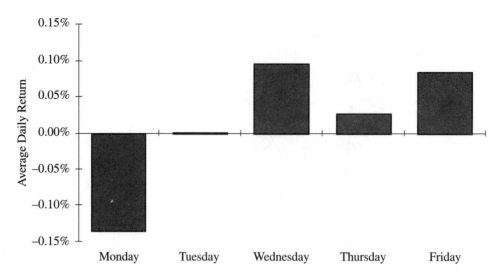

FIGURE 6.16   Average Daily Returns by Day of the Week, 1962–1978
Source: Gibbons and Hess (1981).

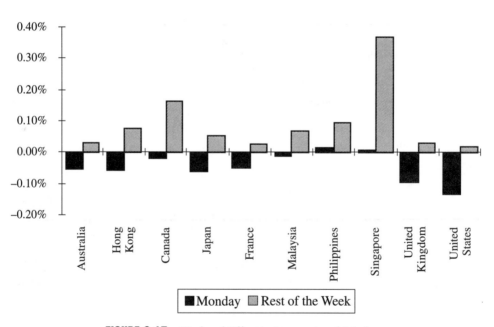

FIGURE 6.17   Weekend Effect in International Markets

prices. Figure 6.19, derived from an early study of insider trading by Jaffe (1974), examines excess returns on two groups of stock, classified on the basis of insider trades. The "buy group" includes stocks where buys exceeded sells by the biggest margin, and the "sell group" includes stocks where sells exceed buys by the biggest margin.

While it seems like the buy group does significantly better than the sell group in this study, advances in information technology have made this information on insider trading available to more and more investors. A more recent study [Seyhun (1998)] of insider trading examined excess returns around both the date the insiders report to the SEC and the date that information becomes available to investors in the official summary. Figure 6.20 presents the contrast between the two event dates.

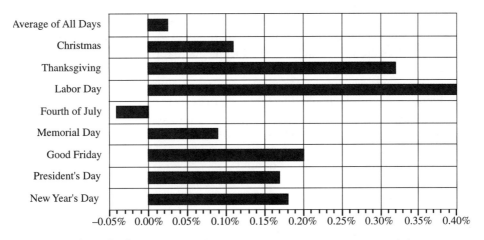

FIGURE 6.18 A Holiday Effect? Average Market Returns on Holidays

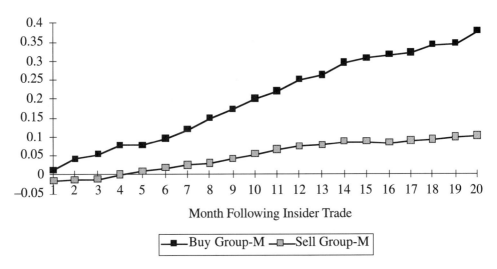

FIGURE 6.19 Cumulative Returns Following Insider Trading: Buy versus Sell Group
Source: Jaffe (1974).

Given the opportunity to buy on the date the insider reports to the SEC, investors could have marginal excess returns, but these returns diminish and become statistically insignificant if investors are forced to wait until the official summary date.

None of these studies examine the question of whether insiders themselves make excess returns. The reporting process, as set up now by the SEC, is biased toward legal and less profitable trades and away from illegal and more profitable trades. Though direct evidence cannot be offered for this proposition, insiders trading illegally on private information must make excess returns.

Analyst Recommendations

Analysts clearly hold a privileged position in the market for information, operating at the nexus of private and public information. Using both types of information, analysts issue buy and sell recommendations to their clients, who trade on this basis.

While both buy and sell recommendations affect stock prices, sell recommendations affect prices much more adversely than buy recommendations affect them positively. Interestingly, Womack (1996) documents that the price effect of buy recommendations tends to be immediate and there is no evidence of price drifts after the announcement, whereas prices continue to trend down after sell recommendations. Figure 6.21 graphs his findings. Stock prices increase by about 3 percent on buy recommendations, whereas they drop by about 4 percent on sell recommendations at the time of the recommendations (three days around reports). In the six months following, prices decline an additional 5 percent for sell recommendations, while leveling off for buy recommendations.

Though analysts provide a valuable service in collecting private information, or maybe *because* they do, there is a negative relationship in the cross section between returns earned by stocks and the number of analysts following the stock. The same kind of relationship exists between another proxy for interest—institutional ownership—and returns. This evidence [Arbel and Strebel (1983)] suggests that neglected stocks—those followed by few analysts and not held widely by institutions—earn higher returns than widely followed and held stocks.

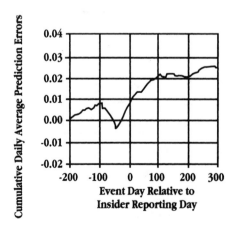
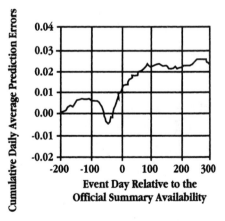

FIGURE 6.20   Abnormal Returns around Reporting Day versus Official Summary Availability Day

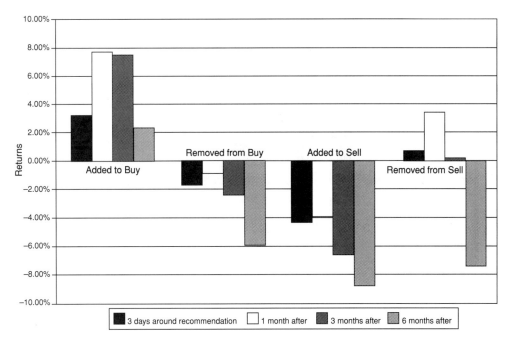

FIGURE 6.21 Market Reaction to Recommendations, 1989–1990
Source: Womack (1996).

Money Managers

Professional money managers operate as the experts in the field of investments. They are supposed to be better informed, have lower transaction costs, and be better investors overall than smaller investors. The earliest study of mutual funds by Jensen (1968) suggested that this supposition might not hold in practice. His findings, summarized in Figure 6.22 as excess returns on mutual funds, were that the average portfolio manager actually underperformed the market between 1955 and 1964.

These results have been replicated with mild variations in their conclusions. In the studies that are most favorable for professional money managers, they break even against the market after adjusting for transaction costs, and in those that are least favorable they underpeform the market even before adjusting for transaction costs.

The results, when categorized on a number of different bases, do not offer much solace. For instance, Figure 6.23 shows excess returns from 1983 to 1990 and the percentage of money managers beating the market, categorized by investment style. Money managers in every investment style underperform the market index.

Figure 6.24 looks at the payoff to active portfolio management by measuring the added value from trading actively during the course of the year, and finds that returns drop between 0.5 percent and 1.5 percent a year as a consequence.

Finally, we find no evidence of continuity in performance. It classified money managers into quartiles and examined the probabilities of movement from one quartile to another each year from 1983 to 1990. The results are summarized in Table 6.4.

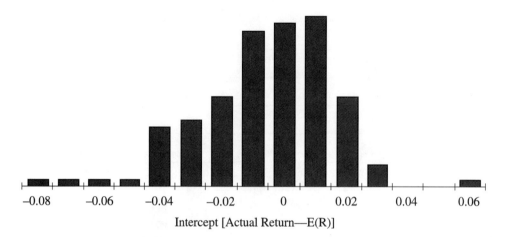

Intercept [Actual Return—E(R)]

FIGURE 6.22   Mutual Fund Performance, 1955–1964—the Jensen Study
Source: Jensen (1968).

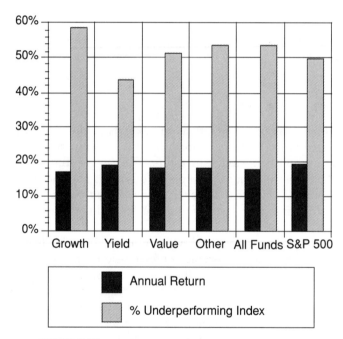

FIGURE 6.23   Performance of Equity Funds, 1983–1990

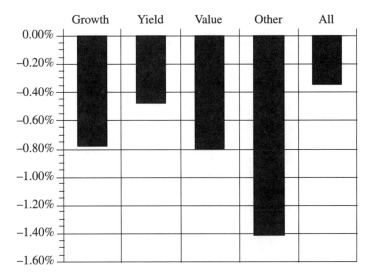

FIGURE 6.24 The Payoff to Active Money Management: Equity Funds
Note: This chart measures the difference between actual return on equity funds and return on hypothetical portfolio frozen at beginning of period.

TABLE 6.4 Probabilities of Transition from One Quartile to Another

	Ranking Next Period			
Ranking This Period	1	2	3	4
1	26%	24%	23%	27%
2	20%	26%	29%	25%
3	22%	28%	26%	24%
4	32%	22%	22%	24%

Table 6.4 indicates that a money manager who was ranked in the first quartile in a period had a 26 percent chance of being ranked in the first quartile in the next period and a 27 percent chance of being ranked in the bottom quartile. There is some evidence of reversal in the portfolio managers in the lowest quartile, though some of that may be a reflection of the higher-risk portfolios that they put together.

CONCLUSION

The question of whether markets are efficient will always be a provocative one, given the implications that efficient markets have for investment management and research. If an efficient market is defined as one where the market price is an unbiased estimate of the true value, it is quite clear that some markets will always be more efficient than others and that markets will always be more efficient to some investors than to others. The capacity of a market to correct inefficiencies quickly

MARKET INEFFICIENCIES AND MONEY MANAGER PERFORMANCE

The evidence on markets is contradictory. On the one hand, there seem to be numerous patterns in stock prices—stock prices reverse course in the long term and returns are higher in January—and evidence of market anomalies—small-market-cap firms with low price-to-book and price-to-earnings ratios seem to handily beat the market. On the other hand, there seems to be little evidence of money managers being able to exploit these findings to beat the market.

There are a number of possible explanations. The most benign one is that the inefficiences show up mostly in hypothetical studies and that the transaction cost and execution problems associated with converting these inefficiencies into portfolios overwhelm the excess returns. A second possible explanation is that the studies generally look at the long term; many are over 20 to 50 years. Over shorter periods, there is substantially more uncertainty about whether small stocks will outperform large stocks and whether buying losers will generate excess returns. There are no investment strategies that are sure bets for short periods. Pradhuman (2000) illustrates this phenomenon by noting that small-cap stocks have underperformed large-cap stocks in roughly one out of every four years in the past 50 years. Bernstein (1998) notes that while value investing (buying low PE and low price-to-book value stocks) may earn excess returns over long periods, growth investing has outperformed value investing over many five-year periods during the past three decades. A third explanation is that portfolio managers do not consistently follow any one strategy but jump from one strategy to another, both increasing their expenses and reducing the likelihood that the strategy can generate excess returns in the long term.

will depend, in part, on the ease of trading, the transaction costs, and the vigilance of profit-seeking investors in that market.

While market efficiency can be tested in a number of different ways, the two most widely used tests to test efficiency are event studies, which examine market reactions to information events, and portfolio studies, which evaluate the returns of portfolios created on the basis of observable characteristics. It does make sense to be vigilant, because bias can enter these studies, intentionally or otherwise, in a number of different ways and can lead to unwarranted conclusions and, worse still, wasteful investment strategies.

There is substantial evidence of irregularities in market behavior related to systematic factors such as size, price-earnings ratios, and price–book value ratios, as well as to time—the January and the weekend effects. While these irregularities may be inefficiencies, there is also the sobering evidence that professional money managers, who are in a position to exploit these inefficiencies, have a very difficult time consistently beating financial markets. Read together, the persistence of the irregularities and the inability of money managers to beat the market are testimony to the gap between empirical tests on paper and real-world money management in some cases, and the failure of the models of risk and return in others.

QUESTIONS AND SHORT PROBLEMS

1. Which of the following is an implication of market efficiency? (There may be more than one right answer.)
   a. Resources are allocated among firms efficiently (i.e., put to best use).
   b. No investor will do better than the market in any time period.
   c. No investor will do better than the market consistently.
   d. No investor will do better than the market consistently after adjusting for risk.
   e. No investor will do better than the market consistently after adjusting for risk and transaction costs.
   f. No group of investors will do better than the market consistently after adjusting for risk and transaction costs.

2. Suppose you are following a retailing stock that has a strong seasonal pattern to sales. Would you expect to see a seasonal pattern in the stock price as well?

3. Tests of market efficiency are often referred to as joint tests of two hypotheses—the hypothesis that the market is efficient and an expected returns model. Explain. Is it ever possible to test market efficiency alone (i.e., without jointly testing an asset pricing model)?

4. You are in a violent argument with a chartist. He claims that you are violating the fundamental laws of economics by trying to find intrinsic value. "Price is determined by demand and supply, not by some intrinsic value." Is finding an intrinsic value inconsistent with demand and supply?

5. You are testing the effect of merger announcements on stock prices. (This is an event study.) Your procedure goes through the following steps:
   Step 1: You choose the 20 biggest mergers of the year.
   Step 2: You isolate the date the merger became effective as the key day around which you will examine the data.
   Step 3: You look at the returns for the five days after the effective merger date.
   By looking at these returns (0.13%) you conclude that you could not have made money on merger announcements. Are there any flaws that you can detect in this test? How would you correct for them? Can you devise a stronger test?

6. In an efficient market, the market price is defined to be an "unbiased estimate" of the true value. This implies that (choose one):
   a. The market price is always equal to true value.
   b. The market price has nothing to do with true value.
   c. Markets make mistakes about true value, and investors can exploit these mistakes to make money.
   d. Market prices contain errors, but the errors are random and therefore cannot be exploited by investors.
   e. No one can beat the market.

7. Evaluate whether the following actions are likely to increase stock market efficiency, decrease it, or leave it unchanged, and explain why.
   a. The government imposes a transaction tax of 1% on all stock transactions.
   Increase efficiency ____   Decrease efficiency ____   Leave unchanged ____
   b. The securities exchange regulators impose a restriction on all short sales to prevent rampant speculation.
   Increase efficiency ____   Decrease efficiency ____   Leave unchanged ____

   c. An options market, trading call and put options, is opened up, with options traded on many of the stocks listed on the exchange.
   Increase efficiency _____   Decrease efficiency _____   Leave unchanged _____
   d. The stock market removes all restrictions on foreign investors acquiring and holding stock in companies.
   Increase efficiency _____   Decrease efficiency _____   Leave unchanged _____

8. The following is a graph of cumulative abnormal returns around the announcement of asset divestitures by major corporations.

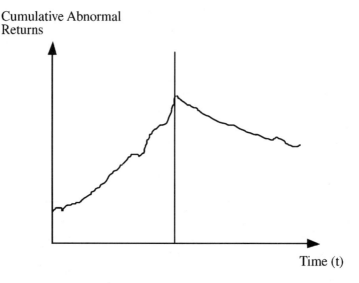

How best would you explain the:
a. Market behavior before the announcement?
b. Market reaction to the announcement?
c. Market reaction after the announcement?

9. What is the phenomenon of the size effect in stock performance? How does it relate to the turn-of-the-year effect? Can you suggest any good reasons why small stocks, after adjusting for beta, still do better than large stocks? What strategy would you follow to exploit this anomaly? What factors do you have to keep in mind?

10. A study examining market reactions to earnings surprises found that prices tend to drift after earnings surprises. What does this tell you about the market's capacity to learn from events and new information? What cross-sectional differences would you expect to find in this learning behavior? (Would you expect to see a greater price drift in some types of firms than in others? Why?) How would you try to exploit this anomaly? What possible costs would you have to keep in mind?

11. One explanation of the turn-of-the-year or January effect has to do with sales and purchases related to the tax year.
a. Present the tax effect hypothesis.
b. Studies have shown that the January effect occurs internationally, even in countries where the tax year does not start in January. Speculate on a good reason for this.

12. The following are the expected price appreciation and dividend yield components of returns on two portfolios—a high dividend yield portfolio and a low dividend yield portfolio.

Portfolio	Expected Price Appreciation	Expected Dividend Yield
High yield	9%	5%
Low yield	12%	1%

You are a taxable investor who faces a tax rate of 40% on dividends. What would your tax rate on capital gains need to be for you to be indifferent between these two portfolios?

13. Answer true or false to the following questions:
    a. Low price-earnings stocks, on average, earn returns in excess of expectations, while high price-earnings stocks earn less than expected. This is primarily because lower PE ratio stocks have lower risk.
       True _____ False _____
    b. The small firm effect, which refers the positive excess returns earned, on average, by small firms, is primarily caused by a few small firms that make very high positive returns.
       True _____ False _____
    c. Investors generally cannot make money on analyst recommendations, because stock prices are not affected by these recommendations.
       True _____ False _____

14. You are examining the performance of two mutual funds. AD Value Fund has been in existence since January 1, 1988, and invests primarily in stocks with low price-earnings ratios and high dividend yields. AD Growth Fund has also been in existence since January 1, 1988, but it invests primarily in high-growth stocks, with high PE ratios and low or no dividends. The performance of these funds over the past five years is summarized as follows:

	Average from 1988 to 1992		
	Price Appreciation	Dividend Yield	Beta
NYSE Composite	13%	3%	1.0
AD Value	11%	5%	0.8
AD Growth	15%	1%	1.2

The average risk-free rate during the period was 6%. The current risk-free rate is 3%.
    a. How well or badly did these funds perform after adjusting for risk?
    b. Assume that the front-end load on each of these funds is 5% (i.e., if you put $1,000 in each of these funds today, you would only be investing $950 after the initial commission). Assume also that the excess returns you have calculated in part (a) will continue into the future and that you choose to invest in the fund that outperformed the market. How many years would you have to hold this fund to break even?

CHAPTER 7

Riskless Rates and Risk Premiums

All models of risk and return in finance are built around a rate that investors can make on riskless investments and the risk premium or premiums that investors should charge for investing in the average-risk investment. In the capital asset pricing model (CAPM), where there is only one source of market risk captured in the market portfolio, this risk premium becomes the premium that investors would demand when investing in that portfolio. In multifactor models, there are multiple risk premiums, each one measuring the premium demanded by investors for exposure to a specific market risk factor. This chapter examines how best to measure a riskless rate and to estimate a risk premium or premiums for use in these models.

As noted in Chapter 4, risk is measured in terms of default risk for bonds, and this default risk is captured in a default spread that firms have to pay over and above the riskless rate. This chapter closes by considering how best to estimate these default spreads and factors that may cause these spreads to change over time.

THE RISK-FREE RATE

Most risk and return models in finance start off with an asset that is defined as risk free, and use the expected return on that asset as the risk-free rate. The expected returns on risky investments are then measured relative to the risk-free rate, with the risk creating an expected risk premium that is added to the risk-free rate. But what makes an asset risk free? And what do we do when we cannot find such an asset? These are the questions that will be dealt with in this section.

Requirements for an Asset to Be Risk Free

Chapter 4 considered some of the requirements for an asset to be risk free. In particular, an asset is risk free if we know the expected returns on it with certainty (i.e., the actual return is always equal to the expected return). Under what conditions will the actual returns on an investment be equal to the expected returns? There are two basic conditions that have to be met. The first is that *there can be no default risk*. Essentially, this rules out any security issued by a private firm, since even the largest and safest firms have some measure of default risk. The only securities that have a chance of being risk free are government securities, not because governments are better run than corporations, but because they control the printing of currency. At least in nominal terms, they should be able to fulfill their promises.

Even this assumption, straightforward though it might seem, does not always hold up, especially when governments refuse to honor claims made by previous regimes and when they borrow in currencies other than their own.

There is a second condition that riskless securities need to fulfill that is often forgotten. For an investment to have an actual return equal to its expected return, *there can be no reinvestment risk*. To illustrate this point, assume that you are trying to estimate the expected return over a five-year period and that you want a risk-free rate. A six-month Treasury bill rate, while default free, will not be risk free, because there is the reinvestment risk of not knowing what the Treasury bill rate will be in six months. Even a five-year Treasury bond is not risk free, since the coupons on the bond will be reinvested at rates that cannot be predicted today. The risk-free rate for a five-year time horizon has to be the expected return on a default-free (government) five-year zero coupon bond. This clearly has painful implications for anyone doing corporate finance or valuation, where expected returns often have to be estimated for periods ranging from 1 to 10 years. A purist's view of risk-free rates would then require different risk-free rates for each period, and different expected returns.

As a practical compromise, however, it is worth noting that the present value effect of using year-specific risk-free rates tends to be small for most well-behaved term structures.[1] In these cases, we could use a duration matching strategy, where the duration of the default-free security used as the risk-free asset is matched up to the duration[2] of the cash flows in the analysis. If, however, there are very large differences, in either direction, between short-term and long-term rates, it does pay to stick with year-specific risk-free rates in computing expected returns.

Practical Implications When a Default-Free Entity Exists

In most developed markets, where the government can be viewed as a default-free entity, at least when it comes to borrowing in the local currency, the implications are simple. When doing investment analysis on longer-term projects or valuations, the risk-free rate should be the long-term government bond rate. If the analysis is shorter-term, the short-term government security rate can be used as the risk-free rate. The choice of a risk-free rate also has implications for how risk premiums are estimated. If, as is often the case, historical risk premiums are used, where the excess return earned by stocks over and above a government security rate over a past period is used as the risk premium, the government security chosen has to be same one as that used for the risk-free rate. Thus, the historical risk premium used in the United States should be the excess return earned by stocks over Treasury bonds, and not Treasury bills, for purposes of long-term analysis.

---

[1]Well-behaved term structures would include a normal upward-sloping yield curve, where long-term rates are at most 2 to 3 percent higher than short-term rates.

[2]In investment analysis, where we look at projects, these durations are usually between 3 and 10 years. In valuation, the durations tend to be much longer, since firms are assumed to have infinite lives. The durations in these cases are often well in excess of 10 years and increase with the expected growth potential of the firm.

Cash Flows and Risk-Free Rates: The Consistency Principle

The risk-free rate used to come up with expected returns should be measured consistently with how the cash flows are measured. Thus, if cash flows are estimated in nominal U.S. dollar terms, the risk-free rate will be the U.S. Treasury bond rate. This also implies that it is not where a firm is domiciled that determines the choice of a risk-free rate, but the currency in which the cash flows on the firm are estimated. Thus, Nestlé can be valued using cash flows estimated in Swiss francs, discounted back at an expected return estimated using a Swiss long-term government bond rate, or it can be valued in British pounds, with both the cash flows and the risk-free rate being in British pounds. Given that the same firm can be valued in different currencies, will the final results always be consistent? If we assume purchasing power parity, then differences in interest rates reflect differences in expected inflation. Both the cash flows and the discount rate are affected by expected inflation; thus, a low discount rate arising from a low risk-free rate will be exactly offset by a decline in expected nominal growth rates for cash flows, and the value will remain unchanged.

If the difference in interest rates across two currencies does not adequately reflect the difference in expected inflation in these currencies, the values obtained using the different currencies can be different. In particular, firms will be valued more highly when the currency used is the one with low interest rates relative to inflation. The risk, however, is that the interest rates will have to rise at some point to correct for this divergence, at which point the values will also converge.

Real versus Nominal Risk-Free Rates

Under conditions of high and unstable inflation, valuation is often done in real terms. Effectively, this means that cash flows are estimated using real growth rates and without allowing for the growth that comes from price inflation. To be consistent, the discount rates used in these cases have to be real discount rates. To get a real expected rate of return, we need to start with a real risk-free rate. While government bills and bonds offer returns that are risk free in nominal terms, they are not risk free in real terms, since expected inflation can be volatile. The standard approach of subtracting an expected inflation rate from the nominal interest rate to arrive at a real risk-free rate provides at best an estimate of the real risk-free rate.

Until recently, there were few traded default-free securities that could be used to estimate real risk-free rates, but the introduction of inflation-indexed Treasuries has filled this void. An inflation-indexed Treasury security does not offer a guaranteed nominal return to buyers, but instead provides a guaranteed real return. Thus, an inflation-indexed Treasury that offers a 3 percent real return will yield approximately 7 percent in nominal terms if inflation is 4 percent and only 5 percent in nominal terms if inflation is only 2 percent.

The only problem is that real valuations are seldom called for or done in the United States, which has stable and low expected inflation. The markets where we would most need to do real valuations, unfortunately, are markets without inflation-indexed default-free securities. The real risk-free rates in these markets can be estimated by using one of two arguments:

1. The first argument is that as long as capital can flow freely to those economies with the highest real returns, there can be no differences in real risk-free rates across markets. Using this argument, the real risk-free rate for the United States, estimated from the inflation-indexed Treasury, can be used as the real risk-free rate in any market.
2. The second argument applies if there are frictions and constraints in capital flowing across markets. In that case, the expected real return on a economy, in the long term, should be equal to the expected real growth rate, again in the long term, of that economy, for equilibrium. Thus, the real risk-free rate for a mature economy like Germany should be much lower than the real risk-free rate for a economy with greater growth potential, such as Hungary.

Risk-Free Rates When There Is No Default-Free Entity

Our discussion, hitherto, has been predicated on the assumption that governments do not default, at least on local borrowing. There are many emerging market economies where this assumption might not be viewed as reasonable. Governments in these markets are perceived as capable of defaulting even on local borrowing. When this is coupled with the fact that many governments do not borrow long-term locally, there are scenarios where obtaining a local risk-free rate, especially for the long term, becomes difficult. Under these cases, there are compromises that give us reasonable estimates of the risk-free rate:

■ Look at the largest and safest firms in that market, and use the rate that they pay on their long-term borrowings in the local currency as a base. Given that these firms, in spite of their size and stability, still have default risk, you would use a rate that is marginally lower than the corporate borrowing rate.[3]

■ If there are long-term dollar-denominated forward contracts on the currency, you can use interest rate parity and the Treasury bond rate (or riskless rate in any other base currency) to arrive at an estimate of the local borrowing rate.

$$\text{Forward rate}_{FC,\$}^{t} = \text{Spot rate}_{FC,\$} \frac{(1 + \text{Interest rate}_{FC})^{t}}{(1 + \text{Interest rate}_{\$})^{t}}$$

where Forward rate$_{FC,\$}^{t}$ = Forward rate for foreign currency units/\$ in period t
Spot rate$_{FC,\$}$ = Spot rate for foreign currency units/\$
Interest rate$_{FC}$ = Interest rate in foreign currency
Interest rate$_{\$}$ = Interest rate in U.S. dollars

For instance, if the current spot rate is 38.10 Thai baht per U.S. dollar, the 10-year forward rate is 61.36 baht per dollar, and the current 10-year U.S. Treasury bond rate is 5 percent, the 10-year Thai risk-free rate (in nominal baht) can be estimated as follows:

$$61.36 = 38.10(1 + \text{Interest rate}_{\text{Thai baht}})^{10}/1.05^{10}$$

---

[3]I would use 1 percent less than the corporate borrowing rate as my risk-free rate. This is roughly an AA default spread in the United States.

Solving for the Thai interest rate yields a 10-year risk-free rate of 10.12 percent. The biggest limitation of this approach, however, is that long-term forward rates are difficult to come by for periods beyond a year for many of the emerging markets, where we would be most interested in using them.[4]

■ You could adjust the local currency government borrowing rate by the estimated default spread on the bond to arrive at a riskless local rate. The default spread on the government bond can be estimated using the local currency ratings[5] that are available for many countries. For instance, assume that the Indian government bond rate is 12 percent and that the rating assigned to the Indian government is A. If the default spread for A-rated bonds is 2 percent, the riskless Indian rupee rate would be 10 percent.

$$\text{Riskless rupee rate} = \text{Indian government bond rate} - \text{Default spread}$$
$$= 12\% - 2\% = 10\%$$

EQUITY RISK PREMIUM

The notion that risk matters, and that riskier investments should have a higher expected return than safer investments, to be considered good investments, is intuitive. Thus, the expected return on any investment can be written as the sum of the risk-free rate and an extra return to compensate for the risk. The disagreement, in both theoretical and practical terms, remains on how to measure this risk, and how to convert the risk measure into an expected return that compensates for risk. This section looks at the estimation of an appropriate risk premium to use in risk and return models, in general, and in the capital asset pricing model, in particular.

Competing Views on Risk Premiums

In Chapter 4, we considered several competing models of risk ranging from the capital asset pricing model to multifactor models. Notwithstanding their different conclusions, they all share some common views about risk. First, they all define risk in terms of variance in actual returns around an expected return; thus, an investment is riskless when actual returns are always equal to the expected return. Second, they all argue that risk has to be measured from the perspective of the marginal investor in an asset, and that this marginal investor is well diversified. Therefore, the argument goes, it is only the risk that an investment adds on to a diversified portfolio that should be measured and compensated. In fact, it is this view

---

[4]In cases where only a one-year forward rate exists, an approximation for the long-term rate can be obtained by first backing out the one-year local currency borrowing rate, taking the spread over the one-year Treasury bill rate, and then adding this spread to the long-term Treasury bond rate. For instance, with a one-year forward rate of 39.95 on the Thai bond, we obtain a one-year Thai baht riskless rate of 9.04 percent (given a one-year T-bill rate of 4 percent). Adding the spread of 5.04 percent to the 10-year Treasury bond rate of 5 percent provides a 10-year Thai baht rate of 10.04 percent.

[5]Ratings agencies generally assign different ratings for local currency borrowings and dollar borrowing, with higher ratings for the former and lower ratings for the latter.

of risk that leads models of risk to break the risk in any investment into two components. There is a firm-specific component that measures risk that relates only to that investment or to a few investments like it, and a market component that contains risk that affects a large subset or all investments. It is the latter risk that is not diversifiable and should be rewarded.

While all risk and return models agree on this fairly crucial distinction, they part ways when it comes to how measure this market risk. Table 7.1 summarizes four models and the way each model attempts to measure risk.

In the first three models, the expected return on any investment can be written as:

$$\text{Expected return} = \text{Risk-free rate} + \sum_{j=1}^{j=k} \beta_j (\text{Risk premium}_j)$$

where β_j = Beta of investment relative to factor j
Risk premium$_j$ = Risk premium for factor j

Note that in the special case of a single-factor model, like the CAPM, each investment's expected return will be determined by its beta relative to the single factor.

Assuming that the risk-free rate is known, these models all require two inputs. The first is the beta or betas of the investment being analyzed, and the second is the appropriate risk premium(s) for the factor or factors in the model. While the issue of beta estimation will be examined in the next chapter, this section will concentrate on the measurement of the risk premium.

TABLE 7.1 Comparing Risk and Return Models

Model	Assumptions	Measure of Market Risk
Capital asset pricing model (CAPM)	There are no transaction costs or private information. Therefore, the diversified portfolio includes all traded investments, held in proportion to their market value.	Beta measured against this market portfolio
Arbitrage pricing model (APM)	Investments with the same exposure to market risk have to trade at the same price (no arbitrage).	Betas measured against multiple (unspecified) market risk factors
Multifactor model	There is the same no-arbitrage assumption as with the APM.	Betas measured against multiple specified macroeconomic factors
Proxy model	Over very long periods, higher returns on investments must be compensation for higher market risk.	Proxies for market risk, for example, include market capitalization and price–book value ratios.

What We Would Like to Measure   As far as the risk premium is concerned, we would like to know for each factor, what investors, on average, require as a premium over the risk-free rate for an investment with average risk.

Without any loss of generality, let us consider the estimation of the beta and the risk premium in the capital asset pricing model. Here, the risk premium should measure what investors, on average, demand as extra return for investing in the market portfolio relative to the risk-free asset.

Historical Risk Premiums

In practice, we usually estimate the risk premium by looking at the historical premium earned by stocks over default-free securities over long time periods. The historical premium approach is simple. The actual returns earned on stocks over a long time period are estimated, and compared to the actual returns earned on a default-free (usually government) security. The difference, on an annual basis, between the two returns is computed and represents the historical risk premium. This approach might yield reasonable estimates in markets like the United States, with a large and diversified stock market and a long history of returns on both stocks and government securities. However, they yield meaningless estimates for the risk premium in other countries, where the equity markets represent a small proportion of the overall economy, and the historical returns are available only for short periods.

While users of risk and return models may have developed a consensus that historical premium is, in fact, the best estimate of the risk premium looking forward, there are surprisingly large differences in the actual premiums we observe being used in practice. For instance, the risk premium estimated in the U.S. markets by different investment banks, consultants, and corporations range from 4 percent at the lower end to 12 percent at the upper end. Given that we almost all use the same database of historical returns, provided by Ibbotson Associates,[6] summarizing data from 1926, these differences may seem surprising. There are, however, three reasons for the divergence in risk premiums:

1. *Time period used.* While there are many who use all the data going back to 1926, there are almost as many using data over shorter time periods, such as 50, 20 or even 10 years to come up with historical risk premiums. The rationale presented by those who use shorter periods is that the risk aversion of the average investor is likely to change over time, and that using a shorter time period provides a more updated estimate. This has to be offset against a cost associated with using shorter time periods, which is the greater noise in the risk premium estimate. In fact, given the annual standard deviation in stock prices[7] between 1926 and 2000 of 20 per-

---

[6]See "Stocks, Bonds, Bills and Inflation," an annual edition that reports on annual returns on stocks, Treasury bonds, and Treasury bills, as well as inflation rates from 1926 to the present (www.ibbotson.com).

[7]For the historical data on stock returns, bond returns, and bill returns check under "Updated Data" in www.stern.nyu.edu/~adamodar.

cent, the standard error[8] associated with the risk premium estimate can be estimated as follows for different estimation periods in Table 7.2.

Note that to get reasonable standard errors, we need very long time periods of historical returns. Conversely, the standard errors from 10-year and 20-year estimates are likely to almost as large or larger than the actual risk premium estimated. This cost of using shorter time periods seems, in our view, to overwhelm any advantages associated with getting a more updated premium.

2. *Choice of risk-free security.* The Ibbotson database reports returns on both Treasury bills (T-bills) and Treasury bonds (T-bonds), and the risk premium for stocks can be estimated relative to each. Given that the yield curve in the United States has been upward-sloping for most of the past seven decades, the risk premium is larger when estimated relative to shorter-term government securities (such as Treasury bills). *The risk-free rate chosen in computing the premium has to be consistent with the risk-free rate used to compute expected returns.* Thus, if the Treasury bill rate is used as the risk-free rate, the premium has to be the premium earned by stocks over that rate. If the Treasury bond rate is used as the risk-free rate, the premium has to be estimated relative to that rate. For the most part, in corporate finance and valuation, the risk-free rate will be a long-term default-free (government) bond rate and not a Treasury bill rate. Thus, the risk premium used should be the premium earned by stocks over Treasury bonds.

3. *Arithmetic and geometric averages.* The final sticking point when it comes to estimating historical premiums relates to how the average returns on stocks, Treasury bonds, and Treasury bills are computed. The arithmetic average return measures the simple mean of the series of annual returns, whereas the geometric average looks at the compounded return.[9] Conventional wisdom argues for the use of the arithmetic average. In fact, if annual returns are uncorrelated over time, and our objective were to estimate the risk premium for the next year, the arithmetic average is the best unbiased estimate of the premium. In reality, however, there are strong arguments that can be made for the use of geometric averages. First, empiri-

TABLE 7.2 Standard Errors in Risk Premium Estimates

Estimation Period	Standard Error of Risk Premium Estimate
5 years	$20\% \sqrt{5} = 8.94\%$
10 years	$20\% \sqrt{10} = 6.32\%$
25 years	$20\% \sqrt{25} = 4.00\%$
50 years	$20\% \sqrt{50} = 2.83\%$

---

[8]These estimates of the standard error are probably understated, because they are based on the assumption that annual returns are uncorrelated over time. There is substantial empirical evidence that returns are correlated over time, which would make this standard error estimate much larger.

[9]The compounded return is computed by taking the value of the investment at the start of the period (Value$_0$) and the value at the end (Value$_N$), and then computing the following:

$$\text{Geometric average} = \left(\frac{\text{Value}_N}{\text{Value}_0} \right)^{1/N} - 1$$

cal studies seem to indicate that returns on stocks are negatively correlated over time.[10] Consequently, the arithmetic average return is likely to overstate the premium. Second, while asset pricing models may be single-period models, the use of these models to get expected returns over long periods (such as 5 or 10 years) suggests that the single period may be much longer than a year. In this context, the argument for geometric average premiums becomes even stronger.

In summary, the risk premium estimates vary across users because of differences in time periods used, the choice of Treasury bills or bonds as the risk-free rate and the use of arithmetic as opposed to geometric averages. The effect of these choices is summarized in Table 7.3, which uses returns from 1928 to 2000. Note that the premiums can range from 4.5 percent to 12.67 percent, depending on the choices made. In fact, these differences are exacerbated by the fact that many risk premiums that are in use today were estimated using historical data three, four, or even ten years ago.

---

 histretSP.xls: There is a dataset on the Web that summarizes historical returns on stocks, T-bonds and T-bills in the United States going back to 1928.

Historical Risk Premiums: Other Markets   If it is difficult to estimate a reliable historical premium for the U.S. market, it becomes doubly so when looking at markets with short and volatile histories. This is clearly true for emerging markets, but it is also true for the European equity markets. While the economies of Germany, Italy, and France may be mature, their equity markets do not share the same characteristic. They tend to be dominated by a few large companies; many businesses remain private; and trading, until recently, tended to be thin except on a few stocks.

There are some practitioners who still use historical premiums for these markets. To capture some of the danger in this practice, Table 7.4 summarizes historical risk premiums[11] for major non-U.S. markets for 1970 to 1996.

TABLE 7.3   Historical Risk Premiums for the United States

	Stocks versus Treasury Bills		Stocks versus Treasury Bonds	
	Arithmetic	Geometric	Arithmetic	Geometric
1928–2000	8.41%	7.17%	6.53%	5.51%
1962–2000	6.41%	5.25%	5.30%	4.52%
1990–2000	11.42%	7.64%	12.67%	7.09%

Source: Federal Reserve Bank.

---

[10]In other words, good years are more likely to be followed by poor years, and vice versa. The evidence on negative serial correlation in stock returns over time is extensive, and can be found in Fama and French (1988). While they find that the one-year correlations are low, the five-year serial correlations are strongly negative for all size classes.

[11]This data is also from Ibbotson Associates, and can be obtained from their web site: www.ibbotson.com.

HISTORICAL RISK PREMIUM APPROACH: SOME CAVEATS

Given how widely the historical risk premium approach is used, it is surprising how flawed it is and how little attention these flaws have attracted. Consider first the underlying assumption that investors' risk premiums have not changed over time and that the average risk investment (in the market portfolio) has remained stable over the period examined. We would be hard-pressed to find anyone who would be willing to sustain this argument with fervor.

The obvious fix for this problem, which is to use a more recent time period, runs directly into a second problem, which is the large standard error associated with risk premium estimates. While these standard errors may be tolerable for very long time periods, they clearly are unacceptably high when shorter periods are used.

Finally, even if there is a sufficiently long time period of history available and investors' risk aversion has not changed in a systematic way over that period, there is a final problem. Markets that exhibit this characteristic, and let us assume that the U.S. market is one such example, represent so-called survivor markets. In other words, assume that one had invested in the 10 largest equity markets in the world in 1928, of which the United States was one. In the period extending from 1928 to 2000, investments in none of the other equity markets would have earned as large a premium as the U.S. equity market, and some of them (like Austria) would have resulted in investors earning little or even negative returns over the period. Thus, the survivor bias will result in historical premiums that are larger than expected premiums for markets like the United States, even assuming that investors are rational and factor risk into prices.

TABLE 7.4 Historical Risk Premiums in Non-U.S. Markets

Country	Equity			Bonds	
	Beginning	Ending	Annual Return	Annual Return	Risk Premium
Australia	100	898.36	8.47%	6.99%	1.48%
Canada	100	1,020.70	8.98%	8.30%	0.68%
France	100	1,894.26	11.51%	9.17%	2.34%
Germany	100	1,800.74	11.30%	12.10%	−0.80%
Hong Kong	100	14,993.06	20.39%	12.66%	7.73%
Italy	100	423.64	5.49%	7.84%	−2.35%
Japan	100	5,169.43	15.73%	12.69%	3.04%
Mexico	100	2,073.65	11.88%	10.71%	1.17%
Netherlands	100	4,870.32	15.48%	10.83%	4.65%
Singapore	100	4,875.91	15.48%	6.45%	9.03%
Spain	100	844.80	8.22%	7.91%	0.31%
Switzerland	100	3,046.09	13.49%	10.11%	3.38%
United Kingdom	100	2,361.53	12.42%	7.81%	4.61%

Data source: Ibbotson Associates.

Note that a couple of the countries have negative historical risk premiums, and a few others have risk premiums under 1 percent. Before an attempt is made to come up with rationale for why this might be so, it is worth noting that the standard errors on each and every one of these estimates is larger than 5 percent, largely because the estimation period includes only 26 years.

If the standard errors on these estimates make them close to useless, consider how much more noise there is in estimates of historical risk premiums for emerging market equity markets, which often have a reliable history of 10 years or less, and very large standard deviations in annual stock returns. Historical risk premiums for emerging markets may provide for interesting anecdotes, but they clearly should not be used in risk and return models.

Modified Historical Risk Premium   While historical risk premiums for markets outside the United States cannot be used in risk models, we still need to estimate a risk premium for use in these markets. To approach this estimation question, let us start with the basic proposition that the risk premium in any equity market can be written as:

Equity risk premium = Base premium for mature equity market + Country premium

The country premium could reflect the extra risk in a specific market. This boils down our estimation to answering two questions:

1. What should the base premium for a mature equity market be?
2. Should there be a country premium, and if so, how do we estimate the premium?

To answer the first question, one can argue that the U.S. equity market is a mature market and that there is sufficient historical data in the United States to make a reasonable estimate of the risk premium. In fact, reverting back to our discussion of historical premiums in the U.S. market, we will use the geometric average premium earned by stocks over Treasury bonds of 5.51 percent between 1928 and 2000. We chose the long time period to reduce standard error, the Treasury bond to be consistent with our choice of a risk-free rate, and geometric averages to reflect our desire for a risk premium that we can use for longer-term expected returns.

On the issue of country premiums, there are some who argue that country risk is diversifiable and that there should be no country risk premium. After looking at the basis for their argument, and then considering the alternative view that there should be a country risk premium, we will present approaches for estimating country risk premiums, one based on country bond default spreads and one based on equity market volatility.

Should There Be a Country Risk Premium?   Is there more risk in investing in a Malaysian or Brazilian stock than there is in investing in the United States? The answer, to most, seems to be obviously affirmative. That, however, does not answer the question of whether there should be an additional risk premium charged when investing in those markets.

Note that the only risk that is relevant for purposes of estimating a cost of equity is market risk or risk that cannot be diversified away. The key question then becomes whether the risk in an emerging market is diversifiable or nondiversifiable risk. If, in fact, the additional risk of investing in Malaysia or Brazil can be diversified away, then there should be no additional risk premium charged. If it cannot, then it makes sense to think about estimating a country risk premium.

But diversified away by whom? Equity in a Brazilian or Malaysian firm can be held by hundreds or thousands of investors, some of whom may hold only domestic stocks in their portfolio, whereas others may have more global exposure. For purposes of analyzing country risk, we look at the marginal investor—the investor most likely to be trading on the equity. If that marginal investor is globally diversified, there is at least the potential for global diversification. If the marginal investor does not have a global portfolio, the likelihood of diversifying away country risk declines substantially. Stulz (1999) made a similar point using different terminology. He differentiated between segmented markets, where risk premiums can be different in each market, because investors cannot or will not invest outside their domestic markets, and open markets, where investors can invest across markets. In a segmented market, the marginal investor will be diversified only across investments in that market, whereas in an open market, the marginal investor has the opportunity (even if he or she does not take it) to invest across markets.

Even if the marginal investor is globally diversified, there is a second test that has to be met for country risk not to matter. All or much of country risk should be country specific. In other words, there should be low correlation across markets. Only then will the risk be diversifiable in a globally diversified portfolio. If, however, the returns across countries have significant positive correlation, country risk has a market risk component, is not diversifiable, and can command a premium. Whether returns across countries are positively correlated is an empirical question. Studies from the 1970s and 1980s suggested that the correlation was low, and this was an impetus for global diversification. Partly because of the success of that sales pitch and partly because economies around the world have become increasingly intertwined over the past decade, more recent studies indicate that the correlation across markets has risen. This is borne out by the speed with which troubles in one market, say Russia, can spread to a market with little or no obvious relationship to it, say Brazil.

So where do we stand? We believe that while the barriers to trading across markets have dropped, investors still have a home bias in their portfolios and that markets remain partially segmented. While globally diversified investors are playing an increasing role in the pricing of equities around the world, the resulting increase in correlation across markets has resulted in a portion of country risk being nondiversifiable or market risk. The next section will consider how best to measure this country risk and build it into expected returns.

Measuring Country Risk Premiums   If country risk matters and leads to higher premiums for riskier countries, the obvious follow-up question becomes how we measure this additional premium. This section will look at two approaches. The first builds on default spreads on country bonds issued by each country, whereas the second uses equity market volatility as its basis.

Default Risk Spreads   While there are several measures of country risk, one of the simplest and most easily accessible is the rating assigned to a country's debt by a ratings agency; Standard & Poor's (S&P), Moody's Investors Service, and Fitch

IBCA all rate countries. These ratings measure default risk (rather than equity risk) but they are affected by many of the factors that drive equity risk—the stability of a country's currency, its budget and trade balances, and its political stability, for instance.[12] The other advantage of ratings is that they come with default spreads over the riskless rate. For instance, Table 7.5 summarizes the ratings and default spreads for Latin American countries as of June 2000.

The market spreads measure the difference between dollar-denominated bonds issued by the country and the U.S. Treasury bond rate. While this is a market rate and reflects current expectations, country bond spreads are extremely volatile and can shift significantly from day to day. To counter this volatility, typical spreads have been estimated by averaging the default spreads of all countries in the world with the specified rating over and above the appropriate riskless rate. These spreads tend to be less volatile and more reliable for long-term analysis.

Analysts who use default spreads as measures of country risk typically add them on to both the cost of equity and debt of every company traded in that country. For instance, the cost of equity for a Brazilian company, estimated in U.S. dollars, will be 4.83 percent higher than the cost of equity of an otherwise similar U.S. company. If we assume that the risk premium for the United States and other mature equity markets is 5.51%, the cost of equity for a Brazilian company with a beta of 1.2 can be estimated as follows (with a U.S. Treasury bond rate of 5 percent).

TABLE 7.5   Ratings and Default Spreads (in Basis Points): Latin America

Country	Rating[a]	Typical Spread[b]	Market Spread[c]
Argentina	B1	450	433
Bolivia	B1	450	469
Brazil	B2	550	483
Colombia	Ba2	300	291
Ecuador	Caa2	750	727
Guatemala	Ba2	300	331
Honduras	B2	550	537
Mexico	Baa3	145	152
Paraguay	B2	550	581
Peru	Ba3	400	426
Uruguay	Baa3	145	174
Venezuela	B2	550	571

[a]Ratings are foreign currency ratings from Moody's Investors Service.

[b]Typical spreads are estimated by looking at the default spreads on bonds issued by all countries with this rating, over and above a riskless rate (U.S. Treasury or German euro rate).

[c]Market spread measures the spread difference between dollar-denominated bonds issued by this country and the U.S. Treasury bond rate.

---

[12]The process by which country ratings are obtained in explained on the S&P web site at www.ratings.standardpoor.com/criteria/index.htm.

$$\text{Cost of equity} = \text{Risk-free rate} + \text{Beta} \times (\text{U.S. risk premium}) + \text{Default spread}$$
$$= 5\% + 1.2(5.51\%) + 4.83\% = 16.34\%$$

In some cases, analysts add the default spread to the U.S. risk premium and multiply it by the beta. This increases the cost of equity for high-beta companies and lowers it for low-beta firms.

While ratings provide a convenient measure of country risk, there are costs associated with using them as the only measure. First, ratings agencies often lag markets when it comes to responding to changes in the underlying default risk. Second, the ratings agency focus on default risk may obscure other risks that could still affect equity markets. What are the alternatives? There are numerical country risk scores that have been developed by some services as much more comprehensive measures of risk. The *Economist*, for instance, has a score that runs from 0 to 100 (where 0 is no risk, and 100 is most risky) that it uses to rank emerging markets. Alternatively, country risk can be estimated from the bottom up by looking at economic fundamentals in each country. This, of course, requires significantly more information than the other approaches. Finally, default spreads measure the risk associated with bonds issued by countries and not the equity risk in these countries. Since equities in any market are likely to be more risky than bonds, you could argue that default spreads understate equity risk premiums.

Relative Standard Deviations   There are some analysts who believe that investors in equity markets choose between these markets based on their assessed riskiness and that the risk premiums should reflect the differences in equity risk. A conventional measure of equity risk is the standard deviation in stock prices; higher standard deviations are generally associated with more risk. If you scale the standard deviation of one market against another, you obtain a measure of relative risk.

$$\text{Relative standard deviation}_{\text{country X}} = \text{Standard deviation}_{\text{country X}}/\text{Standard deviation}_{\text{U.S.}}$$

This relative standard deviation, when multiplied by the premium used for U.S. stocks, should yield a measure of the total risk premium for any market.

THE DANGER OF DOUBLE COUNTING RISK

When assessing country risk, there is a substantial chance that the same risk may be counted more than once in a valuation. For instance, there are analysts who use the dollar-denominated bonds issued by a country—the Brazilian C-bond, for instance—as the risk-free rate when estimating cost of equity for Brazilian companies. The interest rate on this bond already incorporates the default spreads discussed in the preceding section. If the risk premium is also adjusted upward to reflect country risk, there has been a double counting of the risk. This effect is made worse when betas are adjusted upward and cash flows are adjusted downward (a process called "haircutting") because of country risk.

Equity risk premium$_{\text{country X}}$ = Risk premum$_{\text{U.S.}}$ × Relative standard deviation$_{\text{country X}}$

Assume, for the moment, that you are using a mature market premium for the United States of 5.51 percent and that the annual standard deviation of U.S. stocks is 20 percent. If the annual standard deviation of Indonesian stocks is 35 percent, the estimate of a total risk premium for Indonesia would be:

$$\text{Equity risk premium}_{\text{Indonesia}} = 5.51\% \times (35\%/20\%) = 9.64\%$$

The country risk premium can be isolated as follows:

$$\text{Country risk premium}_{\text{Indonesia}} = 9.64\% - 5.51\% = 4.13\%$$

While this approach has intuitive appeal, there are problems with using standard deviations computed in markets with widely different market structures and liquidity. There are very risky emerging markets that have low standard deviations for their equity markets because the markets are illiquid. This approach will understate the equity risk premiums in those markets. The second problem is related to currencies, since the standard deviations are usually measured in local currency terms; the standard deviation in the U.S. market is a dollar standard deviation, whereas the standard deviation in the Indonesian market is a rupiah standard deviation. This is a relatively simple problem to fix, though, since the standard deviations can be measured in the same currency—you could estimate the standard deviation in dollar returns for the Indonesian market.

Default Spreads + Relative Standard Deviations   The country default spreads that come with country ratings provide an important first step, but still only measure the premium for default risk. Intuitively, we would expect the country equity risk premium to be larger than the country default risk spread. To address the issue of how much higher, one can look at the volatility of the equity market in a country relative to the volatility of the country bond used to estimate the spread. This yields the following estimate for the country equity risk premium:

$$\text{Country risk premium} = \text{Country default spread} \times \left(\frac{\sigma_{\text{equity}}}{\sigma_{\text{country bond}}} \right)$$

To illustrate, consider the case of Brazil. In March 2000, Brazil was rated B2 by Moody's, resulting in a default spread of 4.83 percent. The annualized standard deviation in the Brazilian equity index over the previous year was 30.64 percent, while the annualized standard deviation in the Brazilian dollar-denominated C-bond was 15.28 percent. The resulting country equity risk premium for Brazil is as follows:

$$\text{Brazil's country risk premium} = 4.83\%(30.64\%/15.28\%) = 9.69\%$$

Note that this country risk premium will increase if the country rating drops or if the relative volatility of the equity market increases.

Why should equity risk premiums have any relationship to country bond spreads? A simple explanation is that an investor who can make 11 percent on a dollar-denominated Brazilian government bond would not settle for an expected return of 10.5 percent (in dollar terms) on Brazilian equity. Playing devil's advocate, however, a critic could argue that the interest rate on a country bond, from which default spreads are extracted, is not really an expected return since it is based on the promised cash flows (coupon and principal) on the bond rather than the expected cash flows. In fact, if we wanted to estimate a risk premium for bonds, we would need to estimate the expected return based on expected cash flows, allowing for the default risk. This would result in a much lower default spread and equity risk premium.

Both this approach and the previous one use the standard deviation in equity of a market to make a judgment about country risk premium, but they measure it relative to different bases. This approach uses the country bond as a base, whereas the previous one uses the standard deviation in the U.S. market. This approach assumes that investors are more likely to choose between Brazilian bonds and Brazilian equity, whereas the previous one approach assumes that the choice is across equity markets.

Choosing between the Approaches The three approaches to estimating country risk premiums will generally give you different estimates, with the bond default spread and relative equity standard deviation approaches yielding lower country risk premiums than the melded approach that uses both the country bond default spread and the equity standard deviation. We believe that the larger country risk premiums that emerge from the last approach are the most realistic for the immediate future, but that country risk premiums will decline over time. Just as companies mature and become less risky over time, countries can mature and become less risky as well.

One way to adjust country risk premiums over time is to begin with the premium that emerges from the melded approach and to adjust this premium down toward either the country bond default spread or the country premium estimated from equity standard deviations. Another way of presenting this argument is to note that the differences between standard deviations in equity and bond prices narrow over longer periods, and the resulting relative volatility will generally be smaller.[13] Thus, the equity risk premium will converge on the country bond spread as we look at longer-term expected returns. For example, the country risk premium for Brazil would be 9.69 percent for the next year but decline over time to either the 4.83 percent (country default spread) or 4.13 percent (relative standard deviation).

Estimating Asset Exposure to Country Risk Premiums Once country risk premiums have been estimated, the final question that has to be addressed relates to the exposure of individual companies within that country to country risk. There are three alternative views of country risk:

1. *Assume that all companies in a country are equally exposed to country risk.* Thus, for Brazil, with its estimated country risk premium of 9.69 percent, each

---

[13]Jeremy Siegel reports on the standard deviation in equity markets in his book *Stocks for the Very Long Run*, and notes that they tend to decrease with time horizon.

company in the market will have an additional country risk premium of 9.69 percent added to its expected returns. For instance, the cost of equity for Aracruz Celulose, a paper and pulp manufacturer listed in Brazil with a beta of 0.72, in U.S. dollar terms would be (assuming a U.S. Treasury bond rate of 5 percent and a mature market (U.S.) risk premium of 5.51 percent):

$$\text{Expected cost of equity} = 5.00\% + 0.72(5.51\%) + 9.69\% = 18.66\%$$

Note that the risk-free rate used is the U.S. Treasury bond rate and that the 5.51 percent is the equity risk premium for a mature equity market (estimated from historical data in the U.S. market). The biggest limitation of this approach is that it assumes that all firms in a country, no matter what their business or size, are equally exposed to country risk. To convert this dollar cost of equity into a cost of equity in the local currency, all that we need to do is to scale the estimate by relative inflation. To illustrate, if the Brazilian inflation rate is 10 percent and the U.S. inflation rate is 3 percent, the cost of equity for Aracruz in Brazilian real (BR) terms can be written as:

$$\text{Expected cost of equity}_{BR} = 1.1866(1.10/1.03) - 1 = 0.2672 \text{ or } 26.72\%$$

This will ensure consistency across estimates and valuations in different currencies.

  2. *Assume that a company's exposure to country risk is proportional to its exposure to all other market risk, which is measured by the beta.* For Aracruz, this would lead to a cost of equity estimate of:

$$\text{Expected cost of equity} = 5.00\% + 0.72(5.51\% + 9.69\%) = 15.94\%$$

This approach does differentiate between firms, but it assumes that betas that measure exposure to all other market risk measure exposure to country risk as well. Thus, low-beta companies are less exposed to country risk than high-beta companies.

  3. *The most general, and our preferred approach, is to allow for each company to have an exposure to country risk that is different from its exposure to all other market risk.* Measuring this exposure with λ, the cost of equity for any firm is estimated as follows:

$$\text{Expected return} = R_f + \text{Beta(Mature equity risk premium)} \\ + \lambda(\text{Country risk premium})$$

How can we best estimate λ? This question is considered in far more detail in the next chapter, but we would argue that commodity companies that get most of their revenues in U.S. dollars[14] by selling into a global market should be less exposed than manufacturing companies that service the local market. Using this rationale, Aracruz, which derives 80 percent or more of its revenues in the global paper market in U.S. dollars, should be less exposed than the typical Brazilian firm to country

---

[14]While I have categorized the revenues into dollar revenues and revenues in dollars, the analysis can be generalized to look at revenues in stable currencies (e.g., the dollar, euro, etc.) and revenues in risky currencies.

risk.[15] Using a λ of 0.25, for instance, we get a cost of equity in U.S. dollar terms for Aracruz of:

$$\text{Expected return} = 5\% + 0.72(5.51\%) + 0.25(9.69\%) = 11.39\%$$

Note that the third approach essentially converts our expected return model to a two-factor model, with the second factor being country risk, with λ measuring exposure to country risk. This approach also seems to offer the most promise in analyzing companies with exposures in multiple countries like Coca-Cola and Nestlé. While these firms are ostensibly developed market companies, they have substantial exposure to risk in emerging markets, and their costs of equity should reflect this exposure. We could estimate the country risk premiums for each country in which they operate and a λ relative to each country, and use these to estimate a cost of equity for either company.

 ctryprem.xls: There is a dataset on the Web that contains the updated ratings for countries and the risk premiums associated with each.

Alternative Approach: Implied Equity Premiums

There is an alternative to estimating risk premiums that does not require historical data or corrections for country risk, but does assume that the market, overall, is correctly priced. Consider, for instance, a very simple valuation model for stocks:

$$\text{Value} = \frac{\text{Expected dividends next period}}{(\text{Required return on equity} - \text{Expected growth rate})}$$

This is essentially the present value of dividends growing at a constant rate. Three of the four inputs in this model can be obtained externally—the current level of the market (value), the expected dividends next period, and the expected growth rate in earnings and dividends in the long term. The only unknown is then the required return on equity; when we solve for it, we get an implied expected return on stocks. Subtracting the risk-free rate will yield an implied equity risk premium.

To illustrate, assume that the current level of the S&P 500 index is 900, the expected dividend yield on the index is 2 percent, and the expected growth rate in earnings and dividends in the long term is 7 percent. Solving for the required return on equity yields the following:

$$900 = (.02 \times 900)/(r - .07)$$

Solving for r,

$$r = (18 + 63)/900 = 9\%$$

---

[15] λ_{Aracruz} = % from local market$_{\text{Aracruz}}$/% from local market$_{\text{average Brazilian firm}}$ = 0.20/0.80 = 0.25.

If the current risk-free rate is 6 percent, this will yield a premium of 3 percent.

This approach can be generalized to allow for high growth for a period, and extended to cover cash flow–based, rather than dividend, models. To illustrate this, consider the S&P 500 index as of December 31, 1999. The index was at 1,469, and the dividend yield on the index was roughly 1.68 percent. In addition, the consensus estimate[16] of growth in earnings for companies in the index was approximately 10 percent for the next five years. Since this is not a growth rate that can be sustained forever, we employ a two-stage valuation model, where we allow growth to continue at 10 percent for five years, and then lower the growth rate to the treasury bond rate of 6.5 percent after that.[17] The following table summarizes the expected cash flows for the next five years of high growth and the first year of stable growth thereafter:

Year	Cash Flow on Index
1	27.23
2	29.95
3	32.94
4	36.24
5	39.86
6	42.45

Cash flow in the first year = (Dividend yield)(Index)$(1 + g)$ = $(.0168)(1,469)(1.10)$.

If we assume that these are reasonable estimates of the cash flows and that the index is correctly priced, then:

$$\text{Level of the index} = 1,469 = 27.23/(1 + r) + 29.95/(1 + r)^2 + 32.94/(1 + r)^3 + 36.24/(1 + r)^4 + [39.86 + 42.45/(r - .065)]/(1 + r)^5$$

Note that the last term in the equation is the terminal value of the index, based on the stable growth rate of 6.5 percent, discounted back to the present. Solving for r in this equation yields us the required return on equity of 8.6 percent. The Treasury bond rate on December 31, 1999, was approximately 6.5 percent, yielding an implied equity premium of 2.10 percent.

The advantage of this approach is that it is market-driven and current, and does not require any historical data. Thus, it can be used to estimate implied equity premiums in any market. It is, however, bounded by whether the model used for the valuation is the right one and the availability and reliability of the inputs to that model. For instance, the equity risk premium for the Argentine market on September 30, 1998, was estimated from the following inputs. The index (Merval) was at 687.50, and the current dividend yield on the index was 5.6 percent. Earnings in companies in the index are expected to grow 11 percent (in U.S. dollar terms) over

---

[16]We used the average of the analyst estimates for individual firms (bottom-up). Alternatively, we could have used the top-down estimate for the S&P 500 earnings (from economists).

[17]The Treasury bond rate is the sum of expected inflation and the expected real rate. If we assume that real growth is equal to the real rate, the long-term stable growth rate should be equal to the Treasury bond rate.

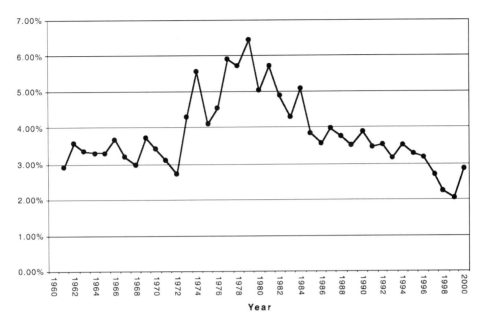

FIGURE 7.1 Implied Premium for U.S. Equity Market

the next five years, and 6 percent thereafter. These inputs yield a required return on equity of 10.59 percent, which when compared to the U.S. Treasury bond rate of 5.14 percent on that day results in an implied equity premium of 5.45 percent. For simplicity, we have used nominal dollar expected growth rates[18] and Treasury bond rates, but this analysis could have been done entirely in the local currency.

The implied equity premiums change over time as stock prices, earnings, and interest rates change. In fact, the contrast between these premiums and the historical premiums is best illustrated by graphing out the implied premiums in the S&P 500 going back to 1960 in Figure 7.1. In terms of mechanics, smoothed historical growth rates in earnings and dividends were used as projected growth rates, and a two-stage dividend discount model was used. Looking at these numbers, the following conclusions would be drawn:

- ■ The implied equity premium has seldom been as high as the historical risk premium. Even in 1978, when the implied equity premium peaked, the estimate of 6.5 percent was well below what many practitioners use as the risk premium in their risk and return models. In fact, the average implied equity risk premium has been about 4 percent over the past 40 years. This is probably because of the survivor bias that pushes up historical risk premiums.
- ■ The implied equity premium did increase during the 1970s as inflation increased. This does have interesting implications for risk premium estimation.

---

[18]The input that is most difficult to estimate for emerging markets is a long-term expected growth rate. For Argentine stocks, I used the average consensus estimate of growth in earnings for the largest Argentine companies that have American depository receipts (ADRs) listed on them. This estimate may be biased as a consequence.

Instead of assuming that the risk premium is a constant and unaffected by the level of inflation and interest rates, which is what we do with historical risk premiums, it may be more realistic to increase the risk premium as expected inflation and interest rates increase. In fact, an interesting avenue of research would be to estimate the fundamentals that determine implied risk premiums.

■ Finally, the risk premium has been on a downward trend since the early 1980s, and the risk premium at the end of 1999 was a historical low. Part of the decline can be attributed to a decline in inflation uncertainty and lower interest rates, and part of it, arguably, may reflect other changes in investor risk aversion and characteristics over the period. There is, however, the very real possibility that the risk premium is low because investors had overpriced equity. In fact, the market correction in 2000 pushed the implied equity risk premium up to 2.87 percent by the end of 2000.

As a final point, there is a strong tendency toward mean reversion in financial markets. Given this tendency, it is possible that we can end up with a far better estimate of the implied equity premium by looking at not just the current premium but also at historical data. There are two ways in which we can do this:

■ We can use the average implied equity premium over longer periods, say 10 to 15 years. Note that we do not need as many years of data here as we did with the historical premium estimate, because the standard errors tend to be smaller.

■ A more rigorous approach would require relating implied equity risk premiums to fundamental macroeconomic data over the period. For instance, given that implied equity premiums tend to be higher during periods with higher inflation rates (and interest rates), we ran a regression of implied equity premiums against Treasury bond rates and a term structure variable between 1960 and 2000:

$$\text{Implied equity premium} = 1.87\% + 0.2903(\text{T-bond rate}) - 0.1162(\text{T-bond} - \text{T-bill})$$
$$[5.94] \qquad\qquad\qquad [1.10]$$

The regression has significant explanatory power, with an R-squared of 49 percent, and the t statistics (in brackets under the coefficients) indicate the statistical significance of the independent variables used. Substituting the current Treasury bond rate and bond-bill spread into this equation should yield an updated estimate[19] of the implied equity premium.

---

 histimpl.xls: **This dataset on the Web shows the inputs used to calculate the premium in each year for the U.S. market.**

---

[19]On June 30, 2001, for instance, I substituted in the Treasury bond rate of 5 percent and a spread of 1.0 percent between the T-bond and T-bill rate into the regression equation to get:

$$.0182 + 0.2903(.05) - 0.1162(.01) = .032 \text{ or } 3.20\%$$

HISTORICAL VERSUS IMPLIED EQUITY PREMIUMS: EFFECT OF MARKET VIEWS

As you can see from the preceding discussion, historical premiums can be very different from implied equity premiums. At the end of 2000, the historical risk premium for stocks over bonds in the United States was 5.51%, whereas the implied equity risk premium was 2.87%. When doing discounted cash flow valuation, you have to decide which risk premium you will use in the valuation, and your choice will be determined by both your market views and your valuation mission.

Market Views: If you believe that the *market is right in the aggregate,* though it may make mistakes on individual stocks, the risk premium you should use is the implied equity risk premium (2.87% at the end of 2000). If you believe that the market often makes mistakes in the aggregate and that *risk premiums in markets tend to move back to historical norms* (mean reversion), you should go with the historical premium (5.5% at the end of 2000). A way to split the difference is to assume that *markets are right across time,* though they may make mistakes at individual points in time. If you make this assumption, you should use an average implied equity risk premium over time. The average implied equity risk premium from 1960 to 2000 is 4%. While this book will use the historical premium a few times in our valuations, we will stick with the average implied premium of 4% in most of the valuations.

Valuation Mission: If your valuation requires you to market neutral, you should use the implied equity risk premium. This is often the case if you are an equity research analyst or if you have to value a company for an acquisition.

---

 implprem.xls: This spreadsheet allows you to estimate the implied equity premium in a market.

DEFAULT SPREADS ON BONDS

The interest rates on bonds are determined by the default risk that investors perceive in the issuer of the bonds. This default risk is often measured with a bond rating and the interest rate that corresponds to the rating is estimated by adding a default spread to the riskless rate. In Chapter 4, we examined the process used by rating agencies to rate firms. This chapter considers how to estimate default spreads for a given ratings class and why these spreads may change over time.

Estimating Default Spreads

The simplest way to estimate default spreads for each ratings class is to find a sampling of bonds within that ratings class and obtain the current market interest rate on these bonds. Why do we need a sampling rather than just one bond? A bond can be misrated or mispriced. Using a sample reduces or eliminates this problem. In obtaining this sample, you should try to focus on the most liquid bonds with as few special features attached to them as possible. Corporate bonds are often illiquid and the interest rates on such bonds may not reflect current market rates. The presence of special features on bonds such as convertibility can affect the pricing of these bonds and consequently the interest rates estimated on them.

Once a sample of bonds within each ratings class has been identified, you need to estimate the interest rate on these bonds. There are two measures that are widely used. The first is the yield on the bond, which is the coupon rate divided by the market price. The second is the yield to maturity on the bond, which is the interest rate that makes the present value of the coupons and face value of the bond equal to the market price. In general, it is the yield to maturity that better measures the market interest rate on the bond.

Having obtained the interest rates on the bonds in the sample, you have two decisions to make. The first relates to weighting. You could compute a simple average of the interest rates of the bonds in the sample or a weighted average, with the weights based upon the trading volume—more liquid bonds will be weighted more than less liquid bonds. The second relates to the index Treasury rate, since the average interest rate for a ratings class is compared to this rate to arrive at a default spread. In general, the maturity of the Treasury should match the average maturity of the corporate bonds chosen to estimate the average interest rate. Thus, the average interest rate for five-year BBB-rated corporate bonds should be compared to the average interest rate for five-year Treasuries to derive the spread for the BBB-rated bonds.

While publications like *Barron's* have historically provided interest rates on at least higher-rated bonds (BBB or higher), an increasing number of online services provide the same information today for all rated bonds. Table 7.6 is extracted from one such online service in early 2001 for 10-year bonds.

TABLE 7.6 Default Spreads by Ratings Class—January 2001 (T-Bond Rate = 5%)

Rating	Spread	Interest Rate on Debt
AAA	0.75%	5.75%
AA	1.00%	6.00%
A+	1.50%	6.50%
A	1.80%	6.80%
A–	2.00%	7.00%
BBB	2.25%	7.25%
BB	3.50%	8.50%
B+	4.75%	9.75%
B	6.50%	11.50%
B–	8.00%	13.00%
CCC	10.00%	15.00%
CC	11.50%	16.50%
C	12.70%	17.70%
D	14.00%	19.00%

Source: bondsonline.com.

Determinants of Default Spreads

Table 7.6 provides default spreads at a point in time, but default spreads not only vary across time, but they also can vary for bonds with the same rating but different maturities. This section considers how default spreads vary across time and for bonds with varying maturities.

Default Spreads and Bond Maturity Empirically, the default spread for corporate bonds of a given ratings class seems to increase with the maturity of the bond. Figure 7.2 presents the default spreads estimated for a AAA-, BBB-, and CCC-rated bond for maturities ranging from 1 to 10 years in January 2001.

For every rating, the default spread seems to widen for the longer maturities, and it widens more for the lower-rated bonds. Why might this be? It is entirely possible that default risk is multiplied as we look at longer maturities. A bond investor buying a 10-year bond in a CCC-rated company may feel more exposed to default risk than a bondholder buying a higher-rated bond.

Default Spreads over Time The default spreads presented in Table 7.6, after a year of declining markets and a slowing economy, were significantly higher than the default spreads a year earlier. This phenomenon is not new. Historically, default spreads for every ratings class have increased during recessions and decreased during economic booms. Figure 7.3 graphs the spread between 10-year Moody's Baa-rated bonds and the 10-year Treasury bond rate each year from 1960 to 2000. The default spreads did increase during periods of low economic growth; note the increase during 1973–1974

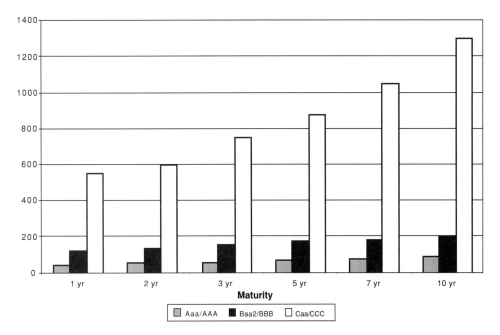

FIGURE 7.2 Default Spreads by Maturity—January 2001
Source: bondsonline.com.

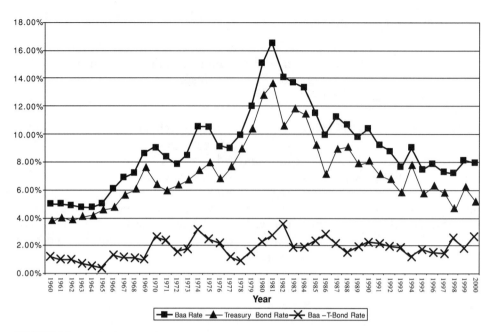

FIGURE 7.3 Default Spread—Baa versus Treasury Bond Rates from 1960 to 2000
Source: Federal Reserve.

and 1979–1981 in particular. In fact, a regression of default spreads each year against real economic growth that year bears out this conclusion:

$$\text{Default spread}_{\text{BBB-Treasury}} = 0.47 - 0.04 \text{ GNP growth}_{\text{real}} \qquad R^2 = 41\%$$
[259]

After years of high real growth, default spreads tend to shrink.

The practical implication of this phenomenon is that default spreads for bonds have to be reestimated at regular intervals, especially if the economy shifts from low to high growth or vice versa.

 ratings.xls: This dataset on the Web summarizes default spreads by bond rating class for the most recent period.

CONCLUSION

The risk-free rate is the starting point for all expected return models. For an asset to be risk free, it has to be free of both default and reinvestment risk. Using these criteria, the appropriate risk-free rate to use to obtain expected returns should be a default-free (government) zero coupon rate that is matched up to when the cash flow that is being discounted occurs. In practice, however, it is usually appropriate to match up the duration of the risk-free asset to the duration of the cash flows being analyzed. In valuation, this will lead us toward long-term government bond rates as risk-free rates. It is also important that the risk-free rate be consistent with the cash flows being discounted. In particular, the currency in which the risk-free rate is denominated and whether it is a real or nominal risk-free rate should be determined by the currency in which the cash flows are estimated and whether the estimation is done in real or nominal terms.

The risk premium is a fundamental and critical component in portfolio management, corporate finance, and valuation. Given its importance, it is surprising that more attention has not been paid in practical terms to estimation issues. This chapter considered the conventional approach to estimating risk premiums, which is to use historical returns on equity and government securities, and evaluated some of its weaknesses. It also examined how to extend this approach to emerging markets, where historical data tends to be both limited and volatile. The alternative to historical premiums is to estimate the equity premium implied by equity prices. This approach does require that we start with a valuation model for equities, and estimate the expected growth and cash flows, collectively, on equity investments. It has the advantage of not requiring historical data and reflecting current market perceptions.

QUESTIONS AND SHORT PROBLEMS

1. Assume that you are valuing an Indonesian firm in U.S. dollars. What would you use as the riskless rate?
2. Explain why a six-month Treasury bill rate is not an appropriate riskless rate in discounting a five-year cash flow.
3. You have been asked to estimate a riskless rate in Indonesian rupiah. The Indonesian government has rupiah-denominated bonds outstanding, with an interest rate of 17%. S&P has a rating of BB on these bonds, and the typical spread for a BB-rated country is 5% over a riskless rate. Estimate the rupiah riskless rate.
4. You are valuing an Indian company in rupees. The current exchange rate is Rs 45 per dollar and you have been able to obtain a 10-year forward rate of Rs 70 per dollar. If the U.S. Treasury bond rate is 5%, estimate the riskless rate in Indian rupees.
5. You are attempting to do a valuation of a Chilean company in real terms. While you have been unable to get a real riskless rate in Latin America, you know that inflation-indexed Treasury bonds in the United States are yielding 3%. Could you use this as a real riskless rate? Why or why not? What are the alternatives?
6. Assume you have estimated the historical risk premium, based on 50 years of data, to be 6%. If the annual standard deviation in stock prices is 30%, estimate the standard error in the risk premium estimate.
7. When you use a historical risk premium as your expected future risk premium, what are the assumptions that you are making about investors and markets? Under what conditions would a historical risk premium give you too high a number (to use as an expected premium)?
8. You are trying to estimate a country equity risk premium for Poland. You find that S&P has assigned an A rating to Poland and that Poland has issued euro-denominated bonds that yield 7.6% in the market currently. (Germany, a AAA-rated country, has euro-denominated bonds outstanding that yield 5.1%.)
   a. Estimate the country risk premium, using the default spread on the country bond as the proxy.

    b. If you were told that the standard deviation in the Polish equity market was 25% and that the standard deviation in the Polish euro bond was 15%, estimate the country risk premium.

9. The standard deviation in the Mexican Equity Index is 48%, and the standard deviation in the S&P 500 is 20%. You use an equity risk premium of 5.5% for the United States.

    a. Estimate the country equity risk premium for Mexico using relative equity standard deviations.

    b. Now assume that you are told that Mexico is rated BBB by Standard & Poor's and that it has dollar-denominated bonds outstanding that trade at a spread of about 3% above the Treasury bond rate. If the standard deviation in these bonds is 24%, estimate the country risk premium for Mexico.

10. The S&P 500 is at 1,400. The expected dividends and cash flows next year on the stocks in the index are expected to be 5% of the index. If the expected growth rate in dividends and cash flows over the long term are expected to be 6% and the riskless rate is 5.5%, estimate the implied equity risk premium.

11. The Bovespa (Brazilian equity index) is at 15,000. The dividends on the index last year were 5% of the index value, and analysts expect them to grow 15% a year in real terms for the next five years. After the fifth year, the growth is expected to drop to 5% in real terms in perpetuity. If the real riskless rate is 6%, estimate the implied equity risk premium in this market.

12. As stock prices go up, implied equity risk premiums will go down. Is this statement always true? If not, when is it not true?

CHAPTER 8

Estimating Risk Parameters and Costs of Financing

The preceding chapter laid the groundwork for estimating the costs of equity and capital for firms by looking at how best to estimate a riskless rate that operates as a base for all costs, an equity risk premium for estimating the cost of equity, and default spreads for estimating the cost of debt. It did not, however, consider how to estimate the risk parameters for individual firms. This chapter examines the process of estimating risk parameters for individual firms, for estimating both the cost of equity and the cost of debt.

For the cost of equity, we look at the standard process of estimating the beta for a firm and consider alternative approaches. For the cost of debt, we examine bond ratings as measures of default risk and the determinants of these ratings.

The chapter closes by bringing together the risk parameter estimates for individual firms and the economy-wide estimates of the risk-free rate and risk premiums to estimate a cost of capital for the firm. To do this, the sources of capital have to be weighted by their relative market values.

THE COST OF EQUITY AND CAPITAL

Firms raise money from both equity investors and lenders to fund investments. Both groups of investors make their investments expecting to make a return. Chapter 4 argued that the expected return for equity investors would include a premium for the equity risk in the investment. We label this expected return the cost of equity. Similarly, the expected return that lenders hope to make on their investments includes a premium for default risk, and we call that expected return the cost of debt. If we consider all of the financing that the firm takes on, the composite cost of financing will be a weighted average of the costs of equity and debt, and this weighted cost is the cost of capital.

The chapter begins by estimating the equity risk in a firm and using the equity risk to estimate the cost of equity, and follows up by measuring the default risk to estimate a cost of debt. It will conclude by determining the weights we should attach to each of these costs to arrive at a cost of capital.

COST OF EQUITY

The cost of equity is the rate of return investors require on an equity investment in a firm. The risk and return models described in Chapter 4 need a riskless rate and a risk premium (in the CAPM) or premiums (in the APM and multifactor models), which were estimated in the last chapter. They also need measures of a firm's exposure to market risk in the form of betas. These inputs are used to arrive at an expected return on an equity investment:

$$\text{Expected return} = \text{Riskless rate} + \text{Beta(Risk premium)}$$

This expected return to equity investors includes compensation for the market risk in the investment and is the cost of equity. This section will concentrate on the estimation of the beta of a firm. While much of the discussion is directed at the CAPM, it can be extended to apply to the arbitrage pricing and multifactor models, as well.

Betas

In the CAPM, the beta of an investment is the risk that the investment adds to a market portfolio. In the APM and multifactor model, the betas of the investment relative to each factor have to be measured. There are three approaches available for estimating these parameters: One is to use historical data on market prices for individual investments; the second is to estimate the betas from the fundamental characteristics of the investment; and the third is to use accounting data. All three approaches are described in this section.

Historical Market Betas   The conventional approach for estimating the beta of an investment is a regression of returns on the investment against returns on a market index. For firms that have been publicly traded for a length of time, it is relatively straightforward to estimate returns that an investor would have made on investing in the firms' equity in intervals (such as a week or a month) over that period. In theory, these stock returns on the assets should be related to returns on a market portfolio (i.e., a portfolio that includes all traded assets) to estimate the betas of the assets. In practice, we tend to use a stock index such as the S&P 500 as a proxy for the market portfolio, and we estimate betas for stocks against the index.

Regression Estimates of Betas   The standard procedure for estimating betas is to regress stock returns (R_j) against market returns (R_m):

$$R_j = a + b\,R_m$$

where a = Intercept from the regression
       b = Slope of the regression = Covariance(R_j, R_m)/σ_m^2

The slope of the regression corresponds to the beta of the stock and measures the riskiness of the stock.

The intercept of the regression provides a simple measure of performance of the investment during the period of the regression, when returns are measured against the expected returns from the capital asset pricing model. To see why, consider the following rearrangement of the capital asset pricing model:

$$R_j = R_f + \beta(R_m - R_f)$$
$$= R_f(1 - \beta) + \beta R_m$$

Compare this formulation of the return on an investment to the return equation from the regression:

$$R_j = a + b R_m$$

Thus, a comparison of the intercept a to $R_f(1 - \beta)$ should provide a measure of the stock's performance, at least relative to the capital asset pricing model.[1] In summary, then:

> If a > $R_f(1 - \beta)$ . . . Stock did better than expected during regression period.
> a = $R_f(1 - \beta)$ . . . Stock did as well as expected during regression period.
> a < $R_f(1 - \beta)$ . . . Stock did worse than expected during regression period.

The difference between a and $R_f(1 - \beta)$ is called Jensen's alpha[2] and provides a measure of whether the investment in question earned a return greater than or less than its required return, given both market performance and risk. For instance, a firm that earned 15 percent during a period when firms with similar betas earned 12 percent, will have earned an excess return of 3 percent; its intercept will also exceed $R_f(1 - \beta)$ by 3 percent.

The third statistic that emerges from the regression is the R-squared (R^2) of the regression. While the statistical explanation of the R-squared is that it provides a measure of the goodness of fit of the regression, the economic rationale is that it provides an estimate of the proportion of the risk of a firm that can be attributed to market risk; the balance $(1 - R^2)$ can then be attributed to firm-specific risk.

The final statistic worth noting is the standard error of the beta estimate. The slope of the regression, like any statistical estimate, may be different from the true value, and the standard error reveals just how much error there could be in the estimate. The standard error can also be used to arrive at confidence intervals for the "true" beta value from the slope estimate.

---

[1]The regression is sometimes calculated using returns in excess of the riskless rate for both the stock and the market. In that case, the intercept of the regression should be zero if the actual returns equal the expected returns from the CAPM, greater than zero if the stock does better than expected, and less than zero if it does worse than expected.
[2]The terminology is confusing, since the intercept of the regression is sometimes also called the alpha and is sometimes compared to zero as a measure of risk-adjusted performance. The intercept can be compared to zero only if the regression is run with excess returns for both the stock and the index; the riskless rate has to be subtracted from the raw return in each month for both.

ILLUSTRATION 8.1: Estimating a Regression Beta for Boeing

Boeing Company is a dominant firm in both the aerospace and defense businesses, and has been traded on the New York Stock Exchange (NYSE) for decades. In assessing risk parameters for Boeing, we compute the returns on the stock and the market index in two steps:

1. The returns to a stockholder in Boeing are computed month by month from January 1996 to December 2000. These returns include both dividends and price appreciation and are defined as follows:

$$\text{Stock return}_{Boeing, j} = (\text{Price}_{Boeing, j} - \text{Price}_{Boeing, j-1} + \text{Dividends}_j)/\text{Price}_{Boeing, j-1}$$

where $\text{Stock return}_{Boeing, j}$ = Returns to a stockholder in Boeing in month j
                 $\text{Price}_{Boeing, j}$ = Price of Boeing stock at the end of month j
                 Dividends_j = Dividends on Boeing stock in month j

Dividends are added to the returns of the month in which stockholders are entitled to the dividend.[3]

2. The returns on the S&P 500 market index are computed for each month of the period, using the level of the index at the end of each month and the monthly dividend on stocks in the index.

$$\text{Market return}_j = (\text{Index}_j - \text{Index}_{j-1} + \text{Dividends}_j)/\text{Index}_{j-1}$$

where Index_j is the level of the index at the end of month j and Dividends_j is the dividends paid on the index in month j. While the S&P 500 and the NYSE Composite are the most widely used indexes for U.S. stocks, they are, at best, imperfect proxies for the market portfolio in the CAPM, which is supposed to include all assets.

Figure 8.1 graphs monthly returns on Boeing against returns on the S&P 500 index from January 1996 to December 2000.

The regression statistics for Boeing are as follows:

(a) Slope of the regression = 0.56. This is Boeing's beta, based on monthly returns from 1996 to 2000. Using a different time period for the regression or different return intervals (weekly or daily) for the same period can result in a different beta.

(b) Intercept of the regression = 0.54%. This is a measure of Boeing's performance, when it is compared with $R_f(1 - \beta)$. The monthly riskless rate (since the returns used in the regression are monthly returns) between 1996 and 2000 averaged 0.4%, resulting in the following estimate for the performance:

$$R_f(1 - \beta) = 0.4\%(1 - 0.56) = 0.18\%$$
$$\text{Intercept} - R_f(1 - \beta) = 0.54\% - 0.18\% = 0.36\%$$

This analysis suggests that Boeing performed 0.36% better than expected, when expectations are based on the CAPM, on a monthly basis between January 1996 and December 2000. This results in an annualized excess return of approximately 4.41%.

$$\text{Annualized excess return} = (1 + \text{Monthly excess return})^{12} - 1$$
$$= (1 - .0036)^{12} - 1 = 4.41\%$$

Note, however, that this does not imply that Boeing would be a good investment in the future.

---

[3]The stock has to be bought by a day called the ex-dividend day in order for investors to be entitled to dividends. The returns in a period include dividends if the ex-dividend day is in that period.

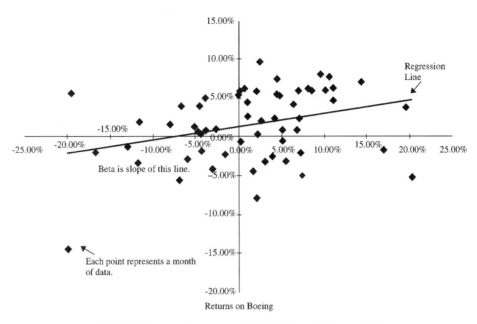

FIGURE 8.1 Boeing versus S&P 500 from 1996 to 2000

The performance measure also does not provide a breakdown of how much of this excess return can be attributed to the performance of the entire sector (aerospace and defense) and how much is specific to the firm. To make that breakdown, we would need to compute the excess over the same period for other firms in the aerospace and defense industry and compare them with Boeing's excess return. The difference would then be attributable to firm-specific actions. In this case, for instance, the average annualized excess return on other aerospace/defense firms between 1996 and 2000 was −0.85%, suggesting that the firm-specific component of performance for Boeing is actually 5.26% [firm-specific Jensen's alpha = 4.41% − (−0.85%)].

(c) R-squared of the regression = 9.43%. This statistic suggests that 9.43% of the risk (variance) in Boeing comes from market sources, and that the balance of 90.57% of the risk comes from firm-specific components. The latter risk should be diversifiable and therefore will not be rewarded with a higher expected return. Boeing's R-squared is lower than the median R-squared of companies listed on the New York Stock Exchange, which was approximately 19% in 2000.

(d) Standard Error of Beta Estimate = 0.23. This statistic implies that the true beta for Boeing could range from 0.33 to 0.79 (subtracting and adding one standard error to beta estimate of 0.56) with 67% confidence and from 0.10 to 1.02 (subtracting and adding two standard errors to beta estimate of 0.56) with 95% confidence. While these ranges may seem large, they are not unusual for most U.S. companies. This suggests that we should consider estimates of betas from regressions with caution.

Using a Service Beta Most of us who use betas obtain them from an estimation service; Merrill Lynch, Barra, Value Line, Standard & Poor's, Morningstar, and Bloomberg are some of the well-known services. All these services begin with the regression beta just described and adjust them to reflect what they feel are better estimates of future risk. Although many of these services do not reveal their estimation procedures, Bloomberg is an exception. Figure 8.2 is the beta calculation page

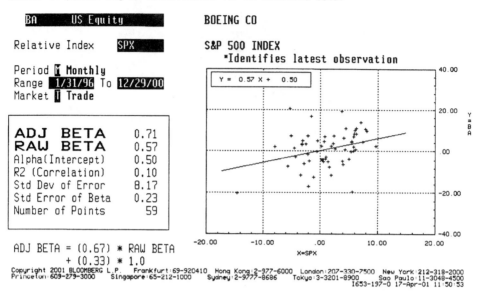

FIGURE 8.2   Beta Estimate for Boeing

from Bloomberg for Boeing, using the same period as our regression (January 1996 to December 2000).

While the time period used is identical to the one used in our earlier regression, there are subtle differences between this regression and the one in Figure 8.1. First, Bloomberg uses price appreciation in the stock and the market index in estimating betas and ignores dividends.[4] The fact that dividends are ignored does not make much difference for a company like Boeing, but it could make a difference for a company that either pays no dividends or pays significantly higher dividends than the market. This explains the mild differences in the intercept (.50% versus .54%) and the beta (.57 versus .56).

Second, Bloomberg also computes what it calls an adjusted beta, which is estimated as follows:

$$\text{Adjusted beta} = \text{Raw beta}(0.67) + 1.00(0.33)$$

These weights (0.67 and 0.33) do not vary across stocks, and this process pushes all estimated betas toward 1. Most services employ similar procedures to adjust betas toward 1. In doing so, they are drawing on empirical evidence that suggests that the betas for most companies, over time, tend to move toward the average beta, which is 1. This may be explained by the fact that firms get more diversified in their product mix and client base as they get larger. While we agree with the notion that betas move toward 1 over time, the weighting process used by most services strikes us as arbitrary and not particularly useful.

---

[4]This is done purely for computational convenience.

Estimation Choices for Beta Estimation There are three decisions that must be made in setting up the regression described earlier. The first concerns the length of the estimation period. Most estimates of betas, including those by Value Line and Standard & Poor's, use five years of data, while Bloomberg uses two years of data. The trade-off is simple: A longer estimation period provides more data, but the firm itself might have changed in its risk characteristics over the time period. Boeing, during the period of our analysis, acquired both Rockwell and McDonnell Douglas, changing its business mix and its basic risk characteristics.

The second estimation issue relates to the return interval. Returns on stocks are available on an annual, a monthly, a weekly, a daily, and even an intraday basis. Using daily or intraday returns increases the number of observations in the regression, but it exposes the estimation process to a significant bias in beta estimates related to nontrading.[5] For instance, the betas estimated for small firms, which are more likely to suffer from nontrading, are biased downward when daily returns are used. Using weekly or monthly returns can reduce the nontrading bias significantly.[6] In this case, using weekly returns for two years yields a beta estimate for Boeing of only 0.88, while the monthly beta estimate is 0.96.

The third estimation issue relates to the choice of a market index to be used in the regression. The standard practice used by most beta estimation services is to estimate the betas of a company relative to the index of the market in which its stock trades. Thus, the betas of German stocks are estimated relative to the Frankfurt DAX, British stocks relative to the FTSE, Japanese stocks relative to the Nikkei, and U.S. stocks relative to the NYSE Composite or the S&P 500. While this practice may yield an estimate that is a reasonable measure of risk for the domestic investor, it may not be the best approach for an international or cross-border investor, who would be better served with a beta estimated relative to an international index. For instance, Boeing's beta between 1996 and 2000 estimated relative to the Morgan Stanley Capital International (MSCI) index that is composed of stocks from different global markets yields a beta of 0.82.

To the extent that different services use different estimation periods, use different market indexes, and adjust the regression beta differently, they will often provide different beta estimates for the same firm at the same point in time. While these beta differences are troubling, note that the beta estimate delivered by each of these services comes with a standard error, and it is very likely that all the betas reported for a firm fall within the range of standard errors from the regressions.

Historical Beta Estimation for Companies in Smaller (or Emerging) Markets The process for estimating betas in markets with fewer stocks listed on them is no different from the process described earlier, but the estimation choices on return intervals, the market index, and the return period can make a much bigger difference in the estimate.

---

[5]The nontrading bias arises because the returns in nontrading periods are zero (even though the market may have moved up or down significantly in those periods). Using these nontrading period returns in the regression will reduce the correlation between stock returns and market returns and the beta of the stock.
[6]The bias can also be reduced using statistical techniques suggested by Dimson and Scholes-Williams.

INDEX DOMINATION AND BETA ESTIMATES

There are a number of indexes that are dominated by one or a few stocks. One of the most striking cases was the Helsinki Stock Exchange (HEX) in the late 1990s. Nokia, the telecommunications giant, represented 75 percent of the Helsinki Index in terms of market value. Not surprisingly, a regression of Nokia against the HEX yielded the results shown in Figure 8.3.

The regression looks impeccable. In fact, the noise problem that we noted with Boeing, arising from the high standard errors, disappears. The beta estimate has a standard error of 0.03, but the results are deceptive. The low standard error is the result of a regression of Nokia on itself, since it dominates the index. The beta is meaningless to a typical investor in Nokia, who is likely to be diversified, if not globally, at least across European stocks. Worse still, the betas of all other Finnish stocks against the HEX become betas estimated against Nokia. In fact, the beta of every other Finnish stock at the time of this regression was less than 1. How is this possible, you might ask, if the average beta is 1? It is the weighted average beta that is 1, and if Nokia (which comprises three-quarters of the index) has a beta greater than 1 (which it does), every other stock in the index could well end up with a beta less than 1.

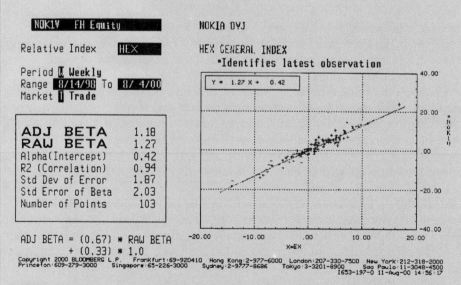

FIGURE 8.3 Beta Estimate for Nokia

▓ When liquidity is limited, as it often is in many stocks in emerging markets, the betas estimated using short return intervals tend to be much more biased. In fact, using daily or even weekly returns in these markets will tend to yield betas that are not good measures of the true market risk of the company.

▓ In many emerging markets, both the companies being analyzed and the market itself change significantly over short periods of time. Using five years of returns, as we did for Boeing, for a regression may yield a beta for a company (and market) that bears little resemblance to the company (and market) as it exists today.

▓ Finally, the indexes that measure market returns in many smaller markets tend to be dominated by a few large companies. For instance, the Bovespa (the Brazilian index) was dominated for several years by Telebras, which represented almost half the index. Nor is this just a problem with emerging markets. The DAX, the equity index for Germany, is dominated by Allianz, Deutsche Bank, Siemens, and Daimler. When an index is dominated by one or a few companies, the betas estimated against that index are unlikely to be true measures of market risk. In fact, the betas are likely to be close to 1 for the large companies that dominate the index and wildly variable for all other companies.

ILLUSTRATION 8.2:   Estimating a Beta for Titan Cement Company

Titan Cement is a cement and construction company in Greece. Reproduced in Figure 8.4 is the beta estimate for Titan from April 1999 to April 2001 (using weekly returns) obtained from a beta service (Bloomberg). Note that the index used is the Athens Stock Exchange Index. Based on this regression, we arrive at the following equation:

$$\text{Returns}_{\text{Titan Cement}} = 0.31\% + 0.93\ \text{Returns}_{\text{ASE}} \qquad \text{R-squared} = 57\%$$
$$[0.08]$$

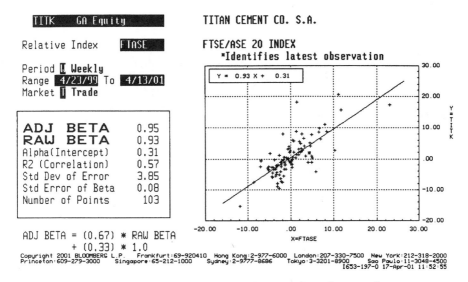

FIGURE 8.4   Beta Estimate for Titan Cement: Athens Stock Exchange Index

HISTORICAL BETA

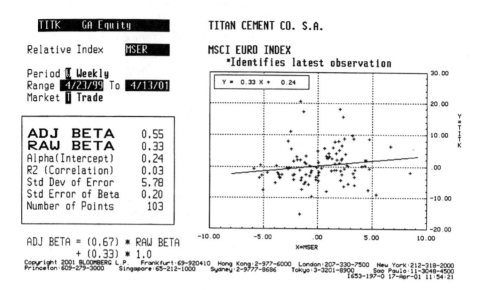

FIGURE 8.5   Beta Estimate for Titan Cement: MSCI European Index

HISTORICAL BETA

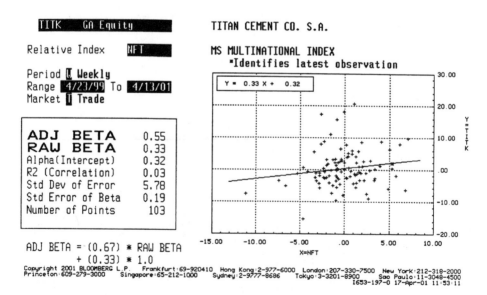

FIGURE 8.6   Beta Estimate for Titan Cement: MSCI Global Index

The beta for Titan Cement, based upon this regression, is 0.93. The standard error of the estimate, shown in brackets below, is only 0.08, but the caveats about narrow indexes applies to the Athens Stock Exchange Index.

Drawing on the arguments in the previous section, if the marginal investor in Titan Cement is, in fact, an investor diversified across European companies, the appropriate index would have been a European stock index. The Bloomberg beta calculation with the MSCI European index is reported in Figure 8.5. Note the decline in beta to 0.33 and the increase in the standard error of the beta estimate.

In fact, if the marginal investor is globally diversified, Titan Cement's beta (as well as Boeing's beta in Illustration 8.1) should have been estimated against a global index. Using the Morgan Stanley Capital International (MSCI) global index, we get a regression beta of 0.33 in Figure 8.6. In fact, the beta estimate and the standard error look very similar to the ones estimated against the European index.

Estimating the Historical Beta for Private Firms   The historical approach to estimating betas works only for assets that have been traded and have market prices. Private companies do not have a market price history. Consequently, we cannot estimate a regression beta for these companies. Nevertheless, we still need estimates of cost of equity and capital for these companies.

You might argue that this is not an issue if you do not value private companies; but you will still be confronted with this issue even when valuing publicly traded firms. Consider, for instance, the following scenarios:

■ If you have to value a private firm for an initial public offering, you will need to estimate discount rates for the valuation.
■ Even after a firm has gone public, there will be a period of time lasting as long as two years when there will be insufficient data for a regression.
■ If you are called upon to value the division of a publicly traded firm that is up for sale, you will not have past prices to draw on to run a regression.
■ Finally, if your firm has gone through significant restructuring—divestitures or recapitalization—in the recent past, regression betas become meaningless because the company itself has changed its risk characteristics.

Thus regression betas are either unavailable or meaningless in a significant number of valuations.

Some analysts assume that discounted cash flow valuation is not feasible in these scenarios; instead they use multiples. Others make assumptions about discount rates based on rules of thumb. Neither approach is appealing. The next section develops an approach for estimating betas that is general enough to apply to all of these companies.

 risk.xls. **This spreadsheet allows you to run a regression of stock returns against market returns and estimate risk parameters.**

The Limitations of Regression Betas   Much of what has been presented in this section represents an indictment of regression betas. In the case of Boeing, the biggest problem was that the beta had high standard error. In fact, this is not a problem unique to Boeing. Figure 8.7 presents the distribution of standard errors on beta estimates for U.S. companies.

With the Nokia regression, we seem to cure the standard error problem but at a very large cost. The low standard errors reflect the domination of the index by a stock and result in betas that may be precise but bear no resemblance to true risk.

Changing the market index, the return period, and the return interval offers no respite. If the index becomes a more representative index, the standard errors on betas will increase, reflecting the fact that more of the risk in the stock is firm-specific. If the beta changes as the return period or interval changes, it creates more uncertainty about the true beta of the company.

In short, regression betas will almost always be either too noisy or skewed by estimation choices to be useful measures of the equity risk in a company. The cost of equity is far too important an input into a discounted cash flow valuation to be left to statistical chance.

Fundamental Betas   A second way to estimate betas is to look at the fundamentals of the business. The beta for a firm may be estimated from a regression, but it is determined by decisions the firm has made on what business to be in and how much operating leverage to use in the business, and by the degree to which the firm uses financial leverage. This section examines an alternative way of estimating betas, where we are less reliant on historical betas and more cognizant of their fundamental determinants.

Determinants of Betas   The beta of a firm is determined by three variables: (1) the type of business or businesses the firm is in, (2) the degree of operating leverage of the firm, and (3) the firm's financial leverage. Although we will use these determinants to find betas in the capital asset pricing model, the same analysis can be used to calculate the betas for the arbitrage pricing and the multifactor models as well.

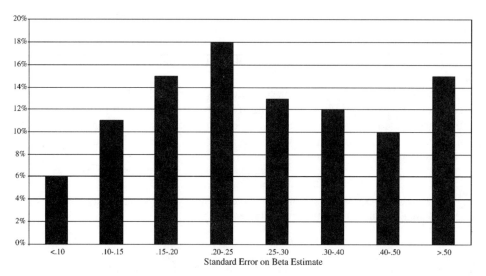

FIGURE 8.7   Distribution of Standard Errors on Beta Estimates
Data Source: Bloomberg.

Type of Business   Since betas measure the risk of a firm relative to a market index, the more sensitive a business is to market conditions, the higher its beta. Thus, other things remaining equal, cyclical firms can be expected to have higher betas than noncyclical firms. Companies involved in housing and automobiles, two sectors of the economy that are very sensitive to economic conditions, should have higher betas than companies in food processing and tobacco, which are relatively insensitive to business cycles.

This view can be extended to a company's products. The degree to which a product's purchase is discretionary will affect the beta of the firm manufacturing the product. Firms whose products are much more discretionary to their customers—they can defer or delay buying these products—should have higher betas than firms whose products are viewed as necessary or less discretionary. Thus, the beta of Procter & Gamble, which sells diapers and daily household products, should be lower than the beta of Gucci, which manufactures luxury products.

Degree of Operating Leverage   The degree of operating leverage is a function of the cost structure of a firm and is usually defined in terms of the relationship between fixed costs and total costs. A firm that has high fixed costs relative to total costs is said to have high operating leverage. A firm with high operating leverage will also have higher variability in operating income than would a firm producing a similar product with low operating leverage. Other things remaining equal, the higher variance in operating income will lead to a higher beta for the firm with high operating leverage.

Can firms change their operating leverage? While some of a firm's cost structure is determined by the business it is in (an energy utility has to build expensive power plants, and airlines have to buy or lease expensive planes), firms in the United States have become increasingly inventive in lowering the fixed cost component in their total costs. For instance, firms have made cost structures more flexible by:

■ Negotiating labor contracts that emphasize flexibility and allow the firm to make its labor costs more sensitive to its financial success.
■ Entering into joint venture agreements, where the fixed costs are borne by someone else.
■ Subcontracting manufacturing and outsourcing, which reduce the need for expensive plant and equipment.

While the arguments for such actions may be couched in terms of offering competitive advantage and flexibility, they do also reduce the operating leverage of the firm and its exposure to market risk.

While operating leverage affects betas, it is difficult to measure the operating leverage of a firm, at least from the outside, since fixed and variable costs are often aggregated in income statements. It is possible to get an approximate measure of the operating leverage of a firm by looking at changes in operating income as a function of changes in sales.

Degree of operating leverage = % change in operating profit/% change in sales

For firms with high operating leverage, operating income should change more than proportionately when sales change.

SIZE, GROWTH, AND BETAS

Generally, smaller firms with higher growth potential are viewed as riskier than larger, more stable firms. While the rationale for this argument is clear when talking about total risk, it becomes more difficult to see when looking at market risk or betas. Should a smaller software firm have a higher beta than a larger software firm? One reason to believe that it should is operating leverage. If there is a setup cost associated with investing in infrastructure or economies of scale, smaller firms will have higher fixed costs than larger firms, leading in turn to higher betas for these firms.

   With growth firms, the argument for higher betas rests on the notion of discretionary versus nondiscretionary purchases. For a high-growth firm to deliver on its growth, new customers have to adopt the product or existing customers have to buy more of the product. Whether they do so will depend, in large part, on how well-off they feel. This, in turn, will make the profits of high-growth firms much more dependent on how well the economy is doing, thus increasing their betas.

Degree of Financial Leverage   Other things remaining equal, an increase in financial leverage will increase the beta of the equity in a firm. Intuitively, we would expect that the fixed interest payments on debt result in increasing income in good times and decreasing income in bad times. Higher leverage increases the variance in net income and makes equity investment in the firm riskier. If all the firm's risk is borne by the stockholders (i.e., the beta of debt is zero),[7] and debt has a tax benefit to the firm, then,

$$\beta_L = \beta_u[1 + (1 - t)(D/E)]$$

where β_L = Levered beta for equity in the firm
         β_u = Unlevered beta of the firm (i.e., the beta of the firm without any debt)
           t = Corporate tax rate
       D/E = Debt-to-equity ratio (market value)

Intuitively, we expect that as leverage increases (as measured by the debt-to-equity ratio), equity investors bear increasing amounts of market risk in the firm, leading to higher betas. The tax factor in the equation measures the tax deductibility of interest payments.

   The unlevered beta of a firm is determined by the types of the businesses in which

---

[7] This formula was originally developed by Hamada in 1972. There are two common modifications. One is to ignore the tax effects and compute the levered beta as:

$$\beta_L = \beta_u(1 + D/E)$$

If debt has market risk (i.e., its beta is greater than zero), the original formula can be modified to take this into account. If the beta of debt is β_D, the beta of equity can be written as:

$$\beta_L = \beta_u[1 + (1 - t)(D/E)] - \beta_D(1 - t)D/E$$

it operates and its operating leverage. It is often also referred to as the asset beta, since it is determined by the assets owned by the firm. Thus, the levered beta, which is also the beta for an equity investment in a firm, is determined both by the riskiness of the business it operates in by the amount of financial leverage risk it has taken on.

Since financial leverage multiplies the underlying business risk, it stands to reason that firms that have high business risk should be reluctant to take on financial leverage. It also stands to reason that firms that operate in stable businesses should be much more willing to take on financial leverage. Utilities, for instance, have historically had high debt ratios but have not had high betas, mostly because their underlying businesses have been stable and fairly predictable.

ILLUSTRATION 8.3: Effects of Leverage on Betas: Boeing

From the regression for the period from 1996 to 2000, Boeing had a historical beta of 0.56. Since this regression uses stock prices of Boeing over this period, we began by estimating the average debt-to-equity ratio between 1996 and 2000, using market values for debt and equity.

Average debt-to-equity ratio between 1996 and 2000 = 15.56%

The beta over the 1996–2000 period reflects this average leverage. To estimate the unlevered beta over the period, a marginal tax rate of 35% is used:

$$\text{Unlevered beta} = \text{Current beta} / [1 + (1 - \text{Tax rate})(\text{Average debt/Equity})]$$
$$= 0.56/[1 + (1 - 0.35)(0.1556)] = 0.51$$

The unlevered beta for Boeing over the 1996–2000 period is 0.51. The levered beta at different levels of debt can then be estimated:

$$\text{Levered beta} = \text{Unlevered beta} \times [1 + (1 - \text{Tax rate})(\text{Debt/Equity})]$$

For instance, if Boeing were to increase its debt equity ratio to 10%, its equity beta will be:

$$\text{Levered beta (@10\% D/E)} = 0.51 \times [1 + (1 - 0.35)(0.10)] = 0.543$$

If the debt equity ratio were raised to 25%, the equity beta would be:

$$\text{Levered beta (@25\% D/E)} = 0.51 \times [1 + (1 - 0.35)(0.25)] = 0.59$$

The following table summarizes the beta estimates for different levels of financial leverage ranging from 0% to 90% debt.

Debt to Capital	Debt/Equity Ratio	Beta	Effect of Leverage
0%	0.00%	0.51	0.00
10%	11.11%	0.55	0.04
20%	25.00%	0.59	0.08
30%	42.86%	0.65	0.14
40%	66.67%	0.73	0.22
50%	100.00%	0.84	0.33
60%	150.00%	1.00	0.50
70%	233.33%	1.28	0.77
80%	400.00%	1.83	1.32
90%	900.00%	3.48	2.98

As Boeing's financial leverage increases, the beta increases concurrently.

levbeta.xls. **This spreadsheet allows you to estimate the unlevered beta for a firm and compute the betas as a function of the leverage of the firm.**

Bottom-Up Betas   Breaking down betas into their business risk and financial leverage components provides us with an alternative way of estimating betas, in which we do not need past prices on an individual firm or asset to estimate its beta.

To develop this alternative approach, we need to introduce an additional property of betas that proves invaluable. The beta of two assets put together is a weighted average of the individual asset betas, with the weights based on market value. Consequently, the beta for a firm is a weighted average of the betas of all the different businesses it is in. We can estimate the beta for a firm in five steps:

Step 1: Identify the business or businesses the firm operates in.

Step 2: Find other publicly traded firms in each business and obtain their regression betas, which we use to compute an average beta for the firms.

Step 3: Estimate the average unlevered beta for the business by unlevering the average beta for the firms by their average debt to equity ratio. Alternatively, we could estimate the unlevered beta for each firm and then compute the average of the unlevered betas. The first approach is preferable because unlevering an erroneous regression beta is likely to compound the error.

$$\text{Unlevered beta}_{\text{business}} = \text{Beta}_{\text{comparable firms}}/[1 + (1 - t)(\text{D/E ratio}_{\text{comparable firms}})]$$

Step 4: Estimate an unlevered beta for the firm being analyzed, taking a weighted average of the unlevered betas for the businesses it operates in, using the proportion of firm value derived from each business as the weights. If values are not available, use operating income or revenues as weights. This weighted average is called the bottom-up unlevered beta.

$$\text{Unlevered beta}_{\text{firm}} = \sum_{j=1}^{j=k} \left(\text{Unlevered beta}_j \times \text{Value weight}_j \right)$$

where the firm is assumed to operating in k different businesses.

Step 5: Finally, estimate the current market values of debt and equity at the firm and use this debt to equity ratio to estimate a levered beta.

The betas estimated using this processs are called bottom-up betas.

The Case for Bottom-Up Betas   At first sight, the use of bottom-up betas may seem to leave us exposed to all of the problems noted with regression betas. After all, the betas for other publicly traded firms in the business are obtained from regressions. Notwithstanding this, bottom-up betas represent a significant improvement on regression betas for the following reasons:

- While each regression beta is estimated with standard error, the average across a number of regression betas has much lower standard error. The intuition is simple. A high standard error on a beta estimate indicates that it can be significantly higher or lower than the true beta. Averaging across these betas results in an average beta that is far more precise than the individual betas that went into it. In fact, if the estimation errors on individual firm betas are uncorrelated across firms, the savings in standard error can be stated as a function of the average standard error or beta estimates and the number of firms in the sample.

$$\text{Standard error}_{\text{bottom-up beta}} = \frac{\text{Average standard error}_{\text{comparable firms}}}{\sqrt{n}}$$

where n is the number of firms in the sample. Thus, if the average standard error in beta estimates for software firms is 0.50 and the number of software firms is 100, the standard error of the average beta is only 0.05 ($0.50/\sqrt{100}$).
- A bottom-up beta can be adapted to reflect actual changes in a firm's business mix and expected changes in the future. Thus if a firm divested a major portion of its operations last week, the weights on the businesses can be modified to reflect the divestiture. The same can be done with acquisitions. In fact, a firm's strategic plans to enter new businesses in the future can be brought into the beta estimates for future periods.
- Firms do change their debt ratios over time. While regression betas reflect the average debt-to-equity ratio maintained by the firm during the regression period, bottom-up betas use the current debt-to-equity ratio. If a firm plans to change its debt-to-equity ratio in the future, the beta can be adjusted to show these changes.
- Finally, bottom-up betas wean us from our dependence on historical stock prices. While we do need these prices to get betas for comparable firms, all we need for the firm being analyzed is a breakdown of the businesses it is in. Thus, bottom-up betas can be estimated for private firms, divisions of business, and stocks that have just started trading in financial markets.

Computational Details While the idea behind bottom-up betas is fairly simple, there are several computational details that are deserving of attention.

- *Defining comparable firms.* First, we have to decide how narrowly we want to define a business. Consider, for instance, a firm that manufactures entertainment software. We could define the business as entertainment software and consider only companies that primarily manufacture entertainment software to be comparable firms. We could go even further and define comparable firms as firms manufacturing entertainment software with revenues similar to that of the company being analyzed. While there are benefits to narrowing the comparable firm definition, there is a large cost. Each additional criterion added to the definition of "comparable" will mean that fewer firms make the list, and the savings in standard error that comprise the biggest benefit to bottom-up betas become smaller. A commonsense principle should therefore come into play. If there are hundreds of firms in a business, as there are in the software sector, you can afford to be more selective. If there are relatively few firms, not only do you have to become less selective, you might have to broaden the definition of comparable to bring other firms into the mix.

■ *Estimating betas.* Once the comparable firms in a business have been defined, you have to estimate the betas for these firms. Although it would be best to estimate the beta for each of these firms against a common and well-diversified equity index, it is usually easier to use service betas that are available for each of these firms. These service betas may be estimated against different indexes. For instance, if you define your business to be global telecommunications and obtain betas for global telecom firms from Bloomberg, these betas will be estimated against the local indexes. This is usually not a fatal problem, especially with large samples, since errors in the estimates tend to average out.

■ *Averaging method.* The average beta for the firms in the sector can be computed in one of three ways. We could use market-weighted averages, but the savings in standard error that touted in the earlier section will be muted, especially if there are one or two very large firms in the sample. We could estimate the simple average of the betas of the companies, thus weighting all betas equally. The process weighs in the smallest firms in the sample disproportionately (to their market value), but the savings in standard error are likely to be maximized.

■ *Controlling for differences.* In essence, when we use betas from comparable firms, we are assuming that all firms in the business are equally exposed to business risk and have similar operating leverage. Note that the process of levering and unlevering of betas allows us to control for differences in financial leverage. If there are significant differences in operating leverage—cost structure—across companies, the differences in operating leverage can be controlled for as well. This would require estimation of a business beta, where the effects of operating leverage are taken out from the unlevered beta:

$$\text{Business beta} = \text{Unlevered beta}/[1 + (\text{Fixed costs}/\text{Variable costs})]$$

Note the similarity to the adjustment for financial leverage; the only difference is that both fixed and variable costs are eligible for the tax deduction, and the tax rate is therefore no longer a factor. The business beta can then be relevered to reflect the differences in operating leverage across firms.

---

 betas.xls: **This dataset on the Web has updated betas and unlevered betas by business sector in the United States.**

ILLUSTRATION 8.4: Estimating a Bottom-Up Beta for Vans Shoes—January 2001

Vans Shoes is a shoe manufacturing firm with a market capitalization of $191 million. To estimate the bottom-up beta for Vans Shoes, consider the betas of all publicly traded shoe companies in the following table:

Company Name	Beta	Market D/E	Tax Rate	Fixed/Variable
Barry (R.G.)	1.00	40.51%	36.89%	75.66%
Brown Shoe	0.80	106.64%	37.06%	61.41%
Candie's Inc.	1.20	75.86%	0.00%	29.78%
Converse Inc.	0.60	653.46%	0.00%	39.64%
Deckers Outdoor Corp.	0.80	82.43%	0.00%	62.52%
Florsheim Group Inc.	0.65	96.79%	32.47%	79.03%
K-Swiss Inc.	0.65	0.69%	40.94%	56.92%
Kenneth Cole 'A'	1.05	0.29%	39.50%	56.97%
LaCrosse Footwear Inc.	0.55	81.15%	39.25%	30.36%
Maxwell Shoe Inc.	0.75	2.24%	33.28%	20.97%
Nike Inc. 'B'	0.90	9.47%	39.50%	46.07%
Reebok Int'l.	1.05	171.90%	32.28%	35.03%
Rocky Shoes & Boots Inc.	0.80	93.51%	0.00%	26.89%
Saucony Inc.	0.15	34.93%	31.11%	49.33%
Shoe Carnival	0.85	2.18%	39.97%	35.03%
Stride Rite Corp.	0.80	0.00%	36.80%	48.23%
Timberland Co. 'A'	1.10	15.23%	32.00%	49.50%
Vulcan Int'l.	0.65	3.38%	5.61%	11.92%
Wellco Enterprises Inc.	0.60	48.89%	0.00%	11.52%
Weyco Group	0.30	11.91%	35.74%	24.69%
Wolverine World Wide	1.35	44.37%	32.62%	32.31%
Average (Simple)	*0.79*	*75.04%*	*25.95%*	*42.08%*
Vans Shoes		*9.41%*	*34.06%*	*31.16%*

In addition to the betas for each firm, the table reports the market debt-to-equity ratio, the effective tax rate, and a measure of operating leverage obtained by dividing selling, general, and administrative (SG&A) expenses (which we consider fixed) by other operating expenses (which we consider variable). We can estimate the unlevered beta for the business using the averages for these values:

Average beta = 0.79

Average debt-to-equity ratio = 75.04%

Using the average tax rate of 25.95%, we can estimate the unlevered beta.

Unlevered beta = 0.79/[1 + (1 − .2595).7504] = .5081

The beta for Vans Shoes can then be obtained using the firm's tax rate of 34.06% and its market debt to equity ratio of 9.41%.

Levered beta$_{Vans}$ = 0.5081[1 + (1 − .3406).0941] = .5397

This levered beta is based on the implicit assumption that all shoe manufacturers have similar operating leverage. In fact, we could adjust the unlevered beta for the average fixed cost/variable cost ratio for the business and then relever back at the operating leverage for Vans Shoes:

Average fixed cost/Variable cost ratio = 42.08%

Business beta = Unlevered beta/(1 + Fixed costs/Variable costs)
= .5081/1.4208 = .3576

We can then use Vans' fixed cost to variable cost ratio of 31.16% to estimate an adjusted unlevered and levered beta.

$$\text{Unlevered beta}_{\text{Vans}} = 0.3576(1 + .3116) = .4691$$
$$\text{Levered beta} = .4691[1 + (1 - .3406).0941] = .4981$$

By having a debt-to-equity ratio and an operating leverage that is lower than the average for the industry, Vans Shoes ends up with a beta much lower than that of the industry.

ILLUSTRATION 8.5: Estimating a Bottom-Up Beta for Boeing—September 2000

Boeing has undergone a significant change in both its business mix and its financial leverage over the past five years. Not only did it acquire Rockwell and McDonnell Douglas, giving it a major foothold in the defense business, but it borrowed substantial amounts to make these acquisitions. Since these events have occurred over time, the historical regression beta does not fully reflect the effects of these changes. To estimate Boeing's beta today, we broke its business into two areas:

1. *Commercial aircraft*, which is Boeing's core business of manufacturing commercial jet aircraft and providing related support services.
2. *Information, space and defense systems (ISDS)*, which include research, development, production, and support of military aircraft, helicopters, and missile systems.

Each of these areas of business has very different risk characteristics, and the unlevered beta for each business was estimated by looking at comparable firms in each business. The following table summarizes these estimates.

Segment	Revenues	Value/Sales Ratio for Segment	Estimated Value	Unlevered Beta	Segment Weight	Weighted Beta
Commercial aircraft	$26,929	1.12	$30,160	0.91	70.39%	0.6405
ISDS	$18,125	0.70	$12,688	0.80	29.61%	0.2369
Boeing	$45,054		$42,848		100.00%	0.8774

For commercial aircraft there are no truly comparable firms. We looked at Boeing's own beta prior to its expansion in the defense business and computed the unlevered beta using this estimate. For ISDS, we used 17 firms that derived the bulk of their revenues from defense contracting, and computed the average beta and debt-to-equity ratio for these firms. The unlevered beta was computed using these averages. The values for each of the divisions were estimated using the revenues from each segment[8] and a typical revenue multiple[9] for that type of business. The unlevered beta for Boeing as a company in 2000 can be estimated by taking a value-weighted average of the betas of each of the different business areas. This is reported in the last column to be 0.8774.

The equity beta can then be estimated using the current financial leverage for Boeing as a firm. Combining the market value of equity of $55.20 billion and the value of debt of $7.85 billion, and using a 35% tax rate for the firm, we arrive at the current beta for Boeing.

$$\text{Equity beta for Boeing} = 0.8774[1 + (1 - .35)(7.85/55.2)] = 0.9585$$

This is very different from the historical beta of 0.56 that we obtained from the regression, but it is, in our view, a much truer reflection of the risk in Boeing.

---

[8]Note that Boeing breaks its business down in its financial statements into these two segments. We could have used operating income or EBITDA and a typical multiple to arrive at value.

[9]To estimate these multiples, we looked at the market value of publicly traded firms relative to their revenues. This is a ratio of enterprise value to revenues.

ILLUSTRATION 8.6:   Estimating a Bottom-Up Beta for Titan Cements—January 2000

To estimate a beta for Titan Cement, we began by defining comparable firms as other cement companies in Greece but found only one comparable firm. When we expanded the list to include cement companies across Europe, we increased our sample to nine firms. Since we did not see any reason to restrict our comparison to just European firms, we decided to look at the average beta for cement companies globally. There were 108 firms in this sample, with an average beta of 0.99, an average tax rate of 34.2%, and an average debt-to-equity ratio of 27.06%. We used these numbers to arrive at an unlevered beta of 0.84.

$$\text{Unlevered beta for cement companies} = 0.99/[1 + (1 - .342)(.2706)] = 0.84$$

We then used Titan's market values of equity (566.95 million Gdr) and debt (13.38 million Gdr) to estimate a levered beta for its equity:

$$\text{Levered beta} = 0.84 [1 + (1 - .2414)(13.38/566.95)] = 0.86$$

We used Titan's tax rate of 24.14% in this calculation.

HOW WELL DO BETAS TRAVEL?

Often, when analyzing firms in small or emerging markets, we have to estimate betas by looking at firms in the same business but traded on other markets. This is what we did when estimating the beta for Titan Cement. Is this appropriate? Should the beta for a steel company in the United States be comparable to that of a steel company in Indonesia? We see no reason why it should not be. But the company in Indonesia has much more risk, you might argue. We do not disagree, but the fact that we use similar betas does not mean that we believe that the costs of equity are identical across all steel companies. In fact, using the approach described in the preceding chapter, the risk premium used to estimate the cost of equity for the Indonesian company will incorporate a country risk premium, whereas the cost of equity for the U.S. company will not. Thus, even if the betas used for the two companies are identical, the cost of equity for the Indonesian company will be much higher.

There are a few exceptions to this proposition. Recall that one of the key determinants of betas is the degree to which a product or service is discretionary. It is entirely possible that products or services that are discretionary in one market (and command high betas) may be nondiscretionary in another market (and have low betas). For instance, phone service is viewed as a nondiscretionary product in most developing markets, but is a discretionary product in emerging markets. Consequently, the average beta estimated by looking at telecom firms in developed markets will understate the true beta of a telecom firm in an emerging market. For the latter beta, the comparable firms should be restricted to include only telecom firms in emerging markets.

Calculating Betas after a Major Restructuring   The bottom-up process of estimating betas provides a solution when firms go through major restructurings that change both their business mix and their leverage. In these cases, the regression betas are misleading because they do not reflect fully the effects of these changes. Boeing's beta estimated using the bottom-up approach is likely to provide a more precise estimate than the historical beta from a regression of Boeing's stock prices, given Boeing's acquisitions of Rockwell and McDonnell Douglas and its increase in leverage. In fact, a firm's beta can be estimated using the bottom-up approach even before the restructuring becomes effective. Illustration 8.7, for instance, estimates Boeing's beta just before and after its acquisition of McDonnell Douglas, allowing for the changes in both the business mix and the leverage.

ILLUSTRATION 8.7:   Beta of a Firm after an Acquisition: Boeing and McDonnell Douglas

---

In 1997, Boeing announced that it was acquiring McDonnell Douglas, another company involved in the aerospace and defense business. At the time of the acquisition, the two firms had the following market values and betas:

Company	Beta	Debt	Equity	Firm Value
Boeing	0.95	$3,980	$32,438	$36,418
McDonnell Douglas	0.90	$2,143	$12,555	$14,698

Note that the market values of equity used for the two firms reflect the market values after the acquisition announcement and reflect the acquisition price agreed on for McDonnell Douglas shares.

In order to evaluate the effects of the acquisition on Boeing's beta, we first examine the effects of the merger on the business risk of the combined firm by estimating the unlevered betas of the two companies and calculating the combined firm's unlevered beta.

$$\text{Boeing's unlevered beta} = 0.95/[1 + (1 - .35) \times (3,980/32,438)] = 0.88$$
$$\text{McDonnell Douglas' unlevered beta} = 0.90/[1 + (1 - .35) \times (2,143/12,555)] = 0.81$$

The unlevered beta for the combined firm can be calculated as the weighted average of the two unlevered betas, with the weights based on the market values of the two firms.

$$\text{Unlevered beta for combined firm} = 0.88(36,418/51,116) + 0.81(14,698/51,116)$$
$$= 0.86$$

Boeing's acquisition of McDonnell Douglas was accomplished by issuing new stock in Boeing to cover the value of McDonnell Douglas' equity of $12,555 million. Since no new debt was used to finance the deal, the debt outstanding in the firm after the acquisition is just the sum of the debt outstanding at the two companies before the acquisition.

$$\text{Debt} = \text{McDonnell Douglas' old debt} + \text{Boeing's old debt}$$
$$= \$3,980 + \$2,143 = \$6,123 \text{ million}$$

$$\text{Equity} = \text{Boeing's old equity} + \text{New equity used for acquisition}$$
$$= \$32,438 + \$12,555 = \$44,993 \text{ million}$$

The debt/equity ratio can then be computed as follows:

$$\text{D/E ratio} = 6,123/44,993 = 13.61\%$$

This debt/equity ratio in conjunction with the new unlevered beta for the combined firm yields a new beta of:

$$\text{New beta} = 0.86[1 + (1 - .35)(.1361)] = 0.94$$

Accounting Betas   A third approach is to estimate the market risk parameters from accounting earnings rather than from traded prices. Thus, changes in earnings at a division or a firm, on a quarterly or an annual basis, can be related to changes in earnings for the market, in the same periods, to arrive at an estimate of a accounting beta to use in the CAPM. While the approach has some intuitive appeal, it suffers from three potential pitfalls. First, accounting earnings tend to be smoothed out relative to the underlying value of the company, as accountants spread expenses and income over multiple periods. This results in betas that are "biased down," especially for risky firms, or "biased up" for safer firms. In other words, betas are likely to be closer to 1 for all firms using accounting data.

Second, accounting earnings can be influenced by nonoperating factors, such as changes in depreciation or inventory methods, and by allocations of corporate expenses at the divisional level. Finally, accounting earnings are measured, at most, once every quarter, and often only once every year, resulting in regressions with few observations and not much explanatory power (low R-squared, high standard errors).

ILLUSTRATION 8.8:   Estimating Accounting Betas: Defense Division of Boeing—1995

Having operated in the defense business for decades, Boeing has a record of its profitability. These profits are reported in the following table, together with earnings changes for companies in the S&P 500 going back to 1980.

Year	S&P 500	Boeing's Defense Business
1980	−2.10%	−12.70%
1981	−6.70%	−35.56%
1982	−45.50%	27.59%
1983	37.00%	159.36%
1984	41.80%	13.11%
1985	−11.80%	−26.81%
1986	7.00%	−16.83%
1987	41.50%	20.24%
1988	41.80%	18.81%
1989	2.60%	−29.70%
1990	−18.00%	−40.00%
1991	−47.40%	−35.00%
1992	64.50%	10.00%
1993	20.00%	−7.00%
1994	25.30%	11.00%

Regressing the changes in profits in the defense division ($\Delta \text{Earnings}_{defense}$) against changes in profits for the S&P 500 ($\Delta \text{Earnings}_{S\&P}$) yields the following:

$$\Delta \text{Earnings}_{defense} = -0.03 + 0.65 \, \Delta \text{Earnings}_{S\&P}$$

Based on this regression, the beta for the defense division is 0.65.

---

 accbeta.xls: **This spreadsheet allows you to estimate the accounting beta on a division or firm.**

spearn.xls: This dataset on the Web has earnings changes, by year, for the S&P 500 going back to 1960.

Market, Bottom-Up, and Accounting Betas: Which One Do We Use?   For most publicly traded firms, betas can be estimated using accounting data or market data or from the bottom-up approach. Since the betas will almost never be the same, using these different approaches, the question is, which one do we use? We would almost never use accounting betas, for all the reasons specified earlier. We are almost as reluctant to use historical market betas for individual firms because of the standard errors in beta estimates, the failures of the local indexes (as is the case with most emerging market companies) and the inability of these regressions to reflect the effects of major changes in the business mix and financial risk at the firm. Bottom-up betas, in our view, provide us with the best beta estimates for three reasons:

1. They allow us to consider changes in business and financial mix, even before they occur.
2. They use average betas across large numbers of firms, which tend to be less noisy than individual firm betas.
3. They allow us to calculate betas by area of business for a firm, which is useful both in the context of investment analysis and in valuation.

Measuring Country Risk Exposure (Lambda)   Chapter 7 introduced the concept of country risk exposure and the notion of lambda—a measure of a company's exposure to country risk. In this section, we would like to consider intuitively what factors determine this exposure and how best to estimate lambda. A company's exposure to country risk is affected by almost every aspect of its operations, beginning with where its factories are located and who its customers are and continuing with what currency its contracts are denominated in and how well it manages its exposure to exchange rate risk. Much of this information, however, is internal information and not available to someone valuing the firm from the outside. As a practical matter, then, we can estimate lambda using one of the following approaches:

- *Revenue breakdown.* The simplest way of estimating lambda is to use the proportion of a firm's revenues that are generated in a country and scale this to the proportion of the revenues generated by the average firm in that country.

$$\lambda = \frac{\text{Proportion of revenues in country}_{\text{firm}}}{\text{Proportion of revenues in country}_{\text{average firm}}}$$

  Thus, a firm that generates only 40 percent of its revenues in Indonesia when the average firm in Indonesia generates 80 percent of its revenues domestically will have a lambda of 0.5 for Indonesian country risk. Note, though, that if the remaining 60 percent of its revenues are in Thailand, you would have to estimate a lambda for Thai country risk and add that component to the cost of equity.
- *Regression versus country bond.* A second approach to estimating lambdas would be to run regressions of stock returns for each firm in the emerging market against the returns on the country bond. In Brazil, for instance, this would involve regressing returns on each Brazilian stock against returns on the Brazilian country bond (the C-bond). The slope of this regression should measure

how sensitive a stock is to changes in country risk (since country bond returns are direct measures of country risk) and thus yield a measure of lambda. For instance, assuming that regressing Embraer's stock returns against returns on the C-bond yields a slope of 0.30 and that the average slope across all Brazilian stocks is 0.75, the lambda would be 0.40 (0.30/0.75).

From Betas to Cost of Equity

Having estimated the riskless rate and the risk premium(s) in Chapter 7 and the beta(s) in this chapter, we can now estimate the expected return from investing in equity at any firm. In the CAPM, this expected return can be written as:

$$\text{Expected return} = \text{Riskless rate} + \text{Beta} \times \text{Expected risk premium}$$

where the riskless rate would be the rate on a long-term government bond, the beta would be either the historical, fundamental, or accounting betas described earlier, and the risk premium would be either the historical premium or an implied premium.

In the arbitrage pricing and multifactor model, the expected return would be written as follows:

$$\text{Expected return} = \text{Riskless rate} + \sum_{j-1}^{j=n} \beta_j \times \text{Risk premium}_j$$

where the riskless rate is the long-term government bond rate; β_j is the beta relative to factor j, estimated using historical data or fundamentals; and risk premium$_j$ is the risk premium relative to factor j, estimated using historical data.

The expected return on an equity investment in a firm, given its risk, has strong implications for both equity investors in the firm and the managers of the firm. For equity investors, it is the rate they need to earn to be compensated for the risk they have taken in investing in the equity of the firm. If, after analyzing an investment, they conclude they cannot make this return, they would not buy this investment; alternatively, if they decide they can make a higher return, they would make the investment. For managers in the firm, the return investors need to make to break even on their equity investments becomes the return they have to try to deliver to keep these investors from becoming restive and rebellious. Thus, it becomes the rate they have to beat in terms of returns on their equity investments in projects. In other words, this is the cost of equity to the firm.

ILLUSTRATION 8.9:   Estimating the Cost of Equity for Boeing—December 2000

Now that we have an estimate of beta of 0.9585 for Boeing, based on the bottom-up estimates, we can estimate its cost of equity. To make the estimate, we used the prevailing Treasury bond rate of 5% and a historical risk premium of 5.51%.

$$\text{Cost of equity} = 5.00\% + 0.9585(5.51\%) = 10.28\%$$

There are two points making about this estimate. The first is that the cost of equity would have been significantly lower if we had chosen to use the implied equity premium on December 31, 2000, which was about 2.87% (see Chapter 7).

$$\text{Cost of equity} = 5.00\% + 0.9585(2.87\%) = 7.75\%$$

The second point is that we are not considering the exposure that Boeing has to emerging market risk from its business. If the exposure is significant, we should be adding a country risk premium to the cost of equity estimate.

ILLUSTRATION 8.10:   Estimating the Cost of Equity for Embraer—March 2001

Embraer is a Brazilian aerospace firm. To estimate its cost of equity, we first estimated the unlevered beta by looking at aerospace firms globally.

Unlevered beta for aerospace firms = 0.87

Embraer's debt-to-equity ratio at the time of this analysis was 2.45%,[10] resulting in a levered beta for Embraer:

Levered beta for Embraer = 0.87[1 + (1 − .33).0245] = 0.88

To estimate the cost of equity for Embraer in U.S. dollar terms, we began with the Treasury bond rate of 5% at the time of the analysis, but incorporated the country risk associated with Brazil into the risk premium. Using the approach described in Chapter 7, we estimated a country risk premium of 10.24% in March 2001. In conjunction with a mature market risk premium of 5.51% estimated for the United States, this yields a cost of equity of 18.93%.

Cost of equity for Embraer = 5% + 0.88(5.51% + 10.24%) = 18.86%

Again, there are several points that are worth making on this estimate. The first is that this cost of equity can be expected to change over time as Brazil matures as a market and country risk declines. The second is that we have assumed that betas measure exposure to country risk. A company like Embraer that derives the bulk of its revenues outside Brazil could argue that it is less exposed to country risk. We could have derived λ as a measure of exposure to country risk for Embraer by looking at the proportion of its revenues that it derives in Brazil and comparing it to the proportion of revenues derived by a typical company in Brazil. In 2000, for instance, this would have yielded the following:

$$\lambda_{Embraer} = \frac{\text{Proportion of revenues from Brazil}_{Embraer}}{\text{Proportion of revenues from Brazil}_{typical\ Brazilian\ firm}} = \frac{9\%}{60\%} = 0.15$$

Using this measure of exposure to country risk, Embraer would have had a much lower cost of equity.

Cost of equity in U.S. dollars = Risk-free rate + Beta(Mature market risk premium)
+ λ(Country risk premium)
= 5% + 0.88(5.51%) + 0.15(10.24%) = 11.39%

The final point is that the cost of equity in dollar terms can be converted into a nominal Brazilian real (BR) cost of equity fairly simply by considering the differences in expected inflation rates in Brazil and the United States. For instance, if the expected inflation rate in Brazil is 10% and the expected inflation rate in the United States is 2%, the cost of equity in nominal BR is as follows:

Cost of equity$_{nominal\ BR}$ = (1 + Cost of equity$_\$$)(Inflation rate$_{Brazil}$/Inflation rate$_{U.S.}$) − 1
= (1.1139)(1.10/1.02) − 1 = 20.12%

Implicitly, we assume that real risk-free rates around that world are the same with this approach and that the risk premium scales up with inflation as well. The alternative is to estimate a cost of equity from scratch, beginning with a nominal BR risk-free rate (which was 14% at the time of this analysis) and adding the premiums from before:

Cost of equity$_{nominal\ BR}$ = Risk-free rate + Beta(Mature market risk premium)
+ λ(Country risk premium)
= 14% + 0.88(5.51%) + 0.15(10.24%) = 20.39%

Substituting in a real risk-free rate in the equation would yield a real cost of equity.

---

[10]We used net debt (the difference between gross debt and cash) in making this estimate. We discuss later in the chapter when this practice is appropriate and when it is not.

COST OF EQUITY AND A SMALL FIRM PREMIUM

Chapter 6 presented evidence of a small firm premium—small market-cap stocks earn higher returns than large market-cap stocks with equivalent betas. The magnitude and persistence of the small firm premium can be viewed as evidence that the capital asset pricing model understates the risk of smaller companies, and that a cost of equity based purely on a CAPM beta will therefore yield too low a number for these firms. There are some analysts who argue that you should therefore add a premium to the estimated cost of equity for smaller firms. Since small cap stocks have earned about 2 percent more than large cap stocks over the past few decades, you could consider this a reasonable estimate for the small firm premium. To estimate the cost of equity for a small cap stock with a beta of 1.2 (assuming a risk-free rate of 5.1 percent and a market risk premium of 4 percent), for instance, you would do the following:

$$\begin{aligned}
\text{Cost of equity for small cap stock} &= \text{Risk-free rate} + \text{Beta} \\
&\quad \times \text{Market risk premium} \\
&\quad + \text{Small cap premium} \\
&= 5.1\% + 1.2 \times 4\% + 2\% \\
&= 11.9\%
\end{aligned}$$

We would introduce two notes of caution with this approach. First, it opens the door to a series of adjustments that you could make to the cost of equity, reflecting the numerous inefficiencies cited in Chapter 6. For instance, you could estimate a low PE premium, a low price-to-book premium, and a high dividend yield premium and add them all to the cost of equity. If our objective in valuation is to uncover market mistakes, it would be a mistake to start off with the presumption that markets are right in their assessments in the first place. Second, a better way of considering the small firm premium would be to identify the reasons for the premium and then develop more direct measures of risk. For instance, assume that the higher risk of small cap stocks comes from the higher operating leverage that these firms have, relative to their larger competitors. You could adjust the betas for operating leverage (as we did a few pages ago for Vans Shoes) and use the higher betas for small firms.

FROM COST OF EQUITY TO COST OF CAPITAL

While equity is undoubtedly an important and indispensable ingredient of the financing mix for every business, it is but one ingredient. Most businesses finance some or much of their operations using debt or some security that is a combination of equity and debt. The costs of these sources of financing are generally very different from the cost of equity, and the cost of financing for a firm should reflect their costs as well, in proportion to their use in the financing mix. Intuitively, the cost of capital is the weighted average of the costs of the different components of financing—including debt, equity, and hybrid securities—used by a firm to fund its financial requirements. This section examines the process of estimating the cost of financing other than equity, and the weights for computing the cost of capital.

Calculating the Cost of Debt

The cost of debt measures the current cost to the firm of borrowing funds to finance projects. In general terms, it is determined by the following variables:

- *The riskless rate.* As the riskless rate increases, the cost of debt for firms will also increase.
- *The default risk (and associated default spread) of the company.* As the default risk of a firm increases, the cost of borrowing money will also increase. Chapter 7 looked at how the default spread has varied across time and can vary across maturity.
- *The tax advantage associated with debt.* Since interest is tax deductible, the after-tax cost of debt is a function of the tax rate. The tax benefit that accrues from paying interest makes the after-tax cost of debt lower than the pretax cost. Furthermore, this benefit increases as the tax rate increases.

$$\text{After-tax cost of debt} = \text{Pretax cost of debt}(1 - \text{Tax rate})$$

This section will focus on how best to estimate the default risk in a firm and to convert that default risk into a default spread that can be used to come up with a cost of debt.

Estimating the Default Risk and Default Spread of a Firm The simplest scenario for estimating the cost of debt occurs when a firm has long-term bonds outstanding that are widely traded. The market price of the bond in conjunction with its coupon and maturity can serve to compute a yield that is used as the cost of debt. For instance, this approach works for a firm like AT&T that has dozens of outstanding bonds that are liquid and trade frequently.

Many firms have bonds outstanding that do not trade on a regular basis. Since these firms are usually rated, we can estimate their costs of debt by using their ratings and associated default spreads. Thus, Boeing with an AA rating can be expected to have a cost of debt approximately 1.00 percent higher than the Treasury bond rate, since this is the spread typically paid by AA-rated firms.

Some companies choose not to get rated. Many smaller firms and most private businesses fall into this category. While ratings agencies have sprung up in many emerging markets, there are still a number of markets where companies are not rated on the basis of default risk. When there is no rating available to estimate the cost of debt, there are two alternatives:

1. *Recent borrowing history.* Many firms that are not rated still borrow money from banks and other financial institutions. By looking at the most recent borrowings made by a firm, we can get a sense of the types of default spreads being charged the firm and use these spreads to come up with a cost of debt.
2. *Estimate a synthetic rating.* An alternative is to play the role of a ratings agency and assign a rating to a firm based on its financial ratios; this rating is called a synthetic rating. To make this assessment, we begin with rated firms and examine the financial characteristics shared by firms within each ratings class. To illustrate, Table 8.1 lists the range of interest coverage ratios for small manufacturing firms in each S&P ratings class.[11]

---

[11]This table was developed in early 2001 by listing out all rated firms with market capitalization lower than $2 billion and their interest coverage ratios, and then sorting firms based on their bond ratings. The ranges were adjusted to eliminate outliers and to prevent overlapping ranges.

TABLE 8.1 Interest Coverage Ratios and Ratings: Low-Market-Cap Firms

Interest Coverage Ratio	Rating	Spread
More than 12.5	AAA	0.75%
9.5 to 12.5	AA	1.00%
7.5 to 9.5	A+	1.50%
6 to 7.5	A	1.80%
4.5 to 6	A-	2.00%
3.5 to 4.5	BBB	2.25%
3 to 3.5	BB	3.50%
2.5 to 3	B+	4.75%
2 to 2.5	B	6.50%
1.5 to 2	B-	8.00%
1.25 to 1.5	CCC	10.00%
0.8 to 1.25	CC	11.50%
0.5 to 0.8	C	12.70%
Less than 0.5	D	14.00%

Source for raw data: Compustat.

Now consider a small firm that is not rated but has an interest coverage ratio of 6.15. Based on this ratio, a synthetic rating of A would be assessed for the firm.

The interest coverage ratios tend to be lower for larger firms for any given rating. Table 8.2 summarizes these ratios.

This approach can be expanded to allow for multiple ratios and qualitative

TABLE 8.2 Interest Coverage Ratios and Ratings: High-Market-Cap Firms

Interest Coverage Ratio	Rating	Spread
More than 8.5	AAA	0.75%
6.5 to 8.5	AA	1.00%
5.5 to 6.5	A+	1.50%
4.25 to 5.5	A	1.80%
3 to 4.25	A-	2.00%
2.5 to 3	BBB	2.25%
2 to 2.5	BB	3.50%
1.75 to 2	B+	4.75%
1.5 to 1.75	B	6.50%
1.25 to 1.5	B-	8.00%
0.8 to 1.25	CCC	10.00%
0.65 to 0.8	CC	11.50%
0.2 to 0.65	C	12.70%
Less than 0.2	D	14.00%

Source: Compustat.

EXTENDING THE SYNTHETIC RATINGS APPROACH

By basing the rating on the interest coverage ratio alone, we run the risk of missing the information that is available in the other financial ratios used by ratings agencies. The approach can be extended to incorporate other ratios. The first step would be to develop a score based on multiple ratios. For instance, the Altman Z score, which is used as a proxy for default risk, is a function of five financial ratios that are weighted to generate a Z score. The ratios used and their relative weights are usually based on empirical evidence on past defaults. The second step is to relate the level of the score to a bond rating, much as is done in Tables 8.1 and 8.2 with interest coverage ratios.

In making this extension, though, note that complexity comes at a cost. While credit or Z scores may, in fact, yield better estimates of synthetic ratings than those based on interest coverage ratios, changes in ratings arising from these scores are much more difficult to explain than those based on interest coverage ratios. That is a reason to prefer the flawed but simpler ratings derived from interest coverage ratios.

---

variables as well. Once a synthetic rating is assessed, it can be used to estimate a default spread which when added to the risk-free rate yields a pretax cost of debt for the firm.

Estimating a Tax Rate To estimate the after-tax cost of debt, consider the fact that interest expenses are tax deductible to the firm. While the computation is fairly simple and requires that the pretax cost be multiplied by (1 – Tax rate), the question of what tax rate to use can be a difficult one to answer because there are so many choices. For instance, firms often report an effective tax rate, estimated by dividing the taxes due by the taxable income. The effective tax rate, though, is usually very different from the marginal tax rate, which is the rate at which the last dollar of income is taxed. Since interest expenses save you taxes at the margin (they are deducted from your last dollar of income), the right tax rate to use is the marginal tax rate.

The other caveat to keep in mind is that interest creates a tax benefit only if a firm has enough income to cover the interest expenses. Firms that have operating losses will not get a tax benefit from interest expenses, at least in the year of the loss. The after-tax cost of debt will be equal to the pretax cost of debt in that year. If you expect the firm to make money in future years, you would need to adjust the after-tax cost of debt for taxes in those years.

The book will return to this issue and examine it in more detail in Chapter 10, where we look at the same issue in the context of estimating after-tax cash flows.

ILLUSTRATION 8.11:   Estimating the Cost of Debt: Boeing in December 2000

Boeing is rated AA by S&P. Using the typical default spreads for AA-rated firms, we could estimate the pretax cost for Boeing by adding the default spread of 1.00%[12] to the riskless rate of 5%.

$$\text{Pretax cost of debt}_{\text{actual rating}} = 5\% + 1\% = 6\%$$

Boeing has an effective tax rate of 27%, but we use a marginal tax rate of 35%, which is the federal marginal corporate tax rate in the United States, to estimate the after-tax cost of debt for Boeing.

$$\text{After-tax cost of debt} = 6.00\%(1 - .35) = 3.90\%$$

We could also compute a synthetic rating for Boeing based on its interest coverage ratio from 1999. Based on its operating income of $1,720 million in 1999 and interest expense of $453 million in that year, we would have estimated an interest coverage ratio:

$$\text{Interest coverage ratio}_{\text{Boeing}} = 1,720/453 = 3.8$$

Using Table 8.2, we would have assigned a synthetic rating of A– to Boeing. Based on default spreads prevailing in December 2000, this would have resulted in a default spread of 2.00% and a pretax cost of debt of 7.00% for the firm.

Estimating the Cost of Debt for an Emerging Market Firm   In general, there are three problems that we run into when assessing the cost of debt for emerging market firms. The first is that most of these firms are not rated, leaving us with no option but to estimate the synthetic rating (and associated costs). The second is that the synthetic ratings may be skewed by differences in interest rates between the emerging market and the United States. Interest coverage ratios will usually decline as interest rates increase and it may be far more difficult for a company in an emerging market to achieve the interest coverage ratios of companies in developed markets. Finally, the existence of country default risk hangs over the cost of debt of firms in that market.

The second problem can be fixed fairly simply by either modifying the tables developed using U.S. firms or restating the interest expenses (and interest coverage ratios) in dollar terms. The question of country risk is a thornier one. Conservative analysts often assume that companies in a country cannot borrow at a rate lower than the country itself can borrow at. With this reasoning, the cost of debt for an emerging market company will include the country default spread for the country.

$$\text{Cost of debt}_{\text{emerging market company}} = \text{Riskless rate} + \text{Country default spread}_{\text{emerging market}}$$
$$+ \text{Company default spread}_{\text{synthetic rating}}$$

The counter to this argument is that companies may be safer than the countries in which they operate, and that they bear only a portion or perhaps even none of the country default spread.

---

[12]The default spread was obtained from Table 8.2.

ILLUSTRATION 8.12:   Estimating the Cost of Debt: Embraer in March 2001

To estimate Embraer's cost of debt, we first estimated a synthetic rating for the firm. Based on its operating income of $810 million and interest expenses of $28 million in 2000, we arrived at an interest coverage ratio of 28.73 and an AAA rating. While the default spread for AAA-rated bonds was only 0.75% at the time, there is the added consideration that Embraer is a Brazilian firm. Since the Brazilian dollar-denominated government bond had a default spread of 5.37% at the time of the analysis, you could argue that every Brazilian company should pay this premium in addition to its own default spread. With this reasoning, the pretax cost of debt for Embraer in U.S. dollars (assuming a Treasury bond rate is 5%) can be calculated:

$$\text{Cost of debt} = \text{Risk-free rate} + \text{Default spread for country} + \text{Default spread for firm}$$
$$= 5\% + 5.37\% + 0.75\% = 11.12\%$$

Using a marginal tax rate of 33%, we can estimate an after-tax cost of debt for Embraer:

$$\text{After-tax cost of debt} = 11.12\%(1 - .33) = 7.45\%$$

With this approach, the cost of debt for a firm can never be lower than the cost of debt for the country in which it operates. Note, though, that Embraer gets a significant portion of its revenues in dollars from contracts with non-Brazilian airlines. Consequently, it could reasonably argue that it is less exposed to risk than is the Brazilian government and should therefore command a lower cost of debt.

 ratings.xls: This spreadsheet allows you to estimate the synthetic rating and cost of debt for any firm.

Calculating the Cost of Hybrid Securities

While debt and equity represent the fundamental financing choices available for firms, there are some types of financing that share characteristics with both debt and equity. These are called hybrid securities. This section considers how best to estimate the costs of such securities.

Cost of Preferred Stock   Preferred stock shares some of the characteristics of debt (the preferred dividend is prespecified at the time of the issue and is paid out before common dividend) and some of the characteristics of equity (the preferred dividend is not tax deductible). If preferred stock is viewed as perpetual (as it usually is), the cost of preferred stock can be written as follows:

$$k_{ps} = \text{Preferred dividend per share/Market price per preferred share}$$

This approach assumes the dividend is constant in dollar terms forever and that the preferred stock has no special features (convertibility, callability, etc.). If such special features exist, they will have to be valued separately to estimate the cost of preferred stock. In terms of risk, preferred stock is safer than common equity, because preferred dividends are paid before dividends on common equity. It is, however, riskier than debt since interest payments are made prior to preferred dividend payments. Consequently, on a pretax basis, it should command a higher cost than debt and a lower cost than equity.

ILLUSTRATION 8.13: **Calculating the Cost of Preferred Stock: General Motors**

In March 1995, General Motors had preferred stock that paid a dividend of $2.28 annually and traded at $26.38 per share. The cost of preferred stock can be estimated as follows:

Cost of preferred stock = Preferred dividend per share/Preferred stock price = $2.28/$26.38 = 8.64%

At the same time, GM's cost of equity, using the CAPM, was 13%, its pretax cost of debt was 8.25%, and its after-tax cost of debt was 5.28%. Not surprisingly, its preferred stock was less expensive than equity, but much more expensive than debt.

Calculating the Cost of Other Hybrid Securities A convertible bond is a bond that can be converted into equity at the option of the bondholder. A convertible bond can be viewed as a combination of a straight bond (debt) and a conversion option (equity). Instead of trying to calculate the cost of these hybrid securities individually, we can break down hybrid securities into their debt and equity components and treat the components separately.

ILLUSTRATION 8.14: **Breaking Down a Convertible Bond into Debt and Equity Components: Amazon.com, Inc.**

In 1999, Amazon.com, Inc., the online retailer, issued convertible bonds with a coupon rate of 4.75% and a 10-year maturity. Since the firm was losing money, it was rated CCC+ by S&P and would have had to pay 11% if it had issued straight bonds at the same time. The bonds were issued at a price that was 98% of par, and the total par value of the convertible bond issue was $1.25 billion. The convertible bond can be broken down into straight bond and conversion option components.

Straight bond component = Value of a straight 4.75% coupon bond due in 10 years
with 11% interest rate
= $636 (assuming semiannual coupons)

Conversion option = $980 − $636 = $344

The straight bond component of $636 is treated as debt, and has the same cost as the rest of debt. The conversion option of $344 is treated as equity, with the same cost of equity as other equity issued by the firm. For the entire bond issue of $1.25 billion, the value of debt is $811 million, and the value of equity is $439 million.

Calculating the Weights of Debt and Equity Components

Now that we have the costs of debt, equity, and hybrid securities, we have to estimate the weights that should be attached to each. Before we discuss how best to estimate weights, we define what we include in debt. We then make the argument that weights used should be based on market value and not book value. This is so because the cost of capital measures the cost of issuing securities—stocks as well as bonds—to finance projects, and these securities are issued at market value, not at book value.

What Is Debt?   The answer to this question may seem obvious since the balance sheet for a firm shows the outstanding liabilities of a firm. There are, however, limitations with using these liabilities as debt in the cost of capital computation. The first is that some of the liabilities on a firm's balance sheet, such as accounts payable and supplier credit, are not interest-bearing. Consequently, applying an after-tax cost of debt to these items can provide a misleading view of the true cost of capital for a firm. The second is that there are items off the balance sheet that create fixed commitments for the firm and provide the same tax deductions that interest payments on debt do. The most prominent of these off-balance sheet items are operating leases. Chapter 3 contrasted operating and capital leases and noted that operating leases are treated as operating expenses rather than financing expenses. Consider, though, what an operating lease involves. A retail firm leases a store space for 12 years and enters into a lease agreement with the owner of the space agreeing to pay a fixed amount each year for that period. We do not see much difference between this commitment and borrowing money from a bank and agreeing to pay off the bank loan over 12 years in equal annual installments.

There are therefore two adjustments we will make when we estimate how much debt a firm has outstanding.

1. We will consider only interest-bearing debt rather than all liabilities. We would include both short-term and long-term borrowings in debt.
2. We will also capitalize operating leases and treat them as debt.

Capitalizing Operating Leases   Converting operating lease expenses into a debt equivalent is straightforward. The operating lease commitments in future years, which are revealed in the footnotes to the financial statements for U.S. firms, should be discounted back at a rate that reflects their status as unsecured and fairly risky debt. As an approximation, using the firm's current pretax cost of borrowing as the discount rate yields a good estimate of the value of operating leases.

Outside the United States, firms do not have to reveal their operating lease commitments in future periods. When this is the case, you can get a reasonably close estimate of the debt value of operating leases by estimating the present value of an annuity equal to the current year's payment for a period that reflects a typical lease period (8 to 10 years).

There is one final issue relating to capitalization. Earlier in this chapter it was stated that the interest coverage ratio could be used to estimate a synthetic rating for a firm that is not rated. For firms with little in terms of conventional debt and substantial operating leases, the interest coverage ratio used to estimate a synthetic rating has to be adapted to include operating lease expenses.

Modified interest coverage ratio = (EBIT + Current year's operating lease expense)
/(Interest expenses
+ Current year's operating lease expense)

This ratio can then be used in conjunction with Tables 8.1 and 8.2 to estimate a synthetic rating.

ILLUSTRATION 8.15:   The Debt Value of Operating Leases: Boeing in December 2000

Boeing has both conventional debt and operating lease commitments. This illustration will estimate the "debt value" of Boeing's operating leases by taking the present value of operating lease expenses over time. To compute the present value of operating leases in the following table (in $millions), we use the pretax cost of borrowing for the firm, estimated in Illustration 8.11 to be 6%.

Year	Operating Lease Expense	Present Value at 6%
1	$205	$193.40
2	$167	$146.83
3	$120	$100.75
4	$ 86	$ 68.12
5	$ 61	$ 45.58
6 to15	$ —	$ 0.00
Present value of operating lease expenses		$556.48

Thus, Boeing has $556 million more in debt than is reported in the balance sheet.

 Oplease.xls: This spreadsheet allows you to convert operating lease expenses into debt.

Book Value versus Market Value Debt Ratios   There are three standard arguments against using market value, and none of them is convincing. First, there are some financial managers who argue that book value is more reliable than market value because it is not as volatile. While it is true that book value does not change as much as market value, this is more a reflection of book value's weakness rather than its strength, since the true value of the firm changes over time as both firm-specific and market information is revealed. We would argue that market value, with its volatility, is a much better reflection of true value than is book value.[13]

Second, the defenders of book value also suggest that using book value rather than market value is a more conservative approach to estimating debt ratios. This assumes that market value debt ratios are always lower than book value debt ratios, an assumption not based on fact. Furthermore, even if the market value debt ratios are lower than the book value ratios, the cost of capital calculated using book value ratios will be lower than those calculated using market value ratios, making them less conservative estimates, not more. To illustrate this point, assume that the market value debt ratio is 10 percent, while the book value debt ratio is 30 percent, for a firm with a cost of equity of 15 percent and an after-tax cost of debt of 5 percent. The cost of capital can be calculated as follows:

With market value debt ratios: 15%(.9) + 5%(.1) = 14%

With book value debt ratios: 15%(.7) + 5%(.3) = 12%

[13]There are some who argue that stock prices are much more volatile than the underlying true value. Even if this argument is justified (and it has not conclusively been shown to be so), the difference between market value and true value is likely to be much smaller than the difference between book value and true value.

Third, it is claimed that lenders will not lend on the basis of market value, but this claim again seems to be based more on perception than on fact. Any homeowner who has taken a second mortgage on a house that has appreciated in value knows that lenders do lend on the basis of market value. It is true, however, that the greater the perceived volatility in the market value of an asset, the lower is the borrowing potential on that asset.

Estimating the Market Values of Equity and Debt   The market value of equity is generally the number of shares outstanding times the current stock price. If there are other equity claims in the firm such as warrants and management options, these should also be valued and added to the value of the equity in the firm.

The market value of debt is usually more difficult to obtain directly, since very few firms have all their debt in the form of bonds outstanding trading in the market. Many firms have nontraded debt, such as bank debt, which is specified in book value terms but not market value terms. A simple way to convert book value debt into market value debt is to treat the entire debt on the books as one coupon bond, with a coupon set equal to the interest expenses on all the debt and the maturity set equal to the face-value weighted average maturity of the debt, and then to value this coupon bond at the current cost of debt for the company. Thus, the market value of $1 billion in debt, with interest expenses of $60 million and a maturity of six years, when the current cost of debt is 7.5 percent, can be estimated as follows:

$$\text{Estimated market value of debt} = 60 \left(\frac{1 - \dfrac{1}{1.075^6}}{.075} \right) + \frac{1,000}{1.075^6} = \$930$$

ILLUSTRATION 8.16:   Difference between Market Value and Book Value Debt Ratios: Boeing in June 2000

This illustration contrasts the book values of debt and equity with the market values. For debt, we estimate the market value of debt using the book value of debt, the interest expense on the debt, the average maturity of the debt, and the pretax cost of debt for each firm. For Boeing, the book value of debt is $6,972 million, the interest expense on the debt is $453 million, the average maturity of the debt is 13.76 years, and the pretax cost of debt is 6.00%. The estimated market value is:

$$\text{Estimated MV of Boeing debt} = 453 \left(\frac{1 - \dfrac{1}{1.06^{13.76}}}{.06} \right) + \frac{6,972}{(1.06)^{13.76}} = \$7,291$$

To this, we need to add the present value of operating leases of $556 million to arrive at a total market value for debt of $7,847 million.

The book value of equity for Boeing was $12,316 million while the market value of equity was $55,197 million. The debt ratios in market value and book value terms are computed as follows:

	Market Value	Book Value
Debt to equity	7,847/55,197 = 14.22%	6,972/12,316 = 56.61%
Debt/(Debt + Equity)	7,847/(7,847 + 55,197) = 12.45%	6,972/(6,972 + 12,316) = 36.15%

The market debt ratio is significantly lower than the book debt ratio.

GROSS DEBT VERSUS NET DEBT

Gross debt refers to all debt outstanding in a firm. Net debt is the difference between gross debt and the cash balance of the firm. For instance, a firm with $1.25 billion in interest-bearing debt outstanding and a cash balance of $1 billion has a net debt balance of $250 million. The practice of netting cash against debt is common in both Latin America and Europe, and debt ratios are usually estimated using net debt.

It is generally safer to value a firm based on gross debt outstanding and to add the cash balance outstanding to the value of operating assets to arrive at the firm value. The interest payment on total debt is then entitled to the tax benefits of debt, and we can assess the effect of whether the company invests its cash balances efficiently on value.

In some cases, especially when firms maintain large cash balances as a matter of routine, analysts prefer to work with net debt ratios. If we choose to use net debt ratios, we have to be consistent all the way through the valuation. To begin, the beta for the firm should be estimated using a net debt-to-equity ratio rather than a gross debt-to-equity ratio. The cost of equity that emerges from the beta estimate can be used to estimate a cost of capital, but the market value weight on debt should be based on net debt. Once we discount the cash flows of the firm at the cost of capital, we should not add back cash. Instead, we should subtract the net debt outstanding to arrive at the estimated value of equity.

Implicitly, when we net cash against debt to arrive at net debt ratios, we are assuming that cash and debt have roughly similar risk. While this assumption may not be outlandish when analyzing highly rated firms, it becomes much shakier when debt becomes riskier. For instance, the debt in a BB-rated firm is much riskier than the cash balance in the firm, and netting out one against the other can provide a misleading view of the firm's default risk. In general, using net debt ratios will overstate the value of riskier firms.

 wacccalc.xls: This spreadsheet allows you to convert book values of debt into market values.

Estimating the Cost of Capital

Since a firm can raise its money from three sources—equity, debt, and preferred stock—the cost of capital is defined as the weighted average of each of these costs. The cost of equity (k_e) reflects the riskiness of the equity investment in the firm, the after-tax cost of debt (k_d) is a function of the default risk of the firm, and the cost of preferred stock (k_{ps}) is a function of its intermediate standing in terms of risk between debt and equity. The weights on each of these components should reflect their market value proportions, since these proportions best measure how the existing firm is being financed. Thus if E, D, and PS are the market values of equity, debt, and preferred stock respectively, the cost of capital can be written as follows:

$$\text{Cost of capital} = k_e[E/(D + E + PS)] + k_d[D/(D + E + PS)] + k_{ps}[PS/(D + E + PS)]$$

ILLUSTRATION 8.17:   Estimating Cost of Capital: Boeing in December 2000

Having estimated the costs of debt and equity in earlier illustrations, and the market value debt ratio in Illustration 8.16, we can put them together to arrive at a cost of capital for Boeing.

Cost of equity = 10.28% (from Illustration 8.9)
Cost of debt = 3.90% (from Illustration 8.11)
Market value debt ratio = 12.45% (from Illustration 8.16)
Cost of capital = 10.28%(.8755) + 3.90%(.1245) = 9.49%

ILLUSTRATION 8.18:   Estimating Cost of Capital: Embraer in March 2001

To estimate a cost of capital for Embraer, we again draw on the estimates of cost of equity and cost of debt we obtained in prior illustrations. The cost of capital will be estimated using net debt all the way through (for the levered betas, interest coverage ratios, and debt ratios) and in U.S. dollars:

Cost of equity = 18.86% (from Illustration 8.10)
After-tax cost of debt = 7.45% (from Illustration 8.12)
Market value of debt = 1,328 million BR
Cash and marketable securities = 1,105 million BR
Market value of equity = 9,084 million BR

The cost of capital for Embraer is estimated as follows:

Net debt = 1,328 million BR − 1,105 million BR = 223 million BR

Cost of capital = 18.86%[9,084/(9,084 + 223)] + 7.45%[223/(9,084 + 223)] = 18.59%

To convert this into a nominal BR cost of capital, we would apply the differential inflation rates (10% in Brazil and 2% in the United States).

$$\text{Cost of capital}_{\text{nominal BR}} = (1 + \text{Cost of capital}_{\$})(\text{Inflation rate}_{\text{Brazil}}/\text{Inflation rate}_{\text{U.S.}}) - 1$$
$$= (1.1859)(1.10/1.02) - 1 = 27.89\%$$

BEST PRACTICES AT FIRMS

We have spent this chapter discussing what firms should do when it comes to estimating the cost of capital. What do they actually do? Bruner, Eades, Harris, and Higgins surveyed 27 well-regarded corporations, and their findings are summarized in Table 8.3.

CONCLUSION

When we analyze the investments of a firm or assess its value, we need to know the cost that the firm faces in raising equity, debt, and capital. The risk and return models described in earlier chapters can be used to estimate the costs of equity and capital for a firm.

Building on the premise that the cost of equity should reflect the riskiness of equity to investors in the firm, there are three basic inputs we need to estimate the

TABLE 8.3 Current Practices for Estimating Cost of Capital

Cost of Capital Item	Current Practices
Cost of equity	• 81% of firms used the capital asset pricing model to estimate the cost of equity, 4% used a modified capital asset pricing model, and 15% were uncertain about how they estimated the cost of equity.
	• 70% of firms used 10-year Treasuries or longer as the riskless rate, 7% used 3- to 5-year Treasuries, and 4% used the Treasury bill rate.
	• 52% used a published source for a beta estimate, while 30% estimated it themselves.
	• There was wide variation in the market risk premium used, with 37% using a premium between 5% and 6%.
Cost of debt	• 52% of firms used a marginal borrowing rate and a marginal tax rate, while 37% used the current average borrowing rate and the effective tax rate.
Weights for debt and equity	• 59% used market value weights for debt and equity in the cost of capital, 15% used book value weights, and 19% were uncertain about what weights they used.

Source: Bruner, Eades, Harris, and Higgins (1998).

cost of equity for any firm. The riskless rate is the expected return on an investment with no default risk and no reinvestment risk. Since much of the analysis in corporate finance is long term, the riskless rate should be the interest rate on a long-term government bond. The risk premium measures what investors demand as a premium for investing in risky investments instead of riskless investments. This risk premium, which can vary across investors, can be estimated either by looking at past returns on stocks and government securities or by looking at how the market prices stocks currently. The beta for a firm is conventionally measured using a regression of returns on the firm's stock against returns on a market index. This approach yields imprecise beta estimates, and we are better off estimating betas by examining the betas of the businesses that the firm operates in.

The cost of capital is a weighted average of the costs of the different components of financing, with the weights based on the market values of each component. The cost of debt is the market rate at which the firm can borrow, adjusted for any tax advantages of borrowing. The cost of preferred stock, however, is the preferred dividend yield.

The cost of capital is useful at two levels. On a composite basis, it is what these firms have to make collectively on their investments to break even. It is also the appropriate discount rate to use to discount expected future cash flows to arrive at an estimate of firm value.

QUESTIONS AND SHORT PROBLEMS

1. In December 1995, Boise Cascade's stock had a beta of 0.95. The Treasury bill rate at the time was 5.8%, and the Treasury bond rate was 6.4%. The firm had debt outstanding of $1.7 billion and a market value of equity of $1.5 billion; the corporate marginal tax rate was 36%.

    a. Estimate the expected return on the stock for a short-term investor in the company.

    b. Estimate the expected return on the stock for a long-term investor in the company.

    c. Estimate the cost of equity for the company.

2. Continuing problem 1, Boise Cascade also had debt outstanding of $1.7 billion and a market value of equity of $1.5 billion; the corporate marginal tax rate was 36%.

    a. Assuming that the current beta of 0.95 for the stock is a reasonable one, estimate the unlevered beta for the company.

    b. How much of the risk in the company can be attributed to business risk and how much to financial leverage risk?

3. Biogen Inc., a biotechnology firm, had a beta of 1.70 in 1995. It had no debt outstanding at the end of that year.

    a. Estimate the cost of equity for Biogen if the Treasury bond rate is 6.4%.

    b. What effect will an increase in long-term bond rates to 7.5% have on Biogen's cost of equity?

    c. How much of Biogen's risk can be attributed to business risk?

4. Genting Berhad is a Malaysian conglomerate with holdings in plantations and tourist resorts. The beta estimated for the firm relative to the Malaysian stock exchange is 1.15, and the long-term government borrowing rate in Malaysia is 11.5%. (The Malaysian risk premium is 12%.)

    a. Estimate the expected return on the stock.

    b. If you were an international investor, what concerns, if any, would you have about using the beta estimated relative to the Malaysian Index? If you do have concerns, how would you modify the beta?

5. You have just done a regression of monthly stock returns of HeavyTech Inc., a manufacturer of heavy machinery, on monthly market returns over the past five years and have come up with the following regression:

$$R_{HeavyTech} = 0.5\% + 1.2\,R_M$$

The variance of the stock is 50%, and the variance of the market is 20%. The current T-bill rate is 3% (it was 5% one year ago). The stock is currently selling for $50, down $4 over the past year; it has paid a dividend of $2 during the past year and expects to pay a dividend of $2.50 over the next year. The NYSE Composite has gone down 8% over the past year, with a dividend yield of 3%. HeavyTech Inc. has a tax rate of 40%.

    a. What is the expected return on HeavyTech over the next year?

    b. What would you expect HeavyTech's price to be one year from today?

    c. What would you have expected HeavyTech's stock returns to be over the plast year?

    d. What were the actual returns on HeavyTech over the past year?

    e. HeavyTech has $100 million in equity and $50 million in debt. It plans to issue $50 million in new equity and retire $50 million in debt. Estimate the new beta.

6. Safecorp, which owns and operates grocery stores across the United States, currently has $50 million in debt and $100 million in equity outstanding. Its stock has a beta of 1.2. It is planning a leveraged buyout (LBO), where it will increase its debt-to-equity ratio of 8. If the tax rate is 40%, what will the beta of the equity in the firm be after the LBO?

7. Novell, which had a market value of equity of $2 billion and a beta of 1.50, announced that it was acquiring WordPerfect, which had a market value of equity of $1 billion and a beta of 1.30. Neither firm had any debt in its financial structure at the time of the acquisition, and the corporate tax rate was 40%.
   a. Estimate the beta for Novell after the acquisition, assuming that the entire acquisition was financed with equity.
   b. Assume that Novell had to borrow the $1 billion to acquire WordPerfect. Estimate the beta after the acquisition.

8. You are analyzing the beta for Hewlett Packard (HP) and have broken down the company into four broad business groups, with market values and betas for each group.

Business Group	Market Value of Equity	Beta
Mainframes	$2.0 billion	1.10
Personal Computers	$2.0 billion	1.50
Software	$1.0 billion	2.00
Printers	$3.0 billion	1.00

   a. Estimate the beta for Hewlett Packard as a company. Is this beta going to be equal to the beta estimated by regressing past returns on HP stock against a market index? Why or why not?
   b. If the Treasury bond rate is 7.5%, estimate the cost of equity for Hewlett Packard. Estimate the cost of equity for each division. Which cost of equity would you use to value the printer division?
   c. Assume that HP divests itself of the mainframe business and pays the cash out as a dividend. Estimate the beta for HP after the divestiture. (HP had $1 billion in debt outstanding.)

9. The following table summarizes the percentage changes in operating income, percentage changes in revenue, and betas for four pharmaceutical firms.

Firm	% Change in Revenue	% Change in Operating Income	Beta
PharmaCorp	27%	25%	1.00
SynerCorp	25%	32%	1.15
BioMed	23%	36%	1.30
Safemed	21%	40%	1.40

   a. Calculate the degree of operating leverage for each of these firms.
   b. Use the operating leverage to explain why these firms have different betas.

10. A prominent beta estimation service reports the beta of Comcast Corporation, a major cable TV operator, to be 1.45. The service claims to use weekly returns on the stock over the prior five years and the NYSE Composite as the market index to estimate betas. You replicate the regression using weekly returns over the same period and arrive at a beta estimate of 1.60. How would you reconcile the two estimates?

11. Battle Mountain is a mining company with gold, silver, and copper in mines in South America, Africa, and Australia. The beta for the stock is estimated to be 0.30. Given the volatility in commodity prices, how would you explain the low beta?

12. You have collected returns on AnaDone Corporation (AD Corp.), a large, diversified manufacturing firm, and the NYSE index for five years:

Year	AD Corp.	NYSE
1981	10%	5%
1982	5%	15%
1983	-5%	8%
1984	20%	12%
1985	-5%	-5%

a. Estimate the intercept (alpha) and slope (beta) of the regression.

b. If you bought stock in AD Corp. today, how much would you expect to make as a return over the next year? (The six-month T-bill rate is 6%.)

c. Looking back over the past five years, how would you evaluate AD Corp.'s performance relative to the market?

d. Assume now that you are an undiversified investor and that you have all of your money invested in AD Corp. What would be a good measure of the risk that you are taking on? How much of this risk would you be able to eliminate if you diversify?

e. AD Corp. is planning to sell off one of its divisions. The division under consideration has assets that comprise half of the book value of AD Corp. and 20% of the market value. Its beta is twice the average beta for AD Corp. (before divestment). What will the beta of AD Corp. be after divesting this division?

13. You run a regression of monthly returns of Mapco Inc., an oil- and gas-producing firm, on the S&P 500 index, and come up with the following output for the period 1991 to 1995:

Intercept of the regression = 0.06%
Slope of the regression = 0.46
Standard error of X-coefficient = 0.20
R-squared = 5%

There are 20 million shares outstanding, and the current market price is $2 per share. The firm has $20 million in debt outstanding. (The firm has a tax rate of 36%.)

a. What would an investor in Mapco's stock require as a return if the T-bond rate is 6%?

b. What proportion of this firm's risk is diversifiable?

c. Assume now that Mapco has three divisions of equal size (in market value terms). It plans to divest itself of one of the divisions for $20 million in cash and acquire another for $50 million (it will borrow $30 million to complete this acquisition). The division it is divesting is in a business line where the average unlevered beta is 0.20, and the division it is acquiring is in a business line where the average unlevered beta is 0.80. What will the beta of Mapco be after this acquisition?

14. You have just run a regression of monthly returns of American Airlines (AMR Corporation) against the S&P 500 over the past five years. You have misplaced some of the output and are trying to derive it from what you have.

a. You know the R-squared of the regression is 0.36, and that your stock has a variance of 67%. The market variance is 12%. What is the beta of AMR?

b. You also remember that AMR was not a very good investment during the period of the regression and that it did worse than expected (after adjusting for risk) by 0.39% a month for the five years of the regression. During this period, the average risk-free rate was 4.84%. What was the intercept on the regression?

c. You are comparing AMR Inc. to another firm, which also has an R-squared of 0.48. Will the two firms have the same beta? If not, why not?

15. You have run a regression of monthly returns on Amgen, a large biotechnology firm, against monthly returns on the S&P 500 index, and come up with the following output:

$$R_{stock} = 3.28\% + 1.65\ R_{market} \qquad R^2 = 0.20$$

The current one-year Treasury bill rate is 4.8% and the current 30-year bond rate is 6.4%. The firm has 265 million shares outstanding, selling for $30 per share.

a. What is the expected return on this stock over the next year?

b. Would your expected return estimate change if the purpose was to get a discount rate to value the company?

c. An analyst has estimated, correctly, that the stock did 51.10% better than expected, annually, during the period of the regression. Can you estimate the annualized risk-free rate that she used for her estimate?

d. The firm has a debt/equity ratio of 3% and faces a tax rate of 40%. It is planning to issue $2 billion in new debt and acquire a new business for that amount, with the same risk level as the firm's existing business. What will the beta be after the acquisition?

16. You have just run a regression of monthly returns on MAD Inc., a newspaper and magazine publisher, against returns on the S&P 500, and arrived at the following result:

$$R_{MAD} = -0.05\% + 1.20\ R_{S\&P}$$

The regression has an R-squared of 22%. The current T-bill rate is 5.5%, and the current T-bond rate is 6.5%. The risk-free rate during the period of the regression was 6%. Answer the following questions relating to the regression:

a. Based on the intercept, how well or badly did MAD do, relative to expectations, during the period of the regression.

b. You now realize that MAD Inc. went through a major restructuring at the end of last month (which was the last month of your regression), and made the following changes:

■ The firm sold off its magazine division, which had an unlevered beta of 0.6, for $20 million.

■ It borrowed an additional $20 million, and bought back stock worth $40 million.

After the sale of the division and the share repurchase, MAD Inc. had $40 million in debt and $120 million in equity outstanding. If the firm's tax rate is 40%, reestimate the beta after these changes.

17. Time Warner Inc., the entertainment conglomerate, has a beta of 1.61. Part of the reason for the high beta is the debt left over from the leveraged buyout of Time by Warner in 1989, which amounted to $10 billion in 1995. The market value of equity at Time Warner in 1995 was also $10 billion. The marginal tax rate was 40%.

a. Estimate the unlevered beta for Time Warner.

b. Estimate the effect of reducing the debt ratio by 10% each year for the next two years on the beta of the stock.

18. Chrysler, the automotive manufacturer, had a beta of 1.05 in 1995. It had $13 billion in debt outstanding in that year, and 355 million shares trading at $50 per share. The firm had a cash balance of $8 billion at the end of 1995. The marginal tax rate was 36%.
   a. Estimate the unlevered beta of the firm.
   b. Estimate the effect of paying out a special dividend of $5 billion on this unlevered beta.
   c. Estimate the beta for Chrysler after the special dividend.

19. You are trying to estimate the beta of a private firm that manufactures home appliances. You have managed to obtain betas for publicly traded firms that also manufacture home appliances.

Firm	Beta	Debt	MV of Equity
Black & Decker	1.40	$2,500	$3,000
Fedders Corp.	1.20	$ 5	$ 200
Maytag Corp.	1.20	$ 540	$2,250
National Presto	0.70	$ 8	$ 300
Whirlpool	1.50	$2,900	$4,000

   The private firm has a debt equity ratio of 25% and faces a tax rate of 40%. The publicly traded firms all have marginal tax rates of 40% as well.
   a. Estimate the beta for the private firm.
   b. What concerns, if any, would you have about using betas of comparable firms?

20. As the result of stockholder pressure, RJR Nabisco is considering spinning off its food division. You have been asked to estimate the beta for the division, and decide to do so by obtaining the beta of comparable publicly traded firms. The average beta of comparable publicly traded firms is 0.95, and the average debt-to-equity ratio of these firms is 35%. The division is expected to have a debt ratio of 25%. The marginal corporate tax rate is 36%.
   a. What is the beta for the division?
   b. Would it make any difference if you knew that RJR Nabisco had a much higher fixed cost structure than the comparable firms used here?

21. Southwestern Bell, a phone company, is considering expanding its operations into the media business. The beta for the company at the end of 1995 was 0.90, and the debt-to-equity ratio was 1. The media business is expected to be 30% of the overall firm value in 1999, and the average beta of comparable firms is 1.20; the average debt-to-equity ratio for these firms is 50%. The marginal corporate tax rate is 36%.
   a. Estimate the beta for Southwestern Bell in 1999, assuming that it maintains its current debt-to-equity ratio.
   b. Estimate the beta for Southwestern Bell in 1999, assuming that it decides to finance its media operations with a debt-to-equity ratio of 50%.

22. The chief financial officer of Adobe Systems, a growing software manufacturing firm, has approached you for some advice regarding the beta of his company. He subscribes to a service that estimates Adobe Systems' beta each year, and he has noticed that the beta estimates have gone down every year since 1991—from 2.35 in 1991 to 1.40 in 1995. He would like the answers to the following questions:

    a. Is this decline in beta unusual for a growing firm?

    b. Why would the beta decline over time?

    c. Is the beta likely to keep decreasing over time?

23. You are analyzing Tiffany & Company, an upscale retailer, and find that the regression estimate of the firm's beta is 0.75; the standard error for the beta estimate is 0.50. You also note that the average unlevered beta of comparable specialty retailing firms is 1.15.

    a. If Tiffany has a debt/equity ratio of 20%, estimate the beta for the company based on comparable firms. (The tax rate is 40%.)

    b. Estimate a range for the beta from the regression.

    c. Assume that Tiffany is rated BBB and that the default spread for BBB-rated firms is 1% over the Treasury bond rate. If the Treasury bond rate is 6.5%, estimate the cost of capital for the firm.

24. You have been asked to estimate the cost of capital for NewTel, a telecom firm. The firm has the following characteristics:

    ■ There are 100 million shares outstanding, trading at $250 per share.

    ■ The firm has a book value of debt with a maturity of six years of $10 billion, and interest expenses of $600 million on the debt. The firm is not rated, but it had operating income of $2.5 billion last year. (Firms with an interest coverage ratio of 3.5 to 4.5 were rated BBB, and the default spread was 1%.)

    ■ The tax rate for the firm is 35%.

The Treasury bond rate is 6%, and the unlevered beta of other telecom firms is 0.80.

    a. Estimate the market value of debt for this firm.

    b. Based on the synthetic rating, estimate the cost of debt for this firm.

    c. Estimate the cost of capital for this firm.

CHAPTER 9

Measuring Earnings

To estimate cash flows, we usually begin with a measure of earnings. Free cash flows to the firm, for instance, are based on after-tax operating earnings. Free cash flow to equity estimates, on the other hand, commence with net income. While we obtain measures of operating and net income from accounting statements, the accounting earnings for many firms bear little or no resemblance to the true earnings of the firm.

This chapter begins by considering the philosophical difference between the accounting and financial views of firms. We then consider how the earnings of a firm, at least as measured by accountants, have to be adjusted to get a measure of earnings that is more appropriate for valuation. In particular, we examine how to treat operating lease expenses, which we argue are really financial expenses, and research and development expenses, which we consider to be capital expenses. The adjustments affect not only our measures of earnings but our estimates of book value of capital. We also look at extraordinary items (both income and expenses) and one-time charges, the use of which has expanded significantly in recent years as firms have shifted toward managing earnings more aggressively. The techniques used to smooth earnings over periods and beat analyst estimates can skew reported earnings, and, if we are not careful, the values that emerge from them.

ACCOUNTING VERSUS FINANCIAL BALANCE SHEETS

When analyzing a firm, what are the questions to which we would like to know the answers? A firm, as defined here, includes both investments already made—assets-in-place—and investments yet to be made—growth assets. In addition, a firm can either borrow the funds it needs to make these investments, in which case it is using debt, or raise it from its owners in the form of equity. Figure 9.1 summarizes this description of a firm in the form of a financial balance sheet.

Note that while this summary does have some similarities with the accounting balance sheet, there are key differences. The most important one is that here we explicitly consider growth assets when we look at what a firm owns.

When doing a financial analysis of a firm, we would like to be able to answer a number of questions relating to each of these items. Figure 9.2 lists the questions. As we will see in this chapter, accounting statements allow us to acquire some information about each of these questions, but they fall short in terms of both the timeliness with which they provide it and the way in which they measure asset value, earnings, and risk.

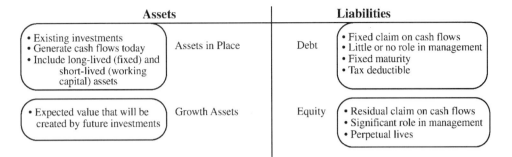

FIGURE 9.1   A Financial Balance Sheet

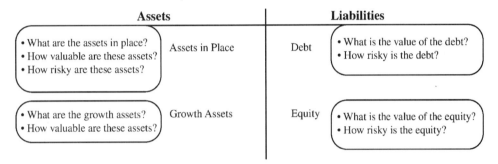

FIGURE 9.2   Key Financial Questions

ADJUSTING EARNINGS

The income statement for a firm provides measures of both the operating and equity income of the firm in the form of the earnings before interest and taxes (EBIT) and net income. When valuing firms, there are two important considerations in using this measure. One is to obtain as updated an estimate as possible, given how much these firms change over time. The second is that reported earnings at these firms may bear little resemblance to true earnings because of limitations in accounting rules and the firms' own actions.

Importance of Updating Earnings

Firms reveal their earnings in their financial statements and annual reports to stockholders. Annual reports are released only at the end of a firm's financial year, but you are often required to value firms all through the year. Consequently, the last annual report that is available for a firm being valued can contain information that is several months old. In the case of firms that are changing rapidly over time, it is dangerous to base value estimates on information that is this old. Instead, use more recent information. Since firms in the United States are required to file quarterly reports with the Securities and Exchange Commission (10-Qs) and reveal these reports to the public, a more recent estimate of key items in the financial statements can be obtained by aggregating the numbers over the most recent four quarters. The estimates of revenues and earnings that emerge from this exercise are called trailing 12-month revenues and earnings and can be very different from the values for the same variables in the most recent annual report.

There is a price paid for the updating. Unfortunately, not all items in the annual report are revealed in the quarterly reports. You have to either use the numbers in the last annual report (which does lead to inconsistent inputs) or estimate their values at the end of the last quarter (which leads to estimation error). For example, firms do not reveal details about options outstanding (issued to managers and employees) in quarterly reports, while they do reveal them in annual reports. Since you need to value these options, you can use the options outstanding as of the last annual report, or assume that the options outstanding today have changed to reflect changes in the other variables. (For instance, if revenues have doubled, the options have doubled as well.)

For younger firms, it is critical that you stay with the most updated numbers you can find, even if these numbers are estimates. These firms are often growing exponentially, and using numbers from the last financial year will lead to misleading estimates of value. Even those that are not growing are changing substantially from quarter to quarter, and updated information might give you a chance to capture these changes.

There are several financial markets where firms still file financial reports only once a year, thus denying us the option of using quarterly updates. When valuing firms in these markets, analysts may have to draw on unofficial sources to update their valuations.

ILLUSTRATION 9.1: Updated Earnings for Ariba—June 2000

Assume that you were valuing Ariba, a firm specializing in business-to-business (B2B) e-commerce in June 2000. The last 10-K was as of September 1999 and the firm had released two quarterly reports (10-Qs), one in December 1999 and one in March 2000. To illustrate how much the fundamental inputs to the valuation have changed in the six months, the information in the last 10-K is compared to the trailing 12-month information in the latest 10-Q for revenues, operating income, R&D expenses, and net income (in thousands of dollars).

	Six Months Ending March 2000	Six Months Ending March 1999	Annual September 1999	Trailing 12-Month
Revenues	$ 63,521	$16,338	$45,372	$ 92,555
EBIT	−$140,604	−$ 8,315	−$31,421	−$163,710
R&D	$ 11,567	$ 3,849	$11,620	$ 19,338
Net income	−$136,274	−$ 8,128	−$29,300	−$157,446

Trailing 12-month = Annual September 1999 − Six-month March 1999 + Six-month March 2000.

The trailing 12-month revenues are twice the revenues reported in the latest 10-K, and the firm's operating loss and net loss have both increased more than fivefold. Ariba in March 2000 was a very different firm from Ariba in September 1999. Note that these are not the only inputs that have changed. The number of shares outstanding in the firm has changed dramatically as well, from 35.03 million shares in September 1999 to 179.24 million shares in the latest 10-Q (March 2000) to 235.8 million shares in June 2000.

Correcting Earnings Misclassification

1. Operating expenses are expenses that generate benefits for the firm only in the current period. For instance, the fuel used by an airline in the course of its flights is an operating expense, as is the labor cost for an automobile company associated with producing vehicles.
2. Capital expenses are expenses that generate benefits over multiple periods. For example, the expense associated with building and outfitting a new factory for an automobile manufacturer is a capital expense, since it will generate several years of revenues.
3. Financial expenses are expenses associated with nonequity capital raised by a firm. Thus, the interest paid on a bank loan would be a financial expense.

The operating income for a firm, measured correctly, should be equal to its revenues less its operating expenses. Neither financial nor capital expenses should be included in the operating expenses in the year that they occur, though capital expenses may be depreciated or amortized over the period that the firm obtains benefits from the expenses. The net income of a firm should be its revenues less both its operating and financial expenses. No capital expenses should be deducted to arrive at net income.

The accounting measures of earnings can be misleading because operating, capital, and financial expenses are sometimes misclassified. This section will consider the two most common misclassifications and how to correct for them. The first is the inclusion of capital expenses such as research and development (R&D) in the operating expenses, which skews the estimation of both operating and net income. The second adjustment is for financial expenses such as operating leases expenses that are treated as operating expenses. This affects the measurement of operating income and free cash flows to the firm.

The third factor to consider is the effect of the phenomenon of so-called "managed earnings" at these firms. Firms sometimes use accounting techniques to post earnings that beat analyst estimates, resulting in misleading measures of earnings.

Capital Expenses Treated as Operating Expenses While in theory capital income is not computed after operating expenses, the reality is that there are a number of expenses that are treated as operating expenses. For instance, a significant shortcoming of accounting statements is the way in which they treat research and development expenses. Using the rationale that the products of research are too uncertain and difficult to quantify, accounting standards have generally required that all R&D expenses be expensed in the period in which they occur. This has several consequences, but one of the most profound is that the value of the assets created by research does not show up on the balance sheet as part of the total assets of the firm. This, in turn, creates ripple effects for the measurement of capital and profitability ratios for the firm. We will consider how to capitalize R&D expenses in the first part of the section and extend the argument to other capital expenses in the second part of the section.

Capitalizing R&D Expenses Research expenses, notwithstanding the uncertainty about future benefits, should be capitalized. To capitalize and value research assets, we make an assumption about how long it takes for research and development to be converted, on average, into commercial products. This is called the amortizable life of these assets. This life will vary across firms and reflect the time involved in converting research into products. To illustrate, research and development expenses at a pharmaceutical company should have fairly long amortizable lives, since the approval process for new drugs is long. In contrast, research and development expenses at a software firm, where products tend to emerge from research much more quickly, should be amortized over a shorter period.

Once the amortizable life of research and development expenses has been estimated, the next step is to collect data on R&D expenses over past years ranging back over the amortizable life of the research asset. Thus, if the research asset has an amortizable life of five years, the R&D expenses in each of the five years prior to the current one have to be obtained. For simplicity, it can be assumed that the amortization is uniform over time, which leads to the following estimate of the residual value of research asset today:

$$\text{Value of the research asset} = \sum_{t=-(n-1)}^{t=0} R\&D_t \frac{(n+t)}{n}$$

Thus, in the case of the research asset with a five-year life, you cumulate one-fifth of the R&D expenses from four years ago, two-fifths of the R&D expenses from three years ago, three-fifths of the R&D expenses from two years ago, four-fifths of the R&D expenses from last year, and this year's entire R&D expense to arrive at the value of the research asset. This augments the value of the assets of the firm and, by extension, the book value of equity.

Adjusted book value of equity = Book value of equity + Value of the research asset

Finally, the operating income is adjusted to reflect the capitalization of R&D expenses. First, the R&D expenses that were subtracted out to arrive at the operating income are added back to the operating income, reflecting their recategorization as capital expenses. Next, the amortization of the research asset is treated the same way that depreciation is and netted out to arrive at the adjusted operating income:

Adjusted operating income = Operating income + R&D expenses
– Amortization of research asset

The adjusted operating income will generally increase for firms that have R&D expenses that are growing over time. The net income will also be affected by this adjustment:

Adjusted net income = Net income + R&D expenses – Amortization of research asset

While we would normally consider only the after-tax portion of this amount, the fact that R&D is entirely tax deductible eliminates the need for this adjustment.[1]

---

[1]If only amortization were tax deductible, the tax benefit from R&D expenses would be:

Amortization × Tax rate

This extra tax benefit we get from the entire R&D being tax deductible is as follows:

(R&D – Amortization) × Tax rate

If we subtract out (R&D – Amortization)(1 – Tax rate) and then add the differential tax benefit that is computed above, (1 – Tax rate) drops out of the equation.

R&DConv.xls: **This spreadsheet allows you to convert R&D expenses from operating to capital expenses.**

ILLUSTRATION 9.2: Capitalizing R&D Expenses: Amgen in March 2001

Amgen is a biotechnology firm. Like most pharmaceutical firms, it has a substantial amount of R&D expenses, and we will attempt to capitalize it in this section. The first step in this conversion is determining an amortizable life for R&D expenses. How long will it take, on an expected basis, for research to pay off at Amgen? Given the length of the approval process for new drugs by the Food and Drug Administration, we will assume that this amortizable life is 10 years.

The second step in the analysis is collecting research and development expenses from prior years, with the number of years of historical data being a function of the amortizable life. The following table provides this information for each of the years:

Year	R&D Expenses
Current	$845.00
−1	$822.80
−2	$663.30
−3	$630.80
−4	$528.30
−5	$451.70
−6	$323.63
−7	$255.32
−8	$182.30
−9	$120.94
−10	Firm not in existence

Dollars in millions.

The current year's information reflects the R&D in the last financial year (which was calendar year 2000).

The portion of the expenses in prior years that would have been amortized already and the amortization this year from each of these expenses is considered. To make estimation simpler, these expenses are amortized linearly over time; with a 10-year life, 10% is amortized each year. This allows you to estimate the value of the research asset created at each of these firms, and the amortization of R&D expenses in the current year. The procedure is illustrated in the following table:

Year	R&D Expense	Unamortized Portion of Research Asset		Amortization This Year
Current	$845.00	1.00	$845.00	
−1	$822.80	0.90	$740.52	$82.28
−2	$663.30	0.80	$530.64	$66.33
−3	$630.80	0.70	$441.56	$63.08
−4	$528.30	0.60	$316.98	$52.83
−5	$451.70	0.50	$225.85	$45.17
−6	$323.63	0.40	$129.45	$32.36
−7	$255.32	0.30	$ 76.60	$25.53
−8	$182.30	0.20	$ 36.46	$18.23
−9	$120.94	0.10	$ 12.09	$12.09
−10	$ 0.00	0.00	$ 0.00	$ —

Note: The firm has been in existence only nine years prior to the current year.

Note that none of the current year's expenditure has been amortized because it is assumed to occur at the end of the year but that 50 percent of the expense from five years ago has been amortized. The sum of the dollar values of unamortized R&D from prior years is $3.355 billion. This can be viewed as the value of Amgen's research asset and would be also added to the book value of equity for computing return on equity and capital measures. The sum of the amortization in the current year for all prior year expenses is $397.91 million.

The final step in the process is the adjustment of the operating income to reflect the capitalization of research and development expenses. We make the adjustment by adding back R&D expenses to the operating income (to reflect its reclassification as a capital expense) and subtract out the amortization of the research asset, estimated in the last step. For Amgen, which reported operating income of $1,549 million in its income statement for 2000, the adjusted operating earnings would be:

$$\text{Adjusted operating earnings} = \text{Operating earnings} + \text{Current year's R\&D expense}$$
$$- \text{Amortization of research asset}$$
$$= 1,549 + 845 - 398 = \$1,996 \text{ million}$$

The stated net income of $1,139 million can be adjusted similarly.

$$\text{Adjusted net income} = \text{Net income} + \text{Current year's R\&D expense} - \text{Amortization of research asset}$$
$$= 1,139 + 845 - 398 = \$1,586 \text{ million}$$

You might wonder why there is no tax effect, but we will return to this question in the next chapter.

Both the book value of equity and capital are augmented by the value of the research asset. Since measures of return on capital and equity are based on the prior year's values, we computed the value of the research asset at the end of 1999, using the same approach that we used in 2000.

$$\text{Value of research asset}_{1999} = \$2,909 \text{ million}$$

$$\text{Adjusted book value of equity}_{1999} = \text{Book value of equity}_{1999} + \text{Value of research asset}$$
$$= 3,024 \text{ million} + 2,909 \text{ million} = \$5,933 \text{ million}$$

$$\text{Adjusted book value of capital}_{1999} = \text{Book value of capital}_{1999} + \text{Value of research asset}$$
$$= 3,347 \text{ million} + 2,909 \text{ million} = \$6,256 \text{ million}$$

The returns on equity and capital are reported with both the unadjusted and adjusted numbers:

	Unadjusted	*Adjusted for R&D*
Return on equity	1,139/3,024 = 37.67%	1,586/5,933 = 26.73%
Pretax return on capital	1,549/3,347 = 46.28%	1,996/6,256 = 31.91%

While the profitability ratios for Amgen remain impressive even after the adjustment, they decline significantly from the unadjusted numbers. This is likely to happen for most firms that earn high returns on equity and capital and have substantial R&D expenses.[2]

---

[2]If the return on capital earned by a firm is well below the cost of capital, the adjustment could result in a higher return.

Capitalizing Other Operating Expenses While R&D expenses are the most prominent example of capital expenses being treated as operating expenses, there are other operating expenses that arguably should be treated as capital expenses. Consumer product companies such as Gillette and Coca-Cola could argue that a portion of advertising expenses should be treated as capital expenses, since they are designed to augment brand name value. For a consulting firm, the cost of recruiting and training its employees could be considered a capital expense, since the consultants who emerge are likely to be the heart of the firm's assets and provide benefits over many years. For many new technology firms, including e-tailers such as Amazon.com, the biggest operating expense item is selling, general, and administrative expenses (SG&A). These firms could argue that a portion of these expenses should be treated as capital expenses, since they are designed to increase brand name awareness and bring in new customers. America Online (AOL), for instance, used this argument to justify capitalizing the expenses associated with the free trial CDs that it bundled with magazines in the United States.

While this argument has some merit, you should remain wary about using it to justify capitalizing these expenses. For an operating expense to be capitalized, there should be substantial evidence that the benefits from the expense accrue over multiple periods. Does a customer who is enticed to buy from Amazon, based on an advertisement or promotion, continue as a customer for the long term? There are some analysts who claim that this is indeed the case, and attribute significant value added to each new customer.[3] It would be logical, under those circumstances, to capitalize these expenses using a procedure similar to that used to capitalize R&D expenses.

- Determine the period over which the benefits from the operating expense (such as SG&A) will flow.
- Estimate the value of the asset (similar to the research asset) created by these expenses. If the expenses are SG&A expenses, this would be the SG&A asset.
- Adjust the operating income for the expense and the amortization of the created asset.

$$\text{Adjusted operating income} = \text{Operating income} \\ + \text{SG\&A expenses for the current period} \\ - \text{Amortization of SG\&A asset}$$

A similar adjustment has to be made to net income:

$$\text{Adjusted net income} = \text{Net income} + \text{SG\&A expenses for the current period} \\ - \text{Amortization of SG\&A asset}$$

As with the research asset, the capitalization of these expenses will create an asset that augments the book value of equity (and capital).

---

[3]As an example, Jamie Kiggen, an equity research analyst at Donaldson, Lufkin & Jenrette, valued an Amazon customer at $2,400 in an equity research report in 1999. This value was based on the assumption that the customer would continue to buy from Amazon.com and on an expected profit margin from such sales.

ILLUSTRATION 9.3: Should You Capitalize SG&A Expense? Analyzing Amazon.com and America Online

Let use consider SG& A expenses at Amazon and America Online. To make a judgment on whether you should capitalize this expense, you need to get a sense of what these expenses are and how long the benefits accruing from these expenses last. For instance, assume that an Amazon promotion (the expense of which would be included in SG&A) attracts new customers to the web site, and that customers, once they try Amazon, continue, on average, to be customers for three years. You would then use a three year amortizable life for SG&A expenses, and capitalize them the same way you capitalized R&D: by collecting historical information on SG&A expenses, amortizing them each year, estimating the value of the selling asset and then adjusting operating income.

We do believe, on balance, that selling, general, and administrative expenses should continue to be treated as operating expenses and not capitalized for Amazon for two reasons. First, retail customers are difficult to retain, especially online, and Amazon faces serious competition not only from other online retailers but also from traditional retailers like Wal-Mart, setting up their online operations. Consequently, the customers that Amazon might attract with its advertising or sales promotions are unlikely to stay for an extended period just because of the initial inducements. Second, as the company has become larger, its selling, general, and administrative expenses seem increasingly directed toward generating revenues in current periods rather than future periods.

In contrast, consider the SG&A expenses at America Online. Especially when the firm was smaller, these expenses primarily related to the cost of the CDs that AOL would package with magazines to get readers to try its service. The company's statistics indicated that a customer who tried the service remained a subscriber to it for about three years, on average. This makes a case for treating the expense as a capital expense stronger, with an amortizable life of three years.

ILLUSTRATION 9.4: Capitalizing Recruitment and Training Expenses: Cyber Health Consulting

Cyber Health Consulting (CHC) is a firm that specializes in offering management consulting services to health-care firms. CHC reported operating income (EBIT) of $51.5 million and net income of $23 million in the most recent year. However, the firm's expenses include the cost of recruiting new consultants ($5.5 million) and the cost of training ($8.5 million). A consultant who joins CHC stays with the firm, on average, four years.

To capitalize the cost of recruiting and training, we obtained these costs from each of the prior four years. The following table reports on these human capital expenses, and amortizes each of these expenses over four years.

Year	Training and Recruiting Expenses	Unamortized Portion		Amortization This Year
Current	$14.00	100%	$14.00	
−1	$12.00	75%	$ 9.00	$3.00
−2	$10.40	50%	$ 5.20	$2.60
−3	$ 9.10	25%	$ 2.28	$2.28
−4	$ 8.30	—	$ 0.00	$2.08
Value of human capital asset =			$30.48	$9.95

The adjustments to operating and net income are as follows:

Adjusted operating income = Operating income + Training and recruiting expenses
$$- \text{Amortization of expense this year}$$
$$= \$51.5 + \$14 - \$9.95 = \$55.55 \text{ million}$$

Net income = Net income + Training and recruiting expenses − Amortization of expense this year
$$= \$23 \text{ million} + \$14 \text{ million} - \$9.95 \text{ million} = \$27.05 \text{ million}$$

As with R&D expenses, the fact that training and recruiting expenses are fully tax deductible dispenses with the need to consider the tax effect when adjusting net income.

Adjustments for Financing Expenses The second adjustment is for financing expenses that accountants treat as operating expenses. The most significant example is operating lease expenses, which are treated as operating expenses, in contrast to capital leases, which are presented as debt.

Converting Operating Leases into Debt In Chapter 8, the basic approach for converting operating leases into debt was presented. You discount future operating lease commitments back at the firm's pretax cost of debt. The present value of the operating lease commitments is then added to the conventional debt of the firm to arrive at the total debt outstanding.

Adjusted debt = Debt + Present value of lease commitments

Once operating leases are recategorized as debt, the operating incomes can be adjusted in two steps. First, the operating lease expense is added back to the operating income, since it is a financial expense. Next, the depreciation on the leased asset is subtracted out to arrive at adjusted operating income:

Adjusted operating income = Operating income + Operating lease expenses
– Depreciation on leased asset

If you assume that the depreciation on the leased asset approximates the principal portion of the debt being repaid, the adjusted operating income can be computed by adding back the imputed interest expense on the debt value of the operating lease expense:

Adjusted operating income = Operating income
+ Debt value of operating lease expense
× Interest rate on debt

ILLUSTRATION 9.5: Adjusting Operating Income for Operating Leases: The Gap in 2001

As a specialty retailer, the Gap has hundreds of stores that are leased, with the leases being treated as operating leases. For the most recent financial year, the Gap has operating lease expenses of $705.8 million. The following table presents the operating lease commitments for the firm over the next five years and the lump sum of commitments beyond that point in time.

Year	Commitment
1	$774.60
2	$749.30
3	$696.50
4	$635.10
5	$529.70
6 and beyond	$5,457.90

The Gap has a pretax cost of debt of 7%. To compute the present value of the commitments, you have to make a judgment on the lump sum commitment in year 6. Based on the average annual lease commitment over the first five years ($677 million), we arrive at an annuity of eight years:[4]

Approximate life of annuity (for year 6 lump sum) = $5,458/677 = 8.06

---

[4]The value is rounded to the nearest integer.

The present values of the commitments at the 7% pretax cost of debt are estimated in the following table:

Year	Commitment	Present Value
1	$774.60	$ 723.93
2	$749.30	$ 654.47
3	$696.50	$ 568.55
4	$635.10	$ 484.51
5	$529.70	$ 377.67
6 and beyond	$682.24	$2,904.59
Debt value of leases		$5,713.72

The present value of operating leases is treated as the equivalent of debt, and is added on to the conventional debt of the firm. The Gap has interest-bearing debt of $1.56 billion on its balance sheet. The cumulated debt for the firm is:

Adjusted debt = Interest-bearing debt + Present value of lease commitments
= $1,560 million + $5,714 million = $7,274 million

To adjust the operating income for the Gap, we first use the full adjustment. To compute depreciation on the leased asset, we assume straight-line depreciation over the lease life[5] (13 years) on the value of the leased asset which is equal to the debt value of the lease commitments:

Straight-line depreciation = Value of leased asset/Lease life = $5,714/13 = $440 million

The Gap's stated operating income of $1,365 million is adjusted as follows:

Adjusted operating income = Operating income + Operating lease expense in current year
− Depreciation on leased asset
= $1,365 million + $706 − $440 = $1,631 million

The approximate adjustment is also estimated below, where we add the added imputed interest expense using the pretax cost of debt:

Adjusted operating income = Operating income + Debt value of leases × Pretax cost of debt
= $1,365 + $5,714 × .07 = $1,765 million

 Oplease.xls: **This spreadsheet allows you to convert operating lease expenses into debt.**

---

[5]The lease life is computed by adding the estimated annuity life of eight years for the lump sum to the initial five years.

> ### WHAT ABOUT OTHER COMMITMENTS?
>
> The argument made about leases can be made about other long-term commitments where a firm has no escape hatches or cancellations options, or where the payment is not connected to performance/earnings. For instance, consider a professional sports team that signs a star player to a 10-year contract, agreeing to pay $5 million a year. If the payment is not contingent on performance, this firm has created the equivalent of debt by signing this contract.
>
> The upshot of this argument is that firms that have no debt on their balance sheet may still be highly levered and subject to default risk as a consequence. For instance, Mario Lemieux, a star player for the Pittsburgh Penguins, the professional ice hockey team, was given partial ownership of the team because of its failure to meet contractual commitments it had made to him.

Accounting Earnings and True Earnings

Firms have become particularly adept at meeting and beating analyst estimates of earnings each quarter. While beating earnings estimates can be viewed as a positive development, some firms adopt accounting techniques that are questionable to accomplish this objective. When valuing these firms, you have to correct operating income for these accounting manipulations to arrive at the correct operating income.

The Phenomenon of Managed Earnings   In the 1990s, firms like Microsoft and Intel set the pattern for technology firms. In fact, Microsoft beat analyst estimates of earnings in 39 of the 40 quarters during the decade, and Intel posted a record almost as impressive. As the market values of these firms skyrocketed, other technology firms followed in their footsteps in trying to deliver earnings that were higher than analyst estimates by at least a few pennies. The evidence is overwhelming that the phenomenon is spreading. For an unprecedented 18 quarters in a row from 1996 to 2000, more firms beat consensus earnings estimates than missed them.[6] In another indication of the management of earnings, the gap between the earnings reported by firms to the Internal Revenue Service and that reported to equity investors has been growing over the last decade.

Given that these analyst estimates are expectations, what does this tell you? One possibility is that analysts consistently under estimate earnings and never learn from their mistakes. While this is a possibility, it seems extremely unlikely to persist over an entire decade. The other is that technology firms particularly have far more discretion in how they measure and report earnings and are using this discretion to beat estimates. In particular, the treatment of research expenses as operating expenses gives these firms an advantage when it comes to managing earnings.

Does managing earnings really increase a firm's stock price? It might be possible to beat analysts quarter after quarter, but are markets as gullible? They are not, and the advent of so-called whispered earnings estimates is in reaction to the consistent delivery of earnings that are above expectations. What are whispered earnings? Whispered earnings are implicit earnings estimates that firms have to beat to

---

[6]I/B/E/S estimates.

surprise the market, and these estimates are usually a few cents higher than analyst estimates. For instance, on April 10, 1997, Intel reported earnings per share of $2.10 per share, higher than analyst estimates of $2.06 per share, but saw its stock price drop 5 points because the whispered earnings estimate had been $2.15. In other words, markets had built into expectations the amount by which Intel had beaten earnings estimates historically.

Why Do Firms Manage Earnings?   Firms generally manage earnings because they believe that they will be rewarded by markets for delivering earnings that are smoother and come in consistently above analyst estimates. As evidence, they point to the success of firms like Microsoft and Intel, and the brutal punishment meted out for firms that do not meet expectations.

Many financial managers also seem to believe that investors take earnings numbers at face value, and work at delivering bottom lines that reflect this belief. This may explain why any efforts by the Financial Accounting Standards Board (FASB) to change the way earnings are measured are fought with vigor, even when the changes make sense. For instance, any attempts by FASB to value the options granted by firms to their managers at a fair value and charge them against earnings or change the way mergers are accounted for have been consistently opposed by technology firms.

It may also be in the best interests of the managers of firms to manage earnings. Managers know that they are more likely to be fired when earnings drop significantly relative to prior periods. Furthermore, there are firms where managerial compensation is still built around profit targets, and meeting these targets can lead to lucrative bonuses.

Techniques for Managing Earnings   How do firms manage earnings? One aspect of good earnings management is the care and nurturing of analyst expectations, a practice that Microsoft perfected during the 1990s. Executives at the firm monitored analyst estimates of earnings, and stepped in to lower expectations when they believed that the estimates were too high.[7] There are several other techniques that are used, and some of the most common will be considered in this section. Not all the techniques are hurtful to the firm, and some may indeed be considered prudent management.

- ■ *Planning ahead.* Firms can plan investments and asset sales to keep earnings rising smoothly.
- ■ *Revenue recognition.* Firms have some leeway when it comes when revenues have to be recognized. As an example, Microsoft, in 1995, adopted an extremely conservative approach to accounting for revenues from its sale of Windows 95, and chose not to show large chunks of revenues that they were entitled (though not obligated) to show.[8] In fact, the firm had accumulated $1.1

---

[7]Microsoft preserved its credibility with analysts by also letting them know when their estimates were too low. Firms that are consistently pessimistic in their analyst presentations lose their credibility and consequently their effectiveness in managing earnings.

[8]Firms that bought Windows 95 in 1995 also bought the right to upgrades and support in 1996 and 1997. Microsoft could have shown these as revenues in 1995.

billion in unearned revenues by the end of 1996 that it could borrow on to supplement earnings in a weaker quarter.

- *Book revenues early.* In an opposite phenomenon, firms sometimes ship products during the final days of a weak quarter to distributors and retailers and record the revenues. Consider the case of MicroStrategy, a technology firm that went public in 1998. In the last two quarters of 1999, the firm reported revenue growth of 20 percent and 27 percent respectively, but much of that growth was attributable to large deals announced just days after each quarter ended, with some revenues attributed to the just-ended quarter.[9] In a more elaborate variant of this strategy, two technology firms, both of which need to boost revenues, can enter into a transaction swapping revenues.

- *Capitalize operating expenses.* Just as with revenue recognition, firms are given some discretion in whether they classify expenses as operating or capital expenses, especially for items like software R&D. AOL's practice of capitalizing and writing off the cost of the CDs and disks it provided with magazines, for instance, allowed it to report positive earnings through much of the late 1990s.

- *Write-offs.* A major restructuring charge can result in lower income in the current period, but it provides two benefits to the firm taking it. Since operating earnings are reported both before and after the restructuring charge, it allows the firm to separate the expense from operations. It also makes beating earnings easier in future quarters. To see how restructuring can boost earnings, consider the case of IBM. By writing off old plants in the year they are closed, IBM was able to drop depreciation expenses to 5 percent of revenue in 1996 from an average of 7 percent in 1990–1994. The difference, in 1996 revenue, was $1.64 billion, or 18 percent of the company's $9.02 billion in pretax profit last year. Technology firms have been particularly adept at writing off a large portion of acquisition costs as "in-process R&D" to register increases in earnings in subsequent quarters. Lev and Deng (1997) studied 389 firms that wrote off in-process R&D between 1990 and 1996[10]; these write-offs amounted, on average, to 72 percent of the purchase price on these acquisitions, and increased the acquiring firm's earnings 22 percent in the fourth quarter after the acquisition.

- *Use reserves.* Firms are allowed to build up reserves for bad debts, product returns, and other potential losses. Some firms are conservative in their estimates in good years, and use the excess reserves that they have built up during these years to smooth out earnings in other years.

- *Income from investments.* Firms with substantial holdings of marketable securities or investments in other firms often have these investments recorded on their books at values well below their market values. Thus, liquidating these investments can result in large capital gains which can boost income in the period.

---

[9]*Forbes* magazine carried an article on March 6, 2000, on MicroStrategy, with this excerpt: "On Oct. 4 MicroStrategy and NCR announced what they described as a $52.5 million licensing and technology agreement. NCR agreed to pay MicroStrategy $27.5 million to license its software. MicroStrategy bought an NCR unit which had been a competitor for what was then $14 million in stock, and agreed to pay $11 million in cash for a data warehousing system. Microstrategy reported $17.5 million of the licensing money as revenue in the third quarter, which had closed four days earlier."

[10]Only three firms wrote off in-process R&D during the prior decade (1980–1989).

Adjustments to Income   To the extent that firms manage earnings, you have to be cautious about using the current year's earnings as a base for projections. This section will consider a series of adjustments that we might need to make to stated earnings before using the number as a basis for projections. We will begin by considering the often subtle differences between one-time, recurring, and unusual items. We will follow up by examining how best to deal with the debris left over by acquisition accounting. Then we will consider how to deal with income from holdings in other companies and investments in marketable securities. Finally, we will look at a series of tests that may help us gauge whether the reported earnings of a firm are reliable indicators of its true earnings.

Extraordinary, Recurring, and Unusual Items   The rule for estimating both operating and net income is simple. The operating income that is used as a base for projections should reflect continuing operations and should not include any items that are one-time or extraordinary. Putting this statement to practice is often a challenge because there are four types of extraordinary items:

1. *One-time expense or income that is truly one-time.* A large restructuring charge that has occurred only once in the past 10 years would be a good example. These expenses can be backed out of the analysis and the operating and net income calculated without them.

2. *Expenses and income that do not occur every year but seem to recur at regular intervals.* Consider, for instance, a firm that has taken a restructuring charge every 3 years for the past 12 years. While not conclusive, this would suggest that the extraordinary expenses are really ordinary expenses that are being bundled by the firm and taken once every three years. Ignoring such an expense would be dangerous because the expected operating income in future years would be overstated. What would make sense would be to take the expense and spread it out on an annual basis. Thus, if the restructuring expense every three years has amounted to $1.5 billion, on average, the operating income for the current year should be reduced by $0.5 billion to reflect the annual charge due to this expense.

3. *Expenses and income that recur every year but with considerable volatility.* The best way to deal with such items is to normalize them by averaging the expenses across time and reducing this year's income by this amount.

4. *Items that recur every year that change signs—positive in some years and negative in others.* Consider, for instance, the effect of foreign currency translations on income. For a firm in the United States, the effect may be negative in years in which the dollar gets stronger and positive in years in which the dollars gets weaker. The most prudent thing to do with these expenses would be to ignore them.

To differentiate between these items requires that you have access to a firm's financial history. For young firms, this may not be available, making it more difficult to draw the line between expenses that should be ignored, expenses that should be normalized and expenses that should be considered in full.

Adjusting for Acquisitions and Divestitures   Acquisition accounting can wreak havoc on reported earnings for years after an acquisition. The most common by-product of acquisitions, if purchase accounting is used, is the amortization of goodwill. This amortization can reduce reported net income in subsequent periods, though operating income should be unaffected. Should we consider amortization to be an operating expense? We think not, since it is both a noncash and often a non-tax-deductible charge. The safest route to follow with goodwill amortization is to look at earnings prior to the amortization.

In recent years, technology companies have used an unusual ploy to get the goodwill created when a premium is paid over book value off their books. Using the argument that the bulk of the market value paid for technology companies comes from the value of the research done by the firm over time, they have written off what they called in-process R&D to preserve consistency. After all, they argue, the R&D they do internally is expensed. As with amortization of goodwill, writing off in-process R&D creates a noncash and non-tax-deductible charge and we should look at earnings prior to their write-off.

When firms divest assets, they can generate income in the form of capital gains. Infrequent divestitures can be treated as one-time items and ignored, but some firms divest assets on a regular basis. For such firms, it is best to ignore the income associated with the divestiture, but to consider the cash flows associated with divestiture, net of capital gains taxes, when estimating net capital expenditures. For instance, a firm with $500 million in capital expenditures, $300 million in depreciation, and $120 million in divestitures every year would have a net capital expenditure of $80 million.

$$\text{Net capital expenditures} = \text{Capital expenditures} - \text{Depreciation} - \text{Divestiture proceeds}$$
$$= \$500 - \$300 - \$120 = \$80 \text{ million}$$

Income from Investments and Cross Holdings   Investments in marketable securities generate two types of income. The first takes the form of interest or dividends and the second is the capital gains (losses) associated with selling securities at prices that are different from their cost bases. In the 1990s, when the stock market was booming, several technology firms used the latter to augment income and beat analyst estimates. In our view, neither type of income should be considered part of the earnings used in valuation for any firm other than a financial service firm that defines its business as the buying and selling of securities (such as a hedge fund). The interest earned on marketable securities should be ignored when valuing the firm, since it is far easier to add the market value of these securities at the end of the process rather than mingle them with other assets. For instance, assume that you have a firm that generates $100 million in after-tax cash flows, but also assume that 20 percent of these cash flows come from holdings of marketable securities with a current market value of $500 million. The remaining 80 percent of the cash flows come operating assets, these cash flows are expected to grow at 5 percent a year in perpetuity, and the cost of capital (based on the risk of these assets) is 10 percent. The value of this firm can be most easily estimated as follows:

Value of operating assets of the firm = $80(1.05)/(.10 − .05)	$1,680 million
Value of marketable securities	$ 500 million
Value of firm	$2,180 million

If we had chosen to discount the entire after-tax cash flow of $100 million, we would have had to adjust the cost of capital downward (to reflect the lower risk of the marketable securities). The adjustment, done right, should yield the same value as that estimated.[11] The capital gain or loss from the sale of marketable securities should be ignored for a different reason. If you incorporate this gain into your income and use it in your forecasts, you are not only counting on being able to sell your securities for higher prices each period in the future but you risk double counting the value of these securities, if you are adding them to the value of the operating assets to arrive at an estimate of value.

Firms that have a substantial number of cross holdings in other firms will often report increases or decreases to earnings reflecting these holdings. The effect on earnings will vary depending on how the holding is categorized. Chapter 3 differentiated between three classifications:

1. A minority passive holding, where only the dividends received from the holding are recorded in income.
2. A minority active interest, where the portion of the net income (or loss) from the subsidiary is shown in the income statement as an adjustment to net income (but not to operating income).
3. A majority active interest, where the income statements are consolidated and the entire operating income of the subsidiary (or holding) are shown as part of the operating income of the firm. In such cases, the net income is usually adjusted for the portion of the subsidiary owned by others (minority interests).

The safest route to take with the first two types of holdings is to ignore the income shown from the holding when valuing a firm, to value the holding separately and to add it to the value obtained for the other assets. As a simple example, consider a firm (Holding Inc.) that generates $100 million in after-tax cash flows from its operating assets and assume that these cash flows will grow at 5 percent a year forever. In addition, assume that the firm owns 10 percent of another firm (Subsidiary Inc.) with after-tax cash flows of $50 million growing at 4 percent a year forever. Finally, assume that the cost of capital for both firms is 10 percent. The firm value for Holding Inc. can be estimated as follows:

Value of operating assets of Holding Inc. = 100(1.05)/(.10 − .05) $2,100 million
Value of operating assets of Subsidiary Inc. = 50(1.04)/(.10 − .04) $ 867 million
Value of Holding Inc. = $2,100 + .10(867) $2,187 million

When earnings are consolidated, you can value the combined firm with the consolidated income statement and then subtract out the value of the minority holdings. To do this, though, you have to assume that the two firms are in the same business and are of equivalent risk since the same cost of capital will be applied to both firm's cash flows. Alternatively, you can strip the entire operating income of the subsidiary from the consolidated operating income and follow the process just laid out to value the holding.

---

[11]This will happen only if the marketable securities are fairly priced and you are earning a fair market return on them. If they are not, you can get different values from the approaches.

ILLUSTRATION 9.6: Adjusting Earnings for One-Time Charges

Between 1997 and 1999, Xerox's reported earnings included a significant number of one-time, extraordinary, and unusual items. The summary of the earnings is provided in the following table:

	1999	1998	1997
Sales	$10,346	$10,696	$ 9,881
Service and rentals	$ 7,856	$ 7,678	$ 7,257
Finance income	$ 1,026	$ 1,073	$ 1,006
Total revenues	*$19,228*	*$19,447*	*$18,144*
Costs and expenses			
Cost of sales	$ 5,744	$ 5,662	$ 5,330
Cost of service and rentals	$ 4,481	$ 4,205	$ 3,778
Inventory charges	$ 0	$ 113	$ 0
Equipment financing interest	$ 547	$ 570	$ 520
Research and development expenses	$ 979	$ 1,040	$ 1,065
SG&A expenses	$ 5,144	$ 5,321	$ 5,212
Restructuring charge and asset impairment	$ 0	$ 1,531	$ 0
Other, net	$ 297	$ 242	$ 98
Total expenses	*$17,192*	*$18,684*	*$16,003*
Earnings before taxes, equity income and minority interests	$ 2,036	$ 763	$ 2,141
– Income taxes	$ 631	$ 207	$ 728
+ Equity in net income of unconsolidated affiliates	$ 68	$ 74	$ 127
– Minority interests in earnings of subsidiaries	$ 49	$ 45	$ 88
Net Income from continuing operations	*$ 1,424*	*$ 585*	*$ 1,452*
– Discontinued operations	$ 0	$ 190	$ 0
Net income	*$ 1,424*	*$ 395*	*$ 1,452*

There are a few obvious adjustments to income that represent one-time charges and a host of other issues. Let us consider first the obvious adjustments:

- The inventory charge and restructuring charges seem to represent one-time charges, though there is the possibility that they represent more serious underlying problems that can create charges in future periods. The charge for discontinued operations also affects only one year's income. These expenses should be added back to arrive at adjusted operating income and net income.
- The other (net) expenses line item is a recurring but volatile item. We would average this expense when forecasting future income.
- To arrive at adjusted net income we would also reverse the last two adjustments by subtracting out the equity in net income of subsidiaries (reflecting Xerox's minority holdings in other firms) and adding back the earnings in minority interests (reflecting minority interests in Xerox's majority holdings).

The following table adjusts the net income in each of the years for the changes suggested:

	1999	1998	1997
Net income from continuing operations	$1,424	$ 585	$1,452
– Equity in net income of unconsolidated affiliates	$ 68	$ 74	$ 127
+ Minority interests in earnings of subsidiaries	$ 49	$ 45	$ 88
+ Restructuring charge (1 – Tax rate)	$ 0	$1,116	$ 0
+ Inventory charge (1 – Tax rate)	$ 0	$ 82	$ 0
+ Other, net (1 – Tax rate)	$ 205	$ 176	$ 65
– Normalized other, net (1 – Tax rate)	$ 147	$ 155	$ 140
Adjusted net income	$1,463	$1,776	$1,338

The restructuring and inventory charges were tax deductible and the after-tax portion was added back; the tax rate was computed based on taxes paid and taxable income for that year.

$$\text{Tax rate in 1998} = \text{Taxes paid/Taxable income} = 207/763 = 27.13\%$$

We also add back the after-tax portion of the other expenses (net) and subtract out the average annual expense over the three years:

$$\text{Average annual other expenses} = (297 + 242 + 98)/3 = \$212 \text{ million}$$

Similar adjustments would need to be made to operating income. Xerox nets out interest expenses against interest income on its Capital subsidiary to report finance income. You would need to separate interest expenses from interest income to arrive at an estimate of operating income for the firm.

What are the other issues? The plethora of one-time charges suggests that there may be ongoing operational problems at Xerox that may cause future charges. In fact, it is not surprising that Xerox had to delay its 10-K filing for 2000 because of accounting issues.

CONCLUSION

Financial statements remain the primary source of information for most investors and analysts. There are differences, however, in how accounting and financial analysis approach answering a number of key questions about the firm.

This chapter begins our analysis of earnings by looking at the accounting categorization of expenses into operating, financing and capital expenses. While operating and financing expenses are shown in income statements, capital expenditures are spread over several time periods and take the form of depreciation and amortization. Accounting standards misclassify operating leases and research and development expenses as operating expenses (when the former should be categorized as financing expenses and the latter as capital expenses). We suggest ways in which earnings can be corrected to better measure the impact of these items.

In the second part of the chapter, we consider the effect of one-time, nonrecurring, and unusual items on earnings. While the underlying principle is that earnings should include only normal expenses, this is put to the test by the attempts on the part of companies to move normal operating expenses into the nonrecurring column and nonoperating income into operating earnings.

WARNING SIGNS IN EARNINGS REPORTS

The most troubling thing about earnings reports is that we are often blind-sided not by the items that get reported (such as extraordinary charges) but by the items that are hidden in other categories. We would suggest the following checklist that should be reviewed about any earnings report to gauge the possibility of such shocks:

- Is earnings growth outstripping revenue growth by a large magnitude year after year? This may well be a sign of increased efficiency, but when the differences are large and continue year after year, you should wonder about the source of these efficiencies.
- Do one-time or nonoperating charges to earnings occur frequently? The charge itself might be categorized differently each year—an inventory charge one year, a restructuring charge the next, and so on. While this may be just bad luck, it may also reflect a conscious effort by a company to move regular operating expenses into these nonoperating items.
- Do any of the operating expenses, as a percent of revenues, swing wildly from year to year? This may suggest that this expense item (say SG&A) includes nonoperating expenses that should really be stripped out and reported separately.
- Does the company manage to beat analyst estimates quarter after quarter by a cent or two? Not every company is a Microsoft. Companies that beat estimates year after year probably are involved in earnings management and are moving earnings across time periods. As growth levels off, this practice can catch up with them.
- Do a substantial proportion of the revenues come from subsidiaries or related holdings? While the sales may be legitimate, the prices set may allow the firm to move earnings from unit to the other and give a misleading view of true earnings at the firm.
- Are accounting rules for valuing inventory or depreciation changed frequently?
- Are acquisitions followed by miraculous increases in earnings? An acquisition strategy is difficult to make successful in the long term. A firm that claims instant success from such as strategy requires scrutiny.
- Is working capital ballooning out as revenues and earning surge? This can sometimes let us pinpoint those firms that generate revenues by lending to their own customers.

None of these factors, by themselves, suggest that we lower earnings for these firms, but combinations of the factors can be viewed as a warning signal that the earnings statement needs to be held up to higher scrutiny.

QUESTIONS AND SHORT PROBLEMS

1. Derra Foods is a specialty food retailer. In its balance sheet, the firm reports $1 billion in book value of equity and no debt, but it has operating leases on all its stores. In the most recent year, the firm made $85 million in operating lease payments, and its commitments to make lease payments for the next five years and beyond are:

Year	Operating Lease Expense
1	$90 million
2	$90 million
3	$85 million
4	$80 million
5	$80 million
6–10	$75 million annually

   If the firm's current cost of borrowing is 7%, estimate the debt value of operating leases. Estimate the book value debt-to-equity ratio.
2. Assume that Derra Foods, in the preceding problem, reported earnings before interest and taxes (with operating leases expensed) of $200 million. Estimate the adjusted operating income, assuming that operating leases are capitalized.
3. FoodMarkets Inc. is a grocery chain. It reported a book debt-to-capital ratio of 10% and a return on capital of 25% on a book value of capital invested of $1 billion. Assume that the firm has significant operating leases. If the operating lease expense in the current year is $100 million and the present value of lease commitments is $750 million, reestimate FoodMarkets' debt to capital and return on capital. (You can assume a pretax cost of debt of 8%.)
4. Zif Software is a firm with significant research and development expenses. In the most recent year, the firm had $100 million in R&D expenses. R&D expenses are amortizable over five years, and over the past five years they are:

Year	R&D Expenses
–5	$ 50 million
–4	$ 60 million
–3	$ 70 million
–2	$ 80 million
–1	$ 90 million
Current year	$100 million

   Assuming a linear amortization schedule (over five years), estimate:
   a. The value of the research asset.
   b. The amount of R&D amortization this year.
   c. The adjustment to operating income.
5. Stellar Computers has a well-earned reputation for earning a high return on capital. The firm had a return on capital of 100% on capital invested of $1.5 billion, in 1999. Assume that you have estimated the value of the research asset to be $1 billion. In addition, the R&D expense this year is $250 million, and the amortization of the research asset is $150 million. Reestimate Stellar Computers' return on capital.

CHAPTER 10

From Earnings to Cash Flows

The value of an asset comes from its capacity to generate cash flows. When valuing a firm, these cash flows should be after taxes, prior to debt payments and after reinvestment needs. When valuing equity, the cash flows should also be after debt payments. There are thus three basic steps to estimating these cash flows. The first is to estimate the earnings generated by a firm on its existing assets and investments, a process we examined in the preceding chapter. The second step is to estimate the portion of this income that would go toward taxes. The third is to develop a measure of how much a firm is reinvesting back for future growth.

This chapter will examine the last two steps. It will begin by investigating the difference between effective and marginal taxes, as well as the effects of substantial net operating losses carried forward. To examine how much a firm is reinvesting, we will break it down into reinvestment in tangible and long-lived assets (net capital expenditures) and short-term assets (working capital). We will use a much broader definition of reinvestment to include investments in R&D and acquisitions as part of capital expenditures.

THE TAX EFFECT

To compute the after-tax operating income, you multiply the earnings before interest and taxes by an estimated tax rate. This simple procedure can be complicated by three issues that often arise in valuation. The first is the wide differences you observe between effective and marginal tax rates for these firms, and the choice you face between the two in valuation. The second issue arises usually with firms with large losses, leading to net operating losses that are carried forward and can save taxes in future years. The third issue arises from the capitalizing of research and development and other expenses. The fact that these expenditures can be expensed immediately lead to much higher tax benefits for the firm.

Effective versus Marginal Tax Rate

You are faced with a choice of several different tax rates. The most widely reported tax rate in financial statements is the effective tax rate, which is computed from the reported income statement as follows:

$$\text{Effective tax rate} = \text{Taxes due} / \text{Taxable income}$$

The second choice on tax rates is the marginal tax rate, which is the tax rate the firm faces on its last dollar of income. This rate depends on the tax code and reflects what firms have to pay as taxes on their marginal income. In the United States, for instance, the federal corporate tax rate on marginal income is 35 percent; with the addition of state and local taxes, most firms face a marginal corporate tax rate of 40 percent or higher.

While the marginal tax rates for most firms in the United States should be fairly similar, there are wide differences in effective tax rates across firms. Figure 10.1 provides a distribution of effective tax rates for firms in the United States in January 2001. Note that a number of firms report effective tax rates of less than 10 percent as well as that a number of firms have effective tax rates that exceed 50 percent. In addition, it is worth noting that this figure does not include about 2,000 firms that did not pay taxes during the most recent financial year or that have a negative effective tax rate.[1]

Reasons for Differences between Marginal and Effective Tax Rates Given that most of the taxable income of publicly traded firms is at the highest marginal tax bracket, why would a firm's effective tax rate be different from its marginal tax rate? There are at least three reasons:

1. Many firms, at least in the United States, follow different accounting standards for tax and for reporting purposes. For instance, firms often use straight line depreciation for reporting purposes and accelerated depreciation for tax pur-

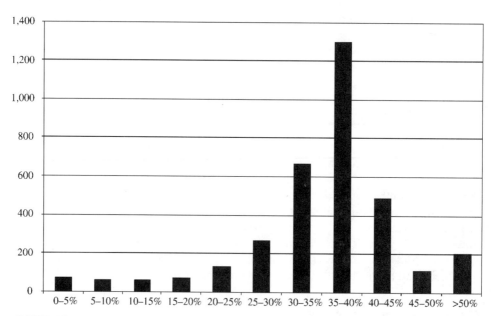

FIGURE 10.1 Effective Tax Rates for U.S. Firms: January 2001
Source: Value Line.

---

[1]A negative effective tax rate usually arises because a firm is reporting an income in its tax books (on which it pays taxes) and a loss in its reporting books.

poses. As a consequence, the reported income is significantly higher than the taxable income, on which taxes are based.[2]

2. Firms sometimes use tax credits to reduce the taxes they pay. These credits, in turn, can reduce the effective tax rate below the marginal tax rate.

3. Finally, firms can sometimes defer taxes on income to future periods. If firms defer taxes, the taxes paid in the current period will be at a rate lower than the marginal tax rate. In a later period, however, when the firm pays the deferred taxes, the effective tax rate will be higher than the marginal tax rate.

Marginal Tax Rates for Multinationals When a firm has global operations, its income is taxed at different rates in different locales. When this occurs, what is the marginal tax rate for the firm? There are three ways in which we can deal with different tax rates.

1. The first is to use a weighted average of the marginal tax rates, with the weights based on the income derived by the firm from each of these countries. The problem with this approach is that the weights will change over time, if income is growing at different rates in different countries.

2. The second is to use the marginal tax rate of the country in which the company is incorporated, with the implicit assumption being that the income generated in other countries will eventually have to be repatriated to the country of origin, at which point the firm will have to pay the marginal tax rate.

3. The third and safest approach is to keep the income from each country separate and apply a different marginal tax rate to each income stream.

Effects of Tax Rate on Value In valuing a firm, should you use the marginal or the effective tax rates? If the same tax rate has to be applied to earnings every period, the safer choice is the marginal tax rate, because none of the three reasons noted can be sustained in perpetuity. As new capital expenditures taper off, the difference between reported and tax income will narrow; tax credits are seldom perpetual and firms eventually do have to pay their deferred taxes. There is no reason, however, why the tax rates used to compute the after-tax cash flows cannot change over time. Thus, in valuing a firm with an effective tax rate of 24 percent in the current period and a marginal tax rate of 35 percent, you can estimate the first year's cash flows using the marginal tax rate of 24 percent and then increase the tax rate to 35 percent over time. It is critical that the tax rate used in perpetuity to compute the terminal value be the marginal tax rate.

When valuing equity, we often start with net income or earnings per share, which are after-tax earnings. While it looks like we can avoid dealing with the estimating of tax rates when using after-tax earnings, appearances are deceptive. The current after-tax earnings of a firm reflect the taxes paid this year. To the extent that tax planning or deferral caused this payment to be very low (low effective tax rates) or very high (high effective tax rates), we run the risk of assuming that the firm can continue to do this in the future if we do not adjust the net income for changes in the tax rates in future years.

---

[2]Since the effective tax rate is based on the taxes paid (which comes from the tax statement) and the reported income, the effective tax rate will be lower than the marginal tax rate for firms that change accounting methods to inflate reported earnings.

ILLUSTRATION 10.1:   Effect of Tax Rate Assumptions on Value

Convoy Inc. is a telecommunications firm that generated $150 million in pretax operating income and reinvested $30 million in the most recent financial year. As a result of tax deferrals, the firm has an effective tax rate of 20%, while its marginal tax rate is 40%. Both the operating income and the reinvestment are expected to grow 10% a year for five years, and 5% thereafter. The firm's cost of capital is 9% and is expected to remain unchanged over time. We will estimate the value of Convoy using three different assumptions about tax rates—the effective tax rate forever, the marginal tax rate forever, and an approach that combines the two rates.

APPROACH 1:   Effective Tax Rate Forever

We first estimate the value of Convoy assuming that the tax rate remains at 20% forever:

Tax Rate	20% Current Year	20% 1	20% 2	20% 3	20% 4	20% 5	20% Terminal Year
EBIT	$150.00	$165.00	$181.50	$199.65	$219.62	$241.58	$253.66
EBIT(1 − t)	$120.00	$132.00	$145.20	$159.72	$175.69	$193.26	$202.92
− Reinvestment	$ 30.00	$ 33.00	$ 36.30	$ 39.93	$ 43.92	$ 48.32	$ 50.73
Free cash flow to firm (FCFF)	$ 90.00	$ 99.00	$108.90	$119.79	$131.77	$144.95	$152.19
Terminal value						$3,804.83	
Present value		$ 90.83	$ 91.66	$ 92.50	$ 93.35	$2,567.08	
Firm value	$2,935.42						

This value is based on the implicit assumption that deferred taxes will never have to be paid by the firm.

APPROACH 2:   Marginal Tax Rate Forever

We next estimate the value of Convoy assuming that the tax rate is the marginal tax rate of 40% forever:

Tax Rate	20% Current Year	40% 1	40% 2	40% 3	40% 4	40% 5	40% Terminal Year
EBIT	$150.00	$165.00	$181.50	$199.65	$219.62	$241.58	$253.66
EBIT(1 − t)	$120.00	$ 99.00	$108.90	$119.79	$131.77	$144.95	$152.19
− Reinvestment	$ 30.00	$ 33.00	$ 36.30	$ 39.93	$ 43.92	$ 48.32	$ 50.73
FCFF	$ 90.00	$ 66.00	$ 72.60	$ 79.86	$ 87.85	$ 96.63	$101.46
Terminal value						$2,536.55	
Present value		$ 60.55	$ 61.11	$ 61.67	$ 62.23	$1,711.39	
Firm value	$1,956.94						

This value is based on the implicit assumption that the firm cannot defer taxes from this point on. In fact, an even more conservative reading would suggest that we should reduce this value by the amount of the cumulated deferred taxes from the past. Thus, if the firm has $200 million in deferred taxes from prior years, and expects to pay these taxes over the next four years in equal annual installments of $50 million, we would first compute the present value of these tax payments:

Present value of deferred tax payments = $50 million(PV of annuity, 9%, 4 years) = $161.99 million

The value of the firm would then be $1,794.96 million.

Firm value after deferred taxes = $1,956.94 − $161.99 million = $1,794.96 million

APPROACH 3: Blended Tax Rates

In the final approach, we will assume that the effective tax will remain 20% for five years and we will use the marginal tax rate to compute the terminal value:

Tax Rate	20% Current Year	20% 1	20% 2	20% 3	20% 4	20% 5	40% Terminal Year
EBIT	$150.00	$165.00	$181.50	$199.65	$219.62	$241.58	$253.66
EBIT(1 − t)	$120.00	$132.00	$145.20	$159.72	$175.69	$193.26	$152.19
− Reinvestment	$ 30.00	$ 33.00	$ 36.30	$ 39.93	$ 43.92	$ 48.32	$ 50.73
FCFF	$ 90.00	$ 99.00	$108.90	$119.79	$131.77	$144.95	$101.46
Terminal value						$2,536.55	
Present value		$ 90.83	$ 91.66	$ 92.50	$ 93.35	$1,742.79	
Firm value	$2,111.12						

Note, however, that the use of the effective tax rate for the first five years will increase the deferred tax liability to the firm. Assuming that the firm ended the current year with a cumulated deferred tax liability of $200 million, we can compute the deferred tax liability by the end of the fifth year:

$$\text{Expected deferred tax liability} = \$200 + (\$165 + \$181.5 + \$199.65 + \$219.62 + \$241.58)$$
$$\times (.40 - .20) = \$401.47 \text{ million}$$

We will assume that the firm will pay this deferred tax liability after year 5, but spread the payments over 10 years, leading to a present value of $167.45 million.

$$\text{Present value of deferred tax payments} = (\$401.47/10)(\text{PV of annuity, 9\%, 10 years})/1.09^5$$
$$= \$167.45 \text{ million}$$

Note that the payments do not start until the sixth year, and hence get discounted back an additional five years. The value of the firm can then be estimated:

$$\text{Value of firm} = \$2,111.12 - \$167.45 = \$1,943.67 \text{ million}$$

---

 taxrate.xls: **This dataset on the Web summarizes average effective tax rates by industry group in the United States for the most recent quarter.**

Effect of Net Operating Losses

For firms with large net operating losses carried forward or continuing operating losses, there is the potential for significant tax savings in the first few years that they generate positive earnings. There are two ways of capturing this effect.

One is to change tax rates over time. In the early years, these firms will have a zero tax rate, as losses carried forward offset income. As the net operating losses decrease, the tax rates will climb toward the marginal tax rate. As the tax rates used to estimate the after-tax operating income change, the rates used to compute the after-tax cost of debt in the cost of capital computation also need to change. Thus, for a firm with net operating losses carried forward, the tax rate used for both the computation of after-tax operating income and cost of capital will be zero during the years when the losses shelter income.

The other approach is often used when valuing firms that already have positive earnings but have a large net operating loss carried forward. Analysts will often value the firm, ignoring the tax savings generated by net operating losses, and then add to this amount the expected tax savings from net operating losses. Often, the expected tax savings are estimated by multiplying the tax rate by the net operating loss. The limitation of doing this is that it assumes that the tax savings are both guaranteed and instantaneous. To the extent that firms have to generate earnings to create these tax savings, and there is uncertainty about earnings, it will over estimate the value of the tax savings.

There are two final points that need to be made about operating losses. To the extent that a potential acquirer can claim the tax savings from net operating losses sooner than the firm generating these losses, there can be potential for tax synergy that we will examine in the chapter on acquisitions. The other is that there are countries where there are significant limitations in how far forward operating losses can be taken. If this is the case, the value of these net operating losses may be reduced.

ILLUSTRATION 10.2: The Effect of Net Operating Loss on Value: Commerce One

This illustration considers the effect of both net operating losses (NOLs) carried forward and expected losses in future periods on the tax rate for Commerce One, a pioneer in the B2B business, in 2001. Commerce One reported an operating loss of $340 million in 2000 and had an accumulated net operating loss of $454 million by the end of that year.

While things do look bleak for the firm, we will assume that revenues will grow significantly over the next decade and that the firm's operating margin will converge on the industry average of 16.36% for mature business service firms. The following table summarizes our projections of revenues and operating income for Commerce One for the next 10 years:

Year	Revenues	Operating Income or Loss	NOL at End of Year	Taxable Income	Taxes	Tax Rate
Current	$ 402	−$ 340	$454	$ 0	$ 0	0.00%
1	$ 603	−$ 206	$660	$ 0	$ 0	0.00%
2	$ 1,205	−$ 107	$767	$ 0	$ 0	0.00%
3	$ 2,170	$ 81	$686	$ 0	$ 0	0.00%
4	$ 3,472	$ 349	$337	$ 0	$ 0	0.00%
5	$ 4,860	$ 642	$ 0	$ 305	$107	16.63%
6	$ 6,561	$ 970	$ 0	$ 970	$339	35.00%
7	$ 8,530	$1,328	$ 0	$1,328	$465	35.00%
8	$10,236	$1,634	$ 0	$1,634	$572	35.00%
9	$11,259	$1,820	$ 0	$1,820	$637	35.00%
10	$11,822	$1,922	$ 0	$1,922	$673	35.00%

Note that Commerce One continues to lose money over the next two years, and adds to its net operating losses. In years 3 and 4, its operating income is positive but it still pays no taxes because of its accumulated net operating losses from prior years. In year 5, it is able to reduce its taxable income by the remaining net operating loss ($337 million), but it begins paying taxes for the first time. We will assume a 35% tax rate and use this as our marginal tax rate beyond year 5. The benefits of the net operating losses are thus built into the cash flows and the value of the firm.

The Tax Benefits of R&D Expensing

The preceding chapter argued that R&D expenses should be capitalized. If we decide to do so, there is a tax benefit that we might be missing. Firms are allowed to deduct their entire R&D expense for tax purposes. In contrast, they are allowed to deduct only the depreciation on their capital expenses. To capture the tax benefit, therefore, you would add the tax savings on the difference between the entire R&D expense and the amortized amount of the research asset to the after-tax operating income of the firm:

$$\text{Additional tax benefit}_{\text{R\&D expensing}} = (\text{Current year's R\&D expense} \\ - \text{Amortization of research asset}) \times \text{Tax rate}$$

A similar adjustment would need to be made for any other operating expense that you choose to capitalize. In Chapter 9, we noted that the adjustment to pretax operating income from capitalizing R&D:

$$\text{Adjusted operating earnings} = \text{Operating earnings} + \text{Current year's R\&D expense} \\ - \text{Amortization of research asset}$$

To estimate the after-tax operating income, we would multiply this value by (1 – Tax rate) and add on the additional tax benefit from above:

$$\begin{aligned}
\text{Adjusted after-tax operating earnings} = &(\text{Operating earnings} \\
&+ \text{Current year's R\&D expense} \\
&- \text{Amortization of research asset}) \\
&\times (1 - \text{Tax rate}) \\
&+ (\text{Current year's R\&D expense} \\
&- \text{Amortization of research asset}) \times \text{Tax rate} \\
= &\text{Operating earnings}(1 - \text{Tax rate}) \\
&+ \text{Current year's R\&D expense} \\
&- \text{Amortization of research asset}
\end{aligned}$$

In other words, the tax benefit from R&D expensing allows us to add the difference between R&D expense and amortization directly to the after-tax operating income (and to net income).

ILLUSTRATION 10.3: Tax Benefit from Expensing: Amgen in 2001

In Chapter 9, we capitalized R&D expenses for Amgen and estimated the value of the research asset to Amgen and adjusted operating income. Reviewing Illustration 9.2, we see the following adjustments:

Current year's R&D expense = $845 million
Amortization of research asset this year = $398 million

To estimate the tax benefit from expensing for Amgen, first assume that the tax rate for Amgen is 35% and note that Amgen can deduct the entire $845 million for tax purposes:

Tax deduction from R&D expense = R&D × Tax rate = 845 × .35 = $295.75 million

If only the amortization had been eligible for a tax deduction in 2000, the tax benefit would have been:

Tax deduction from R&D amortization = $398 million × .35 = $139.30 million

By expensing instead of capitalizing, Amgen was able to derive a much larger tax benefit ($295.75 million versus $139.30 million). The differential tax benefit can be written as:

Differential tax benefit = $295.75 – $139.30 = $156.45 million

Thus, Amgen derives a tax benefit of $156 million because it can expense R&D expenses rather than capitalize them. Completing the analysis, we computed the adjusted after-tax operating income for Amgen. Note that in Illustration 9.2, we estimated the adjusted pretax operating income to be the following:

$$\text{Adjusted pretax operating earnings} = \text{Operating earnings} + \text{Current year's R\&D expense}$$
$$- \text{Amortization of research asset}$$
$$= 1,549 + 845 - 398 = \$1,996 \text{ million}$$

The adjusted after-tax operating income can be written as follows:

$$\text{Adjusted after-tax operating earnings} = \text{After-tax operating earnings} + \text{Current year's R\&D expense}$$
$$- \text{Amortization of research asset}$$
$$= 1,549(1 - .35) + 845 - 398 = \$1,454 \text{ million}$$

Tax Books and Reporting Books   It is no secret that many firms in the United States maintain two sets of books—one for tax purposes and one for reporting purposes—and that this practice not only is legal but also is widely accepted. While the details vary from company to company, the income reported to stockholders generally is much higher than the income reported for tax purposes. When valuing firms, we generally have access only to the former and not the latter and this can affect our estimates in a number of ways:

- Dividing the taxes paid, which is computed on the tax income, by the reported income, which is generally much higher, will yield a tax rate that is lower than the true tax rate. If we use this tax rate as the forecasted tax rate, we could over value the company. This is another reason for shifting to marginal tax rates in future periods.
- If we base the projections on the reported income, we will overstate expected future income. The effect on cash flows is likely to be muted. To see why, consider one very common difference between reporting and tax income: Straight-line depreciation is used to compute the former and accelerated depreciation is used for the latter. Since we add depreciation back to after-tax income to get to cash flows, the drop in depreciation will offset the increase in earnings. The problem, however, is that we understate the tax benefits from depreciation.
- Some companies capitalize expenses for reporting purposes (and depreciate them in subsequent periods) but expense them for tax purposes. Here again, using the income and the capital expenditures from reporting books will result in an understatement of the tax benefits from the expensing.

Thus the problems created by firms having different standards for tax and accounting purposes are much greater if we focus on reported earnings (as is the case when we use earnings multiples) than when we use cash flows. If we did have a choice, however, we would base our valuations on the tax books rather than the reporting books.

DEALING WITH TAX SUBSIDIES

Firms sometimes obtain tax subsidies from the government for investing in specified areas or types of businesses. These tax subsidies can either take the form of reduced tax rates or tax credits. Either way, these subsidies should increase the value of the firm. The question, of course, is how best to build in the effects into the cash flows. Perhaps the simplest approach is to first value the firm, ignoring the tax subsidies, and to then add on the value increment from the subsidies.

For instance, assume that you are valuing a pharmaceutical firm with operations in Puerto Rico, which entitle the firm to a tax break in the form of a lower tax rate on the income generated from these operations. You could value the firm using its normal marginal tax rate, and then add to that value the present value of the tax savings that will be generated by the Puerto Rican operations. There are three advantages with this approach:

1. It allows you to isolate the tax subsidy and consider it only for the period over which you are entitled to it. When the effects of these tax breaks are consolidated with other cash flows, there is a danger that they can be viewed as perpetuities.
2. The discount rate used to compute the tax breaks can be different from the discount rate used on the other cash flows of the firm. Thus, if the tax break is a guaranteed tax credit by the government, you could use a much lower discount rate to compute the present value of the cash flows.
3. Building on the theme that there are few free lunches, it can be argued that governments provide tax breaks for investments only because firms are exposed to higher costs or more risk in these investments. By isolating the value of the tax breaks, firms can then consider whether the trade off operates in their favor. For example, assume that you are a sugar manufacturer that is offered a tax credit by the government for being in the business. In return, the government imposes sugar price controls. The firm can compare the value created by the tax credit with the value lost because of the price controls and decide whether it should fight to preserve its tax credit.

REINVESTMENT NEEDS

The cash flow to the firm is computed after reinvestments. Two components go into estimating reinvestment. The first is net capital expenditures, which is the difference between capital expenditures and depreciation. The other is investments in non-cash working capital.

Net Capital Expenditures

In estimating net capital expenditures, we generally deduct depreciation from capital expenditures. The rationale is that the positive cash flows from depreciation pay for at least a portion of capital expenditures, and that it is only the excess that represents a drain on the firm's cash flows. While information on capital spending and depreciation are usually easily accessible in most financial statements, forecasting these expenditures can be difficult for three reasons. The first is that firms often incur capital spending in chunks—a large investment in one year can be followed by small investments in subsequent years. The second is that the accounting definition of capital spending does not incorporate those capital expenses that are treated as operating expenses such as R&D expenses. The third is that acquisitions are not classified by accountants as capital expenditures. For firms that grow primarily through acquisition, this will result in an understatement of the net capital expenditures.

Lumpy Capital Expenditures and the Need for Smoothing   Firms seldom have smooth capital expenditure streams. Firms can go through periods when capital expenditures are very high (as is the case when a new product is introduced or a new plant built), followed by periods of relatively light capital expenditures. Consequently, when estimating the capital expenditures to use for forecasting future cash flows, you should normalize capital expenditures. There are at least two ways in which you can normalize capital expenditures.

The simplest normalization technique is to average capital expenditures over a number of years. For instance, you could estimate the average capital expenditures over the last four or five years for a manufacturing firm and use that number rather the capital expenditures from the most recent year. By doing so, you could capture the fact that the firm may invest in a new plant every four years. If instead, you had used the capital expenditures from the most recent year, you would either have over estimated capital expenditures (if the firm built a new plant that year) or under estimated it (if the plant had been built in an earlier year).

There are two measurement issues that you will need to confront. One relates to the number of years of history that you should use. The answer will vary across firms and will depend on how infrequently the firm makes large investments. The other is on the question of whether averaging capital expenditures over time requires us to average depreciation as well. Since depreciation is spread out over time, the need for normalization should be much smaller. In addition, the tax benefits received by the firm reflect the actual depreciation in the most recent year, rather than an average depreciation over time. Unless depreciation is as volatile as capital expenditures, it makes more sense to leave depreciation untouched.

For firms with a limited history or firms that have changed their business mix over time, averaging over time is either not an option or will yield numbers that are not indicative of its true capital expenditure needs. For these firms, industry averages for capital expenditures are an alternative. Since the sizes of firms can vary across an industry, the averages are usually computed with capital expenditures as a percent of a base input—revenues and total assets are common choices. We prefer to look at capital expenditures as a percent of depreciation, and average this statistic for the industry. In fact, if there are enough firms in the sample, you could look at the average for a subset of firms that are at the same stage of the life cycle as the firm being analyzed.

ILLUSTRATION 10.4: Estimating Normalized Net Capital Expenditures: Reliance Industries

Reliance Industries is one of India's largest firms and is involved in a multitude of of businesses ranging from chemicals to textiles. The firm makes substantial investments in these businesses, and the following table summarizes the capital expenditures and depreciation for the period 1997 to 2000:

Year	Capital Expenditures	Depreciation	Net Capital Expenditures
1997	INR 24,077	INR 4,101	INR 19,976
1998	INR 23,247	INR 6,673	INR 16,574
1999	INR 18,223	INR 8,550	INR 9,673
2000	INR 21,118	INR 12,784	INR 8,334
Average	INR 21,666	INR 8,027	INR 13,639

The firm's capital expenditures have been volatile, but its depreciation has been trending upward. There are two ways in which we can normalize the net capital expenditures. One is to take the average net capital expenditure over the four year period, which would result in net capital expenditures of INR 13,639 million. The problem with doing this, however, is that the depreciation implicitly being used in the calculation is INR 8,027 million, which is well below the actual depreciation of INR 12,784. A better way to normalize capital expenditures is to use the average capital expenditure over the four-year period (INR 21,166) and depreciation from the current year (INR 12,784) to arrive at a normalized net capital expenditure value:

Normalized net capital expenditures = 21,166 – 12,784 = INR 8,382 million

Note that the normalization did not make much difference in this case because the actual net capital expenditures in 2000 amounted to INR 8,334 million.

Capital Expenses Treated as Operating Expenses   In Chapter 9, we discussed the capitalization of expenses such as R&D and personnel training, where the benefits last over multiple periods, and examined the effects on earnings. There should also clearly be an impact on our estimates of capital expenditures, depreciation, and, consequently, net capital expenditures.

- If we decide to recategorize some operating expenses as capital expenses, we should treat the current period's value for this item as a capital expenditure. For instance, if we decide to capitalize R&D expenses, the amount spent on R&D in the current period has to be added to capital expenditures.

Adjusted capital expenditures = Capital expenditures
+ R&D expenses in current period

- Since capitalizing an operating expense creates an asset, the amortization of this asset should be added to depreciation for the current period. Thus, capitalizing R&D creates a research asset, which generates an amortization in the current period.

Adjusted depreciation and amortization = Depreciation and amortization
+ Amortization of the research asset

■ If we are adding the current period's expense to the capital expenditures and the amortization of the asset to the depreciation, the net capital expenditures of the firm will increase by the difference between the two:

Adjusted net capital expenditure = Net capital expenditures
+ R&D expenses in current period
− Amortization of the research asset

Note that the adjustment that we make to net capital expenditure mirrors the adjustment we make to operating income. Since net capital expenditures are subtracted from after-tax operating income, we are, in a sense, nullifying the impact on cash flows of capitalizing R&D.

ILLUSTRATION 10.5:   Effect of Capitalizing R&D: Amgen

In Illustration 9.2 we capitalized Amgen's R&D expense and created a research asset. In Illustration 10.2 we considered the additional tax benefit generated by the fact that a company can expense the entire amount. In this illustration, we complete the analysis by looking at the impact of capitalization on net capital expenditures.

Reviewing the numbers again, Amgen had an R&D expense of $845 million in 2000. Capitalizing the R&D expenses, using an amortizable life of 10 years, yields a value for the research asset of $3,355 million and an amortization for the current year (2000) of $398 million. In addition, note that Amgen reported capital expenditures of $438 million in 2000 and depreciation and amortization amounting to $212 million. The adjustments to capital expenditures, depreciation, and amortization and net capital expenditures are:

Adjusted capital expenditures = Capital expenditures + R&D expenses in current period
= $438 million + $845 million = $1,283 million

Adjusted depreciation and amortization = Depreciation and amortization
+ Amortization of the research asset
= $212 million + $398 million = $610 million

Adjusted net capital expenditure = Net capital expenditures + R&D expenses in current period
− Amortization of the research asset
= ($438 million − $212 million) + $845 million − $398 million
= $673 million

Viewed in conjunction with the adjustment to after-tax operating income in Illustration 10.2, the change in net capital expenditure is exactly equal to the change in after-tax operating income. Capitalizing R&D thus has no effect on the free cash flow to the firm. Though the bottom-line cash flow does not change, the capitalization of R&D significantly changes the estimates of earnings and reinvestment. Thus it helps us better understand how profitable a firm is and how much it is reinvesting for future growth.

Acquisitions   In estimating capital expenditures, we should not distinguish between internal investments (which are usually categorized as capital expenditures in cash flow statements) and external investments (which are acquisitions). The capital expenditures of a firm, therefore, need to include acquisitions. Since firms seldom make acquisitions every year, and each acquisition has a different price tag, the point about normalizing capital expenditures applies even more strongly to this item. The capital expenditure projections for a firm that makes an acquisition of $100 million approximately every five years should therefore include about $20 million, adjusted for inflation, every year.

Should you distinguish between acquisitions funded with cash versus those funded with stock? We do not believe so. While there may be no cash spent by a firm in the latter case, the firm is increasing the number of shares outstanding. In fact, one way to think about stock-funded acquisitions is that the firm has skipped a step in the funding process. It could have issued the stock to the public, and used the cash to make the acquisitions. Another way of thinking about this issue is that a firm that uses stock to fund acquisitions year after year and is expected to continue to do so in the future will increase the number of shares outstanding. This, in turn, will dilute the value per share to existing stockholders.

ILLUSTRATION 10.6:   Estimating Net Capital Expenditures: Cisco Systems in 1999

Cisco Systems increased its market value a hundredfold during the 1990s, largely based on its capacity to grow revenues and earnings at an annual rate of 60% to 70%. Much of this growth was created by acquisitions of small companies with promising technologies and Cisco's success at converting them into commercial successes. To estimate net capital expenditures for Cisco, we begin with the estimates of capital expenditure ($584 million) and depreciation ($486 million) in the 10-K. Based on these numbers, we would have concluded that Cisco's net capital expenditures in 1999 were $98 million.

The first adjustment we make to this number is to incorporate the effect of research and development expenses. We used a five-year amortizable life and estimated the value of the research asset and the amortization in 1999 in the following table:

Year	R&D Expense	Unamortized at Year-End		Amortization This Year
Current	$1,594.00	100.00%	$1,594.00	
−1	$1,026.00	80.00%	$ 820.80	$205.20
−2	$ 698.00	60.00%	$ 418.80	$139.60
−3	$ 399.00	40.00%	$ 159.60	$ 79.80
−4	$ 211.00	20.00%	$ 42.20	$ 42.20
−5	$ 89.00	0.00%	$ —	$ 17.80
Value of the research asset			$3,035.40	
Amortization this year				$484.60

The net capital expenditures for Cisco were adjusted by adding back the R&D expenses in the most recent financial year ($1,594 million) and subtracting the amortization of the research asset ($485 million).

The second adjustment is to bring in the effect of acquisitions that Cisco made during the last financial year. The following table summarizes the acquisitions made during the year and the price paid on these acquisitions:

Acquired	Method of Acquisition	Price Paid
GeoTel	Pooling	$1,344
Fibex	Pooling	318
Sentient	Pooling	103
American Internet Corporation	Purchase	58
Summa Four	Purchase	129
Clarity Wireless	Purchase	153
Selsius Systems	Purchase	134
PipeLinks	Purchase	118
Amteva Technologies	Purchase	159
Total		$2,516

Dollars in millions.

Note that both purchase and pooling transactions are included, and that the sum total of these acquisitions is added to net capital expenditures in 1999. We are assuming, given Cisco's track record, that its acquisitions in 1999 are not unusual and reflect Cisco's reinvestment policy. The amortization associated with these acquisitions is already included as part of depreciation by the firm.[3] The following table summarizes the final net capital expenditures for Cisco in 1999.

Capital expenditures	$584.00
– Depreciation	$486.00
Net cap ex (from financials)	$98.00
+ R&D expenditures	$1,594.00
– Amortization of R&D	$484.60
+ Acquisitions	$2,516.00
Adjusted net cap ex	$3,723.40

IGNORING ACQUISITIONS IN VALUATION: A POSSIBILITY?

Incorporating acquisitions into net capital expenditures and value can be difficult, and especially so for firms that do large acquisitions infrequently. Predicting whether there will be acquisitions, how much they will cost, and what they will deliver in terms of higher growth can be close to impossible. There is one way in which you can ignore acquisitions, but it does come with a cost. If you assume that firms pay a fair price on acquisitions (i.e., a price that reflects the fair value of the target company) and you assume that the target company stockholders claim any or all synergy or control value, acquisitions have no effect on value no matter how large they might be and how much they might seem to deliver in terms of higher growth. The reason is simple: A fair-value acquisition is an investment that earns its required return—a zero net present value investment.

If you choose not to consider acquisitions when valuing a firm, you have to remain internally consistent. The portion of growth that is due to acquisitions should not be considered in the valuation. A common mistake that is made in valuing companies that have posted impressive historic growth numbers from an acquisition-based strategy is to extrapolate from this growth and ignore acquisitions at the same time. This will result in an overvaluation of your firm, since you have counted the benefits of the acquisitions but have not paid for them.

What is the cost of ignoring acquisitions? Not all acquisitions are fairly priced, and not all synergy and control value ends up with the target company stockholders. Ignoring the costs and benefits of acquisitions will result in an undervaluation of a firm like Cisco that has established a reputation for generating value from acquisitions. However, ignoring acquisitions can overvalue firms that routinely overpay on acquisitions.

 capex.xls: This dataset on the Web summarizes capital expenditures, as a percent of revenues and firm value, by industry group in the United States for the most recent quarter.

---

[3]It is only the tax-deductible amortization that really matters. To the extent that amortization is not tax deductible, you would look at the EBIT before the amortization and not consider it while estimating net capital expenditures.

Investment in Working Capital

The second component of reinvestment is the cash that needs to be set aside for working capital needs. Increases in working capital tie up more cash and hence generate negative cash flows. Conversely, decreases in working capital release cash and positive cash flows.

Defining Working Capital   Working capital is usually defined to be the difference between current assets and current liabilities. However, we will modify that definition when we measure working capital for valuation purposes.

- We will back out cash and investments in marketable securities from current assets. This is because cash, especially in large amounts, is invested by firms in Treasury bills, short-term government securities, or commercial paper. While the return on these investments may be lower than what the firm may make on its real investments, they represent a fair return for riskless investments. Unlike inventory, accounts receivable and other current assets, cash then earns a fair return and should not be included in measures of working capital. Are there exceptions to this rule? When valuing a firm that has to maintain a large cash balance for day-to-day operations or a firm that operates in a market in a poorly developed banking system, you could consider the cash needed for operations as a part of working capital.
- We will also back out all interest-bearing debt—short-term debt and the portion of long-term debt that is due in the current period—from the current liabilities. This debt will be considered when computing cost of capital and it would be inappropriate to count it twice.

The noncash working capital varies widely across firms in different sectors and often across firms in the same sector. Figure 10.2 shows the distribution of noncash working capital as a percent of revenues for U.S. firms in January 2001.

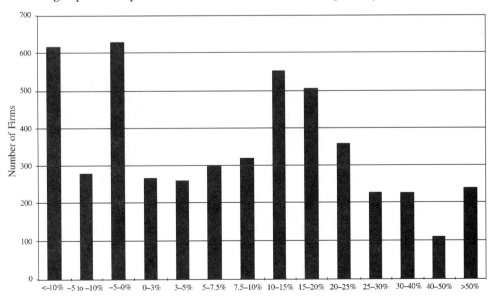

FIGURE 10.2   Noncash Working Capital as Percent of Revenues
Source: Value Line.

ILLUSTRATION 10.7:   Working Capital versus Noncash Working Capital: Marks and Spencer

Marks and Spencer operates retail stores in the United Kingdom and has substantial holdings in retail firms in other parts of the world. The following table breaks down the components of working capital for the firm for 1999 and 2000 and reports both the total working capital and noncash working capital in each year:

	1999	2000
Cash and near cash	282	301
Marketable securities	204	386
Trade debtors (accounts receivable)	1,980	2,186
Stocks (Inventory)	515	475
Other current assets	271	281
Total current assets	3,252	3,629
Noncash current assets	2,766	2,942
Trade creditors (accounts payable)	215	219
Short-term debt	913	1,169
Other short-term liabilities	903	774
Total current liabilities	2,031	2,162
Nondebt current liabilities	1,118	993
Working capital	1,221	1,467
Noncash working capital	1,648	1,949

The noncash working capital is substantially higher than the working capital in both years. We would suggest that the former is a much better measure of cash tied up in working capital.

Estimating Expected Changes in Noncash Working Capital   While we can estimate the noncash working capital change fairly simply for any year using financial statements, this estimate has to be used with caution. Changes in noncash working capital are unstable, with big increases in some years followed by big decreases in the following years. To ensure that the projections are not the result of an unusual base year, you should tie the changes in working capital to expected changes in revenues or costs of goods sold at the firm over time. The noncash working capital as a percent of revenues can be used, in conjunction with expected revenue changes each period, to estimate projected changes in noncash working capital over time. You can obtain the noncash working capital as a percent of revenues by looking at the firm's history or at industry standards.

Should you break working capital down into more detail? In other words, is there a payoff to estimating individual items, such as accounts receivable, inventory, and accounts payable separately? The answer will depend on both the firm being analyzed and how far into the future working capital is being projected. For firms where inventory and accounts receivable behave in very different ways as revenues grow, it clearly makes sense to break down into detail. The cost, of course, is that it increases the number of inputs needed to value a firm. In addition, the payoff to breaking working capital down into individual items will become smaller as we go further into the future. For most firms, estimating a composite number for noncash working capital is easier to do and often more accurate than breaking it down into more detail.

ILLUSTRATION 10.8:   Estimating Noncash Working Capital Needs: The Gap

As a specialty retailer, the Gap has substantial inventory and working capital needs. At the end of the 2000 financial year (which concluded in January 2001), the Gap reported $1,904 million in inventory and $335 million in other noncash current assets. At the same time, the accounts payable amounted to $1,067 million and other non-interest-bearing current liabilities of $702 million. The noncash working capital for the Gap in January 2001 can be estimated as follows:

$$\text{Noncash working capital} = \$1,904 + \$335 - \$1,067 - \$702 = \$470 \text{ million}$$

The following table reports on the noncash working capital at the end of the previous year and the total revenues in each year:

	1999	2000	Change
Inventory	$ 1,462	$ 1,904	$ 442
Other noncash current assets	$ 285	$ 335	$ 50
Accounts payable	$ 806	$ 1,067	$ 261
Other noninterest-bearing current liabilities	$ 778	$ 702	-$ 76
Noncash working capital	$ 163	$ 470	$ 307
Revenues	$11,635	$13,673	$2,038
Working capital as % of revenues	1.40%	3.44%	15.06%

The noncash working capital increased by $307 million from last year to this one. When forecasting the noncash working capital needs for the Gap, there are five choices:

1. One is to use the change in noncash working capital from the year ($307 million) and to grow that change at the same rate as earnings are expected to grow in the future. This is probably the least desirable option because changes in noncash working capital from year to year are extremely volatile, and last year's change may in fact be an outlier.
2. The second is to base our changes on noncash working capital as a percent of revenues in the most recent year and expected revenue growth in future years. In the case of the Gap, that would indicate that noncash working capital changes in future years will be 3.44% of revenue changes in that year. This is a much better option than the first one, but the noncash working capital as a percent of revenues can also change from one year to the next.
3. The third is to base our changes on the marginal noncash working capital as a percent of revenues in the most recent year, computed by dividing the change in noncash working capital in the most recent year and the change in revenues in the most recent year, and expected revenue growth in future years. In the case of the Gap, this would lead to noncash working capital changes being 15.06% of revenues in future periods. This approach is best used for firms whose business is changing and where growth is occurring in areas different from the past. For instance, a brick-and-mortar retailer that is growing mostly online may have a very different marginal working capital requirement than the total.
4. The fourth is to base our changes on the noncash working capital as a percent of revenues over a historical period. For instance, noncash working capital as a percent of revenues between 1997 and 2000 averaged out to 4.5% of revenues. The advantage of this approach is that it smooths out year-to-year shifts, but it may not be appropriate if there is a trend (upward or downward) in working capital.
5. The final approach is to ignore the working capital history of the firm and to base the projections on the industry average for noncash working capital as a percent of revenues. This approach is most appropriate when a firm's history reveals a working capital that is volatile and unpredictable. It is also the best way of estimating noncash working capital for very small firms that

may see economies of scale as they grow. While these conditions do not apply for the Gap, we can still estimate noncash working capital requirements using the average noncash working capital as a percent of revenues for specialty retailers is 7.54%.

To illustrate how much of a change each of these assumptions can have on working capital requirements, the following table forecasts expected changes in noncash working capital (WC) using each of them. In making these estimates, we have assumed a 10% growth rate in revenues and earnings for the Gap for the next five years.

	Current	1	2	3	4	5
Revenues	$13,673.00	$15,040.30	$16,544.33	$18,198.76	$20,018.64	$22,020.50
Change in revenues		$ 1,367.30	$ 1,504.03	$ 1,654.43	$ 1,819.88	$ 2,001.86
1. Change in noncash WC	$ 307.00	$ 337.70	$ 371.47	$ 408.62	$ 449.48	$ 494.43
2. Current: WC/revenues	3.44%	$ 47.00	$ 51.70	$ 56.87	$ 62.56	$ 68.81
3. Marginal: WC/revenues	15.06%	$ 205.97	$ 226.56	$ 249.22	$ 274.14	$ 301.56
4. Historical average	4.50%	$ 61.53	$ 67.68	$ 74.45	$ 81.89	$ 90.08
5. Industry average	7.54%	$ 103.09	$ 113.40	$ 124.74	$ 137.22	$ 150.94

The noncash working capital investment varies widely across the five approaches that have been described here.

Negative Working Capital (or Changes)   Can the change in noncash working capital be negative? The answer is clearly yes. Consider, though, the implications of such a change. When noncash working capital decreases, it releases tied-up cash and increases the cash flow of the firm. If a firm has bloated inventory or gives out credit too easily, managing one or both components more efficiently can reduce working capital and be a source of positive cash flows into the immediate future—three, four, or even five years. The question, however, becomes whether it can be a source of cash flows for longer than that. At some point in time, there will be no more inefficiencies left in the system, and any further decreases in working capital can have negative consequences for revenue growth and profits. Therefore, it appears that for firms with positive working capital, decreases in working capital are feasible only for short periods. In fact, once working capital is being managed efficiently, the working capital changes from year to year should be estimated using working capital as a percent of revenues. For example, consider a firm that has noncash working capital that represents 10 percent of revenues and that you believe that better management of working capital could reduce this to 6 percent of revenues. You could allow working capital to decline each year for the next four years from 10 percent to 6 percent, and, once this adjustment is made, begin estimating the working capital requirement each year as 6 percent of additional revenues. The following table provides estimates of the change in noncash working capital on this firm, assuming that current revenues are $1 billion and that revenues are expected to grow 10 percent a year for the next 15 years.

Year	Current	1	2	3	4	5
Revenues	$1,000.00	$1,100.00	$1,210.00	$1,331.00	$1,464.10	$1,610.51
Noncash WC as % of revenues	10%	9%	8%	7%	6%	6%
Noncash working capital	$ 100.00	$ 99.00	$ 96.80	$ 93.17	$ 87.85	$ 96.63
Change in noncash WC		–$ 1.00	–$ 2.20	–$ .63	–$ 5.32	$ 8.78

Can working capital itself be negative? Again, the answer is yes. Firms whose current liabilities exceed noncash current assets have negative noncash working capital. This is a thornier issue than negative changes in working capital. A firm that has a negative working capital is, in a sense, using supplier credit as a source of capital, especially if the negative working capital becomes larger as the firm becomes larger. A number of firms, with Wal-Mart being the most prominent example, have used this strategy to grow. While this may seem like a cost-efficient strategy, there are potential downsides. The first is that supplier credit is generally not really free. To the extent that delaying paying supplier bills may lead to the loss of cash discounts and other price breaks, firms are paying for the privilege. Thus a firm that decides to adopt this strategy will have to compare the costs of this capital to more traditional forms of borrowing.

The second downside is that a negative noncash working capital has generally been viewed both by accountants and ratings agencies as a source of default risk. To the extent that a firm's rating drops and interest rates paid by the firm increase, there may be costs created for other capital by using supplier credit as a source. As a practical question, you still have an estimation problem on your hands when forecasting working capital requirements for a firm that has negative noncash working capital. As in the previous scenario, with negative changes in noncash working capital, there is no reason why firms cannot continue to use supplier credit as a source of capital in the short term. In the long term, however, we should not assume that noncash working capital will become more and more negative over time. At some point in the future we have to assume either that the change in noncash working capital is zero or that pressure will build for increases in working capital.

---

 wcdata.xls: This dataset on the Web summarizes noncash working capital needs by industry group in the United States for the most recent quarter.

CONCLUSION

When valuing a firm, the cash flows that are discounted should be after taxes and reinvestment needs but before debt payments. This chapter considered some of the challenges in coming up with this number for firms.

The chapter began with the corrected and updated version of income described in Chapter 9. To state this income in after-tax terms, you need a tax rate.

Firms generally state their effective tax rates in their financial statements, but these effective tax rates can be different from marginal tax rates. While the effective tax rate can be used to arrive at the after-tax operating income in the early years, the tax rate used should converge on the marginal tax rate in future periods. For firms that are losing money and not paying taxes, the net operating losses that they are accumulating will protect some of their future income from taxation.

The reinvestment that firms make in their own operations is then considered in two parts. The first part is the net capital expenditure of the firm which is the difference between capital expenditures (a cash outflow) and depreciation (effectively a cash inflow). In this net capital expenditure, we include the capitalized operating expenses (such as R&D) and acquisitions. The second part relates to investments in noncash working capital, mainly inventory and accounts receivable. Increases in noncash working capital represent cash outflows to the firm, while decreases represent cash inflows. Noncash working capital at most firms tends to be volatile and may need to be smoothed out when forecasting future cash flows.

QUESTIONS AND SHORT PROBLEMS

1. You are valuing GenFlex, a small manufacturing firm, which reported paying taxes of $12.5 million on taxable income of $50 million and reinvesting $15 million in the most recent year. The firm has no debt outstanding, the cost of capital is 11%, and the marginal tax rate for the firm is 35%. Assuming that the firm's earnings and reinvestment are expected to grow 10% a year for three years and 5% a year forever after that, estimate the value of this firm:
   a. Using the effective tax rate to estimate after-tax operating income.
   b. Using the marginal tax rate to estimate after-tax operating income.
   c. Using the effective tax rate for the next three years and the marginal tax rate in year 4.

2. You are trying to estimate the free cash flow to the firm for RevTech, a technology firm. The firm reported $80 million in earnings before interest and taxes, capital expenditures of $30 million, and depreciation of $20 million in the most recent year. There are two additional complications:
   - The firm had R&D expenses of $50 million in the most recent year. You believe that a three-year amortizable life is appropriate for this firm and the R&D expenses for the past three years have amounted to $20 million, $30 million, and $40 million respectively.
   - The firm also made two acquisitions during the year—a cash-based acquisition for $45 million and a stock-based acquisition for $35 million.
   If the firm has no working capital requirements and a tax rate of 40%, estimate the free cash flow to the firm in the most recent year.

3. Lewis Clark, a firm in the travel business, reported earnings before interest and taxes of $60 million last year, but you have uncovered the following additional items of interest:

- The firm had operating lease expenses of $50 million last year and has a commitment to make equivalent payments for the next eight years.
- The firm reported capital expenditures of $30 million and depreciation of $50 million last year. However, the firm also made two acquisitions, one funded with cash for $50 million and another funded with a stock swap for $30 million. The amortization of these acquisitions is already included in the current year's depreciation.
- The total working capital increased from $180 million at the start of the year to $200 million at the end of the year. However, the firm's cash balance was a significant portion of this working capital and increased from $80 million at the start of the year to $120 million at the end. (The cash is invested in T-bills.)
- The tax rate is 40%, and the firm's pretax cost of debt is 6%.

Estimate the free cash flows to the firm last year.

4. The following is the balance sheet for Ford Motor Company as of December 31, 1994 (in millions).

Assets		Liabilities	
Cash	$ 19,927	Accounts payable	$ 11,635
Receivables	$132,904	Debt due within 1 year	$ 36,240
Inventory	$ 10,128	Other current liabilities	$ 2,721
Current assets	*$ 91,524*	*Current liabilities*	*$ 50,596*
Fixed assets	$ 45,586	Short-term debt	$ 36,200
		Long-term debt	$ 37,490
		Equity	$ 12,824
Total assets	$137,110	Total liabilities	$137,110

The firm had revenues of $154,951 million in 1994 and cost of goods sold of $103,817 million.
  a. Estimate the net working capital.
  b. Estimate the noncash working capital.
  c. Estimate noncash working capital as a percent of revenues.

5. Continuing problem 4, assume that you expect Ford's revenues to grow 10% a year for the next five years.
  a. Estimate the expected changes in noncash working capital each year, assuming that noncash working capital as a percent of revenues remains at 1994 levels.
  b. Estimate the expected changes in noncash working capital each year, assuming that noncash working capital as a percent of revenues will converge on the industry average of 4.3% of revenues.

6. Newell Stores is a retail firm that reported $1 billion in revenues, $80 million in after-tax operating income, and noncash working capital of −$50 million last year.
  a. Assuming that working capital as a percent of revenues remains unchanged next year and that there are no net capital expenditures, estimate the free cash flow to the firm if revenues are expected to grow 10%.
  b. If you are projecting free cash flows to the firm for the next 10 years, would you make the same assumptions about working capital? Why or why not?

CHAPTER 11

Estimating Growth

The value of a firm is the present value of expected future cash flows generated by the firm. The most critical input in valuation, especially for high-growth firms, is the growth rate to use to forecast future revenues and earnings. This chapter considers how best to estimate these growth rates for firms, including those with low revenues and negative earnings.

There are three basic ways of estimating growth for any firm. One is to look at the growth in a firm's past earnings—its historical growth rate. While this can be a useful input when valuing stable firms, there are both dangers and limitations in using this growth rate for high-growth firms. The historical growth rate can often not be estimated, and even if it can, it cannot be relied on as an estimate of expected future growth.

The second is to trust the equity research analysts that follow the firm to come up with the right estimate of growth for the firm, and to use that growth rate in valuation. While many firms are widely followed by analysts, the quality of growth estimates, especially over longer periods, is poor. Relying on these growth estimates in a valuation can lead to erroneous and inconsistent estimates of value.

The third is to estimate the growth from a firm's fundamentals. A firm's growth ultimately is determined by how much is reinvested into new assets and the quality of these investments, with investments widely defined to include acquisitions, building distribution channels, or even expanding marketing capabilities. By estimating these inputs, you are, in a sense, estimating a firm's fundamental growth rate.

THE IMPORTANCE OF GROWTH

A firm can be valuable because it owns assets that generate cash flows now or because it is expected to acquire such assets in the future. The first group of assets is categorized as assets in place and the second as growth assets. Figure 11.1 presents a financial balance sheet for a firm. Note that an accounting balance sheet can be very different from a financial balance sheet, since accounting for growth assets tends to be both conservative and inconsistent.

For high-growth firms, accounting balance sheets do a poor job of summarizing the values of the assets of the firm because they completely ignore the largest component of value, which is future growth. The problems are exacerbated for firms that invest in research, because the book value will not include the most important asset at these firms—the research asset.

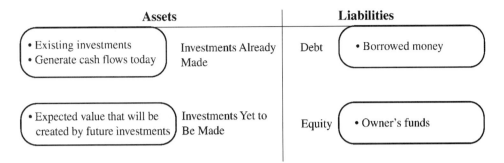

Assets			Liabilities

- Existing investments
- Generate cash flows today — Investments Already Made

Debt — • Borrowed money

- Expected value that will be created by future investments — Investments Yet to Be Made

Equity — • Owner's funds

FIGURE 11.1 Financial View of a Firm

HISTORICAL GROWTH

When estimating the expected growth for a firm, we generally begin by looking at the firm's history. How rapidly have the firm's operations, as measured by revenues or earnings, grown in the recent past? While past growth is not always a good indicator of future growth, it does convey information that can be valuable while making estimates for the future. This section begins by looking at measurement issues that arise when estimating past growth, and then considers how past growth can be used in projections.

Estimating Historical Growth

Given a firm's earnings history, estimating historical growth rates may seem like a simple exercise but there are several measurement problems that may arise. In particular, the average growth rates can be different, depending on how the average is estimated and whether you allow for compounding in the growth over time. Estimating growth rates can also be complicated by the presence of negative earnings in the past or in the current period.

Arithmetic versus Geometric Averages The average growth rate can vary depending on whether it is an arithmetic average or a geometric average. The arithmetic average is the simple average of past growth rates, while the geometric mean takes into account the compounding that occurs from period to period:

$$\text{Arithmetic average} = \frac{\sum_{t=-n}^{t=-1} g_t}{n}$$

where g_t = Growth rate in year t

$$\text{Geometric average} = \left(\frac{\text{Earnings}_0}{\text{Earnings}_{-n}} \right)^{(1/n)} - 1$$

where Earnings_t = Earnings in year t

The two estimates can be very different, especially for firms with volatile earnings. The geometric average is a much more accurate measure of true growth in past earnings, especially when year-to-year growth has been erratic.

In fact, the point about arithmetic and geometric growth rates also applies to revenues, though the difference between the two growth rates tend to be smaller for revenues than for earnings. For firms with volatile earnings and revenues, the caveats about using arithmetic growth carry even more weight.

ILLUSTRATION 11.1:   Differences between Arithmetic and Geometric Averages: Motorola

The following table reports the revenues, EBITDA, EBIT, and net income for Motorola for each year from 1994 to 1999. The arithmetic and geometric average growth rates in each series are reported at the bottom of the table.

Year	Revenues	Percent Change	EBITDA	Percent Change	EBIT	Percent Change	Net Income	Percent Change
1994	$22,245		$4,151		$2,604		$1,560	
1995	$27,037	21.54%	$4,850	16.84%	$2,931	12.56%	$1,781	14.17%
1996	$27,973	3.46%	$4,268	−12.00%	$1,960	−33.13%	$1,154	−35.20%
1997	$29,794	6.51%	$4,276	0.19%	$1,947	−0.66%	$1,180	2.25%
1998	$29,398	−1.33%	$3,019	−29.40%	$ 822	−57.78%	$ 212	−82.03%
1999	$30,931	5.21%	$5,398	78.80%	$3,216	291.24%	$ 817	285.38%
Arithmetic average		7.08%		10.89%		42.45%		36.91%
Geometric average		6.82%		5.39%		4.31%		−12.13%
Standard deviation		8.61%		41.56%		141.78%		143.88%

Geometric average = $(\text{Earnings}_{1999}/\text{Earnings}_{1994})^{1/5} - 1$

The arithmetic average growth rate is higher than the geometric average growth rate for all four items, but the difference is much larger with net income and operating income (EBIT) than it is with revenues and EBITDA. This is because the net and operating income are the most volatile of the numbers, with a standard deviation in year-to-year changes of almost 140%. Looking at the net and operating income in 1994 and 1999, it is also quite clear that the geometric averages are much better indicators of true growth. Motorola's operating income grew only marginally during the period, and this is reflected in its geometric average growth rate, which is 4.31%, but not in its arithmetic average growth rate, which indicates much faster growth. Motorola's net income dropped by almost 50% during the period. This is reflected in its negative geometric average growth rate but its arithmetic average growth rate is 36.91%.

Linear and Log-Linear Regression Models   The arithmetic mean weights percentage changes in earnings in each period equally and ignores compounding effects in earnings. The geometric mean considers compounding but focuses on the first and the last earnings observations in the series—it ignores the information in the intermediate observations and any trend in growth rates that may have developed over the period. These problems are at least partially overcome by using ordinary least squares (OLS)[1] regressions of earnings per share (EPS) against time. The linear version of this model is:

$$\text{EPS}_t = a + bt$$

where EPS_t = Earnings per share in period t
$\quad\quad$ t = Time period t

---

[1]An ordinary least squares (OLS) regression estimates regression coefficients by minimizing the squared differences of predicted values from actual values.

The slope coefficient on the time variable is a measure of earnings change per time period. The problem, however, with the linear model is that it specifies growth in terms of dollar EPS and is not appropriate for projecting future growth, given compounding.

The log-linear version of this model converts the coefficient into a percentage change:

$$\ln(EPS_t) = a + bt$$

where $\ln(EPS_t)$ = Natural logarithm of earnings per share in period t
t = Time period t

The coefficient b on the time variable becomes a measure of the percentage change in earnings per unit time.

ILLUSTRATION 11.2: Linear and Log-Linear Models of Growth: General Electric

The earnings per share from 1991 until 2000 is provided for General Electric (GE) in the following table with the percentage changes and the natural logs of the earnings per share computed each year:

Year	Calendar Year	EPS	Percent Change in EPS	ln(EPS)
1	1991	0.42		−0.8675
2	1992	0.41	−2.38%	−0.8916
3	1993	0.4	−2.44%	−0.9163
4	1994	0.58	45.00%	−0.5447
5	1995	0.65	12.07%	−0.4308
6	1996	0.72	10.77%	−0.3285
7	1997	0.82	13.89%	−0.1985
8	1998	0.93	13.41%	−0.0726
9	1999	1.07	15.05%	0.0677
10	2000	1.27	18.69%	0.2390

There are a number of ways in which we can estimate the growth rate in earnings per share at GE between 1991 and 2000. One is to compute the arithmetic and geometric averages:

Arithmetic average growth rate in earnings per share = 13.79%
Geometric average growth rate in earnings per share = $(1.27/0.42)^{1/9} - 1 = 13.08\%$

The second is to run a linear regression of earnings per share against a time variable (where the earliest year is given a value of 1, the next year a value of 2 and so on):

Linear regression: EPS = 0.2033 + 0.0952 EPS R^2 = 94.5%
                   [4.03]   [11.07]

This regression would indicate that the earnings per share increased 9.52 cents a year from 1991 to 2000. We can convert it into a percent growth in earnings per share by dividing this change by the average earnings per share over the period:

Growth rate in earnings per share = Coefficient on linear regression/Average EPS
                   = 0.0952/0.727 = 13.10%

Finally, you can regress ln(EPS) against the time variable:

$$\text{Log-linear regression: } \ln(\text{EPS}) = -1.1288 + 0.1335\,t \qquad R^2 = 95.8\%$$
$$[19.53] \quad [14.34]$$

The coefficient on the time variable here can be viewed as a measure of compounded percent growth in earnings per share; GE's earnings per share grew at 13.35% a year based on this regression.

The numbers are close using all the approaches because there is so little variability in the growth rate of earnings per share at GE. For companies with more volatile earnings, the differences will be much larger.

Negative Earnings Measures of historical growth are distorted by the presence of negative earnings numbers. The percentage change in earnings on a year-by-year basis is defined as:

$$\% \text{ change in EPS in period } t = (\text{EPS}_t - \text{EPS}_{t-1})/\text{EPS}_{t-1}$$

If EPS_{t-1} is negative, this calculation yields a meaningless number. This extends into the calculation of the geometric mean. If the EPS in the initial time period is negative or zero, the geometric mean is not meaningful.

Similar problems arise in log-linear regressions, since the EPS has to be greater than zero for the log transformation to exist. There are at least two ways of trying to get meaningful estimates of earnings growth for firms with negative earnings. One is to run the linear regression of EPS against time specified in the previous regression:

$$\text{EPS} = a + bt$$

The growth rate can then be approximated as follows:

$$\text{Growth rate in EPS} = b/\text{Average EPS over the time period of the regression}$$

This assumes that the average EPS over the time period is positive. Another approach to estimating growth for these firms uses the higher of the two numbers (EPS_t or EPS_{t-1}) in the denominator:

$$\% \text{ change in EPS} = (\text{EPS}_t - \text{EPS}_{t-1})/\text{Max}(\text{EPS}_t, \text{EPS}_{t-1})$$

Alternatively, you could use the absolute value of EPS in the previous period.

Note that these approaches to estimating historical growth do not provide any information on whether these growth rates are useful in predicting future growth. It is not incorrect, and, in fact, it may be appropriate to conclude that the historical growth rate is not meaningful when earnings are negative and to ignore it in predicting future growth.

ILLUSTRATION 11.3: Negative Earnings: Commerce One and Aracruz Celulose

The problems with estimating earnings growth when earnings are negative can be seen even for firms that have only negative earnings. For instance, Commerce One, the B2B firm reported operating earnings (EBIT) of –$53 million in 1999 and –$340 million in 2000. Clearly, the firm's earnings deteriorated, but estimating a standard earnings growth rate would lead us to the following growth rate:

Earnings growth for Commerce One in 2000 = [–340 – (–53)]/–53 = 5.41 or 541%

Now consider Aracruz, a Brazilian paper and pulp company, susceptible like other firms in the industry to the ebbs and flows of commodity prices. The following table reports the earnings per share at the firm from 1995 to 2000.

Year	EPS in Brazilian Reals
1995	0.302
1996	0.041
1997	0.017
1998	–0.067
1999	0.065
2000	0.437

The negative net income (and earnings per share) numbers in 1998 make the estimation of a growth rate in 1999 problematic. For instance, the firm has a loss per share of 0.067 BR in 1998 and and a profit per share of 0.065 BR in 1999. The growth rate in earnings per share estimated using the conventional equation, would be:

Earnings growth rate in 1999 = [$0.065 – (–$0.067)]/(–$0.067) = –197%

This growth rate, a negative number, makes no sense given the improvement in earnings during the year. There are two fixes to this problem. One is to replace the actual earnings per share in the denominator with the absolute value:

Earnings growth rate in 1999$_{absolute\ value}$ = [$0.065 – (–$0.067)]/($0.067) = 192%

The other is to use the higher of the earnings per share from the two years yielding:

Earnings growth rate in 1999$_{higher\ value}$= [$0.065 – (–$0.067)]/($0.065) = 203%

While the growth rate is now positive, as you would expect it to be, the values for the growth rates themselves are not very useful for making estimates for the future.

Time Series Models to Predict Earnings per Share Time series models use the same historical information as the simpler models described in the previous section. They attempt to extract better predictions from this data, however, through the use of sophisticated statistical techniques.

Box-Jenkins Models Box and Jenkins developed a procedure for analyzing and forecasting univariate time series data using an autoregressive integrated moving average model. Autoregressive integrated moving average (ARIMA) models model a value in a time series as a linear combination of past values and past errors (shocks). Since historical data is used, these models are appropriate as long as the data does not show deterministic behavior, such as a time trend or a dependence on outside events or variables. ARIMA models are usually denoted by the notation:

$$ARIMA(p, d, q)$$

where p = Degree of the autoregressive part
       d = Degree of differencing
       q = Degree of the moving average process

The mathematical model can then be written as follows:

$$w_t = \phi_1 w_{t-1} + \phi_2 w_{t-2} + \ldots + \phi_p w_{t-p} + \theta_0 - \theta_1 a_{t-1} - \theta_2 a_{t-2} - \ldots - \theta_q a_{t-q} + \varepsilon_t$$

where

w_t = Original data series or difference of degree d of the original data
$\phi_1, \phi_2 \ldots \phi_p$ = Autoregressive parameters
θ_0 = Constant term
$\theta_1, \theta_2, \ldots \theta_q$ = Moving average parameters
ε_t = Independent disturbances, random error

ARIMA models can also adjust for seasonality in the data, in which case the model is denoted by the notation:

$$SARIMA(p, d, q) \times (p, d, q)_{s=n}$$

where s = Seasonal parameter of length n

Time Series Models in Earnings   Most time series models used in forecasting earnings are built around quarterly earnings per share. In a survey paper, Bathke and Lorek (1984) point out that three time-series models have been shown to be useful in forecasting quarterly earnings per share. All three models are seasonal autoregressive integrated moving average (SARIMA) models, since quarterly earnings per share have a strong seasonal component. The first model, developed by Foster (1977), allows for seasonality in earnings and is a follows:

$$Model\ 1:\ SARIMA(1, 0, 0) \times (0, 1, 0)_{s=4}$$
$$EPS_t = \phi_1 EPS_{t-1} + EPS_{t-4} - \phi_1 EPS_{t-5} + \theta_0 + \varepsilon_t$$

This model was extended by Griffin and Watts to allow for a moving average parameter:

$$Model\ 2:\ SARIMA(0, 1, 1) \times (0, 1, 1)_{s=4}$$
$$EPS_t = EPS_{t-1} + EPS_{t-4} - EPS_{t-5} - \theta_1 \varepsilon_{t-1} - \Theta \varepsilon_{t-4} - \Theta\theta_1 \varepsilon_{t-5} + \varepsilon_t$$

where θ_1 = First-order moving average [MA(1)] parameter
       Θ = First-order seasonal moving average parameter
       ε_t = Disturbance realization at the end of quarter t

The third time series model, developed by Brown and Rozeff (1979), is similar in its use of seasonal moving average parameter:

$$\text{Model 3: SARIMA}(1, 0, 0) \times (0, 1, 1)_{s=4}$$
$$\text{EPS}_t = \phi_1 \text{EPS}_{t-1} + \text{EPS}_{t-4} - \phi_1 \text{EPS}_{t-5} + \theta_0 - \Theta \varepsilon_{t-4}$$

How Good Are Time Series Models at Predicting Earnings?   Time series models do better than naive models (using past earnings) in predicting earnings per share in the next quarter. The forecast error (i.e., the difference between the actual earnings per share and forecasted earnings per share) from the time series models is, on average, smaller than the forecast error from naive models (such as simple averages of past growth). The superiority of the models over naive estimates declines with longer term forecasts, suggesting that the estimated time series parameters are not stationary.

Among the time series models themselves, there is no evidence that any one model is dominant, in terms of minimizing forecast error, for every firm in the sample. The gain from using the firm-specific best models, relative to using the same model for every firm is relatively small.

Limitations in Using Time Series Models in Valuation   There are several concerns in using time series models for forecasting earnings in valuation. First, time series models require a lot of data, which is why most of them are built around quarterly earnings per share. In most valuations, the focus is on predicting annual earnings per share and not on quarterly earnings. Second, even with quarterly earnings per share, the number of observations is limited for most firms to 10 to 15 years of data (40 to 60 quarters of data), leading to large estimation errors[2] in time series model parameters and in the forecasts. Third, the superiority of earnings forecasts from time series models declines as the forecasting period is extended. Given that earnings forecasts in valuation have to be made for several years rather than a few quarters, the value of time series models may be limited. Finally, studies indicate that analyst forecasts dominate even the best time series models in forecasting earnings.

In conclusion, time series models are likely to work best for firms that have a long history of earnings and where the parameters of the models have not shifted significantly over time. For the most part, however, the cost of using these models is likely to exceed their benefits, at least in the context of valuation.

Usefulness of Historical Growth

Is the growth rate in the past a good indicator of growth in the future? Not necessarily. In this section we consider how good historical growth is as a predictor of future growth for all firms, and why the changing size and volatile businesses of many firms can undercut growth projections.

Higgledy Piggledy Growth   Past growth rates are useful in forecasting future growth, but they have considerable noise associated with them. In a study of the

---

[2]Time series models generally can be run as long as there at least 30 observations, but the estimation error declines as the number of observations increases.

relationship between past growth rates and future growth rates, Little (1960) coined the term "higgledy-piggledy growth" because he found little evidence that firms that grew fast in one period continued to grow fast in the next period. In the process of running a series of correlations between growth rates in consecutive periods of different length, he frequently found negative correlations between growth rates in the two periods, and the average correlation across the two periods was close to zero (0.02).

If past growth is not a reliable indicator of future growth at many firms, it becomes even less so at smaller firms. The growth rates at smaller firms tend to be more volatile than growth rates at other firms in the market. The correlation between growth rates in earnings in consecutive time periods (five-year, three-year, and one-year) for firms in the United States, categorized by market value, is reported in Figure 11.2.

While the correlations tend to be higher across the board for one-year growth rates than for three-year or five-year growth rates in earnings, they are also consistently lower for smaller firms than they are for the rest of the market. This would suggest that you should be more cautious about using past growth, especially in earnings, for forecasting future growth at these firms.

Revenue Growth versus Earnings Growth   In general, revenue growth tends to be more persistent and predictable than earnings growth. This is because accounting choices have a far smaller effect on revenues than they do on earnings. Figure 11.3 compares the correlations in revenue and earnings growth over one-year, three-

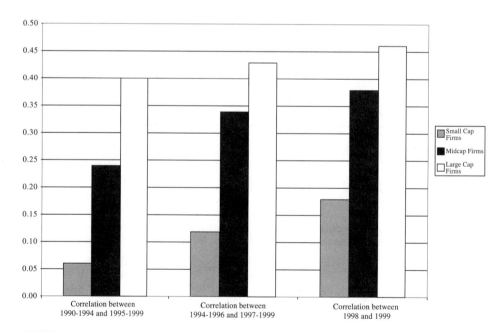

FIGURE 11.2 Correlations in Earnings Growth by Market Capitalization
Source: Compustat.

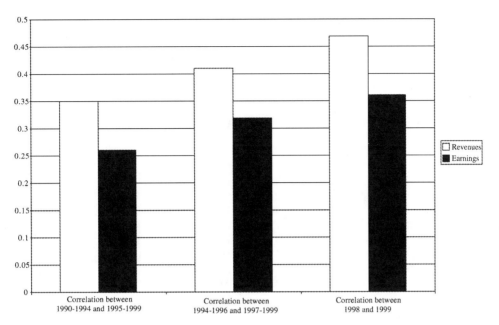

FIGURE 11.3 Correlation in Revenues and Earnings
Source: Compustat.

year, and five-year periods at U.S. firms. Revenue growth is consistently more correlated over time than earnings growth. The implication is that historical growth in revenues is a far more useful number when it comes to forecasting than historical growth in earnings.

Effects of Firm Size Since the growth rate is stated in percentage terms, the role of the size of the firm has to be weighed in the analysis. It is easier for a firm with $10 million in earnings to generate a 50 percent growth rate than it is for a firm with $500 million in earnings. Since it becomes harder for firms to sustain high growth rates as they become larger, past growth rates for firms that have grown dramatically in size may be difficult to sustain in the future. While this is a problem for all firms, it is a particular problem when analyzing small and growing firms. While the fundamentals at these firms, in terms of management, products, and underlying markets, may not have changed, it will still be difficult to maintain historical growth rates as the firms double or triple in size.

The true test for a small firm lies in how well it handles growth. Some firms such as Cisco Systems have been able to continue to deliver their products and services efficiently as they have grown. In other words, they have been able to scale up successfully. Other firms have had much more difficulty replicating their success as they become larger. In analyzing small firms, therefore, it is important that you look at plans to increase growth but it is even more critical that you examine the systems in place to handle this growth.

ILLUSTRATION 11.4: Cisco: Earnings Growth and Size of the Firm

Cisco's evolution from a firm with $28 million in revenues and net income of about $4 million in 1989 to revenues in excess of $12 billion and net income of $2.096 billion in 1999 is reported in the following table:

Year	Revenues	Percent Change	EBIT	Percent Change	Net Income	Percent Change
1989	$ 28		$ 7		$ 4	
1990	$ 70	152.28%	$ 21	216.42%	$ 14	232.54%
1991	$ 183	162.51%	$ 66	209.44%	$ 43	210.72%
1992	$ 340	85.40%	$ 129	95.48%	$ 84	95.39%
1993	$ 649	91.10%	$ 264	103.70%	$ 172	103.77%
1994	$ 1,243	91.51%	$ 488	85.20%	$ 315	83.18%
1995	$ 2,233	79.62%	$ 794	62.69%	$ 457	45.08%
1996	$ 4,096	83.46%	$1,416	78.31%	$ 913	99.78%
1997	$ 6,440	57.23%	$2,135	50.78%	$1,049	14.90%
1998	$ 8,488	31.80%	$2,704	26.65%	$1,355	29.17%
1999	$12,154	43.19%	$3,455	27.77%	$2,096	54.69%
Arithmetic average		87.81%		95.64%		96.92%
Geometric average		83.78%		86.57%		86.22%

While this table presents the results of a phenomenally successful decade for Cisco, it does suggest that you should be cautious about assuming that the firm will continue to grow at a similar rate in the future for two reasons. First, the growth rates have been tapering off as the firm becomes larger. Second, if you assume that Cisco will maintain its historic growth (estimated using the geometric average) over the last decade for the next five years, the revenue and earnings growth that the firm will have to post will be unsustainable. For instance, if operating income grew at 86.57% for the next five years, Cisco's operating income in five years will be $78 billion. Third, Cisco's growth has come primarily from acquisitions of small firms with promising technologies and using its capabilities to commercially develop these technologies. In 1999, for instance, Cisco acquired 15 firms and these acquisitions accounted for almost 80% of its reinvestment that year. If you assume that Cisco will continue to grow at historical rates, you are assuming that the number of acquisitions also will grow at the same rate. Thus Cisco would have to acquire almost 80 firms five years from now to maintain historical growth.

histgr.xls: **This dataset on the Web summarizes historical growth rates in earnings and revenues by industry group for the United States.**

HISTORICAL GROWTH AT HIGH-GROWTH AND YOUNGER FIRMS

The presence of negative earnings, volatile growth rates over time, and the rapid changes that high-growth firms go through over time make historical growth rates unreliable indicators of future growth for these firms. Notwithstanding this, you can still find ways to incorporate information from historical growth into estimates of future growth, if you follow these general guidelines:

- Focus on revenue growth, rather than earnings growth, to get a measure of both the pace of growth and the momentum that can be carried forward into future years. Revenue growth is less volatile than earnings growth and is much less likely to be swayed by accounting adjustments and choices.
- Rather than look at average growth over the last few years, look at growth each year. This can provide information on how the growth is changing as the firm becomes larger, and help when making projections for the future.
- Use historical growth rates as the basis for projections only in the near future (next year or two), since technologies can change rapidly and undercut future estimates.
- Consider historical growth in the overall market and in other firms that are serving it. This information can be useful in deciding what the growth rates of the firm that you are valuing will converge on over time.

ANALYST ESTIMATES OF GROWTH

Equity research analysts provide not only recommendations on the firms they follow but also estimates of earnings and earnings growth for the future. How useful are these estimates of expected growth from analysts and how, if at all, can they be used in valuing firms? This section considers the process that analysts follow to estimated expected growth and follows up by examining why such growth rates may not be appropriate when valuing some firms.

Who Do Analysts Follow?

The number of analysts tracking firms varies widely across firms. At one extreme are firms like GE, Cisco, and Microsoft that are followed by dozens of analysts. At the other extreme, there are hundreds of firms that are not followed by any analysts. Figure 11.4 shows the divergence across firms in the United States, in terms of the number of analysts following them.

Why are some firms more heavily followed than others? These seem to be some of the determinants:

- *Market capitalization.* The larger the market capitalization of a firm, the more likely it is to be followed by analysts.

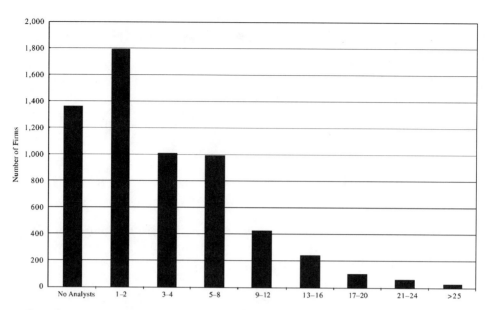

FIGURE 11.4 Number of Analysts Estimating Earnings per Share: U.S. Firms in January 2001
Source: Morningstar.

■ *Institutional holding.* The greater the percent of a firm's stock that is held by institutions, the more likely it is to be followed by analysts. The open question, though, is whether analysts follow institutions or whether institutions follow analysts. Given that institutional investors are the biggest clients of equity research analysts, the causality probably runs both ways.

■ *Trading volume.* Analysts are more likely to follow liquid stocks. Here again, though, it is worth noting that the presence of analysts and buy (or sell) recommendations on a stock may play a role in increasing trading volume.

Information in Analyst Forecasts

There is a simple reason to believe that analyst forecasts of growth should be better than using historical growth rates. Analysts, in addition to using historical data, can avail themselves of five other types of information that may be useful in predicting future growth:

1. *Firm-specific information that has been made public since the last earnings report.* Analysts can use information that has come out about the firm since the last earnings report, to make predictions about future growth. This information can sometimes lead to significant reevaluation of the firm's expected cash flows.

2. *Macroeconomic information that may impact future growth.* The expected growth rates of all firms are affected by economic news on GNP growth, interest rates, and inflation. Analysts can update their projections of future growth as new information comes out about the overall economy and about changes in fiscal and monetary policy. Information, for instance, that shows the economy growing at a faster rate than forecast will result in analysts increasing their estimates of expected growth for cyclical firms.

3. *Information revealed by competitors on future prospects.* Analysts can also condition their growth estimates for a firm on information revealed by competitors on pricing policy and future growth. For instance, a negative earnings report by one telecommunications firm can lead to a reassessment of earnings for other telecommunications firms.

4. *Private information about the firm.* Analysts sometimes have access to private information about the firms they follow that may be relevant in forecasting future growth. This avoids answering the delicate question of when private information becomes illegal inside information. There is no doubt, however, that good private information can lead to significantly better estimates of future growth. In an attempt to restrict this type of information leakage, the SEC issued new regulations in 2000 preventing firms from selectively revealing information to a few analysts or investors. Outside the United States, however, firms routinely convey private information to analysts following them.

5. *Public information other than earnings.* Models for forecasting earnings that depend entirely on past earnings data may ignore other publicly available information that is useful in forecasting future earnings. It has been shown, for instance, that other financial variables such as earnings retention, profit margins, and asset turnover are useful in predicting future growth. Analysts can incorporate information from these variables into their forecasts.

Quality of Earnings Forecasts

If firms are followed by a large number of analysts[3] and these analysts are indeed better informed than the rest of the market, the forecasts of growth that emerge from analysts should be better than estimates based on either historical growth or other publicly available information. But is this presumption justified? Are analyst forecasts of growth superior to other forecasts?

The general consensus from studies that have looked at short-term forecasts (one quarter ahead to four quarters ahead) of earnings is that analysts provide better forecasts of earnings than models that depend purely on historical data. The mean relative absolute error, which measures the absolute difference between the actual earnings and the forecast for the next quarter, in percentage terms, is smaller for analyst forecasts than it is for forecasts based on historical data. Two other studies shed further light on the value of analysts' forecasts. Crichfield, Dyckman, and Lakonishok (1978) examined the relative accuracy of forecasts in the "Earnings Forecaster," a publication from Standard & Poor's that summarizes forecasts of earnings from more than 50 investment firms. They measured the squared forecast errors by month of the year and computed the ratio of analyst forecast error to the forecast error from time series models of earnings. They found that the time series models actually outperform analyst forecasts from April until August, but underperform them from September

---

[3]Sell-side analysts work for brokerage houses and investment banks, and their research is offered to clients of these firms as a service. In contrast, buy-side analysts work for institutional investors, and their research is generally proprietary.

through January. They hypothesized that this is because there is more firm-specific information available to analysts during the latter part of the year. The other study, by O'Brien (1988), compared consensus analyst forecasts from the Institutions Brokers Estimate System (I/B/E/S) with time series forecasts from one quarter ahead to four quarters ahead. The analyst forecasts outperformed the time series model for one-quarter-ahead and two-quarter-ahead forecasts, did as well as the time series model for three-quarter-ahead forecasts, and did worse than the time series model for four-quarter-ahead forecasts. Thus, the advantage gained by analysts from firm-specific information seems to deteriorate as the time horizon for forecasting is extended.

In valuation, the focus is more on long-term growth rates in earnings than on next quarter's earnings. There is little evidence to suggest that analysts provide superior forecasts of earnings when the forecasts are over three or five years. An early study by Cragg and Malkiel compared long-term forecasts by five investment management firms in 1962 and 1963 with actual growth over the following three years to conclude that analysts were poor long-term forecasters. This view is contested by Vander Weide and Carleton (1988), who found that the consensus prediction of five-year growth in the I/B/E/S is superior to historically oriented growth measures in predicting future growth. There is an intuitive basis for arguing that analyst predictions of growth rates must be better than time series or other historical data–based models simply because they use more information. The evidence indicates, however, that this superiority in forecasting is surprisingly small for long-term forecasts and that past growth rates play a significant role in determining analyst forecasts.

There is one final consideration. Analysts generally forecast earnings per share, and most services report these estimates. When valuing a firm, you need forecasts of operating income and the growth in earnings per share will usually not be equal to the growth in operating income. In general, the growth rate in operating income should be lower than the growth rate in earnings per share. Thus, even if you decide to use analyst forecasts, you will have to adjust them to reflect the need to forecast operating income growth.

How Do You Use Analyst Forecasts in Estimating Future Growth?

The information in the growth rates estimated by other analysts can and should be incorporated into the estimation of expected future growth. There are four factors that determine the weight assigned to analyst forecasts in predicting future growth:

1. *Amount of recent firm-specific information.* Analyst forecasts have an advantage over historical data–based models because they incorporate more recent information about the firm and its future prospects. This advantage is likely to be greater for firms where there have been significant changes in management or business conditions in the recent past, for example, a restructuring or a shift in government policy relating to the firm's underlying business.

2. *Number of analysts following the stock.* Generally speaking, the larger the number of analysts following a stock, the more informative is their consensus forecast, and the greater should be the weight assigned to it in analysis. The informational gain from having more analysts is diminished somewhat by the well-established fact that

most analysts do not act independently and that there is a high correlation across analysts' revisions of expected earnings.

3. *Extent of disagreement between analysts.* While consensus earnings growth rates are useful in valuation, the extent of disagreement between analysts measured by the standard deviation in growth predictions is also a useful measure of the reliability of the consensus forecasts. Givoly and Lakonsihok found that the dispersion of earnings is correlated with other measures of risk such as beta and is a good predictor of expected returns.

4. *Quality of analysts following the stock.* This is the hardest of the variables to quantify. One measure of quality is the size of the forecast error made by analysts following a stock, relative to models that use only historical data—the smaller this relative error, the larger the weight that should be attached to analyst forecasts. Another measure is the effect on stock prices of analyst revisions—the more informative the forecasts, the greater the effect on stock prices. There are some who argue that the focus on consensus forecasts misses the point that some analysts are better than others in predicting earnings, and that their forecasts should be isolated from the rest and weighted more.

Analyst forecasts may be useful in coming up with a predicted growth rate for a firm, but there is a danger to blindly following consensus forecasts. Analysts often make significant errors in forecasting earnings, partly because they depend on the same data sources (which might have been erroneous or misleading) and partly because they sometimes overlook significant shifts in the fundamental characteristics of the firm. The secret to successful valuation often lies in discovering inconsistencies between analysts' forecasts of growth and a firm's fundamentals. The next section examines this relationship in more detail.

FUNDAMENTAL DETERMINANTS OF GROWTH

With both historical and analyst estimates, growth is an exogenous variable that affects value but is divorced from the operating details of the firm. The soundest way of incorporating growth into value is to make it endogenous (i.e., to make it a function of how much a firm reinvests for future growth and the quality of its reinvestment). This section begins by considering the relationship between fundamentals and growth in equity income, and then moves on to look at the determinants of growth in operating income.

Growth in Equity Earnings

When estimating cash flows to equity, we usually begin with estimates of net income, if we are valuing equity in the aggregate, or earnings per share, if we are valuing equity per share. This section begins by presenting the fundamentals that determine expected growth in earnings per share and then move on to consider a more expanded version of the model that looks at growth in net income.

Growth in Earnings per Share The simplest relationship determining growth is one based on the retention ratio (percentage of earnings retained in the firm) and the return on equity on its projects. Firms that have higher retention ratios and earn higher returns on equity should have much higher growth rates in earnings per share than firms that do not share these characteristics. To establish this, note that:

$$g_t = (NI_t - NI_{t-1})/NI_{t-1}$$

where g_t = Growth rate in net income
      NI_t = Net income in year t

Given the definition of return on equity, the net income in year t − 1 can be written as:

$$NI_{t-1} = \text{Book value of equity}_{t-2} \times ROE_{t-1}$$

where ROE_{t-1} = Return on equity in year t − 1

The net income in year t can be written as:

$$NI_t = (\text{Book value of equity}_{t-2} + \text{Retained earnings}_{t-1}) \times ROE_t$$

Assuming that the return on equity is unchanged (i.e., $ROE_t = ROE_{t-1} = ROE$):

$$
\begin{aligned}
g_t &= \text{Retained earnings}_{t-1}/NI_{t-1} \times ROE \\
&= \text{Retention ratio} \times ROE \\
&= b \times ROE
\end{aligned}
$$

where b is the retention ratio. Note that the firm is not being allowed to raise equity by issuing new shares. Consequently, the growth rate in net income and the growth rate in earnings per share are the same in this formulation.

ILLUSTRATION 11.5:   Growth in Earnings per Share

This illustration considers the expected growth rate in earnings based on the retention ratio and return on equity for three firms—Consolidated Edison, a regulated utility that provides power to New York City and its environs; Procter & Gamble, a leading brand-name consumer product firm; and Reliance Industries, a large Indian manufacturing firm. The following table summarizes the returns on equity, retention ratios, and expected growth rates in earnings for the three firms:

	Return on Equity	Retention Ratio	Expected Growth Rate
Consolidated Edison	11.63%	29.96%	3.49%
Procter & Gamble	29.37%	49.29%	14.48%
Reliance Industries	19.43%	82.57%	16.04%

Reliance has the highest expected growth rate in earnings per share, assuming that it can maintain its current return on equity and retention ratio. Procter & Gamble also can be expected to post a healthy growth rate, notwithstanding the fact that it pays out more than 50% of its earnings as dividends because of its high return on equity. Con Ed, on the other hand, has a very low expected growth rate because its return on equity and retention ratio are anemic.

Growth in Net Income If we relax the assumption that the only source of equity is retained earnings, the growth in net income can be different from the growth in earnings per share. Intuitively, note that a firm can grow net income significantly by issuing new equity to fund new projects, while earnings per share stagnates. To derive the relationship between net income growth and fundamentals, we need a measure of investment that goes beyond retained earnings. One way to obtain such a measure is to estimate directly how much equity the firm reinvests back into its businesses in the form of net capital expenditures and investments in working capital.

$$\text{Equity reinvested in business} = \text{Capital expenditures} - \text{Depreciation} \\ + \text{Change in working capital} \\ - (\text{New debt issued} - \text{Debt repaid})$$

Dividing this number by the net income gives us a much broader measure of the equity reinvestment rate:

$$\text{Equity reinvestment rate} = \text{Equity reinvested/Net income}$$

Unlike the retention ratio, this number can be well in excess of 100 percent because firms can raise new equity. The expected growth in net income can then be written as:

$$\text{Expected growth in net income} = \text{Equity reinvestment rate} \times \text{Return on equity}$$

ILLUSTRATION 11.6: Growth in Net Income

To estimate growth in operating income based on fundamentals, we look at three firms—Coca-Cola, Nestlé, and Sony. The following table estimates the components of equity reinvestment and uses it to estimate the reinvestment rate for each of the firms. We also present the return on equity and the expected growth rate in net income at each of these firms:

	Net Income	Net Cap Ex	Change in Working Capital	Net Debt Issued (Paid)	Equity Reinvestment Rate	ROE	Expected Growth Rate
Coca-Cola	$2177 m	468	852	−$104.00	65.41%	23.12%	15.12%
Nestlé	SFr 5763 m	2,470	368	272	44.53%	21.20%	9.44%
Sony	JY 30.24 b	26.29	−4.1	3.96	60.28%	1.80%	1.09%

The pluses and minuses of this approach are visible in the table. The approach much more accurately captures the true reinvestment in the firm by focusing not on what was retained but on what was reinvested. The limitation of the approach is that the ingredients that go into the reinvestment—capital expenditures, working capital change, and net debt issued—are all volatile numbers. Note that Coca-Cola paid off debt last year, while reinvesting back into the business and Sony's working capital dropped. In fact, it would probably be much more realistic to look at the average reinvestment rate over three or five years, rather than just the current year. We will return to examine this question in more depth when we look at growth in operating income.

Determinants of Return on Equity Both earnings per share and net income growth are affected by the return on equity of a firm. The return on equity is affected by the leverage decisions of the firm. In the broadest terms, increasing leverage will lead to a higher return on equity if the after-tax return on capital exceeds the after-tax interest rate paid on debt. This is captured in the following formulation of return on equity:

$$ROE = ROC + D/E[ROC - i(1 - t)]$$

where ROC = EBIT(1 − t)/(BV of debt + BV of equity)
D/E = BV of debt/BV of equity
i = Interest expense on debt/BV of debt
t = Tax rate on ordinary income

The derivation is simple and is provided in a footnote.[4] Using this expanded version of ROE, the growth rate can be written as:

$$g = b\{ROC + D/E[ROC - i(1 - t)]\}$$

The advantage of this formulation is that is allows explicitly for changes in leverage and the consequent effects on growth.

ILLUSTRATION 11.7: Breaking Down Return on Equity

To consider the components of return on equity, the following table looks at Consolidated Edison, Procter & Gamble, and Reliance Industries, three firms whose returns on equity were shown in Illustration 11.5:

	Return on Capital	Book D/E	Book Interest Rate	Tax Rate	Return on Equity
Consolidated Edison	8.76%	75.72%	7.76%	35.91%	11.63%
Procter & Gamble	17.77%	77.80%	5.95%	36.02%	28.63%
Reliance Industries	10.24%	94.24%	8.65%	2.37%	11.94%

Comparing these numbers to those reported in Illustration 11.5, you will note that the return on equity is identical for Con Ed but significantly lower here for the other two firms. This is because both Procter & Gamble and Reliance Industries posted significant nonoperating profits. We have chosen to consider only operating income in the return on capital computation. To the extent that firms routinely report nonoperating income, you could modify the return on capital.

The decomposition of return on equity for Reliance suggests a couple of areas of concern. One is that the high return on equity in Illustration 11.5 reported by the firm is driven by three factors—high leverage, a significant nonoperating profit, and a low tax rate. If the firm loses its tax breaks and the sources of nonoperating income dry up, the firm could very easily find itself with a return on capital that is lower than its book interest rate. If this occurs, leverage could bring down the return on equity of the firm.

---

[4]ROC + D/E[ROC − i(1 − t)] = [NI + Int(1 − t)]/(D + E) + D/E{[NI + Int(1 − t)]/(D + E)
  − Int(1 − t)/D}
  = {[NI + Int(1 − t)]/(D + E)}(1 + D/E) − Int(1 − t)/E
  = NI/E + Int(1 − t)/E − Int(1 − t)/E = NI/E = ROE

AVERAGE AND MARGINAL RETURNS

The return on equity is conventionally measured by dividing the net income in the most recent year by the book value of equity at the end of the previous year. Consequently, the return on equity measures the quality of both older projects that have been on the books for a substantial period and new projects from more recent periods. Since older investments represent a significant portion of the earnings, the average returns may not shift substantially for larger firms that are facing a decline in returns on new investments, either because of market saturation or competition. In other words, poor returns on new projects will have a lagged effect on the measured returns. In valuation, it is the returns that firms are making on their newer investments that convey the most information about a quality of a firm's projects. To measure these returns, we could compute a marginal return on equity by dividing the change in net income in the most recent year by the change in book value of equity in the prior year:

$$\text{Marginal return on equity} = \Delta \text{ Net income}_t / \Delta \text{ Book value of equity}_{t-1}$$

For example, Reliance Industries reported net income of Rs 24,033 million in 2000 on book value of equity of Rs 123,693 million in 1999, resulting in an average return on equity of 19.43%:

$$\text{Average return on equity} = 24{,}033/123{,}693 = 19.43\%$$

The marginal return on equity is computed as follows:

$$\text{Change in net income from 1999 to 2000} = 24{,}033 - 17{,}037$$
$$= \text{Rs } 6{,}996 \text{ million}$$

$$\text{Change in book value of equity from 1998 to 1999} = 123{,}693 - 104{,}006$$
$$= \text{Rs } 19{,}687 \text{ million}$$

$$\text{Marginal return on equity} = 6{,}996/19{,}687 = 35.54\%$$

The Effects of Changing Return on Equity   So far, this section has operated on the assumption that the return on equity remains unchanged over time. If we relax this assumption, we introduce a new component to growth—the effect of changing return on equity on existing investment over time. Consider, for instance, a firm that has a book value of equity of $100 million and a return on equity of 10 percent. If this firm improves its return on equity to 11 percent, it will post an earnings growth rate of 10 percent even if it does not reinvest any money. This additional growth can be written as a function of the change in the return on equity:

$$\text{Addition to expected growth rate} = (\text{ROE}_t - \text{ROE}_{t-1})/\text{ROE}_{t-1}$$

where ROE_t is the return on equity in period t. This will be in addition to the fundamental growth rate computed as the product of the return on equity and the retention ratio.

While increasing return on equity will generate a spurt in the growth rate in the period of the improvement, a decline in the return on equity will create a more than proportional drop in the growth rate in the period of the decline.

It is worth differentiating at this point between returns on equity on new investments and returns on equity on existing investments. The additional growth that we are estimating above comes not from improving returns on new investments but by changing the return on existing investments. For lack of a better term, you could consider it "efficiency-generated growth."

ILLUSTRATION 11.8: Effects of Changing Return on Equity: Con Ed

---

In Illustration 11.5 we looked at Con Ed's expected growth rate based on its return on equity of 11.63% and its retention ratio of 29.96%. Assume that the firm will be able to improve its overall return on equity (on both new and existing investments) to 13% next year and that the retention ratio remains at 29.96%. The expected growth rate in earnings per share next year can then be written as:

$$\text{Expected growth rate in EPS} = \text{ROE}_t \times \text{Retention ratio} + (\text{ROE}_t - \text{ROE}_{t-1})/\text{ROE}_{t-1}$$
$$= .13 \times .2996 + (.13 - .1163)/.1163$$
$$= .1567 \text{ or } 15.67\%$$

After next year, the growth rate will subside to a more sustainable 3.89% (.13 × .2996).

How would the answer be different if the improvement in return on equity were only on new investments but not on existing assets? The expected growth rate in earnings per share can then be written as:

$$\text{Expected growth rate in EPS} = \text{ROE}_t \times \text{Retention ratio} = .13 \times .2996 = .0389$$

Thus, there is no additional growth created in this case. What if the improvement had been only on existing assets and not on new investments? Then, the expected growth rate in earnings per share can be written as:

$$\text{Expected growth rate in EPS} = \text{ROE}_t \times \text{Retention ratio} + (\text{ROE}_t - \text{ROE}_{t-1})/\text{ROE}_{t-1}$$
$$= .1163 \times .2996 + (.13 - .1163)/.1163$$
$$= .1526 \text{ or } 15.26\%$$

Growth in Operating Income

Just as equity income growth is determined by the equity reinvested back into the business and the return made on that equity investment, you can relate growth in operating income to total reinvestment made into the firm and the return earned on capital invested.

We will consider three separate scenarios, and examine how to estimate growth in each, in this section. The first is when a firm is earning a high return on capital that it expects to sustain over time. The second is when a firm is earning a positive return on capital that is expected to increase over time. The third is the most general scenario, where a firm expects operating margins to change over time, sometimes from negative values to positive levels.

Stable Return on Capital Scenario When a firm has a stable return on capital, its expected growth in operating income is a product of the reinvestment rate (i.e., the proportion of the after-tax operating income that is invested in net capital expenditures and noncash working capital), and the quality of these reinvestments, measured as the return on the capital invested.

$$\text{Expected growth}_{EBIT} = \text{Reinvestment rate} \times \text{Return on capital}$$

$$\text{where } \text{Reinvestment rate} = \frac{\text{Capital expenditure} - \text{Depreciation} + \Delta \text{ Noncash WC}}{\text{EBIT}(1 - \text{Tax rate})}$$

$$\text{Return on capital} = \text{EBIT}(1 - t)/\text{Capital invested}$$

Both measures—the reinvestment rate and return on capital—should be forward looking, and the return on capital should represent the expected return on capital on future investments. In the rest of this section, we consider how best to estimate the reinvestment rate and the return on capital.

Reinvestment Rate The reinvestment rate measures how much a firm is plowing back to generate future growth. The reinvestment rate is often measured using the most recent financial statements for the firm. Although this is a good place to start, it is not necessarily the best estimate of the future reinvestment rate. A firm's reinvestment rate can ebb and flow, especially in firms that invest in relatively few large projects or acquisitions. For these firms, looking at an average reinvestment rate over time may be a better measure of the future. In addition, as firms grow and mature, their reinvestment needs (and rates) tend to decrease. For firms that have expanded significantly over the last few years, the historical reinvestment rate is likely to be higher than the expected future reinvestment rate. For these firms, industry averages for reinvestment rates may provide a better indication of the future than using numbers from the past. Finally, it is important that we continue treating R&D expenses and operating lease expenses consistently. The R&D expenses, in particular, need to be categorized as part of capital expenditures for purposes of measuring the reinvestment rate.

Return on Capital The return on capital is often based on the firm's return on capital on existing investments, where the book value of capital is assumed to measure the capital invested in these investments. Implicitly, we assume that the current accounting return on capital is a good measure of the true returns earned on existing investments, and that this return is a good proxy for returns that will be made on future investments. This assumption, of course, is open to question for the following reasons:

- The book value of capital might not be a good measure of the capital invested in existing investments, since it reflects the historical cost of these assets and accounting decisions on depreciation. When the book value understates the capital invested, the return on capital will be overstated; when book value overstates the capital invested, the return on capital will be understated. This problem is exacerbated if the book value of capital is not adjusted to reflect the value of the research asset or the capital value of operating leases.
- The operating income, like the book value of capital, is an accounting measure of the earnings made by a firm during a period. All the problems in using unadjusted operating income described in Chapter 9 continue to apply.
- Even if the operating income and book value of capital are measured correctly, the return on capital on existing investments may not be equal to the marginal return on capital that the firm expects to make on new investments, especially as you go further into the future.

Given these concerns, we should consider not only a firm's current return on capital, but any trends in this return as well as the industry average return on capital. If the current return on capital for a firm is significantly higher than the industry average, the forecasted return on capital should be set lower than the current return to reflect the erosion that is likely to occur as competition responds.

Finally, any firm that earns a return on capital greater than its cost of capital is earning an excess return. The excess returns are the result of a firm's competitive advantages or barriers to entry into the industry. High excess returns locked in for very long periods imply that this firm has a permanent competitive advantage.

ILLUSTRATION 11.9:   Measuring the Reinvestment Rate, Return on Capital, and Expected Growth Rate: Embraer and Amgen

This illustration estimates the reinvestment rate, return on capital, and expected growth rate for Embraer, the Brazilian aerospace firm, and Amgen. We begin by presenting the inputs for the return on capital computation:

	EBIT	EBIT(1 − t)	Book Value of Debt	Book Value of Equity	Return on Capital
Embraer	B$ 945	B$ 716.54	B$1,321.00	B$ 697	35.51%
Amgen	$1,996	$1,500	$ 323	$ 5,933	23.98%

We use the effective tax rate for computing after-tax operating income and the book value of debt and equity from the end of the prior year. For Amgen, we use the operating income and book value of equity, adjusted for the capitalization of the research asset, as described in Illustration 9.2. The after-tax returns on capital are computed in the last column.

We follow up by estimating capital expenditures, depreciation, and the change in noncash working capital from the most recent year:

	EBIT (1 − t)	Capital Expenditures	Depreciation	Change in Working Capital	Reinvestment	Reinvestment Rate
Embraer	B$ 716.54	B$ 182.10	B$150.16	−173.00	−141.06	−19.69%
Amgen	$1,500.32	$1,283.00	$610.00	$121.00	$794.00	52.92%

Here again, we treat R&D as a capital expenditure and the amortization of the research asset as part of depreciation for computing the values for Amgen. In the last column, we compute the reinvestment rate by dividing the total reinvestment (capital expenditures—Depreciation + Change in working capital) by the after-tax operating income. Note that Embraer's reinvestment rate is negative because of noncash working capital dropped by $173 million in the most recent year.

Finally, we compute the expected growth rate by multiplying the after-tax return on capital by the reinvestment rate:

	Reinvestment Rate	Return on Capital	Expected Growth Rate
Embraer	−19.69%	35.51%	−6.99%
Amgen	52.92%	23.98%	12.69%

If Amgen can maintain the return on capital and reinvestment rate that they had last year, it would be able to grow at 12.69% a year. Embraer's growth rate is negative because its reinvestment rate is negative. In the illustration that follows, we will look at the reinvestment rate in more detail.

ILLUSTRATION 11.10:   Current, Historical Average and Industry Averages

The reinvestment rate is a volatile number and often shifts significantly from year to year. Consider Embraer's reinvestment rate over the past five years:

	1996	1997	1998	1999	2000	Total
EBIT	75.75	91.86	230.51	588.63	945.00	
Tax rate	0.00%	0.00%	8.15%	0.00%	24.17%	
EBIT(1 − t)	75.75	91.86	211.72	588.63	716.32	1,684.46
Capital expenditures	334.57	9.90	27.62	45.64	182.11	
Depreciation	52.90	60.95	100.07	127.50	150.16	
Change in noncash working capital	−3.00	52.00	279.00	608.00	−205.00	
Reinvestment	278.67	0.95	206.55	526.14	−173.05	839.26
Reinvestment Rate	367.88%	1.03%	97.56%	89.38%	−24.16%	49.82%

The reinvestment rate over the past five years has ranged from −24% in 2000 to 368% in 1996. We computed the reinvestment rate over the five years by dividing the total reinvestment over the five years by the total after-tax operating income over the past five years.[5]

We also computed Embraer's return on capital each year for the past five years:

	1996	1997	1998	1999	2000	Total
EBIT(1 − t)	75.75	91.86	211.72	588.63	716.50	1,684.46
Book value of capital (beginning)	404	578	724	1,234	2,018	4,958
Return on capital	18.75%	15.89%	29.24%	47.70%	35.51%	33.97%

While the return on capital also shifts significantly over time, the average return on capital of 33.97% is close to the current return on capital.

Clearly, the estimates of expected growth are a function of what you assume about future investments. For Embraer, if we assume that the current return on capital and reinvestment rate are the best indicators for the future, we would obtain a negative growth rate. If, on the other hand, we assume that the average reinvestment rate and return on capital were better measures for the future, our expected growth rate would be:

$$\text{Expected growth rate} = \text{Reinvestment rate} \times \text{Return on capital}$$
$$= .4982 \times .3397 = .1693 \text{ or } 16.93\%$$

In the case of Embraer, we believe that this estimate is a much more reasonable one given what we know about the firm and its growth potential.

---

 fundgrEB.xls: **This dataset on the Web summarizes reinvestment rates and return on capital by industry group in the United States for the most recent quarter.**

---

[5]This tends to work better than averaging the reinvestment rate over five years. The reinvestment rate tends to be much more volatile than the dollar values.

<hr>

NEGATIVE REINVESTMENT RATES: CAUSES AND CONSEQUENCES

The reinvestment rate for a firm can be negative if its depreciation exceeds its capital expenditures or if the working capital declines substantially during the course of the year. For most firms, this negative reinvestment rate will be a temporary phenomenon reflecting lumpy capital expenditures or volatile working capital. For these firms, the current year's reinvestment rate (which is negative) can be replaced with an average reinvestment rate over the past few years. (This is what we did for Embraer in Illustration 11.10.) For some firms, though, the negative reinvestment rate may be a reflection of the policies of the firms and how we deal with it will depend on why the firm is embarking on this path:

- Firms that have overinvested in capital equipment or working capital in the past may be able to live off past investment for a number of years, reinvesting little and generating higher cash flows for that period. If this is the case, we should use the negative reinvestment rate in forecasts and estimate growth based on improvements in return on capital. Once the firm has reached the point where it is efficiently using its resources, though, we should change the reinvestment rate to reflect expected growth.
- The more extreme scenario is a firm that has decided to liquidate itself over time, by not replacing assets as they become run down and by drawing down working capital. In this case, the expected growth should be estimated using the negative reinvestment rate. Not surprisingly, this will lead to a negative expected growth rate and declining earnings over time.

<hr>

Positive and Changing Return on Capital Scenario   The analysis in the last section is based on the assumption that the return on capital remains stable over time. If the return on capital changes over time, the expected growth rate for the firm will have a second component, which will increase the growth rate if the return on capital increases and decrease the growth rate if the return on capital decreases.

$$\text{Expected growth rate} = ROC_t \times \text{Reinvestment rate} + (ROC_t - ROC_{t-1})/ROC_{t-1}$$

For example, a firm that sees its return on capital improve from 10 to 11 percent while maintaining a reinvestment rate of 40 percent will have an expected growth rate of:

$$\text{Expected growth rate} = .11 \times .40 + (.11 - .10)/.10 = 14.40\%$$

In effect, the improvement in the return on capital increases the earnings on existing assets and this improvement translates into an additional growth of 10 percent for the firm.

Marginal and Average Returns on Capital   So far, we have looked at the return on capital as the measure that determines return. In reality, however, there are two measures of returns on capital. One is the return earned by firm collectively on all of its investments, which we define as the average return on capital. The other is the return earned by a firm on just the new investments it makes in a year, which is the marginal return on capital.

Changes in the marginal return on capital do not create a second-order effect, and the value of the firm is a product of the marginal return on capital and the reinvestment rate. Changes in the average return on capital, however, will result in the additional impact on growth chronicled earlier.

Candidates for Changing Average Return on Capital   What types of firms are likely to see their return on capital change over time? One category would include firms with poor returns on capital that improve their operating efficiency and margins, and consequently their return on capital. In these firms, the expected growth rate will be much higher than the product of the reinvestment rate and the return on capital. In fact, since the return on capital on these firms is usually low before the turnaround, small changes in the return on capital translate into big changes in the growth rate. Thus, an increase in the return on capital on existing assets from 1 percent to 2 percent doubles the earnings (resulting in a growth rate of 100 percent).

The other category would include firms that have very high returns on capital on their existing investments but are likely to see these returns slip as competition enters the business, not only on new investments but also on existing investments.

ILLUSTRATION 11.12:   Estimating Expected Growth with Changing Return on Capital: Titan Cement and Motorola

---

In 2000, Titan Cement, a Greek cement company, reported operating income of 55,467 million drachmas on capital invested of 135,376 million drachmas. Using its effective tax rate of 24.5%, we estimate a return on capital for the firm of 30.94%:

$$\text{Return on capital} = 55,467(1 - .245)/135,376 = 30.94\%$$

Assume that the firm will see its return on capital drop on both its existing assets and its new investments to 29% next year and that its reinvestment rate will stay at 35%. The expected growth rate next year can be estimated as follows:

$$\text{Expected growth rate} = .29 \times .35 + (.29 - .3094)/.3094 = 3.88\%$$

In contrast, consider Motorola. The firm had a reinvestment rate of 52.99% and a return on capital of 12.18% in 1999. Assume that Motorola's return on capital will increase towards the industry average of 22.27%, as the firm sheds the residue of its ill-fated Iridium investment and returns to its roots. Assume that Motorola's return on capital will increase from 12.18% to 17.22% over the next five years.[6] For simplicity, also assume that the change occurs linearly over the next five years. The expected growth rate in operating income each year for the next five years can then be estimated as follows:[7]

$$\begin{aligned}
\text{Expected growth rate} &= ROC_{marginal} \times \text{Reinvestment rate}_{current} \\
&\quad + \{[1 + (ROC_{in\ 5\ years} - ROC_{current})/ROC_{current}]^{1/5} - 1\} \\
&= .1722 \times .5299 + \{[1 + (.1722 - .1218)/.1218]^{1/5} - 1\} \\
&= .1630 \text{ or } 16.30\%
\end{aligned}$$

The improvement in return on capital over the next five years will result in a higher growth rate in operating earnings at Motorola over that period. Note that this calculation assumes that the return on capital on new investments next year will be 17.22%.

---

[6]Note that 17.22% is exactly halfway between the current return on capital and the industry average (22.27 percent).
[7]You are allowing for a compounded growth rate over time. Thus, if earnings are expected to grow 25 percent over three years, you estimate the expected growth rate each year to be: expected growth rate each year = $(1.25)^{1/3} - 1$

chgrowth.xls: This spreadsheet allows you to estimate the expected growth rate in operating income for a firm where the return on capital is expected to change over time.

Negative Return on Capital Scenario   The third and most difficult scenario for estimating growth is when a firm is losing money and has a negative return on capital. Since the firm is losing money, the reinvestment rate is also likely to be negative. To estimate growth in these firms, we have to move up the income statement and first project growth in revenues. Next, we use the firm's expected operating margin in future years to estimate the operating income in those years. If the expected margin in future years is positive, the expected operating income will also turn positive, allowing us to apply traditional valuation approaches in valuing these firms. We also estimate how much the firm has to reinvest to generate revenue growth growth, by linking revenues to the capital invested in the firm.

Growth in Revenues   Many high-growth firms, while reporting losses, also show large increases in revenues from period to period. The first step in forecasting cash flows is forecasting revenues in future years, usually by forecasting a growth rate in revenues each period. In making these estimates, there are five points to keep in mind.

1. The rate of growth in revenues will decrease as the firm's revenues increase. Thus, a tenfold increase in revenues is entirely feasible for a firm with revenues of $2 million but unlikely for a firm with revenues of $2 billion.
2. Compounded growth rates in revenues over time can seem low, but appearances are deceptive. A compounded annual growth rate in revenues of 40 percent over 10 years will result in a 40-fold increase in revenues over the period.
3. While growth rates in revenues may be the mechanism that you use to forecast future revenues, you do have to keep track of the dollar revenues to ensure that they are reasonable, given the size of the overall market that the firm operates in. If the projected revenues for a firm 10 years out would give it a 90 or 100 percent share (or greater) of the overall market in a competitive marketplace, you clearly should reassess the revenue growth rate.
4. Assumptions about revenue growth and operating margins have to be internally consistent. Firms can post higher growth rates in revenues by adopting more aggressive pricing strategies but the higher revenue growth will then be accompanied by lower margins.
5. In coming up with an estimate of revenue growth, you have to make a number of subjective judgments about the nature of competition, the capacity of the firm that you are valuing to handle the revenue growth and the marketing capabilities of the firm.

ILLUSTRATION 11.12: Estimating Revenues at Commerce One

This illustration considers Commerce One, the B2B pioneer. The following table forecasts revenues for the firm for the next 10 years, as well as for Ashford.com, an online jewelry and brand-name product retailer.

	Commerce One		Ashford.com	
Year	Expected Growth Rate	Revenues	Expected Growth Rate	Revenues
Current		$ 402		$ 70.00
1	50.00%	$ 603	80.00%	$126.00
2	100.00%	$ 1,205	60.00%	$201.60
3	80.00%	$ 2,170	40.00%	$282.24
4	60.00%	$ 3,472	30.00%	$366.91
5	40.00%	$ 4,860	20.00%	$440.29
6	35.00%	$ 6,561	17.00%	$515.14
7	30.00%	$ 8,530	14.00%	$587.26
8	20.00%	$10,236	11.00%	$651.86
9	10.00%	$11,259	8.00%	$704.01
10	5.00%	$11,822	5.00%	$739.21

Estimates of growth for the firms in the initial years are based on the growth in revenues over the past year, but we did lower the growth rate for Commerce One in the first year because of the fact that the economy was weak at the time of the valuation and business spending had slowed.

As a check, we also examined how much the revenues at each of these firms would be in 10 years relative to more mature companies in the sector now.

- We compared revenues at Commerce One in 10 years to those of Electronic Data Systetms (EDS), a leading provider of business services. EDS had revenues of $18.73 billion in 1999, which would make Commerce One a leading player in this sector but not by an overwhelming margin.
- Zale Corporation, the largest retailer of jewelry in the United States, had revenues of about $1.7 billion in 2000. Our projected growth rate for Ashford.com would give it revenues of $739 million in 10 years.

Operating Margin Forecasts Before considering how best to estimate the operating margins, let us begin with an assessment of where many high-growth firms, early in the life cycle, stand when the valuation begins. They usually have low revenues and negative operating margins. If revenue growth translates low revenues into high revenues and operating margins stay negative, these firms not only will be worth nothing but are unlikely to survive. For firms to be valuable, the higher revenues eventually have to deliver positive earnings. In a valuation model, this translates into positive operating margins in the future. A key input in valuing a high-growth firm then is the operating margin you would expect it to have as it matures.

In estimating this margin, you should begin by looking at the business that the firm is in. While many new firms claim to be pioneers in their businesses and some believe that they have no competitors, it is more likely that they are the first to find a new way of delivering a product or service that was previously delivered through other channels. Thus, Amazon.com might have been one of the first firms to sell books online, but Barnes & Noble and Borders preceded Amazon as book retailers.

In fact, one can consider online retailers as logical successors to catalog retailers such as L. L. Bean and Lillian Vernon. Similarly, Yahoo! might have been one of the first (and most successful) Internet portals, but it is following the lead of newspapers that have used content and features to attract readers and used their readership to attract advertising. Using the average operating margin of competitors in the business may strike some as conservative. After all, they would point out, Amazon can hold less inventory than Borders and does not have the burden of carrying the operating leases that Barnes & Noble does (on its stores) and should, therefore, be more efficient about generating its revenues. This may be true, but it is unlikely that the operating margins for Internet retailers can be persistently higher than their brick-and-mortar counterparts. If they were, you would expect to see a migration of traditional retailers to online retailing and increased competition among online retailers on price and products, driving the margin down.

While the margin for the business in which a firm operates provides a target value, there are still two other estimation issues that you need to confront. Given that the operating margins in the early stages of the life cycle are negative, you first have to consider how the margin will improve from current levels to the target values. Generally, the improvements in margins will be greatest in the earlier years (at least in percentage terms) and then taper off as the firm approaches maturity. The second issue is one that arises when talking about revenue growth. Firms may be able to post higher revenue growth with lower margins but the trade-off has to be considered. While firms generally want both higher revenue growth and higher margin, the margin and revenue growth assumptions have to be consistent.

ILLUSTRATION 11.13: Estimating Operating Margins

To estimate the operating margins for Commerce One, we begin by estimating the operating margins of other firms in the business services/software sector. In 2000, the average pretax operating margin for firms in this sector was 16.36%. For Ashford.com, we will use the average pretax operating margin of jewelry and brand-name product retailers, which is 10.86%.

We will assume that both Commerce One and Ashford.com will move toward their target margins, with greater marginal improvements[8] in the earlier years and smaller ones in the later years. The following table summarizes the expected operating margins over time for both firms:

Year	Commerce One Margin	Ashford.com Margin
Current	−84.62%	−228.57%
1	−34.13%	−119.74%
2	−8.88%	−60.38%
3	3.74%	−28.00%
4	10.05%	−10.33%
5	13.20%	−0.70%
6	14.78%	4.55%
7	15.57%	7.42%
8	15.97%	8.98%
9	16.16%	9.84%
10	16.26%	10.30%
11	16.36%	10.86%

[8]The margin each year is computed as follows: (Margin this year + Target margin)/2.

Since we estimated revenue growth in the last section and the margins in this one, we can now estimate the pretax operating income at each of the firms over the next 10 years:

	Commerce One			Ashford.com		
Year	Revenues	Operating Margin	EBIT	Revenues	Operating Margin	EBIT
Current	$ 402	−84.62%	−$ 340	$ 70.00	−228.57%	−$160.00
1	$ 603	−34.13%	−$ 206	$126.00	−119.74%	−$150.87
2	$ 1,205	−8.88%	−$ 107	$201.60	−60.38%	−$121.72
3	$ 2,170	3.74%	$ 81	$282.24	−28.00%	−$ 79.02
4	$ 3,472	10.05%	$ 349	$366.91	−10.33%	−$ 37.92
5	$ 4,860	13.20%	$ 642	$440.29	−0.70%	−$ 3.08
6	$ 6,561	14.78%	$ 970	$515.14	4.55%	$ 23.46
7	$ 8,530	15.57%	$1,328	$587.26	7.42%	$ 43.58
8	$10,236	15.97%	$1,634	$651.86	8.98%	$ 58.56
9	$11,259	16.16%	$1,820	$704.01	9.84%	$ 69.25
10	$11,822	16.26%	$1,922	$739.21	10.30%	$ 76.15

As the margins move toward target levels and revenues grow, the operating income at each of the firms also increases.

MARKET SIZE, MARKET SHARE, AND REVENUE GROWTH

Estimating revenue growth rates for a young firm in a new business may seem like an exercise in futility. While it is difficult to do, there are ways in which you can make the process easier.

One way is to work backward by first considering the share of the overall market that you expect your firm to have once it matures, and then determining the growth rate you would need to arrive at this market share. For instance, assume that you are analyzing an online toy retailer with $100 million in revenues currently. Assume also that the entire toy retail market had revenues of $70 billion last year. Assuming a 3 percent growth rate in this market over the next 10 years and a market share of 5 percent for your firm, you would arrive at expected revenues of $4.703 billion for the firm in 10 years, and a compounded revenue growth rate of 46.98%.

$$\text{Expected revenues in 10 years} = \$70 \text{ billion} \times 1.03^{10} \times .05$$
$$= \$4.703 \text{ billion}$$

$$\text{Expected compounded growth rate} = (4{,}703/100)^{1/10} - 1 = 0.4698$$

The other approach is to forecast the expected growth rate in revenues over the next three to five years based on past growth rates. Once you estimate revenues in year 3 or 5, you can then forecast a growth rate based on the rate at which companies with similar revenues grow currently. For instance, assume that the online toy retailer had revenue growth of 200 percent last year (revenues went from $33 million to $100 million). You could forecast growth rates of 120 percent, 100 percent, 80 percent, and 60 percent for the next four years, leading to revenues of $1.267 billion in four years. You could then look at the average growth rate posted by retail firms with revenues between $1 billion and $1.5 billion last year and use that as the growth rate commencing in year 5.

Sales-to-Capital Ratio   High revenue growth is clearly a desirable objective, especially when linked with positive operating margins in future years. Firms do, however, have to invest to generate both revenue growth and positive operating margins in future years. This investment can take traditional forms (plant and equipment) but it should also include acquisitions of other firms, partnerships, investments in distribution and marketing capabilities, and research and development.

To link revenue growth with reinvestment needs, we look at the revenues that every dollar of capital that we invest generates. This ratio, called the sales-to-capital ratio, allows us to estimate how much additional investment the firm has to make to generate the projected revenue growth. This investment can be in internal projects, acquisitions, or working capital. To estimate the reinvestment needs in any year then, you divide the revenue growth that you have projected (in dollar terms) by the sales to capital ratio. Thus, if you expect revenues to grow by $1 billion and you use a sales-to-capital ratio of 2.5, you would estimate a reinvestment need for this firm of $400 million ($1 billion/2.5). Lower sales-to-capital ratios increase reinvestment needs (and reduce cash flows) while higher sales-to-capital ratios decrease reinvestment needs (and increase cash flows).

To estimate the sales-to-capital ratio, we look at both a firm's past and the business it operates in. To measure this ratio historically, we look at changes in revenue each year and divide it by the reinvestment made that year. We also look at the average ratio of sales to book capital invested in the business in which the firm operates.

Linking operating margins to reinvestment needs is much more difficult to do, since a firm's capacity to earn operating income and sustain high returns comes from the competitive advantages that it acquires, partly through internal investment and partly through acquisitions. Firms that adopt a two-track strategy in investing, where one track focuses on generating higher revenues and the other on building up competitive strengths, should have higher operating margins and values than firms that concentrate on only revenue growth.

Link to Return on Capital   One of the dangers that you face when using a sales-to-capital ratio to generate reinvestment needs is that you might underestimate or overestimate your reinvestment needs. You can keep tabs on whether this is happening and correct it when it does by also estimating the after-tax return on capital on the firm each year through the analysis. To estimate the return on capital in a future year, you use the estimated after-tax operating income in that year and divide it by the total capital invested in that firm in that year. The former number comes from your estimates of revenue growth and operating margins, while the latter can be estimated by aggregating the reinvestments made by the firm all the way through the future year. For instance, a firm that has $500 million in capital invested today and is required to reinvest $300 million next year and $400 million the year after will have capital invested of $1.2 billion at the end of the second year.

For firms losing money today, the return on capital will be a negative number when the estimation begins but improve as margins improve. If the sales-to-capital ratio is set too high, the return on capital in the later years will be too high, while if it is set too low, it will be too low. Too low or high relative to what, you ask? There are two comparisons that are worth making. The first is to the average return on capital for mature firms in the business in which your firm operates—mature specialty and brand-name retailers in the case of Ashford.com. The second is to the firm's own cost of capital. A projected return on capital of 40 percent for a firm with a cost of capital of 10 percent in a sector where returns on capital hover around 15 percent is an indicator that the firm is investing too little for the projected revenue growth and operating margins. Decreasing the sales-to-capital ratio until the return on capital converges on 15 percent would be prudent.

ILLUSTRATION 11.14: Estimated Sales-to-Capital Ratios

To estimate how much Commerce One and Ashford.com have to invest to generate the expected revenue growth, we estimate the current sales-to-capital ratio for each firm, the marginal sales to capital ratio in the last year, and the average sales-to-capital ratio for the businesses that each operates in:

	Commerce One	Ashford.com
Firm's sales to capital	3.13	1.18
Marginal sales to capital: most recent year	2.70	1.60
Industry average sales to capital	3.18	3.24
Sales-to-capital ratio used in valuation	2.00	2.50

We used a sales-to-capital ratio of 2.50 for Ashford.com, approximately midway through its marginal sales to capital ratio from last year and the industry average. For Commerce One, we set the sales-to-capital ratio well below the industry average and the firm's marginal sales-to-capital ratio. We feel that as competition increases, Commerce One will have to invest increasing amounts in technology and in acquisitions to grow.

Based on these estimates of the sales-to-capital ratio for each firm, we can now estimate how much each firm will have to reinvest each year for the next 10 years:

	Commerce One		Ashford.com	
Year	Increase in Revenue	Reinvestment	Increase in Revenue	Reinvestment
1	$ 201	$100	$56	$22
2	$ 603	$301	$76	$30
3	$ 964	$482	$81	$32
4	$1,302	$651	$85	$34
5	$1,389	$694	$73	$29
6	$1,701	$851	$75	$30
7	$1,968	$984	$72	$29
8	$1,706	$853	$65	$26
9	$1,024	$512	$52	$21
10	$ 563	$281	$35	$14

As a final check, we estimate the return on capital each year for the next 10 years for both firms:

Year	Commerce One	Ashford.com
1	−160.23%	−254.67%
2	−46.80%	−149.09%
3	15.30%	−70.62%
4	34.46%	−26.31%
5	32.17%	−1.73%
6	26.74%	11.31%
7	26.91%	18.36%
8	25.34%	22.00%
9	23.44%	23.72%
10	22.49%	24.34%
Industry average	20.00%	20.00%

The returns on capital at both firms converge to sustainable levels, at least relative to industry averages, by the terminal year. This suggests that our estimates of sales-to-capital ratios are reasonable.

margins.xls: This dataset on the Web summarizes operating and net margins, by industry, for the United States.

QUALITATIVE ASPECTS OF GROWTH

The emphasis on quantitative elements—return on capital and reinvestment rates for profitable firms, and margins, revenue growth, and sales-to-capital ratios for unprofitable firms—may strike some as skewed. After all, growth is determined by a number of subjective factors—the quality of management, the strength of a firm's marketing, its capacity to form partnerships with other firms, and the management's strategic vision, among many others. Where, you might ask, is there room in the growth equations that have been presented in this chapter for these factors?

The answer is that qualitative factors matter, and that they all ultimately have to show up in one or more of the quantitative inputs that determine growth. Consider the following:

- The quality of management plays a significant role in the returns on capital that you assume firms can earn on their new investments and in how long they can sustain these returns. Thus, the fact that a firm has a well-regarded management team may be one reason why you allow a firm's return on capital to remain well above the cost of capital.
- The marketing strengths of a firm and its choice of marketing strategy are reflected in the operating margins and turnover ratios that you assume for firms. Thus, it takes faith in a Coca-Cola's capacity to market its products effectively to assume a high turnover ratio and a high target margin. In fact, you can consider various marketing strategies, which trade off lower margins for higher turnover ratios, and consider the implications for value. The brand name of a firm's products and the strength of its distribution system also affect these estimates.
- Defining reinvestment broadly to include acquisitions, research and development, and investments in marketing and distribution allows you to consider different ways in which firms can grow. For some firms like Cisco, reinvestment and growth come from acquisitions, while for other firms such as GE it may take the form of more traditional investments in plant and equipment. The effectiveness of these reinvestment strategies is captured in the return on capital that you assume for the future, with more effective firms having higher returns on capital.
- The strength of the competition that firms face is in the background but it does determine how high excess returns (return on capital less cost of capital) will be, and how quickly they will fade toward zero.

Thus, every qualitative factor is quantified and the growth implications are considered. What if you cannot quantify the effects? If you cannot, you should remain skeptical about whether these factors truly affect value. What about those qualitative factors that do not affect the return on capital, margin or reinvestment rate? At the risk of sounding dogmatic, these factors cannot affect value.

Why is it necessary to impose this quantitative structure on growth estimate? One of the biggest dangers in valuing technology firms is that story telling can be used to justify growth rates that are neither reasonable nor sustainable. Thus, you might be told that Ashford.com will grow at 60 percent a year because the online retailing market is huge and that Coca-Cola will grow 20 percent a year because it has a great brand name. While there is truth in these stories, a consideration of how these qualitative views translate into the quantitative elements of growth is an essential step towards consistent valuations.

Can different investors consider the same qualitative factors and come to different conclusions about the implications for returns on capital, margins, and reinvestment rates, and consequently, about growth? Absolutely. In fact, you would expect differences in opinion about the future and different estimates of value. The payoff to knowing a firm and the sector it operates better than other investors is that your estimates of growth and value will be better than theirs. Unfortunately, this does not guarantee that your investment returns will be better than theirs.

CONCLUSION

Growth is the key input in every valuation, and there are three sources for growth rates. One is the past, though both estimating and using historical growth rates can be difficult for most firms with their volatile and sometimes negative earnings. The second source is analyst estimates of growth. Though analysts may be privy to information that is not available to the rest of the market, this information does not result in growth rates that are superior to historical growth estimates. Furthermore, the analyst emphasis on earnings per share growth can be a problem when forecasting operating income. The third and soundest way of estimating growth is to base it on a firm's fundamentals.

The relationship of growth to fundamentals will depend on what growth rate we are estimating. To estimate growth in earnings per share, we looked at return on equity and retention ratios. To estimate growth in net income, we replaced the retention ratio with the equity reinvestment rate. To evaluate growth in operating income, we used return on capital and reinvestment rate. While the details vary from approach to approach, there are some common themes that emerge from these approaches. The first is that growth and reinvestment are linked, and estimates of one have to be linked with estimates of the other. Firms that want to grow at high rates over long periods have to reinvest to create that growth. The second is that the quality of growth can vary widely across firms, and the best measure of the quality of growth is the returns earned on investments. Firms that earn higher returns on equity and capital not only will generate higher growth, but that growth will add more to their value.

QUESTIONS AND SHORT PROBLEMS

1. Walgreen Company reported the following earnings per share from 1989 to 1994.

Year	EPS
1989	$1.28
1990	$1.42
1991	$1.58
1992	$1.78
1993	$1.98
1994	$2.30

a. Estimate the arithmetic average and geometric average growth rate in earnings per share between 1989 and 1994. Why are they different? Which is more reliable?

b. Estimate the growth rate using a linear growth model.

c. Estimate the growth rate using a log-linear growth model.

2. BIC Corporation reported a return on equity of 20% and paid out 37% of its earnings as dividends in the most recent year.

a. Assuming that these fundamentals do not change, estimate the expected growth rate in earnings per share.

b. Now assume that you expect the return on equity to increase to 25% on both new and existing investments next year. Estimate the expected growth rate in earnings per share.

3. You are trying to estimate the expected growth in net income at Metallica Corporation, a manufacturing firm that reported $150 million in net income in the just-completed financial year; the book value of equity at the beginning of the year was $1 billion. The firm had capital expenditures of $160 million, depreciation of $100 million, and an increase in working capital of $40 million during the year. The debt outstanding increased by $40 million during the year. Estimate the equity reinvestment rate and expected growth in net income.

4. You are trying to estimate a growth rate for HipHop Inc., a record producer and distributor. The firm earned $100 million in after-tax operating income on capital invested of $800 million last year. In addition, the firm reported net capital expenditures of $25 million and an increase in noncash working capital of $15 million.

a. Assuming that the firm's return on capital and reinvestment rate remain unchanged, estimate the expected growth in operating income next year.

b. How would your answer to (a) change if you were told that the firm's return on capital next year will increase by 2.5%? (Next year's return on capital = This year's return on capital + 2.5%.)

5. InVideo Inc. is an online retailer of videos and DVDs. The firm reported an operating loss of $10 million on revenues of $100 million in the most recent financial year. You expect revenue growth to be 100% next year, 75% in year 2, 50% in year 3, and 30% in years 4 and 5. You also expect the pretax operating margin to improve to 8% of revenues by year 5. Estimate the expected revenues and operating income (or loss) each year for the next five years.

6. SoftTech Inc. is a small manufacturer of entertainment software that reported revenues of $25 million in the most recent financial year. You expect the firm to grow significantly over time and capture 8% of the overall entertainment software market in 10 years. If the total revenues from entertainment software in the most recent year amounted to $2 billion and you expect an annual growth rate of 6% in these revenues for the next 10 years, estimate the compounded annual revenue growth rate at SoftTech for the next 10 years.

CHAPTER 12

Closure in Valuation: Estimating Terminal Value

In the previous chapter, we examined the determinants of expected growth. Firms that reinvest substantial portions of their earnings and earn high returns on these investments should be able to grow at high rates. But for how long? This chapter brings closure to firm valuation by considering this question.

As a firm grows, it becomes more difficult for it to maintain high growth and it eventually will grow at a rate less than or equal to the growth rate of the economy in which it operates. This growth rate, labeled stable growth, can be sustained in perpetuity, allowing us to estimate the value of all cash flows beyond that point as a terminal value for a going concern. The key question that we confront is the estimation of when and how this transition to stable growth will occur for the firm that we are valuing. Will the growth rate drop abruptly at a point in time to a stable growth rate or will it occur more gradually over time? To answer these questions, we will look at a firm's size (relative to the market that it serves), its current growth rate, and its competitive advantages.

We also consider an alternate route, which is that firms do not last forever and that they will be liquidated at some point in the future. We will consider how best to estimate liquidation value and when it makes more sense to use this approach rather than the going concern approach.

CLOSURE IN VALUATION

Since you cannot estimate cash flows forever, you generally impose closure in discounted cash flow valuation by stopping your estimation of cash flows sometime in the future and then computing a terminal value that reflects the value of the firm at that point.

$$\text{Value of a firm} = \sum_{t=1}^{t=n} \frac{CF_t}{(1+k_c)^t} + \frac{\text{Terminal value}_n}{(1+k_c)^n}$$

You can find the terminal value in one of three ways. One is to assume a liquidation of the firm's assets in the terminal year and estimate what others would pay for the assets that the firm has accumulated at that point. The other two approaches value the firm as a going concern at the time of the terminal value estimation. One applies a multiple to earnings, revenues, or book value to estimate the value in the terminal year. The other assumes that the cash flows of the firm will grow at a constant rate forever—a stable growth rate. With stable growth, the terminal value can be estimated using a perpetual growth model.

Liquidation Value

In some valuations, we can assume that the firm will cease operations at a point in time in the future and sell the assets it has accumulated to the highest bidders. The estimate that emerges is called a liquidation value. There are two ways in which the liquidation value can be estimated. One is to base it on the book value of the assets, adjusted for any inflation during the period. Thus, if the book value of assets 10 years from now is expected to be $2 billion, the average age of the assets at that point is five years and the expected inflation rate is 3 percent, the expected liquidation value can be estimated as:

$$\text{Expected liquidation value} = \text{Book value of assets}_{\text{term year}}(1 + \text{Inflation rate})^{\text{average life of assets}}$$
$$= \$2 \text{ billion}(1.03)^5 = \$2.319 \text{ billion}$$

The limitation of this approach is that it is based on accounting book value and does not reflect the earning power of the assets.

The alternative approach is to estimate the value based on the earning power of the assets. To make this estimate, we would first have to estimate the expected cash flows from the assets and then discount these cash flows back to the present, using an appropriate discount rate. In the example above, for instance, if we assumed that the assets in question could be expected to generate $400 million in after-tax cash flows for 15 years (after the terminal year) and the cost of capital was 10 percent, our estimate of the expected liquidation value would be:

$$\text{Expected liquidation value} = \$400 \text{ million(PV of annuity, 15 years @ 10\%)}$$
$$= \$3.042 \text{ billion}$$

When valuing equity, there is one additional step that needs to be taken. The estimated value of debt outstanding in the terminal year has to be subtracted from the liquidation value to arrive at the liquidation proceeds for equity investors.

Multiple Approach

In this approach, the value of a firm in a future year is estimated by applying a multiple to the firm's earnings or revenues in that year. For instance, a firm with expected revenues of $6 billion 10 years from now will have an estimated terminal value in that year of $12 billion, if a value-to-sales multiple of 2 is used. If valuing equity, we use equity multiples such as price-earnings ratios to arrive at the terminal value.

While this approach has the virtue of simplicity, the multiple has a huge effect on the final value and where it is obtained can be critical. If, as is common, the multiple is estimated by looking at how comparable firms in the business today are priced by the market, the valuation becomes a relative valuation, rather than a discounted cash flow valuation. If the multiple is estimated using fundamentals, it converges on the stable growth model that will be described in the next section.

All in all, using multiples to estimate terminal value, when those multiples are estimated from comparable firms, results in a dangerous mix of relative and discounted cash flow valuation. While there are advantages to relative valuation, and we will consider these in a later chapter, a discounted cash flow valuation should provide you with an estimate of intrinsic value, not relative value. Consequently, the only consistent way of estimating terminal value in a discounted cash flow model is to use either a liquidation value or to use a stable growth model.

Stable Growth Model

In the liquidation value approach, you are assuming that your firm has a finite life and that it will be liquidated at the end of that life. Firms, however, can reinvest some of their cash flows back into new assets and extend their lives. If you assume that cash flows, beyond the terminal year, will grow at a constant rate forever, the terminal value can be estimated as follows:

$$\text{Terminal value}_t = \text{Cash flow}_{t+1}/(r - \text{Stable growth})$$

The cash flow and the discount rate used will depend on whether you are valuing the firm or valuing equity. If we are valuing equity, the terminal value of equity can be written as:

$$\text{Terminal value of equity}_n = \text{Cash flow to equity}_{n+1}/(\text{Cost of equity}_{n+1} - g_n)$$

The cash flow to equity can be defined strictly as dividends (in the dividend discount model) or as free cash flow to equity. If valuing a firm, the terminal value can be written as:

$$\text{Terminal value}_n = \text{Free cash flow to firm}_{n+1}/(\text{Cost of capital}_{n+1} - g_n)$$

where the cost of capital and the growth rate in the model are sustainable forever.

In this section, we will begin by considering how high a stable growth rate can be, how to best estimate when your firm will be a stable growth firm, and what inputs need to be adjusted as a firm approaches stable growth.

Constraints on Stable Growth   Of all the inputs into a discounted cash flow valuation model, none can affect the value more than the stable growth rate. Part of the reason for it is that small changes in the stable growth rate can change the terminal value significantly, and the effect gets larger as the growth rate approaches the discount rate used in the estimation. Not surprisingly, analysts often use it to alter the valuation to reflect their biases.

The fact that a stable growth rate is constant forever, however, puts strong constraints on how high it can be. Since no firm can grow forever at a rate higher than the growth rate of the economy in which it operates, the constant growth rate cannot be greater than the overall growth rate of the economy. In making a judgment on what the limits on stable growth rate are, we have to consider the following three questions:

1. *Is the company constrained to operate as a domestic company, or does it operate (or have the capacity to operate) multinationally?* If a firm is a purely domestic company, either because of internal constraints (such as those imposed by management) or external (such as those imposed by a government), the growth rate in the domestic economy will be the limiting value. If the company is a multinational or has aspirations to be one, the growth rate in the global economy (or at least those parts of the globe that the firm operates in) will be the limiting value. Note that the difference will be small for a U.S. firm, since the U.S economy still represents a large portion of the world economy. It may, however, mean that you could use a stable growth rate that is slightly higher (say 0.5 to 1 percent) for a Coca-Cola than for a Consolidated Edison.

2. *Is the valuation being done in nominal or real terms?* If the valuation is a nominal valuation, the stable growth rate should also be a nominal growth rate (i.e., include an expected inflation component). If the valuation is a real valuation, the stable growth rate will be constrained to be lower. Again, using Coca-Cola as an example, the stable growth rate can be as high as 5.5 percent if the valuation is done in nominal U.S. dollars but only 3 percent if the valuation is done in real dollars.

3. *What currency is being used to estimate cash flows and discount rates in the valuation?* The limits on stable growth will vary depending on what currency is used in the valuation. If a high-inflation currency is used to estimate cash flows and discount rates, the stable growth rate will be much higher, since the expected inflation rate is added on to real growth. If a low-inflation currency is used to estimate cash flows, the stable growth rate will be much lower. For instance, the stable growth rate that would be used to value Titan Cement, the Greek cement company, will be much higher if the valuation is done in drachmas than in euros.

While the stable growth rate cannot exceed the growth rate of the economy in which a firm operates, it can be lower. There is nothing that prevents us from assuming that mature firms will become a smaller part of the economy and it may, in fact, be the more reasonable assumption to make. Note that the growth rate of an economy reflects the contributions of both young, higher-growth firms and mature, stable-growth firms. If the former grow at a rate much higher than the growth rate of the economy, the latter have to grow at a rate that is lower.

Setting the stable growth rate to be less than or equal to the growth rate of the economy is not only the consistent thing to do but it also ensures that the growth rate will be less than the discount rate. This is because of the relationship between the riskless rate that goes into the discount rate and the growth rate of the economy. Note that the riskless rate can be written as:

Nominal riskless rate = Real riskless rate + Expected inflation rate

In the long term, the real riskless rate will converge on the real growth rate of the economy, and the nominal riskless rate will approach the nominal growth rate of the economy. In fact, a simple rule of thumb on the stable growth rate is that it generally should not exceed the riskless rate used in the valuation.

CAN THE STABLE GROWTH RATE BE NEGATIVE?

The previous section noted that the stable growth rate has to be less than or equal to the growth rate of the economy. But can it be negative? There is no reason why not since the terminal value can still be estimated. For instance, a firm with $100 million in after-tax cash flows growing at –5% a year forever and a cost of capital of 10 percent has a value of:

Value of firm = 100(1 – .05)/[.10 – (–.05)] = $633 million

Intuitively, though, what does a negative growth rate imply? It essentially allows a firm to partially liquidate itself each year until it just about disappears. Thus, it is an intermediate choice between complete liquidation and the going concern that gets larger each year forever.

This may be the right choice to make when valuing firms in industries that are being phased out because of technological advances (such as the manufacturers of typewriters, with the advent of the personal computer) or where an external and critical customer is scaling back purchases for the long term (as was the case with defense contractors after the end of the cold war).

Key Assumptions about Stable Growth In every discounted cash flow valuation, there are three critical assumptions you need to make on stable growth. The first relates to when the firm that you are valuing will become a stable growth firm, if it is not one already. The second relates to what the characteristics of the firm will be in stable growth, in terms of return on investments and costs of equity and capital. The final assumption relates to how the firm that you are valuing will make the transition from high growth to stable growth.

Length of the High Growth Period The question of how long a firm will be able to sustain high growth is perhaps one of the more difficult questions to answer in a valuation, but two points are worth making. One is that it is not a question of whether but when firms hit the stable growth wall. All firms ultimately become stable growth firms, in the best case, because high growth makes a firm larger, and the firm's size will eventually become a barrier to further high growth. In the worst-case scenario, firms may not survive and will be liquidated. The second is that high growth in valuation, or at least high growth that creates value,[1] comes from firms earning excess returns on their marginal investments. In other words, increased value comes from firms having a return on capital that is well in excess of the cost of capital (or a return on equity that exceeds the cost of equity). Thus, when you assume that a firm will experience high growth for the next 5 or 10 years, you are also implicitly assuming that it will earn excess returns (over and above the required return) during that period. In a competitive market, these excess returns will eventually draw in new competitors, and the excess returns will disappear.

---

[1] Growth without excess returns will make a firm larger but not add value.

You should look at three factors when considering how long a firm will be able to maintain high growth.

1. *Size of the firm.* Smaller firms are much more likely to earn excess returns and maintain these excess returns than otherwise similar larger firms. This is because they have more room to grow and a larger potential market. Small firms in large markets should have the potential for high growth (at least in revenues) over long periods. When looking at the size of the firm, you should look not only at its current market share, but also at the potential growth in the total market for its products or services. A firm may have a large market share of its current market, but it may be able to grow in spite of this because the entire market is growing rapidly.

2. *Existing growth rate and excess returns.* Momentum does matter, when it comes to projecting growth. Firms that have been reporting rapidly growing revenues are more likely to see revenues grow rapidly at least in the near future. Firms that are earning high returns on capital and high excess returns in the current period are likely to sustain these excess returns for the next few years.

3. *Magnitude and sustainability of competitive advantages.* This is perhaps the most critical determinant of the length of the high growth period. If there are significant barriers to entry and sustainable competitive advantages, firms can maintain high growth for longer periods. If, on the other hand, there are no or minor barriers to entry, or if the firm's existing competitive advantages are fading, you should be far more conservative about allowing for long growth periods. The quality of existing management also influences growth. Some top managers have the capacity to make the strategic choices that increase competitive advantages and create new ones.[2]

COMPETITIVE ADVANTAGE PERIOD (CAP)

The confluence of high growth and excess returns that is the source of value has led to the coining of the term competitive advantage period (CAP) to capture the joint effect. This term, popularized by Michael Mauboussin at Credit Suisse First Boston, measures the period for which a firm can be expected to earn excess returns. The value of such a firm can then be written as the sum of the capital invested today and the present value of the excess returns that the firm will earn over its life. Since there are no excess returns after the competitive advantage period, there is no additional value added.

In an inventive variant, analysts sometimes try to estimate how long the competitive advantage period will have to be to sustain a current market value, assuming that the current return on capital and cost of capital remain unchanged. The resulting market implied competitive advantage period (MI-CAP) can then be either compared across firms in a sector or evaluated on a qualitative basis.

---

[2]Jack Welch at GE and Roberto Goizueta at Coca-Cola are good examples of CEOs who made a profound difference in the growth of their firms.

ILLUSTRATION 12.1:   Length of High Growth Period

To illustrate the process of estimating the length of the high growth period, we will consider a number of companies and make subjective judgments about how long each one will be able to maintain high growth:

CONSOLIDATED EDISON

Background: The firm has a monopoly in generating and selling power in the environs of New York. In return for the monopoly, though, the firm is restricted in both its investment policy and its pricing policy. A regulatory commission determines how much Con Ed can raise prices and it makes this decision based on the returns made by Con Ed on its investments; if the firm is making high returns on its investments, it is unlikely to be allowed to increase prices. Finally, the demand for power in New York is stable, as the population levels off.

Implication: The firm is already a stable growth firm. There is little potential for either high growth or excess returns.

PROCTER & GAMBLE

Background: Procter & Gamble comes in with some obvious strengths. Its valuable brand names have allowed it to earn high excess returns (as manifested in its high return on equity of 29.37% in 2000) and sustain high growth rates in earnings over the past few decades. The firm faces two challenges. One is that it has a significant market share in a mature market in the United States, and that its brand names are less recognized and therefore less likely to command premiums abroad. The other is the increasing assault on brand names in general by generic manufacturers.

Implication: Brand name can sustain excess returns and growth higher than the stable growth rate for a short period—we will assume five years. Beyond that, we will assume that the firm will be in stable growth albeit with some residual excess returns. If the firm is able to extend its brand names overseas, its potential for high growth will be significantly higher.

AMGEN

Background: Amgen has a stable of drugs, on which it has patent protection, that generate cash flows currently, and several drugs in its R&D pipeline. While it is the largest biotechnology firm in the world, the market for biotechnology products is expanding significantly and will continue to do so. Finally, Amgen has had a track record of delivering high earnings growth.

Implication: The patents that Amgen has will protect it from competition, and the long lead time to drug approval will ensure that new products will take a while getting to the market. We will allow for 10 years of high growth and excess returns.

There is clearly a strong subjective component to making a judgment on how long high growth will last. Much of what was said about the interrelationships between qualitative variables and growth toward the end of Chapter 11 has relevance for this discussion as well.

Characteristics of Stable Growth Firm   As firms move from high growth to stable growth, you need to give them the characteristics of stable growth firms. A firm in stable growth is different from that same firm in high growth on a number of dimensions. In general, you would expect stable growth firms to have average risk, use more debt, have lower (or no) excess returns, and reinvest less than high growth firms. In this section, we will consider how best to adjust each of these variables.

Equity Risk   When looking at the cost of equity, high growth firms tend to be more exposed to market risk (and have higher betas) than stable growth firms. Part of the reason for this is that they tend to be niche players supplying discretionary products, and part of the reason is high operating leverage. Thus, young technology or telecomm firms will have high betas. As these firms mature, you would expect them to have less exposure to market risk and betas that are closer to 1—the average for the market. One option is to set the beta in stable growth to one for all firms, arguing that firms in stable growth should all be average risk. Another is to allow for small differences to persist even in stable growth with firms in more volatile businesses having higher betas than firms in stable businesses. We would recommend that, as a rule of thumb, stable period betas not exceed 1.2.[3]

But what about firms that have betas well below 1, such as commodity companies? If you are assuming that these firms will stay in their existing businesses, there is no harm in assuming that the beta remains at existing levels. However, if your estimates of growth in perpetuity will require them to branch out into other business, you should adjust the beta upward toward 1.[4]

 betas.xls: This dataset on the Web summarizes the average levered and unlevered betas, by industry group, for firms in the United States.

Project Returns   High-growth firms tend to have high returns on capital (and equity) and earn excess returns. In stable growth, it becomes much more difficult to sustain excess returns. There are some who believe that the only assumption consistent with stable growth is to assume no excess returns; the return on capital is set equal to the cost of capital. While, in principle, excess returns in perpetuity are not feasible, it is difficult in practice to assume that firms will suddenly lose the capacity to earn excess returns. Since entire industries often earn excess returns over long periods, assuming a firm's returns on equity and capital will move toward industry averages will yield more reasonable estimates of value.

 eva.xls: This dataset on the Web summarizes the returns on capital (equity), costs of capital (equity), and excess returns, by industry group, for firms in the United States.

Debt Ratios and Costs of Debt   High growth firms tend to use less debt than stable growth firms. As firms mature, their debt capacity increases. When valuing firms, this will change the debt ratio that we use to compute the cost of capital. When valuing equity, changing the debt ratio will change both the cost of equity and the expected cash flows. The question of whether the debt ratio for a firm should

---

[3]Two-thirds of U.S. firms have betas that fall between 0.8 and 1.2. That becomes the range for stable period betas.

[4]If you are valuing a commodity company and assuming any growth rate that exceeds inflation, you are assuming that your firm will branch into other businesses and you have to adjust the beta accordingly.

be moved toward a more sustainable level in stable growth cannot be answered without looking at the incumbent managers' views on debt, and how much power stockholders have in these firms. If managers are willing to change their financing policy, and stockholders retain some power, it is reasonable to assume that the debt ratio will move to a higher level in stable growth; if not, it is safer to leave the debt ratio at existing levels.

As earnings and cash flows increase, the perceived default risk in the firm will also change. A firm that is currently losing $10 million on revenues of $100 million may be rated B, but its rating should be much better if your forecasts of $10 billion in revenues and $1 billion in operating income come to fruition. In fact, internal consistency requires that you reestimate the rating and the cost of debt for a firm as you change its revenues and operating income.

On the practical question of what debt ratio and cost of debt to use in stable growth, you should look at the financial leverage of larger and more mature firms in the industry. One solution is to use the industry average debt ratio and cost of debt as the debt ratio and cost of debt for the firm in stable growth.

---

 wacc.xls: This dataset on the Web summarizes the debt ratios and costs of debt, by industry group, for firms in the United States.

Reinvestment and Retention Ratios   Stable growth firms tend to reinvest less than high-growth firms, and it is critical that we capture the effects of lower growth on reinvestment and that we ensure that the firm reinvests enough to sustain its stable growth rate in the terminal phase. The actual adjustment will vary depending on whether we are discounting dividends, free cash flows to equity, or free cash flows to the firm.

In the dividend discount model, note that the expected growth rate in earnings per share can be written as a function of the retention ratio and the return on equity.

$$\text{Expected growth rate} = \text{Retention ratio} \times \text{Return on equity}$$

Algebraic manipulation can allow us to state the retention ratio as a function of the expected growth rate and return on equity:

$$\text{Retention ratio} = \text{Expected growth rate}/\text{Return on equity}$$

If we assume, for instance, a stable growth rate of 5 percent (based on the growth rate of the economy) for Procter & Gamble (P&G) and a return on equity of 15 percent, based on industry averages), we would be able to compute the retention ratio that the firm in stable growth:

$$\text{Retention ratio} = 5\%/15\% = 33.33\%$$

Procter & Gamble will have to reinvest 33.33 percent of its earnings into the firm to generate its expected growth of 5 percent; it can pay out the remaining 66.67 percent.

In a free cash flow to equity model, where we are focusing on net income growth, the expected growth rate is a function of the equity reinvestment rate, and the return on equity:

Expected growth rate = Equity reinvestment rate × Return on equity

The equity reinvestment rate can then be computed as follows:

Equity reinvestment rate = Expected growth rate/Return on equity

If, for instance, we assume that Coca-Cola will have a stable growth rate of 5.5 percent and that its return on equity in stable growth of 18 percent, we can estimate an equity reinvestment rate:

Equity reinvestment rate = 5.5%/18% = 30.56%

Finally, looking at free cash flows to the firm, we estimated the expected growth in operating income as a function of the return on capital and the reinvestment rate:

Expected growth rate = Reinvestment rate × Return on capital

Again, algebraic manipulation yields the following measure of the reinvestment rate in stable growth:

Reinvestment rate in stable growth = Stable growth rate/ROC_n

where the ROC_n is the return on capital that the firm can sustain in stable growth. This reinvestment rate can then be used to generate the free cash flow to the firm in the first year of stable growth.

Linking the reinvestment rate retention ratio to the stable growth rate also makes the valuation less sensitive to assumptions about the stable growth rate. While increasing the stable growth rate, holding all else constant, can dramatically increase value, changing the reinvestment rate as the growth rate changes will create an offsetting effect. The gains from increasing the growth rate will be partially or completely offset by the loss in cash flows because of the higher reinvestment rate. Whether value increases or decreases as the stable growth increases will entirely depend on what you assume about excess returns. If the return on capital is higher than the cost of capital in the stable growth period, increasing the stable growth rate will increase value. *If the return on capital is equal to the stable growth rate, increasing the stable growth rate will have no effect on value.* This can be proved quite easily:

$$\text{Terminal value} = \frac{EBIT_{n+1}(1-t)(1-\text{Reinvestment rate})}{\text{Cost of capital}_n - \text{Stable growth rate}}$$

Substituting in the stable growth rate as a function of the reinvestment rate, from the equation, you get:

$$\text{Terminal value} = \frac{\text{EBIT}_{n+1}(1-t)(1-\text{Reinvestment rate})}{\text{Cost of capital}_n - (\text{Reinvestment rate} \times \text{Return on capital})}$$

Setting the return on capital equal to the cost of capital, you arrive at:

$$\text{Terminal value} = \frac{\text{EBIT}_{n+1}(1-t)(1-\text{Reinvestment rate})}{\text{Cost of capital}_n - (\text{Reinvestment rate} \times \text{Cost of capital})}$$

Simplifying, the terminal value can be stated as:

$$\text{Terminal value}_{\text{ROC=WACC}} = \frac{\text{EBIT}_{n+1}(1-t)}{\text{Cost of capital}_n}$$

You could establish the same proposition with equity income and cash flows, and show that a return on equity equal to the cost of equity in stable growth nullifies the positive effect of growth.

 divfund.xls: **This dataset on the Web summarizes retention ratios, by industry group, for firms in the United States.**

 capex.xls: **This dataset on the Web summarizes the reinvestment rates, by industry group, for firms in the United States.**

ILLUSTRATION 12.2:   Stable Growth Rates and Excess Returns

Alloy Mills is a textile firm that is currently reporting after-tax operating income of $100 million. The firm has a return on capital currently of 20% and reinvests 50% of its earnings back into the firm, giving it an expected growth rate of 10% for the next five years:

Expected growth rate = 20% × 50% = 10%

After year 5 the growth rate is expected to drop to 5% and the return on capital is expected to stay at 20%. The terminal value can be estimated as follows:

Expected operating income in year 6 = 100(1.10)^5(1.05) = $169.10 million
Expected reinvestment rate from year 5 = g/ROC = 5%/20% = 25%
Terminal value in year 5 = $169.10(1 − .25)/(.10 − .05) = $2,537 million

The value of the firm today would then be:

Value of firm today = $55/1.10 + $60.5/1.10^2 + $66.55/1.10^3 + $73.21/1.10^4
    + $80.53/1.10^5 + $2,537/1.10^5 = $2,075 million

If we did change the return on capital in stable growth to 10% while keeping the growth rate at 5%, the effect on value would be dramatic:

Expected operating income in year 6 = $100(1.10)^5(1.05)$ = $169.10 million
Expected reinvestment rate from year 5 = g/ROC = 5%/10% = 50%
Terminal value in year 5 = $169.10(1 − .5)/(.10 − .05)$ = $1,691 million
Value of firm today = $55/1.10 + $60.5/1.10^2 + $66.55/1.10^3 + $73.21/1.10^4$
$\qquad$ + $80.53/1.10^5 + $1,691/1.10^5$ = $1,300 million

Now consider the effect of lowering the growth rate to 4% while keeping the return on capital at 10% in stable growth:

Expected operating income in year 6 = $100(1.10)^5(1.04)$ = $167.49 million
Expected reinvestment rate in year 6 = g/ROC = 4%/10% = 40%
Terminal value in year 5 = $167.49(1 − .4)/(.10 − .04)$ = $1,675 million
Value of firm today = $55/1.10 + $60.5/1.10^2 + $66.55/1.10^3 + $73.21/1.10^4$
$\qquad$ + $96.63/1.10^5 + $1,675/1.10^5$ = $1,300 million

Note that the terminal value decreases by $16 million but the cash flow in year 5 also increases by $16 million because the reinvestment rate at the end of year 5 drops to 40%. The value of the firm remains unchanged at $1,300 million. In fact, changing the stable growth rate to 0% has no effect on value:

Expected operating income in year 6 = $100(1.10)^5$ = $161.05 million
Expected reinvestment rate in year 6 = g/ROC = 0%/10% = 0%
Terminal value in year 5 = $161.05(1 − .0)/(.10 − .0)$ = $1,610.5 million
Value of firm today = $55/1.10 + $60.5/1.10^2 + $66.55/1.10^3 + $73.21/1.10^4$
$\qquad$ + $161.05/1.10^5 + $1,610.5/1.10^5$ = $1,300 million

---

ILLUSTRATION 12.3:   Stable Growth Inputs

To illustrate how the inputs to valuation change as we go from high growth to stable growth, we will consider three firms—Procter & Gamble, with the dividend discount model; Coca-Cola, with a free cash flow to equity model; and Embraer, the Brazilian aerospace firm with a free cash flow to firm model.

Consider Procter & Gamble first in the context of the dividend discount model. While we will do the valuation in the next chapter, note that there are only three real inputs to the dividend discount model—the payout ratio (which determines dividends), the expected return on equity (which determines the expected growth rate), and the beta (which affects the cost of equity). In Illustration 12.1, we argued that Procter & Gamble would have a five-year high-growth period. The following table summarizes the inputs into the dividend discount model for the valuation of Procter & Gamble.

	High Growth Period	Stable Growth Period
Payout ratio	45.67%	66.67%
Return on equity	25.00%	15.00%
Expected growth rate	13.58%	5.00%
Beta	0.85	1.00

Note that the payout ratio and the beta for the high-growth period are based on the current year's values. The return on equity for the next five years is set at 25%, which is below the current return on equity but reflects the competitive pressures that Procter & Gamble has been under recently. The expected growth rate of 13.58% for the next five years is the product of the return on equity and retention ratio. In stable growth, we adjust the beta to one, though the adjustment has little effect on value since the beta is already close to 1. We assume that the stable growth rate will be 5%, just slightly below the nominal growth rate in the global economy. We also assume that the return on equity will drop to 15%, about halfway between the cost of equity and the average return on equity earned by brand-name companies similar to Procter & Gamble today. This reflects our assumption that returns on equity will decline for the entire industry as competition from generics eats into profit margins. The retention ratio decreases to 33.33%, as both growth and return on equity drop.

To analyze Coca-Cola in a free cash flow to equity model, the following table summarizes our inputs for high growth and stable growth:

	High Growth	Stable Growth
Return on equity	27.83%	20.00%
Equity reinvestment rate	39.32%	27.50%
Expected growth	10.94%	5.50%
Beta	0.8	0.80

In high growth, the high equity reinvestment rate and high return on equity combine to generate an expected growth rate of 10.94% a year. In stable growth, we reduce the return on equity for Coca-Cola to the industry average for beverage companies and estimate the expected equity reinvestment rate based on a stable growth rate of 5.5%. The beta for the firm is left unchanged at its existing level, since Coca-Cola's management has been fairly disciplined in staying focused on the core businesses.

Finally, let us consider Amgen. The following table reports on the return on capital, reinvestment rate, and debt ratio for the firm in high growth and stable growth periods.

	High Growth	Stable Growth
Return on capital	23.24%	20.00%
Reinvestment rate	56.27%	25.00%
Expected growth	13.08%	5.00%
Beta	1.35	1.00

The firm has a high return on capital currently, and we assume that this return will decrease slightly in stable growth to 20% as the firm becomes larger and patents expire. Since the stable growth rate drops to 5%, the resulting reinvestment rate at Amgen will decrease to 25%. We will also assume that the beta for Amgen will converge on the market average.

For all of the firms, it is worth noting that we are assuming that excess returns continue in perpetuity by setting the return on capital above the cost of capital. While this is potentially troublesome, the competitive advantages that these firms have built up historically or will build up over the high-growth phase will not disappear in an instant. The excess returns will fade over time, but moving them to or toward industry averages in stable growth seems like a reasonable compromise.

Transition to Stable Growth   Once you have decided that a firm will be in stable growth at a point in time in the future, you have to consider how the firm will change as it approaches stable growth. There are three distinct scenarios. In the first, the firm will be maintain its high growth rate for a period of time and then become a stable growth firm abruptly; this is a two-stage model. In the second, the firm will maintain its high growth rate for a period and then have a transition period where its characteristics change gradually toward stable growth levels; this is a three-stage model. In the third, the firm's characteristics change each year from the initial period to the stable growth period; this can be considered an n-stage model.

Which of these three scenarios gets chosen depends on the firm being valued. Since the firm goes in one year from high growth to stable growth in the two-stage model, this model is more appropriate for firms with moderate growth rates, where the shift will not be too dramatic. For firms with very high growth rates in operating income, a transition phase allows for a gradual adjustment not just of growth rates but also of risk characteristics, returns on capital and reinvestment rates towards stable growth levels. For very young firms or for firms with negative operating margins, allowing for changes in each year (in an n-stage model) is prudent.

ILLUSTRATION 12.4:   Choosing a Growth Pattern

Consider the three firms analyzed in Illustration 12.3. We assumed a growth rate of 13.58% and a high-growth period of five years for P&G, a growth rate of 10.94% and a high-growth period of 10 years for Coca-Cola, and a growth rate of 13.08% and a high-growth period of 10 years for Amgen. For Procter & Gamble, we will use a two-stage model—growth of 13.58% for five years and 5% thereafter. For both Coca-Cola and Amgen, we will allow for a transition phase between years 6 and 10 where the inputs will change gradually from high growth to stable growth levels. Figure 12.1 reports on how the payout ratio and expected growth change at Coca-Cola, from years 6 through 10, as well as the change in the return on capital and reinvestment rate at Amgen over the same period.

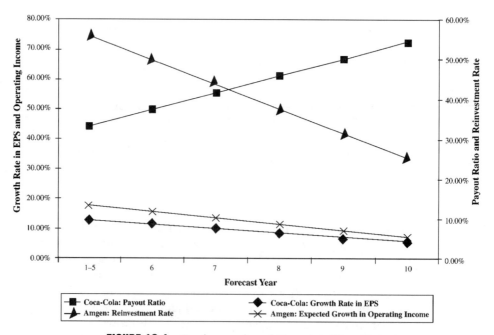

FIGURE 12.1   Fundamentals and Growth in Transition

> ## EXTRAORDINARY GROWTH PERIODS WITHOUT A HIGH GROWTH RATE OR A NEGATIVE GROWTH RATE
>
> Can you have extraordinary growth periods for firms that have expected growth rates that are less than or equal to the growth rate of the economy? The answer is yes, for some firms. This is because stable growth requires not just that the growth rate be less than the growth rate of the economy, but that the other inputs into the valuation are also appropriate for a stable growth firm. Consider, for instance, a firm whose operating income is growing at 4 percent a year but whose current return on capital is 20 percent and whose beta is 1.5. You would still need a transition period where the return on capital declined to more sustainable levels (say 12 percent) and the beta moved toward 1.
>
> By the same token, you can have an extraordinary growth period, where the growth rate is less than the stable growth rate and then moves up to the stable growth rate. For instance, you could have a firm that is expected to see its earnings grow at 2 percent a year for the next five years (which would be the extraordinary growth period) and 5 percent thereafter.

THE SURVIVAL ISSUE

Implicit in the use of a terminal value in discounted cash flow valuation is the assumption that the value of a firm comes from it being a going concern with a perpetual life. For many risky firms, there is the very real possibility that they might not be in existence in 5 or 10 years, with volatile earnings and shifting technology. Should the valuation reflect this chance of failure, and, if so, how can the likelihood that a firm will not survive be built into a valuation?

Life Cycle and Firm Survival

There is a link between where a firm is in the life cycle and survival. Young firms with negative earnings and cash flows can run into serious cash flow problems and end up being acquired by firms with more resources at bargain basement prices. Why are young firms more exposed to this problem? The negative cash flows from operations, when combined with significant reinvestment needs, can result in a rapid depletion of cash reserves. When financial markets are accessible and additional equity (or debt) can be raised at will, raising more funds to meet these funding needs is not a problem. However, when stock prices drop and access to markets becomes more limited, these firms can be in trouble.

A widely used measure of the potential for a cash flow problem for firms with negative earnings is the cash burn ratio, which is estimated as the cash balance of the firm divided by its earnings before interest, taxes, depreciation, and amortization (EBITDA).

$$\text{Cash burn ratio} = \text{Cash balance/EBITDA}$$

where EBITDA is a negative number and the absolute value of EBITDA is used to estimate this ratio. Thus a firm with a cash balance of $1 billion and EBITDA of −$1.5 billion will burn through its cash balance in eight months.

Likelihood of Failure and Valuation

One view of survival is that the expected cash flows that you use in a valuation reflect cash flows under a wide range of scenarios from very good to abysmal and the probabilities of the scenarios occurring. Thus, the expected value already has built into it the likelihood that the firm will not survive. Any market risk associated with survival or failure is assumed to be incorporated into the cost of capital. Firms with a high likelihood of failure will therefore have higher discount rates and lower present values.

Another view of survival is that discounted cash flow valuations tend to have an optimistic bias and that the likelihood that the firm will not survive is not considered adequately in the value. With this view, the discounted cash flow value that emerges from the analysis in the prior section overstates the value of operating assets and has to be adjusted to reflect the likelihood that the firm will not survive to deliver its terminal value or even the positive cash flows that you have forecast in future years.

Should You or Should You Not Discount Value for Survival?

For firms that have substantial assets in place and relatively small probabilities of distress, the first view is the more appropriate one. Attaching an extra discount for nonsurvival is double counting risk.

For younger and smaller firms, it is a tougher call and depends on whether expected cash flows consider the probability that these firms may not make it past the first few years. If they do, the valuation already reflects the likelihood that the firms will not survive past the first few years. If they do not, you do have to discount the value for the likelihood that the firm will not survive the near future. One way to estimate this discount is to use the cash burn ratio, described earlier, to estimate a probability of failure, and adjust the operating asset value for this probability:

$$\text{Adjusted value} = \text{Discounted cash flow value}(1 - \text{Probability of distress}) + \text{Distressed sale value}(\text{Probability of distress})$$

For a firm with a discounted cash flow value of $1 billion on its assets, a distress sale value of $500 million and a 20 percent probability of distress, the adjusted value would be $900 million:

$$\text{Adjusted value} = \$1,000(.8) + \$500(.2) = \$900 \text{ million}$$

There are two points worth noting here. It is not the failure to survive per se that causes the loss of value but the fact that the distressed sale value is at a discount on the true value. The second is that this approach revolves around estimating the probability of failure. This probability is difficult to estimate because it will depend upon both the magnitude of the cash reserves of the firm (relative to its cash needs) and the state of the market. In buoyant equity markets, even firms with little or no cash can survive because they can access markets for more funds. Under more negative market conditions, even firms with significant cash balances may find themselves under threat.

> ### ESTIMATING THE PROBABILITY OF DISTRESS
>
> There are two ways in which we can estimate the probability that a firm will not survive. One is to draw on the past, look at firms that have failed, compare them to firms that did not, and look for variables that seem to set them apart. For instance, firms with high debt ratios and negative cash flows from operations may be more likely to fail than firms without these characteristics. In fact, you can use statistical techniques such as probits to estimate the probability that a firm will fail. To run a probit, you would begin, for instance, with all listed firms in 1990 and their financial characteristics, identify the firms that failed during the 1991–1999 time period and then estimate the probability of failure as a function of variables that were observable in 1990. The output, which resembles regression output, will then let you estimate the probability of default for any firm today.
>
> The other way of estimating the probability of default is to use the bond rating for the firm, if it is available. For instance, assume that Commerce One has a B rating. An empirical examination of B-rated bonds over the past few decades reveals that the likelihood of default with this rating is 25 percent.[5] While this approach is simpler, it is limiting insofar as it can be used only for rated firms, and it assumes that the standards used by ratings agencies have not changed significantly over time.

CLOSING THOUGHTS ON TERMINAL VALUE

The role played by the terminal value in discounted cash flow valuations has often been the source of much of the criticism of the discounted cash flow approach. Critics of the approach argue that too great a proportion of the discounted cash flow value comes from the terminal value and that it is easy to manipulate the terminal value to yield any number you want. They are wrong on both counts.

It is true that a large portion of the value of any stock or equity in a business comes from the terminal value, but it would be surprising if it were not so. When you buy a stock or invest in the equity in a business, consider how you get your returns. Assuming that your investment is a good investment, the bulk of the returns come not while you hold the equity (from dividends or other cash flows) but when you sell it (from price appreciation). The terminal value is designed to capture the latter. Consequently, the greater the growth potential in a business, the higher the proportion of the value that comes from the terminal value.

Is it easy to manipulate the terminal value? We concede that terminal value is manipulated often and easily, but it is because analysts either use multiples to get these values or because they violate one or both of two basic propositions in stable growth models. One is that the growth rate cannot exceed the growth rate of the

---

[5]Professor Altman at NYU's Stern School of Business estimates these probabilities as part of an annual series that he updates. The latest version is available from the Stern School of Business working paper series.

economy. The other is that firms have to reinvest in stable growth to generate the growth rate. In fact, as we showed earlier in the chapter, it is not the stable growth rate that drives value as much as what we assume about excess returns in perpetuity. When excess returns are zero, changes in the stable growth rate have no impact on value.

CONCLUSION

The value of a firm is the present value of its expected cash flows over its life. Since firms have infinite lives, you apply closure to a valuation by estimating cash flows for a period and then estimating a value for the firm at the end of the period—a terminal value. Many analysts estimate the terminal value using a multiple of earnings or revenues in the final estimation year. If you assume that firms have infinite lives, an approach that is more consistent with discounted cash flow valuation is to assume that the cash flows of the firm will grow at a constant rate forever beyond a point in time. When the firm that you are valuing will approach this growth rate, which you label a stable growth rate, is a key part of any discounted cash flow valuation. Small firms that are growing fast and have significant competitive advantages should be able to grow at high rates for much longer periods than larger and more mature firms, without these competitive advantages. If you do not want to assume an infinite life for a firm, you can estimate a liquidation value based on what others will pay for the assets that the firm has accumulated during the high-growth phase.

QUESTIONS AND SHORT PROBLEMS

1. Ulysses Inc. is a shipping company with $100 million in earnings before interest and taxes that is expected to have earnings growth of 10% for the next five years. At the end of the fifth year, you estimate the terminal value using a multiple of 8 times operating income (which is the average for the sector).
   a. Estimate the terminal value of the firm.
   b. If the cost of capital for Ulysses is 10%, the tax rate is 40%, and you expect the stable growth rate to be 5%, what is the return on capital that you are assuming in perpetuity if you use a multiple of 8 times operating income.
2. Genoa Pasta manufactures Italian food products and currently earns $80 million in earnings before interest and taxes. You expect the firm's earnings to grow 20 percent a year for the next six years and 5% thereafter. The firm's current after-tax return on capital is 28%, but you expect it to be halved after the sixth year. If the cost of capital for the firm is expected to be 10% in perpetuity, estimate the terminal value for the firm. (The tax rate for the firm is 40%.)
3. Lamps Galore Inc. manufactures table lamps and earns an after-tax return on capital of 15% on its current capital invested (which is $100 million). You expect the firm to reinvest 80% of its after-tax operating income back into the business for the next four years and 30% thereafter (the stable growth period). The cost of capital for the firm is 9%.
   a. Estimate the terminal value for the firm (at the end of the fourth year).
   b. If you expected the after-tax return on capital to drop to 9% after the fourth year, what would your estimate of terminal value be?

4. Bevan Real Estate Inc. is a real estate holding company with four properties. You estimate that the income from these properties, which is currently $50 million after taxes, will grow 8% a year for the next 10 years and 3% thereafter. The current market value of the properties is $500 million, and you expect this value to appreciate at 3% a year for the next 10 years.
   a. Estimate the terminal value of the properties, based on the current market value and the expected appreciation rate in property values.
   b. Assuming that your projections of income growth are right, what is the terminal value as a multiple of after-tax operating income in the tenth year?
   c. If you assume that no reinvestment is needed after the tenth year, estimate the cost of capital that you are implicitly assuming with your estimate of the terminal value.

5. Latin Beats Corporation is a firm that specializes in Spanish music and videos. In the current year, the firm reported $20 million in after-tax operating income, $15 million in capital expenditures, and $5 million in depreciation. The firm expects all three items to grow at 10% for the next five years. Beyond the fifth year, the firm expects to be in stable growth and grow at 4% a year in perpetuity. You assume that earnings, capital expenditures, and depreciation will grow at 4% in perpetuity and that your cost of capital is 12%. (There is no working capital.)
   a. Estimate the terminal value of the firm.
   b. What reinvestment rate and return and capital are you implicitly assuming in perpetuity when you do this?
   c. What would your terminal value have been if you had assumed that capital expenditures offset depreciation in stable growth?
   d. What return on capital are you implicitly assuming in perpetuity when you set capital expenditures equal to depreciation?

6. Crabbe Steel owns a number of steel plants in Pennsylvania. The firm reported after-tax operating income of $40 million in the most recent year on capital invested of $400 million. The firm expects operating income to grow 7% a year for the next three years, and 3% thereafter.
   a. If the firm's cost of capital is 10% and you expect the firm's current return on capital to continue in perpetuity, estimate the value at the end of the third year.
   b. If you expect operating income to stay fixed after year 3 (what you earn in year 3 is what you will earn every year thereafter), estimate the terminal value.
   c. If you expect operating income to drop 5% a year in perpetuity after year 3, estimate the terminal value.

7. How would your answers to the preceding problem change if you were told that the cost of capital for the firm is 8%?

CHAPTER 13

Dividend Discount Models

In the strictest sense, the only cash flow you receive from a firm when you buy publicly traded stock in it is a dividend. The simplest model for valuing equity is the dividend discount model—the value of a stock is the present value of expected dividends on it. While many analysts have turned away from the dividend discount model and view it as outmoded, much of the intuition that drives discounted cash flow valuation is embedded in the model. In fact, there are companies where the dividend discount model remains a useful tool for estimating value.

This chapter explores the general model as well as specific versions of it tailored for different assumptions about future growth. It also examines issues in using the dividend discount model and the results of studies that have looked at its efficacy.

THE GENERAL MODEL

When an investor buys stock, he or she generally expects to get two types of cash flows—dividends during the period the stock is held and an expected price at the end of the holding period. Since this expected price is itself determined by future dividends, the value of a stock is the present value of dividends through infinity:

$$\text{Value per share of stock} = \sum_{t=1}^{t=\infty} \frac{E(DPS_t)}{(1+k_e)^t}$$

where DPS_t = Expected dividends per share
  k_e = Cost of equity

The rationale for the model lies in the present value rule—the value of any asset is the present value of expected future cash flows, discounted at a rate appropriate to the riskiness of the cash flows being discounted.

There are two basic inputs to the model—expected dividends and the cost on equity. To obtain the expected dividends, we make assumptions about expected future growth rates in earnings and payout ratios. The required rate of return on a stock is determined by its riskiness, measured differently in different models—the market beta in the capital asset pricing model (CAPM) and the factor betas in the arbitrage and multifactor models. The model is flexible enough to allow for time-varying discount rates, where the time variation is because of expected changes in interest rates or risk across time.

VERSIONS OF THE MODEL

Since projections of dollar dividends cannot be made through infinity, several versions of the dividend discount model have been developed based on different assumptions about future growth. We will begin with the simplest—a model designed to value stock in a stable growth firm that pays out what it can afford to in dividends—and then look at how the model can be adapted to value companies in high growth that may be paying little or no dividends.

The Gordon Growth Model

The Gordon growth model can be used to value a firm that is in "steady state" with dividends growing at a rate that can be sustained forever.

The Model   The Gordon growth models relates the value of a stock to its expected dividends in the next time period, the cost of equity, and the expected growth rate in dividends.

$$\text{Value of stock} = \frac{DPS_1}{k_e - g}$$

where DPS_1 = Expected dividends next year
k_e = Cost of equity
g = Growth rate in dividends forever

What Is a Stable Growth Rate?   While the Gordon growth model provides a simple approach to valuing equity, its use is limited to firms that are growing at a stable growth rate. There are two insights worth keeping in mind when estimating a stable growth rate. First, since the growth rate in the firm's dividends is expected to last forever, the firm's other measures of performance (including earnings) can also be expected to grow at the same rate. To see why, consider the consequences in the long term of a firm whose earnings grow 6 percent a year forever, while its dividends grow at 8 percent. Over time, the dividends will exceed earnings. If a firm's earnings grow at a faster rate than dividends in the long term, the payout ratio, in the long term, will converge toward zero, which is also not a steady state. Thus, though the model's requirement is for the expected growth rate in dividends, analysts should be able to substitute in the expected growth rate in earnings and get precisely the same result, if the firm is truly in steady state.

The second issue relates to what growth rate is reasonable as a stable growth rate. As noted in Chapter 12, this growth rate has to be less than or equal to the growth rate of the economy in which the firm operates. This does not, however, imply that analysts will always agree about what this rate should be even if they agree that a firm is a stable growth firm for three reasons:

1. Given the uncertainty associated with estimates of expected inflation and real growth in the economy, there can be differences in the benchmark growth rate used by different analysts (i.e., analysts with higher expectations

of inflation in the long term may project a nominal growth rate in the economy that is higher).

2. The growth rate of a company cannot be greater than the stable growth rate but can be less. Firms can become smaller over time relative to the economy.

3. There is another instance in which an analyst may be stray from a strict limit imposed on the stable growth rate. If a firm is likely to maintain a few years of "above-stable" growth rates, an approximate value for the firm can be obtained by adding a premium to the stable growth rate, to reflect the above-average growth in the initial years. Even in this case, the flexibility that the analyst has is limited. The sensitivity of the model to growth implies that the stable growth rate cannot be more than 1 percent or 2 percent above the growth rate in the economy. If the deviation become larger, the analyst will be better served using a two-stage or a three-stage model to capture the supernormal or above-average growth, and restricting the Gordon growth model to when the firm becomes truly stable.

Limitations of the Model   The Gordon growth model is extremely sensitive to the inputs for the growth rate. Used incorrectly, it can yield misleading or even absurd results since as the growth rate converges on the discount rate, the value goes to infinity. Consider a stock with an expected dividend per share next period of $2.50, a cost of equity of 15 percent, and an expected growth rate of 5 percent forever. The value of this stock is:

$$\text{Value} = 2.50/(.15 - .05) = \$25$$

Note, however, the sensitivity of this value to estimates of the growth rate in Figure 13.1. As the growth rate approaches the cost of equity, the value per share ap-

---

DOES A STABLE GROWTH RATE HAVE TO BE CONSTANT OVER TIME?

The assumption that the growth rate in dividends has to be constant over time is a difficult assumption to meet, especially given the volatility of earnings. If a firm has an average growth rate that is close to a stable growth rate, the model can be used with little real effect on value. Thus a cyclical firm that can be expected to have year-to-year swings in growth rates, but has an average growth rate that is 5 percent, can be valued using the Gordon growth model, without a significant loss of generality. There are two reasons for this result. First, since dividends are smoothed even when earnings are volatile, they are less likely to be affected by year-to-year changes in earnings growth. Second, the mathematical effects on present value of using year-specific growth rates rather than a constant growth rate are small.

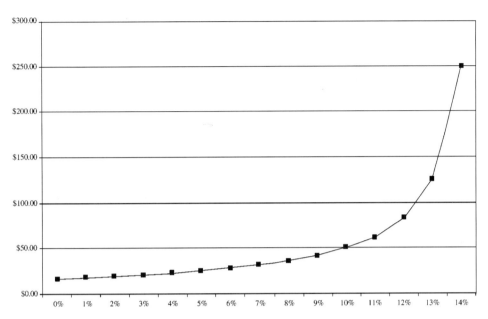

FIGURE 13.1 Value per Share and Expected Growth Rate

proaches infinity. If the growth rate exceeds the cost of equity, the value per share becomes negative.

This issue is tied to the question of what comprises a stable growth rate. If an analyst follows the constraints discussed in the previous chapter in estimating stable growth rates, this will never happen. In this example, for instance, an analyst who uses a 14 percent growth rate and obtains a $250 value would have been violating a basic rule on what comprises stable growth.

Firms Model Works Best For In summary, the Gordon growth model is best suited for firms growing at a rate equal to or lower than the nominal growth in the economy and which have well established dividend payout policies that they intend to continue into the future. The dividend payout of the firm has to be consistent with the assumption of stability, since stable firms generally pay substantial dividends.[1] In particular, this model will underestimate the value of the stock in firms that consistently pay out less than they can afford to and accumulate cash in the process.

---

[1]The average payout ratio for large stable firms in the United States is about 60%.

ILLUSTRATION 13.1:   Regulated Firm: Consolidated Edison in May 2001

Consolidated Edison is the electric utility that supplies power to homes and businesses in New York City and its environs. It is a monopoly whose prices and profits are regulated by the state of New York.

RATIONALE FOR USING THE MODEL

- The firm is in stable growth based on its size and the area that it serves. Its rates are also regulated; it is unlikely that the regulators will allow profits to grow at extraordinary rates.
- The firm is in a stable business and regulation is likely to restrict expansion into new businesses.
- The firm is in stable leverage.
- The firm pays out dividends that are roughly equal to FCFE.
  - Average annual FCFE between 1996 and 2000 = $551 million
  - Average annual dividends between 1996 and 2000 = $506 million
  - Dividends as % of FCFE = 91.54%

BACKGROUND INFORMATION

Earnings per share in 2000 = $3.13
Dividend payout ratio in 2000 = 69.97%
Dividends per share in 2000 = $2.19
Return on equity = 11.63%

ESTIMATES

We first estimate the cost of equity, using a bottom-up levered beta for electric utilities of 0.90, a risk-free rate of 5.40% and a market risk premium of 4%:

$$\text{Con Ed beta} = 0.90$$

$$\text{Cost of equity} = 5.4\% + 0.90 \times 4\% = 9\%$$

We estimate the expected growth rate from fundamentals:

$$\text{Expected growth rate} = (1 - \text{Payout ratio})\text{Return on equity}$$
$$= (1 - .6997).1163 = 3.49\%$$

VALUATION

We now use the Gordon growth model to value the equity per share at Con Ed:

$$\text{Value of equity} = \text{Expected dividends next year}/(\text{Cost of equity} - \text{Expected growth rate})$$
$$= \$2.19(1.0349)/(.09 - .0349) = \$41.15$$

Con Ed was trading for $36.59 on the day of this analysis (May 14, 2001). Based on this valuation, the stock would have been undervalued.

IMPLIED GROWTH RATE

The value for Con Ed is different from the market price, and this is likely to be the case with almost any company that you value. There are three possible explanations for this deviation. One is that you are right and the market is wrong. While this may be the correct explanation, you should probably make sure that the other two explanations do not hold—that the market is right and you are wrong or that the difference is too small to draw any conclusions.

To examine the magnitude of the difference between the market price and your estimate of value, you can hold the other variables constant and change the growth rate in your valuation until the value converges on the price. Figure 13.2 estimates value as a function of the expected growth rate (assuming a beta of 0.90 and current dividends per share of $2.19). Solving for the expected growth rate that provides the current price, we get:

$$\$36.59 = \$2.19(1 + g)/(.09 - g)$$

The growth rate in earnings and dividends would have to be 2.84% a year to justify the stock price of $36.59. This growth rate is called an implied growth rate. Since we estimate growth from fundamentals, this allows us to estimate an implied return on equity:

$$\text{Implied return on equity} = \text{Implied growth rate/Retention ratio}$$
$$= .0284/.3003 = 9.47\%$$

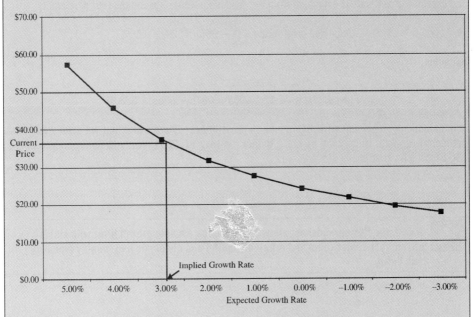

FIGURE 13.2 Value per Share versus Growth

ILLUSTRATION 13.2:   Real Estate Investment Trust: Vornado REIT

Real estate investment trusts (REITs) were created in the early 1970s by a law that allowed these entities to invest in real estate and pass the income, tax-free, to their investors. In return for the tax benefit, however, REITs are required to return 95% of their earnings as dividends. Thus, they provide an interesting case study in dividend discount model valuation. Vornado Realty Trust owns and has investments in real estate in the New York area including Alexander's, the Hotel Pennsylvania, and other ventures.

RATIONALE FOR USING THE MODEL

Since the firm is required to pay out 95% of its earnings as dividends, the growth in earnings per share will be modest,[2] making it a good candidate for the Gordon growth model.

BACKGROUND INFORMATION

In 2000, Vornado paid dividends per share of $2.12 on earnings per share of $2.22. The estimated payout ratio is:

$$\text{Expected payout ratio} = 2.12/2.22 = 95.50\%$$

The firm had a return on equity of 12.29%.

ESTIMATES

We use the average beta for real estate investment trusts of 0.69, a risk-free rate of 5.4% and a risk premium of 4% to estimate a cost of equity:

$$\text{Cost of equity} = 5.4\% + 0.69(4\%) = 8.16\%$$

The expected growth rate is estimated from the dividend payout ratio and the return on equity:

$$\text{Expected growth rate} = (1 - .955)(.1229) = 0.55\%$$

VALUATION

$$\text{Value per share} = 2.12(1.0055)/(.0816 - .0055) = \$28.03$$

It is particularly important with REITs when estimating per-share value that we steer away from net income growth, which may be much higher. On May 14, 2001, Vornado Realty was trading at $36.57, which would make it overvalued.

 DDMst.xls: **This spreadsheet allows you to value a stable growth firm, with stable firm characteristics (beta and return on equity) and dividends that roughly match cash flows.**

---

[2]Growth in net income may be much higher, since REITs can still issue new equity for investing in new ventures.

Two-Stage Dividend Discount Model

The two-stage growth model allows for two stages of growth—an initial phase where the growth rate is not a stable growth rate and a subsequent steady state where the growth rate is stable and is expected to remain so for the long term. While, in most cases, the growth rate during the initial phase is higher than the stable growth rate, the model can be adapted to value companies that are expected to post low or even negative growth rates for a few years and then revert back to stable growth.

The Model   The model is based on two stages of growth, an extraordinary growth phase that lasts n years, and a stable growth phase that lasts forever after that:

Extraordinary growth rate: g% each year for n years   Stable growth: g_n forever

Value of the stock = PV of dividends during extraordinary phase
+ PV of terminal price

$$P_0 = \sum_{t=1}^{t=n} \frac{DPS_t}{\left(1+k_{e,hg}\right)^t} + \frac{P_n}{\left(1+k_{e,hg}\right)^n}$$

$$\text{where } P_n = \frac{DPS_{n+1}}{\left(k_{e,st} - g_n\right)}$$

where DPS_t = Expected dividends per share in year t
k_e = Cost of equity (hg: high growth period; st: stable growth period)
P_n = Price at the end of year n
g = Extraordinary growth rate for the first n years
g_n = Growth rate forever after year n

In the case where the extraordinary growth rate (g) and payout ratio are unchanged for the first n years, this formula can be simplified as follows:

$$P_0 = \frac{DPS_0 \times \left(1+g\right) \times \left[1 - \frac{\left(1+g\right)^n}{\left(1+k_{e,hg}\right)^n} \right]}{k_{e,hg} - g} + \frac{DPS_{n+1}}{\left(k_{e,st} - g_n\right)\left(1+k_{e,hg}\right)^n}$$

where the inputs are as defined previously.

Calculating the Terminal Price   The same constraint that applies to the growth rate for the Gordon growth model (i.e., that the growth rate in the firm is comparable to the nominal growth rate in the economy) applies for the terminal growth rate (g_n) in this model as well.

In addition, the payout ratio has to be consistent with the estimated growth rate. If the growth rate is expected to drop significantly after the initial growth phase, the payout ratio should be higher in the stable phase than in the growth phase. A stable firm can pay out more of its earnings in dividends than a growing firm. One way of estimating this new payout ratio is to use the fundamental growth model described in Chapter 12:

$$\text{Expected growth} = \text{Retention ratio} \times \text{Return on equity}$$
$$= (1 - \text{Payout ratio}) \times \text{Return on equity}$$

Algebraic manipulation yields the following stable period payout ratio:

$$\text{Stable payout ratio} = 1 - \text{Stable growth rate/Stable period return on equity}$$

Thus a firm with a 5 percent growth rate and a return on equity of 15 percent will have a stable period payout ratio of 66.67 percent.

The other characteristics of the firm in the stable period should be consistent with the assumption of stability. For instance, it is reasonable to assume that a high growth firm has a beta of 2.0, but unreasonable to assume that this beta will remain unchanged when the firm becomes stable. In fact, the rule of thumb that we developed in the last chapter—that stable period betas betas be between 0.8 and 1.2—is worth repeating here. Similarly, the return on equity, which can be high during the initial growth phase, should come down to levels commensurate with a stable firm in the stable growth phase. What is a reasonable stable period return on equity? The industry average return on equity and the firm's own stable period cost of equity provide useful information to make this judgment.

Limitations of the Model   There are three problems with the two-stage dividend discount model; the first two would apply to any two-stage model, and the third is specific to the dividend discount model.

1. The first practical problem is in defining the length of the extraordinary growth period. Since the growth rate is expected to decline to a stable level after this period, the value of an investment will increase as this period is made longer. While we did develop criteria that might be useful in making this judgment in Chapter 12, it is difficult in practice to convert these qualitative considerations into a specific time period.
2. The second problem with this model lies in the assumption that the growth rate is high during the initial period and is transformed overnight to a lower stable rate at the end of the period. While these sudden transformations in growth can happen, it is much more realistic to assume that the shift from high growth to stable growth happens gradually over time.
3. The focus on dividends in this model can lead to skewed estimates of value for firms that are not paying out what they can afford to in dividends. In particular, we will underestimate the value of firms that accumulate cash and pay out too little in dividends.

Firms Model Works Best For   Since the two-stage dividend discount model is based on two clearly delineated growth stages—high growth and stable growth—it is best suited for firms that are in high growth and expect to maintain that growth rate for a specific time period, after which the sources of the high growth are expected to disappear. One scenario, for instance, where this may apply is when a company has patent rights to a very profitable product for the next few years, and is expected to enjoy supernormal growth during this period. Once the patent expires, it is expected to settle back into stable growth. Another scenario where it may be reasonable to make this assumption about growth is when a firm is in an industry that is enjoying supernormal growth because there are significant barriers to entry (either legal or as a consequence of infrastructure requirements), which can be expected to keep new entrants out for several years.

The assumption that the growth rate drops precipitously from its level in the initial phase to a stable rate also implies that this model is more appropriate for firms with modest growth rates in the initial phase. For instance, it is more reasonable to assume that a firm growing at 12 percent in the high growth period will see its growth rate drops to 6 percent after than it is for a firm growing at 40 percent in the high-growth period.

Finally, the model works best for firms that maintain a policy of paying out residual cash flows (i.e., cash flows left over after debt payments and reinvestment needs have been met) as dividends.

ILLUSTRATION 13.3: Valuing a Firm with the Two-Stage Dividend Discount Model: Procter & Gamble

Procter & Gamble (P&G) manufactures and markets consumer products all over the world. Some of its best-known brand names include Pampers diapers, Tide detergent, Crest toothpaste, and Vicks cough/cold medicines.

RATIONALE FOR USING THE MODEL

- *Why two-stage?* While P&G is a firm with strong brand names and an impressive track record on growth, it faces two problems. The first is the saturation of the domestic U.S. market, which represents about half of P&G's revenues. The second is the increased competition from generics across all of its product lines. We will assume that the firm will continue to grow but restrict the growth period to five years.
- *Why dividends?* P&G has a reputation for paying high dividends, and it has not accumulated large amounts of cash over the previous decade.

BACKGROUND INFORMATION

Earnings per share in 2000 = $3.00
Dividends per share in 2000 = $1.37
Payout ratio in 2000 = 1.37/3.00 = 45.67%
Return on equity in 2000 = 29.37%

ESTIMATES

We will first estimate the cost of equity for P&G, based on a bottom-up beta of 0.85 (estimated using the unlevered beta for consumer product firms and P&G's debt-to-equity ratio), a risk-free rate of 5.4%, and a risk premium of 4%:

$$\text{Cost of equity} = 5.4\% + 0.85(4\%) = 8.8\%$$

To estimate the expected growth in earnings per share over the five-year high growth period, we use the retention ratio in the most recent financial year (2000) but lower the expected return on equity to 25%:

$$\text{Expected growth rate} = \text{Retention ratio} \times \text{Return on equity}$$
$$= (1 - 1.37/3.00)(.25) = 13.58\%$$

In stable growth, we will estimate that the beta for the stock will rise to 1, leading to a cost of equity of 9.40%:

$$\text{Cost of equity in stable growth} = 5.4\% + 4\% = 9.4\%$$

The expected growth rate will be assumed to be equal to the growth rate of the economy (5%) and the return on equity will drop to 15%, which is lower than the current industry average (17.4%) but higher than the cost of equity estimated above. The retention ratio in stable growth can then be written as:

$$\text{Retention ratio in stable growth} = g/ROE = 5\%/15\% = 33.33\%$$

The payout ratio in stable growth is therefore 66.67%.

ESTIMATING THE VALUE

The first component of value is the present value of the expected dividends during the high growth period. Based on the current earnings ($3.00), the expected growth rate (13.58%), and the expected dividend payout ratio (45.67%), the expected dividends can be computed for each year in the high-growth period:

Year	EPS	DPS	Present Value
1	$3.41	$1.56	$1.43
2	$3.87	$1.77	$1.49
3	$4.40	$2.01	$1.56
4	$4.99	$2.28	$1.63
5	$5.67	$2.59	$1.70
Sum			$7.81

The present value is computed using the cost of equity of 8.8% for the high-growth period.

$$\text{Cumulative present value of dividends during high growth (@8.8\%)} = \$7.81$$

The present value of the dividends can also be computed in shorthand using the following computation:

$$\text{PV of dividends} = \frac{\$1.37 \times 1.1358 \times \left(1 - \dfrac{1.1358^5}{1.088^5}\right)}{.088 - .1358} = \$7.81$$

The value at the end of the high-growth phase (end of year 5), can be estimated using the constant growth model.

$$\text{Terminal price} = \text{Expected dividends per share}_{n+1}/(k_{e,st} - g_n)$$
$$\text{Expected earnings per share}_6 = 3.00 \times 1.1358^5 \times 1.05 = \$5.96$$
$$\text{Expected dividends per share}_6 = \text{EPS}_6 \times \text{Stable period payout ratio}$$
$$= \$5.96 \times 0.6667 = \$3.97$$
$$\text{Terminal price} = \text{Dividends}_6/(k_{e,st} - g) = \$3.97/(.094 - .05) = \$90.23$$

The present value of the terminal price can be then written as:

$$\text{PV of terminal price} = \frac{\$90.23}{1.088^5} = \$59.18$$

The cumulated present value of dividends and the terminal price can then be calculated as follows:

$$P_0 = \frac{\$1.37 \times 1.1358 \times \left(1 - \dfrac{1.1358^5}{1.088^5}\right)}{.088 - .1358} + \frac{\$90.23}{1.088^5} = \$7.81 + \$59.18 = \$66.99$$

P&G was trading at $63.90 at the time of this analysis on May 14, 2001.

DDM2st.xls: This spreadsheet allows you to value a growth firm, with an initial period of high growth and stable growth thereafter, using expected dividends.

A TROUBLESHOOTING GUIDE: WHAT IS WRONG WITH THIS VALUATION? (TWO-STAGE DDM)

If This Is Your Problem	*This May Be the Solution*
• If you get a extremely low value from the two-stage DDM, the likely culprits are:	
The stable period payout ratio is too low for a stable firm (< 40%).	If using fundamentals, use a higher ROE. If entering directly, enter a higher payout.
The beta in the stable period is too high for a stable firm.	Use a beta closer to 1.
The two-stage model is being used when the three-stage model is more appropriate.	Use a three-stage model.
• If you get an extremely high value:	
The growth rate in the stable growth period is too high for a stable firm.	Use a growth rate closer to GNP growth, and make sure that your retention ratio is consistently estimated.

Modifying the Model to Include Stock Buybacks In recent years, firms in the United States have increasingly turned to stock buybacks as a way of returning cash to stockholders. Figure 13.3 presents the cumulative amounts paid out by firms in the form of dividends and stock buybacks from 1960 to 1998. The trend toward stock buybacks is very strong, especially in the 1990s.

What are the implications for the dividend discount model? Focusing strictly on dividends paid as the only cash returned to stockholders exposes us to the risk that we might be missing significant cash returned to stockholders in the form of stock buybacks. The simplest way to incorporate stock buybacks into a dividend discount model is to add them on to the dividends and compute a modified payout ratio:

Modified dividend payout ratio = (Dividends + Stock buybacks)/Net income

While this adjustment is straightforward, the resulting ratio for any one year can be skewed by the fact that stock buybacks, unlike dividends, are not smoothed out. In other words, a firm may buy back $3 billion in stock in one year, and not buy back stock for the next three years. Consequently, a much better estimate of the modified payout ratio can be obtained by looking at the average value over a

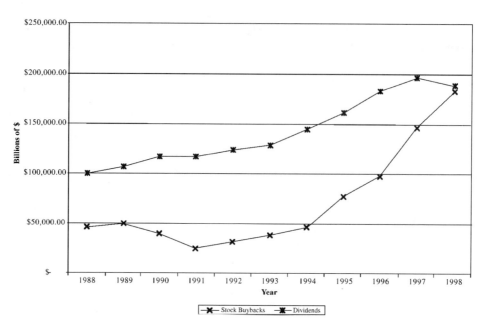

FIGURE 13.3   Stock Buybacks and Dividends: Aggregate for U.S. Firms, 1989–1998
Source: Compustat.

four- or five-year period. In addition, firms may sometimes buy back stock as a way of increasing financial leverage. We could adjust for this by netting out new debt issued from the earlier calculation:

$$\text{Modified dividend payout} = (\text{Dividends} + \text{Stock buybacks} - \text{Long-term debt issues})/\text{Net income}$$

Adjusting the payout ratio to include stock buybacks will have ripple effects on estimated growth and the terminal value. In particular, the modified growth rate in earnings per share can be written as:

$$\text{Modified growth rate} = (1 - \text{Modified payout ratio}) \times \text{Return on equity}$$

Even the return on equity can be affected by stock buybacks. Since the book value of equity is reduced by the market value of equity bought back, a firm that buys back stock can reduce its book equity (and increase its return on equity) dramatically. If we use this return on equity as a measure of the marginal return on equity (on new investments), we will overstate the value of a firm. Adding back stock buybacks in recent years to the book equity and reestimating the return on equity can sometimes yield a more reasonable estimate of the return on equity on investments.

ILLUSTRATION 13.4:   Valuing a Firm with Modified Dividend Discount Model: Procter & Gamble

Consider our earlier valuation of Procter & Gamble that used the current dividends as the basis for projections. Note that over the past four years P&G has had significant stock buybacks each period. The following table summarizes the dividends and buybacks:

	1997	1998	1999	2000	Total
Net income	3,415	3,780	3,763	3,542	14,500
Dividends	1,329	1,462	1,626	1,796	6,213
Buybacks	2,152	391	1,881	−1021	3,403
Dividends + buybacks	3,481	1,853	3,507	775	9,616
Payout ratio	38.92%	38.68%	43.21%	50.71%	42.85%
Modified payout ratio	101.93%	49.02%	93.20%	21.88%	66.32%
Buybacks	1,652	1,929	2,533	1,766	
Net long-term debt issued	−500	1,538	652	2,787	
Buybacks net of debt	2,152	391	1,881	−1,021	

Over the four-year period, P&G had significant buybacks but it also increased its leverage dramatically in the last three years. Summing up the total cash returned to stockholders over the past four years, we arrive at a payout ratio of 66.32 percent. If we substitute this payout ratio into the valuation in Illustration 13.3, the expected growth rate over the next five years drops to 8.42%:

Expected growth rate = (1 − Modified payout ratio)ROE = (1 − .6632)(.25) = 8.42%

We will still assume a five-year high-growth period and that the parameters in stable growth remain unchanged. The value per share can be estimated as follows:

$$P_0 = \frac{\$3.00 \times .6632 \times (1.0842) \times \left(1 - \dfrac{(1.0842)^5}{(1.0880)^5}\right)}{.0880 - .0842} + \frac{\$71.50}{(1.0880)^5} = \$56.75$$

Note that the drop in earnings growth reduces earnings in the terminal year and the terminal value.

This value is lower than that obtained in Illustration 13.3, and it reflects our expectation that P&G does not have as many new profitable new investments (earning a return on equity of 25%).

Valuing an Entire Market Using the Dividend Discount Model   All our examples of the dividend discount model so far have involved individual companies, but there is no reason why we cannot apply the same model to value a sector or even the entire market. The market price of the stock would be replaced by the cumulative market value of all of the stocks in the sector or market. The expected dividends would be the cumulated dividends of all these stocks, and could be expanded to include stock buybacks by all firms. The expected growth rate would be the growth rate in cumulated earnings of the index. There would be no need for a beta or betas, since you are looking at the entire market (which should have a beta of 1), and you could add the risk premium (or premiums) to the risk-free rate to estimate a cost of equity. You could use a two-stage model, where this growth rate is greater than the growth rate of the economy, but you should be cautious about setting the growth rate too high or the growth period too long, because it will be difficult for cumulated earnings growth of all firms in an economy to run ahead of the growth rate in the economy for extended periods.

Consider a simple example. Assume that you have an index trading at 700, and that the average dividend yield of stocks in the index is 5 percent. Earnings and dividends can be expected to grow at 4 percent a year forever, and the riskless rate is 5.4 percent. If you use a market risk premium of 4 percent, the value of the index can be estimated as follows:

Cost of equity = Riskless rate + Risk premium = 5.4% + 4% = 9.4%

Expected dividends next year = (Dividend yield × Value of the index)
$$(1 + \text{expected growth rate})$$
$$= (.05 \times 700)(1.04) = 36.4$$

Value of the index = Expected dividends next year
/(Cost of equity − Expected growth rate)
$$= 36.4/(.094 - .04) = 674$$

At its existing level of 700, the market is slightly overpriced.

ILLUSTRATION 13.5:   Valuing the S&P 500 Using a Dividend Discount Model: January 1, 2001

On January 1, 2001, the S&P 500 index was trading at 1,320. The dividend yield on the index was only 1.43%, but including stock buybacks increases the yield to 2.50%. Analysts were estimating that the earnings of the stocks in the index would increase 7.5% a year for the next five years. Beyond year 5, the expected growth rate is expected to be 5%, the nominal growth rate in the economy. The Treasury bond rate was 5.1%, and we will use a market risk premium of 4%, leading to a cost of equity of 9.1%:

Cost of equity = 5.1% = 4% = 9.1%

The expected dividends (and stock buybacks) on the index for the next five years can be estimated from the current dividends and expected growth of 7.50%:

Current dividends = 2.50% of 1,320 = 33.00

	1	2	3	4	5
Expected dividends	$35.48	$38.14	$41.00	$44.07	$47.38
Present value	$32.52	$32.04	$31.57	$31.11	$30.65

The present value is computed by discounting back the dividends at 9.1%. To estimate the terminal value, we estimate dividends in year 6 on the index:

Expected dividends in year 6 = $47.38(1.05) = $49.74

Terminal value of the index = Expected dividends$_6$/(r − g) = $49.74/(.091 − .05) = $1,383.11

Present value of terminal value = $1,383.11/1.091^5 = $894.81

The value of the index can now be computed:

Value of index = Present value of dividends during high growth + Present value of terminal value
$$= \$32.52 + \$32.04 + \$31.57 + \$31.11 + \$30.65 + \$894.81 = \$1,052.69$$

Based on this, we would have concluded that the index was overvalued at 1,320.

The Value of Growth

Investors pay a price premium when they acquire companies with high growth potential. This premium takes the form of higher price-earnings or price–book value ratios. While no one will contest the proposition that growth is valuable, it is possible to pay too much for growth. In fact, empirical studies that show low price-earnings ratio stocks earning return premiums over high price-earnings ratio stocks in the long term support the notion that investors overpay for growth. This section uses the two-stage dividend discount model to examine the value of growth, and it provides a benchmark that can be used to compare the actual prices paid for growth.

Estimating the Value of Growth   The value of the equity in any firm can be written in terms of three components:

$$P_0 = \left\{ \frac{DPS_0 \times (1+g) \times \left[1 - \dfrac{(1+g)^n}{(1+r)^n}\right]}{k_{e,hg} - g} + \frac{DPS_{n+1}}{\left(k_{e,st} - g_n\right)\left(1 + k_{e,hg}\right)^n} - \frac{DPS_1}{k_{e,st} - g_n} \right\}$$

$$\underbrace{\phantom{\frac{DPS_0 \times (1+g) \times \left[1 - \dfrac{(1+g)^n}{(1+r)^n}\right]}{k_{e,hg} - g} + \frac{DPS_{n+1}}{\left(k_{e,st} - g_n\right)\left(1 + k_{e,hg}\right)^n} - \frac{DPS_1}{k_{e,st} - g_n}}}_{\text{Extraordinary growth}}$$

$$+ \underbrace{\left(\frac{DPS_1}{k_{e,st} - g_n} - \frac{DPS_0}{k_{e,st}} \right)}_{\text{Stable growth}} + \underbrace{\frac{DPS_0}{k_{e,st}}}_{\text{Assets in place}}$$

where DPS_t = Expected dividends per share in year t

k_e = Cost of equity

g_n = Growth rate forever after year n

Value of extraordinary growth = Value of the firm with extraordinary growth in first n years – Value of the firm as a stable growth firm[3]

Value of stable growth = Value of the firm as a stable growth firm – Value of firm with no growth

Assets in place = Value of firm with no growth

In making these estimates, though, we have to remain consistent. For instance, to value assets in place, you would have to assume that the entire earnings could be paid out in dividends, while the payout ratio used to value stable growth should be a stable period payout ratio.

---

[3]The payout ratio used to calculate the value of the firm as a stable firm can be either the current payout ratio, if it is reasonable, or the new payout ratio calculated using the fundamental growth formula.

ILLUSTRATION 13.6:   **The Value of Growth: P&G in May 2001**

In Illustration 13.3, we valued P&G using a two-stage dividend discount model at $66.99. We first value the assets in place using current earnings ($3.00) and assume that all earnings are paid out as dividends. We also use the stable growth cost of equity as the discount rates.

$$\text{Value of assets in place} = \text{Current EPS}/r = \$3.00/.094 = \$31.91$$

To estimate the value of stable growth, we assume that the expected growth rate will be 5% and that the payout ratio is the stable period payout ratio of 66.67%:

$$\text{Value of stable growth} = \text{Current EPS} \times \text{Stable payout ratio} \times (1 + g_n)/(r - g_n)$$
$$- \text{Value of assets in place}$$
$$= (\$3.00 \times 0.6667 \times 1.05)/(.094 - .05) - \$31.91 = \$15.81$$

$$\text{Value of extraordinary growth} = \$66.99 - \$31.91 - \$15.81 = \$19.26$$

Note that $66.99 was our estimate of value per share in Illustration 13.3.

DETERMINANTS OF THE VALUE OF GROWTH

- *Growth rate during extraordinary period.* The higher the growth rate in the extraordinary period, the higher is the estimated value of growth. If the growth rate in the extraordinary growth period had been raised to 20% for the Procter & Gamble valuation, the value of extraordinary growth would have increased from $19.26 to $39.45. Conversely, the value of high growth companies can drop precipitously if the expected growth rate is reduced, either because of disappointing earnings news from the firm or as a consequence of external events.
- *Length of the extraordinary growth period.* The longer the extraordinary growth period, the greater the value of growth. At an intuitive level, this is fairly simple to illustrate. The value of $19.26 obtained for extraordinary growth in P&G is predicated on the assumption that high growth will last for five years. If this is revised to last 10 years, the value of extraordinary growth will increase to $43.15.
- *Profitability of projects.* The profitability of projects determines both the growth rate in the initial phase and the terminal value. As projects become more profitable, they increase both growth rates, and the resulting value from extraordinary growth will be greater.
- *Riskiness of the firm/equity.* The riskiness of a firm determines the discount rate at which cash flows in the initial phase are discounted. Since the discount rate increases as risk increases, the present value of the extraordinary growth will decrease.

H Model for Valuing Growth

The H model is a two-stage model for growth, but unlike the classic two-stage model, the growth rate in the initial growth phase is not constant but declines linearly over time to reach the stable growth rate in steady state. This model was presented in Fuller and Hsia (1984).

The Model   The model is based on the assumption that the earnings growth rate starts at a high initial rate (g_a) and declines linearly over the extraordinary growth period (which is assumed to last 2H periods) to a stable growth rate (g_n). It also assumes that the dividend payout and cost of equity are constant over time, and are not affected by the shifting growth rates. Figure 13.4 graphs the expected growth over time in the H model.

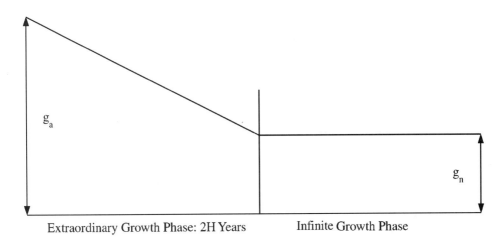

FIGURE 13.4 Expected Growth in the H Model

The value of expected dividends in the H model can be written as follows:

$$P_0 = \frac{DPS_0 \times (1 + g_n)}{k_e - g_n} + \frac{DPS_0 \times H \times (g_a - g_n)}{k_e - g_n}$$

Stable growth   Extraordinary growth

where P_0 = Value of the firm now per share

DPS_t = DPS in year t

k_e = Cost of equity

g_a = Growth rate initially

g_n = Growth rate at end of 2H years, applies forever after that

Limitations This model avoids the problems associated with the growth rate dropping precipitously from the high-growth to the stable growth phase, but it does so at a cost. First, the decline in the growth rate is expected to follow the strict structure laid out in the model—it drops in linear increments each year based on the initial growth rate, the stable growth rate, and the length of the extraordinary growth period. While small deviations from this assumption do not affect the value significantly, large deviations can cause problems. Second, the assumption that the payout ratio is constant through both phases of growth exposes the analyst to an inconsistency—as growth rates decline, the payout ratio usually increases.

Firms Model Works Best For The allowance for a gradual decrease in growth rates over time may make this a useful model for firms that are growing rapidly right now, but where the growth is expected to decline gradually over time as the firms get larger and the differential advantage they have over their competitors declines. The assumption that the payout ratio is constant, however, makes this an inappropriate model to use for any firm that has low or no dividends currently. Thus, the model, by requiring a combination of high growth and high payout, may be quite limited[4] in its applicability.

ILLUSTRATION 13.7:   Valuing with the H Model: Alcatel

Alcatel, a French telecommunications firm, paid dividends per share of 0.72 Ffr on earnings per share of 1.25 Ffr in 2000. The firm's earnings per share had grown at 12% over the prior five years but the growth rate is expected to decline linearly over the next 10 years to 5%, while the payout ratio remains unchanged. The beta for the stock is 0.8, the risk-free rate is 5.1%, and the market risk premium is 4%.

$$\text{Cost of equity} = 5.1\% + 0.8 \times 4\% = 8.30\%$$

The stock can be valued using the H model:

$$\text{Value of stable growth} = \frac{0.72 \times (1.05)}{.083 - .05} = 22.91 \text{ Ffr}$$

$$\text{Value of extraordinary growth} = \frac{0.72 \times (10/2) \times (.12 - .05)}{.083 - .05} = 7.64 \text{ Ffr}$$

$$\text{Value of stock} = 22.91 + 7.64 = 30.55 \text{ Ffr}$$

The stock was trading at 33.40 Ffr in May 2001.

 DDMH.xls: This spreadsheet allows you to value a firm, with an initial period when the high growth declines to stable growth, using expected dividends.

Three-Stage Dividend Discount Model

The three-stage dividend discount model combines the features of the two-stage model and the H model. It allows for an initial period of high growth, a transitional period where growth declines, and a final stable growth phase. It is the most general of the models because it does not impose any restrictions on the payout ratio.

The Model   This model assumes an initial period of stable high growth, a second period of declining growth, and a third period of stable low growth that lasts forever. Figure 13.5 graphs the expected growth over the three time periods.

The value of the stock is then the present value of expected dividends during the high-growth and the transitional periods, and of the terminal price at the start of the final stable growth phase.

---

[4]Proponents of the model would argue that using a steady-state payout ratio for firms that pay little or no dividends is likely to cause only small errors in the valuation.

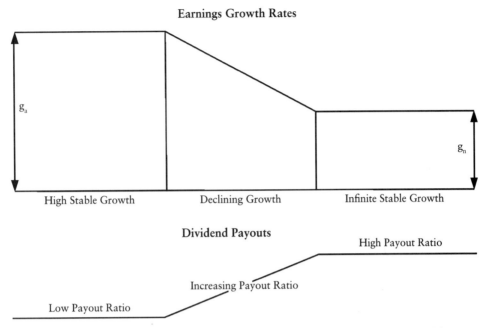

FIGURE 13.5 Expected Growth in the Three-Stage Dividend Discount Model

$$P_0 = \sum_{t=1}^{t=n1} \frac{EPS_0 \times \left(1+g_a\right)^t \times \Pi_a}{\left(1+k_{e,hg}\right)^t} + \sum_{t=n1+1}^{t=n2} \frac{DPS_t}{\left(1+k_{e,t}\right)^t} + \frac{EPS_{n2}\left(1+g_n\right) \times \Pi_n}{\left(k_{e,st}-g_n\right)\left(1+r\right)^n}$$

$\qquad\qquad$ High-growth phase $\qquad\qquad$ Transition $\qquad$ Stable growth phase

where $\quad EPS_t$ = Earnings per share in year t
$\qquad DPS_t$ = Dividends per share in year t
$\qquad g_a$ = Growth rate in high-growth phase (lasts n1 periods)
$\qquad g_n$ = Growth rate in stable phase
$\qquad \Pi_a$ = Payout ratio in high-growth phase
$\qquad \Pi_n$ = Payout ratio in stable growth phase
$\qquad k_e$ = Cost of equity in high growth (hg), transition (t), and stable
$\qquad\qquad$ growth (st)

Assumptions This model removes many of the constraints imposed by other versions of the dividend discount model. In return, however, it requires a much larger number of inputs—year-specific payout ratios, growth rates, and betas. For firms where there is substantial noise in the estimation process, the errors in these inputs can overwhelm any benefits that accrue from the additional flexibility in the model.

Firms Model Works Best For This model's flexibility makes it a useful model for any firm that in addition to changing growth over time is expected to change on other dimensions as well—in particular, payout policies and risk. It is best suited for firms that are growing at an extraordinary rate now and are expected to maintain this rate for an initial period, after which the differential advantage of the firm is expected to deplete leading to gradual declines in the growth rate to a stable growth rate. Practically speaking, this may be the more appropriate model to use for a firm whose earnings are growing at very high rates,[5] are expected to continue growing at those rates for an initial period, but are expected to start declining gradually toward a stable rate as the firm become larger and loses its competitive advantages.

ILLUSTRATION 13.8:   Valuing with the Three-Stage DDM Model: Coca-Cola

Coca-Cola, the owner of the most valuable brand name in the world according to Interbrand (a consulting firm), was able to increase its market value tenfold in the 1980s and 1990s. Growth has leveled off in the past few years, but the firm is still expanding into both other products and other markets.

RATIONALE FOR USING THE THREE-STAGE DIVIDEND DISCOUNT MODEL

- *Why three-stage?* Coca-Cola is still in high growth, but its size and dominant market share will cause growth to slide in the second phase of the high-growth period. The high-growth period is expected to last five years, and the transition period is expected to last an additional five years.
- *Why dividends?* The firm has had a track record of paying out large dividends to its stockholders, and these dividends tend to mirror free cash flows to equity.
- The financial leverage is stable.

BACKGROUND INFORMATION

Current earnings/dividends

> Earnings per share in 2000 = $1.56
> Dividends per share in 2000 = $0.69
> Payout ratio in 2000 = 44.23%
> Return on equity = 23.37%

ESTIMATE

Cost of Equity: We will begin by estimating the cost of equity during the high-growth phase, expected. We use a bottom-up levered beta of 0.80 and a risk-free rate of 5.4%. We use a risk premium of 5.6%, significantly higher than the mature market premium of 4% that we have used in the valuations so far, to reflect Coca-Cola's exposure in Latin America, Eastern Europe, and Asia. The cost of equity can then be estimated for the high-growth period.

$$\text{Cost of equity}_{\text{high growth}} = 5.4\% + 0.8(5.6\%) = 9.88\%$$

In stable growth, we assume that the beta will remain 0.80, but reduce the risk premium to 5% to reflect the expected maturing of many emerging markets.

$$\text{Cost of equity}_{\text{stable growth}} = 5.4\% + 0.8(5.0\%) = 9.40\%$$

During the transition period, the cost of equity will linearly decline from 9.88% in year 5 to 9.40% in year 10.

---

[5]The definition of a "very high" growth rate is largely subjective. As a rule of thumb, growth rates over 25 percent would qualify as very high when the stable growth rate is 6 to 8 percent.

Expected Growth and Payout Ratios: The expected growth rate during the high-growth phase is estimated using the current return on equity of 23.37% and payout ratio of 44.23%.

Expected growth rate = Retention ratio × Return on equity = (1 − 0.4423)(0.2337) = 13.03%

During the transition phase, the expected growth rate declines linearly from 13.03% to a stable growth rate of 5.5%. To estimate the payout ratio in stable growth, we assume a return on equity of 20% for the firm:

$$\text{Stable period payout ratio} = 1 - \frac{g}{\text{ROE}} = 1 - \frac{5.5\%}{20\%} = 72.5\%$$

During the transition phase, the payout ratio adjusts upward from 44.23% to 72.5% in linear increments.

ESTIMATING THE VALUE

These inputs are used to estimated expected earnings per share (EPS), dividends per share (DPS), and costs of equity for both the high-growth transition, and the stable periods. The present values are also shown in the last column of the following table:

Year	Expected Growth	EPS	Payout Ratio	DPS	Cost of Equity	Present Value
High-Growth Stage						
1	13.03%	$1.76	44.23%	$0.78	9.88%	$0.71
2	13.03%	$1.99	44.23%	$0.88	9.88%	$0.73
3	13.03%	$2.25	44.23%	$1.00	9.88%	$0.75
4	13.03%	$2.55	44.23%	$1.13	9.88%	$0.77
5	13.03%	$2.88	44.23%	$1.27	9.88%	$0.79
Transition Stage						
6	11.52%	$3.21	49.88%	$1.62	9.78%	$0.91
7	10.02%	$3.53	55.54%	$1.96	9.69%	$1.02
8	8.51%	$3.83	61.19%	$2.34	9.59%	$1.11
9	7.01%	$4.10	66.85%	$2.74	9.50%	$1.18
10	5.50%	$4.33	72.50%	$3.14	9.40%	$1.24

Since the costs of equity change each year, the present value has to be calculated using the cumulated cost of equity. Thus in year 7 the present value of dividends is:

$$\text{PV of year 7 dividend} = \frac{\$1.96}{(1.0988)^5(1.0978)(1.0969)} = \$1.02$$

The terminal price at the end of year 10 can be calculated based on the earnings per share in year 11, the stable growth rate of 5%, a cost of equity of 9.40%, and the payout ratio of 72.50%:

$$\text{Terminal price} = \frac{\$4.33(1.055)(0.725)}{0.094 - 0.055} = \$84.83$$

The components of value are as follows:

Present value of dividends in high-growth phase	$ 3.76
Present value of dividends in transition phase	$ 5.46
Present value of terminal price at end of transition	$33.50
Value of Coca-Cola stock	$42.72

Coca-Cola was trading at $46.29 on May 21, 2001.

DDM3st.xls: This spreadsheet allows you to value a firm with a period of high growth followed by a transition period where growth declines to a stable growth rate.

A TROUBLESHOOTING GUIDE: WHAT IS WRONG WITH THIS MODEL? (THREE-STAGE DDM)

If This Is Your Problem	*This May Be the Solution*
• If you are getting too low a value from this model:	
The stable period payout ratio is too low for a stable firm (< 40%).	If using fundamentals, use a higher ROE. If entering directly, enter a higher payout.
The beta in the stable period is too high for a stable firm.	Use a beta closer to 1.
• If you get an extremely high value:	
The growth rate in the stable growth period is too high for stable firm.	Use a growth rate closer to gross national product (GNP) growth.
The period of growth (high + transition) is too high.	Use shorter high growth and transition periods.

ISSUES IN USING THE DIVIDEND DISCOUNT MODEL

The dividend discount model's primary attraction is its simplicity and its intuitive logic. There are many analysts, however, who view its results with suspicion because of limitations that they perceive it to possess. The model, they claim, is not really useful in valuation except for a limited number of stable, high-dividend-paying stocks. This section examines some of the areas where the dividend discount model is perceived to fall short.

Valuing Non-Dividend-Paying or Low-Dividend-Paying Stocks

The conventional wisdom is that the dividend discount model cannot be used to value a stock that pays low or no dividends. It is wrong. If the dividend payout ratio is adjusted to reflect changes in the expected growth rate, a reasonable value can be obtained even for non-dividend-paying firms. Thus, a high-growth firm, paying no dividends currently, can still be valued based on dividends that it is expected to pay out when the growth rate declines. If the payout ratio is not adjusted to reflect changes in the growth rate, however, the dividend discount model will underestimate the value of non-dividend-paying or low-dividend-paying stocks.

Is the Model Too Conservative in Estimating Value?

A standard critique of the dividend discount model is that it provides too conservative an estimate of value. This criticism is predicated on the notion that the value is determined by more than the present value of expected dividends. For instance, it is argued that the dividend discount model does not reflect the value of "unutilized assets." There is no reason, however, that these unutilized assets cannot be valued separately and added on to the value from the dividend discount model. Some of the assets that are supposedly ignored by the dividend discount model, such as the value of brand names, can be dealt with fairly simply within the context of the model.

A more legitimate criticism of the model is that it does not incorporate other ways of returning cash to stockholders (such as stock buybacks). If you use the modified version of the dividend discount model, this criticism can also be countered.

Contrarian Nature of the Model

The dividend discount model is also considered by many to be a contrarian model. As the market rises, fewer and fewer stocks, they argue, will be found to be undervalued using the dividend discount model. This is not necessarily true. If the market increase is due to an improvement in economic fundamentals, such as higher expected growth in the economy and/or lower interest rates, there is no reason, a priori, to believe that the values from the dividend discount model will not increase by an equivalent amount. If the market increase is not due to fundamentals, the dividend discount model values will not follow suit, but that is more a sign of strength than weakness. The model is signaling that the market is overvalued relative to dividends and cash flows, and the cautious investor will pay heed.

TESTS OF THE DIVIDEND DISCOUNT MODEL

The ultimate test of a model lies in how well it works at identifying undervalued and overvalued stocks. The dividend discount model has been tested and the results indicate that it does, in the long term, provide for excess returns. It is unclear, however, whether this is because the model is good at finding undervalued stocks or because it proxies for well-known empirical irregularities in returns relating to price-earnings ratios and dividend yields.

Simple Test of the Dividend Discount Model

A simple study of the dividend discount model was conducted by Sorensen and Williamson, where they valued 150 stocks from the S&P 400 in December 1980 using the dividend discount model. They used the difference between the market price at that time and the model value to form five portfolios based on the degree of under or over valuation. They made fairly broad assumptions in using the dividend discount model:

- The average of the earnings per share between 1976 and 1980 was used as the current earnings per share.
- The cost of equity was estimated using the CAPM.

■ The extraordinary growth period was assumed to be five years for all stocks, and the I/B/E/S consensus forecast of earnings growth was used as the growth rate for this period.
■ The stable growth rate, after the extraordinary growth period, was assumed to be 8 percent for all stocks.
■ The payout ratio was assumed to be 45 percent for all stocks.

The returns on these five portfolios were estimated for the following two years (January 1981 to January 1983) and excess returns were estimated relative to the S&P 500 index using the betas estimated at the first stage and the CAPM. Figure 13.6 illustrates the excess returns earned by the portfolio that was undervalued by the dividend discount model relative to both the market and the overvalued portfolio.

The undervalued portfolio had a positive excess return of 16 percent per annum between 1981 and 1983, while the overvalued portfolio had a negative excess return of 15 percent per annum during the same time period. Other studies that focus only on the dividend discount model come to similar conclusions. In the long term, undervalued and overvalued stocks from the dividend discount model outperform and underperform, respectively, the market index on a risk-adjusted basis.

Caveats on the Use of the Dividend Discount Model

The dividend discount model provides impressive results in the long term. There are, however, three considerations in generalizing the findings from these studies:

The Dividend Discount Model Does Not Beat the Market Every Year The dividend discount model outperforms the market over five-year time periods, but there have been individual years where the model has significantly underperformed the mar-

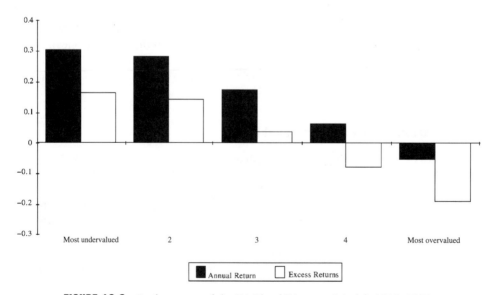

FIGURE 13.6 Performance of the Dividend Discount Model, 1981–1983

ket. Haugen reports on the results of a fund that used the dividend discount model to analyze 250 large capitalization firms and to classify them into five quintiles from the first quarter of 1979 to the last quarter of 1991. The betas of these quintiles were roughly equal. The valuation was done by six analysts who estimated an extraordinary growth rate for the initial high-growth phase, the length of the high-growth phase, and a transitional phase for each of the firms. The returns on the five portfolios, as well as the returns on all 250 stocks and the S&P 500 from 1979 to 1991, are reported in Table 13.1. The undervalued portfolio earned significantly higher returns than the overvalued portfolio and the S&P 500 for the 1979–1991 period, but it underperformed the market in 6 of the 13 years and the overvalued portfolio in 4 of the 13 years.

Is the Model Just Proxying for Low PE Ratios and Dividend Yields? The dividend discount model weights expected earnings and dividends in near periods more than earnings and dividends in far periods, and is biased toward finding low price-earnings ratio stocks with high dividend yields to be undervalued and high price-earnings ratio stocks with low or no dividend yields to be overvalued. As noted in Chapter 6, studies of market efficiency indicate that low-PE-ratio stocks have outperformed (in terms of excess returns) high-PE-ratio stocks over extended time periods. Similar conclusions have been drawn about high-dividend-yield stocks relative to low-dividend-yield stocks. Thus, the valuation findings of the model are consistent with empirical irregularities observed in the market.

It is unclear how much the model adds in value to investment strategies that use PE ratios or dividend yields to screen stocks. Jacobs and Levy (1988b) indicate that the marginal gain is relatively small.

TABLE 13.1 Returns on Quintiles: Dividend Discount Model

	Quintile						
	Undervalued	2	3	4	Over-valued	250 Stocks	S&P 500
1979	35.07%	25.92%	18.49%	17.55%	20.06%	23.21%	18.57%
1980	41.21%	29.19%	27.41%	38.43%	26.44%	31.86%	32.55%
1981	12.12%	10.89%	1.25%	−5.59%	−8.51%	28.41%	24.55%
1982	19.12%	12.81%	26.72%	28.41%	35.54%	24.53%	21.61%
1983	34.18%	21.27%	25.00%	24.55%	14.35%	24.10%	22.54%
1984	15.26%	5.50%	6.03%	−4.20%	−7.84%	3.24%	6.12%
1985	38.91%	32.22%	35.83%	29.29%	23.43%	33.80%	31.59%
1986	14.33%	11.87%	19.49%	12.00%	20.82%	15.78%	18.47%
1987	0.42%	4.34%	8.15%	4.64%	−2.41%	2.71%	5.23%
1988	39.61%	31.31%	17.78%	8.18%	6.76%	20.62%	16.48%
1989	26.36%	23.54%	30.76%	32.60%	35.07%	29.33%	31.49%
1990	−17.32%	−8.12%	−5.81%	2.09%	−2.65%	−6.18%	−3.17%
1991	47.68%	26.34%	33.38%	34.91%	31.64%	34.34%	30.57%
1979–1991	1,253%	657%	772%	605%	434%	722%	654%

Attribute	Average Excess Return per Quarter: 1982–1987
Dividend discount model	0.06% per quarter
Low P/E ratio	0.92% per quarter
Book/price ratio	0.01% per quarter
Cash flow/price	0.18% per quarter
Sales/price ratio	0.96% per quarter
Dividend yield	−0.51% per quarter

This suggests that using low PE ratios to pick stocks adds 0.92 percent to your quarterly returns, whereas using the dividend discount model adds only a further 0.06 percent to quarterly returns. If, in fact, the gain from using the dividend discount model is that small, screening stocks on the basis of observables (such as PE ratio or cash flow measures) may provide a much larger benefit in terms of excess returns.

Tax Disadvantages from High-Dividend Stocks Portfolios created with the dividend discount model are generally characterized by high dividend yield, which can create a tax disadvantage if dividends are taxed at a rate greater than capital gains or if there is a substantial tax timing liability associated with dividends.[6] Since the excess returns uncovered in the studies presented above are pretax to the investor, the introduction of personal taxes may significantly reduce or even eliminate these excess returns.

In summary, the dividend discount model's impressive results in studies looking at past data have to be considered with caution. For a tax-exempt investment with a long time horizon, the dividend discount model is a good tool (though it may not be the only one) to pick stocks. For a taxable investor, the benefits are murkier, since the tax consequences of the strategy have to be considered. For investors with shorter time horizons, the dividend discount model may not deliver on its promised excess returns because of the year-to-year volatility in its performance.

CONCLUSION

When you buy stock in a publicly traded firm, the only cash flow you receive directly from this investment in expected dividends. The dividend discount model builds on this simple proposition and argues that the value of a stock then has to be the present value of expected dividends over time. Dividend discount models can range from simple growing perpetuity models such as the Gordon growth model, where a stock's value is a function of its expected dividends next year, the cost of equity, and the stable growth rate, to complex three-stage models, where payout ratios and growth rates change over time. While the model is often criticized as being of limited value, it has proven to be surprisingly adaptable and useful in a wide range of circumstances. It may be a conservative model that finds fewer and fewer undervalued firms as market prices rise relative to fundamentals (earnings, dividends, etc.); but that can also be viewed as a strength. Tests of the model also seem to indicate its usefulness in gauging value, though much of its effectiveness may be derived from its finding low-PE-ratio, high-dividend-yield stocks to be undervalued.

---

[6]Investors do not have a choice of when they receive dividends, whereas they have a choice on the timing of capital gains.

QUESTIONS AND SHORT PROBLEMS

1. Respond true or false to the following statements relating to the dividend discount model:
   a. The dividend discount model cannot be used to value a high-growth company that pays no dividends.
   True _____ False _____
   b. The dividend discount model will undervalue stocks, because it is too conservative.
   True _____ False _____
   c. The dividend discount model will find more undervalued stocks when the overall stock market is depressed.
   True _____ False _____
   d. Stocks that are undervalued using the dividend discount model have generally made significant positive excess returns over long time periods (five years or more).
   True _____ False _____
   e. Stocks that pay high dividends and have low price-earnings ratios are more likely to come out as undervalued using the dividend discount model.
   True _____ False _____

2. Ameritech Corporation paid dividends per share of $3.56 in 1992, and dividends are expected to grow 5.5% a year forever. The stock has a beta of 0.90, and the Treasury bond rate is 6.25%. (Risk premium is 5.5%.)
   a. What is the value per share, using the Gordon growth model?
   b. The stock was trading for $80 per share. What would the growth rate in dividends have to be to justify this price?

3. Church & Dwight, a large producer of sodium bicarbonate, reported earnings per share of $1.50 in 1993 and paid dividends per share of $0.42. In 1993, the firm also reported the following:

   Net income = $30 million
   Interest expense = $0.8 million
   Book value of debt = $7.6 million
   Book value of equity = $160 million

   The firm faced a corporate tax rate of 38.5%. (The market value debt-to-equity ratio is 5%. The Treasury bond rate is 7%.)
   The firm expected to maintain these financial fundamentals from 1994 to 1998, after which it was expected to become a stable firm, with an earnings growth rate of 6%. The firm's financial characteristics were expected to approach industry averages after 1998. The industry averages were as follows:

   Return on capital = 12.5%
   Debt/equity ratio = 25%
   Interest rate on debt = 7%

   Church & Dwight had a beta of 0.85 in 1993, and the unlevered beta was not expected to change over time.
   a. What is the expected growth rate in earnings, based on fundamentals, for the high-growth period (1994 to 1998)?

    b. What is the expected payout ratio after 1998?

    c. What is the expected beta after 1998?

    d. What is the expected price at the end of 1998?

    e. What is the value of the stock, using the two-stage dividend discount model?

    f. How much of this value can be attributed to extraordinary growth? To stable growth?

4. Oneida Inc, the world's largest producer of stainless steel and silverplated flat-ware, reported earnings per share of $0.80 in 1993, and paid dividends per share of $0.48 in that year. The firm was expected to report earnings growth of 25% in 1994, after which the growth rate was expected to decline linearly over the following six years to 7% in 1999. The stock was expected to have a beta of 0.85. (The Treasury bond rate is 6.25%, and the risk premium is 5.5%.)

    a. Estimate the value of stable growth, using the H model.

    b. Estimate the value of extraordinary growth, using the H model.

    c. What are the assumptions about dividend payout in the H model?

5. Medtronic Inc., the world's largest manufacturer of implantable biomedical devices, reported earnings per share in 1993 of $3.95, and paid dividends per share of $0.68. Its earnings were expected to grow 16% from 1994 to 1998, but the growth rate was expected to decline each year after that to a stable growth rate of 6% in 2003. The payout ratio was expected to remain unchanged from 1994 to 1998, after which it would increase each year to reach 60% in steady state. The stock was expected to have a beta of 1.25 from 1994 to 1998, after which the beta would decline each year to reach 1.00 by the time the firm becomes stable. (The Treasury bond rate is 6.25%, and the risk premium is 5.5%.)

    a. Assuming that the growth rate declines linearly (and the payout ratio increases linearly) from 1999 to 2003, estimate the dividends per share each year from 1994 to 2003.

    b. Estimate the expected price at the end of 2003.

    c. Estimate the value per share, using the three-stage dividend discount model.

6. Yuletide Inc. is a manufacturer of Christmas ornaments. The firm earned $100 million last year and paid out 20% of its earnings as dividends. The firm also has bought back $180 million of stock over the past four years, in varying amounts each year. The firm is in stable growth, expects to grow 5% a year in perpetuity, and has a cost of equity of 12%.

    a. Assuming that the dividend payout ratio will not change over time, estimate the value of equity.

    b. How would your answer change if your dividend payout ratio is modified to include stock buybacks?

CHAPTER 14

Free Cash Flow to Equity Discount Models

The dividend discount model is based on the premise that the only cash flows received by stockholders are dividends. Even if we use the modified version of the model and treat stock buybacks as dividends, we may misvalue firms that consistently fail to return what they can afford to their stockholders.

This chapter uses a more expansive definition of cash flows to equity as the cash flows left over after meeting all financial obligations, including debt payments, and after covering capital expenditure and working capital needs. It discusses the reasons for differences between dividends and free cash flows to equity, and presents the discounted free cash flow to equity model for valuation.

MEASURING WHAT FIRMS CAN RETURN TO THEIR STOCKHOLDERS

Given what firms are returning to their stockholders in the form of dividends or stock buybacks, how do we decide whether they are returning too much or too little? We measure how much cash is available to be paid out to stockholders after meeting reinvestment needs and compare this amount to the amount actually returned to stockholders.

Free Cash Flows to Equity

To estimate how much cash a firm can afford to return to its stockholders, we begin with the net income—the accounting measure of the stockholders' earnings during the period—and convert it to a cash flow by subtracting out a firm's reinvestment needs. First, any capital expenditures, defined broadly to include acquisitions, are subtracted from the net income, since they represent cash outflows. Depreciation and amortization, on the other hand, are added back in because they are noncash charges. The difference between capital expenditures and depreciation (net capital expenditures) is usually a function of the growth characteristics of the firm. High-growth firms tend to have high net capital expenditures relative to earnings, whereas low-growth firms may have low, and sometimes even negative, net capital expenditures.

Second, increases in working capital drain a firm's cash flows, while decreases in working capital increase the cash flows available to equity investors. Firms that are growing fast, in industries with high working capital requirements (retailing, for instance), typically have large increases in working capital. Since we are interested in the cash flow effects, we consider only changes in noncash working capital in this analysis.

Finally, equity investors also have to consider the effect of changes in the levels of debt on their cash flows. Repaying the principal on existing debt represents a cash outflow, but the debt repayment may be fully or partially financed by the issue of new debt, which is a cash inflow. Again, netting the repayment of old debt against the new debt issues provides a measure of the cash flow effects of changes in debt.

Allowing for the cash flow effects of net capital expenditures, changes in working capital, and net changes in debt on equity investors, we can define the cash flows left over after these changes as the free cash flow to equity (FCFE):

Free cash flow to equity = Net income – (Capital expenditures – Depreciation)
– (Change in noncash working capital)
+ (New debt issued – Debt repayments)

This is the cash flow available to be paid out as dividends.

This calculation can be simplified if we assume that the net capital expenditures and working capital changes are financed using a fixed mix[1] of debt and equity. If δ is the proportion of the net capital expenditures and working capital changes that is raised from debt financing, the effect on cash flows to equity of these items can be represented as follows:

Equity cash flows associated with meeting capital expenditure needs
$$= -(\text{Capital expenditures} - \text{Depreciation})(1 - \delta)$$

Equity cash flows associated with meeting working capital needs
$$= -(\Delta \text{ Working capital})(1 - \delta)$$

Accordingly, the cash flow available for equity investors after meeting capital expenditure and working capital needs is:

Free cash flow to equity = Net income – (Capital expenditures – Depreciation)
$$\times (1 - \delta) - (\Delta \text{ Working capital})(1 - \delta)$$

Note that the net debt payment item is eliminated, because debt repayments are financed with new debt issues to keep the debt ratio fixed. It is particularly useful to assume that a specified proportion of net capital expenditures and working capital needs will be financed with debt if the target or optimal debt ratio of the firm is used to forecast the free cash flow to equity that will be available in future periods. Alternatively, in examining past periods, we can use the firm's average debt ratio over the period to arrive at approximate free cash flows to equity.

---

[1]The mix has to be fixed in book value terms. It can be varying in market value terms.

WHAT ABOUT PREFERRED DIVIDENDS?

In both the long and short formulations of free cash flows to equity described in the preceding section, we have assumed that there are no preferred dividends paid. Since the equity that we value is only common equity, you would need to modify the formulas slightly for the existence of preferred stock and dividends. In particular, you would subtract the preferred dividends to arrive at the free cash flow to equity:

Free cash flow to equity = Net income – (Capital expenditures
– Depreciation) – (Change in noncash WC)
– (Preferred dividends + New preferred stock issued)
+ (New debt issued – Debt repayments)

In the short form, you would obtain the following:

Free cash flow to equity = Net income – Preferred dividend
– (Capital expenditures – Depreciation)
$\times (1 - \delta) - (\Delta \text{ Working capital})(1 - \delta)$

The debt ratio (δ) would then have to include the expected financing from new preferred stock issues.

ILLUSTRATION 14.1:   Estimating Free Cash Flows to Equity: The Home Depot and Boeing

In this illustration, we estimate the free cash flows to equity for the Home Depot, the home improvement retail giant, and Boeing. We begin by estimating the free cash flow to equity for the Home Depot each year from 1989 to 1998 in the table, using the full calculation described in the last section.

Year	Net Income	Depreciation	Capital Spending	Change in Noncash Working Capital	Net Debt Issued	FCFE
1989	$ 111.95	$ 21.12	$ 190.24	$ 6.20	$181.88	$118.51
1990	$ 163.43	$ 34.36	$ 398.11	$ 10.41	$228.43	$ 17.70
1991	$ 249.15	$ 52.28	$ 431.66	$ 47.14	–$ 1.94	($179.31)
1992	$ 362.86	$ 69.54	$ 432.51	$ 93.08	$802.87	$709.68
1993	$ 457.40	$ 89.84	$ 864.16	$153.19	–$ 2.01	($472.12)
1994	$ 604.50	$129.61	$1,100.65	$205.29	$ 97.83	($474.00)
1995	$ 731.52	$181.21	$1,278.10	$247.38	$497.18	($115.57)
1996	$ 937.74	$232.34	$1,194.42	$124.25	$470.24	$321.65
1997	$1,160.00	$283.00	$1,481.00	$391.00	–$ 25.00	($454.00)
1998	$1,615.00	$373.00	$2,059.00	$131.00	$238.00	$ 36.00
Average	$ 639.36	$146.63	$ 942.99	$140.89	$248.75	($ 49.15)

As the table indicates, the Home Depot had negative free cash flows to equity in 5 of the 10 years, largely as a consequence of significant capital expenditures. The average net debt issued during the period was $248.75 million, and the average net capital expenditure and working capital needs amounted to $937.25 million ($942.99 – 146.63 + 140.89), resulting in a debt ratio of 26.54%. Using the approximate formulation for FCFE yields the following results for FCFE for the same period:

Year	Net Income	Net Capital Expenditures (1 – DR)	Change in Noncash Working Capital (1 – DR)	FCFE
1989	$ 111.95	$ 124.24	$ 4.55	($ 16.84)
1990	$ 163.43	$ 267.21	$ 7.65	($111.43)
1991	$ 249.15	$ 278.69	$ 34.63	($ 64.17)
1992	$ 362.86	$ 266.64	$ 68.38	$ 27.85
1993	$ 457.40	$ 568.81	$112.53	($223.95)
1994	$ 604.50	$ 713.32	$150.81	($259.63)
1995	$ 731.52	$ 805.77	$181.72	($255.98)
1996	$ 937.74	$ 706.74	$ 91.27	$139.72
1997	$1,160.00	$ 880.05	$287.23	($ 7.28)
1998	$1,615.00	$1,238.53	$ 96.23	$280.24
Average	$ 639.36	$ 585.00	$103.50	($ 49.15)

DR = Average debt ratio during the period = 26.54%

Note that the approximate formulation yields the same average FCFE for the period. Since new debt issues are averaged out over the 10 years in the approach, it also smooths out the annual FCFE, since actual debt issues are much more unevenly spread over time.

A similar estimation of FCFE was done for Boeing from 1989 to 1998 in the following table:

Year	Net Income	Net Capital Expenditures (1 – DR)	Change in Noncash Working Capital (1 – DR)	FCFE
1989	$ 973.00	$423.80	$333.27	$ 215.93
1990	$1,385.00	$523.55	$113.59	$ 747.86
1991	$1,567.00	$590.44	($ 55.35)	$1,031.92
1992	$ 552.00	$691.34	($555.26)	$ 415.92
1993	$1,244.00	$209.88	$268.12	$ 766.00
1993	$ 856.00	($200.08)	$ 6.34	$1,049.74
1995	$ 393.00	($232.95)	($340.77)	$ 966.72
1996	$1,818.00	($155.68)	($ 21.91)	$1,995.59
1997	($ 178.00)	$516.63	($650.98)	($ 43.65)
1998	$1,120.00	$754.77	$107.25	$ 257.98
Average	$ 973.00	$312.17	($ 79.57)	$ 740.40

DR = Average debt ratio during the period = 42.34%

During the period, Boeing financed a high proportion of its reinvestment needs with debt, and its market debt ratio increased from about 1% to approximately 20%. The average free cash flow to equity during the period was $740.40 million. Note that the 1997 and 1998 capital expenditures include the amount spent by Boeing to acquire McDonnell Douglas.

Comparing Dividends to Free Cash Flows to Equity

The conventional measure of dividend policy—the dividend payout ratio—gives us the value of dividends as a proportion of earnings. Our approach measures the total cash returned to stockholders as a proportion of the free cash flow to equity:

Dividend payout ratio = Dividends/Earnings

Cash to stockholders to FCFE ratio = (Dividends + Equity repurchases)/FCFE

The ratio of cash to stockholders to FCFE shows how much of the cash available to be paid out to stockholders is actually returned to them in the form of dividends and stock buybacks. If this ratio, over time, is equal or close to 1, the firm is paying out all that it can to its stockholders. If it is significantly less than 1, the firm is paying out less than it can afford to and is using the difference to increase its cash balance or to invest in marketable securities. If it is significantly over 1, the firm is paying out more than it can afford and is either drawing on an existing cash balance or issuing new securities (stocks or bonds).

We can observe the tendency of firms to pay out less to stockholders than they have available in free cash flows to equity by examining cash returned to stockholders paid as a percentage of free cash flow to equity. In 1998, for instance, the average dividend to free cash flow to equity ratio across all firms on the New York Stock Exchange was 51.55%. Figure 14.1 shows the distribution of cash returned as a percent of FCFE across all firms.

A percentage less than 100 percent means that the firm is paying out less in dividends than it has available in free cash flows and that it is generating surplus cash. For those firms, this cash surplus appears as an increase in the cash balance. A percentage greater than 100 percent indicates that the firm is paying out more in dividends than it has available in cash flow. These firms have to finance these dividend payments either out of existing cash balances or by making new stock issues.

The implications for valuation are simple. If we use the dividend discount model and do not allow for the buildup of cash that occurs when firms pay out less than they can afford, we will underestimate the value of equity in firms. If we use the model to value firms that pay out more dividends than they have available, we will overvalue the firm. The rest of this chapter is designed to correct for this limitation.

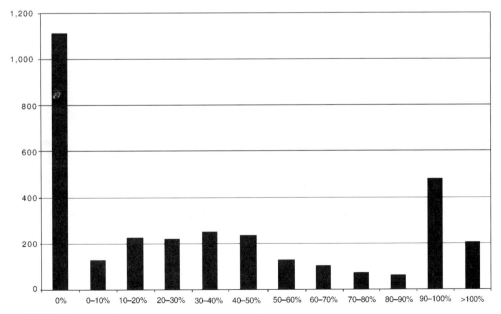

FIGURE 14.1   Cash Returned as Percent of FCFE
Source: Compustat database 1998.

dividends.xls: This spreadsheet allows you to estimate the free cash flow to equity and the cash returned to stockholders for a period of up to 10 years.

 divfcfe.xls: This dataset on the Web summarizes dividends, cash returned to stockholders, and free cash flows to equity, by sector, in the United States.

Why Firms May Pay Out Less than Is Available

Many firms pay out less to stockholders, in the form of dividends and stock buybacks, than they have available in free cash flows to equity. The reasons vary from firm to firm.

Desire for Stability   Firms are generally reluctant to change dividends, and dividends are considered "sticky" because the variability in dividends is significantly lower than the variability in earnings or cash flows. The unwillingness to change dividends is accentuated when firms have to reduce dividends, and empirically, increases in dividends outnumber cuts in dividends by at least a five-to-one margin in most periods. As a consequence of this reluctance to cut dividends, firms will often refuse to increase dividends even when earnings and FCFE go up, because they are uncertain about their capacity to maintain these higher dividends. This leads to a lag between earnings increases and dividend increases. Similarly, firms frequently keep dividends unchanged in the face of declining earnings and FCFE. Figure 14.2 reports the number of dividend changes (increases, decreases, no changes) between 1989 and 1998.

The number of firms increasing dividends outnumbers those decreasing dividends seven to one. The number of firms, however, that do not change dividends

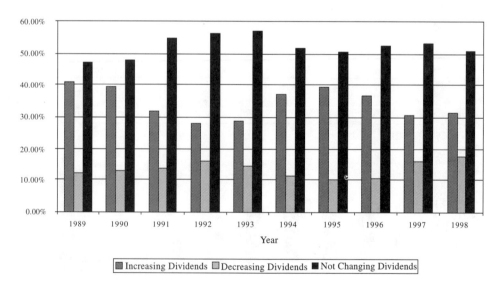

FIGURE 14.2   Dividend Changes, 1989–1998
Source: Compustat.

outnumbers firms that do about four to one. Dividends are also less variable than either FCFE or earnings, but this reduced volatility is a result of keeping dividends significantly below the FCFE.

Future Investment Needs   A firm might hold back on paying its entire FCFE as dividends if it expects substantial increases in capital expenditure needs in the future. Since issuing stocks is expensive (from a flotation cost standpoint), it may choose to keep the excess cash to finance these future needs. Thus, to the degree that a firm may be unsure about its future financing needs, it may retain some cash to take on unexpected investments or meet unanticipated needs.

Tax Factors   If dividends are taxed at a higher tax rate than capital gains, a firm may choose to retain the excess cash and pay out much less in dividends than it has available. This is likely to be accentuated if the stockholders in the firm are in high tax brackets, as is the case with many family-controlled firms. If, however, investors in the firm like dividends or tax laws favor dividends, the firm may pay more out in dividends than it has available in FCFE, often borrowing or issuing new stock to do so.

Signaling Prerogatives   Firms often use dividends as signals of future prospects, with increases in dividends being viewed as positive signals and decreases as negative signals. The empirical evidence is consistent with this signaling story, since stock prices generally go up on dividend increases and down on dividend decreases. The use of dividends as signals may lead to differences between dividends and FCFE.

Managerial Self-interest   The managers of a firm may gain by retaining cash rather than paying it out as a dividend. The desire for empire building may make increasing the size of the firm an objective on its own. Or management may feel the need to build up a cash cushion to tide over periods when earnings may dip; in such periods, the cash cushion may reduce or obscure the earnings drop and may allow managers to remain in control.

FCFE VALUATION MODELS

The free cash flow to equity model does not represent a radical departure from the traditional dividend discount model. In fact, one way to describe a free cash flow to equity model is that it represents a model where we discount potential dividends rather than actual dividends. Consequently, the three versions of the FCFE valuation model presented in this section are simple variants on the dividend discount model, with one significant change—free cash flows to equity replace dividends in the models.

Underlying Principle

When we replace the dividends with FCFE to value equity, we are doing more than substituting one cash flow for another. We are implicitly assuming that the FCFE will be paid out to stockholders. There are two consequences:

1. There will be no future cash buildup in the firm, since the cash that is available after debt payments and reinvestment needs is paid out to stockholders each period.
2. The expected growth in FCFE will include growth in income from operating assets and not growth in income from increases in marketable securities. This follows directly from the last point.

How does discounting free cash flows to equity compare with the modified dividend discount model, where stock buybacks are added back to dividends and discounted? You can consider stock buybacks to be the return of excess cash accumulated largely as a consequence of not paying out their FCFE as dividends. Thus, FCFE represents a smoothed-out measure of what companies can return to their stockholders over time in the form of dividends and stock buybacks.

Estimating Growth in FCFE

Free cash flows to equity, like dividends, are cash flows to equity investors and you could use the same approach that you used to estimate the fundamental growth rate in dividends per share:

$$\text{Expected growth rate} = \text{Retention ratio} \times \text{Return on equity}$$

The use of the retention ratio in this equation implies that whatever is not paid out as dividends is reinvested back into the firm. There is a strong argument to be made, though, that this is not consistent with the assumption that free cash flows to equity are paid out to stockholders, which underlies FCFE models. It is far more consistent to replace the retention ratio with the equity reinvestment rate, which measures the percent of net income that is invested back into the firm.

$$\text{Equity reinvestment rate} = 1 - (\text{Net cap ex} + \text{Change in working capital} - \text{Net debt issues})/\text{Net income}$$

The return on equity may also have to be modified to reflect the fact that the conventional measure of the return includes interest income from cash and marketable securities in the numerator and the book value of equity also includes the value of the cash and marketable securities. In the FCFE model, there is no excess cash left in the firm and the return on equity should measure the return on noncash investments. You could construct a modified version of the return on equity that measures this:

$$\text{Noncash ROE} = \frac{\text{Net income} - \text{After-tax income from cash and marketable securities}}{\text{Book value of equity} - \text{Cash and marketable securities}}$$

The product of the equity reinvestment rate and the modified ROE will yield the expected growth rate in FCFE:

$$\text{Expected growth in FCFE} = \text{Equity reinvestment rate} \times \text{Noncash ROE}$$

Constant Growth FCFE Model

The constant growth FCFE model is designed to value firms that are growing at a stable growth rate and are hence in steady state.

The Model The value of equity, under the constant growth model, is a function of the expected FCFE in the next period, the stable growth rate, and the required rate of return.

$$\text{Value} = \frac{\text{FCFE}_1}{k_e - g_n}$$

where Value = Value of stock today
  FCFE_1 = Expected FCFE next year
  k_e = Cost of equity of the firm
  g_n = Growth rate in FCFE for the firm forever

Caveats The model is very similar to the Gordon growth model in its underlying assumptions and works under some of the same constraints. The growth rate used in the model has to be reasonable, relative to the nominal growth rate in the economy in which the firm operates. As a general rule, a stable growth rate cannot exceed the growth rate of the economy in which the firm operates.

The assumption that a firm is in steady state also implies that it possesses other characteristics shared by stable firms. This would mean, for instance, that capital expenditures are not disproportionately large, relative to depreciation, and the firm is of average risk. (If the capital asset pricing model is used, the beta of the equity should be close to 1.) To estimate the reinvestment for a stable growth firm, you can use one of two approaches:

You can use the typical reinvestment rates for firms in the industry to which the firm belongs. A simple way to do this is to use the average capital expenditure to depreciation ratio for the industry (or better still, just stable firms in the industry) to estimate a normalized capital expenditure for the firm.

Alternatively, you can use the relationship between growth and fundamentals to estimate the required reinvestment. The expected growth in net income can be written as:

Expected growth rate in net income = Equity reinvestment rate × Return on equity

This allows us to estimate the equity reinvestment rate:

Equity reinvestment rate = Expected growth rate/Return on equity

To illustrate, a firm with a stable growth rate of 4 percent and a return on equity of 12 percent would need to reinvest about one-third of its net income back into net capital expenditures and working capital needs. Put another way, the free cash flows to equity should be two-thirds of net income.

Best Suited for Firms This model, like the stable growth dividend discount model, is best suited for firms growing at a rate comparable to or lower than the nominal growth in the economy. It is, however, the better model to use than the dividend discount model for stable firms that pay out dividends that are unsustainably high (because they exceed FCFE by a significant amount) or are significantly lower than the FCFE. Note, though, that if the firm is stable, and pays out its FCFE as dividend, the value obtained from this model will be the same as the one obtained from the Gordon growth model.

ILLUSTRATION 14.2:   FCFE Stable Growth Model: Singapore Airlines

RATIONALE FOR USING THE MODEL

- Singapore Airlines is a large firm in a mature industry. Given the competition for air passengers and the limited potential for growth, it seems reasonable to assume stable growth for the future. Singapore Airline's revenues have grown about 3% a year for the past five years.
- Singapore Airlines has maintained a low book debt ratio historically, and its management seems inclined to keep leverage low.

BACKGROUND INFORMATION

In the financial year ended March 2001, Singapore Airlines reported net income of S$1,164 million on revenues of S$7,816 million, and earned a noncash return on equity of 10% for the year. The capital expenditures during the year amounted to S$2,214 million, but the average capital expenditures between 1997 and 2000 were S$1,520 million. The depreciation in 2000 was S$1,205 million. The noncash working capital increased by $303 million in 2000. The book value debt to capital ratio at the end of 2000 was 5.44%.

ESTIMATION

We begin by estimating a normalized free cash flow to equity for the current year. We will assume that earnings will grow 5% over the next year. To estimate net capital expenditures, we will use the average capital expenditures between 1997 and 2000 (to smooth out the year-to-year jumps) and the depreciation from the most recent year. Finally, we will assume that the 5.44% of future reinvestment needs will come from debt, reflecting the firm's current book debt ratio:[2]

Net income next year	$1,164 million
Net cap ex (1 − Debt ratio) = (1,520 − 1,205)(1 − .0544)	$298 million
Change in working capital (1 − Debt ratio) = 303 (1 − .0544)	$287 million
Normalized FCFE for current year	$579 million

As a check, we also computed the equity reinvestment rate that Singapore Airlines would need to maintain to earn a growth of 5%, based on its return on equity of 10%:

$$\text{Equity reinvestment rate} = g/\text{ROE} = 50\%$$

With this reinvestment rate, the free cash flows to equity would have been half the net income. The reinvestment we used in the calculation above is very close to this value:

$$\text{Equity reinvestment rate used} = (289 + 287)/1,164 = 50.2\%$$

---

[2]In making estimates for the future, you can go with either book or market debt ratios, depending on what you think about the firm's financing policy.

To estimate the cost of equity, we used the bottom-up unlevered beta for airlines (0.81), Singapore Airlines' market debt to equity ratio of 3.63% and tax rate of 38%.

$$\text{Levered beta} = 0.81[1 + (1 - .38)(.0363)] = 0.83$$

Using a riskless rate of 6% based on a 10-year S$-denominated bond issued by the Singapore government, and using a risk premium of 5% (4% for mature market risk plus 1% for additional country risk), we estimate a cost of equity:

$$\text{Cost of equity} = 6\% + 0.83 \times (5\%) = 10.14\%$$

VALUATION

With the normalized FCFE estimated above, a perpetual growth rate of 5%, and a cost of equity of 10.14%, we can estimate the value of equity:

$$\text{Value of equity} = \text{Expected FCFE next year}/(\text{Cost of equity} - \text{Expected growth})$$
$$= 579(1.05)/(.1014 - .05) = \text{S\$11,833 million}$$

The equity in the firm had a market value of S$14,627 million in May 2001.

 FCFEst.xls: **This spreadsheet allows you to value the equity in a firm in stable growth, with all of the inputs of a stable growth firm.**

LEVERAGE, FCFE, AND EQUITY VALUE

Embedded in the FCFE computation seems to be the makings of a free lunch. Increasing the debt ratio increases free cash flow to equity because more of a firm's reinvestment needs will come from borrowing and less is needed from equity investors. The released cash can be paid out as additional dividends or used for stock buybacks. In the case for Singapore Airlines, for instance, the free cash flow to equity is shown as a function of the debt to capital ratio in Figure 14.3.

If the free cash flow to equity increases as the leverage increases, does it follow that the value of equity will also increase with leverage? Not necessarily. The discount rate used is the cost of equity, which is estimated based on a beta or betas. As leverage increases, the beta will also increase, pushing up the cost of equity. In fact, in the levered beta equation that we introduced in Chapter 8 the levered beta is:

Levered beta = Unlevered beta [1 + (1 − Tax rate)(Debt/Equity)]

This, in turn, will have a negative effect on equity value. The net effect on value will then depend on which effect—the increase in cash flows or the increase in betas—dominates. Figure 14.4 graphs out the value of Singapore Airlines as a function of the debt-to-capital ratio. The value of equity is maximized at a debt ratio of 30 percent, but beyond that level debt's costs outweigh its benefits.

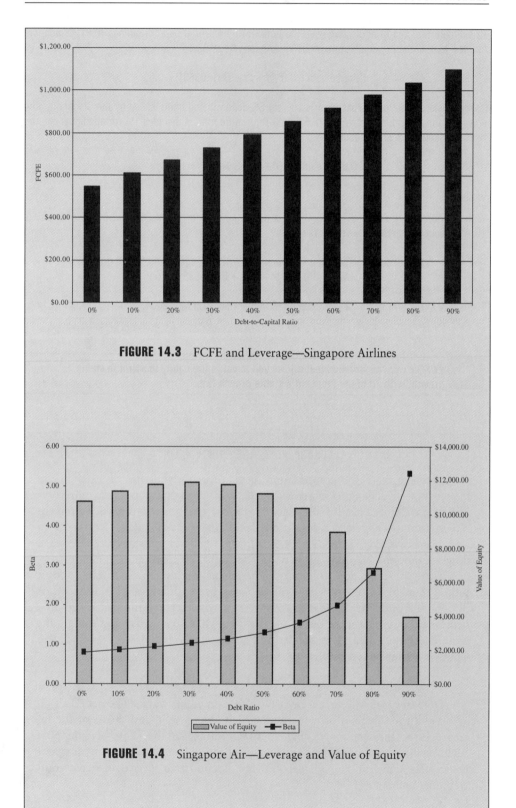

FIGURE 14.3   FCFE and Leverage—Singapore Airlines

FIGURE 14.4   Singapore Air—Leverage and Value of Equity

A TROUBLESHOOTING GUIDE: WHAT IS WRONG WITH THIS VALUATION? (CONSTANT GROWTH FCFE MODEL)

If This Is Your Problem	*This May Be the Solution*
• If you get a low value from this model, it may be because:	
Capital expenditures are too high relative to depreciation.	Use a smaller cap ex or use the two-stage model.
Working capital as a percent of revenues is too high.	Normalize this ratio, using historical averages.
The beta is high for a stable firm.	Use a beta closer to 1.
• If you get too high a value, it is because:	
Capital expenditures are lower than depreciation.	Estimate an appropriate reinvestment rate = g/ROE.
Working capital ratio as percent of revenue is negative.	Set equal to zero.
The expected growth rate is too high for a stable firm.	Use a growth rate less than or equal to GNP growth.

Two-Stage FCFE Model

The two-stage FCFE model is designed to value a firm that is expected to grow much faster than a stable firm in the initial period and at a stable rate after that.

The Model   The value of any stock is the present value of the FCFE per year for the extraordinary growth period plus the present value of the terminal price at the end of the period.

$$\text{Value} = \text{PV of FCFE} + \text{PV of terminal price}$$

$$= \sum_{t=1}^{t=n} \text{FCFE}_t / (1 + k_{e,hg})^t + P_n / (1 + k_{e,hg})^n$$

where FCFE_t = Free cash flow to equity in year t
  P_n = Price at the end of the extraordinary growth period
  k_e = Cost of equity in high growth (hg) and stable growth (st) periods

The terminal price is generally calculated using the infinite growth rate model:

$$P_n = \text{FCFE}_{n+1} / (k_{e,st} - g_n)$$

where g_n = Growth rate after the terminal year forever

Calculating the Terminal Price   The same caveats that apply to the growth rate for the stable growth rate model, described in the previous section, apply here as well. In addition, the assumptions made to derive the free cash flow to equity after the terminal year have to be consistent with this assumption of stability. For instance, while capital spending may be much greater than depreciation in the initial high-growth phase, the difference should narrow as the firm enters its stable growth phase. We can use the two approaches described for the stable growth model—industry average capital expenditure requirements or the fundamental growth equation (equity reinvestment rate = g/ROE) to make this estimate.

The beta and debt ratio may also need to be adjusted in stable growth to reflect the fact that stable growth firms tend to have average risk (betas closer to 1) and use more debt than high-growth firms.

ILLUSTRATION 14.3:   Capital Expenditure, Depreciation, and Growth Rates

Assume you have a firm that is expected to have earnings growth of 20% for the next five years and 5% thereafter. The current earnings per share is $2.50. Current capital spending is $2.00, and current depreciation is $1.00. If we assume that capital spending and depreciation grow at the same rate as earnings and there are no working capital requirements or debt:

Earnings in year 5 = $2.50 \times (1.20)^5$	$6.22
Capital spending in year 5 = $2.00 \times (1.20)^5$	$4.98
Depreciation in year 5 = $1.00 \times (1.20)^5$	$2.49
Free cash flow to equity in year 5 = $6.22 + $2.49 − $4.98	$3.73

If we use the infinite growth rate model, but fail to adjust the imbalance between capital expenditures and depreciation, the free cash flow to equity in the terminal year is:

$$\text{Free cash flow to equity in year 6} = 3.73 \times 1.05 = \$3.92$$

This free cash flow to equity can then be used to compute the value per share at the end of year 5, but it will understate the true value. There are two ways in which you can adjust for this:

1. Adjust capital expenditures in year 6 to reflect industry average capital expenditure needs: Assume, for instance, that capital expenditures are 150% of depreciation for the industry in which the firm operates. You could compute the capital expenditures in year 6 as follows:

$$\text{Depreciation in year 6} = 2.49(1.05) = \$2.61$$

$$\text{Capital expenditures in year 6} = \text{Depreciation in year 6}$$
$$\times \text{Industry average capital expenditures as \% of depreciation}$$
$$= \$2.61 \times 1.50 = \$3.92$$

$$\text{FCFE in year 6} = \$6.53 + \$2.61 - \$3.92 = \$5.23$$

2. Estimate the equity reinvestment rate in year 6, based on expected growth and the firm's return on equity. For instance, if we assume that this firm's return on equity will be 15% in stable growth, the equity reinvestment rate would need to be:

$$\text{Equity reinvestment rate} = g/ROE = 5\%/15\% = 33.33\%$$

$$\text{Net capital expenditures in year 6} = \text{Equity reinvestment rate} \times \text{Earnings per share}$$
$$= .3333 \times \$6.53 = \$2.18$$

$$\text{Capital expenditures in year 6} = \text{Net capital expenditures} + \text{Depreciation}$$
$$= \$2.18 + \$2.61 = \$4.79$$

$$\text{FCFE in year 6} = \$6.53 + \$2.61 - \$4.79 = \$4.35$$

Firms Model Works Best For   This model makes the same assumptions about growth as the two-stage dividend discount model (i.e., that growth will be high and constant in the initial period and drop abruptly to stable growth after that). It is different because of its emphasis on FCFE rather than dividends. Consequently, it provides much better results than the dividend discount model when valuing firms which either have dividends which are unsustainable (because they are higher than FCFE) or which pay less in dividends than they can afford to (i.e., dividends are less than FCFE).

ILLUSTRATION 14.4:   Two-Stage FCFE Model: Nestlé

Nestlé has operations all over the world, with 97% of its revenues coming from markets outside Switzerland, where it is headquartered. The firm, like many large European corporations, has a weak corporate governance system, and stockholders have little power over managers.

RATIONALE FOR USING THE MODEL

- *Why two-stage?* Nestlé has a long and impressive history of growth, and while we believe that its growth will be moderate, we assume that it will be able to maintain high growth for 10 years.
- *Why FCFE?* Given its weak corporate governance structure and a history of accumulating cash, the dividends paid by Nestlé bear little resemblance to what the firm could have paid out.

BACKGROUND INFORMATION

Current net income = Sfr 5,763 million
Current capital spending = Sfr 5,058 million
Current depreciation = Sfr 3,330 million
Current revenues = Sfr 81,422 million
Noncash working capital= Sfr 5,818 million
Change in working capital = Sfr 368 million
Net debt issues = Sfr 272 million

Earnings per share = Sfr 148.33
Capital expenditures/share = Sfr 130.18
Depreciation/share = Sfr 85.71
Revenue/share = Sfr 2,095.64
Working capital/share = Sfr 149.74
Change in working capital/share = Sfr 9.47

ESTIMATES

We will begin by estimating the cost of equity for Nestlé during the high growth period in Swiss francs. We will use the 10-year Swiss government Sfr bond rate of 4% as the risk-free rate. To estimate the risk premium, we used the breakdown of Nestlé's revenues by region:

Region	Revenues (in Billions Sfr)	Weight	Risk Premium
North America	20.21	24.82%	4.00%
South America	4.97	6.10%	12.00%
Switzerland	1.27	1.56%	4.00%
Germany/France/United Kingdom	21.25	26.10%	4.00%
Italy/Spain	7.39	9.08%	5.50%
Asia	6.70	8.23%	9.00%
Rest of Western Europe	15.01	18.44%	4.00%
Eastern Europe	4.62	5.67%	8.00%
Total	81.42	100.00%	5.26%

The risk premiums for each region represent an average of the risk premiums of the countries in the region. Using a bottom-up beta of 0.85 for Nestlé, we estimated a cost of equity of:

Cost of equity = 4% + 0.85(5.26%) = 8.47%

To estimate the expected growth rate in free cash flows to equity, we first computed the free cash flows to equity in the current year:

FCFE = Net income − (Cap ex − Depreciation) − Change in working capital + Net debt issues
= 5,763 − (5,058 − 3,330) − 368 + 272 = Sfr 3,939 million

The equity reinvestment rate can be estimated from this value:

Equity reinvestment rate = 1 − FCFE/Net income = 1 − 3,939/5,763 = 31.65%

The return on equity in 2000 was estimated using the net income from 2000 and the book value of equity from the end of the previous year:

Return on equity = 5,763/25,078 = 22.98%

The expected growth rate in FCFE is a product of the equity reinvestment rate and the return on equity:

Expected growth in FCFE = Equity reinvestment rate × Return on equity = .3165 × .2298 = 7.27%

We will assume that net capital expenditures and working capital will grow at the same rate as earnings and that the firm will raise 33.92% of its reinvestment needs from debt (which is its current book value debt-to-capital ratio).

In stable growth, we assume a growth rate of 4%. We also assume that the cost of equity remains unchanged but that the return on equity drops to 15%. The equity reinvestment rate in stable growth can be estimated as follows:

Equity reinvestment in stable growth = g/ROE = 4%/15% = 26.67%

VALUATION

The first component of value is the present value of the expected FCFE during the high-growth period, (see table) assuming earnings, net capital expenditures, and working capital grow at 7.27% and 33.92% of reinvestment needs come from debt:

Year	Earnings per Share	Net Cap Ex per Share	Change in Working Capital per Share	Reinvestment per Share	Equity Reinvestment per Share	FCFE per Share	Present Value
1	159.12	47.71	10.89	58.60	38.72	120.39	110.99
2	170.69	51.18	11.68	62.86	41.54	129.15	109.76
3	183.10	54.90	12.53	67.44	44.56	138.54	108.55
4	196.42	58.90	13.44	72.34	47.80	148.62	107.35
5	210.71	63.18	14.42	77.60	51.28	159.43	106.17
6	226.03	67.77	15.47	83.25	55.01	171.02	105.00
7	242.47	72.70	16.60	89.30	59.01	183.46	103.84
8	260.11	77.99	17.80	95.80	63.30	196.81	102.69
9	279.03	83.67	19.10	102.76	67.91	211.12	101.56
10	299.32	89.75	20.49	110.24	72.85	226.48	100.44
			Sum of present value of FCFE				1,056.34

Note that the change in working capital each year is computed based on the existing working capital of Sfr 149.74 per share, and that the present value is computed using the cost of equity of 8.47%.

To estimate the terminal value, we first estimate the free cash flows to equity in year 11:

Expected earnings per share in year 11 = $EPS_{10}(1 + g) = 299.32(1.04) = 311.30$
Equity reinvestment in year 11 = $EPS_{11} \times$ Stable equity reinvestment rate = $311.30 \times .2667 = 83.02$
Expected FCFE in year 11 = EPS_{11} – Equity reinvestment$_{11}$ = $311.30 - 83.02 = 228.28$
Terminal value of equity per share = $FCFE_{11}/($Cost of equity$_{11} - g) = 228.28/(.0847 - .04) = 5,105.88$

The value per share can be estimated as the sum of the present value of FCFE during the high growth phase and the present value of the terminal value of equity:

Value per share = PV of dividend during high-growth phase + Terminal price/$(1 + k_e)^n$
= $1,056.34 + 5,105.88/1.0847^{10} = 3,320.65$ Sfr

The stock was trading at 3,390 Sfr per share in May 2001 at the time of this valuation.

 FCFE2st.xls: **This spreadsheet allows you to value a firm with a temporary period of high growth in FCFE, followed by stable growth.**

REINVESTMENT ASSUMPTIONS, TERMINAL VALUE, AND EQUITY VALUE

We have repeatedly emphasized the importance of linking growth assumptions to assumptions about reinvestment, and especially so in stable growth. A very common assumption in many discounted cash flow valuations is that capital expenditures offset depreciation in stable growth. When combined with the assumption of no working capital changes, this translates into zero reinvestment. While this may be a reasonable assumption for a year or two, it is not consistent with the assumption that operating income will grow in perpetuity. How much of a difference can one assumption make? In the Nestlé valuation, we reestimated terminal value of equity per share assuming no reinvestment:

Estimated terminal value of equity per share = $311.30/(.0847 - .04) = 6,962.57$

Keeping all of our other assumptions intact, this results in a value of equity per share of 4,144 Sfr per share—an increase in value of approximately 22 percent.

E Model—A Three-Stage FCFE Model

The E model is designed to value firms that are expected to go through three stages of growth—an initial phase of high growth rates, a transitional period where the growth rate declines, and a steady-state period where growth is stable.

The Model The E model calculates the present value of expected free cash flow to equity over all three stages of growth:

$$P_0 = \sum_{t=1}^{t=n1} \frac{FCFE_t}{\left(1+k_e\right)^t} + \sum_{t=n1+1}^{t=n2} \frac{FCFE_t}{\left(1+k_e\right)^t} + \frac{P_{n2}}{\left(1+k_e\right)^{n2}}$$

where P_0 = Value of the stock today

       $FCFE_t$ = FCFE in year t

        k_e = Cost of equity

       P_{n2} = Terminal price at the end of transitional period = $FCFE_{n2+1}/(k_e - g_n)$

       n1 = End of initial high-growth period

       n2 = End of transition period

Caveats in Using Model   Since the model assumes that the growth rate goes through three distinct phases—high growth, transitional growth, and stable growth—it is important that assumptions about other variables are consistent with these assumptions about growth.

Capital Spending versus Depreciation   It is reasonable to assume that as the firm goes from high growth to stable growth, the relationship between capital

---

A TROUBLESHOOTING GUIDE: WHAT IS WRONG WITH THIS VALUATION? (TWO-STAGE FCFE MODEL)

If This Is Your Problem	*This May Be the Solution*
• If you get a extremely low value from the two-stage FCFE, the likely culprits are:	
Earnings are depressed due to some reason (economy, etc.).	Use normalized earnings.
Capital expenditures are significantly higher than depreciation in stable growth phase.	Reduce the difference for stable growth period. (Compute the appropriate reinvestment rate— you might need a higher ROE.)
The beta in the stable period is too high for a stable firm.	Use a beta closer to 1.
Working capital as percent of revenue is too high to sustain.	Use a working capital ratio closer to industry.
The use of the two-stage model when the three-stage model is more appropriate.	Use a three-stage model.
• If you get an extremely high value:	
Earnings are inflated above normal levels.	Use normalized earnings.
Capital expenditures offset or lag depreciation during high-growth period.	Compute the appropriate reinvestment rate = g/ROE.
The growth rate in the stable growth period is too high for stable firm.	Use a growth rate closer to GNP growth.

spending and depreciation will change. In the high-growth phase, capital spending is likely to much larger than depreciation. In the transitional phase, the difference is likely to narrow and the difference between capital spending and depreciation will be lower still in stable growth, reflecting the lower expected growth rate. (See Figure 14.5.)

Risk As the growth characteristics of a firm change, so do its risk characteristics. In the context of the CAPM, as the growth rate declines the beta of the firm can be expected to change. The tendency of betas to converge toward one in the long term has been confirmed by empirical observation of portfolios of firms with high betas. Over time, as these firms get larger and more diversified, the average betas of these portfolios move toward 1.

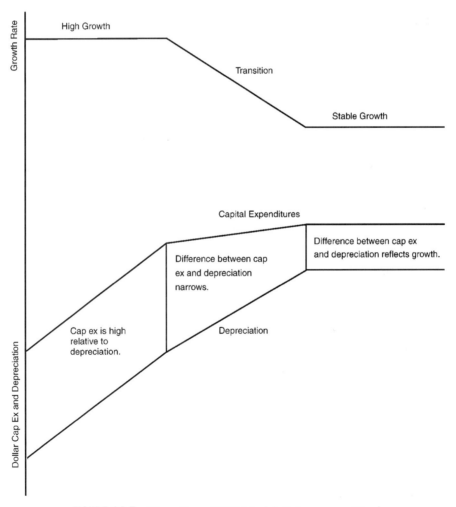

FIGURE 14.5 Three-Stage FCFE Model: Reinvestment Needs

Firms Model Works Best For   Since the model allows for three stages of growth and for a gradual decline from high to stable growth, it is the appropriate model to use to value firms with very high growth rates currently. The assumptions about growth are similar to the ones made by the three-stage dividend discount model, but the focus is on FCFE instead of dividends, making it more suited to value firms whose dividends are significantly higher or lower than the FCFE.

ILLUSTRATION 14.5:   Three-Stage FCFE Model: Tsingtao Breweries (China)

Tsingtao Breweries produces and distributes beer and other alcoholic beverages in China and around the world under the Tsingtao brand name. The firm has 653.15 million shares listed on the Shanghai and Hong Kong exchanges.

RATIONALE FOR USING THE THREE-STAGE FCFE MODEL

- *Why three-stage?* Tsingtao is a small firm serving a huge and growing market—China, in particular, and the rest of Asia in general. The firm's current return on equity is low, and we anticipate that it will improve over the next five years. As it increases, earnings growth will be pushed up.
- *Why FCFE?* Corporate governance in China tends to be weak and dividends are unlikely to reflect free cash flow to equity. In addition, the firm consistently funds a portion of its reinvestment needs with new debt issues.

BACKGROUND INFORMATION

In 2000, Tsingtao Breweries earned 72.36 million CY (Chinese yuan) in net income on a book value of equity of 2,588 million CY, giving it a return on equity of 2.80%. The firm had capital expenditures of 335 million CY and depreciation of 204 million CY during the year, and noncash working capital dropped by 1.2 million CY during the year. The total reinvestment in 2000 was therefore:

Total reinvestment = Capital expenditures – Depreciation + Change in noncash working capital
= 335 – 204 – 1.2 = 129.8 million

The working capital changes over the past four years have been volatile, and we normalize the change using noncash working capital as a percent of revenues in 2000:

Normalized change in noncash working capital = (Noncash working capital$_{2000}$/Revenues$_{2000}$)
$\times$ (Revenues$_{2000}$ – Revenues$_{1999}$)
= (180/2,253) $\times$ (2,253 – 1,598) = 52.3 million CY

The normalized reinvestment in 2000 can then be estimated as follows:

Normalized reinvestment = Capital expenditures – Depreciation
+ Normalized change in noncash working capital
= 335 – 204 + 52.3 = 183.3 million CY

As with working capital, debt issues have been volatile. We estimate the firm's book debt to capital ratio of 40.94% at the end of 2000 and use it to estimate the normalized equity reinvestment in 2000:

Equity reinvestment in 2000 = Reinvestment(1 – Debt ratio) = 183.3(1 – .4094) = 108.27 million CY

As a percent of net income,

Equity reinvestment rate in 2000 = 108.27/72.36 = 149.97%

ESTIMATION

To estimate free cash flows to equity for the high-growth period, we make the assumption that the return on equity, which is 2.80% today, will drift up to 12% by the fifth year. In addition, we will assume that new investments from now on will earn a return on equity of 12%. Finally, we will assume that the equity reinvestment rate will remain at its current level (149.97%) each year for the next five years. The expected growth rate over the next five years can then be estimated as follows:

$$\text{Expected growth rate—next five years} = \text{Equity reinvestment rate} \times \text{ROE}_{new}$$
$$+ [(\text{ROE}_{new} - \text{ROE}_{today})/\text{ROE}_{today}]^{1/5} - 1$$
$$= 1.4997 \times .12 + \{[(.12 - .028)/.028]^{1/5} - 1\} = 44.91\%$$

After year 5, we will assume that the expected growth rate declines linearly each year from years 6 through 10 to reach a stable growth rate of 10% in year 10. (Note that the growth rate is in nominal CY; the higher stable growth rate reflects the higher expected inflation in that currency.) As the growth rate declines, the equity reinvestment rate also drops off to a stable period equity reinvestment rate of 50%, estimated using the 10% stable growth rate and an assumed return on equity in stable growth of 20%.

$$\text{Stable period equity reinvestment rate} = g/\text{ROE} = 10\%/20\% = 50\%$$

To estimate the cost of equity, we used a risk-free rate of 10% (in nominal CY), a risk premium of 6.28% (4% for mature market risk and 2.28% as the country risk premium for China) and a beta of 0.75 (reflecting the bottom-up beta for breweries):

$$\text{Cost of equity} = 10\% + 0.75(6.28\%) = 14.71\%$$

In stable growth, we assume that the beta will drift up to 0.80 and that the country risk premium will drop to 0.95%:

$$\text{Cost of equity} = 10\% + 0.80(4.95\%) = 13.96\%$$

The cost of equity adjusts in linear increments from 14.71% in year 5 to 13.96% in year 10.

VALUATION To value Tsingtao, we will begin by projecting the free cash flows to equity during the high growth and transition phases, using an expected growth rate of 44.91% in net income and an equity reinvestment rate of 149.97% for the first five years. The next five years represent a transition period, where the growth drops in linear increments from 44.91% to 10% and the equity reinvestment rate drops from 149.97% to 50%. The resulting free cash flows to equity are shown in the following table:

Year	Expected Growth	Net Income	Equity Reinvestment Rate	FCFE	Cost of Equity	Present Value
Current		CY72.36	149.97%			
1	44.91%	CY104.85	149.97%	(CY52.40)	14.71%	(CY45.68)
2	44.91%	CY151.93	149.97%	(CY75.92)	14.71%	(CY57.70)
3	44.91%	CY220.16	149.97%	(CY110.02)	14.71%	(CY72.89)
4	44.91%	CY319.03	149.97%	(CY159.43)	14.71%	(CY92.08)
5	44.91%	CY462.29	149.97%	(CY231.02)	14.71%	(CY116.32)
6	37.93%	CY637.61	129.98%	(CY191.14)	14.56%	(CY84.01)
7	30.94%	CY834.92	109.98%	(CY83.35)	14.41%	(CY32.02)
8	23.96%	CY1,034.98	89.99%	CY103.61	14.26%	CY34.83
9	16.98%	CY1,210.74	69.99%	CY363.29	14.11%	CY107.04
10	10.00%	CY1,331.81	50.00%	CY665.91	13.96%	CY172.16

Sum of the present values of FCFE during high growth = ($186.65)

To estimate the terminal value of equity, we use the net income in the year 11, reduce it by the equity reinvestment needs in that year, and then assume a perpetual growth rate to get to a value.

Expected stable growth rate =10%
Equity reinvestment rate in stable growth = 50%
Cost of equity in stable growth = 13.96%
Expected FCFE in year 11 = Net income$_{11}$ × (1 − Stable period equity reinvestment rate)
$$= CY1,331.81(1.10)(1 - .5) = CY732.50 \text{ million}$$
Terminal value of equity in Tsingtao Breweries = FCFE$_{11}$/(Stable period cost of equity
$$- \text{Stable growth rate}) = 732.5/(.1396 - .10)$$
$$= CY18,497 \text{ million}$$

To estimate the value of equity today, we sum up the present value of the FCFE over the high-growth period and add to it the present value of the terminal value of equity:

Value of equity = PV of FCFE during the high-growth period + PV of terminal value
$$= -CY186.65 + CY18,497/(1.1471^5 \times 1.1456 \times 1.1441 \times 1.1426$$
$$\times 1.1411 \times 1.1396) = CY4,596 \text{ million}$$

Value of equity per share = Value of equity/Number of shares = CY4,596/653.15 = CY7.04 per share

The stock was trading at 10.10 yuan per share, which would make it overvalued based on this valuation.

NEGATIVE FCFE, EQUITY DILUTION, AND VALUE PER SHARE

Unlike dividends, free cash flows to equity can be negative. This can occur either because net income is negative or because a firm's reinvestment needs are significant; this is the case with Tsingtao in Illustration 14.5. The resulting net capital expenditure and working capital needs may be much larger than the net income. In fact, this is likely to occur fairly frequently with high-growth firms.

The FCFE model is flexible enough to deal with this issue. The free cash flows to equity will be negative as the firm reinvests substantial amounts to generate high growth. As the growth declines, the reinvestment needs also drop off and free cash flows to equity turn positive.

Intuitively, though, consider what a negative free cash flow to equity implies. It indicates that the firm does not generate enough cash flows from current operations to meet its reinvestment needs. Since the free cash flow to equity is after net debt issues, the firm will have to issue new equity in years where the cash flow is negative. This expected dilution in future years will reduce the value of equity per share today. In the FCFE model, the negative free cash flows to equity in the earlier years will reduce the estimated value of equity today. Thus the dilution effect is captured in the present value, and no additional consideration is needed of new stock issues in future years and the effect on value per share today.

A TROUBLESHOOTING GUIDE: WHAT IS WRONG WITH THIS VALUATION? (THREE-STAGE FCFE MODEL)

If This Is Your Problem	*This May Be the Solution*
• If you get a extremely low value from the three-stage FCFE, the likely culprits are:	
Capital expenditures are significantly higher than depreciation in stable growth phase.	Reduce net cap ex in stable growth. Cap ex grows slower than depreciation during transition period.
The beta in the stable period is too high for a stable firm.	Use a beta closer to 1.
Working capital as percent of revenue is too high to sustain.	Use working capital ratio closer to industry average.
• If you get an extremely high value:	
Capital expenditures offset depreciation during high-growth period.	Capital expenditures should be set higher.
Capital expenditures are less than depreciation.	(Calculate reinvestment rate = g/ROC)
Growth period (high growth and transition) is too long.	Use a shorter growth period.
The growth rate in the stable growth period is too high for stable firm.	Use a growth rate closer to GNP growth.

 FCFE3st.xls: This spreadsheet allows you to value a firm with a temporary period of high growth in FCFE, followed by a transition period, followed by stable growth.

FCFE VALUATION VERSUS DIVIDEND DISCOUNT MODEL VALUATION

The discounted cash flow model that uses FCFE can be viewed as an alternative to the dividend discount model. Since the two approaches sometimes provide different estimates of value, it is worth examining when they provide similar estimates of value, when they provide different estimates of value, and what the difference tells us about the firm.

When They Are Similar

There are two conditions under which the value from using the FCFE in discounted cash flow valuation will be the same as the value obtained from using the dividend discount model. The first is the obvious one, where the dividends are equal to the FCFE. The second condition is more subtle, where the FCFE is greater than dividends, but the excess cash (FCFE minus dividends) is invested in projects with net present value of zero. (For instance, investing in financial assets that are fairly priced should yield a net present value of zero.)

When They Are Different

There are several cases where the two models will provide different estimates of value. First, when the FCFE is greater than the dividend and the excess cash either earns below-market interest rates or is invested in negative net present value projects, the value from the FCFE model will be greater than the value from the dividend discount model. There is reason to believe that this is not as unusual as it would seem at the outset. There are numerous case studies of firms, which having accumulated large cash balances, by paying out low dividends relative to FCFE, have chosen to use this cash to finance unwise takeovers (where the price paid is greater than the value received from the takeover). Second, the payment of smaller dividends than can be afforded to be paid out by a firm lowers debt-to-equity ratios and may lead the firm to become underleveraged, causing a loss in value.

In the cases where dividends are greater than FCFE, the firm will have to issue either new stock or new debt to pay these dividends leading to at least three negative consequences for value. One is the flotation cost on these security issues, which can be substantial for equity issues, creates an unnecessary expenditure that decreases value. Second, if the firm borrows the money to pay the dividends, the firm may become overlevered (relative to the optimal) leading to a loss in value. Finally, paying too much in dividends can lead to capital rationing constraints where good projects are rejected, resulting in a loss of wealth.

There is a third possibility and it reflects different assumptions about reinvestment and growth in the two models. If the same growth rate is used in the dividend discount and FCFE models, the FCFE model will give a higher value than the dividend discount model whenever FCFE are higher than dividends and a lower value when dividends exceed FCFE. In reality, the growth rate in FCFE should be different from the growth rate in dividends, because the free cash flow to equity is assumed to be paid out to stockholders. This will affect the reinvestment rate of the firm. In addition, the return on equity used in the FCFE model should reflect the return on equity on noncash investments, whereas the return on equity used in the dividend discount model should be the overall return on equity. Table 14.1 summarizes the differences in assumptions between the two models.

In general, when firms pay out much less in dividends than they have available in FCFE, the expected growth rate and terminal value will be higher in the dividend discount model, but the year-to-year cash flows will be higher in the FCFE model. The net effect on value will vary from company to company.

TABLE 14.1 Differences between DDM and FCFE Models

	Dividend Discount Model	FCFE Model
Implicit assumption	Only dividends are paid. Remaining portions of earnings are invested back into the firm, some in operating assets and some in cash and marketable securities.	The FCFE is paid out to stockholders. The remaining earnings are invested only in operating assets.
Expected growth	Measures growth in income from both operating and cash assets. In terms of fundamentals, it is the product of the retention ratio and the return on equity.	Measures growth only in income from operating assets. In terms of fundamentals, it is the product of the equity reinvestment rate and the noncash return on equity.
Dealing with cash and marketable securities	The income from cash and marketable securities is built into earnings and ultimately into dividends. Therefore, cash and marketable securities do not need to be added in.	You have two choices: 1. Build in income from cash and marketable securities into projections of income, and estimate the value of equity. 2. Ignore income from cash and marketable securities, and add their value to equity value in model.

What Does It Mean When They Are Different?

When the value using the FCFE model is different from the value using the dividend discount model, with consistent growth assumptions, there are two questions that need to be addressed: What does the difference between the two models tell us? Which of the two models is the appropriate one to use in evaluating the market price?

The more common occurrence is for the value from the FCFE model to exceed the value from the dividend discount model. The difference between the value from the FCFE model and the value using the dividend discount model can be considered one component of the value of controlling a firm—it measures the value of controlling dividend policy. In a hostile takeover, the bidder can expect to control the firm and change the dividend policy (to reflect FCFE), thus capturing the higher FCFE value.

As for which of the two values is the more appropriate one for use in evaluating the market price, the answer lies in the openness of the market for corporate control. If there is a sizable probability that a firm can be taken over or its management changed, the market price will reflect that likelihood, and the appropriate benchmark to use is the value from the FCFE model. As changes in corporate control become more difficult because of a firm's size and/or legal or market restrictions on takeovers, the value from the dividend discount model will provide the appropriate benchmark for comparison.

ILLUSTRATION 14.6: Comparing the DDM and FCFE Models: Coca-Cola

In Chapter 13, we valued Coca-Cola using a three-stage dividend discount model at $42.72 a share. Here, we will value Coca-Cola using a three-stage free cash flow to equity model.

RATIONALE FOR USING THREE-STAGE FCFE MODEL

- *Why three-stage?* Coca-Cola's strong brand name will allow it to overcome some of the constraints that may exist on its high growth rate—the saturation of its domestic market and its high market share in these markets. However, we believe that this growth will come under assault from competition in future years, leading us to allow for a transition to stable growth.
- *Why FCFE?* While the firm does have a history of returning cash to stockholders, we wanted to examine the differences in value, if any, estimated with the dividend and FCFE models.
- The firm has used debt a little more liberally in the past few years, but it remains a firm that uses equity for much of its reinvestment needs.

BACKGROUND INFORMATION

Net income = $3,879.77
Number of shares outstanding = 2,487.03
Current capital expenditures = $992.00
Current depreciation = $773.00
Increase in noncash working capital in most recent year = $852.00
Net debt issued (paid) during the year = ($585.00)

Based on these values, we can estimate the free cash flows to equity in the most recent year as follows:

$$\text{Free cash flow to equity} = \text{Net income} - (\text{Cap expenditures} - \text{Depreciation})$$
$$- \text{Change in noncash working capital} + \text{Net debt issued}$$
$$= 3,878 - (992 - 773) - 852 + (-585) = \$2,222 \text{ million}$$

The return on equity in the most recent year was estimated to be 23.37% in the dividend discount model. We reestimated the return on equity excluding the income from cash and marketable securities from net income[3] and the value of the cash and marketable securities from book equity:

$$\text{Modified return on equity} = (\text{Net income} - \text{After-tax interest income from cash})$$
$$/(\text{Book value of equity} - \text{Cash and marketable securities})$$
$$= (2,177 - 91)/(9,317 - 1,822) = 27.83\%$$

ESTIMATION

We assume that the cost of equity for Coca-Cola will be 9.99% for the five-year high-growth period, declining in linear increments to 9.40% in year 10 and stable growth beyond. The slightly higher cost of equity results from the use of beta of 0.82 in the high-growth period. (In the DDM we used a beta of 0.80.)

    The capital expenditures, working capital requirements and the debt ratio for Coca-Cola have been volatile over the past five years. To normalize changes over time, we decided to do the following:

    First, we computed the net capital expenditures as a percent of earnings before interest and taxes each year for the past five years:

---

[3]As in the dividend discount model, we used a normalized net income ($2,177 million) just for this computation. The rest of the valuation is based on the actual net income prior to extraordinary items.

	–5	–4	–3	–2	Current	Average
Net cap ex	$1,391.00	$1,485.00	$1,996.00	$2,332.00	$ 219.00	$1,484.60
EBIT	$4,833.00	$5,001.00	$4,967.00	$3,982.00	$5,134.00	$4,783.40
Average net cap ex/EBIT =						31.04%

Normalized net capital expenditure = Average net cap ex as % of EBIT over past five years
$$\times \text{ EBIT in most recent year} = .3104 \times 5{,}134 = \$1{,}593 \text{ million}$$

Then we estimated noncash working capital as a percent of revenues in the most recent year and used this to estimate the change in noncash working capital over the last year:

Noncash working capital in current year = $223 million
Revenues in current year = $20,458 million
Revenues last year = $19,805 million
Normalized change in noncash working capital last year = (223/20,458)(20,458 – 19,805)
$$= \$7.12 \text{ million}$$

Finally, we normalized the net debt issued by assuming that Coca-Cola would continue to fund its reinvestment needs with its market debt-to-capital ratio. To estimate the market debt-to-capital ratio, we used the total interest bearing debt outstanding at the end of 2000 and the current market value of equity:

Debt ratio = Interest-bearing debt/(Interest-bearing debt + Market value of equity)
$$= 5{,}651/(5{,}651 + 115{,}125) = 4.68\%$$

Normalized debt issued in current year = (Normalized net capital expenditures
+ Normalized change in noncash working capital)
$$\times \text{ Debt ratio} = (1{,}593 + 7.12) \times (.0468) = \$74.89 \text{ million}$$

The normalized free cash flow to equity can then be computed:

Normalized FCFE = Net income – Normalized net cap ex – Normalized change in working capital
+ Normalized net debt issued = 3,878 – 1,593 – 7.12 + 74.89 = $2,353 million

This normalized FCFE also lets us compute the equity reinvestment rate for the firm:

Equity reinvestment rate = 1 – FCFE/Net income = 1 – 2,353/3,878 = 39.3%

With the current return on equity of 27.83%, this yields an expected growth rate in noncash net income at Coca-Cola of 10.94%.

Expected growth = Equity reinvestment rate × Return on equity = .393 × .2783 = .1094

In stable growth, we assume that the return on equity drops to 20% and that the growth rate in perpetuity in net income is 5.5%. The equity reinvestment rate can then be estimated as follows:

Equity reinvestment rate in stable growth = g/ROE = 5.5%/20% = 27.5%

VALUATION

To value Coca-Cola, we will begin by projecting the free cash flows to equity during the high growth and transition phases, using an expected growth rate of 10.94% in noncash net income and an equity reinvestment rate of 39.3% for the first five years.

Noncash net income = Net income – After-tax interest income from cash and marketable securities
$$= \$3{,}878 \text{ million} – \$91 \text{ million} = \$3{,}789 \text{ million}$$

The next five years represent a transition period, where the growth drops in linear increments from 10.94% to 5% and the equity reinvestment rate drops from 39.3% to 25%. The resulting free cash flows to equity are shown in the following table:

Year	Expected Growth	Net Income	Equity Reinvestment Rate	FCFE	Cost of Equity	Present Value
1	10.94%	$4,203.28	39.32%	$2,550.42	9.99%	$ 2,318.73
2	10.94%	$4,663.28	39.32%	$2,829.53	9.99%	$ 2,338.80
3	10.94%	$5,173.61	39.32%	$3,139.18	9.99%	$ 2,359.03
4	10.94%	$5,739.79	39.32%	$3,482.72	9.99%	$ 2,379.44
5	10.94%	$6,367.93	39.32%	$3,863.86	9.99%	$ 2,400.03
6	9.85%	$6,995.48	36.96%	$4,410.06	9.87%	$ 2,493.13
7	8.77%	$7,608.71	34.59%	$4,976.57	9.76%	$ 2,563.34
8	7.68%	$8,192.87	32.23%	$5,552.37	9.64%	$ 2,608.54
9	6.59%	$8,732.68	29.86%	$6,124.69	9.52%	$ 2,627.34
10	5.50%	$9,212.97	27.50%	$6,679.40	9.40%	$ 2,619.11
			Sum of the present values of FCFE during high growth			$24,707.49

To estimate the terminal value of equity, we use the net income in the terminal year (year 11), reduce it by the equity reinvestment needs in that year, and then assume a perpetual growth rate to get to a value.

Expected stable growth rate = 5.5%
Equity reinvestment rate in stable growth = 27.5%
Cost of equity in stable growth = 9.40%
Expected FCFE in year 11 = Net income$_{11}$ × (1 − Stable period equity reinvestment rate)
$\quad$ = $9,213(1.055)(1 − .275) = $7,047 million
Value of equity in Coca-Cola = FCFE$_{11}$/(Stable period cost of equity − Stable growth rate)
$\quad$ = 7,047/(.094 − .055) = $180,686

To estimate the value of equity today, we sum up the present value of the FCFE over the high-growth period and add to it the present value of the terminal value of equity:

Value of equity = PV of FCFE during the high-growth period + PV of terminal value
$\quad$ = $24,707 + $180,686/(1.0999^5 × 1.0987 × 1.0976 × 1.0964 × 1.0952 × 1.094)
$\quad$ = $95,558 million

Adding in the value of the cash and marketable securities that Coca-Cola had on hand at the end of 2001, we obtain the total value of equity:

Value of equity including cash = $95,588 + $1,892 = $97,447 million

$\quad$ Value of equity per share = Value of equity/Number of shares = $97,447/2,487.03 = $39.19

The FCFE model yields a slightly lower value than the dividend discount model value of $42.72 a share. This may seem surprising since the FCFE each year for the high-growth period are greater than the dividends, but this effect is more than offset by the decline in the expected growth rate, which is generated by the equity reinvestment rate being lower than the retention ratio. This valuation is probably more realistic than the dividend discount model because it keeps investments in cash and marketable securities separate from investments in operating assets. The dividend discount model overstates the expected growth rate because it does not consider the fact that the low return earned by cash investments will bring the return on equity down over time (and growth down with it).

CONCLUSION

The primary difference between the dividend discount models described in the previous chapter and the free cash flow to equity models described in this one lies in the definition of cash flows; the dividend discount model uses a strict definition of cashflow to equity (i.e., the expected dividends on the stock), while the FCFE model uses an expansive definition of cash flow to equity as the residual cash flow after meeting all financial obligations and investment needs. When firms have dividends that are different from the FCFE, the values from the two models will be different. In valuing firms for takeovers or in valuing firms where there is a reasonable chance of changing corporate control, the value from the FCFE model provides the better estimate of value.

QUESTIONS AND SHORT PROBLEMS

1. Respond true or false to the following statements relating to the calculation and use of FCFE:
   a. The free cash flow to equity will generally be more volatile than dividends.
      True _____ False _____
   b. The free cash flow to equity will always be higher than dividends.
      True _____ False _____
   c. The free cash flow to equity will always be higher than net income.
      True _____ False _____
   d. The free cash flow to equity can never be negative.
      True _____ False _____
2. Kimberly-Clark, a household product manufacturer, reported earnings per share of $3.20 in 1993 and paid dividends per share of $1.70 in that year. The firm reported depreciation of $315 million in 1993, and capital expenditures of $475 million. (There were 160 million shares outstanding, trading at $51 per share.) This ratio of capital expenditures to depreciation is expected to be maintained in the long term. The working capital needs are negligible. Kimberly-Clark had debt outstanding of $1.6 billion, and intended to maintain its current financing mix (of debt and equity) to finance future investment needs. The firm was in steady state and earnings were expected to grow 7% a year. The stock had a beta of 1.05. (The Treasury bond rate was 6.25%, and the risk premium was 5.5%.)
   a. Estimate the value per share, using the dividend discount model.
   b. Estimate the value per share, using the FCFE model.
   c. How would you explain the difference between the two models, and which one would you use as your benchmark for comparison to the market price?
3. Ecolab Inc. sells chemicals and systems for cleaning, sanitizing, and maintenance. It reported earnings per share of $2.35 in 1993, and expected earnings growth of 15.5% a year from 1994 to 1998, and 6% a year after that. The capital expenditure per share was $2.25, and depreciation was $1.125 per share in 1993. Both were expected to grow at the same rate as earnings from 1994 to 1998. Working capital was expected to remain at 5% of revenues, and revenues, which were $1 billion in 1993, were expected to increase 6% a year from 1994 to 1998, and 4% a year after that. The firm had has a debt ratio [D/(D + E)] of 5%, but planned to finance future investment needs (including working capital investments) using a debt ratio of 20%. The stock was expected to have a beta of 1 for the period of

the analysis, and the Treasury bond rate was 6.50%. (There were 63 million shares outstanding, and the market risk premium was 5.5%.)

a. Assuming that capital expenditures and depreciation offset each other after 1998, estimate the value per share. Is this a realistic estimate?

b. Assuming that capital expenditures continue to be 200% of depreciation even after 1998, estimate the value per share.

c. What would the value per share have been, if the firm had continued to finance new investments with its old financing mix (5%)? Is it fair to use the same beta for this analysis?

4. Dionex Corporation, a leader in the development and manufacture of ion chromography systems (used to identify contaminants in electronic devices), reported earnings per share of $2.02 in 1993, and paid no dividends. These earnings were expected to grow 14% a year for five years (1994 to 1998) and 7% a year after that. The firm reported depreciation of $2 million in 1993 and capital spending of $4.20 million, and had 7 million shares outstanding. The working capital was expected to remain at 50% of revenues, which were $106 million in 1993, and were expected to grow 6% a year from 1994 to 1998 and 4% a year after that. The firm was expected to finance 10% of its capital expenditures and working capital needs with debt. Dionex had a beta of 1.20 in 1993, and this beta was expected to drop to 1.10 after 1998. (The Treasury bond rate was 7%, and the market risk premium was 5.5%.)

a. Estimate the expected free cash flow to equity from 1994 to 1998, assuming that capital expenditures and depreciation grow at the same rate as earnings.

b. Estimate the terminal price per share (at the end of 1998). Stable firms in this industry have capital expenditures which are 150% of revenues, and maintain working capital at 25% of revenues.

c. Estimate the value per share today, based on the FCFE model.

5. Biomet Inc., which designs, manufactures, and markets reconstructive and trauma devices, reported earnings per share of $0.56 in 1993, on which it paid no dividends (it had revenues per share in 1993 of $2.91). It had capital expenditures of $0.13 per share in 1993, and depreciation in the same year of $0.08 per share. The working capital was 60% of revenues in 1993 and were expected to remain at that level from 1994 to 1998, while earnings and revenues were expected to grow 17% a year. The earnings growth rate was expected to decline linearly over the following five years to a rate of 5% in 2003. During the high-growth and transition periods, capital spending and depreciation were expected to grow at the same rate as earnings, but capital spending would be 120% of depreciation when the firm reaches steady state. Working capital was expected to drop from 60% of revenues during the 1994–1998 period to 30% of revenues after 2003. The firm had no debt currently, but planned to finance 10% of its net capital investment and working capital requirements with debt.

The stock was expected to have a beta of 1.45 for the high-growth period (1994–1998), and it was expected to decline to 1.10 by the time the firm goes into steady state (in 2003). The Treasury bond rate is 7%, and the market risk premium is 5.5%.

a. Estimate the value per share, using the FCFE model.

b. Estimate the value per share, assuming that working capital stays at 60% of revenues forever.

    c. Estimate the value per share, assuming that the beta remains unchanged at 1.45 forever.

6. Will the following firms be likely to have a higher value from the dividend discount model, a higher value from the FCFE model, or the same value from both models?

    a. A firm that pays out less in dividends than it has available in FCFE, but which invests the balance in treasury bonds.

    b. A firm that pays out more in dividends than it has available in FCFE, and then issues stock to cover the difference.

    c. A firm that pays out, on average, its FCFE as dividends.

    d. A firm that pays out less in dividends that it has available in FCFE, but which uses the cash at regular intervals to acquire other firms with the intent of diversifying.

    e. A firm that pays out more in dividends than it has available in FCFE, but borrows money to cover the difference. (The firm is overlevered to begin with.)

7. You have been asked to value Oneida Steel, a midsize steel company. The firm reported $80 million in net income, $50 million in capital expenditures, and $20 million in depreciation in the just-completed financial year. The firm reported that its noncash working capital increased by $20 million during the year and that total debt outstanding increased by $10 million during the year. The book value of equity at Oneida Steel at the beginning of the last financial year was $400 million. The cost of equity is 10%.

    a. Estimate the equity reinvestment rate, return on equity, and expected growth rate for Oneida Steel. (You can assume that the firm will continue to maintain the same debt ratio that it used last year to finance its reinvestment needs.)

    b. If this growth rate is expected to last five years and then drop to a 4% stable growth rate after that and the return on equity after year 5 is expected to be 12%, estimate the value of equity today, using the projected free cash flows to equity.

8. Luminos Corporation, a manufacturer of lightbulbs, is a firm in stable growth. The firm reported net income of $100 million on a book value of equity of $1 billion. However, the firm also had a cash balance of $200 million on which it earned after-tax interest income of $10 million last year. (This interest income is included in the net income, and the cash is part of the book value of equity.) The cost of equity for the firm is 9%.

    a. Estimate the noncash return on equity at Luminos Corporation.

    b. If you expect the cash flows from the operating assets of Luminos to increase 3% a year in perpetuity, estimate the value of equity at Luminos.

CHAPTER 15

Firm Valuation: Cost of Capital and Adjusted Present Value Approaches

The preceding two chapters examined two approaches to valuing the equity in the firm—the dividend discount model and the free cash flow to equity (FCFE) valuation model. This chapter develops another approach to valuation where the entire firm is valued, by either discounting the cumulated cash flows to all claim holders in the firm by the weighted average cost of capital (the cost of capital approach) or by adding the marginal impact of debt on value to the unlevered firm value—the adjusted present value (APV) approach.

In the process of looking at firm valuation, we also look at how leverage may or may not affect firm value. We note that in the presence of default risk, taxes, and agency costs, increasing leverage can sometimes increase firm value and sometimes decrease it. In fact, we argue that the optimal financing mix for a firm is the one that maximizes firm value.

FREE CASH FLOW TO THE FIRM

The free cash flow to the firm (FCFF) is the sum of the cash flows to all claim holders in the firm, including stockholders, bondholders, and preferred stockholders. There are two ways of measuring the free cash flow to the firm.

One is to add up the cash flows to the claim holders, which would include cash flows to equity (defined either as free cash flow to equity or dividends), cash flows to lenders (which would include principal payments, interest expenses, and new debt issues), and cash flows to preferred stockholders (usually preferred dividends):

FCFF = Free cash flow to equity + Interest expense(1 – Tax rate)
+ Principal repayments – New debt issues + Preferred dividends

Note, however, that we are reversing the process that we used to get to free cash flow to equity, where we subtracted out payments to lenders and preferred stockholders to estimate the cash flow left for stockholders. A simpler way of getting to free cash flow to the firm is to estimate the cash flows prior to any of these claims. Thus we could begin with the earnings before interest and taxes, net out taxes and reinvestment needs, and arrive at an estimate of the free cash flow to the firm:

FCFF = EBIT(1 – Tax rate) + Depreciation – Capital expenditure – Δ Working capital

Since this cash flow is prior to debt payments, it is often referred to as an unlevered cash flow. Note that this free cash flow to the firm does not incorporate any of the tax benefits due to interest payments. This is by design, because the use of the after-tax cost of debt in the cost of capital already considers this benefit, and including it in the cash flows would double count it.

FCFF and Other Cash Flow Measures

The differences between FCFF and FCFE arise primarily from cash flows associated with debt—interest payments, principal repayments, and new debt issues—and other nonequity claims, such as preferred dividends. For firms at their desired debt level, which finance their capital expenditures and working capital needs with this mix of debt and equity and use debt issues to finance principal repayments, the free cash flow to the firm will exceed the free cash flow to equity.

One measure that is widely used in valuation is the earnings before interest, taxes, depreciation, and amortization (EBITDA). The free cash flow to the firm is a closely related concept but it takes into account the potential tax liability from the earnings as well as capital expenditures and working capital requirements.

Three measures of earnings are also often used to derive cash flows. The amount of earnings before interest and taxes (EBIT) or operating income comes directly from a firm's income statements. Adjustments to EBIT yield the net operating profit or loss after taxes (NOPLAT) or the net operating income (NOI). The net operating income is defined to be the income from operations prior to taxes and non-operating expenses.

Each of these measures is used in valuation models, and each can be related to the free cash flow to the firm. Each, however, makes some assumptions about the relationship between depreciation and capital expenditures that are made explicit in Table 15.1.

Growth in FCFE versus Growth in FCFF

Will equity cash flows and firm cash flows grow at the same rate? Consider the starting point for the two cash flows. Equity cash flows are based on net income or earnings per share—measures of equity income. Firm cash flows are based on operating income (i.e., income prior to debt payments). As a general rule, you would expect growth in operating income to be lower than growth in net income, because financial leverage can augment the latter. To see why, let us go back to the fundamental growth equations laid out in Chapter 11:

Expected growth in net income = Equity reinvestment rate × Return on equity

Expected growth in operating income = Reinvestment rate × Return on capital

TABLE 15.1   Free Cash Flows to the Firm: Comparison to Other Measures

Cash Flow Used	Definition	Use in Valuation
FCFF	Free cash flow to firm	Discounting free cash flow to the firm at the cost of capital will yield the value of the operating assets of the firm. To this, you would add on the value of nonoperating assets to arrive at firm value.
FCFE	FCFF – Interest (1 – t) – Principal repaid + New debt issued – Preferred dividend	Discounting free cash flows to equity at the cost of equity will yield the value of equity in a business.
EBITDA	FCFF + EBIT(t) + Capital expenditures + Change in working capital	If you discount EBITDA at the cost of capital to value an asset, you are assuming that there are no taxes and that the firm will actively disinvest over time. It would be inconsistent to assume a growth rate or an infinite life for this firm.
EBIT (1 – t) (NOPLAT is a slightly modified version of this estimate and it removes any non-operating items that might affect the reported EBIT.)	FCFF + Capital expenditures – Depreciation + Change in working capital	If you discount after-tax operating income at the cost of capital to value a firm, you are assuming no reinvestment. The depreciation is reinvested back into the firm to maintain existing assets. You can assume an infinite life but no growth.

We also defined the return on equity in terms of the return on capital:

$$\text{Return on equity} = \text{Return on capital} + \frac{\text{Debt}}{\text{Equity}}$$

$$\times (\text{Return on capital} - \text{After-tax cost of debt})$$

When a firm borrows money and invests in projects that earn more than the after-tax cost of debt, the return on equity will be higher than the return on capital. This, in turn, will translate into a higher growth rate in equity income at least in the short term.

In stable growth, though, the growth rates in equity income and operating income have to converge. To see why, assume that you have a firm whose revenues and operating income and growing at 5 percent a year forever. If you assume that the same firm's net income grows at 6 percent a year forever, the net income will catch up with operating income at some point in time in the future and exceed revenues at a later point in time. In stable growth, therefore, even if return on equity exceeds the return on capital, the expected growth will be the same in all measures of income.[1]

FIRM VALUATION: THE COST OF CAPITAL APPROACH

The value of the firm is obtained by discounting the free cash flow to the firm at the weighted average cost of capital. Embedded in this value are the tax benefits of debt (in the use of the after-tax cost of debt in the cost of capital) and expected additional risk associated with debt (in the form of higher costs of equity and debt at higher debt ratios). Just as with the dividend discount model and the FCFE model, the version of the model used will depend on assumptions made about future growth.

Stable Growth Firm

As with the dividend discount and FCFE models, a firm that is growing at a rate that it can sustain in perpetuity—a stable growth rate—can be valued using a stable growth model.

The Model   A firm with free cash flows to the firm growing at a stable growth rate can be valued using the following equation:

$$\text{Value of firm} = \frac{\text{FCFF}_1}{\left(\text{WACC} - g_n\right)}$$

where FCFF_1 = Expected FCFF next year
  WACC = Weighted average cost of capital
  g_n = Growth rate in the FCFF forever

The Caveats   There are two conditions that need to be met in using this model. First, the growth rate used in the model has to be less than or equal to the growth rate in the economy—nominal growth, if the cost of capital is in nominal terms, or real growth, if the cost of capital is a real cost of capital. Second, the characteristics of the firm have to be consistent with assumptions of stable growth. In particular, the reinvestment rate used to estimate free cash flows to the firm should be consistent with the stable growth rate. The best way of enforcing this consistency is to derive the reinvestment rate from the stable growth rate:

$$\text{Reinvestment rate in stable growth} = \frac{\text{Growth rate}}{\text{Return on capital}}$$

If reinvestment is estimated from net capital expenditures and change in working capital, the net capital expenditures should be similar to those other firms in the

---

[1]The equity reinvestment rate and firm reinvestment rate will adjust to ensure that this happens. The equity reinvestment rate will be a lower number than the firm reinvestment rate in stable growth for any levered firm.

industry (perhaps by setting the ratio of capital expenditures to depreciation at industry averages) and the change in working capital should generally not be negative. A negative change in working capital creates a cash inflow, and while this may, in fact, be viable for a firm in the short term, it is dangerous to assume it in perpetuity.[2] The cost of capital should also be reflective of a stable growth firm. In particular, the beta should be close to 1—the rule of thumb presented in the earlier chapters that the beta should be between 0.8 and 1.2 still holds. While stable growth firms tend to use more debt, this is not a prerequisite for the model, since debt policy is subject to managerial discretion.

Limitations   Like all stable growth models, this one is sensitive to assumptions about the expected growth rate. This is accentuated, however, by the fact that the discount rate used in valuation is the WACC, which is significantly lower than the cost of equity for most firms. Furthermore, the model is sensitive to assumptions made about capital expenditures relative to depreciation. If the inputs for reinvestment are not a function of expected growth the free cash flow to the firm can be inflated (deflated) by reducing (increasing) capital expenditures relative to depreciation. If the reinvestment rate is estimated from the return on capital, changes in the return on capital can have significant effects on firm value.

ILLUSTRATION 15.1:   Valuing a Firm with a Stable Growth FCFF Model: Tube Investments of India

Tube Investments of India (TI) is a diversified manufacturing firm, with its headquarters in South India. In 1999, the firm reported operating income of Rs 632.2 million and faced a tax rate of 30% on income. The firm had a book value of equity of Rs 3,432.1 million and book value of debt of Rs 1,377.2 million at the end of 1998. The firm's return on capital can be estimated as follows:

$$\text{Return on capital} = \text{EBIT}(1 - t)/(\text{Book value of debt} + \text{Book value of equity})$$
$$= 632.2(1 - .3)/(3,432.1 + 1,377.2) = 9.20\%$$

The firm is in stable businesses and expects to grow only 5% a year.[3] Assuming that it maintains its current return on capital, the reinvestment rate for the firm will be:

$$\text{Reinvestment rate} = g/\text{ROC} = 5\%/9.20\% = 54.35\%$$

The firm's expected free cash flow to the firm next year can be estimated as follows:

Expected EBIT(1 – t) next year = 632.2(1 – .30)(1.05)	464.7
– Expected reinvestment next year = EBIT(1 – t)(Reinvestment rate) = 464.7(.5435)	252.5
Expected free cash flow to the firm	212.2

To estimate the cost of capital, we use a bottom-up beta (adjusted to 1.17 to reflect TI's additional leverage), a nominal rupee risk-free rate of 10.50%, and a risk premium of 9.23% (4% for the

---

[2]Carried to its logical extreme, this will push net working capital to a very large (potentially infinite) negative number.

[3]Note that while this resembles growth rates we have used for other firms, it is a low growth rate given that this valuation is in Indian rupees. As a simple check, note that the risk-free rate used is 10.50 percent.

mature market premium and 5.23% for country risk in India). The cost of equity can then be estimated as follows:

$$\text{Cost of equity} = 10.5\% + 1.17(9.23\%) = 21.30\%$$

The pretax cost of debt for Tube Investments is 12%, which in conjunction with its market debt-to-capital ratio of 44.19% yields a cost of capital of 15.60%:

$$\text{Cost of capital} = \text{Cost of equity}[E/(D + E)] + \text{After-tax cost of debt}[D/E + E)]$$
$$= 21.30\%(.5581) + 12\%(1 - .3)(.4419) = 15.60\%$$

With the perpetual growth of 5%, the expected free cash flow to the firm shown (Rs 212.2 million) and the cost of capital of 15.60%, we obtain a value for the firm of:

$$\text{Value of the operating assets of firm} = 212.2/(.156 - .05) = \text{Rs } 2{,}002 \text{ million}$$

Adding back cash and marketable securities with a value of Rs 1,365.3 million and subtracting out the debt outstanding of Rs 1,807.3 million yields a value for the equity of Rs 1,560 million and a value per share of Rs 63.36 (based on the 24.62 million shares outstanding). The stock was trading at Rs 92.70 at the time of this valuation.

An interesting aspect of this valuation is that the return on capital used to compute the reinvestment rate is significantly lower than the cost of capital. In other words, we are locking in this firm into investing in negative excess return projects forever. If we assume that the firm will find a way to earn its cost of capital of 15.6% on investments, the reinvestment rate would be much lower:

$$\text{Reinvestment rate}_{\text{ROC=cost of capital}} = g/ROC = .05/.156 = 32.05\%$$

Value of operating assets = 464.7 (1 − .3205)/(.156 − .05)	= Rs 2,979 million
+ Value of cash and marketable securities	= Rs 1,365 million
− Debt	= Rs 1,807 million
Value of equity	= Rs 2,537 million
Value per share	= 2,537/24.62 = Rs 103.04 per share

General Version of the FCFF Model

Rather than break the free cash flow model into two-stage and three-stage models and risk repeating what was said in the preceding chapter, we present the general version of the model in this section. We follow up by examining a range of companies—a traditional manufacturing firm, a firm with operating leases, and a firm with substantial R&D investments—to illustrate the differences and similarities between this approach and the FCFE approach.

The Model   The value of the firm, in the most general case, can be written as the present value of expected free cash flows to the firm:

$$\text{Value of firm} = \sum_{t=1}^{t=\infty} \frac{\text{FCFF}_t}{(1 + \text{WACC})^t}$$

where FCFF_t = Free cash flow to firm in year t
WACC = Weighted average cost of capital

MARKET VALUE WEIGHTS, COST OF CAPITAL, AND CIRCULAR REASONING

To value a firm, you first need to estimate a cost of capital. Every textbook is categorical that the weights in the cost of capital calculation be market value weights. The problem, however, is that the cost of capital is then used to estimate new values for debt and equity that might not match the values used in the original calculation. One defense that can be offered for this inconsistency is that if you bought all of the debt and equity in a publicly traded firm, you would pay current market value and not your estimated value, and your cost of capital reflects this.

For those who are bothered by this inconsistency, there is a way out. You could do a conventional valuation using market value weights for debt and equity, but then use the estimated values of debt and equity from the valuation to reestimate the cost of capital. This, of course, will change the values again, but you could feed the new values back and estimate cost of capital again. Each time you do this, the differences between the values you use for the weights and the values you estimate will narrow, and the values will converge sooner rather than later.

How much of a difference will it make in your ultimate value? The greater the difference between market value and your estimates of value, the greater the difference this iterative process will make. In the valuation of Tube Investments, we began with a market price of Rs 92.70 per share and estimated a value of Rs 63.36. If we substituted back this estimated value and iterated to a solution, we would arrive at an estimate of value of $70.66 per share.[4]

If the firm reaches steady state after n years and starts growing at a stable growth rate g_n after that, the value of the firm can be written as:

$$\text{Value of firm} = \sum_{t=1}^{t=n} \frac{\text{FCFF}_t}{(1+\text{WACC}_{hg})^t} + \frac{\left[\text{FCFF}_{n+1}/(\text{WACC}_{st} - g_n)\right]}{(1+\text{WACC}_{hg})^n}$$

where WACC = Cost of capital (hg: high growth; st: stable growth)

Firms Model Best Suited For   Firms that either have very high leverage or are in the process of changing their leverage are best valued using the FCFF approach. The calculation of FCFE is much more difficult in these cases because of the volatility induced by debt payments (or new issues), and the value of equity, which is a small slice of the total value of the firm, is more sensitive to assumptions about growth and risk. It is worth noting, though, that in theory the two approaches should yield the same value for the equity. Getting them to agree in practice is an entirely different challenge and we will return to examine it later in this chapter.

---

[4]In Microsoft Excel, it is easy to set this process up. You should first go into calculation options and put a check in iteration box. You can then make the cost of capital a function of your estimated values for debt and equity.

Problems   There are three problems that we see with the free cash flow to the firm model. The first is that the free cash flows to equity are a much more intuitive measure of cash flows than cash flows to the firm. When asked to estimate cash flows, most of us look at cash flows after debt payments (free cash flows to equity), because we tend to think like business owners and consider interest payments and the repayment of debt as cash outflows. Furthermore, the free cash flow to equity is a real cash flow that can be traced and analyzed in a firm. The free cash flow to the firm is the answer to a hypothetical question: What would this firm's cash flow be if it had no debt (and associated payments)?

The second is that its focus on predebt cash flows can sometimes blind us to real problems with survival. To illustrate, assume that a firm has free cash flows to the firm of $100 million but that its large debt load makes its free cash flows to equity equal to –$50 million. This firm will have to raise $50 million in new equity to survive, and if it cannot, all cash flows beyond this point are put in jeopardy. Using free cash flows to equity would have alerted you to this problem, but free cash flows to the firm are unlikely to reflect this.

The final problem is that the use of a debt ratio in the cost of capital to incorporate the effect of leverage requires us to make implicit assumptions that might not be feasible or reasonable. For instance, assuming that the market value debt ratio is 30 percent will require a growing firm to issue large amounts of debt in future years to reach that ratio. In the process, the book debt ratio might reach stratospheric proportions and trigger covenants or other negative consequences. In fact, we count the expected tax benefits from future debt issues implicitly in the value of equity today.

ILLUSTRATION 15.2:   Valuing the Gap (July 2001): Dealing with Operating Leases

---

The Gap is one of the largest specialty retailers in the world and sells its products at Gap, GapKids, babyGap, Banana Republic, and Old Navy stores. While it has operations around the world, it gets the bulk of its revenues from the United States.

RATIONALE FOR USING THE MODEL

- *Why two-stage?* While the Gap is one of the largest and most successful specialty retailers in the world, its dependence on the mature U.S. market for growth restricts its capacity to maintain high growth in the future. We will assume a high-growth period of five years and then put the firm into stable growth.
- *Why FCFF?* The Gap has a significant operating lease commitments, and the firm has increased its leverage aggressively over the past few years.

BACKGROUND INFORMATION

In 2000, the Gap reported operating income $1,445 million on revenues of $13,673 million. The firm also reported capital expenditures of $1,859 million and depreciation of $590 million for the year, and its noncash working capital increased by $323 million during the year. The operating lease expenses for the year were $705.8 million, and the following table reports the lease commitments for future years (in $millions):

Year	Commitment
1	$ 774.60
2	$ 749.30
3	$ 696.50
4	$ 635.10
5	$ 529.70
6 and beyond	$5,457.90

To convert these operating lease expenses into debt, we first compute a pretax cost of debt for the firm based on its rating of A. The default spread for A-rated firms is 1.80%, which when added to the risk-free rate of 5.4%, yields a pretax cost of debt of 7.2%. Treating the commitment in year 6 and beyond as an annuity of $682.24 million for eight years, we estimate a debt value for the operating leases:

Year	Commitment	Present Value
1	$774.60	$ 722.57
2	$749.30	$ 652.03
3	$696.50	$ 565.38
4	$635.10	$ 480.91
5	$529.70	$ 374.16
6 and beyond	$682.24	$2,855.43
Debt value of leases		$5,650.48

This amount is added on to the debt outstanding on the balance sheet of $1,809.90 million to arrive at a total value for debt of $7,460.38 million. The Gap's market value of equity at the time of this valuation was $28,795 million, yielding a market debt to capital ratio of:

Market debt to capital = Debt/(Debt + Market value of equity) = $7,460/($7,460 + $28,795) = 20.58%

The operating income is also adjusted to reflect this shift by adding the imputed interest expense on the debt value of operating leases:

Adjusted operating income = Operating income + Debt value of operating leases × Pretax cost of debt
= 1,445 + 5,650 × .072 = $1,851 million

Multiplying by (1 − Tax rate), using a marginal tax rate of 35%, we get an after-tax operating income of $1,203 million:

Adjusted after-tax operating income = Adjusted operating income(1 − Tax rate)
= 1,851(1 − .35) = $1,203 million

Dividing this value by the book value (BV) of debt (including capitalized operating leases) and the book value of equity at the end of the previous year yields an adjusted return on capital of 13.61% in 2000 for the firm:

$ROC_{2000} = EBIT_{2000}(1 − t)/(BV \text{ of debt}_{1999} + BV \text{ of equity}_{1999})$
= 1,203/(6,604 + 2,233) = 13.61%

We will assume that the firm will be able to maintain this return on capital in perpetuity.

VALUATION

We will begin with a cost of equity estimate for the Gap, using a bottom-up beta of 1.20 (based on the betas of specialty retailers) for the high-growth period, a risk-free rate of 5.4%, and a mature market premium of 4%. In stable growth, we will lower the beta to 1.00, keeping the risk-free rate and risk premium unchanged.

$$\text{Cost of equity}_{\text{high growth}} = 5.4\% + 1.2(4\%) = 10.2\%$$
$$\text{Cost of equity}_{\text{stable growth}} = 5.4\% + 1.0(4\%) = 9.4\%$$

To estimate the cost of capital during the high-growth and stable growth phases, we will assume that the pretax cost of debt will remain at 7.2% in perpetuity and that the current market debt ratio of 20.58% will remain the debt ratio:

$$\text{Cost of capital}_{\text{high growth}} = 10.2\%(.7942) + 7.2\% (1 - .35)(.2058) = 9.06\%$$
$$\text{Cost of capital}_{\text{stable growth}} = 9.4\%(.7942) + 7.2\% (1 - .35)(.2058) = 8.43\%$$

To estimate the expected growth in operating earnings during the high-growth period, we will assume that the firm will continue to earn 13.61% as its return on capital and that its reinvestment rate will equal its average reinvestment rate over the past four years:[5]

$$\text{Average reinvestment rate over past four years} = 93.53\%$$

$$\text{Expected growth rate} = \text{Reinvestment rate} \times \text{Return on capital} = .9353 \times 1,361 = 12.73\%$$

The following table summarizes the expected cash flows for the high-growth period:

Year	EBIT(1 – t)	Reinvestment Rate	Reinvestment	FCFF	Present Value
Current	$1,203				
1	$1,356	93.53%	$1,269	$ 88	$ 80
2	$1,529	93.53%	$1,430	$ 99	$ 83
3	$1,732	93.53%	$1,620	$112	$ 86
4	$1,952	93.53%	$1,826	$126	$ 89
5	$2,190	93.53%	$2,049	$142	$ 92
Sum of present values of cash flows					$430

Note that the cash flows during the high-growth period are discounted back at 9.06%. To estimate the terminal value at the end of year 5, we assume that this cash flow will grow forever at 5%. The reinvestment rate can then be estimated and used to measure the free cash flow to the firm in year 6:

$$\text{Expected growth rate} = 5\%$$

$$\text{Reinvestment rate in stable growth} = g/\text{Stable period ROC} = 5\%/13.61\% = 36.73\%$$

$$FCFF_6 = EBIT_5(1 - t)(1 + \text{Stable period } g)(1 - \text{Reinvestment rate})$$
$$= 2,190(1.05)(1 - .3673) = 1,455$$

The terminal value is:

$$\text{Terminal value} = FCFF_6/(\text{Stable period cost of capital} - \text{Stable growth rate})$$
$$= 1,455/(.0843 - .05) = \$42,441 \text{ million}$$

Discounting the terminal value to the present and adding it to the present value (PV) of the cash flows over the high-growth period yields a value for the operating assets of the firm:

$$\text{Value of operating assets} = \text{PV of cash flows during high growth} + \text{PV of terminal value}$$
$$= \$430 + \$42,441/1.0906^5 = \$27,933 \text{ million}$$

Adding back the firm's cash and marketable securities (estimated to be $409 million at the end of 2000) and subtracting out the value of the debt yields a value for the equity in the firm:

$$\text{Value of the equity} = \text{Value of the operating assets} + \text{Cash and marketable securities} - \text{Debt}$$
$$= 27,933 + 409 - 7,460 = \$20,882 \text{ million}$$

Note that the debt subtracted includes the present value of operating leases. At its prevailing market value of equity of $27,615 million, the Gap is overvalued.

---

[5]The Gap has had volatile capital expenditures and working capital changes. This is our attempt to average out this volatility.

ILLUSTRATION 15.3:   Valuing Amgen: Effects of R&D

As a leading biotechnology firm, Amgen has substantial research and development expenses that were capitalized earlier in this book. In this valuation, we will consider the implications of this capitalization for firm and equity values.

RATIONALE FOR USING MODEL

- *Why three-stage?* Amgen, in spite of being one of the largest biotechnology firms in the world, has significant potential for future growth because of drugs that it has in commercial production and other drugs in the pipeline. We will assume that the firm will continue to grow for 10 years, five at a high-growth rate followed by five years in transition to stable growth.
- *Why FCFF?* The firm has little debt on its books currently but will come under increasing pressure to increase its leverage as its cash flows become larger and more stable.

BACKGROUND INFORMATION

In 2000, Amgen reported operating income $1,549 million on revenues of $3,629 million. The firm also reported capital expenditures of $437 million and depreciation of $212 million for the year, and its noncash working capital (WC) increased by $146 million during the year. Recapping the analysis of Amgen's R&D from Chapter 9, we will use a 10-year amortizable life to estimate the value of the research asset:

Year	R&D Expense	Unamortized Portion		Amortization This Year
Current	$845.00	1.00	$ 845.00	
−1	$822.80	0.90	$ 740.52	$ 82.28
−2	$663.30	0.80	$ 530.64	$ 66.33
−3	$630.80	0.70	$ 441.56	$ 63.08
−4	$528.30	0.60	$ 316.98	$ 52.83
−5	$451.70	0.50	$ 225.85	$ 45.17
−6	$323.63	0.40	$ 129.45	$ 32.36
−7	$255.32	0.30	$ 76.60	$ 25.53
−8	$182.30	0.20	$ 36.46	$ 18.23
−9	$120.94	0.10	$ 12.09	$ 12.09
−10	$ 0.00	0.00	$ 0.00	$ 0.00
Value of research asset			$3,355.15	$397.91

The operating income is adjusted by adding back the current year's R&D expense and subtracting out the amortization of the research asset.

Adjusted operating income = Operating income + Current year's R&D − Amortization of research asset
= $1,549 + $845 − $398 = $1,996 million

To get to the after-tax operating income, we also consider the tax benefits from expensing R&D (as opposed to just the amortization of the research asset):

Adjusted after-tax operating income = Adjusted operating income(1 − Tax rate)
+ (Current year R&D − Amortization)Tax rate
= 1,996(1 − .35) + (845 − 398)(.35) = $1,454 million

The current year's R&D expense is added to the capital expenditures for the year, and the amortization to the depreciation. In conjunction with an increase in working capital of $146 million, we estimate an adjusted reinvestment rate for the firm of 56.27%.

Adjusted capital expenditures = 437 + 845 = $1,282 million
Adjusted depreciation = 212 + 398 = $610 million
Adjusted reinvestment rate = (Capital expenditures − Depreciation + Change in working capital)
/Adjusted EBIT(1 − t) = (1,282 − 610 + 146)/1,454 = 56.27%

To estimate the return on capital, we estimated the value of the research asset at the end of the previous year and added it to the book value of equity. The resultant return on capital for the firm is:

Return on capital = Adjusted EBIT(1 − t)/(Adjusted book value of equity, including research asset) + Book value of debt) = 1,454/(5,932 + 323) = 23.24%

VALUATION

To value Amgen, we will begin with the estimates for the five-year high growth period. We use a bottom-up beta estimate of 1.35, a risk-free rate of 5.4%, and a risk premium of 4% to estimate the cost of equity:

Cost of equity = 5.4% + 1.35(4%) = 10.80%

We estimate a synthetic rating of AAA for the firm, and use it to come up with a pretax cost of borrowing of 6.15% by adding a default spread of 0.75% to the Treasury bond rate of 5.4%. With a marginal tax rate of 35% and a debt ratio of 0.55%, the firm's cost of capital closely tracks its cost of equity:

Cost of capital = 10.80%(.9945) + .0615(1 − .35)(.0055) = 10.76%

To estimate the expected growth rate during the high growth period, we will assume that the firm can maintain its current return on capital and reinvestment rate estimated in the preceding section:

Expected growth rate = Reinvestment rate × Return on capital = .5627 × .2324 = 13.08%

Before we consider the transition period, we estimate the inputs for the stable growth period. First, we assume that the beta for Amgen will drop to 1, and that the firm will raise its debt ratio to 10%. Keeping the cost of debt unchanged, we estimate a cost of capital of:

Cost of equity = 5.4% + 1(4%) = 9.4%

Cost of capital = 9.4%(.9) + 6.15%(1 − .35)(.1) = 8.86%

We assume that the stable growth rate will be 5% and that the firm will have a return on capital of 20% in stable growth. This allows us to estimate the reinvestment rate in stable growth:

Reinvestment rate in stable growth = g/ROC = 5%/20% = 25%

During the transition period, we adjust growth, the reinvestment rate, and the cost of capital from high-growth levels to stable growth levels in linear increments. The following table summarizes the inputs and cash flows for both the high-growth and transition periods (in $millions):

Year	Expected Growth	EBIT(1 − t)	Reinvestment Rate	FCFF	Cost of Capital	Present Value
Current	$1,454					
1	13.08%	$1,644	56.27%	$ 719	10.76%	$ 649
2	13.08%	$1,859	56.27%	$ 813	10.76%	$ 663
3	13.08%	$2,102	56.27%	$ 919	10.76%	$ 677
4	13.08%	$2,377	56.27%	$1,040	10.76%	$ 691
5	13.08%	$2,688	56.27%	$1,176	10.76%	$ 705
6	11.46%	$2,996	50.01%	$1,498	10.38%	$ 814
7	9.85%	$3,291	43.76%	$1,851	10.00%	$ 914
8	8.23%	$3,562	37.51%	$2,226	9.62%	$1,003
9	6.62%	$3,798	31.25%	$2,611	9.24%	$1,077
10	5.00%	$3,988	25.00%	$2,991	8.86%	$1,133
	Sum of the present value of the FCFF during high growth =					$8,327

Finally, we estimate the terminal value, based on the estimated growth rate, cost of capital, and reinvestment rate:

$$FCFF_{11} = EBIT_{11}(1 − t)(1 − \text{Reinvestment rate}) = 3,988 (1.05)(1 − .25) = \$3,140 \text{ million}$$

$$\text{Terminal value}_{10} = FCFF_{11}/(\text{Cost of capital in stable growth} − \text{Growth rate})$$
$$= 3,140/(.0886 − .05) = \$81,364 \text{ million}$$

Adding the present value of the terminal value to the present value of the free cash flows to the firm in the first 10 years, we get:

Value of the operating assets of the firm = $8,327 million + $81,364/(1.1076^5 \times 1.1038 \times 1.10$
$$\times 1.0962 \times 1.0924 \times 1.0886)$$
$$= \$39,161 \text{ million}$$

Adding the value of cash and marketable securities ($2.029 million) and subtracting debt ($323 million) yields a value for the equity of $40,867 million. At the time of this valuation in May 2001, the equity was trading at a market value of $58,000 million.

ILLUSTRATION 15.4:   Valuing Embraer: Dealing with Country Risk

Embraer is a Brazilian aerospace firm that manufactures and sells both commercial and military aircraft. In this valuation, we will consider the implications of valuing the firm in the context of country risk and uncertainty about expected inflation.

RATIONALE FOR USING MODEL

- *Why two-stage?* Embraer has done exceptionally well in the past few years despite the fact that it operates in a mature business with strong competition from giants such as Boeing and Airbus. We believe that it can sustain growth for a long period (10 years) and that there will be a transition to stable growth in the second half of this growth period.
- *Why FCFF?* The firm's debt ratio has been volatile. While it does not use much debt to fund its operations currently, it does have the capacity to raise more debt now, especially in the United States.
- *Why real cash flows?* We had two choices when it came to valuation—to work with U.S. dollars or to work in real cash flows. We avoided working with nominal BR, largely because of the difficulties associated with getting a risk-free rate in that currency.

BACKGROUND INFORMATION

In 2000, Embraer reported operating income of 810.32 million BR on revenues of 4,560 million BR, and faced a marginal tax rate of 33% on its income. At the end of 2000, the firm had net debt (debt minus cash) of 215.5 million BR on which its net interest expenses for 2000 were 28.20 million BR. The firm's noncash working capital at the end of 2000 amounted to 915 million BR, an increase of 609.7 million BR over the previous year's amount.

The firm's capital expenditures were 233.5 million BR, and depreciation was 127.5 million for the year, yielding a reinvestment rate of 131.83% for the year:

$$\text{Reinvestment rate}_{2000} = (233.5 - 127.5 + 609.7)/[810.32 \times (1 - .33)] = 131.83\%$$

Normalizing the noncash working capital component[6] yields a change in noncash working capital of 239.59 million BR and a normalized reinvestment rate of:

$$\text{Normalized reinvestment rate}_{2000} = (233.5 - 127.5 + 239.59)/[810.32 \times (1 - .33)] = 63.65\%$$

---

[6]The normalized change in noncash working capital was computed as follows:

$$\text{Normalized change} = (\text{Noncash WC}_{2000}/\text{Revenues}_{2000}) \times (\text{Revenues}_{2000} - \text{Revenues}_{1999})$$

Based on the capital invested of 1,470 million BR in the firm at the beginning of 2000, the return on capital at Embraer in 2000 was 36.94%:

$$\text{Return on capital} = 810.32(1 - .33)/1,470 = 36.94\%$$

VALUATION

We first have to estimate a country risk premium for Brazil. Drawing on the approach developed in Chapter 7, we estimate a country risk premium for Brazil of 10.24%:

Country rating for Brazil = B1
Default spread on Brazilian government C-bond (U.S. dollar–denominated) = 5.37%

To estimate the country equity risk premium, we estimated the standard deviation in weekly returns over the last two years in both the Bovespa (the Brazilian equity index) and the C-bond:

Standard deviation in the Bovespa = 32.6%
Standard deviation in the C-bond = 17.1%
Country risk premium = Default spread(Standard deviation$_{equity}$/Standard deviation$_{C\text{-bond}}$)
  = 5.37%(32.6/17.1) = 10.24%

To make an estimate of Embraer's beta, we used a bottom-up unlevered beta of 0.87 and Embraer's market net debt-to-equity ratio (to stay consistent with use of net debt in the valuation) of 2.45%:

$$\text{Levered beta} = 0.87[1 + (1 - .33)(.0245)] = 0.88$$

Finally, to estimate the cost of equity, we used a real riskless rate of 4.5% and a mature market risk premium of 4% (in addition to the country risk premium of 10.24%):

$$\text{Cost of equity} = 4.5\% + 0.88(4\% + 10.24\%) = 17.03\%$$

We estimate a synthetic rating of AAA for Embraer, and use it to come up with a pretax cost of borrowing of 10.62% by adding a default spread of 0.75% to the real riskless rate of 4.5%, and then adding the country default spread of 5.37%:[7]

Pretax cost of debt = Real risk-free rate + Country default spread + Company default spread
  = 4.5% + 5.37% + 0.75% = 10.62%

With a marginal tax rate of 33% and a net debt to capital ratio of 2.40%, the firm's cost of capital is:

$$\text{Cost of capital} = 17.03\%(.976) + .1062(1 - .35)(.024) = 16.79\%$$

To estimate the expected growth rate during the high-growth period, we will assume that the firm can maintain its current return on capital and use the normalized reinvestment rate:

Expected growth rate = Normalized reinvestment rate × Return on capital
  = .6365 × .3694 = 23.51%

---

[7]This is a conservative estimate. It is entirely possible that the market will not assess Embraer with all of the country risk, and may view Embraer as safer than the Brazilian government.

In stable growth, we assume that the beta for Embraer will rise slightly to 0.90, that its net debt ratio will remain unchanged at 2.40% and that the country risk premium will drop to 5.37% (which is the bond default spread). We also assume that the pretax cost of debt will decline to 7.50%.

$$\text{Cost of equity} = 4.5\% + 0.9(4\% + 5.37\%) = 12.93\%$$

$$\text{Cost of capital} = 12.93\%(.976) + 7.5\%(1 - .33)(.024) = 12.74\%$$

We assume that the stable real growth rate will be 3% and that the firm will have a return on capital of 15% in stable growth. This is a significant drop from its current return on capital but reflect the returns of more mature firms in the business. This allows us to estimate the reinvestment rate in stable growth:

$$\text{Reinvestment rate in stable growth} = g/ROC = 3\%/15\% = 20\%$$

During the transition period, we adjust growth, reinvestment rate, and the cost of capital from high-growth levels to stable-growth levels in linear increments. The following table summarizes the inputs and cash flows for both the high-growth and transition periods:

Year	Expected Growth	EBIT(1 − t)	Reinvestment Rate	FCFF	Cost of Capital	Present Value
Current		BR 543				
1	23.51%	BR 671	63.65%	BR 244	16.79%	BR 209
2	23.51%	828	63.65%	301	16.79%	221
3	23.51%	1,023	63.65%	372	16.79%	233
4	23.51%	1,264	63.65%	459	16.79%	247
5	23.51%	1,561	63.65%	567	16.79%	261
6	19.41%	1,864	54.92%	840	15.98%	333
7	15.31%	2,149	46.19%	1,156	15.17%	398
8	11.21%	2,390	37.46%	1,495	14.36%	450
9	7.10%	2,559	28.73%	1,824	13.55%	484
10	3.00%	2,636	20.00%	2,109	12.74%	496
	Sum of the present value of the FCFF during high growth					BR 3,333

Finally, we estimate the terminal value, based on the growth rate, cost of capital, and reinvestment rate estimated previously:

$$FCFF_{11} = EBIT_{11}(1 - t)(1 - \text{Reinvestment rate}) = 2,636(1.03)(1 - .2) = 2,172 \text{ million BR}$$

$$\text{Terminal value}_{10} = FCFF_{11}/(\text{Cost of capital in stable growth} - \text{Growth rate})$$
$$= 2,172/(.1274 - .03) = 22,295 \text{ million BR}$$

Adding the present value of the terminal value to the present value of the free cash flows to the firm in the first 10 years, we get:

$$\text{Value of the operating assets of the firm} = 3,333 \text{ million BR} + 22,295/(1.1679^5 \times 1.1598 \times 1.1517$$
$$\times 1.1436 \times 1.1355 \times 1.1274)$$
$$= 8,578 \text{ million BR}$$

We do not add back cash and marketable securities, because we are using net debt (and the cash has therefore already been netted out against debt). Adding the value of nonoperating assets ($510 million) and subtracting out net debt ($223 million) yields a value for the equity of 8,865 million BR and a per-share value of 14.88 BR. At the time of this valuation in March 2001, the equity was trading at a market price of 15.2 BR per share.

Doing a valuation is only the first part of the process. Presenting it to others is the second part and perhaps just as important. Valuations can be complicated, and it is easy to lose your audience (and yourself) in the details. Presenting a big picture of the valuation often helps. In Figure 15.1, for instance, the valuation of a Embraer is presented in a picture. The valuation contains all of the details presented in the Amgen and Gap valuations, but they are presented in a more concise format and the connections between the various inputs are much more visible.

 fcffginzu.xls: **This spreadsheet allows you to estimate the value of a firm using the FCFF approach.**

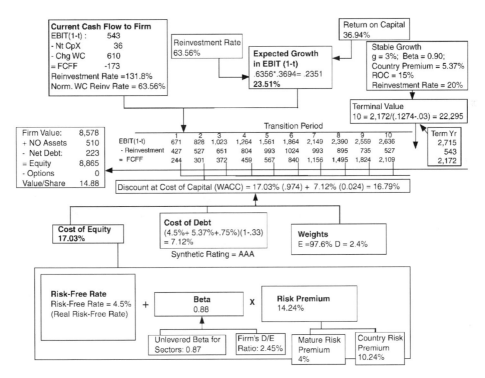

FIGURE 15.1 Embraer

NET DEBT VERSUS GROSS DEBT

In valuing Embraer, we used net debt where cash was netted out against debt. In all of the earlier valuations, we used gross debt. What is the difference between the two approaches, and will the valuations from the two approaches agree?

A comparison of the Embraer and the earlier valuations reveals the differences in the way we approach the calculation of key inputs to the valuation, summarized as follows:

	Gross Debt	*Net Debt*
Levered beta	Unlevered beta is levered using gross debt to market equity ratio.	Unlevered beta is levered using net debt to market equity ratio.
Cost of capital	Debt-to-capital ratio used is based on gross debt.	Debt-to-capital ratio used is based on net debt.
Treatment of cash and debt	Cash is added to value of operating assets and gross debt is subtracted to get to equity value.	Cash is not added back to operating assets and net debt is subtracted to get to equity value.

While working with net debt in valuation is not difficult to do, the more interesting question is whether the value that emerges will be the same as the value that would have been estimated using gross debt. In general the answer is no, and the reason usually lies in the cost of debt used in the net debt valuation. Intuitively, what you are doing when you use net debt is break the firm into two parts—a cash business, which is funded 100 percent with riskless debt, and an operating business funded partly with risky debt. Carrying this to its logical conclusion, the cost of debt you would have for the operating business would be significantly higher than the firm's current cost of debt. This is because the current lenders to the firm will factor in the firm's cash holdings when setting the cost of debt.

To illustrate, assume that you have a firm with an overall value of $1 billion—$200 million in cash and $800 million in operating assets—with $400 million in debt and $600 million in equity. The firm's cost of debt is 7 percent, a 2 percent default spread over the risk-free rate of 5 percent; note that this cost of debt is set based on the firm's substantial cash holdings. If you net debt against cash, the firm would have $200 million in net debt and $600 million in equity. If you use the 7 percent cost of debt to value the firm now, you will overstate its value. Instead, the cost of debt you should use in the valuation is 9 percent:

$$\text{Cost of debt on net debt} = (\text{Pretax cost of debt}_{\text{gross debt}} \times \text{Gross debt}$$
$$- \text{Risk rate}_{\text{net debt}} \times \text{Cash})/(\text{Gross debt} - \text{Cash})$$
$$= (.07 \times 400 - .05 \times 200)/(400 - 200) = .09$$

In general, we would recommend using gross debt rather than net debt for two other reasons. First, the net debt can be a negative number if cash exceeds the gross debt. If this occurs, you should set the net debt to zero and consider the excess cash just as you would cash in a gross debt valuation. Second, maintaining a stable net debt ratio in a growing firm will require that cash balances increase as the firm value increases.

Will Equity Value Be the Same under Firm and Equity Valuation?

This model, unlike the dividend discount model or the FCFE model, values the firm rather than equity. The value of equity, however, can be extracted from the value of the firm by subtracting the market value of outstanding debt. Since this model can be viewed as an alternative way of valuing equity, two questions arise: Why value the firm rather than equity? Will the values for equity obtained from the firm valuation approach be consistent with the values obtained from the equity valuation approaches described in the previous chapter?

The advantage of using the firm valuation approach is that cash flows relating to debt do not have to be considered explicitly since the FCFF is a predebt cash flow, while they have to be taken into account in estimating FCFE. In cases where the leverage is expected to change significantly over time, this is a significant savings, since estimating new debt issues and debt repayments when leverage is changing can become increasingly messy the further into the future you go. The firm valuation approach does, however, require information about debt ratios and interest rates to estimate the weighted average cost of capital.

The value for equity obtained from the firm valuation and equity valuation approaches will be the same if you make consistent assumptions about financial leverage. Getting them to converge in practice is much more difficult. Let us begin with the simplest case—a no-growth, perpetual firm. Assume that the firm has $166.67 million in earnings before interest and taxes and a tax rate of 40 percent. Assume that the firm has equity with a market value of $600 million, with a cost of equity of 13.87 percent, and debt of $400 million, with a pretax cost of debt of 7 percent. The firm's cost of capital can be estimated as follows:

$$\text{Cost of capital} = 13.87\%(700/1{,}000) + 7\%(1 - .4)(300/1{,}000) = 10\%$$

$$\text{Value of the firm} = \text{Earnings before interest and taxes}(1 - t)/\text{Cost of capital}$$
$$= 166.67(1 - .4)/.10 = \$1{,}000$$

Note that the firm has no reinvestment and no growth. We can value equity in this firm by subtracting the value of debt:

$$\text{Value of equity} = \text{Value of firm} - \text{Value of debt} = \$1{,}000 - \$400 = \$600 \text{ million}$$

Now let us value the equity directly by estimating the net income:

$$\text{Net income} = (\text{EBIT} - \text{Pretax cost of debt} \times \text{Debt})(1 - t)$$
$$= (166.67 - .07 \times 400)(1 - .4) = \$83.202 \text{ million}$$

The value of equity can be obtained by discounting this net income at the cost of equity:

$$\text{Value of equity} = \text{Net income}/\text{Cost of equity} = 83.202/.1387 = \$600 \text{ million}$$

Even this simple example works because of the following three assumptions made implicitly or explicitly during the valuation:

1. The values for debt and equity used to compute the cost of capital were equal to the values obtained in the valuation. Notwithstanding the circularity in reasoning—you need the cost of capital to obtain the values in the first place—it indicates that a cost of capital based on market value weights will not yield the

same value for equity as an equity valuation model if the firm is not fairly priced in the first place.

2. There are no extraordinary or nonoperating items that affect net income but not operating income. Thus, to get from operating to net income all we do is subtract interest expenses and taxes.

3. The interest expenses are equal to the pretax cost of debt multiplied by the market value of debt. If a firm has old debt on its books, with interest expenses that are different from this value, the two approaches will diverge.

If there is expected growth, the potential for inconsistency multiplies. You have to ensure that you borrow enough money to fund new investments to keep your debt ratio at a level consistent with what you are assuming when you compute the cost of capital.

---

 fcffvsfcfe.xls: This spreadsheet allows you to compare the equity values obtained using FCFF and FCFE models.

FIRM VALUATION: THE ADJUSTED PRESENT VALUE APPROACH

The adjusted present value (APV) approach begins with the value of the firm without debt. As debt is added to the firm, the net effect on value is examined by considering both the benefits and the costs of borrowing. To do this, it is assumed that the primary benefit of borrowing is a tax benefit, and that the most significant cost of borrowing is the added risk of bankruptcy.

Mechanics of APV Valuation

We estimate the value of the firm in three steps:

1. Estimate the value of the firm with no leverage.
2. Consider the present value of the interest tax savings generated by borrowing a given amount of money.
3. Evaluate the effect of borrowing the amount on the probability that the firm will go bankrupt, and the expected cost of bankruptcy.

Value of Unlevered Firm   The first step in this approach is the estimation of the value of the unlevered firm. This can be accomplished by valuing the firm as if it had no debt (i.e., by discounting the expected free cash flow to the firm at the unlevered cost of equity). In the special case where cash flows grow at a constant rate in perpetuity,

$$\text{Value of unlevered firm} = E(FCFF_1)/(\rho_u - g)$$

where $FCFF_1$ is the expected after-tax operating cash flow to the firm, ρ_u is the unlevered cost of equity, and g is the expected growth rate. In the more general case, you can value the firm using any set of growth assumptions you believe are reasonable for the firm.

The inputs needed for this valuation are the expected cash flows, growth rates, and the unlevered cost of equity. To estimate the unlevered cost of equity, we can draw on our earlier analysis and compute the unlevered beta of the firm:

$$\beta_{unlevered} = \beta_{current}/[1 + (1 - t)D/E]$$

where $\beta_{unlevered}$ = Unlevered beta of the firm
$\beta_{current}$ = Current equity beta of the firm
    t = Tax rate for the firm
  D/E = Current debt/equity ratio

This unlevered beta can then be used to arrive at the unlevered cost of equity.

Expected Tax Benefit from Borrowing   The second step in this approach is the calculation of the expected tax benefit from a given level of debt. This tax benefit is a function of the tax rate and interest payments of the firm and is discounted at the cost of debt to reflect the riskiness of this cash flow. If the tax savings are viewed as a perpetuity,

$$\text{Value of tax benefits} = (\text{Tax rate} \times \text{Cost of debt} \times \text{Debt})/\text{Cost of debt}$$
$$= \text{Tax rate} \times \text{Debt} = t_c D$$

The tax rate used here is the firm's marginal tax rate, and it is assumed to stay constant over time. If we anticipate the tax rate changing over time, we can still compute the present value of tax benefits over time, but we cannot use the perpetual growth equation cited earlier. In addition, you would have to modify this equation if the current interest expenses do not reflect the current cost of debt.

Estimating Expected Bankruptcy Costs and Net Effect   The third step is to evaluate the effect of the given level of debt on the default risk of the firm and on expected bankruptcy costs. In theory, at least, this requires the estimation of the probability of default with the additional debt and the direct and indirect cost of bankruptcy. If π_a is the probability of default after the additional debt and BC is the present value of the bankruptcy cost, the present value (PV) of expected bankruptcy cost can be estimated:

$$\text{PV of expected bankruptcy cost} = \text{Probability of bankruptcy} \times \text{PV of bankruptcy cost}$$
$$= \pi_a BC$$

This step of the adjusted present value approach poses the most significant estimation problems, since neither the probability of bankruptcy nor the bankruptcy cost can be estimated directly.

There are two basic ways in which the probability of bankruptcy can be estimated indirectly. One is to estimate a bond rating and use the empirical estimates of default probabilities for the rating. For instance, Table 15.2, extracted from a study by Altman and Kishore, summarizes the probability of default over 10 years by bond rating class in 1998.[8]

---

[8]This study estimated default rates over 10 years only for some of the ratings classes. We extrapolated the rest of the ratings.

TABLE 15.2   Default Rates by
Bond Rating Classes

Bond Rating	Default Rate
D	100.00%
C	80.00%
CC	65.00%
CCC	46.61%
B–	32.50%
B	26.36%
B+	19.28%
BB	12.20%
BBB	2.30%
A–	1.41%
A	0.53%
A+	0.40%
AA	0.28%
AAA	0.01%

Source: Altman and Kishore (1998).

The other way is to use a statistical approach such as a probit to estimate the probability of default, based on the firm's observable characteristics, at each level of debt.

The bankruptcy cost can be estimated, albeit with considerable error, from studies that have looked at the magnitude of this cost in actual bankruptcies. Research that has looked at the direct cost of bankruptcy concludes that they are small[9] relative to firm value. The indirect costs of bankruptcy can be substantial, but the costs vary widely across firms. Shapiro and Titman speculate that the indirect costs could be as large as 25 to 30 percent of firm value but provide no direct evidence of the costs.

ILLUSTRATION 15.5:   Valuing a Firm with the APV Approach: Tube Investments

Illustration 15.1 valued Tube Investments using a cost of capital approach. Here, we reestimate the value of the firm using an adjusted present value approach in three steps:

STEP 1: UNLEVERED FIRM VALUE

To estimate the unlevered firm value, we first compute the unlevered beta. Tube Investments' beta is 1.17, its current market debt to equity ratio is 79%, and the firm's tax rate is 30%:

$$\text{Unlevered beta} = 1.17/[1 + (1 - .3)(.79)] = 0.75$$

---

[9]In Warner's study of railroad bankruptcies, the direct cost of bankruptcy seems to be about 5 percent.

Using the rupee risk-free rate of 10.5% and the risk premium of 9.23% for India, we estimate an unlevered cost of equity:

$$\text{Unlevered cost of equity} = 10.5\% + 0.75(9.23\%) = 17.45\%$$

Using the free cash flow to the firm estimated in Illustration 15.1 of Rs 212.2 million and the stable growth rate of 5%, we estimate the unlevered firm value:

$$\text{Unlevered firm value} = 212.2/(.1745 - .05) = \$1,704.6 \text{ million}$$

STEP 2: TAX BENEFITS FROM DEBT

The tax benefits from debt are computed based un Tube Investments' existing dollar debt of Rs 1,807.3 million and the tax rate of 30%:

$$\text{Expected tax benefits in perpetuity} = \text{Tax rate(Debt)} = .30(1,807.3) = \text{Rs } 542.2 \text{ million}$$

STEP 3: EXPECTED BANKRUPTCY COSTS

To estimate this, we made two assumptions. One, based on the firm's existing synthetic rating, is that the probability of default at its existing debt level is 10%. The other is that the cost of bankruptcy is 40% of unlevered firm value.

$$\text{Expected bankruptcy cost} = \text{Probability of bankruptcy} \times \text{Cost of bankruptcy} \times \text{Unlevered firm value}$$
$$= .10 \times .40 \times 1,704.6 = \text{Rs } 68.2 \text{ million}$$

The value of the operating assets of the firm can now be estimated:

$$\text{Value of the operating assets} = \text{Unlevered firm value} + \text{PV of tax benefits} - \text{Expected bankruptcy costs}$$
$$= 1,704.6 + 542.2 - 68.2 = \text{Rs } 2,178.6 \text{ million}$$

Adding to this the value of cash and marketable securities of Rs 1,365.3 million, we obtain a value for the firm of Rs 3,543.9 million. In contrast, we valued the firm at Rs 3,367.3 million with the cost of capital approach.

Cost of Capital versus APV Valuation

In an APV valuation, the value of a levered firm is obtained by adding the net effect of debt to the unlevered firm value.

$$\text{Value of levered firm} = \text{FCFF}_o(1 + g)/(\rho_u - g) + t_c D - \pi_a BC$$

In the cost of capital approach, the effects of leverage show up in the cost of capital, with the tax benefit incorporated in the after-tax cost of debt and the bankruptcy costs in both the levered beta and the pretax cost of debt. Will the two approaches yield the same value? Not necessarily. The first reason for differences is that the models consider bankruptcy costs very differently, with the adjusted present value approach providing more flexibility in allowing you to consider indirect bankruptcy costs. To the extent that these costs do not show up or show up inadequately in the pretax cost of debt, the APV approach will yield a more conservative estimate of value. The second reason is that the APV approach considers the tax

> ### APV WITHOUT BANKRUPTCY COSTS
>
> There are many who believe that adjusted present value is a more flexible way of approaching valuation than traditional discounted cash flow models. This may be true in a generic sense, but APV valuation in practice has significant flaws. The first and most important is that most practitioners who use the adjusted present value model ignore expected bankruptcy costs. Adding the tax benefits to unlevered firm value to get to levered firm value makes debt seem like an unmixed blessing. Firm value will be overstated, especially at very high debt ratios, where the cost of bankruptcy is clearly not zero.

benefit from a dollar debt value, usually based on existing debt. The cost of capital approach estimates the tax benefit from a debt ratio that may require the firm to borrow increasing amounts in the future. For instance, assuming a market debt to capital ratio of 30 percent in perpetuity for a growing firm will require it to borrow more in the future, and the tax benefit from expected future borrowings is incorporated into value today.

EFFECT OF LEVERAGE ON FIRM VALUE

Both the cost of capital approach and the APV approach make the value of a firm a function of its leverage. It follows directly, then, that there is some mix of debt and equity at which firm value is maximized. The rest of this chapter considers how best to make this link.

Cost of Capital and Optimal Leverage

In order to understand the relationship between the cost of capital and optimal capital structure, we rely on the relationship between firm value and the cost of capital. The earlier section noted that the value of the entire firm can be estimated by discounting the expected cash flows to the firm at the firm's cost of capital.

The firm value can then be written as follows:

$$\text{Value of firm} = \sum_{t=1}^{t=n} \frac{\text{CF to firm}_t}{(1+\text{WACC})^t}$$

and is a function of the firm's cash flows and its cost of capital. If we assume that the cash flows to the firm are unaffected by the choice of financing mix, and the cost of capital is reduced as a consequence of changing the financing mix, the value of the firm will increase. If the objective in choosing the financing mix for the firm is the maximization of firm value, we can accomplish it, in this case, by minimizing the cost of capital. In the more general case where the cash flows to the firm are a function of the debt-equity mix, the optimal financing mix is the mix that maximizes firm value.[10]

---

[10]In other words, the value of the firm might not be maximized at the point that cost of capital is minimized, if firm cash flows are much lower at that level.

ILLUSTRATION 15.6: WACC, Firm Value, and Leverage

Assume that you are given the costs of equity and debt at different debt levels for Strunks Inc., a leading manufacturer of chocolates and other candies, and that the cash flows to this firm are currently $200 million. Strunks is in a relatively stable market, and these cash flows are expected to grow at 6% forever and to be unaffected by the debt ratio of the firm. The cost of capital schedule is provided in the following table, along with the value of the firm at each level of debt.

D/(D + E)	Cost of Equity	Cost of Debt	WACC	Firm Value
0%	10.50%	4.80%	10.50%	$4,711
10%	11.00%	5.10%	10.41%	$4,807
20%	11.60%	5.40%	10.36%	$4,862
30%	12.30%	5.52%	10.27%	$4,970
40%	13.10%	5.70%	10.14%	$5,121
50%	14.00%	6.30%	10.15%	$5,108
60%	15.00%	7.20%	10.32%	$4,907
70%	16.10%	8.10%	10.50%	$4,711
80%	17.20%	9.00%	10.64%	$4,569
90%	18.40%	10.20%	11.02%	$4,223
100%	19.70%	11.40%	11.40%	$3,926

Note that:

Value of firm = Cash flows to firm × (1 + g)/(Cost of capital − g) = $200 × 1.06/(Cost of capital − .06)

The value of the firm increases as the cost of capital decreases, and decreases as the cost of capital increases. This is illustrated in Figure 15.2. While this illustration makes the choice of an optimal financing mix seem easy, it obscures problems that may arise in its practice. First, we typically do not have the benefit of having the entire schedule of costs of financing prior to an analysis. In most cases, the only level of debt at which we have information on the cost of debt and equity financing is the current level. Second, the analysis assumes implicitly that the level of operating income of the firm is unaffected by the financing mix of the firm and, consequently, by the default risk (or bond rating) for the firm. While this may be reasonable in some cases, it might not be in others. Firms that borrow too much might find that there are indirect bankruptcy costs that affect revenues and operating income.

Steps in Cost of Capital Approach We need three basic inputs to compute the cost of capital—the cost of equity, the after-tax cost of debt, and the weights on debt and equity. The costs of equity and debt change as the debt ratio changes, and the primary challenge of this approach is in estimating each of these inputs.

Let us begin with the cost of equity. We argued that the beta of equity will change as the debt ratio changes. In fact, we estimated the levered beta as a function of the market debt to equity ratio of a firm, the unlevered beta and the firm's marginal tax rate:

$$\beta_{levered} = \beta_{unlevered}[1 + (1 - t)\text{Debt/Equity}]$$

Thus, if we can estimate the unlevered beta for a firm, we can use it to estimate the levered beta of the firm at every debt ratio. This levered beta can then be used to compute the cost of equity at each debt ratio.

$$\text{Cost of equity} = \text{Risk-free rate} + \beta_{\text{levered}}(\text{Risk premium})$$

The cost of debt for a firm is a function of the firm's default risk. As firms borrow more, their default risk will increase and so will the cost of debt. If we use bond ratings as our measure of default risk, we can estimate the cost of debt in three steps. First, estimate a firm's dollar debt and interest expenses at each debt ratio; as firms increase their debt ratio, both dollar debt and interest expenses will rise. Second, at each debt level, compute a financial ratio or ratios that measures default risk and use the ratio(s) to estimate a rating for the firm; again, as firms borrow more, this rating will decline. Third, a default spread, based on the estimated rating, is added to the risk-free rate to arrive at the pretax cost of debt. Applying the marginal tax rate to this pretax cost yields an after-tax cost of debt.

Once we estimate the costs of equity and debt at each debt level, we weight them based on the proportions used of each to estimate the cost of capital. While we have not explicitly allowed for a preferred stock component in this process, we can have preferred stock as a part of capital. However, we have to keep the preferred stock portion fixed, while changing the weights on debt and equity. The debt ratio at which the cost of capital is minimized is the optimal debt ratio.

In this approach, the effect on firm value of changing the capital structure is isolated by keeping the operating income fixed and varying only the cost of capital. In practical terms, this requires us to make two assumptions. First, the debt ratio is decreased by raising new equity and retiring debt; conversely, the debt ratio is increased by borrowing money and buying back stock. This process is called recapitalization. Second, the pretax operating income is assumed to be unaffected by the firm's financing mix and, by extension, its bond rating. If the operating income

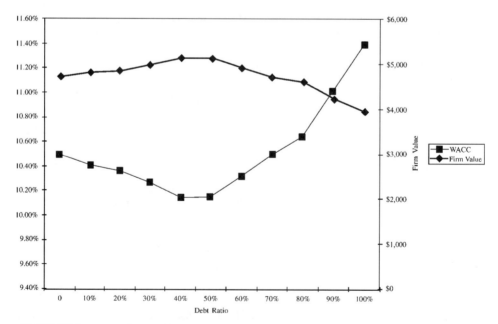

FIGURE 15.2 Cost of Capital and Firm Value
Source: Corporate Finance: Theory and Practice, Second Edition, by Aswath Damodaran, copyright © 2001 by John Wiley & Sons, Inc. This material is used by permission of John Wiley & Sons, Inc.

changes with a firm's default risk, the basic analysis will not change, but minimizing the cost of capital may not be the optimal course of action, since the value of the firm is determined by both the cash flows and the cost of capital. The value of the firm will have to be computed at each debt level and the optimal debt ratio will be that which maximizes firm value.

ILLUSTRATION 15.7:   Analyzing the Capital Structure for Boeing—March 1999

The cost of capital approach can be used to find the optimal capital structure for a firm, as in this case for Boeing in March 1999. Boeing had $6,972 million in debt on its books at that time, with an estimated market value, inclusive of operating leases, of $8,194 million.[11] The market value of equity at the same time was $32,595 million; the market price per share was $32.25, and there were 1,010.7 million shares outstanding. Proportionally, 20.09% of the overall financing mix was debt, and the remaining 79.91% was equity.

The beta for Boeing's stock in March 1999 was 1.01. The Treasury bond rate at that time was 5%. Using an estimated market risk premium of 5.5%, we estimated the cost of equity for Boeing to be 10.58%:

$$\text{Cost of equity} = \text{Risk-free rate} + \text{Beta} \times (\text{Market premium})$$
$$= 5.00\% + 1.01(5.5\%) = 10.58\%$$

Boeing's senior debt was rated AA. Based on this rating, the estimated pretax cost of debt for Boeing is 5.50%. The tax rate used for the analysis is 35%.

$$\text{Value of firm} = 8,194 + 32,595 = \$40,789 \text{ million}$$

$$\text{After-tax cost of debt} = \text{Pretax interest rate}(1 - \text{Tax rate}) = 5.50\%(1 - 0.35) = 3.58\%$$

The cost of capital was calculated using these costs and the weights based on market value:

$$\text{WACC} = \text{Cost of equity}[\text{Equity}/(\text{Equity} + \text{Debt})] + \text{After-tax cost of debt}[\text{Debt}/(\text{Debt} + \text{Equity})]$$
$$= 10.58\% \times [32,595/40,789] + 3.58\% \times [8,194/40,789] = 9.17\%$$

Boeing's Cost of Equity and Leverage

The cost of equity for Boeing at different debt ratios can be computed using the unlevered beta of the firm, and the debt-equity ratio at each level of debt. We use the levered betas that emerge to estimate the cost of equity. The first step in this process is to compute the firm's current unlevered beta, using the current market debt to equity ratio and a tax rate of 35%.

$$\text{Unlevered beta} = \text{Current beta}/[1 + (1 - t)\text{Debt/Equity}]$$
$$= 1.014/[1 + (1 - 0.35)(8,194/32,595)] = 0.87$$

The recomputed betas are reported in the following table. We use the Treasury bond rate of 5% and the market premium of 5.5% to compute the cost of equity.

---

[11]The details of this calculation are in Chapter 7.

Debt Ratio	Beta	Cost of Equity
0%	0.87	9.79%
10%	0.93	10.14%
20%	1.01	10.57%
30%	1.11	11.13%
40%	1.25	11.87%
50%	1.51	13.28%
60%	1.92	15.54%
70%	2.56	19.06%
80%	3.83	26.09%
90%	7.67	47.18%

In calculating the levered betas in this table, we assumed that all market risk is borne by the equity investors; this may be unrealistic especially at higher levels of debt. We also adjusted the tax rate beyond a debt ratio of 50% to reflect the loss of tax benefits. We could also consider an alternative estimate of levered betas that apportions some of the market risk to the debt:

$$\beta_{levered} = \beta_u[1 + (1 - t)D/E] - \beta_{debt}(1 - t)D/E$$

The beta of debt is based on the rating of the bond and is estimated by regressing past returns on bonds in each rating class against returns on a market index. The levered betas estimated using this approach will generally be lower than those estimated with the conventional model.

BOEING'S COST OF DEBT AND LEVERAGE

We assume that bond ratings are determined solely by the interest coverage ratio, which is defined as:

Interest coverage ratio = Earnings before interest and taxes/Interest expense

We chose the interest coverage ratio for three reasons. First, it is a ratio used by both Standard & Poor's and Moody's to determine ratings.[12] Second, there is significant correlation not only between the interest coverage ratio and bond ratings, but also between the interest coverage ratio and other ratios used in analysis, such as the debt coverage ratio and the funds flow ratios. Third, the interest coverage ratio changes as a firm changes is financing mix and decreases as the debt ratio increases. The ratings agencies would argue, however, that subjective factors, such as the perceived quality of management, are part of the ratings process. One way to build these factors into the analysis would be to modify the ratings obtained from the financial ratio analysis across the board to reflect the ratings agencies' subjective concerns.[13]

The data in the following table were obtained based on an analysis of the interest coverage ratios of large manufacturing firms in different ratings classes.

---

[12]S&P lists interest coverage ratio first among the nine ratios that it reports for different ratings classes on its web site.

[13]For instance, assume that a firm's current rating is AA, but that its financial ratios would result in an A rating. It can then be argued that the ratings agencies are, for subjective reasons, rating the company one notch higher than the rating obtained from a purely financial analysis. The ratings obtained for each debt level can then be increased by one notch across the board to reflect these subjective considerations.

Interest Coverage Ratio	Rating
> 8.5	AAA
6.50–8.50	AA
5.50–6.50	A+
4.25–5.50	A
3.00–4.25	A–
2.50–3.00	BBB
2.00–2.50	BB
1.75–2.00	B+
1.50–1.75	B
1.25–1.50	B–
0.80–1.25	CCC
0.65–0.80	CC
0.20–0.65	C
< 0.65	D

Source: Compustat.

Using this table as a guideline, a firm with an interest coverage ratio of 1.65 would have a rating of B for its bonds.

The relationship between bond ratings and interest rates in February 1999 was obtained by looking at the typical default spreads for bonds in different ratings classes.[14] The following table summarizes the interest rates/rating relationship and reports the spreads for these bonds over Treasury bonds and the resulting interest rates, using the Treasury bond rate of 5%.

Rating	Spread	Interest Rate on Debt
AAA	0.20%	5.20%
AA	0.50%	5.50%
A+	0.80%	5.80%
A	1.00%	6.00%
A–	1.25%	6.25%
BBB	1.50%	6.50%
BB	2.00%	7.00%
B+	2.50%	7.50%
B	3.25%	8.25%
B–	4.25%	9.25%
CCC	5.00%	10.00%
CC	6.00%	11.00%
C	7.50%	12.50%
D	10.00%	15.00%

Source: bondsonline.com.

The following table summarizes Boeing's income statement for the financial year 1998. It shows that Boeing had earnings before interest, taxes, depreciation, and amortization (EBITDA) of $3,237 million, and paid interest expenses of $453 million.

---

[14]These default spreads were estimated from bondsonline.com, a service that provides, among other data on fixed income securities, updated default spreads for each ratings class.

Sales and other operating revenues	$56,154.00
– Operating costs and expenses	$52,917.00
EBITDA	$ 3,237.00
– Depreciation	$ 1,517.00
EBIT	$ 1,720.00
+ Extraordinary income	$ 130.00
EBIT with extraordinary income	$ 1,850.00
– Interest expenses	$ 453.00
Earnings before taxes	$ 1,397.00
– Income Taxes	$ 277.00
Net earnings (loss)	$ 1,120.00

Based on the earnings before interest and taxes (EBIT) of $1,720 million and interest expenses of $453 million, Boeing has an interest coverage ratio of 3.80 and should command a rating of A–. Boeing's earnings before interest, taxes, and depreciation for the year were $3,237 million. The actual rating of the firm, which is AA, reflects the ratings agency view that Boeing had subpar years in both 1997 and 1998, and is capable of earning more on a regular basis. In our analysis, we adjust the EBIT and EBITDA for the imputed interest expenses on Boeing's operating leases;[15] this results in an increase of $31 million in both numbers—to $1,751 million in EBIT and $3,268 million in EBITDA.

Finally, to compute Boeing's ratings at different debt levels, we redo the operating income statement at each level of debt, compute the interest coverage ratio at that level of debt, and find the rating that corresponds to that level of debt. For example, the following table estimates the interest expenses, interest coverage ratios, and bond ratings for Boeing at 0% and 10% debt ratios, at the existing level of operating income.

Debt/(Debt + Equity)	0.00%	10.00%
Debt/Equity	0.00%	11.11%
$ Debt	$0	$4,079
EBITDA	$3,268	$3,268
Depreciation	$1,517	$1,517
EBIT	$1,751	$1,751
Interest expense	$0	$227
Pretax int. coverage	∞	7.80
Likely rating	AAA	AA
Interest rate	5.20%	5.50%
Effective tax rate	35.00%	35.00%

The dollar debt is computed to be 10% of the current value of the firm by adding the market values of debt and equity:

Dollar debt at 10% debt ratio = Debt ratio(Market value of equity + Market value of debt)
= .10(32,595 + 8,194) = $4,079 million

There is circular reasoning involved in estimating the interest expense. The interest rate is needed to calculate the interest coverage ratio, and the coverage ratio is necessary to compute the interest rate. To get around the problem, we began our analysis by assuming that you could borrow $4.079 billion at the AAA rate of 5.20%; we then computed an interest expense and interest coverage ratio using that rate, and estimated a new rating of AA for Boeing. We recomputed the interest expense using the AA rate of 5.50% as our cost of debt.[16] This process is repeated for each level of debt from 10% to 90%, and the after-tax costs of debt are obtained at each level of debt in the following table:

---

[15]The details of this adjustment are provided in Chapter 9.
[16]Since the interest expense rises, it is possible for the rating to drop again. Thus a third iteration might be necessary in some cases.

Debt Ratio	$ Debt	Interest Expense	Interest Coverage Ratio	Bond Rating	Pretax Cost of Debt	Tax Rate	After-Tax Cost of Debt
0.00%	$ 0	$0	∞	AAA	5.20%	35.00%	3.38%
10.00%	$ 4,079	$224	7.80	AA	5.50%	35.00%	3.58%
20.00%	$ 8,158	$510	3.43	A–	6.25%	35.00%	4.06%
30.00%	$12,237	$857	2.04	BB	7.00%	35.00%	4.55%
40.00%	$16,316	$1,632	1.07	CCC	10.00%	35.00%	6.50%
50.00%	$20,394	$2,039	0.86	CCC	10.00%	30.05%	7.00%
60.00%	$24,473	$2,692	0.65	CC	11.00%	22.76%	8.50%
70.00%	$28,552	$3,569	0.49	C	12.50%	17.17%	10.35%
80.00%	$32,631	$4,079	0.43	C	12.50%	15.02%	10.62%
90.00%	$36,710	$4,589	0.38	C	12.50%	13.36%	10.83%

There are two points to make about this computation. We assume that at every debt level, all existing debt will be refinanced at the new interest rate that will prevail after the capital structure change. For instance, Boeing's existing debt, which has a AA rating, is assumed to be refinanced at the interest rate corresponding to a BB rating when Boeing moves to a 30% debt ratio. This is done for two reasons. The first is that existing debt holders might have protective puts that enable them to put their bonds back to the firm and receive face value.[17] The second is that the refinancing eliminates "wealth expropriation" effects—the effects of stockholders expropriating wealth from bondholders when debt is increased, and vice versa when debt is reduced. If firms can retain old debt at lower rates while borrowing more and becoming riskier, the lenders of the old debt will lose wealth. Locking in current rates on existing bonds and recalculating the optimal debt ratio will allow for this wealth transfer.[18]

While it is conventional to leave the marginal tax rate unchanged as the debt ratio is increased, we adjust the tax rate to reflect the potential loss of the tax benefits of debt at higher debt ratios, where the interest expenses exceed the earnings before interest and taxes. To illustrate this point, note that the amount of earnings before interest and taxes at Boeing is $1,751 million. As long as interest expenses are less than $1,751 million, interest expenses remain fully tax deductible and earn the 35% tax benefit. For instance, at a 40% debt ratio, the interest expenses are $1,632 million and the tax benefit is therefore 35% of this amount. At a 50% debt ratio, however, the interest expenses balloon to $2,039 million, which is greater than the earnings before interest and taxes of $1,751 million. Considering the tax benefit on the interest expenses up to this amount:

$$\text{Tax benefit} = \$1,751 \text{ million} \times .35 = \$612.85 \text{ million}$$

As a proportion of the total interest expenses, the tax benefit is now less than 35%:

$$\text{Effective tax rate} = \$613/\$1,751 = 30.05\%$$

This, in turn, raises the after-tax cost of debt. This is a conservative approach, since losses can be carried forward. Given that this is a permanent shift in leverage, it does make sense to be conservative.

---

[17] If they do not have protective puts, it is in the best interests of the stockholders not to refinance the debt (as in the leveraged buyout of RJR Nabisco) if debt ratios are increased.

[18] This will have the effect of reducing interest cost when debt is increased, and thus interest coverage ratios. This will lead to higher ratings, at least in the short term, and a higher optimal debt ratio.

LEVERAGE AND COST OF CAPITAL

Now that we have estimated the cost of equity and the cost of debt at each debt level, we can compute Boeing's cost of capital. This is done for each debt level in the following table. The cost of capital, which is 9.79% when the firm is unlevered, decreases as the firm initially adds debt, reaches a minimum of 9.16% at 30% debt, and then starts to increase again.

Debt Ratio	Beta	Cost of Equity	Cost of Debt (After-Tax)	Cost of Capital
0%	0.87	9.79%	3.38%	9.79%
10%	0.93	10.14%	3.58%	9.48%
20%	1.01	10.57%	4.06%	9.27%
30%	1.11	11.13%	4.55%	9.16%
40%	1.25	11.87%	6.50%	9.72%
50%	1.48	13.15%	7.00%	10.07%
60%	1.88	15.35%	8.50%	11.24%
70%	2.56	19.06%	10.35%	12.97%
80%	3.83	26.09%	10.62%	13.72%
90%	7.67	47.18%	10.83%	14.47%

The optimal debt ratio is shown graphically in Figure 15.3.

To illustrate the robustness of this solution to alternative measures of levered betas, we reestimate the costs of debt, equity, and capital under the assumption that debt bears some market risk, and the results are summarized in the following table.

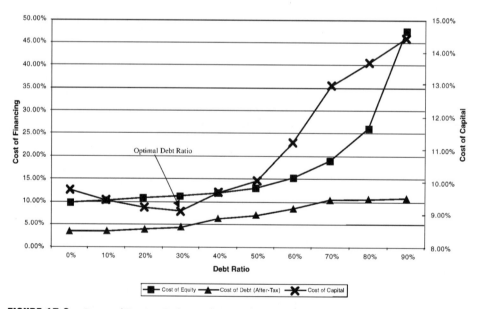

FIGURE 15.3 Costs of Equity, Debt, and Capital: Boeing
Source: Corporate Finance: Theory and Practice, Second Edition, by Aswath Damodaran, copyright © 2001 by John Wiley & Sons, Inc. This material is used by permission of John Wiley & Sons, Inc.

Debt Ratio	Beta	Cost of Equity	Beta of Debt	Bond Rating	Interest Rate on Debt	Tax Rate	Cost of Debt (After-Tax)	Cost of Capital
0%	0.89	9.92%	0.02	AAA	5.20%	35.00%	3.38%	9.92%
10%	0.96	10.26%	0.05	AA	5.50%	35.00%	3.58%	9.59%
20%	1.02	10.62%	0.11	A–	6.25%	35.00%	4.06%	9.31%
30%	1.10	11.04%	0.18	BB	7.00%	35.00%	4.55%	9.09%
40%	1.11	11.08%	0.45	CCC	10.00%	35.00%	6.50%	9.25%
50%	1.24	11.80%	0.45	CCC	10.00%	29.81%	7.02%	9.41%
60%	1.24	11.80%	0.68	C	12.50%	19.87%	10.02%	10.73%
70%	1.44	12.94%	0.68	C	12.50%	17.03%	10.37%	11.14%
80%	1.86	15.24%	0.68	C	12.50%	14.91%	10.64%	11.56%
90%	3.11	22.13%	0.68	C	12.50%	13.25%	10.84%	11.97%

If the debt holders bear some market risk,[19] the cost of equity is lower at higher levels of debt and Boeing's optimal debt ratio is still 30%, which is unchanged from the optimal calculated under the conventional calculation of the levered beta.

FIRM VALUE AND COST OF CAPITAL

The reason for minimizing the cost of capital is that it maximizes the value of the firm. To illustrate the effects of moving to the optimal on Boeing's firm value, we use the model described earlier in the chapter designed to value a firm in stable growth:

$$\text{Firm value} = \text{Expected FCFF}_{\text{next year}}/(\text{WACC} - g)$$

where g is the stable growth rate.

We begin by computing Boeing's current free cash flow using its current earnings before interest and taxes of $1,753 million, its tax rate of 35%, and its reinvestments in 1998 in working capital and net fixed assets:

EBIT(1 – Tax rate)	$1,138
+ Depreciation and amortization	$1,517
– Capital expenditures	$1,584
– Change in working capital	$ (105)
Free cash flow to the firm	$1,176

The market value of the firm at the time of this analysis was obtained by adding up the estimated market values of debt and equity:

Market value of equity	$32,595
+ Market value of debt	$ 8,194
= Value of the firm	$40,789

---

[19]To estimate the beta of debt, we used the default spread at each level of debt, and assumed that half this risk is market risk. Thus, at a C rating, the default spread is 9 percent. Based on the market risk premium of 5.5 percent and the risk-free rate of 5 percent that we used elsewhere, we estimated the beta at a C rating to be:

Imputed debt beta at a C rating = (9%/5.5%) × 0.5 = 0.68

Based on the current cost of capital of 9.17%, we solve for the implied growth rate:

Growth rate = (Firm value × Cost of capital − CF to firm)/(Firm value + CF to firm)
= (40,789 × .0917 − 1,176)/(40,789 + 1,176) = .0611 or 6.11%

Now assume that Boeing shifts to 30% debt and a WACC of 9.16%. The firm can now be valued using the following parameters:

Cash flow to firm = $1,176 million
WACC = 9.16%
Growth rate in cash flows to firm = 6.11%
Firm value = (1,176 × 1.0611)/(.0916 − .0611) = $40,990 million

The value of the firm[20] will increase from $40,789 million to $40,990 million if the firm moves to the optimal debt ratio:

Increase in firm value = $40,990 million − $ 40,789 million = $201 million

With 1,010.7 million shares outstanding, assuming that stockholders can evaluate the effect of this refinancing, we can calculate the increase in the stock price:

Increase in stock price = Increase in firm value/Number of shares outstanding
= $201/1,010.7 = $0.20

Since the current stock price is $32.25, the stock price can be expected to increase to $32.45, which translates into a 0.62% increase in the price. The change is negligible because the change in the cost of capital is small. The firm value and cost of capital at different debt ratios are summarized in Figure 15.4.

Since the asset side of the balance sheet is kept fixed and changes in capital structure are made by borrowing funds and repurchasing stock, this analysis implies that the stock price would increase to $32.45 on the announcement of the repurchase. Implicit in this analysis is the assumption that the increase in firm value will be spread evenly across both stockholders who sell their stock back to the firm and those who do not. To the extent that stock can be bought back at the current price of $32.25 or some value lower than $32.45, the change in stock price will be larger. For instance, if Boeing could have bought stock back at the existing price of $32.25, the increase in value per share would be $0.23.[21]

---

 captstr.xls: **This spreadsheet allows you to compute the optimal debt ratio firm value for any firm, using the same information used for Boeing. It has updated interest coverage ratios and default spreads built in.**

---

[20]This approach works best for firms with growth rates close to or below the growth rate of the economy, since this is a model that assumes perpetual growth. When this is not the case (i.e., when implied growth is much higher than 6 percent, we would suggest a modified approach, in which the present value of savings in firm value each year from going to the lower cost of capital is computed using a stable growth rate capped at about 6 percent. In the case of Boeing, this calculation would have yielded the following:

Savings each year = $40,789(.0917 − .0916) = $6.14 million
Present value of savings = $6.14/(.0916 − .06) = $206 million
Increase in value per share = $206 million/1,010.7 = $0.20

[21]To compute this change in value per share, we first compute how many shares we would buy back with the additional debt taken on of $4.043 billion (debt at 30 percent optimal minus current debt) and the stock price of $32.25. We then divide the increase in firm value of $202 million by the remaining shares outstanding:

Change in stock price = $202 million/[1,010.7 − (4,043/32.25)] = $0.23 per share

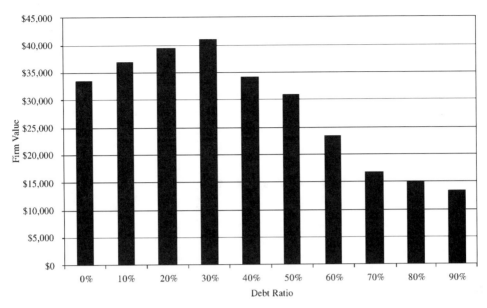

FIGURE 15.4   Debt Ratios and Firm Value

Source: Corporate Finance: Theory and Practice, Second Edition, by Aswath Damodaran, copyright © 2001 by John Wiley & Sons, Inc. This material is used by permission of John Wiley & Sons, Inc.

DEFAULT RISK, OPERATING INCOME, AND OPTIMAL LEVERAGE

The Boeing analysis just completed assumed that operating income would remain constant while the debt ratios changed. While this assumption simplifies the analysis substantially, it is not realistic. The operating income, for many firms, will drop as the default risk increases; this, in fact, is the cost we label as an indirect bankruptcy cost. The drop is likely to become more pronounced as the default risk falls below an acceptable level; for instance, a bond rating below investment grade may trigger significant losses in revenues and increases in expenses.

A general model for optimal capital structure would allow both operating income and cost of capital to change as the debt ratio changes. We have already described how we can estimate cost of capital at different debt ratios, but we could also attempt to do the same with operating income. For instance, we could estimate how the operating income for the Boeing would change as debt ratios and default risk changes by looking at the effects of rating downgrades on the operating income of other retailers.

If both operating income and cost of capital change, the optimal debt ratio may no longer be the point at which the cost of capital is minimized. Instead, the optimal has to be defined as that debt ratio at which the value of the firm is maximized.

ADJUSTED PRESENT VALUE AND FINANCIAL LEVERAGE

In the adjusted present value (APV) approach, we begin with the value of the firm without debt. As we add debt to the firm, we consider the net effect on value by considering both the benefits and the costs of borrowing. The value of the levered firm can then be estimated at different levels of the debt, and the debt level that maximizes firm value is the optimal debt ratio.

Steps in the Adjusted Present Value Approach

The unlevered firm value is not a function of expected leverage and can be estimated as described in the earlier section—by discounting the free cash flows to the firm at the unlevered cost of equity. In fact, if you do not want to estimate this value and take the market value of the firm as correct, you could back out the unlevered firm value by subtracting out the tax benefits and adding back the expected bankruptcy cost from the existing debt.

Current firm value = Value of unlevered firm + Present value of tax benefits
− Expected bankruptcy cost

Value of unlevered firm = Current firm value − Present value of tax benefits
+ Expected bankruptcy cost

The only components that change as a firm changes its leverage are the expected tax benefits and the expected bankruptcy costs. To obtain these values as you change leverage, you would go through the following five steps:

1. *Estimate the dollar debt outstanding at each debt ratio.* This process mirrors what was done in the cost of capital approach. Keeping firm value fixed, consider how much debt the firm will have at 20 percent debt, 30 percent debt, and so on.
2. *Estimate the tax benefits of debt by multiplying the dollar debt by the tax rate.* This essentially assumes that the debt is permanent and that the tax benefits will continue in perpetuity.
3. *Estimate the rating, interest rate, and interest expense at each debt ratio.* This process again replicates what was done in the cost of capital approach.
4. *Use the rating to estimate a probability of default.* Note that Table 15.2 provides these probabilities for each rating.
5. *Estimate the expected bankruptcy cost* by multiplying the probability of bankruptcy by the bankruptcy cost, stated as a percent of unlevered firm value.

We compute the value of the levered firm at different levels of debt. The debt level that maximizes the value of the levered firm is the optimal debt ratio.

ILLUSTRATION 15.8: Using the Adjusted Present Value Approach to Calculate Optimal Debt Ratio for Boeing in 1999

This approach can be applied to estimating the optimal capital structure for Boeing. The first step is to estimate the value of the unlevered firm. To do so, we start with the firm value of Boeing in 1999 and net the effect of the tax savings and bankruptcy costs arising from the existing debt.

$$\text{Value of Boeing in 1999} = \text{Value of equity} + \text{Value of debt}$$
$$= \$32,595 + \$8,194 = \$40,789$$

We compute the present value of the tax savings from the existing debt, assuming that the interest payments on the debt constitute a perpetuity.

$$\text{PV of tax savings from existing debt} = \text{Existing debt} \times \text{Tax rate}$$
$$= \$8,194 \times 0.35 = \$2,868 \text{ million}$$

Based on Boeing's current rating of AA, we estimate a probability of bankruptcy of 0.28% from Table 15.2. The bankruptcy cost is assumed to be 30% of the unlevered firm value.[22] The cost is high because the perception of default risk is likely to be very damaging for a firm like Boeing, whose customers depend on it for long-term service and support, and whose sales contracts are often spread out over a decade or more.

$$\text{Present value of expected bankruptcy cost} = \text{Probability of default} \times \text{Bankruptcy cost}$$
$$= 0.28\% \times [0.30 \times (40,789 - 2,868)] = \$32$$

We then compute the value of Boeing as an unlevered firm.

$$\text{Value of Boeing as unlevered firm} = \text{Current market value} - \text{PV of tax savings}$$
$$+ \text{Expected bankruptcy cost}$$
$$= \$40,789 - \$2,868 + \$32 = \$37,953 \text{ million}$$

The next step in the process is to estimate the tax savings at different levels of debt in the following table. While we use the standard approach of assuming that the present value is calculated over a perpetuity, we reduce the tax rate used in the calculation, if interest expenses exceed the earnings before interest and taxes. The adjustment to the tax rate was described more fully earlier in the cost of capital approach.

Debt Ratio	$ Debt	Tax Rate	Tax Benefits
0%	$ 0	35.00%	$ 0
10%	$ 4,079	35.00%	$1,428
20%	$ 8,158	35.00%	$2,855
30%	$12,237	35.00%	$4,283
40%	$16,316	35.00%	$5,710
50%	$20,394	30.05%	$6,128
60%	$24,473	22.76%	$5,571
70%	$28,552	17.17%	$4,903
80%	$32,631	15.02%	$4,903
90%	$36,710	13.36%	$4,903

---

[22]This estimate is based on the Warner study, which estimates bankruptcy costs for large companies to be 15 percent of the value, and on the qualitative analysis of indirect bankruptcy costs in Shapiro and Cornell.

The final step in the process is to estimate the expected bankruptcy cost, based on the bond ratings, the probabilities of default, and the assumption that the bankruptcy cost is 30% of unlevered firm value. The following table summarizes these probabilities and the expected bankruptcy cost, computed based on the unlevered firm value.

Debt Ratio	Bond Rating	Probability of Default	Expected Bankruptcy Cost
0%	AA	0.28%	$ 32
10%	AA	0.28%	$ 32
20%	A–	1.41%	$ 161
30%	BB	12.20%	$1,389
40%	CCC	50.00%	$5,693
50%	CCC	50.00%	$5,693
60%	CC	65.00%	$7,401
70%	C	80.00%	$9,109
80%	C	80.00%	$9,109
90%	C	80.00%	$9,109

The value of the levered firm is estimated in the following table by aggregating the effects of the tax savings and the expected bankruptcy costs:

Debt Ratio	Unlevered Firm Value	Tax Benefits	Expected Bankruptcy Cost	Value of Levered Firm
0%	$37,953	$ 0	$ 32	$37,921
10%	$37,953	$1,428	$ 32	$39,349
20%	$37,953	$2,855	$ 161	$40,648
30%	$37,953	$4,283	$1,389	$40,847
40%	$37,953	$5,710	$5,693	$37,970
50%	$37,953	$6,128	$5,693	$38,388
60%	$37,953	$5,571	$7,401	$36,123
70%	$37,953	$4,903	$9,109	$33,747
80%	$37,953	$4,903	$9,109	$33,747
90%	$37,953	$4,903	$9,109	$33,747

The firm value is optimized at between 20% and 30% debt, which is consistent with the results of the cost of capital approach. These results are, however, very sensitive to both the estimate of bankruptcy cost as a percent of firm value and the probabilities of default.

 apv.xls: This spreadsheet allows you to compute the value of a firm, with leverage, using the adjusted present value approach.

Benefits and Limitations of the Adjusted Present Value Approach

The advantage of the APV approach is that it separates the effects of debt into different components and allows the analyst to use different discount rates for each component. In addition, we do not assume that the debt ratio stays unchanged forever, which is an implicit assumption in the cost of capital approach. Instead, we have the flexibility to keep the dollar value of debt fixed and to calculate the benefits and costs of the fixed dollar debt.

VALUING THE PIECES RATHER THAN THE WHOLE

The adjusted present value model values debt separately from the operating assets, and firm value is the sum of the two components. In fact, one of the biggest benefits of discounted cash flow valuation is that breaking up cash flows into individual components and valuing them separately should not change the value. Thus, you could value a firm like General Electric (GE) by valuing each of its divisions separately and adding them up, or Coca-Cola by valuing its operations in each country separately and summing those up.

The advantage of piecewise valuation is that you can estimate cash flows and discount rates separately for each piece and thus get more precise estimates of value. For example, you would use very different assumptions about operating margins, reinvestment needs, and costs of capital when valuing the appliance and aircraft engine divisions of GE. Similarly, you could apply different country risk premiums for each country that Coca-Cola operates in to value the firm. Since this is always the case, you might ask why we do not do this for all firms. The problem is with the information. Many firms do not break down their earnings and cash flows in sufficient detail to allow for piecewise valuation. Even firms that do, like GE, often have large centralized expenses that get allocated, often arbitrarily, to individual divisions.

The benefits of breaking a firm down into pieces clearly increase as a firm becomes more diverse in its operations. These benefits have to be weighed against the costs associated with more imprecise information and greater estimation problems.

These advantages have to be weighed against the difficulty of estimating probabilities of default and the cost of bankruptcy. In fact, many analyses that use the adjusted present value approach ignore the expected bankruptcy costs, leading them to the conclusion that firm value increases as firms borrow money. Not surprisingly, this will yield the conclusion that the optimal debt ratio for a firm is 100 percent debt.

In general, with the same assumptions, the APV and the cost of capital conclusions give identical answers. However, the APV approach is more practical when firms are evaluating a dollar amount of debt, while the cost of capital approach is easier when firms are analyzing debt proportions.[23]

CONCLUSION

This chapter develops an alternative approach to discounted cash flow valuation. The cash flows to the firm are discounted at the weighted average cost of capital to obtain the value of the firm, which when reduced by the market value

---

[23]See Inselbag and Kaufold (1997).

of outstanding debt yields the value of equity. Since the cash flow to the firm is a cash flow prior to debt payments, this approach is more straightforward to use when there is significant leverage or when leverage changes over time, though the weighted average cost of capital, used to discount free cash flows to the firm, has to be adjusted for changes in leverage. Finally, the costs of capital can be estimated at different debt ratios and used to estimate the optimal debt ratio for a firm.

The alternative approach to firm valuation is the APV approach, where the effect on value of debt (tax benefits minus bankruptcy costs) is added to the unlevered firm value. This approach can also be used to estimate the optimal debt ratio for the firm.

QUESTIONS AND SHORT PROBLEMS

1. Respond true or false to the following statements about the free cash flow to the firm:
    a. The free cash flow to the firm is always higher than the free cash flow to equity.
       True _____ False _____
    b. The free cash flow to the firm is the cumulated cash flow to all investors in the firm, though the form of their claims may be different.
       True _____ False _____
    c. The free cash flow to the firm is a predebt, pretax cash flow.
       True _____ False _____
    d. The free cash flow to the firm is an after-debt, after-tax cash flow.
       True _____ False _____
    e. The free cash flow to the firm cannot be estimated for a firm with debt without knowing interest and principal payments.
       True _____ False _____
2. Union Pacific Railroad reported net income of $770 million in 1993 after interest expenses of $320 million. (The corporate tax rate was 36%.) It reported depreciation of $960 million in that year, and capital spending was $1.2 billion. The firm also had $4 billion in debt outstanding on the books, rated AA (carrying a yield to maturity of 8%) and trading at par (up from $3.8 billion at the end of 1992). The beta of the stock was 1.05, and there were 200 million shares outstanding (trading at $60 per share), with a book value of $5 billion. Union Pacific's working capital requirements were negligible. (The Treasury bond rate was 7%, and the risk premium was 5.5%.)
    a. Estimate the free cash flow to the firm in 1993.
    b. Estimate the value of the firm at the end of 1993.
    c. Estimate the value of equity at the end of 1993, and the value per share, using the FCFF approach.
3. Lockheed Corporation, one of the largest defense contractors in the United States, reported EBITDA of $1,290 million in 1993, prior to interest expenses of $215 million and depreciation charges of $400 million. Capital expenditures in 1993 amounted to $450 million, and working capital was 7% of revenues (which were $13,500 million). The firm had debt outstanding of $3.068 billion

(in book value terms), trading at a market value of $3.2 billion and yielding a pretax interest rate of 8%. There were 62 million shares outstanding, trading at $64 per share, and the most recent beta was 1.10. The tax rate for the firm was 40%. (The Treasury bond rate was 7%, and the risk premium was 5.5%.)

The firm expected revenues, earnings, capital expenditures and depreciation to grow at 9.5% a year from 1994 to 1998, after which the growth rate was expected to drop to 4%. (Capital spending will be 120% of depreciation in the steady state period.) The company also planned to lower its debt/equity ratio to 50% for the steady state (which will result in the pretax interest rate dropping to 7.5%).

a. Estimate the value of the firm.

b. Estimate the value of the equity in the firm, and the value per share.

4. In the face of disappointing earnings results and increasingly assertive institutional stockholders, Eastman Kodak was considering a major restructuring in 1993. As part of this restructuring, it was considering the sale of its health division, which earned $560 million in earnings before interest and taxes in 1993, on revenues of $5.285 billion. The expected growth in earnings was expected to moderate to 6% between 1994 and 1998, and to 4% after that. Capital expenditures in the health division amounted to $420 million in 1993, while depreciation was $350 million. Both were expected to grow 4% a year in the long term. Working capital requirements were negligible.

The average beta of firms competing with Eastman Kodak's health division was 1.15. While Eastman Kodak had a debt ratio [D/(D + E)] of 50%, the health division could sustain a debt ratio [D/(D + E)] of only 20%, which was similar to the average debt ratio of firms competing in the health sector. At this level of debt, the health division could expect to pay 7.5% on its debt, before taxes. (The tax rate is 40%, the Treasury bond rate is 7%, and the risk premium is 5.5%.)

a. Estimate the cost of capital for the division.

b. Estimate the value of the division.

c. Why might an acquirer pay more than this estimated value for the division?

5. You are analyzing a valuation done on a stable firm by a well-known analyst. Based on the expected free cash flow to firm next year of $30 million and an expected growth rate of 5%, the analyst has estimated a value of $750 million. However, he has made the mistake of using the book values of debt and equity in his calculation. While you do not know the book value weights he used, you know that the firm has a cost of equity of 12% and an after-tax cost of debt of 6%. You also know that the market value of equity is three times the book value of equity, while the market value of debt is equal to the book value of debt. Estimate the correct value for the firm.

6. Santa Fe Pacific, a major rail operator with diversified operations, had earnings before interest, taxes, and depreciation of $637 million in 1993, with depreciation amounting to $235 million (offset by capital expenditure of an equivalent amount). The firm was in steady state and expected to grow 6% a year in perpetuity. Santa Fe Pacific had a beta of 1.25 in 1993, and debt outstanding of $1.34 billion. The stock price was $18.25 at the end of 1993, and there were 183.1 million shares outstanding. The expected ratings and the costs of debt at different levels of debt for Santa Fe are shown in the following table:

D/(D + E)	Rating	Cost of Debt (Pretax)
0%	AAA	6.23%
10%	AAA	6.23%
20%	A+	6.93%
30%	A–	7.43%
40%	BB	8.43%
50%	B+	8.93%
60%	B–	10.93%
70%	CCC	11.93%
80%	CCC	11.93%
90%	CC	13.43%

The earnings before interest and taxes were expected to grow 3% a year in perpetuity, with capital expenditures offset by depreciation. (The tax rate is 40%, and the Treasury bond rate is 7% and the market risk premium is 5.5%.)

a. Estimate the cost of capital at the current debt ratio.

b. Estimate the costs of capital at debt ratios ranging from 0% to 90%.

c. Estimate the value of the firm at debt ratios ranging from 0% to 90%.

7. You have been asked to estimate the value of Cavanaugh Motels, a motel chain. The firm reported earnings of $200 million before interest and taxes in the most recent year and paid 40% of its taxable income in taxes. The book value of capital at the firm is $1.2 billion, and the firm expects to grow 4% a year in perpetuity. The firm has a beta of 1.2, a pretax cost of debt of 6%, equity with a market value of $1 billion, and debt with a market value of $500 million. (The risk-free rate is 5%, and the market risk premium is 5.5%.)

a. Estimate the value of the firm, using the cost of capital approach.

b. If you were told the probability of default at this firm at its current debt level is 10% and that the cost of bankruptcy is 25% of unlevered firm value, estimate the value of the firm using the adjusted present value approach.

c. How would you reconcile the two estimates of value?

8. Bethlehem Steel, one of the oldest and largest steel companies in the United States, is considering the question of whether it has any excess debt capacity. The firm has $527 million in market value of debt outstanding and $1.76 billion in market value of equity. The firm has earnings before interest and taxes of $131 million, and faces a corporate tax rate of 36%. The company's bonds are rated BBB, and the cost of debt is 8%. At this rating, the firm has a probability of default of 2.3%, and the cost of bankruptcy is expected to be 30% of firm value.

a. Estimate the unlevered value of the firm from the current market value of the firm.

b. Estimate the levered value of the firm, using the adjusted present value approach, at a debt ratio of 50%. At that debt ratio, the firm's bond rating will be CCC, and the probability of default will increase to 46.61% of unlevered firm value.

CHAPTER 16

Estimating Equity Value per Share

Chapter 15 considered how best to estimate the value of the operating assets of the firm. To get from that value to the firm value, you have to consider the value of cash, marketable securities, and other nonoperating assets held by a firm. In particular, you have to value holdings in other firms and deal with a variety of accounting techniques used to record such holdings. To get from firm value to equity value, you have to determine what should be subtracted from firm value (i.e., the value of the nonequity claims in the firm).

Once you have valued the equity in a firm, it may appear to be a relatively simple exercise to estimate the value per share. It seems that all you need to do is divide the value of the equity by the number of shares outstanding. But, in the case of some firms, even this simple exercise can become complicated by the presence of management and employee options. This chapter discusses the magnitude of this option overhang on valuation and then consider ways of incorporating the effect into the value per share.

VALUE OF NONOPERATING ASSETS

Firms have a number of assets on their books that can be categorized as nonoperating assets. The first and most obvious one is cash and near-cash investments—investments in riskless or very low-risk investments that most companies with large cash balances make. The second is investments in equities and bonds of other firms, sometimes for investment reasons and sometimes for strategic ones. The third is holdings in other firms, private and public, which are categorized in a variety of ways by accountants. Finally, there are assets that firms own that do not generate cash flows but nevertheless could have value—say, undeveloped land in New York City or Tokyo.

Cash and Near-Cash Investments

Investments in short-term government securities or commercial paper, which can be converted into cash quickly and with very low cost, are considered near-cash investments. This section considers how best to deal with these investments in valuation.

Operating Cash Requirements   If a firm needs cash for its operations—an operating cash balance—and this cash does not earn a fair market return you should consider such cash part of working capital requirements rather than as a source of additional value. Any cash and near-cash investments that exceed the operating cash requirements can be then added to the value of operating assets. How much cash does a firm need for its operations? The answer depends on both the firm and the economy in which the firm operates. A small retail firm in an emerging market, where cash transactions are more common than credit card transactions, may require an operating cash balance that is substantial. In contrast, a manufacturing firm in a developed market may not need any operating cash. If the cash held by a firm is interest-bearing and the interest earned on the cash reflects a fair rate of return,[1] you would not consider that cash to be part of working capital. Instead, you would add it to the value of operating assets to value the firm.

Dealing with Nonoperating Cash Holdings   There are two ways in which we can deal with cash and marketable securities in valuation. One is to lump them in with the operating assets and value the firm (or equity) as a whole. The other is to value the operating assets and the cash and marketable securities separately.

Consolidated Valuation   Is it possible to consider cash as part of the total assets of the firm, and to value it on a consolidated basis? The answer is yes, and it is, in a sense, what we do when we forecast the total net income for a firm and estimate dividends and free cash flows to equity from those forecasts. The net income will then include income from investments in government securities, corporate bonds, and equity investments. While this approach has the advantage of simplicity and can be used when financial investments comprise a small percent of the total assets, it becomes much more difficult to use when financial investments represent a larger proportion of total assets for two reasons:

First, the cost of equity or capital used to discount the cash flows has to be adjusted on an ongoing basis for the cash. In specific terms, you would need to use an unlevered beta that represents a weighted average of the unlevered beta for the operating assets of the firm and the unlevered beta for the cash and marketable securities. For instance, the unlevered beta for a steel company where cash represents 10 percent of the value would be a weighted average of the unlevered beta for steel companies and the beta of cash (which is usually zero). If the 10 percent were invested in riskier securities, you would need to adjust the beta accordingly. While this can be done if you use bottom-up betas, you can see that it would be much more difficult to do if you obtain a beta from a regression.[2]

Second, as the firm grows, the proportion of income that is derived from operating assets is likely to change. When this occurs, you have to adjust the inputs to the valuation model—cash flows, growth rates, and discount rates—to maintain consistency.

What will happen if you do not make these adjustments? You will tend to misvalue the financial assets. To see why, assume that you were valuing the aforementioned steel company with 10 percent of its value coming from cash. This cash is invested in government securities and earns an appropriate rate—say 5 percent. If

---

[1]Note that if the cash is invested in riskless assets such as Treasury bills, the riskless rate is a fair rate of return.

[2]The unlevered beta that you can back out of a regression beta reflects the average cash balance (as a percent of firm value) over the period of the regression. Thus, if a firm maintains this ratio at a constant level, you might be able to arrive at the correct unlevered beta.

this income is added on to the other income of the firm and discounted back at a cost of equity appropriate for a steel company—say 11 percent—the value of the cash will be discounted. A billion dollars in cash will be valued at $800 million, for instance, because the discount rate used is incorrect.

Separate Valuation It is safer to separate cash and marketable securities from operating assets and to value them individually. We do this almost always when we use the firm valuation approaches described in the preceding chapter. This is because we use operating income to estimate free cash flows to the firm, and operating income generally does not include income from financial assets. If, however, this is not the case and some of the investment income has found its way into the operating income, you would need to back it out before you did the valuation. Once you value the operating assets, you can add the value of the cash and marketable securities to it to arrive at firm value.

Can this be done with the FCFE valuation models described in Chapter 14? While net income includes income from financial assets, we can still separate cash and marketable securities from operating assets if we wanted to. To do this, we would first back out the portion of the net income that represents the income from financial investments (interest on bonds, dividends on stock) and use this adjusted net income to estimate free cash flows to equity. These free cash flows to equity would be discounted back using a cost of equity that would be estimated using a beta that reflected only the operating assets. Once the equity in the operating assets has been valued, you could add the value of cash and marketable securities to it to estimate the total value of equity. In fact, we used this approach to value Coca-Cola in Chapter 14.

ILLUSTRATION 16.1: Consolidated versus Separate Valuation

To examine the effects of a cash balance on firm value, consider a firm with investments of $1,200 million in noncash assets and $200 million in cash. For simplicity, let us assume the following:

- The noncash assets have a beta of 1, and are expected to earn $120 million in net income each year in perpetuity, and there are no reinvestment needs.
- The cash is invested at the riskless rate, which we assume to be 4.5%.
- The market risk premium is assumed to be 5.5%.

Under these conditions, we can value the equity using both the consolidated and separate approaches.

Let us first consider the consolidated approach. Here, we will estimate a cost of equity for all of the assets (including cash) by computing a weighted average beta of the noncash and cash assets:

$$\text{Beta of the firm} = \text{Beta}_{\text{noncash assets}} \times \text{Weight}_{\text{noncash assets}} + \text{Beta}_{\text{cash assets}} \times \text{Weight}_{\text{cash assets}}$$
$$= 1.00 \times (1{,}200/1{,}400) + 0 \times (200/1{,}400) = 0.8571$$

$$\text{Cost of equity for the firm} = 4.5\% + 0.8571(5.5\%) = 9.21\%$$

$$\text{Expected earnings for the firm} = \text{Net income from operating assets} + \text{Interest income from cash}$$
$$= (120 + .045 \times 200) = \$129 \text{ million (which is also the FCFE since there are no reinvestment needs)}$$

$$\text{Value of the equity} = \text{FCFE/Cost of equity} = 129/.0921 = \$1{,}400 \text{ million}$$

The equity is worth $1,400 million.

Now, let us try to value them separately, beginning with the noncash investments:

$$\text{Cost of equity for noncash investments} = \text{Riskless rate} + \text{Beta} \times \text{Risk premium}$$
$$= 4.5\% + 1.00 \times 5.5\% = 10\%$$

$$\text{Expected earnings from operating assets} = \$120 \text{ million (which is the FCFE from these assets)}$$

$$\text{Value of noncash assets} = \text{Expected earnings/Cost of equity for noncash assets}$$
$$= 120/.10 = \$1{,}200 \text{ million}$$

To this we can add the value of the cash, which is $200 million, to get a value for the equity of $1,400 million.

To see the potential for problems with the consolidated approach, note that if you had discounted the total FCFE of $129 million at the cost of equity of 10% (which reflects only the operating assets) you would valued the firm at $1,290 million. The loss in value of $110 million can be traced to the mishandling of cash:

$$\text{Interest income from cash} = 4.5\% \times 200 = \$9 \text{ million}$$

If you discount the cash at 10%, you would value the cash at $90 million instead of the correct value of $200 million—hence the loss in value of $110 million.

Should You Ever Discount Cash? In Illustration 16.1, cash was reduced in value for the wrong reason—a riskless cash flow was discounted at a discount rate that reflects risky investments. However, there are two conditions under which you might legitimately apply a discount to a cash balance:

1. The cash held by a firm is invested at a rate that is lower than the market rate, given the riskiness of the investment.
2. The management is not trusted with the large cash balance because of its past track record on investments.

Cash Invested at Below-Market Rates The first and most obvious condition occurs when much or all the cash balance does not earn a market interest rate. If this is the case, holding too much cash will clearly reduce the firm's value. While most firms in the United States can invest in government bills and bonds with ease today, the options are much more limited for small businesses in the United States and for firms in many emerging markets. When this is the case, a large cash balance earning less than a fair return can destroy value over time.

ILLUSTRATION 16.2: Cash Invested at Below-Market Rates

Illustration 16.1 assumed that cash was invested at the riskless rate. Assume, instead, that the firm was able to earn only 3% on its cash balance, while the riskless rate is 4.5%. The estimated value of the cash kept in the firm would then be:

$$\text{Estimated value of cash invested at } 3\% = (.03 \times 200)/.045 = 133.33$$

The firm would have been worth only $1,333 million instead of $1,400 million. The cash returned to stockholders would have a value of $200 million. In this scenario, returning the cash to stockholders would yield them a surplus value of $66.67 million. In fact, liquidating any asset that has a return less than the required return would yield the same result, as long as the entire investment can be recovered on liquidation.[3]

---

[3]While this assumption is straightforward with cash, it is less so with real assets, where the liquidation value may reflect the poor earning power of the asset. Thus, the potential surplus from liquidation may not be as easily claimed.

Distrust of Management While making a large investment in low-risk or no-risk marketable securities by itself is value neutral, the burgeoning cash balance can tempt managers to accept large investments or make acquisitions even if these investments earn substandard returns. In some cases, managers may take these action to prevent the firm from becoming a takeover target.[4] To the extent that stockholders anticipate such substandard investments, the current value of the firm will reflect the cash at a discounted level. The discount is likely to be largest at firms with few investment opportunities and poor management, and there will be no discount in firms with significant investment opportunities and good management.

ILLUSTRATION 16.3: Discount for Poor Investments in the Future

---

Return now to the firm described in Illustration 16.1, where the cash is invested at the riskless rate of 4.5%. Normally, we would expect this firm to trade at a total value of $1,400 million. Assume, however, that the managers of this firm have a history of poor acquisitions and that the presence of a large cash balance increases the probability from 0% to 30% that they will try to acquire another firm. Further, assume that the market anticipates that they will overpay by $50 million on this acquisition. The cash will then be valued at $185 million, with the discount estimated as follows:

$$\text{Estimated discount on cash balance} = \Delta \, \text{Probability}_{acquisition} \times \text{Expected overpayment}_{acquisition}$$
$$= 0.30 \times \$50 \text{ million} = \$15 \text{ million}$$
$$\text{Value of cash} = \text{Cash balance} - \text{Estimated discount}$$
$$= \$200 \text{ million} - \$15 \text{ million} = \$185 \text{ million}$$

The firm will therefore be valued at $1,385 million instead of $1,400 million. The two factors that determine this discount—the incremental likelihood of a poor investment and the expected net present value of the investment—are likely to be based on investors' assessments of management quality.

Investments in Risky Securities

So far this chapter has looked at how to value cash and near-cash investments. In some cases, firms invest in risky securities, which can range from investment-grade bonds to high-yield bonds to publicly traded equity in other firms. This section examines the motivation, consequences, and accounting for such investments.

Reasons for Holding Risky Securities Why do firms invest in risky securities? Some firms do so for the allure of the higher returns they can expect to make investing in stocks and corporate bonds, relative to Treasury bills. In recent years, there has also been a trend for firms to take equity positions in other firms to further their strategic interests. Still other firms take equity positions in firms they view as undervalued by the market; and finally, investing in risky securities is part of doing business for banks, insurance companies, and other financial service companies.

---

[4]Firms with large cash balances are attractive targets, since the cash balance reduces the cost of making the acquisition.

To Make a Higher Return   Near-cash investments such as Treasury bills and commercial paper are liquid and have little or no risk, but they also earn low returns. When firms have substantial amounts invested in marketable securities, they can expect to earn considerably higher returns by investing in riskier securities. For instance, investing in corporate bonds will yield a higher interest rate than investing in Treasury bonds, and the rate will increase with the riskiness of the investment. Investing in stocks will provide an even higher expected return, though not necessarily a higher actual return, than investing in corporate bonds. Figure 16.1 summarizes returns on risky investments—corporate bonds, high-yield bonds, and equities—and compares them to the returns on near-cash investments between 1990 and 2000.

However, while investing in riskier investments may earn a higher return for the firm, it does not make the firm more valuable. In fact, using the same reasoning that we used to analyze near-cash investments, we can conclude that investing in riskier investments and earning a fair market return (which would reward the risk) has to be value neutral.

To Invest in Undervalued Securities   A good investment is one that earns a return greater than its required return. That principle, developed in the context of investments in projects and assets, applies just as strongly to financial investments. A firm that invests in undervalued stocks is accepting positive net present value investments, since the return it will make on these equity investments will exceed the cost of equity on these investments. Similarly, a firm that invests in underpriced corporate bonds will also earn an excess return and a positive net present value.

How likely is it that a firm will find undervalued stocks and bonds to invest in? It depends on how efficient markets are and how good the managers of the firm are at finding undervalued securities. In unique cases, a firm may be more adept at find-

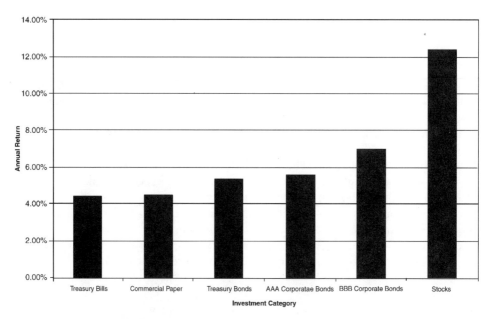

FIGURE 16.1   Returns on Investments—1990–2000

ing good investments in financial markets than it is at competing in product markets. Consider the case of Berkshire Hathaway, a firm that has been a vehicle for Warren Buffett's investing acumen over the past few decades. At the end of the second quarter of 1999, Berkshire Hathaway had $69 billion invested in securities of other firms. Among its holdings were investments of $12.4 billion in Coca-Cola, $6.6 billion in American Express, and $3.9 billion in Gillette. While Berkshire Hathaway also has real business interests, including ownership of a well-regarded insurance company (GEICO), investors in the firm get a significant portion of their value from the firm's passive equity investments.

Notwithstanding Berkshire Hathaway's success, most firms in the United States steer away from looking for bargains among financial investments. Part of the reason for this is their realization that it is difficult to find undervalued securities in financial markets. Part of the reluctance on the part of firms to make equity investments in other firms can be traced to a recognition that investors in firms like Procter & Gamble and Coca-Cola invest in these firms because of their competitive advantages in product markets (brand name, marketing skills, etc.) and not for their perceived skill at picking stocks.

Strategic Investments   During the 1990s, Microsoft accumulated a huge cash balance in excess of $20 billion. It used this cash to make a series of investments in the equity of software, entertainment, and Internet-related firms. It did so for several reasons.[5] First, doing so gave Microsoft a say in the products and services these firms were developing and preempted competitors from forming partnerships with the firms. Second, it allowed Microsoft to work on joint products with these firms. In 1998 alone, Microsoft announced investments in 14 firms, including ShareWave, General Magic, RoadRunner, and Qwest Communications. In an earlier investment in 1995, Microsoft invested in NBC to create the MSNBC network in order to give it a foothold in the television and entertainment business.

Can strategic investments be value enhancing? As with all investments, it depends on how much is invested and what the firm receives as benefits in return. If the side benefits and synergies that are touted in these investments exist, investing in the equity of other firms can earn much higher returns than the hurdle rate and can create value. It is clearly a much cheaper option than acquiring the entire equity of the firm.

Business Investments   Some firms hold marketable securities not as discretionary investments, but because it is the nature of their business. For instance, insurance companies and banks often invest in marketable securities in the course of their business, the former to cover expected liabilities on insurance claims and the latter in the course of trading. While these financial service firms have financial assets of substantial value on their balance sheets, these holdings are not comparable to those of the firms described so far. In fact, they are more akin to the raw material used by manufacturing firms than to discretionary financial investments.

---

[5]One of Microsoft's oddest investments was in one of its primary competitors, Apple Computer, early in 1998. The investment may have been intended to fight the antitrust suit brought against Microsoft by the Justice Department.

Dealing with Marketable Securities in Valuation   Marketable securities can include corporate bonds, with default risk embedded in them, and traded equities, which have even more risk associated with them. As the marketable securities held by a firm become more risky, the choices on how to deal with them become more complex. You have three ways of accounting for marketable securities:

1. The simplest and most direct approach is to estimate the current market value of these marketable securities and add the value to the value of operating assets. For firms valued on a going-concern basis, with a large number of holdings of marketable securities, this may be the only practical option.
2. The second approach is to estimate the current market value of the marketable securities and net out the effect of capital gains taxes that may be due if those securities were sold today. This capital gains tax bite depends on how much was paid for these assets at the time of the purchase and the value today. This is the best way of estimating value when valuing a firm on a liquidation basis or when the firm has provided a clear indication that it plans to sell its holdings.
3. The third and most difficult way of incorporating the value of marketable securities into firm value is to value the firms (using a discounted cash flow approach) that issued these securities and estimate the value of these securities. This approach tends to work best for firms that have relatively few, but large, holdings in other publicly traded firms.

ILLUSTRATION 16.4:   Microsoft's Cash and Marketable Securities

---

Over the past decade, Microsoft has accumulated a huge cash balance, largely as a consequence of holding back on free cash flows to equity that could have been paid to stockholders. In 1999 and 2000, for instance, the firm reported the following holdings of near-cash investments (in $millions):

	1999	2000
Cash and equivalents:		
Cash	$ 635	$ 849
Commercial paper	$ 3,805	$ 1,986
Certificates of deposit	$ 522	$ 1,017
U.S. government and agency securities	$ 0	$ 729
Corporate notes and bonds	$ 0	$ 265
Money market preferreds	$ 13	$ 0
Total cash and equivalents	$ 4,975	$ 4,846
Short-term investments:		
Commercial paper	$ 1,026	$ 612
U.S. government and agency securities	$ 3,592	$ 7,104
Corporate notes and bonds	$ 6,996	$ 9,473
Municipal securities	$ 247	$ 1,113
Certificates of deposit	$ 400	$ 650
Total short-term investments	$12,261	$18,952
Cash and short-term investments	*$17,236*	*$23,798*

When valuing Microsoft in 2000, we should clearly consider the $23.798 billion investment as part of the firm's value. The interesting question is whether there should be a discount reflecting investor's fears about poor investments in the future. Over its life, Microsoft has not been punished for holding on to cash, largely as a consequence of its impeccable track record in delivering ever-increasing profits on the one hand and high stock returns on the other. While 1999 and 2000 were not good years for the firm, investors will probably give the firm the benefit of the doubt at least for the near future. We would add the cash balance at face value to the value of Microsoft's operating assets.

The more interesting component is the $17.7 billion that Microsoft shows as investments in riskier securities in 2000. Microsoft reports the following information about these investments (in $millions):

	Cost Basis	Unrealized Gains	Unrealized Losses	Recorded Basis
Debt securities recorded at market:				
Within one year	$ 498	$ 27	$ 0	$ 525
Between 2 and 10 years	$ 388	$ 11	-$ 3	$ 396
Between 10 and 15 years	$ 774	$ 14	-$ 93	$ 695
Beyond 15 years	$ 4,745		-$ 933	$ 3,812
Total debt securities recorded at market	$ 6,406	$ 52	-$1,029	$ 5,429
Equities:				
Common stock and warrants	$ 5,815	$5,655	-$1,697	$ 9,773
Preferred stock	$ 2,319			$ 2,319
Other investments	$ 205		$ 205	
Total equities and other investments	$14,745	$5,707	-$2,726	$17,726

Microsoft has generated a paper profit of almost $3 billion on its original cost of $14.745 billion, and reports a current value of $17.726 billion. Most of these investments are traded in the market and are recorded at market value. The easiest way to deal with these investments is to add the market value to the value of the operating assets of the firm to arrive at firm value. The most volatile item is the investment in common stock of other firms. The value of these holdings has almost doubled, as reflected in the recorded basis of $9,773 million. Should we reflect this at current market value when we value Microsoft? The answer is generally yes. However, if these investments are overvalued, you risk building in this overvaluation into your valuation. The alternative is to value each of the equities that the firm has invested in, but this will become increasingly cumbersome as the number of equity holdings increases.

In summary, then, you would add the values of both the near-cash investments of $23.798 billion and the equity investments of $17.726 billion to the value of the operating assets of Microsoft.

Premiums or Discounts on Marketable Securities?   As a general rule, you should not attach a premium or discount for marketable securities. Thus, you would add the entire value of $17,726 million to the value of Microsoft. There is an exception to this rule, though, and it relates to firms that make it their business to buy and sell financial assets. These are the closed-end mutual funds, of which there are several hundred listed on the U.S. stock exchanges, and investment companies, such as Fidelity and T. Rowe Price. Closed-end mutual funds sell shares to investors and use the funds to invest in financial assets. The number of shares in a closed-end fund remains fixed, and the share price changes. Since the investments of a closed-end fund are in publicly traded securities, this sometimes creates a phenomenon where the market value of the shares in a closed-end fund is greater than or less than the market value of the securities owned by the fund. For these firms, it is appropriate to attach a discount or premium to the marketable securities to reflect their capacity to generate excess returns on these investments.

A closed-end mutual fund that consistently finds undervalued assets and delivers much higher returns than expected (given the risk) should be valued at a premium on the value of its marketable securities. The amount of the premium will depend on how large the excess return is and how long you would expect the firm to continue to make these excess returns. Conversely, a closed-end fund that delivers returns that are much lower than expected should trade at a discount on the value of the marketable securities held by the fund. The stockholders in this fund would clearly be better off if it were liquidated, but that may not be a viable option.

ILLUSTRATION 16.5:   Valuing a Closed-End Fund

The Pierce Regan Asia fund is a closed-end fund with investments in traded Asian stocks, valued at $4 billion at today's market prices. The fund has earned a return of 13% over the past 10 years, but based on the riskiness of its investments and the performance of the Asian market over the period, it should have earned 15%. Looking forward, your expected return for the Asian market for the future is 12%, but you anticipate that the Pierce Regan fund will continue to underperform the market by 2%.

To estimate the discount you would expect to see on the fund, let us begin by assuming that the fund will continue in perpetuity earning 2% less than the return on the market index. The discount would then be:

$$\text{Estimated discount} = \text{Excess return} \times \text{Fund value/Expected return on the market}$$
$$= (.10 - .12)(4,000)/.12 = \$667 \text{ million}$$

On a percent basis, the discount represents 16.67% of the market value of the investments.

If you assume that the fund will either be liquidated or begin earning the expected return at a point in time in the future—say 10 years from now—the expected discount will become smaller.

Holdings in Other Firms

In this category, we consider a broader category of nonoperating assets, where we look at holdings in other companies, public as well as private. We begin by looking at the differences in accounting treatment of different holdings and how this treatment can affect the way they are reported in financial statements.

Accounting Treatment   The way in which these assets are valued depends on the way the investment is categorized and the motive behind the investment. In general, an investment in the securities of another firm can be categorized as a minority passive investment. a minority active investment, or a majority active investment, and the accounting rules vary depending on the categorization.

Minority Passive Investments   If the securities or assets owned in another firm represent less than 20 percent of the overall ownership of that firm, an investment is treated as a minority passive investment. These investments have an acquisition value, which represents what the firm originally paid for the securities, and often a market value. Accounting principles require that these assets be subcategorized into one of three groups—investments that will be held to maturity, investments that are available for sale, and trading investments. The valuation principles vary for each.

- For investments that will be held to maturity, the valuation is at historical cost or book value, and interest or dividends from this investment are shown in the income statement.

- For investments that are available for sale, the valuation is at market value, but the unrealized gains or losses are shown as part of the equity in the balance sheet and not in the income statement. Thus, unrealized losses reduce the book value of the equity in the firm, and unrealized gains increase the book value of equity.
- For trading investments, the valuation is at market value, and the unrealized gains and losses are shown in the income statement.

Firms are allowed an element of discretion in the way they classify investments and through this choice in the way they value these assets. This classification ensures that firms such as investment banks, whose assets are primarily securities held in other firms for purposes of trading, revalue the bulk of these assets at market levels each period. This is called marking to market, and provides one of the few instances in which market value trumps book value in accounting statements.

Minority Active Investments   If the securities or assets owned in another firm represent between 20 percent and 50 percent of the overall ownership of that firm, an investment is treated as a minority active investment. While these investments have an initial acquisition value, a proportional share (based on ownership proportion) of the net income and losses made by the firm in which the investment was made, is used to adjust the acquisition cost. In addition, the dividends received from the investment reduce the acquisition cost. This approach to valuing investments is called the equity approach.

The market value of these investments is not considered until the investment is liquidated, at which point the gain or loss from the sale relative to the adjusted acquisition cost is shown as part of the earnings in that period.

Majority Active Investments   If the securities or assets owned in another firm represent more than 50 percent of the overall ownership of that firm, an investment is treated as a majority active investment.[6] In this case, the investment is no longer shown as a financial investment but is instead replaced by the assets and liabilities of the firm in which the investment was made. This approach leads to a consolidation of the balance sheets of the two firms, where the assets and liabilities of the two firms are merged and presented as one balance sheet. The share of the firm that is owned by other investors is shown as a minority interest on the liability side of the balance sheet. A similar consolidation occurs in the other financial statements of the firm as well, with the statement of cash flows reflecting the cumulated cash inflows and outflows of the combined firm. This is in contrast to the equity approach, used for minority active investments, in which only the dividends received on the investment are shown as a cash inflow in the cash flow statement.

Here again, the market value of this investment is not considered until the ownership stake is liquidated. At that point, the difference between the market price and the net value of the equity stake in the firm is treated as a gain or loss for the period.

---

[6]Firms have evaded the requirements of consolidation by keeping their share of ownership in other firms below 50 percent.

Valuing Cross Holdings in Other Firms Given that the holdings in other firms can be accounted for in three different ways, how do you deal with each in valuation? The best way to deal with each of them is exactly the same. You would value the equity in each holding separately, and estimate the value of the proportional holding. This value would then be added to the value of the equity of the parent company. Thus, to value a firm with minority holdings in three other firms, you would value the equity in each of these firms, take the percent share of the equity in each, and add it to the value of equity in the parent company.

When income statements are consolidated, you would first need to strip the income, assets, and debt of the subsidiary from the parent company's financials before you do any of the above. If you do not do so, you will double count the value of the subsidiary.

Why, you might ask, do we not value the consolidated firm? You could, and in some cases, because of the absence of information, you might have to. The reason we would suggest separate valuations is because the parent and the subsidiaries may have very different characteristics—costs of capital, growth rates, and reinvestment rates. Valuing the combined firm under these circumstances may yield misleading results. There is another reason: Once you have valued the consolidated firm, you will have to subtract the portion of the equity in the subsidiary that the parent company does not own. If you have not valued the subsidiary separately, it is not clear how you would do this. Note that the conventional practice of netting out the minority interest does not accomplish this, because minority interest reflects book rather than market value.

As a firm's holdings become more numerous, estimating the values of the holdings will become more onerous. If the holdings are publicly traded, substituting the market values of the holdings for estimated value is an alternative worth exploring. While you risk building into your valuation any mistakes the market might be making in valuing these holdings, this approach is more time efficient.

ESTIMATING THE VALUE OF HOLDINGS IN PRIVATE COMPANIES

When a publicly traded firm has a cross holding in a private company, it is often difficult to obtain information on the private company and to value it. Consequently, you might have to make your best estimate of how much this holding is worth based on the limited information that you have available. One way to do this is to estimate the multiple of book value at which firms in the same business (as the private business in which you have holdings) typically trade at and apply this multiple to the book value of the holding in the private business. Assume, for instance, that you are trying to estimate the value of the holdings of a pharmaceutical firm in five privately held biotechnology firms, and that these holdings collectively have a book value of $50 million. If biotechnology firms typically trade at 10 times book value, the estimated market value of these holdings would be $500 million.

In fact, this approach can be generalized to estimate the value of complex holdings where you lack the information to estimate the value for each holding or there are too many such holdings. For example, you could be valuing a Japanese firm with dozens of cross holdings. You could estimate a value for the cross holdings by applying a multiple of book value to their cumulative book value.

ILLUSTRATION 16.6: Valuing Holdings in Other Companies

Segovia Entertainment operates in a wide range of entertainment businesses. The firm reported $300 million in operating income (EBIT) on capital invested of $1,500 million in the current year; the total debt outstanding is $500 million. A portion of the operating income ($100 million), capital invested ($400 million), and debt outstanding ($150 million) represent Segovia's holdings in Seville Television, a television station owner. Segovia owns only 51% of Seville, but Seville's financials are consolidated with those of Segovia.[7] In addition, Segovia owns 15% of LatinWorks, a record and CD company. These holdings have been categorized as minority passive investments, and the dividends from the investments are shown as part of Segovia's net income but not as part of its operating income. Latin-Works reported operating income of $80 million on capital invested of $250 million in the current year; the firm has $100 million in debt outstanding. We will assume the following:

- The cost of capital for Segovia Entertainment, without considering its holdings in either Seville or LatinWorks, is 10%. The firm is in stable growth, with operating income (again not counting the holdings) growing 5% a year in perpetuity.
- Seville Television has a cost of capital of 9% and is in stable growth, with operating income growing 5% a year in perpetuity.
- LatinWorks has a cost of capital of 12% and is in stable growth, with operating income growing 4.5% a year in perpetuity.
- None of the firms has a significant balance of cash and marketable securities.
- The tax rate for all of these firms is 40%.

We can value Segovia Entertainment in three steps:

STEP 1: Value the equity in the operating assets of Segovia without counting any of the holdings. To do this, we first have to cleanse the operating income of the consolidation:

Operating income from Segovia's operating assets = Consolidated income − Income from Seville = $300 − $100 = $200 million

Capital invested in Segovia's operating assets = Consolidated capital − Capital from Seville = $1,500 − $400 = $1,100 million

Debt in Segovia's operating assets = Consolidated debt − Debt from Seville = $500 − $150 = $350 million

Return on capital invested in Segovia's operating assets = 200(1 − .4)/1,100 = 10.91%

Reinvestment rate = g/ROC = 5%/10.91% = 45.83%

Value of Segovia's operating assets = EBIT(1 − t)(1 − Reinvestment rate)(1 + g)/(Cost of capital − g) = 200(1 − .4)(1 − .4583)(1.05)/(.10 − .05) = $1,365 million

Value of equity in Segovia's operating assets = Value of operating assets − Value of Segovia's debt = 1,365 − 350 = $1,015 million

STEP 2: Value the 51% of equity in Seville Enterprises:

Operating income from Seville's operating assets = $100 million

Capital invested in Seville's operating assets = $400 million

Debt invested in Seville = $150 million

Return on capital invested in Seville's operating assets = 100(1 − .4)/400 = 15%

Reinvestment rate = g/ROC = 5%/15% = 33.33%

Value of Seville's operating assets = EBIT(1 − t)(1 − Reinvestment rate)(1 + g)/(Cost of capital − g) = 100(1 − .4)(1 − .3333)(1.05)/(.09 − .05) = $1,050 million

---

[7]Consolidation in the U.S. requires that you consider 100 percent of the subsidiary, even if you own less. There are other markets in the world where consolidation requires only that you consider the portion of the firm that you own.

Value of Seville's equity = Value of operating assets − Debt = 1,050 − 150 = $900 million

Value of Segovia's equity stake in Seville = .51(900) = $459 million

STEP 3: Value the 15% stake in LatinWorks:

Operating income from LatinWorks' operating assets = $75 million

Capital invested in LatinWorks' operating assets = $250 million

Return on capital invested in LatinWorks' operating assets = 75(1 − .4)/250 = 18%

Reinvestment rate = g/ROC = 4.5%/18% = 25%

Value of LatinWorks' operating assets = EBIT(1 − t)(1 − Reinvestment rate)(1 + g)/(Cost of capital − g) = 75(1 − .4)(1 − .25)(1.045)/(.12 − .045) = $470.25 million

Value of LatinWorks' equity = Value of operating assets − Debt = 470.25 − 100 = $370.25 million

Value of Segovia's equity stake in LatinWorks = .15(370.25) = $55 million

The value of Segovia as a firm can now be computed (assuming that it has no cash balance):

Value of equity in Segovia = Value of equity in Segovia + 51% of equity in Seville
+ 15% of equity in LatinWorks
= $1,015 + $459 + $55 = $1,529 million

To provide a contrast, consider what would have happened if we had used the consolidated income statement and Segovia's cost of capital to do this valuation. We would have valued Segovia and Seville together as follows:

Operating income from Segovia's consolidated assets = $300 million

Capital invested in Segovia's consolidated assets = $1,500 million

Consolidated debt = $500 million

Return on capital invested in Segovia's operating assets = 300(1 − .4)/1,500 = 12%

Reinvestment rate = g/ROC = 5%/12% = 41.67%

Value of Segovia's operating assets = EBIT(1 − t)(1 − Reinvestment rate)(1 + g)/(Cost of capital − g) = 300(1 − .4)(1 − .4167)(1.05)/(.10 − .05) = $2,205 million

Value of equity in Segovia = Value of operating assets − Consolidated debt − Minority interests in Seville + Minority interest in LatinWorks = 2,205 − 500 − 122.5 + 22.5 = $1,605 million

Note that the minority interests in Seville are computed as 49% of the book value of equity at Seville.

Book value of equity in Seville = Capital invested in Seville − Seville's debt
= 400 − 150 = 250 million

Minority interest = (1 − Parent company holding)Book value of equity
= (1 − .51)250 = $122.5 million

The minority interests in LatinWorks are computed as 15% of the book value of equity in LatinWorks, which is $250 million (capital invested minus debt outstanding). It would be pure chance if this value were equal to the true value of equity, as first estimated, of $1,529 million.

You can see from the discussion that you need a substantial amount of information to value holdings correctly. This information may be difficult to come by when the holdings are in private companies.

VALUE OF TRANSPARENCY

The difficulty we often face in identifying and valuing holdings in other companies highlights a cost faced by firms that have complicated cross-holding structures and that make little or no effort to explain what they own to investors. In fact, many companies seem to adopt a strategy of making it difficult for their own stockholders to see what they own lest they be questioned about the wisdom of their choices. Not surprisingly, the market values of these firms often understate the value of these hidden holdings.

Many firms outside the United States use, as an excuse, the argument that the disclosure laws are not as strict in their countries as they are in the United States, but disclosure laws provide a floor for information that has to be revealed to markets and not a ceiling. For instance, InfoSys, an Indian software company, has one of the most informative financial reports of any company anywhere in the world. In fact, the firm has reaped substantial financial rewards because of its openness, as investors are better able to gauge how the firm is doing and tend to be much more willing to listen to management views.

So, what can undervalued firms with cross holdings do to improve their value? First, they can break down complicated holdings structures that impede understanding and valuation. Second, they can adopt a strategy of revealing as much as they can to investors about their holdings—private as well as public. Third, they need to stick with this strategy when they have bad news to report. A firm that is generous with positive information and stingy with negative information will rapidly lose credibility as an information source. Finally, if all else fails, they can consider divesting or spinning off their holdings.

Other Nonoperating Assets

Firms can have other nonoperating assets, but they are likely to be of less importance than those listed in the previous section. In particular, firms can have unutilized assets that do not generate cash flows and have book values that bear little resemblance to market values. An example would be prime real estate holdings that have appreciated significantly in value since the firm acquired them but produce little if any cash flows. An open question also remains about overfunded pension plans. Do the excess funds belong to stockholders, and, if so, how do you incorporate the effect into value?

Unutilized Assets The strength of discounted cash flow models is that they estimate the value of assets based on expected cash flows that these assets generate. In some cases, however, this can lead to assets of substantial value being ignored in the final valuation. For instance, assume that a firm owns a plot of land that has not been developed, and that the book value of the land reflects its original acquisition price. The land obviously has significant market value but does not generate any cash flow for the firm yet. If a conscious effort is not made to bring the expected cash flows from developing the land into the valuation, the value of the land will be left out of the final estimate.

How do you reflect the value of such assets in firm value? An inventory of all such assets (or at least the most valuable ones) is a first step, followed up by estimates of market value for each of the assets. These estimates can be obtained by looking at what the assets would fetch in the market today or by projecting the cash flows that could be generated if the assets were developed and discounting the cash flows at the appropriate discount rate.

The problem with incorporating unutilized assets into firm value is an informational one. Firms do not reveal their unutilized assets as part of their financial statements. While it may sometimes be possible for investors and analysts to find out about such assets, it is far more likely that they will be uncovered only when you have access to information about what the firm owns and uses.

Pension Fund Assets   Firms with defined pension liabilities sometimes accumulate pension fund assets in excess of these liabilities. While the excess does belong to stockholders, they usually face a tax liability if they claim it. The conservative rule in dealing with overfunded pension plans would be to assume that the social and tax costs of reclaiming the excess funds are so large that few firms would ever even attempt to do it. The more realistic approach would be to add the after-tax portion of the excess funds into the valuation.

As an illustration, consider a firm that reports pension fund assets that exceed its liabilities by $1 billion. Since a firm that withdraws excess assets from a pension fund is taxed at 50% on these withdrawals (in the United States), you would add $500 million to the estimated value of the operating assets of the firm. This would reflect the 50% of the excess assets that the firm will be left with after paying the taxes.

---

 cash.xls: **This dataset on the Web summarizes the value of cash and marketable securities by industry group in the United States for the most recent quarter.**

FIRM VALUE AND EQUITY VALUE

Once you have estimates of the values of the operating assets, cash and marketable securities, and the other nonoperating assets owned by a firm, you can estimate the value of the firm as the sum of the three components. To get to the value of the equity from the firm value, you subtract out the nonequity claims on the firm. Nonequity claims would include debt and preferred stock, though the latter are often treated as equity in financial statements.

What Nonequity Claims Should Be Subtracted?

The general rule that you should use is that the debt you subtract from the value of the firm should be at least equal to the debt that you use to compute the cost of capital. Thus, if you decide to capitalize operating leases as debt, as we did with the Gap in the preceding chapter, to compute the cost of capital, you should subtract the debt value of operating leases from the value of operating assets to estimate the value of equity. If the firm you are valuing has preferred stock, you would use the market value of the stock (if it is traded) or estimate a market value (if it is not)[8] and deduct it from firm value to get to the value of common equity.

There may be other claims on the firm that do not show up in debt that you should subtract from firm value.

■ *Expected liabilities on lawsuits.* You could be analyzing a firm that is the defendant in a lawsuit, where it potentially could have to pay tens of millions of dollars in damages. You should estimate the probability that this will occur, and use this probability to estimate the expected liability. Thus, if there is a 10 percent chance that you could lose a case that you are defending, and the expected damage award is $1 billion, you would reduce the value of the firm by $100 million (probability × expected damages). If the expected liability is not anticipated until several years from now, you would compute the present value of the payment.

■ *Unfunded pension and health care obligations.* If a firm has significantly underfunded a pension or a health plan, it will need to set aside cash in future years to meet these obligations. While it would not be considered debt for cost of capital purposes, it should be subtracted from firm value to arrive at equity value.

■ *Deferred tax liability.* The deferred tax liability that shows up on the financial statements of many firms reflects the fact that firms often use tax-deferral strategies that reduce their taxes in the current year while increasing their taxes in future years. Of the three items listed here, this one is the least clearly defined, since it is not clear when or even whether the obligation will come due. Ignoring it may be foolhardy, though, since the firm could find itself making these tax payments in the future. The most sensible way of dealing with this item is to consider it an obligation, but one that will come due only when the firm's growth rate moderates. Thus, if you expect your firm to be in stable growth in 10 years, you would discount the deferred tax liability back 10 years and deduct this amount from firm value to get to equity value.

What about Future Claims?

As you forecast earnings growth for your firm, you generally also assume that the firm will increase its debt as it grows. A question that arises then is whether you should be subtracting the value of these future debt issues when estimating equity value today. The answer is no, since the value of the equity is a current value and these future claims do not exist today. To illustrate, assume that you have a firm with no debt today and that you assume that it will have a 30 percent debt ratio in stable growth. Assume further that your estimate of the terminal value for this firm is $10 billion in five years. You are implicitly assuming that your firm will borrow

---

[8]Estimating market value for preferred stock is relatively simple. Preferred stock generally is perpetual, and the estimated market value of the preferred stock is therefore:

$$\text{Value of preferred stock} = \text{Preferred dividend}/\text{Cost of preferred stock}$$

The cost of preferred stock should be higher than the pretax cost of debt, since debt has a prior claim on the cash flows and assets of the firm.

$3 billion in five years to raise its debt ratio to 30 percent. This higher debt ratio may affect your firm value today, but the value of equity today is the firm value less the current debt (which is zero).

MANAGEMENT AND EMPLOYEE OPTIONS

Firms use options to reward managers as well as other employees. There are two effects that these options have on value per share. One is created by options that have already been granted. These options, most of which have exercise prices well below the stock price, reduce the value of equity per share, since a portion of the existing equity in the firm has to be set aside to meet these eventual option exercises. The other is the likelihood that these firms will use options on a continuing basis to reward employees or to compensate them. These expected option grants reduce the portion of the expected future cash flows that accrue to existing stockholders.

Magnitude of the Option Overhang

The use of options in management compensation packages is not new to firms. Many firms in the 1970s and 1980s initiated option-based compensation packages to induce top managers to think like stockholders in their decision making. In most cases, though, the drain on value created by these options was small enough that it could be ignored without affecting the value per share substantially. In the past decade, however, the surge in both the number and the value of technology firms has highlighted the importance of dealing with these options in valuation.

What is different about technology firms? One is that management contracts at these firms are much more heavily weighted toward options than are those at other firms. The second is that the paucity of cash at these firms has meant that options are granted not just to top managers but to employees all through the organization, making the total option grants much larger. The third is that some of the smaller firms have used options to meet operating expenses and pay for supplies.

Figure 16.2 summarizes the number of options outstanding as a percent of outstanding stock at technology firms and compares them to options outstanding at nontechnology firms. As Figure 16.2 makes clear, the overhang is larger for younger new-technology firms.

Characteristics of Option Grants Firms that use employee options usually restrict when and whether these options can be exercised. It is standard, for instance, that the options granted to an employee cannot be exercised until they are vested. For this to occur, the employee usually has to remain for a period that is specified with the contract. While firms do this to keep employee turnover low, it also has implications for the value of these options. Firms that issue options do not face any tax consequences in the year in which they make the issue. When the options are exercised, however, they are allowed to treat the difference between the stock price and the exercise price as an employee expense. This tax deductibility also has implications for option value.

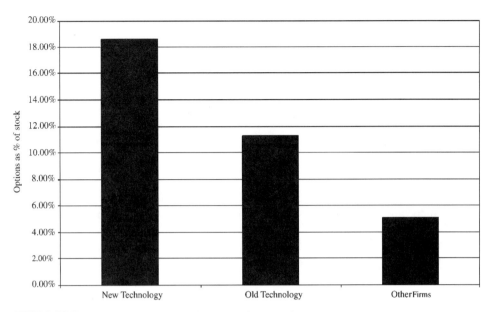

FIGURE 16.2 Options as Percent of Outstanding Stock
Source: Securities and Exchange Commission.

Options in Existence

Given the large number of options outstanding at many firms, our first task is to consider ways in which we can incorporate their effect into value per share. The section begins by presenting the argument for why these outstanding options matter when computing value per share, and then considers four ways in which we can incorporate their effect on value.

Why Options Affect Value per Share Why do existing options affect value per share? Note that not all options do. In fact, options issued and listed by the options exchanges have no effect on the value per share of the firms on which they are issued. The options issued by firms themselves do have an effect on value per share, since there is a chance that they will be exercised in the near or far future. Given that these options offer the right to individuals to buy stock at a fixed price, they will be exercised only if the stock price rises above that exercise price. When they are exercised, the firm has two choices, both of which have negative consequences for existing stockholders. It can issue additional shares to cover the option exercise. But this increases the number of shares outstanding and reduces the value per share to existing stockholders.[9] Alternatively, it can use cash flows from operations to

---

[9]This would be dilution in the true sense of the word, rather than the term that is used to describe any increase in the number of shares outstanding. The reason there is dilution is because the additional shares are issued only to the option holders at a price below the current price. In contrast, the dilution that occurs in a rights issue where every stockholder gets the right to buy additional shares at a lower price is value neutral. The shares will trade at a lower price but everyone will have more shares outstanding.

buy back shares in the open market and use these shares to meet the option exercise. This reduces the cash flows available to current equity investors in future periods, and makes their equity less valuable today.

Ways of Incorporating Existing Options into Value   There are four approaches that are used to incorporate that effect of options that are already outstanding into the value per share. However, the first three approaches can lead to misleading estimates of value.

Use Fully Diluted Number of Shares to Estimate Per-Share Value   The simplest way to incorporate the effect of outstanding options on value per share is to divide the value of equity by the number of shares that will be outstanding if all options are exercised today—the fully diluted number of shares. While this approach has the virtue of simplicity, it will lead to too low an estimate of value per share for two reasons:

1. It considers all options outstanding, not just ones that are in-the-money and vested. To be fair, there are variants of this approach where the shares outstanding are adjusted to reflect only in-the-money and vested options.
2. It does not incorporate the expected proceeds from exercise, which will comprise a cash inflow to the firm.

Finally, this approach does not build in the time premium on the options into the valuation.

Estimate Expected Option Exercises in the Future and Build In Expected Dilution   In this approach, you forecast when in the future options will be exercised and build in the expected cash outflows associated with the exercise by assuming that the firm will go out and buy back stock to cover the exercise. The biggest limitation of this approach is that it requires estimates of what the stock price will be in the future and when options will be exercised on the stock. Given that your objective is to examine whether the price today is correct, forecasting future prices to estimate the current value per share seems circular. In general, this approach is neither practical nor particularly useful in coming up with reasonable estimates of value.

Use Treasury Stock Approach   This approach is a variant of the fully diluted approach. Here the number of shares is adjusted to reflect options that are outstanding, but the expected proceeds from the exercise (exercise price times number of options) are added to the value of equity. The limitations of this approach are that, like the fully diluted approach, it does not consider the time premium on the options and there is no effective way of dealing with vesting. Generally this approach, by underestimating the value of options granted, will overestimate the value of equity per share.

ILLUSTRATION 16.7: Fully Diluted Approach to Estimating Value per Share: Commerce One

Commerce One, as a young and fast-growing B2B business, used options liberally in the period 1998 to 2000 to compensate employees. The following table summarizes the options granted, exercised, and canceled each year and also provides information on the total number of options outstanding at the firm at the end of each of these years:

Commerce One Options (in '000s)

	Granted	Exercised	Canceled	Outstanding
1998	7,336	462	1,338	11,334
1999	26,288	7,431	2,995	17,195
2000	29,023	8,033	2,275	45,911

At the end of 2000, Commerce One had options on 45.911 million shares outstanding, with a wide range of exercise prices and expiration dates. The following table summarizes the details of these options:

Exercise Price Range	Number of Options	Remaining Life	Average Exercise Price	Exercisable and Vested	Average Exercise Price
$0.00–$0.40	4,771,451	7.26	$ 0.19	1,889,590	$ 0.13
$0.67–$3.50	7,414,524	8.38	$ 2.33	1,672,662	$ 2.32
$4.71–$24.61	5,498,253	8.75	$ 15.42	1,036,632	$ 14.07
$25.31–$28.81	2,746,602	9.73	$ 27.88	274,724	$ 27.56
$30.00–$33.00	4,851,300	9.29	$ 32.70	1,053,513	$ 32.80
$34.17–$54.69	5,032,969	9.38	$ 42.75	631,181	$ 42.48
$54.88–$62.81	7,926,752	9.39	$ 59.75	919,951	$ 56.86
$64.19–$75.07	5,000,268	9.36	$ 72.12	837,853	$ 73.15
$78.50–$101.81	2,103,829	9.2	$ 86.94	387,099	$ 89.94
$104.44	565,275	9.16	$104.44	117,755	$104.44
Total or average	45,911,223	8.92	$ 35.49	8,820,960	$ 28.16

To apply the fully diluted approach to estimate the per share value, we first estimated the total value of equity for Commerce One using a discounted cash flow model. The value obtained was $4,941 million.[10] At the end of 2000, Commerce One had 228.32 million shares outstanding. To estimate the value of equity per share, we used the total number of shares that would be outstanding if all options were exercised:

Value of equity per share = Value of equity/(Shares outstanding + Shares in options)
= 4,941/(228.32 + 45.911) = $18.02

Note, though, that some of these options are not vested or exercisable. If only exercisable options were considered, we would estimate a value of equity per share that is higher:

Value of equity per share = Value of equity/(Shares outstanding + Exercisable options)
= 4,941/(228.32 + 8.82) = $20.84

---

[10]The details of this valuation are in Chapter 23.

The biggest advantage of this approach is that it does not require a value per share (or stock price) to incorporate the option value into per-share value. As you will see with the last (and recommended) approach, there is a circularity that is created when the stock price is an input when estimating value per share.

ILLUSTRATION 16.8:   Treasury Stock Approach: Commerce One

To estimate the value per share with the treasury stock approach for Commerce One, we consider the expected proceeds for the exercise of the options today. To simplify calculations, we use the total number of options outstanding and the weighted average exercise price from the tables in Illustration 16.7:

$$\text{Expected proceeds from option exercise} = \text{Number of options} \times \text{Weighted exercise price}$$
$$= 45.911 \times 35.49 = \$1,629 \text{ million}$$

We add the expected proceeds from option exercise to the value of equity that we estimated for Commerce One, and then divide by the total number of shares outstanding to estimate the value of equity per share:

$$\text{Value per share} = (\text{Value of equity} + \text{Expected proceeds})/(\text{Shares outstanding}$$
$$+ \text{Shares underlying options})$$
$$= (4,941 + 1,629)/(228.32 + 45.911) = \$23.96$$

Here again, we could have used the modified approach of looking only at in-the-money options, which would have given us the following:

$$\text{Expected proceeds from option exercise} = \text{Number of exercisable options} \times \text{Weighted exercise price}$$
$$= 8.82 \times \$28.16 = \$248 \text{ million}$$

$$\text{Value per share} = (\text{Value of equity} + \text{Expected proceeds from in-the-money options})$$
$$/(\text{Shares outstanding} + \text{Exercisable options})$$
$$= (4,941 + 248)/(228.32 + 8.82) = \$21.88$$

Note that the value per share using this approach is higher than the value per share using the fully diluted approach. The difference is greatest when options have a higher exercise price, relative to the current stock price. The estimated value per share still ignores the time premium of the options.

Value Options Using Option Pricing Model   The correct approach to dealing with options is to estimate the value of the options today, given today's value per share and the time premium on the option. Once this value has been estimated, it is subtracted from the equity value, and then divided by the number of shares outstanding to arrive at value per share.

$$\text{Value of equity per share} = (\text{Value of equity} - \text{Value of options outstanding})$$
$$/\text{Primary number of shares outstanding}$$

In valuing these options, however, there are four measurement issues that you have to confront. One relates to the fact that not all of the options outstanding are vested and some of the nonvested options might never be vested. The second relates to the stock price to use in valuing these options. As the description in the preceding paragraph makes clear, the value per share is an input to the process as well as the output. The third issue is taxation. Since firms are allowed to deduct a portion of the expense associated with option exercises, there may be a potential tax saving when the options are exercised. The final issue relates to private firms or firms on the verge of a public offering. Key inputs to the option pricing model, including the stock price and the variance, cannot be obtained for these firms, but the options have to be valued nevertheless.

Dealing with Vesting As noted earlier in the chapter, firms granting employee options usually require that the employee receiving the options stay with the firm for a specified period, for the option to be vested. Consequently, when you examine the options outstanding at a firm, you are looking at a mix of vested and nonvested options. The nonvested options should be worth less than the vested options, but the probability of vesting will depend upon how in-the-money the options are and the period left for an employee to vest. While there have been attempts to develop option pricing models that allow for the possibility that employees may leave a firm before vesting and forfeit the value of their options,[11] the likelihood of such an occurrence when a manager's holdings are substantial should be small. Carpenter (1998) developed a simple extension of the standard option pricing model to allow for early exercise and forfeiture, and used it to value executive options.

Which Stock Price? The answer to this question may seem obvious. Since the stock is traded, and you can obtain a stock price, it would seem that you should be using the current stock price to value options. However, you are valuing these options to arrive at a value per share that you will then compare to the market price to decide whether a stock is under- or overvalued. Thus, using the current market price to arrive at the value of the options and then using this option value to estimate an entirely different value per share seems inconsistent.

There is a solution. You can value the options using the estimated value per share. This creates circular reasoning in your valuation. In other words, you need the option value to estimate value per share and value per share to estimate the option value. We would recommend that the value per share be initially estimated using the treasury stock approach, and that you then converge on the proper value per share by iterating.[12]

There is another related issue. When options are exercised, they increase the number of shares outstanding, and by doing so, there can have an effect on the stock price. In conventional option pricing models, the exercise of the option does not affect the stock price. These models have to be adapted to allow for the dilutive effect of option exercise. This can be done fairly simply by adjusting the current stock price for the expected effects of dilution (as we did with warrants in Chapter 5).

---

[11]Cuny and Jorion (1995) examine the valuation of options when there is the possibility of forfeiture.

[12]The value per share, obtained using the treasury stock approach, will become the stock price in the option pricing model. The option value that results from using this price is used to compute a new value per share, which is fed back into the option pricing model, and so on.

Taxation   When options are exercised, the firm can deduct for tax purposes the difference between the stock price at the time and the exercise price as an employee expense. This potential tax benefit reduces the drain on value created by having options outstanding. One way in which you could estimate the tax benefit is to multiply the difference between the stock price today and the exercise price by the tax rate; clearly, this would make sense only if the options are in-the-money. While this does not allow for the expected price appreciation over time, it has the benefit of simplicity. An alternative way of estimating the tax benefit is to compute the after-tax value of the options:

After-tax value of options = Value from option pricing model(1 – Tax rate)

This approach is also straightforward and allows you to consider the tax benefits from option exercise in valuation. One of the advantages of this approach is that it can be used to consider the potential tax benefit even when options are out-of-the-money.

Nontraded Firms   A couple of key inputs to the option pricing model—the current price per share and the variance in stock prices—cannot be obtained if a firm is not publicly traded. There are two choices in this scenario. One is to revert to the treasury stock approach to estimate the value of the options outstanding and abandon the option pricing models. The other is to stay with the option pricing models and to estimate the value per share, from the discounted cash flow model. The variance of similar firms that are publicly traded can be used to estimate the value of the options.

WHAT ABOUT OTHER OPTIONS?

While we have considered the effects of management options specifically in this section, everything that has been said here about management and employee options applies to other equity options issued by the firm as well. In particular, warrants issued to raise equity capital and conversion options in convertible securities (bonds and preferred stock) also dilute the value of the common stock in a firm. Consequently, you would need to reduce the value of equity by the value of these options as well. Generally speaking, though, warrants and conversions tend to be easier to value than management options because they are traded. The market values of the warrants and the conversion options can be used as measures of their estimated values.

ILLUSTRATION 16.9: Option Value Approach: Commerce One

We use an option pricing model and adjust for dilution to value all outstanding options at Commerce One. To estimate the value of the options, we first estimate the standard deviation in stock prices[13] over the previous two years. Weekly returns are used to make this estimate, and this estimate is annualized.[14] All options, vested as well as nonvested, are valued, and there is no adjustment for nonvesting.

Inputs to the Black-Scholes Model: Commerce One Options

Current stock price	$8.28
Weighted average exercise price per option	$35.49
Weighted average maturity of options	8.92 years
Standard deviation in stock price	135%
Riskless rate	5.40%
Number of options outstanding	45.911
Number of shares outstanding	228.32
Value of options outstanding	$349
After-tax value of options outstanding	349(1 − .35) = $227 million

In estimating the after-tax value of the options at Commerce One, we have used their prospective marginal tax rate of 35%. If the options are exercised prior to these firms reaching their marginal tax rates, the tax benefit is lower since the expenses are carried forward and offset against income in future periods.

The value per share can now be computed by subtracting the value of the options outstanding from the value of equity and dividing by the primary number of shares outstanding. Again, using Commerce One, we estimate a value for equity per share:

$$\text{Value of equity per share} = (\text{Value of equity} - \text{Value of options outstanding})$$
$$/\text{Number of shares outstanding}$$
$$= (4{,}941 - 227)/228.32 = \$20.65 \text{ per share}$$

The inconsistency averred to earlier is clear when you compare the value per share that is estimated here ($20.65) to the price per share ($8.28) used to estimate the value of the options. (Commerce One's value per share is $20.65, whereas the price per share used in the option valuation is $8.28.) If you choose to iterate, you would revalue the options using the estimated value of $20.65, which would increase the value of the options and lower the value per share, leading to a second iteration and a third one and so on. The values converge to yield a consistent estimate.

$$\text{Estimated value of options with estimated value per share} = \$835 \text{ million}$$

$$\text{Value per share} = (\text{Value of equity} - \text{Value of options outstanding})/\text{Number of shares outstanding}$$
$$= [4{,}941 - 835 \times (1 - .35)]/228.32 = \$19.26 \text{ per share}$$

The options are also valued using the same value per share.

---

[13]The variance estimate is actually on the natural log of the stock prices. This allows you to cling to at least the possibility of a normal distribution. Neither stock prices nor stock returns can be normally distributed since prices cannot fall below zero and returns cannot be lower than −100 percent.

[14]All of the inputs to the Black-Scholes model have to be in annual terms. To annualize a weekly variance, you multiply by 52.

> ### THE REPRICING OF OPTIONS: EFFECTS ON VALUE
>
> In recent years, firms that have seen their stock price drop have often reset
> their exercise prices on options closer to the market price to make them more
> attractive to management. This practice is obviously hazardous to stockhold-
> ers since it increases the value of the option overhang. In fact, if this practice is
> flagrant at a firm, you should value the options with an exercise price of zero,
> which would make them each worth as much as a regular share. In effect, the
> fully diluted estimate of value per share will be the value you get even if you
> used the option pricing model.

Future Option Grants

While incorporating options that are already outstanding is fairly straightforward,
incorporating the effects of future option grants is much more complicated. In this
section, the argument for why these option issues affect value is presented, as well
as how to incorporate these effects into value.

Why Future Options Issues Affect Value   Just as options outstanding currently represent potential dilution or cash outflows to existing equity investors, expected option grants in the future will affect value per share by increasing the number of
shares outstanding in future periods. The simplest way of thinking about this expected dilution is to consider the terminal value in the discounted cash flow model.
As constructed in the last chapter, the terminal value is discounted to the present
and divided by the shares outstanding today to arrive at the value per share. However, expected option issues in the future will increase the number of shares outstanding in the terminal year, and therefore reduce the portion of the terminal value
that belongs to existing equity investors.

Ways of Incorporating Effect into Value per Share   It is much more difficult to incorporate the effect of expected option issues into value than it is to consider existing options. This is because you have to forecast not only how many options will be issued
by a firm in future periods, but also what the terms of these options will be. While this
may be possible for a couple of periods with proprietary information (the firm lets you
know how much it plans to issue and at what terms), it will become more difficult beyond that point. We will consider an approach in which you can obtain an estimate of
the option value, and look at two ways of dealing with this estimate, once obtained.

Estimate Option Value as an Operating or a Capital Expense   You can estimate
the value of options that will be granted in future periods as a percentage of revenues or operating income. By doing so, you can avoid having to estimate the number and terms of future option issues. Estimation will also become easier since you
can draw on the firm's own history (by looking at the value of option grants in previous years as a proportion of firm value) and the experiences of more mature firms
in the sector. Generally, as firms become larger, the value of options granted as a
percent of revenues should become smaller.

Having estimated the value of expected future option issues, you are left with
another choice. You can consider this value each period as an operating expense

and compute the operating income after the expense. You are assuming, then, that option issues form part of annual compensation. Alternatively, you can treat it as a capital expense and amortize it over multiple periods. While the cash flow in the current period is unaffected by this distinction, it has consequences for the return on capital and reinvestment rates that you measure for a firm.

It is important that you do not double count future option issues. The current operating expenses of the firm already include the expenses associated with option exercises in the current period. The operating margins and returns on capital that you might derive by looking at industry averages reflect the effects of option exercise in the current period for the firms in the industry. If the effect on operating income of option exercise in the current period is less than the expected value of new option issues, you have to allow for an additional expense associated with option issues. Conversely, if a disproportionately large number of options were exercised in the last period, you have to reduce the operating expenses to allow for the fact that the expected effect of option issues in future periods will be smaller.

VALUE PER SHARE WHEN VOTING RIGHTS VARY

When you divide the value of the equity by the number of shares outstanding, you assume that the shares all have the same voting rights. If different classes of shares have different voting rights, the value of equity per share has to reflect these differences, with the shares with more voting rights having higher value. Note, though, that the total value of equity is still unchanged. To illustrate, assume that the value of equity in a firm is $500 million and that there are 50 million shares outstanding; 25 million of these shares have voting rights and 25 million do not. Furthermore, assume that the voting shares will have a value 10 percent higher than the nonvoting shares. To estimate the value per share:

Value per nonvoting share = $500 million/(25 million × 1.10 + 25 million)
= $500 million/52.5 million = $9.52

Value per voting share = $9.52(1.10) = $10.48

The key issue that you face in valuation then is in coming up with the discount to apply for nonvoting shares or, alternatively, the premium to attach to voting shares.

Voting Shares versus Nonvoting Shares

What premium should be assigned to the voting shares? You have two choices. One is to look at studies that empirically examine the size of the premium for voting rights and to assign this premium to all voting shares. Lease, McConnell, and Mikkelson (1983) examined 26 firms that had two classes of common stock outstanding, and they concluded that the voting shares traded at a premium relative to nonvoting shares.[15] The premium, on average, amounted to 5.44 percent, and the voting shares sold at a higher price in 88 percent of the months for which data were available. In four firms that also had voting preferred stock, however, the voting common stock traded at a discount of about 1.17 percent relative to nonvoting shares.

The other option is to be more discriminating and vary the premium depending on the firm. Voting rights have value because they give shareholders a say in the

---

[15]The two classes of stock received the same dividend.

ESTIMATING THE PREMIUM FOR VOTING RIGHTS

If one class of shares has significantly more voting rights than another, you would expect it to trade at a higher price. Estimating the premium for voting rights can be fairly complicated. While many analysts prefer to use ad hoc approaches, you can estimate a more precise estimate of the relative value of voting shares by valuing the firm twice—once under incumbent management and once with a new (and better) management. For instance, assume that you value a firm at $800 million with existing management and $1,200 million with new management. The value of control at this firm is $400 million. If you assume that this firm has 10 million voting shares and 10 million nonvoting shares, you could estimate the voting share premium by estimating two per-share values:

Value per share for nonvoting shares = Status quo value
/(Voting + Nonvoting shares)
= 800/(10 + 10) = $40

Value per share for voting shares = Value per share without voting rights
+ (Value of firm with superior
management – Value of firm
status quo)/ Number of voting shares
= $40 + (1,200 – 800)/10 = $80 per share

The voting share premium will decrease as the difference between optimal and current value decreases and also if the likelihood of a hostile takeover lessens.

 warrants.xls: This spreadsheet allows you to value the options outstanding in a firm, allowing for the dilution effect.

management of the firm. To the extent that voting shares can make a difference—by removing incumbent management, forcing management to change policy, or selling to a hostile bidder in a takeover—their price will reflect the possibility of a change in the way the firm is run.[16] Nonvoting shareholders do not participate in these decisions.

CONCLUSION

Incorporating the value of nonoperating assets into firm value can be very simple to do in some cases—cash and near-cash investments—and very complicated in other cases—holdings in private companies. The principle, though, should remain the same. You want to estimate a fair value for these nonoperating assets and bring them into value. As noted, it is often better to value nonoperating assets separately from operating assets, but the absence of information may impede this process.

---

[16]In some cases, the rights of nonvoting stockholders are protected in the specific instance of a takeover by forcing the bidder to buy the nonvoting shares as well.

The existence of options and the possibility of future option grants makes getting from equity value to value per share a complicated exercise. To deal with options outstanding at the time of the valuation, there are four approaches. The simplest is to estimate the value per share by dividing the value of equity by the fully diluted number of shares outstanding. This approach ignores both the expected proceeds from exercising the options and the time value of the options. The second approach of forecasting expected option exercises in the future and estimating the effect on value per share is not only tedious but unlikely to work. In the treasury stock approach, you add the expected proceeds from option exercise to the value of equity and then divide by the fully diluted number of shares outstanding. While this approach does consider the expected proceeds from exercise, it still ignores the option time premium.

In the final and preferred approach, the options are valued using an option pricing model, and the value is subtracted from the value of equity. The resulting estimate is divided by the primary shares outstanding to arrive at the value of equity per share. While the current price of the stock is usually used in option pricing models, the value per share estimated from the discounted cash flow valuation can be substituted to arrive at a more consistent estimate.

To deal with expected option grants in the future, the current operating income has to be dissected to consider how much of an effect option exercises in the current period had on operating expenses. If the options granted during the period had more value than the option expense resulting from exercise of options granted in prior periods, the current operating income has to be adjusted down to reflect the difference. Industry average margins and returns on capital will also have to be adjusted for the same reason.

Once the value per share of equity has been estimated, that value may need to be adjusted for differences in voting rights. Shares with disproportionately high voting rights will sell at a premium relative to shares with low or no voting rights. The difference will be larger for firms that are badly managed and smaller for well-managed firms.

QUESTIONS AND SHORT PROBLEMS

1. ABV Inc. has earnings before interest and taxes of $250 million, expected to grow 5% a year forever; the tax rate is 40%. Its cost of capital is 10%, its reinvestment rate is 33.33%, and it has 200 million shares outstanding. If the firm has $500 million in cash and marketable securities and $750 million in debt outstanding, estimate the value of equity per share.

2. How would your answer to the previous problem change if you were told that ABV had options outstanding for 50 million shares and that each option had a value of $5.

3. If you were told that the average exercise price of the 50 million options in the previous problem was $6, estimate the value per share for ABV using the treasury stock approach.

4. LSI Logic has 1 billion shares outstanding, trading at $25 per share. The firm also has $5 billion in debt outstanding. The cost of equity is 12.5% and the cost of debt, after taxes, is 5%. If the firm has $3 billion in cash outstanding and is fairly valued, estimate how much the firm earned in operating income in the current year. (The return on capital is 15%, the tax rate is 30% and earnings are growing 6% a year in perpetuity.)

5. Lava Lamps Inc. had $800 million in earnings before interest and taxes last year. It has just acquired a 50% stake in General Lamps Inc., which had $400 million in earnings before interest and taxes last year. Because Lava Lamps has a majority active stake, it has been asked to consolidate last year's income statements for the two firms. What earnings before interest and taxes would you see in the consolidated statement?
   a. If both firms have a 5% stable growth rate, a 10% cost of capital, a 40% tax rate, and a return on capital of 11%, estimate the value of equity in Lava Lamps.
   b. How would your answer change if you were told that General Lamps has a 9% cost of capital and a 15% return on capital?

6. Genome Sciences is a biotechnology firm that had after-tax operating income of $300 million last year; these earnings are expected to grow 6% a year forever, the reinvestment rate is 40% and the firm has a cost of capital of 12%. Genome also owns 10% of the stock of Gene Therapies Inc., another publicly traded firm. Gene Therapies has 100 million shares outstanding, trading at $50 per share. If Genome has $800 million in debt outstanding, estimate the value of equity per share in Genome Sciences. (Genome has 50 million shares outstanding.)

7. Fedders Asia Closed End fund is a closed-end equity fund that holds Asian securities with a market value of $1 billion. Over the past 10 years, the fund has earned a return of 9% a year, 3% less than the return earned by index funds investing in Asia. You expect annual returns in the future to be similar to those earned in the past, both for your fund and for index funds in general.
   a. Assuming no growth in the fund and investment in perpetuity, estimate the discount at which you would expect the fund to trade.
   b. How would your answer change if you expect the fund to be liquidated in 10 years?

8. You have been asked to review another analyst's valuation of System Logic Inc., a technology firm. The analyst estimated a value per share of $11 while the stock was trading at $12.50 per share. In making this estimate, however, she divided the value of equity by the fully diluted 1.4 million shares outstanding. Reviewing this number, you discover that the firm has only 1 million shares outstanding and that the remaining 400,000 shares represent options with an average maturity of three years and an average exercise price of $5.
   a. Estimate the correct value per share, using the treasury stock approach.
   b. If the standard deviation in the stock price is 80%, estimate the value of the options using an option pricing model (and the current stock price) and the correct value per share.
   c. Will your value per share increase or decrease if you reestimate the value of the options using your estimated value per share?

CHAPTER **17**

Fundamental Principles of Relative Valuation

In discounted cash flow valuation, the objective is to find the value of assets, given their cash flow, growth, and risk characteristics. In relative valuation, the objective is to value assets based on how similar assets are currently priced in the market. While multiples are easy to use and intuitive, they are also easy to misuse. Consequently, a series of tests are developed in this chapter that can be used to ensure that multiples are correctly used.

There are two components to relative valuation. The first is that, to value assets on a relative basis, prices have to be standardized, usually by converting prices into multiples of earnings, book values, or sales. The second is to find similar firms, which is difficult to do since no two firms are identical and firms in the same business can still differ on risk, growth potential, and cash flows. The question of how to control for these differences, when comparing a multiple across several firms, becomes a key one.

USE OF RELATIVE VALUATION

The use of relative valuation is widespread. Most equity research reports and many acquisition valuations are based on multiples such as price-to-sales ratios and value-to-EBITDA, and a group of comparable firms. In fact, firms in the same business as the firm being valued are called comparable, though as you will see later in this chapter, that is not always true. In this section, the reasons for the popularity of relative valuation are considered first, followed by some potential pitfalls.

Reasons for Popularity

Why is relative valuation so widely used? There are several reasons. First, a valuation based on a multiple and comparable firms can be completed with far fewer explicit assumptions and far more quickly than a discounted cash flow valuation. Second, a relative valuation is simpler to understand and easier to present to clients and customers than a discounted cash flow valuation. Finally, a relative valuation is much more likely to reflect the current mood of the market, since it is an attempt to measure relative and not intrinsic value. Thus, in a market where all Internet stocks see their prices bid up, relative valuation is likely to yield higher values for these stocks than discounted cash flow valuations. In fact, relative valuations will generally yield values that are closer to the market price than discounted cash flow valuations. This is particularly important for those whose job it is to make judgments on relative value, and who are themselves judged on a relative basis. Consider, for instance, managers of growth mutual funds. These managers will be judged based on how their funds do relative to other growth funds. Consequently, they will be rewarded if they pick growth stocks that are undervalued relative to other growth stocks, even if all growth stocks are overvalued.

Potential Pitfalls

The strengths of relative valuation are also its weaknesses. First, the ease with which a relative valuation can be put together, pulling together a multiple and a group of comparable firms, can also result in inconsistent estimates of value where key variables such as risk, growth, or cash flow potential are ignored. Second, the fact that multiples reflect the market mood also implies that using relative valuation to estimate the value of an asset can result in values that are too high when the market is overvaluing comparable firms, or too low when it is undervaluing these firms. Third, while there is scope for bias in any type of valuation, the lack of transparency regarding the underlying assumptions in relative valuations make them particularly vulnerable to manipulation. A biased analyst who is allowed to choose the multiple on which the valuation is based and to pick the comparable firms can essentially ensure that almost any value can be justified.

STANDARDIZED VALUES AND MULTIPLES

The price of a stock is a function both of the value of the equity in a company and the number of shares outstanding in the firm. Thus, a 2-for-1 stock split that doubles the number of units will approximately halve the stock price. Since stock prices are determined by the number of units of equity in a firm, stock prices cannot be compared across different firms. To compare the values of similar firms in the market, you need to standardize the values in some way. Values can be standardized relative to the earnings generated, to the book value or replacement value of the assets employed, to the revenues generated, or to measures that are specific to firms in a sector.

Earnings Multiples

One of the more intuitive ways to think of the value of any asset is as a multiple of the earnings that asset generated. When buying a stock, it is common to look at the price paid as a multiple of the earnings per share generated by the company. This price-earnings ratio can be estimated using current earnings per share, which is called a current PE, or an expected earnings per share in the next year, called a forward PE.

When buying a business, as opposed to just the equity in the business, it is common to examine the value of the firm as a multiple of the operating income or the earnings before interest, taxes, depreciation, and amortization (EBITDA). While, as a buyer of the equity or the firm, a lower multiple is better than a higher one, these multiples will be affected by the growth potential and risk of the business being acquired.

Book Value or Replacement Value Multiples

While markets provide one estimate of the value of a business, accountants often provide a very different estimate of the same business. The accounting estimate of book value is determined by accounting rules and is heavily influenced by the original price paid for assets and any accounting adjustments (such as depreciation) made since. Investors often look at the relationship between the price they pay for a stock and the book value of equity (or net worth) as a measure of how over- or undervalued a stock is; the price–book value (PBV) ratio that emerges can vary widely across industries, depending again on the growth potential and the quality of the investments in each. When valuing businesses, you estimate this ratio using the value of the firm and the book value of all capital (rather than just the equity). For those who believe that book value is not a good measure of the true value of the assets, an alternative is to use the replacement cost of the assets; the ratio of the value of the firm to replacement cost is called Tobin's Q, discussed in Chapter 19.

Revenue Multiples

Both earnings and book value are accounting measures and are determined by accounting rules and principles. An alternative measure, which is far less affected by accounting choices, is to use the ratio of the value of an asset to the revenues it generates. For equity investors, this ratio is the price-sales ratio (PS), where the market value of equity is divided by the revenues. For firm value, this ratio can be modified as the value-sales ratio (VS), where the numerator becomes the total value of the firm. This ratio, again, varies widely across sectors, largely as a function of the profit margins in each. The advantage of using revenue multiples, however, is that it becomes far easier to compare firms in different markets, with different accounting systems at work, than it is to compare earnings or book value multiples.

Sector-Specific Multiples

While earnings, book value, and revenue multiples are multiples that can be computed for firms in any sector and across the entire market, there are some multiples that are specific to a sector. For instance, when Internet firms first appeared on the market in the later 1990s, they had negative earnings and negligible revenues and book value. Analysts looking for a multiple to value these firms divided the market value of each of these firms by the number of hits generated by that firm's web site. Firms with a low market value per customer hit were viewed as more undervalued. More recently, e-tailers have been judged by the market value of equity per customer in the firm.

While there are conditions under which sector-specific multiples can be justified, and a few are discussed in Chapter 20, they are dangerous for two reasons. First, since they cannot be computed for other sectors or for the entire market, sector-specific multiples can result in persistent over- or undervaluations of sectors relative to the rest of the market. Thus, investors who would never consider paying 80 times revenues for a firm might not have the same qualms about paying $2,000 for every page hit (on the web site), largely because they have no sense of what high, low, or average is on this measure. Second, it is far more difficult to relate sector-specific multiples to fundamentals, which is an essential ingredient to using multiples well. For instance, does a visitor to a company's web site translate into higher revenues and profits? The answer will not only vary from company to company, but will also be difficult to estimate looking forward.

FOUR BASIC STEPS TO USING MULTIPLES

Multiples are easy to use and easy to misuse. There are four basic steps to using multiples wisely and for detecting misuse in the hands of others. The first step is to ensure that the multiple is defined consistently and that it is measured uniformly across the firms being compared. The second step is to be aware of the cross-sectional distribution of the multiple, not only across firms in the sector being analyzed but also across the entire market. The third step is to analyze the multiple and understand not only what fundamentals determine the multiple but also how changes in these fundamentals translate into changes in the multiple. The final step is finding the right firms to use for comparison, and controlling for differences that may persist across these firms.

Definitional Tests

Even the simplest multiples can be defined differently by different analysts. Consider, for instance, the price-earnings (PE) ratio. Most analysts define it to be the market price divided by the earnings per share but that is where the consensus ends. There are a number of variants on the PE ratio. While the current price is conventionally used in the numerator, there are some analysts who use the average price over the prior six months or year. The earnings per share in the denominator can be the earnings per share from the most recent financial year (yielding the current PE), the last four quarters of earnings (yielding the trailing PE) and expected earnings per share in the next financial year (resulting in a forward PE). In addition, earnings per share can be computed based on primary shares outstanding or fully diluted shares, and can include or exclude extraordinary items. Figure 17.1 provides the PE ratios for Cisco Systems in June 2000 using each of these measures.

Not only can these variants on earnings yield vastly different values for the price-earnings ratio, but the one that gets used by analysts depends on their biases. For instance, in periods of rising earnings, the forward PE yields consistently lower values than the trailing PE, which, in turn, is lower than the current PE. A bullish analyst will tend to use the forward PE to make the case that the stock is trading at a low multiple of earnings, while a bearish analyst will focus on the current PE to make the case that the multiple is too high. The first step when discussing a valuation based on a multiple is to ensure that everyone in the discussion is using the same definition for that multiple.

Consistency   Every multiple has a numerator and a denominator. The numerator can be either an equity value (such as market price or value of equity) or a firm value (such as enterprise value, which is the sum of the values of debt and equity, net of cash). The denominator can be an equity measure (such as earnings per share, net income, or book value of equity) or a firm measure (such as operating income, EBITDA, or book value of capital).

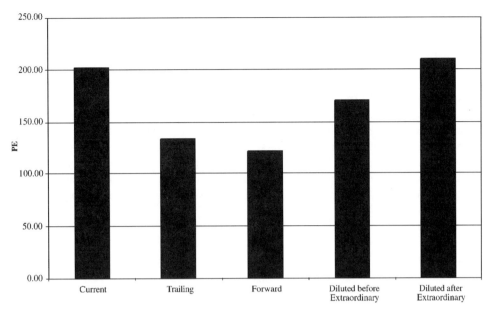

FIGURE 17.1 Estimate of Cisco's PE Ratio
Source: Cisco 10-K.

One of the key tests to run on a multiple is to examine whether the numerator and denominator are defined consistently. *If the numerator for a multiple is an equity value, then the denominator should be an equity value as well. If the numerator is a firm value, then the denominator should be a firm value as well.* To illustrate, the price-earnings ratio is a consistently defined multiple, since the numerator is the price per share (which is an equity value) and the denominator is earnings per share (which is also an equity value). So is the enterprise value to EBITDA multiple, since the numerator and denominator are both firm value measures.

Are there any multiples in use that are inconsistently defined? Consider the price to EBITDA multiple, a multiple that has acquired adherents in the past few years among analysts. The numerator in this multiple is an equity value, and the denominator is a measure of earnings to the firm. The analysts who use this multiple will probably argue that the inconsistency does not matter since the multiple is computed the same way for all of the comparable firms; but they would be wrong. If some firms on the list have no debt and others carry significant amounts of debt, the latter will look cheap on a price-to-EBITDA basis, when in fact they might be overpriced or correctly priced.

Uniformity In relative valuation, the multiple is computed for all of the firms in a group and then compared across these firms to make judgments on which firms are overpriced and which are underpriced. For this comparison to have any merit, the multiple has to be defined uniformly across all of the firms in the group. Thus, if the trailing PE is used for one firm, it has to be used for all of the others as well. In fact, one of the problems with using the current PE to compare firms in a group is that different firms can have different fiscal year-ends. This can lead to some firms having their prices divided by earnings from July to June, with other firms having their prices divided by earnings from January to December. While the differences can be minor in mature sectors, where earnings do not make quantum jumps over six months, they can be large in high-growth sectors.

With both earnings and book value measures, there is another component to be concerned about and that is the accounting standards used to estimate earnings and book values. Differences in accounting standards can result in very different earnings and book value numbers for similar firms. This makes comparisons of multiples across firms in different markets, with different accounting standards, very difficult. Even within the United States, the fact that some firms use different accounting rules (on depreciation and expensing) for reporting purposes and tax purposes and others do not can throw off comparisons of earnings multiples.[1]

Descriptional Tests

When using a multiple, it is always useful to have a sense of what a high value, a low value, or a typical value for that multiple is in the market. In other words, knowing the distributional characteristics of a multiple is a key part of using that multiple to identify under- or overvalued firms. In addition, you need to understand the effects of outliers on averages and unearth any biases in these values, introduced in the process of estimating multiples.

Distributional Characteristics   Many analysts who use multiples have a sector focus and have a good sense of how different firms in their sector rank on specific multiples. What is often lacking, however, is a sense of how the multiple is distributed across the entire market. Why, you might ask, should a software analyst care about price-earnings ratios of utility stocks? Because both software and utility stocks are competing for the same investment dollar, they have to, in a sense, play by the same rules. Furthermore, an awareness of how multiples vary across sectors can be very useful in detecting when the sector you are analyzing is over- or undervalued.

What are the distributional characteristics that matter? The standard statistics—the average and standard deviation—are where you should start, but they represent the beginning of the exploration. The fact that multiples such as the price-earnings ratio can never be less than zero and are unconstrained in terms of a maximum results in distributions for these multiples that are skewed toward the positive values. Consequently, the average values for these multiples will be higher than median values,[2] and the latter are much more representative of the typical firm in the group. While the maximum and minimum values are usually of limited use, the percentile values (10th percentile, 25th percentile, 75th percentile, 90th percentile, and so on) can be useful in judging what a high or low value for the multiple in the group is.

---

[1]Firms that adopt different rules for reporting and tax purposes generally report higher earnings to their stockholders than they do to the tax authorities. When they are compared on a price-earnings basis to firms that do not maintain different reporting and tax books, they will look cheaper (lower PE).

[2]With the median, half of all firms in the group fall below this value and half lie above.

Outliers and Averages   As noted earlier, multiples are unconstrained on the upper end, and firms can have price-earnings ratios of 500 or 2,000 or even 10,000. This can occur not only because of high stock prices but also because earnings at firms can sometimes drop to a few cents. These outliers will result in averages that are not representative of the sample. In most cases, services that compute and report average values for multiples either throw out these outliers when computing the averages or constrain the multiples to be less than or equal to a fixed number. For instance, any firm that has a price-earnings ratio greater than 500 may be given a price-earnings ratio of 500.

When using averages obtained from a service, it is important that you know how the service dealt with outliers in computing the averages. In fact, the sensitivity of the estimated average to outliers is another reason for looking at the median values for multiples.

Biases in Estimating Multiples   With every multiple, there are firms for which the multiple cannot be computed. Consider again the price-earnings ratio. When the earnings per share are negative, the price-earnings ratio for a firm is not meaningful and is usually not reported. When looking at the average price-earnings ratio across a group of firms, the firms with negative earnings will all drop out of the sample because the price-earnings ratio cannot be computed. Why should this matter when the sample is large? The fact that the firms that are taken out of the sample are the firms losing money creates a bias in the selection process. In fact, the average PE ratio for the group will be biased because of the elimination of these firms.

There are three solutions to this problem. The first is to be aware of the bias and build it into the analysis. In practical terms, this will mean adjusting the average PE to reflect the elimination of the money-losing firms. The second is to aggregate the market value of equity and net income (or loss) for all of the firms in the group, including the money-losing ones, and compute the price-earnings ratio using the aggregated values. Figure 17.2 summarizes the average PE ratio, the median PE ratio, and the PE ratio based on aggregated earnings for specialty retailers. Note that the median PE ratio is much lower than the average PE ratio. Furthermore, the PE ratio based on the aggregate values of market value of equity and net income is lower than the average across firms where PE ratios could be computed. The third choice is to use a multiple that can be computed for all of the firms in the group. The inverse of the price-earning ratio, which is called the earnings yield, can be computed for all firms, including those losing money.

Analytical Tests

In discussing why analysts were so fond of using multiples, it was argued that relative valuations require fewer assumptions than discounted cash flow valuations. While this is technically true, it is so only on the surface. In reality, you make just as many assumptions when you do a relative valuation as you make in a discounted cash flow valuation. The difference is that the assumptions in a relative valuation are implicit and unstated, whereas those in discounted cash flow valuation are explicit. The two primary questions that you need to answer before using a multiple are: What are the fundamentals that determine at what multiple a firm should trade? How do changes in the fundamentals affect the multiple?

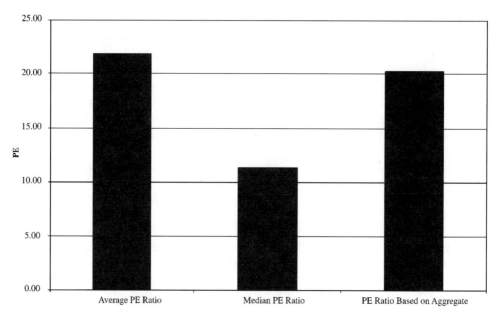

FIGURE 17.2   PE Ratio for Specialty Retailers
Source: Cisco 10-K.

Determinants   In the chapters on discounted cash flow valuation, we observed that the value of a firm is a function of three variables—its capacity to generate cash flows, its expected growth in these cash flows, and the uncertainty associated with these cash flows. Every multiple, whether it is of earnings, revenues, or book value, is a function of the same three variables—risk, growth, and cash flow generating potential. Intuitively, then, firms with higher growth rates, less risk, and greater cash flow generating potential should trade at higher multiples than firms with lower growth, higher risk, and less cash flow potential.

The specific measures of growth, risk, and cash flow generating potential that are used will vary from multiple to multiple. To look under the hood, so to speak, of equity and firm value multiples, you can go back to fairly simple discounted cash flow models for equity and firm value and use them to derive the multiples.

In the simplest discounted cash flow model for equity, which is a stable growth dividend discount model, the value of equity is:

$$\text{Value of equity} = P_0 = \frac{DPS_1}{k_e - g_n}$$

where DPS_1 is the expected dividend in the next year, k_e is the cost of equity, and g_n is the expected stable growth rate. Dividing both sides by the earnings, you obtain the discounted cash flow equation specifying the PE ratio for a stable-growth firm:

$$\frac{P_0}{EPS_0} = PE = \frac{\text{Payout ratio} \times (1 + g_n)}{k_e - g_n}$$

Dividing both sides by the book value of equity, you can estimate the price-book value ratio for a stable growth firm:

$$\frac{P_0}{BV_0} = PBV = \frac{ROE \times Payout\ ratio \times (1 + g_n)}{k_e - g_n}$$

where ROE is the return on equity. Dividing by the sales per share, the price-sales ratio for a stable-growth firm can be estimated as a function of its profit margin, payout ratio, profit margin, and expected growth.

$$\frac{P_0}{Sales_0} = PS = \frac{Profit\ margin \times Payout\ ratio \times (1 + g_n)}{k_e - g_n}$$

You can do a similar analysis to derive the firm value multiples. The value of a firm in stable growth can be written as:

$$Value\ of\ firm = V_0 = \frac{FCFF_1}{k_c - g_n}$$

Dividing both sides by the expected free cash flow to the firm yields the value-to-FCFF multiple for a stable growth firm:

$$\frac{V_0}{FCFF_1} = \frac{1}{k_c - g_n}$$

Since the free cash flow the firm is the after-tax operating income netted against the net capital expenditures and working capital needs of the firm, the multiples of EBIT, after-tax EBIT, and EBITDA can also be estimated similarly.

The point of this analysis is not to suggest that you go back to using discounted cash flow valuation, but to understand the variables that may cause these multiples to vary across firms in the same sector. If you ignore these variables, you might conclude that a stock with a PE of 8 is cheaper than one with a PE of 12, when the true reason may be that the latter has higher expected growth; or you might decide that a stock with a PBV ratio of 0.7 is cheaper than one with a PBV ratio of 1.5, when the true reason may be that the latter has a much higher return on equity.

Relationship Knowing the fundamentals that determine a multiple is a useful first step, but understanding how the multiple changes as the fundamentals change is just as critical to using the multiple. To illustrate, knowing that higher-growth firms have higher PE ratios is not a sufficient insight if you are called on to analyze whether a firm with a growth rate that is twice as high as the average growth rate for the sector should have a PE ratio that is 1.5 times or 1.8 times or 2 times the average price-earnings ratio for the sector. To make this judgment, you need to know how the PE ratio changes as the growth rate changes.

A surprisingly large number of analyses are based on the assumption that there is a linear relationship between multiples and fundamentals. For instance, the price-earnings/growth (PEG) ratio, which is the ratio of the PE to the expected growth rate of a firm and widely used to analyze high-growth firms, implicitly assumes that PE ratios and expected growth rates are linearly related.

One of the advantages of deriving the multiples from a discounted cash flow model, as was done in the last section, is that you can analyze the relationship between each fundamental variable and the multiple by keeping everything else constant and changing the value of that variable. When you do this, you will find that there are very few linear relationships in valuation.

Companion Variable   While the variables that determine a multiple can be extracted from a discounted cash flow model, and the relationship between each variable and the multiple can be developed by holding all else constant and asking what-if questions, there is one variable that dominates when it comes to explaining each multiple. This variable, which is called the companion variable, can usually be identified by looking at how multiples vary across firms in a sector or across the entire market. In the next three chapters, the companion variables for the most widely used multiples from the price-earnings ratio to the value-to-sales multiples are identified and then used in analysis.

Application Tests

When multiples are used, they tend to be used in conjunction with comparable firms to determine the value of a firm or its equity. But what is a comparable firm? While the conventional practice is to look at firms within the same industry or business as comparable firms, this is not necessarily always the correct or the best way of identifying these firms. In addition, no matter how carefully you choose comparable firms, differences will remain between the firm you are valuing and the comparable firms. Figuring out how to control for these differences is a significant part of relative valuation.

What Is a Comparable Firm?   A comparable firm is one with cash flows, growth potential, and risk similar to the firm being valued. It would be ideal if you could value a firm by looking at how an exactly identical firm—in terms of risk, growth, and cash flows—is priced. Nowhere in this definition is there a component that relates to the industry or sector to which a firm belongs. Thus a telecommunications firm can be compared to a software firm, if the two are identical in terms of cash flows, growth, and risk. In most analyses, however, analysts define comparable firms to be other firms in the firm's business or businesses. If there are enough firms in the industry to allow for it, this list is pruned further using other criteria; for instance, only firms of similar size may be considered. The implicit assumption being made here is that firms in the same sector have similar risk, growth, and cash flow profiles and therefore can be compared with much more legitimacy.

This approach becomes more difficult to apply when there are relatively few firms in a sector. In most markets outside the United States, the number of publicly traded firms in a particular sector, especially if it is defined narrowly, is small. It is also difficult to define firms in the same sector as comparable firms if differences in risk, growth, and cash flow profiles across firms within a sector are large. Thus, there may be hundreds of computer software companies listed in the United States, but the differences across these firms are also large. The trade-off is therefore a simple one. Defining an industry more broadly increases the number of comparable firms, but it also results in a more diverse group.

There are alternatives to the conventional practice of defining comparable firms. One is to look for firms that are similar in terms of valuation fundamentals. For instance, to estimate the value of a firm with a beta of 1.2, an expected growth rate in earnings per share of 20 percent, and a return on equity of 40 percent,[3] you would find other firms across the entire market with similar characteristics.[4] The other is to consider all firms in the market as comparable firms and to control for differences on the fundamentals across these firms using statistical techniques such as multiple regressions.

Controlling for Differences across Firms   No matter how carefully you construct your list of comparable firms, you will end up with firms that are different from the firm you are valuing. The differences may be small on some variables and large on others, and you will have to control for these differences in a relative valuation. There are three ways of controlling for these differences: subjective adjustments, modified multiples, and sector or market regressions.

Subjective Adjustments   Relative valuation begins with two choices—the multiple used in the analysis and the group of firms that comprises the comparable firms. The multiple is calculated for each of the comparable firms, and the average is computed. To evaluate an individual firm, you then compare the multiple it trades at to the average computed; if it is significantly different, you make a subjective judgment about whether the firm's individual characteristics (growth, risk, or cash flows) may explain the difference. Thus, a firm may have a PE ratio of 22 in a sector where the average PE is only 15, but you may conclude that this difference can be justified because the firm has higher growth potential than the average firm in the industry. If, in your judgment, the difference on the multiple cannot be explained by the fundamentals, the firm will be viewed as overvalued (if its multiple is higher than the average) or undervalued (if its multiple is lower than the average).

Modified Multiples   In this approach, you modify the multiple to take into account the most important variable determining it—the companion variable. Thus, the PE ratio is divided by the expected growth rate in EPS for a company to determine a growth-adjusted PE ratio or the PEG ratio. Similarly, the PBV ratio is divided by the return on equity (ROE) to find a value ratio, and the price-sales ratio is divided by the net margin. These modified ratios are then compared across companies in a sector. The implicit assumption you make is that these firms are comparable on all the other measures of value, other the one being controlled for. In addition, you are assuming that the relationship between the multiples and fundamentals is linear.

---

[3]The return on equity of 40 percent becomes a proxy for cash flow potential. With a 20 percent growth rate and a 40 percent return on equity, this firm will be able to return half of its earnings to its stockholders in the form of dividends or stock buybacks.

[4]Finding these firms manually may tedious when your universe includes 10,000 stocks. You could draw on statistical techniques such as cluster analysis to find similar firms.

ILLUSTRATION 17.1:   Comparing PE Ratios and Growth Rates across Firms: Beverage Companies

The PE ratios and expected growth rates in EPS over the next five years, based on consensus estimates from analysts, for the firms that are categorized as beverage firms are summarized in the following table:

Company Name	Trailing PE	Expected Growth	Standard Deviation	PEG
Coca-Cola Bottling	29.18	9.50%	20.58%	3.07
Molson Inc. Ltd. 'A'	43.65	15.50%	21.88%	2.82
Anheuser-Busch	24.31	11.00%	22.92%	2.21
Corby Distilleries Ltd.	16.24	7.50%	23.66%	2.16
Chalone Wine Group Ltd.	21.76	14.00%	24.08%	1.55
Andres Wines Ltd. 'A'	8.96	3.50%	24.70%	2.56
Todhunter Int'l.	8.94	3.00%	25.74%	2.98
Brown-Forman 'B'	10.07	11.50%	29.43%	0.88
Coors (Adolph) 'B'	23.02	10.00%	29.52%	2.30
PepsiCo, Inc.	33.00	10.50%	31.35%	3.14
Coca-Cola	44.33	19.00%	35.51%	2.33
Boston Beer 'A'	10.59	17.13%	39.58%	0.62
Whitman Corp.	25.19	11.50%	44.26%	2.19
Mondavi (Robert) 'A'	16.47	14.00%	45.84%	1.18
Coca-Cola Enterprises	37.14	27.00%	51.34%	1.38
Hansen Natural Corp.	9.70	17.00%	62.45%	0.57
Average	22.66	12.60%	33.30%	2.00

Source: Value Line Database.

Is Andres Wines undervalued on a relative basis? A simple view of multiples would lead you to conclude this because its PE ratio of 8.96 is significantly lower than the average for the industry.

In making this comparison, we are assuming that Andres Wines has growth and risk characteristics similar to the average for the sector. One way of bringing growth into the comparison is to compute the PEG ratio, which is reported in the last column. Based on the average PEG ratio of 2.00 for the sector and the estimated growth rate for Andres Wines, you obtain the following value for the PE ratio for Andres:

$$\text{PE ratio} = 2.00 \times 3.50\% = 7.00$$

Based on this adjusted PE, Andres Wines looks overvalued even though it has a low PE ratio. While this may seem like an easy adjustment to resolve the problem of differences across firms, the conclusion holds only if these firms are of equivalent risk. Implicitly, this approach also assumes a linear relationship between growth rates and PE.

Sector Regressions   When firms differ on more than one variable, it becomes difficult to modify the multiples to account for the differences across firms. You can run regressions of the multiples against the variables and then use these regressions to find predicted values for each firm. This approach works reasonably well when the number of comparable firms is large and the relationship between the multiple and the variables is stable. When these conditions do not hold, a few outliers can cause the coefficients to change dramatically and make the predictions much less reliable.

ILLUSTRATION 17.2:   Revisiting the Beverage Sector: Sector Regression

The price-earnings ratio is a function of the expected growth rate, risk, and the payout ratio. None of the firms in the beverage sector pay significant dividends, but they differ in terms of risk and growth. The following table summarizes the price-earnings ratios, standard deviation in stock prices, and expected growth rates for the firms on the list:

Company Name	Trailing PE	Expected Growth	Standard Deviation
Coca-Cola Bottling	29.18	9.50%	20.58%
Molson Inc. Ltd. 'A'	43.65	15.50%	21.88%
Anheuser-Busch	24.31	11.00%	22.92%
Corby Distilleries Ltd.	16.24	7.50%	23.66%
Chalone Wine Group Ltd.	21.76	14.00%	24.08%
Andres Wines Ltd. 'A'	8.96	3.50%	24.70%
Todhunter Int'l.	8.94	3.00%	25.74%
Brown-Forman 'B'	10.07	11.50%	29.43%
Coors (Adolph) 'B'	23.02	10.00%	29.52%
PepsiCo, Inc.	33.00	10.50%	31.35%
Coca-Cola	44.33	19.00%	35.51%
Boston Beer 'A'	10.59	17.13%	39.58%
Whitman Corp.	25.19	11.50%	44.26%
Mondavi (Robert) 'A'	16.47	14.00%	45.84%
Coca-Cola Enterprises	37.14	27.00%	51.34%
Hansen Natural Corp.	9.70	17.00%	62.45%

Source: Value Line Database.

Since these firms differ on both risk and expected growth, a regression of PE ratios on both variables is run:

$$PE = 20.87 - 63.98 \text{ Standard deviation} + 183.24 \text{ Expected growth} \qquad R^2 = 51\%$$
$$[3.01] \quad [2.63] \qquad\qquad\qquad [3.66]$$

The numbers in brackets are t-statistics and suggest that the relationships between PE ratios and both variables in the regression are statistically significant. The R-squared indicates the percentage of the differences in PE ratios that is explained by the independent variables. Finally, the regression itself can be used to get predicted PE ratios for the companies in the list.[5] Thus, the predicted PE ratio for Coca-Cola, based on its standard deviation of 35.51 percent and the expected growth rate of 19 percent, would be:

$$\text{Predicted PE}_{\text{Coca-Cola}} = 20.87 - 63.98(.3551) + 183.24(.19) = 32.97$$

Since the actual PE ratio for Coca-Cola was 44.33, this would suggest that the stock is overvalued, given how the rest of the sector is priced.

If you are uncomfortable with the assumption that the relationship between PE and growth is linear, which is what we have assumed in the preceding regression, you could either run nonlinear regressions or modify the variables in the regression to make the relationship more linear. For instance, using the ln(growth rate) instead of the growth rate in the regression yields much better behaved residuals.

---

[5]Both approaches described assume that the relationship between a multiple and the variables driving value are linear. Since this is not always true, you might have to run nonlinear versions of these regressions.

Market Regressions Searching for comparable firms within the sector in which a firm operates is fairly restrictive, especially when there are relatively few firms in the sector or when a firm operates in more than one sector. Since the definition of a comparable firm is not one that is in the same business but one that has the same growth, risk, and cash flow characteristics as the firm being analyzed, you need not restrict your choice of comparable firms to those in the same industry. The regression introduced in the previous section controls for differences on those variables that you believe cause multiples to vary across firms. Based on the variables that determine each multiple, you should be able to regress PE, PBV, and PS ratios against the variables that should affect them:

$$\text{Price to earnings} = f(\text{Growth, Payout ratios, Risk})$$
$$\text{Price to book value} = f(\text{Growth, Payout ratios, Risk, ROE})$$
$$\text{Price to sales} = f(\text{Growth, Payout ratios, Risk, Margin})$$

It is, however, possible that the proxies that you use for risk (beta), growth (expected growth rate), and cash flow (payout) may be imperfect and that the relationship may not be linear. To deal with these limitations, you can add more variables to the regression (e.g., the size of the firm may operate as a good proxy for risk) and use transformations of the variables to allow for nonlinear relationships.

The first advantage of this approach over the subjective comparison across firms in the same sector is that it does quantify, based on actual market data, the degree to which higher growth or risk should affect the multiples. It is true that these estimates can be noisy, but noise is a reflection of the reality that many analysts choose not to face when they make subjective judgments. Second, by looking at all firms in the market, this approach allows you to make more meaningful comparisons of firms that operate in industries with relatively few firms. Third, it allows you to examine whether all firms in an industry are under- or overvalued by estimating their values relative to other firms in the market.

RECONCILING RELATIVE AND DISCOUNTED CASH FLOW VALUATIONS

The two approaches to valuation—discounted cash flow valuation and relative valuation—will generally yield different estimates of value for the same firm. Furthermore, even within relative valuation, you can arrive at different estimates of value, depending on which multiple you use and what firms you based the relative valuation on.

The differences in value between discounted cash flow valuation and relative valuation come from different views of market efficiency, or, put more precisely, market inefficiency. In discounted cash flow valuation, you assume that markets make mistakes, that they correct these mistakes over time, and that these mistakes can often occur across entire sectors or even the entire market. In relative valuation, you assume that while markets make mistakes on individual stocks, they are correct on average. In other words, when you value Adobe Software relative to other small software companies, you are assuming that the market has priced these companies correctly, on average, even though it might have made mistakes in the pricing of each of them individually. Thus, a stock may be overvalued on a discounted cash flow basis but undervalued on a relative basis, if the firms used in the relative valuation are all overpriced by the market. The reverse would occur, if an entire sector or market were underpriced.

CONCLUSION

In relative valuation, you estimate the value of an asset by looking at how similar assets are priced. To make this comparison, you begin by converting prices into multiples—standardizing prices—and then comparing these multiples across firms that you define as comparable. Prices can be standardized based on earnings, book value, revenue, or sector-specific variables.

While the allure of multiples remains their simplicity, there are four steps in using them soundly. First, you have to define the multiple consistently and measure it uniformly across the firms being compared. Second, you need to have a sense of how the multiple varies across firms in the market. In other words, you need to know what a high value, a low value, and a typical value are for the multiple in question. Third, you need to identify the fundamental variables that determine each multiple and how changes in these fundamentals affect the value of the multiple. Finally, you need to find truly comparable firms and adjust for differences between the firms on fundamental characteristics.

QUESTIONS AND SHORT PROBLEMS

1. You can compute the PE ratio using current earnings, trailing earnings, and forward earnings.
   a. What is the difference between the ratios?
   b. Which one is likely to yield the highest value and why?
2. An analyst has computed a ratio of firm value (which he has defined as the market value of equity plus long-term debt minus cash) to earnings after all interest expenses and taxes.
   a. Explain why this ratio is not consistently estimated.
   b. Explain why this might be a problem when comparing firms using this multiple.
3. The chapter noted that multiples have skewed distributions.
   a. What is meant by skewed distributions?
   b. Why do multiples generally have skewed distributions?
   c. What are the implications for analysts who might use industry averages to compare firms?
4. Generally, we cannot compute PE ratios for firms that have negative earnings. What are the implications for statistics such as industry-average PE ratios?

CHAPTER 18

Earnings Multiples

Earnings multiples remain the most commonly used measures of relative value. This chapter begins with a detailed examination of the price-earnings ratio and then moves on to consider variants of the multiple—the PEG ratio and relative PE. It also looks at value multiples, and, in particular, the value to EBITDA multiple in the second part of the chapter. The four-step process described in Chapter 17 is used to look at each of these multiples.

PRICE-EARNINGS RATIO

The price-earnings multiple (PE) is the most widely used and misused of all multiples. Its simplicity makes it an attractive choice in applications ranging from pricing initial public offerings to making judgments on relative value, but its relationship to a firm's financial fundamentals is often ignored, leading to significant errors in applications. This chapter provides some insight into the determinants of price-earnings ratios and how best to use them in valuation.

Definitions of PE Ratio

The price-earnings ratio is the ratio of the market price per share to the earnings per share:

$$PE = \text{Market price per share/Earnings per share}$$

The PE ratio is consistently defined, with the numerator being the value of equity per share and the denominator measuring earnings per share, which is a measure of equity earnings. The biggest problem with PE ratios is the variations on earnings per share used in computing the multiple. In Chapter 17, we saw that PE ratios could be computed using current earnings per share, trailing earnings per share, forward earnings per share, fully diluted earnings per share, and primary earnings per share.

Especially with high-growth (and high-risk) firms, the PE ratio can be very different depending on which measure of earnings per share is used. This can be explained by two factors:

1. *The volatility in earnings per share at these firms.* Forward earnings per share can be substantially higher (or lower) than trailing earnings per share, which, in turn, can be significantly different from current earnings per share.

2. *Management options.* Since high-growth firms tend to have far more employee options outstanding, relative to the number of shares, the differences between diluted and primary earnings per share tend to be large.

When the PE ratios of firms are compared, it is difficult to ensure that the earnings per share are uniformly estimated across the firms for the following reasons:

- Firms often grow by acquiring other firms, and they do not account for acquisitions the same way. Some do only stock-based acquisitions and use only pooling; others use a mixture of pooling and purchase accounting; still others use purchase accounting and write off all or a portion of the goodwill as in-process R&D. These different approaches lead to different measures of earnings per share and different PE ratios.
- Using diluted earnings per share in estimating PE ratios might bring the shares that are covered by management options into the multiple, but they treat options that are deep in-the-money or only slightly in-the-money as equivalent.
- Firm often have discretion in whether they expense or capitalize items, at least for reporting purposes. The expensing of a capital expense gives firms a way of shifting earnings from period to period, and penalizes those firms that are reinvesting more.

For instance, technology firms that account for acquisitions with pooling and do not invest in R&D can have much lower PE ratios than technology firms that use purchase accounting in acquisitions and invest substantial amounts in R&D.

Cross-Sectional Distribution of PE Ratios

A critical step in using PE ratios is to understand how the cross-sectional multiple is distributed across firms in the sector and the market. In this section, the distribution of PE ratios across the entire market is examined.

Market Distribution   Figure 18.1 presents the distribution of PE ratios for U.S. stocks in July 2000. The current PE, trailing PE, and forward PE ratios are all presented in this figure.

Table 18.1 presents summary statistics on all three measures of the price-earnings ratio, starting with the mean and the standard deviation, and including the median and the 10th and 90th percentile values. In computing these values, the PE ratio is set at 200 if it is greater than 200, to prevent outliers from having too large of an influence on the summary statistics.[1]

Looking at all three measures of the PE ratio, the average is consistently higher than the median, reflecting the fact that PE ratios can be very high numbers but cannot be less than zero. This asymmetry in the distributions is captured in the skewness values. The current PE ratios are also higher than the trailing PE ratios, which, in turn, are higher than the forward PE ratios, reflecting the fact that forward earnings were expected to be higher than trailing earnings.

---

[1]The mean and the standard deviation are the summary statistics that are most likely to be affected by these outliers.

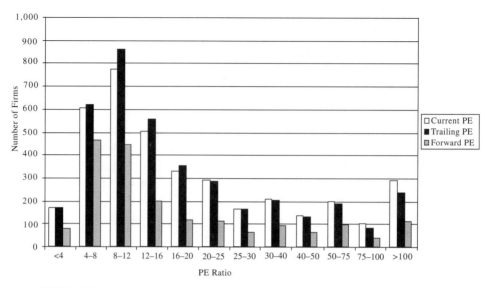

FIGURE 18.1   Current, Trailing, and Forward PE Ratios: U.S. Stocks—July 2000

 pedata.xls: This dataset on the Web summarizes price earnings ratios and
fundamentals by industry group in the United States for the most recent year.

Determinants of the PE Ratio

In Chapter 17 the fundamentals that determine multiples were extracted using a
discounted cash flow model—an equity model like the dividend discount model for
equity multiples and a firm value model for firm multiples. The price-earnings ratio,
being an equity multiple, can be analyzed using a equity valuation model. In this
section, the fundamentals that determine the price-earnings ratio for a high-growth
firm are analyzed.

Discounted Cash Flow Model Perspective on PE Ratios   In Chapter 17 we derived the
PE ratio for a stable growth firm from the stable growth dividend discount model:

TABLE 18.1   Summary Statistics—PE Ratios for U.S. Stocks

	Current PE	Trailing PE	Forward PE
Mean	31.30	28.49	27.21
Standard deviation	44.13	40.86	41.21
Median	14.47	13.68	11.52
Mode	12.00	7.00	7.50
10th percentile	5.63	5.86	5.45
90th percentile	77.87	63.87	64.98
Skewness	17.12	25.96	19.59

$$\frac{P_0}{EPS_0} = PE = \frac{\text{Payout ratio} \times (1 + g_n)}{r - g_n}$$

If the PE ratio is stated in terms of expected earnings in the next time period, this can be simplified to:

$$\frac{P_0}{EPS_1} = \text{Forward PE} = \frac{\text{Payout ratio}}{k_e - g_n}$$

The PE ratio is an increasing function of the payout ratio and the growth rate and a decreasing function of the riskiness of the firm. In fact, we can state the payout ratio as a function of the expected growth rate and return on equity:

$$\text{Payout ratio} = 1 - \text{Expected growth rate/Return on equity} = 1 - g_n/ROE_n$$

Substituting back into the equation,

$$\frac{P_0}{EPS_1} = \text{Forward PE} = \frac{1 - g_n/ROE_n}{k_e - g_n}$$

The price-earnings ratio for a high-growth firm can also be related to fundamentals. In the special case of the two-stage dividend discount model, this relationship can be made explicit fairly simply. When a firm is expected to be in high growth for the next n years and stable growth thereafter, the dividend discount model can be written as follows:

$$P_0 = \frac{EPS_0 \times \text{Payout ratio} \times (1 + g) \times \left[1 - \dfrac{(1+g)^n}{(1+k_{e,hg})^n}\right]}{k_{e,hg} - g}$$
$$+ \frac{EPS_0 \times \text{Payout ratio}_n \times (1+g)^n \times (1+g_n)}{(k_{e,st} - g_n)(1 + k_{e,hg})^n}$$

where EPS_0 = Earnings per share in year 0 (current year)
    g = Growth rate in the first n years
    $k_{e,hg}$ = Cost of equity in high-growth period
    $k_{e,st}$ = Cost of equity in stable-growth period
    Payout = Payout ratio in the first n years
    g_n = Growth rate after n years, forever (stable growth rate)
    $Payout_n$ = Payout ratio after n years for the stable firm

Bringing EPS_0 to the left-hand side of the equation,

$$\frac{P_0}{EPS_0} = \frac{\text{Payout ratio} \times (1+g) \times \left[1 - \frac{(1+g)^n}{(1+k_{e,hg})^n}\right]}{k_{e,hg} - g}$$
$$+ \frac{\text{Payout ratio}_n \times (1+g)^n \times (1+g_n)}{(k_{e,st} - g_n)(1+k_{e,hg})^n}$$

Here again, we can substitute in the fundamental equation relating ROE for payout ratios:

$$\frac{P_0}{EPS_0} = \frac{\left(1 - \frac{g}{ROE_{hg}}\right) \times (1+g) \times \left[1 - \frac{(1+g)^n}{(1+k_{e,hg})^n}\right]}{k_{e,hg} - g}$$
$$+ \frac{\left(1 - \frac{g_n}{ROE_{st}}\right) \times (1+g)^n \times (1+g_n)}{(k_{e,st} - g_n)(1+k_{e,hg})^n}$$

where ROE_{hg} is the return on equity in the high growth period and ROE_{st} is the return on equity in stable growth.

The left-hand side of the equation is the price-earnings ratio. It is determined by:

- *Payout ratio (and return on equity) during the high-growth period and in the stable period.* The PE ratio increases as the payout ratio increases, for any given growth rate. An alternative way of stating the same proposition is that the PE ratio increases as the return on equity increases and decreases as the return on equity decreases.
- *Riskiness (through the discount rate).* The PE ratio becomes lower as riskiness increases.
- *Expected growth rate in earnings in both the high-growth and stable phases.* The PE increases as the growth rate increases, in either period, assuming that the ROE > cost of equity.

This formula is general enough to be applied to any firm, even one that is not paying dividends right now. In fact, the ratio of FCFE to earnings can be substituted for the payout ratio for firms that pay significantly less in dividends than they can afford to.

ILLUSTRATION 18.1: Estimating the PE Ratio for a High-Growth Firm in the Two-Stage Model

Assume that you have been asked to estimate the PE ratio for a firm that has the following characteristics:

Length of high growth = five years

Growth rate in first five years = 25%	Payout ratio in first five years = 20%
Growth rate after five years = 8%	Payout ratio after five years = 50%
Beta = 1.0	Risk-free rate = T-bond rate = 6%
Required rate of return[2] = 6% + 1(5.5%)= 11.5%	Risk premium = 5.5%

$$PE = \frac{0.2 \times (1.25) \times \left[1 - \frac{(1.25)^5}{(1.115)^5}\right]}{(.115 - .25)} + \frac{0.5 \times (1.25)^5 \times (1.08)}{(.115 - .08)(1.115)^5} = 28.75$$

The estimated PE ratio for this firm is 28.75. Note that the return on equity implicit in these inputs can also be computed as follows:

Return on equity in first five years = Growth rate/(1 − Payout ratio) = .25/.8 = 31.25%

Return on equity in stable growth = .08/.5 = 16%

ILLUSTRATION 18.2: Estimating a Fundamental PE Ratio for Procter & Gamble

The following is an estimation of the appropriate PE ratio for Procter & Gamble in May 2001. The assumptions on the growth period, growth rate, and cost of equity are identical to those used in the discounted cash flow valuation of P&G in Chapter 13. The assumptions are:

	High-Growth Period	*Stable-Growth Period*
Length	5 years	Forever after year 5
Cost of equity	8.80%	9.40%
Expected growth rate	13.58%	5.00%
Payout ratio	45.67%	66.67%

The current payout ratio of 45.67% is used for the entire high growth period. After year 5, the payout ratio is estimated based on the expected growth rate of 5% and a return on equity of 15% (based on industry averages):

Stable period payout ratio = 1 − Growth rate/Return on equity = 1 − 5%/15% = 66.67%

The price-earnings ratio can be estimated based on these inputs:

$$PE = \frac{0.4567 \times (1.1358) \times \left[1 - \frac{(1.1358)^5}{(1.0880)^5}\right]}{(.0880 - .1358)} + \frac{0.6667 \times (1.1358)^5 \times (1.05)}{(.094 - .05)(1.0880)^5} = 22.33$$

Based on its fundamentals, you would expect P&G to be trading at 22.33 times earnings. Multiplied by the current earnings per share of $3.00 per share, you get a value per share of $66.99, which is identical to the value obtained in Chapter 13, using the dividend discount model.

---

[2]For purposes of simplicity, the beta and cost of equity are estimated to be the same in both the high-growth and stable-growth periods. They could have been different.

PE Ratios and Expected Extraordinary Growth   The PE ratio of a high growth firm is a function of the expected extraordinary growth rate—the higher the expected growth, the higher the PE ratio for a firm. In Illustration 18.1, for instance, the PE ratio that was estimated to be 28.75, with a growth rate of 25 percent, will change as that expected growth rate changes. Figure 18.2 graphs the PE ratio as a function of the expected growth rate during the high-growth period. As the firm's expected growth rate in the first five years declines from 25 percent to 5 percent, the PE ratio for the firm also decreases from 28.75 to just above 10.

The effect of changes in the expected growth rate varies depending on the level of interest rates. In Figure 18.3, the PE ratios are estimated for different expected growth rates at four levels of riskless rates—4 percent, 6 percent, 8 percent, and 10 percent.

The PE ratio is much more sensitive to changes in expected growth rates when interest rates are low than when they are high. The reason is simple. Growth produces cash flows in the future, and the present value of these cash flows is much smaller at high interest rates. Consequently, the effect of changes in the growth rate on the present value tends to be smaller.

There is a possible link between this finding and how markets react to earnings surprises from high growth firms. When a firm reports earnings that are significantly higher than expected (a positive surprise) or lower than expected (a negative surprise), investors' perceptions of the expected growth rate for this firm can change concurrently, leading to a price effect. You would expect to see much greater price reactions for a given earnings surprise, positive or negative, in a low-interest-rate environment than you would in a high-interest-rate environment.

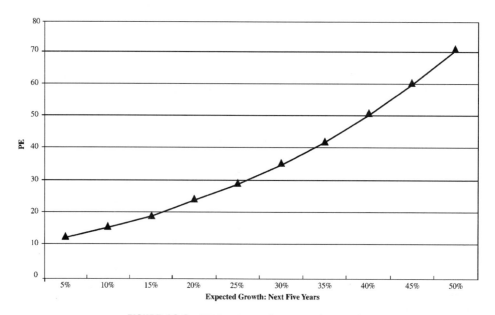

FIGURE 18.2   PE Ratios and Expected Growth

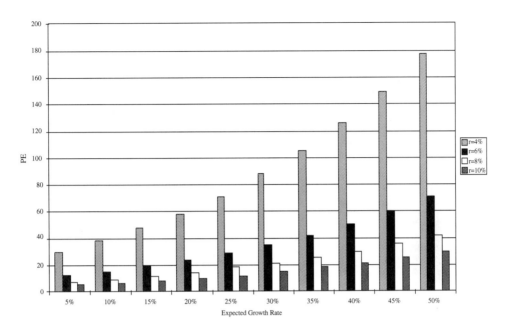

FIGURE 18.3 PE Ratios and Expected Growth: Interest Rate Scenarios

PE Ratios and Risk The PE ratio is a function of the perceived risk of a firm, and the effect shows up in the cost of equity. A firm with a higher cost of equity will trade at a lower multiple of earnings than a similar firm with a lower cost of equity.

Again, the effect of higher risk on PE ratios can be seen using the firm in Illustration 18.1. Recall that the firm, which has an expected growth rate of 25 percent for the next five years and 8% thereafter, has an estimated PE ratio of 28.75, if its beta is assumed to be 1.

$$PE = \frac{0.2 \times (1.25) \times \left[1 - \frac{(1.25)^5}{(1.115)^5}\right]}{(.115 - .25)} + \frac{0.5 \times (1.25)^5 \times (1.08)}{(.115 - .08)(1.115)^5} = 28.75$$

If you assume that the beta is 1.5, the cost of equity increases to 14.25 percent, leading to a PE ratio of 14.87:

$$PE = \frac{0.2 \times (1.25) \times \left[1 - \frac{(1.25)^5}{(1.1425)^5}\right]}{(.1425 - .25)} + \frac{0.5 \times (1.25)^5 \times (1.08)}{(.1425 - .08)(1.1425)^5} = 14.87$$

The higher cost of equity reduces the value created by expected growth.

In Figure 18.4, you can see the impact of changing the beta on the price earnings ratio for four high growth scenarios—8%, 15%, 20%, and 25% for the next five years.

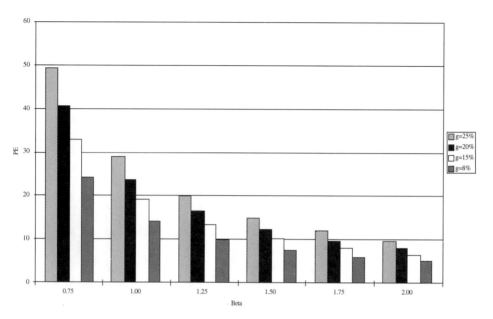

FIGURE 18.4   PE Ratios and Beta: Growth Rate Scenarios

As the beta increases, the PE ratio decreases in all four scenarios. However, the difference between the PE ratios across the four growth classes is lower when the beta is very high, and increases as the beta decreases. This would suggest that at very high risk levels, a firm's PE ratio is likely to increase more as the risk decreases than as growth increases. For many high-growth firms that are viewed as both very risky and having good growth potential, reducing risk may increase value much more than increasing expected growth.

 eqmult.xls: This spreadsheet allows you to estimate the price-earnings ratio for a stable growth or high-growth firm, given its fundamentals.

Using the PE Ratio for Comparisons

Now that we have defined the PE ratio, looked at the cross-sectional distribution, and examined the fundamentals that determine the multiple, we can use PE ratios to make valuation judgments. This section begins by looking at how best to compare the PE ratio for a market over time and follows up by a comparison of PE ratios across different markets. Finally, it uses PE ratios to analyze firms within a sector and then expands the analysis to the entire market. In doing so, note that PE ratios vary across time, markets, industries, and firms because of differences in fundamentals—higher growth, lower risk, and higher payout generally result in higher PE ratios. When comparisons are made, you have to control for these differences in risk, growth rates, and payout ratios.

Comparing a Market's PE Ratio across Time Analysts and market strategists often compare the PE ratio of a market to its historical average to make judgments about whether the market is under- or overvalued. Thus a market that is trading at a PE ratio which is much higher than its historical norms is often considered to be overvalued, whereas one that is trading at a ratio lower is considered undervalued.

While reversion to historic norms remains a very strong force in financial markets, we should be cautious about drawing too strong a conclusion from such comparisons. As the fundamentals (interest rates, risk premiums, expected growth, and payout) change over time, the PE ratio will also change. Other things remaining equal, for instance, we would expect the following:

- An increase in interest rates should result in a higher cost of equity for the market and a lower PE ratio.
- A greater willingness to take risk on the part of investors will result in a lower risk premium for equity and a higher PE ratio across all stocks.
- An increase in expected growth in earnings across firms will result in a higher PE ratio for the market.
- An increase in the return on equity at firms will result in a higher payout ratio for any given growth rate [g = (1 – Payout ratio)ROE] and a higher PE ratio for all firms.

In other words, it is difficult to draw conclusions about PE ratios without looking at these fundamentals. A more appropriate comparison is therefore not between PE ratios across time, but between the actual PE ratio and the predicted PE ratio based on fundamentals existing at that time.

ILLUSTRATION 18.3: PE Ratios across Time

The following are the summary economic statistics at two points in time for the same stock market. The interest rates in the first period were significantly higher than the interest rates in the second period.

	Period 1	*Period 2*
T-bond rate	11.00%	6.00%
Market premium	5.50%	5.50%
Expected inflation	5.00%	4.00%
Expected growth in real GNP	3.00%	2.50%
Average payout ratio	50%	50%
Expected PE ratio	$(0.5 \times 1.08)/(.165 - .08) = 6.35$	$(0.5 \times 1.065)/(.115 - .065) = 10.65$

The PE ratio in the second time period will be significantly higher than the PE ratio in the first period, largely because of the drop in real interest rates (nominal interest rate − expected inflation).

ILLUSTRATION 18.4:   PE Ratios across Time for the S&P 500

Figure 18.5 summarizes the earnings-price (EP) ratios for S&P 500 and Treasury bond rates at the end of each year from 1960 to 2000. There is a strong positive relationship between EP ratios and T-bond rates, as evidenced by the correlation of 0.6854 between the two variables. In addition, there is evidence that the term structure also affects the PE ratio. In the following regression, we regress EP ratios against the level of T-bond rates and the yield spread (T-bond minus T-bill rate), using data from 1965 to 2000.

$$EP = .0188 + 0.7762 \text{ T-bond rate} - 0.4066(\text{T-bond rate} - \text{T-bill rate}) \qquad R^2 = 0.495$$
$$\quad [1.93] \quad [6.08] \qquad\qquad\qquad [-1.37]$$

Other things remaining equal, this regression suggests that:

- Every 1% increase in the T-bond rate increases the EP ratio by 0.7762%. This is not surprising, but it quantifies the impact that higher interest rates have on the PE ratio.
- Every 1% increase in the difference between T-bond and T-bill rates reduces the EP ratio by 0.41%. Flatter or negatively sloping term yield curves seem to correspond to lower PE ratios, and upwardly sloping yield curves to higher PE ratios. While at first sight this may seem surprising, the slope of the yield curve, at least in the United States, has been a leading indicator of economic growth, with more upwardly sloped curves going with higher growth.

Based on this regression, the predicted EP ratio at the beginning of 2001, with the T-bill rate at 4.9% and the T-bond rate at 5.1%, would have been:

$$EP_{2000} = .0188 + 0.7762(.054) - 0.4066(.051 - .049) = .0599 \text{ or } 5.99\%$$
$$PE_{2000} = 1/EP_{2000} = 1/.0599 = 16.69$$

Since the S&P 500 was trading at a multiple of 25 times earnings in early 2001, this would have indicated an overvalued market. This regression can be enriched by adding other variables that should be correlated to the price-earnings ratio, such as expected growth in gross national product (GNP) and payout ratios, as independent variables. In fact, a fairly strong argument can be made that the influx of technology stocks into the S&P 500 over the past decade, the increase in return on equity at U.S. companies over the same period, and a decline in risk premiums could all explain the increase in PE ratios over the period.

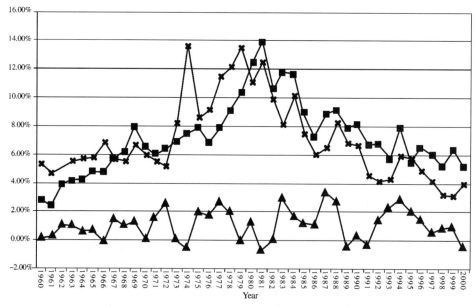

FIGURE 18.5 S&P 500—Earnings Yield, T-bond Rate, and Yield Spread
Source: Federal Reserve.

Comparing PE Ratios across Countries Comparisons are often made between price-earnings ratios in different countries with the intention of finding undervalued and overvalued markets. Markets with lower PE ratios are viewed as undervalued and those with higher PE ratios are considered overvalued. Given the wide differences that exist between countries on fundamentals, it is clearly misleading to draw these conclusions. For instance, you would expect to see the following, other things remaining equal:

- Countries with higher real interest rates should have lower PE ratios than countries with lower real interest rates.
- Countries with higher expected real growth should have higher PE ratios than countries with lower real growth.
- Countries that are viewed as riskier (and thus command higher risk premiums) should have lower PE ratios than safer countries.
- Countries where companies are more efficient in their investments (and earn a higher return on these investments) should trade at higher PE ratios.

ILLUSTRATION 18.5: PE Ratios in Markets with Different Fundamentals

The following are the summary economic statistics for stock markets in two different countries—country 1 and country 2. The key difference between the two countries is that interest rates are much higher in country 1.

	Country 1	Country 2
T-bond rate	10.00%	5.00%
Market premium	4.00%	5.50%
Expected inflation	4.00%	4.00%
Expected growth in real GNP	2.00%	3.00%
Average payout ratio	50%	50%
Expected PE ratio	$(0.5 \times 1.06)/(.14 - .06) = 6.625$	$(0.5 \times 1.07)/(.105 - .07) = 15.29$

In this case, the expected PE ratio in country 2 is significantly higher than the PE ratio in country 1, but it can be justified on the basis of differences in financial fundamentals. (Note that nominal growth = real growth rate + expected inflation.)

ILLUSTRATION 18.6:   Comparing PE Ratios across Markets

This principle can be extended to broader comparisons of PE ratios across countries. The following table summarizes PE ratios across different developed markets in July 2000, together with dividend yields and interest rates (short-term and long-term) at that time:

Country	PE	Dividend Yield	2-Year Rate	10-Year Rate	10-Year – 2-Year
United Kingdom	22.02	2.59%	5.93%	5.85%	–0.08%
Germany	26.33	1.88%	5.06%	5.32%	0.26%
France	29.04	1.34%	5.11%	5.48%	0.37%
Switzerland	19.60	1.42%	3.62%	3.83%	0.21%
Belgium	14.74	2.66%	5.15%	5.70%	0.55%
Italy	28.23	1.76%	5.27%	5.70%	0.43%
Sweden	32.39	1.11%	4.67%	5.26%	0.59%
Netherlands	21.10	2.07%	5.10%	5.47%	0.37%
Australia	21.69	3.12%	6.29%	6.25%	–0.04%
Japan	52.25	0.71%	0.58%	1.85%	1.27%
United States	25.14	1.10%	6.05%	5.85%	–0.20%
Canada	26.14	0.99%	5.70%	5.77%	0.07%

A naive comparison of PE ratios suggests that Japanese stocks, with a PE ratio of 52.25, are overvalued, while Belgian stocks, with a PE ratio of 14.74, are undervalued. There is, however, a strong negative correlation between PE ratios and 10-year interest rates (–.73) and a positive correlation between the PE ratio and the yield spread (.70). A cross-sectional regression of PE ratio on interest rates and expected growth yields the following:

$$\text{PE ratio} = 42.62 - 360.9 \text{ 10-year rate} + 846.61(\text{10-year rate} - \text{2-year rate}) \qquad R^2 = 59\%$$
$$\qquad\quad [2.78] \quad [1.41] \qquad\qquad\qquad\qquad [1.08]$$

The coefficients are of marginal significance, partly because of the small size of the sample. Based on this regression, the predicted PE ratios for the countries are shown in the following table:

Country	Actual PE	Predicted PE	Under- or Overvalued
United Kingdom	22.02	20.83	5.71%
Germany	26.33	25.62	2.76%
France	29.04	25.98	11.80%
Switzerland	19.60	30.58	–35.90%
Belgium	14.74	26.71	–44.81%
Italy	28.23	25.69	9.89%
Sweden	32.39	28.63	13.12%
Netherlands	21.10	26.01	–18.88%
Australia	21.69	19.73	9.96%
Japan	52.25	46.70	11.89%
United States	25.14	19.81	26.88%
Canada	26.14	22.39	16.75%

From this comparison, Belgian and Swiss stocks would be the most undervalued, while U.S. stocks would have been most overvalued.

ILLUSTRATION 18.7: An Example with Emerging Markets

This example is extended to examine PE ratio differences across emerging markets at the end of 2000. In this table, the country risk factor is that estimated by the *Economist* for these emerging markets, scaled from 0 (safest) to 100 (riskiest).

Country	PE Ratio	Interest Rate	GDP Real Growth	Country Risk
Argentina	14	18.00%	2.50%	45
Brazil	21	14.00%	4.80%	35
Chile	25	9.50%	5.50%	15
Hong Kong	20	8.00%	6.00%	15
India	17	11.48%	4.20%	25
Indonesia	15	21.00%	4.00%	50
Malaysia	14	5.67%	3.00%	40
Mexico	19	11.50%	5.50%	30
Pakistan	14	19.00%	3.00%	45
Peru	15	18.00%	4.90%	50
Philippines	15	17.00%	3.80%	45
Singapore	24	6.50%	5.20%	5
South Korea	21	10.00%	4.80%	25
Thailand	21	12.75%	5.50%	25
Turkey	12	25.00%	2.00%	35
Venezuela	20	15.00%	3.50%	45

The regression of PE ratios on these variables provides the following:

PE = 16.16 − 7.94 Interest rates + 154.40 Real growth − 0.112 Country risk $R^2 = 74\%$
    [3.61]   [0.52]   [2.38]   [1.78]

Countries with higher real growth and lower country risk have higher PE ratios, but the level of interest rates seems to have only a marginal impact. The regression can be used to estimate the price earnings ratio for Turkey:

Predicted PE for Turkey = 16.16 − 7.94(.25) + 154.40(.02) − 0.112(35) = 13.354

At a PE ratio of 12, the market can be viewed as slightly undervalued.

Comparing PE Ratios across Firms in a Sector The most common approach to estimating the PE ratio for a firm is to choose a group of comparable firms, to calculate the average PE ratio for this group, and to subjectively adjust this average for differences between the firm being valued and the comparable firms. There are several problems with this approach. First, the definition of a comparable firm is essentially a subjective one. The use of other firms in the industry as the control group is often not the solution because firms within the same industry can have very different business mixes and risk and growth profiles. There is also plenty of potential for bias. One clear example of this is in takeovers, where a high PE ratio for the target firm is justified using the price-earnings ratios of a control group of other firms that have been taken over. This group is designed to give an upwardly biased estimate of the PE ratio and other multiples. Second, even when a legitimate group of comparable firms can be constructed, differences will continue to persist in fundamentals between the firm being valued and this group. It is very difficult to subjectively adjust for differences across firms. Thus, knowing that a firm has much higher growth potential than other firms in the comparable firm list would lead you to estimate a higher PE ratio for that firm, but how much higher is an open question.

The alternative to subjective adjustments is to control explicitly for the one or two variables that you believe account for the bulk of the differences in PE ratios across companies in the sector in a regression. The regression equation can then be used to estimate predicted PE ratios for each firm in the sector and these predicted values can be compared to the actual PE ratios to make judgments on whether stocks are under- or overpriced.

ILLUSTRATION 18.8: Comparing PE Ratios for Global Telecom Firms

The following table summarizes the trailing PE ratios for global telecom firms with American depository receipts (ADRs) listed in the United States in September 2000. The earnings per share used are those estimated using generally accepted accounting principles in the United States and thus should be much more directly comparable than the earnings reported by these firms in their local markets.

Company Name	PE	Growth	Emerging Market Dummy Variable
APT Satellite Holdings ADR	31.00	33.00%	1
Asia Satellite Telecom Holdings ADR	19.60	16.00%	1
British Telecommunications PLC ADR	25.70	7.00%	0
Cable & Wireless PLC ADR	29.80	14.00%	0
Deutsche Telekom AG ADR	24.60	11.00%	0
France Telecom SA ADR	45.20	19.00%	0
Gilat Communications	22.70	31.00%	1
Hellenic Telecommunication Organization SA ADR	12.80	12.00%	1
Korea Telecom ADR	71.30	44.00%	1
Matav RT ADR	21.50	22.00%	1
Nippon Telegraph & Telephone ADR	44.30	20.00%	0
Portugal Telecom SA ADR	20.80	13.00%	0
PT Indosat ADR	7.80	6.00%	1
Royal KPN NV ADR	35.70	13.00%	0
Swisscom AG ADR	18.30	11.00%	0
Tele Danmark AS ADR	27.00	9.00%	0
Telebras ADR	8.90	7.50%	1
Telecom Argentina ADR B	12.50	8.00%	1
Telecom Corporation of New Zealand ADR	11.20	11.00%	0
Telecom Italia SPA ADR	42.20	14.00%	0
Telecomunicaciones de Chile ADR	16.60	8.00%	1
Telefonica SA ADR	32.50	18.00%	0
Telefonos de Mexico ADR L	21.10	14.00%	1
Telekomunikasi Indonesia ADR	28.40	32.00%	1
Telstra ADR	21.70	12.00%	0

The earnings per share represent trailing earnings, and the price-earnings ratios for each firm are reported in the second column. The analyst estimates of expected growth in earnings per share over the next five years are shown in the next column. In the last column, we introduce a dummy variable indicating whether the firm is from an emerging market or a developed one, since emerging market telecom firms are likely to be exposed to far more risk. Not surprisingly, the firms with the lowest PE ratios, such as Telebras and PT Indosat, are from emerging markets.

Regressing the PE ratio for the sector against the expected growth rate and the emerging market dummy yields the following results:

PE ratio = 13.12 + 121.22 Expected growth − 13.85 Emerging market dummy R^2 = 66%
     [3.78] [6.29]   [3.84]

Firms with higher growth have significantly higher PE ratios than firms with lower expected growth. In addition, this regression indicates that an emerging market telecom firm should trade at a much lower PE ratio than one in a developed market. Using this regression to get predicted values, we get:

Company Name	PE	Predicted PE	Under- or Overvalued
APT Satellite Holdings ADR	31.0	39.27	−21.05%
Asia Satellite Telecom Holdings ADR	19.6	18.66	5.05%
British Telecommunications PLC ADR	25.7	21.60	18.98%
Cable & Wireless PLC ADR	29.8	30.09	−0.95%
Deutsche Telekom AG ADR	24.6	26.45	−6.99%
France Telecom SA ADR	45.2	36.15	25.04%
Gilat Communications	22.7	36.84	−38.38%
Hellenic Telecommunication Organization SA ADR	12.8	13.81	−7.31%
Korea Telecom ADR	71.3	52.60	35.55%
Matav RT ADR	21.5	25.93	−17.09%
Nippon Telegraph & Telephone ADR	44.3	37.36	18.58%
Portugal Telecom SA ADR	20.8	28.87	−27.96%
PT Indosat ADR	7.8	6.54	19.35%
Royal KPN NV ADR	35.7	28.87	23.64%
Swisscom AG ADR	18.3	26.45	−30.81%
Tele Danmark AS ADR	27.0	24.03	12.38%
Telebras ADR	8.9	8.35	6.54%
Telecom Argentina ADR B	12.5	8.96	39.51%
Telecom Corporation of New Zealand ADR	11.2	26.45	−57.66%
Telecom Italia SPA ADR	42.2	30.09	40.26%
Telecomunicaciones de Chile ADR	16.6	8.96	85.27%
Telefonica SA ADR	32.5	34.94	−6.97%
Telefonos de Mexico ADR L	21.1	16.23	29.98%
Telekomunikasi Indonesia ADR	28.4	38.05	−25.37%
Telstra ADR	21.7	27.66	−21.55%

Based on the predicted PE ratios, Telecom Corporation of New Zealand is the most undervalued firm in this group and Telecom de Chile is the most overvalued firm.

Comparing PE Ratios across Firms in the Market   In the preceding section, comparable firms were narrowly defined to be other firms in the same business. This section considers ways in which we can expand the number of comparable firms by looking at an entire sector or even the market. There are two advantages in doing this. The first is that the estimates may become more precise as the number of comparable firms increase. The second is that it allows you to pinpoint when firms in a small subgroup are being under- or overvalued relative to the rest of the sector or the market. Since the differences across firms will increase when you loosen the definition of comparable firms, you have to adjust for these differences. The simplest way of doing this is with a multiple regression, with the PE ratio as the dependent variable, and proxies for risk, growth, and payout forming the independent variables.

Past Studies   One of the earliest regressions of PE ratios against fundamentals across the entire market was done by Kisor and Whitbeck in 1963. Using data from the Bank of New York as of June 1962 for 135 stocks, they arrived at the following regression:

$$PE = 8.2 + 1.5 \text{ (Growth rate in earnings)} + 6.7 \text{ (Payout ratio)}$$
$$- .2 \text{ (Standard deviation in EPS changes)}$$

Malkiel and Cragg followed up by estimating the coefficients for a regression of the price-earnings ratio on the growth rate, the payout ratio, and the beta for stocks for the time period from 1961 to 1965.

Year	Equation	R-squared
1961	$PE = 4.73 + 3.28\ g + 2.05\ \pi - 0.85\ \beta$	0.70
1962	$PE = 11.06 + 1.75\ g + 0.78\ \pi - 1.61\ \beta$	0.70
1963	$PE = 2.94 + 2.55\ g + 7.62\ \pi - 0.27\ \beta$	0.75
1964	$PE = 6.71 + 2.05\ g + 5.23\ \pi - 0.89\ \beta$	0.75
1965	$PE = 0.96 + 2.74\ g + 5.01\ \pi - 0.35\ \beta$	0.85

where PE = Price-earnings ratio at the start of the year
        g = Growth rate in earnings
        π = Earnings payout ratio at the start of the year
        β = Beta of the stock

They concluded that while such models were useful in explaining PE ratios, they were of little use in predicting performance. In both these studies, the three variables used—payout, risk, and growth—represent the three variables that were identified as the determinants of PE ratios in an earlier section.

The regressions were updated from 1987 to 1991 in the previous edition of this book using a much broader sample of stocks.[3] The results are summarized as follows:

Year	Regression	R-squared
1987	PE = 7.1839 + 13.05 Payout − 0.6259 Beta + 6.5659 EGR	0.9287
1988	PE = 2.5848 + 29.91 Payout − 4.5157 Beta + 19.9143 EGR	0.9465
1989	PE = 4.6122 + 59.74 Payout − 0.7546 Beta + 9.0072 EGR	0.5613
1990	PE = 3.5955 + 10.88 Payout − 0.2801 Beta + 5.4573 EGR	0.3497
1991	PE = 2.7711 + 22.89 Payout − 0.1326 Beta + 13.8653 EGR	0.3217

where EGR is a historical growth rate in EPS. Note the volatility in the R-squared over time and the changes in the coefficients on the independent variables. For in-

---

[3]These regressions look at all stocks listed on the Compustat database. The growth rate over the previous five years was used as the expected growth rate, and the betas were estimated from the CRSP tape.

stance, the R-squared in the regressions reported declines from 0.93 in 1987 to 0.32 in 1991, and the coefficients change dramatically over time. Part of the reason for these shifts is that earnings are volatile, and price-earnings ratios reflect this volatility. The low R-squared for the 1991 regression can be ascribed to the recession's effects on earnings in that year. These regressions are clearly not stable, and the predicted values are likely to be noisy.

Updated Market Regressions   The data needed to run market regressions is much more easily available today than it was for these earlier studies. In this section, the results of two regressions are presented. In the following regression, run in July 2000 the PE ratio was regressed against payout ratios, betas, and expected growth for all firms in the market:[4]

$$PE = -17.22 + 155.65 \text{ (Expected growth rate)} + 16.44 \text{ (Beta)} + 10.93 \text{ (Payout ratio)}$$
$$[7.06] \quad [6.42] \qquad\qquad\qquad [6.77] \qquad\quad [5.02]$$
$$R\text{-}squared = 24.9\% \qquad Number\ of\ observations = 2,498$$

With the sample size expanding to about 2,500 firms, this regression represents the broadest measure of relative value.

This regression has a low R-squared, but it is more a reflection of the noise in PE ratios than it is on the regression methodology. As you will see, the market regressions for price-to-book value and price-to-sales ratios tend to be better behaved and have a higher R-squared than PE ratio regressions. The other disquieting finding is that the coefficients on the variables do not always have the signs you would expect them to have. For instance, higher-risk stocks (higher betas) have higher PE ratios, when fundamentals would lead you to expect the opposite.

Problems with the Regression Methodology   The regression methodology is a convenient way of compressing large amounts of data into one equation capturing the relationship between PE ratios and financial fundamentals. But it does have its limitations. First, the independent variables are correlated with each other.[5] For example, high-growth firms tend to have high risk and low payout ratios, as is clear from Table 18.2, which summarizes the correlation between beta, growth, and payout ratios for all U.S. firms. Note the negative correlation between payout ratios and growth, and the positive correlation between beta and growth. This multicollinearity makes the coefficients of the regressions unreliable (increase standard error) and may explain the wrong signs on the coefficients and the large changes in these coefficients from period to period. Second, the regression is based on a linear relationship between PE ratios and the fundamentals, and that might not be appropriate. An analysis of the residuals from a regression may suggest transformations of the independent variables (squared or natural logs) that work better in explaining PE ratios. Third, the basic relationship between PE ratios and financial variables itself is not stable, and if it shifts from year to year, the predictions from the regression equation may not be reliable for extended periods. For

---

[4]The t-statistics are reported in brackets below the coefficients.

[5]In a multiple regression, the independent variables should be independent of each other.

TABLE 18.2 Correlations between Independent Variables

	PE	Growth	Beta	Payout Ratio
PE	1.000			
Growth rate	0.288	1.000		
Beta	0.141	0.292[1]	1.000	
Payout ratio	−0.087	−0.404[1]	−0.183[1]	1.000

[1]Significant at 1% level.

all these reasons, the regression approach is useful but it has to be viewed as one more tool in the search for true value.

ILLUSTRATION 18.9:   Valuing Procter & Gamble (P&G) Using the Market Regression

In an earlier illustration, we estimated a PE ratio for P&G from fundamentals. To value P&G using the broader regressions, you would first have to estimate the values, for P&G, of the independent variables in the regression:

P&G's beta = 0.85
P&G's payout ratio = 45.67%
P&G's expected growth rate = 13.58%

Note that these variables have been defined consistently with the variables in the regression. Thus, the growth rate over the next five years, the beta over the past five years, and the payout ratio over the most recent four quarters are used to make the prediction. Based on the price-earnings ratio regression for all stocks in the market, you would get a predicted PE ratio of:

$$\text{Predicted PE}_{P\&G} = -17.22 + 155.65(\text{Growth}) + 16.44(\text{Beta}) + 10.93(\text{Payout})$$
$$= -17.22 + 155.65(.1358) + 16.44(0.85) + 10.93(.4567) = 22.88$$

Based on the market regression, you would expect P&G to be trading at 22.88 times earnings.

 pereg.htm: **This dataset on the Web reports the results of the latest regression of PE ratios against fundamentals, using all firms in the market.**

NORMALIZING EARNINGS FOR PE RATIOS

The dependence of PE ratios on current earnings makes them particularly vulnerable to the year-to-year swings that often characterize reported earnings. In making comparisons, therefore, it may make much more sense to use normalized earnings. The process used to normalize earnings varies widely, but the most common approach is a simple averaging of earnings across time. For a cyclical firm, for instance, you would average the earnings per share across a cycle. In doing so, you should adjust for inflation. If you do decide to normalize earnings for the firm you are valuing, consistency demands that you normalize it for the comparable firms in the sample as well.

THE PEG RATIO

Portfolio managers and analysts sometimes compare PE ratios to the expected growth rate to identify undervalued and overvalued stocks. In the simplest form of this approach, firms with PE ratios less than their expected growth rate are viewed as undervalued. In its more general form, the ratio of PE ratio to growth (PEG) is used as a measure of relative value, with a lower value believed to indicate that a firm is undervalued. For many analysts, especially those tracking firms in high-growth sectors, these approaches offer the promise of a way of controlling for differences in growth across firms, while preserving the inherent simplicity of a multiple.

Definition of PEG Ratio

The PEG ratio is defined to be the price-earnings ratio divided by the expected growth rate in earnings per share:

$$PEG\ ratio = PE\ ratio / Expected\ growth\ rate$$

For instance, a firm with a PE ratio of 20 and a growth rate of 10 percent is estimated to have a PEG ratio of 2. Consistency requires the growth rate used in this estimate be the growth rate in earnings per share rather than operating income, because PEG ratio is an equity multiple.

Given the many definitions of the PE ratio, which one should you use to estimate the PEG ratio? The answer depends on the base on which the expected growth rate is computed. If the expected growth rate in earnings per share is based on earnings in the most recent year (current earnings), the PE ratio that should be used is the current PE ratio. If it is based on trailing earnings, the PE ratio used should be the trailing PE ratio. The forward PE ratio should never be used in this computation, since it may result in a double counting of growth. To see why, assume that you have a firm with a current price of $30 and current earnings per share of $1.50. The firm is expected to double its earnings per share over the next year (forward earnings per share will be $3.00) and then have earnings growth of 5 percent a year for the following four years. An analyst estimating growth in earnings per share for this firm, with the current earnings per share as a base, will estimate a growth rate of 19.44%:

$$Expected\ earnings\ growth = [(1 + Growth\ rate_{year\ 1})(1 + Growth\ rate_{years\ 2-5})^4]^{1/5} - 1$$
$$= [2.00(1.05)^4]^{1/5} - 1 = .1944$$

If you used the forward PE ratio and this estimate of earnings growth to estimate the PEG ratio, you would get:

$$PEG\ ratio\ based\ on\ forward\ PE = Forward\ PE / Expected\ growth_{next\ 5\ years}$$
$$= (Price / Forward\ EPS) / Expected\ growth_{next\ 5\ years}$$
$$= (\$30/\$3)/19.44 = 0.51$$

On a PEG ratio basis, this firm seems to be cheap. Note, however, that the growth in the first year has been counted twice—the forward earnings are high because of the doubling of earnings, leading to a low forward PE ratio, and the growth rate is high for the same reason. A consistent estimate of the PEG ratio would require using a current PE and the expected growth rate over the next five years:

$$\text{PEG ratio based on current PE} = (\text{Price/Current EPS})/\text{Expected growth rate}_{\text{next 5 years}}$$
$$= (\$30/\$1.50)/19.44 = 1.03$$

Alternatively, you could compute the PEG ratio based on forward earnings per share and the growth rate from years 2 through 5:

$$\text{PEG ratio based on forward PE} = (\text{Price/Forward EPS})/\text{Expected growth}_{\text{years 2-5}}$$
$$= (\$30/\$3)/5 = 2.0$$

If this approach is used, the PEG ratio would have to be estimated uniformly for all of the other comparable firms as well, using the forward PE and the expected growth rate from years 2 through 5.

Building on the theme of uniformity, the PEG ratio should be estimated using the same growth estimates for all firms in the sample. You should not, for instance, use five-year growth rates for some firms and one-year growth rates for others. One way of ensuring uniformity is to use the same source for earnings growth estimates for all the firms in the group. For instance, I/B/E/S and Zacks both provide consensus estimates from analysts of earnings per share growth over the next five years for most U.S. firms. Alternatively, you could estimate expected growth rates for each company in the group.

Cross-Sectional Distribution of PEG Ratios

Now that the PEG ratio has been defined, the cross-sectional distribution of PEG ratios across all U.S. firms is examined in Figure 18.6. In estimating these PEG ratios, the analyst estimates of growth in earnings per share over the next five years is used in conjunction with the current PE. Any firm, therefore, that has negative earnings per share or lacks an analyst estimate of expected growth is dropped from the sample. This may be a source of bias, since larger and more liquid firms are more likely to be followed by analysts.

PEG ratios are most widely used in analyzing technology firms. Figure 18.7 contains the distribution of PEG ratios for technology stocks, using analyst estimates of growth again to arrive at the PEG ratios. Note that of the 448 firms for which PE ratios were estimated, only 335 have PEG ratios available; the 113 firms for which analyst estimates of growth were not available have been dropped from the sample.

Finally, Table 18.3 includes the summary statistics for PEG ratios for technology stocks and non-technology stocks.[6] The average PEG ratio for technology stocks is much higher than the average PEG ratio for nontechnology stocks. In addition, the average is much higher than the median for both groups.

---

[6]The PEG ratio is capped at 10.

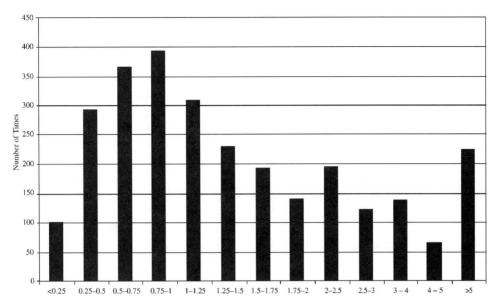

FIGURE 18.6 PEG Ratios: U.S. Stock—July 2000
Source: Value Line.

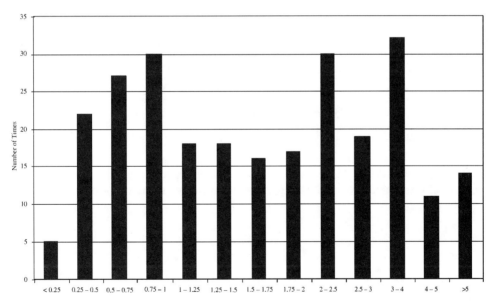

FIGURE 18.7 PEG Ratios for Technology Stocks: United States—July 2000
Source: Value Line.

TABLE 18.3   PEG Ratios: Technology Stocks versus Nontechnology Stocks

	Technology Stocks	Nontechnology Stocks	All Stocks
Mean	5.83	2.99	3.31
Standard error	1.03	0.36	0.34
Median	2.03	1.13	1.18
Standard deviation	18.05	17.68	17.74
Skewness	7.81	22.09	20.33
Range	198.62	569.73	569.73
Minimum	0.08	0.00	0.00
Maximum	198.70	569.73	569.73
Number of firms	309	2,454	2,763

 pedata.xls: **This dataset on the Web summarizes the PEG ratios by industry for firms in the United States.**

Determinants of the PEG Ratio

The determinants of the PEG ratio can be extracted using the same approach used to estimate the determinants of the PE ratio. The value per share in a two-stage dividend discount model can be written as:

$$
P_0 = \frac{EPS_0 \times \text{Payout ratio} \times (1+g) \times \left[1 - \dfrac{(1+g)^n}{(1+k_{e,hg})^n}\right]}{k_{e,hg} - g}
$$
$$
+ \frac{EPS_0 \times \text{Payout ratio}_n \times (1+g)^n \times (1+g_n)}{(k_{e,st} - g_n)(1+k_{e,hg})^n}
$$

Dividing both sides of the equation by the earnings per share (EPS_0) first and the expected growth rate over the high growth period (g) next, you can estimate the PEG ratio:

$$
PEG = \frac{\text{Payout ratio} \times (1+g) \times \left[1 - \dfrac{(1+g)^n}{(1+k_{e,hg})^n}\right]}{g(k_{e,hg} - g)}
$$
$$
+ \frac{\text{Payout ratio}_n \times (1+g)^n \times (1+g_n)}{g(k_{e,st} - g_n)(1+k_{e,hg})^n}
$$

Even a cursory glance at this equation suggests that analysts who believe that using the PEG ratio neutralizes the growth effect are mistaken. Instead of disappearing, the growth rate becomes even more deeply entangled in the multiple. In fact, as the growth rate increases, the effects on the PEG ratio can be both positive and negative and the net effect can vary depending on the level of the growth rate.

ILLUSTRATION 18.10:   Estimating the PEG Ratio for a Firm

Assume that you have been asked to estimate the PEG ratio for a firm that has the same characteristics as the firm described in Illustration 18.1:

Growth rate in first five years = 25%   Payout ratio in first five years = 20%
Growth rate after five years = 8%   Payout ratio after five years = 50%
Beta = 1.0   Risk-free rate = T-bond rate = 6%
Required rate of return = 6% + 1(5.5%)= 11.5%

The PEG ratio can be estimated as follows:

$$PEG = \frac{0.2 \times (1.25) \times \left[1 - \frac{(1.25)^5}{(1.115)^5}\right]}{.25(.115 - .25)} + \frac{0.5 \times (1.25)^5 \times (1.08)}{.25(.115 - .08)(1.115)^5} = 1.15$$

The PEG ratio for this firm, based on fundamentals, is 1.15.

EXPLORING THE RELATIONSHIP WITH FUNDAMENTALS

Consider first the effect of changing the growth rate during the high-growth period (next five years) from 25%. Figure 18.8 presents the PEG ratio as a function of the expected growth rate. As the growth rate increases, the PEG ratio initially decreases, but then starts increasing again. This U-shaped relationship between PEG ratios and growth suggests that comparing PEG ratios across firms with widely different growth rates can be complicated.

Next, consider the effect of changing the riskiness (beta) of this firm on the PEG ratio. Figure 18.9 presents the PEG ratio as a function of the beta. Here, the relationship is clear. As the risk increases, the PEG ratio of a firm decreases. When comparing the PEG ratios of firms with different risk

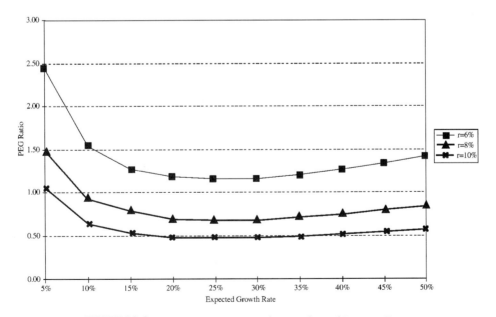

FIGURE 18.8   PEG Ratios, Expected Growth, and Interest Rates

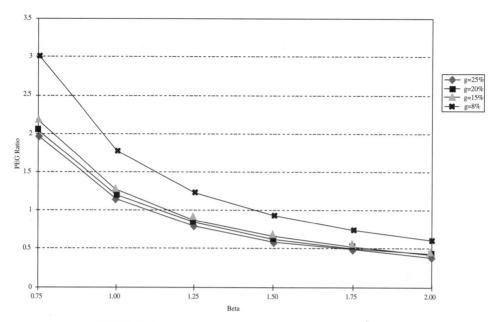

FIGURE 18.9   PEG Ratios and Beta: Different Growth Rates

levels, even within the same sector, this would suggest that riskier firms should have lower PEG ratios than safer firms.

Finally, not all growth is created equal. A firm that is able to grow at 20% a year while paying out 50% of its earnings to stockholders has higher-quality growth than another firm with the same growth rate that reinvests all of its earnings back. Thus the PEG ratio should increase as the payout ratio increases, for any given growth rate, as is evidenced in Figure 18.10.

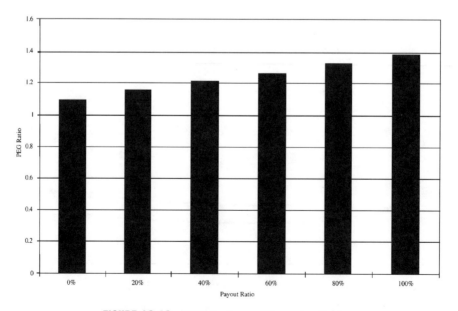

FIGURE 18.10   PEG Ratios and Retention Ratios

The growth rate and the payout ratio are linked by the firm's return on equity. In fact, the expected growth rate of a firm can be written as:

Expected growth rate = Return on equity(1 − Payout ratio)

The PEG ratio should therefore be higher for firms with higher returns on equity, for a given growth rate.

---

 eqmult.xls: **This spreadsheet allows you to estimate the PEG ratio for a stable-growth or high-growth firm, given its fundamentals.**

Using the PEG Ratio for Comparisons

As with the PE ratio, the PEG ratio is used to compare the valuations of firms that are in the same business. As noted in the preceding section, the PEG ratio is a function of the risk, growth potential, and payout ratio of a firm. This section looks at ways of using the PEG ratio and examines some of the problems in comparing PEG ratios across firms.

Direct Comparisons Most analysts who use PEG ratios compute them for firms within a business (or comparable firm group) and compare these ratios. Firms with lower PEG ratios are usually viewed as undervalued, even if growth rates are different across the firms being compared. This approach is based on the incorrect perception that PEG ratios control for differences in growth. In fact, direct comparisons of PEG ratios work only if firms are similar in terms of growth potential, risk, and payout ratios (or returns on equity). If this were the case, however, you could just as easily compare PE ratios across firms.

When PEG ratios are compared across firms with different risk, growth, and payout characteristics, and judgments are made about valuations based on this comparison, you will tend to find that:

- Lower-growth firms will have higher PEG ratios and look more overvalued than higher-growth firms, because PEG ratios tend to decrease as the growth rate decreases (see Figure 18.7).
- Higher-risk firms will have lower PEG ratios and look more undervalued than lower-risk firms, because PEG ratios tend to decrease as a firm's risk increases (see Figure 18.8).
- Firms with lower returns on equity (or lower payout ratios) will have lower PEG ratios and look more undervalued than firms with higher returns on equity and higher payout ratios (see Figure 18.9).

In short, firms that look undervalued based on direct comparison of the PEG ratios may in fact be firms with higher risk, higher growth, or lower returns on equity that are, in fact, correctly valued.

Controlled Comparisons When comparing PEG ratios across firms, then, it is important that you control for differences in risk, growth, and payout ratios when making the comparison. While you can attempt to do this subjectively, the complicated relationship between PEG ratios and these fundamentals can pose a challenge. A far more promising route is to use the regression approach suggested for PE ratios, and to relate the PEG ratios of the firms being compared to measures of risk, growth potential, and the payout ratio.

As with the PE ratio, the comparable firms in this analysis can be defined narrowly (as other firms in the same business), more expansively as firms in the same sector, or as all firms in the market. In running these regressions, all the caveats that were presented for the PE regression continue to apply. The independent variables continue to be correlated with each other and the relationship is both unstable and likely to be nonlinear. In fact, Figure 18.11, which provides a scatter plot of PEG ratios against growth rates for all U.S. stocks in July 2000, indicates the degree of nonlinearity.

In running the regression, especially when the sample contains firms with very different levels of growth, you should transform the growth rate to make the relationship more linear. A scatter plot of PEG ratios against the natural log of the expected growth rate, for instance, yields a much more linear relationship, as evidenced in Figure 18.12.

The results of the regression of PE ratios against ln(expected growth), beta,

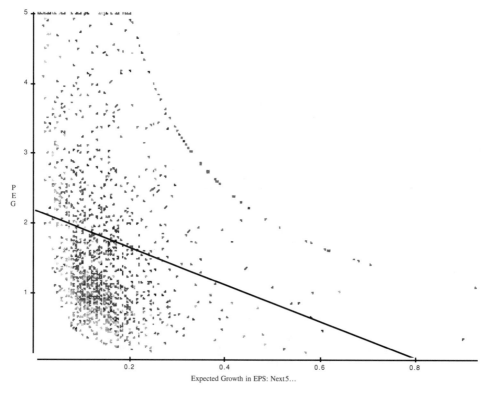

FIGURE 18.11   PEG Ratios versus Expected Growth Rates
Source: Value Line.

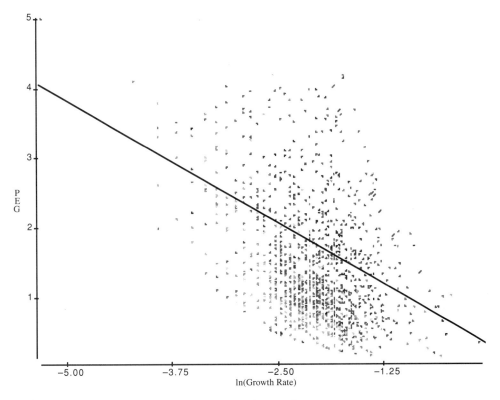

FIGURE 18.12 PEG Ratios versus ln(Expected Growth Rate)
Source: Value Line.

and payout ratio are reported below for the entire market and for technology stocks in July 2000.

Entire Market
PEG ratio = −0.25 − 0.44 ln(Growth) + 0.95 (Beta) + 0.71 (Payout)
[1.76] [10.40]   [9.66]   [7.95]
R-squared = 9.0%   Number of firms = 2,594

Only Technology Stocks
PEG ratio = 1.24 + 0.80 ln(Growth) + 2.45 (Beta) − 1.96 (Payout)
[1.27] [2.20]   [4.15]   [0.73]
R-squared = 11.0%   Number of firms = 274

The low R-squared is indicative of the problems with this multiple and the difficulties you will run into in using it in comparisons across firms.

ILLUSTRATION 18.11:   Estimating and Using the PEG Ratio for Data Networking Firms

The following table summarizes the PEG ratios of the firms that are considered data networking firms as of June 2000:

Company Name	PE	Beta	Projected Growth	PEG
3Com Corp.	37.20	1.35	11.00%	3.38
ADC Telecom.	78.17	1.40	24.00%	3.26
Alcatel ADR	51.50	0.90	24.00%	2.15
Ciena Corp.	94.51	1.70	27.50%	3.44
Cisco Systems	133.76	1.43	35.20%	3.80
Comverse Technology	70.42	1.45	28.88%	2.44
E-TEK Dynamics	295.56	1.55	55.00%	5.37
JDS Uniphase	296.28	1.60	65.00%	4.56
Lucent Technologies	54.28	1.30	24.00%	2.26
Nortel Networks	104.18	1.40	25.50%	4.09
Tellabs, Inc.	52.57	1.75	22.00%	2.39
Average	*115.31*	*1.44*	*31.00%*	*3.38*

Consider Cisco Systems. Cisco, with a PEG ratio of 3.80, is trading at a higher PEG than the average for the sector, suggesting, at least on a preliminary basis, an overvalued stock. Regressing the PEG ratio against the ln(expected growth rate) in this sector yields:

$$\text{PEG ratio} = 5.06 + 1.33 \ln(\text{Expected growth rate}) \qquad \text{R-squared} = 36.70\%$$

For Cisco, with an expected growth rate of 35.20%, the predicted PEG ratio based on this regression is:

$$\text{Predicted PEG ratio} = 5.06 + 1.33 \ln(.352) = 4.02$$

Cisco's actual PEG ratio is very close to this predicted value.

The predicted PEG ratio for Cisco can also be estimated using the broader regressions, across the technology sector and the market, reported in the previous section:

$$\text{Predicted PEG}_{\text{market}} = -0.25 - 0.44 \ln(.352) + 0.95(1.43) + 0.71(0) = 1.57$$
$$\text{Predicted PEG}_{\text{technology}} = 1.24 + 0.80 \ln(.352) + 2.45(1.43) - 1.96(0) = 3.91$$

Cisco looks overvalued when compared with the rest of the market, but is fairly valued when compared to just technology stocks.

pegreg.xls: **This dataset on the Web summarizes the results of the most recent regression of PEG ratios against fundamentals for U.S. stocks.**

WHOSE GROWTH RATE?

In computing PEG ratios, we are often faced with the question of whose growth rate we will use in estimating the PEG ratios. If the number of firms in the sample is small, you could estimate expected growth for each firm yourself. If the number of firms increases, you will have no choice but to use analyst estimates of expected growth for the firms. Will this expose your analyses to all of the biases in these estimates? Not necessarily. If the bias is uniform—for instance, analysts overestimate growth for all of the firms in the sector—you will still be able to make comparisons of PEG ratios across firms and draw reasonable conclusions.

OTHER VARIANTS ON THE PEG RATIO

While the PE ratio and the PEG ratio may be the most widely used earnings multiples, there are other equity earnings multiples that are also used by analysts. In this section, three variants are considered. The first is the relative PE ratio, the second is a multiple of price to earnings in a future year (say 5 or 10 years from now), and the third is a multiple of price to earnings prior to R&D expenses (used primarily for technology firms).

Relative PE Ratios

Relative price earnings ratios measure a firm's PE ratio relative to the market average. It is obtained by dividing a firm's current PE ratio by the average for the market:

$$\text{Relative PE} = \text{Current PE ratio}_{firm}/\text{Current PE ratio}_{market}$$

Not surprisingly, the distribution of relative PE ratios mimics the distribution of the actual PE ratios, with one difference—the average relative PE ratio is 1.

To analyze relative PE ratios, we will draw on the same model that we used to analyze the PE ratio for a firm in high growth, but we will use a similar model to estimate the PE ratio for the market. Brought together, we obtain the following:

$$\text{Relative PE}_j = \cfrac{\cfrac{\text{Payout ratio}_j \times (1+g_j) \times \left[1 - \cfrac{(1+g_j)^n}{(1+r_j)^n}\right]}{r_j - g_j} + \cfrac{\text{Payout ratio}_{j,n} \times (1+g_j)^n \times (1+g_{j,n})}{(r_j - g_{j,n})(1+r_j)^n}}{\cfrac{\text{Payout ratio}_m \times (1+g_m) \times \left[1 - \cfrac{(1+g_m)^n}{(1+r_m)^n}\right]}{r_m - g_m} + \cfrac{\text{Payout ratio}_{m,n} \times (1+g_m)^n \times (1+g_{m,n})}{(r_m - g_{m,n})(1+r_m)^n}}$$

(j: firm   m: market)

Note that the relative PE ratio is a function of all of the variables that determine the PE ratio—the expected growth rate, the risk of the firm, and the payout ratio—but stated in terms relative to the market. Thus, a firm's relative PE ratio is a function of its relative growth rate in earnings per share (growth rate$_{firm}$/growth rate$_{market}$), its relative cost of equity (cost of equity$_{firm}$/cost of equity$_{market}$), and its relative return on equity (ROE$_{firm}$/ROE$_{market}$). Firms with higher relative growth, lower relative costs of equity, and higher relative returns on equity should trade at higher relative PE ratios.

There are two ways in which relative PEs are used in valuation. One is to compare a firm's relative PE ratio to its historical norms; Ford, for instance, may be viewed as undervalued because its relative PE ratio of 0.24 today is lower than the relative PE that it has historically traded at. The other is to compare relative PE ratios of firms in different markets; this allows comparisons when PE ratios in different markets vary significantly. For instance, we could have divided the PE ratios for each telecom firm in Illustration 18.8 by the PE ratio for the market in which this firm trades locally to estimate relative PE ratios and compared those ratios.

ILLUSTRATION 18.12:   Comparing Relative PE Ratios for Automobile Stocks—December 2000

In December 2000, the S&P 500 was trading at a multiple of 29.09 times earnings. At the same time, Ford, DaimlerChrysler, and GM were trading at 7.05, 8.95, and 6.93 times earnings respectively. Their relative PE ratios are:

Relative PE for Ford = 7.05/29.09 = 0.24
Relative PE for DaimlerChrysler = 8.95/29.09 = 0.30
Relative PE for GM = 6.93/29.09 = 0.24

Does this mean that GM and Ford are more undervalued than DaimlerChrysler? Not necessarily, since there are differences in growth and risk across these firms. In fact, Figure 18.13 graphs the relative PE ratios of the three firms going back to the early 1990s.

In 1993, GM traded at a significantly higher relative PE ratio than the other two firms. In fact, the conventional wisdom until that point in time was that GM was less risky than the other two firms because of its dominance of the auto market and should trade at a higher multiple of earnings. During the 1990s, the premium paid for GM largely disappeared, and the three automobile firms traded at roughly the same relative PE ratios.

Price to Future Earnings

The price-earnings ratio cannot be estimated for firms with negative earnings per share. While there are other multiples, such as the price-to-sales ratio, that can still be estimated for these firms, there are analysts who prefer the familiar ground of PE ratios. One way in which the price-earnings ratio can be modified for use in these firms is to use expected earnings per share in a future year in computing the PE ratio. For instance, assume that a firm has negative earnings per share currently of –$2.00 but is expected to report earnings per share in five years of $1.50 per share. You could divide the price today by the expected earnings per share in five years to obtain PE ratio.

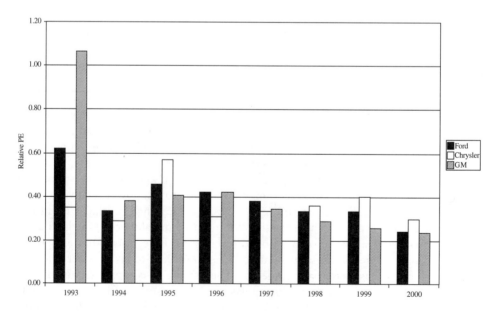

FIGURE 18.13 Relative PE Ratios: Auto Stocks
Source: Value Line.

RELATIVE PE RATIOS AND MARKET GROWTH

As the expected growth rate on the market iincreases, the divergence in PE ratios increases, resulting in a bigger range for relative PE ratios. This can be illustrated very simply, if you consider the relative PE for a company that grows at half the rate of the market. When the market growth rate is 4 percent, this firm will trade at a PE that is roughly 80 percent of the market PE. When the market growth rate increases to 10 percent, the firm will trade at a PE that is 60 percent of the market PE.

This has consequences for analysts who use relative PE ratios. Stocks of firms whose earnings grow at a rate much lower than the market growth rate will often look cheap on a relative PE basis when the market growth rate is high and expensive when the market growth rate is low.

How would such a PE ratio be used? The PE ratio for all of the comparable firms would also have to be estimated using expected earnings per share in five years, and the resulting values can be compared across firms. Assuming that all of the firms in the sample share the same risk, growth, and payout characteristics after year 5, firms with low price-to-future-earnings ratios will be considered undervalued. An alternative approach is to estimate a target price for the negative-earnings firm in five years, dividing that price by earnings in that year and comparing this PE ratio to the PE ratio of comparable firms today.

While this modified version of the PE ratio increases the reach of PE ratios to cover many firms that have negative earnings today, it is difficult to control for differences between the firm being valued and the comparable firms, since you are comparing firms at different points in time.

ILLUSTRATION 18.13:   Analyzing Amazon.com Using Price to Future Earnings per Share

---

Amazon.com has negative earnings per share in 2000. Based on consensus estimates, analysts expect it to lose $0.63 per share in 2001, but it is expected to earn $1.50 per share in 2004. At its current price of $49 per share, this would translate into a price/future earnings per share of 32.67.

In the first approach, this multiple of earnings can be compared to the price/future earnings ratios of comparable firms. If you define comparable firms to be e-tailers, Amazon looks reasonably attractive since the average price/future earnings per share of e-tailers is 65.[7] If, on the other hand, you compared Amazon's price to future earnings per share to the average price to future earnings per share (in 2004) of specialty retailers, the picture is bleaker. The average price to future earnings for these firms is 12, which would lead to a conclusion that Amazon is overvalued. Implicit in both these comparisons is the assumption that Amazon will have similar risk, growth, and cash flow characteristics as the comparable firms in five years. You could argue that Amazon will still have much higher growth potential than other specialty retailers after 2004, and that this could explain the difference in multiples. You could even use differences in expected growth after 2004 to adjust for the differences, but estimates of these growth rates are usually not easily available.

---

[7]The expected earnings per share in 2004 of e-tailers were obtained from consensus estimates of analysts following these firms, and the current price was divided by the expected earnings per share.

In the second approach, we apply the current price-to-earnings ratio for specialty retailers, which is estimated to be 20.31, to the earnings per share of Amazon in 2004 (which is estimated to be $1.50). This would yield a target price of $30.46. Discounting this price back to the present using Amazon's cost of equity of 12.94% results in a value per share:

$$\text{Value per share} = \text{Target price in five years}/(1 + \text{Cost of equity})^5$$
$$= \$30.46/1.1294^5 = \$16.58$$

At its current price of $49, this would again suggest an overvalued stock. Here again, though, you are assuming that Amazon in five years will resemble a specialty retailer today in terms of risk, growth, and cash flow characteristics.

Price to Earnings before R&D Expenses

In the discussion of cash flows and capital expenditures in Chapter 4, it was argued that research and development expenses should be capitalized, since they represent investments for the future. Since accounting standards require that R&D be expensed, rather than capitalized, the earnings of high-growth firms with substantial research expenses is likely to be understated, and the PE ratio is, therefore, likely to be overstated. This will especially be true if you are comparing technology firms, which have substantial research expenditures, to nontechnology firms, which usually do not. Even when comparing only across technology stocks, firms that are growing faster with larger R&D expenses will end up with lower earnings and higher PE ratios than more stable firms in the sector with lower R&D expenses. There are some analysts who argue that the PE ratio should be estimated using earnings prior to R&D expenses:

$$\text{PE}_{\text{pre-R\&D}} = \text{Market value of equity}/(\text{Net income} + \text{R\&D expenses})$$

The PE ratios that emerge from this calculation are likely to be much lower than the PE ratios using conventional definitions of earnings per share.

While the underlying logic behind this approach is sound, adding back R&D to earnings represents only a partial adjustment. To complete the adjustment, you would need to capitalize R&D expenses and compute the amortization of R&D expenses, as was done in Chapter 9. The adjusted PE would then be:

$$\text{PE}_{\text{R\&D adjusted}} = \text{Market value of equity}/(\text{Net income} + \text{R\&D expenses} - \text{Amortization of R\&D})$$

These adjusted PE ratios can then be computed across firms in the sample.

This adjustment to the PE ratio, while taking care of one problem—the expensing of R&D—will still leave you exposed to all of the other problems associated with PE ratios. Earnings will continue to be volatile and affected by accounting choices, and differences in growth, risk, and cash flow characteristics will still cause price-earnings ratios to be different across firms. In addition, you will also have to estimate expected growth in earnings (pre-R&D) on your own, since consensus estimates from analysts will not be available for this growth rate.

Enterprise Value to EBITDA Multiples

Unlike the earnings multiples discussed so far in this chapter, the enterprise value to EBITDA multiple is a firm value multiple. In the past two decades, this multiple has acquired a number of adherents among analysts for a number of reasons. First, there are far fewer firms with negative EBITDA than there are firms with negative earnings per share, and thus fewer firms are lost from the analysis. Second, differences in depreciation methods across different companies—some might use straight line while others use accelerated depreciation—can cause differences in operating income or net income but will not affect EBITDA. Third, this multiple can be compared far more easily than other earnings multiples across firms with different financial leverage (the numerator is firm value and the denominator is a predebt earnings). For all of these reasons, this multiple is particularly useful for firms in sectors that require large investments in infrastructure with long gestation periods. Good examples would be cable firms in the 1980s and cellular firms in the 1990s.

Definition The enterprise value to EBITDA multiple relates the total market value of the firm, net of cash, to the earnings before interest, taxes, depreciation, and amortization of the firm:

$$EV/EBITDA = (\text{Market value of equity} + \text{Market value of debt} - \text{Cash})/EBITDA$$

Why is cash netted out of firm value for this calculation? Since the interest income from the cash is not counted as part of the EBITDA, not netting out the cash will result in an overstatement of the true value to EBITDA multiple. The asset (cash) would be added to value, but the income from the asset is excluded from the income measure (EBITDA).

The enterprise value to EBITDA multiple can be difficult to estimate for firms with cross holdings. To see why, note that cross holdings can be categorized as either majority active, minority active, or minority passive holdings. When a holding is categorized as a minority holding, the operating income of a firm does not reflect the income from the holding. The numerator, on the other hand, includes the market value of equity which should incorporate the value of the minority holdings. Consequently, the value to EBITDA multiple will be too high for these firms, leading a casual observer to conclude that they were overvalued. When a holding is categorized as a majority holding, a different problem arises. The EBITDA includes 100 percent of the EBITDA of the holding, but the numerator reflects only the portion of the holding that belongs to the firm. Thus the value to EBITDA will be too low, leading it to be categorized as an undervalued stock.

The correction for cross holdings is tedious and difficult to do when the holdings are in private firms. With passive investments, you can either subtract the estimated value of the holdings from the numerator or add the portion of the EBITDA of the subsidiary to the denominator. With active investments, you can subtract the proportional share of the value of the holding from the numerator and the entire EBITDA of the holding from the denominator.

ILLUSTRATION 18.14:   Estimating Value to EBITDA with Cross Holdings

In Illustration 16.6, we estimated a discounted cash flow value for Segovia, a firm with two holdings—a 51% stake in Seville Televison and a 15% stake of LatinWorks, a record and CD company. The first holding was categorized as a majority active holding (resulting in consolidation) and the second as a minority passive holding. Here, we will try to estimate an enterprise value to EBITDA multiple for Seville, using the following information:

- The market value of equity at Segovia is $1,529 million and the consolidated debt outstanding at the firm is $500 million. The firm reported $500 million in EBITDA on its consolidated income statement. A portion of the EBITDA ($180 million) and debt outstanding ($150 million) represent Segovia's holdings in Seville Televison.
- Seville Television is a publicly traded firm with a market value of equity of $459 million.
- LatinWorks is a private firm with an EBITDA of $120 million on capital invested of $250 million in the current year; the firm has $100 million in debt outstanding.
- None of the firms have significant cash balances.

If we estimate an enterprise value to EBITDA multiple for Segovia using its consolidated financial statements, we would obtain the following:

$$\text{EV/EBITDA} = (\text{Market value of equity} + \text{Value of debt} - \text{Cash})/\text{EBITDA}$$
$$= (1,529 + 500 - 0)/500 = 4.06$$

This multiple is contaminated by the cross holdings. There are two ways we can correct for these holdings. One is to net out from the market value of equity of Segovia the value of the equity in the holdings and the debt of the consolidated holding from Segovia's debt, and then dividing by the EBITDA of just the parent company. To do this, you would first need to estimate the market value of equity in LatinWorks, which is a private company. We will use the estimate of equity value that we obtained in Illustration 16.6:

Value of equity in Latin Works = 370.25 million

$$\text{EV/EBITDA}_{\text{no holdings}} = \frac{(1,529 - .51 \times 459 - .15 \times 370.25) + (500 - 150)}{500 - 180} = 5.70$$

The alternative is to adjust just the denominator to make it consistent with the numerator. In other words, the EBITDA should include only 51% of the majority active holding's EBITDA and should add in the 15% of the EBITDA in the minority holdings:

$$\text{EV/EBITDA}_{\text{holdings}} = \frac{1,529 + 500}{500 - .49 \times 180 + .15 \times 120} = 4.72$$

The first approach is preferable since it results in multiples that can be more easily compared across firms. The latter yields an enterprise value to EBITDA multiple that is a composite of three different firms.

Description   Figure 18.14 summarizes the enterprise value to EBITDA multiples for U.S. firms in July 2001. As with the price-earnings ratio, you have a heavily skewed distribution. The average EV/EBITDA multiple across U.S. firms in January 2001 was 11.7, while the median value is closer to 8. Note also the large number of

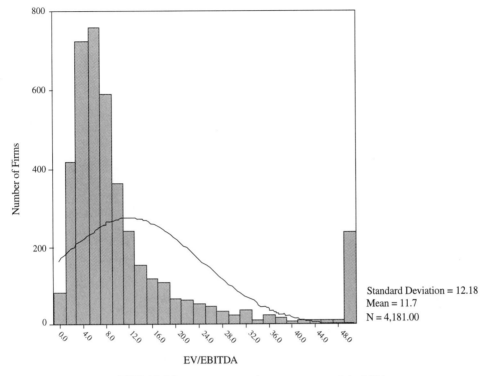

FIGURE 18.14   EV/EBITDA for U.S. Firms—July 2001

firms that trade at very low multiples of EBITDA, suggesting that rules of thumb should be used with caution.

Analysis   To analyze the determinants of enterprise value to EBITDA multiples, we will revert back to a free cash flow to the firm valuation model that we developed in Chapter 15. Specifically, we estimated the value of the operating assets (or enterprise value) of a firm to be:

$$V_0 = \frac{FCFF_1}{WACC - g}$$

We can write the free cash flow to the firm in terms of the EBITDA:

$$
\begin{aligned}
FCFF &= EBIT(1-t) - (Cap\ ex - DA + \Delta\ Working\ capital) \\
&= (EBITDA - DA)(1-t) - (Cap\ ex - DA + \Delta\ Working\ capital) \\
&= EBITDA(1-t) - DA(1-t) - Reinvestment
\end{aligned}
$$

Substituting back into the equation, we get:

$$V_0 = \frac{EBITDA_1(1-t) - DA_1(1-t) - Reinvestment_1}{WACC - g}$$

Dividing both sides by the EBITDA and removing the subscripts yields the following:

$$\frac{V_0}{\text{EBITDA}} = \frac{(1-t) - \dfrac{\text{DA}}{\text{EBITDA}}(1-t) - \dfrac{\text{Reinvestment}}{\text{EBITDA}}}{\text{WACC} - g}$$

The five determinants of the enterprise value to EBITDA multiple are visible in this equation:

1. *Tax rate.* Other things remaining equal, firms with lower tax rates should command higher enterprise value to EBITDA multiples than otherwise similar firms with higher tax rates.
2. *Depreciation and amortization.* Other things remaining equal, firms that derive a greater portion of their EBITDA from depreciation and amortization should trade at lower multiples of EBITDA than otherwise similar firms.
3. *Reinvestment requirements.* Other things remaining equal, the greater the portion of the EBITDA that needs to be reinvested to generate expected growth, the lower the value to EBITDA will be for firms.
4. *Cost of capital.* Other things remaining equal, firms with lower costs of capital should trade at much higher multiples of EBITDA.
5. *Expected growth.* Other things remaining equal, firms with higher expected growth should trade at much higher multiples of EBITDA.

This can be generalized to consider firms in high growth. The variables will remain unchanged but will need to be estimated for each phase of growth.

ILLUSTRATION 18.15:   Analyzing Value to EBITDA Multiples

Castillo Cable is a cable and wireless firm with the following characteristics:

- The firm has a cost of capital of 10% and faces a tax rate of 36% on its operating income.
- The firm has capital expenditures that amount to 45% of EBITDA and depreciation that amounts to 20% of EBITDA. There are no working capital requirements.
- The firm is in stable growth and its operating income is expected to grow 5% a year in perpetuity.

To estimate the enterprise value to EBITDA, we first estimate the reinvestment needs as a percent of EBITDA:

Reinvestment/EBITDA = Cap ex/EBITDA − Depreciation/EBITDA + Δ Working capital/EBITDA
= .45 − .20 − 0 = .25

$$\frac{\text{EV}}{\text{EBITDA}} = \frac{(1-.36) - (0.2)(1-.36) - 0.25}{.10 - .05} = 5.24$$

This multiple is sensitive to the tax rate, as evidenced in Figure 18.15. It is also sensitive to the reinvestment rate (stated as a percent of EBITDA), as shown in Figure 18.16. However, changing the

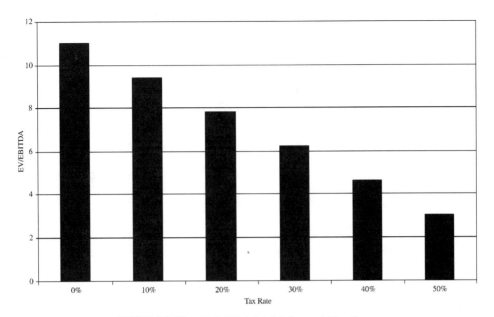

FIGURE 18.15 VEBITDA Multiples and Tax Rates

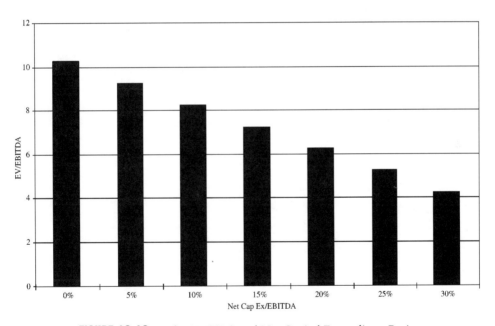

FIGURE 18.16 Value/EBITDA and Net Capital Expenditure Ratios

reinvestment rate while keeping the growth rate fixed is the equivalent of changing the return on capital. In fact, at the existing reinvestment rate and growth rate, we are assuming a return on capital of 10.24%:

$$g = ROC \times \text{Reinvestment rate}$$
$$.05 = ROC \times \text{Net cap ex/EBIT}(1 - t)$$
$$= ROC \times (.45 - .20)/[(1 - .2)(1 - .36)]$$

Solving for the return on capital yields 10.24%. Figure 18.17 looks at the enterprise value to EBITDA multiple as a function of the return on capital.

In short, firms with low returns on capital and high reinvestment rates should trade at low multiples of EBITDA.

 firmmult.xls: **This spreadsheet allows you to estimate firm value multiples for a stable-growth or high-growth firm, given its fundamentals.**

Application Having established the fundamentals that determine the enterprise value to EBITDA multiple, we can now examine how best to apply the multiple. The multiple is most widely used in capital-intensive firms with heavy infrastructure investments. The rationale that is given for using the multiple—that EBITDA is the operating cash flow of the firm—does not really hold up, because many of these firms also tend to have capital expenditure needs that drain cash flows. There are, however, good reasons for using this multiple when depreciation methods vary widely across firms and the bulk of the investment in infrastructure has already been made.

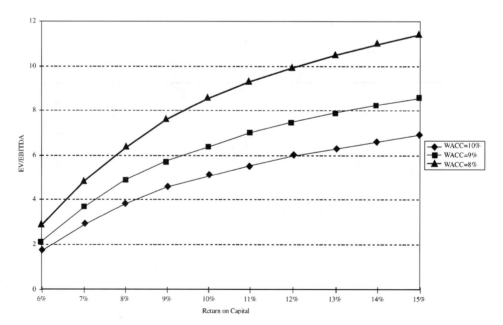

FIGURE 18.17   Value/EBITDA and Net Cap Ex Ratios

ILLUSTRATION 18.16:   Comparing the Value to EBITDA Multiple: Steel Companies

The following table summarizes the enterprise value to EBITDA multiples for steel companies in the United States in March 2001:

Company Name	EV/EBITDA	Tax Rate	ROC	Net Cap Ex/EBITDA	DA/EBITDA
Ampco-Pittsburgh	2.74	26.21%	12.15%	15.72%	20.05%
Bayou Steel	5.21	0.00%	5.95%	12.90%	41.01%
Birmingham Steel	5.60	0.00%	6.89%	−28.64%	51.92%
Carpenter Technology	5.05	33.29%	9.16%	15.51%	28.87%
Castle (A.M.) & Co.	9.26	0.00%	8.92%	9.44%	27.22%
Cleveland-Cliffs	5.14	0.00%	7.65%	51.84%	26.33%
Commercial Metals	2.40	36.86%	16.60%	1.19%	26.44%
Harris Steel	4.26	37.18%	15.00%	3.23%	4.92%
Huntco Inc.	5.40	0.00%	4.82%	−48.84%	53.02%
IPSCO Inc.	5.06	23.87%	9.22%	50.57%	16.88%
Kentucky Elec. Steel Inc.	1.72	37.26%	6.75%	−25.51%	38.78%
National Steel	2.30	0.00%	8.46%	68.49%	53.84%
NN Inc.	6.00	34.35%	15.73%	−15.04%	24.80%
Northwest Pipe Co.	5.14	39.47%	9.05%	8.73%	17.22%
Nucor Corp.	3.88	35.00%	18.48%	15.66%	26.04%
Olympic Steel Inc.	4.46	37.93%	5.80%	−3.75%	26.62%
Oregon Steel Mills	5.32	0.00%	7.23%	−31.77%	49.57%
Quanex Corp.	2.90	34.39%	16.38%	−3.45%	29.50%
Ryerson Tull	7.73	0.00%	5.10%	3.50%	38.36%
Samuel Manu-Tech Inc.	3.13	31.88%	14.90%	−2.91%	21.27%
Schnitzer Steel Inds. 'A'	4.60	8.70%	7.78%	−16.21%	38.74%
Slater STL Inc.	4.48	26.00%	11.25%	0.80%	27.96%
Steel Dynamics	5.83	36.33%	10.09%	33.13%	23.14%
Steel Technologies	3.75	36.87%	9.22%	11.95%	27.69%
Steel-General	4.14	38.37%	9.80%	21.69%	28.75%
Unvl. Stainless & Alloy Prods.	4.28	37.52%	14.51%	12.73%	15.15%
Worthington Inds.	4.80	37.50%	12.54%	0.16%	22.79%

The enterprise value to EBITDA multiples vary widely across these firms, and many of these firms have negative net capital expenditures, partly reflecting the industry's maturity and partly the lumpy nature of reinvestments. Many of them also pay no taxes because they lose money. We regressed the EV/EBITDA multiple against the tax rate and depreciation as a percent of EBITDA:

$$EV/EBITDA = 8.65 - 7.20 \text{ Tax rate} - 8.08 \left(\frac{\text{Depreciation} + \text{Amortization}}{\text{EBITDA}} \right) \quad R^2 = 30\%$$

We did not use expected growth or cost of capital as independent variables because they are very similar across these firms. Using this regression, the predicted value to EBITDA multiple for Birmingham Steel would be:

$$\text{Predicted EV/EBITDA}_{\text{Birmingham Steel}} = 8.65 - 7.20(0.00) - 8.08(.5192) = 4.45$$

At 5.60 times EBITDA, the firm is overvalued.

---

vebitda.xls: **This dataset on the Web summarizes value-to-earnings multiples and fundamentals by industry group in the United States for the most recent year.**

VALUE MULTIPLES: VARIANTS

While enterprise value to EBITDA may be the most widely used value multiple, there are close variants that are sometimes used by analysts—value/EBIT, value/after-tax EBIT, and value/FCFF. Each of these multiples is determined by many of the same variables that determine the EV/EBITDA multiple, but the actual relationship is slightly different. In particular, note that for a stable-growth firm these multiples can be written as follows:

$$\text{Value/FCFF} = 1/(\text{Cost of capital} - \text{Expected growth rate})$$
$$\text{Value/EBIT}(1 - t) = (1 - \text{RIR})/(\text{Cost of capital} - \text{Expected growth rate})$$
$$\text{Value/EBIT} = (1 - t)(1 - \text{RIR})/(\text{Cost of capital} - \text{Expected growth rate})$$

where RIR is the reinvestment rate and t is the tax rate.

In other words, higher costs of capital and lower expected growth decrease all of these multiples. A higher reinvestment rate lowers the last two multiples but does not affect the multiple of FCFF (since FCFF is already after reinvestment). A higher tax rate will affect just the last multiple, since the first two look at earnings after taxes.

CONCLUSION

The price-earnings ratio and other earnings multiples, which are widely used in valuation, have the potential to be misused. These multiples are ultimately determined by the same fundamentals that determine the value of a firm in a discounted cash flow model—expected growth, risk, and cash flow potential. Firms with higher growth, lower risk, and higher payout ratios, other things remaining equal, should trade at much higher multiples of earnings than other firms. To the extent that there are differences in fundamentals across countries, across time, and across companies, the multiples will also be different. A failure to control for these differences in fundamentals can lead to erroneous conclusions based purely on a direct comparison of multiples.

There are several ways in which earnings multiples can be used in valuation. One way is to compare earnings multiples across a narrowly defined group of comparable firms and to control for differences in growth, risk, and cash flows subjectively. Another is to expand the definition of a comparable firm to the entire sector (such as technology) or the market, and to control for differences in fundamentals using statistical techniques.

In the last part of the chapter, we turned our attention from equity multiples to multiples of operating earnings and cash flows. As with the PE ratio, these multiples are a function of growth (in operating income), reinvestment, and risk.

QUESTIONS AND SHORT PROBLEMS

1. National City Corporation, a bank holding company, reported earnings per share of $2.40 in 1993, and paid dividends per share of $1.06. The earnings had grown 7.5% a year over the prior five years, and were expected to grow 6% a year in

the long term (starting in 1994). The stock had a beta of 1.05 and traded for 10 times earnings. The Treasury bond rate was 7%, and the risk premium is 5.5%.

a. Estimate the PE ratio for National City Corporation.

b. What long-term growth rate is implied in the firm's current PE ratio?

2. On March 11, 1994, the New York Stock Exchange Composite was trading at 16.9 times earnings, and the average dividend yield across stocks on the exchange was 2.5%. The Treasury bond rate on that date was 6.95%. The economy was expected to grow 2.5% a year, in real terms, in the long term, and the consensus estimate for inflation, in the long term, was 3.5%. (Market risk premium is 5.5%.)

a. Based on these inputs, estimate the appropriate PE ratio for the exchange.

b. What growth rate in dividends/earnings would justify the PE ratio on March 11, 1994?

c. Would it matter whether this higher growth comes from higher inflation or higher real growth? Why?

3. International Flavors and Fragrances, a leading creator and manufacturer of flavors and fragrances, paid out dividends of $0.91 per share on earnings per share of $1.64 in 1992. The firm was expected to have a return on equity of 20% between 1993 and 1997, after which the firm was expected to have stable growth of 6% a year. (The return on equity was expected to drop to 15% in the stable growth phase.) The dividend payout ratio was expected to remain at the current level from 1993 to 1997. The stock had a beta of 1.10, which was not expected to change. The Treasury bond rate was 7%, and the risk premium is 5.5%.

a. Estimate the PE ratio for International Flavors based on fundamentals.

b. Estimate how much of this PE ratio can be ascribed to the extraordinary growth in earnings that the firm expects to have between 1993 and 1997.

4. Cracker Barrel, which operates restaurants and gift shops, reported dramatic growth in earnings and revenues between 1983 and 1992. During this period, earnings grew from $0.08 per share in 1983 to $0.78 per share in 1993. The dividends paid in 1993 amounted to only $0.02 per share. The earnings growth rate was expected to ease to 15% a year from 1994 to 1998, and to 6% a year after that. The payout ratio was expected to increase to 10% from 1994 to 1998, and to 50% after that. The beta of the stock was 1.55, but it was expected to decline to 1.25 for the 1994–1998 time period and to 1.10 after that. (The Treasury bond rate was 7%, and the risk premium is 5.5%.)

a. Estimate the PE ratio for Cracker Barrel.

b. Estimate how much higher the PE ratio would have been if it had been able to maintain the growth rate in earnings that it had posted between 1983 and 1993. (Assume that the dividend payout ratios are unaffected.)

c. Now assume that disappointing earnings reports in the near future lower the expected growth rate between 1994 and 1998 to 10%. Estimate the PE ratio. (Again, assume that the dividend payout ratio is unaffected.)

5. The S&P 500 was trading at 21.2 times earnings on December 31, 1993. On the same day, the dividend yield on the index was 2.74%, and the Treasury bond rate was 6%. The expected growth rate in real GNP was 2.5%.

a. Assuming that the S&P 500 is correctly priced, what is the inflation rate implied in the PE ratio? (Assume stable growth and a 5.5% risk premium.)

b. By February 1994, Treasury bond rates had increased to 7%. If payout ratios and expected growth remain unchanged, what would the effect on the PE ratio be?

   c. Does an increase in interest rates always imply lower prices (and PE ratios)?

6. The following were the PE ratios of firms in the aerospace/defense industry at the end of December 1993, with additional data on expected growth and risk.

Company	PE Ratio	Expected Growth	Beta	Payout
Boeing	17.3	3.5%	1.10	28%
General Dynamics	15.5	11.5%	1.25	40%
General Motors—Hughes	16.5	13.0%	0.85	41%
Grumman	11.4	10.5%	0.80	37%
Lockheed Corporation	10.2	9.5%	0.85	37%
Logicon	12.4	14.0%	0.85	11%
Loral Corporation	13.3	16.5%	0.75	23%
Martin Marietta	11.0	8.0%	0.85	22%
McDonnell Douglas	22.6	13.0%	1.15	37%
Northrop	9.5	9.0%	1.05	47%
Raytheon	12.1	9.5%	0.75	28%
Rockwell	13.9	11.5%	1.00	38%
Thiokol	8.7	5.5%	0.95	15%
United Industrial	10.4	4.5%	0.70	50%

   a. Estimate the average and median PE ratios. What, if anything, would these averages tell you?

   b. An analyst concludes that Thiokol is undervalued, because its PE ratio is lower than the industry average. Under what conditions is this statement true? Would you agree with it here?

   c. Using a regression, control for differences across firms on risk, growth, and payout. Specify how you would use this regression to spot under- and over-valued stocks. What are the limitations of this approach?

7. The following was the result of a regression of PE ratios on growth rates, betas, and payout ratios for stocks listed on the Value Line Database in April 1993.

$$PE = 18.69 + 0.0695 \text{ Growth} - 0.5082 \text{ Beta} - 0.4262 \text{ Payout} \qquad R^2 = 0.35$$

Thus a stock with an earnings growth rate of 20%, a beta of 1.15, and a payout ratio of 40% would have had an expected PE ratio of:

$$PE = 18.69 + 0.0695 \times 20 - 0.5082(1.15) - 0.4262 \times 0.40 = 19.33$$

You are attempting to value a private firm, with the following characteristics:

- The firm had net profits of $10 million. It did not pay dividends, but had depreciation allowances of $5 million and capital expenditures of $12 million in the most recent year. Working capital requirements were negligible.
- The earnings had grown 25% over the previous five years, and are expected to grow at the same rate over the next five years.
- The average beta of publicly traded firms, in the same line of business, is 1.15, and the average debt-equity ratio of these firms is 25%. (The tax rate is 40%.) The private firm is an all-equity financed firm, with no debt.

   a. Estimate the appropriate PE ratio for this private firm using the regression.

   b. What would some of your concerns be in using this regression in valuation?

CHAPTER 19

Book Value Multiples

The relationship between price and book value has always attracted the attention of investors. Stocks selling for well below the book value of equity have generally been considered good candidates for undervalued portfolios, while those selling for more than book value have been targets for overvalued portfolios. This chapter begins by examining the price–book value ratio in more detail, the determinants of this ratio, and how best to evaluate or estimate the ratio.

In the second part of the chapter, we turn our attention to variants of the price-to-book ratio. In particular, we focus on the value-to-book ratio and Tobin's Q—a ratio of market value of assets to their replacement cost.

PRICE-TO-BOOK EQUITY

The market value of the equity in a firm reflects the market's expectation of the firm's earning power and cash flows. The book value of equity is the difference between the book value of assets and the book value of liabilities, a number that is largely determined by accounting conventions. In the United States, the book value of assets is the original price paid for the assets reduced by any allowable depreciation on the assets. Consequently, the book value of an asset decreases as it ages. The book value of liabilities similarly reflects the at-issue values of the liabilities. Since the book value of an asset reflects its original cost, it might deviate significantly from market value if the earning power of the asset has increased or declined significantly since its acquisition.

Why Analysts Use Book Value and the Downside

There are several reasons why investors find the price–book value ratio useful in investment analysis. The first is that the book value provides a relatively stable, intuitive measure of value that can be compared to the market price. For investors who instinctively mistrust discounted cash flow estimates of value, the book value is a much simpler benchmark for comparison. The second is that, given reasonably consistent accounting standards across firms, price–book value ratios can be compared across similar firms for signs of under- or overvaluation. Finally, even firms with negative earnings, which cannot be valued using price-earnings ratios, can be evaluated using price–book value ratios; there are far fewer firms with negative book value than there are firms with negative earnings.

There are several disadvantages associated with measuring and using price–book value ratios. First, book values, like earnings, are affected by accounting decisions on depreciation and other variables. When accounting standards vary widely across firms, the price–book value ratios may not be comparable. A similar statement can be made about comparing price–book value ratios across countries with different accounting standards. Second, book value may not carry much meaning for service and technology firms that do not have significant tangible assets. Third, the book value of equity can become negative if a firm has a sustained string of negative earnings reports, leading to a negative price–book value ratio.

Definition

The price-to-book ratio is computed by dividing the market price per share by the current book value of equity per share.

$$\text{Price-to-book ratio} = \text{PBV} = \frac{\text{Price per share}}{\text{Book value of equity per share}}$$

While the multiple is fundamentally consistent—the numerator and denominator are both equity values—there is a potential for inconsistency if you are not careful about how you compute book value of equity per share. In particular,

- If there are multiple classes of shares outstanding, the price per share can be different for different classes of shares, and it is not clear how the book equity should be apportioned among shares.
- You should not include the portion of the equity that is attributable to preferred stock in computing the book value of equity, since the market value of equity refers only to common equity.

Some of the problems can be alleviated by computing the price-to-book ratio using the total market value of equity and book value of equity, rather than per-share values.

$$\text{Price-to-book ratio} = \text{PBV} = \frac{\text{Market value of equity}}{\text{Book value of equity}}$$

The safest way to measure this ratio when there are multiple classes of equity is to use the composite market value of all classes of common stock in the numerator and the composite book value of equity in the denominator—you would still ignore preferred stock for this computation.

There are two other measurement issues that you have to confront in computing this multiple. The first relates to the book value of equity, which as an accounting measure gets updated infrequently—once every quarter for U.S. companies and once every year for European companies. While most analysts use the most current book value of equity, there are some who use the average over the previous year or the book value of equity at the end of the latest financial year. Consistency demands that you use the same measure of book equity for all firms in your sample. The second and more difficult problem concerns the value of options outstanding. Technically, you would need to compute the estimated market value of management options and conversion options (in bonds and preferred stock) and add them to the market value of equity before computing the price to book value ratio.[1] If you have a small sample of comparable firms and options represent a large portion of equity value, you should do this. With larger samples and less significant option issues, you can stay with the conventional measure of market value of equity.

Accounting standards can affect book values of equity and price to book ratios and skew comparisons made across firms. For instance, assume that you are comparing the price-to-book ratios of technology firms in two markets, and that one of them allows research expenses to be capitalized and the other does not. You should expect to see lower price-to-book value ratios in the former, since the book value of equity will be augmented by the value of the research asset.

ADJUSTING BOOK EQUITY FOR BUYBACKS AND ACQUISITIONS

In recent years, firms in the United States have increasingly turned to buying back stock as a way of returning cash to stockholders. When a firm buys back stock, the book equity of the firm declines by the amount of the buyback. Although this is precisely what happens when firms pay a cash dividend as well, buybacks tend to be much larger than regular dividends and thus have a bigger impact on book equity. To illustrate, assume that you have a firm that has a market value of equity of $100 million and a book value of equity of $50 million; its price-to-book ratio is 2.00. If the firm borrows $25 million and buys back stock, its book equity will decline to $25 million and its market equity will drop to $75 million. The resulting price-to-book ratio is 3.

With acquisitions, the effect on price-to-book ratios can vary dramatically depending on how the acquisition is accounted for. If the acquiring firm uses purchase accounting, the book equity of the firm will increase by the market value of the acquired firm. If, however, it uses pooling, the book equity will increase by the book value of the acquired firm. Given that the book value is less than the market value for most firms, the price-to-book ratio will be much higher for firms that use pooling on acquisitions than for those that use purchase accounting.

To compare price-to-book ratios across firms when some firms in the sample buy back stocks and some do not or when there are wide differences in both the magnitude and the accounting for acquisitions can be problematic. One way to adjust for the differences is to take out the goodwill from acquisitions and to add back the market value of buybacks to the book equity to come up with an adjusted book value of equity. The price-to-book ratios can then be computed based on this adjusted book value of equity.

---

[1] If you do not do this and compare price to book ratios across firms with widely different amounts of options outstanding, you could misidentify firms with more options outstanding as undervalued—the market value of traded common stock at these firms will be lower because of the option overhang.

Description

To get a sense of what comprises a high, low, or average price to book value ratio, we computed the ratio for every firm listed in the United States, and Figure 19.1 summarizes the distribution of price-to-book ratios in July 2000. Note that this distribution is heavily skewed, as is evidenced by the fact that the average price-to-book-value ratio of firms is 3.25 while the median price-to-book ratio is much lower at 1.85.

Another point worth making about price-to-book ratios is that there are firms with negative book values of equity—the result of continuously losing money—where price to book ratios cannot be computed. In this sample of 5,903 firms, there were 728 firms where this occurred. In contrast, though, 2,045 firms had negative earnings and PE ratios could not be computed for them.

 pbvdata.xls: This dataset on the Web summarizes price-to-book ratios and fundamentals by industry group in the United States for the most recent year.

Analysis

The price–book value ratio can be related to the same fundamentals that determine value in discounted cash flow models. Since this is an equity multiple, we will use an equity discounted cash flow model—the dividend discount model—to explore the determinants. The value of equity in a stable growth dividend discount model can be written as:

$$P_0 = \frac{DPS_1}{k_e - g_n}$$

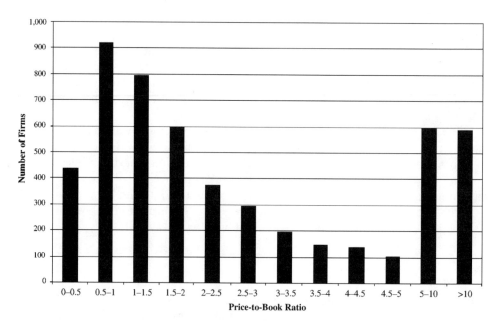

FIGURE 19.1 Price-to-Book Value Ratios—July 2000
Source: Value Line.

where P_0 = Value of equity per share today
DPS_1 = Expected dividends per share next year
   k_e = Cost of equity
   g_n = Growth rate in dividends (forever)

Substituting for DPS_1 = EPS_1(Payout ratio), the value of the equity can be written as:

$$P_0 = \frac{EPS_1 \times \text{Payout ratio}}{k_e - g_n}$$

Defining the return on equity (ROE) = EPS_1/Book value of equity$_0$, the value of equity can be written as:

$$P_0 = \frac{BV_0 \times ROE \times \text{Payout ratio}}{k_e - g_n}$$

Rewriting in terms of the PBV ratio,

$$\frac{P_0}{BV_0} = PBV = \frac{ROE \times \text{Payout ratio}}{k_e - g_n}$$

If we define return on equity using contemporaneous earnings, ROE = EPS_0/Book value of equity$_0$, the price-to-book ratio can be written as:

$$\frac{P_0}{BV_0} = \frac{ROE \times (1 + g) \times \text{Payout ratio}}{k_e - g_n}$$

The PBV ratio is an increasing function of the return on equity, the payout ratio, and the growth rate, and a decreasing function of the riskiness of the firm.

This formulation can be simplified even further by relating growth to the return on equity:

$$g = (1 - \text{Payout ratio}) \times ROE$$

Substituting back into the P/BV equation,

$$\frac{P}{BV} = \frac{(ROE - g_n)}{(k_e - g_n)}$$

The price–book value ratio of a stable firm is determined by the differential between the return on equity and its cost of equity. If the return on equity exceeds the cost of equity, the price will exceed the book value of equity; if the return on equity is lower than the cost of equity, the price will be lower than the book value of equity. The advantage of this formulation is that it can be used to estimate price–book value ratios for private firms that do not pay out dividends.

ILLUSTRATION 19.1:   Estimating the PBV Ratio for a Stable Firm: Volvo

---

Volvo had earnings per share of 11.04 Swedish kroner (Sk) in 2000, and paid out a dividend of 7 Sk per share, which represented 63.41% of its earnings. The growth rate in earnings and dividends, in the long term, is expected to be 5%. The return on equity at Volvo is expected to be 13.66%. The beta for Volvo is 0.80, and the risk-free rate in Swedish kroner is 6.1%. (Market risk premium is 4%.)

> Current dividend payout ratio = 63.41%
> Expected growth rate in earnings and dividends = 5%
> Return on equity = 13.66%
> Cost of equity = 6.1% + 0.80 × 4% = 9.30%
>
> PBV ratio based on fundamentals = ROE × Payout ratio/(Cost of equity − Growth rate)
> = 0.1366 × 0.6341/(.093 − .05) = 2.01

Since the expected growth rate in this case is consistent with that estimated by fundamentals, the price-to-book ratio could also have been estimated from the return differences:

> Fundamental growth rate = (1 − Payout ratio) × ROE = (1 − .6341) × .1366 = .05 or 5%
>
> PBV ratio = (ROE − Growth rate)/(Cost of equity − Growth rate)
> = (.1366 − .05)/(.094 − .05) = 2.01

Volvo was selling at a PBV ratio of 1.10 on the day of this analysis (May 2001), making it significantly undervalued. The alternative interpretation is that the market is anticipating a much lower return on equity in the future and pricing Volvo based on this expectation.

ILLUSTRATION 19.2:   Estimating the Price–Book Value Ratio for a Privatization Candidate: Jenapharm (Germany)

One of the by-products of German reunification was the Treuhandanstalt, the German privatization agency set up to sell hundreds of East German firms to other German companies, individual investors, and the public. One of the handful of firms that seemed to be a viable candidate for privatization was Jenapharm, the most respected pharmaceutical manufacturer in East Germany. Jenapharm, which was expected to have revenues of 230 million DM in 1991, also was expected to report net income of 9 million DM in that year. The firm had a book value of assets of 110 million DM and a book value of equity of 58 million DM at the end of 1990.

The firm was expected to maintain sales in its niche product, a contraceptive pill, and grow at 5% a year in the long term, primarily by expanding into the generic drug market. The average beta of pharmaceutical firms traded on the Frankfurt Stock Exchange was 1.05, though many of these firms had much more diversified product portfolios and less volatile cash flows. Allowing for the higher leverage and risk in Jenapharm, a beta of 1.25 was used for Jenapharm. The 10-year bond rate in Germany at the time of this valuation in early 1991 was 7%, and the risk premium for stocks over bonds is assumed to be 3.5%.

> Expected net income = 9 million DM
> Return on equity = Expected net income/Book value of equity = 9/58 = 15.52%
> Cost of equity = 7% + 1.25(3.5%) = 11.375%
> Price–book value ratio = (ROE − g)/(k_e − g) = (.1552 − .05)/(.11375 − .05) = 1.65
> Estimated MV of equity = BV of equity × Price/BV ratio = 58 × 1.65 = 95.70 million DM

PBV Ratio for a High-Growth Firm

The price–book value ratio for a high-growth firm can also be related to fundamentals. In the special case of the two-stage dividend discount model, this relationship can be made explicit fairly simply. The value of equity of a high-growth firm in the two-stage dividend discount model can be written as:

$$\text{Value of equity} = \text{Present value of expected dividends} + \text{Present value of terminal price}$$

When the growth rate is assumed to be constant after the initial high-growth phase, the dividend discount model can be written as follows:

$$P_0 = \frac{EPS_0 \times \text{Payout ratio} \times (1+g) \times \left[1 - \dfrac{(1+g)^n}{(1+k_{e,hg})^n}\right]}{k_{e,hg} - g}$$
$$+ \frac{EPS_0 \times \text{Payout ratio}_n \times (1+g)^n \times (1+g_n)}{(k_{e,st} - g_n)(1+k_{e,hg})^n}$$

where
g = Growth rate in the first n years
Payout = Payout ratio in the first n years
g_n = Growth rate after n years forever (stable growth rate)
Payout_n = Payout ratio after n years for the stable firm
k_e = Cost of equity (hg: high-growth period; st: stable-growth period)

Rewriting EPS_0 in terms of the return on equity, $EPS_0 = BV_0 \times ROE$, and bringing BV_0 to the left-hand side of the equation, we get:

$$\frac{P_0}{BV_0} = ROE \times \frac{\text{Payout ratio} \times (1+g) \times \left[1 - \dfrac{(1+g)^n}{(1+k_{e,hg})^n}\right]}{k_{e,hg} - g}$$
$$+ ROE \times \frac{\text{Payout ratio}_n \times (1+g)^n \times (1+g_n)}{(k_{e,st} - g_n)(1+k_{e,hg})^n}$$

where ROE is the return on equity and k_e is the cost of equity.

The left-hand side of the equation is the price–book value ratio. It is determined by:

- *Return on equity.* The price–book value ratio is an increasing function of the return on equity.
- *Payout ratio during the high-growth period and in the stable period.* The PBV ratio increases as the payout ratio increases, for any given growth rate.

■ *Riskiness (through the discount rate r).* The PBV ratio becomes lower as riskiness increases; the increased risk increases the cost of equity.
■ *Growth rate in earnings, in both the high-growth and stable phases.* The PBV increases as the growth rate increases, in either period, holding the payout ratio constant.

This formula is general enough to be applied to any firm, even one that is not paying dividends right now. Note, in addition, that the fundamentals that determine the price-to-book ratio are the same as they were for a stable growth firm—the payout ratio, the return on equity, the expected growth rate, and the cost of equity.

Chapter 14 noted that firms may not always pay out what they can afford to and recommended that the free cash flows to equity be substituted in for the dividends in those cases. You can, in fact, modify the equation to state the price-to-book ratio in terms of free cash flows to equity:

$$\frac{P_0}{BV_0} = ROE_{hg} \times \frac{\left[\dfrac{FCFE}{Earnings}\right]_{hg} \times (1+g) \times \left[1 - \dfrac{(1+g)^n}{(1+k_{e,hg})^n}\right]}{k_{e,hg}}$$

$$+ ROE_{st} \times \frac{\left[\dfrac{FCFE}{Earnings}\right]_n \times (1+g)^n \times (1+g_n)}{(k_{e,st} - g_n)(1+k_{e,hg})^n}$$

The only substitution that we have made is the replacement of the payout ratio by the FCFE as a percent of earnings. Note that we have also generalized the equation to allow the return on equity to be different in stable growth.

ILLUSTRATION 19.3: Estimating the PBV Ratio for a High-Growth Firm in the Two-Stage Model

Assume that you have been asked to estimate the PBV ratio for a firm that is expected to be in high growth for the next five years. The firm has the following characteristics:

EPS growth rate in first five years = 20%	Payout ratio in first five years = 20%
EPS growth rate after five years = 8%	Payout ratio after five years = 68%
Beta = 1.0	Risk free rate = T-bond rate = 6%
Return on equity = 25%	
Cost of equity = 6% + 1(5.5%) = 11.5%	

$$PBV = 0.25 \times \left[\frac{(0.2)(1.20)\left(1 - \dfrac{1.20^5}{1.115^5}\right)}{0.115 - 0.20}\right] + 0.25 \times \left[\frac{(0.68)(1.20^5)(1.08)}{(0.115 - 0.08)(1.115^5)}\right] = 7.89$$

The estimated PBV ratio for this firm is 7.89.

ILLUSTRATION 19.4:   Estimating the Price–Book Value Ratio for a High-Growth Firm Using FCFE—Nestlé

In Chapter 14, we valued Nestlé using a two-stage FCFE model. We summarize the inputs we used for that valuation in the following table:

	High Growth	*Stable Growth*
Length	10 years	Forever after year 10
ROE	22.98%	15%
FCFE/Earnings	68.35%	73.33%
Growth rate	7.27%	4%
Cost of equity	8.47%	8.47%

The price–book value ratio, based on these inputs, is calculated as follows:

$$PBV = 0.2298 \times \frac{0.6835 \times (1.0727) \times \left[1 - \frac{(1.0727)^{10}}{(1.0847)^{10}}\right]}{(.0847 - .0727)} + 0.15 \times \frac{0.7333 \times (1.0727)^5 \times (1.04)}{(.0847 - .04)(1.0847)^{10}} = 3.77$$

Nestlé traded at a price–book value ratio of 4.40 in May 2001, which would make it overvalued.

Again, in this valuation, we have preserved consistency by setting the growth rate equal to the product of the return on equity and the equity reinvestment rate (1 − FCFE/Earnings):

$$\text{Growth rate during high growth} = \text{ROE}(1 - \text{FCFE/Earnings})$$
$$= .2298(1 - .6835) = .0727$$

$$\text{Growth rate during stable growth} = \text{ROE}(1 - \text{FCFE/Earnings})$$
$$= .15(1 - .7333) = .04$$

PBV Ratios and Return on Equity

The ratio of price to book value is strongly influenced by the return on equity. A lower return on equity affects the price–book value ratio directly through the formulation specified in the prior section and indirectly by lowering the expected growth or payout.

$$\text{Expected growth rate} = \text{Retention ratio} \times \text{Return on equity}$$

The effects of lower return on equity on the price–book value ratio can be seen by going back to Illustration 19.3 and changing the return on equity for the firm valued in that example.

ILLUSTRATION 19.5:   Return on Equity and Price–Book Value

In Illustration 19.3, we estimated a price to book ratio for the firm of 7.89, based on a return on equity of 25%. This return on equity, in turn, allowed the firm to generate growth rates of 20% in high growth and 8% in stable growth:

$$\text{Growth rate in first five years} = \text{Retention ratio} \times \text{ROE} = 0.8 \times 25\% = 20\%$$
$$\text{Growth rate after year 5} = \text{Retention ratio} \times \text{ROE} = 0.32 \times 25\% = 8\%$$

If the firm's return on equity drops to 12%, the price–book value ratio will reflect the drop. The lower return on equity will also lower expected growth in the initial high-growth period:

$$\text{Expected growth rate (first five years)} = \text{Retention ratio} \times \text{Return on equity}$$
$$= 0.80 \times 12\% = 9.6\%$$

After year 5, either the retention ratio has to increase or the expected growth rate has to be lower than 8%. If the retention ratio is adjusted,

$$\text{New retention ratio after year 5} = \text{Expected growth/ROE} = 8\%/12\% = 66.67\%$$
$$\text{New payout ratio after year 5} = 1 - \text{Retention ratio} = 33.33\%$$

The new price–book value ratio can then be calculated as follows:

$$PBV = (0.12) \times \frac{(0.2)(1.096)\left(1 - \dfrac{(1.096)^5}{(1.115)^5}\right)}{0.115 - 0.096} + (0.12) \times \frac{(0.3333)(1.096)^5(1.08)}{(0.115 - 0.08)(1.115)^5} = 1.25$$

The drop in the ROE has a two-layered impact. First, it lowers the growth rate in earnings and/or the expected payout ratio, thus having an indirect effect on the PBV ratio. Second, it reduces the PBV ratio directly.

The price–book value ratio is also influenced by the cost of equity, with higher costs of equity leading to lower price–book value ratios. The influence of the return on equity and the cost of equity can be consolidated in one measure by taking the difference between the two—a measure of excess equity return. The larger the return on equity relative to the cost of equity, the greater is the price–book value ratio. In Illustrations 19.3 and 19.5, for instance, the firm, which had a cost of equity of 11.5 percent, went from having a return on equity that was 13.5 percent greater than the required rate of return to a return on equity that barely broke even (0.5 percent greater than the required rate of return). Consequently, its price–book value ratio declined from 7.89 to 1.25. Figure 19.2 shows the price–book value ratio as a function of the difference between the return on equity and cost of equity. Note that when the return on equity is equal to the cost of equity, the price is equal to the book value.

Determinants of Return on Equity   The difference between return on equity and the cost of equity is a measure of a firm's capacity to earn excess returns in the business in which it operates. Corporate strategists have examined the determinants of the

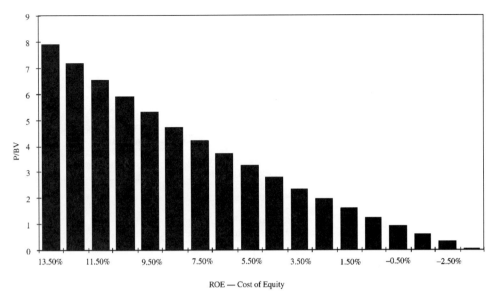

FIGURE 19.2 Price–Book Value as a Function of Return Differential

size and expected duration of these excess profits (and high ROE) using a variety of frameworks. One of the better known is the "five forces of competition" framework developed by Porter. In his approach, competition arises not only from established producers producing the same product but also from suppliers of substitutes and from potential new entrants into the market. Figure 19.3 summarizes the five forces of competition.

In Porter's framework, a firm is able to maintain a high return on equity because there are significant barriers to entry by new firms or because the firm has significant advantages over its competition. The analysis of the return on equity of a firm can be made richer and much more informative by examining the competitive environment in which it operates. There may also be clues in this analysis to the future direction of the return on equity.

 eqmult.xls: **This spreadsheet allows you to estimate the price-earnings ratio for a stable-growth or high-growth firm, given its fundamentals.**

APPLICATIONS OF PRICE–BOOK VALUE RATIOS

There are several potential applications for the principles developed in the preceding section, and we will consider three in this section. We will first look at what causes price-to-book ratios for entire markets to change over time, and when a low (high) price-to-book ratio for a market can be viewed as a sign of undervaluation or overvaluation. We will next compare the price-to-book ratios of firms within a sector, and extend this to look at firms across the market and what you need to

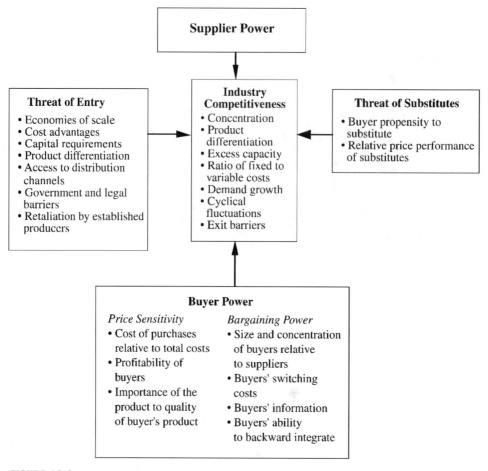

FIGURE 19.3 Forces of Competition and Return on Equity
Source: Porter.

control for in making these comparisons. Finally, we will look at the factors that cause the price-to-book ratio of an individual firm to change over time and how this can be used as a tool for analyzing restructurings.

PBV Ratios for a Market

The price-to-book value ratio for an entire market is determined by the same variables that determine the price-to-book value ratio for an individual firm. Other things remaining equal, therefore, you would expect the price-to-book ratio for a market to go up as the equity return spread (ROE minus cost of equity) earned by firms in the market increases. Conversely, you would expect the price-to-book ratio for the market to decrease as the equity return spread earned by firms decreases.

Chapter 18 noted the increase in the price-earnings ratio for the S&P 500 from 1960 to 2000. Over that period, the price-to-book value ratio for the market has also increased. Figure 19.4 reports on the price-to-book ratio for the S&P 500 and the return on equity for S&P 500 firms. The increase in the price-to-book ratio over

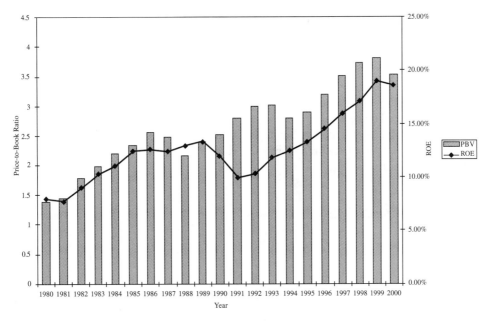

FIGURE 19.4   Price-to-Book Ratios and Return on Equity—S&P 500
Source: S&P.

the past two decades can be at least partially explained by the increase in return on equity over the same period.

Comparisons across Firms in a Sector

Price–book value ratios vary across firms for a number of reasons—different expected growth, different payout ratios, different risk levels, and most importantly, different returns on equity. Comparisons of price–book value ratios across firms that do not take into account these differences are likely to be flawed.

The most common approach to estimating PBV ratios for a firm is to choose a group of comparable firms, to calculate the average PBV ratio for this group, and to base the PBV ratio estimate for a firm on this average. The adjustments made to reflect differences in fundamentals between the firm being valued and the comparable group are usually made subjectively. There are several problems with this approach. First, the definition of a comparable firm is essentially a subjective one. The use of other firms in the industry as the control group is often not a complete solution because firms within the same industry can have very different business mixes and risk and growth profiles. There is also plenty of potential for bias. Second, even when a legitimate group of comparable firms can be constructed, differences will continue to persist in fundamentals between the firm being valued and this group. Adjusting for differences subjectively does not provide a satisfactory solution to this problem, since these judgments are only as good as the analysts making them.

Given the relationship between price–book value ratios and returns on equity, it is not surprising to see firms that have high returns on equity selling for well above book value and firms that have low returns on equity selling at or below book value. The firms that should draw attention from investors are those that provide mismatches of price–book value ratios and returns on equity—low PBV ratios and high ROE, or high PBV ratios and low ROE. There are two ways in which we can bring home these mismatches—a matrix approach and a sector regression.

Matrix Approach If the essence of misvaluation is finding firms that have price-to-book ratios that do not go with their equity return spreads, the mismatch can be brought home by plotting the price-to-book value ratios of firms against their returns on equity. Figure 19.5 presents such a plot.

   If we assume that firms within a sector have similar costs of equity, we could replace the equity return spread with the raw return on equity. Though we often use current returns on equity, in practice, the matrix is based on expected returns on equity in the future.

Regression Approach If the price-to-book ratio is largely a function of the return on equity, we could regress the former against the latter:

$$PBV = a + b \ ROE$$

If the relationship is strong, we could use this regression to obtain predicted price-to-book ratios for all of the firms in the sector, separating out those firms that are undervalued from those that are overvalued.

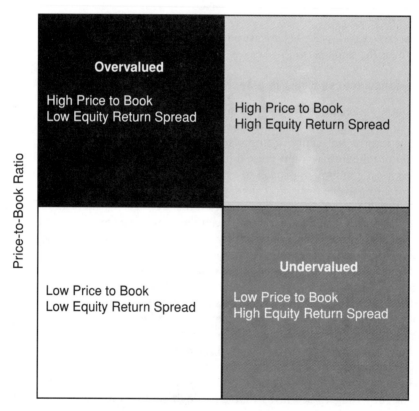

Overvalued

High Price to Book
Low Equity Return Spread

High Price to Book
High Equity Return Spread

Low Price to Book
Low Equity Return Spread

Undervalued

Low Price to Book
High Equity Return Spread

Price-to-Book Ratio

Return on Equity—Cost of Equity

FIGURE 19.5 Price-to-Book Ratios and Return on Equity

This regression can be enriched in two ways. The first is to allow for nonlinear relationships between price-to-book and return on equity; this can be done either by transforming the variables (natural logs, exponentials, etc.) or by running nonlinear regressions. The second is to expand the regression to include other independent variables such as risk and growth.

ILLUSTRATION 19.6:   Comparing Price-to-Book Value Ratios: Integrated Oil Companies

The following table reports on the price-to-book ratios for integrated oil companies listed in the United States in September 2000:

Company Name	Ticker Symbol	Price-to-Book Ratio	Return on Equity	Standard Deviation
Crown Central Petroleum "A"	CNPA	0.29	−14.60%	59.36%
Giant Industries	GI	0.54	7.47%	38.87%
Harken Energy Corp.	HEC	0.64	−5.83%	56.51%
Getty Petroleum Mktg.	GPM	0.95	6.26%	58.34%
Pennzoil–Quaker State	PZL	0.95	3.99%	51.06%
Ashland Inc.	ASH	1.13	10.27%	21.77%
Shell Transport	SC	1.45	13.41%	31.61%
USX–Marathon Group	MRO	1.59	13.42%	45.31%
Lakehead Pipe Line	LHP	1.72	13.28%	19.56%
Amerada Hess	AHC	1.77	16.69%	26.89%
Tosco Corp.	TOS	1.95	15.44%	34.51%
Occidental Petroleum	OXY	2.15	16.68%	39.47%
Royal Dutch Petroleum	RD	2.33	13.41%	29.81%
Murphy Oil Corp.	MUR	2.40	14.49%	27.80%
Texaco Inc.	TX	2.44	13.77%	27.78%
Phillips Petroleum	P	2.64	17.92%	29.51%
Chevron Corp.	CHV	3.03	15.69%	26.44%
Repsol-YPF ADR	REP	3.24	13.43%	26.82%
Unocal Corp.	UCL	3.53	10.67%	34.90%
Kerr-McGee Corp.	KMG	3.59	28.88%	42.47%
Exxon Mobil Corp.	XOM	4.22	11.20%	19.22%
BP Amoco ADR	BPA	4.66	14.34%	27.00%
Clayton Williams Energy	CWEI	5.57	31.02%	26.31%
Average		2.30	12.23%	

The average price-to-book ratio for the sector is 2.30, but the range in price-to-book ratios is large, with Crown Central trading at 0.29 times book value and Clayton Williams Energy trading at 5.57 times book value.

We will begin by plotting price-to-book ratios against returns on equity for these firms in Figure 19.6. While there are no firms that show up in the overvalued quadrant, firms such as Pennzoil (P), Occidental (OXY), Amerada Hess (AHC), and Murphy (MUR) look undervalued relative to the rest of the sector.

Regressing the price-to-book ratio against return on equity for oil companies, we obtained the following:

$$PBV = 1.043 + 10.24 \ ROE \qquad R^2 = 48.6\%$$
$$[2.97] \quad [4.46]$$

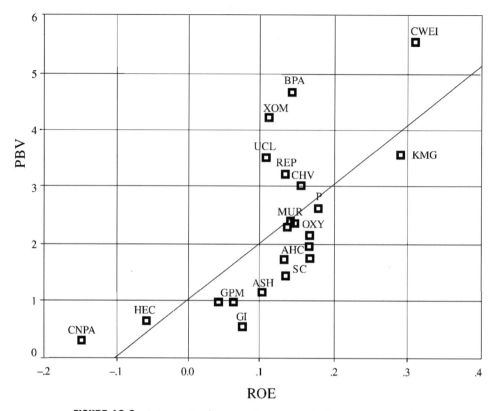

FIGURE 19.6   Price to Book versus Return on Equity: Oil Companies

If we extend this regression to include standard deviation in stock prices as a measure of risk, we get:

$$PBV = 2.21 + 8.22\ ROE - 2.63\ Standard\ deviation \qquad R^2 = 52\%$$
$$[2.16]\ [2.92] \qquad\quad [1.21]$$

This regression can be used to estimate predicted price-to-book ratios for these companies in the following table:

Company Name	Price-to-Book Ratio	Predicted PBV	Under- or Overvalued
Crown Central Petroleum "A"	0.29	−0.56	NMF
Giant Industries	0.54	1.80	−69.74%
Harken Energy Corp.	0.64	0.24	166.59%
Getty Petroleum Mktg.	0.95	1.19	−19.67%
Pennzoil–Quaker State	0.95	1.19	−19.93%
Ashland Inc.	1.13	2.48	−54.28%
Shell Transport	1.45	2.48	−41.56%
USX–Marathon Group	1.59	2.12	−25.11%
Lakehead Pipe Line	1.72	2.78	−38.03%
Amerada Hess	1.77	2.87	−38.33%

Company Name	Price-to-Book Ratio	Predicted PBV	Under- or Overvalued
Tosco Corp.	1.95	2.57	−24.09%
Occidental Petroleum	2.15	2.54	−15.27%
Royal Dutch Petroleum	2.33	2.52	−7.66%
Murphy Oil Corp.	2.40	2.67	−10.07%
Texaco Inc.	2.44	2.61	−6.47%
Phillips Petroleum	2.64	2.90	−9.17%
Chevron Corp.	3.03	2.80	8.20%
Repsol-YPF ADR	3.24	2.60	24.53%
Unocal Corp.	3.53	2.17	63.05%
Kerr-McGee Corp.	3.59	3.46	3.70%
Exxon Mobil Corp.	4.22	2.62	60.99%
BP Amoco ADR	4.66	2.67	74.03%
Clayton Williams Energy	5.57	4.06	36.92%

The most undervalued firm in the group is Giant Industries, with an actual price-to-book ratio of 0.54 and a predicted price-to-book ratio of 1.80, and the most overvalued is Harken Energy, with an actual price-to-book ratio of 0.64 and a predicted price-to-book ratio of 0.24.

Comparing Firms across the Market

In contrast to the comparable firm approach, you could look at how firms are priced across the entire market to predict PBV ratios for individual firms. The simplest way of summarizing this information is with a multiple regression, with the PBV ratio as the dependent variable, and proxies for risk, growth, return on equity, and payout forming the independent variables.

Past Studies The relationship between price–book value ratios and the return on equity has been highlighted in other studies. Wilcox (1984) posited a strong relationship between the price-to-book value ratio (plotted on a logarithmic scale) and return on equity. Using data from 1981 for 949 Value Line stocks, he arrived at the following equation:

$$\log(\text{Price/Book value}) = -1.00 + 7.51(\text{Return on equity})$$

He also found that this regression has much smaller mean squared error that competing models using price-earnings ratios and/or growth rates.

These PBV ratio regressions were updated in the first edition of this book using data from 1987 to 1991. The Compustat database was used to extract information on price–book value ratios, return on equity, payout ratios, and earnings growth rates (for the preceding five years) for all NYSE and AMEX firms with data available in each year. The betas were obtained from the CRSP tape for each year. All firms with negative book values were eliminated from the sample, and the regression of PBV on the independent variables yielded the following for each year:

Year	Regression	R-squared
1987	PBV = 0.1841 + .00200 Payout – 0.3940 Beta + 1.3389 EGR + 9.35 ROE	0.8617
1988	PBV = 0.7113 + 0.00007 Payout – 0.5082 Beta + 0.4605 EGR + 6.9374 ROE	0.8405
1989	PBV = 0.4119 + 0.0063 Payout – 0.6406 Beta + 1.0038 EGR + 9.55 ROE	0.8851
1990	PBV = 0.8124 + 0.0099 Payout – 0.1857 Beta + 1.1130 EGR + 6.61 ROE	0.8846
1991	PBV =1.1065 + 0.3505 Payout – 0.6471 Beta + 1.0087 EGR + 10.51 ROE	0.8601

where PBV = Price/book value ratio at the end of the year
     Payout = Dividend payout ratio at the end of the year
       Beta = Beta of the stock
       EGR = Growth rate in earnings over prior five years
       ROE = Return on equity = Net income/Book value of equity

Updated Regressions In July 2000, we regressed the price-to-book ratios against the fundamentals identified in the preceding section—the return on equity, the payout ratio, the beta, and the expected growth rate over the next five years (from analyst forecasts):

PBV = –.59 + 8.93 ROE + .0809 Payout ratio + .917 Beta + 7.55 Growth rate
    [3.76] [32.22]   [3.06]   [5.68]   [18.37]

The regression has an R-squared of 43.2%.

The strong positive relationship between price to book ratios and returns on equity is not unique to the United States. In fact, Table 19.1 summarizes regressions for other countries of price-to-book ratios against returns on equity. In each of the markets, firms with higher returns on equity have higher price-to-book ratios, though the strength of the relationship is greater in Portugal and India and weaker in Greece and Brazil.

TABLE 19.1   Price to Book and Return on Equity: Market Regressions

Country	Regression Details	Regression Equation
Greece	May 2001 (Entire market: 272 firms)	PBV = 2.11 + 11.63 ROE (R^2 = 17.5%)
Brazil	October 2000 (Entire market: 178 firms)	PBV = 0.77 + 3.78 ROE (R^2 = 17.3%)
Portugal	June 1999 (Entire market: 74 firms)	PBV = –1.94 + 16.34 ROE + 2.83 Beta (R^2 = 78%)
India	November 1997 (50 largest firms)	PBV = –1.68 + 24.03 ROE (R^2 = 51%)

ILLUSTRATION 19.7: Valuing a Private Firm Using the Cross-Sectional Regression

Assume that you had been asked to value a private firm early in 2001 and that you had obtained the following data on the company:

Book value of equity = $100 million
Net income in 2000 = $20 million
Beta based on comparable firms = 1.20

Assume also that the firm reinvested $12 million in 2000 and earnings are expected to grow 25% a year for the next five years. First compute the variables in the desired units:

Payout = 8/20 = 40% (assuming free cash flow to equity is paid out as dividend)
Earnings growth rate = 25%
Return on equity = 20/100 = 20%
Beta = 1.20

Predicted price–book value ratio = $-.59 + 8.93(.20) + .0809(.40) + .917(1.20) + 7.55(.25) = 4.2162$

Predicted market value of firm = $4.2162 \times 100 = 421.62$ million

---

 pbvreg.htm: **This dataset on the Web reports the results of the latest regression of PBV ratios against fundamentals, using all firms in the market.**

CURRENT VERSUS EXPECTED RETURNS ON EQUITY

In all of the comparisons that we have made in this section, we have used a firm's current return on equity to make judgments about valuation. While it is convenient to focus on current returns, the market value of equity is determined by expectations of future returns on equity.

To the extent that there is a strong positive correlation between current ROE and future ROE, using the current return on equity to identify under- or overvalued companies is appropriate. Focusing on the current ROE can be dangerous, however, when the competitive environment is changing, and can lead to significant errors in valuation. In such cases, you should use a forecast return on equity that can be very different from the current return on equity. There are two ways to obtain this forecast:

1. Compute a historical average (over the past three or five years) of the return on equity earned by the firm and substitute this value for the current return on equity, when the latter is volatile.
2. Push the firm's current return on equity toward the industry average to reflect competitive pressures. For instance, assume that you are analyzing a computer software firm with a current return on equity of 35 percent and that the industry average return on equity is 20 percent. The forecast return on equity for this firm would be a weighted average of 20 percent and 35 percent, with the weight on the industry average increasing with the speed with which you expect the firm's return to converge on industry norms.

Comparing a Firm's Price-to-Book Ratio across Time

As a firm's return on equity changes over time, you would expect its price-to-book ratio to also change. Specifically, firms that increase their returns on equity should increase their price-to-book ratios and firms that see their returns on equity deteriorate should see a fall in their price-to-book ratios as well. Another way of thinking about this is in terms of the matrix presented in Figure 19.5, where we argued that firms with low (high) returns on equity should have low (high) price-to-book ratios. Thus, one way to measure the effect of the restructuring of a poorly performing firm (with low return on equity and low price-to-book ratio) is to see where it moves on the matrix. If it succeeds in its endeavor, it should move from the low PBV/low ROE quadrant toward the high PBV/high ROE quadrant. (See Figure 19.7.)

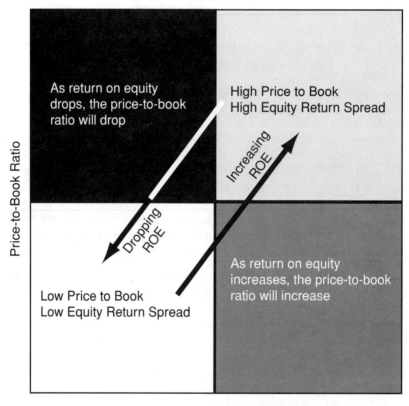

FIGURE 19.7 Changes in ROE and Changes in PBV Ratio

ILLUSTRATION 19.8:   ROE and PBV Ratios: The Case of IBM

IBM provides a classic example of the effects of returns on equity on price–book value ratios. In 1983, IBM had a price which was three times its book value, one of the highest price–book value multiples among the Dow 30 stocks at that time. By 1992, the stock was trading at roughly book value, significantly lower than the average ratio for Dow 30 stocks. This decline in the price–book value ratio was triggered by the decline in return on equity at IBM, from 25% in 1983 and 1984, to negative levels in 1992 and 1993. In the years following Lou Gerstner becoming CEO, the firm has recovered dramatically and was trading at nine times book value in 1999. Figure 19.8 illustrates both PBV and ROE between 1983 and 2000 for IBM.

An investor buying IBM at its low point would have obtained a stock with a low price to book and a low return on equity, but her bet would have paid off. As the return on equity improved, IBM migrated from the bottom-left quadrant to the top-right quadrant in the matrix. As its price-to-book ratio improved, the investor would have seen substantial price appreciation and profits.

USE IN INVESTMENT STRATEGIES

Investors have used the relationship between price and book value in a number of investment strategies ranging from the simple to the sophisticated. Some have used low price–book value ratios as a screen to pick undervalued stocks. Others combine price-to-book value ratios with other fundamentals to make the same judgment. Finally, the sheer persistent of higher returns earned by low price-to-book

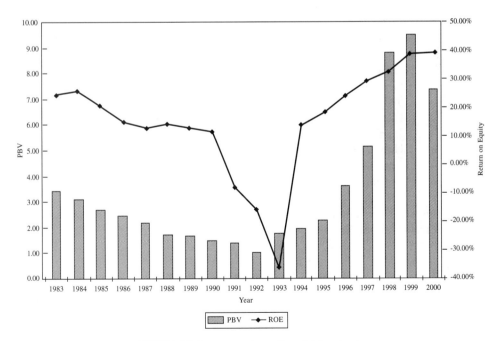

FIGURE 19.8   IBM: The Fall and Rise Again

stocks is viewed by some as an indication that price-to-book value ratio is a proxy for equity risk.

The Link to Excess Returns

Several studies have established a relationship between price–book value ratios and excess returns. Rosenberg, Reid, and Lanstein (1985) found that the average returns on U.S. stocks are positively related to the ratio of a firm's book value to market value. Between 1973 and 1984, the strategy of picking stocks with high book–price ratios (low price–book values) yielded an excess return of 36 basis points a month. Fama and French (1992), in examining the cross section of expected stock returns between 1963 and 1990, established that the positive relationship between book-to-price ratios and average returns persists in both the univariate and multivariate tests, and is even stronger than the small firm effect in explaining returns. When they classified firms on the basis of book-to-price ratios into 12 portfolios, firms in the lowest book-to-price (highest PBV) class earned an average monthly return of 0.30%, while firms in the highest book-to-price (lowest PBV) class earned an average monthly return of 1.83% for the 1963 to 1990 period.

Chan, Hamao, and Lakonishok (1991) found that the book-to-market ratio has a strong role in explaining the cross section of average returns on Japanese stocks. Capaul, Rowley, and Sharpe (1993) extended the analysis of price–book value ratios across other international markets between 1981 and 1992, and concluded that value stocks (stocks with low price–book value ratios) earned excess returns in every market that they analyzed. Their annualized estimates of the return differential earned by stocks with low price–book value ratios, over the market index, were as follows:

Country	Added Return to Low PBV Portfolio
France	3.26%
Germany	1.39%
Switzerland	1.17%
United Kingdom	1.09%
Japan	3.43%
United States	1.06%
Europe	1.30%
Global	1.88%

While this study is dated, the conclusion that lower price-to-book stocks earn higher returns than higher price-to-book stocks looks robust.

Using Price–Book Value Ratios as Investment Screens

The excess returns earned by firms with low price–book value ratios have been exploited by investment strategies that use price–book value ratios as a screen. Benjamin Graham, for instance, in his classic book on security analysis, listed price being less than two-thirds of book value as one of the criteria to be used to pick stocks.

The discussion in the preceding section emphasized the importance of return on equity in determining the price–book value ratio, and noted that only firms with high return on equity and a low price–book value ratio could be considered undervalued. This proposition was tested by screening all NYSE stocks from 1981 to 1990 on the basis of both price–book value ratios and returns on equity and creating two portfolios—an undervalued portfolio with low price–book value ratios (in bottom 25 percent of universe) and high returns on equity (in top 25 percent of universe), and an overvalued portfolio with high price–book value ratios (in top 25 percent of universe) and low returns on equity (in bottom 25 percent)—each year, and then estimating excess returns on each portfolio in the subsequent year. The following table summarizes returns on these two portfolios for each year from 1982 to 1991.

Year	Undervalued Portfolio	Overvalued Portfolio	S&P 500
1982	37.64%	14.64%	40.35%
1983	34.89%	3.07%	0.68%
1984	20.52%	–28.82%	15.43%
1985	46.55%	30.22%	30.97%
1986	33.61%	0.60%	24.44%
1987	–8.80%	–0.56%	–2.69%
1988	23.52%	7.21%	9.67%
1989	37.50%	16.55%	18.11%
1990	–26.71%	–10.98%	6.18%
1991	74.22%	28.76%	31.74%
1982–1991	25.60%	10.61%	17.49%

The undervalued portfolios significantly outperformed the overvalued portfolios in 8 out of 10 years, earning an average of 14.99 percent more per year between 1982 and 1991, and also had an average return significantly higher than the S&P 500.

Price to Book as a Proxy for Risk

The persistence of excess returns earned by firms with lower price-to-book ratios indicates either that the market is inefficient or that the price-to-book ratio is a proxy for equity risk. In other words, if lower price-to-book ratio stocks are viewed by the market as riskier than firms with higher price-to-book ratios, the higher returns earned by these stocks would be a fair return for this risk. In fact, this is the conclusion that Fama and French (1992) reached after examining the returns earned by lower price-to-book stocks.

While you cannot reject this hypothesis out of hand, you would need to put it to the test. What is the additional risk that low price-to-book stocks are exposed to? It is true that some low price-to-book ratio companies are highly levered and may not stay in business. For the most part, though, a portfolio composed of low price-to-book ratio stocks does not seem any more risky than a portfolio of high price-to-book stocks—their leverage and earnings variability are similar.

VALUE-TO-BOOK RATIOS

Instead of relating the market value of equity to the book value of equity, the value-to-book ratio relates the firm value to the book value of capital of the firm. Consequently, it can be viewed as the firm value analogue to the price-to-book ratio.

Definition

The value-to-book ratio is obtained by dividing the market value of both debt and equity by the book value of capital invested in a firm:

$$\text{Value-to-book ratio} = \frac{(\text{Market value of equity} + \text{Market value of debt})}{(\text{Book value of equity} + \text{Book value of debt})}$$

If the market value of debt is unavailable, the book value of debt can be used in the numerator as well. Needless to say, debt has to be consistently defined for both the numerator and denominator. For instance, if you choose to convert operating leases to debt for computing market value of debt, you have to add the present value of operating leases to the book value of debt as well.

There are two common variants of this multiple that do not pass the consistency test. One uses the book value of assets, which will generally exceed the book value of capital by the magnitude of current liabilities, in the denominator. This will result in price-to-book ratios that are biased down for firms with substantial current liabilities. The other uses the enterprise value in the numerator, with cash netted from the market values of debt and equity. Since the book value of equity incorporates the cash holdings of the firm, this will also bias the multiple down. If you decide to use enterprise value in the numerator, you would need to net cash out of the denominator as well.

$$\text{Enterprise value to book} = \frac{(\text{Market value of equity} + \text{Market value of debt} - \text{Cash})}{(\text{Book value of equity} + \text{Book value of debt} - \text{Cash})}$$

In addition, the multiple will need to be adjusted for a firm's cross holdings. The adjustment was described in detail for the enterprise value to EBITDA multiple in Chapter 18 and will require that you net out the portion of the market value and book value of equity that is attributable to subsidiaries.

Description

The distribution of the value-to-book ratio resembles that of the price-to-book ratio. Figure 19.9 presents this distribution for U.S. companies in July 2000. As with the other multiples, it is a heavily skewed distribution. The average value-to-book ratio is 2.93, slightly lower than the average price-to-book ratio computed for the same firms. The median value-to-book ratio is 1.40, which is also lower than the median price-to-book ratio.

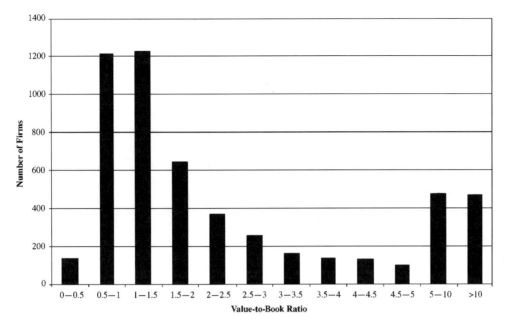

FIGURE 19.9 Value-to-Book Value Ratios
Source: Value Line.

One of the interesting by-products of switching from price-to-book ratios to value-to-book is that we lose no firms in the sample. In other words, the book value of equity can be negative, but the book value of capital is always positive.

 pbvdata.xls: **This dataset on the Web summarizes value to book multiples and fundamentals by industry group in the United States for the most recent year.**

Analysis

The value-to-book ratio is a firm value multiple. To analyze it, we go back to a free cash flow to the firm valuation model, and use it to value a stable growth firm:

$$\text{Value} = \frac{\text{FCFF}_1}{(\text{Cost of capital} - g)}$$

Substituting in FCFF = $\text{EBIT}_1(1 - t)(1 - \text{Reinvestment rate})$, we get:

$$\text{Value} = \frac{\text{EBIT}_1(1 - t)(1 - \text{Reinvestment rate})}{(\text{Cost of capital} - g)}$$

Dividing both sides by the book value of capital, we get:[2]

$$\frac{\text{Value}}{\text{Book value of capital}} = \frac{\text{ROC}(1 - \text{Reinvestment rate})}{(\text{Cost of capital} - g)}$$

The value-to-book ratio is fundamentally determined by its return on capital—firms with high returns on capital tend to have high value-to-book ratios. In fact, the determinants of value-to-book mirror the determinants of price-to-book equity, but we replace equity measures with firm value measures—the ROE with the ROC, the cost of equity with the cost of capital, and the payout ratio with (1 – Reinvestment rate). In fact, if we substitute in the fundamental equation for the reinvestment rate:

$$\text{Reinvestment rate} = g/\text{ROC}$$

$$\frac{\text{Value}}{\text{Book value of capital}} = \frac{(\text{ROC} - g)}{(\text{Cost of capital} - g)}$$

The analysis can be extended to cover high-growth firms, with the value-to-book capital ratio determined by the return on capital, cost of capital, growth rate, and reinvestment—in the high-growth and stable-growth periods:

$$\frac{\text{Value}_0}{\text{BV}_0} = \text{ROC}_{hg}^{*} \times \frac{(1 - \text{RIR}_{hg}) \times (1 + g) \times \left[1 - \dfrac{(1 + g)^n}{(1 + k_{c,hg})^n}\right]}{k_{c,hg} - g}$$

$$+ \, \text{ROC}_{st} \times \frac{(1 - \text{RIR}_{st}) \times (1 + g)^n \times (1 + g_n)}{(k_{c,st} - g_n)(1 + k_{c,hg})^n}$$

where ROC = Return on capital (hg: high-growth period; st: stable-growth period)
   RIR = Reinvestment rate (hg: high-growth period; st: stable-growth period)
   k_c = Cost of capital (hg: high-growth period; st: stable-growth period)

---

 firmmult.xls: **This spreadsheet allows you to estimate firm value multiples for a stable-growth or high-growth firm, given its fundamentals.**

Application

The value-to-book ratios can be compared across firms just as the price-to-book value of equity ratio was in the preceding section. The key variable to control for in making

---

[2]As with the return on equity, if return on capital is defined in terms of contemporaneous earnings (ROC = EBIT_0/Book capital), there will be an extra (1 + g) in the numerator.

this comparison is the return on capital. The value matrix developed for price-to-book ratios can be adapted for the value-to-book ratio in Figure 19.10. Firms with high return on capital will tend to have high value-to-book value ratios, whereas firms with low return on capital will generally have lower value-to-book ratios.

This matrix also yields an interesting link to a widely used value enhancement measure—Economic Value Added (EVA). One of the biggest sales pitches for EVA, which is computed as the product of the return spread (ROC minus cost of capital) and capital invested, is its high correlation with MVA (which is defined as the difference between market value and book value of capital). This is not surprising, since MVA is a variant on the value-to-book ratio and EVA is a variant on the return spread.

Is the link between value-to-book and return on capital stronger or weaker than the link between price-to-book and return on equity? To examine this question, we regressed the value-to-book ratio against return on capital using data on all U.S. firms from January 2001:

$$\text{Value-to-book} = -0.40 + 4.78 \text{ ROC} + 11.48 \text{ Expected growth} + 0.39\ \sigma_{oi} \qquad R^2 = 41\%$$
$$[2.33]\ [24.0] \qquad\quad [16.8] \qquad\qquad\qquad [1.39]$$

where σ_{oi} = Standard deviation in operating income

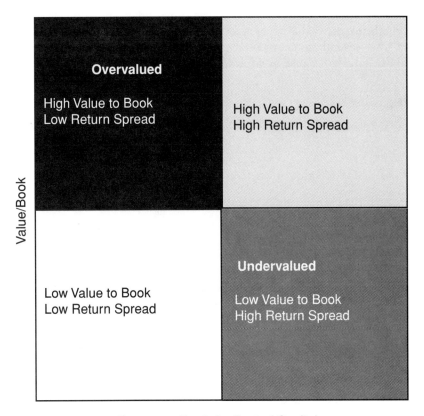

Return on Capital—Cost of Capital

FIGURE 19.10 Valuation Matrix: Value to Book and Excess Returns

The regression yields results similar to those obtained for price-to-book ratios.

If the results from using value-to-book and price-to-book ratios parallel each other, why would you choose to use one multiple over the other? The case for using value-to-book ratios is stronger for firms that have high and/or shifting leverage. Firms can use leverage to increase their returns on equity, but in the process they also increase the volatility in the measure: In good times they report very high returns on equity, and in bad times, very low or negative returns on equity. For such firms, the value to book ratio and the accompanying return on capital will yield more stable and reliable estimates of relative value. In addition, the value-to-book ratio can be computed even for firms that have negative book values of equity and is thus less likely to be biased.

---

 pbvreg.htm: **This dataset on the Web reports the results of the latest regression of PE ratios against fundamentals, using all firms in the market.**

TOBIN'S Q: MARKET VALUE/REPLACEMENT COST

James Tobin presented an alternative to traditional financial measures of value by comparing the market value of an asset to its replacement cost. His measure, called Tobin's Q, has several adherents in academia but still has not broken through into practical use, largely because of informational problems.

Definition

Tobin's Q is estimated by dividing the market value of a firm's assets by the replacement cost of these assets.

Tobin's Q = Market value of assets in place/Replacement cost of assets in place

In cases where inflation has pushed up the replacement cost of the assets or where technology has reduced the cost of the assets, this measure may provide a more updated measure of the value of the assets than accounting book value. The rationale for the measure is simple. Firms that earn negative excess returns and do not utilize their assets efficiently will have a Tobin's Q that is less than 1. Firms that utilize their assets more efficiently will trade at a Tobin's Q that exceeds 1.

While this measure has some advantages in theory, it does have some practical problems. The first is that the replacement value of some assets may be difficult to estimate, especially if assets are not traded on a market. The second is that even where replacement values are available, substantially more information is needed to construct this measure than the traditional price–book value ratio. In practice, analysts often use shortcuts to arrive at Tobin's Q, using book value of assets as a proxy for replacement value and market value of debt and equity as a proxy for the market value of assets. In these cases, Tobin's Q resembles the value-to-book value ratio described in the preceding section.

Description

If we use the strict definition of Tobin's Q, we cannot get a cross-sectional distribution of the multiple because the information to estimate it is neither easily accessible nor even available. This is a serious impediment to using the multiple because we have no sense of what a high, low, or average number for the multiple would be. For instance, assume that you find a firm trading at 1.2 times the replacement cost of the assets. You would have no way of knowing whether you were paying too much or too little for this firm without knowing the summary statistics for the market.

Analysis

The value obtained from Tobin's Q is determined by two variables—the market value of the firm and the replacement cost of assets in place. In inflationary times, where the cost of replacing assets increases over time, Tobin's Q will generally be lower than the unadjusted price–book value ratio, and the difference will increase for firms with older assets. Conversely, if the cost of replacing assets declines much faster than the book value (because of technological changes), Tobin's Q will generally be higher than the unadjusted price–book value ratio.

Tobin's Q is also determined by how efficiently a firm manages its assets and extracts value from them relative to the next best bidder. To see why, note that the market value of an asset will be equal to its replacement cost when assets earn their required return. (If the return earned on capital is equal to the cost of capital, investments have a zero net present value, and the present value of the cash flows from the investment will be equal to the replacement cost.) Carrying this logic forward, Tobin's Q will be less than 1, if a firm earns less than its required return on investments, and more than 1, if it earns positive excess returns.

Applications

Tobin's Q is a practical measure of value for a mature firm with most or all of its assets in place, where replacement cost can be estimated for the assets. Consider, for example, a steel company with little or no growth potential. The market value of this firm can be used as a proxy for the market value of its assets, and you could adjust the book value of the assets owned by the firm for inflation. In contrast, estimating the market value of assets owned would be difficult for a high-growth firm, since the market value of equity for this firm will include a premium for future growth.

Tobin's Q is more a measure of the perceived quality of a firm's management than it is of misvaluation, with poorly managed firms trading at market values that are lower than the replacement cost of the assets that they own. In fact, several studies have examined whether such firms are more likely to be taken over. Lang, Stulz, and Walkling (1991) concluded that firms with low Tobin's Q are more likely to be taken over for purposes of restructuring and increasing value. They also find that shareholders of high q bidders gain significantly more from successful tender offers than shareholders of low q bidders.

CONCLUSION

The relationship between price and book value is much more complex than most investors realize. The price–book value ratio of a firm is determined by its expected payout ratio, its expected growth rate in earnings, and its riskiness. The most important determinant, however, is the return on equity earned by the firm—higher returns lead to higher price–book value ratios, and lower returns lead to lower PBV ratios. The mismatch that should draw investor attention is the one between return on equity and price–book value ratios—high price–book value ratios with low returns on equity (overvalued) and low price–book value ratios with high returns on equity (undervalued).

The value-to-book ratio is the firm value analogue to the price-to-book ratio, and it is a function of the return on capital earned by the firm, its cost of capital, and reinvestment rate. Again, though, firms with low value-to-book ratios and high expected returns on capital can be viewed as undervalued.

QUESTIONS AND SHORT PROBLEMS

1. Answer true or false to the following statements, with a short explanation.
   a. A stock that sells for less than book value is undervalued.
      True _____ False _____
   b. If a company's return on equity drops, its price/book value ratio will generally drop more than proportionately (i.e., if the return on equity drops by half, the price/book value ratio will drop by more than half).
      True _____ False _____
   c. A combination of a low price/book value ratio and a high expected return on equity suggests that a stock is undervalued.
      True _____ False _____
   d. Other things remaining equal, a higher-growth stock will have a higher price/book value ratio than a lower growth stock.
      True _____ False _____
   e. In the Gordon growth model, firms with higher dividend payout ratios will have higher price/book value ratios.
      True _____ False _____
2. NCH Corporation, which markets cleaning chemicals, insecticides, and other products, paid dividends of $2 per share in 1993 on earnings of $4 per share. The book value of equity per share was $40, and earnings are expected to grow 6% a year in the long term. The stock has a beta of 0.85, and sells for $60 per share. (The Treasury bond rate is 7%, and the market risk premium is 5.5%.)
   a. Based on these inputs, estimate the price/book value ratio for NCH.
   b. How much would the return on equity have to increase to justify the price/book value ratio at which NCH sells for currently?
3. You are analyzing the price/book value ratios for firms in the trucking industry, relative to returns on equity and required rates of return. The data on the companies is as follows:

Company	PBV	ROE	Beta
Builders Transport	2.00	11.5%	1.00
Carolina Freight	0.60	5.5%	1.20
Consolidated Freight	2.60	12.0%	1.15
J.B. Hunt	2.50	14.5%	1.00
M.S. Carriers	2.50	12.5%	1.15
Roadway Services	3.00	14.0%	1.15
Ryder System	2.25	13.0%	1.05
Xtra Corporation	2.80	16.5%	1.10

The Treasury bond rate is 7%, and the market risk premium is 5.5%.

a. Compute the average PBV ratio, return on equity, and beta for the industry.

b. Based on these averages, are stocks in the industry under- or overvalued relative to book values?

4. United Healthcare, a health maintenance organization, is expected to have earnings growth of 30% for the next five years and 6% after that. The dividend payout ratio will be only 10% during the high growth phase, but will increase to 60% in steady state. The stock has a beta of 1.65 currently, but the beta is expected to drop to 1.10 in steady state. (The Treasury bond rate is 7.25%.)

a. Estimate the price/book value ratio for United Healthcare, given the inputs above.

b. How sensitive is the price/book value ratio to estimates of growth during the high growth period?

c. United Healthcare trades at a price/book value ratio of 7.00. How long would extraordinary growth have to last (at a 30% annual rate) to justify this PBV ratio?

5. Johnson & Johnson, a leading manufacturer of health care products, had a return on equity of 31.5% in 1993, and paid out 37% of its earnings as dividends. The stock had a beta of 1.25. (The Treasury bond rate is 6%, and the risk premium is 5.5%.) The extraordinary growth is expected to last for 10 years, after which the growth rate is expected to drop to 6% and the return on equity to 15% (the beta will move to 1).

a. Assuming the return on equity and dividend payout ratio continue at current levels for the high growth period, estimate the PBV ratio for Johnson & Johnson.

b. If health care reform passes, it is believed that Johnson & Johnson's return on equity will drop to 20% for the high growth phase. If the company chooses to maintain its existing dividend payout ratio, estimate the new PBV ratio for Johnson & Johnson. (You can assume that the inputs for the steady state period are unaffected.)

6. Assume that you have done a regression of PBV ratios for all firms on the New York Stock Exchange, and arrived at the following result:

PBV = 0.88 + 0.82 Payout + 7.79 Growth – 0.41 Beta + 13.81 ROE $R^2 = 0.65$

where Payout = Dividend payout ratio during most recent period
       Growth = Projected growth rate in earnings over next five years
       Beta = Beta of the stock in most current period

To illustrate, a firm with a payout ratio of 40%, a beta of 1.25, a ROE of 25%, and expected growth rate of 15% would have had a price/book value ratio of:

$$PBV = 0.88 + 0.82(0.4) + 7.79(.15) - 0.41(1.25) + 13.81(.25) = 5.3165$$

a. What use, if any, would you put the R-squared of the regression to?
b. Assume that you have also run a sector regression on a company and estimated a price-to-book ratio based on that regression. Why might your result from the market regression yield a different result from the sector regression?

7. SoftSoap Corporation is a large consumer product firm that reported after-tax operating income of $600 million in the just-completed financial year. At the beginning of the year, the firm reported book value of equity of $4 billion and book value of debt of $1 billion. The market value of equity is $8 billion, the market value of debt is $1 billion, and the firm has a cost of equity of 11% and an after-tax cost of debt of 4%. If the firm is in stable growth, expecting to grow 4% a year in perpetuity, estimate the correct value-to-book value ratio for the firm.

8. Lyondell Inc. is a conglomerate with a value-to-book capital ratio of 2.0. If the firm is in stable growth, expecting to grow 4% a year in perpetuity, and has a cost of capital of 10%, what return on capital is the market assuming in perpetuity for Lyondell?

9. Estimate the value-to-book capital ratio for Zapata Enterprises, a trading firm in high growth, with the following characteristics:

	High Growth	Stable Growth
After-tax return on capital	15%	12%
Expected growth rate	12%	4%
Cost of capital	10%	9%

If high growth is expected to last 10 years, estimate the correct value-to-book ratio for Zapata.

10. If Tobin's Q is computed by dividing the market value of traded equity and debt by the book value of assets, you will overestimate the value for high-growth firms. Explain why.

CHAPTER 20

Revenue Multiples and
Sector-Specific Multiples

While earnings and book value multiples are intuitively appealing and widely used, analysts in recent years have increasingly turned to alternative multiples to value companies. For young firms that have negative earnings, multiples of revenues have replaced multiples of earnings in many valuations. In addition, these firms are being valued on multiples of sector-specific measures such as the number of customers, subscribers, or even web site visitors (for new economy firms). In this chapter, the reasons for the increased use of revenue multiples are examined first, followed by an analysis of the determinants of these multiples and how best to use them in valuation. This is followed by a short discussion of the sector-specific multiples, the dangers associated with their use and the adjustments that might be needed to make them work.

REVENUE MULTIPLES

A revenue multiple measures the value of the equity or a business relative to the revenues that it generates. As with other multiples, other things remaining equal, firms that trade at low multiples of revenues are viewed as cheap relative to firms that trade at high multiples of revenues.

Revenue multiples have proved attractive to analysts for a number of reasons. First, unlike earnings and book value ratios, which can become negative for many firms and thus not meaningful, revenue multiples are available even for the most troubled firms and for very young firms. Thus, the potential for bias created by eliminating firms in the sample is far lower. Second, unlike earnings and book value, which are heavily influenced by accounting decisions on depreciation, inventory, research and development (R&D), acquisition accounting, and extraordinary charges, revenue is relatively difficult to manipulate. Third, revenue multiples are not as volatile as earnings multiples, and hence are less likely to be affected by year-to-year swings in a firm's fortune. For instance, the price-earnings ratio of a cyclical firm changes much more than its price-sales ratios, because earnings are much more sensitive to economic changes than revenues are.

The biggest disadvantage of focusing on revenues is that it can lull you into assigning high values to firms that are generating high revenue growth while losing significant amounts of money. Ultimately, a firm has to generate earnings and cash flows for it to have value. While it is tempting to use price-sales multiples to value firms with negative earnings and book value, the failure to control for differences across firms in costs and profit margins can lead to misleading valuations.

Definition of Revenue Multiple

There are two basic revenue multiples in use. The first, and more popular one, is the multiple of the market value of equity to the revenues of a firm; this is termed the price-to-sales ratio. The second, and more robust, ratio is the multiple of the value of the firm (including both debt and equity) to revenues; this is the value-to-sales ratio.

$$\text{Price-to-sales ratio} = \frac{\text{Market value of equity}}{\text{Revenues}}$$

$$\text{Enterprise value to sales ratio} = \frac{(\text{Market value of equity} + \text{Market value of debt} - \text{Cash})}{\text{Revenues}}$$

As with the EBITDA multiple, we net cash out of firm value, because the income from cash is not part of revenue. The enterprise value-to-sales ratio is a more robust multiple than the price-to-sales ratio because it is internally consistent. It divides the total value of the firm by the revenues generated by that firm. The price-to-sales ratio divides an equity value by revenues that are generated for the firm. Consequently, it will yield lower values for more highly levered firms, and may lead to misleading conclusions when price-to-sales ratios are compared across firms in a sector with different degrees of leverage.

Accounting standards across different sectors and markets are fairly similar when it comes to how revenues are recorded. There have been firms, in recent years though, that have used questionable accounting practices in recording installment sales and intracompany transactions to make their revenues higher. Notwithstanding these problems, revenue multiples suffer far less than other multiples from differences across firms.

Cross-Sectional Distribution

As with the price-earnings ratio, the place to begin the examination of revenue multiples is with the cross sectional distribution of price to sales and value to sales ratios across firms in the United States. Figure 20.1 summarizes this distribution in July 2000.

There are two things worth noting in this distribution. The first is that revenue multiples are even more skewed toward positive values than earnings multiples. The second is that the price-to-sales ratio is generally lower than the value to sales ratio, which should not be surprising since the former includes only equity while the latter considers firm value.

Table 20.1 provides summary statistics on both the price to sales and the value to sales ratios. The average values for both multiples are much higher than the median values, largely as the result of outliers—there are firms that trade at multiples that exceed 100 or more.

Analysis of Revenue Multiples

The variables that determine the revenue multiples can be extracted by going back to the appropriate discounted cash flow models—dividend discount model (or an

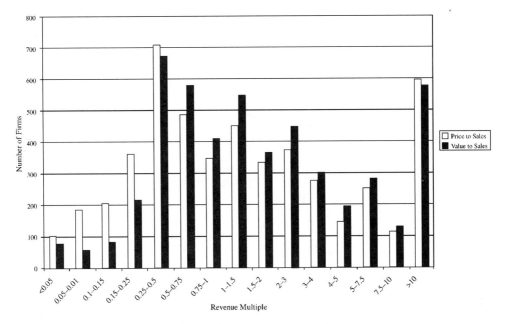

FIGURE 20.1 Revenue Multiples

TABLE 20.1 Summary Statistics on Revenue Multiples: July 2000

	Value-to-Sales Ratio	Price-to-Sales Ratio
Number of firms	4,940	4,940
Average	14.22	13.89
Median	1.06	1.02
Standard deviation	131.32	127.26
10th percentile	0.15	0.27
90th percentile	13.25	12.89

 psdata.xls: **This dataset on the Web summarizes price-to-sales and value-to-sales ratios and fundamentals by industry group in the United States for the most recent year.**

FCFE valuation model) for price-to-sales ratios and a firm valuation model for value-to-sales ratios.

Price-to-Sales Ratios The price-to-sales ratio for a stable firm can be extracted from a stable growth dividend discount model:

$$P_0 = \frac{DPS_1}{k_e - g_n}$$

where
P_0 = Value of equity
DPS_1 = Expected dividends per share next year
k_e = Cost of equity
g_n = Growth rate in dividends (forever)

Substituting in for $DPS_1 = EPS_0(1 + g_n)$(Payout ratio), the value of the equity can be written as:

$$P_0 = \frac{EPS_0 \times \text{Payout ratio} \times (1 + g_n)}{k_e - g_n}$$

Defining the net profit margin = EPS_0/Sales per share, the value of equity can be written as:

$$P_0 = \frac{Sales_0 \times \text{Net margin} \times \text{Payout ratio} \times (1 + g_n)}{k_e - g_n}$$

Rewriting in terms of the price-sales ratio,

$$\frac{P_0}{Sales_0} = PS = \frac{\text{Net margin} \times \text{Payout ratio} \times (1 + g_n)}{k_e - g_n}$$

The PS ratio is an increasing function of the profit margin, the payout ratio, and the growth rate, and a decreasing function of the riskiness of the firm.

The price-sales ratio for a high-growth firm can also be related to fundamentals. In the special case of the two-stage dividend discount model, this relationship can be made explicit fairly simply. With two stages of growth, a high-growth stage and a stable-growth phase, the dividend discount model can be written as follows:

$$P_0 = \frac{EPS_0 \times \text{Payout ratio} \times (1 + g) \times \left[1 - \dfrac{(1 + g)^n}{(1 + k_{e,hg})^n}\right]}{k_{e,hg} - g}$$
$$+ \frac{EPS_0 \times \text{Payout ratio}_n \times (1 + g)^n \times (1 + g_n)}{(k_{e,st} - g_n)(1 + k_{e,hg})^n}$$

where
g = Growth rate in the first n years
$k_{e,hg}$ = Cost of equity in high growth
Payout = Payout ratio in the first n years
g_n = Growth rate after n years forever (stable growth rate)
$k_{e,st}$ = Cost of equity in stable growth
$Payout_n$ = Payout ratio after n years for the stable firm

Rewriting EPS_0 in terms of the profit margin, $EPS_0 = Sales_0 \times$ Profit margin, and bringing $Sales_0$ to the left-hand side of the equation, you get:

$$\frac{\text{Price}}{\text{Sales}} = \text{Net margin} \times \left\{ \frac{\text{Payout ratio} \times (1 + g) \times \left[1 - \dfrac{(1 + g)^n}{(1 + k_{e,hg})^n}\right]}{k_{e,hg} - g} + \frac{\text{Payout ratio}_n \times (1 + g)^n \times (1 + g_n)}{(k_{e,st} - g_n)(1 + k_{e,hg})^n} \right\}$$

The left-hand side of the equation is the price-sales ratio. It is determined by:

- *Net profit margin: net income/revenues.* The price-sales ratio is an increasing function of the net profit margin. Firms with higher net margins, other things remaining equal, should trade at higher price-to-sales ratios.
- *Payout ratio during the high-growth period and in the stable period.* The PS ratio increases as the payout ratio increases, for any given growth rate.
- *Riskiness* (through the discount rate $k_{e,hg}$ in the high-growth period and $k_{e,st}$ in the stable period). The PS ratio becomes lower as riskiness increases, since higher risk translates into a higher cost of equity.
- *Expected growth rate in earnings, in both the high-growth and stable phases.* The PS increases as the growth rate increases, in both the high-growth and stable-growth periods.

You can apply this equation to estimate the price-to-sales ratio, even for a firm that is not paying dividends currently. As with the price to book ratio, you can substitute in the free cash flows to equity for the dividends in making this estimate. Doing so will yield a more reasonable estimate of the price-to-sales ratio for firms that pay out dividends that are far lower than they what can afford to pay out.

$$\frac{Price}{Sales} = Net\ margin \times \left\{ \frac{\left(\frac{FCFE}{Earnings}\right) \times (1+g) \times \left[1 - \frac{(1+g)^n}{(1+k_{e,hg})^n}\right]}{k_{e,hg} - g} + \frac{\left(\frac{FCFE}{Earnings}\right)_n \times (1+g)^n \times (1+g_n)}{(k_{e,st} - g_n)(1+k_{e,hg})^n} \right\}$$

As with the price-to-book ratio, this equation can be modified to allow for different net margins in high-growth and stable-growth periods.

ILLUSTRATION 20.1: Estimating the Price-to-Sales Ratio for a High-Growth Firm in the Two-Stage Model

Assume that you have been asked to estimate the PS ratio for a firm that is expected to be in high growth for the next five years. The following is a summary of the inputs for the valuation:

Growth rate in first five years = 20%	Cost of equity = 6% + 1(5.5%) = 11.5%
Growth rate after five years = 8%	Payout ratio in first five years = 20%
Beta = 1.0	Payout ratio after five years = 50%
Net profit margin = 10%	Risk-free rate = T-bond rate = 6%

This firm's price-to-sales ratio can be estimated as follows:

$$PS = 0.10 \times \left\{ \frac{0.2 \times (1.20) \times \left[1 - \frac{(1.20)^5}{(1.115)^5}\right]}{(.115 - .20)} + \frac{0.50 \times (1.20)^5 \times (1.08)}{(.115 - .08)(1.115)^5} \right\} = 2.35$$

Based on this firm's fundamentals, you would expect its equity to trade at 2.35 times revenues.

ILLUSTRATION 20.2: Estimating the Price-to-Sales Ratio for Unilever

Unilever is a U.K.-based company that sells consumer products globally. To estimate the price-to-sales ratio for Unilever, we used the following inputs in May 2001 for the high growth and stable growth periods. The costs of equity and growth rates are estimated in British pounds.

	High-Growth Period	Stable-Growth Period
Length	5 years	Forever after year 5
Growth rate	8.67%	5%
Net profit margin	5.82%	5.82%
Beta	1.10	1.10
Cost of equity	10.5%	9.4%
Payout ratio	51.17%	66.67%

The risk-free rate used in the analysis is 5% (long-term British government bond rate), and the risk premium is 5% in the high-growth period (due to Unilever's exposure in emerging markets) and 4% in stable growth.

$$PS = 0.0582 \times \left\{ \frac{0.5117 \times (1.0867) \times \left[1 - \frac{(1.0867)^5}{(1.105)^5} \right]}{(.105 - .0867)} + \frac{0.6667 \times (1.0867)^5 \times (1.05)}{(.094 - .05)(1.105)^5} \right\} = 0.99$$

Based on its fundamentals, you would expect Unilever to trade at 0.99 times revenues. The stock was trading at 1.15 times revenues in May 2001.

Value to Sales Ratios To analyze the relationship between value and sales, consider the value of a stable-growth firm:

$$\text{Firm value} = \frac{\text{EBIT}(1-t)(1-\text{Reinvestment rate})}{\text{Cost of capital} - g_n}$$

Dividing both sides by the revenue, you get:

$$\frac{\text{Firm value}}{\text{Sales}} = \frac{[\text{EBIT}(1-t)/\text{Sales}](1-\text{Reinvestment rate})}{\text{Cost of capital} - g_n}$$

$$\frac{\text{Firm value}_0}{\text{Sales}} = \frac{\text{After-tax operating margin}(1-\text{Reinvestment rate})}{\text{Cost of capital} - g_n}$$

Just as the price-to-sales ratio is determined by net profit margins, payout ratios, and costs of equity, the value-to-sales ratio is determined by after-tax operating margins, reinvestment rates, and the cost of capital. Firms with higher operating margins, lower reinvestment rates (for any given growth rate), and lower costs of capital will trade at higher value-to-sales multiples.

This equation can be expanded to cover a firm in high growth by using a two-stage firm valuation model:

$$P_0 = AT \text{ oper margin} \left\{ \frac{(1 - RIR) \times (1 + g) \times \left[1 - \frac{(1 + g)^n}{(1 + k_{c,hg})^n} \right]}{k_{c,hg} - g} + \frac{(1 - RIR_n) \times (1 + g)^n \times (1 + g_n)}{(k_{c,st} - g_n)(1 + k_{c,hg})^n} \right\}$$

where AT oper margin = After-tax operating margin = EBIT$(1 - t)$/Sales
RIR = Reinvestment rate (RIR_n is for stable growth period)
k_c = Cost of capital (hg: high growth and st: stable growth periods)
g = Growth rate in operating income in high-growth and stable-growth periods

Note that the determinants of the value-to-sales ratio remain the same as they were in the stable growth model—the growth rate, the reinvestment rate, the operating margin, and the cost of capital—but the number of estimates increases to reflect the existence of a high-growth period.

ILLUSTRATION 20.3:   Estimating the Value-to-Sales Ratio for Coca-Cola

Coca-Cola has one of the highest operating margins of any large U.S. firm and it should command a high value-to-sales ratio, as a consequence. To estimate the value-to-sales ratio at which Coca-Cola should trade at, we used the following inputs in May 2001.

	High-Growth Period	*Stable-Growth Period*
Length	10 years	Forever after year 10
Growth rate	8.92%	5%
After-tax operating margin	16.31%	16.31%
Cost of capital	9.71%	8.85%
Reinvestment rate	40%	31.25%

The return on capital during the high-growth period is expected to be 22.30% and to drop to 16% during stable growth. Based on these inputs, we can estimate the value-to-sales ratio for Coca-Cola:

$$VS = 0.1631 \times \left\{ \frac{0.60 \times (1.0892) \times \left[1 - \frac{(1.0892)^{10}}{(1.0971)^{10}} \right]}{(.0971 - .0892)} + \frac{0.6875 \times (1.0892)^{10} \times (1.05)}{(.0885 - .05)(1.0971)^{10}} \right\} = 3.79$$

Based on its fundamentals, you would expect Coca-Cola to trade at 3.79 times revenues. The firm was trading at 5.9 times revenues in May 2001.

firmmult.xls: This spreadsheet allows you to estimate the value-to-sales ratio for a stable-growth or high-growth firm, given its fundamentals.

Revenue Multiples and Profit Margins The key determinant of revenue multiples is the profit margin—the net margin for price-to-sales ratios and operating margin for value-to-sales ratios. Firms involved in businesses that have high margins can expect to sell for high multiples of sales. However, a decline in profit margins has a twofold effect. First, the reduction in profit margins reduces the revenue multiple directly. Second, the lower profit margin can lead to lower growth and hence lower revenue multiples.

The profit margin can be linked to expected growth fairly easily if an additional term is defined—the ratio of sales to book value (BV), which is also called a turnover ratio. This turnover ratio can be defined in terms of book equity (Equity turnover = Sales/Book value of equity) or book capital (Capital turnover = Sales/Book value of capital). Using a relationship developed between growth rates and fundamentals, the expected growth rates in equity earnings and operating can be written as a function of profit margins and turnover ratios:

$$\text{Expected growth}_{\text{equity}} = \text{Retention ratio} \times \text{Return on equity}$$
$$= \text{Retention ratio} \times (\text{Net profit/Sales}) \times (\text{Sales/BV of equity})$$
$$= \text{Retention ratio} \times \text{Net margin} \times \text{Sales/BV of equity}$$

For example, in the valuation of Unilever in Illustration 20.2, the expected growth rate of earnings is 8.67%. This growth rate can be derived from Unilever's net margin (5.82%), sales/equity ratio (3.0485), and retention ratio (48.83%):

$$\text{Expected growth rate} = \text{Retention ratio} \times \text{Net margin} \times \text{Sales/BV of equity}$$
$$= .4883 \times .0582 \times 3.0485 = 8.67\%$$

For growth in operating income,

$$\text{Expected growth}_{\text{firm}} = \text{Reinvestment rate} \times \text{Return on capital}$$
$$= \text{Reinvestment rate} \times [\text{EBIT}(1-t)/\text{Sales}]$$
$$\times (\text{Sales/BV of capital})$$
$$= \text{Reinvestment rate} \times \text{After-tax operating margin}$$
$$\times \text{Sales/BV of capital}$$

In the valuation of Coca-Cola in Illustration 20.3, the expected growth rate of operating income is 8.92%. This growth rate can be derived from Coca-Cola's after-tax operating margin (16.31%), sales/capital ratio (1.37), and reinvestment rate (40%):

$$\text{Expected growth}_{\text{firm}} = \text{Reinvestment rate} \times \text{After-tax operating margin}$$
$$\times \text{Sales/BV of capital}$$
$$= 0.4 \times .1631 \times 1.37 = 8.92\%$$

As the profit margin is reduced, the expected growth rate will decrease, if the sales do not increase proportionately.

ILLUSTRATION 20.4:   Estimating the Effect of Lower Margins on Price-Sales Ratios

Consider again the firm analyzed in Illustration 20.1. If the firm's profit margin declines and total revenue remains unchanged, the price-sales ratio for the firm will decline with it. For instance, if the firm's profit margin declines from 10% to 5% and the sales/BV remains unchanged:

$$\text{New growth rate in first five years} = \text{Retention ratio} \times \text{Profit margin} \times \text{Sales/BV}$$
$$= .8 \times .05 \times 2.50 = 10\%$$

The new price-sales ratio can then be calculated as follows:

$$PS = 0.05 \times \left\{ \frac{0.2 \times 1.10 \times \left[1 - \dfrac{1.10^5}{1.115^5} \right]}{(.115 - .10)} + \frac{0.50 \times 1.10^5 \times 1.08}{(.115 - .08)(1.115)^5} \right\} = 0.77$$

The relationship between profit margins and the price-sales ratio is illustrated more comprehensively in the Figure 20.2. The price-sales ratio is estimated as a function of the profit margin, keeping the sales/book value of equity ratio fixed. This linkage of price-sales ratios and profit margins can be utilized to analyze the value effects of changes in corporate strategy as well as the value of a brand name.

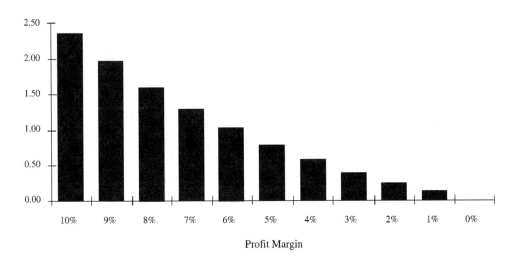

FIGURE 20.2   Price-to-Sales Ratios and Profit Margins

Marketing Strategy and Value   Every firm has a pricing strategy. At the risk of oversimplifying the choice, you can argue that firms have to decide whether they want to go with a low-price, high-volume strategy (volume leader) or with a high-price, lower-volume strategy (price leader). In terms of the variables that link growth to value, this choice will determine the profit margin and turnover ratio to use in valuation.

You could analyze the alternative pricing strategies that are available to a firm by examining the impact that each strategy will have on margins and turnover, and valuing the firm under each strategy. The strategy that yields the highest value for the firm is, in a sense, the optimal strategy.

Note that the effect of price changes on turnover ratios will depend in large part on how elastic or inelastic the demand for the firm's products are. Increases in the price of a product will have a minimal effect on turnover ratios if demand is inelastic. In this case, the value of the firm will generally be higher with a price leader strategy. On the other hand, the turnover ratio could drop more than proportionately if the product price is increased and demand is elastic. In this case, firm value will increase with a volume leader strategy.

ILLUSTRATION 20.5:   Choosing between a High-Margin and a Low-Margin Strategy

---

Assume that a firm has to choose between the two pricing strategies. In the first strategy, the firm will charge higher prices (resulting in higher net margins) and sell less (resulting in lower turnover ratios). In the second strategy, the firm will charge lower prices and sell more. Assume that the firm has done market testing and arrived at the following inputs:

	High Margin, Low Volume	Low Margin, High Volume
Net profit margin	10%	5%
Sales/Book value of equity	2.5	4.0

Assume, in addition, that the firm is expected to pay out 20% of its earnings as dividends over the next five years, and 50% of earnings as dividends after that. The growth rate after year 5 is expected to be 8%. The book value of equity per share is $10. The cost of equity for the firm is 11.5%.

HIGH MARGIN STRATEGY

$$\text{Expected growth rate in first five years}_{\text{high margin}} = \text{Profit margin} \times \text{Sales/BV} \times \text{Retention ratio}$$
$$= 0.10 \times 2.5 \times 0.8 = 20\%$$

$$\text{Price-sales ratio}_{\text{high margin}} = 0.10 \times \left\{ \frac{0.2 \times (1.20) \times \left[1 - \frac{(1.20)^5}{(1.115)^5} \right]}{(.115 - .20)} + \frac{0.50 \times (1.20)^5 \times (1.08)}{(.115 - .08)(1.115)^5} \right\} = 2.35$$

Sales/book value$_{\text{high margin}}$ = 2.50

$$\text{Price}_{\text{high margin}} = \text{Price/Sales} \times \text{Sales/BV} \times \text{BV} = 2.35 \times 2.5 \times 10 = \$58.83$$

LOW MARGIN STRATEGY

Expected growth rate in first five years$_{\text{low margin}}$ = Profit margin × Sales/BV × Retention ratio
$$= 0.05 \times 4 \times 0.8 = 16\%$$

$$\text{Price-sales ratio}_{\text{low margin}} = 0.05 \times \left\{ \frac{0.2 \times (1.16) \times \left[1 - \frac{(1.16)^5}{(1.115)^5} \right]}{(.115 - .16)} + \frac{0.05 \times (1.16)^5 \times (1.08)}{(.115 - .08)(1.115)^5} \right\} = 0.9966$$

Sales/book value$_{\text{low margin}}$ = 4.00

$$\text{Price}_{\text{low margin}} = \text{V/S} \times \text{S/BV} \times \text{BV} = 0.9966 \times 4 \times \$10 = \$39.86$$

The high margin strategy is clearly the better one to follow here, if the objective is value maximization.

ILLUSTRATION 20.6: Examining the Effects of Moving to a Lower-Margin, Higher-Volume Strategy: Philip Morris in 1993

Philip Morris had sales of $59,131 million, earned $4,939 million in net income and had a book value of equity of $12,563 million in 1992. The firm paid 42% of its earnings as dividends in 1992. The beta for the stock was 1.10.

Based on 1992 figures, the inputs for the price/sales ratio calculation would be:

Profit margin = 8.35%	Retention ratio = 58%
Sales/book value of equity = 4.71	Beta for the stock = 1.10
Book value per share = $14.10	Expected return = 7% + 1.1(5.5%) = 13.05%

Expected growth rate over next five years = Retention ratio × Profit margin × Sales/book value
$$= 0.58 \times 0.0835 \times 4.71 = 22.80\%$$

Expected growth rate after five years = 6%   Expected payout ratio after five years = 65%

Price-sales ratio$_{\text{1992 margins}}$ =

$$0.0835 \times \left\{ \frac{0.42 \times (1.2280) \times \left[1 - \frac{(1.2280)^5}{(1.1305)^5} \right]}{(.1305 - .2280)} + \frac{0.65 \times (1.2280)^5 \times (1.06)}{(.1305 - .06)(1.1305)^5} \right\} = 1.46$$

Sales/book value$_{\text{1992 margins}}$ = 4.71

In April 1993, Philip Morris announced that it was cutting prices on its Marlboro brand of cigarettes because of increasing competition from low-priced competitors. This was viewed by many analysts as a precursor of further price cuts and as a signal of a move to a lower-margin strategy. Assume that the profit margin will decline to 7% from 8.35%, as a consequence. If we assume that the sales/book value of equity ratio will remain unchanged at 4.71, we can estimate the expected growth:

Expected growth rate over next five years = Retention ratio × Profit margin × Sales/book value
$$= 0.58 \times 0.07 \times 4.71 = 19.12\%$$

Expected growth rate after five years = 6%   Expected payout ratio after five years = 65%

Price-sales ratio$_{1992 \text{ margins}}$ =

$$0.07 \times \left\{ \frac{0.42 \times (1.1912) \times \left[1 - \dfrac{(1.1912)^5}{(1.1305)^5} \right]}{(.1305 - .1912)} + \frac{0.65 \times (1.1912)^5 \times (1.06)}{(.1305 - .06)(1.1305)^5} \right\} = 1.06$$

As a consequence of the new lower-price strategy, the price-sales ratio will decline from 1.46 to 1.06. Unless the sales/book value ratio increases by an equivalent proportion (27.40%), the value of Philip Morris will decrease. In the case where profit margins decline by this magnitude and the sales/book value is not expected to increase, the value will decline by 27.40%.

The market reacted negatively to the announcement of price cuts, and the stock price dropped approximately 20% on the announcement.

PRICING STRATEGY, MARKET SHARE, AND COMPETITIVE DYNAMICS

All too often firms analyze the effects of changing prices in a static setting, where only the firm is acting and the competition stays still. The problem, though, is that every action (especially when it comes to pricing) generates re-actions from competition, and the net effects can be unpredictable.

Consider, for instance, a firm that cuts prices, hoping to increase market share and sales. If the competition does nothing, the firm may be able to accomplish its objectives. If, on the other hand, the competition reacts by also cutting prices, the firm may find itself with lower margins and the same turnover ratios that it had before the price cut—a recipe for lower firm value. In competitive industries, you have to assume that the latter will happen and plan accordingly.

There are some firms that have focused on maximizing market share as their primary objective function. The linkage between increased market share and market value is a tenuous one, and can be examined using the profit-margin/revenue multiple framework developed in the preceding section. If increasing market share leads to higher margins, either because of economies of scale driving down costs or because of increased market power driving out competitors, it will lead to higher value. If the increase in the market share is accompanied by lower prices and profit margins, the net effect on value can be negative.

Value of a Brand Name   One of the critiques of traditional valuation is that it fails to consider the value of brand names and other intangibles. Hiroyumi Itami, in his book *Mobilizing Invisible Assets*, provides a summary of this criticism. He says:

> *Analysts have tended to define assets too narrowly, identifying only those that can be measured, such as plant and equipment. Yet the intangible assets, such as a particular technology, accumulated consumer information, brand name, reputation, and corporate culture, are invaluable to the firm's competitive power. In fact, these invisible assets are the only real source of competitive edge that can be sustained over time.*

While this criticism is clearly overstated, the approaches used by analysts to value brand names are often ad hoc and may significantly overstate or understate their value. Firms with well known brand names often sell for higher multiples than lesser-known firms. The standard practice of adding on a "brand name premium," often set arbitrarily, to discounted cash flow value, can lead to erroneous estimates. Instead, the value of a brand name can be estimated using the approach that relates profit margins to price-sales ratios.

One of the benefits of having a well-known and respected brand name is that firms can charge higher prices for the same products, leading to higher profit margins and hence to higher price-sales ratios and firm value. The larger the price premium that a firm can charge, the greater is the value of the brand name. In general, the value of a brand name can be written as:

$$\text{Value of brand name} = (V/S_b - V/S_g) \times \text{Sales}$$

where V/S_b = Value-sales ratio of the firm with the benefit of the brand name
   V/S_g = Value-sales ratio of the same firm with the generic product

---

ILLUSTRATION 20.7:   Valuing a Brand Name Using Price-Sales Ratio

---

Consider two firms that produce similar products that compete in the same marketplace: Famous Inc. has a well-known brand name and has an after-tax operating profit margin of 10%, while NoFrills Inc. makes a generic version and has an after-tax operating margin of 5%. Both firms have the same sales-book capital ratio (2.50) and the cost of capital of 11.5%. In addition, both firms are expected to reinvest 80% of their operating income in the next five years and 50% of earnings after that. The growth rate after year 5, for both firms, is 6%. Both firms have total sales of $2.5 billion.

VALUING FAMOUS

$$\text{Expected growth rate}_{\text{Famous}} = \text{Reinvestment rate} \times \text{Operating margin} \times \text{Sales/BV of capital}$$
$$= 0.8 \times 0.10 \times 2.50 = 20\%$$

$$\text{Value/Sales ratio}_{\text{Famous}} = 0.10 \times \left\{ \frac{0.2 \times (1.20) \times \left[1 - \frac{(1.20)^5}{(1.115)^5} \right]}{(.115 - .20)} + \frac{0.50 \times (1.20)^5 \times (1.08)}{(.115 - .08)(1.115)^5} \right\} = 2.35$$

VALUING NOFRILLS

Expected growth rate$_{NoFrills}$ = Reinvestment rate × Operating margin × Sales/BV of capital
= 0.8 × 0.05 × 2.50 = 10%

$$\text{Value/Sales ratio}_{NoFrills} = 0.05 \times \left\{ \frac{0.2 \times (1.10) \times \left[1 - \frac{(1.10)^5}{(1.115)^5} \right]}{(.115 - .10)} + \frac{0.50 \times (1.10)^5 \times (1.08)}{(.115 - .08)(1.115)^5} \right\} = 0.77$$

Total sales = $2.5 billion

Value of brand name = [Value/Sales$_{Famous}$ − Value/Sales$_{NoFrills}$] × Sales
= [2.35 − 0.77] × $2.5 billion = $3.95 billion

ILLUSTRATION 20.8: Valuing a Brand Name: The Coca-Cola Example

In 2000, Coca-Cola reported sales of $20,458 million and after-tax operating income of $3,337 million (thus yielding an after-tax operating margin of 16.31%). In illustration 12.3, we estimated a value to sales ratio of 3.79 for the company based on these inputs. The equation for the value-to-sales ratio is reproduced again:

$$VS = 0.1631 \times \left\{ \frac{0.60 \times (1.0892) \times \left[1 - \frac{(1.0892)^{10}}{(1.0971)^{10}} \right]}{(.0971 - .0892)} + \frac{0.6875 \times (1.0892)^{10} \times (1.05)}{(.0885 - .05)(1.0971)^{10}} \right\} = 3.79$$

One reason for Coca-Cola's high profit margin is its brand name. In contrast, Cott, a Canadian beverage manufacturer that produces and sells generic products, has an after-tax operating margin of 4.82% and a sales-to-capital ratio of 2.06. If Coca-Cola had earned this lower profit margin and matched this sales to capital ratio, the return on capital and expected growth rate during the high-growth period would have been:

Return on capital = After-tax operating margin × Sales/BV of capital
= .0482 × 2.06= 9.92%

Expected growth rate over next 10 years = Reinvestment rate × Return on capital
= .40 × .0992= 3.97%

Assuming that this margin will be maintained in perpetuity, the reinvestment rate needed in stable growth will also increase to sustain a 5% growth rate:

Reinvestment rate in stable growth = g/ROC = .05/.0992 = 50.42%

With the lower growth rate during the high-growth period and a higher reinvestment rate, we obtain a much lower value to sales ratio for Coca-Cola:

$$VS = 0.0482 \times \left\{ \frac{0.60 \times (1.0397) \times \left[1 - \dfrac{(1.0397)^{10}}{(1.0971)^{10}} \right]}{(.0971 - .0397)} + \frac{0.4958 \times (1.0397)^{10} \times (1.05)}{(.0885 - .05)(1.0971)^{10}} \right\} = 0.60$$

The value of the brand name for Coca-Cola can be estimated now as the difference between these two valuations—one with Coca-Cola's current margins and turnover ratios and one with generic margins and turnover ratios:

$$\text{Value of Coca-Cola} = \text{Value/Sales}_{2000 \text{ margins}} \times \text{Sales}_{\text{Coca-Cola}}$$
$$= 3.79 \times \$20,458 = \$77,535 \text{ million}$$

$$\text{Value of Coca-Cola as a generic firm} = \text{Value/Sales}_{\text{generic}} \times \text{Sales}_{\text{Coca-Cola}}$$
$$= 0.60 \times \$20,458 = \$12,274 \text{ million}$$

$$\text{Value of brand name} = (\text{Value/Sales}_{2000 \text{ margins}} - \text{Value/Sales}_{\text{generic}}) \times \text{Sales}_{\text{Coca-Cola}}$$
$$= (3.79 - 0.60) \times \$20,458 \text{ million} = \$65,261 \text{ million}$$

Of Coca-Cola's estimated value of $77,535 million, 84.17% stems from its brand name, which provides it with the market power to earn higher margins and to grow faster.

Using Revenue Multiples in Investment Analysis

The key determinants of the revenue multiples of a firm are its expected margins (net and operating), risk, cash flow, and growth characteristics. To use revenue multiples in analysis and to make comparisons across firms, you would need to control for differences on these characteristics. This section examines different ways of comparing revenue multiples across firms.

AN ASIDE ON BRAND NAME VALUE

It is common to see brand name premiums attached to discounted cash flow valuations. As you can see from the preceding example, this is a mistake. Done right, the value of a brand name is already built into the valuation in a number of places—higher operating margins, higher turnover ratios, and consequently higher returns on capital. These, in turn, have ripple effects, increasing expected growth rates and value. Adding a brand name premium to this value would be double counting.

What about firms that do not exploit a valuable brand name? You might add a premium to the values of these firms, but the premium is not for the brand name but rather for control. In fact, you could estimate similar premiums for any underutilized or mismanaged assets, but you would pay the premiums only if you could acquire control of the firm.

Looking for Mismatches While growth, risk, and cash flow characteristics affect revenue multiples, the key determinants of revenue multiples are profit margins—net profit margin for equity multiples and operating margins for firm value multiples. Thus it is not surprising to find firms with low profit margins and low revenue multiples, and firms with high profit margins and high revenue multiples. However, firms with high revenue ratios and low profit margins as well as firms with low revenue multiples and high profit margins should attract investors' attention as potentially overvalued and undervalued securities respectively. In Figure 20.3, this is presented in a matrix. You can identify under- or overvalued firms in a sector or industry by plotting them on this matrix, and looking for potential mismatches between margins and revenue multiples.

While intuitively appealing, there are at least three practical problems associated with this approach. The first is that data is more easily available on historical (current) profit margins than on expected profit margins. If a firm's current margins are highly correlated with future margins (a firm that has earned high margins historically will continue to do so, and one that have earned low margins historically will also continue to do so), using current margins and current revenue multiples to identify under- or overvalued securities is reasonable. If the current margins of firms are not highly correlated with expected future margins, it is no longer appro-

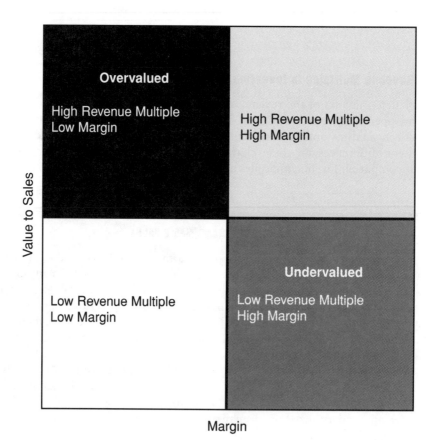

FIGURE 20.3 Value/Sales and Margins

priate to argue that firms are overvalued just because they have low current margins and trade at high price-to-sales ratios. The second problem with this approach is that it assumes that revenue multiples are linearly related to margins. In other words, as margins double, you would expect revenue multiples to double as well. The third problem is that it ignores differences on other fundamentals, especially risk. Thus a firm that looks undervalued because it has a high current margin and is trading at a low multiple of revenues may in fact be a fairly valued firm with very high risk.

ILLUSTRATION 20.9: Revenue Multiples and Margins: Specialty Retailers

In the first comparison, we look at specialty retailers in the United States. In Figure 20.4 the value-to-sales ratios of these firms are plotted against the operating margins of these firms in July 2000 (with the stock symbols for each firm next to each observation).

Firms with higher operating margins tend to have higher value-to-sales ratios, while firms with lower margin have lower value-to-sales ratios. Note, though, that there is a considerable amount of noise even in this subset of firms in the relationship between value-to-sales ratios and operating margins.

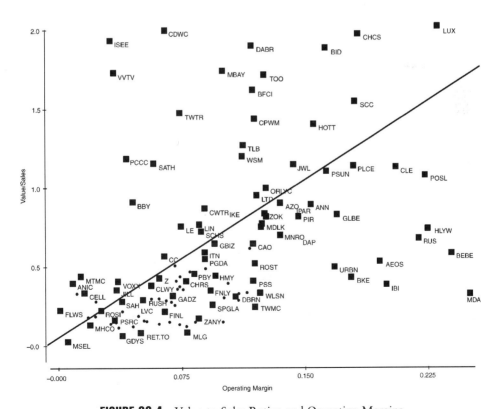

FIGURE 20.4 Value-to-Sales Ratios and Operating Margins

ILLUSTRATION 20.10:   Revenue Multiples and Margins: Internet Retailers

In the second comparison, the price-to-sales ratios in July 2000 of Internet retailers are plotted against the net margins earned by these firms in the most recent year in Figure 20.5.

Here there seems to be almost no relationship between price-to-sales ratios and net margins. This should not be surprising. Most Internet firms have negative net income and net margins. The market values of these firms are based not on what they earn now but what they are expected to earn in the future, and there is little correlation between current and expected future margins.

Statistical Approaches   When analyzing price-earnings and price-to-book value ratios, we used regressions to control for differences in risk, growth, and payout ratios across firms. We could also use regressions to control for differences across firms to analyze revenue multiples. In this section, we begin by applying this approach to comparables defined narrowly as firms in the same business, and then expanded to cover the entire sector and the market.

Comparable Firms in the Same Business   In the last section, we examined firms in the same business looking for mismatches—firms with high margins and low revenue multiples were viewed as undervalued. In a simple extension of this approach, we could regress revenue multiples against profit margins across firms in a sector:

$$\text{Price-to-sales ratio} = a + b(\text{Net profit margin})$$

$$\text{Value-to-sales ratio} = a + b(\text{After-tax operating margin})$$

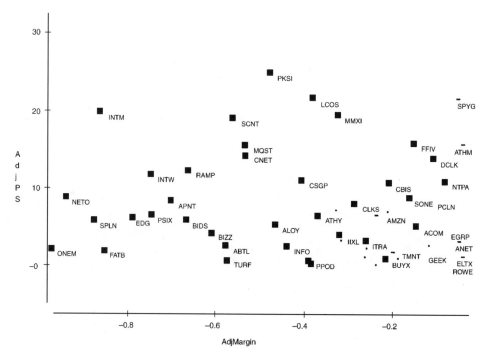

FIGURE 20.5   Price-to-Sales Ratios versus Net Margins: Internet Stocks

These regressions can be used to estimate predicted values for firms in the sample, helping to identify undervalued and overvalued firms.

If the number of firms in the sample is large enough to allow for it, this regression can be extended to add other independent variables. For instance, the standard deviation in stock prices or the beta can be used as an independent variable to capture differences in risk, and analyst estimates of expected growth can control for differences in growth. The regression can also be modified to account for nonlinear relationships between revenue multiples and any or all of these variables.

Can this approach be used for sectors such as the Internet where there seems to be little or no relationship between revenue multiples and fundamentals? It can, but only if you adapt it to consider the determinants of value in these sectors.

ILLUSTRATION 20.11: Regression Approach—Specialty Retailers

Consider again the scatter plot of value to sales ratios and operating margins for retailers in Illustration 20.9. There is clearly a positive relationship and a regression of value to sales ratios against operating margins for specialty retailers yields the following:

$$\text{Value-to-sales ratio} = 0.0563 + 6.6287 \text{ After-tax operating margin} \quad R^2 = 39.9\%$$
$$[0.72] \quad [10.39]$$

This regression has 162 observations and the t statisics are reported in brackets. To estimate the predicted value to sales ratio for Talbots, one of the specialty retailers in the group, which has an 11.22% after-tax operating margin:

$$\text{Predicted value-to-sales ratio} = 0.0563 + 6.6287(.1122) = 0.80$$

With an actual value to sales ratio of 1.27, Talbots can be consider overvalued.

This regression can be modified in two ways. One is to regress the value-to-sales ratio against the ln(operating margins) to allow for the nonlinear relationship between the two variables:

$$\text{Value-to-sales ratio} = 1.8313 + 0.4339 \ln(\text{After-tax operating margin}) \quad R^2 = 22.40\%$$
$$[10.76] \quad [6.89]$$

The other is to expand the regression to include proxies for risk and growth:

$$\text{Value to sales} = -0.6209 + 7.21(\text{Operating Mgn}) - 0.0209\, \sigma_{OpInc} + 3.1460 \text{ Growth}$$
$$[3.47] \quad [10.34] \quad [0.22] \quad [4.91]$$

where Operating Mgn = After-tax operating margin
σ_{OpInc} = Standard deviation in operating income over previous five years
Growth = Expected growth rate in earnings over next five years

This regression has fewer observations (124) than the previous two but a higher R-squared of 50.09%. The predicted value-to-sales ratio for Talbots using this regression is:

$$\text{Predicted value to sales} = -0.6209 + 7.21(.1122) - 0.0209(.7391) + 3.1460(.225) = 0.88$$

Talbots remains overvalued even after adjusting for differences in growth and risk.

ILLUSTRATION 20.12:   Regression Approach—Internet Retailers

In the case of the Internet stocks graphed in Illustration 20.10, the regression of price-to-sales ratios against net margins yields the following:

$$\text{Price-to-sales ratio} = 44.4495 - 0.7331 \text{ (Net margin)} \qquad R^2 = 0.22\%$$
$$[4.39] \qquad [1.20]$$

Not only is the R-squared close to zero, but the relationship between current net margins and price-to-sales ratios is negative. Thus there is little relationship between the pricing of these stocks and their current profitability.

What variables might do a better job of explaining the differences in price-to-sales ratios across Internet stocks? Consider the following propositions.

■ Since this sample contains some firms with very little in revenues and other firms with much higher revenues, you would expect the firms with less in revenues to trade at a much higher multiple of revenues than firms with higher revenues. Thus, Amazon with revenues of almost $2 billion can be expected to trade at a lower multiple of this value than iVillage with revenues of less than $60 million.

■ There is a high probability that some or many of these Internet firms will not survive because they will run out of cash. A widely used measure of this potential for cash problems is the cash burn ratio, which is the ratio of the cash balance to the absolute value of EBITDA (which is usually a negative number). Firms with a low cash burn ratio are at higher risk of running into a cash crunch and should trade at lower multiples of revenues.

■ Revenue growth is a key determinant of value at these firms. Firms that are growing revenues more quickly are likely to reach profitability sooner, other things remaining equal.

The following regression relates price-to-sales ratios to the level of revenues [ln(Revenues)], the cash burn ratio (absolute value of Cash/EBITDA) and revenue growth over the past year for Internet firms:

$$\text{Price-to-sales ratio} = 37.18 - 4.34 \ln(\text{Revenues}) + 0.75(\text{Cash/EBITDA}) + 8.37 \text{ Growth}_{rev}$$
$$[1.85] \quad [0.95] \qquad\qquad\qquad [4.18] \qquad\qquad\qquad [1.06]$$

The regression has 117 observations and an R-squared of 13.83%. The coefficients all have the right signs, but are of marginal statistical significance. You could obtain a predicted price-to-sales ratio for Amazon.com in July 2000 in this regression of:

$$PS_{Amazon.com} = 37.18 - 4.34 \ln(1,920) + 0.75(2.12) + 8.37(1.4810) = 18.364$$

At its actual price-to-sales ratio of 6.69, Amazon looks significantly undervalued relative to other Internet firms.

In any case, the regressions are much too noisy to attach much weight to the predictions. In fact, the low explanatory power with fundamentals and the huge differences in measures of relative value should sound a note of caution on the use of multiples in sectors such as this one, where firms are in transition and changing dramatically from period to period.

Market Regressions   If you can control for differences across firms using a regression, you can extend this approach to look at much broader cross sections of firms. Here, the cross-sectional data is used to estimate the price-to-sales ratio as a function of fundamental variables—profit margin, dividend payout, beta, and growth rate in earnings.

Consider first the technology sector. Regressing the price-to-sales ratio against net margins, growth rate in earnings, payout ratios, and betas in July 2000 yields the following result:

PS = –8.48 + 30.37(Net margin) + 20.98(Growth rate) + 4.68 Beta + 3.79 Payout
[7.19] [10.2]　　　　　　　　[10.0]　　　　　　　　[4.64]　　　[0.85]

There are 273 observations in this regression, and the R-squared is 53.8%.

This approach can be extended to cover the entire market. In the first edition of this book, regressions of price-sales ratios on fundamentals—dividend payout ratio, growth rate in earnings, profit margin, and beta—were run for each year from 1987 to 1991.

Year	Regression	R-squared
1987	PS = 0.7894 + .0008 Payout – 0.2734 Beta + 0.5022 EGR + 6.46 Margin	0.4434
1988	PS = 0.1660 + .0006 Payout – 0.0692 Beta + 0.5504 EGR + 10.31 Margin	0.7856
1989	PS = 0.4911 + .0393 Payout – 0.0282 Beta + 0.2836 EGR + 10.25 Margin	0.4601
1990	PS = 0.0826 + .0105 Payout – 0.1073 Beta + 0.5449 EGR + 10.36 Margin	0.8885
1991	PS = 0.5189 + 0.2749 Payout – 0.2485 Beta + 0.4948 EGR + 8.17 Margin	0.4853

where　　PS = Price-sales ratio at the end of the year
　　　Payout = Payout ratio = Dividends/Earnings at the end of the year
　　　　Beta = Beta of the stock
　　　Margin = Profit margin for the year = Net income/Sales for the year (in %)
　　　　EGR = Earnings growth rate over the previous five years

This regression is updated for the entire market in July 2000 and presented below:

PS = –2.36 + 17.43(Net margin) + 8.72(Growth rate) + 1.45 Beta + 0.37 Payout
[16.5] [35.5]　　　　　　　　[23.9]　　　　　　　[10.1]　　　[3.01]

There are 2,235 observations in this regression and the R-squared is 52.5%.

The regression can also be run in terms of the value-to-sales ratio, with the operating margin, standard deviation in operating income, and reinvestment rate used as independent variables:

VS = –1.67 + 8.82(Operating margin) + 7.66(Growth rate) + 1.50 σ_{oi} + 0.08 RIR
[14.4] [30.7]　　　　　　　　　[19.2]　　　　　　　[8.35]　　[1.44]

where σ_{oi} = Standard deviation in operating income

This regression also has 2,235 observations but the R-squared is slightly lower at 42%.

ILLUSTRATION 20.12:   Valuing Cisco and Motorola Using Sector and Market Regressions— July 2000

These sector and market regressions can be used to estimate predicted price to sales ratios for Cisco and Motorola. In the following table the values of the independent variables are reported for both firms:

	Cisco	Motorola
Net margin	17.25%	2.64%
Expected growth rate (analyst projection over five years)	36.39%	21.26%
Beta	1.43	1.21
Payout ratio	0	35.62%

Using these values, you can estimate predicted price to sales ratios for the two firms from the sector regression (using only technology companies):

$$PS_{Cisco} = -8.48 + 30.37(.1725) + 20.98(.3639) + 4.68(1.43) + 3.79(0) = 11.09$$
$$PS_{Motorola} = -8.48 + 30.37(.0264) + 20.98(.2126) + 4.68(1.21) + 3.79(0.3562) = 3.79$$

You can also estimate predicted price-to-sales ratios from the market regression:

$$PS_{Cisco} = -2.36 + 17.43(.1725) + 8.72(.3639) + 1.45(1.43) + 0.37(0) = 5.89$$
$$PS_{Motorola} = -2.36 + 17.43(.0264) + 8.72(.2126) + 1.45(1.21) + 0.37(0.3562) = 1.84$$

Cisco at its existing price-to-sales ratio of 27.77 looks significantly overvalued relative to both the market and the technology sector. In contrast, Motorola with a price-to-sales ratio of 2.27 is slightly overvalued relative to the rest of the market, but is significantly undervalued relative to other technology stocks.

Multiples of Future Revenues

Chapter 18 examined the use of market value of equity as a multiple of earnings in a future year. Revenue multiples can also be measured in terms of future revenues. Thus, you could estimate the value as a multiple of revenues five years from now. There are some advantages to doing this:

■ For firms that have little in revenues currently but are expected to grow rapidly over time, the revenues in the future—say five years from now—are likely to better reflect the firm's true potential than revenues today.

■ It is easier to estimate multiples of revenues when growth rates have leveled off and the firm's risk profile is stable. This is more likely to be the case five years from now than it is today.

Assuming that revenues five years from now are to be used to estimate value, what multiple should be used on these revenues? You have three choices. One is to use the average multiples of value (today) to revenues today of comparable firms to estimate a value five years from now, and then discount that value back to the present. Consider, for example, a company like Commerce One whose current revenues are only $402 million but which we expect to grow to $4.86 billion in five years. If the average value-to-sales ratio of more mature comparable firms is 1.8, the estimated value of Commerce One can be estimated as follows:

Revenues at Commerce One in five years = $4,860 million

Value of Commerce One in five years = $4,860 × 1.8 = $8,748 million

This could be discounted back at Commerce One's cost of capital of 13.48% to the present to yield a value for the firm today.

$$\text{Value of firm today} = \$8{,}748/1.348^5 = \$4{,}648 \text{ million}$$

The second approach is to forecast the expected revenue in five years for each of the comparable firms, and to divide each firm's current value by these revenues. This multiple of current value to future revenues can be used to estimate the value today. To illustrate, if current value is 1.1 times revenues in five years for comparable firms, the value of Commerce One can be estimated as follows:

Revenues at Commerce One in five years = $4,860 million

Value today = Revenues in five years × (Value today/Revenues$_{\text{in year 5}}$)$_{\text{comparable firms}}$
= 4,860(1.1) = $5,346 million

In the third approach, you can adjust the multiple of future revenues for differences in operating margin, growth and risk for differences between the firm and comparable firms. For instance, Commerce One, five years from now will have an expected operating margin of 14.83% and an expected growth rate of 19.57% over the following five years (years 6 through 10). A regression of value-to-sales ratio against operating margins and expected growth rates run across comparable firms today yields the following:

Value to sales = 1.0834 + 3.0387 Operating margin + 8.1555 Growth $R^2 = 73\%$

Plugging in Commerce One's predicted values for expected growth and operating margins into this regression, we get:

Value to sales$_{\text{Commerce One in 5 years}}$ = 1.0834 + 3.0387(.1483) + 8.1555(.1957) = 3.13

The value of Commerce One in five years can now be estimated using this multiple:

Revenues at Commerce One in five years = $4,860 million

Value of Commerce One in five years = $4,860 × 3.13 = $15,212 million

Value of Commerce One today = $15,212/1.1348^5 = $8,083 million

SECTOR-SPECIFIC MULTIPLES

The value of a firm can be standardized using a number of sector-specific multiples. The value of steel companies can be compared based on market value per ton of steel produced, and the value of electricity generators can be computed on the basis of kilowatt hour (kwh) of power produced. In the past few years, analysts follow-ing new technology firms have become particularly inventive with multiples that range from value per subscriber for Internet service providers to value per web site visitor for Internet portals to value per customer for Internet retailers.

Why Analysts Use Sector-Specific Multiples

The increase in the use of sector-specific multiples in the last few years has opened up a debate about whether they are a good way to compare relative value. There are several reasons why analysts use sector-specific multiples:

- They link firm value to operating details and output. For analysts who begin with these forecasts—predicted number of subscribers for an Internet service provider, for instance—they provide a much more intuitive way of estimating value.
- Sector-specific multiples can often be computed with no reference to account-ing statements or measures. Consequently, they can be estimated for firms where accounting statements are nonexistent, unreliable, or just not compara-ble. Thus, you could compute the value per kwh sold for Latin American power companies and not have to worry about accounting differences across these countries.
- Though this is usually not admitted to, sector-specific multiples are sometimes employed in desperation because none of the other multiples can be estimated or used. For instance, an impetus for the use of sector-specific multiples for new economy firms was that they often had negative earnings and little in terms of book value or revenues.

Limitations

Though it is understandable that analysts sometimes turn to sector-specific multi-ples, there are two significant problems associated with their use:

1. They feed into the tunnel vision that plagues analysts who are sector focused, and thus they allow entire sectors to become overpriced. A cable company trading at $50 a subscriber might look cheap next to another one trading at $125 a subscriber, but it is entirely possible that they are both overpriced or un-derpriced.
2. As will be shown later in this section, the relationship of sector-specific multi-ples to fundamentals is complicated, and consequently it is very difficult to con-trol for differences across firms when comparing them on these multiples.

Definitions of Sector-Specific Multiples

The essence of sector-specific multiples is that the way they are measured vary from sector to sector. In general, though, they share some general characteristics:

- The numerator is usually enterprise value—the market values of both debt and equity netted out against cash and marketable securities.

■ The denominator is defined in terms of the operating units that generate revenues and profits for the firm.

For commodity companies such as oil refineries and gold-mining companies, where revenue is generated by selling units of the commodity, the market value can be standardized by dividing by the value of the reserves that these companies have of the commodity:

$$\text{Value per commodity unit} = \frac{(\text{Market value of equity} + \text{Market value of debt} - \text{Cash})}{\text{Number of units of the commodity in reserves}}$$

Oil companies can be compared on enterprise value per barrel of oil in reserves and gold-mining companies on the basis of enterprise value per ounce of gold in reserves.

For manufacturing firms that produce a homogeneous product (in terms of quality and units), the market value can be standardized by dividing by the number of units of the product that the firm produces or has the capacity to produce:

$$\text{Value per unit product} = \frac{(\text{Market value of equity} + \text{Market value of debt} - \text{Cash})}{\text{Number of units produced (or capacity)}}$$

For instance, steel companies can be compared based on their enterprise value per ton of steel produced or in capacity.

For subscription-based firms such as cable companies, Internet service providers, and information providers (such as TheStreet.com), revenues come from the number of subscribers to the base service provided. Here, the value of a firm can be stated in terms of the number of subscribers:

$$\text{Value per subscriber} = \frac{(\text{Market value of equity} + \text{Market value of debt} - \text{Cash})}{\text{Number of subscribers}}$$

In each of the above cases, you could make an argument for the use of a sector-specific multiple because the units (whether they be barrels of oil, kwh of electricity, or subscribers) generate similar revenues. Sector multiples become much more problematic when the units used to scale value are not homogeneous. Let us consider two examples.

For retailers such as Amazon that generate revenue from customers who shop at their websites, the value of the firm can be stated in terms of the number of regular customers:

$$\text{Value per customer} = \frac{(\text{Market value of equity} + \text{Market value of debt} - \text{Cash})}{\text{Number of customers}}$$

The problem, here, is that amount spent can vary widely across customers, so it is not clear that a firm that looks cheap on this basis is undervalued.

For Internet portals that generate revenue from advertising revenues that are based on traffic to the sites, the revenues can be stated in terms of the number of visitors to the sites:

$$\text{Value per site visitor} = \frac{(\text{Market value of equity} + \text{Market value of debt} - \text{Cash})}{\text{Number of visitors per site}}$$

Here, again, the link between visitors and advertising revenues is neither clearly established nor obvious.

Determinants of Value

What are the determinants of value for these sector-specific multiples? Not surprisingly, they are the same as the determinants of value for other multiples—cash flows, growth, and risk—though the relationship can be complex. The fundamentals that drive these multiples can be derived by going back to a discounted cash flow model stated in terms of these sector-specific variables.

Consider an Internet service provider that has NX existing subscribers, and assume that each subscriber is expected to remain with the provider for the next n years. In addition, assume that the firm will generate net cash flows per customer (revenues from each customer minus cost of serving the customer) of CFX per year for these n years.[1] The value of each existing customer to the firm can then be written as:

$$\text{Value per customer} = VX = \sum_{t=1}^{t=n} \frac{CFX}{(1+r)^t}$$

The discount rate used to compute the value per customer can range from close to the riskless rate, if the customer has signed a contract to remain a subscriber for the next n years, to the cost of capital, if the estimate is just an expectation based on past experience.

Assume that the firm expects to continue to add new subscribers in future years and that the firm will face a cost (advertising and promotion) of C_t for each new subscriber added in period t. If the new subscribers (ΔNX_t) added in period t will generate the a value VX_t per subscriber, the value of this firm can be written as:

$$\text{Value of firm} = NX \times VX + \sum_{t=1}^{t=\infty} \frac{\Delta NX_t \left(VX_t - C_t \right)}{(1+k_c)^t}$$

---

[1]For purposes of simplicity, it has been assumed that the cash flow is the same in each year. This can be generalized to allow cash flows to grow over time.

Note that the first term in this valuation equation represents the value generated by existing subscribers, and that the second is the value of expected growth. The subscribers added generate value only if the cost of adding a new subscriber (C_t) is less than the present value of the net cash flows generated by that subscriber for the firm.

Dividing both sides of this equation by the number of existing subscribers (NX) yields the following:

$$\text{Value per existing subscriber} = \frac{\text{Value of firm}}{\text{NX}} = VX + \frac{\displaystyle\sum_{t=1}^{t=\infty} \frac{\Delta NX_t (VX_t - C_t)}{(1+k_c)^t}}{\text{NX}}$$

In the most general case, then, the value of a firm per subscriber will be a function not only of the expected value that will be generated by existing subscribers, but of the potential for value creation from future growth in the subscriber base. If you assume a competitive market, where the cost of adding new subscribers (C_t) converges on the value that is generated by that customer, the second term in the equation drops out and the value per subscriber becomes just the present value of cash flows that will be generated by each existing subscriber.

$$\text{Value per existing subscriber}_{C=VX} = VX$$

A similar analysis can be done to relate the value of an Internet retailer to the number of customers it has, though it is generally much more difficult to estimate the value that will be created by a customer. Unlike subscribers who pay a fixed fee, retail customers' buying habits are more difficult to predict.

In either case, you can see the problems associated with comparing these multiples across firms. Implicitly, either you have to assume competitive markets and conclude that the firms with the lowest market value per subscriber are the most undervalued, or, alternatively, you have to assume that the value of growth is the same proportion of the value generated by existing customers for all of the firms in your analysis, leading to the same conclusion.

Value can also be related to the number of site visitors, but only if the link between revenues and the number of site visitors is made explicit. For instance, if an Internet portal's advertising revenues are directly tied to the number of visitors at its site, the value of the Internet portal can be stated in terms of the number of visitors to the site. Since sites have to spend money (on advertising) to attract visitors, it is the net value generated by each visitor that ultimately determines value.

ILLUSTRATION 20.13: Estimating the Value per Subscriber: Internet Portal

Assume that you are valuing Golive Online (GOL), an Internet service provider with 1 million existing subscribers. Each subscriber is expected to remain for three years, and GOL is expected to generate $100 in net after-tax cash flow (subscription revenues minus costs of providing subscription service) per subscriber each year. GOL has a cost of capital of 15%. The value added to the firm by each existing subscriber can be estimated as follows:

$$\text{Value per subscriber} = \sum_{t=1}^{t=3} \frac{100}{(1.15)^t} = \$228.32$$

Value of existing subscriber base = $228.32 million

Furthermore, assume that GOL expects to add 100,000 subscribers each year for the next 10 years, and that the value added by each subscriber will grow from the current level ($228.32) at the inflation rate of 3% every year. The cost of adding a new subscriber is $100 currently, assumed to be growing at the inflation rate.

Year	Value Added per Subscriber	Cost of Acquiring Subscriber	Number of Subscribers Added	Present Value at 15%
1	$235.17	$103.00	100,000	$11,493,234
2	$242.23	$106.09	100,000	$10,293,940
3	$249.49	$109.27	100,000	$ 9,219,789
4	$256.98	$112.55	100,000	$ 8,257,724
5	$264.69	$115.93	100,000	$ 7,396,049
6	$272.63	$119.41	100,000	$ 6,624,287
7	$280.81	$122.99	100,000	$ 5,933,057
8	$289.23	$126.68	100,000	$ 5,313,956
9	$297.91	$130.48	100,000	$ 4,759,456
10	$306.85	$134.39	100,000	$ 4,262,817
				$73,554,309

The cumulative value added by new subscribers is $73.55 million. The total value of the firm is the sum of the value generated by existing customers and the value added by new customers:

Value of firm = Value of existing subscriber base + Value added by new customers
= $228.32 million + $73.55 million = $301.87 million

Value per existing subscriber = Value of firm/Number of subscribers
= $301.87 million/1 million = $301.87 per subscriber

Note, though, that a portion of this value per subscriber is attributable to future growth. As the cost of acquiring a subscriber converges on the value added by each subscriber, the value per subscriber will converge on $228.32.

Analysis Using Sector-Specific Multiples

To analyze firms using sector-specific multiples, you have to control for the differences across firms on any or all of the fundamentals that you identified as affecting these multiples in the last part.

With value per subscriber, for instance, you have to control for differences in the value generated by each subscriber. In particular:

■ Firms that are more efficient in delivering a service for a given subscription price (resulting in lower costs) should trade at a higher value per subscriber than comparable firms. This would also apply if a firm has significant economies of scale. In Illustration 20.13, the value per subscriber would be higher if each existing subscriber generated $120 in net cash flows for the firm each year instead of $100.

■ Firms that can add new subscribers at a lower cost (through advertising and promotion) should trade at a higher value per subscriber than comparable firms.

■ Firms with higher expected growth in the subscriber base (in percentage terms) should trade at a higher value per subscriber than comparable firms.

You could make similar statements about value per customer.

With value per site visitor, you have to control for the additional advertising revenue that is generated by each visitor (the greater the advertising revenue, the higher the value per site visitor) and the cost of attracting each visitor (the higher the costs, the lower the value per site visitor).

ILLUSTRATION 20.14:   Comparing Value per Site Visitor

In the following table the market value per site visitor is presented for Internet firms that generate the bulk of their revenues from advertising. The number of visitors per site was from July 1 to July 31, 2000, and the market value is as of July 31, 2000:

Company Name	Firm Value	Visitors	Value per Visitor
Lycos, Inc.	$ 5,396.00	5,858	$0.92
MapQuest.com Inc.	$ 604.80	6,621	$0.09
iVillage Inc.	$ 250.40	7,346	$0.03
CNET Networks	$ 1,984.30	10,850	$0.18
Ask Jeeves Inc.	$ 643.50	11,765	$0.05
Go2Net Inc.	$ 1,468.60	12,527	$0.12
LookSmart, Ltd.	$ 1,795.30	13,374	$0.13
About.com Inc.	$ 541.90	18,282	$0.03
Excite@Home	$ 7,008.20	27,115	$0.26
Yahoo! Inc.	$65,633.40	49,045	$1.34

Source: Media Metrix.

Note the differences in value per site visitor across Yahoo!, Excite, and Lycos. Excite looks much cheaper than either of the other two firms, but the differences could also be attributable to differences across the firms on fundamentals. It could be that Yahoo! earns more in advertising revenues than Excite and Lycos, and that its prospects of earning higher profits in the future are brighter.

CONCLUSION

The price-to-sales multiple and value-to-sales ratio are widely used to value technology firms and to compare value across these firms. An analysis of the fundamentals highlights the importance of profit margins in determining these multiples, in addition to the standard variables—the dividend payout ratio, the cost of equity, and the expected growth rates in net income for price to sales, and the reinvestment rate, cost of capital, and growth in property income for value to sales. Comparisons of revenue multiples across firms have to take into account differences in profit margins. One approach is to look for mismatches—low margins and high revenue multiples suggesting overvalued firms and high margins and low revenue multiples suggesting undervalued firms. Another approach that controls for differences in fundamentals is the cross-sectional regression approach, where revenue multiples are regressed against fundamentals across firms in a business, an entire sector, or the market.

Sector-specific multiples relate value to sector-specific variables, but they have to be used with caution. It is often difficult to compare these multiples across firms without making stringent assumptions about their operations and growth potential.

QUESTIONS AND SHORT PROBLEMS

1. Longs Drug Stores, a large U.S. drugstore chain operating primarily in Northern California, had sales per share of $122 in 1993, on which it reported earnings per share of $2.45 and paid a dividend per share of $1.12. The company is expected to grow 6% in the long term, and has a beta of 0.90. The current T-bond rate is 7%, and the market risk premium is 5.5%.
   a. Estimate the appropriate price-sales multiple for Longs Drug.
   b. The stock is currently trading for $34 per share. Assuming the growth rate is estimated correctly, what would the profit margin need to be to justify this price per share?
2. You are examining the wide differences in price-sales ratios that you can observe among firms in the retail store industry, and trying to come up with a rationale to explain these differences:

Company	Price	Per-Share Sales	Earnings	Expected Growth	Beta	Payout
Bombay Co.	$38	$ 9.70	$0.68	29.00%	1.45	0%
Bradlees	$15	$168.60	$1.75	12.00%	1.15	34%
Caldor	$32	$147.45	$2.70	12.50%	1.55	0%
Consolidated	$21	$ 23.00	$0.95	26.50%	1.35	0%
Dayton Hudson	$73	$272.90	$4.65	12.50%	1.30	38%
Federated	$22	$ 58.90	$1.40	10.00%	1.45	0%
Kmart	$23	$101.45	$1.75	11.50%	1.30	59%
Nordstrom	$36	$ 43.85	$1.60	11.50%	1.45	20%
Penney	$54	$ 81.05	$3.50	10.50%	1.10	41%
Sears	$57	$150.00	$4.55	11.00%	1.35	36%
Tiffany	$32	$ 35.65	$1.50	10.50%	1.50	19%
Wal-Mart	$30	$ 29.35	$1.05	18.50%	1.30	11%
Woolworth	$23	$ 74.15	$1.35	13.00%	1.25	65%

   a. There are two companies that sell for more than revenues, the Bombay Company and Wal-Mart. Why?
   b. What is the variable that is most highly correlated with price-sales ratios?
   c. Which of these companies is most likely to be over/undervalued? How did you arrive at this judgment?

3. Walgreen, a large retail drugstore chain in the United States, reported net income of $221 million in 1993 on revenues of $8,298 million. It paid out 31% of its earnings as dividends, a payout ratio it was expected to maintain between 1994 and 1998, during which period earnings growth was expected to be 13.5%. After 1998, earnings growth was expected to decline to 6%, and the dividend payout ratio was expected to increase to 60%. The beta was 1.15 and was expected to remain unchanged. The Treasury bond rate was 7%, and the risk premium is 5.5%.
   a. Estimate the price/sales ratio for Walgreens, assuming its profit margin remains unchanged at 1993 levels.
   b. How much of this price/sales ratio can be attributed to extraordinary growth?
4. Tambrands, a leading producer of tampons, reported net income of $122 million on revenues of $684 million in 1992. Earnings growth was anticipated to be 11% over the next five years, after which it was expected to be 6%. The firm paid out 45% of its earnings as dividends in 1992, and this payout ratio was expected to increase to 60% during the stable period. The beta of the stock was 1.00.

   During the course of 1993, erosion of brand loyalty and increasing competition for generic brands lead to a drop in net income to $100 million on revenues of $700 million. The sales/book value ratio was comparable to 1992 levels. (The Treasury bond rate in 1992 and 1993 was 7%, and the risk premium is 5.5%.)
   a. Estimate the price-sales ratio, based on 1992 profit margins and expected growth.
   b. Estimate the price-sales ratio, based on 1993 profit margins and expected growth. (Assume that the extraordinary growth period remains five years, but that the growth rate will be impacted by the lower margins.)
5. Gillette Inc. was faced with a significant corporate strategy decision early in 1994 on whether it would continue its high-margin strategy or shift to a lower margin to increase sales revenues in the face of intense generic competition. The two strategies being considered are as follows:

Status Quo High-Margin Strategy
- Maintain profit margins at 1993 levels from 1994 to 2003. (In 1993, net income was $575 million on revenues of $5,750 million.)
- The sales/book value ratio, which was 3 in 1993, can then be expected to decline to 2.5 between 1994 and 2003.

Low-Margin Higher-Sales Strategy
- Reduce net profit margin to 8% from 1994 to 2003.
- The sales/book value ratio will then stay at 1993 levels from 1994 to 2003.

The book value per share at the end of 1993 is $9.75. The dividend payout ratio, which was 33% in 1993, is expected to remain unchanged from 1994 to 2003 under either strategy, as is the beta, which was 1.30 in 1993. (The T-bond rate is 7%, and the risk premium is 5.5%.)

   After 2003, the earnings growth rate is expected to drop to 6%, and the dividend payout ratio is expected to be 60% under either strategy. The beta will decline to 1.0.
   a. Estimate the price-sales ratio under the status quo strategy.
   b. Estimate the price-sales ratio under the low-margin strategy.
   c. Which strategy would you recommend and why?
   d. How much would sales have to drop under the status quo strategy for the two strategies to be equivalent?

6. You have regressed price-sales ratios against fundamentals for NYSE stocks in 1994 and come up with the following regression:

   PS = 0.42 + 0.33 Payout + 0.73 Growth – 0.43 Beta + 7.91 Margin

   For instance, a firm with a 35% payout, a 15% growth rate, a beta of 1.25, and a profit margin of 10% would have had a price-sales ratio of:

   PS = 0.42 + 0.33 × 0.35 + 0.73 × 0.15 – 0.43 × 1.25 + 7.91 × 0.10
   = 0.8985

   a. What do the coefficients on this regression tell you about the independent variable's relationship with the dependent variable? What statistical concerns might you have with this regression?
   b. Estimate the price-sales ratios for all the drugstore chains described in question 2. Why might this answer be different from the one obtained from the regression of only the drugstore firms? Which one would you consider more reliable and why?
7. Ulysses Inc. is a retail firm that reported $1.5 billion in after-tax operating income on $15 billion in revenues in the just-ended financial year; the firm also had a capital turnover ratio of 1.5. The firm's cost of capital is 10%.
   a. If you expect operating income to grow 5% a year in perpetuity, estimate the value-to-sales ratio for the firm.
   b. How would your answer change if you were told that the operating income will grow 10% a year for the next five years and then grow 5% in perpetuity?
8. You have run a regression of value/sales ratios against operating margins for cosmetics firms:

   Value/Sales = 0.45 + 8.5(After-tax operating margin)

   You are trying to estimate the brand name value of Estée Lauder. The firm earned $80 million after interest and after taxes on revenues of $500 million. In contrast, GenCosmetics, a manufacturer of generic cosmetics, had an after-tax operating margin of 5%. Estimate the brand name value for Estée Lauder.
9. You are trying to estimate the brand name value for Steinway, one of the world's best-known piano manufacturers. The firm reported operating income of $30 million on revenues of $100 million in the most recent year; the tax rate is 40%. The book value of capital at the firm is $90 million, and the cost of capital is 10%. The firm is in stable growth and expects to grow 5% a year in perpetuity.
   a. Estimate the value/sales ratio for this firm.
   b. Assume now that the operating profit margin (EBIT/Sales) for generic piano manufacturers is half of the operating profit margin for Steinway. Assuming generic piano manufacturers have the same stable growth rate, capital turnover ratio, and cost of capital as Steinway, what is the value of the Steinway brand name?

CHAPTER 21

Valuing Financial Service Firms

Banks, insurance companies, and other financial service firms pose particular challenges for an analyst attempting to value them for two reasons. The first is the nature of their businesses makes it difficult to define both debt and reinvestment, making the estimation of cash flows much more difficult. The other is that they tend to be heavily regulated, and the effects of regulatory requirements on value have to be considered.

This chapter begins by considering what makes financial service firms unique and ways of dealing with the differences. It then looks at how best we can adapt discounted cash flow models to value financial service firms, and looks at three alternatives—a traditional dividend discount model, a cash flow to equity discount model, and an excess return model. With each, we look at a variety of examples from the financial services arena. We move on to look at how relative valuation works with financial service firms, and what multiples may work best with these firms.

The last part of the chapter examines a series of issues that, if not specific to, are accentuated in financial service firms ranging from the effect of changes in regulatory requirements on risk and value to how best to consider the quality of loan portfolios at banks.

CATEGORIES OF FINANCIAL SERVICE FIRMS

Any firm that provides financial products and services to individuals or other firms can be categorized as a financial service firm. We would categorize financial service businesses into four groups from the perspective of how they make their money. A bank makes money on the spread between the interest it pays to those from who it raises funds and the interest it charges those who borrow from it, and from other services it offers its depositors and its lenders. Insurance companies make their income in two ways. One is through the premiums they receive from those who buy claims from them, and the other is income from the investment portfolios that they maintain to service these claims. An investment bank provides advice and supporting products for non–financial service firms to raise capital from financial markets or to consummate deals such as acquisitions or divestitures. Investment firms provide investment advice or manage portfolios for clients. Their income comes from advisory fees for the advice, and management and sales fees for investment portfolios.

With the consolidation in the financial services sector, an increasing number of firms operate in more than one of these businesses. For example, Citigroup, created by the merger of Travelers and Citicorp, operates in all four businesses. At the same time, however, there remain a large number of small banks, boutique investment banks, and specialized insurance firms that still derive the bulk of their income from one source.

How big is the financial services sector in the United States? Figure 21.1 summarizes the number of publicly traded banks, insurance companies, brokerage houses, and investment firms in the United States at the end of 2000.

Even more striking than the sheer number of financial service firms is their diversity in terms of size and growth. Table 21.1 provides a measure of the range on each measure across different sectors.

In emerging markets, financial service firms tend to have an even higher profile and account for a larger proportion of overall market value than they do in the United States. If we bring these firms into the mix, it is quite clear that no one template will value all financial service firms and that we have to be able to be flexible in how we design the model to allow for all types of financial service firms.

WHAT IS UNIQUE ABOUT FINANCIAL SERVICE FIRMS?

Financial service firms have much in common with non–financial service firms. They attempt to be as profitable as they can, have to worry about competition, and want to grow rapidly over time. If they are publicly traded, they are judged by the total return they make for their stockholders, just as other firms are. This section, though, focuses on those aspects of financial service firms that make them different from other firms and considers the implications for valuation.

Debt: Raw Material or Source of Capital

When we talk about capital for non–financial service firms, we tend to talk about both debt and equity. A firm raises funds from both equity investor and bondholders (and banks) and uses these funds to make its investments. When we value the firm, we value the assets owned by the firm, rather than just the value of its equity.

With a financial service firm, debt takes on a different connotation. Rather than view debt as a source of capital, most financial service firms view it as a raw material. In other words, debt is to a bank what steel is to General Motors, something to be molded into other financial products that can then be sold at a higher

TABLE 21.1 Cross-Sectional Distribution: Financial Service Firms—December 2000

Industry	Number of Firms	Market Value of Equity			
		Average	Maximum	Minimum	Standard Deviation
Banks	211	$ 4,836	$96,910	$10	$12,642
Insurance companies	86	$ 3,975	$90,317	$ 8	$11,663
Investment companies	45	$ 476	$ 2,707	$ 9	$ 500
Securities brokerages	27	$10,524	$97,987	$ 3	$23,672
Thrifts	124	$ 707	$25,751	$ 5	$ 2,533

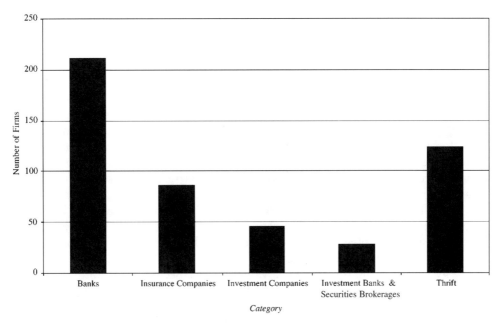

FIGURE 21.1 Financial Service Firms
Source: Value Line.

price and yield a profit. Consequently, capital at financial service firms is more narrowly defined as including only equity capital. This definition of capital is reinforced by the regulatory authorities who evaluate the equity capital ratios of banks and insurance firms.

The definition of what comprises debt also is murkier with a financial service firm than it is with a non–financial service firm. For instance, should deposits made by customers into their checking accounts at a bank be treated as debt by that bank? Especially on interest-bearing deposits, there is little distinction between a deposit and debt issued by the bank. If we do categorize this as debt, the operating income for a bank should be measured prior to interest paid to depositors, which

	Expected Growth Rate			
Industry	Average	Maximum	Minimum	Standard Deviation
Banks	10.60%	19.00%	4.50%	2.82%
Insurance companies	11.24%	37.00%	1.50%	5.31%
Investment companies	9.50%	14.50%	6.50%	3.35%
Securities brokerages	17.56%	32.75%	10.00%	7.19%
Thrifts	11.89%	38.33%	5.00%	5.00%

would be problematic since interest expenses are usually the biggest single expense item for a bank.

The Regulatory Overlay

Financial service firms are heavily regulated all over the world, though the extent of the regulation varies from country to country. In general, these regulations take three forms. First, banks and insurance companies are required to maintain capital ratios to ensure that they do not expand beyond their means and put their claimholders or depositors at risk. Second, financial service firms are often constrained in terms of where they can invest their funds. For instance, the Glass-Steagall Act in the United States restricted commercial banks from investment banking activities and from taking active equity positions in manufacturing firms. Third, entry of new firms into the business is often restricted by the regulatory authorities, as are mergers between existing firms.

Why does this matter? From a valuation perspective, assumptions about growth are linked to assumptions about reinvestment. With financial service firms, these assumptions have to be scrutinized to ensure that they pass regulatory constraints. There might also be implications for how we measure risk at financial service firms. If regulatory restrictions are changing or are expected to change, it adds a layer of uncertainty to the future, which can have an effect on value.

Reinvestment at Financial Service Firms

The preceding section noted that financial service firms are often constrained by regulation in both where they invest their funds and how much they invest. If we define reinvestment, as we have so far in this book, as necessary for future growth, there are other problems associated with measuring reinvestment with financial service firms. Note that Chapter 10 considers two items in reinvestment—net capital expenditures and working capital. Unfortunately, measuring either of these items at a financial service firm can be problematic.

Consider net capital expenditures first. Unlike manufacturing firms that invest in plant, equipment, and other fixed assets, financial service firms invest in intangible assets such as brand name and human capital. Consequently, their investments for future growth often are categorized as operating expenses in accounting statements. Not surprisingly, the statement of cash flows to a bank show little or no capital expenditures and correspondingly low depreciation. With working capital, we run into a different problem. If we define working capital as the different between current assets and current liabilities, a large proportion of a bank's balance sheet would fall into one or the other of these categories. Changes in this number can be both large and volatile and may have no relationship to reinvestment for future growth.

As a result of this difficulty in measuring reinvestment, we run into two practical problems in valuing these firms. The first is that we cannot estimate cash flows without estimating reinvestment. In other words, if we cannot identify net capital expenditures and changes in working capital, we cannot estimate cash flows, either.

The second is that estimating expected future growth becomes more difficult if the reinvestment rate cannot be measured.

GENERAL FRAMEWORK FOR VALUATION

Given the unique role of debt at financial service firms, the regulatory restrictions that they operate under, and the difficulty of identifying reinvestment at these firms, how can we value these firms? In this section, we suggest some broad rules that can allow us to deal with these issues. First, it makes far more sense to value equity directly at financial service firms, rather than the entire firm. Second, we either need a measure of cash flow that does not require us to estimate reinvestment needs or we need to redefine reinvestment to make it more meaningful for a financial service firm.

Equity versus Firm

Early in this book, we noted the distinction between valuing a firm and valuing the equity in the firm. We value firms by discounting expected cash flows prior to debt payments at the weighted average cost of capital. We value equity by discounting cash flows to equity investors at the cost of equity.

Estimating cash flows prior to debt payments or a weighted average cost of capital is problematic when debt and debt payments cannot be easily identified, which, as we argued earlier, is the case with financial service firms. Equity can be valued directly, however, by discounting cash flows to equity at the cost of equity. Consequently, we would argue for the latter approach for financial service firms. We would extend this argument to multiples as well. Equity multiples such as price-to-earnings or price-to-book ratios are a much better fit for financial service firms than value multiples such as value to EBITDA.

Estimating Cash Flows

To value the equity in a firm, we normally estimate the free cash flow to equity. In Chapter 10, we defined the free cash flow to equity thus:

$$\text{Free cash flow to equity} = \text{Net income} - \text{Net capital expenditures} \\ - \text{Change in noncash working capital} \\ - (\text{Debt repaid} - \text{New debt issued})$$

If we cannot estimate the net capital expenditures or noncash working capital, we clearly cannot estimate the free cash flow to equity. Since this is the case with financial service firms, we have two choices. The first is to use dividends as cash flows to equity, and assume that firms over time pay out their free cash flows to equity as dividends. Since dividends are observable, we therefore do not have to confront the question of how much firms reinvest. The second is to adapt the free cash flow to equity measure to allow for the types of reinvestment that financial service firms. For instance, given that banks operate under a capital ratio constraint, it can be argued that these firms have to reinvest equity capital in order to be able to make more loans in the future.

DISCOUNTED CASH FLOW VALUATION

In a discounted cash flow model, we consider the value of an asset to be the present value of the expected cash flows generated by that asset. In this section, we will first consider the use of dividend discount models to value banks and other financial service firms, then move on to analyze cash flow to equity models and conclude with an examination of excess return models.

Dividend Discount Models

Chapter 13 considered how to value the equity in a firm based on dividend discount models. Using the argument that the only cash flows that a stockholder in a publicly traded firm receives are dividends, we valued equity as the present value of the expected dividends. We looked at the range of dividend discount models, from stable to high growth, and considered how best to estimate the inputs. While much of what was said in that chapter applies here as well, we will consider some of the unique aspects of financial service firms in this section.

Basic Models In the basic dividend discount model, the value of a stock is the present value of the expected dividends on that stock. Assuming that equity in a publicly traded firm has an infinite life, we arrive at:

$$\text{Value per share of equity} = \sum_{t=1}^{t=\infty} \frac{DPS_t}{(1+k_e)^t}$$

where DPS_t = Expected dividend per share in period t
$\quad\quad\, k_e$ = Cost of equity

In the special case where the expected growth rate in dividends is constant forever, this model collapses into the Gordon growth model:

$$\text{Value per share of equity in stable growth} = \frac{DPS_1}{(k_e - g)}$$

where g is the expected growth rate in perpetuity.

In the more general case, where dividends are growing at a rate that is not expected to be sustainable or constant forever for a period (called the extraordinary growth period), we can still assume that the growth rate will be constant forever at some point in time in the future. This allows us to then estimate the value of a stock, in the dividend discount model, as the sum of the present values of the dividends over the extraordinary growth period and the present value of the terminal price, which itself is estimated using the Gordon growth model.

$$\text{Value per share of equity in extraordinary growth} = \sum_{t=1}^{t=n} \frac{DPS_t}{(1+k_{e,hg})^t} + \frac{DPS_{n+1}}{(k_{e,st} - g_n)(1+k_{e,hg})^n}$$

The extraordinary growth is expected to last n years, g_n is the expected growth rate after n years, and k_e is the cost of equity (hg: high growth period and st: stable growth period).

Inputs to Model   This section will focus purely on the estimation issues relating to financial service firms when it comes to the inputs to these models. In general, to value a stock using the dividend discount model, we need estimates of the cost of equity, the expected payout ratios, and the expected growth rate in earnings per share over time.

Cost of Equity   In keeping with the way we have estimated the cost of equity for firms so far in this book, the cost of equity for a financial service firm has to reflect the portion of the risk in the equity that cannot be diversified away by the marginal investor in the stock. This risk is estimated using a beta (in the capital asset pricing model) or betas (in a multifactor or arbitrage pricing model).

In our earlier discussions of betas, we argued against the use of regression betas because of the noise in the estimates (standard errors) and the possibility that the firm has changed over the period of the regression. How relevant are these arguments with financial service firms? The regression beta estimates of large and more mature financial service firms often are far more precise than the estimates for firms in other sectors. If regulatory restrictions have remained unchanged over the period and are not expected to change in the future, this may be one of the few sectors where regression betas can continue to be used with some confidence. In periods where the rules are changing and regulatory environments are shifting, the caveat about not using regression betas continues to hold.

There is a second area of difference. When estimating betas for non–financial service firms, we emphasized the importance of unlevering betas (whether they be historical or sector averages) and then relevering them, using a firm's current debt to equity ratio. With financial service firms, we would skip this step for two reasons. First, financial service firms tend to be much more homogeneous in terms of capital structure—they tend to have similar financial leverage. Second, and this is a point made earlier, debt is difficult to measure for financial service firms. In practical terms, this will mean that we will use the average levered beta for comparable firms as the bottom-up beta for the firm being analyzed.

Payout Ratios   The expected dividend per share in a future period can be written as the product of the expected earnings per share in that period and the expected payout ratio. There are two advantages of deriving dividends from expected earnings. The first is that it allows us to focus on expected growth in earnings, which is both more reasonable and more accessible than growth in dividends. The second is that the payout ratio can be changed over time, to reflect changes in growth and investment opportunities.

The payout ratio for a bank, as it is for any other firm, is the dividend divided by the earnings. This said, financial service firms have conventionally paid out more in dividends than other firms in the market, as is clear from Figure 21.2. The dividend payout ratios and dividend yields for banks, insurance companies, investment banks, and investment firms are much higher than similar statistics for the rest of the market.

Why do financial service firms pay out more in dividends than other firms? An obvious response would be that they operate in much more mature businesses than firms in sectors such as telecommunications and software, but this is only part of the story. Even if we control for differences in expected growth rates, financial service firms pay out far more in dividends than other firms for two reasons. One is that banks and insurance companies need to invest far less in capital expenditures, at least as defined by accountants, than other firms. This, in turn, means that far more of the net income of these firms can be paid out as dividends than for a manufacturing firm. A second factor is history. Banks and insurance companies have developed a reputation as reliable payers of high dividends. Over time, they have attracted investors who like dividends, making it difficult for them to change dividend policy.

In recent years, in keeping with a trend that is visible in other sectors as well, financial service firms have increased stock buybacks as a way of returning cash to

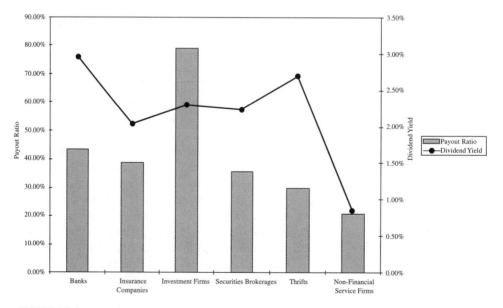

FIGURE 21.2 Payout Ratios and Yields: Financial versus Non–Financial Service Firms
Source: Value Line.

stockholders. In this context, focusing purely on dividends paid can provide a misleading picture of the cash returned to stockholders. An obvious solution is to add the stock buybacks each year to the dividends paid and to compute the composite payout ratio. If we do so, however, we should look at the number over several years, since stock buybacks vary widely across time—a buyback of billions in one year may be followed by three years of relatively meager buybacks, for instance.

Expected Growth   If dividends are based on earnings, the expected growth rate that will determine value is the expected growth rate in earnings. For financial service firms, as with other firms, earnings growth can be estimated in one of three ways:

1. *Historical growth in earnings.* Many banks and insurance companies have very long histories and estimating historical growth is usually feasible. Furthermore, the correlation between past earnings growth and expected future growth is much higher for financial service firms than it is for other firms.

Note, in Figure 21.3, that the correlation between earnings growth over five-year periods is 0.35 for financial service firms, while it is only 0.17 for other firms. This would suggest that historical growth in earnings is a much better predictor of future earnings at these firms. If the regulatory environment is changing, however, we have to be cautious about projecting past growth into the future.

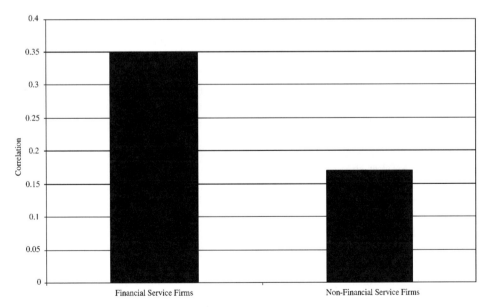

FIGURE 21.3   Correlation between Past and Expected Growth
Source: Compustat.

2. *Analyst estimates in growth in earnings.* Analysts estimate expected growth rates in earnings for many publicly traded firms, though the extent of coverage varies widely. Many large banks and insurance companies are widely followed, allowing us to get these estimates of future growth. As noted in Chapter 11, it is an open question as to whether the long term forecasts from analysts are any better than historical growth for estimating future growth.

3. *Fundamental growth.* In Chapter 11, we suggested that the expected growth in earnings per share can be written as a function of the retention ratio and the return on equity (ROE):

$$\text{Expected growth}_{EPS} = \text{Retention ratio} \times \text{ROE}$$

This equation allows us to estimate the expected growth rate for firms with stable returns on equity. If we consider stock buybacks in addition to dividends when looking at payout, the retention ratio should be defined consistently as well.

If the return on equity is expected to change over time, the expected growth rate in earnings per share can be written as:

$$\text{Expected growth}_{EPS} = \text{Retention ratio} \times \text{ROE}_{t+1} + (\text{ROE}_{t+1} - \text{ROE}_t)/\text{ROE}_t$$

In both formulations, the expected growth rate is a function of the retention ratio, which measures the quantity of reinvestment, and the return on equity, which measures their quality. How well do fundamental growth models work for financial service firms? Surprisingly well. The retention ratio in a bank measures the equity reinvested back into the firms, which in turn, given the regulatory focus on capital ratios, determines, in large part, how much these firms can expand in the future. The return on equity is also a more meaningful measure of investment quality because financial assets are much more likely to be marked up to market.

Stable Growth To get closure with dividend discount models, we have to assume that the financial service firms that we are valuing will be in stable growth at some point in time in the future, where stable growth is defined to be growth that is less than or equal to the growth rate of the economy. In some cases, especially with larger firms in more mature businesses, the expected growth rate today may already be a stable growth rate.

In making the judgment of when a financial service firm will become a stable growth firm, we have to consider three factors. The first is the size of the firm, relative to the market that it serves. Larger financial service firms will find it more difficult to sustain high growth for long periods, especially in mature markets. The second is the nature of the competition. If competition is intense, stable growth will arrive sooner rather than later. If competition is restricted, high growth and excess returns can last for much longer. Finally, the way in which financial service firms are regulated can affect the convergence to stable growth, since regulation can operate both as a help and a hindrance. By restricting new entrants, regulations may help financial service firms maintain high growth for long periods. At the same time, though, regulatory restrictions may prevent firms from entering new and potentially lucrative businesses, and thus reduce the length of the high-growth period.

As noted in prior chapters, it is not only the growth rate that changes in stable growth. The payout ratio has to adjust to reflect the stable growth rate, and can be estimated from the payout ratio:

$$\text{Payout ratio in stable growth} = 1 - g/\text{ROE}_{\text{stable growth}}$$

The risk of the firm should also adjust to reflect the stable growth assumption. In particular, if betas are used to estimate the cost of equity, they should converge toward one in stable growth.

ILLUSTRATION 21.1:   Stable Growth Dividend Discount Model: Citigroup

Citigroup, created by the merger of Citicorp and Travelers Group, is one of the giants in the financial service business. In 1999, Citigroup paid out dividends of $1,973 million on net income of $9,867 million; the return on equity for the year was 22%. The low payout ratio and high return on equity would normally lead us to allow for a period of high growth for the firm, but there are two other factors to consider:

1. Citigroup bought back $4.3 billion of its own stock in 1999 and $4.1 billion in 1998. If we consider the sum of dividends and stock buybacks over both periods as a percent of net income, we arrive at a modified dividend payout ratio of:

$$\text{Modified dividend payout ratio} = \frac{\text{Buybacks}_{1998} + \text{Buybacks}_{1999} + \text{Dividends}_{1998} + \text{Dividends}_{1999}}{\text{Net income}_{1998} + \text{Net income}_{1999}}$$

$$= (4{,}125 + 4{,}294 + 1{,}846 + 1{,}973)/(5{,}807 + 9{,}867) = 78.07\%$$

If we go back over the past four years, rather then just the past two years, the modified payout ratio is 56.40%. Over the same period, the return on equity at the firm has averaged out to 17%.

2. Citigroup has a significant market share in almost every business that it competes it. While overall market growth may be high in some segments—emerging market investment banking, for instance—the firm faces strong competition in each of these segments.

With these factors in mind, we will assume that Citigroup is in stable growth, and that its current earnings (estimated for 2000) of $13.993 billion will grow 5% in perpetuity. In addition, we will assume that the payout ratio looking forward will be 56.40% (the average modified payout ratio over past fouryears) and that the beta for the stock based on its business mix is 1.00. With these inputs, a risk-free rate of 5.1% and a risk premium of 4%, we would value Citigroup as follows:

Cost of equity for Citigroup = 5.1% + 1.00(4%) = 9.1%

Value of Citigroup's equity = $13.993(1.05)(.564)/(.091 − .05) = $202.113 billion

There is an alternative approach we could have used to value Citigroup. Given its return on equity of 17%, we could have estimated a dividend payout ratio and used this ratio to value the stock.

Estimated dividend payout ratio = 1 − g/ROE = 1 − .05/.17 = 70.59%

Value of Citigroup's equity = $13.993(1.05)(.706)/(.091 − .05) = $253 billion

In January 2001, at the time of this valuation, Citigroup had an equity value of $256 billion. Which is the more reasonable value? It depends on whether we believe that the 17% return on equity that Citigroup earned between 1996 and 1999 can be maintained in perpetuity. If the answer is yes, the $253 billion value estimate is the better one. If, however, we assume that Citigroup's return on equity will decline over time, the initial estimate of $202 billion is more credible.

ILLUSTRATION 21.2: A High-Growth Dividend Discount Model: State Bank of India

State Bank of India is India's largest bank, created in the aftermath of a nationalization of all banks in India in 1971. For the two decades that followed, it operated as a monopoly and was entirely government owned. In the 1990s, the Indian governments privatized portions of the bank while retaining control of its management and operations.

In 1999, State Bank of India earned 205 million Indian rupees on a book value of equity of 1,042 million rupees (at the beginning of 1999), resulting in a return on equity of 19.72%. The bank also paid out dividends of Rs 2.50 per share from earnings per share of Rs 38.98; this yields a payout ratio of 6.41%. The high retention ratio suggests that the firm is investing substantial amounts in the expectation of high growth in the future. We will analyze its value over three phases—an initial period of sustained high growth, a transition period where growth drops toward stable growth and a stable-growth phase.

HIGH-GROWTH PHASE

If State Bank can maintain the current return on equity of 19.72% and payout ratio of 6.41%, the expected growth rate in earnings per share will be 18.46%:

$$\text{Expected growth rate} = \text{ROE} \times \text{Retention ratio} = 19.72\%(1 - .0641) = 18.46\%$$

The key question is how long the bank can sustain this growth. Given the large potential size of the Indian market, we assume that this growth will continue for four years. During this period, we also allow for the fact that there will be substantial risk associated with the Indian economy by allowing for a country risk premium in estimating the cost of equity. Using the approach developed earlier in the book, we estimate a risk premium for India based on its rating of BB+ and the relative equity market volatility of the Indian market.

$$\text{Country risk premium for India} = \text{Country default spread} \times \text{Relative equity market volatility}$$
$$= 3.00\% \times 2.1433 = 6.43\%$$

To estimate the cost of equity during the high-growth period—the next four years—we estimate the average beta for Asian commercial banks of 0.80 and assume that State Bank of India will have a similar beta. In conjunction with the risk-free rate in Indian rupees of 12.00%, we estimate a cost of equity of 20.34%.

$$\text{Cost of equity} = \text{Risk-free rate} + \text{Beta}(\text{Mature market premium} + \text{Country risk premium})$$
$$= 12.00\% + 0.80(4.00\% + 6.43\%) = 20.34\%$$

With these estimates of expected growth, payout ratio and the cost of equity, we can estimate the present value of expected dividends per share over the next four years:

	1	2	3	4
Expected growth rate	18.46%	18.46%	18.46%	18.46%
Earnings per share	Rs46.17	Rs54.70	Rs64.79	Rs76.75
Payout ratio	6.41%	6.41%	6.41%	6.41%
Dividends per share	Rs2.96	Rs3.51	Rs4.16	Rs4.92
Cost of equity	20.34%	20.34%	20.34%	20.34%
Present value	Rs2.46	Rs2.42	Rs2.38	Rs2.35

TRANSITION PHASE

We expect State Bank to continue growing beyond year 4 but at a declining rate. Each year, we reduce the expected growth rate linearly from 18.46% to a stable growth rate of 10.00%—these growth rates are all in nominal rupees. As the growth rate declines, we allow the return on equity to decline (as competition increases) to 18% and the payout ratio to rise to reflect the lesser need for reinvestment.[1] To illustrate, the payout ratio in year 8, when the expected growth rate is 10%, can be computed to be:

Payout ratio in year 8 = 1 − Expected growth rate/ROE = 1 − .10/.18 = 0.4444 or 44.44%

We also adjust the country risk premium down from 6.43% to 3.00% to reflect our expectation that there will be less risk in investing in India as the country's economy matures. The following table summarizes expected dividends during the transition phase:

	5	6	7	8
Expected growth rate	16.34%	14.23%	12.11%	10.00%
Earnings per share	Rs89.29	Rs102.00	Rs114.35	Rs125.79
Payout ratio	15.92%	25.43%	34.94%	44.44%
Dividends per share	Rs14.22	Rs25.94	Rs39.95	Rs55.91
Cost of equity	19.66%	18.97%	18.29%	17.60%
Cumulative cost of equity	250.98%	298.60%	353.20%	415.36%
Present value	Rs5.66	Rs8.69	Rs11.31	Rs13.46

Note that the cost of equity in year 8 reflects the lower country risk premium:

Cost of equity in year 8 = 12.00% + 0.80(4.00% + 3.00%) = 17.60%

The beta and the mature market risk premium of 4% have been left unchanged. To compute the present values of the expected dividends over the transition period, we compound the cost of equity and discount the cash flows.[2]

STABLE GROWTH

In stable growth, we assume that State Bank's earnings and dividends will grow in perpetuity at 10% a year and discount them at the stable period cost of equity of 17.60%. The present value of these dividends in perpetuity, which yield the terminal price per share, can be computed to be:

$$\text{Terminal price per share} = \text{Expected earnings per share}_9 \times \text{Payout}_9/(\text{Cost of equity} - g)$$
$$= 125.79(1.10)(.4444)/(.176 - .10) = \text{Rs } 809.18$$

FINAL VALUATION

The final value per share for State Bank can be computed by adding the present values of the dividends during the high-growth phase, the dividends during the transition period and the terminal price at the end of the transition period.

Value per share = PV of dividends: high growth + PV of dividends: transition phase + PV of terminal price
= 2.46 + 2.42 + 2.38 + 2.35 + 5.66 + 8.69 + 11.31 + 13.46 + 809.18/4.1536
= Rs 243.55

Note that the terminal price is discounted back at the compounded cost of equity for the eighth year. In January 2001, at the time of this valuation, State Bank was trading at Rs 235 per share.

---

[1]The adjustment in the payout ratio is linear. The current payout ratio is 6.41 percent and the stable period payout ratio is 44.44 percent. Dividing the difference of 38.03 percent over four years yields an increase in the payout ratio of 9.51 percent each year.

[2]When the cost of equity changes each year, as it does between years 5 and 8, the compounded cost of equity has to be computed. For instance, the cash flow in year 6 will be discounted back using the following compounded cost:

$$\text{Compounded cost} = (1.2034)^4(1.1966)(1.1897)$$

Valuing a Non-Dividend-Paying Financial Service Firm   While many financial service firms do pay dividends, a large number of young, high-growth financial service firms in recent years have chosen not to pay dividends and reinvest all of their earning back into their operations. In fact, some of these firms lose money. While it may seem inappropriate to use the dividend discount model to value such firms, we will argue that the model is flexible enough to deal with them. How, if dividends are zero, will we ever be able to get a positive value for a share? The answer is simple, at least for firms that have positive earnings currently. While dividends are zero currently and are expected to be zero for the foreseeable future, when the firm is growing, the growth will ultimately subside. As the growth drops, the firm's capacity to pay out dividends will increase. In fact, using the fundamental equation for growth from the last section, we can estimate the expected payout ratio in future periods to be:

$$\text{Expected payout ratio} = 1 - g/\text{ROE}$$

The equity will derive its value from expected future dividends.

If earnings are negative currently, the mechanics become a little more involved. We first have to estimate earnings in future periods. Presumably, we would expect earnings to become positive some period in the future. (If we did not, the value of equity would be zero and the valuation exercise would be unnecessary.) Once earnings become positive, the rest of the analysis resembles what we did before.

ILLUSTRATION 21.3:   Valuing a Non-Dividend-Paying Financial Service Firm: NetBank

NetBank is a virtual bank that offers banking services to customers. At the time of this valuation, the bank had just made the turn to profitability and reported net income of $3.05 million on a beginning book value of equity of $38.76 million; this amounted to earnings per share of $0.25. The bank paid no dividends but we anticipate significant growth in earnings both from growth in deposits and economies of scale (which should improve the return on equity). The expected growth rate in earnings is 30% for the next 6 years and it is then expected to decline linearly to a stable growth rate of 5% in the 12th year.

NetBank is not expected to pay dividends during the first six years of high growth. During this period, the bank is also exposed to significant risk. We use a beta of 1.70 to reflect the risk of e-commerce ventures and estimate a cost of equity of 11.80%, based on a Treasury bond rate of 5% and a risk premium of 4%:

$$\text{Cost of equity} = 5\% + 1.70(4\%) = 11.80\%$$

The following table summarizes the expected earnings during this period:

	1	2	3	4	5	6
Expected growth rate	30.00%	30.00%	30.00%	30.00%	30.00%	30.00%
Earnings per share	$0.32	$0.42	$0.54	$0.70	$0.91	$1.19
Payout ratio	0.00%	0.00%	0.00%	0.00%	0.00%	0.00%
Dividends per share	$0.00	$0.00	$0.00	$0.00	$0.00	$0.00
Cost of equity	11.80%	11.80%	11.80%	11.80%	11.80%	11.80%
Present value	$0.00	$0.00	$0.00	$0.00	$0.00	$0.00

In stable growth (after the 12th year), the bank is expected to earn a return on equity of 12% which will allow it to pay out 58.33% of its earnings as dividends during the period:

Expected dividend payout ratio in 12th year = $1 - g/ROE = 1 - 5\%/12\% = 58.33\%$

Between years 6 and 12, as the growth rate tapers off, we will assume that the payout ratio will increase from 0% to 58.33% in linear increments. We will also assume that the risk in the equity will also decline, with the beta dropping from 1.70 to 1.00 in stable growth. The following table summarizes the expected earnings and dividends during this transition period:

	7	8	9	10	11	12
Expected growth rate	25.83%	21.67%	17.50%	13.33%	9.17%	5.00%
Earnings per share	$1.49	$1.82	$2.14	$2.42	$2.64	$2.77
Payout ratio	9.72%	19.44%	29.17%	38.89%	48.61%	58.33%
Dividends per share	$0.15	$0.35	$0.62	$0.94	$1.28	$1.62
Cost of equity	11.33%	10.87%	10.40%	9.93%	9.47%	9.00%
Cumulative cost of equity	217.41%	241.03%	266.10%	292.53%	320.23%	349.05%
Present value	$0.07	$0.15	$0.23	$0.32	$0.40	$0.46

The dividends begin in year 6 and grow at a much faster rate than earnings because the payout ratio increases.

The terminal price at the end of the 12th year can be estimated using the dividends in year 13, the stable period cost of equity and the expected growth rate in perpetuity.

Terminal price per share = $EPS_{12}(1 + g_{stable})$(Payout ratio$_{13}$)/(Cost of equity$_{13}$ – Expected growth rate)
= $2.77(1.05)(.5833)/(.09 - .05) = 42.49

The value per share today can then be computed as the sum of the present values of the dividends during high growth and the present value of the terminal price:

Value per share = $0.07 + $0.15 + $0.23 + $0.32 + $0.40 + $0.46 + $42.49/3.4905 = $13.81

The terminal price per share is discounted at the compounded cost of equity of 3.4905 in year 12. In January 2001, at the time of this valuation, NetBank was trading at $9.50 per share.

Cash Flow to Equity Models

At the beginning of this discussion, we noted the difficulty in estimating cash flows when net capital expenditures and noncash working capital cannot be easily identified. It is possible, however, to estimate cash flows to equity even for financial service firms if we define reinvestment differently.

Defining Cash Flow to Equity   The cash flow to equity is the cash flow left over for equity investors after debt payments have been made and reinvestment needs met. With financial service firms, the reinvestment generally does not take the form of plant, equipment, or other fixed assets. Instead, the investment is in human capital and regulatory capital; the latter is the capital as defined by the regulatory authorities, which, in turn, determines the limits on future growth. There are ways in which we could incorporate both of these items into the reinvestment.

Capitalize Training and Employee Development Expenses   If human capital is a large factor in determining the success or failure of a financial service firm, we could capitalize the expenses associated with developing this capital. The process for doing so closely mirrors the process for capitalizing research and development expenses for technology firms and involves the following steps:

1. *Identify the amortizable life for the asset.* To determine the period over which these expenses will be written off, we have to begin with how long a typical employee that the firm has invested its resources in stays with the firm.
2. *Collect information on employee expenses in prior years.* The amount spent by the firm on employee training and development in prior years is collected, with the number of years matching the amortizable life specified in the first step.
3. *Compute the current year's amortization expense.* The expenses in each of the prior years is amortized. With a linear amortization schedule, the expense will be spread equally over the amortizable life. The sum total of the amortization of all of the expenses in previous years will become the current year's amortization expense.
4. *Adjust the net income for the firm.* The net income for the firm is adjusted for the capitalization of employee expenses:

   Adjusted net income = Reported net income
                     + Employee development expense in the current year
                     − Amortization of the employee expenses (from step 3)

5. *Compute the value of the human capital.* The value of human capital in the firm can be computed by adding up the unamortized portion of the employee development expenses in each of the prior years.

Employee development expenses are more difficult to capitalize than research and development expenses for two reasons. The first is that while research expenses are usually consolidated and reported as one item on a financial statement, employee development expenses tend to be widely spread across the firm and may be included in several different items in an income statement. Disentangling these expenses from employee salary and benefits may be difficult to do. The second is that the patents and licenses that emerge from research belong to the firm, and often give it exclusive rights in commercial use. A firm's employees, on the other hand, are mobile and may, and often do, move to competitors who offer them better terms.

Assuming that we can get over these practical difficulties in valuing human capital, let us consider the factors that determine the value that human capital adds to a firm. The first is the employee turnover ratio; as this ratio rises, the amortizable life for employee expenses will fall and with it the value of human capital. The second relates to the resources spent by the firm in employee development and training; the greater the resources, the greater the value assigned to human capital.

There is a third and often ignored factor. If we consider human capital as an asset, it is the excess returns that we make on the asset that create value. To create excess returns, a firm will have to pay an employee less than what he or she generates in value to the firm. To illustrate, an investment bank will generate value from a bond trader that works for it only if it pays that trader less than what he or she generates in profits for the firm. Why might the trader settle for less? One reason might be that the investment bank has some unique capability that allows the trader to earn these profits; this unique capability might come from proprietary information, client lists, or market position. Another reason might be noneconomic; the trader may have enough goodwill toward the investment bank that he or she might be willing to give up higher compensation elsewhere. Firms that treat their employees well and are loyal to them in bad times are more likely to earn this goodwill and have higher value as a consequence.

Investments in Regulatory Capital   For a financial service firm that is regulated based on capital ratios, equity earnings that are not paid out increase the equity capital of the firm and allow it to expand its activities. For instance, a bank that has a 5% equity capital ratio can make $100 in loans for every $5 in equity capital. When this bank reports net income of $15 million and pays out only $5 million, it is increasing its equity capital by $10 million. This, in turn, will allow it to make $200 million in additional loans and presumably increase its growth rate in future periods.

Using this argument, the portion of net income that does not get paid out can be viewed as reinvestment. It works, however, only if the firm takes advantage of its larger capital base and grows. If it does not, the equity retained is more akin to cash accumulating in the firm rather than reinvestment. One way to measure this usage is to look at the equity capital ratios of the firm over time and compare them to the regulatory constraints. A firm that reports an equity capital ratio that rises over time, well above the regulatory constraint, is not using its equity capital to grow.

Excess Return Models

The third approach to valuing financial service firms is to use an excess return model. In such a model, the value of a firm can be written as the sum of capital invested currently in the firm and the present value of dollar excess returns that the firm expects to make in the future. This section will consider how this model can be applied to valuing equity in a bank.

WHY EARNINGS ARE NOT CASH FLOWS

There are some analysts who value banks by discounting their earnings back to the present. They make the argument that banks have little or no net capital expenditure needs and that working capital needs (inventory, accounts receivable, etc.) are nonexistent. The problem, though, is that they couple the discounting of earnings with an expected growth rate in these earnings. This is clearly not consistent.

To see why, consider a bank that does pay out 100 percent of its earnings as dividends. If this firm issues no new equity, its book equity will stay frozen at current levels forever. If this bank continues to grow its loan portfolio, it will end up with capital ratios that are lower than the regulatory minimum sooner rather than later.

That is why reinvestment has to include investments in regulatory capital, acquisitions, and other such investments that banks need to make to continue to grow. That is also why even mature banks with low growth rates cannot afford to pay out 100 percent of their earnings as dividends.

Basic Model   Given the difficulty associated with defining total capital in a financial service firm, it makes far more sense to focus on just equity when using an excess return model to value a financial service firm. The value of equity in a firm can be written as the sum of the equity invested in a firm's current investments and the expected excess returns to equity investors from these and future investments.

> Value of equity = Equity capital invested currently
> + Present value of expected excess returns to equity investors

The most interesting aspect of this model is its focus on excess returns. A firm that invests its equity and earns just the fair-market rate of return on these investments should see the market value of its equity converge on the equity capital currently invested in it. A firm that earns a below-market return on its equity investments will see its equity market value dip below the equity capital currently invested.

The other point that has to be emphasized is that this model considers expected future investments as well. Thus it is up to the analyst using the model to forecast not only where the financial service firm will direct its future investments but also the returns it will make on those investments.

Inputs to Model   There are two inputs needed to value equity in the excess return model. The first is a measure of equity capital currently invested in the firm. The second and more difficult input is the expected excess returns to equity investors in future periods.

The equity capital invested currently in a firm is usually measured as the book value of equity in the firm. While the book value of equity is an accounting measure and is affected by accounting decisions, it should be a much more reliable measure of equity invested in a financial service firm than in a manufacturing firm for two reasons. The first is that the assets of a financial service firm are often financial assets that are marked up to market; the assets of manufacturing firms are real assets and deviations between book and market value are usually much larger. The second is that depreciation, which can be a big factor in determining book value for manufacturing firms, is often negligible at financial service firms. Notwithstanding this, the book value of equity can be affected by stock buybacks and extraordinary or one-time charges. The book value of equity for financial service firms that buy back stock or take extraordinary charges may understate the equity capital invested in the firm.

The excess returns, defined in equity terms, can be stated in terms of the return on equity and the cost of equity:

Excess equity return = (Return on equity – Cost of equity)(Equity capital invested)

Here again, we are assuming that the return on equity is a good measure of the economic return earned on equity investments. When analyzing a financial service firm, we can obtain the return on equity from the current period and past periods, but the return on equity that is required is the expected future return. This requires an analysis of the firm's strengths and weaknesses as well as the competition faced by the firm. Figure 21.4 summarizes the return on equity, cost of equity, and equity return spread for financial service firms in the United States in January 2001.

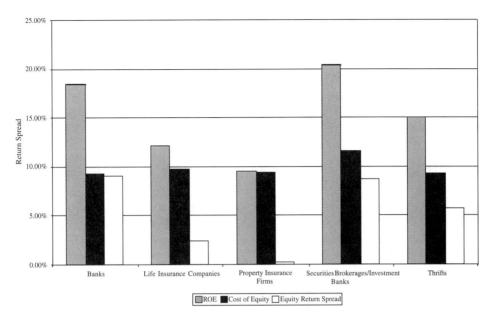

FIGURE 21.4 Return Spreads for Financial Service Firms—January 2001
Source: Value Line.

In making estimates of expected equity return spreads, we have to allow for the fact that the presence of large excess returns is likely to attract competition. These excess returns will fade over time and this should be reflected in the forecasts.

ILLUSTRATION 21.4:   Excess Return Valuation: Morgan Stanley Dean Witter

Morgan Stanley Dean Witter (MSDW) is one of the leading investment banks in the world. In 2000, the firm was earning a return on equity of 30.86% on its equity capital of $17.997 billion. Based on comparable firms, we estimate the beta of the firm to be 1.15, which results in a cost of equity of 9.60% (with a Treasury bond rate of 5% and a risk premium of 4%):

$$\text{Cost of equity} = 5\% + 1.15(4\%) = 9.60\%$$

We assume that the return on equity over the next five years will average 25%, reflecting the competitive pressures as MSDW expands globally and that the cost of equity will be unchanged over that period. In addition, we assume that MSDW will maintain its existing dividend payout ratio of 19.37%. The excess returns to equity investors are computed in the following table:

	1	2	3	4	5
Net income	$4,499.25	$5,406.20	$6,495.98	$7,805.43	$9,378.85
– Equity cost (see below)	$1,727.71	$2,075.98	$2,494.46	$2,997.29	$3,601.48
Excess equity return	$2,771.54	$3,330.22	$4,001.52	$4,808.15	$5,777.37
Cumulated cost of equity	1.09600	1.20122	1.31653	1.44292	1.58144
Present value	$2,528.78	$2,772.38	$3,039.44	$3,332.23	$3,653.23

Estimating Equity Cost Each Year

Beginning BV of equity	$17,997.00	$21,624.82	$25,983.92	$31,221.74	$37,515.38
Cost of equity	9.60%	9.60%	9.60%	9.60%	9.60%
Equity cost	$1,727.71	$2,075.98	$2,494.46	$2,997.29	$3,601.48

Estimating Book Value of Equity

Return on equity	25.00%	25.00%	25.00%	25.00%	25.00%
Net income	$4,499.25	$5,406.20	$6,495.98	$7,805.43	$9,378.85
Dividend payout ratio	19.37%	19.37%	19.37%	19.37%	19.37%
Dividends paid	$871.43	$1,047.10	$1,258.17	$1,511.79	$1,816.53
Retained earnings	$3,627.82	$4,359.11	$5,237.81	$6,293.64	$7,562.31

The net income each year is computed by multiplying the return on equity each year by the beginning book value of equity. The book value of equity each year is augmented by the portion of earnings that is not paid out as dividends—the retained earnings. To put closure on this valuation, we have to make assumptions about excess returns after year 5. If we assume that excess returns are zero, the value of Morgan Stanley's equity would be the sum of the present values of the excess returns computed in the preceding table and the existing book value of equity.

We assumed that the net income would grow 5% a year beyond year 5, that the return on equity would drop to 15% and that the beta for the stock would decline to 1.10.

$$\text{Net income}_6 = \$9,378.85 \times 1.05 = \$9,847.79$$

$$\text{Cost of equity in stable growth period} = 5\% + 1.1(4\%) = 9.40\%$$

$$\text{Book value of equity at beginning of year 6} = \text{Net income}_6/\text{ROE}_6 = \$9,847.79/.15 = \$65,651.92$$

Note that this book value of equity is significantly higher than the book value of equity in year 5 and reflects the much lower return on equity in stable growth.[3] The terminal value of excess returns to equity investors can then be computed as follows:

$$\text{Terminal value of excess returns} = (\text{Net income}_6 - \text{Cost of equity}_6 \times \text{BV of equity}_6)$$
$$/(\text{Cost of equity} - \text{Expected growth rate})$$
$$= (\$9,847.79 - \$65,651.92 \times .094)/(.094 - .05) = \$83,556.98$$

The value of equity can then be computed as the sum of the three components—the book value of equity invested today, the present value of excess equity returns over the next five years, and the present value of the terminal value of excess returns computed above:

Book value of equity invested currently	$17,997.00
PV of equity excess return—next five years	$15,326.06
PV of terminal value of excess returns = $83,556.98/1.096^5$	$52,836.01
Value of equity	$86,159.07
Number of shares	1,120.713
Value per share	$ 76.88

In January 2001, the stock was trading at $70 per share.

---

[3]This is an adjustment that is needed to make the book value of equity consistent with our assumptions about a lower return on equity in stable growth. The alternative is to drop the net income in year 6 to 15 percent of the book value of equity at the beginning of year 6.

ASSET-BASED VALUATION

In asset-based valuation, we value the existing assets of a financial service firm, net out debt and other outstanding claims, and report the difference as the value of equity. For example, with a bank, this would require valuing the loan portfolio of the bank (which would comprise its assets) and subtracting outstanding debt to estimate the value of equity. For an insurance company, you would value the policies that the company has in force and subtract out the expected claims resulting from these policies and other debt outstanding to estimate the value of the equity in the firm.

How would you value the loan portfolio of a bank or the policies of an insurance company? One approach would be to estimate the price at which the loan portfolio can be sold to another financial service firm, but the better approach is to value it based on the expected cash flows. Consider, for instance, a bank with a $1 billion loan portfolio with a weighted average maturity of eight years, on which it earns interest income of $70 million. Furthermore, assume that the default risk on the loans is such that the fair market interest rate on the loans would be 6.50 percent; this fair market rate can be estimated by either getting the loan portfolio rated by a ratings agency or by measuring the potential for default risk in the portfolio. The value of the loans can be estimated as follows:

$$\text{Value of loans} = \$70 \text{ million(PV of annuity, 8 years, 6.5\%)} + \$1,000 \text{ million}/1.065^8$$
$$= \$1,030 \text{ million}$$

This loan portfolio has a fair market value that exceeds its book value because the bank is charging an interest rate that exceeds the market rate. The reverse would be true if the bank charged an interest rate that is lower than the market rate. To value the equity in this book, you would subtract out the deposits, debt, and other claims on the bank.

This approach has merit if you are valuing a mature bank or insurance company with little or no growth potential, but it has two significant limitations. First, it does not assign any value to expected future growth and the excess returns that flow from that growth. A bank, for instance, that consistently is able to lend at rates higher than justified by default risk should be able to harvest value from future loans as well. Second, it is difficult to apply when a financial service firm enters multiple businesses. A firm like Citigroup that operates in multiple businesses would prove to be difficult to value because the assets in each business—insurance, commercial banking, investment banking, portfolio management—would need to be valued separately, with different income streams and different discount rates.

RELATIVE VALUATION

The chapters on relative valuation examined a series of multiples that are used to value firms, ranging from earnings multiples to book value multiples to revenue multiples. This section considers how relative valuation can be used for financial service firms.

Choices in Multiples

Firm value multiples such as value-to-EBITDA or value-to-EBIT cannot be easily adapted to value financial service firms, because neither value nor operating income can be easily estimated for banks or insurance companies. In keeping with our emphasis on equity valuation for financial service firms, the multiples that we will work with to analyze financial service firms are equity multiples. The three most widely used equity multiples are price-earnings ratios, price-to-book value ratios, and price-to-sales ratios. Since sales or revenues are not really measurable for financial service firms, price-to-sales ratios cannot be estimated or used for these firms. This section will look at the use of price-earnings and price-to-book value ratios for valuing financial service firms.

Price-Earnings Ratios

The price-earnings ratio for a bank or insurance companies is measured much the same as it is for any other firm.

$$\text{PE ratio} = \text{Price per share/Earnings per share}$$

Chapter 18 noted that the price earnings ratio is a function of three variables—the expected growth rate in earnings, the payout ratio, and the cost of equity. As with other firms, the price-earnings ratio should be higher for financial service firms with higher expected growth rates in earnings, higher payout ratios, and lower costs of equity.

An issue that is specific to financial service firms is the use of provisions for expected expenses. For instance, banks routinely set aside provisions for bad loans. These provisions reduce the reported income and affect the reported price-earnings ratio. Consequently, banks that are more conservative about categorizing bad loans will report lower earnings and have higher price-earnings ratios, whereas banks that are less conservative will report higher earnings and lower price-earnings ratios.

Another consideration in the use of earnings multiples is the diversification of financial service firms into multiple businesses. The multiple that an investor is willing to pay for a dollar in earnings from commercial lending should be very different than the multiple that the same investor is will to pay for a dollar in earnings from trading. When a firm is in multiple businesses with different risk, growth, and return characteristics, it is very difficult to find truly comparable firms and to compare the multiples of earnings paid across firms. In such a case, it makes far more sense to break the firm's earnings down by business and assess the value of each business separately.

ILLUSTRATION 21.5: Comparing PE Ratios: Insurance Companies

The following table compares the current price-earnings ratios of life insurance companies in January 2001.

Company Name	PE Ratio	Expected Growth Rate	Stock Prices: Standard Deviation
AEGON Ins. Group	32.96	11.50%	36.61%
AFLAC Inc.	34.53	19.00%	43.23%
AmerUs Group Co	12.76	10.00%	33.46%
Delphi Fin'l. 'A'	10.50	10.50%	39.72%
Great West Lifeco Inc.	22.00	15.00%	35.09%
Jefferson-Pilot Corp.	13.93	9.00%	30.49%
Lincoln Nat'l. Corp.	13.01	9.50%	38.07%
MONY Group Inc.	6.22	9.50%	72.16%
Nationwide Financial	2.65	14.53%	42.84%
Penn Treaty American	6.47	15.00%	43.18%
Protective Life	12.36	12.00%	50.64%
Reinsurance Group	29.80	13.30%	50.79%
Torchmark Corp.	13.53	9.50%	37.64%
UICI	9.40	18.00%	63.38%
UNUMProvident Corp.	9.51	6.00%	56.42%

The PE ratios vary widely and range from 2.65 for Nationwide Financial to 34.53 for AFLAC. We also report the consensus estimates by analysts of the growth rate in earnings per share over the next five years and the standard deviation in stock prices over the previous five years. Some of the variation in PE ratios can be explained by differences in the expected growth rate—higher-growth firms tend to have higher PE ratios—and some of it is due to differences in risk—more risky firms have lower PE ratios. Regressing PE ratios against the expected growth rate and the standard deviation yields the following:

PE ratio = 15.72 + 91.67 Expected growth rate − 25.72 Standard deviation $R^2 = 19\%$
    [1.21]   [1.28]   [1.17]

While the regression has limited explanatory power and the coefficients are of marginal statistical significance, it confirms the intuition that higher growth and lower risk firms have higher PE ratios than other firms. Figure 21.5 uses this regression to estimate predicted PE ratios for the companies in the table and reports on whether the firms are under- or overvalued. Based on this regression, Reinsurance Group looks significantly overvalued while Penn Treaty and Nationwide Financial look significantly undervalued.

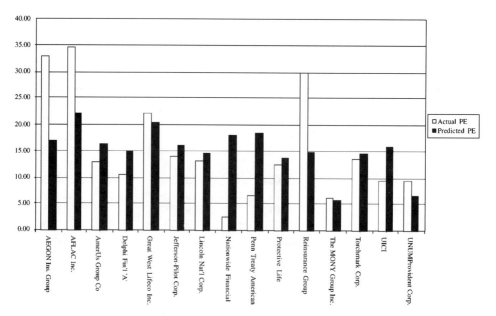

FIGURE 21.5   Actual versus Predicted Price-Earnings Ratios

ILLUSTRATION 21.6:   Earnings Multiples for Business: Citigroup

Citigroup is in multiple businesses—commercial banking, investment banking, and asset management. The following table summarizes the income that Citigroup earned from each business in 2000 and estimates the equity value:

Business	Net Income	PE Ratio for Business	Estimated Value of Equity
Investment banking	$5,800	21.44	$124,352
Commercial banking	$5,200	15.61	$81,172
Asset management	$500	28.70	$14,350
Entire firm	$11,500		$219,874

The value of each business is estimated using the average price-earnings multiple of other firms that operate only in that business. At a market value of $256 billion, Citicorp looks overvalued.

    This approach can be generalized to allow the multiples of earnings used in each business to reflect the differences between that business and other firms that operate only in that business. For instance, if Citigroup's asset management business has higher growth and lower risk than other asset management firms, you would use a higher earnings multiple for the income from the business.

Price-to-Book Value Ratios

The price-to-book value ratio for a financial service firm is the ratio of the price per share to the book value of equity per share.

Price-to-book ratio = Price per share/Book value of equity per share

This definition is identical to the one presented in Chapter 19, and it is determined by the variables specified in that chapter—the expected growth rate in earnings per share, the dividend payout ratio, the cost of equity, and the return on equity. Other thing remaining equal, higher growth rates in earnings, higher payout ratios, lower costs of equity, and higher returns on equity should all result in higher price-to-book ratios. Of these four variables, the return on equity has the biggest impact on the price-to-book ratio, leading us to identify it as the companion variable for the ratio.

If anything, the strength of the relationship between price-to-book ratios and returns on equity should be stronger for financial service firms than for other firms, because the book value of equity is much more likely to track the market value of equity invested in existing assets. Similarly, the return on equity is less likely to be affected by accounting decisions. The strength of the relationship between price-to-book ratios and returns on equity can be seen when we plot the two on a scatter plot for commercial banks in the United States in Figure 21.6.

Banks such as North Fork Bancorp (NFB) and WestAmerica Bancorp (WABC) that have high price-to-book value ratios tend to have high returns on equity. Banks such as City Holding (CHCO) and Eldorado Bancshares (ELBI) that have low re-

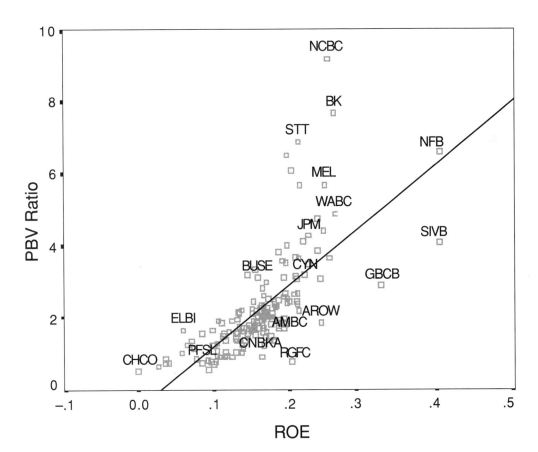

FIGURE 21.6 Price-to-Book Ratios and Returns on Equity: Banks

turns on equity tend to have low price-to-book value ratios. The correlation between price-to-book ratios and returns on equity is .70.

While emphasizing the relationship between price-to-book ratios and returns on equity, we should not ignore the other fundamentals. For instance, banks vary in terms of risk, and we would expect for any given return on equity that riskier banks should have lower price-to-book value ratios. Similarly, banks with much greater potential for growth should have much higher price-to-book ratios, for any given level of the other fundamentals.

ILLUSTRATION 21.7:   Price-to-Book Value Ratios: Investment Banks and Brokerage Houses

The following table reports the price-to-book ratios and returns on equity for security brokerage houses and investment banks:

Company Name	Ticker Symbol	Market Cap	PBV Ratio	ROE
Advest Group	ADV	$283.00	2.09	15.25%
Annaly Mortgage Mgmt.	NLY	$141.40	1.37	16.26%
Bear Stearns	BSC	$6,056.50	1.46	20.92%
Brantley Capital	BBDC	$31.40	0.60	7.44%
Dain Rauscher	DRC	$1,237.60	3.17	23.27%
DLJdirect.com	DIR	$86.30	0.37	0.35%
Edwards (A.G.)	AGE	$3,843.20	2.24	21.98%
Fahnestock Viner 'A'	FVH	$272.10	1.45	22.15%
Firebrand Fin'l. Group Inc.	FFGI	$3.40	0.13	9.26%
Goldman Sachs	GS	$52,108.60	5.14	32.04%
H. D. Vest Inc.	HDVS	$29.80	2.76	27.78%
Jefferies Group	JEF	$683.50	1.72	14.02%
Kirlin Hldg. Corp.	KILN	$12.10	0.68	−6.21%
Legg Mason	LM	$3,287.30	4.37	21.36%
Lehman Bros. Holdings	LEH	$18,771.30	3.36	31.72%
M. H. Meyerson & Co. Inc.	MHMY	$19.30	0.93	14.98%
Merrill Lynch & Co.	MER	$58,235.50	4.71	35.81%
Morgan Keegan Inc.	MOR	$762.30	2.95	18.29%
Morgan Stanley Dean Witter	MWD	$97,986.70	6.15	34.22%
Olympic Cascade Fin'l.	OLY	$8.40	1.05	20.00%
Paulson Capital	PLCC	$16.40	0.65	47.24%
Raymond James Fin'l.	RJF	$1,811.00	3.24	24.33%
Schwab (Charles)	SCH	$37,823.80	16.63	34.21%
Southwest Securities Group	SWS	$442.90	1.52	34.32%
Stifel Finanical Corp.	SF	$79.10	1.34	16.75%

While the relationship between price-to-book ratios and returns on equity is weaker for this sample than it is for commercial banks, higher price-to-book value ratios tend to go with higher returns on equity. Regressing the price-to-book ratios against the return on equity yields the following:

$$\text{Price-to-book ratio} = 0.1338 + 12.41(\text{Return on equity}) \qquad R^2 = 20\%$$
$$[0.11] \quad [2.40]$$

Using this regression yields predicted price-to-book ratios for any firm in the same business. For instance, the predicted price-to-book ratio for Merrill Lynch would be:

$$\text{Predicted price-to-book ratio for Merrill Lynch} = 0.1338 + 12.41(.3581) = 4.58$$

With an actual price-to-book ratio of 4.71, Merrill is close to fairly priced.

ISSUES IN VALUING FINANCIAL SERVICE FIRMS

Up until this point in this chapter, we have emphasized the similarities between financial service firms and other firms. In this section, we will consider some of the special issues that arise in the context of valuing financial service firms and how best to incorporate them into the value.

Provisions for Losses

Banks and insurance companies often set aside provisions to meet future losses. These provisions reduce net income in the current period but are used to meet expected losses in future periods. Thus, a provision for bad debts reduces a bank's income in the current period but allows the bank to cover bad debts when they do occur. In general, while the actual bad debts that occur in any year will not match the provision set aside for that year exactly, the cumulative provisions over time should be equal to the cumulated bad debts over the same period. If this is the case, the provisions smooth out earnings over time, making them lower than the true earnings in years when the economy does well—and default rates are lower—and higher than true earnings in years when the economy does badly and default rates are higher.

There can be a problem, however, when firms consistently set aside more (or less) in provisions than they expect to lose. If they set aside too much, the net income will be understated which will also lower the return on equity and the retention ratio. If expected growth is the product of these two, the value of equity in the firm will be reduced. If too little is set aside, the net income will be overstated (at least for the moment) and you could overestimate the value of equity. The quickest fix for this problem is to look at the provisions set aside over time and the actual losses over time. If the numbers do not match, the provision should be reestimated based on the actual loss ratio, and the net income should be restated. To illustrate, if a bank sets aside 8 percent of its loans into a reserve for bad debts, when its actual bad debt ratio is only 4 percent, the net income should be recomputed using a 4 percent provision for bad debts. This will increase the net income, the return on equity, and the equity value of the bank. The reverse will be true if too little is set aside.

Regulatory Risk and Value

As noted earlier in this chapter, financial service firms are much more likely to be regulated. This regulation can affect the perceived risk of investing in these firms as well as the expected cash flows. Consequently, they should affect the value of these firms. When valuing financial service firms using discounted cash flow models, the regulatory effects can be built explicitly into both the discount rate as well as the expected future cash flows.

- ■ To incorporate regulatory risk into the discount rate, we first need to decide whether such risk is diversifiable in a portfolio. For the most part, we would argue that regulatory risk is diversifiable and should not affect the discount rate. In exceptional cases, where financial service firms dominate a market and the regulatory risk is large, the cost of equity will include a premium for this risk.

■ It is the cash flows, in our view, where regulatory concerns have the biggest impact. The expected growth rate, which was derived from the retention ratio and the return on equity, will be affected by regulatory restrictions on where financial service firms can invest. If the restrictions on investments are severe, for instance, financial service firms may be destined to earn low returns on equity for the foreseeable future, which will negatively affect their values.

If we use relative valuation models and are comparing financial service firms that operate under different regulatory regimes, because they either are from different countries (European banks versus U.S. banks) or are in different businesses (investment banks versus commercial banks), the multiples will vary across firms because of the regulatory differences.

Financing Mix and Value

When analyzing manufacturing firms, we looked at the effect of changing the mix of debt and equity used by the firm for funding on value. With financial service firms, we generally do not examine the financing mix question for two reasons. One is the aforementioned difficulty of defining and measuring debt. The other is that financial service firms tend to use as much debt as they can afford to carry, making it very unlikely that they will be significantly underlevered.

There is the danger, though, that arises from regulatory considerations driving the choice of financial mix. Regulatory requirements are often based on book values of debt and equity and may not always be rational. For instance, if the regulatory capital ratios are set too low for risky loan portfolios, banks that meet regulatory requirements may be borrowing too much. Their values should therefore also be lower.

Subsidies and Constraints

In many markets, banks and insurance companies operate under systems where they derive special benefits because of subsidies and exclusive rights that they are granted, while at the same time being forced to make investments at below-market rates in what are viewed as socially desirable investments. Both subsidies and social investments affect value and can be incorporated into cash flows.

The best approach to bringing in the effect of subsidies into the value is to project the expected positive excess returns or cash flows that will be generated as a consequence of the subsidy or exclusive right and to separate this excess return from the rest of the valuation. The same process can be repeated with social investments, though the effect will usually be negative. The present value of the negative excess returns can be computed and netted from the value of the firm.

There are two advantages in separating the subsidy benefit value and the social investment cost from the rest of the valuation. The first is that it allows us to make specific assumptions that apply only to these items. For instance, the subsidy that the government grants may be expected to last only 10 years and be guaranteed, in which case, we would compute the value of the subsidy using 10 years of expected cash flows and the risk-free rate as the discount rate. The second is that it allows firms to determine whether the trade-off is a favorable one for value, since the social investment requirements are often tied to the subsidy grants. In other words, a bank that is provided a subsidy by the government in return for providing loans at below-market interest rates to small businesses may find that the loss in value associated with the latter exceeds the subsidy benefits.

ILLUSTRATION 21.8: Valuing Subsidies and Social Investment

Consider the valuation of the State Bank of India in Illustration 21.2. Over the past three decades, the State Bank has been given both special privileges (exclusive entry in some markets) and unique responsibilities (such as lending to high-risk businesses at below-market rates). The value of the bank is enhanced by the first and reduced by the latter, and the effect on value of each can be computed. Consider, for instance, the effect of exclusivity in some businesses. By itself, this will allow the bank to earn excess returns in these businesses and the value added will be the present value of these excess returns. On the other side of the coin, the requirement that the bank lend at below-market rates results in a loss in value that come computed as the present value of the negative excess returns in these markets.

Assume, for example, that State Bank is given the exclusive right to lend money to other Indian government enterprises and that the bank uses the exclusivity to charge 1% more than the market interest rate that would be charged these enterprises in a competitive environment. If the bank has 1 billion rupees in loans outstanding to these enterprises, and the fair market interest rate for these enterprises is 10%, the present value of the excess returns in perpetuity can be computed as follows:

Present value of above-market-rate loans = .01 × 1,000/.10 = 100 million rupees

If the exclusivity is expected not to be perpetual, but to disappear after 10 years, the present value of the excess returns will be lower and can be computed as the present value of an annuity over 10 years.

A similar value can be attached to the requirement that the bank lend at below-market rates. For instance, if State Bank is required to loan 800 million rupees to small farmers at 8%, when a fair market interest rate for such loans would be 14%, the effect on value of this requirement can be computed as follows:

Value effect of below-market loans = 800 million × (.08 − .14)/.14 = 343 million rupees

While this value is computed on the assumption that the below-market rates will continue in perpetuity, the analysis can also be modified to allow for shorter periods.

CONCLUSION

The basic principles of valuation apply just as much for financial service firms as they do for other firms. There are, however, a few aspects relating to financial service firms that can affect how they are valued. The first is that debt for a financial service firm is difficult to define and measure, making it difficult to estimate firm value or costs of capital. Consequently, it is far easier to value the equity directly in

---

DEPOSIT INSURANCE AND BANK VALUE

In most countries, the state provides insurance to bank depositors by guaranteeing the deposits up to a specified limit. What effect will such deposit insurance have on value? If banks are charged a fair price for the insurance, it should have no effect on value. In practice, though, deposit insurance can skew value in two ways:

1. In many countries, including the United States, the deposit insurance rate does not vary across banks. Thus, banks with safe loan portfolios are charged the same rate as banks with risky loan portfolios. If the rate set is based on average default, this will result in the former being overcharged and the latter being undercharged. It will also create an incentive system for banks to take on more and more risk. In fact, you can consider deposit insurance to be a put option provided to the bank—the bank can put its deposit liabilities to the insurance agency if the value of its loan portfolio drops below the value of the liabilities. If the put price does not vary with the volatility in the value of the loan portfolio, banks with riskier portfolios will become more valuable (the value of the put will exceed the price paid), and banks with safer portfolios will become less valuable.

2. Even if deposit insurance rates vary across banks, the price of the insurance may not fully reflect the risk of the bank's assets for two reasons. The first is that the risk can change from period to period and the pricing may not keep up. The second is that the insurance may be subsidized by taxpayers, in which case all banks will become more valuable as a result of the insurance.

---

a financial service firm by discounting cash flows to equity at the cost of equity. The second is that capital expenditures and working capital, which are required inputs to estimating cash flows, are often not easily estimated at financial service firms. In fact, much of the reinvestment that occurs at these firms is categorized under operating expenses. To estimate cash flows to equity, therefore, we have to either use dividends (and assume that what is not paid out as dividend is the reinvestment) or modify our definition of reinvestment.

Even if we choose to use multiples, we run into many of the same issues. The difficulties associated with defining debt make equity multiples such as price-earnings or price-to-book value ratios better suited for comparing financial service firms than value multiples. In making these comparisons, we have to control for differences in fundamentals—risk, growth, cash flows, loan quality—that affect value.

Finally, regulatory considerations and constraints overlay financial firm valuations. In some cases, regulatory restrictions on competition allow financial service firms to earn excess returns and increase value. In other cases, the same regulatory authorities may restrict the potential excess returns that a firm may be able to make by preventing the firm from entering a business.

QUESTIONS AND SHORT PROBLEMS

1. You have been asked to assess the value per share of Secure Savings, a mature savings and loan company. The company had earnings per share in the just-completed financial year of $4 per share and paid dividends of $2.40 per share. The book value of equity at the beginning of the year was $40 per share. The beta for the stock is 0.90, the risk-free rate is 6%, and the market risk premium is 4%.
   a. Assuming that the firm will continue to earn its current return on equity in perpetuity and maintain its current dividend payout ratio, estimate the value per share.
   b. If the stock is trading at $40 a share, estimate the implied growth rate.
2. You are now valuing the Southwest Bank, a small bank that is growing rapidly. The bank reported earnings per share of $2 in the just-completed financial year and paid out dividends per share of $0.20. The book value of equity at the beginning of the year was $14. The beta for the stock is 1.10, the risk-free rate is 6% and the risk premium is 4%.
   a. Assuming that it will maintain its current return on equity and payout ratio for the next five years, estimate the expected growth rate in earnings per share.
   b. Assuming that the firm will start growing at a constant rate of 5% a year beyond that point in time, estimate the value per share today. (You can assume that the return on equity will drop to 12% in stable growth and that the beta will become 1.)
3. You have been asked to analyze LongLife Insurance company, a firm in stable growth, with earnings expected to grow 4% in the long term. The firm is trading at a multiple of 1.4 times book value and has a cost of equity of 11%.
   a. If the market is pricing the stock correctly, estimate the return on equity that LongLife is expected to earn in perpetuity.
   b. If the regulatory authorities constrain LongLife to earn a return on equity equal to its cost of equity, what would you expect the price-to-book ratio to be?
4. Now assume that you are comparing the price-to-book ratios of the 13 largest banks in the United States in 2000. The following table summarizes the price-to-book ratios and the returns on equity earned by these firms:

Company Name	PBV	ROE
Wachovia Corp.	2.05	18.47%
PNC Financial Serv.	2.54	21.56%
SunTrust Banks	1.91	15.35%
State Street Corp.	6.63	19.52%
Mellon Financial Corp.	4.59	23.95%
Morgan (J.P.) & Co.	1.74	19.39%
First Union Corp.	1.52	19.66%
FleetBoston Fin'l.	2.25	20.15%
Bank of New York	7.01	25.36%
Chase Manhattan Corp.	2.60	24.60%
Wells Fargo	3.07	17.72%
Bank of America	1.69	19.31%
Bank of Montreal	1.23	18.08%

    a. If you were valuing SunTrust Banks relative to these firms, would you expect it to have a higher or lower price-to-book ratio than the average for the group? Explain why.

    b. If you regress price-to-book ratios against returns on equity, what would your predicted price-to-book ratios be for each of these companies?

5. Signet Bank has asked you to estimate the value of its loan portfolio. The bank has $1 billion in loans outstanding, with an average maturity of six years, and expected interest income of $75 million a year. You have been able to get a synthetic rating of A for the entire loan portfolio, and the current market interest rate on A-rated bonds is 6.5%.

    a. Estimate the value of the loan portfolio.

    b. If Signet Bank has $800 million in debt outstanding, estimate the value of the equity in the bank based on the loans it has in place.

6. Loomis Capital is a boutique investment bank that reported a return on equity of 20% on its book equity of $100 million in the just-completed financial year. The beta for the bank is 1.20, the risk-free rate is 5.2%, and the risk premium is 4%. You assume that the current return on equity and cost of equity will continue unchanged for the next 10 years and that there will be no excess returns after year 10. The payout ratio for the firm is 30%.

    a. Estimate the dollar excess equity returns every year for the next 10 years.

    b. Estimate the value of equity today, using the excess return approach.

    c. How would your answer to (b) change if you were told that the return on equity will drop to 15% after year 10 and remain at that level forever?

CHAPTER 22

Valuing Firms with Negative Earnings

In most of the valuations thus far in this book, we have looked at firms that have positive earnings. In this chapter, we consider a subset of firms with negative earnings or abnormally low earnings that we categorize as troubled firms. We begin by looking at why firms have negative earnings in the first place and look at the ways that valuation has to be adapted to reflect these underlying reasons.

For firms with temporary problems—a strike or a product recall, for instance—we argue that the adjustment process is a simple one, where we back out of current earnings the portion of the expenses associated with the temporary problems. For cyclical firms, where the negative earnings are due to a deterioration of the overall economy, and for commodity firms, where cyclical movements in commodity prices can affect earnings, we argue for the use of normalized earnings in valuation. For firms with long-term strategic problems or operating problems (outdated plants, a poorly trained workforce, or poor investments in the past) the process of valuation becomes more complicated because we have to make assumptions about whether the firm will be able to outlive its problems and restructure itself. Finally, we look at firms that have negative earnings because they have borrowed too much, and consider how best to deal with the potential for default.

NEGATIVE EARNINGS: CONSEQUENCES AND CAUSES

A firm with negative earnings or abnormally low earnings is more difficult to value than a firm with positive earnings. This section looks at why such firms create problems for analysts in the first place, and then follows up by examining the reasons for negative earnings.

Consequences of Negative or Abnormally Low Earnings

Firms that are losing money currently create several problems for the analysts who are attempting to value them. While none of these problems are conceptual, they are significant from a measurement standpoint:

1. *Earnings growth rates cannot be estimated or used in valuation.* The first and most obvious problem is that we can no longer estimate an expected growth rate to earnings and apply it to current earnings to estimate future earnings. When current earnings are negative, applying a growth rate will just make it more negative. In fact, even estimating an earnings growth rate becomes problematic, whether one uses historical growth, analyst projections, or fundamentals.

■ Estimating historical growth when current earnings are negative is difficult, and the numbers, even if estimated, often are meaningless. To see why, assume that a firm's operating earnings have gone from –$200 million last year to –$100 million in the current year. The traditional historical growth equation yields the following:

$$\text{Earnings growth rate} = \text{Earnings}_{\text{today}}/\text{Earnings}_{\text{last year}} - 1$$
$$= (-100/-200) - 1 = -50\%$$

This clearly does not make sense since this firm has improved its earnings over the period. In fact, we looked at this problem in Chapter 11.

■ An alternative approach to estimating earnings growth is to use analyst estimates of projected growth in earnings, especially over the next five years. The consensus estimate of this growth rate across all analysts following a stock is generally available as public information for many U.S. companies and is often used as the expected growth rate in valuation. For firms with negative earnings in the current period, this estimate of a growth rate will not be available or meaningful.

■ A third approach to estimating earnings growth is to use fundamentals. This approach is also difficult to apply for firms that have negative earnings, since the two fundamental inputs—the return made on investments (return on equity or capital) and the reinvestment rate (or retention ratio)—are usually computed using current earnings. When current earnings are negative, both these inputs become meaningless from the perspective of estimating expected growth.

2. *Tax computation becomes more complicated.* The standard approach to estimating taxes is to apply the marginal tax rate on the pretax operating income to arrive at the after-tax operating income:

After-tax operating income = Pretax operating income(1 – Tax rate)

This computation assumes that earnings create tax liabilities in the current period. While this is generally true, firms that are losing money can carry these losses forward in time and apply them to earnings in future periods. Thus analysts valuing firms with negative earnings have to keep track of the net operating losses of these firms and remember to use them to shield income in future periods from taxes.

3. *The going concern assumption may not apply.* The final problem associated with valuing companies that have negative earnings is the very real possibility that these firms will go bankrupt if earnings stay negative, and that the assumption of infinite lives that underlies the estimation of terminal value may not apply in these cases.

The problems are less visible but exist nevertheless for firms that have abnormally low earnings; that is, the current earnings of the firm are much lower than what the firm has earned historically. Though you can compute historical growth and fundamental growth for these firms, they are likely to be meaningless because current earnings are depressed. The historical growth rate in earnings will be negative, and the fundamentals will yield very low estimates for expected growth.

Causes of Negative Earnings

There are several reasons why firms have negative or abnormally low earnings, some of which can be viewed as temporary, some of which are long-term, and some of which relate to where a firm stands in the life cycle.

Temporary Problems　For some firms, negative earnings are the result of temporary problems, sometimes affecting the firm alone, sometimes affecting an entire industry, and sometimes the result of a downturn in the economy.

■ Firm-specific reasons for negative earnings can include a strike by the firm's employees, an expensive product recall, or a large judgment against the firm in a lawsuit. While these will undoubtedly lower earnings, the effect is likely to be one-time and not affect future earnings.

■ Sectorwide reasons for negative earnings can include a downturn in the price of a commodity for a firm that produces that commodity. It is common, for instance, for paper and pulp firms to go through cycles of high paper prices (and profits) followed by low paper prices (and losses). In some cases, the negative earnings may arise from the interruption of a common source of supply for a necessary raw material or a spike in its price. For instance, an increase in oil prices will negatively affect the profits of all airlines.

■ For cyclical firms, a recession will affect revenues and earnings. It is not surprising, therefore, that automobile companies report low or negative earnings during bad economic times.

The common thread for all of these firms is that we expect earnings to recover sooner rather than later as the problem dissipates. Thus we would expect a cyclical firm's earnings to bounce back once the economy revives and an airline's profits to improve once oil prices level off.

Long-Term Problems　Negative earnings are sometimes reflections of deeper and much more long-term problems in a firm. Some of these are the results of poor strategic choices made in the past, some reflect operational inefficiencies, and some are purely financial, the result of a firm borrowing much more than it can support with its existing cash flows.

■ A firm's earnings may be negative because its strategic choices in terms of product mix or marketing policy might have backfired. For such a firm, financial health is generally not around the corner and will require a substantial makeover and, often, new management.

■ A firm can have negative earnings because of inefficient operations. For instance, the firm's plant and equipment may be obsolete or its workforce may be poorly trained. The negative earnings may also reflect poor decisions made in the past by management and the continuing costs associated with such decisions. For instance, firms that have gone on acquisition binges and overpaid on a series of acquisitions may face several years of poor earnings as a consequence.

■ In some cases, a firm that is in good health operationally can end up with negative equity earnings because it has chosen to use too much debt to fund its operations. For instance, many of the firms that were involved in leveraged buyouts in the 1980s reported losses in the first few years after the buyouts.

Life Cycle In some cases, a firm's negative earnings may not be the result of problems in the way it is run but because of where the firm is in its life cycle. Here are three examples:

1. Firms in businesses that require huge infrastructure investments up front will often lose money until these investments are in place. Once they are made and the firm is able to generate revenues, the earnings will turn positive. You can argue that this was the case with the phone companies in the early part of the twentieth century in the United States, the cable companies in the 1980s, and the cellular companies in the early 1990s.
2. Small biotechnology or pharmaceutical firms often spend millions of dollars on research, come up with promising products that they patent, but then have to wait years for Food and Drug Administration (FDA) approval to sell the drugs. In the meantime, they continue to have research and development expenses and report large losses.

MAKING THE CALL: SHORT-TERM VERSUS LONG-TERM PROBLEMS

In practice, it is often difficult to disentangle temporary or short-term problems from long-term ones. There is no simple rule of thumb that works, and accounting statements are not always forthcoming about the nature of the problems. Most firms, when reporting negative earnings, will claim that their problems are transitory and that recovery is around the corner. Analysts have to make their own judgments on whether this is the case, and they should consider the following:

- *The credibility of the management making the claim.* The managers of some firms are much more forthcoming than others in revealing problems and admitting their mistakes, and their claims should be given much more credence.
- *The amount and timeliness of information provided with the claim.* A firm that provides detailed information backing up its claim that the problem is temporary is more credible than a firm that does not provide such information. In addition, a firm that reveals its problems promptly is more believable than one that delays reporting problems until its hand is forced.
- *Confirming reports from other companies in industry.* A cyclical company that claims that its earnings are down because of an economic slowdown will be more believable if other companies in the sector also report similar slowdowns.
- *The persistence of the problem.* If poor earnings persist over multiple periods, it is much more likely that the firm is facing a long-term problem. Thus, a series of restructuring charges should be viewed with suspicion.

3. The third group includes young start-up companies. Often these companies have interesting and potentially profitable ideas, but they lose money until they convert these ideas into commercial products. Until the late 1990s, these companies seldom went public but relied instead on venture capital financing for their equity needs. One of the striking features of the boom in new technology companies from 1997 to 2000 was the number of such firms that chose to bypass the venture capital route and go to the markets directly.

VALUING NEGATIVE EARNINGS FIRMS

The way we deal with negative earnings will depend on why the firm has negative earnings in the first place. This section explores the alternatives that are available for working with negative earnings firms.

Firms with Temporary Problems

When earnings are negative because of temporary or short-term problems, the expectation is that earnings will recover in the near term. Thus, the solutions we devise will be fairly simple ones, which for the most part will replace the current earnings (which are negative) with normalized earnings (which will be positive). How we normalize earnings will vary depending on the nature of the problem.

Firm-Specific Problems   A firm can have a bad year in terms of earnings, but the problems may be isolated to that firm, and be short-term in nature. If the loss can be attributed to a specific event—a strike or a lawsuit judgment, for instance—and the accounting statements report the cost associated with the event, the solution is fairly simple. You should estimate the earnings prior to these costs and use these earnings not only for estimating cash flows but also for computing fundamentals such as return on capital. In making these estimates, though, note that you should remove not just the expense but all of the tax benefits created by the expense as well, assuming that it is tax deductible.

If the cause of the loss is more diffuse or if the cost of the event causing the loss is not separated out from other expenses, you face a tougher task. First, you have to ensure that the loss is in fact temporary and not the symptom of long-term problems at the firm. Next, you have to estimate the normal earnings of the firm. The simplest and most direct way of doing this is to compare each expense item for the firm for the current year with the same item in previous years, scaled to revenues. Any item that looks abnormally high, relative to prior years, should be normalized (by using an average from previous years). Alternatively, you could apply the operating margin that the firm earned in prior years to the current year's revenues and estimate an operating income to use in the valuation.

In general, you will have to consider making adjustments to the earnings of firms after years in which they have made major acquisitions, since the accounting statements in these years will be skewed by large items that are generally nonrecurring and related to the acquisition.

ILLUSTRATION 22.1:   Normalizing Earnings for a Firm after a Poor Year: Daimler-Benz in 1995

In 1995, Daimler-Benz reported an operating loss of DM 2,016 million and a net loss of DM 5,674 million. Much of the loss could be attributed to firm-specific problems including a large write-off of a failed investment in Fokker Aerospace, an aircraft manufacturer. To estimate normalized earnings at Daimler-Benz, we eliminated all charges related to these items and estimated a pretax operating income of DM 5,693 million. To complete the valuation, we made the following additional assumptions:

- Revenues at Daimler had been growing 3% to 5% a year prior to 1995, and we anticipated that the long-term growth rate would be 5% in both revenues and operating income.
- The firm had a book value of capital invested of DM 43,558 million at the beginning of 1995, and was expected to maintain its return on capital (based on the adjusted operating income of DM 5,693 million).
- The firm's tax rate is 44%.[1]

To value Daimler, we first estimated the return on capital at the firm, using the adjusted operating income:

$$\text{Return on capital} = \text{EBIT}(1 - t)/\text{Book value of capital invested}$$
$$= 5,693(1 - 44)/43,558 = 7.32\%$$

Based on the expected growth rate of 5%, this would require a reinvestment rate of 68.31%:

$$\text{Reinvestment rate} = g/\text{ROC} = 5\%/7.32\% = 68.31\%$$

With these assumptions, we were able to compute Daimler's expected free cash flows in 1996:

EBIT$(1 - t) = 5,693(1.05)(1 - .44)$	DM 3,347 million
$-$ Reinvestment $= 5,693(1.05)(.6831)$	DM 2,287 million
Free cash flow to firm	DM 1,061 million

To compute the cost of capital, we used a bottom-up beta of 0.95, estimated using automobile firms listed globally. The long-term bond rate (on a German government bond denominated in DM) was 6%, and Daimler-Benz could borrow long-term at 6.1%. We assumed a market risk premium of 4%. The market value of equity was DM 50,000 million, and there was DM 26,281 million in debt outstanding at the end of 1995.

$$\text{Cost of equity} = 6\% + 0.95(4\%) = 9.8\%$$
$$\text{Cost of debt} = 6.1\%(1 - .44) = 3.42\%$$
$$\text{Debt ratio} = 26,281/(50,000 + 26,281) = 34.45\%$$
$$\text{Cost of capital} = 9.8\%(.6555) + 3.42\%(.3445) = 7.60\%$$

Note that all of the costs are computed in DM terms, to be consistent with our cash flows. The firm value can now be computed, if we assume that earnings and cash flows will grow at 5% a year in perpetuity:

---

[1]Germany has a particularly complicated tax structure since it has different tax rates for retained earnings and dividends, which makes the tax rate a function of a firm's dividend policy.

> Value of operating assets at end of 1995 = Expected FCFF in 1996
> /(Cost of capital − Expected growth rate)
> = 1,061/(.076 − .05) = DM 40,787 million

Adding to this the value of the cash and marketable securities (DM 13,500 million) held by Daimler at the time of this valuation, and netting out the market value of debt ($26,281) yields an estimated value of DM 28,006 million for equity, significantly lower than the market value of DM 50,000 million.

> Value of equity = Value of operating assets + Cash and marketable securities − Debt
> = 40,787 + 13,500 − 26,281 = DM 28,006 million

As in all firm valuations, there is an element of circular reasoning involved in this valuation.[2]

Sectorwide or Market-Driven Problems The earnings of cyclical firms are, by definition, volatile and depend on the state of the economy. In economic booms the earnings of these firms are likely to increase, while in recessions the earnings will be depressed. The same can be said of commodity firms that go through price cycles, where periods of high prices for the commodity are often followed by low prices. In both cases, you can get misleading estimates of value if you use the current year's earnings as your base year earnings.

Valuing Cyclical Firms Cyclical firm valuations can be significantly affected by the level of base year earnings. There are two potential solutions: One is to adjust the expected growth rate in the near periods to reflect cyclical changes, and the other is to value the firm based on normalized rather than current earnings.

Adjust Expected Growth Cyclical firms often report low earnings at the bottom of an economic cycle, but the earnings recover quickly when the economy recovers. One solution, if earnings are not negative, is to adjust the expected growth rate in earnings, especially in the near term, to reflect expected changes in the economic cycle. This would imply using a higher growth rate in the next year or two, if both the firm's earnings and the economy are depressed currently but are expected to recover quickly. The strategy would be reversed if the current earnings are inflated (because of an economic boom), and if the economy is expected to slow down. The disadvantage of this approach is that it ties the accuracy of the estimate of value for a cyclical firm to the precision of the macroeconomic predictions of the analyst doing the valuation. The criticism, though, may not be avoidable since it is difficult to value a cyclical firm without making assumptions about future economic growth. The actual growth rate in earnings in turning-point years (years when the economy goes into or comes out of a recession) can be estimated by looking at the experience of this firm (or similar firms) in prior recessions.

---

[2]The circular reasoning comes in because we use the current market value of equity and debt to compute the cost of capital. We then use the cost of capital to estimate the value of equity and debt. If this is unacceptable, the process can be iterated, with the cost of capital being recomputed using the estimated values of debt and equity, and continued until there is convergence.

ILLUSTRATION 22.2:   Valuing a Cyclical Firm during a Recession—Adjusting the Growth Rate: Chesapeake Corporation in Early 1993

Chesapeake Corporation, a cyclical firm in the paper products industry that makes recycled commercial and industrial tissue, had earnings per share in 1992 of $0.63, down from $2.51 in 1988. If the 1992 earnings per share had been used as the base year's earnings, Chesapeake Corporation would be valued based on the following inputs:

Current earnings per share = $0.63
Current depreciation per share = $2.93
Current capital spending per share = $3.63
Debt ratio for financing capital spending = 45%

Chesapeake had a beta of 1.00 and no significant working capital requirements. The Treasury bond rate was 8.5% at the time of this analysis, and the risk premium of 4% for stocks over bonds is used.

$$\text{Cost of equity} = 8.5\% + 1(4\%) = 12.5\%$$

If we valued Chesapeake based on current earnings and assume a long-term growth rate of 6%, we would have estimated a value per share of $4.

$$\text{Free cash flow to equity in 1992} = \$0.63 - (1 - 0.45)(\$3.63 - \$2.93) = \$0.245$$
$$\text{Value per share} = \$0.245 \times 1.06/(.125 - .06) = \$4.00$$

Chesapeake Corp. was trading at $20 per share in May 1993.

Assume that the economy was expected to recover slowly in 1993 and much faster in 1994. As a consequence, the growth rates in earnings projected for Chesapeake Corporation were as follows:

Year	Expected Growth Rate	Earnings per Share
1993	5%	$0.66
1994	100%	$1.32
1995	50%	$1.98
After 1996	6%	

The capital spending and depreciation were expected to grow at 6%. The free cash flow to equity could be estimated as follows:

	1993	1994	1995	1996
EPS	$0.66	$1.32	$1.98	$2.10
− (Cap ex − Depreciation)(1 − Debt ratio)	$0.41	$0.43	$0.46	$0.49
= FCFE	$0.25	$0.89	$1.53	$1.62

$$\text{Terminal price (at end of 1995)} = \frac{\$1.62}{(.125 - .06)} = \$24.88$$

$$\text{Present value per share} = \$0.25/1.125 + \$0.89/1.125^2 + (\$1.53 + \$24.88)/1.125^3 = \$19.47$$

This value was much closer to the market price of $20.

Normalize Earnings   For cyclical firms, the easiest solution to the problem of volatile earnings over time, and negative earnings in the base period, is to normalize earnings. When normalizing earnings for a firm with negative earnings, we are simply trying to answer the question: "What would this firm earn in a normal year?" Implicit in this statement is the assumption that the current year is not a normal year and earnings will recover quickly to normal levels. This approach, therefore, is most appropriate for cyclical firms in mature businesses. There are a number of ways in which earnings can be normalized:

■ *Average the firm's dollar earnings over prior periods.* The simplest way to normalize earnings is to use the average earnings over prior periods. How many periods should you go back in time? For cyclical firms, you should go back long enough to cover an entire economic cycle—between 5 and 10 years. While this approach is simple, it is best suited for firms that have not changed in scale (or size) over the period. If it is applied to a firm that has become larger or smaller (in terms of the number of units it sells or total revenues) over time, it will result in a normalized estimate that is incorrect.

■ *Average the firm's return on investment or profit margins over prior periods.* This approach is similar to the first one, but the averaging is done on scaled earnings instead of dollar earnings. The advantage of the approach is that it allows the normalized earnings estimate to reflect the current size of the firm. Thus a firm with an average return on capital of 12 percent over prior periods and a current capital invested of $1,000 million would have normalized operating income of $120 million. Using average return on equity and book value of equity yields normalized net income. A close variant of this approach is to estimate the average operating or net margin in prior periods and apply this margin to current revenues to arrive at normalized operating or net income. The advantage of working with revenues is that they are less susceptible to manipulation by accountants.

There is one final question that we have to deal with when normalizing earnings, and it relates to when earnings will be normalized. Replacing current earnings with normalized earnings essentially is equivalent to assuming that normalization will occur instantaneously (i.e., in the very first time period of the valuation). If earnings will not return to normalized levels for several periods, the value obtained by normalizing current earnings will be too high. A simple correction that can be applied is to discount the value back by the number of periods it will take to normalize earnings.

ILLUSTRATION 22.3: Normalizing Earnings for a Cyclical Firm in a Recession: Historical Margin

---

In 1992, toward the end of a recession in Europe and the United States, Volvo reported an operating loss of 2,249 million Swedish kroner (Sk) on revenues of 83,002 million Sk. To value the firm, we first had to normalize earnings. We used Volvo's *average* pretax operating margin from 1988 to 1992 of 4.1% as a measure of the normal margin, and applied it to revenues in 1992 to estimate normalized operating income:

$$\text{Normalized operating income in 1992} = \text{Revenues}_{1992} \times \text{Normalized margin}$$
$$= 83{,}002 \text{ million} \times .041 = 3{,}403 \text{ million Sk}$$

To value the operating assets of the firm, we assumed that Volvo was in stable growth, a reasonable assumption given its size and the competitive nature of the automobile industry, and that the expected growth rate in perpetuity would be 4%. To estimate the firm's reinvestment needs, we assumed that Volvo's return on capital in the future would be equal to the average return on capital that the firm earned between 1988 and 1992, which was 12.2%. This allowed use to estimate a reinvestment rate for the firm of 32.78%.

$$\text{Reinvestment rate in stable growth} = g/ROC = 4\%/12.2\% = 32.78\%$$

The expected free cash flow to the firm in 1993, based on the normalized pretax operating income of 3,403 million Sk, an estimated tax rate of 35%, the expected growth rate of 4%, and the reinvestment rate of 32.78%, can be estimated as follows:

$$\text{Expected free cash flow to the firm in 1993} = EBIT_{1992}(1 + g)(1 - \text{Tax rate})(1 - \text{Reinvestment rate})$$
$$= 3,403(1.04)(1 - .35)(1 - .3278) = 1,546 \text{ million Sk}$$

To estimate the cost of capital for Volvo, we computed weights on the market value of equity of 22,847 million Sk at the end of 1992 and the debt outstanding of 42,641 million Sk. We used a bottom-up beta of 1.20 for Volvo and a pretax cost of debt of 8.00%, reflecting its high leverage at the time of the analysis. The risk-free rate in Swedish kroner was 6.6% and the risk premium used was 4%:

$$\text{Cost of equity} = 6.6\% + 1.2(4\%) = 11.40\%$$
$$\text{Cost of capital} = 11.40\%[.22847/(22,847 + 42,641)] + 8\%(1 - .35)[42,641/(22,847 + 42,641)]$$
$$= 7.36\%$$

The value of the operating assets of Volvo can now be estimated:

$$\text{Value of operating assets} = \text{Expected FCFF in 1993}/(\text{Cost of capital} - \text{Expected growth})$$
$$= 1,546/(.0736 - .04) = 45,977 \text{ million Sk}$$

Adding to this the value of cash and marketable securities (20,760 million Sk) held by the firm at the end of 1992 and subtracting out debt ($42,641) yields an estimated value for equity:

$$\text{Value of equity} = \text{Value of operating assets} + \text{Cash and marketable securities} - \text{Debt}$$
$$= 45,977 + 20,760 - 42,641 = 24,096 \text{ million Sk}$$

Based on this estimate, Volvo was slightly undervalued at the end of 1992, since the market value of equity was $22,847 million.

Implicitly, we are assuming that Volvo's earnings will rebound quickly to normalized levels and that the recession will end in the very near future. If we assume that the recovery will take time, we can incorporate the effect into value by discounting the value estimated in the analysis back by the number of years that it will take Volvo to return to normal earnings. For instance, if we assume that adjustment will take two years, we could discount the value of the firm back two years at the cost of capital and then add cash and subtract the debt outstanding:

Value of the operating assets assuming two-year recovery = $45,977/1.0736^2$	39,889
+ Cash and marketable securities	+ 20,760
− Value of debt outstanding	− 42,641
= Value of equity	18,008

If we assume that the recovery will take two years or more, Volvo's equity is overvalued.

 normearn.xls: **This spreadsheet allows you to normalize the earnings for a firm, using a variety of approaches.**

MACROECONOMIC VIEWS AND VALUATION

The earnings of cyclical firms tend to be volatile, with the volatility linked to how well or badly the economy is performing. One way to incorporate these effects into value is to build in expectations of when future recessions and recoveries will occur into the cash flows. This exercise is fraught with danger, since the error in such predictions is likely to be very large. Economists seldom agree on when a recovery is imminent, and most categorizations of recessions occur after the fact. Furthermore, a valuation that is based on specific macroeconomic forecasts makes it difficult for users to separate how much of the final recommendation (i.e., that the firm is under- or overvalued) comes from the firm being mispriced and how much reflects the analyst's optimism or the pessimism about the overall economy.

The other way to incorporate earnings variability into the valuation is through the discount rate—cyclical firms tend to be more risky and require higher discount rates. This is what we do when we use higher unlevered betas and/or costs of debt for cyclical firms.

Valuing Commodity and Natural Resource Firms Commodity prices are not only volatile but go through cycles—periods of high prices followed by periods with lower prices. Figure 22.1 summarizes the levels of three indexes—an agricultural products index, an energy index, and an overall commodities index each year from 1980 to 2000.

There are two facts that come through from this analysis. The first is that commodity prices are volatile, with long periods of price increases followed by long periods of depressed prices. The other is that there is some correlation across different commodities when it comes to prices, with energy being much more volatile than agricultural products.

Some natural resource companies smooth out their earnings using futures and options contracts, but many let the price changes flow through into their bottom lines. As a consequence, the earnings of commodity companies tend to move up and down with commodity prices. To value natural resource companies—and that group would include not just mining firms but also forest product firms (such as timber) and plantations—you have three choices:

1. One is to try to forecast future commodity prices—the commodity price cycle—and build these forecasts into expected revenues in future years. This may be difficult to do since the cycles are unpredictable. However, you could use prices from the futures market as your forecasted prices.
2. You could value the firms using a normalized commodity price, estimated by looking at the average price of the commodity over a cycle. Thus, the average price of coffee over the past decade can be used to estimate the value of a coffee plantation. The danger, of course, is that the price of coffee may stay well above or below this average price for an extended period, throwing off estimates of value.

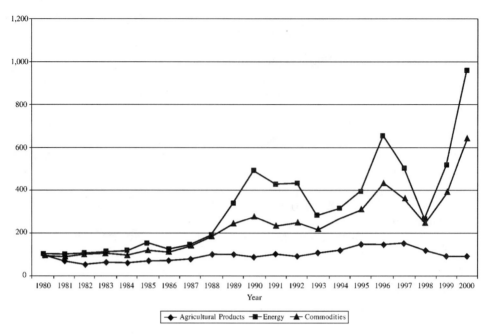

FIGURE 22.1 Commodity Prices
Source: Bloomberg.

3. You could value the firm's current production using the current price for the commodity, low though it might be, and add to it the value of the option that the company possesses, which is to produce more if prices go up and less if they go down. We will look at this approach in more detail in Chapter 28.

ILLUSTRATION 22.4:   Valuing a Commodity Company: Aracruz Celulose

---

Aracruz Celulose is a Brazilian paper and pulp manufacturer and, like all firms in this sector, it is susceptible to the ups and downs of the price of paper and pulp. Figure 22.2 reports on the revenues and operating income at Aracruz over the past decade, and the same graph provides an index of the price of pulp each year. Note the correlation between Aracruz's fortunes and the price of paper and pulp. The years with low or negative earnings for Aracruz generally are also the years when paper prices decline.

In May 2001, when we valued Aracruz, the firm had just emerged from a year of high paper prices and profitability to report 666 million BR of operating income on revenues of 1,342 million BR in 2000; the firm faced a tax rate of 33%. If we use this operating income to value Aracruz, we are assuming that paper prices will continue to remain high. To prevent this from biasing the valuation, we reestimated revenues and operating income in 2000, using the average price of paper over the past decade:

$$\text{Restated revenues} = \text{Revenues}_{2000} \times (\text{Average paper price}_{91-00} / \text{Paper price}_{2000})$$
$$= 1{,}342 \times (102.58/109.39) = 1{,}258 \text{ million BR}$$

$$\text{Restated operating income} = \text{Restated revenues} - \text{Operating expenses}$$
$$= 1{,}258 - (1{,}342 - 666) = 582 \text{ million BR}$$

This operating income was used to compute a normalized return on capital for the firm of 10.55%, based on the book values of debt ($1,549 million) and equity ($2,149 million) invested at the end of the previous year:

$$\text{Normalized return on capital} = \text{Operating income}_{2000}(1-t)$$
$$/(\text{Book value of debt}_{1999} + \text{Book value of equity}_{1999})$$
$$= 582 \times (1 - .33)/(1,549 + 2,149) = 10.55\%$$

We assumed that the firm would maintain this return on capital and grow 10% a year, in real terms, for the next five years and 3% a year in real terms in perpetuity after that. The following table summarizes projections of free cash flows to the firm for Aracruz for the next five years and for the first year of stable growth (six years from now):

	1	2	3	4	5	Terminal Year
Expected growth	10%	10%	10%	10%	10%	3%
Reinvestment rate	94.79%	94.79%	94.79%	94.79%	94.79%	28.44%
EBIT	$644	$712	$787	$870	$961	$1,063
EBIT(1 − t)	$431	$477	$527	$583	$644	$712
− Reinvestment	$409	$452	$500	$552	$611	$203
= FCFF	$22	$25	$27	$30	$34	$510

Note that the reinvestment rate each year is computed based on the expected growth rate and return on capital:

$$\text{Reinvestment rate} = g/\text{Normalized return on capital}$$

As expected growth declines in year 6 (the terminal year), the reinvestment rate also declines.

The cost of capital was estimated in real terms, using a bottom-up beta of 0.70 estimated by looking at paper and pulp firms and an additional risk premium for exposure to Brazilian country

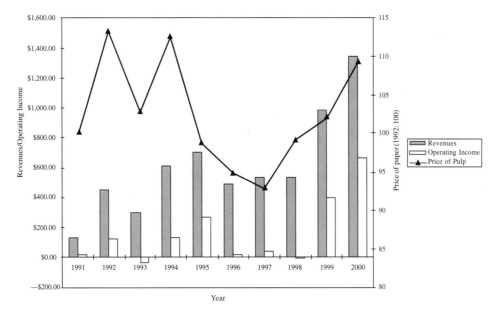

FIGURE 22.2 Aracruz Celulose: Revenues, Profits, and the Price of Pulp
Source: Aracruz Annual Report.

risk—10.24% for the next five years and 5% after five years. This is in addition to the mature market premium of 4%. We use a real risk-free rate of 4%. To estimate the real cost of debt, we assume a pretax real cost of borrowing of 7.5% for Aracruz for both the high-growth and stable-growth periods:

$$\text{Real after-tax cost of debt} = 7.5\%(1 - .33) = 5.03\%$$

The current market values of equity (3,749 million BR) and debt (1,395 million BR) were used to compute a market debt to capital ratio of 27.11%, and the costs of capital for both periods are shown in the following table:

	High Growth	Stable Growth
Beta	0.7	0.7
Risk-free rate	4%	4%
Mature market premium	4%	4%
Country premium	10.24%	5%
Cost of equity	$4\% + 0.7(4\% + 10.24\%) = 13.97\%$	$4\% + 0.7(4\% + 5\%) = 10.30\%$
Cost of debt	5.03%	5.03%
Debt ratio	27.11%	27.11%
Cost of capital	11.54%	8.87%

The terminal value is first estimated using the terminal year's cash flows estimated in the table and the perpetual growth rate of 3%:

$$\text{Terminal value} = \text{FCFF}_{\text{terminal year}}/(\text{Cost of capital}_{\text{stable}} - g)$$
$$= 510/(.0887 - .03) = 8,682 \text{ million BR}$$

The value of the operating assets of the firm can be computed today as the present value of the cash flows for the next five years and the present value of the terminal value, using the high-growth period cost of capital as the discount rate:

$$\text{Value of operating assets} = 22/1.1154 + 25/1.1154^2 + 27/1.1154^3 + 30/1.1154^4$$
$$+ 34/1.1154^5 + 8,682/1.1154^5 = 5,127 \text{ million BR}$$

We added back the value of cash and marketable securities (849 million BR) and subtracted outstanding debt (1,395 million BR) to estimate a value of equity:

$$\text{Value of equity} = 5,127 + 849 - 1,395 = 4,581 \text{ million BR}$$

This would suggest that the firm is undervalued at its current value of 2,149 million BR.

Firms with Long-Term Problems

In all of the valuations presented in the last section, earnings were adjusted either instantaneously to reflect normal levels or very quickly, reflecting our belief that the negative earnings will soon pass. In some cases, though, the negative earnings are a manifestation of more long-term problems at the firm. In such cases, we will be forced to make judgments on whether the problem will be overcome, and if so, when this will occur. This section presents a range of solutions for companies in this position.

MULTIPLES AND NORMALIZED EARNINGS

Would you have to make these adjustments to earnings if you were doing relative valuation rather than discounted cash flow valuation? The answer is generally yes, and when adjustments are not made, you are implicitly assuming normalization of earnings.

To see why, assume that you are comparing steel companies using price-earnings ratios and that one of the firms in your group has just reported very low earnings because of a strike during the past year. If you do not normalize the earnings, this firm will look overvalued relative to the sector, because the market price will probably be based on the expectation that the labor troubles, though costly, are in the past. If you use a multiple such as price-to-sales to make your relative valuation judgments and you compare this firm's price-to-sales ratio to the industry average, you are assuming that the firm's margins will converge on industry averages sooner rather than later.

What if an entire sector's earnings are affected by an event? Would you still need to normalize? We believe so. Though the earnings of all automobile stocks may be affected by a recession, the degree to which they are affected can vary widely depending on differences in operating and financial leverage. Furthermore, you will find yourself unable to compute multiples such as price-earnings ratios for many of the firms in the group that lose money during recessions. Using normalized earnings will yield multiples that are more reliable measures of true value.

Strategic Problems   Firms can sometimes make mistakes in terms of the product mix they offer, the marketing strategies they adopt, or even the markets that they choose to target. They often end up paying a substantial cost in terms of negative or lower earnings and perhaps a permanent loss of market share. Consider the following examples:

■ IBM found its dominant position in the mainframe computer business and the extraordinary profitability of that business challenged by the explosion of the personal computer market in the 1980s. While IBM could have developed the operating system for personal computers early in the process, it ceded that business to an upstart called Microsoft. By 1989, IBM had lost more than half its market value and its return on equity had dropped into the single digits.[3]

■ For decades, Xerox dominated the copier business to the extent that its name became synonymous with the product. In the 1970s and 1980s it was challenged for the market by Asian firms with lower cost structures, like Ricoh and Canon. After initial losses Xerox was able to recoup some of its market share. However, the last part of the 1990s saw a steady decline in Xerox's fortunes as

---

[3]It is worth noting that IBM made a fulsome recovery in the following decades by going back to basics, cutting costs, and refocusing its efforts on business services.

technology (in the form of e-mails, faxes, and low-cost printers) took its toll. By the end of 2000, there were questions about whether Xerox had a future.

■ Under the leadership of Michael Armstrong, AT&T tried to shed its image as a stodgy phone company and become a technology firm. After some initial successes, a series of miscues and poor acquisitions saw the firm enter the new millennium with a vastly reduced market capitalization and no clear vision on where to go next.

When firms have low or negative earnings that can be traced to strategic missteps, you have to determine whether the shift is a permanent one. If it is, you will have to value the firm on the assumption that it will never recover lost ground, and scale down your expectations of revenue growth and expected margins. If, on the other hand, you are more optimistic about the firm's recovery or its entry into new markets, you can assume that the firm will be able to revert to its traditional margins and high growth.

Operating Problems   Firms that are less efficient in the delivery of goods and services than their competitors will also be less profitable and less valuable. But how and why do firms become less efficient? In some cases, the reasons can be traced to a failure to keep up with the times and replenish existing assets and keep up with the latest technology. A steel company whose factories are decades old and whose equipment is outdated will generally bear higher costs for every ton of steel that it produces than its newer competitors. In other cases, the problem may be labor costs. A steel company with plants in the United States faces much higher labor costs than a similar company in Asia.

The variable that best measures operating efficiency is the operating margin, with firms that have operating problems tending to have much lower margins than their competitors. One way to build in the effect of operating improvements over time is to increase the margin toward the industry average, but the speed with which the margins will converge will depend on several factors:

■ *Size of the firm.* Generally, the larger the firm, the longer it will take to eliminate inefficiencies. Not only is inertia a much stronger force in large firms, but the absolute magnitude of the changes that have to be made are much larger. A firm with $10 billion in revenues will have to cut costs by $300 million to achieve a 3% improvement in pretax operating margin, whereas a firm with $100 million in revenues will have to cut costs by $3 million to accomplish the same objective.

■ *Nature of the inefficiency.* Some inefficiencies can be fixed far more quickly than others. For instance, a firm can replace outdated equipment or a poor inventory system quickly, but retraining a labor force will take much more time.

■ *External constraints.* Firms are often restricted in terms of how much and how quickly they can move to fix inefficiencies by contractual obligations and social pressure. For instance, laying off a large portion of the workforce may seem an obvious solution for a firm that is overstaffed, but union contracts and the potential for negative publicity may make firms reluctant to do so.

■ *Management quality.* A management that is committed to change is a critical component of a successful turnaround. In some cases, a replacement of top management may be necessary for a firm to be able to resolve its operating problems.

ILLUSTRATION 22.5: Valuing a Firm with Operating Problems: Marks and Spencer

Marks and Spencer, a multinational retailer headquartered in the United Kingdom, saw its operating income halved from 1996 to 2000, partly because of a high cost structure and partly because of ill-conceived expansion. In 2000, the firm reported £552 million in operating income on revenues of £8,196 million—a pretax operating margin of 6.73%. In contrast, the average pretax operating margin for department stores in the United Kingdom and United States is 12%, and Marks and Spencer's own historical margin (over the previous decade) is 11%. To value Marks and Spencer, we will assume the following:

- Revenues will grow 5% a year in perpetuity. The firm is a large firm in a mature market and it does seem unrealistic to assume much higher growth in revenues.
- The firm reported capital expenditures of £448 million and depreciation of £262 million for the 2000 financial year. In addition, the noncash working capital at the end of the year was £1,948 million. We will assume that net capital expenditures and noncash working capital will continue to grow at the same rate as revenues (i.e., 5% a year forever).
- We will assume that the pretax operating margin of the firm will improve over the next 10 years from 6.73% to 11.50%, with more significant improvements occurring in the next two years, and smaller improvements thereafter.
- We will use a tax rate of 33% to estimate after-tax cash flows. The cost of capital for the firm is estimated using its current market debt to capital ratio of 20%, a cost of equity of 9.52%, and a pretax cost of debt of 6%.

$$\text{Cost of capital} = 9.52(.80) + 6\%(1 - .33)(.2) = 8.42\%$$

The following table summarizes the forecasts of revenues, operating income, and free cash flows to the firm every year for the next six years.

Year	Revenues	Operating Margin	EBIT	EBIT $(1-t)$	Net Cap Ex	Change in Working Capital	FCFF
Current	£ 8,196	6.73%	£ 552	£ 370	£186		
1	£ 8,606	8.32%	£ 716	£ 480	£195	£ 97	£187
2	£ 9,036	9.38%	£ 848	£ 568	£205	£102	£261
3	£ 9,488	10.09%	£ 957	£ 641	£215	£107	£319
4	£ 9,962	10.56%	£1,052	£ 705	£226	£113	£366
5	£10,460	10.87%	£1,137	£ 762	£237	£118	£406
6	£10,983	11.08%	£1,217	£ 815	£249	£124	£442
7	£11,533	11.22%	£1,294	£ 867	£262	£131	£475
8	£12,109	11.31%	£1,370	£ 918	£275	£137	£506
9	£12,715	11.38%	£1,446	£ 969	£289	£144	£537
10	£13,350	11.42%	£1,524	£1,021	£303	£151	£567
Terminal year	$14,018	11.50%	£1,612	£1,080			

After year 10, we assume that revenues and operating income will continue to grow 5% a year forever, and that Marks and Spencer will earn an industry-average return on capital of 15%. This allows us to estimate a stable period reinvestment rate and terminal value:

$$\text{Reinvestment rate in stable growth} = g/\text{ROC} = 5\%/15\% = 33.33\%$$

$$\text{Terminal value} = \text{EBIT}_{11}(1-t)(1 - \text{Reinvestment rate})/(\text{Cost of capital} - g)$$
$$= £1,080(1 - .3333)/(.0842 - .05) = £21,054 \text{ million}$$

Adding the present value of the cash flows in the table to the present value of the terminal value, using the cost of capital of 8.42% as the discount rate, yields a value for the operating assets of £11,879 million. Adding the value of cash and marketable securities at the end of 2000 to this amount, and subtracting the debt yields a value of equity of £10,612 million.

Value of operating assets	£11,879 million
+ Cash & Securities	£687 million
– Debt	£1,954 million
Value of equity	£10,612 million

Dividing by the 2,875 million shares outstanding yields a value per share of £3.69, higher than the stock price of £2.72 prevailing at the time of this analysis in May 2001.

The Special Case of Privatizations   In many privatizations, we are called on to value firms with long financial histories but not very profitable ones. The lack of profitability is not surprising, however, since many of these firms have been run with objectives other than maximizing value or profitability. In some cases, employment in these firms has been viewed as a source of political patronage. Consequently, they end up overstaffed and inefficient.

Will this all change as soon as they are privatized? Not necessarily, and certainly not immediately. The power of unions to preserve existing jobs, the power that governments continue to have on how they are run, and the sheer size of these firms makes change both daunting and slow. While it is reasonable to assume that these firms will, in fact, become more efficient once they are privatized, the speed of the improvement will vary from firm to firm. In general, you would expect the adjustment to be much quicker if the government relinquishes its power to control the management of the firm and if there are strong competitive pressures to become more efficient. It will be slower if the firm is a monopoly and the government continues to handpick the top management of the firm.

GOLDEN SHARES AND THE VALUE OF PRIVATIZED FIRMS

While governments are always eager to receive the cash proceeds from privatizing the firms that they own, they are generally not as eager to give up control of these firms. One way they attempt to preserve power is by maintaining what is called a golden share in the firm that gives them veto power and control over some or many aspects of the firm's management.

For instance, the Brazilian government maintains a golden share in CVRD, allowing it the final decision on whether mines can be closed and other major financial decisions. While governments often view these golden shares as a costless way to privatize and preserve control at the same time, there is a cost that they will bear. Investors valuing firms with golden shares will generally be much less willing to assume radical changes in management and improvements in efficiency. Consequently, the values attached to these firms by the market will be much lower. The more inefficient the firm being privatized and the more restrictive the golden share, the greater will be the loss in value to the government.

ILLUSTRATION 22.6:   Valuing a Privatization: Compahnia Vale Dio Roce (CVRD)

In 1995, the Brazilian government privatized Compahnia Vale Dio Roce (CVRD), Latin America's biggest mining company. In the year the firm was privatized, it reported after-tax operating income of 717 million BR on revenues of 4,714 million BR. Based on the capital invested in the firm at the beginning of the year of 14,722 million BR, the after-tax return on capital earned by the firm was 5.33%.

If we assumed a stable real growth rate of 3% and a real cost of capital of 10%, and valued CVRD on the basis of these inputs, we would have estimated the following value for the firm:

Reinvestment rate = g/ROC = 3%/5.33% = 56.29%

Value of the firm = EBIT(1 – t)(1 + g)(1 – Reinvestment rate)/(Cost of capital – g)
$$= 717(1.03)(1 - .5629)/(.10 - .03)$$
$$= 4,611 \text{ million BR}$$

Note, though, that this assumes that CVRD's return on capital will remain at existing levels in perpetuity. If privatization leads to operating efficiencies at the firm, its margins and return on capital can be expected to improve. For instance, if we valued CVRD using the real return on capital of 7% earned by mining companies in the United States, we would have estimated the following:

Reinvestment rate = g/ROC = 3%/7% = 42.86%

Value of the firm = EBIT(1 – t)(1 + g)(1 – Reinvestment rate)/(Cost of capital – g)
$$= 717(1.03)(1 - .4286)/(.10 - .03)$$
$$= 6,029 \text{ million BR}$$

Is it reasonable to assume this improvement in margins? It depends on which side of the transaction you are on. If you were an investor interested in buying the stock, you might argue that the firm is too entrenched in its ways to make the changes needed for higher profitability, and you would then use the value estimated with current margins. If you are the government and want to obtain the highest value you can, you would argue for the latter.

Financial Leverage   In some cases firms get into trouble because they borrow too much and not because of operating or strategic problems. In these cases, it will be the equity earnings that will be negative while operating earnings will be positive. The solution to the problem depends, in large part, on how distressed the firm really is. If the distress is not expected to push the firm into bankruptcy, there are a variety of potential solutions. If, however, the distress is likely to be terminal, finding a solution is much more difficult.

Overlevered with No Immediate Threat of Bankruptcy   Firms that borrow too much are not always on the verge of bankruptcy. In fact, firms with valuable operating assets and substantial operating cash flows can service much more debt than is optimal for them, even though they might not do so comfortably. So, what are the costs of being overlevered? First, the firm might end up with a large enough exposure to default risk that it affects its operations—customers might not buy its products, suppliers might demand speedier payment, and it might have trouble retaining valued employees. Second, the higher beta and cost of debt that go with the higher leverage may increase the firm's cost of capital and reduce its value. It is therefore in the best interests of the firm to reduce its debt ratio, if not immediately, at least over time.

There are two choices when it comes to valuing levered firms as going concerns:

1. You can estimate free cash flows to the firm and value the firm. If the firm is operationally healthy (the operating margins are both positive and similar to those of comparable firms), the only modification you have to make is to reduce the debt ratio over time—in practical terms, a disproportionate share of the reinvestment each year has to come from equity—and compute costs of capital that change with the debt ratio. If the firm's operating margins have suffered because it borrowed too much, you might need to adjust the operating margins over time toward industry averages as well.

2. You can use the adjusted present value approach and value the firm as an unlevered firm, and add to this unlevered firm value the costs (expected bankruptcy costs) and benefits (tax benefits) of debt. As noted in Chapter 15, though, estimating the expected bankruptcy cost can be difficult to do.

ILLUSTRATION 22.7: Adjust Debt Ratio over Time: Hyundai

Hyundai Corporation is a Korean company that is part of the Hyundai group and handles the trading operations for the firm. Like many other Korean companies, Hyundai borrowed large amounts to fund expansion until the late 1990s. By the end of 2000, Hyundai had debt outstanding of 848 billion Korean won (krw) and had a market value of equity of 163 billion krw, resulting a debt to capital ratio of 83.85%. The high leverage has three consequences:

1. The bottom-up beta for the firm is 2.60, reflecting the firm's high debt-to -equity ratio. With a risk-free rate of 9% in Korean won and the risk premium of 7% (4% as the mature market premium and 3% for Korean country risk) we estimate a cost of equity in Korean won for the firm of 27.20%.

$$\text{Cost of equity} = 9\% + 2.6(7\%) = 27.20\%$$

2. The firm has high default risk, leading to a pretax cost of borrowing in Korean won terms of 12.5%; the tax rate for the firm is 30%.
3. The firm reported pretax operating income of 89.42 billion krw, but the interest expenses of the firm amounted to 99 billion krw, resulting in a loss for the firm. Note, though, that the firm is still obtaining the tax benefits of almost all of its interest payments.[4]

We will assume that the operating income will grow 10% a year for the next six years and 8% a year beyond that point in time. Over that period, we will assume that the firm's capital expenditures (which are currently 12 billion won), depreciation (which is currently 4 billion won), and noncash

---

[4]Without interest expenses, Hyundai would have paid taxes on its operating income of 93 billion won. Because of its interest payments, Hyundai was able to not pay taxes. Of the 99 billion won in interest payments, Hyundai is receiving tax benefits on 93 billion won.

working capital (which is currently 341 billion won) will grow at the same rate as operating income, yielding the following estimates for the cash flows:

	1	2	3	4	5	6
EBIT(1 − t)	$68.86	$75.74	$83.32	$91.65	$100.81	$110.89
+ Depreciation	$ 4.40	$ 4.84	$ 5.32	$ 5.86	$ 6.44	$ 7.09
− Capital spending	$13.20	$14.52	$15.97	$17.57	$ 19.33	$ 21.26
− Chg. working capital	$34.11	$37.52	$41.27	$45.40	$ 49.94	$ 54.93
Free CF to firm	$25.95	$28.54	$31.40	$34.54	$ 37.99	$ 41.79

Over the next six years, we will assume that the firm will reduce its debt ratio from 83.85% to 50%, which will result in the beta decreasing from 2.60 to 1.00 and the pretax cost of debt from 12.5% to 10.5% (we assume that the changes occur linearly over the period). The costs of capital for Hyundai are estimated each year for the next six years:

	1	2	3	4	5	6
Beta	2.60	2.28	1.96	1.64	1.32	1.00
Cost of equity	27.20%	24.96%	22.72%	20.48%	18.24%	16.00%
Cost of debt (after-tax)	8.75%	8.47%	8.19%	7.91%	7.63%	7.35%
Debt ratio	83.85%	77.08%	70.31%	63.54%	56.77%	50.00%
Cost of capital	11.73%	12.25%	12.50%	12.49%	12.22%	11.68%

To estimate the terminal value, we assume a growth rate of 8% in perpetuity, after year 6, and a return on capital of 16%. This allows us to estimate a reinvestment rate and terminal value for the firm at the end of year 6:

Reinvestment rate = 8%/16% = 50%

Terminal value = 110.89(1.08)(1 − .50)/(.1168 − .08) = 1,626 billion krw

Discounting the cash flows over the next six years and the terminal value using the cumulated cost of capital yields the following:

Present value of FCFF in high-growth phase	132.34 billion krw
Present value of terminal value	819.19 billion krw
Value of the operating assets =	951.52 billion krw
+ Cash and marketable securities	80.46 billion krw
− Market value of debt	847.73 billion krw
Market value of equity	184.25 billion krw

Dividing by the number of shares results in an estimated value of equity for the firm of 2,504 won per share, a little higher than the actual trading price of 2,220 won per share.

CAN EQUITY VALUE BE NEGATIVE?

We generally subtract the value of outstanding debt from firm value to get to the value of equity. But can the value of the outstanding debt exceed the value of the firm? If you are using market values for both the firm (obtained by adding the market values of debt and equity) and debt, this will never occur. This is because the market value of equity can never be less than zero. However, if you are using your estimated value for the firm, obtained by discounting cash flows to the firm at the cost of capital, the estimated firm value can be less than the market value of the outstanding debt. When this occurs, there are three possible interpretations:

1. The first and most obvious reading is that you have made a mistake in estimating firm value and that your estimate is too low. In this case, the obvious solution is to redo the firm valuation.
2. The second possibility is that the market value of debt is overstated. This can happen if you are using the book value of debt as a proxy for market value for troubled firms, or if the bond market is making a mistake pricing the debt. Estimating the correct market value of debt will eliminate the problem.[5]
3. The third and most intriguing possibility is that your estimate of firm value and the market value of debt are both correct, in which case the equity value is, in fact, negative. Since the market price of equity cannot be less than zero, the implication is that the equity in this firm is worth nothing. However, as you will see later, equity may still continue to command value, even under these circumstances, if it is viewed as a call option on the firm's assets.

Overlevered with High Probability of Bankruptcy   Discounted cash flow valuation is conditioned on a firm being a going concern, with cash flows continuing into the future. When a firm's financial problems are severe enough to suggest a strong likelihood of bankruptcy, other approaches may need to be used to value a firm and the equity claim in it. There are two possible approaches: One is to estimate a liquidation value for the assets today, and the other is to continue to treat the firm as a going concern and value the equity in it as an option.

Liquidation Value   The liquidation value of a firm is the aggregate of the value that the assets of the firm would command on the market, net of transactions and legal costs. The value of equity can be obtained by subtracting the value of the outstanding debt from the asset value.

Value of equity = Liquidation value of assets − Outstanding debt

---

[5]You could discount the expected cash flows on the debt at a pretax cost of debt that reflects the firm's current standing.

Estimating liquidation value is complicated when the assets of the firm are not easily separated and thus cannot be valued individually. Furthermore, the likelihood that assets will fetch their fair market value will decrease as the urgency of the liquidation increases. A firm in a hurry to liquidate its assets may have to accept a discount on fair market value as a price for speedy execution.

As a note of caution, it is almost never appropriate to treat the book value of the assets as the liquidation value. Most distressed firms earn subpar returns on their assets, and the liquidation value will reflect the earning capacity of the assets rather than the price paid for the assets (which is what the book value measures, net of depreciation).

Option Pricing Models The liquidation value approach presumes that the market value of the assets currently exceeds the face value of outstanding debt. When this assumption is violated, the only approach left to value the equity in a distressed firm may be to use option pricing models. Equity in a heavily levered firm, where the value of the assets is lower than the face value of the debt, can be viewed as an out-of-the-money call option on the underlying firm and can be valued as such. We will return to examine this concept in more detail in Chapter 30.

---

 dbtfund.xls: **This dataset on the Web summarizes book and market value debt ratios by industry group in the United States for the most recent year.**

Life Cycle Earnings As noted earlier in the chapter, it is normal for firms to lose money at certain stages in their life cycles. When valuing such firms, you cannot normalize earnings, as we did with cyclical firms or firms with temporary problems. Instead, you have to estimate the cash flows of the firm over its life cycle, and let them turn positive at the right stage of the cycle. This section will consider in detail one group of firms—those with large infrastructure investments. The other two—pharmaceutical firms that derive the bulk of their value from a patent or patents and young start-up companies—will be considered in more detail in the coming chapters.

Infrastructure Firms If the business that a firm is in requires large infrastructure investments early in the life cycle and the firm has to wait for a long period before it can generate earnings, it is entirely possible that the firm will report large losses in the initial periods when the investments are made. In fact, as an added complication, many of these firms have to borrow large amounts to fund their infrastructure investments, creating a fairly toxic combination—negative earnings and high leverage.

Given this combination, how can an infrastructure firm—a telecom firm or cable company—ever be valuable? Consider one possible path to success. A firm borrows money and makes large investments in infrastructure. Having made these investments, though, it has a secure market where entry is prohibitively expensive. In some cases, the firm may have a legally sanctioned monopoly to provide the service. No further investments are needed in infrastructure but depreciation on the existing investments continues to generate large tax benefits. The net effect is that the firm will be sitting on a cash machine that allows it to not only pay off its debt but ready itself for the next generation of investments. In a sense, phone companies and power companies, as well as some cable and cellular firms, have followed this path to success.

In the 1990s, we saw an explosion both in the number of telecom firms and the capital raised by telecom firms in a variety of ventures. While they followed the timeworn path of high debt and large up-front infrastructure investments laid by their predecessors, we believe that there are two critical ingredients that are missing with this generation of firms. The first is that technology has become a wild card and large investments in infrastructure do not guarantee future profitability or even that a market will exist. The second is that the protection from competition that allowed the old-time technology firms to generate large and predictable profits is unlikely to be there for this new generation of telecom firms. As a consequence, we would predict that far more of these firms will go bankrupt and that they might be well advised to rethink their policies on financial leverage as a consequence.

ILLUSTRATION 22.8:   Valuing an Infrastructure Firm: Global Crossing

Global Crossing provides managed data and voice products over a fiber-optic network. Over its three-year history, the firm has increased revenues from $420 million in 1998 to $3,789 million in 2000, but it has gone from an operating income of $120 million in 1998 to an operating loss of $1,396 million in 2000. In addition, the firm is capital intensive and reported substantial capital expenditures ($4,289 million) and depreciation ($1,381 million) in 2000.

In making the valuation, we assume that there will be no revenue growth in the first year (to reflect a slowing economy) and that revenue growth will be brisk for the next four years and then taper off to a stable growth rate of 5% in the terminal phase, that EBITDA as a percent of sales will move from the current level (of close to 0%) to an industry average of 33% by the end of the tenth year, and that capital expenditures will be ratcheted down over the next two years to maintenance levels. The following table summarizes our assumptions on revenue growth, EBITDA/sales, and reinvestment needs over the next 10 years.

Year	Growth Rate in Revenue	EBITDA/ Revenue	Growth Rate in Capital Spending	Growth Rate in Depreciation	Working Capital as Percent of Revenue
1	0.00%	0.00%	−20%	10%	3.00%
2	30.00%	7.50%	−50%	10%	3.00%
3	25.00%	15.00%	−50%	10%	3.00%
4	20.00%	22.50%	−50%	10%	3.00%
5	10.00%	30.00%	5%	−50%	3.00%
6	10.00%	30.60%	5%	−50%	3.00%
7	10.00%	31.20%	5%	5%	3.00%
8	8.00%	31.80%	5%	5%	3.00%
9	6.00%	32.40%	5%	5%	3.00%
10	5.00%	33.00%	5%	5%	3.00%

For both revenue growth and improvement in EBITDA margins, we assume that the larger changes occur in the earlier years. Note that the changes in depreciation lag the changes in capital spending—the capital spending is cut first and depreciation drops later. Finally, we assume that the firm will need to set aside 3% of the revenue change each year into working capital based on the industry averages.

With these forecasts, we estimated revenues, operating income, and after-tax operating income each year for the high growth period in the following table. To estimate taxes, we consider the net operating losses carried forward into 2001 of $2,075 million and add on the additional losses that we expect in the first few years of the projection.

Year	Revenues	EBITDA	Depreciation	EBIT	NOL at Beginning of Year	Taxes	EBIT $(1-t)$
1	$ 3,789	$ 0	$1,519	−$1,519	$2,075	$ 0	−$1,519
2	$ 4,926	$ 369	$1,671	−$1,302	$3,594	$ 0	−$1,302
3	$ 6,157	$ 924	$1,838	−$ 915	$4,896	$ 0	−$ 915
4	$ 7,389	$1,662	$2,022	−$ 359	$5,810	$ 0	−$ 359
5	$ 8,127	$2,438	$1,011	$1,427	$6,170	$ 0	$1,427
6	$ 8,940	$2,736	$ 505	$2,230	$4,742	$ 0	$2,230
7	$ 9,834	$3,068	$ 531	$2,538	$2,512	$ 9	$2,529
8	$10,621	$3,314	$ 557	$2,756	$ 0	$ 965	$1,792
9	$11,258	$3,580	$ 585	$2,995	$ 0	$1,048	$1,947
10	$11,821	$3,830	$ 614	$3,216	$ 0	$1,125	$2,090
Terminal year	$12,412	$4,096	$ 645	$3,451	$ 0	$1,208	$2,243

The accumulated losses over the first few years shield the firm from paying taxes until the seventh year. After that point, we assume a marginal tax rate of 35%.

Finally, we estimated free cash flows to the firm with our assumptions about capital expenditures and working capital.

Year	EBIT $(1-t)$	Capital Expenditures	Depreciation	Change in Working Capital	FCFF
1	−$1,519	$3,431	$1,519	$ 0	−$3,431
2	−$1,302	$1,716	$1,671	$34	−$1,380
3	−$ 915	$ 858	$1,838	$37	$ 29
4	−$ 359	$ 429	$2,022	$37	$1,197
5	$1,427	$ 450	$1,011	$22	$1,966
6	$2,230	$ 473	$ 505	$24	$2,238
7	$2,259	$ 497	$ 531	$27	$2,536
8	$1,792	$ 521	$ 557	$24	$1,804
9	$1,947	$ 547	$ 585	$19	$1,965
10	$2,090	$ 575	$ 614	$17	$2,113
Terminal year	$2,243	$1,562	$ 645	$18	$1,308

The firm uses debt liberally to fund these investments and had debt outstanding of $7,271 million at the end of 2000. Based on its market capitalization of $11,142 million as the time of this valuation, we estimated a market debt to capital ratio for the firm.

$$\text{Debt to capital} = \frac{7,271}{7,271+11,142} = 39.49\%$$

$$\text{Equity to capital} = \frac{11,142}{7,271+11,142} = 60.51\%$$

Using a bottom-up beta of 2.00 for the equity and a cost of debt of 8.9% based on the current rating for the firm, we can estimate a cost of capital for the next five years. (The risk-free rate is 5.4% and the risk premium is 4%.)

$$\text{Cost of equity} = 5.4\% + 2(4\%) = 13.40\%$$

$$\text{After-tax cost of debt} = 8.9\%(1-0) = 8.9\% \text{ (The firm does not pay taxes)}$$

$$\text{Cost of capital} = 13.40\%(0.6051) + 8.9\%(0.3949) = 11.62\%$$

In stable growth, after year 10, we assume that the beta will decrease to 1.00 and that the pretax cost of debt will decrease to 8%. The adjustment occurs in linear increments from years 6 through 10 as shown in the following table.

	1–5	6	7	8	9	10
Tax rate			0.35%	35%	35%	35%
Beta	2.00	1.80	1.60	1.40	1.20	1.00
Cost of equity	13.40%	12.60%	11.80%	11.00%	10.20%	9.40%
Pretax cost of debt	8.90%	8.72%	8.54%	8.36%	8.18%	8.00%
After-tax cost of debt	8.90%	8.72%	8.51%	5.43%	5.32%	5.20%
Debt ratio	39.49%	39.49%	39.49%	39.49%	39.46%	39.46%
Cost of capital	11.62%	11.07%	10.50%	8.80%	8.27%	7.74%

To estimate the reinvestment rate in the terminal year, we assume that Global Crossing would earn a 9% return on capital in perpetuity after year 10, and that the expected growth rate would be 5%. This yields a reinvestment rate of 55.56%.

$$\text{Reinvestment rate in stable growth} = \frac{5\%}{12\%} = 41.67\%$$

$$\text{Expected FCFF in terminal year} = EBIT_{10}(1+g)(1-t)(1-\text{Reinvestment rate})$$

$$= 3{,}216(1.05)(1-0.35)(1-0.5556)$$

$$= \$997 \text{ million}$$

$$\text{Terminal value} = \frac{FCFF_{11}}{\text{Cost of capital} - g} = \frac{997}{0.0774 - 0.05} = \$36{,}363 \text{ million}$$

Adding the present value of the cash flows over the high-growth period to the present value of the terminal value, we obtain the value of the operating assets.

Value of operating assets	$15,917 million
+ Cash and marketable securities	$ 1,477 million
– Debt	$ 7,271 million
Value of equity	$10,123 million

In May 2001, Global Crossing's market value of equity of $11,143 million suggests that the stock is overvalued.

Firms with Patents   The value of a firm generally comes from two sources—assets in place and expected future growth opportunities. The value of the former is generally captured in current cash flows, while the value of the latter is reflected in the expected growth rate. In the special case of a firm that derives a large portion of its value from a product patent or patents, expected growth will be from developing the patents. Ignoring them in a discounted cash flow valuation will understate the value of the firm.

There are three possible solutions to the problems associated with valuing firms with product options:

1. Value the product options on the open market and add them to the value from discounted cash flow (DCF) valuation. If there is an active market trading in product options, this offers a viable and simple way of valuing these options. In the absence of such a market, or when the product options are not separable and tradable, this approach becomes difficult to apply.
2. Use a higher growth rate than the one justified by existing projects and assets, to capture the additional value from product options. While this keeps the analysis within the traditional discounted cash flow valuation framework, the increase in the growth rate is essentially subjective and it converts contingent cash flows (where the product option will be exercised if and only if it makes economic sense) to expected cash flows.
3. Use an option pricing model to value product options and add the value to that obtained from DCF valuation of assets in place. The advantage of this approach is that it mirrors the cash flow profile of a product option much more precisely.

The primary problem in valuing firms with product options is not that these options are ignored, but that they are often double counted. Analysts all too frequently use a higher growth rate to reflect the product options that a firm owns, but then add on a premium to the DCF value for the same product options. We will return to examine the valuation of these firms in Chapter 28.

Young, Start-Up Firms Many firms begin as ideas in the minds of entrepreneurs and develop into commercial ventures over time. During this transition from idea companies to commercial ventures, it is not unusual for these firms to lose money. This does not make them worthless. In fact, the boom in the market value of new economy companies in the late 1990s brought home the fact that good ideas can have substantial values, though the correction in 2000 also illustrated how volatile these values can be.

Valuing young start-up firms is perhaps the most difficult exercise in valuation and one that was, until very recently, the domain of venture capitalists and private equity investors, who often compensated for uncertainty by demanding extremely high returns on these investments. The challenge becomes much more daunting if a young start-up firm is publicly traded. The next chapter will examine the estimation issues that we face in valuing such a firm.

CONCLUSION

There are many cases where traditional discounted cash flow valuation has to be modified or adapted to provide reasonable estimates of value. Some of these cases are presented in this chapter. Cyclical firms can be difficult to value because their earnings track the economy. The same can be said about commodity firms in relation to the commodity price cycle. A failure to adjust the earnings for these cyclical ups and downs can lead to significant undervaluation of these firms at the depth of a recession and a significant overvaluation at the peak of a boom.

When a firm's earnings are negative because of long-term strategic, operating, or financial problems, the process of valuing these firms becomes more complicated. You have to make a judgment of whether the firm's problems will be solved and, if so, when. For those firms where there is a significant chance of bankruptcy, you might have to consider the liquidation value of the assets. Valuing firms early in their life cycles poses similar problems, but they are accentuated when earnings, cash flow, and book value all turn negative. In most these cases, discounted cash flow valuation is flexible enough to be used to estimate value.

QUESTIONS AND SHORT PROBLEMS

1. Intermet Corporation, the largest independent iron foundry organization in the country, reported a deficit per share of $0.15 in 1993. The earnings per share from 1984 to 1992 were as follows:

Year	EPS
1984	$0.69
1985	$0.71
1986	$0.90
1987	$1.00
1988	$0.76
1989	$0.68
1990	$0.09
1991	$0.16
1992	<$0.07>

The firm had capital expenditures of $1.60 per share and depreciation per share of $1.20 in 1993. Working capital was expected to increase $0.10 per share in 1994. The stock has a beta of 1.2, which is expected to remain unchanged; the company finances its capital expenditure and working capital requirements with 40% debt [D/(D + E)]. The firm was expected, in the long term, to grow at the same rate as the economy (6%).
   a. Estimate the normalized earnings per share in 1994, using the average earnings approach.
   b. Estimate the normalized free cash flow to equity per share in 1994, using the average earnings approach.
2. General Motors Corporation reported a deficit per share in 1993 of $4.85, following losses in the two earlier years. (The average earnings per share is negative.) The company had assets with a book value of $25 billion, and spent almost $7 billion on capital expenditures in 1993, which was partially offset by a depreciation charge of $6 billion. The firm had $19 billion in debt outstanding, on which it paid interest expenses of $1.4 billion. It intended to maintain a debt ratio [D/(D + E)] of 50%. The working capital requirements of the firm were negligible, and the stock has a beta of 1.10. In the last normal period of operations for the firm between 1986 and 1989, the firm earned an average return on capital of 12%. The Treasury bond rate was 7%, and the market risk premium is 5.5%.
   Once earnings are normalized, GM expected them to grow 5% a year forever, and capital expenditures and depreciation to grow at the same rate.
   a. Estimate the value per share for GM, assuming earnings are normalized instantaneously.
   b. How would your valuation be affected if GM is not going to reach its normalized earnings until 1995 (in two years)?

3. Toro Corporation, which manufactures lawn mowers and tractors, had revenues of $635 million in 1992, on which it reported a loss of $7 million (largely as a consequence of the recession). It had interest expenses of $17 million in 1992, and its bonds were rated BBB; a typical BBB-rated company had an interest coverage ratio (EBIT/Interest expenses) of 3.10. The company faced a 40% tax rate. The stock had a beta of 1.10. (The Treasury bond rate was 7%, and the risk premium is 5.5%.)

   Toro spent $25 million on capital expenditures in 1992, and had depreciation of $20 million. Working capital amounted to 25% of sales. The company expected to maintain a debt ratio of 25%. In the long term, growth in revenues and profits was expected to be 4%, once earnings return to normal levels.
   a. Assuming that the bond rating reflects normalized earnings, estimate the normalized earnings for Toro Corporation.
   b. Allowing for the long-term growth rate on normalized earnings, estimate the value of equity for Toro Corporation.
4. Kollmorgen Corporation, a diversified technology company, reported sales of $194.9 million in 1992, and had a net loss of $1.9 million in that year. Its net income had traced a fairly volatile course over the previous five years:

Year	Net Income
1987	$ 0.3 million
1988	$11.5 million
1989	–$ 2.4 million
1990	$ 7.2 million
1991	–$ 4.6 million

   The stock had a beta of 1.20, and the normalized net income was expected to increase 6% a year until 1996, after which the growth rate was expected to stabilize at 5% a year (the beta will drop to 1.00). The depreciation amounted to $8 million in 1992, and capital spending amounted to $10 million in that year. Both items were expected to grow 5% a year in the long term. The firm expected to maintain a debt ratio of 35%. (The Treasury bond rate was 7%, and the risk premium is 5.5%.)
   a. Assuming that the average earnings from 1987 to 1992 represents the normalized earnings, estimate the normalized earnings and free cash flow to equity.
   b. Estimate the value per share.
5. OHM Corporation, an environmental service provider, had revenues of $209 million in 1992 and reported losses of $3.1 million. It had earnings before interest and taxes of $12.5 million in 1992, and had debt outstanding of $104 million (in market value terms). There were 15.9 million shares outstanding, trading at $11 per share. The pretax interest rate on debt owed by the firm was 8.5%, and the stock had a beta of 1.15. The firm's EBIT was expected to increase 10% a year from 1993 to 1996, after which the growth rate is expected to drop to 4% in the long term. The return on capital in stable growth is 10%. (The corporate tax rate was 40%, the Treasury bond rate was 7%, and the market risk premium is 5.5%.)
   a. Estimate the cost of capital for OHM.
   b. Estimate the value of the firm.
   c. Estimate the value of equity (both total and on a per share basis).

6. You have been provided the following information on CEL Inc., a manufacturer of high-end stereo systems.
   - In the most recent year, which was a bad one, the company made only $40 million in net income. It expects next year to be more normal. The book value of equity at the company is $1 billion, and the average return on equity over the previous 10 years (assumed to be a normal period) was 10%.
   - The company expects to make $80 million in new capital expenditures next year. It expects depreciation, which was $60 million this year, to grow 5% next year.
   - The company had revenues of $1.5 billion this year, and it maintained a non-cash working capital investment of 10% of revenues. It expects revenues to increase 5% next year and working capital to decline to 9.5% of revenues.
   - The firm expects to maintain its existing debt policy (in market value terms). The market value of equity is $1.5 billion, and the book value of equity is $500 million. The debt outstanding (in both book and market terms) is $500 million.
   - The cost of equity for the firm is 9%.
   a. Estimate the FCFE next year.
   b. Estimate the value of the equity assuming that the firm can grow 5% a year in perpetuity.
7. Tenet Telecommunications is in serious financial trouble and has just reported an operating loss of $500 million on revenues of $5 billion. The firm also had capital expenditures of $1.8 billion and depreciation of $800 million in the most recent financial year, and no significant noncash working capital requirements. You assume that:
   - Revenues will continue to grow 10% a year for the next five years and 5% in perpetuity after that.
   - EBITDA as a percent of sales will increase in linear increments from existing levels to 20% of revenues in year 5.
   - Capital expenditures can be cut to $600 million each year for the next five years, while depreciation will remain at $800 million each year.
   - The net operating loss carried forward is $700 million.
   - Return on capital in perpetuity after year 5 will be 10%.
   - Cost of capital for the firm is 9% in perpetuity.
   a. Estimate the EBITDA, EBIT, and after-tax EBIT for the firm each year for the next five years, assuming a corporate tax rate of 40%.
   b. Estimate the FCFF each year for the next five years.
   c. Estimate the terminal value of the firm.
   d. Estimate the value of the firm today.
   e. How would your valuation change if you were told that there is a 20% chance that the firm will go bankrupt and that assets will have a distress sale value amounting to 60% of the current book value of $1.25 billion?

CHAPTER 23

Valuing Young or Start-Up Firms

Many of the firms that we have valued in this book are publicly traded firms with established operations. But what about young firms that have just started operations? There are many analysts who argue that these firms cannot be valued because they have no history and in some cases no products or services to sell. This chapter will present a dissenting point of view. While conceding that valuing young firms is more difficult to do than valuing established firms, we will argue that the fundamentals of valuation do not change. The value of a young start-up firm is the present value of the expected cash flows from its operations, though estimates of these expected cash flows may require us to go outside our normal sources of information, which include historical financial statements and the valuation of comparable firms.

INFORMATION CONSTRAINTS

When valuing a firm, you draw on information from three sources. The first is the current financial statements for the firm. You use these to determine how profitable a firm's investments are or have been, how much it reinvests back to generate future growth and for all of the inputs that are required in any valuation. The second is the past history of the firm, in terms of both earnings and market prices. A firm's earnings and revenue history over time let you make judgments on how cyclical a firm's business has been and how much growth it has shown, while a firm's price history can help you measure its risk. Finally, you can look at the firm's competitors or peer group to get a measure of how much better or worse a firm is than its competition, and also to estimate key inputs on risk, growth, and cash flows.

While you would optimally like to have substantial information from all three sources, you may often have to substitute more of one type of information for less of the other if you have no choice. Thus the fact that there exists 75 years or more of history on each of the large automakers in the United States compensates for the fact that there are only three of them.[1] In contrast, there may be only a few years of information on Abercombie and Fitch, but the firm is in a sector (specialty retailing) where there are more than 200 comparable firms. The ease with which you can obtain industry averages and the precision of these averages compensate for the lack of history at the firm.

---

[1]The big three automakers are GM, Chrysler, and Ford. In fact, with Daimler's acquisition of Chrysler, only two are left.

There are some firms, especially in new sectors of the economy, where you might run into information problems. First, these firms usually have not been in existence for more than a year or two, leading to a very limited history. Second, their current financial statements reveal very little about the component of their assets—expected growth—that contributes the most to their value. Third, these firms often represent the first of their kind of business. In many cases, there are no competitors or a peer group against which they can be measured. When valuing these firms, therefore, you may find yourself constrained on all three counts when it comes to information. How have investors responded to this absence of information? Some have decided that these stocks cannot be valued and should not therefore be held in a portfolio. Others have argued that while these stocks cannot be valued with traditional models, the fault lies in the models. They have come up with new and inventive ways, based on the limited information available, of justifying the prices paid for them. We will argue in this chapter that discounted cash flow models can be used to value these firms.

NEW PARADIGMS OR OLD PRINCIPLES: A LIFE CYCLE PERSPECTIVE

The value of a firm is based on its capacity to generate cash flows and the uncertainty associated with these cash flows. Generally speaking, more profitable firms have been valued more highly than less profitable ones. However, young start-up firms often lose money but still sometimes have high values attached to them. This seems to contradict the proposition about value and profitability going hand in hand. There seems to be, at least from the outside, one more key difference between young start-up firms and other firms in the market. A young firm does not have significant investments in land, buildings, or other fixed assets, and seems to derive the bulk of its value from intangible assets.

The negative earnings and the presence of intangible assets are used by analysts as a rationale for abandoning traditional valuation models and developing new ways that can be used to justify investing in young firms. For instance, as noted in Chapter 20, Internet companies in their infancy have been compared based on their value per site visitor, computed by dividing the market value of a firm by the number of visitors to the web site. Implicit in these comparisons are the assumptions that more visitors to your site translate into higher revenues, which, in turn, will lead to greater profits in the future. All too often, though, these assumptions are neither made explicit nor tested, leading to unrealistic valuations.

This search for new paradigms is misguided. The problem with young firms is not that they lose money, have no history, or do not have substantial tangible assets. It is that they are far earlier in their life cycles than established firms, and often have to be valued before they have an established market for their products. In fact, in some cases, the firms being valued have an interesting idea that could be a commercial success but has not been tested yet. The problem, however, is not a conceptual problem but one of estimation. The value of a firm is still the present value of the expected cash flows from its assets, but those cash flows are likely to be much more difficult to estimate.

Figure 23.1 offers a view of the life cycle of the firm and how the availability of information and the source of value changes over that life cycle:

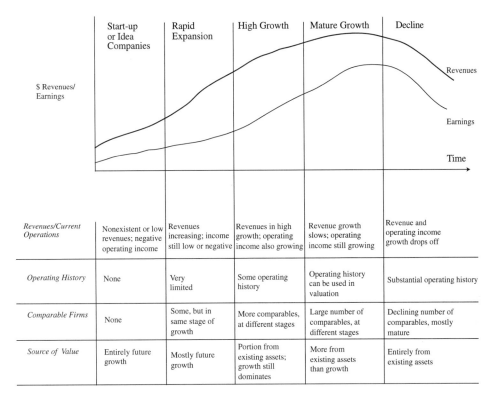

	Start-up or Idea Companies	Rapid Expansion	High Growth	Mature Growth	Decline
Revenues/Current Operations	Nonexistent or low revenues; negative operating income	Revenues increasing; income still low or negative	Revenues in high growth; operating income also growing	Revenue growth slows; operating income still growing	Revenue and operating income growth drops off
Operating History	None	Very limited	Some operating history	Operating history can be used in valuation	Substantial operating history
Comparable Firms	None	Some, but in same stage of growth	More comparables, at different stages	Large number of comparables, at different stages	Declining number of comparables, mostly mature
Source of Value	Entirely future growth	Mostly future growth	Portion from existing assets; growth still dominates	More from existing assets than growth	Entirely from existing assets

FIGURE 23.1   Valuation Issues across the Life Cycle

■ *Start-up.* This represents the initial stage after a business has been formed. The product is generally still untested and does not have an established market. The firm has little in terms of current operations, no operating history, and no comparable firms. The value of this firm rests entirely on its future growth potential. Valuation poses the most challenges at this firm, since there is little useful information to go on. The inputs have to be estimated and are likely to have considerable error associated with them. The estimates of future growth are often based on assessments of the competence of existing managers and their capacity to convert a promising idea into commercial success. This is often the reason why firms in this phase try to hire managers with a successful track record in converting ideas into dollars, because it gives them credibility in the eyes of financial backers.

■ *Expansion.* Once a firm succeeds in attracting customers and establishing a presence in the market, its revenues increase rapidly, though it still might be reporting losses. The current operations of the firm provide useful clues on pricing, margins, and expected growth, but current margins cannot be projected into the future. The operating history of the firm is still limited, and shows large changes from period to period. Other firms generally are in operation, but usually are at the same stage of growth as the firm being valued. Most of the value for this firm also comes from its expected growth. Valuation becomes a little simpler at this stage, but the information is still limited and unreliable, and the inputs to the valuation model are likely to be shifting substantially over time.

■ *High growth.* While the firm's revenues are growing rapidly at this stage, earnings are likely to lag behind revenues. At this stage, both the current operations and operating history of the firm contain information that can be used in valuing the firm. The number of comparable firms is generally highest at this stage, and these firms are more diverse in where they are in the life cycle, ranging from small, high-growth competitors to larger, lower-growth competitors. The existing assets of this firm have significant value, but the larger proportion of value still comes from future growth. There is more information available at this stage, and the estimation of inputs becomes more straightforward.

■ *Mature growth.* As revenue growth starts leveling off, firms generally find two phenomena occurring. The earnings and cash flows continue to increase rapidly, reflecting past investments, and the need to invest in new projects declines. At this stage in the process, the firm has current operations that are reflective of the future, an operating history that provides substantial information about the firm's markets, and a large number of comparable firms at the same stage in the life cycle. Existing assets contribute as much or more to firm value than expected growth, and the inputs to the valuation are likely to be stable.

■ *Decline.* The last stage in this life cycle is decline. Firms in this stage find both revenues and earnings starting to decline, as their businesses mature and new competitors overtake them. Existing investments are likely to continue to produce cash flows, albeit at a declining pace, and the firm has little need for new investments. Thus, the value of the firm depends entirely on existing assets. While the number of comparable firms tends to become smaller at this stage, they are all likely to be either in mature growth or in decline as well. Valuation is easiest at this stage.

Are the principles that drive valuation different at each stage? No. Valuation is clearly more of a challenge in the earlier stages in a life cycle, and estimates of value are much more likely to contain errors for start-up or high-growth firms. But the payoff to valuation is also likely to be highest with these firms for two reasons. The first is that the absence of information scares many analysts away, and analysts who persist and end up with a valuation, no matter how imprecise, are likely to be rewarded. The second is that these are the firms that are most likely to be coming to the market in the form of initial public offerings and new issues, and need estimates of value.

VENTURE CAPITAL VALUATION

Until very recently, young start-up firms raised additional equity primarily from venture capitalists. It is useful to begin by looking at how venture capitalists assess the value of these firms. While venture capitalists sometimes use discounted cash flow models to value firms, they are much more likely to value private businesses using what is called the venture capital method. Here, the earnings of the private firm are forecast in a future year, when the company can be expected to go public. These earnings, in conjunction with an earnings multiple that is estimated by looking at publicly traded firms in the same business, are used to assess the value of the firm at the time of the initial public offering; this is called the exit or terminal value.

For instance, assume that you are valuing InfoSoft, a small software firm, that is expected to have an initial public offering in three years, and that the net income in three years for the firm is expected to be $4 million. If the price-earnings ratio of publicly traded software firms is 25, this would yield an estimated exit value of $100 million. This value is discounted back to the present at what venture capitalists call a target rate of return, which measures what venture capitalists believe is a justifiable return, given the risk that they are exposed to. This target rate of return is usually set at a much higher level than the traditional cost of equity for the firm.[2]

Discounted terminal value = Estimated exit value/$(1 + \text{Target return})^n$

Using the InfoSoft example again, if the venture capitalist requires a target return of 30 percent on his or her investment, the discounted terminal value for InfoSoft would be:

Discounted terminal value for InfoSoft = $100 million/$1.30^3$ = $45.52 million

While this approach works for venture capitalist, it is unlikely to work for investors who are valuing young start-up companies that are publicly traded for two reasons. First, investors generally do not have the luxury of setting target returns of 30 percent or 40 percent, since they compete with other investors for the stock. Furthermore, there is an argument that can be made that a young start-up company should be less risky to an investor who holds a diversified portfolio than to a venture capitalist who might have fewer holdings. Second, venture capitalists have access to the firm's internal projections and usually can play a role in the management of the firm. In contrast, investors have to rely on information that the firm makes publicly available and generally have little or no say in the way the company is run.

The venture capital approach is also exposed to another problem. To the extent that exit multiples are based on how comparable firms are priced today, they can result in serious misevaluations if the market is wrong. For instance, venture capitalists who valued Internet firms in 2000 on the assumption that they would be able to sell these firms at 80 times revenues (which was what the market was pricing small, publicly traded Internet firms at that time) would have overestimated the value of these firms.

---

[2]In 1999, for instance, the target rate of return for private equity investors was in excess of 30 percent.

VENTURE CAPITAL, PRIVATE EQUITY, AND DIVERSIFICATION

Venture capitalists historically have been sector focused—they tend to concentrate their investments in one or two industries. Part of the reason for this is that the demand for venture capital tends to be concentrated in a few sectors at any point in time—new technology stocks in the late 1990s, biotechnology stocks in the late 1980s—and part of the reason is that venture capitalists draw on their knowledge of the industry both to value firms that ask for equity capital and to help in the management of these firms.

There is a cost to not being diversified, however, and it affects how these companies get valued in the first place. The cost of equity in a firm to a diversified investor will be lower than the cost of equity in the same firm to an undiversified investor, and this will result in a lower value being assigned to the firm by the latter.

In recent years, private equity investors have emerged as competition for traditional venture capitalists. Since these investors tend to be more diversified, they can settle for lower costs of equity and thus will attach a much higher value for the same private firm. In the long term, will private equity funds drive out venture capitalists? As long as localized knowledge about an industry matters in valuing firms in that industry, we do not believe so.

GENERAL FRAMEWORK FOR ANALYSIS

To value firms with negative earnings, little or no historical data, and few comparables, the steps involved are essentially the same as in any valuation. This section will look at some of the issues that are likely to come up at each step when valuing young companies.

Step 1: Assess the Firm's Current Standing: The Importance of Updated Information

It is conventional, when valuing firms, to use data from the most recent financial year to obtain the current year's inputs. For firms with negative earnings and high growth in revenues, the numbers tend to change dramatically from period to period. Consequently, it makes more sense to look at the most recent information that one can obtain, at least on revenues and earnings. Using the revenues and earnings from the trailing 12 months, for instance, will provide a much better estimate of value than using earnings from the last financial year. It is true that some items, such as operating leases and options outstanding, may not be updated as frequently. Even so, we would argue for using estimates for these inputs[3] and valuing firms with more recent data.

---

[3]One simple approach is to scale all of the inputs to reflect the growth in revenues that has occurred between the last financial year and the trailing 12 months.

ILLUSTRATION 23.1:   Commerce One: Last Financial Year versus Trailing 12 Months

Commerce One provides services and software to businesses that are interested in setting up electronic marketplaces, a process that arguably reduces costs to these businesses. In May 2001, when we valued Commerce One, its last annual report (10-K) was only three months old and represented information through December 2000. The firm has released one more quarterly report since, containing information for the first quarter of 2001. We constructed trailing 12-month values for each of the key inputs into the valuation. The results are summarized in the following table (in thousands):

	First Quarter 2001	First Quarter 2000	Last 10-K	Trailing 12 Months
Revenues	$ 170,273	$ 35,009	$ 401,796	$537,060
Operating income	–$ 228,739	–$ 45,186	–$ 345,564	–$529,117
Net operating loss carryforward			–$ 447,503	–$676,037
Net income	–$ 228,534	–$ 43,645	–$ 344,947	–$529,836
Capital expenditures	$ 23,386	$ 9,718	$ 79,158	$ 92,826
Depreciation	$ 10,695	$ 1,536	$ 13,815	$ 22,974
Cash and marketable securities	$ 249,373	$ 341,440	$ 249,373	
Investments in other assets	$ 38,213	$ 46,414	$ 38,213	
Book value of equity	$2,604,592	$2,799,411	$2,604,592	
Book value of debt	$ 23,510	$ 6,195	$ 23,510	
Number of shares outstanding	223,820	151,420	168,065	228,320

While only three months have elapsed since the last report, the trailing 12-month numbers are very different from the last annual report. Not only are the income statement numbers—revenues and income—very different, but the number of shares has increased by almost a third since the last annual report. In valuing Commerce One, we will use the updated numbers.

Step 2: Estimate Revenue Growth

Young firms tend to have fairly small amounts of revenues, but the expectation is that these revenues will grow at a substantial rate in the future. Not surprisingly, this is a key input in these valuations, and we would suggest drawing on a number of sources.

■ *Past growth rate in revenues at the firm itself.* Since the firm increases in scale as it grows, it will become more and more difficult to maintain very high growth rates. Thus, a firm that grew 300 percent two years ago and 200 percent last year is likely to grow at a lower rate this year.

■ *Growth rate in the overall market that the firm serves.* It is far easier for firms to maintain high growth rates in markets that are themselves growing at high rates than it is for them to do so in stable markets.

■ *Barriers to entry and competitive advantage possessed by the firm.* For a firm to be able to sustain high growth rates, it has to have some sustainable competitive advantage. This may come from legal protection (as is the case with a patent), a superior product or service, or a brand name, or from being the first mover into a market. If the competitive advantage looks sustainable, high growth is much more likely to last for a long period. If it is not, it will taper off much faster.

We looked at the process of estimating revenue growth in more detail in Chapter 11.

ILLUSTRATION 23.2:   Commerce One: Estimating Revenue Growth

Commerce One has grown at an extraordinary rate since it began operations about three years ago. The revenues of the firm have increased from $2.5 million in 1998 to $33.6 million in 1999 to $401 million in 2000. The compounded revenue growth rate has been 1,166% a year, and the growth rate just in the last year was 1,093%.

The market that Commerce One serves—business software and services—is a very large market, potentially allowing much more room for growth in future years. The primary competition for Commerce One comes both from other B2B firms like Ariba and from larger and more established firms such as Electronic Data Systems (EDS).

As a final consideration, the economy was weak at the time of this valuation, and business spending had slowed down. Consequently, we will be conservative about our estimate of revenue growth for the next year. The following table summarizes our forecasts of revenue growth and dollar revenues at Commerce One for the next 10 years (in millions):

Year	Expected Growth Rate	Revenues
Current		$ 537
1	50.00%	$ 806
2	100.00%	$ 1,611
3	80.00%	$ 2,900
4	60.00%	$ 4,640
5	40.00%	$ 6,496
6	35.00%	$ 8,770
7	30.00%	$11,401
8	20.00%	$13,681
9	10.00%	$15,049
10	5.00%	$15,802
Terminal year (11)	5.00%	$16,592

Note first that all projections are based on the trailing 12-month revenues, rather than revenues last year. Note also that while the growth rate in revenues is expected to decline over time, the dollar increase in revenues each year is larger than the previous year until we get to year 9. By the end of the tenth year, Commerce One's revenues of $15.8 billion would make it a very large player in the business services/software business. As comparison, note that EDS, the largest firm in this business currently, reported revenues of $19.6 billion in 2000.

Step 3: Estimate a Sustainable Operating Margin in Stable Growth

For a firm losing money, high revenue growth alone will accomplish little more than make the losses become larger over time. A key component for a young firm to be valuable is the expectation that the operating margin, while negative now, will become positive in the future. In many ways the true test in valuation is being able to visualize what a young, high-growth firm will look like when growth stabilizes. In the absence of comparables, the difficulty of this task is magnified. Again, a few guidelines help:

■ *Looking at the underlying business that this firm is in, consider its true competitors.* For instance, while Commerce One is considered to be a B2B or e-commerce firm, it is ultimately a provider of business services and software. At least from the perspective of margins, is seems reasonable to argue that Commerce One's margins will approach those of other business service providers.

■ *Deconstruct the firm's current income statement to get a truer measure of its operating margin.* Many young start-up firms that report negative earnings do so not because their operating expenses from generating current revenues are large, but because accounting convention requires them to report capital expenses as operating expenses. Since many of these capital expenses are treated as selling, general, and administrative (SG&A) expenses in income statements, estimating margins and profitability prior to these expenses is a useful exercise in figuring out how profitable a company's products truly are.

ILLUSTRATION 23.3: Estimating Sustainable Margin and Path to Margin: Commerce One

---

In the most recent 12 months, Commerce One reported an operating loss of $529 million on revenues of $537 million. When we capitalize research and development expenses, the operating loss narrows to $427 million. As the firm matures, these margins can be expected to improve, but to what level? The average pretax operating margin of established business service providers in 2000 was 15.73%. Over the 1996–2000 period, the margin has averaged 14.72%. We assumed that Commerce One's margins would reach 14.72% by year 10. There are some who would argue that Commerce One as a B2B business will have higher margins because it does not have the same cost structure as traditional service providers. We do not agree for two reasons. The first is that the high growth rates in revenues that we have assumed will require aggressive pricing from Commerce One and, therefore, lower margins. The second is that as long as anticipated margins for e-commerce firms are higher than they are for traditional competitors, there will be increased competition coming from the latter, pushing margins toward convergence.

To move from current margins to the sustainable margins, we assumed that the marginal improvement will be greater in the first few years, but we do not forecast operating profits until five years from now. The following table summarizes the forecasted operating margins and earnings before interest and taxes for the next 10 years and for the terminal year (year 11):

Year	Revenues	Operating Margin	EBIT
Current	$ 537	−79.45%	−$ 427
1	$ 806	−48.06%	−$ 387
2	$ 1,611	−27.14%	−$ 437
3	$ 2,900	−13.18%	−$ 382
4	$ 4,640	−3.88%	−$ 180
5	$ 6,496	2.32%	$ 151
6	$ 8,770	6.45%	$ 566
7	$11,401	9.21%	$1,050
8	$13,681	11.05%	$1,511
9	$15,049	12.27%	$1,847
10	$15,802	13.09%	$2,068
Terminal year	$16,592	14.72%	$2,442

Note that the growth rate in the terminal year is 5%.

If the improvement in margins is much faster or slower than we forecast, our estimates of value will need to be adjusted upward or downward, respectively.

To get from operating income to after-tax operating income, we generally apply the marginal tax rate, which we assume to be 35% for most U.S. firms. With Commerce One, though, there are two considerations. The first is that the firm is losing money currently and does not pay taxes—

and in fact will not be paying taxes for the next four years. The other is that the losses accumulate and will save the firm taxes even after it starts making money in year 5. At the time of this valuation, Commerce One had already accumulated losses from the past three years amounting to $676 million. The following table summarizes the net operating losses, taxable income, and effective tax rates for the forecast period:

Year	EBIT	NOL at Beginning of Year	Taxable Income	Taxes Paid	Tax Rate
1	−$ 387	$ 676	$ 0	0	0.00%
2	−$ 437	$1,063	$ 0	0	0.00%
3	−$ 382	$1,500	$ 0	0	0.00%
4	−$ 180	$1,883	$ 0	0	0.00%
5	$ 151	$2,063	$ 0	0	0.00%
6	$ 566	$1,912	$ 0	0	0.00%
7	$1,050	$1,346	$ 0	0	0.00%
8	$1,511	$ 297	$1,215	$425	28.13%
9	$1,847	$ 0	$1,847	$646	35.00%
10	$2,068	$ 0	$2,068	$724	35.00%
Terminal year	$2,442	$ 0	$2,442	$855	35.00%

Note that Commerce One starts making money in year 5 but does not start paying taxes until year 8, which is the year in which the net operating losses run out.[4]

Step 4: Estimate Reinvestment to Generate Growth

To grow, firms have to reinvest, and this principle cannot be set aside when you are looking at a young firm. Unlike a mature firm, though, there is likely to be little in the firm's history that will help in determining how much the firm will need to reinvest. As the firm grows, the nature of its reinvestment and the amount reinvested will probably change, and the challenge is to estimate this amount.

Chapter 11 stated that growth in operating income ultimately is a function of how much a firm reinvests and how well it reinvests (measured by the return on capital).

Expected growth = Reinvestment rate × Return on capital

In fact, this equation has been used to estimate growth in most of the valuations done so far in this book. However, we also noted that this equation becomes inoperable when operating earnings are negative, which is the position we are in when valuing young firms. In those cases, the growth in revenues must be estimated first, and the reinvestment must be based on the revenue growth. To make this link, we used a sales-capital ratio, that is, a ratio that specifies how many additional dollars of revenue will be generated by each additional dollar of capital:

Expected reinvestment = Expected change in revenue/(Sales/Capital ratio)

For instance, to grow revenues by $1 billion, with a sales-to-capital ratio of 4, would require a reinvestment of $250 million. The key input required for this formulation is the sales-to-capital ratio, and it can be estimated by looking at the firm's history, limited though it might be, and at industry averages, with the industry defined broadly to reflect the business the firm is in.

---

[4]The tax rate is computed by dividing the taxes by the earnings before interest and taxes.

In steady state, however, the reinvestment needs can be computed using the expected growth rate and the expected return on capital:

$$\text{Expected reinvestment rate}_{stable} = \text{Expected growth}_{stable}/ROC_{stable}$$

An alternative approach is to use the industry-average reinvestment rates (broken up into capital expenditures and working capital needs) to estimate cash flows.

ILLUSTRATION 23.4: Estimating Reinvestment Needs: Commerce One

Even over its brief history, Commerce One has reinvested in a number of different ways—R&D, acquisitions, and traditional capital expenditures—and has reinvested large amounts relative to its size. To estimate future reinvestment needs, we used two pieces of information:

1. In 2000, Commerce One had net capital expenditures, including capitalized R&D, of $160 million and an increase in working capital of $73 million. The revenues for the firm increased from $34 million to $537 million. Based on this, we can estimate a marginal sales/marginal capital ratio for the year:

    Sales/Capital = Change in sales$_{2000}$/Reinvestment$_{2000}$ = (537 − 34)/(160 + 73) = 2.16

2. The average sales-to-capital ratio for the industry—business services and software—is approximately 2.0. This includes more mature firms that are not e-commerce firms like EDS. For smaller firms in the business, the ratio is 2.21.

We assumed that the sales to capital ratio for Commerce One would be 2.20 for the forecast period. In conjunction with the revenues estimated in Illustration 23.2, we were able to estimate the total reinvestment needed each year:

Year	Revenues	Change in Revenues	Reinvestment	Total Capital	EBIT(1 − t)	ROC
Current	$ 537			$2,744	−$ 427	
1	$ 806	$ 269	$ 122	$2,866	−$ 387	−14.11%
2	$ 1,611	$ 806	$ 366	$3,232	−$ 437	−15.26%
3	$ 2,900	$1,289	$ 586	$3,818	−$ 382	−11.83%
4	$ 4,640	$1,740	$ 791	$4,609	−$ 180	−4.72%
5	$ 6,496	$1,856	$ 844	$5,452	$ 151	3.27%
6	$ 8,770	$2,274	$1,033	$6,486	$ 566	10.38%
7	$11,401	$2,631	$1,196	$7,682	$1,050	16.19%
8	$13,681	$2,280	$1,036	$8,718	$1,086	14.14%
9	$15,049	$1,368	$ 622	$9,340	$1,200	13.77%
10	$15,802	$ 752	$ 342	$9,682	$1,344	14.39%

By adding the total reinvestment to the capital invested at the beginning of the period, we estimate the total capital invested in the firm. In the last column, we divide our projected after-tax operating income each year by the capital invested at the end of the previous year to compute the return on capital. By year 10, the return on capital at Commerce One is 14.39%, just a shade below the average return on capital for the industry of 15%.[5] In year 11, which is the first year of stable growth, we assume that Commerce One's return on capital will move to the industry average return on capital. Assuming a stable growth rate of 5% allows us to estimate the reinvestment rate in stable growth:

Reinvestment rate in stable growth = g/ROC = 5%/15% = 33.33%

We will use this reinvestment rate to estimate the terminal value in a few pages.

---

[5]If the return on capital had become much larger than the industry average in year 10, we would have lowered the sales-to-capital ratio used in the valuation.

REINVESTMENT AND GROWTH: LAGGED EFFECTS

In our valuation of Commerce One, we have assumed that reinvestment and growth occur contemporaneously. In other words, the increase in revenues and the reinvestment that creates that increase occur simultaneously. This may seem like a radical assumption, but it is realistic in service businesses or when growth occurs through acquisitions.

If, in fact, there is a lag between reinvestment and growth, it is relatively simple to build this lag into the analysis. In the Commerce One valuation, assuming a one-year lag, you could estimate the reinvestment in year 1 from expected revenue growth in year 2. The length of the lag will depend on both the firm being valued—it will be longer for firms that have to make capital-intensive and infrastructure investments—and the form of the reinvestment—whether it is internal or external (acquisitions).

Step 5: Estimate Risk Parameters and Discount Rates

In the standard approaches for estimating beta, we regress stock returns against market returns. Young start-up firms, even when publicly traded, have little historical data, and we cannot use the conventional approach to estimate risk parameters.[6] In Chapter 7, though, we suggested alternative approaches for estimating betas that are useful to bridge this gap. One is the bottom-up approach. If there are comparable firms that have been listed for two or more years, the current risk parameters for the firm can be estimated by looking at the averages for these firms. If such firms do not exist, risk parameters can be estimated using the financial characteristics of the firm—the volatility in earnings, their size, cash flow characteristics, and financial leverage.[7]

If a young firm has debt, we run into a different problem when estimating the cost of debt. The firm will generally not be rated, thus denying us a chance to estimate a cost of debt based on the rating. We could try estimating a synthetic rating, but the negative operating income will yield a negative interest coverage ratio and a default rating for the firm. One solution is to estimate an expected interest coverage ratio for the firm based on expected operating income in future periods (note that these forecasts were already made in steps 2 and 3) and to use this expected interest coverage ratio to estimate a synthetic rating.

Whatever approach we use to estimate costs of equity and debt, they should not be left unchanged over the estimation period. As the firm matures and moves toward its sustainable margin and stable growth, the risk parameters should also approach those of an average firm—the betas should move toward 1 and the cost of debt should adjust toward a mature firm's cost of debt.

In addition to estimating the cost of equity for these firms, we have to estimate how leverage will change over time. Again, targeting an industry average or an optimal debt ratio for this firm (as it will look in steady state) should yield reasonable estimates for the cost of capital over time.

---

[6]The conventional approach is to regress returns on a stock against returns on a market index over a past period, say two to five years.
[7]For a description of this approach, refer back to Chapter 7.

OPERATING LEVERAGE AND RISK

One argument that can be made for why young firms should have much higher betas than larger, more mature firms in their business is that they have much higher operating leverage. The costs for young firms are for the most part fixed and do not vary with revenues. If you are estimating a bottom-up beta for a young firm by looking at comparable firms, you have two choices:

1. You can use only small, publicly traded firms as your comparable firms. This will work only if there are significant numbers of publicly traded firms in the business.
2. The other and more promising approach is to adjust the bottom-up beta for differences in operating leverage. Chapter 7 noted how betas can be adjusted for differences in fixed cost structures:

   Unlevered beta = Business beta[1 + (Fixed costs/Variable costs)]

ILLUSTRATION 23.5:   Estimating Risk Parameters and Costs of Capital: Commerce One

Commerce One does not have sufficient historical data for us to estimate risk parameters with any degree of accuracy. A regression of stock returns against a market index since the stock's listing in June 1999 yields a beta of 3.06, but the standard error in the estimate is 2.23, rendering it useless.

To estimate the current beta for the firm, we had a choice between using the average unlevered beta of other B2B firms (which is approximately 2.00) and the average unlevered beta of business service providers (0.98). At the moment, Commerce One's fundamental characteristics seem to reflect the former more than the latter; its growth potential is tied to the success of e-commerce. We therefore chose to use an unlevered beta of 2.00 to estimate the current beta for the firm. At the time of this analysis, Commerce One had debt outstanding of $25.1 million and the present value of operating leases at the firm amounted to $131.12 million. Based on the prevailing market price of $8.28, a market value of equity of $1.89 billion and a debt-to-equity ratio of 8.26% were estimated.

$$\text{Debt-to-equity ratio} = (25.1 + 131.12)/1,890 = 8.26\%$$

$$\text{Levered beta} = \text{Unlevered beta}[1 + (1 - t)(D/E)] = 2.00[1 + (1 - 0.00)(.0826)] = 2.17$$

This will be the beta that we use for the first five years, and the tax rate is set to zero to reflect the fact that the firm will not be paying taxes. With a risk-free rate of 5.4% and a risk premium of 4%, we estimate a cost of equity for the first five years:

$$\text{Cost of equity} = 5.4\% + 2.17(4\%) = 14.06\%$$

To estimate the cost of debt, we computed the average operating income over the next seven years using the projections in Illustration 23.3 (obtaining a value of $54 million) and divided this by the current interest expenses (including the operating lease expenses from the current year):

$$\text{Predicted interest coverage ratio} = \text{Average EBIT}/(\text{Interest expense} + \text{Current year's lease expense})$$
$$= 54/(2.5 + 14.41) = 3.17$$

This yields a rating of BB and a default spread of 3.50%, as well as a pretax cost of debt of 8.90% for the next five years. Since the firm pays no taxes over this period, its after-tax cost of debt is equal to the pretax cost.

Beyond year 5, as the firm matures, we feel that Commerce One's risk will approach those of other business service providers and that its beta will decline to 1.2, which will still make it riskier than the typical firm in the sector. The pretax cost of debt will also decline toward an industry average of 7%, while the debt ratio will increase toward the average for the industry of 12%. The following table summarizes resulting estimates of cost of equity, debt, and capital for Commerce One:

Year	Beta	Cost of Equity	Pretax Cost of Debt	Tax Rate	After-Tax Cost of Debt	Debt Ratio	Cost of Capital
1	2.17	14.06%	8.90%	0.00%	8.90%	7.63%	13.67%
2	2.17	14.06%	8.90%	0.00%	8.90%	7.63%	13.67%
3	2.17	14.06%	8.90%	0.00%	8.90%	7.63%	13.67%
4	2.17	14.06%	8.90%	0.00%	8.90%	7.63%	13.67%
5	2.17	14.06%	8.90%	0.00%	8.90%	7.63%	13.67%
6	1.97	13.29%	8.52%	0.00%	8.52%	8.51%	12.88%
7	1.78	12.52%	8.43%	0.00%	8.43%	8.72%	12.16%
8	1.59	11.74%	8.27%	27.93%	5.96%	9.09%	11.22%
9	1.39	10.97%	7.95%	35.00%	5.17%	9.82%	10.40%
10	1.20	10.20%	7.00%	35.00%	4.55%	12.00%	9.52%

Note that the beta declines linearly from the current level of 2.17 in year 5 to 1.20 in year 10 and the pretax cost of debt declines from 8.90% in year 5 to 7% in year 10. The cost of capital beyond year 10 will be 9.52%.

Step 6: Estimate the Value of the Firm

With the inputs on earnings, reinvestment rates, and risk parameters over time, this valuation becomes much more conventional. In many cases, the cash flows in the early years will be negative, in keeping with the negative earnings, but turn positive in later years as margins improve. The bulk of the value will generally be in the terminal value. Consequently, our assumptions about what the firm will look like in stable growth are significant.

Having valued the operating assets of the firm, you need to consider two other factors—the possibility that the firm will not survive to become a going concern and the value of nonoperating assets—to value the firm.

Survival When we value firms using discounted cash flow valuation, we tend to assume that the firm will be a going concern and continue to generate cash flows in perpetuity. This assumption might be suspect when valuing young companies, since many of them will not survive the tests that they will be put to over the next few years. If we ignore this possibility and consider only the best-case scenario of expansion and profitability, we will over estimate the value of these firms. We have two choices when it comes to dealing with this possibility.

1. The first is to build into the expected growth rates and earnings the likelihood of unfavorable outcomes. Thus, the growth rate used in revenues will be the expected growth rate over all scenarios, both optimistic and pessimistic. For young firms, this will become progressively more difficult to do as you get further and further into the future.

2. The second is to estimate a discounted cash flow value across only the scenarios where the firm is a going concern, and then apply a probability that the firm will be a going concern to this value. Chapter 12 suggested a couple of approaches that can help in coming up with this probability including statistical probits and Monte Carlo simulations. Once we have estimated the probability of surviving as a going concern, the value of a firm can then be estimated as follows:

Value of firm = Probability of surviving as a going concern
× Discounted cash flow value of firm
+ (1 − Probability of surviving as a going concern)
× Distress or liquidation sale value

Value of Nonoperating Assets   As with the valuation of any firm, you have to consider cash, marketable securities, and holdings in other companies when you value a firm. The only note of caution that we would add is that young firms can burn through significant cash balances in short periods because their operations drain cash rather than generate it. Thus, the cash balance from the last financial statements, especially if those statements are more than a few months old, can be very different from the current cash balances.

To the extent that young firms often have holdings in other young firms, there is also the danger that investments in other firms may be shown on the books at values that are not reflective of their true value. If there are only one or two large holdings, you should value those holdings using cash flow–based approaches as well.

ILLUSTRATION 23.6:   Estimating Firm Value: Commerce One

Having estimated the cash flows and the discount rates, we are now in a position to estimate the value for Commerce One as a firm. While estimating cash flows, we consider the fact that the firm will have net operating losses to carry forward and that this will reduce their tax burden when they initially start making money. The following table summarizes the cash flows to the firm after reinvestment needs for each of the next 10 years and the discount rate applied to these cash flows.

Year	EBIT (1 − t)	Reinvestment	FCFF	Cost of Capital	Cumulated Cost of Capital	Present Value
1	−$ 388	$ 122	−$ 510	13.67%	1.1367	−$ 449
2	−$ 438	$ 366	−$ 805	13.67%	1.2920	−$ 623
3	−$ 384	$ 586	$ 970	13.67%	1.4686	−$ 660
4	−$ 182	$ 791	$ 973	13.67%	1.6693	−$ 583
5	$ 149	$ 844	−$ 694	13.67%	1.8975	−$ 366
6	$ 565	$1,033	−$ 469	12.88%	2.1419	−$ 219
7	$1,049	$1,196	−$ 147	12.16%	2.4024	−$ 61
8	$1,089	$1,036	$ 52	11.22%	2.6719	$ 19
9	$1,200	$ 622	$ 578	10.40%	2.9498	$ 196
10	$1,344	$ 342	$1,002	9.52%	3.2307	$ 310
	Sum of the present value of the cash flows over high-growth period =					−$2,435

There is one very significant cash flow that is not reported on this table, and that is the terminal value of the firm. To estimate the terminal value at the end of year 10, we first estimated the free cash flow to the firm in year 11:

$$\text{Free cash flow to the firm} = EBIT_{11}(1 - t)(1 - \text{Reinvestment rate}_{stable})$$
$$= \$2,442(1 - .35)(1 - .33) = \$1,058 \text{ million}$$

We use the stable growth rate of 5% and the reinvestment rate of 33.33% that we estimated earlier. The terminal value can now be estimated;

$$\text{Terminal value} = FCFF_{11}/(\text{Cost of capital}_{stable} - \text{Stable growth rate})$$
$$= 1,058/(.0952 - .05) = \$23,404 \text{ million}$$

The value of the operating assets of the firm can be estimated:

$$\text{Value of operating assets} = \text{PV of cash flows during high growth} + \text{PV of terminal value}$$
$$= -\$2,435 + \$23,404/3.2307 = \$4,809 \text{ million}$$

To this, we add the most recent estimate that we have of cash, marketable securities, and other investments:

$$\text{Value of firm} = \text{Value of operating assets} + \text{Cash and marketable securities} + \text{Other investments}$$
$$= \$4,809 \text{ million} + \$249 \text{ million} + \$38 \text{ million} = \$5,097 \text{ million}$$

This would be the value that we would assign the firm as a going concern.

How much of a discount should be applied for the likelihood that Commerce One may not survive? The firm has a cash balance that will cover its operating cash needs for only about six months, which increases the chances of failure, especially if the equity markets remain weak. In addition, we expect the firm to continue to lose money for the next five years, which will increase its need for external financing. On the positive side, the firm is not heavily levered and is not under immediate pressure to meet debt payments. Assume, for instance, that these facts lead you to assign a 25% probability that the firm will not survive and that the distress sale value in the event of failure will be 50% of book value of $2,744 billion. The value of Commerce One can then be estimated as follows:

$$\text{Value of Commerce One} = \text{Going concern value} \times \text{Probability of going concern}$$
$$+ \text{Distress sale value} \times \text{Probability of failure}$$
$$= \$5,097 \times .75 + (\$2,744 \times .5) \times .25 = \$4,166 \text{ million}$$

Clearly, the probability estimate and the distress sale value in this example are arbitrary values, but they can be fine-tuned when the probability of default is high.

Step 7: Estimate the Value of Equity and Per-Share Value

To get from firm value to equity value, we generally subtract out all nonequity claims on the firm. For mature firms, the nonequity claims take the form of bank debt and bonds outstanding. For young firms, there can also be preferred equity claims that have to be valued and subtracted to get to the value of the common equity.

To get from equity value to value per share, you have to consider equity options outstanding on the firm. In Chapter 16, we argued that this is something that needs to be done for all firms, but it becomes particularly important with young start-up firms, because the value of the options outstanding can be a much larger share of the overall equity value. Given the importance of these claims, we would suggest that the options—vested as well as nonvested—be valued using an option pricing model, and that the value of the options be subtracted from the value of the equity to arrive at the value of equity in common stock. This value should then be divided by the actual number of shares outstanding to arrive at the equity value per share.

ILLUSTRATION 23.7:   Valuing Equity per Share: Commerce One

Having estimated the value of Commerce One to be $5.097 million, we first estimate the value of equity by subtracting out the value of the debt claims on the firm. The debt claims that we consider include both the debt outstanding of $25.1 million and the present value of operating lease commitments of $131 million:

Value of Commerce One equity = Value of firm − Debt = 5,097 − (25 + 131) = $4,941 million

As of December 2000, the firm had options outstanding on 45.911 million shares, with a weighted average life of 8.92 years and a weighted exercise price of $35.49. Using a Black-Scholes option pricing model, allowing for dilution, the value of these options were computed using Commerce One's market price of $8.28 per share as of May 2001. The total value of the options outstanding was estimated to be $349 million. Assuming that Commerce One will be able to claim this expense as a tax deduction when the options are exercised, the value of equity in common stock was computed then, as follows:

Value of equity	$4,941 million
− Value of equity in options outstanding = $349(1 − .35)	$ 227 million
= Value of equity in common stock	$4,714 million

Commerce One had 228.32 million shares outstanding as of May 2001, leading to a per-share value of:

Value of equity in common stock	$4,714 million
/ Number of shares outstanding	228.32 million
= Value of equity per share	$ 20.65

This value per share is at variance with the value used to price the options. If we iterated back using this estimated value per share to value the options, we would obtain a value of $835 million (pretax) for the options and a value per share of $19.26.

SHOULD THERE BE A DISCOUNT FOR FLOAT?

Some publicly traded stocks are lightly traded, and the number of shares available for trade (often referred to as the float) is small relative to the total number of shares outstanding.[8] Investors who want to sell their stock quickly in these companies often have a price impact when they sell, and the impact will increase with the size of the holding.

Investors with longer time horizons and a lesser need to convert their holdings into cash quickly have a smaller problem associated with illiquidity than investors with shorter time horizons and a greater need for cash. Investors should consider the possibility that they will need to convert their holdings quickly into cash when they look at lightly traded stocks as potential investments and require much larger discounts on value before they take large positions. Assume, for instance, that an investor is looking at a young firm that she has valued at $19.05 per share. The stock would be underpriced if it were trading at $17, but it might not be underpriced enough for a short-term investor to take a large position in it. In contrast, a long-term investor may find the stock an attractive buy at that price.

---

[8]The float is estimated by subtracting from the shares outstanding the shares that are owned by insiders and 5 percent owners and the rule 144 shares. (Rule 144 refers to restricted stock that cannot be traded.)

VALUE DRIVERS

What are the key inputs that determine the value of a young high-growth firm with negative earnings? In general, the inputs that have the greatest impact on value are the estimates of sustainable margins and revenue growth. To a lesser extent, assumptions about how long it will take the firm to reach a sustainable margin and reinvestment needs in stable growth also have an impact on value.

In practical terms, the bulk of the value of these firms is derived from the terminal value. While this will trouble some, it mirrors how an investor makes returns in these firms. The payoff to these investors takes the form of price appreciation rather than dividends or stock buybacks. Another way of explaining the dependence on terminal value and the importance of the sustainable growth assumption is in terms of assets in place and future growth. The value of any firm can be written as the sum of the two:

Value of firm = Value of assets in place + Value of growth potential

For start-up firms with negative earnings, almost all of the value can be attributed to the second component. Not surprisingly, the firm value is determined by assumptions about the latter.

ILLUSTRATION 23.8:   Value Drivers for Commerce One

There are two key value drivers that affect the value of Commerce One as a firm. The first is the expected compounded growth rate in revenues. We have assumed it to be approximately 40% compounded over the next 10 years. If revenue growth were higher, the value per share would also be higher, as evidenced in Figure 23.2. Note, though, that we are talking about compounded growth. At a 50% compounded growth rate, the value per share would be in excess of $40, but revenues in year 10 would have to be $30 billion. This is in contrast to our base case assumption where revenues grow to $15.8 billion in year 10.

The second is the sustainable operating margin. We assumed that it would converge on the industry average of 14.72%. The value per share is extremely sensitive to this assumption. (See Figure 23.3.) If the pretax operating margin were to be 16% instead of 14.72%, the value per share would increase to $23. For this to happen, however, the competition would essentially have to collapse. If, on the other hand, this market turns out to have fewer barriers to entry than anticipated and competition drives margins to 10%, the value per share will drop to single digits.

In conclusion, it is worth noting that we can justify Commerce One's price per share (of $8.28 at the time of this analysis) under certain circumstances, just as we can justify the market price of any security. For instance, assuming a lower compounded growth rate in revenues for the next 10 years or a lower pretax operating margin or some combination of the two would lead us to a value of $8.28. For any investor or analyst, the follow-up questions then become pragmatic ones: What are the odds of such an occurrence? Do you feel confident enough that this is too pessimistic a view of the world?

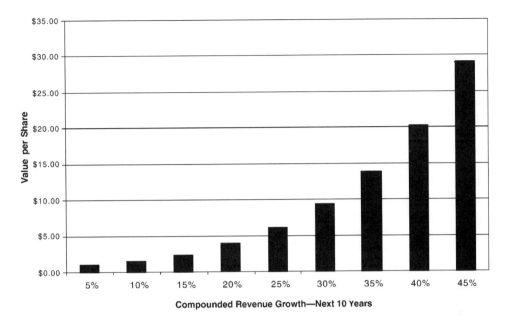

FIGURE 23.2   Revenue Growth and Value per Share: Commerce One

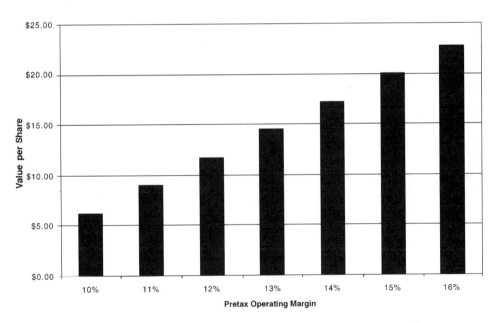

FIGURE 23.3   Value per Share and Sustainable Margins: Commerce One

ESTIMATION NOISE

The framework for valuation provided in this section should not be considered a recipe for precision. *The valuation of a firm with negative earnings, high growth, and limited information will always be noisy.* One way to present this noise is in terms of a valuation range, and the range on the value of these firms will be large. This is often used as an excuse by analysts who do not want to go through the process of valuing such firms. It also provides critics with a simplistic argument against trusting the numbers that emerge from these models.

We have a different view. The noise in the valuation is not a reflection of the quality of the valuation model, or the analyst using it, but of the underlying real uncertainty about the future prospects of the firm. This uncertainty is a fact of life when it comes to investing in these firms. In a valuation, we attempt to grapple with this uncertainty and make our best estimates about the future. Note that those who disdain valuation models for their potential errors end up using far cruder approaches, such as comparing price-sales ratios across firms. The difference, as we see it, is that they choose to sweep the uncertainties under the rug and act as if they do not exist.

There are two other points to make about the precision in these valuations. First, *even if a valuation is imprecise, it provides a powerful tool to answer the question of what has to occur for the current market price of a firm to be justified.* Investors can then decide whether they are comfortable with these assumptions, and make their decisions on buying and selling stock. Second, *even if individual valuations are noisy, portfolios constructed based on these valuations will be more precisely valued.* Thus, an investor who buys 40 stocks that he or she has found to be undervalued using traditional valuation models, albeit with significant noise, should find noise averaging out across the portfolio. The ultimate performance of the portfolio then should reflect the valuation skills, or the absence of them, of the analyst.

IMPLICATIONS FOR INVESTORS

From a valuation perspective, there are a number of useful lessons that emerge for investors in young firms with negative earnings and limited information.

- *Focus on sustainable margins and survival*, rather than quarter-to-quarter or even year-to-year swings in profitability. Understanding what a firm's operating margins will look like when it reaches financial health might be the single most important determinant of whether one is successful investing, in the long term, in such firms. Separating those firms that have a greater chance of surviving and reaching financial health from those that will not survive is a closely connected second determinant. After all, most start-up firms never survive to enjoy their vaunted growth prospects.
- *Earnings reports can be misleading*, especially when reinvestment costs are expensed (as is the case with research, development, and long-term marketing expenses). Thus, when a firm with high-growth potential and poor earnings reports a significant improvement in earnings, investors should examine the report for the reasons. If the earnings are improving because the costs of generat-

ing current revenues are coming down (due to economies of scale or pricing power), this is clearly good news. If, however, the earnings are increasing because the firm has reduced or eliminated discretionary reinvestment expenditures (such as development costs), the net effect on value can be very negative, since future growth is being put at risk.

- *Diversify.* This age-old rule of investing becomes even more critical when investing in stocks that derive the bulk of their value from uncertain future growth. The antidote to estimation noise is often a more diversified portfolio both across firms and across sectors.[9]
- *Keep track of barriers of entry* and competitive advantages; they will, in large part, determine whether the firm will continue to maintain high growth.
- *Be ready to be wrong.* The noise in these valuations is such that no matter how much information is brought into the process and how carefully a valuation is done, the value obtained is an estimate. Thus, investors in these stocks will be spectacularly wrong sometimes, and it is unfair to judge them on individual valuations. They will also be spectacularly right in other cases, and all that we can hope for is that with time as an ally, the successes outweigh the failures.

IMPLICATIONS FOR MANAGERS

If the future growth potential for a firm is uncertain, what are the implications for managers? The first is that the uncertainty about future growth will almost certainly translate into more uncertainty in traditional investment analysis. It is far more difficult to estimate cash flows and discount rates for individual projects in young start-up firms than in more stable sectors. While the reaction of some managers at these firms is to give up and fall back on more intuitive approaches, the managers who persevere and attempt to estimate cash flows will have a much better sense of what they need to do to make new investments pay off.

THE EXPECTATIONS GAME

As the proportion of value determined by future growth increases, expectations become a more critical determinant of how markets react to new information. In fact, the expectations game largely explains why stock prices change in ways that do not seem consistent with the news being announced (good earnings news leading to stock price drops; bad earnings news resulting in stock price increases) and the volatility of young start-up firms in general.

---

[9]The simple rules of diversification that suggest 20 stocks are enough may not apply here. Since these investments tend to come from the same sector and have higher correlations with each other, and since there is so much noise in estimation, more stocks will be needed to accomplish the same degree of diversification that one would have got by buying 20 large-capitalization, mature companies.

Expectations, Information, and Value

The value of a firm is the present value of the expected cash flows on the firm, and implicit in these expected cash flows and the discount rates used to discount the cash flows are investors' views about the firm, its management, and the potential for excess returns. While this is true for all firms, the larger proportion of value that comes from future growth potential at young start-up firms makes them particularly vulnerable to shifts in expectations about the future.

How are these expectations formed? While the past history of these firms and industry averages are sometimes used as the basis for estimates, the firms and the industries themselves both evolve and change over time. The fact that information is both noisy and limited suggests that expectations can change relatively quickly and in response to small shifts in information. An earnings announcement, for instance, that suggests that a firm's strategy is not working as well as anticipated may lead to a reassessment of expectations and a sharp drop in value.

Lessons for Investors

The power of expectations in determining the value of a stock has to be considered when investors choose stocks for their portfolios and when they assess new information about the firm. There are several important implications:

- *Risk is always relative to expectations.* The risk in a firm does not come from whether it performs well or badly but from how it does relative to expectations. Thus, a firm that reports earnings growth of 35 percent a year when it was expected to grow 50 percent a year is delivering bad news and will probably see its stock price drop. In contrast, a firm that reports a 20 percent drop in earnings when it was expected to report a 40 percent drop will generally see its stock price increase.
- *Good companies do not always make good investments.* It is not how well or badly a company is managed that determines stock returns; it is how well or badly managed it is relative to expectations. A company that meets every financial criterion for excellence may be a poor investment if markets are expecting too much of it. Conversely, a firm that is universally viewed as a poorly managed, poorly run company may be a good investment if expectations have been set too low.[10]
- *Small news leads to big price jumps.* As noted in the preceding section, you should expect to see what seem like disproportionate stock price responses to relatively small pieces of information. A report from a high-growth firm that earnings in the most recent quarter were a few cents less than expected may lead to a significant drop in the stock price.

---

[10]The empirical evidence backs up this proposition. Studies of investments seem to indicate that companies that are viewed as well managed underperform companies that are less well regarded as investments.

■ *Focus on information about value drivers.* On a positive note, investors can assess what it is that drives value the most at a firm, and get a sense of what they should focus on when looking at new information. Looking past the aggregate earnings numbers for information on these value drivers may provide clues of both upcoming trouble and potential promise.

Lessons for Managers

If the expectation game affects investors, it is even more critical to managers at young firms. One of the ironies that emerges from this game is that it is far easier to manage a firm that is perceived to be a poor performer than it is to manage one that is perceived to be a star.[11]

■ *Find out what is expected of you.* If you are going to be judged against expectations, it is critical that you gauge what these expectations are. While this translates, for many firms, into keeping track of what analysts are estimating earnings per share or revenue growth to be in the next quarter, there is more to it than this. Understanding why investors value your firm the way they do and what they think are your competitive advantages are much more important in the long term.

■ *Learn to manage expectations.* When firms first go public, managers and insiders sell the idea that their firm has great potential and should be valued highly. While this is perfectly understandable, managers have to change roles after they go public and learn to manage expectations. Specifically, they have to talk down expectations when they feel that their firm is being set up to do things that it cannot accomplish. Again, though, some firms damage their credibility when they talk down expectations incessantly, even when they know the expectations are reasonable.[12]

■ *Do not delay the inevitable.* No matter how well a firm manages expectations, there are times when managers realize that they cannot meet expectations anymore because of changes in the sector or the overall economy. While the temptation is strong to delay revealing this to financial markets, often by shifting earnings from future periods into the current one or using accounting ploys, it is far better to deal with the consequences immediately. This may mean reporting lower earnings than expected and a lower stock price, but firms that delay their day of reckoning tend to be punished much more.

---

[11]Steve Jobs' job at Apple Computer was far easier when he took over in 1998 (when the stock price had hit a 10-year low) than it was two years later, when he had succeeded in changing investor perceptions of the company (and pushed the stock price up tenfold in the process).

[12]Microsoft has developed a reputation for talking down expectations and then beating them on a consistent basis.

CONCLUSION

Valuation, fundamentally, remains the same no matter what type of firm one is analyzing. There are three groups of firms where the exercise of valuation becomes more difficult and estimates of value more noisy. The first group includes firms that have negative earnings. Given the dependence of most models on earnings growth to make projections for the future, analysts have to consider approaches that allow earnings to become positive, at least over time. They can do so by normalizing earnings in the current period, by adjusting margins from current levels to sustainable levels over time, or by reducing leverage. The approach used will depend on why the firm has negative earnings in the first place. The second group of firms where estimates are difficult to make are young firms with little or no financial history. Here, information on comparable firms can substitute for historical data and allow analysts to estimate the inputs needed for valuation. The third group of firms where valuation can be difficult includes unique firms with few or no comparable companies.

If all three problems come together for the same firm—negative earnings, limited history, and few comparables—the difficulty is compounded. This chapter has laid out a broad framework that can be used to value such firms. It should be noted again that the question is not whether these firms can be valued—they certainly can—but whether we are willing to live with noisy estimates of value. To those who argue that these valuations are too noisy to be useful, our counter would be that much of this noise stems from real uncertainty about the future. As we see it, investors who attempt to measure and confront this uncertainty are better prepared for the volatility that comes with investing in these stocks.

QUESTIONS AND SHORT PROBLEMS

1. Intellitech is a technology firm that has been in operating for two years. In the most recent year, the firm reported revenues of $500 million, five times revenues in the previous year. The firm also reported an operating loss of $400 million. You expect revenues to grow 100% next year, 80% the year after, and 40% a year for the following three years, and the pretax operating margin to improve—in linear increments—to 10% by the fifth year. Estimate the revenues and operating income each year for the next five years.

2. You are trying to estimate the trailing 12-month earnings for Fiber Networks. The firm has just reported an operating loss for the first quarter of 2001 of $180 million on revenues of $600 million, a jump from the operating loss of $30 million on revenues of $120 million in the first quarter of 2000. In its annual report for 2000, Fiber Networks reported an operating loss of $330 million on revenues of $1.1 billion. Estimate the operating loss and revenues for the past four quarters.

3. Verispace Software sells inventory management software and reported revenues of $25 million in the most recent financial year. You estimate that the total market for inventory management software to be $25 billion, growing at 5% a year for the foreseeable future. If you expect Verispace to have 10% market share of this market in 10 years, estimate the compounded revenue growth rate over that period.

4. Lumin Telecomm produces specialized telecommunication equipment and has made losses each year over the three years it has been in existence—it has an accumulated net operating loss of $180 million. In the most recent year, the firm reported an operating loss of $90 million on revenues of $1 billion. If you expect the growth rate in revenues to be 20% a year for the next five years, and the pretax operating margin to be –6% next year, –3% two years from now, 0% the year after, 6% in four years, and 10% in five years (tax rate = 40%), estimate:
   a. The revenues and pretax operating income each year for the next five years.
   b. The taxes you would have to pay and your after-tax operating income each year for the next five years.

5. In problem 4, assume that Lumin Telecomm has a beta of 2.0 currently and that you expect it to drop in linear increments to 1.2 by year 5. If the current cost of borrowing is 9% and you expect this to remain unchanged over the next five years, estimate the cost of capital for the firm each year for the next five years. (The risk-free rate is 5.6%, and the risk premium is 4%.) The debt ratio is expected to decline from 70% in the current year to 50% in year 5 in linear increments.

6. You have estimated the value of Vitale Systems, an Internet software firm, to be $700 million as a going concern, seven times its book value. However, you are concerned that Vitale might not survive the next five years and estimate the probability of failure at 40%. If the firm fails, you expect its assets to sell for 1.5 times book value. If there are 30 million shares outstanding, estimate the value per share. (The firm has no debt or options outstanding.)

CHAPTER 24

Valuing Private Firms

So far this book has concentrated on the valuation of publicly traded firms. In this chapter, we turn our attention to the thousands of firms that are private businesses. These businesses range in size from small family businesses to some that rival large publicly traded firms. The principles of valuation remain the same, but there are estimation problems that are unique to private businesses. The information available for valuation tends to be much more limited in terms of both history and depth, since private firms are often not governed by the strict accounting and reporting standards of publicly traded firms. In addition, the standard techniques for estimating risk parameters such as beta and standard deviation require market prices for equity, an input that is lacking for private firms.

When valuing private firms, the motive for the valuation matters and can affect the value. In particular, the value that is attached to a publicly traded firm may be different when it is being valued for sale to an individual, for sale to a publicly traded firm, or for an initial public offering. In particular, whether there should be a discount on value for illiquidity and nondiversifiable risk or a premium for control will depend on the motive for the valuation. Each of these components will be considered over the course of this chapter.

WHAT MAKES PRIVATE FIRMS DIFFERENT?

There are a number of common characteristics shared by private firms with publicly traded firms, but there are four significant differences that can affect how we estimate inputs for valuation.

1. Publicly traded firms are governed by a set of accounting standards that allow us not only to identify what each item in a financial statement includes but also to compare earnings across firms. Private firms, especially if they are not incorporated, operate under far looser standards, and there can be wide differences between firms on how items are accounted for.
2. There is far less information about private firms in terms of both the number of years of data that is typically available and, more importantly, the amount of information available each year. For instance, publicly traded firms have to break down operations by business segments in their filings with the SEC and provide information on revenues and earnings by segment. Private firms do not have to provide this information, and usually do not.

3. A constantly updated price for equity and historical data on this price are very useful pieces of information that we can obtain easily for publicly traded firms but not for private firms. In addition, the absence of a ready market for private firm equity also means that liquidating an equity position in a private business can be far more difficult (and expensive) than liquidating a position in a publicly traded firm.

4. In publicly traded firms, the stockholders tend to hire managers to run the firms, and most stockholders hold equity in several firms in their portfolios. The owner of a private firm tends to be intimately involved with management, and often has all of his or her wealth invested in the firm. The absence of separation between the owner and management can result in an intermingling of personal expenses with business expenses, and a failure to differentiate between management salary and dividends (or their equivalent). The absence of diversification can affect our measurement of risk.

Each of the differences cited can change value by affecting discount rates, cash flows, and expected growth rates.

To examine the issues that arise in the context of valuing private firms, we will consider two firms. The first firm is the New York Yankees, the fabled baseball franchise, and the second is a private software firm called InfoSoft. We will value the Yankees for sale in a private transaction, whereas we will value InfoSoft for sale in an initial public offering (IPO).

ESTIMATING VALUATION INPUTS AT PRIVATE FIRMS

The value of a private firm is the present value of expected cash flows discounted back at an appropriate discount rate. Since this construct is not different from the one we used to value publicly traded firms, the differences between private firms and publicly traded firms have to show up in how we estimate these inputs to the discounted cash flow model.

Discount Rates

If we choose to value equity, we discount cash flows to equity at the cost of equity, whereas if we choose to value the firm, we discount cash flows at the cost of capital. While the fundamental definitions of these costs have not changed, the process of estimating them may have to be changed given the special circumstances surrounding private firms.

Cost of Equity In assessing the cost of equity for publicly traded firms, we looked at the risk of investments through the eyes of the marginal investors in these firms. With the added assumption that these investors were well diversified, we were able to define risk in terms of risk added on to a diversified portfolio or market risk. The beta in the capital asset pricing model (CAPM) and betas (in the multifactor models) that measure this risk are usually estimated using historical stock prices. The absence of historical price information for private firm equity and the failure on the part of many private firm owners to diversify can create serious problems with estimating and using betas for these firms.

Approaches to Estimating Market Betas   The standard process of estimating the beta in the capital asset pricing model involves running a regression of stock returns against market returns. Multifactor models use other statistical techniques, but they also require historical price information. In the absence of such information, as is the case with private firms, there are three ways in which we can estimate betas: accounting betas, fundamental betas, and bottom-up betas.

Accounting Betas   While price information is not available for private firms, accounting earnings information is. We could regress changes in a private firm's accounting earnings against changes in earnings for an equity index (such as the S&P 500) to estimate an accounting beta:

$$\Delta \text{Earnings}_{\text{private firm}} = a + b \, \Delta \text{Earnings}_{\text{S\&P } 500}$$

The slope of the regression (b) is the accounting beta for the firm. Using operating earnings would yield an unlevered beta, whereas using net income would yield a levered or equity beta.

There are two significant limitations with this approach. The first is that private firms usually measure earnings only once a year, leading to regressions with few observations and limited statistical power. The second is that earnings are often smoothed out and subject to accounting judgments, leading to mismeasurement of accounting betas.

ILLUSTRATION 24.1:   Estimating Accounting Betas: InfoSoft

InfoSoft, even though it is a private business, has been in existence since 1992 and has accounting earnings going back to that year. The following table summarizes the quarterly accounting earnings changes at InfoSoft and for the S&P 500 for each quarter between 1992 and the middle of 1998.

Period	InfoSoft	S&P 500	Period	InfoSoft	S&P 500
1992: Q1	7.50%	−1.30%	1995: Q2	24.10%	8.50%
1992: Q2	8.30%	2.20%	1995: Q3	17.50%	6.00%
1992: Q3	8.80%	2.50%	1995: Q4	16.00%	5.00%
1992: Q4	7.90%	3.00%	1996: Q1	27.00%	8.10%
1993: Q1	14.30%	3.60%	1996: Q2	21.30%	7.00%
1993: Q2	16.50%	5.10%	1996: Q3	22.50%	7.20%
1993: Q3	17.10%	5.50%	1996: Q4	20.00%	6.00%
1993: Q4	13.50%	6.20%	1997: Q1	17.10%	5.80%
1994: Q1	11.50%	4.30%	1997: Q2	22.20%	8.00%
1994: Q2	12.30%	4.70%	1997: Q3	17.80%	6.10%
1994: Q3	13.00%	4.50%	1997: Q4	14.50%	4.50%
1994: Q4	11.10%	4.20%	1998: Q1	8.50%	1.30%
1995: Q1	18.60%	7.10%	1998: Q2	3.50%	−0.50%

Note: Earnings changes are over same quarter of previous year.

Regressing the changes in earnings at InfoSoft against changes in profits for the S&P 500 yields the following:

InfoSoft earnings change = 0.05 + 2.15(S&P 500 earnings change)

Based on this regression, the beta for InfoSoft is 2.15. In calculating this beta, we used net income to arrive at an equity beta. Using operating earnings for both the firm and the S&P 500 should yield the equivalent of an unlevered beta.

Fundamental Betas There have been attempts made by researchers to relate the betas of publicly traded firms to observable variables such as earnings growth, debt ratios, and variance in earnings. Beaver, Kettler, and Scholes (1970) examined the relationship between betas and seven variables—dividend payout, asset growth, leverage, liquidity, asset size, earnings variability, and the accounting beta. Rosenberg and Guy (1976) also attempted a similar analysis. The following is a regression that we ran relating the betas of NYSE and AMEX stocks in 1996 to four variables: coefficient of variation in operating income (CV_{OI}), book debt/equity (D/E), historical growth in earnings (g), and the book value of total assets (TA).

$$Beta = 0.6507 + 0.25\ CV_{OI} + 0.09\ D/E + 0.54\ g - 0.000009\ TA \qquad R^2 = 18\%$$

where CV_{OI} = Coefficient of variation in operating income = Standard deviation in operating income/Average operating income

We could measure each of these variables for a private firm and use these to estimate the beta for the firm. While this approach is simple, it is only as good as the underlying regression. The low R-squared suggests that the beta estimates that emerge from it are likely to have large standard errors.

ILLUSTRATION 24.2:   Estimating a Fundamental Beta: InfoSoft

To use the cross-sectional regression reported earlier to estimate a beta for InfoSoft, we have to estimate the values for each of the independent variables for the firm:

Variable	Value
Coefficient of variation in operating income	0.40
Book debt-to-equity ratio	128.57%
Growth in earnings (previous five years)	30%
Book value of total assets	$9 million

Inputting these values into the regression, we obtain a predicted value for the beta:

$$Beta = 0.6507 + 0.25(.40) + 0.09(1.2857) + 0.54(.3) - 0.000009(9) = 1.03$$

This would yield an estimate of 1.03 for InfoSoft's beta. The standard error on this estimate is 0.18, resulting in a range of 0.85 to 1.21 for the beta, with 67% probability.

Bottom-Up Betas When valuing publicly traded firms, we used the unlevered betas of the businesses that the firms operated in to estimate bottom-up betas—the costs of equity were based on these betas. We did so because of the low standard errors on these estimates (due to the averaging across large numbers of firms) and the forward-looking nature of the estimates (because the business mix used to weight betas can be changed). We can estimate bottom-up betas for private firms, and these betas have the same advantages that they do for publicly traded firms. Thus, the beta for a private steel firm can be estimated by looking at the average betas for publicly traded steel companies. Any differences in financial or even operating leverage can be adjusted for in the final estimate.

In making the adjustment of unlevered betas for financial leverage, we do run into a problem with private firms, since the debt-to-equity ratio that should be used is a market value ratio. While many analysts use the book value debt-to-equity ratio to substitute for the market ratio for private firms, we would suggest one of the following alternatives:

■ Assume that the private firm's market leverage will resemble the average for the industry. If this is the case, the levered beta for the private firm can be written as:

$$\beta_{\text{private firm}} = \beta_{\text{unlevered}}[1 + (1 - \text{Tax rate})(\text{Industry average debt/Equity})]$$

■ Use the private firm's target debt-to-equity ratio (if management is willing to specify such a target) or its optimal debt ratio (if one can be estimated) to estimate the beta:

$$\beta_{\text{private firm}} = \beta_{\text{unlevered}}[1 + (1 - \text{Tax rate})(\text{Optimal debt/Equity})]$$

The adjustment for operating leverage is simpler and is based on the proportion of the private firm's costs that are fixed. If this proportion is greater than is typical in the industry, the beta used for the private firm should be higher than the average for the industry.

---

 spearn.xls: **This dataset on the Web has earnings changes, by year, for the S&P 500 going back to 1960.**

ILLUSTRATION 24.3:   Estimating Bottom-Up Betas: New York Yankees and InfoSoft

---

BOTTOM-UP BETA FOR YANKEES

To estimate a bottom-up beta for the Yankees, we first had to define what constituted a comparable firm. We considered three choices:

1. Firms that derive a significant portion of their revenues from baseball (traded baseball teams, baseball cards, and memorabilia).
2. Firms that derive a significant portion of their revenues from professional sports.
3. Firms that derive a significant portion of their revenues from entertainment.

The following table summarizes the number of firms that we obtained with each definition and the levered and unlevered betas for each group.

Comparable Firms	Number of Firms	Levered Beta	Unlevered Beta
Baseball firms	2	0.70	0.64
Sports firms	22	0.98	0.90
Entertainment firms	91	0.87	0.79

We abandoned the estimate obtained by looking at baseball firms because of the fact that there were only two firms that had betas available for them. In choosing between the unlevered beta estimated looking at sports firms and entertainment firms, we decided to go with the former largely because entertainment companies included conglomerates such as Disney and Time Warner with holdings in multiple businesses.

With an unlevered beta estimate of 0.90 for the Yankees from the preceding table, we used a target debt-to-equity ratio of 25%[1] and a private firm tax rate of 40% to arrive at a levered beta estimate of 1.04.

$$\text{Levered beta for Yankees} = 0.90[1 + (1 - .4)(.25)] = 1.04$$

Bottom-Up Beta for InfoSoft

To estimate a beta for InfoSoft, we obtained the betas and market debt-equity ratios for publicly traded software firms. Since there are 264 software firms in the sample, with wide variations in market capitalization and growth prospects, the following table also looks at subclasses of these firms that might be more comparable to InfoSoft.

Grouping	Number of Firms	Beta	D/E Ratio	Unlevered Beta
All software firms	264	1.15	3.70%	1.13
Small-cap software firms	125	1.29	7.09%	1.23
Entertainment software firms	31	1.50	7.56%	1.43

Note that the debt/equity ratios are market value debt/equity ratios. Note also that the difference in the size of the firms should not affect the betas directly, but it might have an indirect effect, since smaller firms tend to have higher operating leverage. We will use an unlevered beta of 1.23 for InfoSoft, based on the average beta of small-cap software firms.

To estimate a levered beta, we have assumed that InfoSoft is close to the industry average for small-cap software firms (7.09%) in terms of financial leverage. We also use the corporate marginal tax rate of 35%, since InfoSoft is being priced to go public, to estimate a beta of 1.29 for InfoSoft.

$$\text{Bottom-up beta for InfoSoft} = 1.23[1 + (1 - .35)(.0709)] = 1.29$$

Adjusting for Nondiversification   Betas measure the risk added by an investment to a diversified portfolio. Consequently, they are best suited for firms where the marginal investor is diversified. With private firms, the owner is often the only investor and thus can be viewed as the marginal investor. Furthermore, in most private firms, the owner tends to have much of his or her wealth invested in the private business and does not have an opportunity to diversify. Consequently, it can be argued that betas will understate the exposure to market risk in these firms.

At the limit, if the owner has all of his or her wealth invested in the private business and is completely undiversified, that owner is exposed to all risk in the firm and not just the market risk (which is what the beta measures). There is a fairly simple adjustment that can allow us to bring in this nondiversifiable risk into the beta computation. To arrive at this adjustment, assume that the standard

---

[1]If you are valuing a private firm, the target debt-to-equity ratio may be supplied to you by management. In this case, we assumed a target debt-to-equity ratio of 25 percent.

deviation in the private firm's equity value (which measures total risk) is σ_j and that the standard deviation in the market index is σ_m. If the correlation between the stock and the index is defined to be ρ_{jm}, the market beta can be written as:

$$\text{Market beta} = \rho_{jm}\sigma_j/\sigma_m$$

To measure exposure to total risk (σ_j), we could divide the market beta by ρ_{jm}. This would yield the following:

$$\text{Market beta}/\rho_{jm} = \sigma_j/\sigma_m$$

This is a relative standard deviation measure, where the standard deviation of the private firm's equity value is scaled against the market index's standard deviation to yield what we will call a total beta.

$$\text{Total beta} = \text{Market beta}/\rho_{jm}$$

The total beta will be higher than the market beta, and will depend on the correlation between the firm and the market—the lower the correlation, the higher the total beta.

You might wonder how a total beta can be estimated for a private firm, where the absence of market prices seems to rule out the calculation of either a market beta or a correlation coefficient. Note, though, that we were able to estimate the market beta of the sector by looking at publicly traded firms in the business. We can obtain the correlation coefficient by looking at the same sample and use it to estimate a total beta for a private firm.

The question of whether the total beta adjustment should be made cannot be answered without examining why the valuation of the private firm is being done in the first place. If the private firm is being valued for sale, whether and how much the market beta should be adjusted will depend on the potential buyer or buyers. If the valuation is for an initial public offering, there should be no adjustment for nondiversification, since the potential buyers are stock market investors. If the valuation is for sale to another individual or private business, the extent of the adjustment will depend on the degree to which the buyer's portfolio is diversified; the more diversified the buyer, the higher the correlation with the market and the smaller the total beta adjustment.

ILLUSTRATION 24.4:   Adjusting Bottom-Up Beta for Nondiversification

---

Consider the estimate of market beta obtained for the New York Yankees in the previous illustration. Using firms that derive the bulk of their revenues from sports as our comparable firms, we obtained an unlevered beta of 0.90 for the Yankees. The average correlation coefficient for these publicly traded firms with the markets is 0.50. (The R-squared is 25%.) The total unlevered beta for the Yankees can be estimated as follows:

$$\text{Total unlevered beta} = 0.90/0.5 = 1.80$$

Using the Yankee's tax rate of 40% and a debt to equity ratio of 25% yields a total levered beta of 2.07.

$$\text{Total levered beta} = 1.80[1 + (1 - .4)(.25)] = 2.07$$

This total beta estimate, in a sense, takes the limiting view that the potential buyer will own only the Yankees. To the extent that the buyer has some diversification, the correlation coefficient will be adjusted upward; if the buyer has a diversified portfolio, the correlation coefficient will approach 1 and the total beta will converge on the market beta.

AN ALTERNATIVE ADJUSTMENT FOR PRIVATE FIRM RISK

There is an alternative approach that is sometimes used to estimate the additional risk premium that should be charged a private firm. In this approach, you compare the historical returns earned by venture capital and private equity funds with the historical returns on publicly traded stocks. The difference between the two can be considered a premium for private company risk. For instance, private equity funds reported an average annual return of 24 percent from 1990 to 2000. In contrast, the average annual return on stocks from 1990 to 2000 was 15 percent. The difference of 9 percent can be viewed as the premium for private firm risk, and it should be added on to the cost of equity estimated with a market beta or betas.

There are three limitations with this approach. First, most venture capitalists and private equity investors do not publicly report their annual returns, and there is a selection bias among those who do; successful private equity funds are more likely to reveal their returns. Second, the standard errors in the annual returns are likely to be very large, and this noise will affect the risk premium estimate as well. Third, all private firms are treated equivalently in this approach, and no attempt is made to assess larger premiums for some firms and smaller premiums for others.

From Cost of Equity to Cost of Capital To get from the cost of equity to the cost of capital, we need two additional inputs—the cost of debt, which measures the rate at which firms can borrow, and the debt ratio that determines the weights in the cost of capital computation. This section considers how best to estimate each of these inputs for a private firm.

Cost of Debt The cost of debt represents the rate at which a firm can borrow money. To estimate it for publicly traded firms, we generally use either the yields on bonds issued by these firms or the ratings for these bonds to get default spreads. Private firms generally are not rated and do not have bonds outstanding. Consequently, we have to use one of the following alternative approaches:

- If the private firm has borrowed money recently (in the past few weeks or months), we can use the interest rate on the borrowing as a cost of debt. Since the cost of debt has to be current, the book interest rate[2] on debt issued in the past is generally not a good measure of the cost of debt.
- If the private firm is being valued for an initial public offering, we can assume that the cost of debt for the private firm will move toward the average cost of debt for the industry to which the firm belongs. We are essentially assuming that the private firm, once public, will structure its debt policy to resemble those of comparable firms.

---

[2]Book interest rate = Interest expenses/Book value of debt.

■ When estimating the cost of debt for publicly traded firms in Chapter 8, we used the interest coverage ratios of these firms to estimate synthetic ratings, and then used the default spreads on these ratings to arrive at the costs of debt. To allow for the fact that private firms tend to be smaller and riskier than most publicly traded firms, we would use the relationship between interest coverage ratios and ratings for a subset of smaller, publicly traded firms, summarized in Table 24.1.

To estimate the cost of debt for a private firm with an interest coverage ratio of 5.1, for instance, we would use a synthetic rating of A– and the default spread associated with that rating. Thus, if firms that are rated A– typically pay 1.25 percent above the riskless rate to borrow, we would add that default spread to the riskless rate to estimate the cost of debt for the private firm.

This approach may underestimate the cost of debt if banks charge higher interest rates for private firms than for otherwise similar publicly traded firms. In that case, you would add an additional spread to reflect this difference, if you were valuing the firm for sale in a private transaction, but not if you were valuing it for sale to a publicly traded firm or an initial public offering.

Debt Ratios   The debt ratio represents the proportion of the market value of a firm that comes from debt financing. For publicly traded firms, we use the market prices of publicly traded stocks and bonds to arrive at this ratio. Since neither input will be available for private firms, we have to consider one of the following options:

■ In estimating levered betas, we suggested that the industry-average or target debt ratios could be used in the computation. Consistency demands that we use the same debt ratio for computing the cost of capital. Thus, if the industry-

TABLE 24.1   Interest Coverage Ratios and Bond Ratings

Interest Coverage Ratio	Rating
> 12.50	AAA
9.50–12.50	AA
7.50–9.50	A+
6.00–7.50	A
4.50–6.00	A–
3.50–4.50	BBB
3.00–3.50	BB
2.50–3.00	B+
2.00–2.50	B
1.50–2.00	B–
1.25–1.50	CCC
0.80–1.25	CC
0.50–0.80	C
< 0.50	D

average debt-to-equity ratio is used to estimate the levered beta, the industry-average debt-to-capital ratio should be used to estimate the cost of capital. If the target debt-to-equity ratio is used for the levered beta computation, the target debt-to-capital ratio should be used in the cost of capital calculation.

■ While market values of equity and debt are not available for private firms, we can use our estimated values of equity and debt from the valuation, though this creates circular reasoning in the analysis. You need the cost of capital (and the debt ratio) to estimate firm and equity value, and you need the equity value to estimate the cost of capital. You could overcome this problem by iterating toward a value—you could start with the book-debt ratio and cost of capital, estimate a firm and equity value, use these values to arrive at a new debt ratio and cost of capital, and reestimate firm and equity value. You would continue until the debt and equity values in the cost of capital computation converge on the estimated values.[3]

ILLUSTRATION 24.5:   Estimating Cost of Debt

We will use different approaches to estimate the cost of debt for the Yankees and InfoSoft. For the Yankees, we will use the interest rate from the most recent loans that the firm has taken:

$$\text{Interest rate on debt} = 7.00\%$$

Using the Yankees' tax rate of 40%, we obtain an after-tax cost of debt:

$$\text{After-tax cost of debt} = 7\%(1 - .4) = 4.2\%$$

For InfoSoft, we will use the interest coverage ratio estimated using the operating income and interest expenses from the most recent year. InfoSoft had earnings before interest and taxes of $2 million and had interest expenses of $265,000.

$$\text{Interest coverage ratio} = \text{EBIT/Interest expenses} = 2,000/265 = 7.55$$

Using Table 24.1, we estimate a synthetic rating of A+ for InfoSoft:

$$\text{Rating based on interest coverage ratio} = \text{A+}$$

The default spread associated with A+-rated bonds in the market at the time of this valuation was 0.80%, and the Treasury bond rate was 6%. Since we are valuing InfoSoft for an initial public offering, we assume that there is no additional private firm spread.

$$\text{Interest rate on debt} = 6\% + 0.80\% = 6.80\%$$

Finally, we attach a corporate marginal tax rate of 35%, rather than InfoSoft's current tax rate (because the initial public offering will change the firm's tax status), to yield an after-tax cost of debt.

$$\text{After-tax cost of debt} = 6.80\%(1 - .35) = 4.42\%$$

---

[3]The values will always converge.

ILLUSTRATION 24.6:   Estimating Cost of Capital

To estimate the cost of capital for the New York Yankees and InfoSoft, we will stay consistent with the assumptions we have made about leverage so far in this chapter. The Yankees, we assumed, would stay close to a management target debt-to-equity ratio of 25%, which translates into a market debt-to-capital ratio of 20%. For InfoSoft, we used the industry-average debt-to-equity ratio of 7.09%, which results in a debt-to-capital ratio of 6.62%.[4]

For the Yankees, given that we are valuing the firm for sale to a private entity, we estimated a total beta of 2.07. Using the Treasury bond rate of 6% prevalent at the time of this valuation and a market risk premium of 4%, we estimate a cost of equity of 14.28%.

$$\text{Cost of equity} = 6\% + 2.07(4\%) = 14.28\%$$

Using the cost of debt of 4.2% estimated in Illustration 24.3, we can estimate the cost of capital:

$$\text{Cost of capital} = 14.28\%(.80) + 4.2\%(.20) = 12.26\%$$

For InfoSoft, where we are pricing an initial public offering, we use the market beta estimate of 1.29. Using the Treasury bond rate of 6% and a risk premium of 4% yields a cost of equity of 11.16%.

$$\text{Cost of equity} = 6\% + 1.29(4\%) = 11.16\%$$

With the after-tax cost of debt of 4.42% estimated in Illustration 24.4 and the industry-average debt ratio of 6.62%, we estimate a cost of capital of 10.71% for InfoSoft.

$$\text{Cost of capital} = 11.16\%(.9338) + 4.42\%(.0662) = 10.71\%$$

Cash Flows

The definitions of the cash flow to equity and cash flow to the firm are identical for both private and publicly traded firms. The cash flow to equity is the cash flow after taxes, debt payments and issues, and reinvestment needs. The cash flow to the firm is the cash flow after taxes and reinvestment needs, but before debt payments. There are three issues that do affect estimation of cash flows with private firms. The first is that many private firms do not adequately consider the salaries for owner-managers, since many owners do not distinguish between income that they receive as dividends and income they receive as salaries. The second is the intermingling of personal and business expenses that often occurs at small private businesses that can cause income to be mismeasured. The third is the effect of taxes on value, since individual tax status and tax rates vary much more widely than corporate tax rates.

Owner Salaries and Equity Cash Flows   In valuing firms, we draw a simple distinction between salaries and dividends. Salaries are compensation for professional

---

[4]Debt to capital = Debt-to-equity ratio/(1 + Debt-to-equity ratio).

services rendered to the firm and should be treated as operating expenses. Dividends or other equity cash withdrawals from the firm are returns on equity capital invested and determine the value of equity. The separation between managers and stockholders in publicly traded firms results in a distinction between salaries (which are paid to managers) and dividends (which are paid to stockholders) that is clear. In a private business, the owner is often the firm's manager and its only equity investor. If the private firm is not incorporated, the income earned by the owner is taxed at the same rate, whether it is categorized as a salary or as a dividend. Consequently, an owner will be indifferent between receiving a salary of $10,000 and a dividend of $90,000 and a salary of $90,000 and a dividend of $10,000. As a consequence, owners do not pay themselves a salary in many small private firms, or even if they do, the salary does not reflect the services they render to the firm.

When valuing a private firm, we generally make forecasts based on the operating income reported by the firm. If that operating income does not reflect a salary adjustment for the owner, it will be overstated and result in a value that is too high. To get a more precise estimate of operating income, we have to estimate the appropriate compensation for the owner-managers, based on the role they play in the firm and the cost of hiring replacements for them. Thus, the owner of a private business might play several roles—cashier, accountant, stockperson, and salesperson, and the management salary would have to include the cost of hiring a person or two to provide the same services.

Intermixing Business and Personal Expenses The intermingling of business and personal expenses is a particular problem in small private business, since owners often have absolute power over many aspects of the business. Many private business owners maintain offices in their residences, have vehicles that they maintain for personal and business use, and share other services between work and home. In some cases, family members are hired to fill phantom positions in order to distribute income or to reduce taxes.

If personal expenses are consolidated with business expenses or are otherwise a part of business expenses, the operating income for a private firm has to be estimated prior to these expenses. The problem with making these adjustments, however, is that private firm owners are usually not forthcoming about the extent of these expenses, and there may be tax consequences.

Tax Effects When valuing publicly traded firms, the tax rate that we use in valuation is defined to be the marginal corporate tax rate. While different firms may face different marginal tax rates, the differences in tax rates across potential buyers of a private firm can be much larger. In fact, the tax rate can vary from the corporate tax rate (if the potential buyer is a corporation) to the highest marginal tax rate for individuals (if the potential buyer is a wealthy individual) to a lower marginal tax rate if the potential buyer is an individual with lower income. The tax rate will affect both the cash flows (through the after-tax operating income) and the cost of capital (through the cost of debt). As a consequence, the value of a private firm can vary across different buyers.

ILLUSTRATION 24.7:   Estimating Operating Income

To estimate the cash flows for the Yankees, we reconstruct the operating income statement based on publicly available information.[5] We begin in the following table by estimating the revenues of the Yankees and contrasting them with the revenues of two other baseball teams:

	Pittsburgh Pirates	Baltimore Orioles	New York Yankees
Net home game receipts	$22,674,597	$ 47,353,792	$ 52,000,000
Road receipts	$ 1,613,172	$ 7,746,030	$ 9,000,000
Concessions and parking	$ 3,755,965	$ 22,725,449	$ 25,500,000
National TV revenues	$15,000,000	$ 15,000,000	$ 15,000,000
Local TV revenues	$11,000,000	$ 18,183,000	$ 90,000,000
National licensing	$ 4,162,747	$ 3,050,949	$ 6,000,000
Stadium advertising	$ 100,000	$ 4,391,383	$ 5,500,000
Other revenues	$ 1,000,000	$ 9,200,000	$ 6,000,000
Total revenues	$59,306,481	$127,650,602	$209,000,000

The expenses are estimated similarly in the next table, with a comparison again to two other teams in professional baseball:

	Pittsburgh Pirates	Baltimore Orioles	New York Yankees
Player salaries	$33,155,366	$ 62,771,482	$ 91,000,000
Team operating expenses	$ 6,239,025	$ 6,803,907	$ 7,853,000
Player development	$ 8,136,551	$ 12,768,399	$ 15,000,000
Stadium and game operations	$ 5,270,986	$ 4,869,790	$ 7,800,000
Other player costs	$ 2,551,000	$ 6,895,751	$ 7,500,000
General and administrative costs	$ 6,167,617	$ 9,321,151	$ 11,000,000
Broadcasting	$ 1,250,000	$ —	$ —
Rent and amortization	$ —	$ 6,252,151	$ —
Total operating expenses	$62,770,545	$109,682,631	$140,153,000

While deducting operating expenses from revenues would normally yield operating income, the operating expenses for the Yankees include $4.5 million in expenses that we are not considering to be part of operations.[6] The following table summarizes these adjustments for the Yankees:

	Pittsburgh Pirates	Baltimore Orioles	New York Yankees
Total revenues	$59,306,481	$127,650,602	$209,000,000
Total operating expenses	$62,770,545	$109,682,631	$140,153,000
EBIT	($ 3,464,064)	$ 17,967,971	$ 68,847,000
Adjustments	$ 1,500,000	$ 2,200,000	$ 4,500,000
Adjusted EBIT	($ 1,964,064)	$ 20,167,971	$ 73,347,000
Taxes (at 40%)	($ 785,626)	$ 8,067,189	$ 29,338,800
EBIT(1 − Tax rate)	($ 1,178,439)	$ 12,100,783	$ 44,008,200

InfoSoft, though a private firm, has essentially been run like a public firm, probably as a lead-in to the initial public offering. The following table reflects the operating income for InfoSoft, and cor-

---

[5]The numbers in the tables are estimates based on the fragments of public information that are available on professional baseball teams and the filings of the only publicly traded professional baseball team—the Cleveland Indians.
[6]Delicately put, these would include what we categorize as personal expenses that the owner-manager charges to the firm, and could include employees who owe their employment status to their relationship to the owner-manager.

rects the operating income for the capitalization of R&D expenses; this is a correction we employed for publicly traded high-technology firms as well. Note that the after-tax operating income incorporates the tax advantage of expensing all of R&D expenses.[7]

Adjusted Operating Income—InfoSoft (in '000s)

Sales and other operating revenues	$20,000.00
– Operating costs and expenses	$13,000.00
– Depreciation	$ 1,000.00
– Research and development expenses	$ 4,000.00
Operating income	$ 2,000.00

Adjusted operating income:	*Pretax*	*After-tax*
Operating income	$2,000.00	$1,300.00
+ R&D expenses	$4,000.00	$4,000.00
– Amortization of research assets	$2,367.00	$2,367.00
Adjusted operating income	$3,633.00	$2,933.00

Growth

The growth rate for a private firm can be estimated by looking at the past (historical growth) or from fundamentals (the reinvestment rate and return on capital). This section will consider some of the issues in estimating private firm growth.

Estimating Growth In estimating growth for publicly traded firms, we noted that we could draw on three sources—historical growth, analyst estimates, and fundamentals. With private firms, we will not find analyst estimates of growth, and historical growth numbers have to be used with caution. The shifting accounting standards that characterize many private firms will mean that reported earnings changes over time may not reflect actual earnings changes. Furthermore, the fact that earnings are measured annually, rather than quarterly, and the reality that private firms tend to be younger than publicly traded firms will mean far less data in the historical growth estimate.

As a consequence of these gaps in past growth and analyst estimates, there is an even greater reliance on fundamentals in private firms. The expected growth rate in operating income is the product of the reinvestment rate and the return on capital, though changes in return on capital in existing assets can create an additional impact.

$$\text{Expected growth rate} = \text{Reinvestment rate} \times \text{Return on capital}$$

In making the estimates of reinvestment rates and returns on capital for private firms, we can draw on the experience of publicly traded firms in the business.

---

[7]If you multiply the operating income of $3,633 by (1 – Tax rate), you would obtain $2,362 million. The higher after-tax operating income we obtain of $2,933 million reflects the additional $571 million in tax benefits from R&D [($4,000 – $2,367) × .35 = 571].

ILLUSTRATION 24.8: Estimating Growth

The process of estimating growth is different for the two firms under consideration in this chapter. With the Yankees we are looking at a valuable asset, but one whose cash flows are unlikely to grow at rate higher than the inflation rate in perpetuity. Consequently, we will assume a growth rate of 3% in nominal terms in perpetuity. While this might seem unduly low for a team that has won the World Series four of the past five years,[8] the current revenues and operating income reflect these successes. Depressing though it might be to fans, the Yankees will not always be world champions, and there will be some lean years ahead. The expected growth rate of 3% can be considered a smoothed growth rate over good times and bad. To estimate how much the team will need to reinvest to generate this growth, we will assume a return on capital of 20%.[9] This yields a reinvestment rate of:

Reinvestment rate = Growth rate/Return on capital = 3%/20% = 15%

To estimate the growth rate at InfoSoft, we follow a more conventional route. We first estimate the return that they earn on their capital invested currently, by dividing the after-tax operating income from the most recent year by the adjusted capital invested[10] at the beginning of the year. We use the adjusted operating income from the preceding table.

$$\text{Return on capital} = EBIT(1 - t)/\text{BV of capital}$$
$$= \$2,933/\$12,933 = 23.67\%$$

We then estimate InfoSoft's reinvestment rate by dividing its reinvestment in capital expenditures (including R&D)[11] and working capital in the most recent year by the after-tax operating income.

$$\text{Reinvestment rate} = (\text{Net cap ex} + R\&D - \text{Amortization} + \Delta WC)/EBIT(1 - t)$$
$$= (\$2,633 + 500)/\$2,933 = 106.82\%$$

The expected growth rate in operating income for InfoSoft for the immediate future is based on the assumption that the return on capital and reinvestment rate will remain unchanged over the next five years.

$$\text{Expected growth rate} = 23.67\% \times 1.0682 = 25.28\%$$

If we had expected the return on capital or the reinvestment rate to change over time, we would have reflected those changes in this growth rate.

Persistence of Growth In valuing publicly traded firms, we generally assumed infinite lives, even though we did allow for the risk that the firm would not survive. With private firms, the perpetual life assumption has to be made with far more caution. Unlike publicly traded firms, where the transition from one CEO to another is common, the transition is much more complicated in a private firm since the

[8]This statement will clearly date this book. As a Yankees fan, I hope it remains true in future years.
[9]This is the weak link in this valuation. Since the book value of capital at the Yankees does not really reflect the true capital invested, it cannot be used to obtain the return on capital. We are assuming that the most valuable franchise in sports earns an excess return, partly due to brand name and partly due to location—it helps to be in the biggest media market in the United States.
[10]The capital invested reflects the value of the research asset.
[11]Reinvestment = Net cap ex + R&D expense − Amortization = $1,000 + $4,000 − $2,367 = $2,633.

owner-manager generally does not want to pass the reins of power to an outsider. Instead, the owner looks to the next generation in his or her family for the successor, a process that is not always successful.

What are the implications for valuation? One is that the terminal value for a private firm will be lower than the terminal value for a publicly traded firm. If we assume, in fact, that the firm will cease operations at some point in time in the future—say when the current owner retires—we would use a liquidation value for the assets as the terminal value. In general, liquidation values are lower than the value of continuing operations. The other is that private firms where owners plan for the transition to the next generation will be worth more than private firms that do not make these arrangements.

Some private firms, especially as they get larger, resemble publicly traded firms in terms of having professional managers. With these firms, the assumption of infinite growth that we used with publicly traded firms can be sustained.

ILLUSTRATION 24.9:   Closure in Valuation and Terminal Values

Neither of the two firms that we are valuing are valued with finite lives. With InfoSoft, the reason is simple. We are assuming a growing and healthy publicly traded firm, based on our projections over the next 5 years. The firm should be worth more based on continuing operations than from liquidation. Consequently, we assume an expected growth rate of 5% beyond year 5 for the firm. As the firm becomes larger, it will become more and more difficult for it to sustain its current return on capital of 23.67%. We will assume that the return on capital will drop to the industry average of 17.20%. These two assumptions yield a reinvestment rate of 29.07% after year 5:

Reinvestment rate = Expected growth rate/Return on capital = 5%/17.2% = 29.07%

While we do value the Yankees for sale in a private transaction, it remains a valuable franchise and should not lack for potential buyers, even if the owner or owners no longer are interested in running it. That is why we assumed a growth rate of 3% in perpetuity.

Illiquidity Discounts

When you take an equity position in an entity, you generally would like to have the option to liquidate that position if you need to. The need for liquidity arises not only because of cash flow considerations but also because you might want to change your portfolio holdings. With publicly traded firms, liquidation is simple and generally has a low cost—the transaction costs for liquid stocks are a small percent of the value. With equity in a private business, liquidation costs as a percent of firm value can be substantial. Consequently, the value of equity in a private business may need to be discounted for this potential illiquidity. This section will consider the determinants of this discount and how best to estimate it.

Determinants of Illiquidity Discount   The illiquidity discount is likely to vary across both firms and buyers, which renders rules of thumb useless. Let us consider first four factors that may cause the discount to vary across firms:

1. *Liquidity of assets owned by the firm.* The fact that a private firm is difficult to sell may be rendered moot if its assets are liquid and can be sold with no significant loss in value. A private firm with significant holdings of cash and marketable securities should have a lower illiquidity discount than one with factories or other assets for which there are relatively few buyers.
2. *Financial health and cash flows of the firm.* A private firm that is financially healthy should be easier to sell than one that is not healthy. In particular, a firm with strong income and positive cash flows should be subject to a smaller illiquidity discount than one with negative income and cash flows.
3. *Possibility of going public in the future.* The greater the likelihood that a private firm can go public in the future, the lower should be the illiquidity discount attached to its value. In effect, the probability of going public is built into the valuation of the private firm. To illustrate, the owner of a private e-commerce firm in 1998 or 1999 would not have had to apply much of an illiquidity discount to his or her firm's value, if any, because of the ease with which these firms could be taken public in those years.
4. *Size of the firm.* If we state the illiquidity discount as a percent of the value of the firm, it should become smaller as the size of the firm increases. In other words, the illiquidity discount should be smaller as a percent of firm value for private firms like Cargill and Koch Industries, which are worth billions of dollars, than it should be for a small firm worth $15 million.

The illiquidity discount is also likely to vary across potential buyers because the desire for liquidity varies with individuals. It is likely that those buyers who have deep pockets and see little or no need to cash out their equity positions will attach much lower illiquidity discounts to value for similar firms than buyers that have less of a safety margin.

Empirical Evidence and Typical Practice How large is the illiquidity discount attached to private firm valuations? This is a very difficult question to answer empirically because the discount itself cannot be observed. Even if we were able to obtain the terms of all private firm transactions, note that what is reported is the price at which private firms are bought and sold. The value of these firms is not reported, and the illiquidity discount is the difference between the value and the price.

In fact, much of the evidence on illiquidity discounts comes from examining restricted stock at publicly traded firms. Restricted securities are securities issued by a publicly traded company, but not registered with the SEC, that can be sold through private placements to investors but cannot be resold in the open market for a two-year holding period, and only limited amounts can be sold after that. When this stock is issued, the issue price is set much lower than the prevailing market price, which is observable, and the difference is viewed as a discount for illiquidity. The results of three studies that have looked at the magnitude of this discount are summarized as follows:

1. Maher examined restricted stock purchases made by four mutual funds in the period 1969–1973 and concluded that they traded at an average discount of 35.43 percent on publicly traded stock in the same companies.
2. Moroney reported a mean discount of 35 percent for acquisitions of 146 restricted stock issues by 10 investment companies, using data from 1970.

3. Silber examined restricted stock issues from 1984 to 1989 and found that the median discount for restricted stock was 33.75 percent.

In summary, then, there seems to be a substantial discount attached, at least on average, when an investment is not liquid. Much of the practice of estimating illiquidity discounts seems to build on these averages. For instance, rules of thumb often set the illiquidity discount at 20 to 30 percent of estimated value, and there seems to be little or no variation across firms.

Silber (1991) also examined factors that explained differences in discounts across different restricted stocks by relating the size of the discount to observable firm characteristics including revenues and the size of the restricted stock offering. He reported the following regression:

$$\ln(\text{RPRS}) = 4.33 + 0.036 \ln(\text{REV}) - 0.142 \ln(\text{RBRT})$$
$$+ 0.174 \text{ DERN} + 0.332 \text{ DCUST}$$

where   RPRS = Restricted stock price/Unrestricted stock price = 1 – Illiquidity discount
REV = Revenues of the private firm (in millions of dollars)
RBRT = Restricted block relative to total common stock in %
DERN = 1 if earnings are positive; 0 if earnings are negative
DCUST = 1 if there is a customer relationship with the investor; 0 otherwise

The illiquidity discount tends to be smaller for firms with higher revenues, decreases as the block offering decreases, and is lower when earnings are positive and when the investor has a customer relationship with the firm.

These findings are consistent with some of the determinants that we identified in the previous section for the illiquidity premium. In particular, the discounts tend to be smaller for large firms (at least as measured by revenues) and for healthy firms (with positive earnings being the measure of financial health). This would suggest that the conventional practice of using constant discounts across private firms is wrong and that we should be adjusting for differences across firms.

Estimating the Illiquidity Discount   If we do decide to adjust the illiquidity discount to reflect the differences across private firms, we are faced with an estimation question. How are we going to measure these differences and build them into an estimate? There are two ways of doing this. The first is to extend the analysis done for restricted securities into the illiquidity discount; in other words, we could adjust the discount factor for the magnitude of a firm's revenues and whether it has positive earnings. The second is to apply some of the empirical work that has been done examining the magnitude of the bid-ask spread for publicly traded firms to estimating illiquidity discounts.

Adjusted Discount Factors   Consider again the regression that Silber presents on restricted stock. Not only does it yield a result specific to restricted stock, but it also provides a measure of how much lower the discount should be as a function of revenues. A firm with revenue of $20 million should have a illiquidity discount that is 1.19 percent lower than a firm with revenues of $10 million. Thus we could establish a benchmark discount for a profitable firm with specified revenues (say $10 million) and adjust this benchmark discount for individual firms that have revenues much higher or lower than this number. The regression can also be used to differentiate between profitable and unprofitable firms. Figure 24.1 presents the difference in illiquidity discounts across both profitable and unprofitable firms with different revenues, using a benchmark discount of 25 percent for a firm with positive earnings and $10 million in revenues.

There are clearly dangers associated with extending a regression run on a small number of restricted stock to estimating discounts for private firms, but it does provide at least a road map for adjusting discount factors.

Bid-Ask Spread Approach The biggest limitation of using studies based on restricted stock is that the samples are small. We would be able to make far more precise estimates if we could obtain a large sample of firms with illiquidity discounts. We would argue that such a sample exists, if we consider the fact that an asset that is publicly traded is not completely liquid. In fact, liquidity varies widely across publicly traded stock. A small company listed over-the-counter is much less liquid than a company listed on the New York Stock Exchange, which in turn is much less liquid than a large-capitalization company that is widely held. In fact, the difference between the bid price and the ask price that we observe on publicly traded assets can be viewed as a measure of the cost of instant liquidity. An investor who buys an asset, changes his or her mind, and decides to sell the asset immediately will pay the bid-ask spread.

While the bid-ask spread might only be a quarter or half a dollar, it looms as a much larger cost when it is stated as a percent of the price per unit. For a stock that is trading at $2, with a bid-ask spread of ¼, this cost is 12.5 percent. For higher-price and very liquid stocks, the illiquidity discount may be less than 0.5 percent of the price, but it is not zero.

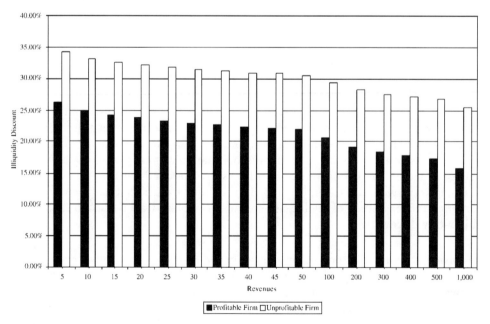

FIGURE 24.1 Illiquidity Discounts: Base Discount of 25 Percent for Profitable Firm with $10 Million in Revenues

What relevance does this have for illiquidity discounts on private companies? Think of equity in a private company as a stock that never trades. On the continuum just described, you would expect the bid-ask spread to be high for such a stock, and this would essentially measure the illiquidity discount.

To make estimates of the illiquidity discounts using the bid-ask spread as the measure, you would need to relate the bid-ask spread of publicly traded stocks to variables that can be measured for a private business. For instance, you could regress the bid-ask spread against the revenues of the firm and a dummy variable reflecting whether the firm is profitable, and extend the regression done on restricted stocks to a much larger sample. You could even consider the trading volume for publicly traded stocks as an independent variable and set it to zero for a private firm. Using data from the end of 2000, for instance, we regressed the bid-ask spread for Nasdaq stocks against revenues, a dummy variable for positive earnings, cash as a percent of firm value, and trading volume.

$$\text{Spread} = 0.145 - 0.0022 \ln(\text{Annual revenues}) - 0.015(\text{DERN})$$
$$- 0.016(\text{Cash/Firm value}) - 0.11(\$ \text{ Monthly trading volume/Firm value})$$

Plugging in the corresponding values—with a trading volume of zero—for a private firm should yield an estimate of the bid-ask spread for the firm.

ILLUSTRATION 24.10: Estimating the Illiquidity Discount for the New York Yankees

We can use both approaches described earlier to estimate the illiquidity discount on the Yankees.

RESTRICTED STOCK APPROACH

To estimate the illiquidity discount for the Yankees, we assume that the base discount for a firm with $10 million in revenues would be 25%. The Yankees' revenues of $209 million should result in a lower discount on the organization's value. We estimate the difference in the illiquidity discount between a firm with $10 million in revenue and $209 million in revenue to be 19.10%. To do this, we first estimated the illiquidity discount in the Silber equation for a firm with $10 million in revenues.

$$\text{Expected illiquidity discount} = \frac{100 - \exp[4.33 + 0.036 \ln(10) - 0.142 \ln(100) + 0.174(1)]}{100} = 48.94\%$$

We then reestimated the illiquidity discount with revenues of $209 million:

$$\text{Expected illiquidity discount} = \frac{100 - \exp[4.33 + 0.036 \ln(209) - 0.142 \ln(100) + 0.174(1)]}{100} = 43.04\%$$

$$\text{Difference in discount} = 48.94\% - 43.04\% = 5.90\%$$

The estimated illiquidity discount for the Yankees would therefore be 19.10%, which is the base discount of 25% adjusted for the revenue difference.

BID-ASK SPREAD APPROACH

We could substitute in the revenues of the Yankees ($209 million) the fact that it has positive earnings and the cash as a percent of revenues held by the firm (3%):

$$\text{Spread} = 0.145 - 0.0022 \ln(\text{Annual revenues}) - 0.015(\text{DERN}) - 0.016(\text{Cash/Firm value})$$
$$- 0.11(\$ \text{ Monthly trading volume/Firm value})$$
$$= 0.145 - 0.0022 \ln(209) - 0.015(1) - 0.016(.03) - 0.11(0) = .1178 \text{ or } 11.78\%$$

---

 liqdisc.xls: **This spreadsheet allows you to estimate the illiquidity discount for private firms using both the restricted stock approach and the bid-ask spread approach.**

VALUATION MOTIVES AND VALUE ESTIMATES

In the preceding section, we considered how best to estimate the inputs to use in valuing a private firm. As we considered each input, though, we noted that the process of estimation might be different depending on the potential buyer of the firm. With betas, for instance, we argued that the market beta should be used if the potential buyer is a publicly traded firm or a stock market investor (in an initial public offering) and that a total beta should be used if the potential buyer is a private party. We made similar arguments about the cost of debt and cash flows. Table 24.2 summarizes the differences in the way we estimate the inputs to valuation for different valuation motives.

The results of using different approaches to estimating discount rates and cash flows, depending on the potential buyer, can have significant effects on value. In general, a private business that is up for sale will be valued much more highly by a publicly traded firm than by a private entity. This can be traced to the fact that the discount rates are higher when we assume that the buyer is not diversified. Thus the owners of private businesses who are interested in selling their businesses will be well served looking for potential buyers who are publicly traded firms. While they might not be able to extract the entire value, they can try to obtain at least a share of the additional value created because the marginal investors are diversified.

The same implications arise when looking at the alternative of going public. The value that a firm can obtain from a public offering will exceed the value that it will receive from a private entity. The values obtained from an initial public offering and sale to a publicly traded firm will be based on similar discount rates, but may vary because of cost and revenue synergies. If the potential for these synergies is large, selling to a publicly traded firm may result in a higher value than going public.

TABLE 24.2   Estimation of Inputs for Valuation: Valuation Motives

	Valuation for Sale to a Private Entity	Valuation for Sale to a Publicly Traded Firm or for an Initial Public Offering
Cost of equity	Based on total beta, with correlation reflecting diversification of potential buyer	Based on market beta, since marginal investor is diversified
Cost of debt	May reflect additional spread associated with being a private business	Based on synthetic rating, estimated by looking at publicly traded firms
Operating cash flows	Private business tax rate used in valuation	Corporate marginal tax rates used in valuation
Firm life	Finite life terminal value or liquidation value	Perpetual life when estimating terminal value
Illiquidity discount	Value discounted for illiquidity	No illiquidity discount

ILLUSTRATION 24.11:   Valuing the New York Yankees for a Private Sale

The inputs for valuing the Yankees as a business are in place. We have estimated the cost of capital of 12.26% in Illustration 24.6, the adjusted after-tax operating income of $44.008 million in Illustration 24.7, and expected growth rate of 3% and reinvestment rate of 15% in Illustration 24.8. These estimates yield a value of $415 million for the Yankees:

$$\text{Value of the Yankees} = \text{EBIT}(1 - t)(1 - \text{Reinvestment rate})(1 + g)/(\text{Cost of capital} - g)$$
$$= \$44.008 \text{ million}(1 - .15)(1.03)/(.1226 - .03) = \$415 \text{ million}$$

Since this a valuation for a private sale, we would apply the illiquidity discount of 11.78% estimated in Illustration 24.10.

$$\text{Value of the Yankees with discount} = \$415 \text{ million}(1 - .1178) = \$366.1 \text{ million}$$

This valuation is a conservative one, and the actual value may well exceed this for two reasons. The first is that publicly traded television and cable companies have expressed interest in the Yankees. Following up, if we substitute in the market beta of 1.03 for the total beta of 2.07, we obtain a cost of capital of 8.95%. This results in a value of $647 million, which no longer has to be discounted for illiquidity:

$$\text{Value to diversified buyer} = \$44.008 \text{ million}(1 - .15)(1.03)/(.0895 - .03) = \$647 \text{ million}$$

The second is the power that sports teams seem to have to extort subsidies and financial assistance from the cities that they represent. For instance, if the Yankees can get New York City to pick up the tab for the reinvestment needs (15% of the after-tax operating income), the value of the Yankees would increase to $762 million.

$$\text{Value with subsidies} = \$44.008 \text{ million}(1.03)/(.0895 - .03) = \$762 \text{ million}$$

Of course, the presence of synergies to the buyer may cause the value to increase even further.

ILLUSTRATION 24.12:   Valuing InfoSoft

The inputs for valuing InfoSoft are summarized in the following table. We assume that InfoSoft will maintain a reinvestment rate of 112.17% and a return on capital of 23.67% for the next five years, allowing its operating earnings to grow 25.28% a year. At the end of five years, we assume that the firm will be in stable growth, growing 5% a year.

Length	High-Growth Phase: Five Years	Stable-Growth Phase: Forever after Year 5
Growth inputs		
Reinvestment rate	106.82%	29.07%
Return on capital	23.67%	17.2%
Expected growth rate	25.28%	5.00%
Cost of capital inputs		
Beta	1.29	1.20
Cost of debt	6.80%	6.80%
Debt ratio	6.62%	6.62%
Cost of capital	10.71%	10.38%

As noted in an earlier section, we use the corporate tax rate of 35% in this valuation because InfoSoft is being valued for an initial public offering. In addition, we added the cash and marketable securities, valued at $500,000, to the value of the operating assets of the firm. The valuation is summarized in Figure 24.2. Based on our assumptions, we would value the equity in InfoSoft at $69.826 million.

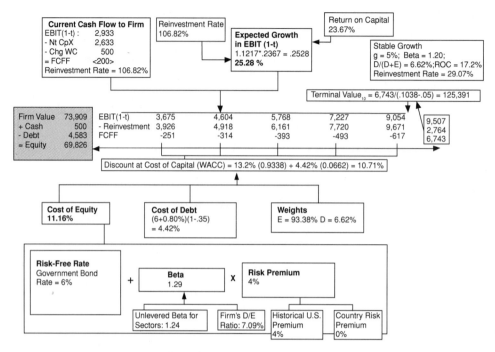

FIGURE 24.2   InfoSoft: A Valuation

Control Issues

When valuing a firm, you always need to consider the competence and strengths of the management of the firm. With private firms, where the owner is also the manager, this consideration carries special weight, since the owner has absolute control. In a publicly traded firm, in contrast, incompetent management can often be replaced, if enough stockholders can be convinced that it is in their best interests to do so.

There are implications for valuation if a portion of a private firm is offered for sale. If that portion provides a controlling interest (i.e., the right to pick the firm's management), it should have a substantially higher value than if it does not provide this power. Normally, this would mean that 51 percent of a private firm's equity should trade at a substantial premium over 49 percent. This applies whether a firm is being sold to a private entity or a publicly traded firm, and may arise in an initial public offering. If, for instance, only nonvoting shares or shares with diluted voting rights are offered to investors in the public offering, they should trade at a discount on shares with full voting rights.

While the intuition about the value of control is simple, estimating how much it is worth is a little more difficult. We will defer a full discussion of the topic until the next chapter, on acquisitions, but we will value it as the difference between two values—the value of the firm run optimally and the value of the firm with the incumbent management. For instance, if the value of a private firm run by incumbent management is $100 million and the value of the firm run optimally is $150 million, the difference in values between the 51 percent and 49 percent shares can be computed as follows:

Value of controlling interest = 51% of optimal value = .51 × 150 = $76.5 million

Value of noncontrolling interest = 49% of status quo value = .49 × 100 = $49 million

The additional 2 percent interest (from 49 to 51 percent) has a disproportionate effect on value because of control. This value of control will be greatest for private firms that are poorly run and will be close to zero for well-run firms.

In fact, the same approach can be used to compute the discount that nonvoting shares will trade at relative to voting shares in initial public offerings. For instance, assume that this private firm creates 10 million voting shares and offers 70 percent to the public. Since the potential for changing management is created by this offering, the value per share will fall between $10 and $15, depending on the probability that is attached to the management change. Thus, if the probability of the management change is 60 percent, the value per share will be $13.

$$\text{Value per share} = \frac{\text{Status quo value}}{\text{Number of shares}} + \frac{(\text{Optimal value} - \text{Status quo value}) \times \text{Probability of change}}{\text{Number of shares}}$$
$$= \$100/10 + [(150 - 100) \times .6]/10 = \$13$$

Now assume that this firm had issued 9 million nonvoting shares, with management retaining 1 million voting shares with complete control. In this case, the nonvoting shares will get little or none of the estimated value change from optimal management. In fact, the values of the two classes can be estimated as follows:

$$\text{Value per nonvoting share} = \frac{\text{Status quo value}}{(\text{Number of voting shares} + \text{Nonvoting shares})}$$
$$= \$100/(9 + 1) = \$10 \text{ per share}$$

$$\text{Value per voting share} = \frac{\text{Status quo value}}{(\text{Number of voting shares} + \text{Nonvoting shares})}$$
$$+ \frac{(\text{Optimal value} - \text{Status quo value}) \times \text{Probability of change}}{\text{Number of voting shares}}$$
$$= \$100/(9 + 1) + [(150 - 100) \times .6]/1 = \$40$$

The voting shares in this case would trade at an enormous premium over the nonvoting shares, but that is because we have assumed that the probability of change is still 60 percent. If the incumbent managers are much more likely to fight a change in management, this probability will drop and reduce the premium with it.

ILLUSTRATION 24.13: Estimating a Per-Share Value for InfoSoft

In the previous illustration, we valued the equity in InfoSoft at $69.826 million. Assume that the firm decides to create 5 million shares—4 million shares will be nonvoting shares and 1 million will be voting shares. In the initial offering, only the nonvoting shares will be sold to the public, and the current owners will retain all of the voting shares.

To value the voting and nonvoting shares, we need to value InfoSoft under optimal management. Assume that the firm would be worth $75 million under optimal management.[12] The value of the voting and nonvoting shares can then be computed:

$$\text{Value per nonvoting share} = \frac{\text{Status quo value}}{(\text{Number of voting shares} + \text{Number of nonvoting shares})}$$
$$= \$69.826/(4+1) = \$13.97$$

Assume that the fact that incumbent managers will retain the voting shares reduces the probability of management change to 25%.

$$\text{Value per voting share} = \frac{\text{Status quo value}}{(\text{Number of voting shares} + \text{Number of nonvoting shares})}$$
$$+ \frac{(\text{Optimal value} - \text{Status quo value}) \times \text{Probability of change}}{\text{Number of voting shares}}$$
$$= \$69.826/(4+1) + (75 - 69.826) \times .25/1 = \$15.26$$

VALUING PRIVATE EQUITY

Earlier in this chapter, we considered how venture capitalists value firms. In the past decade, private equity has emerged as competition to traditional venture capital. Private equity can come from a variety of sources—wealthy individual investors, private equity funds, and corporations with excess funds to invest. Like venture capitalists, private equity investors invest in private firms (often early in the life cycle) in return for a share in the ownership in the firm.

In valuing a private equity stake, we confront many of the issues that we have raised in the chapter:

- While private equity investors tend to be more diversified than venture capitalists, the cost of equity used to value a private equity investment may still be higher than the cost of equity used to value a publicly traded firm. The degree of nondiversification can vary across investors. A publicly traded firm like Microsoft that makes private equity investments should not use a higher cost of equity, whereas an investor who is not diversified may have to make an adjustment similar to the one described for the owners of private firms.
- Private equity investors often provide cash to cash-starved firms in return for a minority stake in the firms. Consequently, the issues of precash versus postcash valuations and the value of control often come up with private equity valuations.

---

[12]InfoSoft was revalued at its optimal debt ratio. We assumed that the existing investment policy was optimal.

PRECASH AND POSTCASH VALUATIONS

When valuing private companies, many analysts draw a distinction between precash and postcash valuations. In general, this is done especially when an infusion of cash is anticipated either from venture capitalists or from an initial public offering. The precash valuation values the firm before the cash influx and the postcash valuation values it after.

There are two reasons why the two valuations may be different. The first is that the firm may face capital rationing constraints without the infusion of the cash, resulting in a scaling down of how much the firm can reinvest. If the firm's return on capital is greater than the cost of capital, this will cause the value to be lower before the cash influx. The second is that the value of cash and marketable securities will be added to the value of the operating assets to arrive at firm value. After a large cash influx, firms may have excess cash to invest in marketable securities, which when added to the value of operating assets will increase value. If the cash is taken out of the firm, though, by the existing owners, you should not add the cash to the value.

Which of these two values should be used to estimate the value per share in a public offering? Since stockholders in the firm will hold stock in the postcash firm, the postcash value should be used. In the case of a venture capitalist, though, the answer may be different. If the venture capitalist has bargaining power—she is the only person who is interested in providing venture capital—she can ask for a share of the firm value based on the precash valuation, arguing that the increase in value is feasible only with the additional venture capital. If two or more venture capitalists are interested in the firm, odds are that the postcash valuations will be the basis for deciding how much of the firm will be yielded to the venture capitalist.

ILLUSTRATION 24.14: Valuing a Private Equity Stake

Assume that you work for a publicly traded firm and have been asked to value a potential stake in a small, privately held firm that wants you to invest $10 million in its equity, which it plans to use to expand operations.

First, you would value the private firm assuming that you do not invest the $10 million. Based on the projected cash flows, assume that you value the equity in the firm at $30 million:

$$\text{Precash valuation} = \$30 \text{ million}$$

Now assume that your investment of $10 million will allow the firm to grow faster and that the present value of the expected cash flows is $50 million for the equity. (This present value does not include the cash inflow of $10 million from the private equity investment.)

$$\text{Postcash valuation} = \$50 \text{ million} + \$10 \text{ million} = \$60 \text{ million}$$

The key question, assuming that you decide to make this investment, is the percentage of the private firm you should demand in return for the $10 million investment. At the minimum, you would demand a share of the postcash valuation:

$$\text{Share of ownership}_{minimum} = \text{Cash invested/Postcash valuation} = 10/60 = 16.66\%$$

However, you would bargain for a larger share. At the limit, you could argue for a share of the precash valuation:

$$\text{Share of ownership}_{maximum} = \text{Cash investment/(Precash valuation + Cash investment)}$$
$$= 10/(30 + 10) = 25\%$$

CONCLUSION

The value of a private firm is the present value of the cash flows it is expected to generate, discounted back at a rate that reflects both the risk in the private firm and the mix of debt and equity it uses. While this statement is identical to the one used to describe the value of a publicly traded firm, there are differences in the way we estimate these inputs for private firms, and even among private firms, depending on the motive for the valuation.

When valuing a private firm for sale to an individual or private entity, we have to consider three specific issues. The first is that the cost of equity, which we have hitherto assumed to be determined purely by the risk that cannot be diversified, might have to be adjusted for the fact that the potential buyer is not well diversified. The second is that equity holdings in private businesses are illiquid, leading to a discount on the estimated value. The discounts on restricted stock issues made by publicly traded firms or the bid-ask spreads of these firms may provide us with useful information on how large this discount should be. The third is that a controlling interest in equity of a private firm can trade at a significant premium over a minority interest.

The valuation of a private firm for sale to a publicly traded firm or initial public offering follows a much more conventional route. We can continue to assume that the cost of equity should be based only on nondiversifiable risk and there is no need for an illiquidity discount. There can still be a control value if less than a controlling interest is sold to the publicly traded firm or if nonvoting shares are issued in the initial public offering.

QUESTIONS AND SHORT PROBLEMS

1. You have been asked to value Barrista Espresso, a chain of espresso coffee shops that have opened on the East Coast of the United States.
   - The company had earnings before interest and taxes of $10.50 million in the most recent year on revenues of $50 million. However, the founders of the company had never charged themselves a salary, which would have amounted to $1 million if based on comparable companies.
   - The tax rate is 36% for all firms, and working capital is 10% of revenues.
   - The capital expenditures in the most recent year amounted to $4.5 million, while depreciation was only $1 million.
   - Earnings, revenues, and net capital expenditures are expected to grow 30% a year for five years, and 6% after that forever.
   - The comparable firms have an average beta of 1.3567 and an average D/E ratio of 13.65%. The average correlation with the market is 0.50. Barrista Espresso is expected to maintain a debt ratio of 12% and face a cost of debt of 8.75%. The risk-free rate is 6%, and the market risk premium is 5.5%.
   a. Estimate the value of Barrista Espresso as a firm.
   b. Estimate the value of equity in Barrista Espresso.
   c. Would your valuation be different if you were valuing the firm for an IPO?
2. You have valued a business, using discounted cash flow models, at $250 million for a private sale. The business, which does make money, had revenues of $200 million in the most recent year. (The average firm has revenues of $10 million.) How much of a liquidity discount would you apply to this firm:

    a. Based on the Silber regression?

    b. Based on correcting the average discount (25%) for the size of the firm?

3. You are valuing a bed-and-breakfast in Vermont with the following information:

- The business had pretax operating income of $100,000 in the most recent year. This income has grown 5% a year for the past three years, and is expected to continue growing at that rate for the foreseeable future.

- About 40% of this operating income can be attributed to the fact that the owner is a master chef. He does not plan to stay on if the business is sold.

- The business is financed equally with debt and equity. The pretax cost of borrowing is 8%. The beta for publicly traded firms in the hospitality business is 1.10. The Treasury bond rate is 7%, the market risk premium is 5.5%, and the tax rate is 40%.

- The capital maintenance expenditure, net of depreciation, was $10,000 in the most recent year, and it is expected to grow at the same rate as operating income.

- The business is expected to have an operating life of 10 years, after which the building will be sold for $500,000, net of capital gains taxes.

    a. Value the business for sale.

    b. How much would the value change if the owner offered to stay on for the next three years?

4. You have been asked by the owner of Tectonics Software, a small firm that produces and sells computer software, to come up with an estimate of value for the firm for an initial public offering. The firm had revenues of $20 million in the most recent year, on which it made earnings before interest and taxes of $2 million. The firm had debt outstanding of $10 million, on which pretax interest expenses amounted to $1 million. The book value of equity is $10 million. The average unlevered beta of publicly traded software firms is 1.20, and the average market value of equity of these firms is, on average, three times the book value of equity. All firms face a 40% tax rate. Capital expenditures amounted to $1 million in the most recent year and were twice the depreciation charge in that year. Both items are expected to grow at the same rate as revenues for the next five years. The return on capital after year 5 is expected to be 15%. The revenues of this firm are expected to grow 20% a year for the next five years and 5% after that, and the operating margins will remain at existing levels. The Treasury bond rate is 6%.

    a. Estimate the cost of capital for the firm.

    b. Estimate the value of the equity in the firm.

    c. If the firm plans to issue 1 million shares, estimate the value per share.

5. How would your answer to (4) change if you were valuing Tectonics Software for sale to a private individual? The individual in question has a portfolio that is not diversified and has a correlation of 0.60 with the market index. In addition, use the following bid-ask spread equation to estimate the illiquidity discount:

$$\text{Bid-ask spread} = 0.14 - 0.015 \ln(\text{Revenues})$$

Estimate the value of equity in the private transaction.

CHAPTER 25

Aquisitions and Takeovers

Firms are acquired for a number of reasons. In the 1960s and 1970s, firms such as Gulf & Western and ITT built themselves into conglomerates by acquiring firms in other lines of business. In the 1980s, corporate giants like Time Inc., Beatrice Foods, and RJR Nabisco were acquired by other firms, their own management, or wealthy raiders, who saw potential value in restructuring or breaking up these firms. The 1990s saw a wave of consolidation in the media business as telecommunications firms acquired entertainment firms, and entertainment firms acquired cable businesses. Through time, firms have also acquired or merged with other firms to gain the benefits of synergy, in the form of either higher growth or lower costs.

Acquisitions seem to offer firms a shortcut to their strategic objectives, but the process has its costs. This chapter examines the four basic steps in an acquisition, starting with establishing an acquisition motive, continuing with the identification and valuation of a target firm, and following up with structuring and paying for the deal. The final, and often the most difficult, step is making the acquisition work after the deal is consummated.

BACKGROUND ON ACQUISITIONS

When we talk about acquisitions or takeovers, we are talking about a number of different types of transactions. These transactions can range from one firm merging with another firm to create a new firm to managers of a firm acquiring the firm from its stockholders and creating a private firm. This section begins by looking at the different forms taken by acquisitions, continues by providing an overview on the acquisition process, and concludes by examining the history of the acquisitions in the United States.

Classifying Acquisitions

There are several ways in which a firm can be acquired by another firm. In a merger, the boards of directors of two firms agree to combine and seek stockholder approval for the combination. In most cases, at least 50 percent of the shareholders of the target and the bidding firm have to agree to the merger. The target firm ceases to exist and becomes part of the acquiring firm; Digital Equipment Corporation was absorbed by Compaq after it was acquired in 1997. In a consolidation, a new firm is created after the merger, and both the acquiring firm and target firm stockholders receive stock in this firm; Citigroup, for instance, was the firm created after the consolidation of Citicorp and Travelers' Group.

In a tender offer, one firm offers to buy the outstanding stock of the other firm at a specific price and communicates this offer in advertisements and mailings to stockholders. By doing so, it bypasses the incumbent management and board of directors of the target firm. Consequently, tender offers are used to carry out hostile takeovers. The acquired firm will continue to exist as long as there are minority stockholders who refuse the tender. From a practical standpoint, however, most tender offers eventually become mergers if the acquiring firm is successful in gaining control of the target firm.

In a purchase of assets, one firm acquires the assets of another, though a formal vote by the shareholders of the firm being acquired is still needed.

There is a one final category of acquisitions that does not fit into any of the four described so far. Here, a firm is acquired by its own management or by a group of investors, usually with a tender offer. After this transaction, the acquired firm can cease to exist as a publicly traded firm and become a private business. These acquisitions are called management buyouts if managers are involved, and leveraged buyouts if the funds for the tender offer come predominantly from debt. This was the case, for instance, with the leveraged buyouts of firms such as RJR Nabisco in the 1980s.

Figure 25.1 summarizes the various transactions and the consequences for the target firm.

Process of an Acquisition

Acquisitions can be friendly or hostile events. In a friendly acquisition, the managers of the target firm welcome the acquisition and in some cases seek it out. In a hostile acquisition, the target firm's management does not want to be acquired.

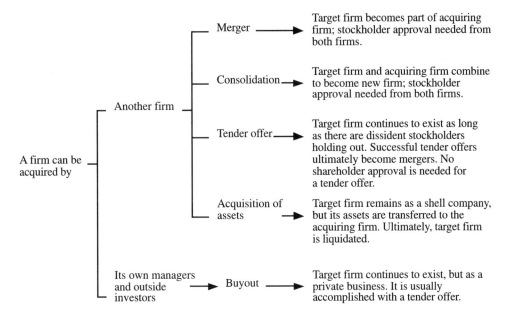

FIGURE 25.1 Classification of Acquisitions
Source: Corporate Finance: Theory and Practice, Second Edition, by Aswath Damodaran, copyright © 2001 by John Wiley & Sons, Inc. This material is used by permission of John Wiley & Sons, Inc.

The acquiring firm offers a price higher than the target firm's market price prior to the acquisition and invites stockholders in the target firm to tender their shares for the price.

In both friendly and hostile acquisitions, the difference between the acquisition price and the market price prior to the acquisition is called the acquisition premium. The acquisition price, in the context of mergers and consolidations, is the price that will be paid by the acquiring firm for each of the target firm's shares. This price is usually based on negotiations between the acquiring firm and the target firm's managers. In a tender offer, it is the price at which the acquiring firm receives enough shares to gain control of the target firm. This price may be higher than the initial price offered by the acquirer, if there are other firms bidding for the same target firm or if an insufficient number of stockholders tender at that initial price. For instance, in 1991 AT&T initially offered to buy NCR for $80 per share, a premium of $25 over the stock price at the time of the offer. AT&T ultimately paid $110 per share to complete the acquisition.

There is one final comparison that can be made, and that is between the price paid on the acquisition and the accounting book value of the equity in the firm being acquired. Depending on how the acquisition is accounted for, this difference will be recorded as goodwill on the acquiring firm's books or not be recorded at all. Figure 25.2 presents the breakdown of the acquisition price into these component parts.

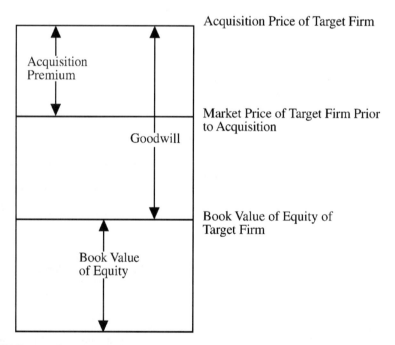

FIGURE 25.2 Breaking Down the Acquisition Price
Source: Corporate Finance: Theory and Practice, Second Edition, by Aswath Damodaran, copyright © 2001 by John Wiley & Sons, Inc. This material is used by permission of John Wiley & Sons, Inc.

EMPIRICAL EVIDENCE ON THE VALUE EFFECTS OF TAKEOVERS

Many researchers have studied the effects of takeovers on the value of both the target firm and the bidder firm. The evidence indicates that the stockholders of target firms are the clear winners in takeovers; they earn significant excess returns[1] not only around the announcement of the acquisitions, but also in the weeks leading up to it. Jensen and Ruback (1983) reviewed 13 studies that look at returns around takeover announcements and reported an average excess return of 30 percent to target stockholders in successful tender offers and 20 percent to target stockholders in successful mergers. Jarrell, Brickley, and Netter (1988) reviewed the results of 663 tender offers made between 1962 and 1985 and noted that premiums averaged 19 percent in the 1960s, 35 percent in the 1970s, and 30 percent between 1980 and 1985. Many of the studies report an increase in the stock price of the target firm prior to the takeover announcement, suggesting either a very perceptive financial market or leaked information about prospective deals.

Some attempts at takeovers fail, either because the bidding firm withdraws the offer or because the target firm fights it off. Bradley, Desai, and Kim (1983) analyzed the effects of takeover failures on target firm stockholders and found that, while the initial reaction to the announcement of the failure is negative, albeit statistically insignificant, a substantial number of target firms are taken over within 60 days of the first takeover failing, eventually earning significant excess returns (50 percent to 66 percent).

The effect of takeover announcements on bidder firm stock prices is not as clear-cut. Jensen and Ruback report excess returns of 4 percent for bidding firm stockholders around tender offers and no excess returns around mergers. Jarrell, Brickley, and Netter, in their examination of tender offers from 1962 to 1985, note a decline in excess returns to bidding firm stockholders from 4.4 percent in the 1960s to 2 percent in the 1970s to –1 percent in the 1980s. Other studies indicate that approximately half of all bidding firms earn negative excess returns around the announcement of takeovers, suggesting that shareholders are skeptical about the perceived value of the takeover in a significant number of cases.

When an attempt at a takeover fails, Bradley, Desai, and Kim (1983) report negative excess returns of 5 percent to bidding firm stockholders around the announcement of the failure. When the existence of a rival bidder is figured in, the studies indicate significant negative excess returns (of approximately 8 percent) for bidder firm stockholders who lose out to a rival bidder within 180 trading days of the announcement, and no excess returns when no rival bidder exists.

STEPS IN AN ACQUISITION

There are four basic and not necessarily sequential steps in acquiring a target firm. The first is the development of a rationale and a strategy for doing acquisitions, and what this strategy requires in terms of resources. The second is the

---

[1]Excess returns represent returns over and above the returns you would have expected an investment to make, after adjusting for risk and market performance.

choice of a target for the acquisition and the valuation of the target firm, with premiums for the value of control and any synergy. The third is the determination of how much to pay on the acquisition, how best to raise funds to do it, and whether to use stock or cash. This decision has significant implications for the choice of accounting treatment for the acquisition. The final step in the acquisition, and perhaps the most challenging one, is to make the acquisition work after the deal is complete.

Developing an Acquisition Strategy

Not all firms that make acquisitions have acquisition strategies, and not all firms that have acquisition strategies stick with them. This section considers a number of different motives for acquisitions and suggests that a coherent acquisition strategy has to be based on one or another of these motives.

Acquire Undervalued Firms Firms that are undervalued by financial markets can be targeted for acquisition by those who recognize this mispricing. The acquirer can then gain the difference between the value and the purchase price as surplus. For this strategy to work, however, three basic components need to come together:

1. *A capacity to find firms that trade at less than their true value.* This capacity would require either access to better information than is available to other investors in the market or a better analytical tools than those used by other market participants.
2. *Access to the funds that will be needed to complete the acquisition.* Knowing a firm is undervalued does not necessarily imply having capital easily available to carry out the acquisition. Access to capital depends on the size of the acquirer—large firms will have more access to capital markets and internal funds than smaller firms or individuals—and upon the acquirer's track record—a history of success at identifying and acquiring undervalued firms will make subsequent acquisitions easier.
3. *Skill in execution.* If the acquirer, in the process of the acquisition, drives the stock price up to and beyond the estimated value, there will be no value gained from the acquisition. To illustrate, assume that the estimated value for a firm is $100 million and that the current market price is $75 million. In acquiring this firm, the acquirer will have to pay a premium. If that premium exceeds 33 percent of the market price, the price exceeds the estimated value, and the acquisition will not create any value for the acquirer.

While the strategy of buying undervalued firms has a great deal of intuitive appeal, it is daunting, especially when acquiring publicly traded firms in reasonably efficient markets, where the premiums paid on market prices can very quickly eliminate the valuation surplus. The odds are better in less efficient markets or when acquiring private businesses.

Diversify to Reduce Risk A strong argument was made in Chapter 4 that diversification reduces an investor's exposure to firm-specific risk. In fact, the risk and return models used in this book have been built on the presumption that the firm-specific risk will be diversified away and hence will not be rewarded. By buying firms in other businesses and diversifying, acquiring firms' managers believe, they can reduce earnings volatility and risk, and increase potential value.

Although diversification has benefits, it is an open question whether it can be accomplished more efficiently by investors diversifying across traded stocks or by firms diversifying by acquiring other firms. If we compare the transaction costs associated with investor diversification with the costs and the premiums paid by firms doing the same, investors in most publicly traded firms can diversify far more cheaply than firms can.

There are two exceptions to this view. The first is in the case of a private firm, where the owner may have all or most of his or her wealth invested in the firm. Here, the argument for diversification becomes stronger, since the owner alone is exposed to all risk. This risk exposure may explain why many family-owned businesses in Asia, for instance, diversified into multiple businesses and became conglomerates. The second, albeit weaker, case is the closely held firm, whose incumbent managers may have the bulk of their wealth invested in the firm. By diversifying through acquisitions, they reduce their exposure to total risk, though other investors (who presumably are more diversified) may not share their enthusiasm.

Create Operating or Financial Synergy   The third reason to explain the significant premiums paid in most acquisitions is synergy. Synergy is the potential additional value from combining two firms. It is probably the most widely used and misused rationale for mergers and acquisitions.

Sources of Operating Synergy   Operating synergies are those synergies that allow firms to increase their operating income, increase growth, or do both. Operating synergies can be categorized into four types:

1. *Economies of scale* that may arise from the merger, allowing the combined firm to become more cost-efficient and profitable.
2. *Greater pricing power* from reduced competition and higher market share, which should result in higher margins and operating income.
3. *Combination of different functional strengths*, as would be the case when a firm with strong marketing skills acquires a firm with a good product line.
4. *Higher growth in new or existing markets*, arising from the combination of the two firms. This would be case when a U.S. consumer products firm acquires an emerging market firm, with an established distribution network and brand name recognition, and uses these strengths to increase sales of its products.

Operating synergies can affect margins and growth, and through these the value of the firms involved in the merger or acquisition.

Sources of Financial Synergy   With financial synergies, the payoff can take the form of either higher cash flows or a lower cost of capital (discount rate). Included are the following:

■ A combination of a firm with excess cash or *cash slack* (and limited project opportunities) and a firm with high-return projects (and limited cash) can yield a payoff in terms of higher value for the combined firm. The increase in value comes from the projects that were taken with the excess cash that otherwise would not have been taken. This synergy is likely to show up most often when large firms acquire smaller firms, or when publicly traded firms acquire private businesses.

■ *Debt capacity* can increase, because when two firms combine, their earnings and cash flows may become more stable and predictable. This, in turn, allows them to borrow more than they could have as individual entities, which creates a tax benefit for the combined firm. This tax benefit can either be shown as higher cash flows or take the form of a lower cost of capital for the combined firm.

■ *Tax benefits* can arise either from the acquisition taking advantage of tax laws or from the use of net operating losses to shelter income. Thus, a profitable firm that acquires a money-losing firm may be able to use the net operating losses of the latter to reduce its tax burden. Alternatively, a firm that is able to increase its depreciation charges after an acquisition will save in taxes, and increase its value.

Clearly, there is potential for synergy in many mergers. The more important issues are whether that synergy can be valued and, if so, how to value it.

Empirical Evidence on Synergy   Synergy is a stated motive in many mergers and acquisitions. Bhide (1993) examined the motives behind 77 acquisitions in 1985 and 1986, and reported that operating synergy was the primary motive in one-third of these takeovers. A number of studies examine whether synergy exists and, if it does, how much it is worth. If synergy is perceived to exist in a takeover, the value of the combined firm should be greater than the sum of the values of the bidding and target firms, operating independently.

$$V(AB) > V(A) + V(B)$$

where   V(AB) = Value of a firm created by combining A and B (synergy)
            V(A) = Value of firm A, operating independently
            V(B) = Value of firm B, operating independently

Studies of stock returns around merger announcements generally conclude that the value of the combined firm does increase in most takeovers and that the increase is significant. Bradley, Desai, and Kim (1988) examined a sample of 236 interfirm tender offers between 1963 and 1984 and reported that the combined value of the target and bidder firms increased 7.48 percent ($117 million in 1984 dollars), on average, on the announcement of the merger. This result has to be interpreted with caution, however, since the increase in the value of the combined firm after a merger is also consistent with a number of other hypotheses explaining acquisitions, including undervaluation and a change in corporate control. It is thus a weak test of the synergy hypothesis.

The existence of synergy generally implies that the combined firm will become more profitable or grow at a faster rate after the merger than will the firms operating separately. A stronger test of synergy is to evaluate whether merged firms improve their performance (profitability and growth) *relative to their competitors*, after takeovers. On this test, as shown later in this chapter, many mergers fail.

Take Over Poorly Managed Firms and Change Management   Some firms are not managed optimally, and other individuals often believe they can run them better than the current managers. Acquiring poorly managed firms and removing incumbent management, or at least changing existing management policy or practices, should make these firms more valuable, allowing the acquirer to claim the increase in value. This value increase is often termed the value of control.

Prerequisites for Success   While this corporate control story can be used to justify large premiums over the market price, the potential for its success rests on the following:

- ■ The poor performance of the firm being acquired should be attributable to the incumbent management of the firm, rather than to market or industry factors that are not under management control.
- ■ The acquisition has to be followed by a change in management practices, and the change has to increase value. Actions that enhance value increase cash flows from existing assets, increase expected growth rates, increase the length of the growth period, or reduce the cost of capital.
- ■ The market price of the acquisition should reflect the status quo—the current management of the firm and their poor business practices. If the market price already has the control premium built into it, there is little potential for the acquirer to earn the premium.

In the past two decades, corporate control has been increasingly cited as a reason for hostile acquisitions.

Empirical Evidence on the Value of Control   The strongest support for the existence of a market for corporate control lies in the types of firms that are typically acquired in hostile takeovers. Research indicates that the typical target firm in a hostile takeover has the following characteristics:

- ■ It has underperformed other stocks in its industry and the overall market, in terms of returns to its stockholders in the years preceding the takeover.
- ■ It has been less profitable than firms in its industry in the years preceding the takeover.
- ■ It has a much lower stock holding by insiders than do firms in its peer groups.

In a comparison of target firms in hostile and friendly takeovers, Bhide illustrates their differences. His findings are summarized in Figure 25.3. As you can see, target firms in hostile takeovers have earned a 2.2 percent lower return on equity, on average, than other firms in their industry; they have earned returns for their stockholders that are 4 percent lower than the market; and only 6.5% of their stock is held by insiders.

There is also evidence that firms make significant changes in the way they operate after hostile takeovers. In his study, Bhide examined the aftermaths of hostile takeovers and noted the following four changes:

1. Many of the hostile takeovers were followed by an increase in debt, which resulted in a downgrading of the debt. The debt was quickly reduced with proceeds from the sale of assets, however.
2. There was no significant change in the amount of capital investment in these firms.
3. Almost 60 percent of the takeovers were followed by significant divestitures, in

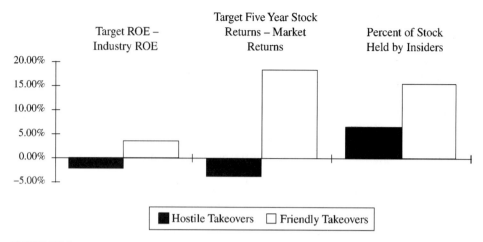

FIGURE 25.3 Target Characteristics—Hostile versus Friendly Takeover
Source: Bhide.

which half or more of the firm was divested. The overwhelming majority of the divestitures were units in business areas unrelated to the company's core business (i.e., they constituted reversal of corporate diversification done in earlier time periods).

4. There were significant management changes in 17 of the 19 hostile takeovers, with the replacement of the entire corporate management team in seven of the takeovers.

Thus, contrary to popular view,[2] most hostile takeovers are not followed by the acquirer stripping the assets of the target firm and leading it to ruin. Instead, target firms refocus on their core businesses and often improve their operating performance.

Cater to Managerial Self-Interest   In most acquisitions, it is the managers of the acquiring firm who decide whether to carry out the acquisition and how much to pay for it, rather than the stockholders of the same firm. Given these circumstances, the motive for some acquisitions may not be stockholder wealth maximization, but rather managerial self-interest, manifested in any of the following motives for acquisitions:

■ *Empire building.* Some top managers' interests seem to lie in making their firms the largest and most dominant firms in their industry or even in the entire market. This objective, rather than diversification, may explain the acquisition strategies of firms like Gulf & Western and ITT[3] in the 1960s and 1970s. Note that both firms had strong-willed CEOs (Charles Bludhorn in the case of Gulf

---

[2]Even if it is not the popular view, it is the populist view that has found credence in Hollywood, in movies like *Wall Street* and *Other People's Money*, and in books such as *Barbarians at the Gate*.

[3]In a delicious irony, ITT itself became the target of a hostile acquisition bid by Hilton Hotels and responded by shedding what it termed its noncore businesses (i.e., all the businesses it had acquired during its conglomerate period).

SHOULD THERE BE AN EGO DISCOUNT?

If managerial self-interest and egos can cause firms to pay too much on acquisitions, should the values of firms run by strong-willed CEOs be discounted? In a sense, this discount is probably already applied if the firm's current return on capital and reinvestment rate reflect the failed acquisitions of the past, and we assume that the firm will continue to generate the same return on capital in the future.

By the same token, though, this is a good reason to revisit a firm valuation when there is a change at the top. If the new CEO does not seem to have the same desire to empire-build or overpay on acquisitions as the old one, the firm's future return on capital can be expected to be much higher than its past return on capital, and its value will rise.

& Western and Harold Geneen in the case of the ITT) during their acquisitive periods.

- *Managerial ego.* It is clear that some acquisitions, especially when there are multiple bidders for the same firm, become tests of machismo[4] for the managers involved. Neither side wants to lose the battle, even though winning might cost their stockholders billions of dollars.
- *Compensation and side benefits.* In some cases, mergers and acquisitions can result in the rewriting of management compensation contracts. If the potential private gains to the managers from the transaction are large, it might blind them to the costs created for their own stockholders.

In a 1981 paper titled "The Hubris Hypothesis," Roll suggested that we might be underestimating how much of the acquisition process and the prices paid can be explained by managerial pride and ego.

Choosing a Target Firm and Valuing Control/Synergy

Once a firm has an acquisition motive, there are two key questions that need to be answered. The first relates to how to best identify a potential target firm for an acquisition, given the motives described in the previous section. The second is the more concrete question of how to value a target firm, again given the different motives that we have outlined in the last section.

Choosing a Target Firm Once a firm has identified the reason for its acquisition program, it has to find the appropriate target firm.

- If the motive for acquisitions is undervaluation, the target firm must be undervalued. How such a firm will be identified depends on the valuation approach

---

[4]An interesting question that is whether these bidding wars will become less likely as more women rise to become CEOs of firms. They might bring in a different perspective on what winning and losing in a merger means.

and model used. With relative valuation, an undervalued stock is one that trades at a multiple (of earnings, book value, or sales) well below that of the rest of the industry, after controlling for significant differences on fundamentals. Thus a bank with a price-to-book value ratio of 1.2 would be an undervalued bank if other banks have similar fundamentals (return on equity, growth, and risk) but trade at much higher price-to-book value ratios. In discounted cash flow valuation approaches, an undervalued stock is one that trades at a price well below the estimated discounted cash flow value.

■ If the motive for acquisitions is diversification, the most likely target firms will be in businesses that are unrelated to and uncorrelated with the business of the acquiring firm. Thus, a cyclical firm should try to acquire countercyclical or at least noncyclical firms to get the fullest benefit from diversification.

■ If the motive for acquisitions is operating synergy, the typical target firm will vary depending on the source of the synergy. For economies of scale, the target firm should be in the same business as the acquiring firm. Thus, the acquisition of Security Pacific by Bank of America was motivated by potential cost savings from economies of scale. For functional synergy, the target firm should be strongest in those functional areas where the acquiring firm is weak. For financial synergy, the target firm will be chosen to reflect the likely source of the synergy—a risky firm with limited or no standalone capacity for borrowing, if the motive is increased debt capacity, or a firm with significant net operating losses carried forward, if the motive is tax benefits.

■ If the motive for the merger is control, the target firm will be a poorly managed firm in an industry where there is potential for excess returns. In addition, its stock holdings will be widely dispersed (making it easier to carry out the hostile acquisition) and the current market price will be based on the presumption that incumbent management will continue to run the firm.

■ If the motive is managerial self-interest, the choice of a target firm will reflect managerial interests rather than economic reasons.

Table 25.1 summarizes the typical target firm, given the motive for the takeover.

TABLE 25.1   Target Firm Characteristics Given Acquisition Motive

If Motive Is	Then the Target Firm
Undervaluation	Trades at a price below the estimated value.
Diversification	Is in a business different from the acquiring firm's business.
Operating synergy	Has the characteristics that create the operating synergy.
	Cost savings: In same business to create economies of scale.
	Higher growth: Has potential to open up new markets or expand existing ones.
Financial synergy	Has the characteristics that create financial synergy.
	Tax savings: Provides a tax benefit to acquirer.
	Debt capacity: Is unable to borrow money or pay high interest rates.
	Cash slack: Has great projects/no funds.
Control	Is a badly managed firm whose stock has underperformed the market.
Manager's interests	Has characteristics that best meet CEO's ego and power needs.

Source: Corporate Finance: Theory and Practice, Second Edition, by Aswath Damodaran, copyright © 2001 by John Wiley & Sons, Inc. This material is used by permission of John Wiley & Sons, Inc.

There are two final points worth making here before moving on to valuation. The first is that firms often choose a target firm and a motive for the acquisition simultaneously, rather than sequentially. That does not change any of the analysis in these sections. The other point is that firms often have more than one motive in an acquisition—say, control and synergy. If this is the case, the search for a target firm should be guided by the dominant motive.

Valuing the Target Firm   The valuation of an acquisition is not fundamentally different from the valuation of any firm, although the existence of control and synergy premiums introduces some complexity into the valuation process. Given the interrelationship between synergy and control, the safest way to value a target firm is in steps, starting with a status quo valuation of the firm, and following up with a value for control and a value for synergy.

Status Quo Valuation   The valuation of the target firm starts by estimating the firm value with existing investing, financing, and dividend policies. This valuation, termed the status quo valuation, provides a base from which control and synergy premiums can be estimated. All of the basic principles presented in the earlier chapters on valuation continue to apply here. In particular, the value of the firm is a function of its cash flows from existing assets, the expected growth in these cash flows during a high-growth period, the length of the high-growth period, and the firm's cost of capital.

ILLUSTRATION 25.1:   A Status Quo Valuation of Digital Equipment Corporation

---

In 1997, Digital Equipment, a leading manufacturer of mainframe computers, was the target of an acquisition bid by Compaq, which was at that time the leading personal computer manufacturer in the world. The acquisition was partly motivated by the belief that Digital was a poorly managed firm and that Compaq would be a much better manager of Digital's assets. In addition, Compaq expected synergies in the form of both cost savings (from economies of scale) and higher growth (from Compaq selling to Digital's customers).

To analyze the acquisition, we begin with a status quo valuation of Digital. At the time of the acquisition, Digital had the following characteristics:

- Digital had earnings before interest and taxes of $391.38 million in 1997, which translated into a pretax operating margin of 3% on revenues of $13,046 million and an after-tax return on capital of 8.51%; the firm had a tax rate of 36%.
- Based on its beta of 1.15, an after-tax cost of borrowing of 5%, and a debt ratio of approximately 10%, the cost of capital for Digital in 1997 was 11.59%. (The Treasury bond rate at the time of the analysis was 6% and we used a risk premium of 5.5%.)

  Cost of equity = 6% + 1.15(5.5%) = 12.33%

  Cost of capital = 12.33%(.9) + 5%(.1) = 11.59%

- Digital had capital expenditures of $475 million[5] and depreciation of $461 million, and working capital is 15% of revenues.
- Operating income, net capital expenditures, and revenues were expected to grow 6% a year for the next five years.
- After year 5, operating income and revenues were expected to grow 5% a year forever. After year 5, capital expenditures were expected to be 110% of depreciation, with depreciation

---

[5]The reinvestment rate is therefore low when we look at net capital expenditures. However, the large working capital investment pushes it up.

growing at 5%. The debt ratio remained at 10%, but the after-tax cost of debt dropped to 4% and the beta dropped to 1.

The value of Digital, based on these inputs, was estimated to be $2,110.41 million.

Year	EBIT(1 – t)	Net Cap Ex	Change in WC	FCFF[6]	Terminal Value	PV
1	$265.51	$14.84	$117.41	$133.26		$ 119.42
2	$281.44	$15.73	$124.46	$141.25		$ 113.43
3	$298.33	$16.67	$131.93	$149.73		$ 107.75
4	$316.23	$17.67	$139.84	$158.71		$ 102.35
5	$335.20	$18.74	$148.23	$168.24	$2,717.35	$1,667.47
Terminal year	$351.96	$64.78	$130.94	$156.25		
Firm value						$2,110.41

Note that the terminal value is computed using the free cash flow to the firm in year 6 and the new cost of capital after year 5:

New cost of equity after year 5 = 6% + 1.00(5.5%) = 11.5%

New cost of capital after year 5 = 11.50%(.9) + 4%(.1) = 10.75%

Terminal value = $156.25/(.1075 – .05) = $2,717.35

Value of Corporate Control Many hostile takeovers are justified on the basis of the existence of a market for corporate control. Investors and firms are willing to pay large premiums over the market price to control the management of firms, especially those that they perceive to be poorly run. This section explores the determinants of the value of corporate control and attempts to value it in the context of an acquisition.

Determinants of the Value of Corporate Control The value of wresting control of a firm from incumbent management is inversely proportional to the perceived quality of that management and its capacity to maximize firm value. In general, the value of control will be much greater for a poorly managed firm that operates at below optimum capacity than for a well-managed firm.

The value of controlling a firm comes from changes made to existing management policy that can increase the firm value. Assets can be acquired or liquidated, the financing mix can be changed and the dividend policy reevaluated, and the firm can be restructured to maximize value. If we can identify the changes that we would make to the target firm, we can value control. The value of control can then be written as:

Value of control = Value of firm optimally managed
– Value of firm with current management

The value of control is negligible for firms that are operating at or close to their optimal value, since a restructuring will yield little additional value. It can be substantial for firms operating at well below optimal, since a restructuring can lead to a significant increase in value.

---

[6]To estimate FCFF in year 1,

FCFF$_1$ = EBIT(1 – t)(1 + g) – Net cap ex(1 + g) – Revenue(g)(WC as % of revenues)
= $391.38(1 – .36)(1.06) – (475 – 461)(1.06) – $13,046(.06)(.15) = $133.26 million

ILLUSTRATION 25.2:   The Value of Control at Digital

We said earlier that one of the reasons Digital was targeted by Compaq was that it was viewed as poorly managed. Assuming that Compaq was correct in its perceptions, we valued control at Digital by making the following assumptions:

- Digital will raise its debt ratio to its optimal of 20%. The beta will increase, but the cost of capital will decrease.

   New beta = 1.25 (Unlevered beta = 1.07; Debt/equity ratio = 25%)
   Cost of equity = 6% + 1.25(5.5%) = 12.88%
   New after-tax cost of debt = 5.25%; the firm is riskier, and its default risk will increase
   Cost of capital = 12.88%(0.8) + 5.25%(0.2) = 11.35%

- Digital will raise its return on capital to 11.35%, which is its cost of capital. (Pretax operating margin will go up to 4%, which is close to the industry average.)
- The reinvestment rate remains unchanged, but the increase in the return on capital will increase the expected growth rate in the next five years to 10%.
- After year 5, the beta will drop to 1, and the after-tax cost of debt will decline to 4%, as in the previous example. The cost of capital will drop to 10% as a consequence.

The effect of these assumptions on the cash flows and present values is listed in the following table:

Year	EBIT(1 – t)	Net Cap Ex	Change in WC	FCFF	Terminal Value	PV
1	$367.38	$15.40	$195.69	$156.29		$ 140.36
2	$404.11	$16.94	$215.26	$171.91		$ 138.65
3	$444.52	$18.63	$236.78	$189.11		$ 136.97
4	$488.98	$20.50	$260.46	$208.02		$ 135.31
5	$537.87	$22.55	$286.51	$228.82	$6,584.62	$3,980.29
Terminal year	$564.77	$77.96	$157.58	$329.23		
Firm value						$4,531.59

The lower cost of capital and higher growth rate increase the firm value from the status quo valuation of $2,110.41 million to $4,531.59 million. We can then estimate the value of control:

Value of firm (optimally managed)	$4,531.59 million
Value of firm (status quo)	$2,110.41 million
Value of control	$2,421.18 million

Valuing Operating Synergy   There is a potential for operating synergy, in one form or the other, in many takeovers. Some disagreement exists, however, over whether synergy can be valued and, if so, what that value should be. One school of thought argues that synergy is too nebulous to be valued and that any systematic attempt to do so requires so many assumptions that it is pointless. If this is true, a firm should not be willing to pay large premiums for synergy it cannot attach a value to.

While valuing synergy requires us to make assumptions about future cash flows and growth, the lack of precision in the process does not mean we cannot obtain an unbiased estimate of value. Thus we maintain that synergy can be valued by answering two fundamental questions:

1. *What form is the synergy expected to take?* Will it reduce costs as a percentage of sales and increase profit margins (e.g., when there are economies of scale)?

Will it increase future growth (e.g., when there is increased market power) or the length of the growth period? Synergy, to have an effect on value, has to influence one of the four inputs into the valuation process—cash flows from existing assets, higher expected growth rates (market power, higher growth potential), a longer growth period (from increased competitive advantages), or a lower cost of capital (higher debt capacity).

2. *When will the synergy start affecting cash flows?* Synergies can sometimes show up instantaneously, but they are more likely to show up over time. Since the value of synergy is the present value of the cash flows created by it, the longer it takes for it to show up, the smaller its value.

Once we answer these questions, we can estimate the value of synergy using an extension of discounted cash flow techniques. First, we value the firms involved in the merger independently, by discounting expected cash flows to each firm at the weighted average cost of capital for that firm. Second, we estimate the value of the combined firm, with no synergy, by adding the values obtained for each firm in the first step. Third, we build in the effects of synergy into expected growth rates and cash flows, and we value the combined firm with synergy. The difference between the value of the combined firm with synergy and the value of the combined firm without synergy provides a value for synergy.

Figure 25.4 summarizes the effects of synergy and control in valuing a target firm for an acquisition. Notice the difference between Figure 25.2, which is based on the market price of the target firm before and after the acquisition, and Figure 25.4, where

Component	Valuation Guidelines	Should You Pay?
Synergy	Value the combined firm with synergy built in. This value may include: • A higher growth rate in revenues: *growth synergy.* • Higher margins because of *economies of scale.* • Lower taxes because of tax benefits: *tax synergy.* • Lower cost of debt: *financing synergy.* • Higher debt ratio because of lower risk: *debt capacity.* Subtract the value of the target firm (with control premium) + value of the bidding firm (preacquisition). This is the value of synergy.	*Which firm is indispensable for synergy?* • If it is the target, you should be willing to pay up to the value of synergy. • If it is the bidder, you should not.
Control Premium	Value the company as if optimally managed. This will usually mean altering investment, financing, and dividend policy: *Investment policy:* Earn higher returns on projects and divest unproductive projects. *Financing policy:* Move to a better financing structure (e.g., optimal capital structure). *Dividend policy:* Return cash for which the firm has no need. Practically, • Look at industry averages as optimal. • Do a full-fledged corporate financial analysis to compute optional debt ratio.	If motive is control or in a standalone valuation, this is the maximum you should pay.
Status Quo Valuation	Value the company as is, with existing inputs for investment, financing, and dividend policy.	If motive is undervaluation, the status quo value is the maximum you should pay.

FIGURE 25.4 Valuing an Acquisition

Source: Corporate Finance: Theory and Practice, Second Edition, by Aswath Damodaran, copyright © 2001 by John Wiley & Sons, Inc. This material is used by permission of John Wiley & Sons, Inc.

we are looking at the value of the target firm with and without the premiums for control and synergy. A fair-value acquisition, which would leave the acquiring firm neither better nor worse off, would require that the total price (in Figure 25.2) be equal to the consolidated value (in Figure 25.4) with the synergy and control benefits built in.

ILLUSTRATION 25.3:   Valuing Synergy: Compaq and Digital

Returning to the Compaq/Digital merger, note that synergy was one of the stated reasons for the acquisition. To value this synergy, we needed to first value Compaq as a standalone firm. To do this, the following assumptions were made:

- Compaq had earnings before interest and taxes of $2,987 million on revenues of $25,484 million. The tax rate for the firm is 36%.
- The firm had capital expenditures of $729 million and depreciation of $545 million in the most recent year; working capital is 15% of revenues.
- The firm had a debt-to-capital ratio of 10%, a beta of 1.25, and an after-tax cost of debt of 5%.
- The operating income, revenues, and net capital expenditures are all expected to grow 10% a year for the next five years.
- After year 5, operating income and revenues are expected to grow 5% a year forever, and capital expenditures are expected to be 110% of depreciation. In addition, the firm will raise its debt ratio to 20%, the after-tax cost of debt will drop to 4%, and the beta will drop to 1.00.

Based on these inputs, the value of the firm can be estimated as follows:

Year	EBIT(1 − t)	Net Cap Ex	Change in WC	FCFF	Terminal Value	PV
1	$2,102.85	$202.40	$382.26	$1,518.19		$ 1,354.47
2	$2,313.13	$222.64	$420.49	$1,670.01		$ 1,329.24
3	$2,544.45	$244.90	$462.53	$1,837.01		$ 1,304.49
4	$2,798.89	$269.39	$508.79	$2,020.71		$ 1,280.19
5	$3,078.78	$296.33	$559.67	$2,222.78	$56,654.81	$33,278.53
Terminal year	$3,232.72	$ 92.16	$307.82	$2,832.74		
Firm value						$38,546.91

The value of Compaq is $38.547 billion.

The value of the combined firm (Compaq and Digital), with no synergy, should be the sum of the values of the firms valued independently. To avoid double counting the value of control, we add the value of Digital, optimally managed, that was estimated in Illustration 25.2, to the value of Compaq to arrive at the value of the combined firm:

Value of Digital (optimally managed)	$4,531.59 million
Value of Compaq (status quo)	$38,546.91 million
Value of combined firm	$43,078.50 million

This would be the value of the combined firm in the absence of synergy.

To value the synergy, we made the following assumptions about the way in which synergy would affect cash flows and discount rates at the combined firm:

- The combined firm will have some economies of scale, allowing it to increase its current after-tax operating margin slightly. The annual dollar savings will be approximately $100 million. This will translate into a slightly higher pretax operating margin:

$$\text{Current operating margin} = (\text{EBIT}_{Compaq} + \text{EBIT}_{Digital})/(\text{Sales}_{Compaq} + \text{Sales}_{Digital})$$
$$= (2,987 + 522)/(25,484 + 13,046) = 9.11\%$$

$$\text{New operating margin} = (2,987 + 522 + 100)/(25,484 + 13,046) = 9.36\%$$

■ The combined firm will also have a slightly higher growth rate of 10.50% in revenues, operating income, and net cap ex over the next five years because of operating synergies.
■ The beta of the combined firm was computed in three steps. We first estimated the unlevered betas for Digital and Compaq:

$$\text{Digital's unlevered beta} = 1.25/[1 + (1 - .36)(.25)] = 1.07$$

$$\text{Compaq's unlevered beta} = 1.25/[1 + (1 - .36)(.10/.90)] = 1.17$$

We then weighted these unlevered betas by the values of these firms to estimate an unlevered beta for the combined firm; Digital has a firm value of $4.5 billion, and Compaq's firm value was $38.6 billion.[7]

$$\text{Unlevered beta for combined firm} = 1.07 \times (4.5/43.1) + 1.17(38.6/43.1) = 1.16$$

We then used the debt-to-equity ratio for the combined firm to estimate a new levered beta and cost of capital for the firm. The debt-to-equity ratio for the combined firm, estimated by cumulating the outstanding debt and market value of equity at the two firms, is 13.64%:

$$\text{New levered beta} = 1.16[1 + (1 - 0.36)(.1364)] = 1.26$$

$$\text{Cost of capital} = 12.93\%(.88) + 5\%(.12) = 11.98\%$$

Based on these assumptions, the cash flows and value of the combined firm, with synergy, can be estimated:

Year	EBIT(1 − t)	Net Cap Ex	Change in WC	FCFF	Terminal Value	PV
1	$2,552.28	$218.79	$606.85	$1,726.65		$ 1,541.95
2	$2,820.27	$241.76	$670.57	$1,907.95		$ 1,521.59
3	$3,116.40	$267.15	$740.98	$2,108.28		$ 1,501.50
4	$3,443.63	$295.20	$818.78	$2,329.65		$ 1,481.68
5	$3,805.21	$326.19	$904.75	$2,574.26	$66,907.52	$39,463.87
Terminal year	$3,995.47	$174.02	$476.07	$3,345.38		
Firm value						$45,510.58

The value of the combined firm, with synergy, is $45,510.58 million. This can be compared to the value of the combined firm without synergy of $43,078.50 million, and the difference is the value of the synergy in the merger.

Value of combined firm (with synergy)	$45,510.58 million
Value of combined firm (with no synergy)	$43,078.50 million
Value of synergy	$2,422.08 million

This valuation is based on the presumption that synergy will be created instantaneously. In reality, it can take years before the firms are able to see the benefits of synergy. A simple way to account for the delay is to consider the present value of synergy. Thus, if it will take Compaq and Digital three years to create the synergy, the present value of synergy can be estimated, using the combined firm's cost of capital as the discount rate:

$$\text{Present value of synergy} = \$2,422 \text{ million}/(1.1198)^3 = \$1,724.86 \text{ million}$$

 synergy.xls: **This spreadsheet allows you to estimate the approximate value of synergy in a merger or acquisition.**

---

[7]The values that we used were the values that we estimated for the two firms.

Valuing Financial Synergy   Synergy can also be created from purely financial factors. We will consider three legitimate sources of financial synergy: better use for excess cash or cash slack, a greater tax benefit from accumulated losses or tax deductions, and an increase in debt capacity and therefore firm value. The discussion begins, however, with diversification, which though a widely used rationale for mergers is not a source of increased value by itself.

Diversification   A takeover motivated only by diversification considerations has no effect on the combined value of the two firms involved in the takeover when the two firms are both publicly traded and when the investors in the firms can diversify on their own. Consider the following example. Dalton Motors, which is an automobile parts manufacturing firm in a cyclical business, plans to acquire Lube & Auto, which is an automobile service firm whose business is noncyclical and high-growth, solely for the diversification benefit. The characteristics of the two firms are as follows:

	Lube & Auto	*Dalton Motors*
Current free cash flow to the firm	$100 million	$200 million
Expected growth rate—next five years	20%	10%
Expected growth rate—after year 5	6%	6%
Debt/(Debt + Equity)	30%	30%
After-tax cost of debt	6%	5.40%
Beta for equity—next five years	1.20	1.00
Beta for equity—after year 5	1.00	1.00

The treasury bond rate is 7 percent, and the market premium is 5.5 percent. The calculations for the weighted average cost of capital and the value of the firms are shown in Table 25.2:

TABLE 25.2   Value of Lube & Auto, Dalton Motors, and Combined Firm

	Lube & Auto	Dalton Motors	Combined Firm
Debt (%)	30%	30%	30%
Cost of debt	6.00%	5.40%	5.65%
Equity (%)	70%	70%	70%
Cost of equity	13.60%	12.50%	12.95%
Cost of capital—year 1	11.32%	10.37%	10.76%
Cost of capital—year 2	11.32%	10.37%	10.76%
Cost of capital—year 3	11.32%	10.37%	10.77%
Cost of capital—year 4	11.32%	10.37%	10.77%
Cost of capital—year 5	11.32%	10.37%	10.77%
Cost of capital after	10.55%	10.37%	10.45%
FCFF in year 1	$ 120.00	$ 220.00	$ 340.00
FCFF in year 2	$ 144.00	$ 242.00	$ 386.00
FCFF in year 3	$ 172.80	$ 266.20	$ 439.00
FCFF in year 4	$ 207.36	$ 292.82	$ 500.18
FCFF in year 5	$ 248.83	$ 322.10	$ 570.93
Terminal value	$5,796.97	$7,813.00	$13,609.97
Present value	$4,020.91	$5,760.47	$ 9,781.38

Source: Corporate Finance: Theory and Practice, Second Edition, by Aswath Damodaran, copyright © 2001 by John Wiley & Sons, Inc. This material is used by permission of John Wiley & Sons, Inc.

The cost of equity and debt for the combined firm is obtained by taking the weighted average of the individual firm's costs of equity (debt); the weights are based on the relative market values of equity (debt) of the two firms. Since these relative market values change over time, the costs of equity and debt for the combined firm also change over time. The value of the combined firm is exactly the same as the sum of the values of the independent firms, indicating that there is no value gain from diversification.

This equality does not imply, however, that the shareholders in the bidding and target firms are indifferent about such takeovers, since the bidding firm pays a significant premium over the market price. To the extent that these firms were correctly valued before the merger (market value of Lube & Auto = \$4,020.91; market value of Dalton Motors = \$5,760.47), the payment of a premium over the market price will transfer wealth from the bidding firm to the target firm.

The absence of added value from this merger may seem puzzling, given the fact that the two firms are in unrelated businesses and thus should gain some diversification benefit. In fact, if the earnings of the two firms are not highly correlated, the variance in earnings of the combined firm should be significantly lower than the variance in earnings of the individual firms operating independently. This reduction in earnings variance does not affect value, however, because it is firm-specific risk, which is assumed to have no effect on expected returns. (The betas, which are measures of market risk, are always value-weighted averages of the betas of the two merging firms.) But what about the impact of reduced variance on debt capacity? Firms with lower variability in earnings can increase debt capacity and thus value. This can be a real benefit of conglomerate mergers, and will be considered separately later in this section.

Cash Slack   Managers may reject profitable investment opportunities if they have to raise new capital to finance them. Myers and Majluf (1984) suggest that since managers have more information than investors about prospective projects, new stock may have to be issued at less than true value to finance these projects, leading to the rejection of good projects and to capital rationing for some firms. It may therefore make sense for a company with excess cash and no investment opportunities to take over a cash-poor firm with good investment opportunities, or vice versa. The additional value of combining these two firms is the present value of the projects that would not have been taken if they had stayed apart, but can now be taken because of the availability of cash.

Cash slack can be a potent rationale for publicly traded firms that have ready access to capital and want to acquire small, private firms that have capital constraints. It may also explain why acquisition strategies concentrating on buying smaller, private firms have worked fairly well in practice. Blockbuster Inc. (video rental), Browning and Ferris (waste disposal), and Service Merchandise (funeral homes) are good examples.

Tax Benefits   Several possible tax benefits accrue from takeovers. If one of the firms has tax deductions that it cannot use because it is losing money, whereas the other firm has income on which it pays significant taxes, combining the two firms can result in tax benefits that can be shared by the two firms. The value of this synergy is the present value of the tax savings that result from this merger. In addition, the assets of the firm being taken over can be written up to reflect new market values in some forms of mergers, leading to higher tax savings from depreciation in future years.

ILLUSTRATION 25.4: Tax Benefits of Writing Up Asset Values after Takeover: Congoleum Inc.

One of the earliest leveraged buyouts (LBOs) occurred in 1979 and involved Congoleum Inc., a diversified firm in shipbuilding, flooring, and automotive accessories. Congoleum's own management bought out the firm. The favorable treatment that would be accorded the firm's assets by tax authorities was a major reason behind the takeover. After the takeover—estimated to cost approximately $400 million—the firm was allowed to write up its assets to reflect their new market values and to claim depreciation on these new values. The estimated change in depreciation and the present value effect of this depreciation tax benefit, based on a tax rate of 48%, discounted at the firm's cost of capital of 14.5%, are shown in the following table:

Year	Depreciation Before	Depreciation After	Change in Depreciation	Tax Savings	Present Value
1980	$ 8.00	$ 35.51	$ 27.51	$13.20	$11.53
1981	$ 8.80	$ 36.26	$ 27.46	$13.18	$10.05
1982	$ 9.68	$ 37.07	$ 27.39	$13.15	$ 8.76
1983	$ 10.65	$ 37.95	$ 27.30	$13.10	$ 7.62
1984	$ 11.71	$ 21.23	$ 9.52	$ 4.57	$ 2.32
1985	$ 12.65	$ 17.50	$ 4.85	$ 2.33	$ 1.03
1986	$ 13.66	$ 16.00	$ 2.34	$ 1.12	$ 0.43
1987	$ 14.75	$ 14.75	$ 0.00	$ 0.00	$ 0.00
1988	$ 15.94	$ 15.94	$ 0.00	$ 0.00	$ 0.00
1989	$ 17.21	$ 17.21	$ 0.00	$ 0.00	$ 0.00
1980–1989	$123.05	$249.42	$126.37	$60.66	$41.76

Note that the increase in depreciation occurs in the first seven years, primarily as a consequence of higher asset values and accelerated depreciation. After year 7, however, the old and new depreciation schedules converge. The present value of the additional tax benefits from the higher depreciation, based amounted to $41.76 million, about 10% of the overall price paid on the transaction.

In recent years, the tax code covering asset revaluations has been significantly tightened. While acquiring firms can still reassess the value of the acquired firm's assets, they can do so only up to fair value.

Debt Capacity If the cash flows of the acquiring and target firms are less than perfectly correlated, the cash flows of the combined firm will be less variable than the cash flows of the individual firms. This decrease in variability can result in an increase in debt capacity and in the value of the firm. The increase in value, however, has to be weighed against the immediate transfer of wealth to existing bondholders in both firms from the stockholders of both the acquiring and target firms. The bondholders in the premerger firms find themselves lending to a safer firm after the takeover. The interest rates they are receiving are based on the riskier premerger firms, however. If the interest rates are not renegotiated, the bonds will increase in price, increasing the bondholders' wealth at the expense of the stockholders.

There are several models available for analyzing the benefits of higher debt ratios as a consequence of takeovers. Lewellen analyzes the benefits in terms of reduced default risk, since the combined firm has less variable cash flows than do the individual firms. He provides a rationale for an increase in the value of debt after the merger, but at the expense of equity investors. It is not clear, therefore, that the value of the firm will increase after the merger. Stapleton evaluates the benefits of higher debt capacity after mergers using option pricing. He shows that the effect of a merger on debt capacity is always positive, even when the earnings of the two firms are perfectly correlated. The debt capacity benefits increase as the earnings of the two firms become less correlated and as investors become more risk averse.

Consider again the merger of Lube & Auto and Dalton Motors. The value of the combined firm was the same as the sum of the values of the independent firms. The fact that the two firms were in different business lines reduced the variance in earnings, but value was not affected, because the capital structure of the firm remained unchanged after the merger and the costs of equity and debt were the weighted averages of the individual firms' costs.

The reduction in variance in earnings can increase debt capacity, which can increase value. If, after the merger of these two firms, the debt capacity for the combined firm were increased to 40 percent from 30 percent (leading to an increase in the beta to 1.21 and no change in the cost of debt), the value of the combined firm after the takeover can be estimated as shown in Table 25.3. As a consequence of the added debt, the value of the firm will increase from $9,781.38 million to $11,429.35 million.

Increase Growth and Price-Earnings Multiples Some acquisitions are motivated by the desire to increase growth and price–cash flow (or price-earnings) multiples. Though the benefits of higher growth are undeniable, the price paid for that growth will determine whether such acquisitions make sense. If the price paid for the growth exceeds the fair market value, the stock price of the acquiring firm will decline even though the expected future growth in its cash flows may increase as a consequence of the takeover.

This can be seen in the previous example. Dalton Motors, with projected

TABLE 25.3   Value of Debt Capacity—Lube & Auto and Dalton Motors

	Lube & Auto	Dalton Motors	Combined Firm— No New Debt	Combined Firm— Added Debt
Debt (%)	30%	30%	30%	40%
Cost of debt	6.00%	5.40%	5.65%	5.65%
Equity (%)	70%	70%	70%	60%
Cost of equity	13.60%	12.50%	12.95%	13.65%
Cost of capital—year 1	11.32%	10.37%	10.76%	10.45%
Cost of capital—year 2	11.32%	10.37%	10.76%	10.45%
Cost of capital—year 3	11.32%	10.37%	10.77%	10.45%
Cost of capital—year 4	11.32%	10.37%	10.77%	10.45%
Cost of capital—year 5	11.32%	10.37%	10.77%	10.45%
Cost of capital after	10.55%	10.37%	10.45%	9.76%
FCFF in year 1	$ 120.00	$ 220.00	$ 340.00	$ 340.00
FCFF in year 2	$ 144.00	$ 242.00	$ 386.00	$ 386.00
FCFF in year 3	$ 172.80	$ 266.20	$ 439.00	$ 439.00
FCFF in year 4	$ 207.36	$ 292.82	$ 500.18	$ 500.18
FCFF in year 5	$ 248.83	$ 322.10	$ 570.93	$ 570.93
Terminal value	$5,796.97	$7,813.00	$13,609.97	$16,101.22
Present value	$4,020.91	$5,760.47	$ 9,781.38	$11,429.35

HOW OFTEN DOES SYNERGY ACTUALLY SHOW UP?

McKinsey & Co. examined 58 acquisition programs between 1972 and 1983 for evidence on two questions: (1) Did the return on the amount invested in the acquisitions exceed the cost of capital? (2) Did the acquisitions help the parent companies outperform the competition? They concluded that 28 of the 58 programs failed both tests, and six failed at least one test. In a follow-up study of 115 mergers in the United Kingdom and the United States in the 1990s, McKinsey concluded that 60 percent of the transactions earned returns on capital less than the cost of capital and that only 23 percent earned excess returns.[8] In 1999, KPMG examined 700 of the most expensive deals between 1996 and 1998 and concluded that only 17 percent created value for the combined firm, 30 percent were value-neutral, and 53 percent destroyed value.[9]

A study looked at the eight largest bank mergers in 1995[10] and concluded that only two (Chase/Chemical, First Chicago/NBD) subsequently outperformed the bank-stock index. The largest, Wells Fargo's acquisition of First Interstate, was a significant failure. Sirower (1996) takes a detailed look at the promises and failures of synergy and draws the gloomy conclusion that synergy is often promised but seldom delivered.

The most damaging piece of evidence on the outcome of acquisitions is the large number of acquisitions that are reversed within fairly short time periods. Mitchell and Lehn note that 20.2 percent of the acquisitions made between 1982 and 1986 were divested by 1988. Studies that have tracked acquisitions for longer time periods (10 years or more) have found the divestiture rate of acquisitions rises to almost 50 percent, suggesting that few firms enjoy the promised benefits from acquisitions. In another study, Kaplan and Weisbach (1992) found that 44 percent of the mergers they studied were reversed, largely because the acquirer paid too much or because the operations of the two firms did not mesh.

growth in cash flows of 10 percent, acquires Lube & Auto, which is expected to grow 20 percent. The fair market value for Lube & Auto is $4,020.91. If Dalton Motors pays more than this amount to acquire Lube & Auto, its stock price will decline, even though the combined firm will grow at a faster rate than Dalton Motors alone. Similarly, Dalton Motors, which sells at a lower multiple of cash flow than Lube & Auto, will increase its value as a multiple of cash flow after the acquisition, but the effect on the stockholders in the firm will still be determined by whether the price paid on the acquisition exceeds the fair value.

---

[8]This study was referenced in an article titled "Merger Mayhem" that appeared in *Barron's* on April 20, 1998.

[9]KPMG measured the success at creating value by comparing the postdeal stock price performance of the combined firm to the performance of the relevant industry segment for a year after the deal was completed.

[10]This study was done by Keefe, Bruyette, and Woods, an investment bank. It was referenced in an article titled "Merger Mayhem" in *Barron's*, April 20, 1998.

TAKEOVER VALUATION: BIASES AND COMMON ERRORS

The process of takeover valuation has potential pitfalls and biases that arise from the desire of the management of both the bidder and target firms to justify their points of view to their stockholders. The bidder firm aims to convince its stockholders that it is getting a bargain (i.e., that it is paying less than what the target firm is truly worth). In friendly takeovers, the target firm attempts to show its stockholders that the price it is receiving is a fair price (i.e., it is receiving at least what it is worth). In hostile takeovers, there is a role reversal, with bidding firms trying to convince target firm stockholders that they are not being cheated out of their fair share, and target firms arguing otherwise. Along the way, there are a number of common errors and biases in takeover valuation.

Use of Comparable Firms and Multiples

The prices paid in most takeovers are justified using the following sequence of actions: The acquirer assembles a group of firms comparable to the one being valued, selects a multiple to value the target firm, computes an average multiple for the comparable firms, and then makes subjective adjustments to this average. Each of these steps provides an opening for bias to enter into the process. Since no two firms are identical, the choice of comparable firms is a subjective one and can be tailored to justify the conclusion we want to reach. Similarly, in selecting a multiple, there are a number of possible choices—price-earnings ratios, price–cash flow ratios, price–book value ratios, and price-sales ratios, among others—and the multiple chosen will be the one that best suits our biases. Finally, once the average multiple has been obtained, subjective adjustments can be made to complete the story. In short, there is plenty of room for a biased firm to justify any price, using reasonable valuation models.

In some acquisition valuations, only firms that have been target firms in acquisitions are used as comparable firms, with the prices paid on the acquisitions being used to estimate multiples. The average multiple paid, which is called a transaction multiple, is then used to justify the price paid in an acquisition. This clearly creates a biased sample, and the values estimated using transactions multiples will generally be too high.

Mismatching Cash Flows and Discount Rates

One of the fundamental principles of valuation is that cash flows should be discounted using a consistent discount rate. Cash flows to equity should be discounted at the cost of equity and cash flows to the firm at the cost of capital; nominal cash flows should be discounted at the nominal discount rate and real cash flows at the real rate; after-tax cash flows should be discounted at the after-tax discount rate and pretax cash flows at the pretax rate. The failure to match cash flows with discount rates can lead to significant under- or overvaluation. Two of the more common mismatches include:

1. *Using the bidding firm's cost of equity or capital to discount the target firm's cash flows.* If the bidding firm raises the funds for the takeover, it is argued, its cost of equity should be used. This argument fails to take into account the fundamental investment principle that it is not who raises the money that determines the cost of equity as much as what the money is raised for. The same firm will face a higher cost of equity for funds raised to finance riskier projects and a lower cost of equity to finance safer projects. Thus the cost of equity in valuing the target will reflect that firm's riskiness (i.e., it is the target firm's cost of equity). Note also that since the cost of equity, as we have defined it, includes only nondiversifiable risk, arguments that the risk will decrease after the merger cannot be used to reduce the cost of equity if the risk being decreased is firm-specific risk.

2. *Using the cost of capital to discount the cash flows to equity.* If the bidding firm uses a mix of debt and equity to finance the acquisition of a target firm, the argument goes, the cost of capital should be used in discounting the target firm's cash flows to equity (cash flows left over after interest and principal payments). By this reasoning, the value of a share in IBM to an investor will depend on how the investor finances his or her acquisition of the share—increasing if the investor borrows to buy the stock (since the cost of debt is less than the cost of equity) and decreasing if the investor buys the stock using his or her own cash. The bottom line is that discounting the cash flows to equity at the cost of capital to obtain the value of equity is always wrong and will result in a significant overvaluation of the equity in the target firm.

Subsidizing the Target Firm

The value of the target firm should not include any portion of the value that should be attributed to the acquiring firm. For instance, assume that a firm with excess debt capacity or a high debt rating uses a significant amount of low-cost debt to finance an acquisition. If we estimated a low cost of capital for the target firm with a high debt ratio and a low after-tax cost of debt, we would overestimate the value of the firm. If the acquiring firm paid this price on the acquisition, it would represent a transfer of wealth from the acquiring firm's stockholders to the target firm's stockholders. Thus, it is not appropriate to use the acquiring firm's cost of debt or debt capacity to estimate the cost of capital for the target firm.

STRUCTURING THE ACQUISITION

Once the target firm has been identified and valued, the acquisition moves forward into the structuring phase. There are three interrelated steps in this phase. The first is the decision on how much to pay for the target firm, given that we have valued it with synergy and control built into the valuation. The second is the determination of how to pay for the deal (i.e., whether to use stock, cash, or some combination of the two) and whether to borrow any of the funds needed. The final step is the choice of the accounting treatment of the deal because it can affect both taxes paid by stockholders in the target firm and how the purchase is accounted for in the acquiring firm's income statement and balance sheets.

Deciding on an Acquisition Price

The preceding section explained how to value a target firm with control and synergy considerations built into the value. This value represents a ceiling on the price that the acquirer can pay on the acquisition rather than a floor. If the acquirer pays the full value, there is no surplus value to claim for the acquirer's stockholders and the target firm's stockholders get the entire value of the synergy and control premiums. This division of value is unfair if the acquiring firm plays an indispensable role in creating the synergy and control premiums.

Consequently, the acquiring firm should try to keep as much of the premium as it can for its stockholders. Several factors, however, will act as constraints. They include:

- *The market price of the target firm, if it is publicly traded, prior to the acquisition.* Since acquisitions have to be based on the current market price, the greater the current market value of equity, the lower the potential for gain to the acquiring firm's stockholders. For instance, if the market price of a poorly managed firm already reflects a high probability that the management of the firm will be changed, there is likely to be little or no value gained from control.
- *The relative scarcity of the specialized resources that the target and the acquiring firm bring to the merger.* Since the bidding firm and the target firm are both contributors to the creation of synergy, the sharing of the benefits of synergy among the two parties will depend in large part on whether the bidding firm's contribution to the creation of the synergy is unique or easily replaced. If it can be easily replaced, the bulk of the synergy benefits will accrue to the target firm. If it is unique, the benefits will be shared much more equitably. Thus, when a firm with cash slack acquires a firm with many high-return projects, value is created. If there are a large number of firms with cash slack and relatively few firms with high-return projects, the bulk of the value of the synergy will accrue to the latter.
- *The presence of other bidders for the target firm.* When there is more than one bidder for a firm, the odds are likely to favor the target firm's stockholders. Bradley, Desai, and Kim (1988) examined an extensive sample of 236 tender offers made between 1963 and 1984 and concluded that the benefits of synergy accrue primarily to the target firms when multiple bidders are involved in the takeover. They estimated the market-adjusted stock returns around the announcement of the takeover for the successful bidder to be 2 percent in single-bidder takeovers and −1.33% in contested takeovers.

Payment for the Target Firm

Once a firm has decided to pay a given price for a target firm, it has to follow up by deciding how it is going to pay for this acquisition. In particular, decisions have to be made about the following aspects of the deal: debt versus equity and cash versus stock.

Debt versus Equity   A firm can raise the funds for an acquisition from either debt or equity. The mix will generally depend on the excess debt capacities of both the acquiring and the target firms. Thus, the acquisition of a target firm that is significantly underlevered may be carried out with a larger proportion of debt than the acquisition of one that is already at its optimal debt ratio. This, of course, is reflected in the value of the firm through the cost of capital. It is also possible that the acquiring firm has excess debt capacity and that it uses its ability to borrow money to carry out the acquisition. Although the mechanics of raising the money may look the same in this case, it is important that the value of the target firm not reflect this additional debt. As noted in the last section, the cost of capital used in valuing the acquisition should not reflect this debt raised. The additional debt has nothing to do with the target firm, and building it into the value will only result in the acquiring firm paying a premium for a value enhancement that rightfully belongs to its own stockholders.

Cash versus Stock   There are three ways in which a firm can use equity in a transaction. The first is to use cash balances that have been built up over time to finance the acquisition. The second is to issue stock to the public, raise cash, and use the cash to pay for the acquisition. The third is to offer stock as payment for the target firm, where the payment is structured in terms of a stock swap—shares in the acquiring firm in exchange for shares in the target firm. The question of which of these approaches is best utilized by a firm cannot be answered without looking at the following factors:

- *The availability of cash on hand*. Clearly, the option of using cash on hand is available only to those firms that have accumulated substantial amounts of cash.
- *The perceived value of the stock*. When stock is issued to the public to raise new funds or when it is offered as payment on acquisitions, the acquiring firm's managers are making a judgment about what the perceived value of the stock is. In other words, managers who believe that their stock is trading at a price significantly below value should not use stock as currency on acquisitions, since what they gain on the acquisitions can be more than lost in the stock issue. However, firms that believe their stocks are overvalued are much more likely to use stock as currency in transactions. The stockholders in the target firm are also aware of this, and may demand a larger premium when the payment is made entirely in the form of the acquiring firm's stock.
- *Tax factors*. When an acquisition is a stock swap, the stockholders in the target firm may be able to defer capital gains taxes on the exchanged shares. Since this benefit can be significant in an acquisition, the potential tax gains from a stock swap may be large enough to offset any perceived disadvantages.

The final aspect of a stock swap is the setting of the terms of the stock swap (i.e., the number of shares of the acquired firm that will be offered per share of the acquiring firm). While this amount is generally based on the market price at the time of the acquisition, the ratio that results may be skewed by the relative mispricing of the two firms' securities, with the more overpriced firm gaining at the expense of the more underpriced (or at least less overpriced) firm. A fairer ratio would be based on the relative values of the two firms' shares. This can be seen quite clearly in the following illustration.

ILLUSTRATION 25.5:   Setting the Exchange Ratio

We will begin by reviewing our valuation for Digital in Figure 25.5. The value of Digital with the synergy and control components is $6,964 million. This is obtained by adding the value of control ($2,421 million) and the value of synergy ($2,422 million) to the status quo value of $2,110 million. Digital also has $1,006 million in debt, and 146.789 million shares outstanding. The maximum value per share for Digital can then be estimated as follows:

Maximum value per share for Digital = (Firm value − Debt)/Number of shares outstanding
= ($6,964 − $1,006)/146.789 = $40.59

The estimated value per share for Compaq is $27, based on the total value of the firm of $38,546.91 million, the debt outstanding of $3.2 billion, and 1,305.76 million shares.

Value per share for Compaq = ($38,546.91 − $3,200)/1,305.76 = $27.00

The appropriate exchange ratio, based on value per share, can be estimated:

$$\text{Exchange ratio}_{\text{Compaq, Digital}} = \text{Value per share}_{\text{Digital}}/\text{Value per share}_{\text{Compaq}}$$
$$= \$40.59/\$27.00 = 1.50 \text{ Compaq shares per Digital share}$$

If the exchange ratio is set above this number, Compaq stockholders will lose to the benefit of Digital stockholders. If it is set below, Digital stockholders will lose to the benefit of Compaq stockholders.

In fact, Compaq paid $30 in cash and offered 0.945 shares of Compaq stock for every Digital share. Assessing the value of this offer,

Value per Digital share (Compaq offer) = $30 + 0.945 ($27.07)	$55.58
Value per Digital share (assessed value)	$40.59
Overpayment by Compaq	$14.99

Based on our assessments of value and control, Compaq overpaid on this acquisition for Digital.

---

 exchratio.xls: This spreadsheet allows you to estimate the exchange ratio on an acquisition, given the value of control and synergy.

Accounting Considerations

There is one final decision that seems to play a disproportionate role in the way in which acquisitions are structured and in setting their terms, and that is the accounting treatment. This section describes the accounting choices and examines why firms choose one over the other.

Purchase versus Pooling   There are two basic choices in accounting for a merger or acquisition. In purchase accounting, the entire value of the acquisition is reflected on the acquiring firm's balance sheet, and the difference between the acquisition price and the restated value of the assets of the target firm[11] is shown as goodwill for the acquiring firm. The goodwill is then written off (amortized) over a

---

[11]The acquiring firm is allowed to restate the assets that are on the books at fair value. This changes the tax basis for the assets, and can affect depreciation in subsequent periods.

Component	Valuation Guidelines	Value
Synergy	Value the combined firm with synergy built in. In the case of Compaq/Digital, the synergy comes from: • Annual cost savings, expected to be $100 million. • Slightly higher growth rate.	$2,422 million
Control Premium	Value Digital as if optimally managed. This was done by assuming: • Higher margins and a return on capital equal to the cost of capital. • Higher debt ratio and a lower cost of capital.	$2,421 million
Status Quo Valuation	Value Digital as is, with existing inputs for investment, financing, and dividend policy.	$2,110 million

FIGURE 25.5 Valuing Digital for Compaq

Source: Corporate Finance: Theory and Practice, Second Edition, by Aswath Damodaran, copyright © 2001 by John Wiley & Sons, Inc. This material is used by permission of John Wiley & Sons, Inc.

period of 40 years, reducing reported earnings in each year. The amortization is not tax deductible and thus does not affect cash flows. If an acquisition qualifies for pooling, the book values of the target and acquiring firms are aggregated. The premium paid over market value is not shown on the acquiring firm's balance sheet.

For an acquisition to qualify for pooling, the merging firms have to meet the following conditions:

■ Each of the combining firms has to be independent; pooling is not allowed when one of the firms is a subsidiary or division of another firm in the two years prior to the merger.

■ Only voting common stock can be issued to cover the transaction; the issue of preferred stock or multiple classes of common stock is not allowed.

■ Stock buybacks or any other distributions that change the capital structure prior to the merger are prohibited.

■ No transactions that benefit only a group of stockholders are allowed.

■ The combined firm cannot sell a significant portion of the existing businesses of the combined companies, other than duplicate facilities or excess capacity.

The question whether an acquisition will qualify for pooling seems to weigh heavily on the managers of acquiring firms. Some firms will not make acquisitions if they do not qualify for pooling, or they will pay premiums to ensure that they do, qualify. Furthermore, as the conditions for pooling make clear, firms are constrained in what they can do after the merger. Firms seem to be willing to accept these constraints, such as restricting stock buybacks and major asset divestitures, just to qualify for pooling.

The bias toward pooling may seem surprising, since this choice does not affect cash flows and value, but it is really not surprising when we consider the source of the bias. Firms are concerned about the effects of the goodwill amortization on their earnings, and about stockholder reactions to the lower earnings. Are firms that use purchase accounting punished by markets when they report lower earnings in subsequent periods? Hong, Kaplan, and Mandelkar (1978) examined the monthly excess returns of 122 firms that acquired other firms between 1954 and 1964 using the pooling technique for 60 months after the acquisition. They compared these findings to 37 acquisitions that used the purchase approach to see if markets were fooled by the pooling technique. They found no evidence that the pooling raised stock prices or that the purchase technique lowered prices. The results are shown in Figure 25.6.

Note that there are no positive excess returns associated with pooling in the 60 months following the merger, nor are there negative excess returns associated with purchase in the same time period. Lindenberg and Ross (1999) studied 387 pooling and 1,055 purchase transactions between 1990 and 1999. They found that the stock price reaction to the acquisition announcement is more positive for purchase transactions than for pooling transactions, and that the market value of firms that use purchase accounting is not adversely affected by the reduction in earnings associated with amortization. They concluded that the earnings multiples of firms that use purchase accounting adjust to offset the decrease in earnings caused by amortization. To illustrate, a 10 percent decrease in earnings because of goodwill amortization is accompanied by a 12.1 percent increase in the price-earnings ratio; the net

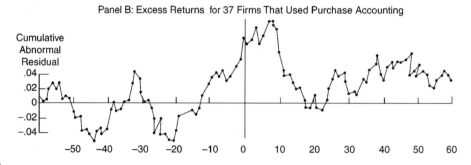

FIGURE 25.6 Pooling versus Purchase Accounting: Effect on Excess Returns

effect is that stock price does not drop. Thus markets seem to discount the negative earnings effect of amortizing goodwill.

There is another consideration, as well. When pooling is used, the shareholders of the acquired firm can transfer their cost basis[12] to the shares they receive in the acquiring firm and not pay capital gains taxes until they sell these shares. When purchase accounting is used, the stockholders of the acquired firm have to recognize the capital gain at the time of the transaction, even if they receive stock in the acquiring firm. Given the substantial premiums paid on acquisitions, this may be a significant factor in why firms choose to use pooling.

In-Process R&D   In the past few years, another accounting choice has entered the mix, especially for acquisitions in the technology sector. Here, firms that qualify can follow up an acquisition by writing off all or a significant proportion of the premium paid on the acquisition as in-process R&D. The net effect is that the firm takes a one-time charge at the time of the acquisition that does not affect operating earnings,[13] and it eliminates or drastically reduces the goodwill that needs to be amortized in subsequent periods. The one-time expense is not tax-deductible and has no cash flow consequences. In acquisitions such as Lotus by IBM and MCI by WorldCom, the in-process R&D charge allowed the acquiring firms to write off a significant portion of the acquisition price at the time of the deal.

The potential to reduce the dreaded goodwill amortization with a one-time charge is appealing for many firms, and studies find that firms try to take maximum advantage of this option. Jeng and Lev (1998) documented this tendency and also noted that firms that qualify for this provision tend to pay significantly larger premiums on acquisitions than firms that do not.

In early 1999, as both the accounting standards board and the SEC sought to crack down on the misuse of in-process R&D, the top executives at high-technology firms fought back, claiming that many acquisitions that were viable now would not be in the absence of this provision. It is revealing of managers' obsession with reported earnings that a provision that has no effects on cash flows, discount rates, and value is making such a difference in whether acquisitions get done.

Final Considerations   The managers of acquiring firms clearly weigh in the accounting effects of acquisitions, even when accounting choices have little or no effect on cash flows. This behavior is rooted in a fear of how much financial markets will punish firms that report lower earnings, largely as a consequence of the write-off of goodwill. Given the transparency of this write-off (firms report earnings before and after goodwill amortization), this fear seems to be misplaced, and the empirical evidence backs that up.

When accounting choices weigh disproportionately in the outcome, the results can be expensive for stockholders in the acquiring firm. In particular,

■ Firms will reject some good acquisitions simply because they fail to meet the pooling test or because in-process R&D cannot be written off.

---

[12]For tax purposes, the cost basis reflects what you originally paid for the shares.
[13]The write-off of in-process R&D is viewed as a nonrecurring charge and is shown separately from operating income.

■ Firms will overpay on acquisitions just to qualify for favorable accounting treatment.

■ To meet the requirements for pooling, firms will often acquire entire companies rather than the divisions that they are interested in and defer asset divestitures that make economic sense.

If the signals emerging from both the SEC and Financial Accounting Standards Board (FASB) have any basis, the rules for both pooling and writing off in-process R&D will be substantially tightened. In fact, it looks likely that firms will not be able to use pooling past 2001 and that they will have to write off goodwill over a much shorter period than the current 40 years.[14] These changes, though bitterly opposed by many top managers, should be welcomed by stockholders.

ANALYZING MANAGEMENT AND LEVERAGED BUYOUTS

The first section, when describing the different types of acquisitions, pointed out two important differences between mergers and buyouts. The first is that, unlike a merger, a buyout does not involve two firms coming together and creating a consolidated entity. Instead, the target firm is acquired by a group of investors that may include the management of the firm. The second is that the target firm in a buyout usually becomes a private business. Some buyouts in the 1980s also used large proportions of debt, leading to their categorization as leveraged buyouts. Each of these differences does have an effect on how we approach the valuation of buyouts.

IMPROVING THE ODDS OF SUCCESS ON MERGERS

The evidence on mergers adding value is murky at best and negative at worst. Considering all the contradictory evidence contained in different studies,[15] we conclude that:

• Mergers of equals (firms of equal size) seem to have a lower probability of succeeding than acquisitions of a smaller firm by a much larger firm.[16]

• Cost-saving mergers, where the cost savings are concrete and immediate, seem to have a better chance of delivering on synergy than mergers based on growth synergy.

• Acquisition programs that focus on buying small private businesses for consolidations have had more success than acquisition programs that concentrate on acquiring publicly traded firms.

• Hostile acquisitions seem to do better at delivering improved postacquisition performance than friendly mergers.

---

[14]Given the formidable lobbying skills of incumbent managers, we would not be surprised to see this change modified or delayed.

[15]Some of this evidence is anecdotal and is based on the study of just a few mergers.

[16]This might well reflect the fact that failures of mergers of equals are much more visible than failures of the small firm/large firm combinations.

Valuation of a Buyout

The fact that buyouts involve only the target firm and that there is no acquiring firm to consider makes valuation much more straightforward. Clearly, there is no potential for synergy and therefore no need to value it. However, the fact that the managers of a firm are also the acquirers of the firm does create two issues. The first is that managers have access to information that investors do not have. This information may allow managers to conclude, with far more certainty than would an external acquirer, that their firm is undervalued. This may be one reason for the buyout. The second is that the management of the firm remains the same after the buyout, but the way in which investment, financing, and dividend decisions are made may change. This happens because managers, once they become owners, may become much more concerned about maximizing firm value.

The fact that firms that are involved in buyouts become private businesses can also have an effect on value. Chapter 24 noted that investments in private businesses are much more difficult to liquidate than investments in publicly traded firms. This can create a significant discount on value. One reason this discount may be smaller in the case of buyouts is that many of them are done with the clear intention, once the affairs of the firm have been put in order, of taking the firm public again.

If going private is expected to increase managers' responsiveness to value maximization in the long term—since they are part owners of the firm—the way to incorporate this in value is to include it in the cash flows. The increased efficiency can be expected to increase cash flows if it increases operating margins. The emphasis on long-term value should be visible in investment choices and should lead to a higher return on capital and higher growth. This advantage has to be weighed against the capital rationing the firm might face because of limited access to financial markets, which might reduce future growth and profits. The net effect will determine the change in value. The empirical evidence on going-private transactions, however, is clear-cut. DeAngelo, DeAngelo, and Rice (1984) reported, for example, an average abnormal return of 30 percent for 81 firms in their sample that went private. Thus financial markets, at least, seem to believe that there is value to be gained for some public firms in going private.

Valuing a Leveraged Buyout

We have seen that leveraged buyouts are financed disproportionately with debt. This high leverage is justified in several ways. First, if the target firm initially has too little debt relative to its optimal debt ratio, the increase in debt can be explained partially by the increase in value moving to the optimal ratio provides. The debt level in most leveraged buyouts exceeds the optimal debt ratio, however, which means that some of the debt will have to be paid off quickly in order for the firm to reduce its cost of capital and its default risk. A second explanation is provided by Michael Jensen, who proposes that managers cannot be trusted to invest free cash flows wisely for their stockholders; they need the discipline of debt payments to maximize cash flows on projects and firm value. A third rationale is that the high debt ratio is temporary and will disappear once the firm liquidates assets and pays off a significant portion of the debt.

The extremely high leverage associated with leveraged buyouts creates two problems in valuation, however. First, it significantly increases the riskiness of the cash flows to equity investors in the firm by increasing the fixed payments to debt holders in the firm. Thus, the cost of equity has to be adjusted to reflect the higher financial risk the firm will face after the leveraged buyout. Second, the expected decrease in this debt over time, as the firm liquidates assets and pays off debt, implies that the cost of equity will also decrease over time. Since the cost of debt and debt ratio will change over time as well, the cost of capital will also change in each period.

In valuing a leveraged buyout, then, we begin with the estimates of free cash flow to the firm, just as we did in traditional valuation. However, instead of discounting these cash flows back at a fixed cost of capital, we discount them back at a cost of capital that will vary from year to year. Once we value the firm, we then can compare the value to the total amount paid for the firm.

ILLUSTRATION 25.6:   Valuing a Leveraged Buyout: Congoleum Inc.

The managers of Congoleum Inc. targeted the firm for a leveraged buyout in 1979.[17] They planned to buy back the stock at $38 per share (it was trading at $24 prior to the takeover) and to finance the acquisition primarily with debt. The breakdown of the cost and financing of the deal is:

Cost of Takeover	
Buy back stock: $38 × 12.2 million shares	$463.60 million
Expenses of takeover	$ 7.00 million
Total cost	$470.60 million

Financing Mix for Takeover	
Equity:	$117.30 million
Debt	$327.10 million
Preferred stock (@13.5%)	$ 26.20 million
Total proceeds	$470.60 million

There were three sources of debt:

1. Bank debt of $125 million, at a 14% interest rate, to be repaid in annual installments of $16.666 million starting in 1980.
2. Senior notes of $115 million, at 11.25% interest rate, to be repaid in equal annual installments of $7.636 million each year from 1981.
3. Subordinated notes of $92 million, at 12.25% interest, to be repaid in equal annual installments of $7.636 million each year from 1989.

The firm also assumed $12.2 million of existing debt, at the advantageous rate of 7.50%; this debt would be repaid in 1982.[18]

The firm projected operating income (EBIT), capital spending, depreciation, and change in working capital from 1980 to 1984 as shown in the following table (in millions of dollars):

[17]The numbers in this illustration were taken from the Harvard Business School case titled "Congoleum." The case is reprinted in Fruhan, Kester, Mason, Piper, and Ruback (1992).

[18]The debt value exceeds the transaction amount, reflecting transaction costs and investment banking fees.

Year	EBIT	Capital Spending	Depreciation	Δ Working Capital
Current	$ 89.80	$ 6.8	$ 7.5	$ 4.0
1980	$ 71.69	$15.0	$35.51	$ 2.0
1981	$ 90.84	$16.2	$36.26	$14.0
1982	$115.73	$17.5	$37.07	$23.3
1983	$133.15	$18.9	$37.95	$11.2
1984	$137.27	$20.4	$21.93	$12.8

The earnings before interest and taxes were expected to grow 8% after 1984, and the capital spending was expected to be offset by depreciation.[19]

Congoleum had a beta of 1.25 in 1979 prior to the leveraged buyout. The Treasury bond rate at the time of the leveraged buyout was 9.5%, and the tax rate was 48%.

We begin the analysis by estimating the expected cash flows to the firm from 1980 to 1985. To obtain these estimates, we subtract the net capital expenditures and changes in working capital (which were provided) from the after-tax operating income.

	1980	1981	1982	1983	1984	1985
EBIT	$71.69	$90.84	$115.73	$133.15	$137.27	$148.25
− EBIT (t)	$34.41	$43.60	$ 55.55	$ 63.91	$ 65.89	$ 71.16
= EBIT (1 - t)	$37.28	$47.24	$ 60.18	$ 69.24	$ 71.38	$ 77.09
+ Depreciation	$35.51	$36.26	$ 37.07	$ 37.95	$ 21.93	$ 21.62
− Capital expenditures	$15.00	$16.20	$ 17.50	$ 18.90	$ 20.40	$ 21.62
− Δ WC	$ 2.00	$14.00	$ 23.30	$ 11.20	$ 12.80	$ 5.00
= FCFF	$55.79	$53.30	$ 56.45	$ 77.09	$ 60.11	$ 72.09

We follow up by estimating the cost of capital for the firm each year, based on our estimates of debt and equity each year. The value of debt for future years is estimated based on the repayment schedule, and it decreases over time. The value of equity in each of the future years is estimated by discounting the expected cash flows in equity beyond that year at the cost of equity. (This explains why the equity in 1980 is greater than the book value of equity.)

	1980	1981	1982	1983	1984	1985
Debt	$327.10	$309.96	$285.17	$260.62	$236.04	$211.45
Equity	$275.39	$319.40	$378.81	$441.91	$504.29	$578.48
Preferred stock	$26.20	$26.20	$26.20	$26.20	$26.20	$26.20
Debt/capital	52.03%	47.28%	41.32%	35.76%	30.79%	25.91%
Equity/capital	43.80%	48.72%	54.89%	60.64%	65.79%	70.88%
Preferred stock/capital	4.17%	4.00%	3.80%	3.60%	3.42%	3.21%
Beta	2.02547	1.87988	1.73426	1.62501	1.54349	1.4745
Cost of equity	20.64%	19.84%	19.04%	18.44%	17.99%	17.61%
After-tax cost of debt	6.53%	6.53%	6.53%	6.53%	6.53%	5.00%
Cost of preferred stock	13.51%	13.51%	13.51%	13.51%	13.51%	13.51%
Cost of capital	13.00%	13.29%	13.66%	14.00%	14.31%	14.21%

An alternative approach to estimating equity that does not require iterations or circular reasoning is to use the book value of equity rather than the estimated market value in calculating debt-equity ratios.[20]

---

[19]We have used the assumptions provided by the investment banker in this case. It is troubling, however, that the firm has an expected growth rate of 8 percent a year forever without reinvesting any money back.
[20]The book value of equity can be obtained as follows:

$$\text{BV of equity}_t = \text{BV of equity}_{t-1} + \text{Net income}_t$$

It is assumed that there will be no dividends paid to equity investors in the initial years of a leveraged buyout.

The cash flows to the firm and the cost of capital in the terminal year (1985), in conjunction with the expected growth rate of 8%,[21] are used to estimate the terminal value of equity (at the end of 1984):

$$\text{Terminal value of firm (end of 1984)} = \text{FCFE}_{1985}/(k_{e,1985} - .08)$$
$$= \$72.09/(.1421 - .08) = \$1{,}161 \text{ million}$$

The expected cash flows to the firm and the terminal value were discounted back to the present at the cost of capital to yield a present value of $820.21 million.[22] Since the acquisition of Congoleum cost only $470.6 million, this acquisition creates value for the acquiring investors.

---

 merglbo.xls: This spreadsheet allows you to evaluate the cash flows and the value of a leveraged buyout.

CONCLUSION

Acquisitions take several forms and occur for different reasons. Acquisitions can be categorized based on what happens to the target firm after the acquisition. A target firm can be consolidated into the acquiring entity (merger), create a new entity in combination with the acquiring firm, or remain independent (buyout).

There are four steps in analyzing acquisitions. First, we specify the reasons for acquisitions and list five: the undervaluation of the target firm, benefit from diversification, the potential for synergy, the value created by changing the way the target firm is run and management self-interest. Second, we choose a target firm whose characteristics make it the best candidate, given the motive chosen in the first step. Third, we value the target firm, assuming it would continue to be run by its current managers and then revalue it assuming better management. We define the difference between these two values as the value of control. We also value each of the different sources of operating and financial synergy and consider the combined value as the value of total synergy. Fourth, we look at the mechanics of the acquisition. We examine how much the acquiring firm should consider paying, given the value estimated in the prior step for the target firm, including control and synergy benefits. We also look at whether the acquisition should be financed with cash or stock, and how the choice of the accounting treatment of the acquisition affects this choice.

Buyouts share some characteristics with acquisitions, but they also vary on a couple of important ones. The absence of an acquiring firm, the fact that the managers of the firm are its acquirers, and the conversion of the acquired firm into a private business all have implications for value. If the buyout is financed predominantly with debt, making it a leveraged buyout, the debt ratio will change in future years, leading to changes in the costs of equity, debt, and capital in those years.

---

[21]While this may seem to be a high growth rate to sustain forever, it would have been appropriate in 1979. Inflation and interest rates were much higher then than in the 1990s.

[22]When the cost of capital changes on a year-to-year basis, the discounting has to be based on a cumulative cost. For instance, the cash flow in year 3 will be discounted back as follows:

$$\text{PV of cash flow in year 3} = 56.45/(1.13)(1.1329)(1.1366)$$

QUESTIONS AND SHORT PROBLEMS

1. The following are the details of two potential merger candidates, Northrop and Grumman, in 1993:

	Northrop	Grumman
Revenues	$4,400.00	$3,125.00
Cost of goods sold (without depreciation)	87.50%	89.00%
Depreciation	$200.00	$74.00
Tax rate	35.00%	35.00%
Working capital	10% of revenue	10% of revenue
Market value of equity	$2,000.00	$1,300.00
Outstanding debt	$160.00	$250.00

Both firms are are expected to grow 5% a year in perpetuity. Capital spending is expected to be 20% of depreciation. The beta for both firms is 1, and both firms are rated BBB, with an interest rate on their debt of 8.5% (The Treasury bond rate is 7%, and the risk premium is 5.5%.)

As a result of the merger, the combined firm is expected to have a cost of goods sold of only 86% of total revenues. The combined firm does not plan to borrow additional debt.
   a. Estimate the value of Grumman, operating independently.
   b. Estimate the value of Northrop, operating independently.
   c. Estimate the value of the combined firm, with no synergy.
   d. Estimate the value of the combined firm, with synergy.
   e. How much is the operating synergy worth?
2. In the Grumman-Northrop example described in the previous question, the combined firm did not take on additional debt after the acquisition. Assume that as a result of the merger the firm's optimal debt ratio increases to 20% of total capital from current levels. (At that level of debt, the combined firm will have an A rating, with an interest rate on its debt of 8%.) If it does not increase debt, the combined firm's rating will be A+ (with an interest rate of 7.75%).
   a. Estimate the value of the combined firm if it stays at its existing debt ratio.
   b. Estimate the value of the combined firm if it moves to its optimal debt ratio.
   c. Who gains this additional value if the firm moves to the optimal debt ratio?
3. In April 1994, Novell, Inc. announced its plan to acquire WordPerfect Corporation for $1.4 billion. At the time of the acquisition, the relevant information about the two companies was as follows:

	Novell	WordPerfect
Revenues	$1,200.00	$600.00
Cost of goods sold (without depreciation)	57.00%	75.00%
Depreciation	$42.00	$25.00
Tax rate	35.00%	35.00%
Capital spending	$75.00	$40.00
Working capital (as % of revenue)	40.00%	30.00%
Beta	1.45	1.25
Expected growth rate in revenues/EBIT	25.00%	15.00%
Expected period of high growth	10 years	10 years
Growth rate after high-growth period	6.00%	6.00%
Beta after high-growth period	1.10	1.10

Capital spending will be 115% of depreciation after the high-growth period. Neither firm has any debt outstanding. The Treasury bond rate is 7%.
   a. Estimate the value of Novell, operating independently.
   b. Estimate the value of WordPerfect, operating independently.
   c. Estimate the value of the combined firm, with no synergy.
   d. As a result of the merger, the combined firm is expected to grow 24% a year for the high-growth period. Estimate the value of the combined firm with the higher growth.
   e. What is the synergy worth? What is the maximum price Novell can pay for WordPerfect?
4. Assume, in the Novell-WordPerfect merger described in the preceding question, that it will take five years for the firms to work through their differences and start realizing their synergy benefits. What is the synergy worth under these circumstances?
5. In 1996, Aetna, a leading player in health insurance, announced its intentions to acquire U.S. Healthcare, the nation's largest health maintenance organization, and provided synergy as a rationale. On the announcement of the merger, Aetna's stock price, which was $57, dropped to $52.50, while U.S. Healthcare's stock price surged from $31 to $37.50. Aetna had 400 million shares, and U.S. Healthcare had 50 million shares outstanding at the time of the announcement.
   a. Estimate the value, if any, that financial markets are attaching to synergy in this merger.
   b. How would you reconcile the market reaction to the rationale presented by management for the acquisition?
6. IH Corporation, a farm equipment manufacturer, has accumulated almost $2 billion in losses over the past seven years of operations and is in danger of not being able to carry forward these losses. EG Corporation, an extremely profitable financial service firm, which had $3 billion in taxable income in its most recent year, is considering acquiring IH Corporation. The tax authorities will allow EG Corporation to offset its taxable income with the carried-forward losses. The tax rate for EG Corporation is 40%, and the cost of capital is 12%.
   a. Estimate the value of the tax savings that will occur as a consequence of the merger.
   b. What is the value of the tax savings if the tax authorities allow EG Corporation to spread the carried-forward losses over four years (i.e., allow $200 million of the carried-forward losses to offset income each year for the next four years)?
7. You are considering a takeover of PMT Corporation, a firm that has significantly underperformed its peer group over the past five years, and you wish to estimate the value of control. The data on PMT Corporation, the peer group, and the best-managed firm in the group are:

	PMT Corporation	Peer Group	Best-Managed Firm
Return on assets (after-tax)	8.00%	12.00%	18.00%
Dividend payout ratio	50.00%	30.00%	20.00%
Debt-equity ratio	10.00%	50.00%	50.00%
Interest rate on debt	7.50%	8.00%	8.00%
Beta	Not available	1.30	1.30

PMT Corporation reported earnings per share of $2.50 in the most recent time period and is expected to reach stable growth in five years, after which the growth rate is expected to be 6% for all firms in this group. The beta during the stable-growth period is expected to be 1 for all firms. There are 100 million shares outstanding, and the Treasury bond rate is 7% (the tax rate is 40% for all firms).

a. Value the equity in PMT Corporation assuming that the current management continues in place.

b. Value the equity in PMT Corporation assuming that it improves its performance to peer group levels.

c. Value the equity in PMT Corporation assuming that it improves its performance to the level of the best managed firm in the group.

8. You are attempting to do a leveraged buyout of Boston Turkey but have run into some roadblocks. You have some partially completed projected cash flow statements and need help to complete them.

	Year 1	Year 2	Year 3	Year 4	Year 5	Terminal Year
Revenues	$1,100,000	$1,210,000	$1,331,000	$1,464,100	$1,610,510	$1,707,141
– Expenses	$ 440,000	$ 484,000	$ 532,400	$ 585,640	$ 644,204	$ 682,856
– Depreciation	$ 100,000	$ 110,000	$ 121,000	$ 133,100	$ 146,410	$ 155,195
= EBIT	$ 560,000	$ 616,000	$ 677,600	$ 745,360	$ 819,896	$ 869,090
– Interest	$ 360,000	$ 324,000	$ 288,000	$ 252,000	$ 216,000	$ 180,000
Taxable income	$ 200,000	$ 292,000	$ 389,600	$ 493,360	$ 603,896	$ 689,090
– Tax	$ 80,000	$ 116,800	$ 155,840	$ 197,344	$ 241,558	$ 275,636
= Net income	$ 120,000	$ 175,200	$ 233,760	$ 296,016	$ 362,338	$ 413,454

The capital expenditures are expected to be $120,000 next year and to grow at the same rate as revenues for the rest of the period. Working capital will be kept at 20% of revenues (revenues this year were $1 million).

The leveraged buyout will be financed with a mix of $1 million of equity and $3 million of debt (at an interest rate of 12%). Part of the debt will be repaid by the end of year 5, and the debt remaining at the end of year 5 will remain on the books permanently.

a. Estimate the cash flows to equity and the firm for the next five years.

b. The cost of equity in year 1 has been computed. Compute the cost of equity each year for the rest of the period (use book value of equity for the calculation).

Item	Year 1
Equity	$1,000,000
Debt	$3,000,000
Debt-equity ratio	3
Beta	2.58
Cost of equity	24.90%

c. Compute the terminal value of the firm.
d. Evaluate whether the leveraged buyout will create value.

9. J & L Chemical is a profitable chemical manufacturing firm. The business, however, is highly cyclical, and the profits of the firm have been volatile. The management of the firm is considering acquiring a food-processing firm to reduce the earnings volatility and exposure to economic cycles.

   a. Would such an action be in the best interests of stockholders? Explain.

   b. Would your analysis be any different if J & L was a private firm? Explain.

   c. Is there any condition under which you would argue for such an acquisition for a publicly traded firm?

CHAPTER 26

Valuing Real Estate

The valuation models developed for financial assets are applicable for real assets as well. Real estate investments comprise the most significant component of real asset investments. For many years, analysts in real estate have used their own variants on valuation models to value real estate. Real estate is too different an asset class, they argue, to be valued with models developed to value publicly traded stocks.

This chapter presents a different point of view: that while real estate and stocks may be different asset classes, the principles of valuation should not differ across the classes. In particular, the value of real estate property should be the present value of the expected cash flows on the property. That said, there are serious estimation issues to confront that are unique to real estate and that will be dealt with in this chapter.

REAL VERSUS FINANCIAL ASSETS

Real estate and financial assets share several common characteristics: Their value is determined by the cash flows they generate, the uncertainty associated with these cash flows, and the expected growth in the cash flows. Other things remaining equal, the higher the level and growth in the cash flows, and the lower the risk associated with the cash flows, the greater is the value of the asset.

There are also significant differences between the two classes of assets. There are many who argue that the risk and return models used to evaluate financial assets cannot be used to analyze real estate because of the differences in liquidity across the two markets and in the types of investors in each market. The alternatives to traditional risk and return models will be examined in this chapter. There are also differences in the nature of the cash flows generated by financial and real estate investments. In particular, real estate investments often have finite lives, and have to be valued accordingly. Many financial assets, such as stocks, have infinite lives. These differences in asset lives manifest themselves in the value assigned to these assets at the end of the estimation period. The terminal value of a stock, 5 or 10 years hence, is generally much higher than the current value because of the expected growth in the cash flows, and because these cash flows are expected to continue forever. The terminal value of a building may be lower than the current value because the usage of the building might depreciate its value. However, the land component will have an infinite life and, in some cases, may be the overwhelming component of the terminal value.

> ### THE EFFECT OF INFLATION: REAL VERSUS FINANCIAL ASSETS
>
> For the most part, real and financial assets seem to move together in response to macroeconomic variables. A downturn in the economy seems to affect both adversely, as does a surge in real interest rates. There is one variable, though, that seems to have dramatically different consequences for real and financial assets, and that is inflation. Historically, higher than anticipated inflation has had negative consequences for financial assets, with both bonds and stocks being adversely impacted by unexpected inflation. Fama and Schwert, for instance, in a study on asset returns report that a 1 percent increase in the inflation rate causes bond prices to drop by 1.54 percent and stock prices by 4.23 percent. In contrast, unanticipated inflation seems to have a positive impact on real assets. In fact, the only asset class that Fama and Schwert tracked that was positively affected by unanticipated inflation was residential real estate.
>
> Why is real estate a potential hedge against inflation? There are a variety of reasons, ranging from more favorable tax treatment when it comes to depreciation to the possibility that investors lose faith in financial assets when inflation runs out of control and prefer to hold real assets. More importantly, the divergence between real estate and financial assets in response to inflation indicates that the risk of real estate will be very different if viewed as part of a portfolio that includes financial assets than if viewed as a standalone investment.

DISCOUNTED CASH FLOW VALUATION

The value of any cash-flow-producing asset is the present value of the expected cash flows on it. Just as discounted cash flow valuation models, such as the dividend discount model, can be used to value financial assets, they can also be used to value cash-flow-producing real estate investments.

To use discounted cash flow valuation to value real estate investments it is necessary to:

- Measure the riskiness of real estate investments, and estimate a discount rate based on the riskiness.
- Estimate expected cash flows on the real estate investment for the life of the asset.

The following section examines these issues.

Estimating Discount Rates

Chapters 6 and 7 presented the basic models that are used to estimate the costs of equity, debt, and capital for an investment. Do those models apply to real estate as well? If so, do they need to be modified? If not, what do we use instead?

This section examines the applicability of risk and return models to real estate investments. In the process, we consider whether the assumption that the marginal investor is well diversified is a justifiable one for real estate investments, and, if so, how best to measure the parameters of the model—risk-free rate, beta, and risk premium—to estimate the cost of equity. We also consider other sources of risk in real estate investments that are not adequately considered by traditional risk and return models and how to incorporate these into valuation.

Cost of Equity The two basic models used to estimate the cost of equity for financial assets are the capital asset and the arbitrage pricing models. In both models, the risk of any asset, real or financial, is defined to be that portion of that asset's variance that cannot be diversified away. This nondiversifiable risk is measured by the market beta in the capital asset pricing model (CAPM) and by multiple factor betas in the arbitrage pricing model (APM). The primary assumptions that both models make to arrive at these conclusions are that the marginal investor in the asset is well diversified and that the risk is measured in terms of the variability of returns.

If one assumes that these models apply for real assets as well, the risk of a real asset should be measured by its beta relative to the market portfolio in the CAPM and by its factor betas in the APM. If we do so, however, we are assuming, as we did with publicly traded stocks, that the marginal investor in real assets is well diversified.

Are the Marginal Investors in Real Estate Well Diversified? Many analysts argue that real estate requires investments that are so large that investors in it may not be able to diversify sufficiently. In addition, they note that real estate investments require localized knowledge, and that those who develop this knowledge choose to invest primarily or only in real estate. Consequently, they note that the use of the capital asset pricing model or the arbitrage pricing model, which assume that only nondiversifiable risk is rewarded, is inappropriate as a way of estimating cost of equity.

There is a kernel of truth to this argument, but it can be countered fairly easily by noting that:

- Many investors who concentrate their holdings in real estate do so by choice. They see it as a way of leveraging their specialized knowledge of real estate. Thus, we would view them the same way we view investors who choose to hold only technology stocks in their portfolios.
- Even large real estate investments can be broken up into smaller pieces, allowing investors the option of holding real estate investments in conjunction with financial assets.
- Just as the marginal investor in stocks is often an institutional investor with the resources to diversify and keep transactions costs low, the marginal investor in many real estate markets today has sufficient resources to diversify.

If real estate developers and private investors insist on higher expected returns because they are not diversified, real estate investments will increasingly be held by real estate investment trusts, limited partnerships, and corporations, which attract more diversified investors with lower required returns. This trend is well in place in the United States and may spread over time to other countries as well.

Measuring Risk for Real Assets in Asset Pricing Models Even if it is accepted that the risk of a real asset is its market beta in the CAPM, and its factor betas in the APM, there are several issues related to the measurement and use of these risk parameters that need to be examined. To provide some insight into the measurement problems associated with real assets, consider the standard approach to estimating betas in the capital asset pricing model for a publicly traded stock. First, the prices of the stock are collected from historical data, and returns are computed on a periodic basis (daily, weekly, or monthly). Second, these stock returns are regressed against returns on a stock index over the same period to obtain the beta. For real estate, these steps are not as straightforward.

Individual Assets: Prices and Risk Parameters   The betas of individual stocks can be estimated fairly simply because stock prices are available for extended time periods. The same cannot be said for individual real estate investments. A piece of property does not get bought and sold very frequently, though similar properties might. Consequently, price indexes are available for classes of assets (for example, downtown Manhattan office buildings), and risk parameters can be estimated for these classes.

Even when price indexes are available for classes of real estate investments, questions remain about the comparability of assets within a class (Is one downtown building the same as any other? How does one control for differences in age and quality of construction? What about location?) and about the categorization itself (office buildings versus residential buildings; single-family versus multifamily residences)?

There have been attempts to estimate market indexes and risk parameters for classes of real estate investments. The obvious and imperfect solution to the nontrading problem in real estate is to construct indexes of real estate investment trusts (REITs) and commingled real estate equity funds (CREFs), which are traded and have market prices. The reason this might not be satisfactory is because the properties owned by real estate investment trusts may not be representative of the real estate property market, and the securitization of real estate may result in differences between real estate and REIT/CREF returns. An alternative and more comprehensive solution is the Frank Russell index of real estate values that is based on approximately 1,000 properties owned by real estate funds. While many of these properties are not traded in every period, the index is based on appraised values for these properties. In addition, Ibbotson and Siegal (I&S) have estimated annual returns on an index of unlevered properties. Finally, Case and Shiller constructed an index using actual transaction prices, rather than appraised values, to estimate the value of residential real estate. Table 26.1 summarizes the returns on real estate indexes, the S&P 500, and an index of bonds.

There are several interesting results that emerge from this table. First, not all real estate series behave the same way. The returns on CREFs have much lower volatility associated with them than REITs, perhaps because CREF values are based on appraisals whereas REITs represent market prices. Second, returns on REITs seem to have more in common with returns on the stock market than returns on other real estate indexes. Third, there is high positive serial correlation in many of the real estate return series, especially those based on appraised data. This can be attributed to the smoothing of appraisals that are used in these series.

The Market Portfolio   In estimating the betas of stocks, we generally use a stock index as a proxy for the market portfolio. In theory, however, the market portfolio should include all assets in the economy in proportion to their market values. This is of particular significance when the market portfolio is used to estimate the risk

TABLE 26.1 Returns on Real Estate, Stocks, and Bonds

	Period	Compound Annual Return	Arithmetic Mean Return	Standard Deviation	Serial Correlation
CREF (commercial)	1969–1987	10.80%	10.90%	2.60%	43.00%
REIT (commercial)	1972–1999	14.20%	15.70%	15.40%	11.00%
I&S (commercial)	1960–1969	8.70%	8.70%	4.90%	73.00%
C&S (residential)	1970–1989	8.50%	8.50%	3.00%	17.00%
Home (residential)	1947–1989	9.80%	9.80%	4.70%	54.00%
Harris (residential)	1926–1989	8.50%	8.50%	5.40%	55.00%
Farm (farmland)	1947–1989	9.90%	9.90%	7.80%	64.00%
S&P 500	1928–2000	10.46%	12.38%	20.02%	–5.00%
T-bonds	1928–2000	4.95%	5.21%	7.68%	16.00%
T-bills	1928–2000	3.97%	3.93%	3.18%	86.00%
Inflation rate	1928–2000	3.21%	3.30%	3.05%	66.00%

Source: Ibbotson, Bloomberg.

parameters of real estate investments. The use of a stock index as the market portfolio will result in the marginalization[1] of real estate investments and the underestimation of risk for these assets.

The differences between a stock and an all-asset portfolio can be large because the market value of real estate investments not included in the stock index is significant. Figure 26.1 summarizes the approximate worldwide market values of different asset classes available to U.S. investors in 2000.

The differences in returns between an all-stock portfolio and a portfolio composed of different asset classes are illustrated in Figure 26.2, which traces returns from 1965 to 1990 on the S&P 500 Index and an index that includes real estate investments.

There is also evidence that real estate investments and stocks do not move together in reaction to larger economic events. (See Table 26.2.) As noted earlier in this chapter, the differences between real asset and financial asset returns widen when inflation rates change. In fact, three of the five real estate indexes are negatively correlated with stocks, and the other two have low correlations. As a consequence, adding real estate investments to a portfolio composed primarily of financial assets will create substantial savings in terms of reduced volatility. In addition, the returns on a market portfolio which includes both financial and real assets can be very different from the returns on a market portfolio that is composed entirely of stocks.

While few economists would argue with the value of incorporating real estate investments into the market portfolio, most are stymied by the measurement problems. These problems, while insurmountable until recently, are becoming more solvable as real estate investments get securitized and traded.

---

[1]When the beta of an asset is estimated relative to a stock index, the underlying assumption is that the marginal investor has the bulk of his or her portfolio (97 percent to 98 percent) in stocks, and measures risk relative to this portfolio.

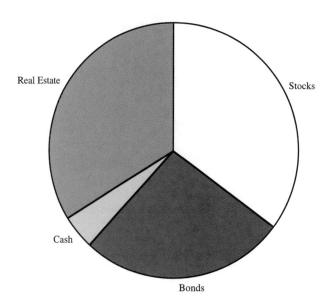

FIGURE 26.1   Market Values of Asset Classes
Source: Ibbotson.

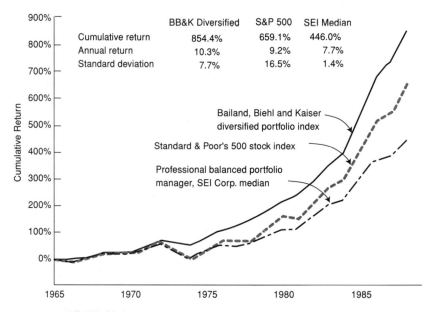

FIGURE 26.2   Returns on Stock Index versus All-Asset Index

TABLE 26.2 Correlations across Asset Classes

	I&S	CREF	Home	C&S	Farm	S&P	T-bonds	T-bills	Inflation
I&S	1.00								
CREF	0.79	1.00							
Home	0.52	0.12	1.00						
C&S	0.26	0.16	0.62	1.00					
Farm	0.06	−0.06	0.51	0.49	1.00				
S&P	0.16	0.25	−0.13	−0.20	−0.10	1.00			
T-bonds	−0.04	0.01	−0.22	−0.54	−0.44	0.11	1.00		
T-bills	0.53	0.42	0.13	−0.56	−0.32	−0.07	0.48	1.00	
Inflation	0.70	0.35	0.77	0.56	0.49	−0.02	−0.17	0.25	1.00

Source: Ibbotson and Brinson (1996).

Some Practical Solutions   If one accepts the proposition that the risk of a real estate investment should be measured using traditional risk and return models, there are some practical approaches that can be used to estimate risk parameters:

- The risk of a class of real estate investments can be obtained by regressing returns on the class (using the Ibbotson series, for instance, on commercial and residential property) against returns on a consolidated market portfolio. The primary problems with this approach are (1) these returns series are based on smoothed appraisals and may understate the true volatility in the market, and (2) the returns are available only for longer return intervals (annual or quarterly).
- The risk parameters of traded real estate securities (REITs and MLPs) can be used as a proxy for the risk in real estate investment. The limitations of this approach are that securitized real estate investments may behave differently from direct investments and that it is much more difficult to estimate risk parameters for different classes of real estate investment (unless one can find REITs that restrict themselves to one class of investments, such as commercial property).
- The demand for real estate is in some cases a derived demand. For instance, the value of a shopping mall is derived from the value of retail space, which should be a function of how well retailing is doing as a business. It can be argued, in such a case, that the risk parameters of a mall should be related to the risk parameters of publicly traded retail stores. Corrections should obviously be made for differences in operating and financial leverage.

Other Risk Factors   Does investing in real estate investments expose investors to more (and different) types of risk than investing in financial assets? If so, how is this risk measured, and is it rewarded? The following are some of the issues related to real estate investments that might affect the measurement of risk and expected returns.

Diversifiable versus Nondiversifiable Risk   As stated earlier, using risk and return models that assume that the marginal investor is well diversified is reasonable even though many investors in real estate choose not to be diversified. Part of the justification for this statement is the presence of firms with diversified investors, such as real estate investment trusts and master limited partnerships, in the real estate market. But what if no such investors exist and the marginal investor in real estate is not well diversified? How would we modify our estimates of cost of equity?

Chapter 24 examined how to adjust the cost of equity for a private business for the fact that its owner was not diversified. In particular, we recommended the use of a total beta that reflected not just the market risk but also the extent of nondiversification on the part of the owner:

Total beta = Market beta/Correlation between owner's portfolio and the market

This measure could be adapted to estimate a total beta for private businesses. For instance, assume that the marginal investor in commercial real estate has a portfolio that has a correlation of 0.50 with the market and that commercial real estate as a property class has a beta of 0.40. The beta you would use to estimate the cost of equity for the investment would be 0.80.

$$\text{Total beta} = 0.40/0.5 = 0.80$$

Using this higher beta would result in a higher cost of equity and a lower value for the real estate investment.

Lack of Liquidity   Another critique of traditional risk measures is that they assume that all assets are liquid (or, at least, that there are no differences in liquidity across assets). Real estate investments are often less liquid than financial assets; transactions occur less frequently, transactions costs are higher, and there are far fewer buyers and sellers. The less liquid an asset, it is argued, the more risky it is.

The link between lack of liquidity and risk is difficult to quantify for several reasons. One is that it depends on the time horizon of the investor. An investor who intends to hold long-term will care less about liquidity than one who is uncertain about his or her time horizon or wants to trade short-term. Another is that it is affected by the external economic conditions. For instance, real estate is much more liquid during economic booms, when prices are rising, than during recessions, when prices are depressed.

The alternative to trying to view the absence of liquidity as an additional risk factor and building into discount rates is to value the illiquid asset conventionally (as if it were liquid) and then applying a illiquidity discount to it. This is often the practice in valuing closely held and illiquid businesses and allows for the illiquidity discount to be a function of the investor and external economic conditions at the time of the valuation. The process of estimating the discount was examined in more detail in Chapter 24.

Exposure to Legal Changes   The values of all investments are affected by changes in the tax law—changes in depreciation methods and changes in tax rates on ordinary income and capital gains. Real estate investments are particularly exposed to changes in the tax law, because they derive a significant portion of their value from depreciation and tend to be highly levered.

Unlike manufacturing or service businesses which can move operations from one locale to another to take advantage of locational differences in tax rates and other legal restrictions, real estate is not mobile and is therefore much more exposed to changes in local laws (such as zoning requirements, property taxes, and rent control).

The question becomes whether this additional sensitivity to changes in tax and local laws is an additional source of risk, and, if so, how this risk should be priced. Again, the answer will depend on whether the marginal investor is diversified not only across asset classes but also across real estate investments in different locations. For instance, a real estate investor who holds real estate in New York, Miami, Los Angeles, and Houston is less exposed to legal risk than one who holds real estate in only one of these locales. The trade-off, however, is that the localized knowledge that allows a real estate investor to do well in one market may not carry well into other markets.

Information Costs and Risk   Real estate investments often require specific information about local conditions that is difficult (and costly) to obtain. The information is also likely to contain more noise. There are some who argue that this higher cost of acquiring information and the greater noise in this information should be built into the risk and discount rates used to value real estate. This argument is not restricted to real estate. It has been used as an explanation for the small stock premium—that is small stocks make higher returns than larger stocks, after adjusting for risk (using the CAPM). Small stocks, it is argued, generally have less information available on them than larger stocks, and the information tends to be more noisy.

DIVERSIFICATION IN REAL ESTATE: TRENDS AND IMPLICATIONS

As we look at the additional risk factors—estimation errors, legal and tax changes, volatility in specific real estate markets—that are often built into discount rates and valuations, the rationale for diversification becomes stronger. A real estate firm that is diversified across holdings in multiple locations will be able to diversify away some of this risk. If the firm attracts investors who are diversified into other asset classes, it diversifies away even more risk, thus reducing its exposure to risk and its cost of equity.

Inexorably, then, you would expect to see diversified real estate investors—real estate corporations, REITs, and MLPs—drive local real estate investors who are not diversified (either across locations or asset classes) out of the market by bidding higher prices for the same properties. If this is true, you might ask, why has it not happened already? There are two reasons. The first is that knowledge of local real estate market conditions is still a critical component driving real estate values, and real estate investors with this knowledge may be able to compensate for their failure to diversify. The second is that a significant component of real estate success still comes from personal connections—to other developers, to zoning boards, and to politicians. Real estate investors with the right connections may be able to get much better deals on their investments than corporations bidding for the same business.

As real estate corporations and REITs multiply, you should expect to see much higher correlation in real estate prices across different regions and a drop-off in the importance of local conditions. Furthermore, you should also expect to see these firms become much more savvy at dealing with the regulatory authorities in different regions.

An Alternative Approach to Estimating Discount Rates: The Survey Approach The problems with the assumptions of traditional risk and return models and the difficulties associated with the measurement of risk for nontraded real assets in these models have led to alternative approaches to estimating discount rates for these real estate investments. In the context of real estate, for instance, the costs of equity and capital are often obtained by surveying potential investors in real estate on what rates of return they would demand for investing in different types of property investments. Table 26.3 summarizes the results of such a survey done by Cushman and Wakefield, a real estate firm, of investors in various real estate properties.

This approach is justified on the following grounds:

- These surveys are not based on some abstract models of risk and return (which may ignore risk characteristics that are unique to the real estate market) but on what actual investors in real want to make as a return.
- These surveys allow for the estimation of discount rates for specific categories of properties (hotels, apartments, etc.) by region, without requiring a dependence on past prices like risk and return models.
- There are relatively few large investors who invest directly in real estate (rather than in securitized real estate). It is therefore feasible to do such a survey.

There are, however, grounds for contesting this approach, as well:

- Surveys, by their very nature, yield different "desired rates of return" for different investors for the same property class. Assuming that a range of desired returns can be obtained for a class of investments, it is not clear where one goes

TABLE 26.3 Survey Results from Cushman Wakefield

Interviewee	Geographic Areas of Investment	Property Type Preference	Overall Rates	
			Going In	Terminal
Apartment Investor	Southwest	Apartments	10%	10–11%
Apartment Investor	Pacific Northwest	Apartments	9.25%	9.25%
Bank (Mortgage Broker)	Pacific Northwest	Apartments	9.25–9.75%	9.5–10.25%
		Office—urban (A)	8.25–8.5%	8.5%
		Office—suburban	9%	9.5%
		Business parks	9–9.5%	9.5–10%
		Industrial	9–9.5%	9.5–10%
		Regional malls	8.25–8.5%	8.5%
		Neighborhood	9.75–10%	10.25%

Source: Cushman and Wakefield Appraisal Division National Investor Survey—May 1991.

next. Presumably, those investors who demand returns at the high end of the scale will find themselves priced out of the market, and those whose desired returns are at the low end of the scale will find plenty of undervalued properties. The question of who the marginal investor in an investment should be is not answered in these surveys.

■ The survey approach bypasses the issue of risk but it does not really eliminate it. Clearly, investors demand the returns that they do on different property classes because they perceive them to have different levels of risk.

■ The survey approach works reasonably well when there are relatively few and fairly homogeneous investors in the market. While this might have been true a decade ago, it is becoming less so as new institutional investors enter the market and the number of investors increases and becomes more heterogeneous.

■ The survey approach also becomes suspect when the investors who are surveyed act as pass-throughs—they invest in real estate, securitize their investments and sell them to others, and move on. If they do so, it is the desired returns of the ultimate investor (the buyer of the securitized real estate) that should determine value, not the desired return of the intermediate investor.

There are several advantages to using a model that measures risk and estimates a discount rate based on the risk measure, rather than using a survey.

■ A risk and return model, properly constructed, sets reasonable bounds for the expected returns. For instance, the expected return on a risky asset in both the CAPM and the APM will exceed the expected return on a riskless asset. There is no such constraint on survey responses.

Internal Rate of Return	Growth Rates		Typical Holding Period
	Income	Expense	
13–15%	0–4.5%	4–5%	6
N/A	5%	4%	5–7
11–12%	4–5%	4–5%	10
11%	4–5%	4–5%	10
11.5–12%	4–5%	4–5%	10
11.5%	4–5%	4–5%	10
11.5%	4–5%	4–5%	10
11%	4–5%	4–5%	10
12–13%	4-5%	4–5%	10

■ A risk and return model, by relating expected return to risk and risk to pre-specified factors, allows an analyst to be proactive in estimating discount rates rather than reactive. For instance, in the context of the CAPM, the expected return on an investment is determined by its beta, which in turn is determined by the cyclicality of the business (in which the investment is made) and the financial leverage taken on. Thus, an analyst who knows how the financial leverage in an investment is expected to change over time can adjust the beta of that investment accordingly and use it in valuation. There is no such mechanism available when the survey approach is used.

■ Where the ultimate investor is not known at the time of the analysis, as is the case in real estate investments that are securitized, a risk and return model provides the framework for estimating the discount rate for a hypothetical marginal investor.

As real estate markets become more accessible to institutional investors and more investments are made with the objective of eventual securitization, the need for a good risk and return model becomes more acute. These same trends will also make real estate investments more like financial investments (by making them more liquid). Sooner rather than later, the same models used to estimate risk and discount rates for financial assets will also be used to estimate risk and discount rates for real estate investments.

From Cost of Equity to Cost of Capital   Once you have estimated a cost of equity, there are two other inputs needed to estimate the cost of capital. The first is the cost of debt, and estimating it is much more straightforward than estimating the cost of equity. You have two choices:

1. If you are raising capital for a new real estate investment, you could use the stated interest rate on bank loans used to fund the investment. In making this estimate, though, you have to be aware of the terms of the bank loan and whether there will be other costs created to the real estate firm. For instance, a requirement that a compensating balance be maintained over the life of the loan will increase the effective cost of debt.

2. You could look at the capacity that the real estate investment has to cover bank payments (this is the equivalent of an interest coverage ratio), estimate a synthetic rating, and use this rating to estimate a pretax cost of debt. In fact, you could modify the numerator to include depreciation, since the investment is a finite life investment and should not require significant reinvestment.

To estimate an after-tax cost of debt, you would use the marginal tax rate of the individual or entity investing in the property.

The debt ratio in most real estate investments is usually estimated by looking at the proportion of the funds raised from debt and equity. Thus, if a property costs $4 million to build and the investor borrows $3 million to fund it, the debt ratio used is 75 percent. While we will stick with this convention, it is worth bearing in mind that the ratios should be based on the value of the property rather than the funding needs. Thus if the value of the property is expected to be $5 million after it is built, the debt ratio used should be 60 percent ($3 million/$5 million). This, of course, requires circular reasoning since the cost of capital is necessary to estimate the value of the property in the first place.

The distinction between cost of equity and the cost of capital, drawn in Chapter 7, is significant. If the cash flows being discounted are predebt cash flows (i.e., cash flows to the firm), the appropriate discount rate is the cost of capital. If you use this approach, you will value the property and if you are the equity investor, you would then subtract out the value of the outstanding debt to arrive at the value of the equity in the real estate investment. If the cash flows being discounted on a real estate deal are cash flows to equity, the appropriate discount rate is the cost of equity. You would then value the equity in the real estate investment directly.

Estimating Cash Flows

Not all real estate investments generate cash flows. For those that do, cash flows can be estimated in much the same way that they can be estimated for financial investments. The ultimate objective is to estimate cash flows after taxes. Just as with financial assets, these cash flows can be estimated to equity investors. This is the cash flow left over after meeting all operating expenses, debt obligations (interest expenses and principal payments), and capital expenditures. The cash flows can also be estimated for all investors (debt as well as equity) in the real estate investment. This is the equivalent of cash flows to the firm, which is the cash flow prior to meeting debt obligations.

Cash Inflows   The cash flows from a real estate investment generally take the form of rents and lease payments. In estimating rents for future years, you have to consider past trends in rents, demand and supply conditions for space provided by the property, and general economic conditions.

In office/multiple residential buildings all space may not be rented at a particular time. Thus, the vacancy rate (i.e., the percentage of the space that will not be rented out at any point in time) has to be projected in conjunction with market rents. Even in tight markets, there will be periods of time where space cannot be rented out, leading to a vacancy rate. Thus, no building, no matter how sought after, can be expected to have a 100 percent occupancy rate. With new buildings, the projections have to factor in how long it will take initially to get occupants to rent/lease space. Clearly, the longer it takes, the smaller is the discounted cash flow value of the building.

In the case of leased property, the terms of the lease can affect the projected lease revenues. If income properties are subject to existing leases, the terms of the lease such as the length of the lease, the contracted lease payments with future increases, additional reimbursable expenses, and provisions on lease renewal will determine cash flow estimates. The leases may also be net leases, where the tenant is responsible for paying taxes, insurance, and maintenance.

Cash Outflows   Expenses on real estate investments include items such as property taxes, insurance, repairs and maintenance, and advertising—which are unrelated to occupancy and are fixed—as well as items such as utility expenses, which are a function of occupancy and are variable. In addition, the following factors will affect projected expenses:

- *Reimbursability.* Some expenses incurred in connection with a property by the owner may be reimbursed by the tenant, as part of a contractual agreement.

■ *Expense stops.* Many office leases include provisions to protect the owner from increases in operating expenses beyond an agreed-on level. Any increases beyond that level have to be paid by the tenant.

In many real estate investments, real estate taxes represent the biggest single item of expenditures, and they can be volatile, not only because the tax laws change but because they are based often on assessed values.

Expected Growth   To estimate future cash flows, we need estimates of the expected growth rate in both rents/leases and expenses. A key factor in estimating the growth rate is the expected inflation rate. In a stable real estate market, the expected growth in cash flows should be close to the expected inflation rate. In tight markets with low vacancy rates, it is possible for the expected growth rate in rents to be higher than the expected inflation rate at least until the market shortages disappear. The reverse is likely to be true in markets with high vacancy rates.

The surveys used to estimate discount rates, reported in Table 26.3, also collect information on investors expectations of expected growth. It is interesting that while there are significant differences between investors on discount rates, the expected growth rates in cash inflows and outflows fall within a tight band. In 1989, for instance, the Cushman and Wakefield survey of investors in a wide range of markets found that they all estimated expected growth in cash flows to be between 4 percent and 6 percent.

How will rent control affect these estimates? By putting a cap on how high the increases can be without limiting the downside, it will generally lower the expected growth rate in cash flows over time. Uncertainty about rent control laws, in terms of both how much the cap will be and whether the laws will be revised, will add to the estimation error in the valuation.

Terminal Value   In all discounted cash flow valuation models, a key input is the estimate of terminal value, that is, the value of the asset being valued at the end of the investment time horizon. There are three basic approaches that can be used to estimate the terminal value:

1. The current value of the property can be assumed to increase at the expected inflation rate to arrive at a terminal value. Thus the terminal value of a property, worth \$10 million now, in 10 years will be \$13.44 million if the expected inflation rate is 3 percent (terminal value = $\$10 \times 1.03^{10}$). The danger of this approach is that it starts off with the assumption that the current value of the asset is reasonable, and tries to then assess the true value of the asset.

2. An alternative to this approach is to assume that the cash flows in the terminal year (the last year of the investment horizon) will continue to grow at a constant rate forever after that. If this assumption is made, the terminal value of the asset is:

$$\text{Terminal value of equity/Asset}_n = \text{Expected CF}_{n+1}/(r - g)$$

where r is the discount rate (cost of equity if it is the terminal value of equity, and cost of capital if it is the terminal value of the asset) and CF_t is the cash flow (cash flow to equity if terminal value is for equity and to firm if terminal value is total terminal value).

Thus if the property described earlier had produced a net cash flow, prior to debt payments, of $1.2 million in year 10, this cash flow was expected to grow 3 percent a year forever after that and the cost of capital was 13 percent, the terminal value of the property can be written as:

$$\text{Terminal value of asset} = FCFF_{11}/(WACC - g)$$
$$= 1.2(1.03)/(.13 - .03) = \$12.36 \text{ million}$$

The assumption of perpetual cash flows may make some analysts uncomfortable, but one way to compensate is to require that more cash be set aside each year to ensure that the property life can be extended. If you use this approach, for instance, you could assume that the cash flow from depreciation be reinvested back into the building in the form of maintenance capital expenditures.

3. A close variation on the infinite growth model is the capitalization rate (cap rate) used by many real estate appraisers to value properties. In its most general form, the cap rate is the rate by which operating income is divided to get the value of the property.

$$\text{Property value} = \text{Operating income after taxes/Capitalization rate}$$

The capitalization rate is, in fact, the inverse of the value-to-EBIT multiple used to value publicly traded companies in Chapter 18.

There are three ways in which capitalization rates are estimated. One is to use the average capitalization rate of similar properties that have sold recently. This is the equivalent of using the industry-average earnings multiple to estimate terminal value in a publicly traded company. The second is to use the surveys mentioned earlier to obtain an estimate of the cap rates used by other real estate investors. The third is to estimate the cap rate from a discounted cash flow model. To see the linkage with the infinite growth model, assume that the net operating income (prior to debt payments) is also the free cash flow to the firm (note that this essentially is the equivalent of assuming that capital maintenance expenditures equal depreciation). Then the capitalization rate can be written as a function of the discount rate and the expected growth rate:

$$\text{Capitalization rate} = (r - g)/(1 + g)$$

where r is the discount rate (the cost of equity if net income is being capitalized and the cost of capital if operating income is being capitalized) and g is the expected growth rate forever. In this example, the capitalization rate would have been:

$$\text{Capitalization rate} = (.13 - .03)/1.03 = 9.70\%$$

If the capitalization rate is being applied to next year's operating income, rather than this year's value, you can ignore the denominator and use a cap rate of 10 percent.

A SPECULATIVE INVESTMENT IN UNDEVELOPED LAND

Developers sometimes buy undeveloped land not with the intention of developing it, but to hold onto in the hope that the value of the land will appreciate significantly over the holding period. An investment in undeveloped land does not generate positive cash flows during the holding period. The only positive cash flow, in fact, is the estimated value of the land at the end of the holding period. If you have to pay property taxes and other expenses during the holding period, you will have negative cash flows during the holding period.

There are two ways you can approach the analysis of this investment. The first is the traditional discounted cash flow approach. You could discount the expected property taxes and other expenses during the holding period and the estimated value of the land at the end of the period back to the present at the cost of capital and see if it exceeds the cost of the land today. In fact, the expected appreciation in the price of the land will have to be greater than the cost of capital and the expected annual property tax rate for this investment to have a positive net present value. To illustrate, if your cost of capital is 10 percent and the annual property tax rate is 2 percent of land value, you would need a price appreciation rate of 12 percent a year for the present value of the inflow to exceed the present value of the outflows.[2]

The other is to view the land as an option, and developing the land as exercising the option. You would then consider the cost of the land as the price of the option. The interesting implication is that you might choose to buy the land even if the expected price appreciation rate is lower than your cost of capital, if there is substantial volatility in land prices. This application will be considered in more detail in Chapter 28.

DCF Valuation Models

Once a discount rate has been chosen and cash flows estimated, the value of an income-producing real asset can be estimated either in whole (by discounting cash flows to the firm at the weighted average cost of capital) or to its equity investors (by discounting cash flows to equity at the cost of equity). The following illustrations provide examples of DCF valuation in real estate.

---

[2]We are assuming that the property taxes are based on the estimated value of the land each year and not the original cost. If it is the latter, the price appreciation rate can be lower.

ILLUSTRATION 26.1: Valuing an Office Building

In this illustration, we will be valuing an office building located at 711 Third Avenue in New York City. The operating details of the building are as follows:

- The building has a capacity of 528,357 square feet of rentable space. While 95% of this space is rented out for the next year, the occupancy rate is expected to climb 0.5% a year for the following four years to reach 97% of capacity in year 5. This is expected to be the occupancy rate in steady state.
- The average rent per square foot[3] was $28.07 in the most recent year and is expected to grow 3% a year in perpetuity. Historically, there has been a credit loss, associated with tenants failing to make payments, of 2.5% of rental revenues.
- The building has a garage that generated $800,000 in income for the most recent year. This income is also expected to grow 3% a year in perpetuity.
- Real estate taxes were $5.24 a square foot in the most recent year, and are expected to grow 4% a year for the next five years and 3% a year thereafter.
- The land under the building is rented under a long-term lease, and the ground rent in the most recent year was $1.5 million. This rent is expected to remain unchanged for the next five years and grow 3% a year thereafter.
- Other expenses, including insurance, maintenance, and utilities, amounted to $6.50 a square foot in the most recent year and are expected grow 3% a year in perpetuity. Approximately 10% of these expenses will be reimbursed by tenants each year (and thus will become a part of the revenues).
- The management fee for the most recent year was $300,000 and is expected to grow 3% a year in perpetuity.
- The depreciation in the building is expected to be $2 million a year for the next five years. The capital maintenance and upgrade expenditures (including leasehold improvements for new tenants) last year amounted to $1.5 million, and are expected to grow 3% a year for the next five years. Beyond year 5, depreciation is expected to increase 3% a year in perpetuity, and capital maintenance expenditures will offset depreciation.

The potential buyer of the building is a corporation that faces a marginal tax rate of 38% and expects to finance the building with a mix of 60% debt and 40% equity. Then debt will take the form of a long-term balloon payment loan with an interest rate of 6.5 percent.

STEP 1: ESTIMATING A COST OF CAPITAL

We begin by trying to estimate a cost of equity. While we had access to a survey that provided typical hurdle rates used by real estate investors for office buildings in New York, we chose to estimate the cost of equity from the capital asset pricing model because the potential buyer is a corporation (whose investors are diversified).[4] To make this estimate, we began with the unlevered beta of 0.62 of equity real estate investment trusts with office properties. We estimated a levered beta using the debt-equity mix proposed for the building:

$$\text{Levered beta} = \text{Unlevered beta}[1 + (1 - \text{Tax rate})(\text{Debt/Equity})]$$
$$= 0.62[1 + (1 - .38)(.6/.4)] = 1.20$$

---

[3]The rents vary depending on location in the building, with lower rents in the basement and lower floors and higher rents on the top floors.
[4]Note that it is the investors in the corporation that need to be diversified and not the corporation itself.

To estimate the cost of equity, we used a risk-free rate of 5.4% and a risk premium of 4%:

$$\text{Cost of equity} = \text{Risk-free rate} + \text{Beta} \times \text{Risk premium}$$
$$= 5.4\% + 1.20(4\%) = 10.20\%$$

Using the interest rate on the bank borrowing as the pretax cost of debt, we estimated a cost of capital:

$$\text{Cost of capital} = 10.20\%(.40) + 6.5\%(1 - .38)(.60) = 6.49\%$$

We assumed that this would be the cost of capital in perpetuity.[5]

Step 2: Estimating Cash Flows on the Building

We used the operating information specified above to estimate the cash flows prior to debt payments on the building for the next five years in the following table.

	Base Year/ Assumption	1	2	3	4	5	Terminal Year
Building space (square feet)		528,357	528,357	528,357	528,357	528,357	
Occupancy		95%	95.50%	96.00%	96.50%	97%	
Rent/square foot	$28.07	$28.91	$29.78	$30.67	$31.59	$32.54	
Rental income		$14,512,115	$15,026,149	$15,557,965	$16,108,166	$16,677,377	$17,177,698
Garage income	$800,000	$ 824,000	$ 848,720	$ 874,182	$ 900,407	$ 927,419	$ 955,242
Reimbursement revenue	10.00%	$ 353,735	$ 364,347	$ 375,277	$ 386,536	$ 398,132	$ 410,076
Credit loss	2.50%	$ 362,803	$ 375,654	$ 388,949	$ 402,704	$ 416,934	$ 429,442
Total revenues		$15,327,047	$15,863,563	$16,418,475	$16,992,404	$17,585,993	$18,113,573
Expenses							
Real estate taxes	$5.24	$ 2,879,334	$ 2,994,508	$ 3,114,288	$ 3,238,860	$ 3,368,414	$ 3,469,466
Ground rent	$1,500,000	$ 1,500,000	$ 1,500,000	$ 1,500,000	$ 1,500,000	$ 1,500,000	$ 1,545,000
Other expenses	$6.50	$ 3,537,350	$ 3,643,471	$ 3,752,775	$ 3,865,358	$ 3,981,319	$ 4,100,758
Management fee	$300,000	$ 309,000	$ 318,270	$ 327,818	$ 337,653	$ 347,782	$ 358,216
Total expenses		$ 8,225,684	$ 8,456,248	$ 8,694,881	$ 8,941,870	$ 9,197,515	$ 9,473,440
Operating income before depreciation		$ 7,101,363	$ 7,407,314	$ 7,723,594	$ 8,050,534	$ 8,388,478	$ 8,640,133
Depreciation	$2,000,000	$ 2,000,000	$ 2,000,000	$ 2,000,000	$ 2,000,000	$ 2,000,000	$ 2,060,000
Operating income		$ 5,101,363	$ 5,407,314	$ 5,723,594	$ 6,050,534	$ 6,388,478	$ 6,580,133
Taxes	38%	$ 1,938,518	$ 2,054,779	$ 2,174,966	$ 2,299,203	$ 2,427,622	$ 2,500,450
Operating income after taxes		$ 3,162,845	$ 3,352,535	$ 3,548,628	$ 3,751,331	$ 3,960,857	$ 4,079,682
+ Depreciation		$ 2,000,000	$ 2,000,000	$ 2,000,000	$ 2,000,000	$ 2,000,000	$ 2,060,000
− Capital maintenance and leasehold improvement	$1,500,000	$ 1,545,000	$ 1,591,350	$ 1,639,091	$ 1,688,263	$ 1,738,911	$ 2,060,000
Cash flow to firm		$ 3,617,845	$ 3,761,185	$ 3,909,538	$ 4,063,068	$ 4,221,946	$ 4,079,682

[5]This implies that the existing loan will be refinanced with a new loan when it comes due.

Since all of the items grow at 3% beyond year 5, we estimated a cash flow for year 6 as the terminal year. The terminal value of the building was calculated based on this cash flow, a perpetual growth rate of 3%, and a cost of capital of 6.49%:

$$\text{Terminal value} = FCFF_6/(\text{Cost of capital} - \text{Expected growth rate})$$
$$= \$4,079,682/(.0649 - .03) = \$116,810,659$$

The present value of the expected cash flows for the next five years and the terminal value, summarized in the following table yields the value of the building:

	1	2	3	4	5
Cash flow to firm	$3,617,845	$3,761,185	$3,909,538	$4,063,068	$ 4,221,946
Terminal value					$116,810,659
Present value @ 6.49%	$3,397,275	$3,316,547	$3,237,186	$3,159,199	$ 90,928,871

The sum of the present value of the cash flows is $101.48 million. This is the estimated value of the building.

ILLUSTRATION 26.2:   Valuing the Equity Stake in a Building

The preceding analysis can be done for just the equity stake in 711 Third Avenue. To do so, we will first estimate the dollar debt that will be borrowed to buy this building. Assuming that the building has a value of $101.48 million (from the previous illustration) and using a debt ratio of 60%, we estimate debt to be $60.89 million.

$$\text{Debt} = \text{Value of building} \times \text{Debt ratio} = 101.48 \times .6 = \$60.89 \text{ million}$$

Since this is a balloon payment loan, the interest payments on the debt will remain the same each year, based on the 6.5% interest rate:

$$\text{Annual interest expenses} = \text{Dollar debt} \times \text{Interest rate} = \$60.89 \times .065 = \$3.96 \text{ million}$$

The appropriate discount rate to use while valuing the equity stake in the building is the cost of equity, estimated to be 10.20% in this analysis.

ESTIMATING CASH FLOWS TO EQUITY

The estimated cash flows to equity are estimated each year by netting out interest expenses from income and adjusting the taxes accordingly. The following table summarizes cash flows to equity each year for the next five years.

	1	2	3	4	5
Building space (square feet)	528,357	528,357	528,357	528,357	528,357
Occupancy	95.00%	95.50%	96.00%	96.50%	97.00%
Rent/square foot	$28.91	$29.78	$30.67	$31.59	$32.54
Rental income	$14,512,115	$15,026,149	$15,557,965	$16,108,166	$16,677,377
Garage income	$ 824,000	$ 848,720	$ 874,182	$ 900,407	$ 927,419
Reimbursement revenue	$ 353,735	$ 364,347	$ 375,277	$ 386,536	$ 398,132
Credit loss	$ 362,803	$ 375,654	$ 388,949	$ 402,704	$ 416,934
Total revenues	$15,327,047	$15,863,563	$16,418,475	$16,992,404	$17,585,993
Expenses					
Real estate taxes	$ 2,879,334	$ 2,994,508	$ 3,114,288	$ 3,238,860	$ 3,368,414
Ground rent	$ 1,500,000	$ 1,500,000	$ 1,500,000	$ 1,500,000	$ 1,500,000
Other expenses	$ 3,537,350	$ 3,643,471	$ 3,752,775	$ 3,865,358	$ 3,981,319
Management fee	$ 309,000	$ 318,270	$ 327,818	$ 337,653	$ 347,782
Interest expenses	$ 3,957,737	$ 3,957,737	$ 3,957,737	$ 3,957,737	$ 3,957,737
Total expenses	$12,183,422	$12,413,986	$12,652,618	$12,899,608	$13,155,252
Net income before depreciation and taxes	$ 3,143,625	$ 3,449,577	$ 3,765,856	$ 4,092,797	$ 4,430,741
Depreciation	$ 2,000,000	$ 2,000,000	$ 2,000,000	$ 2,000,000	$ 2,000,000
Operating income	$ 1,143,625	$ 1,449,577	$ 1,765,856	$ 2,092,797	$ 2,430,741
Taxes	$ 434,578	$ 550,839	$ 671,025	$ 795,263	$ 923,682
Net income	$ 709,048	$ 898,738	$ 1,094,831	$ 1,297,534	$ 1,507,059
+ Depreciation	$ 2,000,000	$ 2,000,000	$ 2,000,000	$ 2,000,000	$ 2,000,000
− Capital maintenance and leasehold improvement	$ 1,545,000	$ 1,591,350	$ 1,639,091	$ 1,688,263	$ 1,738,911
Cash flow to equity	$ 1,164,048	$ 1,307,388	$ 1,455,741	$ 1,609,271	$ 1,768,148

In year 5, we also estimate the terminal value of equity by subtracting the debt due from the terminal value of the building estimated in the previous illustration:

$$\text{Terminal value of equity} = \text{Terminal value of building} - \text{Debt}$$
$$= \$116.81 \text{ million} - \$60.89 \text{ million} = \$55.92 \text{ million}$$

ESTIMATING THE VALUE OF EQUITY

The present value of the cash flows to equity for the next five years and the terminal value are computed in the following table:

	1	2	3	4	5
Cash flow to equity	$1,164,048	$1,307,388	$1,455,741	$1,609,271	$ 1,768,148
Terminal value					$55,922,390
Present value @ 10.20%	$1,056,435	$1,076,833	$1,088,178	$1,091,735	$35,519,318

The value of the equity stake in the building is $39.83 million. Adding this value to the value of the debt raised of $60.89 million gives us an estimate for the value of the building:

$$\text{Estimated value of building} = \$60.89 \text{ million} + \$39.83 \text{ million} = \$100.72 \text{ million}$$

Why is there a difference between this estimate of the property value and the one we arrived at in the previous illustration? The reason is simple. The debt ratio of 60% that we assumed and kept constant when estimating cost of capital will require us to borrow an additional amount each year for the next five years, since the building's value will appreciate by about 3 percent a year. The tax benefits from this additional debt were implicitly built into the valuation of the building in the previous illustration but were ignored while valuing equity in this one. If we consider those tax benefits, we will arrive at the same value.

REAL ESTATE VALUATION IN PRACTICE: A COMPARISON

The building on 711 Seventh Avenue was valued for sale by an appraiser using discounted cash flow valuation. While many of the base assumptions in our valuation were borrowed from that appraisal, the estimate of value in the appraisal was $70 million, about a third below our estimate. The main differences between our valuation and the appraiser's valuation are as follows:

- The appraisal was done entirely in terms of pretax cash flows. Depreciation was therefore not considered and the tax benefits from it were ignored.
- The discount rate used was 11.5 percent, based on a proprietary survey of real estate investors done by the appraiser. While nothing was mentioned in the appraisal, this discount rate presumably was in pretax terms (to ensure consistency with how the cash flows were estimated) and stated as a return on the overall investment (and not just the equity investment). This is higher than the cost of capital we used.
- The terminal value was estimated based on a capitalization rate of 9.0 percent, which was also based on the survey. (The operating income in year 5 was divided by 9.0 percent to arrive at terminal value.)

We believe that using pretax cash flows and pretax discount rates will miss the segment of value that comes from depreciation and interest expenses being tax deductible, and understate the value of the building. Assuming that the discount rate is defined correctly as a pretax cost of capital, the use of surveys to estimate both this number and the terminal multiple makes us uncomfortable, especially given the fact that the buyer of this building is a corporation with diversified investors.

Limitations of Discounted Cash Flow Valuation

There are many reasons given for why discounted cash flow valuation is not appropriate for real estate. First, it is argued the discount rates are difficult, if not impossible, to estimate for most real estate investments. The discussion of this topic has pointed out that this is not necessarily true. Second, it is argued that estimating cash flows for the time horizon is tedious and difficult to do, as is the estimation of the terminal value. However, it would seem that it is much easier to estimate cash flows for real estate than for some financial investments (for instance, a high-growth stock). Third, it is argued that discounted cash flow valuation does not reflect market conditions—that the market is strong or weak at the time of the valuation. This argument could be rejected at two levels. On one level, the cash flows should reflect the market conditions, since they will be higher (higher rents and lower vacancy rates) and grow faster in strong market conditions. On the other level, any additional value being assigned by the market beyond the cash flow levels can be considered to be overvaluation and should not be built into the appraised value in the first place.

COMPARABLE/RELATIVE VALUATION

Just as price-earnings and price-book value ratios are used to value financial assets, real estate investments can be valued using standardized value measures and comparable assets. There are several reasons for doing so:

- It provides a mechanism for valuing non-cash-flow producing assets. For instance, the value of a single family residential building bought as a primary residence can be estimated by looking at similar properties in the same area.
- It takes into account market trends that might not be reflected in the cash flows yet for a number of reasons. Leases might have frozen lease payments in place, while market values have risen, and rent control laws might prevent rents from rising with market values.
- It is also argued that valuing based on comparables is much simpler to do than discounted cash flow valuation since it does not require, at least explicitly, the estimation of discount rates and cash flows.

What Is a Comparable Asset?

The key limitation of all comparable-based approaches is in the definition of comparable. In the case of stocks, differences in growth, risk, and payout ratios between stocks have to be adjusted for before price-earnings ratios are compared. Many analysts choose to restrict their comparisons of stocks to those within the same industry group, to keep it relatively homogeneous. In the case of real estate, differences in income production, size, scale, location, age, and quality of construction have to be accounted for before comparisons are made. Some of these adjustments are simple (such as differences in size) and others are subjective (such as differences in location).

Use of Standardized Value Estimates

When valuing assets based on comparable assets, the value has to be standardized for the comparison. In stocks, this standardization is often done by dividing the price per share by the earnings per share (PE) or the book value per share (PBV). In the case of real estate, this adjustment is made by:

- *Size.* The simplest standardized measure is the price per square foot, which standardizes value using the size of the building. In office rentals, where square footage is a key factor determining rental revenues, this may by a useful adjustment. It does not, however, factor in differences on any of the other dimensions.
- *Income.* The value of an asset can be standardized using its income. For instance, the gross income multiplier (price of property/gross annual income) is an income-standardized value measure. The advantage of this approach is that the income incorporates differences in scale, construction quality, and location.[6] The gross income should be prior to debt payments, since differences in leverage can cause large differences in the income available to equity investors.

---

[6]Buildings of better quality in better locations should command higher rents/leases and higher expected income than other buildings.

Why Comparables May Work Better for Real Estate Than Stocks

One of the difficulties in using comparables to value stocks is that risk and growth characteristics can vary widely across stocks even in the same industry class. In the case of real estate properties in the same locale, the argument can be made that the growth and risk characteristics are very similar across these properties and that the only differences are therefore differences in the capacity to generate income.

ILLUSTRATION 26.3: Valuing a Property Based on Comparables

Consider the property at 711 Third Avenue that was valued using discounted cash flow valuation. The appraisal also noted eight other properties in that part of Manhattan with roughly the same characteristics as the building being appraised that had sold recently. The following table summarizes the details of these properties and the prices that they were sold for:

Property	Size (Square Feet)	Occupancy Rate	Price for Sale	Price per Square Foot	Net Operating Income per Square Foot	Price/ NOI
900 Third Avenue	560,000	99%	$182,000,000	$325.00	26.98	12.05
767 Third Avenue	456,007	95%	$ 95,000,000	$208.33	NA	
350 Madison Avenue	310,000	97%	$ 70,060,000	$226.00	17.6	12.84
888 Seventh Avenue	838,680	96%	$154,500,000	$184.22	NA	
622 Third Avenue	874,434	97%	$172,000,000	$196.70	NA	
150 East 58th Street	507,178	95%	$118,000,000	$232.66	16.52	14.08
1065 Avenue of the Americas	580,000	95%	$ 59,000,000	$101.72	NA	
810 Seventh Avenue	646,000	95%	$141,000,000	$218.27	15.17	14.39
Average		96.13%		$211.61		13.34

The property at 711 Third Avenue has 528,357 square feet of rental space, had an occupancy rate of 95%, and generated net operating income of $6.107 million in the most recent year. Based on the average price per square foot, the value of the property is:

$$\text{Value of 711 Third Avenue} = \text{Square footage} \times \text{Price per square foot}$$
$$= 528,357 \text{ sq. ft.} \times \$211.61 \text{ per square foot} = \$111.807 \text{ million}$$

If we adjust for the fact that the occupancy rate is slightly lower at 711 Third Avenue, we would estimate the following value:

$$\text{Value of 711 Third Avenue} = \text{Square footage} \times (\text{Occupancy rate}_{711 \text{ Third}}/\text{Average occupancy rate})$$
$$\times \text{Price per square foot}$$
$$= 528,357 \text{ sq. ft.} \times (95\%/96.13\%) \times \$211.61 \text{ per square foot}$$
$$= \$110.498 \text{ million}$$

Finally, if we apply to this property the multiple of operating income based on the four properties for which it is available:

$$\text{Value of 711 Third Avenue} = \text{Net operating income} \times \text{Average price/NOI}$$
$$= 6.107 \times 13.34 = \$81.470 \text{ million}$$

Which of these values gets used will depend on whether you view the lower operating income per square foot at 711 Third Avenue as the consequence of poor management or the building's characteristics—location and condition. If it is the former, you might be willing to pay the higher values ($111 million). If it is the latter, you would pay only $81.4 million.

Regression Approach

One of the approaches used to extend the reach of relative valuation for stocks is the regression approach, where price-earnings or price–book value multiples are regressed against independent variables that cause differences in these multiples—risk, growth, and payout. Since the variables causing differences in real estate values in a locale are fairly obvious—vacancy rates, size, and capacity to generate income, among others—it should be relatively simple to extend this approach to analyze properties.

ILLUSTRATION 26.4: Regression Approach

You could regress the price per square foot for the eight properties in Illustration 26.3 against occupancy rates and obtain the following:

$$\text{Price per square foot} = -2{,}535.50 + 2{,}857.86 \ \text{Occupancy rate} \qquad R^2 = 46\%$$
$$[2.07] \qquad [2.25]$$

Using this regression, we would obtain an estimated price per square foot for 711 Seventh Avenue, with its 95% occupancy rate:

$$\text{Price per square foot} = -2{,}535.70 + 2{,}857.86(.95) = \$179.46$$

$$\text{Value of 711 Third Avenue} = 528{,}357 \times \$179.46 = \$94.820 \text{ million}$$

This regression is clearly limited in its power because there only eight observations and the occupancy rates are very similar. If we can obtain information on more properties and include variables on which there are bigger differences—a variable measuring the age of the building, for instance—we would be able to get much stronger predictions.

VALUING REAL ESTATE BUSINESSES

Much of this chapter has focused on valuing real estate properties. This section considers extending this analysis to value a real estate business. To value such a business, you have to consider its sources of income and then look at its organization structure.

Sources of Income

Real estate businesses vary widely in terms of how they generate income, and how you approach valuation will vary as well. In particular, we could categorize real estate firms into four businesses.

1. *Service income.* Some firms generate income from providing just management services or support services to the owners of real estate—for instance, selling, security, or maintenance. Valuing these firms is relatively straightforward and requires assumptions about how fees will be assessed (many management ser-

vice contracts, for instance, are stated as a percent of the gross income on a property) and how much the fee income will increase over time. More efficient firms or firms with better reputations (brand names) may be able to charge higher fees and be worth more.

2. *Real estate construction.* These businesses make their income from real estate construction—building residential or commercial properties. They usually agree to deliver the units at a contractually fixed price and generate profits from being able to construct them at a lower cost. Firms that are more cost-efficient will generally earn higher profits and be worth more. Here again, though, reputation can make a difference, and firms that are associated with quality construction may be able to charge premium prices.

3. *Real estate development.* These businesses usually buy vacant or underutilized land, put up new construction, and sell the units to real estate investors. They generally do not hold on to the properties for purposes of generating ongoing income. The values of these businesses will be determined by their capacity to gauge market demand and complete construction both quickly and at low cost.

4. *Real estate investment.* These are businesses that buy real estate property as income-generating investments. The simplest way of valuing these businesses is to value each of the properties that they own and to aggregate them. However, a premium may be attached to this value if a business has shown the capacity to repeatedly buy undervalued properties.

Thus the factors we should think about when valuing real estate businesses are the same factors we think about in any valuation—the capacity to generate not just cash flows but also excess returns, and the uncertainty associated with these cash flows.

Organizational Structure

There are four basic organizational forms available to real estate business—the real estate investment trust (REIT), master limited partnership (MLP), business trust, and real estate corporation. They differ in two major areas:

Structure of Taxation Single taxation is a characteristic of REITs and MLPs, since both are taxed at the investor level, but not at the firm level. This tax benefit is given to REITs to compensate for certain investment and dividend policy restrictions to which REITs must adhere. MLPs receive single-taxation status only if they invest in certain activities, such as real estate or oil and gas. Otherwise, for tax purposes, MLPs are treated as corporations. This tax advantage does not exist for business trusts and corporations that are taxed at both the entity level on income and at the investor level on dividends.

What are the implications for valuation? When valuing real estate investment trusts and master limited partnerships, the tax rate used to estimate cash flows and discount rates is zero. That does not mean that there are no tax benefits from depreciation or interest expenses, since these benefits still flow through to the ultimate investors. When valuing real estate corporations, the marginal corporate tax rate should be used for estimating cash flows and discount rates.

Restrictions on Investment and Dividend Policy The tax code requires REITs to distribute 95 percent of their taxable income to shareholders, which effectively limits

REITs' use of internal financing. Consequently, REITs must return to the capital markets on a regular basis, which in turn tends to impart discipline and monitoring. The code further requires that a minimum of 75 percent of a REIT's gross income must come from real estate. A REIT must also be a passive investment conduit; that is, less than 30 percent of a REIT's income must come from the operation of real estate held less than four years and income from the sale of securities held less than one year. REITs cannot engage in active real estate operations. They cannot operate a business, develop or trade properties for sale, or sell more than five properties per year. A REIT is prohibited from entering into tax-free exchanges to acquire properties. Although no dividend payout restrictions exist for MLPs, a high payout ratio is likely, since partners are taxed regardless of whether they actually receive the income or the MLP retains it. This fact has to be weighed against the investment opportunities of an MLP. The empirical evidence suggests that MLPs pay out a high proportion of their earnings as dividends. Although MLPs are restricted to engaging in real estate activities (or oil and gas), there are no restrictions on the nature or management of these activities. Consequently, MLPs can actively and directly engage in the real estate trade or business. There are no MLP restrictions on the number of properties that can be sold in any given year. Business trusts and corporations have no restrictions on dividend payout and can engage in any real estate or non–real estate activity except those prohibited in the declaration of trust or corporate charter, respectively.

The implications for valuation are significant. When valuing REITs' and MLPs, you have to assume much of the earnings will be paid out in dividends. If you do not assume external financing, your estimates of expected growth will be low, no matter how well managed the entities are. If you do allow for external financing, you can have high expected growth but the number of shares in the firm will have to increase proportionately, thus limiting the potential price appreciation on a per-share basis. The restrictions on investment policy will constrain how much returns on capital can be changed over time.

CONCLUSION

There is much that is said in this chapter that repeats what was said in earlier chapters on stock valuation. This is because a real estate investment can (and should) be valued with the same approaches used to value financial assets. While the structure and caveats of discounted cash flow models remain unchanged for real estate investments, there are some practical problems that have to be faced and overcome. In particular, real estate investments do not trade regularly and risk parameters (and discount rates) are difficult to estimate. A real estate investment can also be valued using comparable investments, but the difficulties in identifying comparable assets and controlling for differences across them remain significant problems.

QUESTIONS AND SHORT PROBLEMS

1. An analyst who looks at real estate decides to apply the capital asset pricing model to estimate the risk (beta) for real estate. He regresses returns on a real estate index (based on appraised values) against returns on a stock index, and estimates a beta of 0.20 for real estate. Would you agree with this estimate? If you do not, what might be the sources of your disagreement?

2. An alternative way of estimating risk for real estate is to use prices on traded REITs to compute returns, and to regress these returns against a stock index to arrive at a beta estimate. Would this beta be a more reliable estimate of risk? Why or why not?

3. The risk for real estate can be viewed as a derived demand. If this is the case, the risk of real estate can be estimated from the underlying business it supports. Under this view, what would be the appropriate proxy to use for risk in the following types of real estate investments:
   a. Commercial real estate in New York City.
   b. Commercial real estate in Houston, Texas.
   c. Commercial real estate in San Jose, California (Silicon Valley).
   d. Hotel complex in Orlando, Florida.

4. Would your valuation of real estate by affected by who the potential investors in the property are? (For instance, would your analysis be any different if the primary investors were individuals involved primarily in real estate or if they were institutional investors?)

5. How would you factor in the absence of liquidity into your valuation?

6. You have been asked to value an office building in Orlando, Florida, with the following characteristics:
   - The building was built in 1988, and has 300,000 square feet of rentable area.
   - There would be an initial construction and renovation cost of $3.0 million.
   - It will take two years to fill the building. The expected vacancy rates in the first two years are:

Year	Vacancy Rate
1	30%
2	20%
After year 2	10%

   - The market rents in the building were expected to average $15.00 per square foot in the current year based on average rents in the surrounding buildings.
   - The market rents were assumed to grow 5% a year for five years and at 3% a year after that forever.
   - The variable operating expenses were assumed to be $3.00 per square foot, and are expected to grow at the same rate as rents. The fixed operating expense in 1994 amounted to $300,000 and was expected to grow at 3% forever.
   - The real estate taxes are expected to amount to $300,000 in the first year, and grow 3% a year after that. It is assumed that all tenants will pay their pro rate share of increases in real estate taxes that exceed 3% a year.
   - The tax rate on income was assumed to be 42%.
   - The cost of borrowing was assumed to be 8.25%, pretax. It was also assumed that the building would be financed with 30% equity and 70% debt.
   - A survey suggests that equity investors in real estate require a return of 12.5% of their investments.
   a. Estimate the value of the building, based on expected cash flows.
   b. Estimate the value of just the equity stake in this building.

7. You are trying to value the same building based on comparable properties sold in recent years. There have been six property sales of buildings of comparable size in the surrounding area.

Property	Sale Price	Size (Sq. Ft.)	Gross Rent
A	$20,000,000	400,000	$5,000,000
B	$18,000,000	425,000	$4,750,000
C	$22,000,000	450,000	$5,100,000
D	$25,000,000	400,000	$5,500,000
E	$15,000,000	350,000	$4,000,000
F	$12,000,000	300,000	$3,000,000

   a. Estimate the value of the building based on price per square foot.
   b. Estimate the value of the building based on price/gross rent.
   c. What are some of the assumptions you make when you value a building based on comparable buildings?

CHAPTER 27

Valuing Other Assets

One of the fundamental precepts of this book is that all assets, financial as well as real, can be valued systematically using traditional valuation models. The bulk of this book examines the valuation of stocks, but the preceding chapter extended the reach of valuation models to cover real estate. This chapter considers other assets that are usually considered unique and different and attempts to value them using the principles developed in the earlier chapters. Consequently, it examines how to value a wide range of assets, from franchises to a five-star restaurant.

While the assets covered in this chapter have very different characteristics and attract different investors, they can be broadly classified into three categories:

1. Assets that are expected to generate cash flows over time and can be valued with discounted cash flow models.
2. Assets that do not generate cash flows but attain value because they are scarce and are perceived to be valuable (collectibles, coins) and/or generate utility to their owners (antiques, paintings). These assets can be valued using relative valuation.
3. Assets that do not generate cash flows but could be valuable in the event of a contingency—they have option characteristics. These assets can be valued using contingent claim valuation models.

Within each category, there are a surprising number of commonalties both across different assets and with the financial assets described in the earlier chapter.

CASH-FLOW-PRODUCING ASSETS

A number of assets derive their value from their capacity to generate cash flows to their owners. The value of such assets is a function of the expected cash flows in the future and the uncertainty associated with these cash flows. The basic principles of discounted cash flow valuation, described in earlier chapters, apply for any of these assets and require the following steps:

■ Estimate cash flows on the asset for the estimation period. These cash flows can either be predebt (cash flows to the firm) or after-debt cash flows (cash flows to equity).
■ Estimate the value of the asset, if any, at the end of the estimation period. This value will decline over time if the asset loses value with use or has a limited life and may, in some cases, be zero.

- Estimate a discount rate that reflects the riskiness of the cash flows. This discount rate will be the cost of equity if the cash flows discounted are cash flows to equity and the cost of capital if the cash flows are cash flows to the firm.
- Calculate the present value of the cash flows to arrive at the value of the asset or the value of the equity in the assets.

There are several practical problems associated with applying these steps to assets when cash flows are difficult to estimate and risk cannot be easily quantified (and converted into a discount rate). In most cases, these problems are not insurmountable and can be overcome. Since the problems and the solutions vary from case to case, we consider a series of examples, ranging from the valuation of a simple franchise to more complex businesses.

Valuing a Franchise

A franchise gives you the right to market or sell a product or service of a brand-name company. Examples of franchises would include the thousands of McDonald's restaurants around the world, dealerships for the automobile companies, and, loosely defined, even a New York City cab medallion. In each case, the franchisee (the person who buys the franchise) pays the franchisor (McDonald's or Ford) either an up-front price or an annual fee for running the franchise. In return, he or she gets the power of the brand name, corporate support, and advertising backing.

Franchise Value and Excess Returns   The acquisition of a franchise provides the franchisee with the opportunity to earn excess returns for the life of the franchise. While the sources of these above-market returns vary from case to case, they can arise from a number of factors:

- *Brand name value.* The franchise might have a brand name value that enables the franchisee to charge higher prices and attract more customers than an otherwise similar business. Thus, an investor may be willing to pay a significant up-front fee to acquire a McDonald's franchise, in order to take advantage of the brand name value associated with the company.
- *Exclusivity.* In some cases, a franchise has value because it enables a franchisee to produce a product, the rights to which are owned by the franchisor. For instance, an investor may pay a fee to Disney for the right to manufacture Mickey Mouse watches or toys, and hope to recoup the fee by selling more of the product or charging a higher price for it.
- *Legal monopolies.* Sometimes, a franchise may have value because the franchisee is given the exclusive right to provide a service. For instance, a company may pay a large fee for the right to operate concession stands in a baseball stadium knowing that it will face no competition within the stadium. In a milder variant of this, multiple franchises are sometimes sold but the number of franchises is limited to ensure that the franchisees earn excess returns. New York City, for example, sells cab medallions that are a prerequisite for operating a yellow cab in the city, and also has tight restrictions on non–medallion owners offering the same service. Consequently, a market where cab medallions are bought and sold exists.

In essence, the value of a franchise is directly tied to the capacity to generate excess returns. Any action or event that affects these excess returns will affect the value of the franchise.

Special Issues in Valuing Franchises Buying a franchise is often a mixed blessing. While the franchisee gets the backing of a well-known firm with significant resources to back up his or her efforts, there are some costs that may affect the value of the franchise. Among these costs are the following:

■ The problems of the franchisor can spill over onto the franchisee. For instance, when Daewoo, the Korean automaker, borrowed too much and got into financial trouble, its dealers around the world felt the repercussions. Similarly, McDonald's franchisees around the world have been targeted by antiglobalization activists. Thus, an efficient and well-run franchise's value can be affected by actions that it has little or no control over.

■ Since franchisors tend to be large corporations and franchisees tend to be small businesspeople, the former often have much more bargaining power and sometimes take advantage of it to change the terms of franchise agreements in their favor. Franchisees can increase their power by banding together and bargaining as a collective unit.

■ The value of a franchise derives from the exclusive rights it grants the franchisee to sell the products of a firm. This value can be diluted if a franchise is granted to a competitor. For instance, the value of a Days Inn franchise may be diluted if another Days Inn is allowed to open five miles down the highway.

ILLUSTRATION 27.1: Valuing a New York City Cab Medallion—June 1994

BACKGROUND

■ In 1994, New York City had 11,787 cab medallions outstanding.[1] The owner of a cab medallion has the right to operate a yellow cab in the five boroughs of New York City—Manhattan, Brooklyn, the Bronx, Queens, and Staten Island.

■ New York City restricts non–medallion owners from picking up customers on the street, though they can still be summoned in other ways.

■ All yellow cabs in the city are regulated by the Taxi and Limousine Commission, which sets fares and reserves the right to fine owners who do not follow its numerous requirements.

CASH FLOWS ON A CAB MEDALLION

■ The typical New York City cab is a Chevrolet Caprice. The cost of acquiring one in 1994 was approximately $15,000, and it has an expected life of 10 years. The cab can be depreciated over the life down to a salvage value of zero.

■ A cab can be expected to be on the road 330 days of the year, with an expected down time (for maintenance) of 35 days, and make $250 a day prior to meeting operating and maintenance expenses and covering the cost of time for the driver.

---

[1]The number of cab medallions had been frozen at this level since 1937. A proposal in 1995 that sought to raise this number by 400, and faced stiff opposition from existing medallion owners, failed.

- The annual cost of fuel and operating expenses is expected to be 25% of revenues, and the maintenance expenses are expected to amount to $1,500 a year.
- The cost of automobile insurance, covering the cost of collision, theft, and bodily harm, is $2,000 per year.
- The annual fee to be paid to the Taxi and Limousine Commission is $500. Other licensing costs are expected to amount to $500 a year.
- The total cost per day, inclusive of benefits, of the driver of the cab is expected to amount to $100. (This also includes the 35 days where the car is down for maintenance.)

Estimating Risk and Discount Rates

The capacity of a cab to pull in the expected revenues is a function of several variables:

- *State of the city's economy.* The more buoyant the economy of the city, the greater are the potential revenues from owning and operating a cab in it. Since the condition of New York City's economy is, in large part, driven by the state of the financial services sector, there is in all likelihood a positive correlation between cab revenues and financial service sector health.
- *Scarcity of cabs.* The value of a cab medallion is derived directly from the fact that there are a limited number of medallions that are sold. To the extent that the city can either issue more medallions or allows gypsy cabs (unlicensed taxis) to operate within the environs of the city, it can affect the expected revenues.
- *Fare structure.* Since the fare structure is regulated, the expected revenues from owning a cab in the future will be dependent on the generosity of raises that the Taxi and Limousine Commission allows.
- *Other risks.* There are a number of other potential sources of risk including collision and theft that have already been built into the cost structure. To the extent that these are estimates, they could also create swings in the cash flows.

Assuming that the expected revenues already factors in the number of medallions outstanding and the expected changes in the fare structure, the primary source of risk in owning a cab medallion is expected to be from shifts in the city's economy. If the health of the city's economy is a function of the financial service sector, the risk of owning a cab medallion should be similar to the risk of investing in a financial service firm. The average beta of financial service firms headquartered in New York City is 1.25. At the end of 1994, with Treasury bond rates at 8% and using a market risk premium of 5.5%, the cost of equity would have been:

$$\text{Cost of equity} = 8\% + 1.25(5.5\%) = 14.88\%$$

This will be used as the cost of equity in valuing a cab medallion.

Financing Mix

Assume that the medallion will be financed half with equity and half with debt, and that the debt will carry an interest rate of 10% per annum. Allowing for a marginal tax rate (federal, state, and city) of 40%, the cost of capital for valuing the medallion is:

$$\text{Cost of capital} = 14.88\%(0.5) + 10\%(1 - 0.4)(0.5) = 10.44\%$$

Estimating Future Growth and Value

It is assumed that the expected operating income from owning a cab will keep up with expected inflation, which is assumed to be 3%, in the long term. The predebt cash flow from owning a cab medallion is provided in the following table:

Item	Calculation	Amount
Revenues	330 × 250	$82,500
Expenses		
Driver	365 × 100	$36,500
Fuel and operating	25% of revenues	$20,625
Maintenance	$1,500/year	$ 1,500
Depreciation	$1,500/year	$ 1,500
Fees & license costs	$1,000/year	$ 1,000
EBIT		$21,375
Taxes	40% of EBIT	$ 8,550
EBIT (1 – t)		$12,825
+ Depreciation		$ 1,500
– Capital expenditure	For replacement	$ 1,500
Free cash flow from operations		$12,825

The capital expenditure is assumed to be equal to depreciation. Essentially, we are assuming a sinking fund that is set aside to meet the eventual expense of replacing the car at the end of the tenth year.[2]

Based on the expected cash flows from operations of $12,825, the expected growth rate of 3% in the long term, and the cost of capital of 10.44%, the value of owning a medallion is:

Value of a New York City cab medallion = $12,825 × 1.03/(.1044 − .03) = $177,610

OTHER FACTORS

This valuation is based on the presumption that a cab driver is hired to drive the cab. If the driver owns and operates the cab, this is still the appropriate way to approach the valuation, since the time of the driver has to be priced in. Failing to do so will inflate the expected after-tax cash flows and the value of the medallion unjustly. The other issue that is not resolved in this valuation is whether there are any economies of scale involved in owning more than one medallion, in terms of reduced insurance costs or downtime. To the extent that there is, medallions will have higher value to prior owners of medallions rather than to new investors.

Valuing Businesses with a Personal Component

Many businesses derive a significant portion of their value from a key person, who is often the owner, and may be worth significantly less if run by someone else. In these cases, it is important that the consequences of losing this key person be built into the valuation. It is also important that the additional risk associated with the dependence on an individual be factored into the analysis.

There are a number of examples we can offer for businesses with personal components. Consider the following:

- Expensive restaurants are identified closely with the chefs that run their kitchens. Thus when a chef is incapacitated or moves to a competitor the number of customers may drop off dramatically.

---

[2]Setting aside $1,500 a year for 10 years will yield more than $15,000 at the end of the tenth year, but a car will also cost more in 10 years.

FRANCHISE VALUE: CAN THE FRANCHISEE MAKE A DIFFERENCE?

Do not gain the impression that the value of a franchise is entirely attributable to the franchisor and that the franchisee cannot affect the value. Clearly, franchisees can make a difference, which explains why the value of a McDonald's can increase when it passes from one franchisee to another. There are several factors that explain these differences:

- *Efficiency.* Some franchisees do a much better job in controlling costs and generating higher margins than others. To illustrate, a large proportion of low-cost hotels and inns in the United States is owned by a small immigrant group from India. Since the owner's entire family often works at the hotel at low or no pay, employee costs tend to be lower, allowing the owner to turn a larger profit than a passive owner would have.
- *Personal component.* There remains a personal component in many franchises that can make a significant difference to value. For instance, while there are thousands of Ford and GM dealers around the country, relatively few of them account for a significant portion of the total revenues.
- *Economies of scale.* There are economies of scale associated with owning several franchises from the same firm. For instance, you often see franchisees who own more than one franchise of the same company. By pooling several franchises, you might be able to reduce your administrative costs and increase the profitability of each.

■ Many service businesses, ranging from plumbing to dentistry to tax accounting, have a personal component. Hence, when the person providing the service moves on, a large portion of the value of the business could be lost. A dentist who pays a large amount for a thriving dental practice of another dentist may see a drop-off in business after the purchase. This effect will be accentuated if the seller can start a competing business.

■ A mutual fund company may derive its value from its most recognized fund managers. If they move to a competitor or start their own funds, they could take a large portion of the money they manage with them.

So, how should we value these businesses and the component of value that is attributable to the key person? The answer depends on why you are doing the valuation in the first place. If the objective is to value the business for the existing owner, you may separate out the portion of value due to the owner's personal connections and skill, but there are no immediate consequences. If the objective is to value the business for a potential buyer, the simplest way to avoid overpaying is to do two valuations—one with the business as is, with the existing owner, and one without the owner, making reasonable assumptions about the degree to which business will drop off. The latter will be much lower than the former and will represent the price you would be willing to pay.

There are intermediate steps that can be taken to minimize the slippage in value. First, you could contract with the owner to remain with the firm after you buy it, which should reduce the drop-off in customers. Second, you could apprentice or help the owner for a transition period before you buy the business. This will allow customers or patients to get used to you before the business passes hands, and may reduce the number who leave after the transaction. Third, you should ensure that the owner cannot start a competing business and extract business from you for the foreseeable future.

ILLUSTRATION 27.2: Valuing a Dental Practice

Assume that you are a young dentist specializing in pediatric dentistry, and that you are interested in buying a dental practice located in Chatham, New Jersey. The dentist who owns the practice has built it up over the past two decades, and the practice generated $500,000 in revenues last year. The expenditures associated with running this practice last year include the following:

- Employee expenses (including dental hygienists and secretarial help) amounted to $150,000 last year, and are expected to grow 3% a year for the next 10 years.
- The annual rent for the facilities last year was $50,000 and is expected to grow 3% a year for the next 10 years.
- Rentals of medical equipment cost $40,000 last year, and this expense is expected to grow 3% for the next 10 years.
- The cost of medical insurance last year was $60,000 and is expected to grow 3% a year for the next 10 years.
- The tax rate on the income, including state and local taxes, is 40%.
- The cost of capital is 10%.

To value the practice, assume that revenues would have grown 3% a year for the next 10 years if the current dentist continued to run the practice, but that there will be a drop-off of 20% in the first year's revenues if a new dentist comes into the practice. The growth rate of 3% will still occur in the following years but on the lower base revenues.

First, value the practice with the current dentist. To make this estimate, begin by estimating the cash flows in the first year to the practice:

$$\text{Cash flow in year 1} = (\text{Revenues}_1 - \text{Operating expenses}_1)(1 - \text{Tax rate})$$
$$= [500,000(1.03) - (150,000 + 50,000 + 40,000 + 60,000)(1.03)](1 - .40)$$
$$= \$123,600$$

Using the cost of capital as the discount rate and using the growing annuity equation for a 10-year period, you can estimate the value of the practice:

$$\text{Value of practice} = CF_1 \left[\frac{1 - \dfrac{(1+g)^n}{(1+r)^n}}{(r-g)} \right] = \$123,600 \left[\frac{1 - \dfrac{(1.03)^{10}}{(1.10)^{10}}}{(.10-.03)} \right] = \$850,831$$

Assume that the value of the practice fades after 10 years, and therefore attach no terminal value.

Follow up by valuing the practice with a new dentist in place. The cash flow in year 1 will be lower because the revenues will be lower:

$$\text{Cash flow in year 1} = (\text{Revenues}_1 - \text{Operating expenses}_1)(1 - \text{Tax rate})$$
$$= [400,000(1.03) - (150,000 + 50,000 + 40,000 + 60,000)(1.03)](1 - .40)$$
$$= \$61,800$$

$$\text{Value of practice} = \$61,800 \left[\frac{1 - \dfrac{(1.03)^{10}}{(1.10)^{10}}}{(.10-.03)} \right] = \$425,415$$

Notice that the value is halved, and the difference can be viewed as the value of the key person.

As a potential buyer, the new dentist should offer the latter value for the practice. However, if the buyer can arrange for a transition period where the current dentist stays with the practice after the transaction, he or she may be willing to pay a higher price.

ILLUSTRATION 27.3:   Valuing a Five-Star Restaurant: Lutèce in 1994

Lutèce is a renowned restaurant located at 249 East 50th Street in Manhattan. In 1994, Lutèce was sold by its owner/chef Andre Soltner to Ark Restaurants, a publicly traded restaurant chain, for an undisclosed amount. The *New York Times*, blanching as a result of the sale, ran the headline, "Lutèce, a Dining Landmark, Is Sold to a Chain Operator," which was then followed by an article detailing the surprise marriage of the classic French restaurant to Ark, a company largely known for operating theme restaurants. Bryan Miller, the *Times'* former restaurant reviewer and writer of the piece, likened the addition of Lutèce to Ark's portfolio to "hanging a Van Gogh in a community art exhibit."

BACKGROUND

Lutèce was founded in 1961 by Andre Soltner, and quickly acquired a reputation for serving food of exceptional quality. It had received a five-star rating from Mobil for 24 consecutive years and was one of five New York City restaurants that got a four-star rating (the highest) from the *New York Times*. In a sign of slippage, however, its ranking in the *Zagat Survey of New York City Restaurants* dropped to eighth from being perennially at or near the top for much of the 1970s and 1980s.

ESTIMATING CASH FLOWS

The following are some of the background facts on Lutèce:

- The restaurant can seat 92 diners. It has one seating for lunch and two seatings for dinner. It fills in 70% of its seats at lunchtime and 80% of its seats at dinner.
- The restaurant stays open 340 days every year, and is closed for the remaining 25 days.
- The average price of a lunch is $30, and the average price of a dinner is $66. Approximately one-third of this is for liquor.
- There are 42 employees on the staff of the restaurant. The cost of food is approximately 30% of the price of the meal, and the payroll amounts to $1.25 million a year.
- The annual rent for the space used by Lutèce is $600,000.

The following table is an estimation of the after-tax operating cash flows in 1994 for Lutèce:

	Assumption	*Base Year*
Revenues		
Lunch	70% occupancy; $30 per person	$ 656,880
Dinner	80% occupancy; $66 per person	$3,303,168
Total		$3,960,048
Expenses		
Food	30% of revenues	$1,188,014
Staff	$1,250,000 for staff expenses	$1,250,000
Rent		$ 600,000
Total		$3,038,014
EBIT		$ 922,034
Taxes	Assumed tax rate of 40%	$ 368,813
EBIT(1 − t)		$ 553,220

These cash flows are expected to grow 6% a year for three years and 3% a year after that. The following table summarizes the expected cash flows over the next three years.

	Base Year	1	2	3
Revenues	$3,960,048	$4,197,651	$4,449,510	$4,716,481
Expenses	$3,038,014	$3,220,295	$3,413,513	$3,618,324
EBIT	$ 922,034	$ 977,356	$1,035,997	$1,098,157
Taxes	$ 368,813	$ 390,942	$ 414,399	$ 439,263
EBIT(1 − t)	$ 553,220	$ 586,413	$ 621,598	$ 658,894

ESTIMATING DISCOUNT RATES

The acquirer in this case, Ark Restaurants, has a relatively low beta (0.7) and gets only about 10% of its financing needs from debt. Assuming that the underlying risk in investing in Lutèce is similar, the cost of equity can be estimated as follows:

$$\text{Cost of equity} = 8\% + 0.7(5.5\%) = 11.85\%$$

(This assumes that the long-term Treasury bond rate is 8% and a risk premium of 5.5%.)

If Ark Restaurants can borrow money at 9% and faces a 40% tax rate, the cost of capital can be calculated as follows:

$$\text{Cost of capital} = 11.85\%(.90) + 9\%(1 - 0.4)(.10) = 11.20\%$$

ESTIMATING VALUE

The value of Lutèce can be estimated by discounting the cash flows at the weighted average cost of capital. Allowing for a growth rate of 6% over the next three years and 3% after that, the value of the restaurant can be estimated as follows:

$$\text{Value at the end of the high-growth period} = EBIT_4(1 - t)/(WACC - g_n)$$
$$= \$658,894(1.03)/(.112 - .03) = \$8,271,309$$

$$\text{Value of Lutèce} = \$586,413/1.112 + \$621,598/1.112^2 + (\$621,598 + \$8,271,309)/1.112^3$$
$$= \$7,524,559$$

VALUING THE KEY PERSON

There would probably be no argument that some of Lutèce's value derives from Andre Soltner's presence as chef. It would be worth examining how much this value would change if he were to be replaced by somebody else. The simplest way to evaluate this effect is to:

- Estimate the effect on occupancy of replacing Mr. Soltner with another chef, and through this on cash flows. To the extent that occupancy and cash flows decline, the value of the restaurant will decline.
- Calculate the value of the restaurant based on the discounted cash flows.

In extreme cases, where the entire value of an enterprise depends on one person, the value can drop to essentially zero if the key person were to leave or die. In less extreme cases, the value of the key person can be estimated to be the difference in value of the enterprise with and without that person in place.[3]

---

[3]Consider the value of David Letterman to CBS. One estimate in the *New York Times* in 1995 claimed that 20 percent of the profits at CBS could be traced to the success of David Letterman's show. If this is true, CBS may be getting an incredible bargain, even at $5 million a year.

Valuing Trademarks, Copyrights, and Licenses

Trademarks, copyrights, and licenses all give the owner the exclusive right to produce a product or provide a service. Fundamentally, then, their value is derived from the cash flows that can be generated from the exclusive right. To the extent that there is a cost associated with production, the value comes from the excess returns that come from having the exclusive right.

As with other assets, you can value trademarks or copyrights in one of two ways. You can estimate the expected cash flows from owning the asset, attach a discount rate to these cash flows that reflects their uncertainty, and take the present value, which will yield a discounted cash flow valuation of the asset. Alternatively, you can attempt a relative valuation, where you apply a multiple to the revenues or income that you believe that you can generate from the trademark or copyright. The multiple is usually estimated by looking at what similar products have sold for in the past.

In making these estimates, you are likely to run into estimation issues that are unique to these assets. First, you have to consider the fact that a copyright or trademark provides you exclusive rights for a finite period. Consequently, the cash flows you will estimate will be for only this period and there will generally be no terminal value. Second, you have to factor in the expected costs of violations of the copyright and trademark. These costs can include at least two items. The first is the legal and monitoring cost associated with enforcing exclusivity. The second is the fact that no matter how careful you are with the monitoring, you cannot ensure that there will be no violations, and the lost revenues (profits) that arise as a consequence will lower the value of the right.

ILLUSTRATION 27.4: Valuing the Copyright on *Investment Valuation*

Assume that John Wiley & Sons has been approached by another publisher that is interested in buying the copyright to this book (*Investment Valuation*). To estimate the value of the copyright, we will make the following assumptions:[4]

■ The book is expected to generate $150,000 in after-tax cash flows each year for the next three years to Wiley and $100,000 a year for the subsequent two years. These are the cash flows after author royalties, promotional expenses, and production costs.

■ About 40% of these cash flows are from large organizations that make bulk orders and are considered predictable and stable. The cost of capital applied to these cash flows is 7%.

■ The remaining 60% of the cash flows are to the general public, and this segment of the cash flows is considered much more volatile. The cost of capital applied to these cash flows is 10%.

The value of the copyright can be estimated using these cash flows and the cost of capital that has been supplied:

Year	Stable Cash Flows	Present Value @ 7 Percent	Volatile Cash Flows	Present Value @ 10 Percent
1	$60,000	$ 56,075	$90,000	$ 81,818
2	$60,000	$ 52,406	$90,000	$ 74,380
3	$60,000	$ 48,978	$90,000	$ 67,618
4	$40,000	$ 30,516	$60,000	$ 40,981
5	$40,000	$ 28,519	$60,000	$ 37,255
Total		$216,494		$302,053

The value of the copyright, with these assumptions, is $518,547 (the sum of $216,494 and $302,053).

---

[4] I am intentionally making these assumptions as optimistic as I can. I hope you, as the reader, can make the actual cash flows resemble my estimates.

NON-CASH-FLOW-PRODUCING ASSETS

Assets that do not produce cash flows cannot be valued using discounted cash flow models. They derive their value from a combination of factors—a scarcity of supply relative to demand, consumption utility, and individual perceptions. While they can be valued relative to comparables, their values are also much more volatile since they are based entirely on perceptions. There are a wide range of assets that fall under this category, from limited edition Barbie dolls to rare coins to wine.

Special Issues in Valuing Non-Cash-Flow-Producing Assets

The biggest difference between these assets and cash-flow-generating assets is that there is no intrinsic value backing up the price. Consequently, the only way to value these assets is by using relative valuation (i.e., by looking at how similar assets are priced in the market).

The process of using comparables in valuing an asset is fairly straightforward, at least in the abstract. The first step in the process is to collect a group of comparable assets. The second is to estimate a measure of standardized value for this group. The third is to control for differences between assets in this group and the asset being valued to arrive at a measure of reasonable value for the asset. The problems in applying this approach are:

■ Finding comparable assets may be difficult to do for some non-cash-flow-producing assets. While there are indexes compiled on various unconventional assets, there are substantial differences between the assets within each index.
■ The markets for many of these assets are neither liquid nor public. Many transactions are private and the reported prices are therefore unreliable.
■ It is not clear how one controls for differences across assets that are comparable when these differences are not quantitative but relate to perception.
■ The prices of many of these assets are directly related to how scarce the supply of the asset is. For instance, the reason that the Honus Wagner T-206 baseball card is the most highly valued card on the market is because there are only 58 known cards in existence and only one in mint condition.[5] The flip side of this is that any event that alters this balance will affect the price. Thus, a surprise find of another mint-condition Honus Wagner card in someone's attic can cause the price to change dramatically.

Art and Collectibles There are many investors who view investments in art and collectibles as part of their overall portfolios. In that context, it is worth asking the following questions.

■ The first relates to the type of returns that these investments generate for investors over long periods. There are a number of studies that have looked at this question. In one of the more comprehensive analyses of art as an investment, Mei and Moses constructed an index based on repeated sales of artwork between 1875 and 2000, and their results are summarized in Table 27.1.

---

[5]This is the card that sold for $640,000 in 1996 to Michael Gidwitz, an investor from Chicago. The card had been earlier owned by Wayne Gretzky, the hockey great, who bought it for $451,000 in 1991.

TABLE 27.1   Returns from Art versus S&P 500

	Art		Stocks	
	Mean	Standard Deviation	Mean	Standard Deviation
1875–1999	5.60%	25.60%	11.10%	19.00%
1900–1999	4.70%	20.30%	12.20%	19.80%
1950–1999	5.30%	9.30%	14.60%	16.50%

Source: Mei and Moses.

As a stand-alone investment, art has earned low returns historically. In the past 50 years the returns on art have become less volatile, but that may reflect the fact that there have been more transactions in this period than in earlier ones. Does the low return make art a bad investment? Not necessarily. Table 27.2 examines the correlation between the returns on art, stocks, and Treasury bonds. The low correlation between art and stocks may give it a place in a well-diversified portfolio of financial assets, but only at the margin.

■ The second relates to how best to value investments in art and collectibles. In practice, they are almost always valued on a relative basis. Thus a Picasso is usually valued by looking at what other Picassos have sold for recently.

Generally speaking, there are at least three problems that we run into in the context of valuation. The first is that this is not a very liquid market and there are relatively few transactions. Thus, the most recent sale of a Picasso might have three years ago, and a great deal might have changed in the art market since then. The second is that no two Picassos are alike and there are substantial differences (both in style and value) across different paintings. The third problem is that there is the very real possibility of forgery and fraud, and much of it can be detected only by an expert eye. Consequently, the relative valuation of art and collectibles remains the province of expert appraisers, who try to overcome these problems (though not always successfully) and estimate a fair value. Like all analysts, however, they are susceptible to market moods, and bubbles and busts are just as common in this market as they are in others.

So, what are the lessons for individual investors? The first is that while art and collectibles, as a class, may balance a portfolio, you have to spend substantially more time acquiring specialized knowledge to be successful with these investments than you would with financial investments. The second is that you should expect to have much higher transactions costs with investments in art and collectibles, especially at the high end of the market. The third is that you should collect baseball

TABLE 27.2   Correlation between Investments

	Art	S&P 500	T-bonds
Art	1.00		
S&P 500	0.13	1.00	
T-bonds	−0.01	0.05	1.00

Source: Mei and Moses.

cards or old master paintings because you enjoy them and not just as investments. The psychic returns that you receive will then compensate for the substandard financial returns that you may well earn.

Other Assets As any regular visitor to eBay will attest, even the most unconventional assets have to be priced, and the prices often are based on the pricing of comparable assets. Thus, you can attach a value to a baseball card (for instance, a Mickey Mantle rookie card) by looking at the prices at which similar cards have sold. In fact, there are publications that list prices for traded cards, categorized by the condition of the card.

One case where a model for comparables seems to have fared remarkably well is in the area of valuing wine vintages. Professor Orley Ashenfelter at Princeton University has developed a regression model that factors in temperature and rainfall in wine-growing regions to evaluate wine vintages (Bordeaux, California cabernet sauvignon, red Burgundy, sauternes, and port wines) and come up with estimates of value per bottle, which are published in his newsletter titled "Liquid Assets." The analogue from stock valuation would be to compare price-earnings ratios across firms, controlling for risk and growth characteristics.

ASSETS WITH OPTION CHARACTERISTICS

Some assets derive their value not from the cash flows that they generate or from highly valued comparables, but from the potential that they possess to be valuable in the future, contingent on an event occurring. The values of these assets will exceed their discounted cash flow or relative values, with the difference coming from the option component.

One example would be art produced by an unknown artist that could be valuable if the artist is discovered. Another example would be the copyrights and trademarks that we valued using traditional valuation approaches in an earlier section. You might be willing to pay a premium for some copyrights, licenses, or trademarks because of the option component. For instance, a publisher bidding for a book has to consider the possibility that the book could be a runaway success: think of Bloomsbury, the publisher that brought out the first Harry Potter book. A final example would be investing in an off-Broadway show or low-budget movie. While the expected cash flows from the investment may be lower than the cost—making it a poor investment on a discounted cash flow basis—there is a chance, albeit small, that the show could be successful enough to make it to Broadway and perhaps even into a blockbuster movie. In each of these cases, you could value these assets as options; the next three chapters will consider a few applications.

CONCLUSION

This chapter provides an insight into the breadth of use that valuation models can be put to, ranging from valuing a New York City cab medallion to a five-star restaurant. The basic models remain unchanged, but the inputs may be more difficult to get and have more noise associated with them. That should, however, not be viewed as a barrier to their use.

QUESTIONS AND SHORT PROBLEMS

1. Cool Café is a well-regarded restaurant in the Denver area, owned and run by Joanne Arapacio, a star chef specializing in Southwestern cuisine. You are interested in buying the restaurant and have been provided the income statement for the firm for the most recent year is reported below (in '000s):

Revenues	$5,000
– Operating expenses	$3,500
EBIT	$1,500
– Interest expenses	$ 300
– Taxes	$ 480
Net income	$ 720

   The owner did not pay herself a salary last year, but you believe that you will have to pay $200,000 a year for a new chef. The restaurant is in stable growth and is expected to grow 5% a year for the next decade. You estimate the unlevered beta of publicly traded restaurants to be 0.80. The average debt-to-capital ratio for these firms is 30%, and you believe that Cool Café will have to operate at close to this average. The risk-free rate is 6%, the market risk premium is 4% and the cost of debt is 7%.
   a. Estimate the value of Cool Café.
   b. Now assume that you will see a drop-off in revenues of 15% if Joanne Arapacio leaves the restaurant. Assuming that 70% of the current operating expenses are variable and that the remaining 30% of fixed, estimate the value Ms. Arapacio to the restaurant.

2. Sick and tired of the investment banking grind, you decide to quit and buy a franchise for a fast-growing bagel chain in your town. You have been able to get information on what another franchise for the same chain is generating in revenues in the neighboring town:
   ■ The franchise has revenues of $1 million and earnings before interest and taxes of $150,000 last year but the owner did not assess a salary for himself. He does the accounting and oversees the bagel shop, and you believe that hiring someone else to do what he does will cost you $50,000 annually.
   ■ The revenues and operating income are expected to grow 3% a year in perpetuity.
   ■ You expect to pay 35% of your income in taxes and use all of your investment savings to buy the shop. The unlevered beta for franchise food chains is 0.80, and the average correlation with the market is 0.40.
   ■ The owner has a bank loan outstanding of $300,000 and the book value of equity in the business is $200,000. However, the average market debt to capital ratio of publicly traded restaurants is 20% and the average pretax cost of debt for restaurants is 8%.
   ■ The riskless rate is 5% and the market risk premium is 4%.
   Estimate the value of the bagel shop to you.

3. You work for a publishing company and are considering bidding for the copyright to *Cook Light, Cook Right*, a cookbook of low-fat recipes. While the book was out of print last year, you believe that you can generate $120,000 in after-tax cash flows next year, $100,000 the year after, and $80,000 in the following three years. If your cost of capital is 12%, estimate the value of the copyright.

4. You have been asked to value the practice of Dr. Vong, a pediatrician in your town, and are provided with the following facts:

- ■ The practice generated $800,000 in revenues last year, and these revenues are expected to grow 4% a year for the next 10 years.
- ■ Employee expenses (including nurses and secretarial help) amounted to $200,000 last year and are expected to grow 4% a year for the next 10 years.
- ■ The annual rent for the facilities last year was $100,000 and is expected to grow 4% a year for the next 10 years.
- ■ Rentals of medical equipment cost $75,000 last year, and this expense is expected to grow 5% for the next 10 years.
- ■ The cost of medical insurance last year was $75,000 and is expected to grow 7% a year for the next 10 years.
- ■ The tax rate on the income, including state and local taxes, is 40%.
- ■ The cost of capital is 11%.

Assuming that there will be no drop-off in revenues if a new pediatrician takes over the practice, estimate the value of the practice.

5. You are trying to decide how much you should bid on a Ken Griffey Jr. rookie baseball card in good condition on eBay. You notice that there have been eight transactions involving Ken Griffey Jr. cards in the last month on eBay:

Transaction #	Condition of Card	Price Paid for Card
1	Excellent	$800
2	Poor	$200
3	Good	$550
4	Good	$500
5	Excellent	$850
6	Good	$400
7	Poor	$350
8	Excellent	$650

a. Estimate how much you would be willing to pay for the card.
b. Now assume that the seller of the card has been rated poorly by other buyers because he has misrepresented other items he has sold to them. What effect would this information have on how much you would be willing to bid for the card?

6. Assume that you are a wealthy investor with your entire portfolio invested in stocks. Your financial adviser has suggested that you buy some fine art to balance the portfolio and based this suggestion on the low correlation between returns on stocks and returns on fine art (.10).

a. If the standard deviation of stock returns is 20% and the standard deviation in fine art returns is 15%, estimate what the standard deviation of your portfolio would be if you invested 10% of your portfolio in fine art.
b. If the expected return on stocks is 12.5% and the expected return on fine art is only 5%, would you add fine art to your portfolio? Explain why or why not. (The risk-free rate is 6%.)

CHAPTER 28

The Option to Delay
and Valuation Implications

In traditional investment analysis, a project or new investment should be accepted only if the returns on the project exceed the hurdle rate; in the context of cash flows and discount rates, this translates into investing in projects with positive net present values (NPVs). The limitation of this view of the world, which analyzes projects on the basis of expected cash flows and discount rates, is that it fails to consider fully the options that are usually associated with many investments.

This chapter will consider an option that is embedded in many projects, namely the option to wait and take the project in a later period. Why might a firm want to do this? If the present value of the cash flows on the project are volatile and can change over time, a project with a negative net present value today may have a positive net present value in the future. Furthermore, a firm may gain by waiting on a project even after a project has a positive net present value, because the option has a time premium that exceeds the cash flows that can be generated in the next period by accepting the project. This option is most valuable in projects where a firm has the exclusive right to invest in a project and becomes less valuable as the barriers to entry decline.

There are three cases where the option to delay can make a difference when valuing a firm. The first is undeveloped land in the hands of real estate investor or company. The choice of when to develop rests in the hands of the owner and presumably development will occur when real estate values increase. The second is a firm that owns a patent or patents. Since a patent provides a firm with the exclusive rights to produce the patented product or service, it can and should be valued as an option. The third is a natural resource company that has undeveloped reserves that it can choose to develop at a time of its choosing—presumably when the price of the resource is high.

THE OPTION TO DELAY A PROJECT

Projects are typically analyzed based on their expected cash flows and discount rates at the time of the analysis; the net present value computed on that basis is a measure of its value and acceptability at that time. Expected cash flows and discount rates change over time, however, and so does the net present value. Thus, a project that has a negative net present value now may have a positive net present value in the future. In a competitive environment, in which individual firms have no special advantages over their competitors in taking projects, the fact that net present values can be positive in the future may not be significant. In an environment in which a project can be taken by only one firm because of legal restrictions or other barriers to entry to competitors, however, the changes in the project's value over time give it the characteristics of a call option.

Payoff on the Option to Delay

Assume that a project requires an initial up-front investment of X, and that the present value of expected cash inflows from investing in the project, computed today, is V. The net present value of this project is the difference between the two:

$$NPV = V - X$$

Now assume that the firm has exclusive rights to this project for the next n years, and that the present value of the cash inflows may change over that time, because of changes in either the cash flows or the discount rate. Thus, the project may have a negative net present value right now, but it may still be a good project if the firm waits. Defining V again as the present value of the cash flows, the firm's decision rule on this project can be summarized as follows:

If V > X Invest in the project: Project has positive net present value.

V < X Do not invest in the project: Project has negative net present value.

If the firm does not invest in the project over its life, it incurs no additional cash flows, though it will lose what it invested to get exclusive rights to the project. This relationship can be presented in a payoff diagram of cash flows on this project, as shown in Figure 28.1, assuming that the firm holds out until the end of the period for which it has exclusive rights to the project.

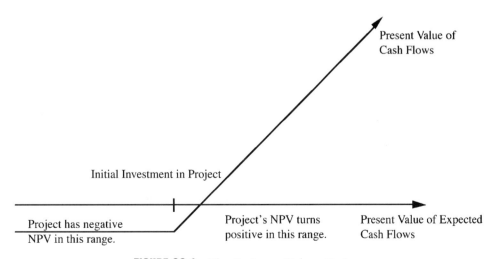

FIGURE 28.1 The Option to Delay a Project

Note that this payoff diagram is that of a call option—the underlying asset is the project, the strike price of the option is the investment needed to take the project, and the life of the option is the period for which the firm has rights to the project. The present value of the cash flows on this project and the expected variance in this present value represent the value and variance of the underlying asset.

Inputs for Valuing the Option to Delay

The inputs needed to apply option pricing theory to valuing the option to delay are the same as those needed for any option. We need the value of the underlying asset, the variance in that value, the time to expiration on the option, the strike price, the riskless rate, and the equivalent of the dividend yield.

Value of the Underlying Asset In the case of product options, the underlying asset is the project to which the firm has exclusive rights. The current value of this asset is the present value of expected cash flows from initiating the project now, not including the up-front investment. This present value can be obtained by doing a standard investment analysis. There is likely to be a substantial amount of error in the cash flow estimates and the present value, however. Rather than being viewed as a problem, this uncertainty should be viewed as the reason the project delay option has value. If the expected cash flows on the project were known with certainty and were not expected to change, there would be no need to adopt an option pricing framework, since there would be no value to the option.

Variance in the Value of the Asset As noted in the prior section, there is likely to be considerable uncertainty associated with the cash flow estimates and the present value that measures the value of the project now. This is partly because the potential market for the product may be unknown, and partly because technological shifts can change the cost structure and profitability of the product. The variance in the present value of cash flows from the project can be estimated in one of three ways.

1. If we have invested in similar projects in the past, the variance in the cash flows from those projects can be used as an estimate. This may be the way that a consumer product company like Gillette might estimate the variance associated with introducing a new blade for its razors.
2. We can assign probabilities to various market scenarios, estimate cash flows and a present value under each scenario, and then calculate the variance across present values. Alternatively, the probability distributions can be estimated for each of the inputs into the project analysis—the size of the market, the market share, and the profit margin, for instance—and simulations used to estimate the variance in the present values that emerge. This approach tends to work best when there are only one or two sources[1] of significant uncertainty about future cash flows.

---

[1] In practical terms, the probability distributions for inputs like market size and market share can often be obtained from market testing.

3. We can use the variance in the value of firms involved in the same business (as the project being considered) as an estimate of the variance. Thus, the average variance in the value of firms involved in the software business can be used as the variance in present value of a software project.

The value of the option is largely derived from the variance in cash flows; the higher the variance, the higher the value of the project delay option. Thus, the value of an option to invest in a project in a stable business will be less than the value of one in an environment where technology, competition, and markets are all changing rapidly.

Exercise Price on Option The option to delay a project is exercised when the firm owning the rights to the project decides to invest in it. The cost of making this initial investment is the exercise price of the option. The underlying assumption is that this cost remains constant (in present value dollars) and that any uncertainty associated with the investment is reflected in the present value of cash flows on the product.

Expiration of the Option and the Riskless Rate The project delay option expires when the rights to the project lapse. Investments made after the project rights expire are assumed to deliver a net present value of zero as competition drives returns down to the required rate. The riskless rate to use in pricing the option should be the rate that corresponds to the expiration of the option. While expiration dates can be estimated easily when firms have the explicit right to a project (through a license or a patent, for instance), they become far more difficult to obtain when the right is less clearly defined. If, for instance, a firm has a competitive advantage on a product or project, the option life can be defined as the expected period over which the advantage can be sustained.

Cost of Delay Chapter 5 noted that an American option generally will not be exercised prior to expiration. When you have the exclusive rights to a project, though, and the net present value turns positive, you would not expect the owner of the rights to wait until the rights expire to exercise the option (invest in the project). Note that there is a cost to delaying investing in a project, once the net present value turns positive. If you wait an additional period, you may gain if the variance pushes value higher but you also lose one period of protection against competition. You have to consider this cost when analyzing the option and there are two ways of estimating it:

1. Since the project rights expire after a fixed period, and excess profits (which are the source of positive present value) are assumed to disappear after that time as new competitors emerge, each year of delay translates into one less year of value-creating cash flows.[2] If the cash flows are evenly distributed over time, and the life of the patent is n years, the cost of delay can be written as:

$$\text{Annual cost of delay} = \frac{1}{n}$$

---

[2]A value-creating cash flow is one that adds to the net present value because it is in excess of the required return for investments of equivalent risk.

Thus, if the project rights are for 20 years, the annual cost of delay works out to $\frac{1}{20}$ or 5% a year. Note, though, that this cost of delay rises each year, to $\frac{1}{19}$ in year 2, $\frac{1}{18}$ in year 3, and so on, making the cost of delaying exercise larger over time.

2. If the cash flows are uneven, the cost of delay can be more generally defined in terms of the cash flow that can be expected to occur over the next period as a percent of the present value today:

$$\text{Cost of delay} = \frac{\text{Cash flow}_{\text{next period}}}{\text{Present value}_{\text{now}}}$$

In either case, the likelihood that a firm will delay investing in a project is higher early in the exclusive rights period rather than later and will increase as the loss in present value from waiting a period increases.

 optvar.xls: **This dataset on the Web summarizes standard deviations in firm value and equity value by industry group in the United States.**

ILLUSTRATION 28.1:   Valuing the Option to Delay a Project

Assume that you are interested in acquiring the exclusive rights to market a new product that will make it easier for people to access their e-mail on the road. If you do acquire the rights to the product, you estimate that it will cost you $50 million up-front to set up the infrastructure needed to provide the service. Based on your current projections, you believe that the service will generate only $10 million in after-tax cash flows each year. In addition, you expect to operate without serious competition for the next five years.

From a static standpoint, the net present value of this project can be computed by taking the present value of the expected cash flows over the next five years. Assuming a discount rate of 15% (based on the riskiness of this project), we obtain the following net present value for the project:

NPV of project = – $50 million + $10 million(PV of annuity, 15%, 5 years)
= – $50 million + $33.5 million = –$16.5 million

This project has a negative net present value.

The biggest source of uncertainty about this project is the number of people who will be interested in the product. While current market tests indicate that you will capture a relatively small number of business travelers as your customers, they also indicate the possibility that the potential market could be much larger. In fact, a simulation of the project's cash flows yields a standard deviation of 42% in the present value of the cash flows, with an expected value of $33.5 million.

To value the exclusive rights to this project, we first define the inputs to the option pricing model:

Value of underlying asset (S) = PV of cash flows from product if introduced now = $33.5 million
Strike price (K) = Initial investment needed to introduce the product = $50 million
Variance in underlying asset's value = $0.42^2 = 0.1764$
Time to expiration = Period of exclusive rights to product = 5 years
Dividend yield = 1/Life of the patent = 1/5 = 0.20

Assume that the five-year riskless rate is 5%. The value of the option can be estimated as follows:

Call value = 33.5 exp$^{(-0.2)(5)}$(0.2250) – 50.0 exp$^{(-0.05)(5)}$(0.0451) = $1.019 million

The rights to this product, which has a negative net present value if introduced today, is $1.019 million. Note, though, as measured by N(d1) and N(d2), the likelihood is low that this project will become viable before expiration.

delay.xls: This spreadsheet allows you to estimate the value of an option to delay an investment.

ARBITRAGE POSSIBILITIES AND OPTION PRICING MODELS

The discussion of option pricing models in Chapter 5 noted that they are based on two powerful constructs—the idea of replicating portfolios and arbitrage. Models such as the Black-Scholes and binomial assume that you can create a replicating portfolio, using the underlying asset and riskless borrowing or lending, that has cash flows identical to those on an option. Furthermore, these models assume that since investors can then create riskless positions by buying the option and selling the replicating portfolio, they have to sell for the same price. If they do not, investors should be able to create riskless positions and walk away with guaranteed profits—the essence of arbitrage. This is why the interest rate used in option pricing models is the riskless rate.

With listed options on traded stocks or assets, arbitrage is clearly feasible, at least for some investors. With options on nontraded assets, it is almost impossible to trade the replicating portfolio, although you can create it on paper. In Illustration 28.1, for instance, you would need to buy 0.225 units (the option delta) of the underlying project (a nontraded asset) to create a portfolio that replicates the call option.

There are some who argue that the impossibility of arbitrage makes it inappropriate to use option pricing models to value real options, whereas others try to adjust for this limitation by using an interest rate higher than the riskless rate in the option pricing model. We do not think that either of these responses is appropriate. Note that while you cannot trade on the replicating portfolios in many real options, you still can create them on paper (as we did in Illustration 28.1) and value the options. The difficulties in creating arbitrage positions may result in prices that deviate by a large amounts from this value, but that is an argument for using real option pricing models and not for avoiding them. Increasing the riskless rate to reflect the higher risk associated with real options may seem like an obvious fix, but doing this will only make call options (such as the one valued in Illustration 28.1) more valuable, not less.

If you want to be more conservative in your estimate of value for real options to reflect the difficulty of arbitrage, you have two choices. One is to use a higher discount rate in computing the present value of the cash flows that you would expect to make from investing in the project today, thus lowering the value of the underlying asset (S) in the model. In Illustration 28.1, using a 20 percent discount rate rather than a 15 percent rate would result in a present value of $29.1 million, which would replace the $33.5 million as S in the model. The other choice is to value the option and then apply an illiquidity discount to it (similar to the one we used in valuing private companies) because you cannot trade it easily.

Problems in Valuing the Option to Delay

While it is quite clear that the option to delay is embedded in many projects, several problems are associated with the use of option pricing models to value these options. First, the underlying asset in this option, which is the project, is not traded, making it difficult to estimate its value and variance. The value can be estimated from the expected cash flows and the discount rate for the project, albeit with error. The variance is more difficult to estimate, however, since we are attempting the estimate a variance in project value over time.

Second, the behavior of prices over time may not conform to the price path assumed by the option pricing models. In particular, the assumption that value follows a diffusion process, and that the variance in value remains unchanged over time, may be difficult to justify in the context of a project. For instance, a sudden technological change may dramatically change the value of a project, either positively or negatively.

Third, there may be no specific period for which the firm has rights to the project. Unlike the case of a patent, for instance, in which the firm has exclusive rights to produce the patented product for a specified period, the firm's rights often are less clearly defined, in terms of both exclusivity and time. For instance, a firm may have significant advantages over its competitors, which may, in turn, provide it with the virtually exclusive rights to a project for a period of time. An example would be a company with strong brand name recognition in retailing or consumer products. The rights are not legal restrictions, however, and will erode over time. In such cases, the expected life of the project itself is uncertain and only an estimate. In the valuation of the rights to the product in the previous section a life of five years for the option was used, but competitors could in fact enter sooner than anticipated. Alternatively, the barriers to entry may turn out to be greater than expected, and allow the firm to earn excess returns for longer than five years. Ironically, uncertainty about the expected life of the option can increase the variance in present value, and through it, the expected value of the rights to the project.

Implications and Extensions of Delay Options

Several interesting implications emerge from the analysis of the option to delay a project as an option. First, a project may have a negative net present value currently based on expected cash flows, but the rights to it may still be valuable because of the option characteristics.

Second, a project may have a positive net present value but still not be accepted right away. This can happen because the firm may gain by waiting and accepting the project in a future period, for the same reasons that investors do not always exercise an option that is in the money. A firm is more likely to wait if it has the rights to the project for a long time, and the variance in project inflows is high. To illustrate, assume a firm has the patent rights to produce a new type of disk drive for computer systems and building a new plant will yield a positive net present value today. If the technology for manufacturing the disk drive is in flux, however, the firm may delay investing in the project in the hopes that the improved technology will increase the expected cash flows and consequently the value of the project. It has to weigh this benefit against the cost of delaying the project, which will be the cash flows that will be forsaken by not investing in it.

Third, factors that can make a project less attractive in a static analysis can actually make the rights to the project more valuable. As an example, consider the effect of uncertainty about the size of the potential market and the magnitude of excess returns. In a static analysis, increasing this uncertainty increases the riskiness of the project and may make it less attractive. When the project is viewed as an option, an increase in the uncertainty may actually make the option more valuable, not less. The chapter will consider two cases, product patents and natural resource reserves, where the project delay option allows value to be estimated more precisely.

Option Pricing Models

Once you have identified the option to delay a project as a call option and identified the inputs needed to value the option, it may seem like a trivial task to actually value the option. There are, however, some serious estimation issues that we have to deal with in valuing these options. Chapter 5 noted that while the more general model for valuing options is the binomial model, many practitioners use the Black-Scholes model, which makes far more restrictive assumptions about price processes and early exercise to value options. With listed options on traded assets, you can do this at fairly low cost. With real options, there can be a substantial cost to this practice for the following reasons:

- Unlike listed options, real options tend to be exercised early, if they are in the money. While there are ways in which the Black-Scholes model can be adjusted to allow for this early exercise, the binomial model allows for much more flexibility.
- The binomal option pricing model allows for a much wider range of price processes for the underlying asset than the Black-Scholes model, which assumes that prices are not only continuous but log-normally distributed. With real options, where the present value of the cash flows is often equivalent to the price, the assumptions of nonnormality and continuous distributions may be difficult to sustain.

The biggest problem with the binomial model is that the prices at each node of the binomial tree have to be estimated. As the number of periods expands, this will become more and more difficult to do. You can, however, use the variance estimate in the Black-Scholes to come up with measures of the magnitude of the up and down movements, which can be used to obtain the binomial tree.

Having made a case for the binomial model, you may find it surprising that we use the Black-Scholes model to value any real options. We do so not only because the model is more compact and elegant to present, but because we believe that it will provide a lower bound on the value in most cases. To provide a frame of reference, we will present the values that we would have obtained using a binomial model in each case.

From Black-Scholes to Binomial   It is a fairly simple exercise to convert the inputs to the Black-Scholes model into a binomial model. To make the adjustment, you have to assume a multiplicative binomial process, where the magnitude of the jumps, in percent terms, remains unchanged from period to period. If you assume symmetric probabilities, the up (u) and down (d) movements can be estimated as a function of the annualized variance in the price process and how many periods you decide to break each year into (t).

$$u = \exp^{\sigma\sqrt{dt}+\left(r-y-\frac{\sigma^2}{2}\right)dt}$$

$$d = \exp^{-\sigma\sqrt{dt}+\left(r-y-\frac{\sigma^2}{2}\right)dt}$$

where dt = 1/Number of periods each year

To illustrate, consider the project delay option valued in Illustration 28.1. The standard deviation in the value was assumed to be 42 percent, the risk-free rate was 5%, and the dividend yield was 20 percent. To convert the inputs into a binomial model, assume that each year is a time period and estimate the up and down movements as follows:

$$u = \exp^{.42\sqrt{1}+\left(.05-.20-\frac{.42^2}{2}\right)\sqrt{t}} = 1.1994$$

$$d = \exp^{-.42\sqrt{1}+\left(.05-.20-\frac{.42^2}{2}\right)1t} = 0.5178$$

The value today is $33.5 million. To estimate the end values for the first branch:

Value with up movement = $33.5(1.1994) = $40.179 million

Value with down movement = $33.5(0.5178) = $17.345 million

You could use these values then to get the three potential values at the second branch. Note that the value of $17.345 million growing at 19.94 percent is exactly equal to the value of $40.179 million dropping by 48.22 percent. The binomial tree for the five periods is shown in Figure 28.2.

You could estimate the value of the option from this binomial tree to be $1.02 million, slightly higher than the estimate obtained from the Black-Scholes model of $1.019 million. The differences will narrow as the option becomes more in-the-money and you shorten the time periods you use in the binomial model.

VALUING A PATENT

A number of firms, especially in the technology and pharmaceutical sectors, can patent products or services. A product patent provides a firm with the right to develop and market a product, and thus can be viewed as an option.

Patents as Call Options

The firm will develop a patent only if the present value of the expected cash flows from the product sales exceed the cost of development, as shown in Figure 28.3. If

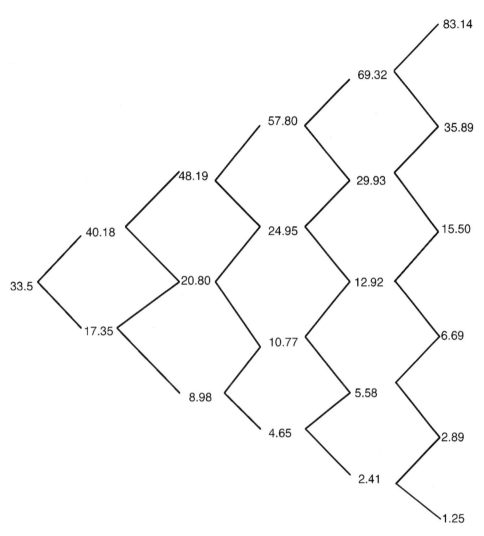

FIGURE 28.2 Binomial Tree for Delay Option

this does not occur, the firm can shelve the patent and not incur any further costs. If I is the present value of the costs of commercially developing the patent and V is the present value of the expected cash flows from development, then:

$$\text{Payoff from owning a product patent} = V - I \quad \text{if } V > I$$
$$= 0 \quad \text{if } V \leq I$$

Thus a product patent can be viewed as a call option, where the product is the underlying asset.

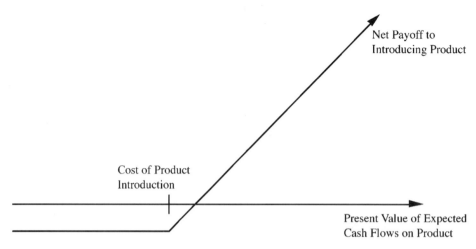

FIGURE 28.3   Payoff to Introducing Product

ILLUSTRATION 28.2:   Valuing a Patent: Avonex in 1997

Biogen is a biotechnology firm with a patent on a drug called Avonex, which has received FDA approval for use In treating multiple sclerosis (MS). Assume you are trying to value the patent and that you have the following estimates for use in the option pricing model:

- An internal analysis of the financial viability of the drug today, based on the potential market and the price that the firm can expect to charge for the drug, yields a present value of cash flows of $3.422 billion prior to considering the initial development cost.
- The initial cost of developing the drug for commercial use is estimated to be $2.875 billion, if the drug is introduced today.
- The firm has the patent on the drug for the next 17 years, and the current long-term Treasury bond rate is 6.7%.
- The average variance in firm value for publicly traded biotechnology firms is 0.224.

We assume that the potential for excess returns exists only during the patent life, and that competition will eliminate excess returns beyond that period. Thus, any delay in introducing the drug, once it becomes viable, will cost the firm one year of patent-protected returns. (For the initial analysis, the cost of delay will be $1/17$, next year it will be $1/16$, the year after $1/15$, and so on.)

Based on these assumptions, we obtain the following inputs to the option pricing model.

Present value of cash flows from introducing the drug now = S = $3.422 billion
Initial cost of developing drug for commercial use (today) = K = $2.875 billion
Patent life = t = 17 years
Riskless rate = r = 6.7% (17-year Treasury bond rate)
Variance in expected present values = σ^2 = 0.224
Expected cost of delay = y = 1/17 = 5.89%

These yield the following estimates for d and N(d):

$$d1 = 1.1362 \quad N(d1) = 0.8720$$
$$d2 = -0.8512 \quad N(d2) = 0.2076$$

Plugging back into the dividend-adjusted Black-Scholes option pricing model,[3] we get:

Value of the patent = 3,422 exp(−0.0589)(17)(0.8720) − 2,875 exp(−0.067)(17)(0.2076) = $907 million

To provide a contrast, the net present value of this project is only $547 million:

$$\text{NPV} = \$3{,}422 \text{ million} - \$2{,}875 \text{ million} = \$547 \text{ million}$$

The time premium of $360 million on this option ($907 − $547) suggests that the firm will be better off waiting rather than developing the drug immediately, the cost of delay notwithstanding. However, the cost of delay will increase over time, and make exercise (development) more likely in future years.

To illustrate, we will value the call option, assuming that all of the inputs, other than the patent life, remain unchanged and changing the patent life. For instance, assume that there are 16 years left on the patent. Holding all else constant, the cost of delay increases as a result of the shorter patent life:

$$\text{Cost of delay} = 1/16$$

The decline in the present value of cash flows (which is S) and increase in the cost of delay (y) reduce the expected value of the patent. Figure 28.4 graphs the option value and the net present value of the project each year.

Based on this analysis, if nothing changes, you would expect Avonex to be worth more as a commercial product than as a patent if there were less than eight years left on the patent, which would also then be the optimal time to commercially develop the product.

---

 product.xls: **This spreadsheet allows you to estimate the value of a patent.**

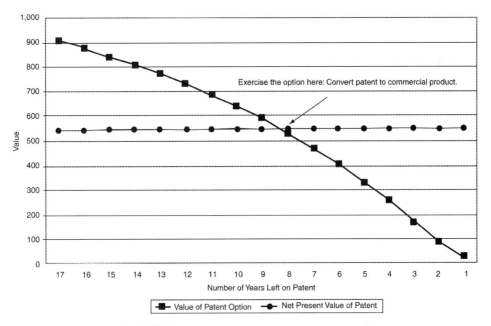

FIGURE 28.4 Patent Value versus Net Present Value

---

[3]With a binomial model, we estimate a value of $915 million for the same option.

COMPETITIVE PRESSURES AND OPTION VALUES

The preceding section has taken the view that a firm is protected from competition for the life of the patent. This is generally true only for the patented product or process, but the firm may still face competition from other firms that come up with their own products to serve the same market. More specifically, Biogen can patent Avonex, but Merck or Pfizer can come up with their own drugs to treat multiple sclerosis and compete with Biogen.

What are the implications for the value of the patent as an option? First, the life of the option will no longer be the life of the patent but the lead time that the firm has until a competing product is developed. For instance, if Biogen knows that another pharmaceutical firm is working on a drug to treat MS and where this drug is in the research pipeline (early research or stage in the FDA approval process), it can use its estimate of how long it will take before the drug is approved for use as the life of the option. This will reduce the value of the option and make it more likely that the drug will be commercially developed earlier rather than later.

The presence of these competitive pressures may explain why commercial development is much quicker with some drugs than with others, and why the value of patents is not always going to be greater than a discounted cash flow valuation. Generally speaking, the greater the number of competing products in the research pipeline, the less likely it is that the option pricing model will generate a value that is greater than the traditional discounted cash flow model.

Valuing a Firm with Patents

If the patents owned by a firm can be valued as options, how can this estimate be incorporated into firm value? The value of a firm that derives its value primarily from commercial products that emerge from its patents can be written as a function of three variables:

1. The cash flows it derives from patents that it has already converted into commercial products.
2. The value of the patents that it already possesses that have not been commercially developed.
3. The expected value of any patents that the firm can be expected to generate in future periods from new patents that it might obtain as a result of its research.

> Value of firm = Value of commercial products + Value of existing patents
> + (Value of new patents that will be obtained in the future
> – Cost of obtaining these patents)

The value of the first component can be estimated using traditional cash flow models. The expected cash flows from existing products can be estimated for their commercial lives and discounted back to the present at the appropriate cost of capital to arrive at the value of these products. The value of the second component can be obtained using the option pricing model described earlier to value each patent.

The value of the third component will be based on perceptions of a firm's research capabilities. In the special case where the expected cost of research and development in future periods is equal to the value of the patents that will be generated by this research, the third component will become zero. In the more general case, firms such as Merck and Pfizer that have a history of generating value from research will derive positive value from this component as well.

How would the estimate of value obtained using this approach contrast with the estimate obtained in a traditional discounted cash flow model? In traditional discounted cash flow valuation, the second and the third components of value are captured in the expected growth rate in cash flows. Firms such as Pfizer are allowed to grow at much higher rates for longer periods because of the technological edge they possess and their research prowess. In contrast, the approach described in this section looks at each patent separately and allows for the option component of value explicitly.

The biggest limitation of the option-based approach is the information that is needed to put it in practice. To value each patent separately, you need access to proprietary information that is usually available only to managers of the firm. In fact, some of the information, such as the expected variance to use in option pricing, may not even be available to insiders and will have to be estimated for each patent separately.

Given these limitations, the real option approach should be used to value small firms with one or two patents and little in terms of established assets. A good example would be Biogen in 1997, which was valued in the preceding section. For firms such as Merck and Pfizer that have significant assets in place and dozens of patents, discounted cash flow valuation is a more pragmatic choice. Viewing new technology as options provides insight into Cisco's successful growth strategy over the previous decade. Cisco has been successful at buying firms with nascent and promising technologies (options) and converting them into commercial success (exercising these options).

ILLUSTRATION 28.3: Valuing Biogen as a Firm

In illustration 28.2, the patent that Biogen owns on Avonex was valued as a call option and the estimated value was $907 million. To value Biogen as a firm two other components of value would have to be considered:

1. Biogen had two commercial products (a drug to treat hepatitis B and a drug called Intron) at the time of this valuation that it had licensed to other pharmaceutical firms. The license fees on these products were expected to generate $50 million in after-tax cash flows each year for the next 12 years. To value these cash flows, which were guaranteed contractually, the pretax cost of debt of the licensing firms (7%) was used:

$$\text{Present value of license fees} = \$50 \text{ million} \left[\frac{1 - 1.07^{-12}}{.07} \right] = \$397.13 \text{ million}$$

2. Biogen continued to fund research into new products, spending about $100 million on R&D in the most recent year. These R&D expenses were expected to grow 20% a year for the next 10 years and 5% thereafter. While it was difficult to forecast the specific patents that would emerge from this research, it was assumed that every dollar invested in research would create $1.25 in value in patents[4] (valued using the option pricing model described earlier) for the next 10 years, and break even after that (i.e., generate $1 in patent value for every $1 invested in R&D). There was a significant amount of risk associated with this component and the cost of capital was estimated to be 15%.[5] The value of this component was then estimated as follows:

$$\text{Value of future research} = \sum_{t=1}^{t=\infty} \frac{\left(\text{Value of patents}_t - \text{R\&D}_t\right)}{(1 + r)^t}$$

The following table summarizes the value of patents generated each period and the R&D costs in that period. Note that there is no surplus value created after the tenth year:

Year	Value of Patents Generated	R&D Cost	Excess Value	Present Value at 15%
1	$150.00	$120.00	$ 30.00	$ 26.09
2	$180.00	$144.00	$ 36.00	$ 27.22
3	$216.00	$172.80	$ 43.20	$ 28.40
4	$259.20	$207.36	$ 51.84	$ 29.64
5	$311.04	$248.83	$ 62.21	$ 30.93
6	$373.25	$298.60	$ 74.65	$ 32.27
7	$447.90	$358.32	$ 89.58	$ 33.68
8	$537.48	$429.98	$107.50	$ 35.14
9	$644.97	$515.98	$128.99	$ 36.67
10	$773.97	$619.17	$154.79	$ 38.26
				$318.30

The total value created by new research is $318.3 million.

The value of Biogen as a firm is the sum of all three components—the present value of cash flows from existing products, the value of Avonex (as an option), and the value created by new research:

Value = CF: commercial products + Value: undeveloped patents + Value: future R&D
= $397.13 million + $907 million + $318.30 million = $1,622.43 million

Since Biogen had no debt outstanding, this value was divided by the number of shares outstanding (35.5 million) to arrive at a value per share:

Value per share = $1,622.43 million/35.5 = $45.70

---

[4]To be honest, this is not an estimate based on any significant facts other than Biogen's history of success in coming up with new products. You can obtain an estimate of this number from the return and cost of capital. For instance, if you assume a return on capital of 15 percent and cost of capital of 10 percent in perpetuity, $1 invested would yield the following:

$$\text{Value of created} = 1 + \frac{(\text{ROC} - \text{Cost of capital})}{\text{Capital invested}} = 1 + \frac{(.15 - .10)}{.10} = \$1.50$$

[5]This discount rate was estimated by looking at the costs of equity of young publicly traded biotechnology firms with little or no revenue from commercial products.

IS THERE LIFE AFTER THE PATENT EXPIRES?

In these valuations it has been assumed that the excess returns are restricted to the patent life and that they disappear the instant the patent expires. In the pharmaceutical sector, the expiration of a patent does not necessarily mean the loss of excess returns. In fact, many firms continue to be able to charge a premium price for their products and earn excess returns even after the patent expires, largely as a consequence of the brand name image that they built up over the project life. A simple way of adjusting for this reality is to increase the present value of the cash flows on the project (S) and decrease the cost of delay (y) to reflect this reality. The net effect is a greater likelihood that firms will delay commercial development while they wait to collect more information and assess market demand.

The other thing that might increase the value of the patent is the capacity that drug companies have shown to lobby legislators to extend the patent life of profitable drugs. If we consider this as a possibility when we value a patent, it will increase the expected life of the patent and its value as an option.

NATURAL RESOURCE OPTIONS

Natural resource companies, such as oil and mining companies, generate cash flows from their existing reserves but also have undeveloped reserves that they can develop if they choose to do so. They will be much more likely to develop these reserves if the price of the resource (oil, gold, copper) increases and these undeveloped reserves can be viewed as call options. This section will begin by looking at the value of an undeveloped reserve and then consider how this can be extended to look at natural resource companies that have both developed and undeveloped reserves.

Undeveloped Reserves as Options

In a natural resource investment, the underlying asset is the natural resource and the value of the asset is based on the estimated quantity and the price of the resource. Thus, in a gold mine, the underlying asset is the value of the estimated gold reserves in the mine, based on the price of gold. In most such investments, there is an initial cost associated with developing the resource; the difference between the value of the estimated reserves and the cost of the development is the profit to the owner of the resource (see Figure 28.5). Defining the cost of development as X, and the estimated value of the resource as V makes the potential payoffs on a natural resource option the following:

$$\text{Payoff on natural resource investment} = V - X \quad \text{if } V > X$$
$$= 0 \quad \quad \text{if } V \leq X$$

Thus the investment in a natural resource option has a payoff function that resembles a call option.

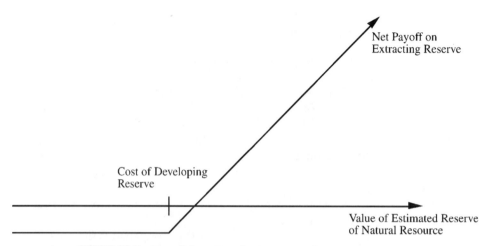

FIGURE 28.5   Payoff from Developing Natural Resource Reserves

Inputs for Valuing a Natural Resource Option   To value a natural resource investment as an option, we need to make assumptions about a number of variables:

- *Available reserves of the resource and estimated value if extracted today.* Since the quantity of the reserve is not known with certainty at the outset, it has to be estimated. In an oil tract, for instance, geologists can provide reasonably accurate estimates of the quantity of oil available in the tract. The value of the reserves is then the product of the estimated reserves and the contribution (price of the resource minus variable cost of extraction) per unit of reserve.
- *Estimated cost of developing the resource.* The estimated cost of developing the resource reserve is the exercise price of the option. In an oil reserve, this would be the fixed cost of installing the rigs to extract oil from the reserve. With a mine, it would be the cost associated with making the mine operational. Since oil and mining companies have done this before in a variety of settings, they can use their experience to come up with a reasonable measure of development cost.
- *Time to expiration of the option.* The life of a natural resource option can be defined in one of two ways. First, if the ownership of the investment has to be relinquished at the end of a fixed period of time, that period will be the life of the option. In many offshore oil leases, for instance, the oil tracts are leased to the oil company for a fixed period. The second approach is based on the inventory of the resource and the capacity output rate, as well as estimates of the number of years it would take to exhaust the inventory. Thus, a gold mine with a mine inventory of 3 million ounces and a capacity output rate of 150,000 ounces a year will be exhausted in 20 years, which is defined as the life of the natural resource option.
- *Variance in value of the underlying asset.* The variance in the value of the underlying asset is determined by the variability in the price of the resource and the variability in the estimate of available reserves. In the special case where the quantity of the reserve is known with certainty, the variance in the underlying asset's value will depend entirely on the variance in the price of the natural resource.
- *Cost of delay.* The net production revenue is the annual cash flow that will be generated, once a resource reserve has been developed, as a percentage of the

market value of the reserve. This is the equivalent of the dividend yield and is treated the same way in calculating option values. An alternative way of thinking about this cost is in terms of a cost of delay. Once a natural resource option is in-the-money (value of the reserves is greater than the cost of developing these reserves), by not developing the reserve the firm is costing itself the net production revenue it could have generated by doing so.

An important issue in using option pricing models to value natural resource options is the effect of development lags on the value of these options. Since oil or gold or any other natural resource reserve cannot be developed instantaneously, a time lag has to be allowed between the decision to extract the resources and the actual extraction. A simple adjustment for this lag is to reduce the value of the developed reserve for the loss of cash flows during the development period. Thus, if there is a one-year lag in development, you can estimate the cash flow you would make over the year as a percent of your reserve value, and discount the current value of the developed reserve at that rate. This is the equivalent of removing the first year's cash flow from your investment analysis and lowering the present value of your cash flows.

ILLUSTRATION 28.4: Valuing an Oil Reserve[6]

Consider an offshore oil property with an estimated oil reserve of 50 million barrels of oil; the cost of developing the reserve is expected to be $600 million, and the development lag is two years. Exxon has the rights to exploit this reserve for the next 20 years, and the marginal value (price per barrel minus marginal cost per barrel) per barrel of oil is currently $12.[7] Once developed, the net production revenue each year will be 5% of the value of the reserves. The riskless rate is 8%, and the variance in oil prices is 0.03.

Given this information, the inputs to the Black-Scholes model can be estimated as follows:

Current value of the asset = S = Value of the developed reserve discounted back the length of the development lag at the dividend yield = $12 \times 50/(1.05)^2 = 544.22

Exercise price = Cost of developing reserve = $600 million

Time to expiration on the option = 20 years

Variance in the value of the underlying asset[8] = 0.03

Riskless rate = 8%

Dividend yield = Net production revenue/Value of reserve = 5%

Based on these inputs, the Black-Scholes model provides the following call value:

$$d1 = 1.0359 \qquad N(d1) = 0.8498$$
$$d2 = 0.2613 \qquad N(d2) = 0.6030$$

$$\text{Call value} = 544.22 \exp^{(-0.05)(20)}(0.8498) - 600 \exp^{(-0.08)(20)}(0.6030) = \$97.08 \text{ million}$$

This oil reserve, though not viable at current prices, is still valuable because of its potential to create value if oil prices go up.[9]

---

[6]The following is a simplified version of the illustration provided by Siegel, Smith, and Paddock to value an offshore oil property.

[7]For simplicity, we will assume that while this marginal value per barrel of oil will grow over time, the present value of the marginal value will remain unchanged at $12 per barrel. If we do not make this assumption, we will have to estimate the present value of the oil that will be extracted over the extraction period.

[8]In this example, we assume that the only uncertainty is in the price of oil, and the variance therefore becomes the variance in ln(oil prices).

[9]With a binomial model, we arrive at an estimate of value of $99.15 million.

natres.xls: This spreadsheet allows you to estimate the value of an undeveloped natural resource reserve.

MULTIPLE SOURCES OF UNCERTAINTY

In the preceding example, we assumed that there was no uncertainty about the quantity of the reserve. Realistically, the oil company has an estimate of the reserve of 50 million barrels but does not know it with certainty. If we introduce uncertainty about the quantity of the reserve into the analysis, there will be two sources of variance and both can affect value. There are two ways we can address this problem:

1. *Combine the uncertainties into one value.* If we consider the value of the reserves to be the product of the price of oil and the oil reserves, the variance in the value should reflect the combined effect of the variances in each input.[10] This would be the variance we would use in the option pricing model to estimate a new value for the reserve.

2. *Keep the variances separate and value the option as a rainbow option.* A rainbow option allows explicitly for more than one source of variance and allows us to keep the variances separate and still value the option. While option pricing becomes more complicated, you may need to do this if you expect the two sources of uncertainty to evolve differently over time—the variance from one source (say, oil prices) may increase over time whereas the variance from the other source (say, oil reserves) may decrease over time.

Valuing a Firm with Undeveloped Reserves

The examples provided above illustrate the use of option pricing theory in valuing individual mines and oil tracts. Since the assets owned by a natural resource firm can be viewed primarily as options, the firm itself can be valued using option pricing models.

Individual Reserves versus Aggregate Reserves   The preferred approach would be to consider each option separately, value it and cumulate the values of the options

---

[10]This is the variance of a product of two variables.

to get the value of the firm. Since this information is likely to be difficult to obtain for large natural resource firms, such as oil companies, which own hundreds of such assets, a variant of this approach is to value the entire firm's undeveloped reserves as one option. A purist would probably disagree, arguing that valuing an option on a portfolio of assets (as in this approach) will provide a lower value than valuing a portfolio of options (which is what the natural resource firm really owns). Nevertheless, the value obtained from the model still provides a reasonable estimate of the value of undeveloped reserves.

Inputs to Option Valuation   If you decide to apply the option pricing approach to estimate the value of aggregate undeveloped reserves, you have to estimate the inputs to the model. In general terms, while the process resembles the one used to value an individual reserve, there are a few differences.

- *Value of underlying asset.* You should cumulate all of the undeveloped reserves owned by a company and estimate the value of these reserves, based on the price of the resource today and the average variable cost of extracting these reserves today. The variable costs are likely to be higher for some reserves and lower for others, and weighting the variable costs at each reserve by the quantity of the resource of that reserve should give you a reasonable approximation of this value. At least hypothetically, we are assuming that the company can decide to extract all of its undeveloped reserves at one time and not affect the price of the resource.
- *Exercise price.* For this input, you should consider what it would cost the company today to develop all of its undeveloped reserves. Again, the costs might be higher for some reserves than for others, and you can use a weighted average cost.
- *Life of the option.* A firm will probably have different lives for each of its reserves. As a consequence, you will have to use a weighted average of the lives of the different reserves.[11]
- *Variance in the value of the asset.* Here, there is a strong argument for looking at only the oil price as the source of variance, since a firm should have a much more precise estimate of its total reserves than it does of any one of its reserves.
- *Dividend yield (cost of delay).* As with an individual reserve, a firm with viable reserves will be giving up the cash flows it could receive in the next period from developing these reserves if it delays exercise. This cash flow, stated as a percent of the value of the reserves, becomes the equivalent of the dividend yield. The development lag reduces the value of this option just as it reduces the value of an individual reserve. The logical implication is that undeveloped reserves will be worth more at oil companies that can develop their reserves quicker than at less efficient companies.

---

[11]If you own some reserves in perpetuity, you should cap the life of the reserve at a large value—say, 30 years—in making this estimate.

ILLUSTRATION 28.4:   Valuing an Oil Company: Gulf Oil in 1984

Gulf Oil was the target of a takeover in early 1984 at $70 per share (It had 165.30 million shares outstanding and total debt of $9.9 billion). It had estimated reserves of 3,038 million barrels of oil and the total cost of developing these reserves at that time was estimated to be $30.38 billion dollars (the development lag is approximately two years). The average relinquishment life of the reserves is 12 years. The price of oil was $22.38 per barrel, and the production costs, taxes, and royalties were estimated at $7 per barrel. The bond rate at the time of the analysis was 9.00%. If Gulf were to choose to develop these reserves, it was expected to have cash flows next year of approximately 5% of the value of the developed reserves. The variance in oil prices is 0.03.

Value of underlying asset = Value of estimated reserves discounted back for period of development lag
$$= 3,038 \times (\$22.38 - \$7)/1.05^2 = \$42,380.44$$

Note that you could have used forecasted oil prices and estimated cash flows over the production period and estimated the value of the underlying asset to be the present value of all of these cash flows. We have used a shortcut of assuming that the current contribution margin of $15.38 a barrel will remain unchanged in present value terms over the production period.

Exercise price = Estimated cost of developing reserves today = $30,380 million
Time to expiration = Average length of relinquishment option = 12 years
Variance in value of asset = Variance in oil prices = 0.03
Riskless interest rate = 9%
Dividend yield = Net production revenue/Value of developed reserves = 5%

Based on these inputs, the Black-Scholes model provides the following value for the call:[12]

$$d1 = 1.6548 \qquad N(d1) = 0.9510$$
$$d2 = 1.0548 \qquad N(d2) = 0.8542$$

Call value = 42,380.44 exp$^{(-0.05)(12)}$(0.9510) − 30,380 exp$^{(-0.09)(12)}$(0.8542) = $13,306 million

This stands in contrast to the discounted cash flow value of $12 billion that you obtain by taking the difference between the present value of the cash flows of developing the reserve today ($42.38 billion) and the cost of development ($30.38 billion). The difference can be attributed to the option possessed by Gulf to choose when to develop its reserves.

The option value ($13.3 billion) represents the value of the undeveloped reserves of oil owned by Gulf Oil. In addition, Gulf Oil had free cash flows to the firm from its oil and gas production of $915 million from already developed reserves and assume that these cashflows are likely to be constant and continue for 10 years (the remaining lifetime of developed reserves). The present value of these developed reserves, discounted at the weighted average cost of capital of 12.5%, yields:

Value of already developed reserves = 915(1 − 1.125^{-10})/.125 = $5,065.83

Adding the value of the developed and undeveloped reserves of Gulf Oil provides the value of the firm.

Value of undeveloped reserves	$13,306 million
Value of production in place	$ 5,066 million
Total value of firm	$18,372 million
Less outstanding debt	$ 9,900 million
Value of equity	$ 8,472 million
Value per share	$ 8,472/165.3 = $51.25

This analysis would suggest that Gulf Oil was overvalued at $70 per share.

---

[12]With a binomial model, we estimate the value of the reserves to be $13.73 billion.

PRICE VOLATILITY AND NATURAL RESOURCE COMPANY VALUATION

An interesting implication of this analysis is that the value of a natural resource company depends not just on the price of the natural resource but also on the expected volatility in that price. Thus, if the price of oil goes from $25 a barrel to $40 a barrel, you would expect all oil companies to become more valuable. If the price drops back to $25, the values of oil companies may not decline to their old levels, since the perceived volatility in oil prices may have changed. If investors believe that the volatility in oil prices has increased, you would expect an increase in values but the increase will be greatest for companies that derive a higher proportion of their value from undeveloped reserves.

If you regard undeveloped reserves as options, discounted cash flow valuation will generally underestimate the value of natural resource companies, because the expected price of the commodity is used to estimate revenues and operating profits. As a consequence, you miss the option component of value. Again, the difference will be greatest for firms with significant undeveloped reserves and with commodities where price volatility is highest.

OTHER APPLICATIONS

While patents and undeveloped reserves of natural resource companies lend themselves best to applying option pricing, there are other assets referenced in earlier chapters that can also be valued as options.

- Chapter 26, in the context of real estate valuation, noted that vacant land could be viewed as an option on commercial development.
- Chapter 27 presented an argument that copyrights and licenses could be viewed as options, even if they are not commercially viable today.

Table 28.1 presents the inputs you would use to value each of these options in an option pricing model. Much of what we have said about the other option applications apply here as well. The value is derived from the exclusivity that you have to commercially develop the asset. That exclusivity is obtained by legal sanction in the case of licenses and copyrights, and from the scarcity of land in the case of undeveloped land.

CONCLUSION

In traditional investment analysis, we compute the net present value of a project's cash flows and conclude that firms should not invest in a project with a negative net present value. This is generally good advice, but it does not imply that the rights to this project are not valuable. Projects that have negative net present values today may have positive net present values in the future, and the likelihood of this occurring is directly a function of the volatility in the present value of the cash flows from the project.

TABLE 28.1   Inputs to Value Other Options to Delay

	Undeveloped Land	License/Copyright
Value of the underlying asset	Present value of the cash flows that would be obtained from commercial development of land today.	Present value of the cash flows that would be obtained from commercially utilizing the license or copyright today.
Variance in value of underlying asset	Variance in the values of commercial property in the area where the real estate is located.	Variance in the present values from commercial utilization of copyright or license (from a simulation).
Exercise price	Cost of commercially developing land today.	Up-front cost of commercially utilizing copyright or license today.
Life of the option	If land is under long-term lease, you could use the lease period. If not, you should set the option life equal to the period when the loan that you used to buy the land comes due.	Period for which you have rights to copyright or license.
Cost of delay	Interest payments you have to make on the loan each year.	Cash flow you could generate in next year as a percent of present value of the cash flows today.

This chapter valued the option to delay an investment and considered the implications of this option for three valuation scenarios—the value of a firm that derives all or a significant portion of value from patents that have not been commercially exploited yet, the value of a natural resource company with undeveloped reserves of the resource, and the value of a real estate firm with undeveloped land. In each case, we showed that using discounted cash flow valuation would result in an understatement of the values of these firms.

QUESTIONS AND SHORT PROBLEMS

1. A company is considering delaying a project with after-tax cash flows of $25 million but that costs $300 million to take on (the life of the project is 20 years, and the cost of capital is 16%). A simulation of the cash flows leads you to conclude that the standard deviation in the present value of cash inflows is 20%. If you can acquire the rights to the project for the next 10 years, what is the value of the rights? (The six-month T-bill rate is 8%, the 10-year bond rate is 12%, and the 20-year bond rate is 14%.)
2. You are examining the financial viability of investing in some abandoned copper mines in Chile, which still have significant copper deposits in them. A geologist survey suggests that there might be 10 million pounds of copper in the mines still, and that the cost of opening up the mines will be $3 million (in present value dollars). The capacity output rate is 400,000 pounds a year, and the price of copper is expected to increase 4% a year. The Chilean government is willing

to grant a 25-year lease on the mine. The average production cost is expected to be 40 cents a pound, and the current price per pound of copper is 85 cents. (The production cost is expected to grow 3% a year, once initiated.) The annualized standard deviation in copper prices is 25%, and the 25-year bond rate is 7%.
   a. Estimate the value of the mine using traditional capital budgeting techniques.
   b. Estimate the value of the mine based on an option pricing model.
   c. How would you explain the difference between the two values?
3. You have been asked to analyze the value of an oil company with substantial oil reserves. The estimated reserves amount to 10 million barrels, and the estimated cost of developing these reserves today is $120 million. The current price of oil is $20 per barrel, and the average production cost is estimated to be $6 per barrel. The company has the rights to these reserves for the next 20 years, and the 20-year bond rate is 7%. The company also proposes to extract 4% of its reserves each year to meet cash flow needs. The annualized standard deviation in the price of the oil is 20%. What is the value of this oil company?
4. You are analyzing a capital budgeting project. The project is expected to have a PV of cash inflows of $250 million and will cost $200 million today to take on. You have done a simulation of the project cash flows, and the simulation yields a variance in present value of cash inflows of 0.04. You have the rights to this project for the next 20 years. The 20-year Treasury bond rate is 8%.
   a. What is the value of the project based on traditional NPV?
   b. What is the value of the project as an option?
   c. Why are the two values different? What factor or factors determine the magnitude of this difference?
5. Cyclops Inc., a high technology company specializing in state-of-the-art visual technology, is considering going public. While the company has no revenues or profits yet on its products, it has a 10-year patent to a product that will enable contact lens users to get no-maintenance lenses that will last for years. While the product is technically viable, it is exorbitantly expensive to manufacture, and the potential market for it will be relatively small currently. (A cash flow analysis of the project suggests that the present value of the cash inflows on the project, if adopted now, would be $250 million, while the cost of the project will be $500 million.) The technology is rapidly evolving, and a simulation of alternative scenarios yields a wide range of present values, with an annualized standard deviation of 60%. The 10-year bond rate is 6%.
   a. Estimate the value of this company.
   b. How sensitive is this value estimate to the variance in project cash flows? What broader lessons would you draw from this analysis?

CHAPTER 29

The Options to Expand and to Abandon: Valuation Implications

The preceding chapter noted that traditional discounted cash flow valuation does not consider the value of the option that many firms have to delay making an investment and consequently understates the value of these firms. This chapter considers two other options that are often embedded in investments (and consequently in the values of the firms that possess them). The first of these is the option to expand an investment not only in new markets but to new products, to take advantage of favorable conditions. We argue that this option may sometimes make young start-up firms significantly more valuable than the present value of their expected cash flows. The second option is the option to abandon or scale down investments, which can reduce the risk and downside from large investments and therefore make them more valuable.

THE OPTION TO EXPAND

Firms sometimes invest in projects because the investments allow them either to make further investments or to enter other markets in the future. In such cases, we can view the initial projects as yielding options allowing the firm to invest in other projects, and we should therefore be willing to pay a price for such options. Put another way, a firm may accept a negative net present value on the initial project because of the possibility of high positive net present values on future projects.

Payoff on the Option to Expand

The option to expand can be evaluated at the time the initial project is analyzed. Assume that this initial project will give the firm the right to expand and invest in a new project in the future. Assessed today, the expected present value of the cash flows from investing in the future project is V, and the total investment needed for this project is X. The firm has a fixed time horizon, at the end of which it has to make the final decision on whether or not to make the future investment. Finally, the firm cannot move forward on this future investment if it does not take the initial project. This scenario implies the option payoffs shown in Figure 29.1. As you can see, at the expiration of the fixed time horizon the firm will expand into the new project if the present value of the expected cash flows at that point in time exceeds the cost of expansion.

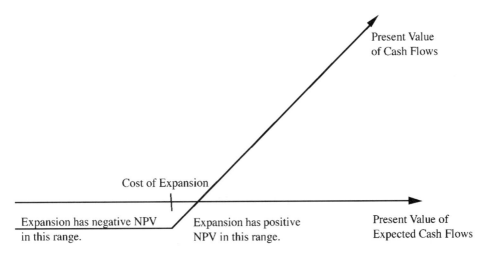

FIGURE 29.1 The Option to Expand a Project

Inputs to Value the Option to Expand   To understand how to estimate the value of the option to expand, let us begin by recognizing that there are two projects usually that drive this option. The first project generally has a negative net present value and is recognized as a poor investment, even by the firm investing in it. The second project is the potential to expand that comes with the first project. It is the second project that represents the underlying asset for the option. The inputs have to be defined accordingly:

- The present value of the cash flows that you would generate if you were to invest in the second project today (the expansion option) is the value of the underlying asset—S in the option pricing model.
- If there is substantial uncertainty about the expansion potential, the present value is likely to be volatile and change over time as circumstances change. It is the variance in this present value that you would want to use to value the expansion option. Since projects are not traded, you have to either estimate this variance from simulations or use the variance in values of publicly traded firms in the business.
- The cost that you would incur up front, if you invest in the expansion today, is the equivalent of the strike price.
- The life of the option is fairly difficult to define, since there is usually no externally imposed exercise period. (This is in contrast to the patents valued in the preceding chapter, which have a legal life that can be used as the option life.) When valuing the option to expand, the life of the option will be an internal constraint imposed by the firm on itself. For instance, a firm that invests on a small scale in China might impose a constraint that it either will expand within five years or pull out of the market. Why might it do so? There may be considerable costs associated with maintaining the small presence or the firm may have scarce resources that have to be committed elsewhere.
- As with other real options, there may be a cost to waiting once the expansion option becomes viable. That cost may take the form of cash flows that will be lost on the expansion project if it is not taken or a cost imposed on the firm until it makes its final decision. For instance, the firm may have to pay a fee every year until it makes its final decision.

ILLUSTRATION 29.1:   Valuing an Option to Expand: Ambev and Guarana

Guarana is a very popular caffeine-based soft drink in Brazil, and Ambev is the Brazilian beverage manufacturer that is the largest producer of Guarana in the world. Assume that Ambev is considering introducing the drink into the United States and that it has decided to do so in two steps:

1. Ambev will initially introduce Guarana in just the large metropolitan areas of the United States to gauge potential demand. The expected cost of this limited introduction is $500 million and the estimated present value of the expected cash flows is only $400 million. In other words, Ambev expects to have a negative net present value of $100 million on this first investment.

2. If the limited introduction turns out to be a success, Ambev expects to introduce Guarana to the rest of the U.S. market. At the moment, though, the firm is not optimistic about this expansion potential and believes that while the cost of the full-scale introduction will be $1 billion, the expected present value of the cash flows is only $750 million (making this a negative net present value investment as well).

At first sight, investing in a poor project to get a chance to invest in an even poorer project may seem like a bad deal, but the second investment does have a redeeming feature. It is an option and Ambev will not make the second investment (of $1 billion) if the expected present value of the cash flows stays below that number. Furthermore, there is considerable uncertainty about the size and potential for this market, and the firm may well find itself with a lucrative investment.

To estimate the value of the second investment as an option, we begin by first identifying the underlying asset—the expansion project—and using the current estimate of expected value ($750 million) as the value of the underlying asset. Since the investment needed for the investment of $1 billion is the exercise price, this option is an out-of-the-money option. The two most problematic assumptions relate to the variance in the value of the underlying asset and the life of the option:

■ We estimated the average standard deviation of 35% in firm values of small, publicly traded beverage companies in the United States and assumed that this would be a good proxy for the standard deviation in the value of the expansion option.

■ We assumed that Ambev would have a five-year window to make its decision. We admit that this is an arbitrary constraint but, in the real world, it may be driven by any of the following:
   Financing constraints (loans will come due).
   Strategic prerogatives (you have to choose where your resources will be invested).
   Personnel decisions (management has to be hired and put in place).

Based on these inputs, we had the following inputs to the option pricing model:

S = Present value of cash flows from expansion option today = $750
K = Exercise price = $1,000
t = 5 years
Standard deviation in value = 35%

We used a riskless rate of 5% and derived the expected up and down movements from the standard deviation:

$$u = 1.4032$$

$$d = 0.6968$$

The binomial tree is presented in Figure 29.2.

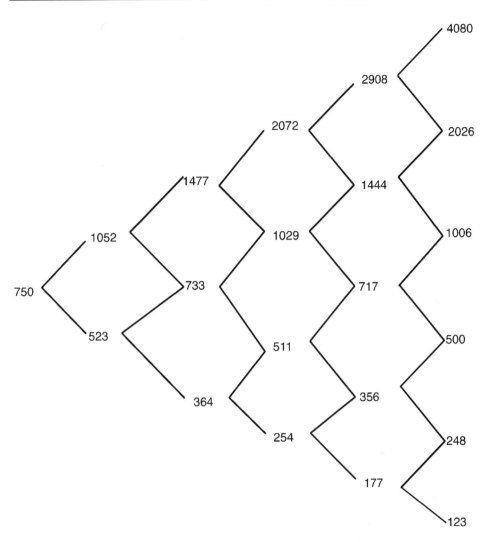

FIGURE 29.2 Binomial Tree—Ambev Expansion Option

Using the replicating portfolio framework described in Chapter 5, we estimate the value of the expansion option to be $203 million. This value can be added on to the net present value of the original project under consideration.

NPV of limited introduction = –500 + 400 = – $100 million

Value of option to expand = $203 million

NPV with option to expand = –$100 million + $203 million = $103 million

Ambev should go ahead with the limited introduction, even though it has a negative net present value, because it acquires an option of much greater value as a consequence.

ESTIMATING VARIANCES FROM MONTE CARLO SIMULATIONS

It has been suggested a couple of times in the last two chapters that the variances to be used in real option pricing models be derived from simulations. A Monte Carlo simulation requires the following three steps:

1. You define probability distributions for each of the key inputs that underlie the cash flows, and the parameters of the distributions—the average and the standard deviation, if it is a normal distribution, for instance.
2. In each simulation, you draw one outcome from each distribution and estimate the present value of the cash flows based on these draws.
3. After repeated simulations you should have a distribution of present values. The mean of this distribution should be the expected value of the project, and the standard deviation of the distribution can be used as the variance in the value to value options on the project.

While the process of running these simulations is straightforward and there are a number of software packages that exist that allow you to do this,[1] we would add the following notes of caution:

- The most difficult step is estimating the probability distributions and parameters for the key variables. It is easier to do when a firm has had experience with similar projects in the past—a retail store considering a new store, for instance—than for a new product or a new market. If the distributions that feed into a simulation are random, the output, impressive though it might look on paper, is meaningless.
- The standard deviation or variance that you want to use in option pricing models is a variance in value over time and not at a point in time. What is the difference, you might ask? Market testing, for instance, provides a distribution for the market potential today and reflects estimation uncertainty. The market itself will evolve over time, and it is the variance in that distribution that we would like to estimate.[2]
- You should estimate the standard deviation in the value of the project—the sum of the present value of the cash flows—rather than the standard deviation in annual income or annual cash flows.

 expand.xls: This spreadsheet allows you to estimate the value of the option to expand a project to cover new markets or new products, using the Black-Scholes model.

[1]Crystal Ball and @Risk are both add-on packages to Excel that allow you to run simulations.
[2]You could, for instance, be fairly certain about the size of the market today—the variance would be low or even zero—but be uncertain about what the market will look like a year from now or three years from now. It is the latter variance that determines the value of the option.

Problems in Valuing the Option to Expand

The practical considerations associated with estimating the value of the option to expand are similar to those associated with valuing the option to delay. In most cases, firms with options to expand have no specific time horizon by which they have to make an expansion decision, making these open-ended options or, at best, options with arbitrary lives. Even in those cases where a life can be estimated for the option, neither the size nor the potential market for the product may be known, and estimating either can be problematic. To illustrate, consider the Ambev example discussed earlier. While we adopted a period of five years, at the end of which Ambev has to decide one way or another on its future expansion in United States, it is entirely possible that this time frame is not specified at the time the initial investment is made. Futhermore, we have assumed that both the cost and the present value of expansion are known at the time of the initial investment. In reality, the firm may not have good estimates for either input before opening the first store, since it does not have much information on the underlying market.

Extensions and Implications of Expansion Options

The option to expand can be used by firms to rationalize investing in projects that have negative net present values but provide significant opportunities to enter new markets or to sell new products. The option pricing approach adds rigor to this argument by estimating the value of this option, and it also provides insight into those occasions when it is most valuable. The option to expand is clearly more valuable for more volatile businesses with higher returns on projects (such as biotechnology or computer software), than it is for stable businesses with lower returns (such as automobile production). We will consider three cases where the expansion option may yield useful insights—strategic acquisitions, research and development expenses, and multistage projects.

Strategic Considerations in Acquisitions In many acquisitions or investments, the acquiring firm believes that the transaction will give it competitive advantages in the future. These competitive advantages include:

- *Entry into a large or growing market.* An investment or acquisition may allow the firm to enter a large or potentially large market much sooner than it otherwise would have been able to do so. A good example of this is the acquisition of a Mexican retail firm by a U.S. firm, with the intent of expanding into the Mexican market.
- *Technological expertise.* In some cases, the acquisition is motivated by the desire to acquire a proprietary technology that will allow the acquirer to either expand its existing market or enter a new market.
- *Brand name.* Firms sometime pay large premiums over market price to acquire firms with valuable brand names, because they believe that these brand names can be used for expansion into new markets in the future.

While all these potential advantages may be used to justify large acquisition premiums, not all of them create valuable options. Even if these advantages can be viewed as valuable expansion options, the value has to be greater than the acquisition premium for stockholders to gain.

Research, Development, and Test Market Expenses   Firms that spend considerable amounts of money on research and development and test marketing are often stymied when they try to evaluate these expenses, since the payoffs are in terms of future projects. At the same time, there is the very real possibility that after the money has been spent the products or projects may turn out not to be viable; consequently, the expenditure must be treated as a sunk cost. In fact, R&D has the characteristics of a call option—the amount spent on the R&D is the cost of the call option, and the projects or products that might emerge from the research provide the payoffs on the options. If these products are viable (i.e., the present value of the cash inflows exceeds the needed investment), the payoff is the difference between the two.

Several logical implications emerge from this view of R&D. First, other things remaining equal, research expenditures should provide much higher value for firms that are in volatile businesses, since the variance in product or project cash flows is positively correlated with the value of the call option. Thus, Minnesota Mining and Manufacturing (3M), which expends a substantial amount on R&D on basic office products such as the Post-it pad, should receive less value for its research than does Amgen, whose research primarily concerns biotechnology products.[3] Second, the value of research and the optimal amount to be spent on research will change over time as businesses mature. The best example is the pharmaceutical industry: Pharmaceutical companies spent most of the 1980s investing substantial amounts in research and earning high returns on new products as health-care costs expanded. In the 1990s, however, as health-care costs started leveling off and the business matured, many of these companies found that they were not getting the same payoffs on research and started cutting back. Some companies moved research dollars from conventional drugs to biotechnology products, where uncertainty about future cash flows remains high.

Multistage Projects/Investments   When entering new businesses or taking new investments, firms sometimes have the option to move in stages. While doing so may reduce potential upside, it also protects the firm against downside risk by allowing it at each stage to gauge demand and decide whether to go on to the next stage. In other words, a standard project can be recast as a series of options to expand, with each option being dependent on the previous one. There are two propositions that follow:

1. Some projects that are unattractive on a full-investment basis may be value-creating if the firm can invest in stages.
2. Some projects that look attractive on a full-investment basis may become even more attractive if taken in stages.

The gain in value from the options created by multistage investments has to be weighed against the cost. Taking investments in stages may allow competitors who decide to enter the market on a full scale to capture the market. It may also lead to

---

[3]This statement is based on the assumption that the quality of research is the same at both firms, though the research is in different businesses, and that the only difference is in the volatility of the underlying businesses.

higher costs at each stage, since the firm is not taking full advantage of economies of scale.

Several implications emerge from viewing this choice between multistage and one-time investments in an option framework. The projects where the gains will be largest from making the investment in multiple stages include:

- *Projects where there are significant barriers to entry to competitors entering the market and taking advantage of delays in full-scale production.* Thus a firm with a patent on a product or other legal protection against competition pays a much smaller price for starting small and expanding as it learns more about the market.
- *Projects where there is uncertainty about the size of the market and the eventual success of the project.* Here, starting small and expanding in stages allows the firm to reduce its losses if the product does not sell as well as anticipated, and to learn more about the market at each stage. This information can be useful in both product design and marketing in subsequent stages.
- *Projects where there is a substantial investment needed in infrastructure and high operating leverage (fixed costs).* Since the savings from doing a project in multiple stages can be traced to the investments needed at each stage, the benefit is likely to be greater in firms where those costs are large. Capital-intensive projects as well as projects that require large initial marketing expenses (a new brand name product for a consumer product company), for example, will gain more from the options created by investing in the projects in multiple stages.

SEQUENTIAL AND COMPOUND OPTIONS: SOME THOUGHTS

A compound option is an option on an option. A simple example would be a call option on a small company that has only one asset—a patent. Last chapter, we argued that a patent could be viewed as an option, and thus the call option on the company becomes a compound option. You can also have a sequence of options where the value of each option is dependent on whether the previous option is exercised. For instance, a five-stage project has sequential options. Whether you reach the fifth stage is obviously a function of whether you make it through the first four stages; the value of the fifth option in the sequence is determined by what happens to the first four options.

Needless to say, option pricing becomes more complicated when you have sequential and compound options. There are two choices. One is to value these options as simple options and accept the fact that the value that you obtain will be an approximation. The other is to modify the option pricing model to allow for the special characteristics of these options. While we do not consider these models in this book, you can modify both the Black-Scholes and binomial models to allow them to price compound and sequential options.

WHEN ARE EXPANSION OPTIONS VALUABLE?

While the argument that some or many investments have valuable strategic or expansion options embedded in them has great allure, there is a danger that this argument can be used to justify poor investments. In fact, acquirers have long justified huge premiums on acquisitions on synergistic and strategic grounds. We need to be more rigorous in our measurement of the value of real options and in our use of real options as justification for paying high prices or making poor investments.

Quantitative Estimation

When real options are used to justify a decision, the justification has to be in more than qualitative terms. In other words, managers who argue for investing in a project with poor returns or paying a premium on an acquisition on the basis of the real options generated by this investment should be required to value these real options and show that the economic benefits exceed the costs. There will be two arguments made against this requirement. The first is that real options cannot be easily valued, since the inputs are difficult to obtain and often noisy. The second is that the inputs to option pricing models can be easily manipulated to back up whatever the conclusion might be. While both arguments have some basis, an estimate is better than no estimate at all, and the process of trying to estimate the value of a real option is, in fact, the first step to understanding what drives its value.

Tests for Expansion Option to Have Value

Not all investments have options embedded in them, and not all options, even if they do exist, have significant value. To assess whether an investment creates valuable options that need to be analyzed and valued, we need to answer three key questions.

1. *Is the first investment a prerequisite for the later investment/expansion? If not, how necessary is the first investment for the later investment/expansion?* Consider our earlier analysis of the value of a patent or the value of an undeveloped oil reserve as options. A firm cannot generate patents without investing in research or paying another firm for the patents, and it cannot get rights to an undeveloped oil reserve without spending on exploration, bidding on it at a government auction, or buying it from another oil company. Clearly, the initial investment here (spending on R&D, bidding at the auction) is required for the firm to have the second investment. Now consider the Ambev investment in a limited introduction and the option to expand into the U.S. market later. The initial investment provides Ambev with information about market potential, without which presumably it is unwilling to expand into the larger market. Unlike the patent and undeveloped reserves examples, the initial investment is not a prerequisite for the second, though management might view it as such. The connection gets even weaker, and the option value lower, when we look at one firm acquiring another to have the option to be able to enter a large market. Acquiring an Internet service provider in order to have a foothold in the Internet retailing market or buying a Chinese brewery to preserve the option to enter the Chinese beer market would be examples of less valuable options.

2. *Does the firm have an exclusive right to the later investment/expansion? If not, does the initial investment provide the firm with significant competitive advantages on subsequent investments?* The value of the option ultimately derives not from the cash flows generated by the second and subsequent investments, but from the excess returns generated by these cash flows. The greater the potential for excess returns on the second investment, the greater the value of the expansion option in the first investment. The potential for excess returns is closely tied to how much of a competitive advantage the first investment provides the firm when it takes subsequent investments. At one extreme, again, consider investing in research and development to acquire a patent. The patent gives the firm that owns it the exclusive rights to produce that product, and if the market potential is large, the right to the excess returns from the project. At the other extreme, the firm might get no competitive advantages on subsequent investments, in which case, it is questionable as to whether there can be any excess returns on these investments. In reality, most investments will fall in the continuum between these two extremes, with greater competitive advantages being associated with higher excess returns and larger option values.

3. *Are the competitive advantages sustainable?* In a competitive marketplace, excess returns attract competitors, and competition drives out excess returns. The more sustainable the competitive advantages possessed by a firm, the greater will be the value of the options embedded in the initial investment. The sustainability of competitive advantages is a function of two forces. The first is the nature of the competition; other things remaining equal, competitive advantages fade much more quickly in sectors where there are aggressive competitors. The second is the nature of the competitive advantage. If the resource controlled by the firm is finite and scarce (as is the case with natural resource reserves and vacant land), the competitive advantage is likely to be sustainable for longer periods. Alternatively, if the competitive advantage comes from being the first mover in a market or from having technological expertise, it will come under assault far sooner. The most direct way of reflecting this competitive advantage in the value of the option is to estimate the period of competitive advantage, and only the excess returns earned over this period count toward the value of the option.

If the answer is yes to all three questions, then the option to expand can be valuable. Applying the last two tests to the Ambev expansion option, you can see the potential problems. While Ambev is the largest producer of Guarana in the world, it does not have a patent on the product. If the initial introduction proves successful, it is entirely possible that Coke and Pepsi could produce their own versions of Guarana for the national market. If this occurs, Ambev will have expended $100 million of its funds to provide market information to its competitors. Thus, if Ambev gets no competitive advantage in the expansion market because of its initial investment, the option to expand ceases to have value and cannot be used to justify the initial investment. Now consider two intermediate scenarios: If Ambev gets a lead time on the expansion investment because of its initial investment, you could build in higher cash flows for that lead time and a fading off to lower cash flows thereafter. This will lower the present value of the cash flows for the expansion and the value of the option. A simpler adjustment would be to cap the present value of the cash flows, the argument being that competition will restrict how large the net present value can become, and value the option with the cap. For instance, if you assume that the present value of the cash flows from the expansion option cannot exceed $2 billion, the value of the expansion option drops to $142 million.[4]

VALUING A FIRM WITH THE OPTION TO EXPAND

Is there an option to expand embedded in some firms that can lead to these firms to trade at a premium over their discounted cash flow values? At least in theory, there is a rationale for making this argument for a small, high-growth firm in a large and evolving market. The discounted cash flow valuation is based on expected cash flows and expected growth and these expectations should reflect the probability that the firm could be hugely successful (or a huge failure). What the expectations might fail to consider is that, in the event of success, the firm could invest more, add new products or expand into new markets and augment this success. This is the real option that is creating the additional value.

Relationship to Discounted Cash Flow Valuation

If the value of this option to expand is estimated, the value of a firm can be written as the sum of two components—a discounted cash flow value based on expected cash flows and a value associated with the option to expand:

$$\text{Value of firm} = \text{Discounted cash flow value} + \text{Option to expand}$$

The option pricing approach adds rigor to this argument by estimating the value of the option to expand, and it also provides insight into those occasions when it is most valuable. In general, the option to expand is clearly more valuable for more volatile businesses with higher returns on projects and greater barriers to competitive entry (such as biotechnology), than in stable businesses with lower returns (such as housing, utilities, or automobile production).

Again, though, you have to be careful not to double count the value of the option. If you use a higher growth rate than would be justified based on expectations because of the option to expand, you have already counted the value of the option in the discounted cash flow valuation. Adding an additional component to reflect the value of the option would be double counting.

Inputs for Valuing Expansion Option   To value a firm with the option to expand, you have to begin by defining the market that the firm has the option to enter and specify the competitive advantages that you believe will give it some degree of exclusivity to make this entry. Once you are convinced that there is this exclusivity, you should then estimate the expected cash flows you would get if you entered the market today and the cost of entering that market. Presumably, the costs will exceed the expected cash flows, or you would have entered the market already. The cost of entering the market will become the exercise price of the option and the expected cash flows from entering the market today will become the value of the underlying asset.

---

[4]You can value the capped call by valuing the expansion option twice in the Black-Scholes model, once with a strike price of $1,000 (yielding the original expansion option value of $218 million) and once with the strike price of $2,000 (yield an option value of $76 million). The difference between the two is the value of the expansion option with a cap on the present value. You could also value it explicitly in the binomial by setting the value to $2,000 whenever it exceeds that number in the binomial tree.

To estimate the variance in the value, you can either run simulations on how the market will evolve over time or use the variances of publicly traded firms that service that market today, and assume that this variance is a good proxy for the volatility in the underlying market. You also have to specify a period by which you have to make the decision of whether to enter the market; this will become the life of the option. You may tie this assumption to the assumptions you made about competitive advantages. For instance, if you have the exclusive license to enter a market for the next 10 years, you would use 10 years as your option life.

ILLUSTRATION 29.2: Considering the Value of the Option to Expand

Rediff.com is an Internet portal serving the Indian subcontinent. In June 2000 the firm had only a few million in revenues, but tremendous growth potential as a portal and electronic marketplace. Using a discounted cash flow model, you could value Rediff.com at $474 million, based on its expected cash flows in the Internet portal business. Assume that in buying Rediff.com, you are in fact buying an option to expand in the online market in India. This market is a small one now, but could potentially be much larger in 5 or 10 years.

In more specific terms, assume that Rediff.com has the option to enter the Internet retailing business in India in the future. The cost of entering this business is expected to be $1 billion, and, based on current expectations, the present value of the cash flows that would be generated by entering this business today is only $500 million. Based on current expectations of the growth in the Indian e-commerce business, this investment clearly does not make sense.

There is substantial uncertainty about future growth in online retailing in India and the overall performance of the Indian economy. If the economy booms and the online market grows faster than expected over the next five years, Rediff.com might be able to create value from entering this market. If you leave the cost of entering the online retailing business at $1 billion, the present value of the cash flows would have to increase above this value for Rediff to enter this business and add value. The standard deviation in the present value of the expected cash flows (which is currently $500 million) is assumed to be 50%.

The value of the option to expand into Internet retailing can now be estimated using an option pricing model, with the following parameters:

S = Present value of the expected cash flows from entering market today = $500 million
K = Cost of entering the market today = $1 billion
σ^2 = Variance in the present value of expected cash flows = $0.5^2 = 0.25$
r = 5.8% (This is a five-year Treasury bond rate; the analysis is being done in U.S. dollar terms)
t = 5 years

The value of the option to expand can be estimated as follows:

$$\text{Option to expand} = 500(0.5786) - 1{,}000\ \exp^{-(0.058)(5)}(0.1789) = \$155.47 \text{ million}$$

Why does the option expire in five years? If the online retail market in India expands beyond this point in time, it is assumed that there will be other potential entrants into this market and that Rediff.com will have no competitive advantages and hence no good reason for entering this market. If the online retail market in India expands sooner than expected, it is assumed that Rediff.com, as one of the few recognized names in the market, will be able to parlay its brand name and the visitors to its portal to establish competitive advantages.

The value of Rediff.com as a firm can now be estimated as the sum of the discounted cash flow value of $474 million and the value of the option to expand into the retail market ($155 million). It is true that the discounted cash flow valuation is based on a high growth rate in revenues, but all of this growth is assumed to occur in the Internet portal business and not in online retailing.

In fact, the option to enter online retailing is only one of several options available to Rediff. Another path it might embark on is to become a development exchange for resources—software developers and programmers in India looking for programming work in the United States and other developed markets. The value of this option can also be estimated using an approach similar to the one just shown.

expand.xls: This spreadsheet allows you to estimate the value of the option to expand an investment or project.

VALUE OF FINANCIAL FLEXIBILITY

When making financial decisions, managers consider the effects of such decisions on their capacity to make new investments or meet unanticipated contingencies in future periods. Practically, this translates into firms maintaining excess debt capacity or larger cash balances than are warranted by current needs in order to meet unexpected future requirements. While maintaining this financing flexibility has value to firms, it also has a cost; the large cash balances might earn below-market returns, and excess debt capacity implies that the firm is giving up some value and has a higher cost of capital.

Determinants of the Value of Financial Flexibility

One reason that a firm maintains large cash balances and excess debt capacity is to have the future option to take unexpected projects with high returns. To value financial flexibility as an option, assume that a firm has expectations about how much it will need to reinvest in future periods, based on its own past history and current conditions in the industry. Assume also that a firm has expectations about how much it can raise from internal funds and its normal access to capital markets in future periods. There is uncertainty about future reinvestment needs; for simplicity, we will assume that the capacity to generate funds is known with certainty to the firm. The advantage (and value) of having excess debt capacity or large cash balances is that the firm can meet any reinvestment needs, in excess of funds available, using its debt capacity. The payoff from these projects, however, comes from the excess returns the firm expects to make on them. To value financial flexibility on an annualized basis, therefore, we will use the measures listed in Table 29.1.

TABLE 29.1 Inputs to Option Valuation: Financing Flexibility

Input to Model	Measure	Estimation Approach
S	Expected annual reinvestment needs as percent of firm value	Use historical average of (Net cap ex + Change in noncash working capital)/Market value of firm
K	Annual reinvestment needs as percent of firm value that can be raised without financing flexibility	If firm does not want to or cannot use external financing: (Net income – Dividend + Depreciation)/ Market value of firm. If firm uses external capital (bank debt, bonds, or equity) regularly: (Net income + Depreciation + Net external financing)/Market value of firm
σ^s	Variance in reinvestment needs	Variance in the reinvestment as percent of firm value (using historical data)
t	1 year	To get an annual estimate of the value of flexibility

ILLUSTRATION 29.3:   Valuing Financial Flexibility at the Home Depot

The Home Depot is a giant retail chain that sells home improvement products, primarily in the United States. This firm traditionally has not been a heavy user of debt and has also grown at an extraordinary rate over the past decade. To estimate the value of financial flexibility for the Home Depot, we began by estimating reinvestments as a percent of firm value from 1989 to 1998 in the following table:

Year	Reinvestment Needs	Firm Value	Reinvestment Needs as Percent of Firm Value	In (Reinvestment Needs)
1989	$ 175	$ 2,758	6.35%	−2.7574751
1990	$ 374	$ 3,815	9.80%	−2.3224401
1991	$ 427	$ 5,137	8.31%	−2.4874405
1992	$ 456	$ 7,148	6.38%	−2.7520951
1993	$ 927	$ 9,239	10.03%	−2.2992354
1994	$1,176	$12,477	9.43%	−2.3617681
1995	$1,344	$15,470	8.69%	−2.4432524
1996	$1,086	$19,535	5.56%	−2.8897065
1997	$1,589	$24,156	6.58%	−2.7214279
1998	$1,817	$30,219	6.01%	−2.8112841

Average reinvestment needs as % of firm value = 7.71%

Standard deviation in ln(Reinvestment needs) = 22.36%

We followed up by estimating internal funds as a percent of firm value, using the sum of net income and depreciation as a measure of internal funds:

Year	Net Income	Depreciation	Firm Value	Internal Funds/ Value
1989	$ 112	$ 21	$ 2,758	4.82%
1990	$ 163	$ 34	$ 3,815	5.16%
1991	$ 249	$ 52	$ 5,137	5.86%
1992	$ 363	$ 70	$ 7,148	6.06%
1993	$ 457	$ 90	$ 9,239	5.92%
1994	$ 605	$130	$12,477	5.89%
1995	$ 732	$181	$15,470	5.90%
1996	$ 938	$232	$19,535	5.99%
1997	$1,160	$283	$24,156	5.97%
1998	$1,614	$373	$30,219	6.58%

Internal funds, on average, were 5.82% of firm value between 1989 and 1998. Since the firm uses almost no external debt, the firm made up the difference between its reinvestment needs (7.71%) and internal fund generation (5.82%) by issuing equity. We will assume, looking forward, that the Home Depot will no longer issue new equity.

The Home Depot's current debt ratio is 4.55%, and its current cost of capital is 9.51%. Using the cost of capital framework developed in Chapter 15, we estimated its optimal debt ratio to be 20%, and its cost of capital at that debt level is 9.17%. Finally, the Home Depot in 1998 earned a return on capital of 16.37%, and we will assume that this is the expected return on new projects as well.

> S = Expected reinvestment needs as percent of firm value = 7.71%
> K = Reinvestment needs that can be financed without flexibility = 5.82%
> t = 1 year
> σ^2 = Variance in ln(Net capital expenditures) = $(.2237)^2$ = .05

With a risk-free rate of 6%, the option value that we estimate using these inputs is .02277. We then convert this option value into a measure of value over time by multiplying the value by the annual excess return and then assuming that the firm forgoes this excess return forever:[5]

$$\text{Value of flexibility} = .02277(\text{Return on capital} - \text{Cost of capital})/\text{Cost of capital}$$
$$= .02277(.1637 - .0951)/.0951 = 1.6425\%$$

On an annual basis, the flexibility generated by the excess debt capacity is worth 1.6425% of firm value at the Home Depot, which is well in excess of the savings (9.51% – 9.17% = 0.34%) in the cost of capital that would be accomplished, if it used up the excess debt capacity.

The one final consideration here is that this estimate does not consider the fact that the Home Depot does not have unlimited financial flexibility. In fact, assume that excess debt capacity of the Home Depot (which is 15.45%, the difference between the optimal debt ratio and the current debt ratio) is the upside limit on financial flexibility. We can value the effect of this limit, by valuing a call with the same parameters as the call described earlier, but with a strike price of 21.27% (15.45% + 5.82%). In this case, the effect of imposing this constraint on the value of flexibility is negligible.

---

 finflex.xls: This spreadsheet allows you to estimate the value of financial flexibility as an option.

Implications of Financial Flexibility Option

Looking at financial flexibility as an option yields valuable insights on when financial flexibility is most valuable. Using the approach developed earlier, for instance, we would argue that:

- Other things remaining equal, firms operating in businesses where projects earn substantially higher returns than their hurdle rates should value flexibility more than those that operate in stable businesses where excess returns are small. This would imply that firms such as Microsoft and Dell, which earn large excess returns on their projects, can use the need for financial flexibility as justification for holding large cash balances and maintaining excess debt capacity.
- Since a firm's ability to fund these reinvestment needs is determined by its capacity to generate internal funds, other things remaining equal, financial flexibility should be worth less to firms with large and stable earnings as a percent of firm value. Firms that have small or negative earnings, and therefore much lower capacity to generate internal funds, will value flexibility more.
- Firms with limited internal funds can still get away with little or no financial flexibility if they can tap external markets for capital—bank debt, bonds, and new equity issues. Other things remaining equal, the greater the capacity (and the willingness) of a firm to raise funds from external capital markets, the less should be the value of flexibility. This may explain why private or small firms,

---

[5]We are assuming that the project that a firm is unable to take because it lacks financial flexibility is lost forever, and that the excess returns on this project would also have lasted forever. Both assumptions are strong and may result in overstatement of the lost value.

which have far less access to capital, will value financial flexibility more than larger firms. The existence of corporate bond markets can also make a difference in how much flexibility is valued. In markets where firms cannot issue bonds and have to depend entirely on banks for financing, there is less access to capital and a greater need to maintain financial flexibility. In the Home Depot example, a willingness to tap external funds—debt or equity—would reduce the value of flexibility substantially.

■ The need for and the value of flexibility is a function of how uncertain a firm is about future reinvestment needs. Firms with predictable reinvestment needs should value flexibility less than firms in businesses where reinvestment needs are volatile on a period-to-period basis.

In our analysis of Home Depot, we considered the firm's gross debt ratio, which cannot be less than 0 percent. If we consider a firm's net debt ratio (gross debt minus cash), we see it is entirely possible for a firm to have a negative net debt ratio. Extending the financing flexibility argument, you could argue that in extreme circumstances—low or negative internal cash flows and no access to capital markets—firms not only will not use their debt capacity (thus driving the gross debt ratio to zero) but will accumulate cash. This may explain why many emerging market firms and young technology firms use no debt and accumulate large cash balances.

THE OPTION TO ABANDON

When investing in new projects, firms worry about the risk that the investment will not pay off, and that actual cash flows will not measure up to expectations. Having the option to abandon a project that does not pay off can be valuable, especially on projects with a significant potential for losses. This section examines the value of the option to abandon and its determinants.

Payoff on the Option to Abandon

The option pricing approach provides a general way of estimating and building in the value of abandonment. To illustrate, assume that V is the remaining value on a project if it continues to the end of its life, and L is the liquidation or abandonment value for the same project at the same point in time. If the project has a remaining life of n years, the value of continuing the project can be compared to the liquidation (abandonment) value. If the value from continuing is higher, the project should be continued; if the value of abandonment is higher, the holder of the abandonment option could consider abandoning the project. The payoffs can be written as:

$$\text{Payoff from owning an abandonment option} = 0 \quad \text{if } V > L$$
$$= L - V \quad \text{if } V \leq L$$

These payoffs are graphed in Figure 29.3, as a function of the expected stock price. Unlike the prior two cases, the option to abandon takes on the characteristics of a put option.

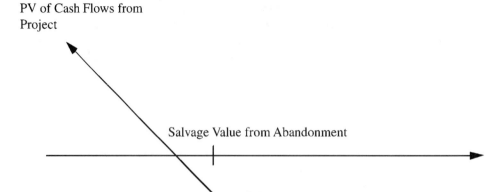

PV of Cash Flows from
Project

Salvage Value from Abandonment

FIGURE 29.3   The Option to Abandon a Project

ILLUSTRATION 29.4:   Valuing an Option to Abandon: Airbus and Lear Aircraft

---

Assume that Lear Aircraft is interested in building a small passenger plane and that it approaches Airbus with a proposal for a joint venture. Each firm will invest $500 million in the joint venture and produce the planes. The investment is expected to have a 30-year life. Airbus works through a traditional investment analysis and concludes that its share of the present value of the expected cash flows would be only $480 million. The net present value of the project would therefore be negative and Airbus would not want to be part of this joint venture.

On rejection of the joint venture, Lear approaches Airbus with a sweetener, offering to buy out Airbus's 50% share of the joint venture any time over the next five years for $400 million. This is less than what Airbus will invest initially but it puts a floor on its losses and thus gives Airbus an abandonment option. To value this option to Airbus, note that the inputs are as follows:

> S = Present value of the share of cash flows from the investment today = $480 million
> K = Abandonment value = $400 million
> t = Period for which abandonment option holds = 5 years

To estimate the variance, assume that Airbus employs a Monte Carlo simulation on the project analysis and estimates a standard deviation in project value of 25%. Finally, note that since the project is a finite-life project, the present value will decline over time, because there will be fewer years of cash flows left. For simplicity, we will assume that this will be proportional to the time left on the project:

> Dividend yield = 1/Remaining life of the project = 1/30 = 3.33%

Inputting these values into the Black-Scholes model and using a 5% riskless rate, we value the put option as follows:

$$\text{Value of abandonment option} = 400 \exp^{(-0.05)(5)}(1 - 0.5776) - 480 \exp^{(-0.033)(5)}(1 - 0.7748)$$
$$= \$40.09 \text{ million}$$

Since this is greater than the negative net present value of the investment, Airbus should enter into this joint venture. On the other hand, Lear needs to be able to generate a positive net present value of at least $40.09 million to compensate for giving up this option.[6]

---

[6]The binomial model yields a value of $46.44 million for this option.

abandon.xls: This spreadsheet allows you to estimate the value of the option to abandon an investment.

Problems in Valuing the Option to Abandon

Illustration 29.4 assumed, rather unrealistically, that the abandonment value was clearly specified and did not change during the life of the project. This may be true in some very specific cases, in which an abandonment option is built into the contract. More often, however, the firm has the option to abandon, and the salvage value from abandonment can only be estimated. Further, the abandonment value may change over the life of the project, making it difficult to apply traditional option pricing techniques. Finally, it is entirely possible that abandoning a project may not bring in a liquidation value but may create costs instead; a manufacturing firm may have to pay severance to its workers, for instance. In such cases, it would not make sense to abandon unless the cash flows on the project are even more negative.

Extensions and Implications of Abandonment Options

The fact that the option to abandon has value provides a rationale for firms to build the operating flexibility to scale back or terminate projects if they do not measure up to expectations. It also indicates that firms that try to generate more revenues by offering their customers the option to walk away from commitments will have to weigh the higher revenues against the cost of the options that have been granted to these customers.

Escape Clauses in Contracts The first and most direct way of creating an abandonment option is to build operating flexibility contractually with other parties that are involved in a project. Thus contracts with suppliers may be written on an annual basis rather than be long-term, and employees may be hired on a temporary basis rather than permanently. The physical plant used for a project may be leased on a short-term basis rather than bought, and the financial investment may be made in stages rather than as an initial lump sum. While there is a cost to building in this flexibility, the gains may be much larger, especially in volatile businesses.

Customer Incentives On the other side of the transaction, offering abandonment options to customers and partners in joint ventures can have a negative impact on value. As an example, assume that a firm that sells its products on multiyear contracts offers customers the option to cancel the contract at any time. While this may increase sales, there is likely to be a substantial cost. In the event of a recession, customers that are unable to meet their obligations are likely to cancel their contracts. Any benefits gained by the initial sale (obtained by offering the inducement of cancellation by the buyer) may be offset by the cost of the option provided to customers.

RECONCILING NET PRESENT VALUE AND REAL OPTION VALUATIONS

Why does an investment sometimes have higher value when you value it using real option approaches than with traditional discounted cash flow models? The answer lies in the flexibility that firms have to change the way they invest in and run a project, based on what they observe in the market. Thus, an oil company will not produce the same amount of oil or drill as many new wells if oil prices go to $15 a barrel as it would if oil prices go up to $35 a barrel.

In traditional net present value, we consider the expected actions and the cash flow consequences of those actions to estimate the value of an investment. If there is a potential for further investments, expansion, or abandonment down the road, all you can do is consider the probabilities of such actions and build them into your cash flows. Analysts often allow for flexibility by using decision trees and mapping out the optimal path, given each outcome. You can then estimate the value of a project today, using the probabilities of each branch and estimating the present value of the cash flows from each branch. For instance, you have a decision tree for a new investment for the Home Depot in Figure 29.4.

This decision tree does bear a significant resemblance to the binomial tree approach that we use to value real options, but there are two differences. The first is that the probabilities of the outcomes are not used directly to value the real option, and the second is that you have only two branches at each node in the binomial tree. Notwithstanding this, you might wonder why the two approaches will yield different values for the project. The answer is surprisingly simple. It lies in the discount rate assumptions we make to compute the value. In the real options approach, you use a replicating portfolio to compute value. In the decision tree, you used the cost of capital for the project as the discount rate all through the process. If the exposure to market risk, which is what determines the cost of capital, changes at each node, you can argue that using the same cost of capital all the way through is incorrect and that you should be modifying the discount rate as you move through time. If you do, you will obtain the same value with both approaches. The real options approach does allow

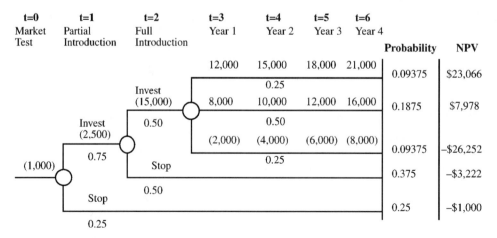

FIGURE 29.4 Decision Tree for the Home Depot Home Shopping

for far more complexity and is simpler to employ with continuous distributions (as opposed to the discrete outcomes that we assume in decision trees).

CONCLUSION

This chapter considers two options that are embedded in many investments—the option to expand an investment and the option to abandon it. When a firm has an option to expand an investment, the value of this expansion option may sometimes allow it to override the fact that the initial investment has a negative net present value. Extending this concept to firm valuation, you may sometimes add a premium to the value obtained from a discounted cash flow valuation for a firm that has the potential to enter new markets or create new products. This expansion option has maximum value when the firm has the exclusive right to make these investments, and the value decreases as the competitive advantages enjoyed by the firm decline.

The option to abandon refers to the right that firms often possess to walk away from poor investments. To the extent that this reduces the firm's exposure to the worst outcomes, it can make the difference between investing in a new project and not investing.

QUESTIONS AND SHORT PROBLEMS

1. NBC has the rights to televise the Winter Olympics in two years, and is trying to estimate the value of these rights for possible sale to another network. NBC expects it to cost $40 million (in present value terms) to televise the Olympics, and based on current assessments expects to have a Nielsen rating[7] of 15 for the games. Each rating point is expected to yield net revenue of $2 million to NBC (in present value terms). There is substantial variability in this estimate, and the standard deviation in the expected net revenues is 30%. The riskless rate is 5%.
   a. What is the net present value of these rights, based on current assessments?
   b. Estimate the value of these rights for sale to another network.
2. You are analyzing Skates Inc., a firm that manufactures skateboards. The firm is currently unlevered and has a cost of equity of 12%. You estimate that Skates would have a cost of capital of 11% at its optimal debt ratio of 40%. The management, however, insists that it will not borrow the money because of the value of maintaining financial flexibility and has provided you with the following information:
   - Over the past 10 years, reinvestment (net capital expenditures + working capital investments) has amounted to 10% of firm value, on an annual basis. The standard deviation in this reinvestment has been 0.30.
   - The firm has traditionally used only internal funding (net income + depreciation) to meet these needs, and these have amounted to 6% of firm value.
   - In the most recent year, the firm earned $180 million in net income on a book value of equity of $1 billion, and it expects to earn these excess returns on new investments in the future.
   - The riskless rate is 5%.

---

[7] There are 99.4 million households in the United States. Each rating point represents 1 percent of roughly 994,000 households.

a. Estimate the value of financial flexibility as a percent of firm value on an annual basis.

b. Based on part a, would you recommend that Skates use its excess debt capacity?

3. Disney is considering entering into a joint venture to build condominiums in Vail, Colorado, with a local real estate developer. The development is expected to cost $1 billion overall and, based on Disney's estimate of the cash flows, generate $900 million in present value cash flows over 25 years. Disney will have a 40% share of the joint venture (requiring it to put up $400 million of the initial investment and entitling it to 40% of the cash flows) but it will have the right to sell its share of the venture back to the developer for $300 million anytime over the next five years. (The project life is 25 years.)

a. If the standard deviation in real estate values in Vail is 30% and the riskless rate is 5%, estimate the value of the abandonment option to Disney.

b. Would you advise Disney to enter into the joint venture?

c. If you were advising the developer, how much would he need to generate in present value cash flows from the investment to make this a good investment?

4. Quality Wireless is considering making an investment in China. While it knows that the investment will cost $1 billion and generate only $800 million in cash flows (in present value terms), the proponents of expansion are arguing that the potential market is huge and that Quality should go ahead with its investment.

a. Under what conditions will the expansion potential have option value?

b. Assume now that there is an option value to expansion that exactly offsets the negative net present value on the initial investment. If the cost of the subsequent expansion in five years is $2.5 billion, what is your current estimate of the present value of the cash flows from expansion? (You can assume that the standard deviation in the present value of the cash flows is 25% and that the riskless rate is 6%.)

5. Reliable Machinery Inc. is considering expanding its operations in Thailand. The initial analysis of the project yields the following results:

■ The project is expected to generate $85 million in after-tax cash flows every year for the next 10 years.

■ The initial investment in the project is expected to be $750 million.

■ The cost of capital for the project is 12%.

If the project generates much higher cash flows than anticipated, you will have the exclusive right for the next 10 years (from a manufacturing license) to expand operations into the rest of Southeast Asia. A current analysis suggests the following about the expansion opportunity:

■ The expansion will cost $2 billion (in current dollars).

■ The expansion is expected to generate $150 million in after-tax cash flows each year for 15 years. There is substantial uncertainty about these cash flows, and the standard deviation in the present value is 40%.

■ The cost of capital for this investment is expected to be 12% as well. The risk-free rate is 6.5%.

a. Estimate the net present value of the initial investment.

b. Estimate the value of the expansion option.

CHAPTER 30

Valuing Equity in Distressed Firms

Chapter 22 examined how discounted cash flow models could be adapted to value firms with negative earnings. Most of the solutions estimated the expected cash flows into the future, and assumed that an improvement in margins or earnings would result in positive cash flows and firm value. In the special case where the firm has substantial amounts of debt, we argued that there is a very real possibility of defaulting on the debt and going bankrupt. In these cases, discounted cash flow valuation may be an inadequate tool for estimating value. This chapter looks at firms with negative earnings, significant assets in place, and substantial debt. We argue that the equity investors in this firm, given limited liability, have the option to liquidate the firm and pay off the debt. This call option on the underlying firm can add value to equity, especially when there is significant uncertainty about the value of the assets.

EQUITY IN HIGHLY LEVERED DISTRESSED FIRMS

In most publicly traded firms, equity has two features. The first is that the equity investors run the firm and can choose to liquidate its assets and pay off other claim holders at any time. The second is that the liability of equity investors in some private firms and almost all publicly traded firms is restricted to their equity investments in these firms. This combination of the option to liquidate and limited liability allows equity to have the features of a call option. In firms with substantial liabilities and negative earnings, the option value of equity may be in excess of the discounted cash flow value.

Payoff on Equity as an Option

The equity in a firm is a residual claim, that is, equity holders lay claim to all cash flows left after other financial claimholders (debt, preferred stock, etc.) have been satisfied. If a firm is liquidated, the same principle applies; equity investors receive the cash that is left in the firm after all outstanding debt and other financial claims have been paid off. With limited liability, if the value of the firm is less than the value of the outstanding debt, equity investors cannot lose more than their investment in the firm. The payoff to equity investors on liquidation can therefore be written as:

$$\text{Payoff to equity on liquidation} = V - D \quad \text{if } V > D$$
$$= 0 \qquad \text{if } V \le D$$

where V = Liquidation value of the firm
        D = Face value of the outstanding debt and other nonequity claims

Equity can thus be viewed as a call option on the firm, where exercising the option requires that the firm be liquidated and the face value of the debt (which corresponds to the exercise price) be paid off. The firm is the underlying asset and the option expires when the debt comes due. The payoffs are shown in Figure 30.1.

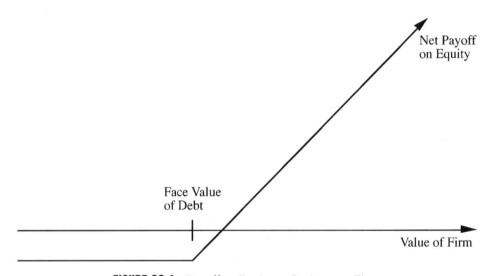

FIGURE 30.1   Payoff on Equity as Option on a Firm

IMPORTANCE OF LIMITED LIABILITY

The argument that equity is a call option holds only if equity has limited liability—that is, the most that an equity investor can lose is what he or she has invested in a firm. This is clearly the case in publicly traded companies. In private companies, however, the owners often have unlimited liability. If these firms get into financial trouble and are unable to make their debt payments, the owner's personal assets can be put at risk. You should not value equity as a call option in these cases.

ILLUSTRATION 30.1:   Valuing Equity as an Option

Assume that you are valuing the equity in a firm whose assets are currently valued at $100 million; the standard deviation in this asset value is 40%. The face value of debt is $80 million (it is zero coupon debt with 10 years left to maturity). The 10-year Treasury bond rate is 10%. We can value equity as a call option on the firm, using the following inputs for the option pricing model:

Value of the underlying asset = S = Value of the firm = $100 million
Exercise price = K = Face value of outstanding debt = $80 million
Life of the option = t = Life of zero coupon debt = 10 years
Variance in the value of the underlying asset = σ^2 = Variance in firm value = 0.16
Riskless rate = r = Treasury bond rate corresponding to option life = 10%

Based on these inputs, the Black-Scholes model provides the following value for the call:

$$d1 = 1.5994 \quad N(d1) = 0.9451$$
$$d2 = 0.3345 \quad N(d2) = 0.6310$$
$$\text{Value of the call} = 100(0.9451) - 80 \text{ exp}^{(-0.10)(10)}(0.6310) = \$75.94 \text{ million}$$

Since the call value represents the value of equity, and the firm value is $100 million, the estimated value of the outstanding debt is:

$$\text{Value of the outstanding debt} = \$100 - \$75.94 = \$24.06 \text{ million}$$

The debt is a 10-year zero coupon bond, and the market interest rate on the bond is:

$$\text{Interest rate on debt} = (\$80/\$24.06)^{1/10} - 1 = 12.77\%$$

Thus the default spread on this bond should be 2.77%.

IMPLICATIONS OF VIEWING EQUITY AS AN OPTION

When the equity in a firm takes on the characteristics of a call option, you have to change the way you think about its value and what determines its value. In this section, we will consider a number of potential implications for equity investors and bondholders in the firm.

When Will Equity Be Worthless?

In discounted cash flow valuation, we argue that equity is worthless if what you own (the value of the firm) is less than what you owe. The first implication of viewing equity as a call option is that equity will have value, even if the value of the firm falls well below the face value of the outstanding debt. While the firm will be viewed as troubled by investors, accountants, and analysts, its equity is not worthless. In fact, just as deep out-of-the-money traded options command value because of the possibility that the value of the underlying asset may increase above the strike price in the remaining lifetime of the option, equity commands value because of the time premium on the option (the time until the bonds mature and come due) and the possibility that the value of the assets may increase above the face value of the bonds before they come due.

ILLUSTRATION 30.2: Firm Value and Equity Value

Revisiting the preceding example, assume that the value of the firm drops to $50 million, below the face value of the outstanding debt ($80 million). Assume that all the other inputs remain unchanged. The parameters of equity as a call option are as follows:

Value of the underlying asset = S = Value of the firm = $50 million
Exercise price = K = Face value of outstanding debt = $80 million
Life of the option = t = Life of zero coupon debt = 10 years
Variance in the value of the underlying asset = σ^2 = Variance in firm value = 0.16
Riskless rate = r = Treasury bond rate corresponding to option life = 10%

Based on these inputs, the Black-Scholes model provides the following value for the call:

$$d1 = 1.0515 \qquad N(d1) = 0.8534$$
$$d2 = -0.2135 \qquad N(d2) = 0.4155$$

$$\text{Value of the call (equity)} = 50(0.8534) - 80\ \exp^{(-0.10)(10)}(0.4155) = \$30.44 \text{ million}$$

$$\text{Value of the bond} = \$50 - \$30.44 = \$19.56 \text{ million}$$

As you can see, the equity in this firm retains value, because of the option characteristics of equity. In fact, equity continues to have value in this example even if the firm value drops to $10 million or below, as shown in Figure 30.2.

Increasing Risk Can Increase Equity Value

In traditional discounted cash flow valuation, higher risk almost always translates into lower value for equity investors. When equity takes on the characteristics of a call option, you should not expect this relationship to continue to hold. Risk can become your ally, when you are an equity investor in a troubled firm. In essence, you have little to lose and much to gain from swings in firm value.

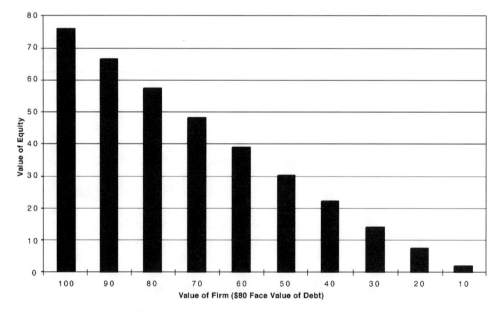

FIGURE 30.2 Value of Equity as Firm Value Changes

ILLUSTRATION 30.3:   Equity Value and Volatility

Let us revisit the valuation in Illustration 30.1. The value of the equity is a function of the standard deviation in firm value, which we assumed to be 40%. If we change this estimate, holding all else constant, the value of the equity will increase as evidenced in Figure 30.3.

Note that the value of equity increases, if we hold firm value constant, as the standard deviation increases. The interest rate on debt also increases as the standard deviation increases.

Probability of Default and Default Spreads

One of the more interesting pieces of output from the option pricing model is the risk-neutral probability of default that you can obtain for the firm. In the Black-Scholes model, you can estimate this value from $N(d2)$, which is the risk-neutral probability that $S > K$, which in this model is the probability that the value of the firm's asset will exceed the face value of the debt.

$$\text{Risk-neutral probability of default} = 1 - N(d2)$$

In addition, the interest rate from the debt allows us to estimate the appropriate default spread to charge on bonds.

You can see the potential in applying this model to bank loan portfolios to extract both the probability of default and to measure whether you are charging an interest rate that is high enough on the debt. In fact, there are commercial services that use fairly sophisticated option pricing models to estimate both values for firms.

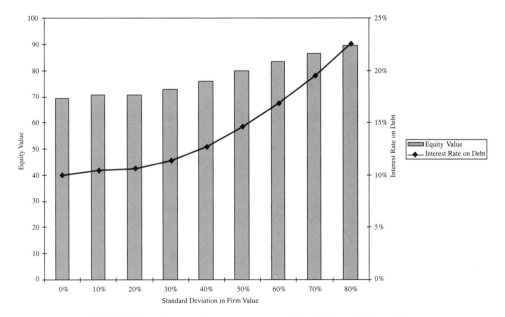

FIGURE 30.3   Equity Value and Standard Deviation in Firm Value

---

ILLUSTRATION 30.4:   **Probabilities of Default and Default Spreads**

We return to Illustration 30.1 and estimate the probability of default as $1 - N(d_2)$ and the default spread as the difference between the interest rate on a firm's debt and the risk-free rate. These values are graphed in Figure 30.4. Note that the probability of default climbs very quickly as the standard deviation in firm value increases and the default spread keeps up with it.

ESTIMATING THE VALUE OF EQUITY AS AN OPTION

The examples we have used thus far to illustrate the application of option pricing to value equity have included some simplifying assumptions. Among them are the following:

- There are only two claimholders in the firm—debt and equity.
- There is only one issue of debt outstanding, and it can be retired at face value.
- The debt has a zero coupon and no special features (convertibility, put clauses, etc.).
- The value of the firm and the variance in that value can be estimated.

Each of these assumptions is made for a reason. First, restricting the claimholders to just debt and equity makes the problem more tractable; introducing other claimholders such as preferred stock makes it more difficult to arrive at a result, albeit not impossible. Second, by assuming only one zero coupon debt issue that can be retired at face value any time prior to maturity, we align the features of the debt

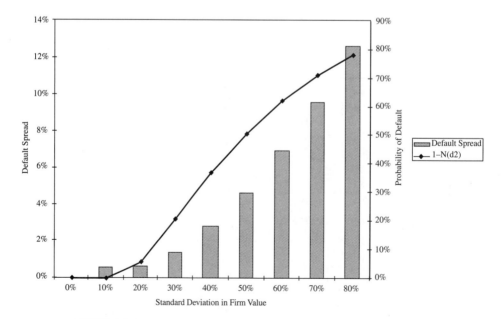

FIGURE 30.4   Risk-Neutral Probability of Default and Default Spread

more closely to the features of the strike price on a standard option. Third, if the debt is coupon debt, or more than one debt issue is outstanding, the equity investors can be forced to exercise (liquidate the firm) at these earlier coupon dates if they do not have the cash flows to meet their coupon obligations.

Finally, knowing the value of the firm and the variance in that value makes the option pricing possible, but it also raises an interesting question about the usefulness of option pricing in equity valuation. If the bonds of the firm are publicly traded, the market value of the debt can be subtracted from the value of the firm to obtain the value of equity much more directly. The option pricing approach does have its advantages, however. Specifically, when the debt of a firm is not publicly traded, option pricing theory can provide an estimate of value for the equity in the firm. Even when the debt is publicly traded, the bonds may not be correctly valued, and the option pricing framework can be useful in evaluating the values of debt and equity. Finally, relating the values of debt and equity to the variance in firm value provides some insight into the redistributive effects of actions taken by the firm.

Inputs for Valuing Equity as an Option

Since most firms do not fall into the neat framework just developed (such as having only one zero coupon bond outstanding), some compromises are needed in order to use this model in valuation.

Value of the Firm   The value of the firm can be obtained in one of four ways. In the first, we cumulate the market values of outstanding debt and equity, assuming that all debt and equity are traded, to obtain firm value. The option pricing model then reallocates the firm value between debt and equity. This approach, while simple, is internally inconsistent. We start with one set of market values for debt and equity and, using the option pricing model, end up with entirely different values for each.

In the second, we estimate the market values of the assets of the firm by discounting expected cash flows at the cost of capital. The one consideration that we need to keep in mind is that the value of the firm in an option pricing model should be the value obtained on liquidation. This may be less than the total firm value, which includes expected future investments, and it may also be reduced to reflect the cost of liquidation. If we estimate the firm value using a discounted cash flow model this would suggest that only existing investments should be considered while estimating firm value.[1] The biggest problem with this approach is that financial distress can affect operating income and thus the value that you obtain by using current operating income may be too low.

In the third approach, we estimate a multiple of revenues by looking at healthy firms in the same business and apply this multiple to the revenues of the firm you are valuing. Implicitly, we are assuming that a potential buyer, in the event of liquidation, will pay this value.

---

[1]Technically, this can be done by putting the firm into stable growth and valuing it as a stable growth firm, where reinvestments are used to either preserve or augment existing assets.

Variance in Firm Value   We can obtain the variance in firm value directly if both stocks and bonds in the firm are traded. Defining σ_e^2 as the variance in the stock price and σ_d^2 as the variance in the bond price, w_e as the market-value weight of equity, and w_d as the market-value weight of debt, we can write the variance in firm value as:[2]

$$\sigma_{firm}^2 = w_e^2\, \sigma_e^2 + w_d^2\, \sigma_d^2 + 2\, w_e\, w_d\, \rho_{ed}\, \sigma_e\, \sigma_d$$

where ρ_{ed} is the correlation between the stock and the bond prices. When the bonds of the firm are not traded, we can use the variance of similarly rated bonds as the estimate of σ_d^2 and the correlation between similarly rated bonds and the firm's stock as the estimate of ρ_{ed}.

When companies get into financial trouble, this approach can yield misleading results as both its stock prices and its bond prices become more volatile. An alternative that often yields more reliable estimates is to use the average variance in firm value for other firms in the sector. Thus the value of equity in a deeply troubled steel company can be estimated using the average variance in firm value of all traded steel companies.

---

 optvar.xls: **This dataset on the Web summarizes standard deviations in equity and firm value, by industry, for firms in the United States.**

Maturity of the Debt   Most firms have more than one debt issue on their books, and much of the debt comes with coupons. Since the option pricing model allows for only one input for the time to expiration, we have to convert these multiple bonds issues and coupon payments into one equivalent zero coupon bond.

- One solution, which takes into account both the coupon payments and the maturity of the bonds, is to estimate the duration of each debt issue and calculate a face-value–weighted average of the durations of the different issues. This value-weighted duration is then used as a measure of the time to expiration of the option.
- An approximation is to use the face-value–weighted maturity of the debt coming for the maturity of the zero coupon bond in the option pricing model.

Face Value of Debt   When a distressed firm has multiple debt issues outstanding, you have three choices when it comes to what you use as the face value of debt:

1. You could add up the principal due on all of the debt of the firm and consider it to be the face value of the hypothetical zero coupon bond that you assume that your firm has issued. The limitation of this approach is that it will understate what the firm will truly have to pay out over the life of the debt, since there will be coupon payments and interest payments during the period.

---

[2]This is an extension of the variance formula for a two-asset portfolio.

2. At the other extreme, you could add the expected interest and coupon payments that will come due on the debt to the principal payments to come up with a cumulated face value of debt. Since the interest payments occur in the near years and the principal payments are due only when the debt comes due, you are mixing cash flows up at different points in time when you do this. This is, however, the simplest approach of dealing with intermediate interest payments coming due.
3. You can consider only the principal due on the debt as the face value of the debt and the interest payments each year, specified as a percent of firm value, can take the place of the dividend yield in the option pricing model. In effect, each year that the firm remains in existence, you would expect to see the value of the firm decline by the expected payments on the debt.

ILLUSTRATION 30.5: Valuing Equity as an Option: Eurotunnel in 1997

Eurotunnel was the firm that was created to build and ultimately profit from the tunnel under the English Channel linking England and France. The tunnel was readied for operations in the early 1990s but was not a commercial success, reporting significant losses each year after opening. In early 1998 Eurotunnel had a book value of equity of –£117 million, and in 1997 the firm had reported earnings before interest and taxes of –£3.45 million and net income of –£611 million on revenues of £456 million. By any measure, it was a firm in financial trouble.

Much of the financing for the tunnel had come from debt, and at the end of 1997 Eurotunnel had debt obligations in excess of £5,000 million, raised from a variety of bond issues and bank debt. Adding the expected interest payments and coupon payments onto the debt brings the total obligations of the firm up to £8,865 million. The following table summarizes the outstanding debt at the firm, with our estimates of the expected duration for each class of debt:

Debt Type	Face Value (Including Cumulated Coupons)	Duration (Years)
Short-term	£935	0.50
100-year	£2,435	6.7
20-year	£3,555	12.6
Longer	£1,940	18.2
Total	£8,865 mil	10.93

The firm's only significant asset is its ownership of the tunnel, and we estimated the value of this asset from its expected cash flows and the appropriate cost of capital. The assumptions were as follows:

■ Revenues will grow 10% a year for five years and 3% thereafter.
■ The cost of goods sold, which was 72% of revenues in 1997, will drop to 60% of revenues by 2002 in linear increments and stay at that level. (This does not include depreciation.)
■ In the most recent year capital expenditures were $45 million and depreciation amounted to $137 million. Capital spending and depreciation will grow 3% a year for the next five years. Beyond year 5, capital expenditures will offset depreciation.
■ There are no working capital requirements.
■ The debt ratio, which was 95.35% at the end of 1997, will drop to 70% by 2002. The cost of debt is 10% for the next 5 years and 8% after that.
■ The beta for the stock will be 2.00 for the next five years, and drop to 0.8 thereafter (as the leverage decreases).

The long-term bond rate at the time of the valuation was 6% and the risk premium was 5.5%. Based on these assumptions, we estimated the cash flows in the following table:

	1	2	3	4	5	Terminal Year
Revenues	$ 501.60	$551.76	$606.94	$667.63	$ 734.39	$756.42
− COGS	$ 361.15	$380.71	$400.58	$420.61	$ 440.64	$453.85
− Depreciation	$ 141.11	$145.34	$149.70	$154.19	$ 158.82	$163.59
EBIT	($ 0.66)	$ 25.70	$ 56.65	$ 92.83	$ 134.94	$138.98
− EBIT × t	$ 0.00	$ 9.00	$ 19.83	$ 32.49	$ 47.23	$ 48.64
EBIT(1 − t)	($ 0.66)	$ 16.71	$ 36.83	$ 60.34	$ 87.71	$ 90.34
+ Depreciation	$ 141.11	$145.34	$149.70	$154.19	$ 158.82	$163.59
− Capital spending	$ 46.35	$ 47.74	$ 49.17	$ 50.65	$ 52.17	$163.59
− Change in working capital	$ 0.00	$ 0.00	$ 0.00	$ 0.00	$ 0.00	$ 0.00
Free CF to firm	$ 94.10	$114.31	$137.36	$163.89	$ 194.36	$ 90.34
Terminal value					$2,402.66	
Present value	$ 87.95	$ 99.86	$112.16	$125.08	$1,852.67	
Value of firm	$2,277.73					

The value of the assets of the firm is £2,278 million.

The final input we estimated was the standard deviation in firm value. Since there are no directly comparable firms, we estimated the standard deviations in Eurotunnel stock and debt using the data over the previous years:

Standard deviation in Eurotunnel stock price (ln) = 41%

Standard deviation in Eurotunnel bond price (ln) = 17%

We also estimated a correlation of 0.50 between Eurotunnel stock and bond prices, and the average market debt-to-capital ratio during the two-year period was 85%. Combining these inputs, we estimated the standard deviation in firm value to be:

$$\sigma^2_{\text{firm}} = (0.15)^2(0.41)^2 + (0.85)^2(0.17)^2 + 2(0.15)(0.85)(0.5)(0.41)(0.17) = 0.0335$$

In summary, the inputs to the option pricing model were as follows:

Value of the underlying asset = S = Value of the firm = £2,312 million
Exercise price = K = Face value of outstanding debt = £8,865 million
Life of the option = t = Weighted average duration of debt = 10.93 years
Variance in the value of the underlying asset = σ^2 = Variance in firm value = 0.0335
Riskless rate = r = Treasury bond rate corresponding to option life = 6%

Based on these inputs, we estimate the following value for the call:

d1 = −0.8582   N(d1) = 0.1955

d2 = −1.4637   N(d2) = 0.0717

Value of the call = 2,278(0.1955) − 8,865 exp$^{(-0.06)(10.93)}$(0.0717) = £116 million

Eurotunnel's equity was trading at £150 million in 1997.

The option pricing framework, in addition to yielding a value for Eurotunnel equity, also yields some valuable insight into the drivers of value for this equity. While it is certainly important that the firm try to bring costs under control and increase operating margins, the two most critical variables determining equity value are the duration of the debt and the variance in firm value. Any action that increases or decreases the debt duration will have a positive or negative effect on equity value. For instance, when the French government put pressure on the bankers who had lent money to Eurotunnel to ease restrictions and allow the firm more time to repay its debt, equity investors benefited as their options became more long-term. Similarly, an action that increases the volatility of expected firm value will increase the value of the option.

equity.xls: This spreadsheet allows you to estimate the value the equity in a troubled firm as an option.

VULTURE INVESTING AND OPTION PRICING

Vulture investing refers to an investment strategy of buying the securities of firms that are in severe financial distress. In a sense, you are investing in deep out-of-the-money options and hoping that some of these options pay off handsomely. Using the option pricing framework allows us to draw some conclusions about when and how this strategy can pay off:

- As with any portfolio of deep out-of-the-money options, you should expect a considerable proportion of the portfolio to end up worthless. The relatively few investments that do pay off, however, will earn huge returns, and you could still end up with a portfolio with impressive returns.
- You should direct your equity investments to equity in deeply troubled firms in volatile sectors. Risk is your ally when you invest in options, and the equity in these firms should be worth more than equity in deeply troubled stable firms.
- If you are buying equity in deeply troubled firms, you should direct your investments toward troubled firms with longer-term debt rather than shorter-term debt. As the life of the option increases, you will see the value of the option also increase.
- If you are investing in the debt issued by financially troubled firms, you cannot be a passive bondholder. You have to take an active role in the management and obtain an equity stake in the companies you invest in, perhaps by making the debt convertible.

CONSEQUENCES FOR DECISION MAKING

Option pricing theory can be applied to illustrate the conflict between stockholders and bondholders when it comes to investment analysis and conglomerate mergers. This section argues that decisions that make stockholders better off are not necessarily value maximizing for the firm and can hurt bondholders.

The Conflict between Bondholders and Stockholders

Stockholders and bondholders have different objective functions, and this can lead to agency problems, whereby stockholders expropriate wealth from bondholders. The conflict can manifest itself in a number of ways. For instance, stockholders have an incentive to invest in riskier projects than bondholders, and to pay more out in dividends than bondholders would like them to. The conflict between bondholders and stockholders can be illustrated dramatically using the option pricing methodology developed in the previous section.

Investing in Risky Projects   Since equity is a call option on the value of the firm, other things remaining equal, an increase in the variance in the firm value will lead to an increase in the value of equity. It is therefore conceivable that stockholders can invest in risky projects with negative net present values, which, while making them better off, may make the bonds and the firm less valuable. To illustrate, consider the firm in Illustration 30.1 with a value of assets of $100 million, a face value of zero coupon 10-year debt of $80 million, and a standard deviation in the value of the firm of 40 percent, valued in the earlier illustration. The equity and debt in this firm were valued as follows:

$$\text{Value of equity} = \$75.94 \text{ million}$$
$$\text{Value of debt} = \$24.06 \text{ million}$$
$$\text{Value of firm} = \$100 \text{ million}$$

Now assume that the stockholders have the opportunity to invest in a project with a net present value of –$2 million; the project is a very risky one that will push up the standard deviation in firm value to 50 percent. The equity as a call option can then be valued using the following inputs:

Value of the underlying asset = S = Value of the firm = $100 million – $2 million = $98 million (the value of the firm is lowered because of the negative net present value project)

Exercise price = K = Face value of outstanding debt = $80 million

Life of the option = t = Life of zero coupon debt = 10 years

Variance in the value of the underlying asset = σ^2 = Variance in firm value = 0.25

Riskless rate = r = Treasury bond rate corresponding to option life = 10%

Based on these inputs, the Black-Scholes model provides the following value for the equity and debt in this firm:

$$\text{Value of equity} = \$77.71$$
$$\text{Value of debt} = \$20.29$$
$$\text{Value of firm} = \$98.00$$

The value of equity rises from $75.94 million to $77.71 million, even though the firm value declines by $2 million. The increase in equity value comes at the expense of bondholders, who find their wealth decline from $24.06 million to $20.19 million.

Conglomerate Mergers   Bondholders and stockholders may also be affected differently by conglomerate mergers, where the variance in earnings and cash flows of the combined firm can be expected to decline because the merging firms have earning streams that are not perfectly correlated. In these mergers, the value of the combined equity in the firm will decrease after the merger because of the decline in variance; consequently, bondholders will gain. Stockholders can reclaim some or all of this lost wealth by utilizing their higher debt capacity and issuing new debt. To illustrate, suppose you are provided with the following information on two firms, Lube & Auto (auto service) and Gianni Cosmetics (a cosmetics manufacturer) that hope to merge.

	Lube & Auto	*Gianni Cosmetics*
Value of the firm	$100 million	$150 million
Face value of debt	$80 million	$50 million (zero coupon debt)
Maturity of debt	10 years	10 years
Standard deviation in firm value	40%	50%

Correlation between firm cash flows is 0.4. The 10-year bond rate is 10%.

We calculate the variance in the value of the firm after the acquisition as follows:

$$\text{Variance in combined firm value} = w_1^2\,\sigma_1^2 + w_2^2\sigma_2^2 + 2w_1 w_2 \rho_{12}\sigma_1\sigma_2$$
$$= (0.4)^2(0.16) + (0.6)^2(0.25)$$
$$+ 2(0.4)(0.6)(0.4)(0.4)(0.5)$$
$$= 0.154$$

We estimate the values of equity and debt in the individual firms and the combined firm using the option pricing model:

	Lube & Auto	*Gianni Cosmetics*	*Combined Firm*
Value of equity in the firm	$ 75.94	$134.48	$207.58
Value of debt in the firm	$ 24.06	$ 15.52	$ 42.42
Value of the firm	$100.00	$150.00	$250.00

The combined value of the equity prior to the merger is $210.42 million; it declines to $207.58 million after that. The wealth of the bondholders increases by an equal amount. There is a transfer of wealth from stockholders to bondholders as a consequence of the merger. Thus conglomerate mergers that are not followed by increases in leverage are likely to result in a wealth transfer from stockholders to bondholders.

IS EQUITY NOT A CALL OPTION IN EVERY FIRM?

Looking at the framework employed in this chapter, you are probably wondering why equity in every firm cannot be viewed as a call option and why therefore we should not add a premium to discounted cash flow values for all firms. It is true that equity is a call option in every firm, but in most firms the value of the firm as a going concern will be greater than the value you obtain from a liquidation option. Consider, for instance, a high-growth firm with very little in assets in place and a high proportion of value from growth potential. If this firm liquidates, it will get the value of its assets in place; this will become the value of the underlying asset in the option pricing model and determine the value of equity as a call option on the firm. This value will be much lower than the value you would obtain if you valued the firm as a going concern and considered the cash flows from expected growth. For some mature firms that derive most of their value from assets in place and substantial debt, the equity value as a call option on liquidation can be the higher value. For other firms, though, the equity value as a going concern will be greater.

CONCLUSION

The value of equity in deeply troubled firms—firms with negative earnings and high leverage—can be viewed as a call option. The option rests in the hands of equity investors, who can choose to liquidate the firm and claim the difference between firm value and debt oustanding. With limited liability, they do not have to make up the difference if firm value falls below the value of the outstanding debt. The equity will retain value even when the value of the assets of the firm is lower than the debt outstanding, because of the time premium on the option.

QUESTIONS AND SHORT PROBLEMS

1. Designate the following statements as true or false:
    a. Equity can be viewed as an option because equity investors have limited liability (limited to their equity investment in the firm).
    True _____ False _____
    b. Equity investors will sometimes take bad projects (with negative net present value) because they can add to the value of the firm.
    True _____ False _____
    c. Investing in a good project (with positive NPV)—which is less risky than the average risk of the firm—can negatively impact equity investors.
    True _____ False _____
    d. The value of equity in a firm is an increasing function of the duration of the debt in the firm (i.e., equity will be more valuable in a firm with longer-term debt than in an otherwise similar firm with short-term debt).
    True _____ False _____
2. XYZ Corporation has $500 million in zero coupon debt outstanding, due in five years. The firm had earnings before interest and taxes of $40 million in the most recent year (the tax rate is 40%). These earnings are expected to grow 5% a year in perpetuity, and the firm paid no dividends. The firm had a return on capital of 12% and a cost of capital of 10%. The annualized standard deviation in firm values of comparable firms is 12.5%. The five-year bond rate is 5%.
    a. Estimate the value of the firm.
    b. Estimate the value of equity, using an option pricing model.
    c. Estimate the market value of debt and the appropriate interest rate on the debt.
3. McCaw Cellular Communications reported earnings before interest and taxes of $850 million in 1993, with a depreciation allowance of $400 million and capital expenditures of $550 million in that year; the working capital requirements were negligible. The earnings before interest and taxes and net cap ex are expected to grow 20% a year for the next five years. The cost of capital is 10% and the return on capital is expected to be 15% in perpetuity after year 5; the growth rate in perpetuity is 5%. The firm has $10 billion in debt outstanding with the following characteristics:

Duration	Debt
1 year	$2 billion
2 years	$4 billion
5 years	$4 billion

The annualized standard deviation in the firm's stock price is 35%, while the annualized standard deviation in the traded bonds is 15%. The correlation between stock and bond prices has been 0.5, and the average debt ratio over the past few years has been 60%. The three-year bond rate is 5%, and the tax rate is 40%.

a. Estimate the value of the firm.

b. Estimate the value of the equity.

c. The stock was trading at $30, and there were 210 million shares outstanding in January 1994. Estimate the implied standard deviation in firm value.

d. Estimate the market value of the debt.

4. You have been asked to analyze the value of equity in a company that has the following features:

■ The earnings before interest and taxes is $25 million, and the corporate tax rate is 40%.

■ The earnings are expected to grow 4% a year in perpetuity, and the return on capital is 10%. The cost of capital of comparable firms is 9%.

■ The firm has two types of debt outstanding—two-year zero coupon bonds with a face value of $250 million and bank debt with 10 years to maturity with a face value of $250 million. (The duration of this debt is four years.)

■ The firm is in two businesses—food processing and auto repair. The average standard deviation in firm value for firms in food processing is 25%, whereas the standard deviation for firms in auto repair is 40%. The correlation between the businesses is 0.5.

■ The riskless rate is 7%.

Use the option pricing model to value equity as an option.

5. You are valuing the equity in a firm with $800 million (face value) in debt with an average duration of six years and assets with an estimated value of $400 million. The standard deviation in asset value is 30%. With these inputs (and a riskless rate of 6%) we obtain the following values (approximately) for d1 and d2:

$$d1 = -0.15 \qquad d2 = -0.90$$

Estimate the default spread (over and above the risk-free rate) that you would charge for the debt in this firm.

CHAPTER 31

Value Enhancement: A Discounted Cash Flow Valuation Framework

In much of this book, we have taken on the role of a passive investor valuing going concerns. In this chapter, we switch roles and look at valuation from the perspective of those who can make a difference in the way a company is run and hence its value. Our focus is therefore on how actions taken by managers and owners can change the value of a firm.

We will use the discounted cash flow framework developed in earlier parts of the book to explore the requirements for an action to be value creating, and then go on to examine the different ways in which a firm can create value. In the process, we will also examine the role that marketing decisions, production decisions, and strategic decisions have in value creation.

VALUE CREATING AND VALUE-NEUTRAL ACTIONS

The value of a firm is the present value of the expected cash flows from both assets in place and future growth, discounted at the cost of capital. For an action to create value, it has to do one or more of the following:

- Increase the cash flows generated by existing investments.
- Increase the expected growth rate in earnings.
- Increase the length of the high-growth period.
- Reduce the cost of capital that is applied to discount the cash flows.

Conversely, an action that does not affect cash flows, the expected growth rate, the length of the high growth period, or the cost of capital cannot affect value.

While this might seem obvious, a number of value-neutral actions taken by firms receive disproportionate attention from both managers and analysts. Consider four examples:

1. Stock dividends and stock splits change the number of units of equity in a firm but do not affect cash flows, growth, or value. These actions can have price effects, though, because they alter investors' perceptions of the future of the company.
2. Accounting changes in inventory valuation and depreciation methods that are restricted to the reporting statements and do not affect tax calculations have no

effect on cash flows, growth, or value. In recent years, firms have spent an increasing amount of time on the management and smoothing of earnings and seem to believe that there is a value payoff to doing this.

3. When making acquisitions, firms often try to structure the deals in such a way that they can pool their assets and not show the market premium paid in the acquisition. When they fail and they are forced to show the difference between market value and book value as goodwill, their earnings are reduced by the amortization of the goodwill over subsequent periods. This amortization is generally not tax deductible, however, and thus does not affect the cash flows of the firm. So, whether a firm adopts purchase or pooling accounting, and the length of time it takes to write off the goodwill, should not really make any difference to value.

4. In the late 1990s, a number of firms that have issued tracking stock on their high-growth divisions. Since these divisions remain under the complete control of the parent company, we would argue that the issue of tracking stock, by itself, should not create value.

Some would take issue with this proposition. When a stock splits or a firm issues tracking stock, they would argue, the stock price often goes up significantly.[1] While this is true, we would emphasize that it is value, not price, that we claim is unaffected by these actions.

While paying stock dividends, splitting stock and issuing tracking stock are value-neutral actions, they can still be useful tools for a firm that perceives itself to be undervalued by the market. These actions can change market perceptions about growth or cash flows and thus act as signals to financial markets. Alternatively, they might provide more information about undervalued assets owned by the firm, and the price may react, as a consequence. In some cases, these actions may even lead to changes in operations; tying the compensation of managers to the price of stock tracking the division in which they work may improve efficiency and thus increase cash flows, growth, and value.

WAYS OF INCREASING VALUE

The value of a firm can be increased by increasing cash flows from assets in place, by increasing expected growth and the length of the growth period, and by reducing the cost of capital. In reality, however, none of these is easily accomplished, and they are likely to reflect all the qualitative factors that financial analysts are often accused of ignoring in valuation. This section will consider how actions taken by a firm on a variety of fronts—marketing, strategic, and financial—can have an effect on value.

Increase Cash Flows from Existing Investments

The first place to look for value is in the firm's existing assets. These assets represent investments the firm has already made and they generate the current operating

---

[1]This is backed up empirically. Stock prices do tend to increase, on average, when stocks are split.

income for the firm. To the extent that these investments earn less than their cost of capital or are earning less than they could if optimally managed, there is potential for value creation.

Poor Investments: Keep, Divest, or Liquidate Every firm has some investments that earn less than the cost of capital used to fund them and sometimes even lose money. At first sight, it would seem to be a simple argument to make that investments that do not earn their cost of capital should be either liquidated or divested. If, in fact, the firm could get back the original capital on liquidation, this statement would be true. But that assumption is not generally true, and there are three different measures of value for an existing investment that we need to consider.

The first is the continuing value, and it reflects the present value of the expected cash flows from continuing the investment through the end of its life. The second is the liquidation or salvage value, which is the net cash flow that the firm will receive if it terminated the project today. Finally, there is the divestiture value, which is the price that will be paid by the highest bidder for this investment.

Whether a firm should continue with an existing project, liquidate the project, or sell it to someone else will depend on which of the three is highest. If the continuing value is the highest, the firm should continue with the project to the end of the project life, even though it might be earning less than the cost of capital. If the liquidation or divestiture value is higher than the continuing value, there is potential for an increase in value from liquidation or divestiture. The value increment can then be summarized:

If liquidation is optimal:

> Expected value increase = Liquidation value − Continuing value

If divestiture is optimal:

> Expected value increase = Divestiture value − Continuing value

How does a divestiture affect a firm's value? To answer this question, we compare the price received on the divestiture to the present value of the expected cash flows that the firm would have received from the divested assets. There are three possible scenarios:

1. If the divestiture value is equal to the present value of the expected cash flows, the divestitures will have no effect on the divesting firm's value.
2. If the divestiture value is greater than the present value of the expected cash flows, the value of the firm will increase on the divestiture.
3. If the divestiture value is less than the present value of the expected cash flows, the value of the firm will decrease on the divestiture.

The divesting firm receives cash in return for the assets and can choose to retain the cash and invest it in marketable securities, invest the cash in other assets or new investments, or return the cash to stockholders in the form of dividends or stock buybacks. This action, in turn, can have a secondary effect on value.

ILLUSTRATION 31.1:   Potential for Value Creation from Divestiture: Boeing

While it is difficult to make judgments about individual investments that firms might have and their capacity to generate continuing value, you can make some observations about the potential for value creation from divestitures and liquidation by looking at the cost of capital of and return on capital earned by different divisions of a firm. For instance, Boeing earned a return on capital of 5.82% in 1998, while its cost of capital was 9.18%. Breaking down Boeing's return by division, we obtain the numbers in the following table:

	Commercial Aircraft	*Information, Space, and Defense*	*Firm*
Operating income	$ 75	$1,576	$ 1,651
Capital invested	$18,673	$9,721	$28,394
After-tax return on capital	0.40%	16.21%	5.82%

At Boeing's annual meeting in 1999, Phil Condit, Boeing's CEO, was candid in admitting that 35% of Boeing's capital was in investments that earned less than the cost of capital. He revealed little, however, about whether it would be feasible to liquidate or divest these investments[2] and get more than continuing value from such actions.

Assume that Boeing is interested in selling its information, space, and defense systems division, and that it has found a potential buyer who is willing to pay $11 billion for the division. The division reported cash flows before debt payments but after reinvestment needs and taxes of $393 million in the most recent year, and the cash flows are expected to grow 5% a year in the long term. The cost of capital for the division is 9%, a little lower than the cost of capital for the entire firm. The division, as a continuing part of Boeing, can be valued as follows:

$$\text{Value of division} = \$393(1.05)/(.09 - .05) = \$10,316 \text{ million}$$

With the divestiture value of $11 billion, the net effect of the divestiture will be an increase in Boeing's value of $684 million.

$$\text{Net effect on value} = \text{Divestiture value} - \text{Continuing value} = \$11,000 \text{ million} - \$10,316 \text{ million}$$
$$= \$684 \text{ million}$$

Improve Operating Efficiency   A firm's operating efficiency determines its operating margin and thus its operating income; more efficient firms have higher operating margins, other things remaining equal, than less efficient firms in the same business. If a firm can increase its operating margin on existing assets, it will generate additional value. There are a number of indicators of the potential to increase margins, but the most important is a measure of how much a firm's operating margin deviates from its industry. Firms whose current operating margins are well below their industry average must locate the source of the difference and try to fix it.

In most firms, the first step in value enhancement takes the form of cost cutting and layoffs. These actions are value enhancing only if the resources that are pruned do not contribute sufficiently either to current operating income or to future

---

[2]In 1999, Lockheed, Boeing's leading competitor in the sector, announced plans to divest itself of approximately 15% of its assets as a remedy for its poor stock price performance.

REASONS FOR DIVESTITURES

Why would a firm sell assets or a division? There are at least three reasons. The first is that the divested assets may have a higher value to the buyer of these assets. For assets to have a higher value, they have to either generate higher cash flows for the buyer or result in lower risk (leading to a lower discount rate). The higher cash flows can occur because the buyer is more efficient at utilizing the assets or because the buyer finds synergies with its existing businesses. The lower discount rate may reflect the fact that the owners of the buying firm are more diversified than the owners of the firm selling the assets. In either case, both sides can gain from the divestiture and share in the increased value.

The second reason for divestitures is less value-driven and more a result of the immediate cash flow needs of the divesting firm. Firms that find themselves unable to meet their current operating or financial expenses may have to sell assets to raise cash. For instance, many leveraged acquisitions in the 1980s were followed by divestitures of assets. The cash generated from these divestitures was used to retire and service debt.

The third reason for divestitures relates to the assets not sold by the firm, rather than the divested assets. In some cases, a firm may find the cash flows and values of its core businesses affected by the fact that it has diversified into unrelated businesses. This lack of focus can be remedied by selling assets or businesses that are peripheral to the main business of a firm.

---

growth. Companies can easily show increases in current operating income by cutting back on expenditures such as research and training, but they may sacrifice future growth in doing so.

ILLUSTRATION 31.2: Operating Margin Comparisons

In Chapter 22, we valued Marks and Spencer in 2000 and noted that its value was depressed because its operating margins had dropped over the previous two years. Figure 31.1 compares the after-tax operating margins at Marks and Spencer in 2000 with the average after-tax margin earned by the firm over the previous five years and the average after-tax margin in 2000 for other firms in the sector.

Marks and Spencer's current margins lag both its own historical levels and the average for the sector. We estimated the effect on value per share at Marks and Spencer of improvements in the operating margin from the current level. Figure 31.2 summarizes the effect of these changes.

While it is not surprising that the value per share is sensitive to changes in the operating margin, you can see that the decline in operating margins from historical levels to the current one have had a significant impact on value. Any value enhancement plan for the firm, therefore, has to be centered on improving operating margins.

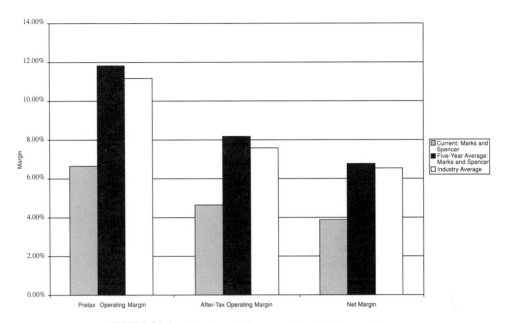

FIGURE 31.1 Marks and Spencer: Margin Comparisons

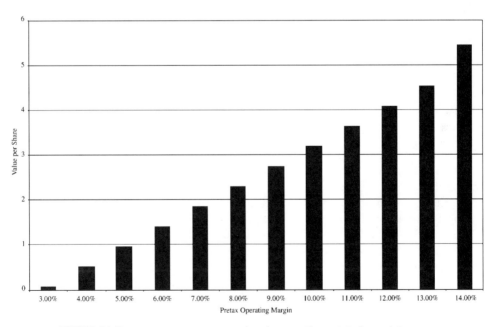

FIGURE 31.2 Operating Margin and Value per Share: Marks and Spencer

SOME THOUGHTS ON COST CUTTING

Firms embark on cost cutting with a great deal of fanfare but seem to have trouble carrying through. Cost cutting is often promised by firms, especially after acquisitions or new management comes into the firm, but seldom delivered. Here are some general conclusions about cost cutting:

- The greater the absolute magnitude of the cost cuts promised, the more likely it is that they will not be delivered.
- Cost cutting is never painless; not only is the human cost associated with layoffs large, but there is an associated loss of morale that can be just as expensive.
- The initial phases of cost cuts go much more smoothly than the later phases. Part of the reason for this is that the easy cost cuts come first and the tough ones come later.
- It is far more difficult to separate those costs that do not generate benefits for the firm from those that do than it seems at the outset, especially if we think of benefits in the long term.
- Cost cutting that is promised in the abstract is less likely to happen than cost cutting that is described in detail. An example would be a bank merger where the branches that will be closed after the merger are specified as opposed to one where the bank just specified that economies of scale will lower costs.

From a valuation perspective, you should first evaluate the credibility of the management that is making the cost cutting claims, and even if you believe the managers you should allow for phasing in the cost cuts over time; the larger the firm and the bigger the cost cuts, the longer the period.

Reduce the Tax Burden   The value of a firm is the present value of its after-tax cash flows. Thus, any action that can reduce the tax burden on a firm for a given level of operating income will increase value. Although there are some aspects of the tax code that offer no flexibility to the firm, the tax rate can be reduced over time by doing any or all of the following:

- Multinational firms that generate earnings in different markets may be able to move income from high-tax locations to low-tax or no-tax locations. For instance, the prices that divisions of these firms charge each other for intracompany sales (transfer prices) can allow profits to be shifted from one part of the firm to another.[3]
- A firm may be able to acquire net operating losses that can be used to shield future income. In fact, this might be why a profitable firm acquires an unprofitable one.

---

[3]Taxes are only one aspect of transfer pricing. Brickley, Smith, and Zimmerman (1995) look at the broader issue of how to best set transfer prices.

■ A firm can use risk management to reduce the average tax rate paid on income over time because the marginal tax rate on income tends to rise, in most tax systems, as income increases. By using risk management to smooth income over time, firms can make their incomes more stable and reduce their exposure to the highest marginal tax rates.[4] This is especially the case when a firm faces a windfall or supernormal profit taxes.

ILLUSTRATION 31.3: Tax Burden and Valuation

In Chapter 22 we valued DaimlerChrysler using a tax rate of 44%, which is much higher than the tax rates used for other companies that we have valued. As a German company, Daimler is clearly much more exposed to high tax rates, but there are two forces that may change this tax rate:

1. With the acquisition of Chrysler and the increasing globalization of its business, DaimlerChrysler has far more options when it comes to moving income to lower-tax locales.
2. As a result of expected changes in German law, the tax rate in Germany will decline over the next five years.

The impact on the value of equity at DaimlerChrysler of changes in the tax rate from 0% to 50% are shown in Figure 31.3. The value of equity changes dramatically as the tax rate changes and would triple from the base case value if the tax rate were zero. This is notwithstanding the fact that the tax benefits from depreciation and interest expenses also decline as the tax rate drops.

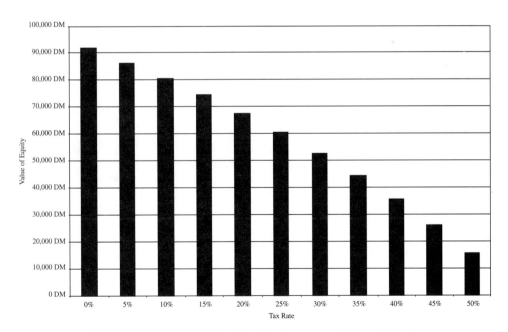

FIGURE 31.3 DaimlerChrysler: Tax Rate versus Value of Equity

---

[4]Stulz (1996) makes this argument for risk management. He also presents other ways in which risk management can be value enhancing.

Reduce Net Capital Expenditures on Existing Investments   The net capital expenditures is the difference between capital expenditures and depreciation, and, as a cash outflow, it reduces the free cash flow to the firm. Part of the net capital expenditure is designed to generate future growth, but part is to maintain existing assets. If a firm can reduce its net capital expenditures on existing assets, it will increase value. During short periods, the capital expenditures can even be lower than depreciation for those assets, creating a cash inflow from net capital expenditures.

There is generally a trade-off between capital maintenance expenditures and the life of existing assets. A firm that does not make any capital expenditures on its assets will generate much higher after-tax cash flows from these assets, but the assets will have a far shorter life. At the other extreme, a firm that reinvests all the cash flows it gets from depreciation into capital maintenance may be able to extend the life of its assets in place significantly. Firms often ignore this trade-off when they embark on cost cutting and reduce or eliminate capital maintenance expenditures. Although these actions increase current cash flows from existing assets, the firm might actually lose value as it depletes these assets at a faster rate.

Reduce Noncash Working Capital   The noncash working capital in a firm is the difference between noncash current assets, generally inventory and accounts receivable, and the nondebt portion of current liabilities, generally accounts payable. Money invested in noncash working capital is tied up and cannot be used elsewhere; thus, increases in noncash working capital are cash outflows, whereas decreases are cash inflows. For retailers and service firms, noncash working capital may be a much larger drain on cash flows than traditional capital expenditures.

The path to value creation seems simple. Reducing noncash working capital as a percent of revenues should increase cash flows and, therefore, value. This assumes, however, that there are no negative consequences for growth and operating income. Firms generally maintain inventory and provide credit because it allows them to sell more. If cutting back on one or both causes lost sales, the net effect on value may be negative.

The availability of updated and reliable data on customers has made it easier for firms to plan and reduced the need for inventory and working capital. In fact, the average noncash working capital as a percent of revenues at major U.S. corporations has dropped from 17.6 percent in 1988 to 14.5 percent in 1998.

ILLUSTRATION 31.4:   Noncash Working Capital: The Home Depot

Consider a large retail firm like the Home Depot. It has significant investments in working capital, and changes in this input can make a significant difference to the value of equity in the firm. Figure 31.4 compares noncash working capital as a percent of revenues, operating income, and book value of capital invested for the Home Depot for 1998 with the previous five years and the average for the sector.

Due to its economies of scale, the Home Depot carries far less working capital than its competitors and this has a positive effect on both cash flows and value. In 1998, we valued the Home Depot using the following inputs for the valuation:

	High-Growth Phase	Stable-Growth Phase
Length	10 years	Forever after year 10
Growth inputs		
Reinvestment rate	88.62%	35.46%
Return on capital	16.37%	14.10%
Expected growth rate	14.51%	5.00%
Cost of capital inputs		
Beta	0.87	0.87
Cost of debt	5.80%	5.50%
Debt ratio	4.55%	30.00%
Cost of capital	9.52%	7.92%
General information		
Tax rate	35%	35%

The value per share obtained, which is summarized in Figure 31.5, was $42.55. We looked at the impact on the Home Depot's value of changing the noncash working capital as a percent of revenues. As noncash working capital increases, the value of equity decreases, and the results are graphed in Figure 31.6. As the noncash working capital increases from 0% to 20% of revenues, the value per share decreases by approximately 20%.

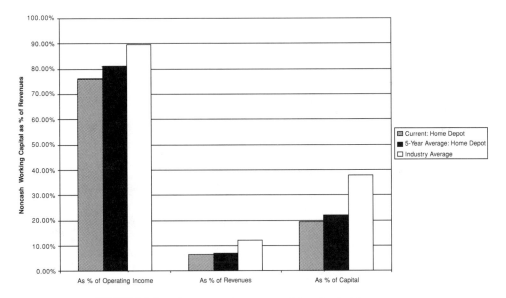

FIGURE 31.4 The Home Depot's Working Capital Investment

 cfbasics.xls: This dataset on the Web summarizes operating margins, tax rates, and noncash working capital as a percent of revenues by industry group for the United States.

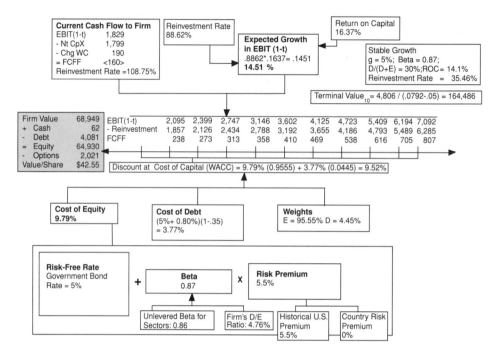

FIGURE 31.5   The Home Depot: A Valuation

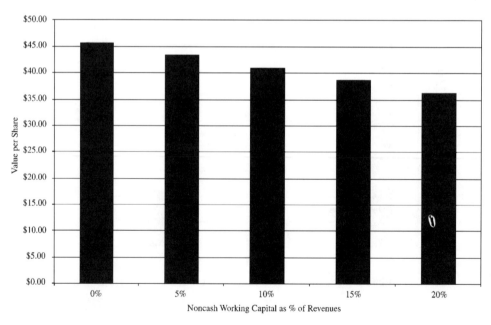

FIGURE 31.6   The Home Depot: Working Capital and Value per Share

Increase Expected Growth

A firm with low current cash flows can still have high value if it is able to grow quickly. For profitable firms, the growth will be defined in terms of earnings but for money-losing firms, you have to consider the nexus of revenue growth and higher margins.

Profitable Firms Higher growth arises from either increases in reinvestment or a higher return on capital. It does not always translate into higher value, though, since higher growth can be offset by changes elsewhere in the valuation. Thus, higher reinvestment rates usually result in higher expected growth but at the expense of lower cash flows, since reinvestment reduces the free cash flows. Higher returns on capital also cause expected growth to increase, but value can still go down if the new investments are in riskier businesses and there is a more than proportionate increase in the cost of capital.

The trade-off from increasing the reinvestment rate is listed in Table 31.1. The positive effect of reinvesting more, higher growth, has to be compared to the negative effect of reinvesting more, the drop in free cash flows.

We could work through the entire valuation and determine whether the present value of the additional cash flows created by higher growth is greater than the present value of the actual reinvestments made, in cash flow terms. There is, however, a far simpler test to determine the effect on value. Note that the net present value of a project measures the value added by the project to overall firm value, and that the net present value is positive only if the internal rate of return on the project exceeds the cost of capital. If we make the assumption that the accounting return on capital on a project is a reasonable estimate for the internal rate of return, then increasing the reinvestment rate will increase value if and only if the return on capital is greater than the cost of capital. If the return on capital is less than the cost of capital, the positive effects of growth will be less than the negative effects of making the reinvestment.

Note that the return on capital that we are talking about is the marginal return on capital (i.e., the return on capital earned on the actual reinvestment), rather than the average return on capital. Given that firms tend to accept their most attractive investment first and their less attractive investments later, the average returns on capital will tend to be greater than the marginal returns on capital. Thus, a firm with a return on capital of 18 percent and a cost of capital of 12 percent may really be earning only 11 percent on its marginal projects. In addition, the marginal return on capital will be much lower if the increase in the reinvestment rate is substantial. Thus, we have to be cautious about assuming large increases in the reinvestment rate while keeping the current return on capital constant.

TABLE 31.1 Trade-Off on Reinvestment Rate

Negative Effects	Positive Effects

Reduces free cash flow to firm:
FCFF = EBIT (1 – Tax rate)
  (1 – Reinvestment rate)
	Increases expected growth:
	Expected growth = Reinvestment rate
	  × Return on capital

A firm that is able to increase its return on capital while keeping the cost of capital fixed will increase its value. The increase in growth will increase value, and there are generally no offsetting effects. If, however, the increase in return on capital comes from the firm entering new businesses that are far riskier than its existing business, there might be an increase in the cost of capital that offsets the increase in growth. The general rule for value creation remains simple, however. As long as the projects, no matter how risky they are, have a marginal return on capital that exceeds their cost of capital, they will create value.

Using the comparison between return on capital and cost of capital, a firm that earns a return on capital that is less than its cost of capital can get an increase in value by accepting higher return investments, but it would get an even greater increase in value by not investing at all and returning the cash to the owners of the business. Liquidation or partial liquidation might be the most value-enhancing strategy for firms trapped in businesses where it is impossible to earn the cost of capital.

ILLUSTRATION 31.5:   Reinvestment Rates, Return on Capital, and Value

In 1998, Boeing earned a return on capital of 6.59% and had a reinvestment rate of 65.98%. If you assume a cost of capital of 9.17% for the firm, you would value the equity in the firm at $13.14 a share. In the same year, the Home Depot had a return on capital of 16.38%, a reinvestment rate of 88.62%, and a cost of capital of 9.51%, resulting in a value per share of $42.55.

	Boeing	Home Depot
Cost of capital	9.17%	9.51%
Return on capital	6.59%	16.38%
Reinvestment rate	65.98%	88.62%
Expected growth rate	4.35%	14.51%
Value per share	$13.14	$42.55

If the Home Depot could increase its reinvestment rates without affecting its returns on capital, the effect on value will be positive, because it is earning excess returns. For Boeing, the effect of increasing the reinvestment rate at the current return on capital will be negative, since the firm's return on capital is less than its cost of capital. Figure 31.7 summarizes the impact on the value of equity of changing the reinvestment rate at both firms, keeping the cost of capital.

To illustrate, we reduced the reinvestment rate at Boeing from 65.98% to 45.98% and examined the percentage effect on value of equity; the change was +4.49%. The effects of a similar change at the Home Depot was negative. The effect of changes in the reinvestment rate were dramatic at the Home Depot, because the high-growth period lasts 10 years.

fundgrEB.xls: **This dataset on the Web summarizes returns on capital and reinvestment rates by industry group for the United States.**

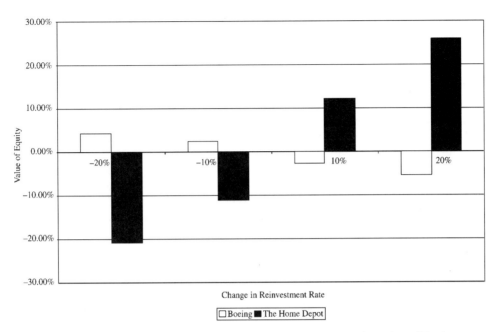

FIGURE 31.7 Effect of Changes in the Reinvestment Rate on the Value of Equity

Negative Earnings Firms For young firms with negative earnings, expected future cash flows are derived from assumptions made about three variables—the expected growth rate in revenues, the target operating margin, and the sales-to-capital ratio. The first two variables determine the operating earnings in future years, and the last variable determines reinvestment needs. Figure 31.8 summarizes the impact of each of these variables on the cash flows.

Other things remaining equal, the expected cash flows in future years will be higher if any of the three variables—revenue growth, target margins, and sales-to-capital ratios—increase. Increasing revenue growth and target margins will increase operating earnings, while increasing the sales-to-capital ratio will reduce reinvestment needs.

In reality, though, firms have to make a trade-off between higher revenue growth and higher margins. When firms increase prices for their products, they improve operating margins but reduce revenue growth. Michael Porter, one of the leading

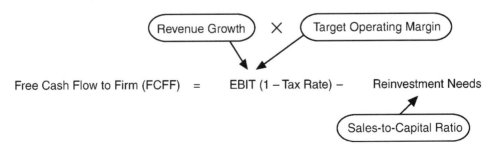

FIGURE 31.8 Determinants of Growth

thinkers in corporate strategy, suggests that when it comes to pricing strategy, there are two basic routes a firm can take.[5] It can choose to be a volume leader, reducing prices and hoping to increase revenues sufficiently to compensate for the lower margins. For this strategy to work, the firm needs a cost advantage over its competitors to prevent pricing wars that may make all firms in the industry worse off. Alternatively, it can attempt to be a price leader, increasing prices and hoping that the effect on volume will be smaller than the increased margins. The extent to which revenue growth will drop depends on how elastic the demand for the product is and how competitive the overall product market is. The net effect will determine value.

While a higher sales-to-capital ratio reduces reinvestment needs and increases cash flow, there are both internal and external constraints on the process. As the sales-to-capital ratio increases, the return on capital on the firm in future years will also increase. If the return on capital substantially exceeds the cost of capital, new competitors will enter the market, making it more difficult to sustain the expected operating margins and revenue growth.

ILLUSTRATION 31.6:   Revenue Growth, Operating Margins, and Sales-to-Capital Ratios

---

In Chapter 23, we valued Commerce One, a firm with an operating loss of $529 million and only $537 million in revenues. Using a compounded revenue growth rate of 40.24%, a target operating margin of 14.72% in 10 years, and a sales-to-capital ratio of 2.20, we estimated a value for the firm of $4.8 billion and value per share of $19.26. Changes in these inputs can have a dramatic effect on the value of the firm, as noted in Chapter 23.

As you would expect, higher revenue growth translates into higher values per share. Figure 31.9 graphs the change in value per share for Commerce One as a function of the change in expected growth rate in revenues over the next decade. Thus, Commerce One's value per share increases by 50% if the compounded revenue growth over the next 10 years is 45% instead of 40%. By the same token, the value per share drops by a third if the growth rate is 35%.

While higher revenue growth clearly increases value, we assumed that the target margin would remain unchanged as the growth rate changes. The target margin is just as important, if not more so, than revenue growth in determining value. Figure 31.10 estimates the value per share, holding revenue growth at 40.24% and changing the target margin. Every 1% change in the target operating margin changes the value by approximately $3 per share.

The trade-off between revenue growth and margins is made more explicit in the following table, which shows value per share as a function of both variables.

Compounded Revenue Growth over Next 10 Years	Target Pretax Operating Margin in 10 years				
	8%	10%	12%	14%	16%
10%	$ 0.00	$ 0.00	$ 0.00	$ 0.47	$ 1.08
20%	$ 0.00	$ 0.18	$ 1.46	$ 2.91	$ 4.29
30%	$ 0.02	$ 2.98	$ 5.74	$ 8.47	$11.18
40%	$ 3.51	$ 8.94	$14.36	$19.77	$25.17
50%	$10.31	$20.74	$31.16	$41.56	$51.97

---

[5]*Competitive Strategy*, by Michael Porter (1980).

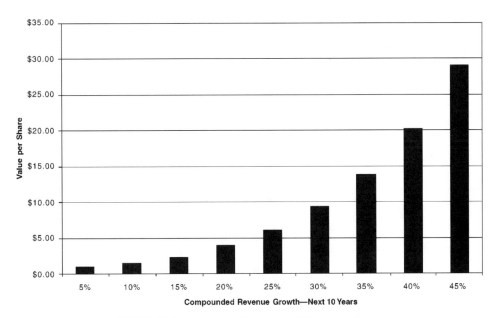

FIGURE 31.9 Revenue Growth and Value per Share

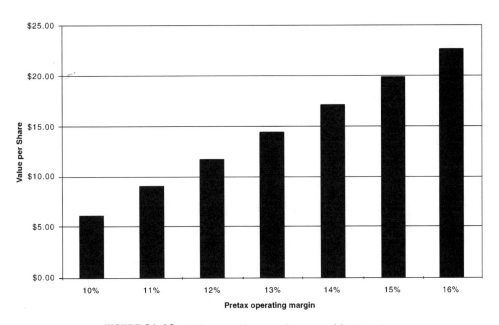

FIGURE 31.10 Value per Share and Sustainable Margins

Commerce One's value varies widely depending on the combination of revenue growth and margins that you assume. In practical terms, this also provides the firm with a sense of the trade-off between higher revenue growth and lower target margins.

Finally, a higher sales-to-capital ratio (which translates into a higher return on capital in 10 years) leads to a higher value per share, because it determines how much Commerce One has to reinvest to generate its expected growth rate. Figure 31.11 presents the effects on value per share of

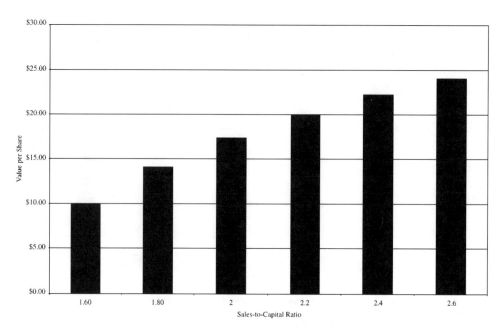

FIGURE 31.11   Value per Share versus Sales-to-Capital Ratio

---

changing the sales-to-capital ratio over the high-growth period for Commerce One. As the sales-to-capital ratio changes, the return on capital in stable growth follows suit, increasing as the sales-to-capital ratio increases. As the sales-to-capital ratio (and the terminal return on capital) increases, the value per share of Commerce One also increases.

Lengthen the Period of High Growth

Every firm, at some point in the future, will become a stable-growth firm, growing at a rate equal to or less than that of the economy in which it operates. In addition, growth creates value only if the firm earns excess returns on its investments. With excess returns, the longer the high-growth period lasts, other things remaining equal, the greater the value of the firm. No firm should be able to earn excess returns for any length of time in a competitive product market, since competitors will be attracted to the business by the excess returns. Thus, implicit in the assumption that there will be high growth with excess returns is the assumption that there also exist some barriers to entry that prevent competing firms from entering the market and eliminating the excess returns that prevail.

One way firms can increase value is by increasing existing barriers to entry and erecting new ones. Another way to express this idea is that companies earning excess returns have significant competitive advantages. Nurturing these advantages can increase value.

Brand Name Advantage   As we noted earlier in the book, the inputs to the traditional discounted cash flow valuation incorporate the effects of brand name. In particular, firms with more valuable brand names are either able to charge higher prices than the competition for the same products (leading to higher margins) or sell more than the competitors at the same price (leading to higher turnover ratios). They usually have higher returns on capital and greater value than their competitors in the industry.

Creating a brand name is a difficult and expensive process that may take years to achieve, but firms can often build on existing brand names and make them valuable. Brand management and advertising can thus contribute in value creation. Consider the extraordinary success that Coca-Cola has had in increasing its market value over the past two decades. Some attribute its success to its high return on equity or capital, yet these returns are not the cause of its success but the consequence of it. The high returns can be traced to the company's relentless focus on making its brand name more valuable globally.[6] Conversely, the managers of a firm who take over a valuable brand name and then dissipate its value will reduce the values of the firm substantially. The near-death experience of Apple Computer in 1996 and 1997, and the travails of Quaker Oats after the Snapple acquisition suggest that managers can quickly squander the advantage that comes from valuable brand names.

Patents, Licenses, and Other Legal Protection The second competitive advantage that companies can possess is a legal one. Firms may enjoy exclusive rights to produce and market a product because they own the patent rights on the product, as is often the case in the pharmaceutical industry. Alternatively, firms may have exclusive licensing rights to service a market, as is the case with utilities in the United States.

The key to value enhancement is not just to preserve but to increase any competitive advantages that the firm possesses. If the competitive advantage comes from its existing patents, the firm has to work at developing new patents that allow it to maintain this advantage over time. While spending more money or research and development (R&D) is clearly one way, the efficiency of reinvestment also applies here. The companies that have the greatest increases in value are not necessarily those that spend the most on R&D, but those that have the most productive R&D departments not only in generating patents but also in converting patents into commercial products.

The competitive advantage from exclusive licensing or a legal monopoly is a mixed blessing and may not lead to value enhancement. When a firm is granted these rights by another entity, say the government, that entity usually preserves the right to control the prices charged and margins earned through regulation. In the United States, for instance, much of the regulation of power and phone utilities was driven by the objective of ensuring that these firms did not earn excess returns. In these circumstances, firms may actually gain in value by giving up their legal monopolies, if they get pricing freedom in return. We could argue that this has already occurred, in great part, in the airline and long-distance telecommunications businesses, and will occur in the future in other regulated businesses. In the aftermath of deregulation, the firms that retain competitive advantages will gain value at the expense of others in the business.

---

[6]Companies like Coca-Cola have taken advantage of the global perception that they represent American culture, and have used it to grow strongly in other markets.

Switching Costs There are some businesses where neither brand name nor a patent provides adequate protection against competition. Products have short life cycles, competition is fierce, and customers develop little loyalty to companies or products. This describes the computer software business in the 1980s, and it still applies to a significant portion of that business today. How, then, did Microsoft succeed so well in establishing its presence in the market? Although many would attribute its success entirely to its ownership of the operating system needed to run the software, there is another reason. Microsoft recognized earlier than most firms that the most significant barrier to entry in the software business is the cost to the end user of switching from its products to those of a competitor. In fact, Microsoft Excel, early in its life, had to overcome the obstacle that most users were working with Lotus spreadsheets and did not want to bear the switching cost. Microsoft made it easy for end users to switch to its products (by allowing Excel to open Lotus spreadsheets, for instance), and it made it more and more expensive for them to switch to a competitor by creating the Microsoft Office Suite. Thus, a user who has Microsoft Office installed on his or her system and who wants to try to switch from Microsoft Word to WordPerfect has to overcome multiple barriers: Will the conversion work well on the hundreds of Word files that exist already? Will the user still be able to cut and paste from Microsoft Excel and PowerPoint into Word Perfect documents? The end result, of course, is that it becomes very difficult for competitors that do not have Microsoft's resources to compete with it in this arena.

There are a number of other businesses where the switching cost concept can be used to augment an argument for value enhancement or debunk it. For instance, there are many who argue that the valuations of Internet companies such as Amazon.com reflect their first-mover advantage—that is, the fact that they are pioneers in the online business. However, the switching costs in online retailing seem to be minimal, and these companies have to come up with a way of increasing switching costs if they want to earn high returns in the future.

Cost Advantages There are several ways in which firms can establish a cost advantage over their competitors and use it as a barrier to entry:

- In businesses where scale can be used to reduce costs, economies of scale can give bigger firms advantages over smaller firms. This is the advantage, for instance, that the Home Depot has used to gain market share at the expense of its smaller and often local competitors.
- Owning or having exclusive rights to a distribution system can provide firms with a cost advantage over its competitors. For instance, American Airlines' ownership of the Sabre airline reservation system gave it an advantage over its competitors in attracting customers.
- Having access to lower-cost labor or resources can also provide cost advantages. Thus Southwest Airlines, with its nonunionized labor force, has an advantage over its unionized competitors, as do natural resource companies with access to reserves that are less expensive to exploit.

These cost advantages will influence value in one of two ways: The firm with the cost advantage may charge the same price as its competitors but have a much higher operating margin. Or the firm may charge lower prices than its competitors and have a much higher capital turnover ratio. In fact, the net effect of increasing margins or turnover ratios (or both) will increase the return on capital, and through it expected growth.

The cost advantage of economies of scale can create high capital requirements that prevent new firms from entering the business. In businesses such as aerospace and automobiles, the competition is almost entirely among existing competitors. The absence of new competitors may allow these firms to maintain above-normal returns, though the competition between existing firms will constrain the magnitude of these returns.

ILLUSTRATION 31.7: Potential for Increasing the Length of the High-Growth Period

This example examines the potential for increasing barriers to entry, and by extension the excess returns and the length of the high-growth period at Cisco Systems and Motorola. The competitive advantages are different for the two firms, and the potential for building on these advantages is different as well.

■ Cisco's most significant differential advantage seems to be its capacity to generate much larger excess returns on its new investments than its competitors. Since most of these investments take the form of acquisitions of other firms, Cisco's excess returns rest on whether it can continue to maintain its success in this area. The primary challenge, however, is that as Cisco continues to grow, it will need to do even more acquisitions each year to maintain the growth rate it had the previous year. It is possible that there might be both external and internal constraints on this process. The number of firms that are potential takeover targets is limited, and the firm may not have the resources to replicate its current success if the number of acquisitions doubles or triples.
■ Motorola's research capabilities and the patents that emerge from the research represent its most significant competitive advantage. However, it is not viewed as the technological leader in either of the two businesses that it operates in. Firms like Nokia are viewed as more innovative when it comes to mobile communications (cellular phones) and Intel is considered the leading innovator among large semiconductor manufacturers.

We begin by valuing each of these firms using their current returns on capital and estimated reinvestment rates as inputs for the high growth period. The following table summarizes the inputs used in the base case valuations and the value per share estimated with these assumptions:

	Cisco		Motorola	
	High Growth	*Stable Growth*	*High Growth*	*Stable Growth*
Beta	1.43	1.00	1.21	1.00
Cost of equity	11.72%	10.00%	10.85%	10.00%
After-tax cost of debt	4.03%	4.03%	4.23%	4.23%
Debt ratio	0.18%	10.00%	6.86%	6.86%
Cost of capital	11.71%	9.40%	10.39%	9.58%
Return on capital	34.07%	16.52%	12.18%	12.18%
Reinvestment rate	106.8%	30.27%	52.99%	41.07%
Expected growth rate	36.39%	5.00%	6.45%	5.00%
Value per share	$44.13		$20.97	

In the base case, we assume 12 years of high growth for Cisco—six years of high growth and six years of transition—and five years of high growth for Motorola. We then consider how much the value per share changes as we change the growth period in Figure 31.12.

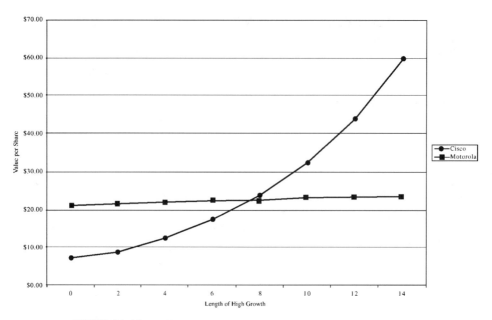

FIGURE 31.12   Value per Share and Length of High-Growth Period

The effect of changing the length of the growth period is very different for the two firms. For Cisco, the value per share changes significantly as the length of the growth period change, increasing as it gets longer. For Motorola, the effect is muted and the value per share is relatively insensitive to changes in the length of the growth period. The reason lies in the excess returns that we are assuming for the two firms over the length of the growth period. For Cisco, the excess returns are very large and thus the impact on value is also large. For Motorola, we assume that the excess returns are relatively small and the effect on value is also much lower.

LEAD TIMES FROM COMPETITIVE ADVANTAGES

A key question that we often face when looking at the effects of a competitive advantage on value is how long a competitive advantage lasts. This is a difficult question to answer because there are a number of firm-specific factors, but there are few interesting studies in corporate strategy that try to address the issue. Levin, Klevorick, Nelson, and Winter (1987) estimate, for instance, that it takes between three and five years to duplicate a patented product or process and between one and three years to duplicate an unpatented product or process. The same study found that patenting is often much less effective at preventing imitation than moving quickly down the learning curve and creating sales and service networks. For example, Intel was able to maintain its competitive advantage even as its computer chips were being cloned by Advanced Micro Devices (AMD) by using the lead time it had to move quickly to the next-generation chips.

Reduce the Cost of Financing

The cost of capital for a firm is a composite cost of debt and equity financing. The cash flows generated over time are discounted to the present at the cost of capital. Holding the cash flows constant, reducing the cost of capital will increase the value of the firm. This section will explore the ways in which a firm may reduce its cost of capital, or more generally, increase its firm value by changing both financing mix and type.

Change Operating Risk   The operating risk of a firm is a direct function of the kinds of products or services it provides and the degree to which these products or services are discretionary to the customer. The more discretionary they are, the greater the operating risk faced by the firm. Both the cost of equity and cost of debt of a firm are affected by the operating risk of the business or businesses in which it operates. In the case of equity, only that portion of the operating risk that is not diversifiable will affect value.

Firms can reduce their operating risk by making their products and services less discretionary to their customers. Advertising clearly plays a role, but finding new uses for a product or service is another way. Reducing operating risk will result in a lowered unlevered beta and a lower cost of debt.

Reduce Operating Leverage   The operating leverage of a firm measures the proportion of its costs that are fixed. Other things remaining equal, the greater the proportion of the costs of a firm that are fixed, the more volatile its earnings will be, and the higher its cost of capital. Reducing the proportion of the costs that are fixed will make firms much less risky and reduce their cost of capital. Firms can reduce their fixed costs by using outside contractors for some services; if business does not measure up, the firm is not stuck with the costs of providing this service. They can also tie expenses to revenues; for instance, tying wages paid to revenues made will reduce the proportion of costs that are fixed.

This basic idea of tying expenses to revenues is often described as making the cost structure more flexible. A more flexible cost structure influences three inputs in a valuation. It leads to a lower unlevered beta (due to the lower operating leverage), reduces the cost of debt (because of the reduction in default risk) and increases the optimal debt ratio. All three reduce the cost of capital and increase firm value.

Change the Financing Mix   A third way to reduce the cost of capital is to change the mix of debt and equity used to finance the firm. As we argued in Chapter 15, debt is always cheaper than equity, partly because lenders bear less risk and partly because of the tax advantage associated with debt. This benefit has to be weighed off against the additional risk of bankruptcy created by the borrowing; this higher risk increases both the beta for equity and the cost of borrowing. The net effect will determine whether the cost of capital will increase or decrease as the firm takes on more debt.

Note, however, that firm value will increase as the cost of capital decreases, if and only if the operating cash flows are unaffected by the higher debt ratio. If, as the debt ratio increases, the riskiness of the firm increases, and this, in turn, affects the firm's operations and cash flows, the firm value may decrease even as cost of capital declines. If this is the case, the objective function when designing the financing mix for a firm has to be restated in terms of firm value maximization rather than cost of capital minimization.

wacc.xls: **This dataset on the Web summarizes debt ratios and costs of capital by industry group for the United States.**

ILLUSTRATION 31.8:   The Effect of Financing Mix on Value

To analyze the effect of changing the financing mix on value, you would need to estimate the costs of equity and debt at each debt ratio. In the following table, the costs of equity and debt are estimated for Motorola for debt ratios from 0% to 90%:

Debt Ratio	Beta	Cost of Equity	Bond Rating	Interest Rate on Debt	Tax Rate	Cost of Debt (After-Tax)	WACC
0%	1.16	10.63%	AAA	6.20%	35.00%	4.03%	10.63%
10%	1.24	10.96%	A–	7.25%	35.00%	4.71%	10.33%
20%	1.34	11.38%	B–	10.25%	35.00%	6.66%	10.43%
30%	1.48	11.91%	CC	12.00%	35.00%	7.80%	10.68%
40%	1.72	12.90%	C	13.50%	26.34%	9.94%	11.72%
50%	2.07	14.28%	C	13.50%	21.07%	10.66%	12.47%
60%	2.63	16.54%	D	16.00%	14.82%	13.63%	14.79%
70%	3.51	20.05%	D	16.00%	12.70%	13.97%	15.79%
80%	5.27	27.07%	D	16.00%	11.11%	14.22%	16.79%
90%	10.54	48.14%	D	16.00%	9.88%	14.42%	17.79%

Note that the cost of equity is estimated based on the levered beta. As the debt ratio increases, the beta increases as well.[7] The cost of debt is estimated based on a synthetic rating that is determined by the interest coverage ratio at each debt ratio. As the debt ratio increases, the interest expense increases leading to a drop in the ratings and higher costs of debt. As Motorola moves from a 0% debt ratio to a 10% debt ratio, the cost of capital decreases (and firm value increases). At a 10% debt ratio, Motorola's cost of capital is 10.33%, which is lower than the current cost of capital of 10.39%. Beyond 10%, though, the trade-off operates against debt, as the cost of capital increases as the debt ratio increases. (The tax rate drops beyond 30% since the interest expenses > EBIT.)

Change Financing Type   A fundamental principle in corporate finance is that the financing of a firm should be designed to ensure, as far as possible, that the cash flows on debt match as closely as possible the cash flows on the asset. By matching cash flows on debt to cash flows on the asset, a firm reduces its risk of default and increases its capacity to carry debt, which, in turn, reduces its cost of capital, and increases value.

Firms that mismatch cash flows on debt and cash flows on assets (by using short-term debt to finance long-term assets, debt in one currency to finance assets in a different currency, or floating-rate debt to finance assets whose cash flows tend to be adversely impacted by higher inflation) will have higher default risk, higher costs of capital, and lower firm value. Firms can use derivatives and swaps to reduce these mismatches and, in the process, increase firm value. Alternatively, they can re-

---

[7]Levered beta = Unlevered beta[1 + (1 – Tax rate)(Debt/Equity)].

WHAT ABOUT MILLER-MODIGLIANI?

One of corporate finance's best-known and most enduring propositions—the Miller-Modigliani theorem—argues that the value of a firm is independent of its capital structure. In other words, changing your financing mix should have no effect on your firm value. How would we reconcile our arguments in this section with the Miller-Modigliani theorem? Note that the original version of the theorem was derived for a world with no taxes and default. With these assumptions, debt creates no tax advantages and no bankruptcy costs and does not affect value. In a world with taxes and default risk, you are much more likely to have to make trade-offs, and debt can increase value, decrease value, or leave it unaffected, depending on how the trade-offs operate.

---

place their existing debt with debt that is more closely matched to their assets. Finally, they can use innovative securities that allow them to pattern cash flows on debt to cash flows on investments. The use of catastrophe bonds by insurance companies and commodity bonds by natural resource firms are good examples.

VALUE ENHANCEMENT CHAIN

We can categorize the range of actions firms can take to increase value in several ways. One is in terms of whether they affect cash flows from assets in place, growth, the cost of capital, or the length of the growth period. There are two other levels at which we can distinguish between actions that create value:

1. *Does an action create a value trade-off or is it a pure value creator?* Very few actions increase value without any qualifications. Among these are the divestitures of assets when the divestiture value exceeds the continuing value, and the elimination of deadweight costs that contribute nothing to the firm's earnings or future growth. Most actions have both positive and negative effects on value, and it is the net effect that determines whether these actions are value enhancing. In some cases, the trade-off is largely internal, and the odds are much better for value creation. An example is a firm changing its mix of debt and equity to reduce the cost of capital. In other cases, however, the net effect on value will be a function of how competitors react to a firm's actions. As an example, changing pricing strategy to increase margins may not work as a value enhancement measure, if competitors react and change prices as well.

2. *How quickly do actions pay off?* Some actions generate an immediate increase in value. Among these are divestitures and cost cutting. Many actions, however, are designed to create value in the long term. Thus, building up a respected brand name clearly creates value in the long term but is unlikely to affect value today.

Table 31.2 summarizes a value enhancement chain, where actions that create value are categorized both on how quickly they create value and on how much control the firm has over the value creation. The first column, "Quick Fixes," lists

TABLE 31.2 The Value Enhancement Chain

More Control   Less Control
Quick Payoff   Payoff in Long Term
→

	Quick Fixes	Odds On	Long Term
Existing investments	• Divest assets/projects with divestiture value > continuing value. • Terminate projects with liquidation value > continuing value. • Eliminate operating expenses that generate no revenues and no growth. • Take advantage of tax law to increase cash flow.	• Reduce net working capital requirements by reducing inventory and accounts receivable or by increasing accounts payable. • Reduce capital maintenance expenditures on assets in place. • Reduce marginal tax rate.	• Change pricing strategy to maximize return on capital and value. • Move to more efficient technology for operations to reduce expenses and improve margins.
Expected growth	• Eliminate new capital expenditures that are expected to earn less than the cost of capital.	• Increase reinvestment rate or marginal return on capital or both in firm's existing businesses.	• Increase reinvestment rate or marginal return on capital or both in new businesses.
Length of high-growth period	• If any of the firm's products or services can be patented and protected, do so.	• Use economies of scale or cost advantages to create higher return on capital.	• Build up brand name. • Increase the cost of switching from product and reduce the cost of switching to it.
Cost of financing	• Use swaps and derivatives to match debt more closely to firm's assets. • Recapitalize to move the firm toward its optimal debt ratio.	• Change financing type and use innovative securities to reflect the types of assets being financed. • Use the optimal financing mix to finance new investments. • Make cost structure more flexible to reduce operating leverage.	• Reduce the operating risk of the firm by making products less discretionary to customers.

actions in which the firm has considerable control over the outcome and the benefit in terms of value creation is immediate. The second column, "Odds On," includes actions that are likely to create value in the near or medium term and where the firm still continues to exercise significant control over the outcome. The third column includes actions designed to create value in the long term. This is where the major strategic initiatives of the firm show up.

ILLUSTRATION 31.9:   A Value Enhancement Plan

Illustration 31.7 valued Motorola at $22.97 using its current return on capital of 12.18% and debt ratio of 6.86% in the valuation. Figure 31.13 summarizes this valuation. Note, though, that the current return on capital is well below what the firm has earned historically and lags the industry average (of 22.36%) by almost 10%. If Motorola could increase its return on capital to 17.22% on its new investments (leaving its existing investments earning 12.18%) and increase its debt ratio to its optimal of 10%, its value per share would increase to $23.86. The restructured valuation is summarized in Figure 31.14.

 valenh.xls: **This spreadsheet allows you to estimate the approximate effect of changing the way a firm is run on its value.**

CLOSING THOUGHTS ON VALUE ENHANCEMENT

Almost all firms claim to be interested in value enhancement, but very few are able to increase value consistently. If value enhancement is as simple as it is made out to be in this chapter, you might wonder why this is so. There are four basic propositions you need to consider in the context of value enhancement:

1. *Value enhancement is hard work, takes time, and may make life uncomfortable for existing managers.* There are no magic bullets that increase value painlessly.

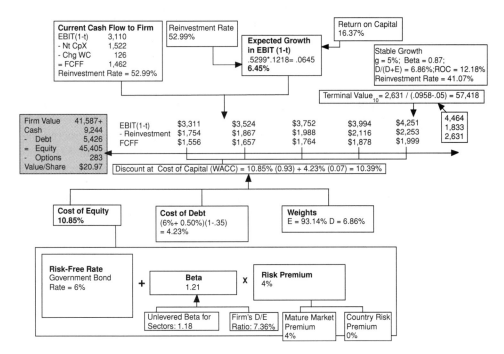

FIGURE 31.13   Motorola: A Status Quo Valuation

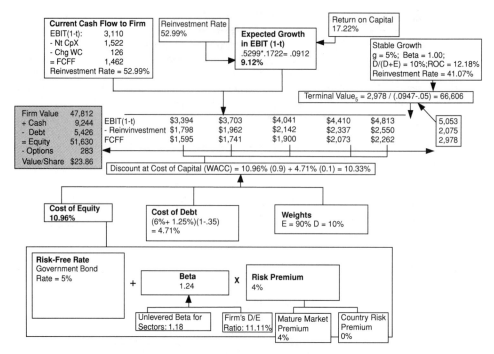

FIGURE 31.14   Motorola: A Restructured Valuation

Increasing cash flows requires hard decisions on layoffs and cost cutting, and in some cases, admitting past mistakes. Increasing the reinvestment rate will require that you analyze new investments with more care and that you invest in the infrastructure you need to manage these investments. Increasing your debt ratio may also create new pressures to make interest payments and to deal with ratings agencies and banks.

2. *For a firm to enhance value, all of its component parts need to buy into the value enhancement plan.* You cannot increase value by edict and you cannot do it from the executive offices (or the finance department). As you probably noticed in the discussion, every part of the firm has a role to play in increasing value. Table 31.3 summarizes the role of each part of the firm in the value enhancement actions that have been described in this chapter. Departments have to cooperate for value enhancement to become a reality.

3. *Value enhancement has to be firm-specific.* No two firms in trouble share the same problems, and using a cookbook approach seldom works in value enhancement. You have to begin by diagnosing the specific problems faced by the firm you are analyzing and tailor a response to these problems. Thus, the value enhancement plan you would devise for a mature firm with cost overruns will be very different from the plan you would devise for a young firm that has a product that no longer meets market needs.

4. *Price enhancement may not always follow value enhancement.* This is perhaps the most disappointing aspect of value enhancement. A firm that takes all the right actions may not necessarily be rewarded immediately by financial mar-

TABLE 31.3 Value Enhancement Actions: Who Is Responsible?

Value-Enhancing Action	Primary Responsibility
Increasing operating efficiency	Operating managers and personnel, from shop-floor stewards to factory managers
Reducing working capital needs	Inventory personnel; credit personnel
Increasing revenue growth	Sales and marketing personnel
Increasing return on capital/reinvestment rate	Strategic teams, with help from financial analysts
Build brand name	Advertising personnel
Other competitive advantages	Strategic analysts
Reduce cost of financing	Finance department

kets. In some cases, markets may even punish such firms because of the effects of these actions on reported earnings. In the long term, markets most likely will recognize value-enhancing actions and reward them, but the manager who took these actions may not be around to share in the rewards.

CONCLUSION

Value enhancement is clearly on the minds of many managers today. Building on the discounted cash flow principles developed in the preceding chapter, the value of a firm can be increased by changing one of the four primary inputs into value: the cash flows from assets in place, the expected growth rate during the high-growth period, the length of the high-growth period and the cost of capital. Conversely, actions that do not change any of these variables cannot create value. Cash flows from assets in place can be increased by cost cutting and more efficient operations, as well as by lowering taxes paid on income and reducing investment needs (capital maintenance and noncash working capital investments). Expected growth can be increased by increasing the reinvestment rate or the return on capital, but increases in the reinvestment rate will generate value only if the return on capital exceeds the cost of capital. High growth, at least the value-creating kind, can be made to last longer by generating new competitive advantages or augmenting existing ones. Finally, the cost of capital can be lowered by moving toward an optimal debt ratio, using debt that is more suited for the assets being financed and by reducing market risk.

QUESTIONS AND SHORT PROBLEMS

1. Marion Manufacturing, a steel company, announces that it will be taking a major restructuring charge that will lower earnings this year by $500 million. Assume that the charge is not tax deductible and has no effects on operations.
   a. What will the effect of this charge be on the value of the firm?
   b. When the firm announces the charge, what effect would you expect it to have on the stock price? Is your answer consistent with your response to question a?

2. Universal Health Care (UHC) is a company whose stock price has declined by 40% in the past year. In the current year, UHC earned $300 million in pretax operating income on revenues of $10 billion. The new CEO of the firm has proposed cost-cutting measures she anticipates will save the firm $100 million in expenses, without any effect on revenues. Assume the firm is growing at a stable rate of 5% a year and that its cost of capital is 10%; neither number is expected to change as a consequence of the cost cutting. The firm's tax rate is 40%. (You can assume that the firm reinvests $100 million each year and that this reinvestment will not change as the firm cuts costs.)
   a. What effect will the cost cutting have on value?
   b. What effect will the cost cutting have on value if the expected growth rate will drop to 4.5% as a consequence? (Some of the costs cut were designed to generate future growth.)

3. Atlantic Cruise Lines operates cruise ships and is headquartered in Florida. The firm had $100 million in pretax operating income in the current year, of which it reinvested $25 million. The firm expects its operating income to grow 4% in perpetuity, and expects to maintain its existing reinvestment rate. Atlantic has a capital structure composed 60% of equity and 40% of debt. Its cost of equity is 12% and it has a pretax cost of borrowing of 8%. The firm currently faces a tax rate of 40%.
   a. Estimate the value of the firm.
   b. Assume now that Atlantic Cruise Lines will move its headquarters to the Cayman Islands. If its tax rate drops to 0% as a consequence, estimate the effect on value of the shift.

4. Furniture Depot is a retail chain selling furniture and appliances. The firm has after-tax operating income of $250 million in the current year on revenues of $5 billion. The firm also has noncash working capital of $1 billion. The net capital expenditures this year of $100 million, and expects revenues, operating income and net capital expenditures to grow 5% a year forever. The firm's cost of capital is 9%.
   a. Assume that noncash working capital remains at the existing percent of revenues, estimate the value of the firm.
   b. Assume now that the firm is able to reduce its noncash working capital requirement by 50%. Estimate the effect on value of this change.
   c. If as a consequence of this noncash working capital change, earnings growth declines to 4.75%, what would the effect on value be of the drop in noncash working capital?

5. General Systems is a firm that manufactures personal computers. As a top manager in the firm, you are considering changes in the way the firm is run. Currently, the firm has after-tax operating income of $50 million on capital invested of $250 million (at the beginning of the year). The firm also reinvests $25 million in net capital expenditures and working capital.
   a. Estimate the expected growth rate in earnings, given the firm's current return on capital and reinvestment rate.
   b. Holding the return on capital constant, what would happen to the expected growth rate if the firm increased its reinvestment rate to 80%?
   c. What would the effect on growth be if, as the reinvestment rate increases to 80%, the return on capital on investments drops by 5%? (For instance, if the return on capital is currently 18%, it will drop to 13%.)

6. Compaq Computers has seen its stock price decline from $45 to $24. The firm is expected to reinvest 50% of its expected after-tax operating income of $2 billion in new investments, and expects to earn a return on capital of 10.69%. The firm is all equity financed and has a cost of equity of 11.5%.
   a. What is the firm's expected growth rate, assuming that it maintains its existing reinvestment rate and return on capital?
   b. Assuming that this growth is perpetual, what is the value of the firm?
   c. How much value is being created or destroyed by the firm's new investments?

7. Referring to problem 6, now assume that Compaq's optimal debt ratio is 20%. Its cost of equity will increase to 12.5%, and its after-tax cost of debt will be 4.5% at the optimal debt ratio.
   a. What is the firm's expected growth rate, assuming it maintains its existing reinvestment rate and return on capital?
   b. Assuming this growth is perpetual, what is the value of the firm?
   c. How much value is being created or destroyed by the firm's new investments?

8. Coca-Cola is considered to have one of the most valuable brand names in the world. The firm has an after-tax operating margin of 20% on revenues of $25 billion. The capital invested in the firm is $10 billion. In addition, Coca-Cola reinvests 50% of its after-tax operating earnings.
   a. Estimate the expected growth in operating earnings, assuming Coca-Cola can sustain these values for the foreseeable future.
   b. Assume generic soft drink manufacturers have after-tax operating margins of only 7.5%. If Coca-Cola maintains its existing reinvestment rate but loses its brand name value, estimate the expected growth rate in operating earning. (You can assume that with the loss in brand name value Coca-Cola's operating margins would drop to 7.5% as well.)

9. BioMask Genetics is a biotechnology firm with only one patent to its name. The after-tax operating earnings in the current year are $10 million, and the firm has no reinvestment needs. The patent will expire in three years, and the firm will have a 15% growth rate in earnings during that period. After year 3, operating earnings are expected to remain constant forever. The firm's management is considering an advertising plan designed to build up the brand name of its patented product. The advertising campaign will cost $50 million (pretax) a year over the next three years; the firm's tax rate is 40%. The firm believes this campaign will allow it to maintain a 15% growth rate for 10 years, as the brand name compensates for the loss of the patent protection. After year 10, the operating earnings are expected to remain constant forever. The firm has a cost of capital of 10%.
   a. Estimate the value of the firm assuming it does not embark on the advertising campaign.
   b. Estimate the value of the firm with the advertising campaign.
   c. Assume there is no guarantee the growth rate will last 10 years as a result of the campaign. What would the probability of success need to be for the campaign to be financially viable?

10. Sunmask is a cosmetics firm that has seen its stock price fall and its earnings decline in the past year. You have been hired as the new CEO of the company, and a careful analysis of Sunmask's current financials reveals the following:

- The firm currently has after-tax operating earnings of $300 million on revenues of $10 billion, and a capital turnover ratio (sales–book value of capital) of 2.5.
- The firm is expected to reinvest 60% of its after-tax operating income.
- The firm is all equity financed and has a cost of capital of 10%.

a. Estimate the value of the firm, assuming existing policies continue forever. (Returns on capital and reinvestment rates remain constant forever as well.)

b. Assume that you can increase operating margins from 3% to 5% without affecting the capital turnover ratio, that you can lower the reinvestment rate to 40%, and that the cost of capital will become 9% if you shift to your optimal debt ratio. How much would your firm value increase if you were able to make these changes?

Value Enhancement: Economic Value Added, Cash Flow Return on Investment, and Other Tools

The discounted cash flow model provides for a rich and thorough analysis of all the different ways in which a firm can increase value, but it can become complex as the number of inputs increases. It is also difficult to tie management compensation systems to a discounted cash flow model, since many of the inputs need to be estimated and can be manipulated to yield the results management wants.

If we assume that markets are efficient, we can replace the unobservable value from the discounted cash flow model with the observed market price and reward or punish managers based on the performance of the stock. Thus, a firm whose stock price has gone up is viewed as having created value, whereas one whose stock price has fallen has destroyed value. Compensation systems based on the stock price, including stock grants and warrants, have become a standard component of most management compensation packages.

While market prices have the advantage of being up-to-date and observable, they are also noisy. Even if markets are efficient, stock prices tend to fluctuate around the true value, and markets sometimes do make mistakes. Thus, a firm may see its stock price go up and its top management rewarded, even as it destroys value. Conversely, the managers of a firm may be penalized as its stock price drops, even though the managers may have taken actions that increase firm value. The other problem with stock prices as the basis for compensation is that they are available only for the entire firm. Thus stock prices cannot be used to analyze the managers of individual divisions of a firm, or for their relative performance.

In the past decade, while firms have become more focused on value creation, they have remained suspicious of financial markets. While they might understand the notion of discounted cash flow value, they are unwilling to tie compensation to a value that is based on dozens of estimates. In this environment, new mechanisms for measuring value that are simple to estimate and use, do not depend too heavily on market movements, and do not require a lot of estimation find a ready market. The two mechanisms that seem to have made the most impact are:

1. *Economic value added (EVA),* which measures the dollar surplus value created by a firm on its existing investment.
2. *Cash flow return on investment (CFROI),* which measures the percentage return made by a firm on its existing investments.

This chapter looks at how each is related to discounted cash flow valuation. It also looks at the conditions under which firms using these approaches to judge performance and evaluate managers may end up making decisions that destroy value rather than create it.

ECONOMIC VALUE ADDED

The economic value added (EVA) is a measure of the dollar surplus value created by an investment or a portfolio of investments. It is computed as the product of the excess return made on an investment or investments and the capital invested in that investment or investments.

$$
\begin{aligned}
\text{Economic value added} &= (\text{Return on capital invested} - \text{Cost of capital}) \\
&\quad \times (\text{Capital invested}) \\
&= \text{After-tax operating income} - (\text{Cost of capital} \\
&\quad \times \text{Capital invested})
\end{aligned}
$$

This section begins by looking at the measurement of economic value added, then considers its links to discounted cash flow valuation, and closes with a discussion of its limitations as a value enhancement tool.

Calculating EVA

The definition of EVA outlines three basic inputs we need for its computation—the return on capital earned on investments, the cost of capital for those investments, and the capital invested in them. In measuring each of these, we will make many of the same adjustments that were discussed in the context of discounted cash flow valuation.

How much capital is there invested in existing assets? One obvious answer is to use the market value of the firm, but market value includes capital invested not just in assets in place but in expected future growth.[1] Since we want to evaluate the quality of assets in place, we need a measure of the market value of just these assets. Given the difficulty of estimating market value of assets in place, it is not surprising that we turn to the book value of capital as a proxy for the market value of capital invested in assets in place. The book value, however, is a number that reflects not just the accounting choices made in the current period, but also accounting decisions made over time on how to depreciate assets, value inventory, and deal with acquisitions. At the minimum, the three adjustments we made to capital invested in the discounted cash flow valuation—converting operating leases into debt, capitalizing R&D expenses, and eliminating the effect of one-time or cosmetic charges—have to be made when computing EVA as well. The older the firm, the more extensive the adjustments that have to be made to book value of capital to get to a reasonable estimate of the market value of capital invested in assets in place. Since this requires that we know and take into account every accounting decision over time, there are cases where the book value of capital is too flawed to be fixable. Here, it is best to estimate the capital invested from the ground up, starting

---

[1] As an illustration, computing the return on capital at Microsoft using the market value of the firm, instead of book value, results in a return on capital of about 3 percent. It would be a mistake to view this as a sign of poor investments on the part of the firm's managers.

EVA COMPUTATION IN PRACTICE

During the 1990s, EVA was promoted most heavily by Stern Stewart, a New York–based consulting firm. The firm's founders, Joel Stern and Bennett Stewart, became the foremost evangelists for the measure. Their success spawned a whole host of imitators from other consulting firms, all of which were variants on the excess return measure.

In the process of applying this measure to real firms, Stern Stewart found that it had to modify accounting measures of earnings and capital to get more realistic estimates of surplus value. In his book *The Quest for Value* Bennett Stewart mentions some of the adjustments that should be made to capital invested, including adjusting for goodwill (recorded and unrecorded). He also suggests adjustments that need to be made to operating income, including the conversion of operating leases into financial expenses.

Many firms that adopted EVA during this period also based management compensation on measured EVA. Consequently, how it was defined and measured became a matter of significant concern to managers at every level.

---

with the assets owned by the firm, estimating the market value of these assets, and cumulating this market value.

To evaluate the return on this invested capital, we need an estimate of the after-tax operating income earned by a firm on these investments. Again, the accounting measure of operating income has to be adjusted for operating leases, R&D expenses, and one-time charges to compute the return on capital.

The third and final component needed to estimate the economic value added is the cost of capital. In keeping with our arguments both in the investment analysis and the discounted cash flow valuation sections, the cost of capital should be estimated based on the market values of debt and equity in the firm, rather than book value. There is no contradiction between using book value for purposes of estimating capital invested and using market value for estimating cost of capital, since a firm has to earn more than its market value cost of capital to generate value. From a practical standpoint, using the book value cost of capital will tend to understate cost of capital for most firms, and will understate it more for more highly levered firms than for lightly levered firms. Understating the cost of capital will lead to overstating the economic value added.

Economic Value Added, Net Present Value, and Discounted Cash Flow Valuation

One of the foundations of investment analysis in traditional corporate finance is the net present value rule. The net present value (NPV) of a project, which reflects the present value of expected cash flows on a project, netted against any investment needs, is a measure of dollar surplus value on the project. Thus, investing in projects with positive net present value will increase the value of the firm, while investing in projects with negative net present value will reduce value. Economic value added is a simple extension of the net present value rule. The net present value of the project is the present value of the economic value added by that project over its life.[2]

$$NPV = \sum_{t=1}^{t=n} \frac{EVA_t}{(1+k_c)^t}$$

where EVA_t is the economic value added by the project in year t, and the project has a life of n years.

This connection between economic value added and NPV allows us to link the value of a firm to the economic value added by that firm. To see this, let us begin with a simple formulation of firm value in terms of the value of assets in place and expected future growth:

Firm value = Value of assets in place + Value of expected future growth

Note that in a discounted cash flow model, the values of both assets in place and expected future growth can be written in terms of the net present value created by each component:

$$\text{Firm value} = \text{Capital invested}_{\text{assets in place}} + NPV_{\text{assets in place}} + \sum_{t=1}^{t=\infty} NPV_{\text{future projects, t}}$$

Substituting the economic value added version of net present value into this equation, we get:

$$\text{Firm value} = \text{Capital invested}_{\text{assets in place}} + \sum_{t=1}^{t=\infty} \frac{EVA_{t,\text{ assets in place}}}{(1+k_c)^t}$$

$$+ \sum_{t=1}^{t=\infty} \frac{EVA_{t,\text{ future projects}}}{(1+k_c)^t}$$

Thus the value of a firm can be written as the sum of three components: the capital invested in assets in place, the present value of the economic value added by these assets, and the expected present value of the economic value that will be added by future investments.

---

[2]This is true, though, only if the expected present value of the cash flows from depreciation is assumed to be equal to the present value of the salvage of the capital invested in the project. A proof of this equality can be found in my paper on value enhancement in the *Contemporary Finance Digest* in 1999.

ILLUSTRATION 32.1:   Discounted Cash Flow Value and Economic Value Added

Consider a firm that has existing assets in which it has capital invested of $100 million. Assume these additional facts about the firm:

- The after-tax operating income on assets in place is $15 million. This return on capital of 15% is expected to be sustained in the future, and the company has a cost of capital of 10%.
- At the beginning of each of the next five years, the firm is expected to make new investments of $10 million each. These investments are also expected to earn 15% as a return on capital, and the cost of capital is expected to remain 10%.
- After year 5, the company will continue to make investments, and earnings will grow 5% a year, but the new investments will have a return on capital of only 10%, which is also the cost of capital.
- All assets and investments are expected to have infinite lives.[3] Thus, the assets in place and the investments made in the first five years will make 15% a year in perpetuity, with no growth.

This firm can be valued using an economic value added approach, as follows:

Capital invested in assets in place	$100
+ EVA from assets in place = (.15 − .10)(100)/.10	$ 50
+ PV of EVA from new investments in year 1 = [(.15 − .10)(10)/.10]	$ 5
+ PV of EVA from new investments in year 2 = [(.15 − .10)(10)/.10]/1.1	$ 4.55
+ PV of EVA from new investments in year 3 = [(.15 − .10)(10)/.10]/1.1^2	$ 4.13
+ PV of EVA from new investments in year 4 = [(.15 − .10)(10)/.10]/1.1^3	$ 3.76
+ PV of EVA from new investments in year 5 = [(.15 − .10)(10)/.10]/1.1^4	$ 3.42
Value of firm	$170.85

Note that the present values are computed assuming that the cash flows on investments are perpetuities and that the investments are made at the beginning of each year. In addition, today value of the economic value added by the investments made in future years are discounted to today, using the cost of capital. To illustrate, the present value of the economic value added by investments made at the beginning of year 2 is discounted back one year. The value of the firm, which is $170.85 million, can be written using the earlier equation as follows:

$$\text{Firm value} = \text{Capital invested}_{\text{assets in place}} + \sum_{t=1}^{t=\infty} \frac{EVA_{t,\text{ assets in place}}}{(1+k_c)^t}$$

$$+ \sum_{t=1}^{t=\infty} \frac{EVA_{t,\text{ future projects}}}{(1+k_c)^t}$$

$$\$170.85 \text{ million} = \$100 \text{ million} + \$50 \text{ million} + \$20.85 \text{ million}$$

The value of existing assets is therefore $150 million, and the value of future growth opportunities is $20.85 million.

Another way of presenting these results is in terms of market value added (MVA). The market value added, in this case, is the difference between the firm value of $170.85 million and the capital invested of $100 million, which yields $70.85 million. This value will be positive only if the return on capital is greater than the cost of capital and will be an increasing function of the spread between the two numbers. The number will be negative if the return on capital is less than the cost of capital.

---

[3]Note that this assumption is purely for convenience, since it makes the net present value easier to compute. This also allows us to assume the depreciation is offset by capital maintenance expenditures.

Note that although the firm continues to grow operating income and makes new investments after the fifth year, these marginal investments create no additional value because they earn the cost of capital. A direct implication is that it is not growth that creates value, but growth in conjunction with excess returns. This provides a new perspective on the quality of growth. A firm can be increasing its operating income at a healthy rate, but if it is doing so by investing large amounts at or below the cost of capital, it will not be creating value and may actually be destroying it.

This firm could also have been valued using a discounted cash flow valuation, with free cash flows to the firm discounted at the cost of capital. The following table shows expected free cash flows and the firm value, using the cost of capital of 10% as the discount rate.

	0	1	2	3	4	5	Terminal Year
EBIT(1 − t) from assets in place	$ 0.00	$15.00	$15.00	$15.00	$15.00	$ 15.00	
EBIT(1 − t) from investments—Year 1		$ 1.50	$ 1.50	$ 1.50	$ 1.50	$ 1.50	
EBIT(1 − t) from investments—Year 2			$ 1.50	$ 1.50	$ 1.50	$ 1.50	
EBIT(1 − t) from investments—Year 3				$ 1.50	$ 1.50	$ 1.50	
EBIT(1 − t) from investments—Year 4					$ 1.50	$ 1.50	
EBIT(1 − t) from investments—Year 5						$ 1.50	
Total EBIT(1 − t)		$16.50	$18.00	$19.50	$21.00	$ 22.50	$23.63
− Net capital expenditures	$ 10.00	$10.00	$10.00	$10.00	$10.00	$ 11.25	$11.81
FCFF		$ 6.50	$ 8.00	$ 9.50	$11.00	$ 11.25	$11.81
PV of FCFF	($ 10)	$ 5.91	$ 6.61	$ 7.14	$ 7.51	$ 6.99	
Terminal value						$236.25	
PV of terminal value						$146.69	
Value of firm	$170.85						
Return on capital	15%	15%	15%	15%	15%	15%	10%
Cost of capital	10%	10%	10%	10%	10%	10%	10%

In looking at this valuation, note the following:

■ The capital expenditures occur at the beginning of each year and thus are shown in the previous year. The investment of $10 million in year 1 is shown in period 0, the year 2 investment in year 1, and so on.

■ In year 5, the net investment needed to sustain growth is computed by using two assumptions—that growth in operating income would be 5% a year beyond year 5, and that the return on capital on new investments starting in year 6 (which is shown in year 5) would be 10%.

Net investment$_5$ = [EBIT$_6$(1 − t) − EBIT$_5$(1 − t)]/ROC$_6$ = ($23.625 − $22.50)/.10 = $11.25 million

The value of the firm obtained by discounting free cash flows to the firm at the cost of capital is $170.85, which is identical to the value obtained using the economic value added approach.

ILLUSTRATION 32.2:   An EVA Valuation of Boeing—1998

The equivalence of traditional DCF valuation and EVA valuation can be illustrated for Boeing. We begin with a discounted cash flow valuation of Boeing and summarize the inputs used:

	High-Growth Phase	*Stable-Growth Phase*
Length	*10 years*	*Forever after year 10*
Growth inputs		
Reinvestment rate	65.98%	59.36%
Return on capital	6.59%	8.42%
Expected growth rate	4.35%	5.00%
Cost of capital inputs		
Beta	1.01	1.00
Cost of debt	5.50%	5.50%
Debt ratio	19.92%	30.00%
Cost of capital	9.18%	8.42%
General information		
Tax rate	35%	35%

The current after-tax operating income for the firm is $1,651 million. With these inputs, the free cash flows to the firm can be estimated:

Year	EBIT(1 − t)	Reinvestment	FCFF	Present Value at 9.18 Percent
Current	$1,651			
1	$1,723	$1,137	$ 586	$537
2	$1,798	$1,186	$ 612	$513
3	$1,876	$1,238	$ 638	$490
4	$1,958	$1,292	$ 666	$469
5	$2,043	$1,348	$ 695	$448
6	$2,132	$1,407	$ 725	$428
7	$2,225	$1,468	$ 757	$409
8	$2,321	$1,532	$ 790	$391
9	$2,422	$1,598	$ 824	$374
10	$2,528	$1,668	$ 860	$357
Terminal year	$2,654	$1,576	$1,078	

The sum of the present value of the cash flows over the growth period is $4,416 million. The terminal value can be estimated based on the cash flow in the terminal year and the cost of capital of 8.42%:

$$\text{Terminal value} = \$1,078/(.0842 - .05) = \$31,529 \text{ million}$$

The discounted cash flow estimate of the value is:

$$\text{Value of Boeing's operating assets} = 4,416 + 31,529/1.0918^{10} = \$17,506 \text{ million}$$

The following table estimates the EVA for Boeing each year for the next 10 years, and the present value of the EVA. To make these estimates, we begin with the current capital invested in the firm of $26,149 million and add the reinvestment each year from the preceding table to it to obtain the capital invested in the following year.

Year	Capital Invested at Beginning of Year	Return on Capital	Cost of Capital	EVA	PV of EVA
1	$26,149	6.59%	9.18%	($678)	($621)
2	$27,286	6.59%	9.18%	($707)	($593)
3	$28,472	6.59%	9.18%	($738)	($567)
4	$29,710	6.59%	9.18%	($770)	($542)
5	$31,002	6.59%	9.18%	($804)	($518)
6	$32,350	6.59%	9.18%	($839)	($495)
7	$33,757	6.59%	9.18%	($875)	($473)
8	$35,225	6.59%	9.18%	($913)	($452)
9	$36,756	6.59%	9.18%	($953)	($432)
10	$38,354	6.59%	9.18%	($994)	($413)
11	$40,022	Present value of EVA over 10 years			($5,107)

The sum of the present values of the EVA is −$5,107 million. To get to the value of the operating assets of the firm, we add two more components:

1. The capital invested in assets in place at the beginning of year 1 (current), which is $26,149 million.
2. The present value of the EVA in perpetuity on assets in place in year 10, which is computed as follows:

$$\frac{[EBIT_{11}(1-t) - Capital\ invested_{11} \times Cost\ of\ capital_{11}]/Cost\ of\ capital_{11}}{(1 + Current\ cost\ of\ capital)^{10}}$$

$$= [(2,653.93 - 40,022 \times .0842)/.0842]/(1.0918)^{10}$$
$$= -\$3,536\ million$$

Note that while the marginal return on capital on new investments is equal to the cost of capital after year 10, the existing investments continue to make 6.59%, which is lower than the cost of capital of 8.42%, in perpetuity.

The total value of the firm can then be computed as follows:

Capital invested in assets in place	$26,149 million
PV of EVA from assets in place	−$ 8,643 million
Value of operating assets	$17,506 million

 fcffeva.xls: This spreadsheet allows you to convert a discounted cash flow valuation into an EVA valuation, and vice versa.

EVA VALUATION VERSUS DCF VALUATION: WHEN THEY WILL DISAGREE

To get the same value from discounted cash flow and EVA valuations, you have to ensure that the following conditions hold:

- The after-tax operating income that you use to estimate free cash flows to the firm should be equal to the after-tax operating income you use to compute Economic Value Added. Thus, if you decide to adjust the operating income for operating leases and research and development expenses when doing discounted cash flow valuation, you have to adjust it for computing EVA as well.
- The growth rate you use to estimate after-tax operating income in future periods should be estimated from fundamentals when doing discounted cash flow valuation. In other words, it should be set to:

Growth rate = Reinvestment rate × Return on capital

If growth is an exogenous input into a DCF model and the relationship between growth rates, reinvestments, and return on capital outlined above does not hold, you will get different values from DCF and EVA valuations.

- The capital invested that is used to compute EVA in future periods should be estimated by adding the reinvestment in each period to the capital invested at the beginning of the period. The EVA in each period should be computed as follows:

$$EVA_t = \text{After-tax operating income}_t - \text{Cost of capital} \times \text{Capital invested}_{t-1}$$

- You have to make consistent assumptions about terminal value in your discounted cash flow and EVA valuations. In the special case, where the return on capital on all investments—existing and new—is equal to the cost of capital after your terminal year, this is simple to do. The terminal value will be equal to your capital invested at the beginning of your terminal year. In the more general case, you will have to ensure that the capital invested at the beginning of your terminal year is consistent with your assumption about return on capital in perpetuity. In other words, if your after-tax operating income in your terminal year is 1.2 billion and you are assuming a return on capital of 10 percent in perpetuity, you will have to set your capital invested at the beginning of your terminal year to be $12 billion.

EVA and Firm Value: Potential Conflicts

Assume that a firm adopts economic value added as its measure of value and decides to judge managers on their capacity to generate greater-than-expected economic value added. What is the potential for abuse? Is it possible for a manager to deliver greater than expected economic value added, while destroying firm value at the same time? If so, how can we protect stockholders against these practices?

To answer these questions, let us go back to the earlier equation where we decomposed firm value into capital invested, the present value of economic value added by assets in place, and the present value of economic value added by future growth.

$$\text{Firm value} = \text{Capital invested}_{\text{assets in place}} + \sum_{t=1}^{t=\infty} \frac{\text{EVA}_{t,\text{ assets in place}}}{(1+k_c)^t}$$

$$+ \sum_{t=1}^{t=\infty} \frac{\text{EVA}_{t,\text{ future projects}}}{(1+k_c)^t}$$

The Capital Invested Game The first two terms in the preceding equation, the capital invested and the present value of economic value added by these investments, are both sensitive to the measurement of capital invested. If capital invested is reduced, keeping the operating income constant, the first term in the equation will drop but the present value of economic value added will increase proportionately. To illustrate, consider the firm valued in Illustration 32.1. Assume that the capital invested is estimated to be $50 million rather than $100 million, and that the operating income on these investments stays at $15 million. This will increase the return on capital on existing assets to 30 percent. The assumptions about future investments remain unchanged. The firm value can then be written as shown in Table 32.1.

The value of the firm is unchanged, but it is redistributed to the economic value added component. When managers are judged on the economic value added, there will be strong incentives to reduce the capital invested, at least as measured for EVA computations.

There are some actions managers can take to reduce capital invested that truly create value. Thus, in the example, if the reduction in capital invested came from closing down a plant that does not (and is not expected to) generate any operating income, the cash flow generated by liquidating the plant's assets will increase value. Some actions, however, are purely cosmetic in terms of their effects on capital invested and thus do not create and may even destroy value. For instance, firms can take one-time restructuring charges that reduce capital, or lease assets rather than buy them because the capital impact of leasing may be smaller.

To illustrate the potential destructiveness of these actions, assume that the managers of the firm in Illustration 32.1 are able to replace half their assets with leased assets. Assume further that the estimated capital invested in these leased as-

TABLE 32.1 EVA Valuation of Firm: EVA and Assets in Place

Capital invested in assets in place	$ 50.00
+ EVA from assets in place = (.30 − .10)(50)/.10	$100.00
+ PV of EVA from new investments in year 1 = [(.15 − .10)(10)/.10]	$ 5.00
+ PV of EVA from new investments in year 2 = [(.15 − .10)(10)/.10]/1.1	$ 4.55
+ PV of EVA from new investments in year 3 = [(.15 − .10)(10)/.10]/1.1^2	$ 4.13
+ PV of EVA from new investments in year 4 = [(.15 − .10)(10)/.10]/1.1^3	$ 3.76
+ PV of EVA from new investments in year 5 = [(.15 − .10)(10)/.10]/1.1^4	$ 3.42
Value of firm	$170.85

sets is only $40 million, which is lower than the capital invested in the replaced assets of $50 million. In addition, assume that the action actually reduces the adjusted annual operating income from these assets from $15 million to $14.8 million. The value of the firm can now be written in Table 32.2. Note that the firm value declines by $2 million, but the economic value added increases by $8 million.

When economic value added is estimated for divisions, the capital invested at the divisional level is a function of a number of allocation decisions made by the firm, with the allocation based on prespecified criteria (such as revenues or number of employees). While we would like these rules to be objective and unbiased, they are often subjective and overallocate capital to some divisions and underallocate it to others. If this misallocation were purely random, we could accept it as error and use changes in economic value added to measure success. Given the natural competition that exists among divisions in a firm for the marginal investment dollar, however, these allocations are also likely to reflect the power of individual divisions to influence the process. Thus, the economic value added will be overestimated for those divisions that are underallocated capital, and underestimated for divisions that are overallocated capital.

The Future Growth Game   The value of a firm is the value of its existing assets and the value of its future growth prospects. When managers are judged on the basis of economic value added in the current year, or on year-to-year changes, the economic value added that is being measured is just that from assets in place. Thus, managers may trade off the economic value added from future growth for higher economic value added from assets in place.

Again, this point can be illustrated simply using the firm in Illustration 32.1. The firm earned a return on capital of 15 percent on both assets in place and future investments. Assume that there are actions the firm can take to increase the return on capital on assets in place to 16 percent, but that this action reduces the return on

TABLE 32.2   Value Reduction with Higher EVA

Capital invested in assets in place	$ 90.00
+ EVA from assets in place = (.1644 − .10)(90)/.10	$ 58.00
+ PV of EVA from new investments in year 1 = [(.15 − .10)(10)/.10]	$ 5.00
+ PV of EVA from new investments in year 2 = [(.15 − .10)(10)/.10]/1.1	$ 4.55
+ PV of EVA from new investments in year 3 = [(.15 − .10)(10)/.10]/1.1^2	$ 4.13
+ PV of EVA from new investments in year 4 = [(.15 − .10)(10)/.10]/1.1^3	$ 3.76
+ PV of EVA from new investments in year 5 = [(.15 − .10)(10)/.10]/1.1^4	$ 3.42
Value of firm	$168.85

TABLE 32.3   Trading Off Future Growth for Higher EVA

Capital invested in assets in place	$100.00
+ EVA from assets in place = (.16 − .10)(100)/.10	$ 60.00
+ PV of EVA from new investments in year 1 = [(.12 − .10)(10)/.10]	$ 2.00
+ PV of EVA from new investments in year 2 = [(.12 − .10)(10)/.10]/1.1	$ 1.82
+ PV of EVA from new investments in year 3 = [(.12 − .10)(10)/.10]/1.1^2	$ 1.65
+ PV of EVA from new investments in year 4 = [(.12 − .10)(10)/.10]/1.1^3	$ 1.50
+ PV of EVA from new investments in year 5 = [(.12 − .10)(10)/.10]/1.1^4	$ 1.37
Value of firm	$168.34

capital on future investments to 12 percent. The value of this firm can then be estimated in Table 32.3. Note that the value of the firm has decreased, but the economic value added in year 1 is higher now than it was before. In fact, the economic value added at this firm for each of the next five years is graphed in Figure 32.1 for both the original firm and this one. The growth trade-off, while leading to a lower firm value, results in economic value added in each of the first three years that is larger than it would have been without the trade-off.

Compensation mechanisms based on EVA are sometimes designed to punish managers who give up future growth for current EVA. Managers are partly compensated based on the economic value added this year, but another part is held back in a compensation bank and is available to the manager only after a period (say three or four years). There are significant limitations with these approaches. First, the limited tenure that managers have with firms implies that this measure can at best look at economic value added only over the next three or four years. The real costs of the growth trade-off are unlikely to show up until much later. Second, these approaches are really designed to punish managers who increase economic value added in the current period while reducing economic value added in future periods. In the more subtle case, where the economic value added continues to increase but at a rate lower than it otherwise would have, it is difficult to devise a punishment for managers who trade off future growth. In the preceding example, for instance, the economic value added with the growth trade-off increases over time. The increases are smaller than they would have been without the trade-off, but that number would not have been observed, anyway.

The Risk Shifting Game The value of a firm is the sum of the capital invested and the present value of the economic value added. The latter term is therefore a function not just of the dollar economic value added but also of the cost of capital. A

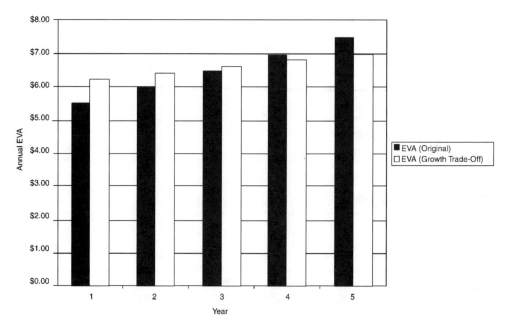

FIGURE 32.1 Annual EVA: With and Without Growth Trade-Off

firm can invest in projects to increase its economic value added but still end up with a lower value, if these investments increase its operating risk and cost of capital.

Again, using the firm in Illustration 32.1, assume that the firm is able to increase its return on capital on both assets in place and future investments from 15 percent to 16.25 percent and from 10 percent to 11 percent after year 5. Simultaneously, assume that the cost of capital increases to 11 percent. The economic value added in each year for the next five years is contrasted with the original economic value added in each year in Figure 32.2. While the economic value added in each year is higher with the high-risk strategy, the value of the firm is shown in Table 32.4. Note that the risk effect dominates the higher excess dollar returns, and the value of the firm decreases.

This risk shifting can be dangerous for firms that adopt economic value added based on objective functions. When managers are judged based on year-to-year economic value added changes, there will be a tendency to shift into riskier investments. This tendency will be exaggerated if the measured cost of capital does not reflect the changes in risk or lags it.[4]

In closing, economic value added is an approach skewed toward assets in place and away from future growth. It should not be surprising, therefore, that when economic value added is computed at the divisional level of a firm, the higher-growth divisions end up with the lowest economic value added, and in some cases with negative economic value added. Again, while these divisional managers may still be judged based on changes in economic value added from year to year, the temptation

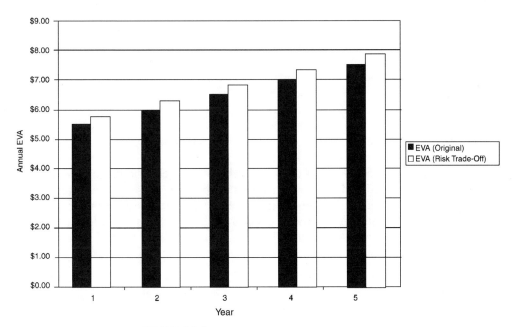

FIGURE 32.2 EVA: Higher Risk and Return

---

[4]In fact, beta estimates that are based on historical returns will lag changes in risk. With a five-year return estimation period, for instance, the lag might be as long as three years and the full effect will not show up for five years after the change.

TABLE 32.4   EVA with High-Risk Strategy

Capital invested in assets in place	$100.00
+ EVA from assets in place = (.1625 − .11) (100)/.11	$ 47.73
+ PV of EVA from investments in year 1 = [(.1625 − .11)(10)/.11]	$ 4.77
+ PV of EVA from investments in year 2 = [(.1625 − .10)(10)/.11]/1.11	$ 4.30
+ PV of EVA from investments in year 3 = [(.1625 − .11)(10)/.11]/1.11^2	$ 3.87
+ PV of EVA from investments in year 4 = [(.1625 − .11)(10)/.11]/1.11^3	$ 3.49
+ PV of EVA from investments in year 5 = [(.1625 − .11)(10)/.11]/1.11^4	$ 3.14
Value of firm	$167.31

at the firm level to reduce or eliminate capital invested in these divisions will be strong, since it will make the firm's overall economic value added look much better.

EVA and Market Value

Will increasing economic value added cause market value to increase? While an increase in economic value added will generally lead to an increase in firm value, barring the growth and risk games described earlier, it may or may not increase the stock price. This is so because the market value has built into it expectations of future economic value added. Thus a firm like Microsoft is priced on the assumption that it will earn large and increasing economic value added over time. Whether a firm's market value increases or decreases on the announcement of higher economic value added will depend in large part on what the expected change in economic value added was. For mature firms, where the market might have expected no increase or even a decrease in economic value added, the announcement of an increase will be good news and cause the market value to increase. For firms that are perceived to have good growth opportunities and are expected to report an increase in economic value added, the market value will decline if the announced increase in economic value added does not measure up to expectations. This should be no surprise to investors, who have recognized this phenomenon with earnings per share for decades; the earnings announcements of firms are judged against expectations, and the earnings surprise is what drives prices.

We would therefore not expect any correlation between the magnitude of the economic value added and stock returns, or even between the change in economic value added and stock returns. Stocks that report the biggest increases in economic value added should not necessarily earn high returns for their stockholders.[5] These priors are confirmed by a study done by Richard Bernstein at Merrill Lynch, who examined the relationship between EVA and stock returns, and concluded that:

- A portfolio of the 50 firms which had the highest absolute levels[6] of economic value added earned an annual return on 12.9% between February 1987 and February 1997, while the S&P index returned 13.1% a year over the same period.

---

[5]A study by Kramer and Pushner found that differences in operating income (NOPAT) explained differences in market value better than differences in EVA. O'Byrne (1996), however, finds that changes in EVA explain more than 55 percent of changes in market value over five-year periods.

[6]See Quantitative Viewpoint, Merrill Lynch, December 19, 1997.

EVA FOR HIGH-GROWTH FIRMS

The fact that the value of a firm is a function of the capital invested in assets in place, the present value of economic value added by those assets, and the economic value added by future investments points to some of the dangers of using it as a measure of success or failure for high-growth and especially high-growth technology firms. In particular, there are three problems:

1. We have already noted many of the problems associated with how accountants measure capital invested at technology firms. Given the centrality of capital invested to economic value added, these problems have a much bigger effect when firms use EVA than when you use discounted cash flow valuation.
2. When 80 percent to 90 percent of your value comes from future growth potential, the risks of managers trading off future growth for current EVA are magnified. It is also very difficult to monitor these trade-offs at young firms.
3. The constant change that these firms go through also makes them much better candidates for risk shifting. In this case, the negative effect (of a higher discount rate) can more than offset the positive effect of a higher economic value added.

Finally, it is unlikely that there will be much correlation between actual changes in economic value added at technology firms and changes in market value. The market value is based on expectations of economic value added in future periods, and investors expect an economic value added that grows substantially each year. Thus if the economic value added increases, but by less than expected, you could see its market value drop on the report.

 eva.xls: **This dataset on the Web summarizes economic value added by industry group for the United States.**

■ A portfolio of the 50 firms that had the highest growth rates[7] in economic value added over the previous year earned an annual return of 12.8% over the same time period.

Equity Economic Value Added

While EVA is usually calculated using total capital, it can easily be modified to be an equity measure:

Equity EVA = (Return on equity – Cost of equity)(Equity invested in project or firm)
= Net income – Cost of equity(Equity invested)

Again, a firm that earns a positive equity EVA is creating value for its stockholders while a firm with a negative equity EVA is destroying value for its stockholders.

---

[7]See Quantitative Viewpoint, Merrill Lynch, February 3, 1998.

Why might a firm use this measure rather than the traditional measure? Chapter 21, when looking at financial service firms, noted that defining debt (and therefore capital) may open you open to measurement problems, since so much of the firm could potentially be categorized as debt. Consequently, it was argued that financial service firms should be valued using equity valuation models and multiples. Extending that argument to economic value added holds that equity EVA is a much better measure of performance for financial service firms than the traditional EVA measure.

It must be added that much or all of the issues raised in the context of the traditional EVA measure affect the equity EVA measure as well. Banks and insurance companies can play the capital invested, growth, and risk games to increase equity EVA just as other firms can with traditional EVA.

CASH FLOW RETURN ON INVESTMENT

The cash flow return on investment (CFROI) for a firm is the internal rate of return on existing investments, based on real cash flows. Generally, it should be compared to the real cost of capital to make judgments about the quality of these investments.

Calculating CFROI

The cash flow return on investment for a firm is calculated using four inputs. The first is the gross investment (GI) the firm has in its existing assets, obtained by adding back cumulated depreciation and inflation adjustments to the book value. The second input is the gross cash flow (GCF) earned in the current year on that asset, which is usually defined as the sum of the after-tax operating income of a firm and the noncharges against earnings, such as depreciation and amortization. The third input is the expected life of the assets (n) in place at the time of the original investment, which varies from sector to sector but reflects the earning life of the investments in question. The expected salvage value (SV) of the assets at the end of this life, in current dollars, is the final input. This is usually assumed to be the portion of the initial investment, such as land and building, that is not depreciable, adjusted to current dollar terms. The CFROI is the internal rate of return of these cash flows (i.e., the discount rate that makes the net present value of the gross cash flows and salvage value equal to the gross investment), and it can thus be viewed as a composite internal rate of return in current dollar terms.

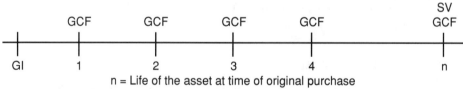

n = Life of the asset at time of original purchase
CFROI is the internal rate of return that makes the PV of GCF + SV = GI

An alternative formulation of the CFROI allows for setting aside an annuity to cover the expected replacement cost of the asset at the end of the project life. This annuity is called the economic depreciation and is computed as follows:

$$\text{Economic depreciation} = \frac{\text{Replacement cost in current dollars}(k_c)}{\left[(1+k_c)^n - 1\right]}$$

where n is the expected life of the asset, k_c is the cost of capital, and the expected replacement cost of the asset is defined in current dollar terms to be the difference between the gross investment and the salvage value. The CFROI for a firm or a division can then be written as follows:

$$CFROI = \frac{\text{Gross cash flow} - \text{Economic depreciation}}{\text{Gross investment}}$$

For instance, assume that you have existing assets with a book value of $2,431 million, a gross cash flow of $390 million, an expected salvage value (in today's dollar terms) of $607.8 million, and a life of 10 years.

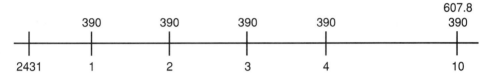

CFROI = Internal rate of return = 11.71%

The conventional measure of CFROI is 11.71%, and the real cost of capital is 8%. The estimate using the alternative approach is computed as follows:

$$\text{Economic depreciation} = \frac{(\$2.431 \text{ billion} - \$0.6078 \text{ billion})(.08)}{(1.08^{10} - 1)} = \$125.86 \text{ million}$$

$$CFROI = (\$390.00 \text{ million} - \$125.86 \text{ million})/\$2,431 \text{ million}$$
$$= 10.87\%$$

The difference in the reinvestment rate assumption accounts for the difference in CFROI estimated using the two methods. In the first approach, intermediate cash flows get reinvested at the internal rate of return, while in the second, at least the portion of the cash flows that are set aside for replacement get reinvested at the cost of capital. In fact, if we estimated that the economic depreciation using the internal rate of return of 11.71 percent, the two approaches would yield identical results.[8]

Cash Flow Return on Investment, Internal Rate of Return, and Discounted Cash Flow Value

If net present value provides the genesis for the economic value added approach to value enhancement, the internal rate of return is the basis for the CFROI approach. In investment analysis, the internal rate of return on a project is computed using the initial investment on the project and all cash flows over the project's life:

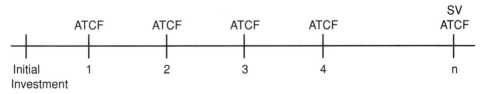

---

[8]With an 11.71 percent rate, the economic depreciation works out to $105.37 million, and the CFROI to 11.71 percent.

where the ATCF is the after-tax cash flow on the project, and SV is the expected salvage value of the project assets. This analysis can be done entirely in nominal terms, in which case the internal rate of return is a nominal IRR and is compared to the nominal cost of capital, or in real terms, in which case it is a real IRR and is compared to the real cost of capital.

At first sight, the CFROI seems to do the same thing. It uses the gross investment in the project (in current dollars) as the equivalent of the initial investment, assumes that the gross current-dollar cash flow is maintained over the project life and computes a real internal rate of return. There are, however, some significant differences.

The internal rate of return does not require the after-tax cash flows to be constant over a project's life, even in real terms. The CFROI approach assumes that real cash flows on assets do not increase over time. This may be a reasonable assumption for investments in mature sectors, but will understate project returns if there is real growth. Note, however, that the CFROI approach can be modified to allow for real growth.

The second difference is that the internal rate of return on a project or asset is based on incremental future cash flows. It does not consider cash flows that have occurred already, since these are viewed as "sunk." The CFROI, on the other hand, tries to reconstruct a project or asset, using both cash flows that have occurred already and cash flows that are yet to occur. To illustrate, consider the project described in the previous section. At the time of the original investment, assuming that the inputs for initial investment, after-tax cash flows, and salvage value are unchanged, both the internal rate of return and the CFROI of this project would have been 11.71 percent. The CFROI is, however, being computed three years into the project life and remains at 11.71 percent since none of the original inputs have changed. The IRR of this project will change, though. It will now be based on the current market value of the asset, the expected cash flows over the remaining life of the asset, and a life of seven years. Thus, if the market value of the asset has increased to $2.5 billion, the internal rate of return on this project would be computed to be only 6.80 percent.

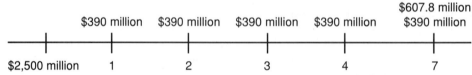

Given the real cost of capital of 8 percent, this would mean that the CFROI is greater than the cost of capital, while the internal rate of return is lower. Why is there a difference between the two measures, and what are the implications? The reason for the difference is that IRR is based entirely on expected future cash flows, whereas the CFROI is not. A CFROI that exceeds the cost of capital is viewed as a sign that a firm is deploying its assets well. If the IRR is less than the cost of capital, that interpretation is false, because the owners of the firm would be better off selling the asset and getting the market value for it rather than continuing its operation.

To link the cash flow return on investment with firm value, let us begin with a simple discounted cash flow model for a firm in stable growth:

$$\text{Firm value} = \frac{FCFF_1}{(k_c - g_n)}$$

where FCFF is the expected free cash flow to the firm k_c is the cost of capital, and g_n is the stable growth rate. Note that this can be rewritten, approximately, in terms of the CFROI as follows:

$$\text{Firm value} = \frac{[(\text{CFROI} \times \text{GI} - \text{DA})(1-t) - (\text{CX} - \text{DA}) - \Delta \text{WC}]}{(k_c - g_n)}$$

where CFROI is the cash flow return on investment, GI is the gross investment, DA is the depreciation and amortization, CX is the capital expenditure and ΔWC is the change in working capital. To illustrate, consider a firm with a CFROI of 30%, a gross investment of \$100 million, capital expenditures of \$15 million, depreciation of \$10 million, and no working capital requirements. If we assume a 10% cost of capital, a 40% tax rate, and a 5% stable growth rate, it would be valued as follows:

$$\text{Firm value} = \frac{[(.30 \times 100 - 10)(1 - .4) - (15 - 10) - 0]}{(.10 - .05)} = \$140 \text{ million}$$

More important than the mechanics, however, is the fact that firm value, while a function of the CFROI, is also a function of the other variables in the equation—the gross investment, the tax rate, the growth rate, the cost of capital, and the firm's reinvestment needs.

Again, sophisticated users of CFROI do recognize the fact that value comes from the CFROI not just on assets in place but also on future investments. In fact, Holt Associates, one of CFROI's leading proponents, allows for a fade factor in CFROI, where the current CFROI fades toward the real cost of capital over time. The fade factor is estimated empirically by looking at firms in different CFROI classes and tracking them over time. Thus, a firm that has a current CFROI of 20 percent and real cost of capital of 8 percent will be projected to have lower CFROI over time. The value of the firm, in this more complex format, can then be written as a sum of the following:

■ The present value of the cash flows from assets in place over their remaining life, which can be written as:

$$\sum_{t=1}^{t=n} \frac{\text{CFROI}_{aip} \times \text{GI}_{aip}}{(1+k_c)^t}$$

where CFROI_{aip} is the CFROI on assets in place, GI_{aip} is the gross investment in assets in place, and k_c is the real cost of capital.

■ The present value of the excess cash flows from future investments, which can be written in real terms as

$$\sum_{t=1}^{t=\infty} \frac{\text{CFROI}_{t,NI} \times \Delta \text{GI}_t}{(1+k_c)^t} - \Delta \text{GI}_t$$

where $\text{CFROI}_{t,NI}$ is the CFROI on new investments made in year t and ΔGI_t is the new investment made in year t. Note that if $\text{CFROI}_{t,NI} = k_c$, this present value is equal to zero.

Thus, a firm's value will depend on the CFROI it earns on assets in place and both the abruptness and the speed with which this CFROI fades toward the cost of capital. Thus, a firm can therefore potentially increase its value by doing either of the following:

- Increasing the CFROI from assets in place for a given gross investment.
- Reducing the speed at which the CFROI fades toward the real cost of capital.

Note that this is no different from our earlier analysis of firm value in the discounted cash flow approach in Chapter 31, in terms of cash flows from existing investments (increase current CFROI), the length of the high growth period (reduce fade speed), and the growth rate during the growth period (keep excess returns from falling as steeply).

---

 cfroi.xls: This spreadsheet allows you to estimate the cash flow return on investment for a firm or project.

CFROI and Firm Value: Potential Conflicts

The relationship between CFROI and firm value is less intuitive than the relationship between EVA and firm value, partly because it is a percentage return. Notwithstanding this fundamental weakness, managers can take actions that increase CFROI while reducing firm value.

- *Reduce gross investment.* If the gross investment in existing assets is reduced, the CFROI may be increased. Since it is the product of CFROI and gross investment that determines value, it is possible for a firm to increase CFROI and end up with a lower value.

CFROI INNOVATIONS: THE FADE FACTOR AND IMPLIED COST OF CAPITAL

The biggest contribution made by practitioners who use CFROI has been the work that they have done on how returns on capital fade over time toward the cost of capital. Madden (1999) makes the argument that not only is this phenomenon widespread but it is at least partially predictable. He presents evidence done by Holt Associates, a leading proponent of CFROI, which sorted the largest 1,000 firms by CFROI from highest to lowest, and tracked them over time to find a convergence toward an average. It should be noted that this book has used fade factors, without referring to them as such, in the chapters on discounted cash flow valuation. The fade to a lower return on capital occurred either precipitously in the terminal year or over a transition period. It was mentioned that the return on capital could converge to the cost of capital or to the industry average.

To compute the cost of capital, CFROI practitioners look to the market instead of the risk and return models that we have used to compute DCF value. Using the current market values of stocks and their estimates of expected aggregate cash flows, they compute internal rates of return that they use as the cost of capital in analysis. Chapter 7 used a very similar approach to estimate an implied risk premium, though this premium was used as an input into traditional risk and return models.

- *Sacrifice future growth.* CFROI, even more than EVA, is focused on existing assets and does not look at future growth. To the extent that managers increase CFROI at the expense of future growth, the value can decrease while CFROI goes up.
- *Trade off risk.* While the CFROI is compared to the real cost of capital to pass judgment on whether a firm is creating or destroying value, it represents only a partial correction for risk. The value of a firm is still the present value of expected future cash flows. Thus a firm can increase its spread between the CFROI and cost of capital but still end up losing value if the present value effect of having a higher cost of capital dominates the higher CFROI.

In general, then, an increase in CFROI does not, by itself, indicate that the firm value has increased, since it might have come at the expense of lower growth and/or higher risk.

CFROI and Market Value

There is a relationship between CFROI and market value. Firms with high CFROI generally have high market value. This is not surprising, since it mirrors what we noted earlier about economic value added. However, it is *changes* in market value that create returns, not market value per se. When it comes to market value changes, the relationship between CFROI and value changes tends to be much weaker. Since market values reflect expectations, there is no reason to believe that firms that have high CFROI will earn excess returns.

The relationship between changes in CFROI and excess returns is more intriguing. To the extent that any increase in CFROI is viewed as a positive surprise, firms with the biggest increases in CFROI should earn excess returns. In reality, however, the actual change in CFROI has to be measured against expectations; if CFROI increases, but less than expected, the market value should drop; if CFROI drops but by less than expected, the market value should increase.

A POSTSCRIPT ON VALUE ENHANCEMENT

The value of a firm has three components. The first is its capacity to generate cash flows from existing assets, with higher cash flows translating into higher value. The second is its willingness to reinvest to create future growth, and the quality of these reinvestments. Other things remaining equal, firms that reinvest well and earn significant excess returns on these investments will have higher value. The final component of value is the cost of capital, with higher costs or capital resulting in lower firm values. To create value, then, a firm has to:

- Generate higher cash flows from existing assets, without affecting its growth prospects or its risk profile.
- Reinvest more and with higher excess returns, without increasing the riskiness of its assets.
- Reduce the cost of financing its assets in place or future growth, without lowering the returns made on these investments.

All value enhancement measures are variants on these simple themes. Whether these approaches measure dollar excess returns, as does economic value added, or percentage excess returns, like CFROI, they have acquired followers because they seem simpler and less subjective than discounted cash flow valuation. This simplicity comes at a cost, since these approaches make subtle assumptions about other components of value that are often not visible or not recognized by many users. Approaches that emphasize economic value added and reward managers for increasing the same often assume that increases in economic value added are not being accomplished at the expense of future growth or by increasing risk. Practitioners who judge performance based on the cash flow return on investment make similar assumptions.

Is there something of value in the new value enhancement measures? Absolutely, but only in the larger context of valuation. One of the inputs we need for traditional valuation models is the return on capital (to get expected growth). Making the adjustments to operating income suggested by those who use economic value added and augmenting it with a cash flow return, with CFROI, may help us come up with a better estimate of this number. The terminal value computation in traditional valuation models, where small changes in assumptions can lead to large changes in value, becomes much more tractable if we think in terms of excess returns on investments rather than just growth and discount rates. Finally, the empirical evidence that has been collected by practitioners who use CFROI on fade factors can be invaluable in traditional valuation models, where practitioners sometimes make the mistake of assuming that current returns will continue forever.

CONCLUSION

This chapter considers two widely used value enhancement measures. Economic value added measures the dollar excess return on existing assets. The cash flow return on investment is the internal rate of return on existing assets, based on the original investment in these assets and the expected future cash flows. While both approaches can lead to conclusions consistent with traditional discounted cash flow valuation, their simplicity comes at a cost. Managers can take advantage of measurement limitations in both approaches to make their firms look better with either approach while reducing firm value. In particular, they can trade off less growth in the future for higher economic value added today and shift to riskier investments.

As we look at various approaches to value enhancement, we should consider a few facts. The first is that no value enhancement mechanism will work at generating value unless there is a commitment on the part of managers to making value maximization their primary objective. If managers put other goals first, then no value enhancement mechanism will work. Conversely, if managers truly care about value maximization, they can make almost any mechanism work in their favor. The second is that while it is sensible to connect whatever value enhancement measure we have chosen to management compensation, there is a downside. Managers, over time, will tend to focus their attention on making themselves look better on that measure even if that can be accomplished only by reducing firm value. Finally, there are no magic bullets that create value. Value creation is hard work in competitive markets and almost involves a trade-off between costs and benefits. Everyone has a role in value creation, and it certainly is not the sole domain of financial analysts. In fact, the value created by financial engineers is smaller and less significant than the value created by good strategic, marketing, production, or personnel decisions.

QUESTIONS AND SHORT PROBLEMS

1. Everlast Batteries Inc. has hired you as a consultant. The firm had after-tax operating earnings in 1998 of $180 million and net income of $100 million, and it paid a dividend of $50 million. The book value of equity at the end of 1998 was $1.25 billion, and the book value of debt was $350 million. The firm raised $50 million of new debt during 1998. The market value of equity at the end of 1998 was twice the book value of equity, and the market value of debt was the same as the book value of debt. The firm has a cost of equity of 12% and an after-tax cost of debt of 5%.
   a. Estimate the return on capital earned by Everlast Batteries.
   b. Estimate the cost of capital earned by Everlast Batteries.
   c. Estimate the economic value added by Everlast Batteries.
2. Assume, in the preceding problem, that Everlast Batteries is in stable growth, and that it expects its economic value added to grow at 5% a year forever.
   a. Estimate the value of the firm.
   b. How much of this value comes from excess returns?
   c. What is the market value added (MVA) of this firm?
   d. How would your answers to a, b, and c change if you were told that there would be no economic value added after year 5?
3. Stereo City is a retailer of stereos and televisions. The firm has operating income of $150 million, after operating lease expenses of $50 million. The firm has operating lease commitments for the next five years and beyond:

Year	Operating Lease Commitment
1	55
2	60
3	60
4	55
5	50
Years 6–15	40 each year

   The book value of equity is $1 billion, and the firm has no debt outstanding. The firm has a cost of equity of 11% and a pretax cost of borrowing of 6%. The tax rate is 40%.
   a. Estimate the capital invested in the firm, before and after adjusting for operating leases.
   b. Estimate the return on capital, before and after adjusting for operating leases.
   c. Estimate the economic value added, before and after adjusting for operating leases. (The market value of equity is $2 billion.)
4. Sevilla Chemicals earned $1 billion in after-tax operating income on capital invested of $5 billion last year. The firm's cost of equity is 12%, its debt-to-capital ratio is 25%, and the after-tax cost of debt is 4.5%.
   a. Estimate the economic value added by Sevilla Chemicals last year.
   b. Assume now that the entire chemical industry earned $40 billion after taxes on capital invested of $180 billion, and that the cost of capital for the industry is 10%. Estimate the economic value added by the entire industry.
   c. Based on economic value added, how did Sevilla do relative to the industry?
5. Jeeves Software is a small software firm in high growth. The firm is all equity financed. In the current year, the firm earned $20 million in after-tax operating income on capital invested of $60 million. The firm's cost of equity is 15%.

   a. Assume that the firm will be able to grow its economic value added 15% a year for the next five years, and that there will be no excess returns after year 5. Estimate the value of the firm. How much of this value comes from the EVA and how much from capital invested?

   b. Now, assume the firm is able to reduce its capital invested this year by $20 million by selling its assets and leasing them back. Assuming operating income and cost of capital do not change as a result of the sale-lease-back, estimate the value of the firm now. How much of the value of the firm now comes from EVA and how much from capital invested?

6. Healthy Soups is a company that manufactures canned soups made without preservatives. The firm has assets that have a book value of $100 million. The assets are five years old and have been depreciated $50 million over that period. In addition, the inflation rate over those five years has averaged 2% a year. The assets are currently earning $15 million in after-tax operating income. They have a remaining life of 10 years, and the depreciation each year is expected to be $5 million. At the end of these 10 years, the assets will have an expected salvage value, in current dollars, of $50 million.

   a. Estimate the CFROI of Healthy Foods, using the conventional CFROI approach.

   b. Estimate the CFROI of Healthy Foods, using the economic depreciation approach.

   c. If Healthy Foods has a cost of capital in nominal terms of 10%, and the expected inflation rate is 2%, evaluate whether Healthy Foods' existing investments are value-creating or value-destroying.

CHAPTER 33

Valuing Bonds

T he value of a bond is the present value of the promised cash flows on the bond, discounted at an interest rate that reflects the default risk in these cash flows. Since the cash flows on a straight bond are fixed at issue, the value of a bond is inversely related to the interest rate that investors demand for that bond. The interest rate charged on a bond is determined by both the general level of interest rates and the default premium specific to the entity issuing the bond. This chapter examines the determinants of both the general level of interest rates and the magnitude of the default premiums on specific bonds. The general level of interest rates incorporates expected inflation and a measure of real return, and reflects the term structure, with bonds of different maturities carrying different interest rates. The default premiums vary across time, depending in large part on the health of the economy and investors' risk preferences.

Bonds often have special features embedded in them that have to be factored into the value. Some of these features are options—for the bondholder to convert into stock (convertible bonds), for the bond issuer to call the bond back if interest rates go down (callable bonds), and for the bondholder to put the bond back to the issuer at a fixed price under specific circumstances (putable bonds). Other bond characteristics, such as interest rate caps and floors, have option features. Some of these options reside with the issuer of the bond, some with the buyer of the bond, but they all have to be priced. Option pricing models can be used to value these special features, and price complex fixed income securities. Some special features in bonds such as the existence of sinking funds, subordination of further debt, and the type of collateral used may affect the prices of bonds as well.

BOND PRICES AND INTEREST RATES

The value of a straight bond is determined by the level of and changes in interest rates. As interest rates rise, the price of a bond will decrease, and vice versa. This inverse relationship between bond prices and interest rates arises directly from the present value relationship that governs bond prices.

The Present Value Relationship

The value of a bond is the present value of the promised cash flows on that bond, discounted at an interest rate that reflects the default risk associated with the cash flows. There are two features that set bonds apart from equity investments. First, the promised cash flows on a bond (i.e., the coupon payments and the face value of the bond) are usually set at issue and do not change during the life of the bond. Even when they do change, as in floating rate bonds, the changes are generally linked to changes in interest rates. Second, bonds usually have fixed lifetimes, unlike stocks, since most bonds specify a maturity date.[1] As a consequence, the present value of a straight bond with fixed coupons and specified maturity is determined entirely by changes in the discount rate, which incorporates both the general level of interest rates and the specific default risk of the bond being valued.

The present value of a bond, expected to mature in N time periods, with coupons every period can be written as:

$$\text{PV of bond} = \sum_{t=1}^{t=N} \frac{\text{Coupon}_t}{(1+r)^t} + \frac{\text{Face value}}{(1+r)^N}$$

where Coupon_t = Coupon expected in period t
            Face value = Face value of the bond
                        r = Discount rate for the cash flows

The discount rate used to calculate the present value of the bond will vary from bond to bond, depending on default risk, with higher rates used for riskier bonds and lower rates for safer ones.

If the bond is traded, and a market price is therefore available for it, the internal rate of return can be computed for the bond (i.e., the discount rate at which the present value of the coupons and the bond's face value is equal to the market price). This internal rate of return is called the yield to maturity on the bond.

There are several details relating to both the magnitude and the timing of cash flows that can affect the value of a bond and its yield to maturity. First, the coupon payment on a bond may be semiannual, in which case the discounting has to allow for the semiannual cash flows. (The first coupon will be discounted back half a year, the second one year, the third a year and a half, and so on.) Second, once a bond has been issued, it accrues coupon interest between coupon payments, and this accrued interest has to be added on to the price of the bond when valuing the bond.

ILLUSTRATION 33.1:   Valuing a Straight Bond at Issue

The following is a valuation of a 30-year U.S. government bond at the time of issue. The coupon rate on the bond is 7.5%, and the market interest rate is 7.75%. The price of the bond can be calculated thus:

$$\text{PV of bond} = \sum_{t=1}^{t=30} \frac{75.00}{(1.0775)^t} + \frac{1,000}{(1.0775)^{30}} = \$971.18$$

This is based on annual coupons. If the calculation is based on semiannual coupons, the value of the bond is:

$$\text{PV of bond} = \sum_{t=0.5}^{t=30} \frac{37.50}{(1.0775)^t} + \frac{1,000}{(1.0775)^{30}} = \$987.62$$

---

[1]Console bonds are the exception to this rule, since they are perpetuities.

ILLUSTRATION 33.2: Valuing a Seasoned Straight Bond

The following is a valuation of a seasoned government bond with slightly less than 20 years left to expiration and a coupon rate of 11.75%. The next coupon is due in two months. The current 20-year bond rate is 7.5%. The value of the bond can be calculated as follows:

$$\text{PV of bond} = \sum_{t=0.5}^{t=19.5} \frac{58.75}{(1.075)^t} + \frac{58.75}{(1.075)^{2/12}} + \frac{1,000}{(1.075)^{19.67}} = \$1,505.31$$

This bond trades at well above face value because of its high coupon rate. Note that the second term of the equation is the present value of the next coupon.

A Measure of Interest Rate Risk in Bonds

When the fact that the promised cash flows on a bond are fixed at issue is combined with the present value relationship governing bond prices, there is a clear rationale for why interest changes affect bond prices so directly. Any increase in interest rates, either at the economy-wide level or because of an increase in the default risk of the company issuing the bond, will lower the present value of the stream of expected cash flows and hence the value of the bond. Any decrease in interest rates will have the opposite impact.

The effect of interest rate changes on bond prices will vary from bond to bond and will depend on a number of characteristics of the bond:

- *Maturity of the bond.* Holding coupon rates and default risk constant, increasing the maturity of a straight bond will increase its sensitivity to interest rate changes. The present value of cash flows changes much more for cash flows further in the future, as interest rates change, than for cash flows that are nearer in time. Figure 33.1 illustrates the present values of six bonds—a 5-year,

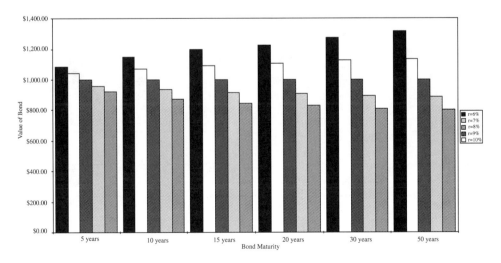

FIGURE 33.1 Bond Values and Interest Rates

a 10-year, a 15-year, a 20-year, a 30-year, and a 50-year bond—all with 8 percent coupons for a range of interest rates.

The longer-term bonds are much more sensitive to interest rate changes than the shorter-term bonds. For instance, an increase in interest rates from 8 percent to 10 percent results in a decline in value of 7.61 percent for the 5-year bond and of 19.83 percent for the 50-year bonds.

■ *Coupon rate of the bond.* Holding maturity and default risk constant, increasing the coupon rate of a straight bond will decrease its sensitivity to interest rate changes. Since higher coupons result in more cash flows earlier in the bond's life, the present value will change less as interest rates change. At the extreme, if the bond is a zero coupon bond, the only cash flow is the face value at maturity, and the present value is likely to vary much more as a function of interest rates. Figure 33.2 illustrates the percentage changes in bond prices for six 30-year bonds with coupon rates ranging from 0 percent to 10 percent as the market interest rate of 8 percent changes.

The bonds with the lower coupons are much more sensitive, in percentage terms, to interest rate changes than those with higher coupons.

While the maturity and the coupon rate are the key determinants of how sensitive the price of a bond is to interest rate changes, a number of other factors impinge on this sensitivity. Any special features that the bond has, including convertibility and callability, make the maturity of the bond less definite and can therefore affect the bond price's sensitivity to interest rate changes. If there is any

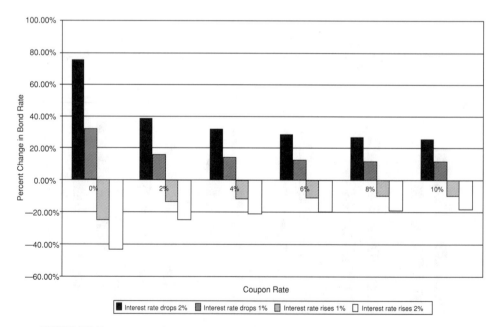

FIGURE 33.2   Percent Change in Bond Price—Interest Rate Changes from 8 Percent

relationship between the level of interest rates and the default premiums on bonds, the default risk of a bond can affect its price sensitivity.

A More Formal Measure of Interest Rate Risk—Duration

Since the interest rate risk of a bond is a significant component of its total risk, a more formal measure of interest risk is needed, which consolidates the effects of maturity, coupon rates, and the bond's special features. To arrive at this measure, consider the present value relationship developed earlier in this chapter:

$$\text{PV of bond} = \sum_{t=1}^{t=N} \frac{\text{Coupon}_t}{(1+r)^t} + \frac{\text{Face value}}{(1+r)^N}$$

Differentiating the bond price with respect to interest rate should provide a formal measure of bond price sensitivity to interest rate changes:

$$\text{Duration of bond} = \frac{dP/P}{dr/r} = \frac{\left[\sum_{t=1}^{t=N} \frac{t \times \text{Coupon}_t}{(1+r)^t} + \frac{N \times \text{Face value}}{(1+r)^N} \right]}{\left[\sum_{t=1}^{t=N} \frac{\text{Coupon}_t}{(1+r)^t} + \frac{\text{Face value}}{(1+r)^N} \right]}$$

The bond price differential, $(dP/P)/(dr/r)$, is called the duration of the bond, and measures the interest rate sensitivity of the bond.

The duration of a bond is a weighted maturity of all the cash flows on the bond including the coupons, where the weights are based on both the timing and the magnitude of the cash flows. Larger and earlier cash flows are weighted more than smaller and later cash flows. By incorporating the magnitude and timing of all the cash flows on the bond, duration encompassed all the variables that affect bond price sensitivity in one measure. The higher the duration of a bond, the more sensitive it is to changes in interest rates.

The duration of a bond will always be less than the maturity for a coupon bond, and equal to the maturity for a zero coupon bond with no special features. In general, the duration of a bond will decrease as the coupon rate on the bond increases.

The measure of duration described here is called Macaulay duration and it is the simplest version, based on yields to maturity. It is based on the assumption of a flat term structure. There are modified versions of duration, which are more flexible in their assumptions about the term structure and its shifts over time.

ILLUSTRATION 33.3:   Estimating Durations for Coupon Bonds

This example estimates the duration of a seasoned government bond with 20 years left to expiration and a coupon rate of 11.75%. The interest rate is 7.5%. The duration of the bond, assuming annual coupon payments, can be calculated as follows:

t	Cash Flow	PV of Cash Flow	$t \times$ PV of Cash Flow
1	$ 117.50	$ 109.30	$ 109.30
2	$ 117.50	$ 101.68	$ 203.35
3	$ 117.50	$ 94.58	$ 283.75
4	$ 117.50	$ 87.98	$ 351.94
5	$ 117.50	$ 81.85	$ 409.23
6	$ 117.50	$ 76.14	$ 456.81
7	$ 117.50	$ 70.82	$ 495.77
8	$ 117.50	$ 65.88	$ 527.06
9	$ 117.50	$ 61.29	$ 551.57
10	$ 117.50	$ 57.01	$ 570.10
11	$ 117.50	$ 53.03	$ 583.36
12	$ 117.50	$ 49.33	$ 591.99
13	$ 117.50	$ 45.89	$ 596.58
14	$ 117.50	$ 42.69	$ 597.65
15	$ 117.50	$ 39.71	$ 595.67
16	$ 117.50	$ 36.94	$ 591.05
17	$ 117.50	$ 34.36	$ 584.17
18	$ 117.50	$ 31.97	$ 575.38
19	$ 117.50	$ 29.74	$ 564.98
20	$1,117.50	$ 263.07	$ 5,261.48
		$1,433.27	$14,501.21

Duration of the bond = $14,501/1,433 = 10.12

DETERMINANTS OF INTEREST RATES

The interest rate used to discount cash flows on a bond is determined by a number of variables—the general level of interest rates in the economy, the term structure of interest rates, and the default risk of the bond. Figure 33.3 provides the building blocks for arriving at the interest rate on a straight corporate bond.

The first block is the level of short-term default-free interest rates, and it captures the overall level of rates in the economy. The second block is a maturity premium, which reflects the difference between longer-term default free rates and short-term rates, and is generally positive. The third block is a default premium, which is related to the default risk of the bond in question and is always positive. This section takes a closer look at these blocks.

Level of Interest Rates

The short-term default-free rate can be decomposed into two components—an expected inflation rate during the period and an expected real rate of return.

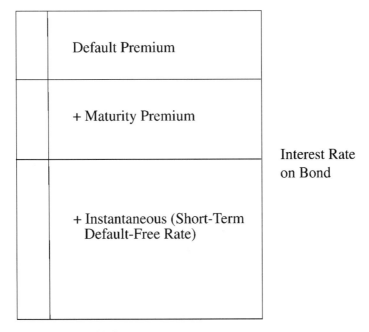

FIGURE 33.3 Building Blocks for Interest Rates

Short-term default-free rate = Expected inflation + Expected real rate of return

This identity is known as the Fisher equation and essentially implies that changes in short-term rates can be traced to changes in either expected inflation or the expected real rate of return. The more precise version of the Fisher equation allows for the compounding effect:

$$(1 + r) = (1 + I)(1 + R)$$

where r = Nominal interest rate
       I = Expected inflation
       R = Expected real rate of return

It should be emphasized that the Fisher equation is an identity, and there is no question of it being proved or disproved. The real questions that arise from the equation arise as a consequence of specific assumptions about the real rate and expected inflation.

Expected Inflation   Expected inflation is clearly the dominant variable determining interest rates. Generally speaking, a forecaster who can predict changes in inflation well should also have a good track record in predicting interest rate changes. The first step in forecasting inflation is understanding its determinants.

Determinants of Inflation   There is consensus on the determinants of inflation, though there is little agreement about the effects of specific actions on inflation.

To understand both the determinants of inflation and the sources of disagreement between the different schools of thought on inflation, consider another identity:

$$P = M \, V/Y$$

where   P = Price level
        M = Money supply in the economy
        V = Velocity of money circulation in the economy
        Y = Real output in the economy

The velocity of money measures how often the currency, used to define the money supply M, circulates in the economy, and how much is created in terms of transactions for every unit of currency created. Thus, if $1 in additional currency created $3 in transactions, the velocity of money is 3. While the money supply used in the equation can be defined in a number of different ways ranging from just currency to broader aggregates, the velocity has to be defined consistently.

This identity can be stated in terms of changes as follows:

$$dP = (dM)(dV)/dY$$

The left-hand side of this identity is the inflation rate, and the right-hand side provides the three determinants of the inflation rate:

1. *Change in the money supply.* If the money supply increases, with no concurrent change in real output and money velocity, the inflation rate will increase. This is the basis for the argument by many monetarists, who believe that there is no linkage between real output and money supply and that money velocity is stable over long periods, that loose monetary policy (increasing money supply) is the reason for high inflation. While some monetarists will concede that monetary policy can have short-term effects on real output, most argue that it cannot impact real output in the long term. They also argue that while money velocity may change over time, that these changes occur over the very long term, and are unlikely to have a major impact on inflation.

2. *Change in money velocity.* If the money velocity increases, with no concurrent change in money supply and real output, the inflation rate will decrease. Economists have long debated why money velocity changes over time. One determinant is technology, since changes in the way people save (from checking accounts to money market accounts) and in the way they spend (from cash transactions to credit card transactions) affect the money velocity. Another is the faith the public has in the currency. In hyperinflationary environments, individuals are much less willing to hold currency (because it depreciates in value so quickly) and therefore attempt to convert the currency into real goods. This unwillingness to hold currency translates into higher money velocity. Thus, if the central bank is viewed as having eased the reins on money supply, there is often a concurrent increase in money velocity, leading to a surge in inflation.

3. *Change in real output.* If the real output increases, with no concurrent increase in money supply and money velocity, the inflation rate will decrease. This is of-

ten the basis of the argument used by Keynesians for easing monetary policy during economic downturns. Increasing the money supply, they argue, results in a concomitant increase in real output, since there is excess capacity, and the effects on inflation are therefore muted or nonexistent.

Measuring Inflation A true measure of inflation would consider changes in the prices of all goods and services used in an economy, weighted by their usage values. The reported measures of inflation, at either the consumer or the producer level, attempt to do so, but often lag changes in true inflation because of a number of reasons. The first is that not all goods and services are traded in a marketplace, and prices are not easily available and goods are not always standardized. Thus it is easy to gauge the inflation in medical prescription prices, but much more difficult to gauge the inflation in the prices of medical services. The second is that all inflation indexes are based on samplings of prices of goods, rather than the universe of all goods traded. Even if the sample is not biased, there is the possibility of sampling error that enters into the numbers. The third is the issue of weighting on the basis of usage value. Due to practical considerations of time and resources, the weights are not adjusted every time the inflation index is computed to allow for changes in usage. Instead index weights are adjusted infrequently, leading to biases in the measured inflation. Thus the inflation indexes that kept the usage of gasoline by households constant in the late 1970s while oil prices were climbing (and people were cutting back on the use of gasoline) tended to overstate the inflation rate. The final consideration is about the level at which inflation is to be measured, since counting goods at every level of the process (from commodity to manufactured good to retailed good) would result in double or even triple counting the same good. Different inflation indexes examine inflation at different stages in the process, and can therefore lead to different conclusions about whether inflation is increasing, decreasing, or staying unchanged.

Forecasting Inflation Since changes in inflation signal changes in interest rates, economists and analysts have expended considerable time and resources forecasting inflation, with mixed results. The forecasting approaches used range from the naive to the sophisticated and are based on everything from gut feeling to elaborate models. The output from these models can be contrasted with predictions based purely on past inflation—either the inflation in the last time period or time-series models that examine trends and shifts in past inflation—and the results for the most part are mixed. Elaborate forecasting models do no better than time-series models in the short term, but may better capture changes in inflation in the long term because they consider information beyond what's available in past inflation rates.

The introduction of inflation-adjusted Treasury bonds a few years ago has provided an interesting alternative for those who would rather rely on markets than on economists for their inflation estimates. In particular, if we view the market interest rate on an inflation-indexed Treasury bond as a riskless real rate and the market interest rate on a nominal Treasury bond of equal maturity as a nominal rate, the expected inflation rate can be estimated as follows:

$$\text{Expected inflation rate} = \frac{(1 + \text{Nominal rate})}{(1 + \text{Real rate})} - 1$$

For instance, if the nominal rate is 5.1 percent and the real rate is 2.7%, you can estimate the expected inflation rate as follows:

$$\text{Expected inflation rate} = (1.051/1.027) - 1 = .0233 \text{ or } 2.33\%$$

Testing the Fisher Equation   As mentioned earlier, the Fisher equation is an identity that cannot be proved or disproved. There have, however, been numerous attempts to impose additional constraints on the model, to test the usefulness of the model in explaining changes in interest rates over time. These studies go back to Fisher's own work on interest rates and inflation, where he found that the correlation between the rate of inflation and the commercial paper rate was low in both his sample periods—1890 to 1914 and 1915 to 1927.

Fama (1975) made the assumption that real rates do not change much over time and that changes in interest rates should therefore almost entirely be caused by changes in inflation. He tested this proposition by regressing interest rates against expected inflation:

$$I_t = a + b\,R_t$$

where R_t = Nominal interest rate during period t
$\quad\quad I_t$ = Expected inflation during period t

Fama argued that if his initial assumption about constant real rates was true, this regression would yield the following:

- ■ The intercept would be equal to the constant real rate over the period.
- ■ The slope of the regression would be one, since all changes in interest rates would be a consequence of changes in inflation.

Lacking an adequate measure of expected inflation, Fama used the one-month Treasury bill rate at the start of each month as a measure of expected inflation during the month, and the one- and three-month Treasury bill rates as measures of nominal rates. His results, for the period 1953 to 1971, were as follows:
Consumer price index regressed against one-month T-bills:

$$I_t = 0.0007 + 0.98\,R_t \quad\quad R^2 = 0.29$$
$$[0.0003] \quad [0.10]$$

Consumer price index regressed against three-month T-bills:

$$I_t = 0.0023 + 0.92\,R_t \quad\quad R^2 = 0.48$$
$$[0.0011] \quad [0.11]$$

Based on this regression, Fama concluded that the hypothesis of constant real rates was supported and that the slope was statistically indistinguishable from one, suggesting that there was a one-to-one relationship between changes in interest rates and expected inflation.

The studies that followed have generally not been as encouraging. Wood, for instance, updated Fama's regression, after adding a lagged measure of inflation to it, and contrasted the results for two periods—1953 to 1971 and 1974 to 1981.

$$I_t = a + b\,R_t + c\,I_{t-1}$$

Period	Regression	R-Squared
1953–1971	$I_t = 0.0006 + 0.84\,R_t + 0.09\,I_{t-1}$ [0.0003] [0.111] [0.064]	0.309
1974–1981	$I_t = -0.0023 + 0.25\,R_t + 0.47\,I_{t-1}$ [0.0008] [0.12] [0.11]	0.371

The coefficient on nominal interest rates (R_t), which was close to 1 for the 1953–1971 time period used by Fama in his study, drops to 0.25 for the 1974–1981 time period.

The reason for the surprisingly good results from 1953 to 1971 may be traceable to the fact that inflation was very stable during this period, and that changes in inflation tended to be small. Thus, it seems likely that the hypothesis of stable real rates and a one-to-one relationship between interest rates and inflation will be rejected in any period or any economy where there is volatility in interest rates and inflation. Since the importance of forecasting increases with the volatility of interest rates and inflation, the cautionary notes on forecasting short-term interest rates based only upon expected inflation should be taken to heart.

Expected Real Rate of Return   The other component of the Fisher equation is the expected real rate of return. On an intuitive level, the expected real rate of return is the rate at which individuals are willing to trade off current consumption for future consumption. Given the preference for present consumption, the expected real rate of return should be positive, but can vary widely across time and across economies. If individuals in a society have a strong desire for current consumption, the expected real rate of return will have to be high to induce them to defer consumption.

Realized Real Rates of Return   Since the expected real rate of return is based on the preference functions of individuals, which are difficult to observe, we are reduced to observing realized real rates of return, which can be defined to be:

Realized real rate of return = Nominal interest rate$_t$ – Actual inflation$_t$

where Nominal interest rate$_t$ = Nominal interest rate at the beginning of period t
       Actual inflation$_t$ = Actual inflation during period t

While the expected real rate of return should be positive, the realized real rate of return can be positive or negative, depending on the period under observation. During the 1970s, for instance, bond investors in the United States earned negative real rates of return as actual inflation outstripped expected inflation.

Expected Real Return and Expected Real Growth   Ultimately, real returns to investors in an economy comes from real growth in the economy. One way to approach the estimation of expected real return is to estimate the expected real

ROLE OF THE CENTRAL BANK

Central banks do not set interest rates, but they certainly can influence them in two ways. On a short-term basis, central banks can tighten or loosen their reins on the money supply and try to slow an overheated economy or regenerate a sluggish economy. In either case, though, we should not attribute more power to central banks than they actually have. The only interest rate that the Federal Reserve in the United States, for instance, directly controls is the federal funds rate. By raising or lowering this rate it can hope to affect other rates, but the market does not always cooperate. It is generally true that market interest rates tend to move with the federal funds rate, but there are two caveats: The first is that markets tend to lead the Federal Reserve, as bond investors build in expectations of changes in Fed policy; and the second is that the correlation tends to be strongest for short-term rates (Treasury bills and commercial paper) and weaker for longer-term rates.

On a long-term basis, central banks can have a much bigger impact on interest rates through their conduct of monetary policy and the resolution that they show about fighting inflation. It is no coincidence that high inflation occurs most often when central banks are undisciplined when it comes to monetary policy and show no resolve when it comes to taking tough measures to fight inflation.

growth rate in the economy. Thus the expected real return in an economy growing in the long term at 2.5 percent a year should be approximately 2.5 percent. If the expected real return increases above the long-term growth rate in the economy, the imbalance will lead to a depletion of savings and a shortfall in investments. Alternatively, if the real return decreases below the long-term growth rate, the imbalance will lead to an accumulation of savings and overinvestment.

Maturity Premium

The maturity premium refers to the difference in interest rates between a short-term (or instantaneous) default-free interest rate and an interest rate for a longer-maturity default-free bond. In the following section, the maturity premium is clarified further and a number of different theories designed to explain the magnitude of the maturity premium are examined.

The Yield Curve   The relationship between maturity and interest rates is usually captured by a yield curve, which graphs yields on bonds against bond maturities. Figure 33.4 summarizes the Treasury yield curve in January and June 2001.

In January 2001 the yield curve was slightly downward-sloping, but by June 2001 the yield curve had reverted; short-term rates dropped while long-term rates increased slightly. While the yield curve has generally been upward-sloping over much of this century, there have been periods where the yield curve has been downward-sloping. Figure 33.5 shows the yield curves from 1980 to 2001. In the early 1980s, short-term rates were higher than long-term rates for a period. Over the past two decades, rates have dropped at both ends of the spectrum.

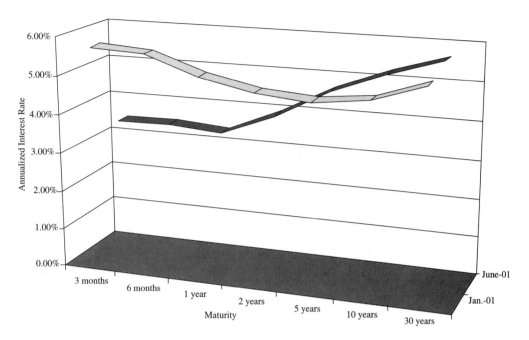

FIGURE 33.4   Yield Curves—January 2001 and June 2001
Source: Federal Reserve.

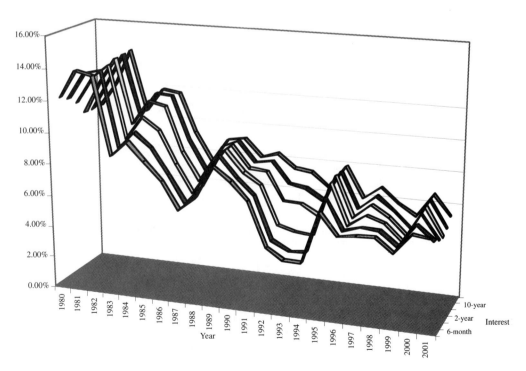

FIGURE 33.5   Yield Curves: 1980–2001
Source: Federal Reserve.

While the yield curves are generally constructed using the yields to maturity of government bonds, the presence of coupons on these bonds affects the calculated yield to maturity. This limitation can be overcome in one of two ways. The first is to construct a yield curve using only zero coupon government bonds of different maturities. The second is to extract spot interest rates from the yields to maturity of coupon bonds, and to plot the spot rates against maturities. The following example illustrates the process of extracting spot rates.

ILLUSTRATION 33.4:   Yields to Maturity and Spot Rates

The following table provides prices and yields to maturity on one- to five-year bonds, and extracts spot rates from the yields to maturity:

Maturity	Yield to Maturity	Spot Rate
1 year	4.00%	4.00%
2 year	4.25%	4.26%
3 year	4.40%	4.41%
4 year	4.50%	4.51%
5 year	4.58%	4.60%

The spot rate is estimated from the two-year rate as follows:

$$\text{Price of two-year bond} = \text{Coupon}_1/(1 + {}_0r_1) + (\text{Face value} + \text{Coupon}_2)/(1 + {}_0r_2)^2$$

Assuming the bond is priced at par,

$$1{,}000 = 42.50/1.04 + 1{,}042.50/(1 + {}_0r_2)^2$$

Solving for ${}_0r_2$,

$${}_0r_2 = \sqrt{1{,}042.50/(1{,}000 - 42.50/1.04)} - 1 = 4.26\%$$

The other rates are extracted using a similar process,

$$1{,}000 = 44/1.04 + 44/1.0426^2 + 1{,}044/(1 + {}_0r_3)^3 \qquad {}_0r_3 = 4.41\%$$
$$1{,}000 = 45/1.04 + 45/1.0426^2 + 45/1.0441^3 + 1{,}045/(1 + {}_0r_4)^4 \qquad {}_0r_4 = 4.51\%$$
$$1{,}000 = 45.80/1.04 + 45.80/1.0426^2 + 45.80/1.0441^3 + 45.80/1.0451^4 + 1{,}045.80/(1 + {}_0r_5)^5 \quad {}_0r_5 = 4.60\%$$

The difference between yields to maturity and spot rates increases as the bond maturity increases.

Spot and Forward Rates   The spot rate on a multiperiod bond is an average rate that applies over the periods. The forward rate is a one-period rate for a future period, and can be extracted from the spot rates. For instance, if ${}_0S_2$ is the two-period spot rate, and ${}_0S_1$ is the one-period spot rate, the forward rate for the second period, ${}_1F_2$, can be obtained as follows:

$${}_1F_2 = (1 + {}_0S_2)^2/(1 + {}_0S_1) - 1$$

The forward rate for period 3 can be extracted using the spot rates for periods 2 and 3, and in general, the forward rate for period n can be written as:

$$_{n-1}F_n = (1 + {_0}S_n)^n/(1 + {_0}S_{n-1})^{n-1} - 1$$

If the yield curve for spot rates is upward-sloping, the yield curve using forward rates will be even more so. Alternatively, if the spot rate yield curve is downward-sloping, the forward rate yield curve will be even more so. The following illustration builds on the previous one, and extracts forward rates from spot rates.

ILLUSTRATION 33.5: Spot Rates and Forward Rates

The forward rates are extracted from the spot rates for one- to five-year bonds. This is illustrated in the following table:

	Yield to Maturity	Spot Rate	Forward Rate
1	4.00%	4.00%	4.00%
2	4.25%	4.26%	4.52%
3	4.40%	4.41%	4.71%
4	4.50%	4.51%	4.81%
5	4.58%	4.60%	4.96%

Forward rate for year 2 = $1.0426^2/1.04 - 1 = 4.52\%$
Forward rate for year 3 = $1.0441^3/1.0426^2 - 1 = 4.71\%$
Forward rate for year 4 = $1.0451^4/1.0441^3 - 1 = 4.81\%$
Forward rate for year 5 = $1.0458^5/1.0451^4 - 1 = 4.96\%$

Determinants of the Maturity Premium   The magnitude of the maturity premium is determined by a number of factors including expectations about inflation, investor preferences for liquidity, and demands from specific market segments. Each of these factors is examined in more detail in the following section.

Expected Inflation   Expectations about future inflation are a key determinant of longer-term rates. In general, if inflation is expected to go up in future periods, longer-term rates will be higher than shorter-term rates. Alternatively, if inflation is expected to go down in future period, longer-term rates will be lower than shorter-term rates.

An extreme version of this story is the pure expectations hypothesis, where the term structure is driven entirely be expectations about inflation. Under this hypothesis, the yield curve will be upward-sloping, if investors expect inflation to rise in future periods, flat if investors expect inflation to remain unchanged in future periods, and downward-sloping if investors expect inflation to decline in future periods. This is illustrated in Figure 33.6.

The pure expectations hypothesis can also be stated in terms of forward rates

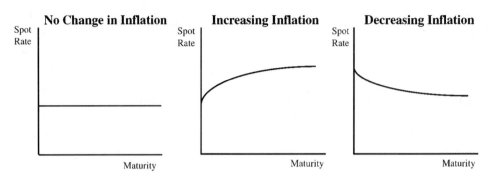

FIGURE 33.6 Pure Expectations Hypothesis

and expected spot rates. If the hypothesis is correct, the forward rate for period n should be the best predictor of the expected spot rate in that period; that is,

$$_{n-1}F_n = \text{Exp}(_{n-1}S_n)$$

where
$_{n-1}F_n$ = Forward rate for period n
$\text{Exp}(_{n-1}S_n)$ = Expected one-period spot rate in period n

While the pure expectations hypothesis may be extreme in assuming that forward rates are determined entirely by expected spot rates, it does highlight the importance of expected inflation in determining the maturity premium.

Liquidity Preference The liquidity preference theory is not an alternative to the pure expectations theory but builds on it by taking into account uncertainty and risk aversion. In the form in which it was originally developed by Hicks (1946), the uncertainty was seen as accruing to the lender who concurrently charged a liquidity premium for lending for longer time periods. This uncertainty can also be stated in terms of bond prices, with long-term bonds being viewed as more volatile than short-term bonds, as interest rates change. Under this theory, holding expectations of inflation constant, longer-term rates will be higher than shorter-term rates. Stated in terms of forward rates and expected spot rates,

$$_{n-1}F_n = \text{Exp}(_{n-1}S_n) + L_t$$

where L_t = Liquidity premium corresponding to a bond maturity of t periods

Figure 33.7 illustrates how the liquidity premium builds on top of the pure expectations hypothesis.

While the traditional theory assumes a positive liquidity premium (L_t), the assumption that all lenders prefer to lend short-term over long-term may not be always appropriate. For instance, a lender with fixed liabilities 20 years from now may view a 20-year zero coupon bond as less risky than a Treasury bill, because it matches cash inflows to cash outflows. The question therefore becomes an empirical one: Does the average lender prefer to lend short-term or long-term?

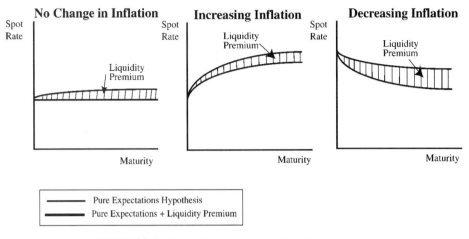

FIGURE 33.7   Term Structure with Liquidity Premium

McCulloch (1975) attempted to estimate term premiums for different time periods, and found positive term premiums, suggesting that lenders prefer short-term lending to long-term lending. Van Horne (1965) found term premiums increasing, albeit at a decreasing rate, with bond maturity.

Demands from Specific Market Segments   The price of bonds, like any other security, is determined by demand and supply. If the market is segmented and there are sizable groups of investors whose demand is for a specific maturity, the term structure will be affected by these groups. Again, considering the extreme case, where investors will lend and borrow only for specific maturities, the interest rate at each maturity will be determined by demand and supply at that maturity. This is illustrated in Figure 33.8. Under this scenario, the term structure can take any shape, depending on the demand and supply at each maturity.

The assumption that investors will lend or borrow only for specific maturities, and not substitute other maturities even when it is extremely favorable for them to do so is an extreme one. In reality, market segments do exist and do affect the term structure, but only at the margin and for one or two maturities. For instance, the demand from Japanese investors in the late 1980s for just-issued 30-year bonds resulted in a slight kink in the term structure, where 30-year bond rates were slightly lower than 29-year bond rates, even though the rest of the yield curve was upward-sloping.

Empirical Evidence on Maturity Premiums   Empirical studies of the term structure have examined several questions including the relative frequency of upward- and downward-sloping term structures, the magnitude of liquidity premiums, and the presence of market segments. The evidence can be summarized as follows:

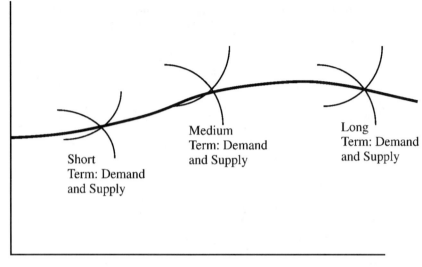

FIGURE 33.8 Market Segmentation and Term Structure

■ The yield curve, at least in this century, has been more likely to be upward-sloping than downward-sloping. Examining yield curves at the beginning of each year from 1900 to 2000, the yield curve has been downward-sloping in only 29 of the 100 years. This is inconsistent with a pure expectations hypothesis, where downward-sloping yield curves should be just as likely as flat or upward-sloping yield curves.[2] It is, however, consistent with a combination of an expectations and liquidity preference hypotheses, where positive liquidity premiums are demanded over and above expected inflation.

■ The term structure is much more likely to be downward-sloping when the level of interest rates is high relative to historical rates. The following table[3] summarizes the frequency of downward-sloping yield curves as a function of the level of interest rates.

Period	One-Year Corporate Bond Rate	Slope of Yield Curve		
		Positive	Flat	Negative
1900–1970	Above 4.40%	0	0	20
	3.25% to 4.40%	10	10	5
	Below 3.25%	26	0	0
1971–2000	Above 8.00%	4	2	3
	Below 8.00%	13	6	0

---

[2]Prior to the abandonment of the gold standard in the 1930s, negatively sloped yield curves were just as likely to occur as positively sloped yield curves.
[3]Some of the data table is extracted from Wood (1985).

This evidence is consistent with the expectations and liquidity preference hypotheses, but it is also consistent with a hypothesis that interest rates move within a normal range. When they approach the upper end or lower end of the normal range, the yield curve is more likely to be downward-sloping or upward-sloping, respectively.

■ Studies have generally found that expectations about future interest rates are important in shaping the term structure. Meiselman computed high positive correlations between forecasting errors and changes in various forward rates, and stable term premiums. In contrast, there are many researchers who argue that the volatility in interest rates is much too great to be explained by just expectations about future rates and constant term premiums. Shiller (1979) concluded that the greater the volatility in interest rates, the larger the term premiums.

■ Attempts by the government to alter the shape of the yield curve by adjusting the maturity of issues have largely been unsuccessful in the long term. For instance, Operation Twist in 1962 was designed to make the yield curve flatter by lowering long-term rates and raising short-term rates by issuing short-term debt to finance deficits.[4] Though the yield curve did flatten, long-term yields did not decline. This can be viewed as evidence of the weakness of the market segmentation hypothesis.

■ There is evidence that the shape of the term structure has strong predictive power for future changes in the real economy, with more upward sloping yield curves being associated with higher real growth. Harvey (1991) examined the G-7 countries (Canada, France, Germany, Italy, Japan, United Kingdom, United States) and concluded that 54 percent of world economic growth could be explained by the term structure.

Default Premium

While there is no possibility of default for bond issues made by the U.S. Treasury, corporate bonds or state/local bonds can default on interest or principal payments. The same can be said about bonds issued by sovereigns with default risk. If there is any possibility of default on a bond, there will be a default premium in addition to the maturity premium on the bond. The default premium will increase with the perceived default risk of the bond and is generally also a function of the maturity and terms of the specific bond. Chapter 7 examined this issue in detail as part of the discussion of how best to estimate the cost of debt for a firm. Reviewing that discussion, the conclusions were:

■ The most direct measure of default risk is the default rate, which measures defaulted issues as a percentage of the par value of debt outstanding. Hickman

---

[4]A similar, though less formal, attempt was made in 1993 by the U.S. Treasury Department to raise short-term rates and lower long-term rates by issuing more short-term bonds and fewer long-term bonds. It was successful at raising short-term rates, but long-term rates increased concomitantly.

investigated the default experience of fixed-income corporate bonds between 1900 and 1943, as a function of the bond rating.

	Ratings					
Size of Issue	*I*	*II*	*III*	*IV*	*V–IX*	*No Rating*
> $5 million	5.9%	6.0%	13.4%	19.1%	42.4%	28.6%
≤ $5 million	10.2%	15.5%	9.9%	25.2%	32.6%	27.0%

Hickman's study has been extended by several researchers, and data availability has made this easier to do. Altman computes default rates for high-yield bonds from 1970 to the present on an annual basis and relates them to bond ratings.

■ Default spreads on bonds tend to increase during economic downturns and decrease during economic booms.

■ Default spreads are generally larger for longer-term bonds than they are for shorter-term bonds, for any given level of default risk. There may be specific circumstances, though, where the reverse is true. Johnson defines a "crisis-at-maturity" scenario, usually in the midst of a recession or a depression, where a firm is perceived to have insufficient funds to meet its immediate debt servicing needs, though it is expected to revert to health in the long term. In this scenario, the default premiums will be lower for longer-maturity bonds than for shorter-maturity bonds. Johnson found evidence of inverted default premium term structures during 1934, in the midst of the Depression.

SPECIAL FEATURES IN BONDS AND PRICING EFFECTS

The preceding section examined the question of how to price a government or a corporate bond based on the expected coupons and the appropriate interest rate for the bond. Most bonds, though, have other features added on, some of which make the bonds more valuable and some less valuable. This section considers how best to value these special features.

Convertibility

A convertible bond is a bond that can be converted into a predetermined number of shares, at the option of the bondholder. While it generally does not pay to convert at the time of the bond issue, conversion becomes a more attractive option as stock prices increase. Firms generally add conversion options to bonds to lower the interest rate paid on the bonds.

Conversion Option   In a typical convertible bond, the bondholder is given the option to convert the bond into a specified number of shares of stock. The conversion ratio measures the number of shares of stock for which each bond may be ex-

CORPORATE BONDS IN
EMERGING MARKETS

In the framework developed here, you build up to the rate on a corporate bond by adding a default spread to the government bond rate. This process works only when the government is viewed as having no default risk. When governments have default risk, as is often the case in emerging markets, the process becomes more complicated. To estimate the appropriate interest rate on a corporate bond in an emerging market, you have to begin by estimating a riskless rate. The best way to do it is to build it up from the Fisher equation—add an expected inflation rate to the real rate of return in that market. The latter can be set equal to the expected real growth rate in the economy, but the former can be a volatile number in high inflation markets. An alternative approach is to begin with the government bond rate and subtract the estimated default spread for the government; this default spread can be obtained using the rating for the government.

You could also estimate the corporate bond rate for a company in an emerging market in a different currency—U.S. dollars or euros. In this case, the riskless rate will be defined in that currency—the Treasury bond rate in the U.S. for dollars and the German government bond rate in euros. The default spread for the company can then be added on to this riskless rate to estimate the corporate bond rate.

There is one final point that needs to be confronted with corporate bonds in emerging markets, and it relates to whether you should incorporate the country default risk spread into the corporate bond rate. For instance, should the interest rate on a bond issued by Embraer, the Brazilian aerospace firm, incorporate the default spread on Brazilian government bonds? For smaller firms, the answer should generally be yes. For larger firms with substantial operations outside the country, we have a little more leeway. These firms may be able to borrow at rates lower than the sovereign rate.

changed. The market conversion value is the current value of the shares for which the bonds can be exchanged. The conversion premium is the excess of the bond value over the conversion value of the bond.

Thus a convertible bond with a par value of $1,000, which is convertible into 50 shares of stock, has a conversion ratio of 50. The conversion ratio can also be used to compute a conversion price—the par value divided by the conversion ratio, yielding a conversion price of $20. If the current stock price is $25, the market conversion value is $1,250 (50 × $25). If the convertible bond is trading at $1,300, the conversion premium is $50.

The effect of including a conversion option in a bond is illustrated in Figure 33.9.

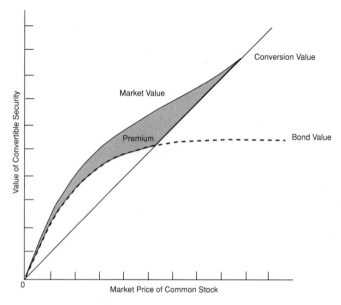

FIGURE 33.9   Bond Value and Conversion Option

Determinants of Value   The conversion option is a call option on the underlying stock, and its value is therefore determined by the variables that affect call option values—the underlying stock price, the conversion ratio (which determines the strike price), the life of the convertible bond, the variance in the stock price, and the level of interest rates. The payoff diagrams on a call option and on the conversion option in a convertible bond are illustrated in Figure 33.10. Like a call option, the value of the conversion option will increase with the price of the underlying stock, the variance of the stock, and the life of the conversion option, and decrease with the exercise price (determined by the conversion option).

The effects of increased risk in the firm can cut both ways in a convertible bond—it will decrease the value of the straight bond portion while increasing the value of the conversion option. These offsetting effects will generally mean that

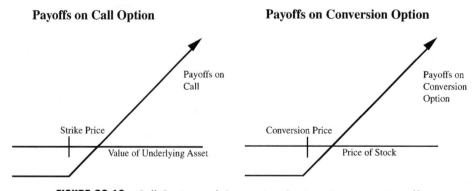

FIGURE 33.10   Call Option and Conversion Option: Comparing Payoffs

convertible bonds will be less exposed to changes in the firm's risk than are other types of securities.

Option pricing models can be used to value the conversion option with three caveats: Conversion options are long-term, making the assumptions about constant variance and constant dividend yields much shakier; conversion options result in stock dilution; and conversion options are often exercised before expiration, making it dangerous to use European option pricing models. These problems can be partially alleviated by using a binomial option pricing model, allowing for shifts in variance and early exercise and factoring in the dilution effect. These changes are described in more detail in Chapter 5. The following illustration provides an example of the use of option pricing models in valuing a conversion option in a convertible bond.

The value of a convertible bond is also affected by a feature shared by most convertible bonds that allow for the adjustment of the conversion ratio (and price) if the firm issues new stock below the conversion price or has a stock split or dividend. In some cases, the conversion price has to be lowered to the price at which new stock is issued. This is designed to protect the convertible bondholder from misappropriation by the firm.

Effect of Forced Conversion Companies that issue convertible bonds sometimes have the right to force conversion if the stock price rises to a specified level. This right to force conversion caps the profit that can be made on the conversion option, and hence affects its value. Figure 33.11 illustrates the effect of forced conversion on the expected payoffs.

The value of a capped call with an exercise price of K_1 and a cap of K_2 can be calculated as follows:

$$\text{Value of capped call } (K_1, K_2) = \text{Value of call}(K_1) - \text{Value of call}(K_2)$$

This is because the cash flows on a capped call can be replicated by buying the call with a strike price of K_1 and selling the call with a strike price of K_2.

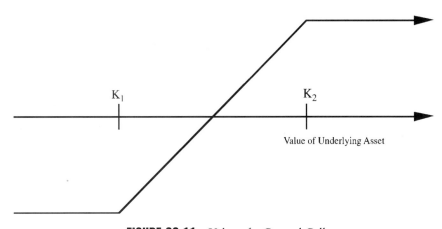

FIGURE 33.11 Value of a Capped Call

ILLUSTRATION 33.6:   Valuing a Conversion Option/Convertible Bond

In December 1994, General Signal had convertible bonds outstanding with the following features:

- The bonds will mature in June 2002. There were 100,000 convertible bonds outstanding.
- They had a face value of $1,000 and were convertible into 25.32 shares per bond until June 2002.
- The coupon rate on the bonds was set at 5.75%.
- The company was rated A–. Straight bonds of similar rating and similar maturity were yielding 9.00%.
- The stock price in December 1994 was $32.50. The volatility (standard deviation in log stock prices) based on historical data was 50.00%.
- There were 47.35 million shares oustanding. Exercising the convertible bonds will create 2.532 million additional shares (100,000 × 25.32 shares).

The two components of the convertible bond can be valued as follows.

STRAIGHT BOND COMPONENT

If this bond had been a straight bond, with a coupon rate of 5.75% and a yield to maturity of 9.00% (based on the bond rating), the value of this straight bond would have been:

$$\text{PV of bond} = \sum_{t=.5}^{t=7.5} \frac{28.75}{(1.09)^t} + \frac{1,000}{(1.09)^{7.5}} = \$834.79$$

This is based on semiannual coupon payments (of $28.75 for semiannual periods).

VALUING THE CONVERSION OPTION

The value of the conversion option is estimated using the Black-Scholes model, with the following parameters for the conversion option:

Type of option = Call   Number of calls per bond = 25.32
Stock price = $32.50   Strike price = $1,000/25.32 = $39.49
Time to expiration = 7.5 years   Standard deviation in ln(stock prices) = 0.50
Riskless rate = 7.75% (rate on 7.5-year Treasury bond)
Dividend yield on stock = 3.00%

Allowing for the dilution inherent in the exercise and using the warrant valuation model from Chapter 5 we get:

Value of one call = $13.57
Value of the conversion option = $13.57 × 25.32 = $343.51

VALUE OF CONVERTIBLE BOND

The value of the convertible bond is the sum of the straight bond and conversion option components:

Value of convertible bond = Value of straight bond + Value of conversion option
= $834.79 + $343.51 = $1,178.30

This valuation is based on the assumption that the conversion option is unconstrained and that the bonds are not callable. The effects of introducing these changes into the analysis will be examined in the following sections.

Callability

The issuer of a callable bond reserves the right to call back the bond and pay a fixed price (generally at a premium over the par value) for it. Thus, if interest rates decline (bond prices rise) after the initial issue, the firm can refund the bonds at the fixed price instead of the market value. Adding the call option to a bond should make it less attractive to buyers, since it reduces the potential upside on the bond. As interest rates go down, and the bond price increases, the bonds are more likely to be called back.

The distinction between a straight bond and a callable bond are illustrated in the Figure 33.12. The difference on the upside between straight and callable bonds is quite clearly illustrated in the figure. As interest rates decline, the values of the two bonds diverge, whereas they converge as interest rates increase.

There are several common features shared by most callable bonds. Most callable bonds come with an initial period of call protection, during which the bonds cannot be called back. Such bonds are called deferred callable bonds. The call price on most callable bonds is set at an initial level above par value plus one annual coupon payment, but declines as time passes and approaches the par value.

Valuing the Callability Option The issuer's right to call back a bond if interest rates drop (or bond prices rise) to an attractive level is a call option on the bond and can be valued as such. The payoffs on a callable bond are shown in Figure 33.13.

The value of the callable feature on a callable bond will increase as interest rates decline, and as the volatility of interest rates increases. Since the callable feature is held by the issuer of the bond, the value of a callable bond can be written as:

Value of callable bond = Value of straight bond − Value of call feature in bond

A callable bond should therefore sell for less than an otherwise similar straight bond.

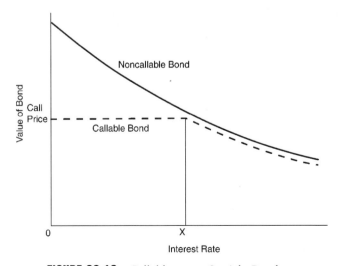

FIGURE 33.12 Callable versus Straight Bonds

Payoffs on Call Option   **Payoffs on Call Feature on Bond**

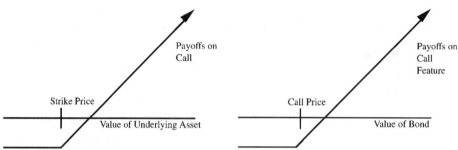

FIGURE 33.13 Payoffs on Call Feature on Bond to Seller of Bond

Traditional Analysis The traditional approach to analyzing callable bonds is to estimate yields to call as well as yields to maturity. The former is based on the assumption
that the bond will be called at the first call date, while the latter assumes holding the
bond until maturity. The two yields are compared, and the investor chooses the lower
of the two as a measure of the expected return on the bond. This approach can also be
extended to calculate the yield to all possible call dates, and picking the lowest of these
yields as the expected yield on the callable bond. This yield is called the yield to worst.
    While this approach may give the investor some sense of the potential down-
side from the callability of the bond, it suffers from all the standard problems of the
yield to maturity calculation. First, it assumes that the investor can reinvest all
coupons until the bond is called at the yield to call, which is not a realistic assumption since calls are much more likely if interest rates go down. Second, it assumes
that the bond will be called on the call date, which takes away the option characteristics of the call feature.

ILLUSTRATION 33.7 Estimating Yields to Maturity and Call on a Callable Bond

Consider a corporate bond with 20 years to maturity and a 12% coupon rate that is callable in two
years at 105% of the face value. The bond is trading at 98 currently. The yields to maturity and the
yields to call on the corporate bond are as follows:

$$\text{Yield to maturity:} \sum_{t=0.5}^{t=20} \frac{60.00}{(1+r)^t} + \frac{1,000}{(1+r)^{20}} = \$980: \text{ Solve for } r$$

The yield to maturity is approximately 12.65%.
    The yield to call can be similarly calculated:

$$\text{Yield to call:} \sum_{t=0.5}^{t=2} \frac{60.00}{(1+r)^t} + \frac{1,050}{(1+r)^2} = \$980: \text{ Solve for } r$$

The yield to call is approximately 13.61%. You would use the lower of these two values (12.65%) as
your expected yield on this bond.

Price/Yield Relationship for a Callable Bond The price/yield relationship on a callable bond is different because the potential that the bond will be called back puts an upper limit on the price, making the relationship between price and yield convex for some range of the yields. The difference is illustrated in Figure 33.14.

The section of the price/yield relationship on the callable bond when the yield falls below y^* has negative convexity—that is, the price appreciation on this bond will be less than the price depreciation for a given change (down or up) in interest rates.

Determinants of Value—Option Pricing Approach The call feature in a callable bond can be valued using option pricing models. It is a series of call options on the underlying bond, and its value is determined by the level and volatility of interest rates. There are some modifications that need to be made to the standard option pricing models before they can be applied in this context.

Once the call feature is valued as a series of option, the yield on a callable bond can be adjusted for the option features, and the difference between this adjusted yield and a noncallable bond of equivalent maturity is called the option adjusted spread. This approach is a more realistic way of considering the effects of the call feature on expected yields than the traditional yield to call approach.

The following illustration values the call feature on a callable bond.

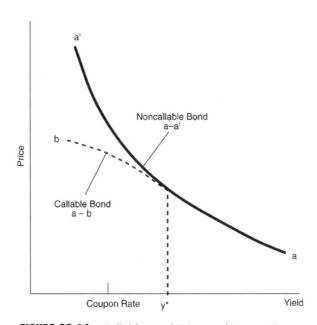

FIGURE 33.14 Callable Bond Prices and Interest Rates

ILLUSTRATION 33.8: Valuing a Callable Bond

The following analysis values a 17-year callable bond with a coupon rate of 12% by valuing the straight bond, the call feature on the straight bond, and the value of the callable bond as a function of the yield on the bond. The actual option valuation was done using a binomial option pricing model, an interest rate volatility of 12%, and a short-term interest rate of 6%.

Yield	Value of Straight Bond	Value of Call Feature	Value of Callable Bond
20.51%	$ 60.00	$ 0.00	$ 60.00
19.55%	$ 63.00	$ 0.00	$ 63.00
18.66%	$ 66.00	$ 0.00	$ 66.00
17.59%	$ 70.00	$ 0.00	$ 70.00
16.63%	$ 74.00	$ 0.00	$ 74.00
15.54%	$ 79.00	$ 0.02	$ 78.98
14.56%	$ 84.00	$ 0.06	$ 83.94
13.51%	$ 90.00	$ 0.22	$ 89.78
12.57%	$ 96.00	$ 0.67	$ 95.33
11.46%	$104.00	$ 2.11	$101.89
10.59%	$111.00	$ 4.60	$106.40
9.59%	$120.00	$ 9.80	$110.20
8.60%	$130.00	$17.81	$112.19
7.73%	$140.00	$27.21	$112.79

While the value of the straight bond increases as the yield drops, the callable bond's value stops increasing because the call feature becomes more and more valuable as the yield becomes lower. In fact, the value of the callable bond is maximized at $112.94.

Valuing a Callable-Convertible Bond Many convertible bonds have embedded call features. The presence of two options in the bond, one possessed by the buyer of the bond and the other possessed by the seller of the bond, and the interaction between the two options imply that the two options have to be valued together. Brennan and Schwartz (1977, 1980) provide an analysis of convertible bonds with call features, default risk, and stock price dilution. The simplest approach for illustrating the interaction between the various options is a binomial option pricing model.

Empirical Evidence on Call Feature When a convertible bond is callable, holders of the convertible bond lose the opportunity to make further returns on the bond as stock prices increase. Companies can establish a variety of call policies such as calling the instant the market value of the convertible rises above the call price or waiting until the market value is well in excess of the call price. Ingersoll (1977) argues that a bond should be called when its conversion value equals its call price. Given that a 30-day notice has to be given to bondholders of a call, firms may prefer to build a cushion to protect against risk during this period.

The empirical evidence however suggests that firms do not usually follow the optimal policy. Ingersoll, for instance, found that between 1968 and 1975 the average conversion value was 43.9 percent above the call price for bonds and 38.5 percent for preferred stocks. The call policy chosen by a firm and communicated to financial markets implicitly through its actions has an effect on the value of the convertible bond.

Mortgage-Backed Securities

Mortgage-backed securities, which came of age in the 1980s, securitized residential mortgages by packaging them and issuing marketable securities of various types on them—either as flow-through investments, where holders receive a share of the total cash flows on the pool of mortgages, or as derivative products, where holders receive customized packages of cash flows depending on their preferences. The latter, called collateralized mortgage obligations (CMOs), in their simplest form divide cash flows on the mortgage pool into four tranches, with cash flows on each tranche starting as the cash flows on the prior tranche are completed. Figure 33.15 illustrates this type of security.

In recent years, CMOs have been refined further, and even more specialized products have been created including stripped mortgage-backed securities (where cash flows are divided on the basis of principal and interest), floating rate classes, and inverse floaters (where the interest rate on the security increases as the index rate decreases).

Mortgages can be prepaid by borrowers if interest rates decline. This prepayment option that resides with borrowers affects the cash flows, and therefore the value, of all mortgage-backed securities.

Prepayment Option   The homeowner may prepay a loan for any number of reasons, but the level of interest rates is a critical variable. If interest rates decline sufficiently, the potential gain from prepayment may exceed the cost of prepayment.

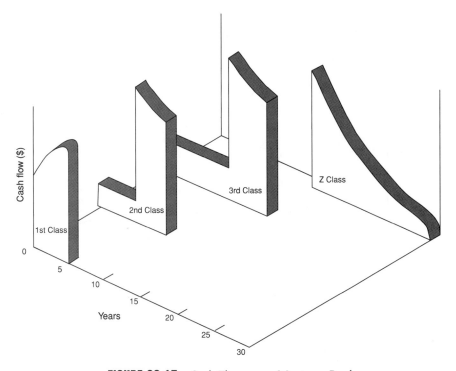

FIGURE 33.15   Cash Flows on a Mortgage Pool

Figure 33.16 illustrates the percentage of homeowners who prepay as a function of the difference between interest rate and the coupon rate, based on historical data.

If the level of interest rates were the only determinant of prepayment and homeowners were rational about prepayment decisions, the prepayment option could be valued very similarly to the call option in a callable bond (as a function of the level and volatility of interest rates).

There are, however, other variables besides the level of interest rates that determine whether homeowners prepay. For instance, there is a correlation between prepayment and the age of a mortgage, irrespective of interest rates. Furthermore, some homeowners may never prepay their mortgages no matter how much interest rates drop. There are also seasonal factors that affect prepayment. Consequently, option pricing models alone fall short in pricing prepayment options in mortgage-backed securities.

A number of researchers have attempted to develop models that explain prepayment as a basis for pricing the prepayment option, with characteristics such as age and coupon rate as inputs, in addition to specific characteristics of the borrowers in the pool. In cases where a specific rather than a generic pool of mortgages is being priced, the historical payment record of the specific pool is useful and is often the basis for estimating prepayments.[5]

Valuing the Prepayment Option   The effect of the prepayment option on value will vary with the type of mortgage-backed security. Consider, for instance, the price behavior of interest-only and principal-only securities as interest rates change. As interest rates

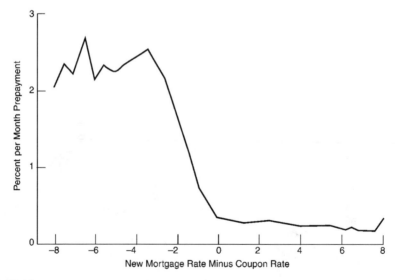

FIGURE 33.16   Prepayment History
Source: Sean Becketti, "The Prepayment Risk of Mortgage-Backed Securities," *Economic Review of the Federal Reserve Bank of Kansas City* (February 1989), 53.

---

[5]A number of variables have been found to be useful in explaining prepayments—the market price of a house relative to the original purchase price and geographical differences, for instance.

increase, the interest payments on the interest-only securities go up, leading to a higher value for the security, at least initially, though the present value effects (which are negative) start to dominate beyond a certain point. As interest rates decrease, the prepayments lead to lower interest payments and a lower value for the security. The principal-only securities behave more like conventional bonds, increasing in value as interest rates decline and decreasing in value as they increase. Figure 33.17 illustrates this relationship.

Interest Rate Caps and Floors

A floating rate bond is a bond that has an interest rate linked up to an index—either a government bond rate (Treasury bond or bill) or the LIBOR. The rationale for issuing such bonds is to reduce the interest rate risk for both the issuer and the buyer of the bond. Most floating rate bond issuers, however, cap their floating rate obligations to ensure that interest rates do not rise above a prespecified rate (the cap). Some floating rate bonds offer buyers some compensation by providing a floor, below which interest rates will not decline. If a floating rate bond has a cap and a floor, a collar is created.

Caps, Floors, and Collars   The presence of a cap on a floating rate bond can be illustrated best by contrasting a bond with a cap with a floating rate bond without one, as shown in Figure 33.18. The cap on a floating rate bond has the same effect as a call option on interest rates with a strike price of K_c, with the issuer of the bond holding the option. A call option on interest rates translates into a put option on the underlying bond.[6] The price of a floating rate bond with a cap can then be written as:

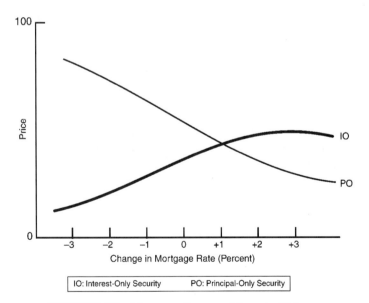

FIGURE 33.17   Mortgage Rates and Security Values

---

[6]The translation is not one to one. A call option on interest rates is the equivalent of a options on the underlying bill or bond, where $\alpha = 1/$Exercise price of equivalent bill.

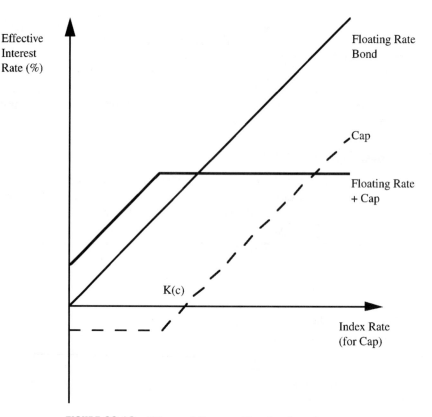

FIGURE 33.18   Effects of Caps on Floating Rate Loans

Price of floating rate bond with cap = Price of floating rate bond without cap
– Value of put on bond

The presence of a floor on interest rates can also be illustrated using a similar comparison of a bond with a floor with a bond without one in Figure 33.19. The floor on a floating rate bond has the same effect as adding a put option on interest rates with a strike price of K_f, with the buyer of the bond holding the put. A put option on interest rates can be translated into a call option on the underlying bond. The price of a floating rate bond with a floor can then be written as:

Price of floating rate bond with floor = Price of floating rate bond without floor
+ Value of call on bond

Finally, the presence of both a cap and a floor can be illustrated in Figure 33.20. The presence of a collar on a floating rate bond creates two options—a call option with a strike price of K_c for the issuer of the bond and a put option with a strike price of K_f for the buyer of the bond. These options on interest rates can be stated again in terms of options on the underlying bond.

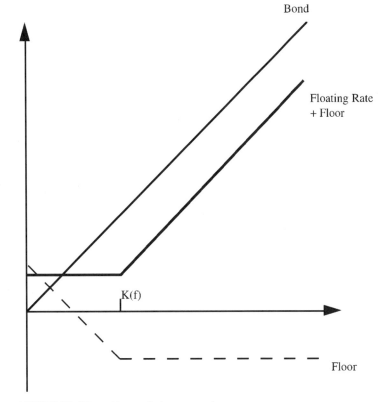

FIGURE 33.19 Effects of Floors on Floating Rate Loans

Price of floating rate bond with collar = Price of floating rate bond without collar
+ Value of call on bond
− Value of put on bond

Valuing Caps and Floors Option pricing models can be used to value caps, floors, and collars with some caveats. The key assumption in the Black-Scholes model of constant volatility over the life of the option is likely to be violated for floating rate options, both because of the long-term nature of these options and because the variance in the bond price is likely to change as the bond maturity declines. There have been attempts to use yield instead of price, and assume that it conforms to a lognormal distribution.

Stapleton and Subrahmanyam (1990) noted that the value of a cap on interest rates can be written as a series of put options on the price of an equivalent bill or bond. Briys, Crouhy, and Schobel (1991) provided a framework for pricing caps, floors, and collars. They argued that caps and floors can be modeled as a series of independent options on zero coupon bonds. They allowed for the fact that bond prices do not follow the geometric Brownian motion used by Black and Scholes (1972), but adopted a different stochastic process to price caps, floors, and collars.

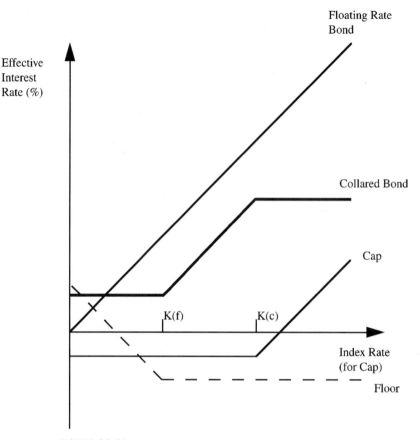

FIGURE 33.20 Effects of Collars on Floating Rate Loans

Other Features

There are a number of other bond features that affect the value of the bond: a sinking fund provision where the firm plans to retire a specified face value of the bonds outstanding each year, provisions relating to the subordination of future debt issues, and bond covenants on investment and dividend policy.

Sinking Funds Most industrial bond issues come with sinking fund provisions, requiring the issuer to retire a specified portion of the bond issue each year, starting a period of time (5 or 10 years) after the initial issue. The sinking fund provision can take one of two forms:

VALUING OPTIONS EMBEDDED IN BONDS

A corporate bond can often have three or four options embedded in it, and to value the bonds you have to value the options. While conventional option pricing models can be used to value fixed income options, you should note the following:

- The assumption of constant volatility that we often use to value options on stocks cannot be used to value options on bonds. Bonds are finite-life instruments and their volatility will decrease as they approach maturity. You will have to model the change in volatility over time to price the option.
- When multiple options exist in a bond, you will have to examine the relationship between the options to price them. For instance, consider a callable-convertible bond. While both callability and convertibility are options—one is held by the bond issuer and the other by the bond buyer—the exercise of one of these options voids the other. This will become a factor in when the options will be exercised and how much they are worth.
- The key underlying variable for some bond options—such as interest rate caps and floors—is the interest rate process, and how it is modeled can have a significant impact on the value of the options.

---

1. A trustee collects a cash payment from the bond issuer, and calls bonds for redemption at the sinking-fund call price, usually based on a lottery.
2. The bond issuer can buy back bonds in the open market and deliver the specified number of bonds to the trustee in the periods specified.

If the bond issuer has the option to do the latter, bonds will be bought back and delivered if the market price is less than the call price, and cash will be delivered to the trustee to make the call if the market price is greater than the call price.

Sinking funds usually relate to a single issue, but they can sometimes cover multiple issues ("funnel sinking fund"). Most sinking funds also allow the bond issuer to accelerate call backs if it is in the issuer's favor to do so (i.e., interest rates have gone down since the issue).

A sinking fund has two effects, one of which benefits the issuer of the bond and the other of which benefits the buyer of the bond. The issuer of the bond gets a delivery option, because he or she has an option to either deliver the cash for the call price or to buy the bonds at the market price. The value of this call option (similar to the option in a callable bond) will increase with the volatility of interest rates and decrease with the level of interest rates. The buyer of the bond has less default risk because of the requirement that some of the debt be retired each period. The net effect will determine whether a sinking fund provision adds or detracts from the value of a bond.

The empirical evidence on the sinking fund provision is mixed. While some of the earlier studies concluded that a sinking fund provision added to bond value, Ho and Lee (1989) found that its net value is insignificant overall, but that it adds more value as default risk increases.

Subordination of Further Debt and Collateral Existing debt holders are negatively affected by the issue of new debt, especially if the new debt has superior claims on the assets of the issuer. Therefore, some bond issues have subordination clauses, which put restrictions on the issue of additional debt. Additional debt might have to be subordinated to existing debt; that is, in the event of bankruptcy, subordinated debt will be paid off after existing debt is fully paid. The presence of subordination clauses in a bond agreement should make it less risky, and therefore more valuable.

Some bonds are issued with specific collateral issued behind them, with a specific asset of the firm backing up the promised payments on the bond. If the collateral is property, the bond is called a mortgage bond, whereas if it is securities, it is a collateral trust bond. Other bonds are issued without specific collateral and are called unsecured bonds. Other things remaining equal, secured bonds should be viewed as less risky and more valuable than equivalent unsecured bonds.

Effect of Bond Covenants Most bond issues are accompanied by a set of covenants that restrict the investment and dividend policies of the firm. These covenants are designed to protect bondholders from stockholders, who might try to expropriate wealth from them by investing in much riskier projects, especially if the firm is highly levered, or paying significantly higher dividends than expected.

Bond covenants should reduce the risk of expropriation on a bond and increase the value of the bond.

CONCLUSION

The price of a bond is the present value of the cash flows on the bond—coupons and face value—discounted back at an appropriate interest rate. To estimate that interest rate, the chapter began with the instantaneous riskless interest rate and added a maturity premium and a default premium to it.

Bonds become increasingly complex as special features are added to them, since these special features affect the cash flows, risk, and value of these bonds. Many of these special features have option characteristics—the chance to convert the bond into other securities or assets, the option to call the bond back if interest rates go down, and the option to put the bond back to the issuer if contractual obligations are not met. Traditional option pricing models can be used to value these options, some of which reside with the buyer (thus increasing the value of the bond) and some of which are held by the seller (which would reduce value). The presence of more than one of these options in the same bond (for example, a callable-convertible bond) does add to the complexity of the pricing process, but it can be overcome.

QUESTIONS AND SHORT PROBLEMS

1. Estimate the value of a just-issued 20-year government bond with an 8% coupon rate if interest rates are at 9%. How much will this value change if interest rates go up by 2%? If they go down by 2%? (Coupons are paid semiannually.)
2. Estimate the value of seasoned government bond with a 7.5% coupon rate and 12 years to maturity, if interest rates are at 8.0%. (Coupons are paid semiannually, and the next coupon is due in three months.)
3. Estimate the duration of a government bond with a coupon rate of 10% and a five-year maturity, if the yield to maturity on the bond is 8%. (You can assume, for purposes of simplicity, that the coupons are paid annually.)
4. Why are longer-term bonds more sensitive to a given change in interest rates than shorter-term bonds? Why are zero coupon bonds more sensitive than coupon bonds of equal maturity?
5. If the nominal interest rate is 8%, and expected inflation is 5%, estimate the expected real rate of return. Why might the actual real rate of return deviate from this expectation?
6. You are provided with the following information on government bonds of different maturities:

Maturity	Yield to Maturity
1 year	5.0%
2 years	5.5%
3 years	6.0%
4 years	6.5%
5 years	7.0%

You can assume that the bonds are trading at par, and that therefore the coupon rates are equal to the yields to maturity.
   a. Plot the yield curve using the yields to maturity.
   b. Estimate the spot rates for the different maturities.
   c. Estimate the forward rates for each of the five years.
7. If lenders demand a liquidity premium for lending long term, yield curves will always be upward-sloping. Is this statement true? Why or why not?
8. Some studies that looked at low-rated bonds in the 1980s found that the default premiums received on these bonds were much larger than the default rates on them. (In other words, investors in these bonds made more over the period, even after adjusting for actual defaults, than investors in higher-rated or default-free bonds.) They then concluded that the default premiums were too high. Would you agree? Why or why not?
9. You are analyzing a convertible bond with a face value of $1,000 and an annual coupon of 4%, which is convertible into 30 shares of stock anytime over

the next 20 years. The current stock price is $27, and the convertible is trading at $1,177. Estimate the following:
   a. The conversion ratio and conversion price.
   b. The conversion premium.
   c. The value of the conversion option if the interest rate on straight bonds issued by the same company is 8%.

10. ITC Corporation has convertible bonds outstanding with the following features:
   ■ The bonds mature in 15 years; there are 100,000 bonds outstanding.
   ■ Each bond can be converted into 50 shares of stock at any time until expiration.
   ■ The coupon rate on the bond is 5%; straight bonds issued by the company are yielding 10%.
   ■ The current stock price is $15 per share, and the standard deviation in ln (stock prices) is 40%.
   ■ There are 20 million shares outstanding.
   a. Value the conversion option.
   b. Estimate the value of the straight bond portion.
   c. If these bonds were issued at par, who would be gaining? Who would be losing?
   d. What impact would forced conversion have on the value of this convertible bond?

11. A company has two issues of bonds outstanding; they both have the same maturities and coupon rates, but differ in one respect: The first issue (issue A) is callable, while the second is not. Respond true or false to the following statements:
   a. The callable bonds will trade for a higher price than the noncallable bonds.
      True _____   False _____
   b. The callable bonds have a shorter duration than the noncallable bonds.
      True _____   False _____
   c. The callable bonds will have a higher yield than the noncallable bonds.
      True _____   False _____
   d. The callable bonds will be more sensitive to interest rate changes than the noncallable bonds.
      True _____   False _____

12. You are evaluating the yield on a callable bond with a 10-year maturity and a 9% coupon rate. The bonds can be called back at 110% of par in three years. The bond is trading at $950.
   a. Estimate the yield to maturity.
   b. Estimate the yield to call.
   c. Which of the two would you use in analyzing the bond?

13. Collateralized mortgage obligations (CMOs) provide investors with the opportunity to invest in cash flows from mortgage obligations. These cash flows are affected by mortgage prepayments. Assume that you have valued (and bought) CMOs on the assumption that homeowners will prepay as soon as it is rational for them to do so. What would be the effect on your returns if:
   a. Homeowners consistently waited too long before prepaying mortgages?
   b. Homeowners consistently prepaid mortgages at the right time?

14. Answer true or false to the following statements, and explain:
   a. A floating rate loan with no cap or floor has very low or no duration.
      True _____   False _____

   b. A floating rate loan with a cap will have a higher interest rate than a similar floating rate loan with no cap.
   True _____ False _____

   c. A floating rate loan with a floor will have a higher interest rate than a similar floating rate loan with no floor.
   True _____ False _____

   d. A loan with a sinking fund provision will have a lower interest rate than a similar loan with no sinking fund provision.
   True _____ False _____

CHAPTER 34

Valuing Futures and Forward Contracts

A futures contract is a contract between two parties to exchange assets or services at a specified time in the future at a price agreed on at the time of the contract. In most conventionally traded futures contracts, one party agrees to deliver a commodity or security at some time in the future, in return for an agreement from the other party to pay an agreed-on price on delivery. The former is the seller of the futures contract, while the latter is the buyer.

This chapter explores the pricing of futures contracts on a number of different assets—perishable commodities, storable commodities, and financial assets—by setting up the basic arbitrage relationship between the futures contract and the underlying asset. It also examines the effects of transactions costs and trading restrictions on this relationship and on futures prices. Finally, the chapter reviews some of the evidence on the pricing of futures contracts.

FUTURES, FORWARD, AND OPTION CONTRACTS

Futures, forward, and option contracts are all viewed as derivative contracts because they derive their value from an underlying asset. There are, however, some key differences in the workings of these contracts.

How a Futures Contract Works

There are two parties to every futures contract: the seller of the contract, who agrees to deliver the asset at the specified time in the future, and the buyer of the contract, who agrees to pay a fixed price and take delivery of the asset. (See Figure 34.1.)

While a futures contract may be used by a buyer or seller to hedge other positions in the same asset, price changes in the asset after the futures contract agreement is made provide gains to one party at the expense of the other. If the price of the underlying asset increases after the agreement is made, the buyer gains at the expense of the seller. If the price of the asset drops, the seller gains at the expense of the buyer.

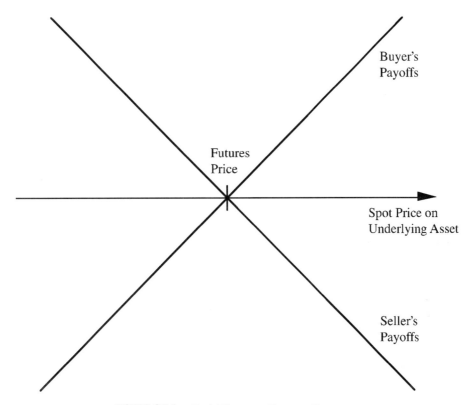

FIGURE 34.1 Cash Flows on Futures Contracts

Futures versus Forward Contracts

While futures and forward contracts are similar in terms of their final results, a forward contract does not require that the parties to the contract settle up until the expiration of the contract. Settling up usually involves the loser (i.e., the party that guessed wrong on the direction of the price) paying the winner the difference between the contract price and the actual price. In a futures contract, the differences are settled every period, with the winner's account being credited with the difference, while the loser's account is reduced. This process is called marking to the market. While the net settlement is the same under the two approaches, the timing of the settlements is different and can lead to different prices for the two types of contracts. The difference is illustrated in the following example, using a futures contract in gold.

ILLUSTRATION 34.1: Futures versus Forward Contracts: Gold Futures Contract

Assume that the three-period futures contract on gold has a price of $415. The following table summarizes the cash flow (CF) to the buyer and seller of this contract on a futures and forward contract over the next three time periods, as the price of gold changes over the next three periods.

Time Period	Gold Price	Buyer's CF: Forward	Seller's CF Forward	Buyer's CF: Futures	Seller's CF: Futures
1	$420	$ 0	$ 0	$ 5	−$ 5
2	$430	$ 0	$ 0	$10	−$10
3	$425	$10	−$10	−$ 5	$ 5
Net		$10	−$10	$10	−$10

The net cash flow from the seller to the buyer if $10 in both cases, but the timing of the cash flows is different. On the forward contract, the settlement occurs at maturity. On the futures contract, the profits or losses are recorded each period.

Futures and Forward Contracts versus Option Contracts

While the difference between a futures and a forward contract may be subtle, the difference between these contracts and option contracts is much greater. In an options contract, the buyer is not obligated to fulfill his or her side of the bargain, which is to buy the asset at the agreed-on strike price in the case of a call option and to sell the asset at the strike price in the case of a put option. Consequently, the buyer of an option will exercise the option only if it is in his or her best interest to do so (i.e., if the asset price exceeds the strike price in a call option and vice versa in a put option). The buyer of the option, of course, pays for this privilege up front. In a futures contract, both the buyer and the seller are obligated to fulfill their sides of the agreement. Consequently, the buyer does not gain an advantage over the seller and should not have to pay an up-front price for the futures contract itself. Figure 34.2 summarizes in a payoff diagram the differences in payoffs on the two types of contracts to a buyer.

TRADED FUTURES CONTRACTS—INSTITUTIONAL DETAILS

A futures contract is an agreement between two parties. In a traded futures contract, an exchange acts as an intermediary and guarantor, and also standardizes and regulates how the contract is created and traded.

This section will examine some of the institutional features of traded futures contracts.

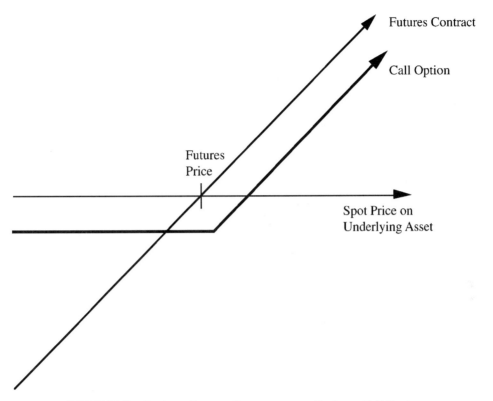

FIGURE 34.2 Buying a Futures Contract versus Buying a Call Option

Standardization

Traded futures contracts are standardized to ensure that contracts can be easily traded and priced. The standardization occurs at a number of levels:

- *Asset quality and description.* The type of asset that can be covered by the contract is clearly defined. For instance, a crude oil contract traded on the New York Mercantile Exchange requires the delivery of specific domestic crude oil with 0.42 percent sulfur or less. A Treasury bond futures contract traded on the Chicago Board of Trade (CBOT) requires the delivery of bonds with a face value of $100,000 with a maturity of greater than 15 years.[1]

---

[1] The reason the exchange allows equivalents is to prevent investors from buying a significant portion of the specified Treasury bonds and cornering the market.

■ *Asset quantity.* Each traded futures contract on an asset provides for the delivery of a specified quantity of the asset. For instance, a gold futures contract traded on the Chicago Board of Trade requires the delivery of 100 ounces of gold at the contract's expiration.

The purpose of the standardization is to ensure that the futures contracts on an asset are perfect substitutes for each other. This allows for liquidity and also allows parties to a futures contract to get out of positions easily.

Price Limits

Futures exchanges generally impose price movement limits on most futures contracts. For instance, the daily price movement limit on orange juice futures contract on the New York Board of Trade is 5 cents per pound or $750 per contract (which covers 15,000 pounds). If the price of the contract drops or increases by the amount of the price limit, trading is generally suspended for the day, though the exchange reserves the discretion to reopen trading in the contract later in the day. The rationale for introducing price limits is to prevent panic buying and selling on an asset based on faulty information or rumors, and to prevent overreaction to real information. If investors are allowed more time to react to extreme information, it is argued, the price reaction will be more rational and reasoned.

Margin Requirements for Trading

In a futures agreement, there is no payment made by the buyer to the seller, nor does the seller have to show proof of physical ownership of the asset at the time of the agreement. In order to ensure, however, that the parties to the futures contract fulfill their sides of the agreement, they are required to deposit funds in a margin account. The amount that has to be deposited at the time of the contract is called the initial margin. As prices move subsequently, the contracts are marked to market, and the profits or losses are posted to the investor's account. The investor is allowed to withdraw any funds in the margin account in excess of the initial margin. Table 34.1 summarizes price limits and contract specifications for many traded futures contracts as of June 2001.

If the investor has a string of losses because of adverse price movements, his or her margin will decrease. To ensure that there are always funds in the account, the investor is expected to maintain a maintenance margin, which is generally lower than the initial margin. If the funds in the margin account fall below the maintenance margin, the investor will receive a margin call to replenish the funds in the account. These extra funds that have to be brought in is known as a variation margin. Maintenance margins can vary across contracts and even across different customers. Table 34.2, for instance, shows the relationship between maintenance and initial margins for a sampling of futures contracts from the Chicago Mercantile Exchange.

TABLE 34.1 Futures Contracts: Description, Price Limits, and Margins

Contract	Exchange	Specifications	Tick Value	Initial Margin/ Contract	Daily Limit/ Unit
Softs					
Coffee	NYBOT	37,500 lbs.	$18.75/.05¢	$ 2,450	None
Sugar	NYBOT	112,000 lbs.	$11.20/.01¢	$ 840	None
Cocoa	NYBOT	10 metric tons	$10/1¢	$ 980	None
Cotton	NYBOT	50,000 lbs.	$ 5/.01¢	$ 1,000	3¢
Orange juice	NYBOT	15,000 lbs.	$ 7.50/.05¢	$ 700	5¢
Metals					
Gold	NYMEX	100 troy oz.	$10/10¢	$ 1,350	$75
Kilo gold	CBOT	1 gross kgm.	$ 3.22/10¢	$ 473	$50
Silver	NYMEX	5,000 troy oz.	$25/.5¢	$ 1,350	$1.50
5,000 oz. silver	CBOT	5,000 troy oz.	$ 5/.1¢	$ 270	$1
Copper	NYMEX	25,000 lbs.	$12.50/.05¢	$ 4,050	$0.20
Platinum	NYMEX	50 troy oz.	$ 5/10¢	$ 2,160	$25
Palladium	NYMEX	100 troy oz.	$ 5/5¢	$67,500	None
Energy					
Crude	NYMEX	1,000 barrels	$10/1¢	$ 3,375	$7.50 first
Unleaded	NYMEX	42,000 gallons	$ 4.20/.01¢	$ 3,375	20¢ first
Heating oil	NYMEX	42,000 gallons	$ 4.20/.01¢	$ 3,375	20¢ first
Natural gas	NYMEX	10,000 mm Btu	$10/.01¢	$ 4,725	$1
Agriculture					
Live cattle	CME	40,000 lbs.	$10/2.5¢	$ 810	1.5¢
Feeder cattle	CME	50,000 lbs.	$12.50/2.5¢	$ 945	1.5¢
Lean hogs	CME	40,000 lbs.	$10/2.5¢	$ 999	2¢
Pork bellies	CME	40,000 lbs.	$10/2.5¢	$ 1,620	3¢
Lumber	CME	110,000 ft.	$11/10¢	$ 1,013	$10
Currencies					
Eurocurrency	CME	125,000 euros	$12.50/.01¢	$ 2,349	400 ticks
Swiss franc	CME	125,000 Sfr	$12.50/.01¢	$ 1,755	400 ticks
Japanese yen	CME	12,500,000 yen	$12.50/.0001¢	$ 2,835	400 ticks
British pound	CME	62,500 Bp	$ 6.25/.02¢	$ 1,418	800 ticks
Canadian dollar	CME	100,000 C$	$10/.01¢	$ 608	400 ticks
Australian dollar	CME	100,000 A$	$10/.01¢	$ 1,215	400 ticks
Mexican peso	CME	500,000 pesos	$12.50/.0025¢	$ 2,500	2000 ticks
Dollar index	NYBOT	$1,000 times dollar index	$10/.01¢	$ 1,995	2 pts.
Interest Rates					
T-bond	CBOT	$100,000 face value	$31.25/$\frac{1}{32}$	$ 2,363	None
T-note (10)	CBOT	$100,000 face value	$31.25/$\frac{1}{32}$	$ 1,620	None
T-note (5)	CBOT	$100,000 face value	$31.25/$\frac{1}{32}$	$ 1,080	None
Muni bond	CBOT	$1,000 times the closing value of The Bond Buyer™ 40 Index	$31.25/$\frac{1}{32}$	$ 1,350	None
MIDAM bond	MIDAM	$50,000 face value	$15.62/$\frac{1}{32}$	$ 878	3 pts.
T-bills	CME	$1,000,000	$25/.05¢	$ 540	None
Eurodollars	CME	$1,000,000	$25/.05¢	$ 810	None

(Continued)

TABLE 34.1   *(Continued)*

Contract	Exchange	Specifications	Tick Value	Initial Margin/ Contract	Daily Limit/ Unit
Indexes					
S&P 500	CME	$250 times S&P 500 index	$25/.10 pts.	$21,563	None
NYSE index	NYBOT	$250 times S&P 500 index	$25/.05 pts.	$19,000	None
Nasdaq 100	CME	$100 times Nasdaq	$ 5/.05 pts.	$33,750	None
Mini Nasdaq	CME	$20 times Nasdaq	$10/.50 Pts.	$ 6,750	None
Mini S&P	CME	$50 times S&P 500 index	$12.50/.25 pts	$ 4,313	None
Dow Jones Futures	CBOT	$10 times Dow Jones index	$10/1 pt.	$ 6,750	None
Value Line	KCBT	$100 times Value Line index	$25/.05 pts.	$ 3,500	None
Nikkei	CME	$5 times Nikkei index	$25/5 pts.	$ 6,750	None
GSCI	CME	$250 times GSCI	$12.50/.05 pts.	$ 3,750	None
CRB	NYBOT		$25/.05 pts.	$ 1,500	None
Grains					
Soybeans	CBOT	5,000 bushels	$12.50/.25¢	$ 945	50¢
Soymeal	CBOT	100 tons	$10/10¢	$ 810	$20
Bean oil	CBOT	60,000 lbs.	$ 6/.01¢	$ 473	2¢
Wheat	CBOT	5,000 bushels	$12.50/.25¢	$ 743	30¢
Corn	CBOT	5,000 bushels	$12.50/.25¢	$ 473	20¢
Oats	CBOT	50,00 bushels	$12.50/.25¢	$ 270	20¢

CBOT: Chicago Board of Trade.
KCBT: Kansas City Board of Trade.
NYBOT: New York Board of Trade.
NYMEX: New York Mercantile Exchange.
CME: Chicago Mercantile Exchange.
MIDAM: Mid American Exchange.

TABLE 34.2   Initial versus Maintenance Margins

Agriculture Group	Maintenance Margin (per Contract)	Initial Margin Markup Percentage	Initial Margin (per Contract)
Corn	$350	135%	$473
Oats	$200	135%	$270
Rough rice	$500	135%	$675
Soybeans	$700	135%	$945
Soybean meal	$600	135%	$810
Soybean oil	$350	135%	$473
Wheat	$550	135%	$743

ILLUSTRATION 34.2:   Calculating Initial and Maintenance Margins

Assume that you buy 100 wheat futures contracts on the CME and that the spot price of wheat today is $3.15. Your initial margin can be computed based on the $743 per contract specified by the exchange:

$$\text{Initial margin} = \$743 \times 100 \text{ contracts} = \$74{,}300$$

Assume that the price of wheat drops to $3.14 per bushel tomorrow. The contract will be marked to market, resulting is a loss to you:

$$\text{Loss from marking to market} = \text{Change in price} \times \text{Bushels per contract} \times \text{Number of contracts}$$
$$= (\$3.15 - \$3.14) \times 5{,}000 \times 100 = \$5{,}000$$

The equity in your account is now:

$$\text{Equity after marking to market} = \$74{,}300 - \$5{,}000 = \$69{,}300$$

You are still safely above the maintenance margin requirement, but a series of price drops can cause your equity to drop below the maintenance margin:

$$\text{Maintenance margin} = \$550 \times 100 = \$55{,}000$$

If you drop below this level, you will get a margin call. Failure to meet the margin call will result in the position being liquidated.

PRICE LIMITS: EFFECTS ON LIQUIDITY

The logic of price limits is that they act as a brake on the market and prevent panic buying or selling. Implicit in their use is the assumption that trading can sometimes exacerbate volatility and cause prices to swing to unjustifiably high or low levels. The problem with price limits, however, is that they do not discriminate between rational price movements (caused by shifts in the underlying demand or supply of a commodity) and irrational ones. Consequently, price limits can limit liquidity when investors need it the most and slow down the process of price adjustment.

An interesting way to frame the question on price limits is to ask whether you would be willing to pay more or less for an asset that has price limits associated with trading than for an asset without those price limits. The trade-off between lower volatility (from restrictions on trading) and less liquidity will determine how you answer the question.

PRICING OF FUTURES CONTRACTS

Most futures contracts can be priced on the basis of arbitrage: that is, a price or range of prices can be derived at which investors will not be able to create positions involving the futures contract and the underlying asset that make riskless profits with no initial investment. The following sections examine the pricing relationships for a number of futures contracts.

Perishable Commodities

Perishable commodities offer the exception to the rule that futures contracts are priced on the basis of arbitrage, since the commodity has to be storable for arbitrage to be feasible. On a perishable futures contract, the futures price will be influenced by:

- *Expected spot price of the underlying commodity.* If the spot price on the underlying commodity is expected to increase before the expiration of the futures contract, the futures prices will be greater than the current spot price of the commodity. If the spot price is expected to decrease, the futures price will be lower than the spot price.
- *Any risk premium associated taking the futures position.* Since there is a buyer and a seller on a futures contract, the size and the direction of the risk premium will be vary from case to case, and will depend on whether the buyer is viewed as providing a service to the seller or vice versa. In an agricultural futures contract, where farmers or producers are the primary sellers of futures contracts, and individual investors are the buyers, it can be argued that the latter are providing a service to the former, and thus should be rewarded. In this scenario, the futures price will be lower than the expected spot price.

Futures price = Spot price − Expected risk premium

In this type of relationship between futures and spot prices, prices are said to exhibit "normal backwardation."

In a futures contract, where buyers of the futures contract are industrial users (a good example would be Hershey's, a chocolate manufacturer, buying sugar futures to lock in favorable prices), and the sellers are individual investors, the buyers are being provided the service, and the sellers could demand a reward, leading to a risk premium that is positive. In this case, the futures price will be greater than the expected spot price, and futures prices are said to exhibit "normal contango."

In most modern commodity futures markets, neither sellers nor buyers are likely to be dominated by users or producers, and the net benefit can accrue to either buyers or sellers and there is no a priori reason to believe that risk premiums have to be positive or negative. In fact, if buyers and sellers are both speculating on the price, rather than hedging output or input needs, the net benefit can be zero, leading to a zero risk premium. In such a case the futures price should be equal to the expected spot price.

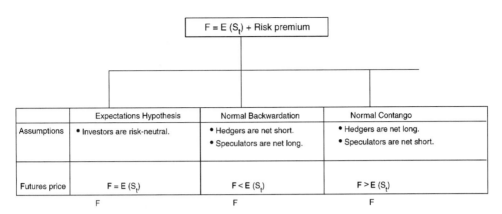

FIGURE 34.3 Futures on Perishable Commodities

These three possible scenarios for the futures price, relative to the expected spot price, are graphed in Figure 34.3. The empirical evidence from commodity futures markets is mixed. An early study by Houthaker (1957) found that futures prices for commodities were generally lower than the expected spot prices, a finding that is consistent with normal backward action. Telser (1958), however, reported contradictory evidence from the wheat and corn futures markets.

Storable Commodities

The distinction between storable and perishable goods is that storable goods can be acquired at the spot price and stored till the expiration of the futures contract, which is the practical equivalent of buying a futures contract and taking delivery at expiration. Since the two approaches provide the same result, in terms of having possession of the commodity at expiration, the futures contract, if priced right, should cost the same as a strategy of buying and storing the commodity. The two additional costs of the latter strategy are:

1. Since the commodity has to be acquired now, rather than at expiration, there is an added financing cost associated with borrowing the funds needed for the acquisition now.

    $$\text{Added interest cost} = \text{Spot price} \times [(1 + \text{Interest rate})^{\text{life of futures contract}} - 1]$$

2. If there is a storage cost associated with storing the commodity until the expiration of the futures contract, this cost has to be reflected in the strategy as well. In addition, there may be a benefit to having physical ownership of the commodity. This benefit is called the convenience yield and will reduce the futures price. The net storage cost is defined to be the difference between the total storage cost and the convenience yield.

If F is the futures contract price, S is the spot price, r is the annualized interest rate, t is the life of the futures contract, and k is the annual storage costs; net of the convenience yield, (as a percentage of the spot price) for the commodity, the two equivalent strategies and their costs can be written as follows:

Strategy 1: Buy the futures contract; take delivery at expiration; pay $F.

Strategy 2: Borrow the spot price of the commodity (S) and buy the commodity; pay the additional costs:

$$\text{Interest cost} = S[(1 + r)^t - 1]$$

$$\text{Cost of storage, net of convenience yield} = Skt$$

If the two strategies have the same costs,

$$F^* = S + S[(1 + r)^t - 1] + Skt$$
$$= S[(1 + r)^t + kt]$$

This is the basic arbitrage relationship between futures and spot prices. Any deviation from this arbitrage relationship should provide an opportunity for arbitrage (i.e., a strategy with risk and no initial investment, will provide positive profits). These arbitrage opportunities are described in Figure 34.4.

This arbitrage is based on several assumptions. First, investors are assumed to borrow and lend at the same rate, which is the riskless rate. Second, when the futures contract is underpriced, it is assumed that the buyer of the futures contract (the arbitrageur) can sell short on the commodity and that he or she can recover from the owner of the commodity the storage costs that are saved as a conse-

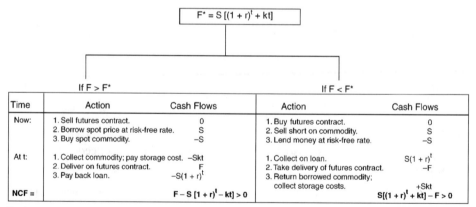

Key inputs
$F^* = $ Theoretical futures price $r = $ Riskless rate of interest (annualized)
$F = $ Actual futures price $t = $ Time to expiration on the futures contract
$S = $ Spot price of commodity $k = $ Annualized carrying cost, net of convenience yield (as % of spot price)

Key assumptions
1. The investor can lend and borrow at the riskless rate.
2. There are no transaction costs associated with buying or selling short the commodity.
3. The short seller can collect all storage costs saved because of the short selling.

FIGURE 34.4 Storable Commodity Futures: Pricing and Arbitrage

quence. To the extent that these assumptions are unrealistic, the bounds on prices within which arbitrage is not feasible expand. Assume, for instance, that the rate of borrowing is r_b and the rate of lending is r_a, and that short seller cannot recover any of the saved storage costs and has to pay a transactions cost of t_s. The futures price will then fall within a bound:

$$(S - t_s)(1 + r_a)^t < F^* < S[(1 + r_b)^t + kt]$$

If the futures price falls outside this bound, there is a possibility of arbitrage, and this is illustrated in Figure 34.5.

Stock Index Futures

Futures on stock indexes have become an important and growing part of most financial markets. Today, you can buy or sell futures on the Dow Jones, the S&P 500, the Nasdaq, and the Value Line indexes.

An index future entitles the buyer to any appreciation in the index over and above the index futures price, and the seller to any depreciation in the index from the same benchmark. To evaluate the arbitrage pricing of an index future, consider the following strategies:

> *Strategy 1:* Sell short on the stocks in the index for the duration of the index futures contract; invest the proceeds at the riskless rate. (This strategy requires that the owners of the stocks be compensated for the dividends they would have received on the stocks.)
>
> *Strategy 2:* Sell the index futures contract.

Modified Assumptions
1. Investor can borrow at r_b ($r_b > r$) and lend at r_a ($r_a < r$).
2. The transactions cost associated with selling short is t_s (where t_s is the dollar transactions cost).
3. The short seller does not collect any of the storage costs saved by the short selling.

$$F_h^* = S[(1 + r_b)^t + kt]$$
$$F_l^* = (S - t_s)(1 + r_a)$$

If $F > F_h^*$ If $F < F_l^*$

Time	Action	Cash Flows	Action	Cash Flows
Now:	1. Sell futures contract.	0	1. Buy futures contract.	0
	2. Borrow spot price at r_b.	S	2. Sell short on commodity.	$S - t_s$
	3. Buy spot commodity.	$-S$	3. Lend money at r_a.	$-(S - t_s)$
At t:	1. Collect commodity from storage.	$-Skt$	1. Collect on loan.	$(S - t_s)(1 + r_a)^t$
	2. Deliver on futures contract.	F	2. Take delivery of futures contract.	$-F$
	3. Pay back loan.	$-S(1 + r_b)^t$	3. Return borrowed commodity; collect storage costs.	0
NCF =		$F - S[(1 + r_b)^t - kt] > 0$		$(S - t_s)(1 + r_a)^t - F > 0$

F_h = Upper limit for arbitrage bound on futures prices F_l = Lower limit for arbitrage bound on futures prices

FIGURE 34.5 Storable Commodity Futures: Pricing and Arbitrage with Modified Assumptions

Both strategies require the same initial investment, have the same risk, and should provide the same proceeds. Again, if S is the spot price of the index, F is the futures prices, y is the annualized dividend yield on the stock, and r is the riskless rate, the cash flows from the two contracts at expiration can be written as:

$$F^* = S(1 + r - y)^t$$

If the futures price deviates from this arbitrage price, there should be an opportunity for arbitrage. This is illustrated in Figure 34.6.

This arbitrage is conditioned on several assumptions. First, it, like the commodity futures arbitrage, assumes that investors can lend and borrow at the riskless rate. Second, it ignores transactions costs on both buying stock and selling short on stocks. Third, it assumes that the dividends paid on the stocks in the index are known with certainty at the start of the period. If these assumptions are unrealistic, the index futures arbitrage will be feasible only if prices fall outside a band, the size of which will depend on the seriousness of the violations in the assumptions.

Assume that investors can borrow money at r_b and lend money at r_a, and that the transactions costs of buying stock is t_c and selling short is t_s. The band within which the futures price must stay can be written as:

$$(S - t_s)(1 + r_a - y)^t < F^* < (S + t_c)(1 + r_b - y)^t$$

The arbitrage that is possible if the futures price strays outside this band is illustrated in Figure 34.7.

In practice, one of the issues that you have to factor in is the seasonality of dividends since the dividends paid by stocks tend to be higher in some months than others. Figure 34.8 graphs out dividends paid as a percent of the S&P 500 index on

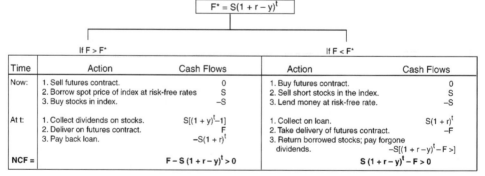

Key Inputs

F^* = Theoretical futures price
F = Actual futures price
S = Spot level of index
r = Riskless rate of interest (annualized)
t = Time to expiration on the futures contract
y = Dividend yield over lifetime of futures contract as % of current index level

Key assumptions
1. The investor can lend and borrow at the riskless rate.
2. There are no transaction costs associated with buying or selling short stocks.
3. Dividends are known with certainty.

FIGURE 34.6 Stock Index Futures: Pricing and Arbitrage

Modified Assumptions
1. Investor can borrow at r_b ($r_b > r$) and lend at r_a ($r_a < r$).
2. The transaction cost associated with selling short is t_S (where t_S is the dollar transaction cost) and the transaction cost associated with buying the stocks in the index is t_C.

$$F_h^* = (S + t_c)\,(1 + r_b - y)^t$$
$$F_l^* = (S - t_s)\,(1 + r_a - y)^t$$

If $F > F_h^*$ If $F < F_l^*$

Time	Action	Cash Flows	Action	Cash Flows
Now:	1. Sell futures contract.	0	1. Buy futures contract.	0
	2. Borrow spot price at r_b.	$S + t_c$	2. Sell short stocks in the index.	$S - t_s$
	3. Buy stocks in the index.	$-S - t_c$	3. Lend money at r_a.	$-(S - t_s)$
At t:	1. Collect dividends on stocks.	$S[(1 + y)^t - 1]$	1. Collect on loan.	$(S - t_s)(1 + r_a)^t$
	2. Deliver on futures contract.	F	2. Take delivery of futures contract.	$-F$
	3. Pay back loan.	$-(S + t_c)(1 + r_b)^t$	3. Return borrowed stocks: pay forgone dividends.	$-S[(1 + y)^t - 1]$
NCF =		$F - (S + t_c)\,(1 + r_b - y)^t > 0$		$(S - t_s)\,(1 + r_a - y)^t - F > 0$

F_h = Upper limit for arbitrage bound on futures prices F_l = Lower limit for arbitrage bound on futures prices

FIGURE 34.7   Stock Index Futures: Pricing and Arbitrage with Modified Assumptions

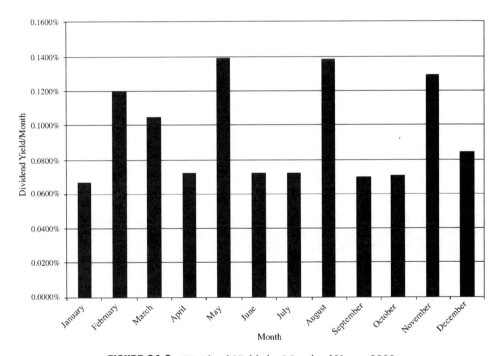

FIGURE 34.8   Dividend Yields by Month of Year—2000

U.S. stocks in 2000 by month of the year. Thus, dividend yields seem to peak in February, May, August, and November.

Treasury Bond Futures

The Treasury bond futures traded on the CBOT require the delivery of any government bond with a maturity greater than 15 years, with a no-call feature for at least the first 15 years. Since bonds of different maturities and coupons will have different prices, the CBOT has a procedure for adjusting the price of the bond for its characteristics. The conversion factor itself is fairly simple to compute, and is based on the value of the bond on the first day of the delivery month, with the assumption that the interest rate for all maturities equals 8 percent per annum (with semiannual compounding). The following example calculates the conversion factor for a 9 percent coupon bond with 20 years to maturity.

ILLUSTRATION 34.3: Calculation Conversion Factors for T-Bond Futures

Consider a 9% coupon bond with 20 years to maturity. Working in terms of a $100 face value of the bond, the value of the bond can be written as follows, using the interest rate of 8%:

$$\text{PV of bond} = \sum_{t=.5}^{t=20} \frac{4.50}{(1.08)^t} + \frac{100}{(1.08)^{20}} = \$111.55$$

The conversion factor for this bond is 111.55. Generally speaking, the conversion factor will increase as the coupon rate increases and with the maturity of the delivered bond.

THE DELIVERY OPTION AND THE WILD CARD PLAY

This feature of Treasury bond futures (i.e., that any one of a menu of Treasury bonds can be delivered to fulfill the obligation on the bond) provides an advantage to the seller of the futures contract. Naturally, the cheapest bond on the menu, after adjusting for the conversion factor, will be delivered. This delivery option has to be priced into the futures contract.

    There is an additional option embedded in Treasury bond futures contracts that arises from the fact that the T-bond futures market closes at 2 P.M., whereas the bonds themselves continue trading until 4 P.M. The seller does not have to notify the clearing house until 8 P.M. about his or her intention to deliver. If bond prices decline after 2 P.M., the seller can notify the clearinghouse of intention to deliver the cheapest bond that day. If not, the seller can wait for the next day. This option is called the wild card play.

VALUING A T-BOND FUTURES CONTRACT

The valuation of a Treasury bond futures contract follows the same lines as the valuation of a stock index future, with the coupons of the Treasury bond replacing the dividend yield of the stock index. The theoretical value of a futures contract should be:

$$F^* = (S - PVC)(1 + r)^t$$

where   F* = Theoretical futures price for Treasury bond futures contract
        S = Spot price of Treasury bond
      PVC = Present value of coupons during life of futures contract
        r = Risk-free interest rate corresponding to futures life
        t = Life of the futures contract

If the futures price deviates from this theoretical price, there should be the opportunity for arbitrage. These arbitrage opportunities are illustrated in Figure 34.9.

This valuation ignores the two options just described—the option to deliver the cheapest-to-deliver bond and the option to have a wild card play. These give an advantage to the seller of the futures contract and should be priced into the futures contract. One way to build this into the valuation is to use the cheapest deliverable bond to calculate both the current spot price and the present value of the coupons. Once the futures price is estimated, it can be divided by the conversion factor to arrive at the standardized futures price.

Currency Futures

In a currency futures contract, you enter into a contract to buy a foreign currency at a price fixed today. To see how spot and futures currency prices are related, note that holding the foreign currency enables the investor to earn the risk-free interest rate (R_f) prevailing in that currency while the domestic currency earn the domestic risk-free rate (R_d). Since investors can buy currency at spot rates and assuming that there are no restrictions on investing at the risk-free rate, we can derive the relationship between the spot and futures prices. Interest rate parity relates the differential between futures and spot prices to interest rates in the domestic and foreign market.

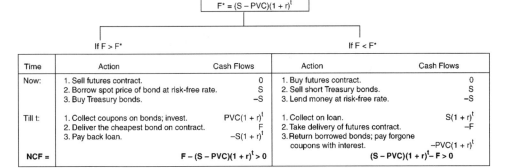

FIGURE 34.9   Treasury Bond Futures: Pricing and Arbitrage

$$\frac{\text{Futures price}_{d,f}}{\text{Spot price}_{d,f}} = \frac{(1+R_d)}{(1+R_f)}$$

where futures price$_{d,f}$ is the number of units of the domestic currency that will be received for a unit of the foreign currency in a futures contract, and spot price$_{d,f}$ is the number of units of the domestic currency that will be received for a unit of the same foreign currency in a spot contract. For instance, assume that the one-year interest rate in the United States is 5 percent, and the one-year interest rate in Germany is 4 percent. Furthermore, assume that the spot exchange rate is $0.65 per deutsche mark. The one-year futures price, based on interest rate parity, should be as follows:

$$\frac{\text{Futures price}_{d,f}}{\$0.65} = \frac{(1.05)}{(1.04)}$$

resulting in a futures price of $0.65625 per deutsche mark.

Why does this have to be the futures price? If the futures price were greater than $0.65625, say $0.67, an investor could take advantage of the mispricing by selling the futures contract, completely hedging against risk and ending up with a return greater than the risk-free rate. When a riskless position yields a return that exceeds the risk-free rate, it is called an arbitrage position. The actions the investor would need to take are summarized in Table 34.3, with the cash flows associated with each action in parentheses next to the action. This arbitrage results in a riskless profit of $0.0143, with no initial investment. The process of arbitrage will push down the futures price toward the equilibrium price.

TABLE 34.3 Arbitrage When Forward Contracts Are Mispriced

Forward Rate Mispricing	Actions to Take Today	Actions at Expiration of Forward Contract
If futures price > $0.65625	1. Sell a futures contract at $0.67 per deutsche mark ($0.00). 2. Borrow the spot price in the U.S. domestic markets @ 5% (+$0.65). 3. Convert the dollars into deutsche marks at spot price (−$0.65/+1 DM). 4. Invest deustche marks in the German market @ 4% (−1 DM).	1. Collect on deutsche mark investment (+1.04 DM). 2. Convert into dollars at futures price (−1.04/+$0.6968). 3. Repay dollar borrowing with interest ($0.6825). Profit = $0.6968 − $0.6825 = $0.0143
If futures price < $0.65625	1. Buy a futures price at $0.64 per deutsche mark ($0.00). 2. Borrow the spot rate in the German market @ 4% (+1 DM). 3. Convert the deutsche marks into dollars at spot rate (−1 DM/+$0.65). 4. Invest dollars in the U.S. market @ 5% (−$0.65).	1. Collect on dollar investment (+$0.6825). 2. Convert into dollars at futures price (−$0.6825/1.0664 DM). 3. Repay DM borrowing with interest (1.04). Profit = 1.0664 − 1.04 = .0264 DM

If the futures price were lower than $0.65625, the actions would be reversed, with the same final conclusion. Investors would be able to take no risk, invest no money, and still end up with a positive cash flow at expiration. Table 34.3 lays out the actions that would lead to a riskless profit of .0264 DM.

EFFECTS OF SPECIAL FEATURES IN FUTURES CONTRACTS

The arbitrage relationship provides a measure of the determinants of futures prices on a wide range of assets. There are, however, some special features that affect futures prices. One is the fact that futures contracts require marking to the market, while forward contracts do not. Another is the existence of trading restrictions such as price limits on futures contracts. The following section examines the pricing effects of each of these special features.

Futures versus Forward Contracts

As described earlier in this section, futures contracts require marking to market while forward contracts do not. If interest rates are constant and the same for all maturities, there should be no difference between the value of a futures contract and the value of an equivalent forward contract. When interest rates vary unpredictably, forward prices can be different from futures prices. This is because of the reinvestment assumptions that have to be made for intermediate profits on a futures contract and the borrowing rate assumptions that have to be made for intermediate losses. The effect of this interest rate–induced volatility on futures prices will depend on the relationship between spot prices and interest rates. If they move in opposite directions (as is the case with stock indexes and Treasury bonds), the interest rate risk will make futures prices greater than forward prices. If they move together (as is the case with some real assets), the interest rate risk can actually counter price risk and make futures prices less than forward prices. In most real-world scenarios, and in empirical studies, the difference between futures and forward prices is fairly small and can be ignored.

There is another difference between futures and forward contracts that can cause their prices to deviate and it relates to credit risk. Since the futures exchange essentially guarantees traded futures contracts, there is relatively little credit risk, since the exchange itself would have to default for buyers or sellers of contracts not to be paid. Forward contracts are between individual buyers and sellers. Consequently, there is potential for significant default risk, which has to be taken into account when valuing a forward contract.

Trading Restrictions

The existence of price limits and margin requirements on futures contracts are generally ignored in the valuation and arbitrage conditions described in this chapter. It is, however, possible that these restrictions on trading, if onerous enough, could impact value. The existence of price limits, for instance, has two effects. One is that it might reduce the volatility in prices by protecting against market overreaction to information, and thus make futures contracts more valuable. The other is that it make futures contracts less liquid, and this may make them less valuable. The net effect could be positive or negative.

CONCLUSION

The value of a futures contract is derived from the value of the underlying asset. The opportunity for arbitrage will create a strong linkage between the futures and spot prices, and the actual relationship will depend on the level of interest rates, the cost of storing the underlying asset, and any yield that can be made be holding the asset. In addition, the institutional characteristics of the futures markets, such as price limits and marking to market, as well as delivery of options, can affect the futures price.

QUESTIONS AND SHORT PROBLEMS

1. The following futures prices of gold are from the *Wall Street Journal* futures page. The current cash (spot) price of gold is $403.25. Make your best estimates of the implied interest rates (from the arbitrage relationship) in the futures prices. (You can assume zero carrying costs for gold.)

Contract Expiring In	Trading At
1 month	$404.62
2 months	$406.11
3 months	$407.70
6 months	$412.51
12 months	$422.62

2. You are a portfolio manager who has just been exposed to the possibilities of stock index futures. Respond to the following situations:
   a. Assume that you have the resources to buy and hold the stocks in the S&P 500. You are given the following data (assume that this is January 1):

   Level of the S&P 500 index = 258.90
   June S&P 500 futures contract = 260.15
   Annualized rate on T-bill expiring June 26 (expiration date) = 6%
   Annualized dividend yield on S&P 500 stocks = 3%

   Assume that dividends are paid out continuously over the year. Is there potential for arbitrage? How would you go about setting up the arbitrage?
   b. Assume now that you are known for your stock selection skills. You have 10,000 shares of Texaco in your portfolio (now selling for 38) and are extremely worried about the direction of the market until June. You would like to protect yourself against market risk by using the December S&P 500 futures contract (which is at 260.15). If Texaco's beta is 0.8, how would you go about creating this protection?
3. Assume that you are a mutual fund manager with a total portfolio value of $100 million. You estimate the beta of the fund to be 1.25. You would like to hedge against market movements by using stock index futures. You observe that the S&P 500 June futures are selling for 260.15 and that the index is at 258.90. Answer the following questions:
   a. How many stock index futures would you have to sell to protect against market risk?

   b. If the risk-free rate is 6% and the market risk premium is 8%, what return would you expect to make on the mutual fund (assuming you don't hedge)?

   c. How much would you expect to make if you hedge away all market risk?

4. Given the following information on gold futures prices, the spot price of gold, the riskless interest rate, and the carrying cost of gold, construct an arbitrage position. (Assume that it is December 1987 now.)

> December 1988 futures contract price = 515.60/troy oz.
> Spot price of gold = 481.40/troy oz.
> Interest rate (annualized) = 6%
> Carrying cost (annualized) = 2%

   a. What would you have to do right now to set up the arbitrage?

   b. What would you have to do in December to unwind the position? How much arbitrage profit would you expect to make?

   c. Assume now that you can borrow at 8%, but you can lend at only 6%. Establish a price band for the futures contract within which arbitrage is not feasible.

5. The following is a set of prices for stock index futures on the S&P 500.

Maturity	Futures Price
March	246.25
June	247.75

The current level of the index is 245.82, and the current annualized T-bill rate is 6%. The annualized dividend yield is 3%. (Today is January 14. The March futures expire on March 18, and the June futures on June 17.)

   a. Estimate the theoretical basis and actual basis in each of these contracts.

   b. Using one of the two contracts, set up an arbitrage. Also show how the arbitrage will be resolved at expiration. (You can assume that you can lend or borrow at the risk-free rate and that you have no transaction costs or margins.)

   c. Assume that a good economic report comes out on the wire. The stock index goes up to 247.82 and the T-bill rate drops to 5%. Assuming arbitrage relationships hold and that the dollar dividends paid do not change, how much will the March future go up by?

6. You are provided the following information:

> Current price of wheat = $19,000 for 5,000 bushels
> Riskless rate = 10% (annualized)
> Cost of storage = $200 a year for 5,000 bushels
> One-year futures contract price = $20,400 (for a contract for 5,000 bushels)

   a. What is F* (the theoretical price)?

   b. How would you arbitrage the difference between F and F*? (Specify what you will do now and at expiration, and what your arbitrage profits will be.)

   c. If you can sell short (cost $100 for 5,000 bushels) and cannot claim any of the storage cost for yourself on short sales,[2] at what rate would you have to be able to lend for this arbitrage to be feasible?

---

[2]In theory, we make the unrealistic assumption that a person who short sells (i.e., borrows somebody else's property and sells it now) will be able to collect the storage costs saved by the short sales from the other party to the transaction.

CHAPTER 35

Overview and Conclusion

The problem in valuation is not that there are not enough models to value an asset, it is that there are too many. Choosing the right model to use in valuation is as critical to arriving at a reasonable value as understanding how to use the model. This chapter attempts to provide an overview of the valuation models introduced in this book, and a general framework that can be used to pick the right model for any task.

CHOICES IN VALUATION MODELS

In the broadest possible terms, firms or assets can be valued in one of four ways: asset-based valuation approaches where you estimate what the assets owned by a firm are worth currently, discounted cash flow valuation approaches that discount cash flows to arrive at a value of equity or the firm, relative valuation approaches that base value on how comparable assets are priced, and option pricing approaches that use contingent claim valuation. Within each of these approaches, there are further choices that help determine the final value.

There are at least two ways in which you can value a firm using asset-based valuation techniques. One is liquidation value, where you consider what the market will be willing to pay for assets if the assets were liquidated today. The other is replacement cost, where you evaluate how much it would cost you to replicate or replace the assets that a firm has in place today.

In the context of discounted cash flow valuation, cash flows to equity can be discounted at the cost of equity to arrive at a value of equity, or cash flows to the firm can be discounted at the cost of capital to arrive at the value for the firm. The cash flows to equity themselves can be defined in the strictest sense as dividends or in a more expansive sense as free cash flows to equity. These models can be further categorized on the basis of assumptions about growth into stable-growth, two-stage, three-stage and n-stage models. Finally, the measurement of earnings and cash flows may be modified to match the special characteristics of the firm/asset—current earnings for firms/assets that have normal earnings, or normalized earnings for firms/assets whose current earnings may be distorted either by temporary factors or cyclical effects.

In the context of multiples, you can use either equity or firm value as your measure of value and relate it to a number of firm-specific variables—earnings, book value, and sales. The multiples themselves can be estimated by using comparable firms in the same business or from cross-sectional regressions that use the broader universe. For other assets, such as real estate, the price can similarly be expressed as a function of gross income or per square foot of space. Here the comparables would be other properties in the same locale with similar characteristics.

Contingent claim models can also be used in a variety of scenarios. When you consider the option that a firm has to delay making investment decisions, you can value a patent or an undeveloped natural resource reserve as an option. The option to expand may make young firms with potentially large markets trade at a premium on their discounted cash flow values. Finally, equity investors may derive value from the option to liquidate troubled firms with substantial debt. (See Figure 35.1.)

WHICH APPROACH SHOULD YOU USE?

The values that you obtain from the four approaches can be very different, and deciding which one to use can be a critical step. This judgment, however, will depend on several factors, some of which relate to the business being valued but many of which relate to you as the analyst.

Asset or Business Characteristics

The approach you use to value a business will depend on how marketable its assets are, whether it generates cash flows, and how unique it is in terms of its operations.

Marketability of Assets Liquidation valuation and replacement cost valuation are easiest to do for firms that have assets that are separable and marketable. (See Figure 35.2.) For instance, you can estimate the liquidation value for a real estate company because its properties can be sold individually, and you can estimate the value of each property easily. The same can be said about a closed-end mutual fund. At the other extreme, consider a brand-name consumer product like Gillette. Its assets

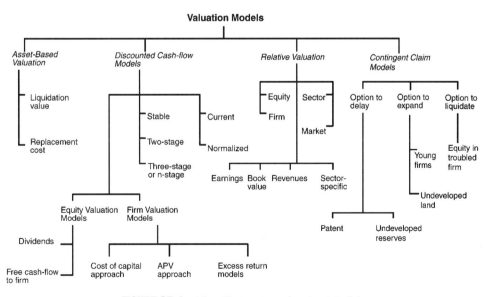

FIGURE 35.1 The Choices in Valuation Models

Mature businesses · Growth businesses
Separable and marketable assets · · · · · · · · · · · · · · · · Linked and nonmarketable assets

Liquidation and · Other valuation models
replacement cost valuation

FIGURE 35.2 Asset Marketability and Valuation Approaches

are not only intangible but difficult to separate out. For instance, you cannot separate the razor business easily from the shaving cream business, and brand name value is inherent in both businesses.

You can also use this same analysis to see why the liquidation or replacement cost value of a high-growth business may bear little resemblance to true value. Unlike assets in place, growth assets cannot be easily identified or sold.

Cash Flow Generating Capacity You can categorize assets into three groups based on their capacity to generate cash flows: assets that are either generating cash flows currently or are expected to do so in the near future, assets that are not generating cash flows currently but could in the future in the event of a contingency, and assets that will never generate cash flows. (See Figure 35.3.)

1. The first group includes most publicly traded companies, and these firms can be valued using discounted cash flow models. Note that a distinction is not drawn between negative and positive cash flows, and young start-up companies that generate negative cash flow can still be valued using discounted cash flow models.
2. The second group includes assets such as drug patents, promising (but not viable) technology, undeveloped oil or mining reserves, and undeveloped land. These assets may generate no cash flows currently and could generate large cash flows in the future but only under certain conditions—if the FDA approves the drug patent, if the technology becomes commercially viable, if oil prices and commercial property values go up. While you could estimate expected values using discounted cash flow models by assigning probabilities to these events, you will understate the value of the assets if you do so. You should value these assets using option pricing models.
3. Assets that are never expected to generate cash flows include your primary residence, a baseball card collection, or fine art. These assets can only be valued using relative valuation models.

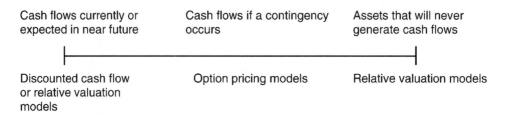

Cash flows currently or · · · · · Cash flows if a contingency · · · · · Assets that will never
expected in near future · · · · · · occurs · generate cash flows

Discounted cash flow · · · · · · · Option pricing models · · · · · · · · Relative valuation models
or relative valuation
models

FIGURE 35.3 Cash Flows and Valuation Approaches

Uniqueness (or Presence of Comparables)   In a market where thousands of stocks are traded and tens of thousands of assets are bought and sold every day, it may be difficult to visualize an asset or business that is so unique that you cannot find comparable assets. On a continuum, though, some assets and businesses are part of a large group of similar assets, with no or very small differences across the assets. (See Figure 35.4.) These assets are tailor-made for relative valuation, since assembling comparable assets (businesses) and controlling for differences is simple. The further you move from this ideal, the less reliable is relative valuation. For businesses that are truly unique, discounted cash flow valuation will yield much better estimates of value.

Analyst Characteristics and Beliefs

The valuation approach that you choose to use will depend on your time horizon, the reason that you are doing the valuation in the first place, and what you think about markets—whether they are efficient, and if they are not, what form the inefficiency takes.

Time Horizon   At one extreme, in discounted cash flow valuation you consider a firm as a going concern that may last into perpetuity. At the other extreme, with liquidation valuation, you are estimating value on the assumption that the firm will cease operations today. With relative valuation and contingent claim valuation, you take an intermediate position between the two. (See Figure 35.5.) Not surprisingly, then, you should be using discounted cash flow valuation if you have a long time horizon, and relative valuation if you have a shorter time horizon. This may explain why discounted cash flow valuation is more prevalent when valuing a firm for an acquisition, and relative valuation is more common in equity research and portfolio management.

Reason for Doing the Valuation   Analysts value businesses for a number of reasons, and the valuation approach used will vary depending on the reason. (See Figure 35.6.) If you are an equity research analyst following steel companies,

FIGURE 35.4   Uniqueness of Asset and Valuation Approaches

FIGURE 35.5   Investor Time Horizon and Valuation Approaches

Market neutral   Can take view on market
Judged on relative basis   Judged on absolute basis

Relative valuation   Discounted cash flow value
                                                        Option pricing models

FIGURE 35.6   Market Neutrality and Valuation Approaches

your job description is simple. You are asked to find the most under- and over-valued companies in the sector, and not take a stand on whether the sector over-all is under- or overvalued. You can see why multiples would be your weapon of choice when valuing companies. This effect is likely to be exaggerated if the way you are judged and rewarded is on a relative basis (i.e., your recommendations are compared to those made by other steel company analysts). But if you are an individual investor setting money aside for retirement or a private busi-nessperson valuing a business for purchase, you want to estimate intrinsic value. Consequently, discounted cash flow valuation is likely to be more appropriate for your needs.

Beliefs about Markets   Embedded in each approach are assumptions about mar-kets and how they work or fail to work. (See Figure 35.7.) With discounted cash flow valuation, you are assuming that market prices deviate from intrinsic value but that they correct themselves over long periods. With relative valuation, you are assuming that markets are on average right, and that while individual firms in a sector or market may be mispriced, the sector or overall market is fairly priced. With asset-based valuation models, you are assuming that the markets for real and financial assets can deviate and that you can take advantage of these differences. Fi-nally, with option pricing models, you are assuming that markets are not very effi-cient at assessing the value of flexibility that firms have, and that option pricing models will therefore give you an advantage. In each and every one of these cases, though, you are assuming that markets will eventually recognize their mistakes and correct them.

CHOOSING THE RIGHT DISCOUNTED CASH FLOW MODEL

The model used in valuation should be tailored to match the characteristics of the asset being valued. The unfortunate truth is that the reverse is often true. Time and

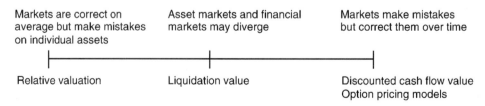

Markets are correct on   Asset markets and financial   Markets make mistakes
average but make mistakes   markets may diverge   but correct them over time
on individual assets

Relative valuation   Liquidation value   Discounted cash flow value
                                                                   Option pricing models

FIGURE 35.7   Views on Market and Valuation Approaches

BRIDGING THE PHILOSOPHICAL DIVIDE

Philosophically, there is a big gap between discounted cash flow valuation and relative valuation. In discounted cash flow valuation, we take a long-term perspective, evaluate a firm's fundamentals in detail, and try to estimate a firm's intrinsic value. In relative valuation, we assume that the market is right on average and estimate the value of a firm by looking at how similar firms are priced. There is something of value in both approaches, and it would be useful if we could borrow the best features of relative valuation while doing discounted cash flow valuation, or vice versa.

Assume that your instincts lead you to discounted cash flow valuation, but that you are expected, as an analyst, to be market-neutral. You can stay market-neutral in a discounted cash flow framework if you use the implied risk premium for the market (described in Chapter 7) to estimate the cost of equity for the valuation. You can also bring in information about comparable firm margins and betas when estimating fundamentals for your firm. Your estimate of intrinsic value will then be market-neutral and include information about comparables.

Alternatively, assume that you prefer relative valuation. Your analysis can carry the rigor of a discounted cash flow valuation if you can bring in the details of the fundamentals into your comparisons. The chapters on relative valuation attempted to do this by noting the link between multiples and fundamentals, and also by examining how best to control for these differences in the analysis.

---

resources are wasted trying to make assets fit a prespecified valuation model, either because it is considered to be the best model or because not enough thought goes into the process of model choice. There is no one best model. The appropriate model to use in a particular setting will depend on a number of the characteristics of the asset or firm being valued.

Choosing a Cash Flow to Discount

With consistent assumptions about growth and leverage, you should get the same value for your equity using the firm approach (where you value the firm and subtract outstanding debt) and the equity approach (where you value equity directly). If this is the case, you might wonder why you would pick one approach over the other. The answer is purely pragmatic. For firms that have stable leverage (i.e., they have debt ratios that are not expected to change during the period of the valuation), there is little to choose between the models in terms of the inputs needed for valuation. You use a debt ratio to estimate free cash flows to equity in the equity valuation model, and to estimate the cost of capital in the firm valuation model. Under these circumstances, you should stay with the model that you are more intuitively comfortable with.

For firms that have unstable leverage (i.e., they have too much or too little debt and want to move toward their optimal or target debt ratio during the period of the valuation), the firm valuation approach is much simpler to use because it does not require cash flow projections from interest and principal payments and is much less sensitive to errors in estimating leverage changes. The calculation of the cost of capital requires an estimate of the debt ratio, but the cost of capital itself does not change as much as a consequence of changing leverage as does the cash flow to equity. If you prefer to work with assumptions about dollar debt rather than debt ratios, you can switch to the adjusted present value approach.

In valuing equity, you can discount dividends or free cash flows to equity. You should consider using the dividend discount model under the following circumstances:

- You cannot estimate cash flows with any degree of precision either because you have insufficient or contradictory information about debt payments and reinvestments or because you have trouble defining what comprises debt. This was the rationale for using dividend discount models for valuing financial service firms in Chapter 21.
- There are significant restrictions on stock buybacks and other forms of cash return, and you have little or no control over what the management of a firm does with the cash. In this case, the only cash flows you can expect to get from your equity investment are the dividends that managers choose to pay out.

In all other cases, you will get much more realistic estimates of a firm's value using the free cash flow to equity, which may be greater than or lower than the dividend.

Should You Use Current or Normalized Earnings?

Most valuations begin with the current financial statements of the firm and use the reported earnings in those statements as the base for projections. There are some firms, though, where you may not be able to do this, either because the firm's earnings are negative or because these earnings are abnormally high or low (a firm's earnings are abnormal if they do not fit in with the firm's own history of earnings).

When earnings are negative or abnormal, you can sometimes replace current earnings with a normalized value, estimated by looking at the company's history or industry averages, and value the firm based on these normalized earnings. This is the easiest route to follow if the causes for the negative or abnormal earnings are temporary or transitory, as in the following cases:

- A cyclical firm will generally report depressed earnings during an economic downturn and high earnings during an economic boom. Neither may capture properly the true earnings potential of the firm.
- A firm may report abnormally low earnings in a period during which it takes an extraordinary charge.
- A firm in the process of restructuring may report low earnings during the restructuring period as the changes made to improve firm performance are put into effect.

The presumption here is that earnings will quickly bounce back to normal levels and that little will be lost by assuming that this will occur immediately.

For some firms, though, the negative or low earnings may reflect factors that are unlikely to disappear quickly. There are at least three groups of firms where the negative earnings are likely to be a long-term phenomenon and may even threaten the firm's survival:

1. *Firms with long-term operating, strategic, or financial problems* can have extended periods of negative or low earnings. If you replace current earnings with normalized earnings and value these firms, you will overvalue them.
   - If a firm seems to be in a hopeless state and likely to go bankrupt, the only models that are likely to provide meaningful measures of value are the option pricing model (if financial leverage is high) or a model based on liquidation value.
   - If the firm is troubled but unlikely to go bankrupt, you will have to nurse it back to financial health. In practical terms, you will have to adjust the operating margins over time to healthier levels and value the firm based on its expected cash flows.
2. *An infrastructure firm* may report negative earnings in its initial periods of growth, not because it is unhealthy but because the investments it has made take time to pay off. The cash flows to the firm and equity are often also negative, because the capital expenditure needs for this type of firm tend to be disproportionately large relative to depreciation. For these firms to have value, capital expenditure has to drop once the infrastructure investments have been made and operating margins have to improve. The net result will be positive cash flows in future years and a value for the firm today.
3. *Young start-up companies* often report negative earnings early in their life cycles, as they concentrate on turning interesting ideas into commercial products. To value such companies, you have to assume a combination of high revenue growth and improving operating margins over time.

Growth Patterns

In general, when valuing a firm, you can assume that your firm is already in stable growth, assume a period of constant high growth and then drop the growth rate to stable growth (two-stage growth), or allow for a transition phase to get to stable growth (three-stage or n-stage models). There are several factors you should consider in making this judgment:

Growth Momentum   The choice of growth pattern will be influenced by the level of current growth in earnings and revenues. You can categorize firms, based on growth in recent periods, into three groups.

1. Stable-growth firms report earnings and revenues growing at or below the nominal growth rate in the economy that they operate in.
2. Moderate-growth firms report earnings and revenues growing at a rate moderately higher than the nominal growth rate in the economy; as a rule of thumb, consider any growth rate within 8 to 10 percent of the growth rate of the economy as a moderate growth rate.
3. High-growth firms report earnings and revenues growing at a rate much higher than the nominal growth rate in the economy.

For firms growing at the stable rate, the steady state models that assume constant growth provide good estimates of value. For firms growing at a moderate rate, the two-stage discounted cash flow model should provide enough flexibility in terms of capturing changes in the underlying characteristics of the firm, while a three-stage or n-stage model may be needed to capture the longer transitions to stable growth that are inherent in high-growth-rate firms.

Source of Growth (Barriers to Entry)   The higher expected growth for a firm can come from either general competitive advantages acquired over time such as a brand name or reduced costs of production (from economies of scale) or specific advantages that are the result of legal barriers to entry—licenses or product patents. The former are likely to erode over time as new competitors enter the marketplace, while the latter are more likely to disappear abruptly when the legal barriers to entry are removed. The expected growth rate for a firm that has specific sources of growth is likely to follow the two-stage process where growth is high for a certain period (for instance, the period of the patent) and drops abruptly to a stable rate after that. The expected growth rate for a firm that has general sources of growth is more likely to decline gradually over time as new competitors come in. The speed with which this competitive advantage is expected to be lost is a function of several factors, including:

■ *Nature of the competitive advantage.* Some competitive advantages, such as brand name in consumer products, seem to be more difficult to overcome and consequently are likely to generate growth for longer periods. Other competitive advantages, such as a first-mover advantage, seem to erode much faster.
■ *Competence of the firm's management.* More competent management will be able to slow, though not stop, the loss of competitive advantage over time by creating strategies that find new markets in which to exploit the firm's current competitive advantage and that attempt to find new sources of competitive advantage.
■ *Ease of entry into the firm's business.* The greater the barriers to industry in entering the firm's business, because of either capital requirements or technological factors, the slower will be the loss of competitive advantage.

These factors are summarized and presented in Figure 35.8, with the appropriate discounted cash flow model indicated for each combination of the factors.

CHOOSING THE RIGHT RELATIVE VALUATION MODEL

Many analysts choose to value assets using relative valuation models. In making this choice, two basic questions have to be answered: Which multiple will be used in the valuation? Will this multiple be arrived at using the sector or the entire market?

Which Multiple Should I Use?

The chapters on multiples presented a variety of multiples. Some were based on earnings, some on book value, and some on revenues. For some multiples, current values were used, and for others forward or forecast values were used. Since the

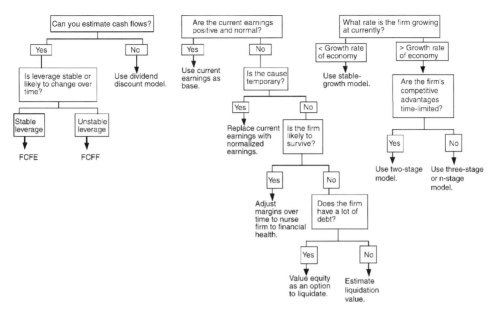

FIGURE 35.8 Discounted Cash Flow Models

STATUS QUO VERSUS OPTIMAL MANAGEMENT

The chapters on valuing acquisitions and troubled firms noted that the value of a firm can be substantially higher if you assume that it is optimally run than if it is run by incumbent management. A question that you are often faced with in valuation is whether you should value the firm with incumbent management or with the optimal management. The answer is simple in some cases and complicated in others:

- If you are interested in acquiring the firm and intend to change the management, you should value the firm with the optimal management policies in place. Whether you will pay that amount in the acquisition will depend on your bargaining power and how long you think it will take you to change the way the firm is run.
- If you are a small investor looking at buying stock in the firm, you cannot change incumbent management yourself but you can still pay a premium if you believe that there is a possibility of change. If there are strong mechanisms for corporate governance—hostile takeovers are common and poor managers get replaced quickly—you can assume that the value will quickly converge on the optimal value. If, however, it is difficult to dislodge incumbent management, you should value the firm based on their continued stewardship of the firm.
- If you are an institutional investor, you fall between these two extremes. While you may not intend to take over the firm and change the way it is run, you could play a role in making this change happen.

values you obtain are likely to be different using different multiples, deciding which multiple to use can make a big difference to your estimate of value. There are three ways you can answer this question: One is to adopt the cynical view that you should use the multiple that reflects your biases, the second is to value your firm with different multiples and try to use all of the values that you obtain; and the third is to pick the best multiple and base your valuation on it.

The Cynical View You can always use the multiple that best fits your story. Thus, if you are trying to sell a company, you will use the multiple which gives you the highest value for your company. If you are buying the same company, you will choose the multiple that yields the lowest value. While this clearly crosses the line from analysis into manipulation, it is a more common practice than you might realize. Even if you never plan to employ this practice, you should consider ways in which you can protect yourself from being victimized by it. First, you have to recognize that conceding the choice of multiple and comparables to an analyst is the equivalent of letting him or her write the rules of the game. You should play an active role in deciding which multiple should be used to value a company and what firms will be viewed as comparable firms. Second, when presented with a value based on one multiple, you should always ask what the value would have been if an alternative multiple had been used.

The Bludgeon View You can always value a company using a dozen or more multiples and then use all of the values, different thought they might be, in your final recommendation. There are three ways in which can present the final estimate of value. The first is in terms of a range of values, with the lowest value that you obtained from a multiple being the lower end of the range and the highest value being the upper limit. The problem with this approach is that the range is usually so large that it becomes useless for any kind of decision making. The second approach is a simple average of the values obtained from the different multiples. While this approach has the virtue of simplicity, it gives equal weight to the values from each multiple even though some multiples may yield more precise answers than others. The third approach is a weighted average, with the weight on each value reflecting the precision of the estimate. This weight can either be a subjective one or a statistical measure—you can, for instance, use the standard error on a prediction from a regression.

The Best Multiple While we realize that you might be reluctant to throw away any information, the best estimates of value are usually obtained by using the one multiple that is best suited for your firm. There are three ways in which you can find this multiple:

1. *Fundamentals approach.* You should consider using the variable that is most highly correlated with your firm's value. For instance, current earnings and value are much more highly correlated in consumer product companies than in technology companies. Using price-earnings ratios makes more sense for the former than for the latter.
2. *Statistical approach.* You could run regressions of each multiple against the fundamentals that we determined affected the value of the multiple in earlier

chapters, and use the R-squared of the regression as a measure of how well that multiple works in the sector. The multiple with the highest R-squared is the multiple that you can best explain using fundamentals and should be the multiple you use to value companies in that sector.

3. *Conventional multiple approach.* Over time, we usually see a specific multiple become the most widely used one for a specific sector. For instance, price-to-sales ratios are the most commonly used multiple to analyze retail companies.

Table 35.1 summarizes the most widely used multiples by sector. In an ideal world, you should see all three approaches converge—the fundamental that best explains value should also have the highest R-squared and be the conventional multiple used in the sector. In fact, when the multiple in use conventionally does not reflect fundamentals, which can happen if the sector is in transition or evolving, you will get misleading estimates of value.

Market or Sector Valuation

In most relative valuations, you value a firm relative to other firms in the industry in which the firm operates, and attempt to answer a simple question: Given how other firms in the business (sector) are priced by the market, is this firm under- or overvalued? Within this approach, you can define comparable firms either narrowly, as being firms that not only operate in the business in which your firm operates but also look like your firm in terms of size or market served, or broadly, in which case you will have far more comparable firms. If you are attempting to control for differences across firms subjectively, you should stick with the narrower group. But if you plan to control for differences statistically—with a regression, for instance—you should go with the broader definition.

The chapters on relative valuation presented an alternative approach to relative valuation, where firms were valued relative to the entire market. When you do this,

TABLE 35.1 Most Widely Used Multiples by Sector

Sector	Multiple Used	Rationale/Comments
Cyclical manufacturing	PE, relative PE	Often with normalized earnings.
High tech, high growth	PEG	Big differences in growth across firms make it difficult to compare PE ratios.
High growth/negative earnings	PS, VS	Assume future margins will be positive.
Infrastructure	VEBITDA	Firms in sector have losses in early years, and reported earnings can vary depending on depreciation method.
REIT	P/CF	Restrictions on investment policy and large depreciation charges make cash flows better measure than equity earnings.
Financial services	PBV	Book value often marked to market.
Retailing	PS	If leverage is similar across firms.
	VS	If leverage is different.

you are not only using a much larger universe of questions, but asking a different question: Given how other firms in the market are priced, is this firm under- or overvalued? A firm can be undervalued relative to its sector but overvalued relative to the market if the entire sector is mispriced.

The approach you use to relative valuation will depend again on what your task is defined to be. If you want to stay narrowly focused on your sector and make judgments on which stocks are under- or overvalued, you should stick with sector-based relative valuation. If you have more leeway and are trying to find under- or overvalued stocks across the market, you should look at the second approach—perhaps in addition to the first one.

WHEN SHOULD YOU USE THE OPTION PRICING MODELS?

The chapters on applying option pricing models to valuation presented a number of scenarios where option pricing may yield a premium on traditional discounted cash flow valuation. You should keep in mind the following general propositions when using option pricing models:

CAN A FIRM BE UNDERVALUED AND OVERVALUED AT THE SAME TIME?

If you value a firm using both discounted cash flow and relative valuation models, you may very well get different answers using the two: The firm may be undervalued using relative valuation models but overvalued using discounted cash flow models. What do we make of these differences, and why do they occur? If a firm is overvalued using a discounted cash flow model and undervalued using relative valuation, it is usually an indication that the sector is overvalued relative to its fundamentals. For instance, in March 2000 we valued Amazon at $30 a share using a discounted cash flow model, when it was trading at $70 a share; it was clearly overvalued. At the same time, a comparison of Amazon to other dot-com firms suggested that it was undervalued relative to these firms.

If a firm is undervalued using a discounted cash flow model and overvalued using relative valuation, it indicates that the sector is undervalued. By March 2001 Amazon's stock price had dropped to $15, but the values of all Internet stocks had dropped by almost 90 percent. In March 2001 a discounted cash flow valuation suggested that Amazon was undervalued, but a relative valuation indicated that it was now overvalued relative to the sector.

As an investor, you can use both discounted cash flow and relative valuation to value a company. Optimally, you would like to buy companies that are undervalued using both approaches. That way, you benefit from market corrections both across time (which is the way you make money in discounted cash flow valuation) and across companies.

■ *Use options sparingly.* Restrict your use of options to where they make the biggest difference in valuation. In general, options will affect value the most at smaller firms that derive the bulk of their value from assets that resemble options. Therefore, valuing patents as options to estimate firm value makes more sense for a small biotechnology firm than it does for a drug giant like Merck. While Merck may have dozens of patents, it derives much of its value from a portfolio of developed drugs and the cash flows they generate.

■ *Opportunities are not always options.* You should be careful not to mistake opportunities for options. Analysts often see a firm with growth potential and assume that there must be valuable options embedded in the firm. For opportunities to become valuable options, you need some degree of exclusivity for the firm in question; this can come from legal restrictions on competition or a significant competitive edge.

■ *Do not double count options.* All too often, analysts incorporate the effect of options on fundamentals and in company value and then proceed to add on premiums to reflect the same options. Consider, for instance, the undeveloped oil reserves owned by an oil company. While it is legitimate to value these reserves as options, you should not add this value to a discounted cash flow valuation of the company if your expected growth rate in the valuation is set higher because of the firm's undeveloped reserves.

CONCLUSION

The analyst faced with the task of valuing a firm/asset or its equity has to choose among three different approaches—discounted cash flow valuation, relative valuation, and option pricing models—and within each approach, between different models. This choice will be driven largely by the characteristics of the firm/asset being valued—the level of its earnings, its growth potential, the sources of earnings growth, the stability of its leverage, and its dividend policy. Matching the valuation model to the asset or firm being valued is as important a part of valuation as understanding the models and having the right inputs.

Once you decide to go with one or another of these approaches, you have further choices to make—whether to use equity or firm valuation in the context of discounted cash flow valuation, which multiple you should use to value firms or equity, and what type of option is embedded in a firm.

references

Chapter 1   Introduction to Valuation

Buffett, W. E., and L. A. Cunningham. 2001. *The essays of Warren Buffett: Lessons of corporate America*. Minneapolis, MN: Cunningham Group.

Cottle, S., R. Murray, and F. Bloch. 1988. *Security analysis*. New York: McGraw-Hill.

Graham, B., D. L. Dodd, and S. Cottle. 1962. *Security analysis*, 4th ed. New York: McGraw-Hill.

Chapter 2   Approaches to Valuation

Black, F., and M. Scholes. 1972. The valuation of option contracts and a test of market efficiency. *Journal of Finance* 27:399–417.

Damodaran, A. 1994. *Damodaran on Valuation*. New York: John Wiley & Sons.

Hooke, J. C. 2001. *Security analysis on Wall Street*. New York: John Wiley & Sons.

Chapter 3   Understanding Financial Statements

Choi, F. D. S., and R. M. Levich. 1990. *The capital market effects of international accounting diversity*. New York: Dow Jones–Irwin.

Stickney, C. P. 1993. *Financial statement analysis*. Fort Worth, TX: Dryden Press.

White, G. I., A. Sondhi, and D. Fried. 1997. *The analysis and use of financial statements*. New York: John Wiley & Sons.

Williams, J. R. 1998. *GAAP guide*. New York: Harcourt Brace.

Chapter 4   The Basics of Risk

Amihud, Y., B. Christensen, and H. Mendelson. 1992. Further evidence on the risk-return relationship. Working paper. New York University.

Bernstein, P. 1992. *Capital ideas*. New York: Free Press.

Bernstein, P. 1996. *Against the Gods*. New York: John Wiley & Sons.

Chan, L. K., and J. Lakonishok. 1993. Are the reports of beta's death premature? *Journal of Portfolio Management* 19:51–62.

Chen, N., R. Roll, and S. A. Ross. 1986. Economic forces and the stock market. *Journal of Business* 59:383–404.

Elton, E. J., and M. J. Gruber. 1995. *Modern portfolio theory and investment management*. New York: John Wiley & Sons.

Fama, E. F., and K. R. French. 1992. The cross-section of expected returns. *Journal of Finance* 47:427–466.

Jensen, M. C. 1969. Risk, the pricing of capital assets, and the evaluation of investment portfolios. *Journal of Business* 42:167–247.

Kothari, S. P., and J. Shanken. 1995. In defense of beta. *Journal of Applied Corporate Finance* 8(1):53–58.

Lintner, J. 1965. The valuation of risk assets and the selection of risky investments in stock portfolios and capital budgets. *Review of Economics and Statistics* 47:13–37.

Markowitz, H. M. 1991. Foundations of portfolio theory. *Journal of Finance* 46(2):469–478.

Roll, R. 1977. A critique of the asset pricing theory's tests: Part I: On past and potential testability of theory. *Journal of Financial Economics* 4:129–176.

Ross, S. A. 1976. The arbitrage theory of capital asset pricing. *Journal of Economic Theory* 13(3):341–360.

Seyhun, H. N. 1986. Insiders' profits, costs of trading and market efficiency. *Journal of Financial Economics* 16:189–212.

Sharpe, W. F 1964. Capital asset prices: A theory of market equilibrium under conditions of risk. *Journal of Finance* 19:425–442.

Weston, J. F., and T. E. Copeland. 1992. *Managerial finance*. Forth Worth: Dryden Press.

Chapter 5   Option Pricing Theory and Models

Black, F., and M. Scholes. 1972. The valuation of option contracts and a test of market efficiency. *Journal of Finance* 27:399–417.

Cox, J. C., and M. Rubinstein. 1985. *Options markets*. Upper Saddle River, NJ: Prentice Hall.

Cox, J. C., and S. A. Ross. 1976. The valuation of options for alternative stochastic processes. *Journal of Financial Economics* 3:145–166.

Cox, J. C., S. A. Ross, and M. Rubinstein. 1979. Option pricing: A simplified approach. *Journal of Financial Economics* 7:229–264.

Geske, R. 1979. The valuation of compound options. *Journal of Finance* 7:63–82.

Hull, J. C. 1999. *Options, futures and other derivatives*. Upper Saddle River, NJ: Prentice Hall.

Hull, J. C. 1995. *Introduction to futures and options markets*. Upper Saddle River, NJ: Prentice Hall.

Merton, R. C. 1973. The theory of rational option pricing. *Bell Journal of Economics* 4(1):141–183.

Merton, R. C. Option pricing when the underlying stock returns are discontinuous. *Journal of Financial Economics* 3:125–144.

Chapter 6   Market Efficiency—Definitions, Tests, and Evidence

Alexander, S. S. 1964. Price movements in speculative markets: Trends or random walks? In *The Random Character of Stock Market Prices*. Cambridge, MA: MIT Press.

Arbel, A., and P. J. Strebel. 1983. Pay attention to neglected stocks. *Journal of Porfolio Management* 9:37–42.

Banz, R. 1981. The relationship between return and market value of common stocks. *Journal of Financial Economics* 9:3–18.

Basu, S. 1977. The investment performance of common stocks in relation to their price-earnings: A test of the efficient market hypothesis. *Journal of Finance* 32:663–682.

Basu, S. 1983. The relationship between earnings yield, market value and return for NYSE common stocks: Further evidence. *Journal of Financial Economics* 12:129–156.

Bernstein, R. 1995. *Style investing*. New York: John Wiley & Sons.

Capaul, C., I. Rowley, and W. F. Sharpe. 1993. International value and growth stock returns. *Financial Analysts Journal* 49:27–36.

Carhart, M. M. 1997. On the persistence of mutual fund performance. *Journal of Finance* 52:57–82.

Chambers, A. E., and S. H. Penman. 1984. Timeliness of reporting and the stock price reaction to earnings announcements. *Journal of Accounting Research* 22:21–47.

Chan, L. K., Y. Hamao, and J. Lakonishok. 1991. Fundamentals and stock returns in Japan. *Journal of Finance* 46:1739–1789.

Chan, S. H., J. Martin, and J. Kensinger. 1990. Corporate research and development expenditures and share value. *Journal of Financial Economics* 26:255–276.

Conrad, J. 1989. The price effect of option introduction. *Journal of Finance* 44:487–498.

Cootner, P. H. 1961. Common elements in futures markets for commodities and bonds. *American Economic Review* 51(2):173–183.

Cootner, P. H. 1962. Stock prices: Random versus systematic changes. *Industrial Management Review* 3:24–45.

Damodaran, A. 1989. The weekend effect in information releases: A study of earnings and dividend announcements. *Review of Financial Studies* 2:607–623.

DeBondt, W. F. M., and R. Thaler. 1985 Does the stock market overreact? *Journal of Finance* 40:793–805.

DeBondt , W. F. M., and R. Thaler. 1987. Further evidence on investor overreaction and stock market seasonality. *Journal of Finance* 42:557–581.

Dimson, E., and P. R. Marsh. 1984. An analysis of brokers' and analysts' unpublished forecasts of UK stock returns. *Journal of Finance* 39:1257–1292.

Dimson, E., and P. R. Marsh. 1986. Event studies and the size effect: The case of UK press recommendations. *Journal of Financial Economics* 17:113–142.

Dimson, E., and P. R. Marsh. 2001. Murphy's law and market anomalies. *Journal of Portfolio Management* 25:53–69.

Fama, E. F. 1965. The behavior of stock market prices. *Journal of Business* 38:34–105.

Fama, E. F. 1970. Efficient capital markets: A review of theory and empirical work. *Journal of Finance* 25:383–417.

Fama, E. F., and K. R. French. 1988. Permanent and temporary components of stock prices. *Journal of Political Economy* 96:246–273.

Fama, E. F., and K. R. French. 1992. The cross-section of expected returns. *Journal of Finance* 47:427–466.

Fama, E. F., and M. Blume. 1966. Filter rules and stock market trading profits. *Journal of Business* 39:226–241.

Gibbons, M. R., and P. Hess. 1981. Day of the week effects and asset returns. *Journal of Business* 54:579–596.

Gultekin, M. N., and B. N. Gultekin. 1983. Stock market seasonality: International evidence. *Journal of Financial Economics* 12:469–481.

Haugen, R. A. 1990. *Modern investment theory*. Englewood Cliffs, NJ: Prentice Hall.

Haugen, R. A., and Lakonishok, J. 1988. *The incredible January effect*. Homewood IL: Dow Jones–Irwin.

Jaffe, J. 1974. Special information and insider trading. *Journal of Business* 47:410–428.

Jegadeesh, N., and S. Titman. 1993. Returns to buying winners and selling losers: Implications for stock market efficiency. *Journal of Finance* 48(1):65–91.

Jegadeesh, N., and S. Titman. 2001. Profitability of momentum strategies: An evaluation of alternative explanations. *Journal of Finance* 56(2):699–720.

Jennergren, L. P. 1975. Filter tests of Swedish share prices. In *International Capital Markets*, 55–67. New York: North-Holland.

Jennergren, L. P., and P. E. Korsvold. 1974. Price formation in the Norwegian and Swedish stock markets—Some random walk tests. *Swedish Journal of Economics* 76:171–185.

Jensen, M. 1968. The performance of mutual funds in the period 1945–64. *Journal of Finance* 2:389–416.

Jensen, M., and G. A. Bennington. 1970. Random walks and technical theories, some additional evidence. *Journal of Finance* 25:469–482.

Kaplan, R. S., and R. Roll. 1972. Investor evaluation of accounting information: Some empirical evidence. *Journal of Business* 45:225–257.

Keim, D. 1983. Size related anomalies and stock return seasonality: Further empirical evidence. *Journal of Financial Economics* 12.

McConnell, J. J., and C. J. Muscarella. 1985. Corporate capital expenditure decisions and the market value of the firm. *Journal of Financial Economics* 14:399–422.

Michaely, R., and K. L. Womack. 1999. Conflict of interest and the credibility of underwriter analyst recommendations. *Review of Financial Studies* 12:653–686.

Niederhoffer, V., and M. F. M. Osborne. 1966. Market making and reversal on the stock exchange. *Journal of the American Statistical Association* 61:891–916.

Peters, E. E. 1991. *Chaos and order in the capital markets*. New York: John Wiley & Sons.

Pradhuman, S. 2000. *Small cap dynamics*. Princeton, NJ: Bloomberg Press.

Praetz, P. D. 1972. The distribution of share price changes. *Journal of Business* 45(1):49–55.

Reinganum, M. R. 1983. The anomalous stock market behavior of small firms in January: Empirical tests for tax-loss effects. *Journal of Financial Economics* 12.

Rendleman, R. J., C. P. Jones, and H. A. Latene. 1982. Empirical anomalies based on unexpected earnings and the importance of risk adjustments. *Journal of Financial Economics* 10:269–287.

Richards, R. M., and J. D. Martin. 1979. Revisions in earnings forecasts: How much response? *Journal of Portfolio Management* 5:47–52.

Ritter, J., and N. Chopra. 1989. Portfolio rebalancing and the turn of the year effect. *Journal of Finance* 44:149–166.

Roll, R. 1983. Vas ist das? *Journal of Portfolio Management* 9:18–28.

Roll, R. 1984. A simple implicit measure of the bid-ask spread in an efficient market. *Journal of Finance* 39:1127–1139.

Rosenberg, B., K. Reid, and R. Lanstein. 1985. Persuasive evidence of market inefficiency. *Journal of Portfolio Management* 11:9–17.

Seyhun, H. N. 1998. *Investment intelligence from insider trading*. Cambridge, MA: MIT Press.

Shiller, R. 1999. *Irrational exuberance*. Princeton, NJ: Princeton University Press.

Sunder, S. 1973. Relationship between accounting changes and stock prices: Problems of measurement and some empirical evidence. In *Empirical Research in Accounting: Selected Studies* 1–45. Toronto: Lexington.

Sunder, S. 1975. Stock price and risk related accounting changes in inventory valuation. *Accounting Review* 305–315.

Womack, K. 1996. Do brokerage analysts' recommendations have investment value? *Journal of Finance* 51:137–167.

Woodruff, C. S., and A. J. Senchack, Jr. 1988. Intradaily price-volume adjustments of NYSE stocks to unexpected earnings. *Journal of Finance* 43(2):467–491.

Chapter 7   Riskless Rates and Risk Premiums

Altman, E. I. 1968. Financial ratios, discriminant analysis and the prediction of corporate bankruptcy. *Journal of Finance* 23:589–609.

Altman, E. I., and V. Kishore. 2000. The default experience of U.S. bonds. Working paper. Salomon Center, New York University.

Booth, L. 1999. Estimating the equity risk premium and equity costs: New way of looking at old data. *Journal of Applied Corporate Finance* 12(1):100–112.

Bruner, R. F., K. M. Eades, R. S. Harris, and R.C. Higgins. 1998. Best practices in estimating the cost of capital: Survey and synthesis. *Financial Practice and Education* 14–28.

Chan, K. C., G. A. Karolyi, and R. M. Stulz. 1992. Global financial markets and the risk premium on U.S. equity. *Journal of Financial Economics* 32:132–167.

Damodaran, A. 1999. *Estimating the equity risk premium*. Working paper. www.stern.nyu.edu/~adamodar/New_Home_Page/papers.html.

Elton, E., M. J. Gruber, and J. Mei. 1994. Cost of capital using arbitrage pricing theory: A case study of nine New York utilities. *Financial Markets, Institutions and Instruments* 3:46–73.

Fama, E. F., and K. R. French. 1988. Permanent and temporary components of stock prices. *Journal of Political Economy* 96:246–273.

Godfrey, S., and R. Espinosa. 1996. A practical approach to calculating the cost of equity for investments in emerging markets. *Journal of Applied Corporate Finance* 9(3):80–81.

Ibbotson, R. G., and G. P. Brinson. 1993. *Global investing*. New York: McGraw-Hill.

Indro, D. C., and W. Y. Lee. 1997. Biases in arithmetic and geometric averages as estimates of long-run expected returns and risk premium. *Financial Management* 26:81–90.

Pettit, J. 1999. Corporate capital costs: A practitioner's guide. *Journal of Applied Corporate Finance* 12(1):113–120.

Rosenberg, B., and V. Marathe. 1979. Tests of capital asset pricing hypotheses. *Research in Finance* 1:115–124.

Stocks, bonds, bills and inflation. 1999. Chicago: Ibbotson Associates.

Stulz, R. M.. 1999. Globalization, corporate finance, and the cost of capital. *Journal of Applied Corporate Finance* 12(1).

Chapter 8   Estimating Risk Parameters and Costs of Financing

Blume, M. 1979. Betas and their regression tendencies: Some further evidence. *Journal of Finance* 34(1):265–267.

Brown, S. J., and J. B. Warner. 1980. Measuring security price performance. *Journal of Financial Economics* 8(3):205–258.

Brown, S. J., and J. B. Warner. 1985. Using daily stock returns: The case of event studies. *Journal of Financial Economics* 14(1):3–31.

Bruner, R. F., K. M. Eades, R. S. Harris and R. C. Higgins. 1998. Best practices in estimating the cost of capital: Survey and synthesis. *Financial Practice and Education* 14–28.

Dimson, E. 1979. Risk measurement when shares are subject to infrequent trading. *Journal of Financial Economics* 7(2):197–226.

Hamada, R. S. 1972. The effect of the firm's capital structure on the systematic risk of common stocks. *Journal of Finance* 27:435–452.

Scholes, M., and J. T. Williams. 1977. Estimating betas from nonsynchronous data. *Journal of Financial Economics* 5(3):309–327.

Chapter 9   Measuring Earnings

Aboody, D., and B. Lev. 1998. The value relevance of intangibles: The case of software capitalization. *Journal of Accounting Research* 36(0):161–191.

Bernstein, L. A., and J. G. Siegel. 1979. The concept of earnings quality. *Financial Analysts Journal* 35:72–75.

Damodaran, A. 1999. *The treatment of operating leases.* Working paper. www.stern.nyu.edu/~adamodar/New_Home_Page/papers.html.

Damodaran, A. 1999. *The treatment of R&D.* Working paper. www.stern.nyu.edu/~adamodar/New_Home_Page/papers.html.

Deng, Z., and B. Lev. 1998. The valuation of acquired R&D. Working paper. New York University.

Chapter 10   From Earnings to Cash Flows

Brennan, M. J. 1970. Taxes, market valuation and corporation financial policy. *National Tax Journal* 417–427.

Graham, J. R. 2000. How big are the tax benefits of debt? *Journal of Finance* 55(5):1901–1941.

Graham, J. R. Proxies for the corporate marginal tax rate. *Journal of Financial Economics* 42(2):187–221.

Chapter 11   Estimating Growth

Arnott, R. D. 1985. The use and misuse of consensus earnings. *Journal of Portfolio Management* 11:18–27.

Bathke, A. W., Jr., and K. S. Lorek. 1984. The relationship between time-series models and the security market's expectation of quarterly earnings. *Accounting Review* 163–176.

Box, G., and G. Jenkins. 1976. *Time series analysis: Forecasting and control.* Oakland, CA: Holden-Day.

Brown, L. D., and M. S. Rozeff. 1979. Univariate time series models of quarterly accounting earnings per share: A proposed model. *Journal of Accounting Research* 178–189.

Brown, L. D., and M. S. Rozeff. 1980. Analysts can forecast accurately! *Journal of Portfolio Management* 6:31–34.

Collins, W., and W. Hopwood. 1980. A multivariate analysis of annual earnings forecasts generated from quarterly forecasts of financial analysts and univariate time series models. *Journal of Accounting Research* 20:390–406.

Cragg, J. G., and B. G. Malkiel. 1968. The consensus and accuracy of predictions of the growth of corporate earnings. *Journal of Finance* 23:67–84.

Crichfield, T., T. Dyckman, and J. Lakonishok. 1978. An evaluation of security analysts forecasts. *Accounting Review* 53:651–668.

Foster, G. 1977. Quarterly accounting data: Time series properties and predictive ability results. *Accounting Review* 52:1–31.

Fried, D., and D. Givoly. 1982. Financial analysts forecasts of earnings: A better surrogate for earnings expectations. *Journal of Accounting and Economics* 4:85–107.

Fuller, R. J., L. C. Huberts, and M. Levinson. 1992. It's not higgledy-piggledy growth! *Journal of Portfolio Management* 18:38–46.

Givoly, D., and J. Lakonishok. 1984. The quality of analysts' forecasts of earnings. *Financial Analysts Journal* 40:40–47.

Hawkins, E. H., S. C. Chamberlin, and W. E. Daniel. 1984. Earnings expectations and security prices. *Financial Analysts Journal* 40:24–27, 30–38, 74.

Little, I. M. D. 1960. *Higgledy piggledy growth*. Oxford: Institute of Statistics.

O'Brien, P. 1988. Analysts' forecasts as earnings expectations. *Journal of Accounting and Economics* 10:53–83.

Vander Weide, J. H., and W. T. Carleton 1988. Investor growth expectations: Analysts vs. history. *Journal of Portfolio Management* 14:78–83.

Watts, R. 1975. *The time series behavior of quarterly earnings*. Working paper. University of Newcastle.

Chapter 12   Closure in Valuation: Estimating Terminal Value

Altman, E. I. 1968. Financial ratios, discriminant analysis and the prediction of corporate bankruptcy. *Journal of Finance* 23:589–609.

Grant, R. M., 1998. *Contemporary strategy analysis*. Malden, MA: Blackwell.

Mauboussin, M., and P. Johnson. 1997. Competitive advantage period: The neglected value driver. *Financial Management* 26(2):67–74.

Porter, M. E. 1980. *Competitive strategy: Techniques for analyzing industries and competitors*. New York: Free Press.

Chapter 13   Dividend Discount Models

Bethke, W. M., and S.E. Boyd. 1983. Should dividend discount models be yield-tilted? *Journal of Portfolio Management* 9:23–27.

Estep, T. 1987. Security analysis and stock selection: Turning financial information into return forecasts. *Financial Analysts Journal* 43:34–43.

Estep, T. 1985. A new method for valuing common stocks. *Financial Analysts Journal* 41:26, 27, 30–33.

Fuller, R. J., and C. Hsia. 1984. A simplified common stock valuation model. *Financial Analysts Journal* 40:49–56.

Gordon, M. 1962. *The investment, financing and valuation of the corporation.* Homewood, IL: Irwin.

Haugen, R. 1997. *Modern investment theory.* Upper Saddle River, NJ: Prentice Hall.

Jacobs, B. I., and K. N. Levy. 1988a. Disentangling equity return irregularities: New insights and investment opportunities. *Financial Analysts Journal* 44:18–44.

Jacobs, B. I., and K. N. Levy. 1988b. On the value of "value." *Financial Analysts Journal* 44:47–62.

Litzenberger, R. H., and K. Ramaswamy. 1979. The effect of personal taxes and dividends on capital asset prices: Theory and empirical evidence. *Journal of Financial Economics* 7:163–196.

Sorensen, E. H., and D. A. Williamson. 1985. Some evidence on the value of the dividend discount model. *Financial Analysts Journal* 41:60–69.

Chapter 14   Free Cash Flow to Equity Discount Models

Damodaran, A. 2001. *Corporate finance: Theory and practice*, 2d ed. New York: John Wiley & Sons.

Chapter 15   Firm Valuation: Cost of Capital and Adjusted Present Value Approaches

Altman, E. I., and V. Kishore. 2000. *The default experience of U.S. bonds.* Working paper, Salomon Center, New York University.

Barclay, M. J., C. W. Smith, and R. L. Watts. 1995. The determinants of corporate leverage and dividend policies. *Journal of Applied Corporate Finance* 7(4):4–19.

Bhide, A. 1993. Reversing corporate diversification. In *The new corporate finance—Where theory meets practice*, ed. D. H. Chew Jr. New York: McGraw-Hill.

Damodaran, A. 2001. *Corporate finance: Theory and practice*, 2d ed. New York: John Wiley & Sons.

Davis, D., and K. Lee. 1997. A practical approach to capital structure for banks. *Journal of Applied Corporate Finance* 10(1):33–43.

Denis, D. J., and D. K. Denis. 1993. Leveraged recaps in the curbing of corporate overinvestment. *Journal of Applied Corporate Finance* 6(1):60–71.

Graham, J. 1996. Debt and the marginal tax rate. *Journal of Financial Economics* 41:41–73.

Inselbag, I., and H. Kaufold. 1997. Two DCF approaches and valuing companies under alternative financing strategies. *Journal of Applied Corporate Finance* 10(1):115–122.

Jensen, M. C. 1986. Agency costs of free cash flow, corporate finance, and takeovers. *American Economic Review* 76:323–329.

Kaplan, S. N. 1989. Campeau's acquisition of Federated: Value destroyed or value added? *Journal of Financial Economics* 25:191–212.

Mackie-Mason, J. 1990. Do taxes affect corporate financing decisions? *Journal of Finance* 45:1471–1494.

Miller, M. 1977. Debt and taxes. *Journal of Finance* 32:261–275.

Modigliani, F., and M. Miller. 1958. The cost of capital, corporation finance and the theory of investment. *American Economic Review* 48:261–297.

Myers, S. C. 1976. Determinants of corporate borrowing. *Journal of Financial Economics* 5:147–175.

Myers, S. C., and N. S. Majluf. 1984. Corporate financing and investment decisions when firms have information that investors do not have. *Journal of Financial Economics* 13:187–221.

Opler, T., M. Saron, and S. Titman. 1997. Designing capital structure to create stockholder value. *Journal of Applied Corporate Finance* 10:21–32.

Palepu, K. G. 1986. Predicting takeover targets: A methodological and empirical analysis. *Journal of Accounting and Economics* 8(1):3–35.

Palepu, K. G. 1990. Consequences of leveraged buyouts. *Journal of Financial Economics* 26:247–262.

Pinegar, J. M., and L. Wilbricht. 1989. What managers think of capital structure theory: A survey. *Financial Management* 18(4):82–91.

Shapiro, A. 1989. *Modern corporate finance.* New York: Macmillan.

Smith, A. J. 1990. Corporate ownership structure and performance: The case of management buyouts. *Journal of Financial Economics* 27:143–164.

Smith, C. W. 1986. Investment banking and the capital acquisition process. *Journal of Financial Economics* 15:3–29.

Titman, S. 1984. The effect of capital structure on a firm's liquidation decision. *Journal of Financial Economics* 13:137–151.

Warner, J. N. 1977. Bankruptcy costs: Some evidence. *Journal of Finance* 32:337–347.

Chapter 16   Estimating Equity Value per Share

Carpenter, J. 1998. The exercise and valuation of executive stock options. *Journal of Financial Economics* 48:127–158.

Cuny, C. C., and P. Jorion. 1995. Valuing executive stock options with endogenous departure. *Journal of Accounting and Economics* 20:193–205.

Damodaran, A. 1999. *Dealing with cash, marketable securities and cross holdings.* Working paper. www.stern.nyu.edu/~adamodar/New_Home_Page/papers.html.

Lease, R. C., J. J. McConnell, and W. H. Mikkelson. 1983. The market value of control in publicly-traded corporations. *Journal of Financial Economics* 11:439–471.

Chapter 17   Fundamental Principles of Relative Valuation

Damodaran, A. 2001. *It's all relative: First principles of relative valuation.* Working paper. www.stern.nyu.edu/~adamodar/New_Home_Page/papers.html.

Chapter 18   Earnings Multiples

Cragg, J. G., and B. G. Malkiel. 1968. The consensus and accuracy of predictions of the growth of corporate earnings. *Journal of Finance* 23:67–84.

Goodman, D. A., and J. W. Peavy, III. 1983. Industry relative price-earnings ratios as indicators of investment returns. *Financial Analysts Journal* 39:60–66.

Kisor, M., Jr., and V. S. Whitbeck. 1963. A new tool in investment decision-making. *Financial Analysts Journal* 19:55–62.

Leibowitz, M. L., and S. Kogelman. 1992. Franchise value and the growth process. *Financial Analysts Journal* 48:53–62.

Levy, H., and Z. Lerman. 1985. Testing P/E ratio filters with stochastic dominance. *Journal of Portfolio Management* 11:31–40.

Peters, D. J. 1991. Valuing a growth stock. *Journal of Portfolio Mangement* 17:49–51.

Chapter 19   Book Value Multiples

Capaul, C., I. Rowley, and W. F. Sharpe. 1993. International value and growth stock returns. *Financial Analysts Journal* 49:27–36.

Chan, L. K., Y. Hamao, and J. Lakonishok. 1991. Fundamentals and stock returns in Japan. *Journal of Finance* 46:1739–1789.

Fama, E. F., and K. R. French. 1992. The cross-section of expected returns. *Journal of Finance* 47:427–466.

Jacobs, B. I., and K. N. Levy. 1988. On the value of "value." *Financial Analysts Journal* 44:47–62.

Lang, L. H. P., R. M. Stulz, and R. A. Walkling. 1991. A test of the free cash flow hypothesis: The case of bidder returns. *Journal of Financial Economics* 29:315–335.

Porter, M. E. 1980. *Competitive strategy: Techniques for analyzing industries and competitors.* New York: Free Press.

Rosenberg, B., K. Reid, and R. Lanstein. 1985. Persuasive evidence of market inefficiency. *Journal of Portfolio Management* 11:9–17.

Wilcox, J. W. 1984. The P/B-ROE valuation model. *Financial Analysts Journal* 40:58–66.

Chapter 20   Revenue Multiples and Sector-Specific Multiples

Itami, H. 1987. *Mobilizing invisible assets.* Cambridge, MA: Harvard University Press.

Jacobs, B. I., and K. N. Levy. 1988. Disentangling equity return irregularities: New insights and investment opportunities. *Financial Analysts Journal* 44:18–44.

Senchack, A. J., Jr., and J. D. Martin. 1987. The relative performance of the PSR and PER investment strategies. *Financial Analysts Journal* 43:46–56.

Chapter 21   Valuing Financial Service Firms

Copeland, T. E., T. Koller, and J. Murrin. 1999. *Valuation: Measuring and managing the value of companies.* New York: John Wiley & Sons.

Chapter 22   Valuing Firms with Negative Earnings

Damodaran, A. 2001. *Dealing with negative earnings.* Working paper. www.stern.nyu.edu/~adamodar/New_Home_Page/papers.html.

Chapter 23   Valuing Young or Start-Up Firms

Damodaran, A. 2001. *The dark side of valuation.* Upper Saddle River, NJ: Prentice Hall.

Chapter 24   Valuing Private Firms

Beaver, W. H., P. Kettler, and M. Scholes. 1970. The association between market determined and accounting determined risk measures. *Accounting Review* 45(4):654–682.

Kim, S. H., T. Crick, and S. H. Kim. 1986. Do executives practice what academics preach? *Management Accounting* 68:49–52.

Maher, J. M. 1976. Discounts for lack of marketability for closely held business interests. *Tax Magazine* 1:562–571.

Moroney, R. E. 1973. Most courts overvalue closely held stocks. *Tax Magazine* 1:144–155.

Pratt, S., R. F. Reilly, and R. P. Schweihs. 2000. *Valuing a business: The analysis and appraisal of closely held companies.* New York: McGraw-Hill.

Rosenberg, B., and J. Guy. 1976. Beta and investment fundamentals; Beta and investment fundamentals—II. *Financial Analysts Journal* 32(3):60–72; 32(4):62–70.

Rosenberg, B., and J. Guy. 1995. Prediction of beta from investment fundamentals. *Financial Analysts Journal* 51(1):101–112.

Silber, W. L. 1991. Discounts on restricted stock: The impact of illiquidity on stock prices. *Financial Analysts Journal* 47:60–64.

Chapter 25   Acquisitions and Takeovers

Bhide, A. 1989. The causes and consequences of hostile takeovers. *Journal of Applied Corporate Finance* 2:36–59.

Bhide, A. 1993. Reversing corporate diversification. In *The new corporate finance—Where theory meets practice*, ed. D. H. Chew Jr. New York: McGraw-Hill.

Bradley, M., A. Desai, and E. H. Kim. 1983. The rationale behind interfirm tender offers. *Journal of Financial Economics* 11:183–206.

Bradley, M., A. Desai, and E. H. Kim. 1988. Synergistic gains from corporate acquisitions and their division between the stockholders of target and acquiring firms. *Journal of Financial Economics* 21:3–40.

Dann, L. Y., and H. DeAngelo. 1983. Standstill agreements, privately negotiated stock repurchases, and the market for corporate control. *Journal of Financial Economics* 11:275–300.

Dann, L. Y., and H. DeAngelo. 1988. Corporate financial policy and corporate control: A study of defensive adjustments in asset and ownership structure. *Journal of Financial Economics* 20:87–128.

DeAngelo, H., and E. M. Rice. 1983. Antitakeover charter amendments and stockholder wealth. *Journal of Financial Economics* 11:329–360.

DeAngelo, H., L. DeAngelo, and E. M. Rice. 1984. Going private: The effects of a change in corporate ownership structure. *Midland Corporate Finance Journal* 35–43.

Deng, Z., and B. Lev. 1998. *The valuation of acquired R&D.* Working paper. New York University.

Dubofsky, P., and P. R. Varadarajan. 1987. Diversification and measures of performance: Additional empirical evidence. *Academy of Management Journal* 597–608.

Fruhan, W. E., W. C. Kester, S. P. Mason, T. R. Piper, and R. S. Ruback. 1992. *Congoleum: Case problems in finance.* Homestead, IL: Irwin.

Gaughan, P. A. 1999. *Mergers, Acquisitions and Corporate Restructurings.* New York: John Wiley & Sons.

Healy, P. M., K.G . Palepu, and R.S . Ruback. 1992. Does corporate performance improve after mergers? *Journal of Financial Economics* 31:135–176.

Hong, H., R. S. Kaplan, and G. Mandelkar. 1978. Pooling vs. purchase: The effects of accounting for mergers on stock prices. *Accounting Review* 53(1):31–47.

Jarrell, G. A., J. A. Brickley, and J. M. Netter. 1988. The market for corporate control: The empirical evidence since 1980. *Journal of Economic Perspectives* 2:49–68.

Jensen, M.C. 1986. Agency costs of free cashflow, corporate finance and takeovers. *American Economic Review* 76:323–329.

Jensen, M. C., and R. S. Ruback. 1983. The market for corporate control. *Journal of Financial Economics* 11:5–50.

Kaplan, S., and M. S. Weisbach. 1992. The success of acquisitions: The evidence from divestitures. *Journal of Finance* 47:107–138.

Karpoff, J. M., and P. H. Malatesta. 1990. The wealth effects of second-generation state takeover legislation. *Journal of Financial Economics* 25:291–322.

KPMG. 1999. *Unlocking shareholder value: The keys to success.* New York: KPMG Global Research Report.

Krallinger, J. C. 1997. *Mergers and acquisitions: Managing the transaction.* New York: McGraw-Hill.

Lewellen, W. G. 1971. A pure financial rationale for the conglomerate merger. *Journal of Finance* 26:521–537.

Lindenberg, E., and M. P. Ross. 1999. To purchase or to pool: Does it matter? *Journal of Applied Corporate Finance* 12:32–47.

Linn, S., and J. J. McConnell. 1983. An empirical investigation of the impact of anti-takeover amendments on common stock prices. *Journal of Financial Economics* 11:361–399.

Michel, A., and I. Shaked. 1984. Does business diversification affect performance? *Financial Management* 13:5–14.

Mitchell, M. L., and K. Lehn. 1990. Do bad bidders make good targets? *Journal of Applied Corporate Finance* 3:60–69.

Myers, S. C., and N. S. Majluf. 1984. Corporate financing and investment decisions when firms have information that investors do not have. *Journal of Financial Economics* 13:187–221.

Nail, L. A., W. L. Megginson, and C. Maquieira. 1998. Wealth creation versus wealth redistributions in pure stock-for-stock mergers. *Journal of Financial Economics* 48:3–33.

Parrino, J. D., and R. S. Harris. Takeovers, management replacement and post-acquisition operating performance: Some evidence from the 1980s. *Journal of Applied Corporate Finance* 11:88–97.

Roll, R. 1986. The hubris hypothesis of corporate takeovers. *Journal of Business* 59:197–216.

Sirower, M. L. 1996. *The synergy trap.* New York: Simon & Schuster.

Stapleton, R. C. 1985. A note on default fisk, leverage and the MM theorem. *Journal of Financial Economics* 2:377–381.

Varadarajan, P. R., and V. Ramanujam. 1987. Diversification and performance: A reexamination using a new two-dimensional conceptualization of diversity in firms. *Academy of Management Journal* 30:369–380.

Weston, J. F., K. S. Chung, and J. A. Siu. 1998. *Takeovers, restructuring and corporate governance.* New York: Simon & Schuster.

Chapter 26   Valuing Real Estate

Fama, E. F., and G. W. Schwert. 1977. Asset returns and inflation. *Journal of Financial Economics* 5:115–146.

Ibbotson, R. G., and G. P. Brinson. 1993. *Global investing.* New York: McGraw-Hill.

Chapter 27   Valuing Other Assets

Mei, J., and M. Moses. 2001. *Art as an investment and the underperformance of masterpieces: Evidence from 1875–2000.* Working paper. Stern School of Business, New York University.

Chapter 28   The Option to Delay and Valuation Implications

Avellaneda, M., and P. Lawrence. 2000. *Quantitative modeling of derivative securities.* New York: Chapman & Hall.

Brennan, M. J., and E. S. Schwartz. 1985. Evaluating natural resource investments. *Journal of Business* 58:135–158.

Siegel, D., J. Smith, and J. Paddock. 1993. Valuing offshore oil properties with option pricing models. In *The new corporate finance,* ed. D. H. Chew Jr. New York: McGraw-Hill.

Chapter 29   The Options to Expand and to Abandon: Valuation Implications

Amram, M., and N. Kulantilaka. 1998. *Real options: Managing strategic investments in an uncertain world.* New York: Oxford University Press.

Copeland, T. E., and V. Antikarov. 2001. *Real options: A practitioners guide.* New York: Texere.

Mauboussin, M. 1998. *Get real.* Credit Suisse First Boston.

Chapter 30   Valuing Equity in Distressed Firms

Copeland, T. E., and V. Antikarov. 2001. *Real options: A practitioners guide.* New York: Texere.

Chapter 31   Value Enhancement: A Discounted Cash Flow Valuation Framework

Brickley, J., C. Smith, and J. Zimmerman. 1995. The economics of organizational architecture. *Journal of Applied Corporate Finance* 8:19–31.

Copeland, T. E., T. Koller, and J. Murrin. 1999. *Valuation: Measuring and managing the value of companies.* New York: John Wiley & Sons.

Damodaran, A. 1999. Value enhancement: Back to the future. *Contemporary Finance Digest* 3:2–47.

Fruhan, W. E. 1979. *Financial strategy: Studies in the creation, transfer and destruction of shareholder value.* Homewood, IL: Irwin.

Grant, R. M. 1998. *Contemporary strategy analysis.* Malden, MA: Blackwell.

Levin, R. C., A. K. Klevorick, R. R. Nelson, and S. G. Winter. 1987. Appropriating the returns from industrial research and development. Brookings Paper on Economic Activity.

McConnell, J. J., and C. J. Muscarella. 1985. Corporate capital expenditure decisions and the market value of the firm. *Journal of Financial Economics* 14:399–422.

Porter, M. E. 1980. *Competitive strategy: Techniques for analyzing industries and competitors.* New York: Free Press.

Rappaport, A. 1998. *Creating shareholder value.* New York: Free Press.

Schipper, K., and A. Smith. 1983. Effects of recontracting on shareholder wealth: The case of voluntary spin-offs. *Journal of Financial Economics* 12:437–468.

Schipper, K., and A. Smith. 1986. A comparison of equity carve-outs and seasoned equity offerings: Share price effects and corporate restructuring. *Journal of Financial Economics* 15:153–186.

Shapiro, A. 1985. Corporate strategy and the capital budgeting decision. *Midland Corporate Finance Journal* 3:22–36.

Shapiro, A. 1989. *Modern corporate finance.* New York: Macmillan.

Stulz, R. 1996. Does the cost of capital differ across countries? An agency perspective. *European Financial Management* 2:11–22.

Weston, J. F., and T. E. Copeland. 1992. *Managerial finance,* 9th ed. Orlando, FL: Harcourt Brace Jovanovich.

Woolridge, R. 1993. Competitive decline and corporate restructuring. In *The new corporate finance,* ed. D. H. Chew Jr. New York: McGraw-Hill.

Chapter 32   Value Enhancement: Economic Value Added, Cash Flow Return on Investment, and Other Tools

Bernstein, R. 1997. *EVA and market returns.* Quantitative Viewpoint, Merrill Lynch, December 19, 1997.

Bernstein, R. 1997. *EVA and market returns.* Quantitative Viewpoint, Merrill Lynch, February 3, 1998.

Brickley, J., C. Smith, and J. Zimmerman. 1995. Transfer pricing and the control of internal corporate transactions. *Journal of Applied Corporate Finance* 8(2):60–67.

Damodaran, A. 1999. Value enhancement: Back to the future. *Contemporary Finance Digest* 3:2–47.

Ehrbar, A. 1998. *EVA: The real key to creating wealth.* New York: John Wiley & Sons.

Kramer, J. R., and G. Pushner. 1997. An empirical analysis of economic value added as a proxy for market value added. *Financial Practice and Education* 7:41–49.

Madden, B. L. 1998. *CFROI cash flow return on investment valuation: A total system approach to valuing a firm.* Woburn, MA: Butterworth-Heinemann.

O'Byrne, S. F. 1996. EVA and market value. *Journal of Applied Corporate Finance* 9(1):116–125.

O'Byrne, S. F., and S. D. Young. 2000. *EVA and value-based management.* New York: McGraw-Hill.

Stewart, G. B. 1991. *The quest for value.* New York: HarperBusiness.

Stulz, R. 1996. Rethinking risk management. *Journal of Applied Corporate Finance* 9(3):8–24.

Chapter 33   Valuing Bonds

Altman, E. I., and V. Kishore. 2000. The default experience of U.S. bonds. Working paper. Salomon Center, New York University.

Atkinson, T. R. 1967. *Trends in corporate bond quality.* Cambridge, MA: National Bureau of Economic Research.

Black, F., and M. Scholes. 1972. The valuation of option contracts and a test of market efficiencies. *Journal of Finance* 27:399–417.

Brennan, M. J., and E. S. Schwartz. 1977. Savings bonds, retractable bonds and callable bonds. *Journal of Financial Economics* 5:67–88.

Brennan, M. J., and E. S. Schwartz. 1980. Analyzing convertible bonds. *Journal of Financial and Quantitative Analysis* 15:907–929.

Briys, E., M. Crouhy, and R. Schobel. 1991. The pricing of default-free interest rate cap, floor and collar agreements. *Journal of Finance* 46:1879–1892.

Fabozzi, F. J. 1994. *Investment management.* Englewood Cliffs, NJ: Prentice Hall.

Fama, E. F. 1975. Short term interest rates as predictors of inflation. *American Economic Review* 65:269–282.

Figlewski, S., W. L. Silber, and M. G. Subrahmanyam, eds. 1990. *Financial options.* Homewood, IL: Business One Irwin.

Fraine, H. G., and R. H. Mills. 1961. Effect of defaults and credit deterioration on yields of corporate bonds. *Journal of Finance* 16:423–434.

Harvey, C. R. 1991. The term structure and world economic growth. *Journal of Fixed Income* 1:4–17.

Hempel, G. H. 1971. *The postwar quality of state and local debt.* Cambridge, MA: National Bureau of Economic Research.

Hickman, W. B. 1958. *Corporate bond quality and investor experience.* Cambridge, MA: National Bureau of Economic Research.

Hicks, J. R. 1946. *The value of capital.* New York: Oxford University Press.

Ho, T. S. Y., and S. B. Lee. 1989. Pricing of the call and sinking fund provisions on corporate bonds under interest rate risk: Empirical evidence. *International Journal of Finance* 2:1–17.

Ingersoll, J. 1977. An examination of corporate call policies on convertible securities. *Journal of Finance* 32:463–478.

Johnson, R. E. 1967. Term structures of corporate bond yields as a function of the risk of default. *Journal of Finance* 22:313–345.

McCulloch, J. H. 1975. An estimate of the liquidity premium. *Journal of Political Economy* 83:95–119.

Meiselman, D. 1962. *The term structure of interest rates.* Englewood Cliffs, NJ: Prentice Hall.

Park, S. Y., and M. G. Subrahmanyam. 1990. Option features of corporate securities. In *Financial Options,* ed. S. Figlewski et al. Homewood, IL: Business One Irwin.

Sarig, O., and A. Warga. 1989. Some empirical estimates of the term structure of interest rates. *Journal of Finance* 44:1351–1360.

Shiller, R. J. 1979. The volatility of long-term interest rates and expectations models of the term structure. *Journal of Political Economy* 87:1190–1219.

Stapleton, R. C., and M. G. Subrahmanyam. 1990. Interest rate caps and floors. In *Financial options,* ed. S. Figlewski et al. Homewood, IL: Business One Irwin.

Van Horne, J. C. 1965. Interest-rate risk and the term structure of interest rates. *Journal of Political Economy* 73:344–351.

Wood, J. H., and N. L. Wood. 1985. *Financial markets.* Orlando, FL: Harcourt Brace Jovanovich

Chapter 34   Valuing Futures and Forward Contracts

Houthaker, H. S. 1957. Can speculators forecast prices? *Review of Economics and Statistics* 39:73–87.

Hull, J. C. 1999. *Options, futures and derivative securities.* Upper Saddle River, NJ: Prentice Hall.

Telser, L. G. 1958. Futures trading and the storage of cotton and wheat. *Journal of Political Economy* 3:233–255.

Chapter 35   Overview and Conclusion

Damodaran, A. 2001. *Choosing the right valuation model.* Working paper. www.stern.nyu.edu/~adamodar/New_Home_Page/papers.html.

index